MySQL

Fifth Edition

Developer's Library

ESSENTIAL REFERENCES FOR PROGRAMMING PROFESSIONALS

Developer's Library books are designed to provide practicing programmers with unique, high-quality references and tutorials on the programming languages and technologies they use in their daily work.

All books in the *Developer's Library* are written by expert technology practitioners who are especially skilled at organizing and presenting information in a way that's useful for other programmers.

Key titles include some of the best, most widely acclaimed books within their topic areas:

PHP & MySQL Web Development
Luke Welling & Laura Thomson
ISBN 978-0-672-32916-6

Python Essential Reference
David Beazley
ISBN-13: 978-0-672-32978-4

MySQL
Paul DuBois
ISBN-13: 978-0-321-83387-7

PostgreSQL
Korry Douglas
ISBN-13: 978-0-672-32756-8

Linux Kernel Development
Robert Love
ISBN-13: 978-0-672-32946-3

C++ Primer Plus
Stephen Prata
ISBN-13: 978-0-321-77640-2

Developer's Library books are available in print and in electronic formats at most retail and online bookstores, as well as by subscription from Safari Books Online at **safari.informit.com**

**Developer's
Library**
informit.com/devlibrary

MySQL

Fifth Edition

Paul DuBois

♦♦Addison-Wesley

Upper Saddle River, NJ • Boston • Indianapolis • San Francisco
New York • Toronto • Montreal • London • Munich • Paris • Madrid
Cape Town • Sydney • Tokyo • Singapore • Mexico City

MySQL, Fifth Edition

ISBN-13: 978-0-321-83387-7

ISBN-10: 0-321-83387-2

Library of Congress Cataloging-in-Publication Data will be inserted once available.

Printed in the United States of America

First Printing March 2013

Trademarks

All terms mentioned in this book that are known to be trademarks or service marks have been appropriately capitalized. Pearson cannot attest to the accuracy of this information. Use of a term in this book should not be regarded as affecting the validity of any trademark or service mark.

Warning and Disclaimer

Every effort has been made to make this book as complete and as accurate as possible, but no warranty or fitness is implied. The information provided is on an "as is" basis. The author and the publisher shall have neither liability nor responsibility to any person or entity with respect to any loss or damages arising from the information contained in this book.

Bulk Sales

Pearson offers excellent discounts on this book when ordered in quantity for bulk purchases or special sales. For more information, please contact

U.S. Corporate and Government Sales
1-800-382-3419
corpsales@pearsontechgroup.com

For sales outside of the U.S., please contact

International Sales
international@pearsoned.com

Acquisitions Editor
Mark Taber

Managing Editor
Sandra Schroeder

Senior Project Editor
Tonya Simpson

Copy Editor
Water Crest Publishing

Indexer
Heather McNeill

Proofreader
Jess DeGabriele

Technical Editor
Stephen Frein

Publishing Coordinator
Vanessa Evans

Designer
Chuti Prasertsith

Compositor
Bumpy Design

Contents at a Glance

Introduction **1**

Part I: General MySQL Use

1 Getting Started with MySQL **11**

2 Using SQL to Manage Data **95**

3 Data Types **179**

4 Views and Stored Programs **261**

5 Query Optimization **277**

Part II: Using MySQL Programming Interfaces

6 Introduction to MySQL Programming **307**

7 Writing MySQL Programs Using C **319**

8 Writing MySQL Programs Using Perl DBI **395**

9 Writing MySQL Programs Using PHP **485**

Part III: MySQL Administration

10 Introduction to MySQL Administration **537**

11 The MySQL Data Directory **543**

12 General MySQL Administration **563**

13 Security and Access Control **645**

14 Database Maintenance, Backups, and Replication **699**

Part IV: Appendixes

A Software Required to Use This Book **735**

B Data Type Reference **747**

C Operator and Function Reference **763**

D System, Status, and User Variable Reference **835**

E SQL Syntax Reference **897**

F MySQL Program Reference **999**

Index **1073**

> **Note:** *Appendixes G, H, and I are located online and are accessible either by registering this book at **informit.com/register** or by visiting **www.kitebird.com/mysql-book**.*

G C API Reference **Web: 1073**

H Perl DBI API Reference **Web: 1129**

I PHP API Reference **Web: 1157**

Table of Contents

Introduction   1

Why Choose MySQL?   2

What You Can Expect from This Book   4

Road Map to This Book   4

Part I: General MySQL Use   4

Part II: Using MySQL Programming Interfaces   5

Part III: MySQL Administration   5

Part IV: Appendixes   6

How to Read This Book   6

Versions of Software Covered in This Book   7

Conventions Used in This Book   9

Additional Resources   9

Part I: General MySQL Use

1   Getting Started with MySQL   11

1.1   How MySQL Can Help You   11

1.2   A Sample Database   14

1.2.1   The U.S. Historical League Project   15

1.2.2   The Grade-Keeping Project   17

1.2.3   How the Sample Database Applies to You   17

1.3   Basic Database Terminology   18

1.3.1   Structural Terminology   18

1.3.2   Query Language Terminology   20

1.3.3   MySQL Architectural Terminology   21

1.4   A MySQL Tutorial   22

1.4.1   Obtaining the Sample Database Distribution   23

1.4.2   Preliminary Requirements   23

1.4.3   Establishing and Terminating Connections to the MySQL Server   25

1.4.4   Executing SQL Statements   27

1.4.5   Creating a Database   30

1.4.6   Creating Tables   31

1.4.7   Adding New Rows   49

1.4.8   Resetting the sampdb Database to a Known State   53

1.4.9   Retrieving Information   54

1.4.10   Deleting or Updating Existing Rows   85

1.5   Tips for Interacting with mysql   87

   1.5.1   Simplifying the Connection Process   87

   1.5.2   Issuing Statements with Less Typing   90

1.6   Where to Now?   94

2   Using SQL to Manage Data   95

2.1   The Server SQL Mode   96

2.2   MySQL Identifier Syntax and Naming Rules   97

2.3   Case Sensitivity in SQL Statements   99

2.4   Character Set Support   101

   2.4.1   Specifying Character Sets   102

   2.4.2   Determining Character Set Availability and Current Settings   103

   2.4.3   Unicode Support   104

2.5   Selecting, Creating, Dropping, and Altering Databases   105

   2.5.1   Selecting Databases   105

   2.5.2   Creating Databases   106

   2.5.3   Dropping Databases   107

   2.5.4   Altering Databases   107

2.6   Creating, Dropping, Indexing, and Altering Tables   107

   2.6.1   Storage Engine Characteristics   108

   2.6.2   Creating Tables   113

   2.6.3   Dropping Tables   121

   2.6.4   Indexing Tables   122

   2.6.5   Altering Table Structure   127

2.7   Obtaining Database Metadata   130

   2.7.1   Obtaining Metadata with SHOW   130

   2.7.2   Obtaining Metadata with INFORMATION_SCHEMA   132

   2.7.3   Obtaining Metadata from the Command Line   135

2.8   Performing Multiple-Table Retrievals with Joins   136

   2.8.1   Inner Joins   137

   2.8.2   Qualifying References to Columns from Joined Tables   139

   2.8.3   Left and Right (Outer) Joins   139

2.9   Performing Multiple-Table Retrievals with Subqueries   143

   2.9.1   Subqueries with Relative Comparison Operators   144

   2.9.2   IN and NOT IN Subqueries   145

   2.9.3   ALL, ANY, and SOME Subqueries   146

2.9.4   EXISTS and NOT EXISTS Subqueries   147

2.9.5   Correlated Subqueries   148

2.9.6   Subqueries in the FROM Clause   149

2.9.7   Rewriting Subqueries as Joins   149

2.10   Performing Multiple-Table Retrievals with UNION   151

2.11   Multiple-Table Deletes and Updates   154

2.12   Performing Transactions   156

2.12.1   Using Transactions to Ensure Safe Statement Execution   157

2.12.2   Using Transaction Savepoints   161

2.12.3   Transaction Isolation   162

2.13   Foreign Keys and Referential Integrity   164

2.14   Using FULLTEXT Searches   170

2.14.1   Natural Language FULLTEXT Searches   172

2.14.2   Boolean Mode FULLTEXT Searches   174

2.14.3   Query Expansion FULLTEXT Searches   175

2.14.4   Configuring the FULLTEXT Search Engine   176

3   **Data Types   179**

3.1   Data Value Categories   181

3.1.1   Numeric Values   181

3.1.2   String Values   182

3.1.3   Temporal (Date and Time) Values   191

3.1.4   Spatial Values   191

3.1.5   Boolean Values   192

3.1.6   The NULL Value   192

3.2   MySQL Data Types   192

3.2.1   Data Type Overview   193

3.2.2   Specifying Column Types in Table Definitions   194

3.2.3   Specifying Column Default Values   196

3.2.4   Numeric Data Types   196

3.2.5   String Data Types   204

3.2.6   Temporal (Date and Time) Data Types   218

3.3   How MySQL Handles Invalid Data Values   228

3.4   Working with Sequences   230

3.4.1   General AUTO_INCREMENT Properties   230

3.4.2   Storage Engine-Specific AUTO_INCREMENT Properties   232

3.4.3   Issues to Consider with AUTO_INCREMENT Columns   235

3.4.4   Tips for Working with `AUTO_INCREMENT` Columns   235

3.4.5   Generating Sequences Without `AUTO_INCREMENT`   237

3.5   Expression Evaluation and Type Conversion   239

3.5.1   Writing Expressions   240

3.5.2   Type Conversion   247

3.6   Choosing Data Types   255

3.6.1   What Kind of Values Will the Column Hold?   257

3.6.2   Do Your Values Lie Within Some Particular Range?   259

4   Views and Stored Programs   261

4.1   Using Views   262

4.2   Using Stored Programs   265

4.2.1   Compound Statements and Statement Delimiters   266

4.2.2   Stored Functions and Procedures   268

4.2.3   Triggers   272

4.2.4   Events   274

4.3   Security for Views and Stored Programs   275

5   Query Optimization   277

5.1   Using Indexing   277

5.1.1   Benefits of Indexing   278

5.1.2   Costs of Indexing   281

5.1.3   Choosing Indexes   281

5.2   The MySQL Query Optimizer   285

5.2.1   How the Optimizer Works   286

5.2.2   Using `EXPLAIN` to Check Optimizer Operation   290

5.3   Choosing Data Types for Efficient Queries   296

5.4   Choosing Table Storage Formats for Efficient Queries   299

5.5   Loading Data Efficiently   300

5.6   Scheduling, Locking, and Concurrency   303

Part II: Using MySQL Programming Interfaces

6   Introduction to MySQL Programming   307

6.1   Why Write Your Own MySQL Programs?   307

6.2   APIs Available for MySQL   310

6.2.1   The C API   311

6.2.2   The Perl DBI API   311

6.2.3   The PHP API   313

6.3   Choosing an API   314

   6.3.1   Execution Environment   314

   6.3.2   Performance   315

   6.3.3   Development Time   316

   6.3.4   Portability   317

7   Writing MySQL Programs Using C   319

7.1   Compiling and Linking Client Programs   320

7.2   Connecting to the Server   323

7.3   Handling Errors and Processing Command Options   327

   7.3.1   Checking for Errors   327

   7.3.2   Getting Connection Parameters at Runtime   330

   7.3.3   Incorporating Option Processing into a Client Program   344

7.4   Processing SQL Statements   348

   7.4.1   Handling Statements That Modify Rows   350

   7.4.2   Handling Statements That Return a Result Set   351

   7.4.3   A General-Purpose Statement Handler   354

   7.4.4   Alternative Approaches to Statement Processing   356

   7.4.5   `mysql_store_result()` Versus `mysql_use_result()`   357

   7.4.6   Using Result Set Metadata   359

   7.4.7   Encoding Special Characters and Binary Data   364

7.5   An Interactive Statement-Execution Program   368

7.6   Writing Clients That Include SSL Support   370

7.7   Using Multiple-Statement Execution   375

7.8   Using Server-Side Prepared Statements   377

7.9   Using Prepared `CALL` Support   389

8   Writing MySQL Programs Using Perl DBI   395

8.1   Perl Script Characteristics   396

8.2   Perl DBI Overview   396

   8.2.1   DBI Data Types   396

   8.2.2   A Simple DBI Script   397

   8.2.3   Handling Errors   402

   8.2.4   Handling Statements That Modify Rows   406

   8.2.5   Handling Statements That Return a Result Set   407

   8.2.6   Quoting Special Characters in Statement Strings   416

8.2.7   Placeholders and Prepared Statements   419
8.2.8   Binding Query Results to Script Variables   422
8.2.9   Specifying Connection Parameters   423
8.2.10 Debugging   426
8.2.11 Using Result Set Metadata   430
8.2.12 Performing Transactions   434
8.3 Putting DBI to Work   436
8.3.1   Generating the Historical League Directory   436
8.3.2   Sending Membership Renewal Notices   442
8.3.3   Historical League Member Entry Editing   448
8.3.4   Finding Historical League Members with Common Interests   454
8.3.5   Putting the Historical League Directory Online   455
8.4 Using DBI in Web Applications   459
8.4.1   Setting Up Apache for CGI Scripts   460
8.4.2   A Brief CGI.pm Primer   461
8.4.3   Connecting to the MySQL Server from Web Scripts   468
8.4.4   A Web-Based Database Browser   471
8.4.5   A Grade-Keeping Project Score Browser   475
8.4.6   Historical League Common-Interest Searching   479

9 Writing MySQL Programs Using PHP   485
9.1 PHP Overview   487
9.1.1   A Simple PHP Script   489
9.1.2   Using PHP Library Files for Code Encapsulation   492
9.1.3   A Simple Data-Retrieval Page   497
9.1.4   Processing Statement Results   500
9.1.5   Testing for NULL Values in Query Results   504
9.1.6   Using Prepared Statements   505
9.1.7   Using Placeholders to Handle Data Quoting Issues   505
9.1.8   Handling Errors   507
9.2 Putting PHP to Work   509
9.2.1   An Online Score-Entry Application   510
9.2.2   Creating an Interactive Online Quiz   522
9.2.3   Historical League Online Member Entry Editing   528

Part III: MySQL Administration

10   Introduction to MySQL Administration   537
10.1   MySQL Components   538
10.2   General MySQL Administration   539
10.3   Access Control and Security   540
10.4   Database Maintenance, Backups, and Replication   540

11   The MySQL Data Directory   543
11.1   The Data Directory Location   544
11.2   Structure of the Data Directory   545
    11.2.1   How the MySQL Server Provides Access to Data   546
    11.2.2   Representation of Databases in the Filesystem   547
    11.2.3   Representation of Tables in the Filesystem   548
    11.2.4   Representation of Views and Triggers in the Filesystem   549
    11.2.5   How SQL Statements Map onto Table File Operations   549
    11.2.6   Operating System Constraints on Database Object Names   550
    11.2.7   Factors That Affect Maximum Table Size   551
    11.2.8   Implications of Data Directory Structure for System Performance   553
    11.2.9   MySQL Status and Log Files   554
11.3   Relocating Data Directory Contents   556
    11.3.1   Relocation Methods   557
    11.3.2   Relocation Precautions   558
    11.3.3   Assessing the Effect of Relocation   558
    11.3.4   Relocating the Entire Data Directory   559
    11.3.5   Relocating Individual Databases   559
    11.3.6   Relocating Individual Tables   560
    11.3.7   Relocating the InnoDB System Tablespace   561
    11.3.8   Relocating Status and Log Files   561

12   General MySQL Administration   563
12.1   Securing a New MySQL Installation   564
    12.1.1   Establishing Passwords for the Initial MySQL Accounts   564
    12.1.2   Setting Up Passwords for Additional Servers   569
12.2   Arranging for MySQL Server Startup and Shutdown   570
    12.2.1   Running the MySQL Server On Unix   570
    12.2.2   Running the MySQL Server On Windows   575
    12.2.3   Specifying Server Startup Options   577

12.2.4   Controlling How the Server Listens for Connections   579

12.2.5   Stopping the Server   580

12.2.6   Regaining Control of the Server When You Cannot Connect to It   581

12.3   Using System and Status Variables   583

12.3.1   Checking and Setting System Variable Values   584

12.3.2   Checking Status Variable Values   588

12.4   The Plugin Interface   589

12.5   Storage Engine Configuration   593

12.5.1   Selecting Storage Engines   593

12.5.2   Selecting a Default Storage Engine   594

12.5.3   Configuring the InnoDB Storage Engine   594

12.6   Globalization Issues   601

12.6.1   Configuring Time Zone Support   601

12.6.2   Selecting the Default Character Set and Collation   603

12.6.3   Selecting the Language for Error Messages   604

12.6.4   Selecting the Locale   604

12.7   Server Tuning   605

12.7.1   General-Purpose System Variables for Server Tuning   606

12.7.2   Storage Engine Tuning   609

12.7.3   Using the Query Cache   614

12.7.4   Hardware Optimizations   616

12.8   Server Logs   617

12.8.1   The Error Log   620

12.8.2   The General Query Log   621

12.8.3   The Slow Query Log   621

12.8.4   The Binary Log   622

12.8.5   The Relay Log   624

12.8.6   Using Log Tables   624

12.8.7   Log Management   625

12.9   Running Multiple Servers   632

12.9.1   General Multiple Server Issues   632

12.9.2   Configuring and Compiling Different Servers   635

12.9.3   Strategies for Specifying Startup Options   636

12.9.4   Using `mysqld_multi` for Server Management   637

12.9.5   Running Multiple Servers on Windows   639

12.9.6   Running Clients of Multiple Servers   641

12.10   Updating MySQL   642

13 Security and Access Control   645

13.1   Securing Filesystem Access to MySQL   646

13.1.1   How to Steal Data   647

13.1.2   Securing Your MySQL Installation   648

13.2   Managing MySQL User Accounts   654

13.2.1   High-Level MySQL Account Management   655

13.2.2   Granting Privileges   660

13.2.3   Displaying Account Privileges   671

13.2.4   Revoking Privileges   671

13.2.5   Changing Passwords or Resetting Lost Passwords   672

13.2.6   Avoiding Access-Control Risks   673

13.2.7   Pluggable Authentication and Proxy Users   676

13.3   Grant Table Structure and Contents   679

13.3.1   Grant Table Scope-of-Access Columns   683

13.3.2   Grant Table Privilege Columns   683

13.3.3   Grant Table Authentication Columns   684

13.3.4   Grant Table SSL-Related Columns   685

13.3.5   Grant Table Resource Management Columns   685

13.4   How the Server Controls Client Access   686

13.4.1   Scope Column Contents   687

13.4.2   Statement Access Verification   689

13.4.3   Scope Column Matching Order   690

13.4.4   A Privilege Puzzle   691

13.5   Setting Up Secure Connections Using SSL   694

14 Database Maintenance, Backups, and Replication   699

14.1   Principles of Preventive Maintenance   699

14.2   Performing Database Maintenance with the Server Running   701

14.2.1   Locking Individual Tables for Read-Only or Read/Write Access   702

14.2.2   Locking All Databases for Read-Only Access   705

14.3   General Preventive Maintenance   705

14.3.1   Using the Server's Auto-Recovery Capabilities   706

14.3.2   Scheduling Preventive Maintenance   706

14.4   Making Database Backups   707

14.4.1   Storage Engine Portability Characteristics   709

14.4.2   Making Text Backups with `mysqldump`   711

14.4.3   Making Binary Database Backups   714

14.4.4   Backing Up InnoDB Tables   715

14.5   Copying Databases to Another Server   716

14.5.1   Copying Databases Using a Backup File   716

14.5.2   Copying Databases from One Server to Another   717

14.6   Checking and Repairing Database Tables   718

14.6.1   Checking Tables with CHECK TABLE   719

14.6.2   Repairing Tables with REPAIR TABLE   720

14.6.3   Using mysqlcheck to Check and Repair Tables   720

14.7   Using Backups for Data Recovery   722

14.7.1   Recovering Entire Databases   722

14.7.2   Recovering Individual Tables   723

14.7.3   Re-Executing Statements in Binary Log Files   723

14.7.4   Coping with InnoDB Auto-Recovery Problems   725

14.8   Setting Up Replication Servers   726

14.8.1   How Replication Works   727

14.8.2   Establishing a Master-Slave Replication Relationship   728

14.8.3   Binary Logging Formats   731

14.8.4   Using a Replication Slave for Making Backups   731

Part IV: Appendixes

A   Software Required to Use This Book   735

A.1   Obtaining the sampdb Sample Database Distribution   735

A.2   Obtaining MySQL and Related Software   736

A.3   MySQL Installation Notes   737

A.3.1   Creating a Login Account for the MySQL User   738

A.3.2   Installing MySQL   739

A.3.3   Setting Your PATH Environment Variable   739

A.3.4   Initializing the Data Directory and Grant Tables   740

A.3.5   Starting the Server   741

A.3.6   Initializing Other System Tables   742

A.4   Perl DBI Installation Notes   743

A.5   PHP and PDO Installation Notes   743

B   Data Type Reference   747

B.1   Numeric Types   748

B.1.1   Integer Types   749

B.1.2   Fixed-Point Types   751

B.1.3   Floating-Point Types   751

B.1.4   BIT Type   752

B.2   String Types   753

    B.2.1   Binary String Types   755

    B.2.2   Nonbinary String Types   756

    B.2.3   ENUM and SET Types   758

B.3   Temporal (Date and Time) Types   759

C   Operator and Function Reference   763

C.1   Operators   764

    C.1.1   Operator Precedence   764

    C.1.2   Grouping Operators   765

    C.1.3   Arithmetic Operators   766

    C.1.4   Comparison Operators   768

    C.1.5   Bit Operators   773

    C.1.6   Logical Operators   774

    C.1.7   Cast Operators   775

    C.1.8   Pattern-Matching Operators   776

C.2   Functions   780

    C.2.1   Comparison Functions   781

    C.2.2   Cast Functions   783

    C.2.3   Numeric Functions   784

    C.2.4   String Functions   789

    C.2.5   Date and Time Functions   802

    C.2.6   Summary Functions   817

    C.2.7   Security and Compression Functions   821

    C.2.8   Advisory Locking Functions   824

    C.2.9   IP Address Functions   826

    C.2.10   XML Functions   828

    C.2.11   Spatial Functions   828

    C.2.12   Miscellaneous Functions   829

D   System, Status, and User Variable Reference   835

D.1   System Variables   835

    D.1.1   InnoDB System Variables   870

D.2   Status Variables   881

    D.2.1   InnoDB Status Variables   888

    D.2.2   Query Cache Status Variables   891

    D.2.3   SSL Status Variables   892

D.3   User-Defined Variables   894

E SQL Syntax Reference   897

E.1   SQL Statement Syntax (Noncompound Statements)   898

E.2   SQL Statement Syntax (Compound Statements)   987

　　E.2.1   Control Structure Statements   987

　　E.2.2   Declaration Statements   989

　　E.2.3   Cursor Statements   991

　　E.2.4   Condition-Handling Statements   992

E.3   Comment Syntax   996

F MySQL Program Reference   999

F.1   Displaying a Program's Help Message   1000

F.2   Specifying Program Options   1001

　　F.2.1   Standard MySQL Program Options   1003

　　F.2.2   Option Files   1007

　　F.2.3   Environment Variables   1011

F.3   `myisamchk`   1013

　　F.3.1   Standard Options Supported by `myisamchk`   1014

　　F.3.2   Options Specific to `myisamchk`   1015

　　F.3.3   Variables for `myisamchk`   1018

F.4   `mysql`   1019

　　F.4.1   Standard Options Supported by `mysql`   1021

　　F.4.2   Options Specific to `mysql`   1021

　　F.4.3   Variables for `mysql`   1025

　　F.4.4   `mysql` Commands   1026

　　F.4.5   `mysql` Prompt Definition Sequences   1028

F.5   `mysql.server`   1030

　　F.5.1   Options Supported by `mysql.server`   1030

F.6   `mysql_config`   1030

　　F.6.1   Options Specific to `mysql_config`   1031

F.7   `mysql_install_db`   1031

　　F.7.1   Standard Options Supported by `mysql_install_db`   1032

　　F.7.2   Options Specific to `mysql_install_db`   1032

F.8   `mysql_upgrade`   1033

　　F.8.1   Standard Options Supported by `mysql_upgrade`   1033

　　F.8.2   Options Specific to `mysql_upgrade`   1033

F.9   `mysqladmin`   1034

　　F.9.1   Standard Options Supported by `mysqladmin`   1034

F.9.2   Options Specific to `mysqladmin`   1034

F.9.3   Variables for `mysqladmin`   1035

F.9.4   `mysqladmin` Commands   1035

F.10 `mysqlbinlog`   1038

F.10.1   Standard Options Supported by `mysqlbinlog`   1038

F.10.2   Options Specific to `mysqlbinlog`   1038

F.10.3   Variables for `mysqlbinlog`   1041

F.11 `mysqlcheck`   1041

F.11.1   Standard Options Supported by `mysqlcheck`   1042

F.11.2   Options Specific to `mysqlcheck`   1042

F.12 `mysqld`   1045

F.12.1   Standard Options Supported by `mysqld`   1046

F.12.2   Options Specific to `mysqld`   1046

F.12.3   Variables for `mysqld`   1056

F.13 `mysqld_multi`   1056

F.13.1   Standard Options Supported by `mysqld_multi`   1057

F.13.2   Options Specific to `mysqld_multi`   1057

F.14 `mysqld_safe`   1058

F.14.1   Standard Options Supported by `mysqld_safe`   1058

F.14.2   Options Specific to `mysqld_safe`   1058

F.15 `mysqldump`   1060

F.15.1   Standard Options Supported by `mysqldump`   1060

F.15.2   Options Specific to `mysqldump`   1061

F.15.3   Data Format Options for `mysqldump`   1067

F.15.4   Variables for `mysqldump`   1068

F.16 `mysqlimport`   1068

F.16.1   Standard Options Supported by `mysqlimport`   1068

F.16.2   Options Specific to `mysqlimport`   1069

F.16.3   Data Format Options for `mysqlimport`   1070

F.17 `mysqlshow`   1070

F.17.1   Standard Options Supported by `mysqlshow`   1071

F.17.2   Options Specific to `mysqlshow`   1071

F.18 `perror`   1072

F.18.1   Standard Options Supported by `perror`   1072

Note: *Appendixes G, H, and I are located online and are accessible either by registering this book at **informit.com/register** or by visiting **www.kitebird.com/mysql-book**.*

G   C API Reference   1073

G.1   Compiling and Linking   1074

G.2   C API Data Structures   1075

   G.2.1   Scalar Data Types   1075

   G.2.2   Nonscalar Data Structures   1076

   G.2.3   Accessor Macros   1087

G.3   C API Functions   1088

   G.3.1   Client Library Initialization and Termination Routines   1088

   G.3.2   Connection Management Routines   1089

   G.3.3   Error-Reporting Routines   1101

   G.3.4   Statement Construction and Execution Routines   1102

   G.3.5   Result Set Processing Routines   1104

   G.3.6   Multiple Result Set Routines   1113

   G.3.7   Information Routines   1113

   G.3.8   Transaction Control Routines   1116

   G.3.9   Prepared Statement Routines   1116

   G.3.10   Administrative Routines   1125

   G.3.11   Threaded Client Routines   1126

   G.3.12   Debugging Routines   1127

H   Perl DBI API Reference   1129

H.1   Writing Scripts   1130

H.2   DBI Methods   1130

   H.2.1   DBI Class Methods   1132

   H.2.2   Database-Handle Methods   1137

   H.2.3   Statement-Handle Methods   1142

   H.2.4   General Handle Methods   1146

   H.2.5   MySQL-Specific Administrative Methods   1147

H.3   DBI Utility Functions   1148

H.4   DBI Attributes   1149

   H.4.1   Database-Handle Attributes   1149

   H.4.2   General Handle Attributes   1149

   H.4.3   MySQL-Specific Database-Handle Attributes   1150

   H.4.4   Statement-Handle Attributes   1152

H.4.5   MySQL-Specific Statement-Handle Attributes   1154

H.4.6   Dynamic Attributes   1155

H.5   DBI Environment Variables   1156

I   **PHP API Reference   1157**

I.1   Writing PHP Scripts   1157

I.2   PDO Classes   1158

I.3   PDO Methods   1159

I.3.1   PDO Class Methods   1159

I.3.2   PDOStatement Object Methods   1166

I.3.3   PDOException Object Methods   1172

I.3.4   PDO Constants   1173

Index   1175

About the Author

Paul DuBois is a writer, database administrator, and leader in the open source and MySQL communities. He has contributed to the online documentation for MySQL and is the author of *MySQL and Perl for the Web* (New Riders), *MySQL Cookbook, Using csh and tcsh,* and *Software Portability with imake* (O'Reilly). He is currently a technical writer with the MySQL documentation team at Oracle Corporation.

Acknowledgments

My technical reviewer, Stephen Frein, provided good insights and suggestions for improvement. In addition, because this edition would not have been possible without the previous ones, my continued thanks go to everyone listed in those editions who served as technical reviewer or who patiently answered my questions.

The staff at Pearson responsible for this edition were Mark Taber, acquisitions editor; Tonya Simpson, project editor; Sarah Kearns, copy editor; Kim Scott, compositor; Jess DeGabriele, proofreader; Heather McNeill, indexer; and Chuti Prasertsith, cover designer. My thanks to each of them.

Thanks to my wife Karen for her support and encouragement throughout the production of this edition.

We Want to Hear from You!

As the reader of this book, *you* are our most important critic and commentator. We value your opinion and want to know what we're doing right, what we could do better, what areas you'd like to see us publish in, and any other words of wisdom you're willing to pass our way.

You can email or write directly to let us know what you did or didn't like about this book—as well as what we can do to make our books stronger.

Please note that we cannot help you with technical problems related to the topic of this book, and that due to the high volume of mail we receive, we might not be able to reply to every message.

When you write, please be sure to include this book's title and author, as well as your name and phone or email address.

Email: feedback@developers-library.info

Mail: Reader Feedback
Addison-Wesley Developer's Library
800 East 96th Street
Indianapolis, IN 46240 USA

Reader Services

Visit our website and register this book at **www.informit.com/register** for convenient access to any updates, downloads, or errata that might be available for this book.

Your purchase of this book includes access to a free online edition for 45 days through the Safari Books Online subscription service. Details are on the last page of this book.

Introduction

A relational database management system (RDBMS) is an essential tool in many environments, from uses in business, research, and educational contexts, to content delivery on the Internet. However, despite the importance of a good database system for managing and accessing information resources, many organizations have found them to be out of reach of their financial resources. Historically, database systems have been an expensive proposition, with vendors charging healthy fees both for software and for support. Also, because database engines often had substantial hardware requirements to run with any reasonable performance, the cost was even greater.

Times have changed, on both the hardware and software sides of the picture. Small desktop systems and servers are inexpensive but powerful, and there is a thriving movement devoted to writing high-performance operating systems for them. These operating systems are available free over the Internet or at the cost of an inexpensive CD. They include several BSD Unix derivatives and several distributions of Linux.

Production of free operating systems has proceeded in concert with—and to a large extent has been made possible by—the development of freely available Open Source tools like the gcc GNU C compiler; Apache, the most widely used Web server on the Internet; and well-established general-purpose scripting languages such as Perl, PHP, Python, and Ruby. These all stand in contrast to proprietary solutions that lock you into high-priced products from vendors that don't even provide source code.

Database software has become more accessible, too, and Open Source database systems are freely available. One of the most important is MySQL, a SQL client/server relational database management system originating from Scandinavia. MySQL includes an SQL server, client programs for accessing the server, administrative tools, and a programming interface for writing your own programs.

MySQL's roots begin in 1979, with the UNIREG database tool created by Michael "Monty" Widenius for the Swedish company TcX. In 1994, TcX began searching for an RDBMS with an SQL interface for use in developing Web applications. Commercial servers tested were all found too slow for TcX's large tables, and the freely available mSQL lacked features that TcX required. Consequently, Monty began developing a new server.

In 1995, David Axmark of Detron HB began to push for TcX to release MySQL on the Internet. David also worked on the documentation and on getting MySQL to build with the GNU configuration autotools. MySQL 3.11.1 was unleashed on the world in 1996 in the form of binary distributions for Linux and Solaris. The company MySQL AB was formed to provide distributions of MySQL and to offer commercial services. In 2008, Sun Microsystems acquired MySQL AB, and in 2010, Oracle acquired Sun. Today, MySQL is available in both binary and source form and works on many more platforms.

Initially, MySQL became widely popular because of its speed and simplicity. But there was criticism, too: It lacked features such as transactions and foreign key support. MySQL continued to develop, adding not only those features but others such as replication, subqueries, stored routines, triggers, and views.

These capabilities take MySQL into the realm of enterprise applications. As a result, people who once would have considered only "big iron" database systems for their applications now give serious consideration to MySQL, which runs on anything from modest hardware all the way up to enterprise servers. Its performance rivals any database system you care to put up against it, and it can handle large databases with billions of rows. In the business world, MySQL's presence continues to increase as companies discover it capable of handling their database needs, with the cost for commercial licensing and support a fraction of what they are used to paying.

MySQL lies squarely within the picture that unfolds before us: freely available operating systems running on powerful but inexpensive hardware, putting substantial processing power and capabilities in the hands of businesses and individuals on a wider variety of systems than ever before. This lowering of the economic barriers to computing puts the power of a high-performance RDBMS to work for more organizations than at any time in the past, for very little cost. This is true for individuals as well. For example, I use MySQL with Perl, PHP, and Apache on my Apple laptop running Mac OS X. This enables me to carry my work with me anywhere. Total cost: the cost of the laptop.

Why Choose MySQL?

Several free or low-cost database management systems are available from which to choose, such as MySQL, PostgreSQL, or SQLite. When you compare MySQL with other database systems, think about what's most important to you. Performance, features (such as SQL conformance or extensions), support, licensing conditions, and price all are factors to take into account. Given these considerations, MySQL has many attractive qualities:

- **Speed.** MySQL is fast, and getting faster; see http://www.mysql.com/why-mysql/benchmarks. There have been many improvements recently, particularly within InnoDB (which is now the default storage engine) and the query optimizer.

- **Ease of use.** MySQL is a high-performance but relatively simple database system and is much less complex to set up and administer than larger systems.

- **Query language support.** MySQL understands SQL (Structured Query Language), the standard language of choice for all modern database systems.

- **Capability.** The MySQL server is multi-threaded, so many clients can connect to it at the same time. Each client can use multiple databases simultaneously. You can access MySQL interactively using several interfaces that let you enter queries and view the results: command-line clients, Web browsers, or GUI clients. In addition, programming interfaces are available for many languages, such as C, Perl, Java, PHP, Python, and Ruby. You can also access MySQL using applications that support ODBC and .NET (protocols developed by Microsoft). This gives you the choice of using prepackaged client software or writing your own for custom applications.

- **Connectivity and security.** MySQL is fully networked, and databases can be accessed from anywhere on the Internet, so you can share your data with anyone, anywhere. But MySQL has access control so that one person who shouldn't see another's data cannot. To provide additional security, MySQL supports encrypted connections using the Secure Sockets Layer (SSL) protocol.

- **Portability.** MySQL runs on many varieties of Unix and Linux, as well as on other systems such as Windows. MySQL runs on hardware from small devices such as routers and personal computers up to high-end servers with many CPUs and huge amounts of memory.

- **Availability and cost.** MySQL is an Open Source project available under multiple licensing terms. First, it is available under the terms of the GNU General Public License (GPL). This means that MySQL is available without cost for most in-house uses. Second, for organizations that prefer or require formal arrangements or that do not want to be bound by the conditions of the GPL, commercial licenses are available.

- **Open distribution and source code.** MySQL is easy to obtain; just use your Web browser. If you don't understand how something works, are curious about an algorithm, or want to perform a security audit, you can get the source code and examine it. If you think you've found a bug, please report it; the developers want to know.

What about support? Good question; a database system isn't much use if you can't get help for it. This book is one form of assistance, and I like to think that it's useful in that regard. (That the book has reached its fifth edition suggests that it accomplishes that goal.) There are other resources open to you as well, and you'll find that MySQL has good support:

- The MySQL Reference Manual is included in MySQL distributions, and is easily accessible online. The Reference Manual regularly receives good marks in the MySQL user community. This is important; the value of a good product is diminished if no one can figure out how to use it.

- Technical support contracts and educational resources such as training classes are available from Oracle.

- MySQL mailing lists and forums are invaluable support resources that anyone may access. These have many helpful participants, including several MySQL developers.

The MySQL community, developers and nondevelopers alike, is very responsive. Answers to questions on the mailing lists often arrive within minutes. When bugs are reported, the developers generally fix them quickly, and new releases appear regularly.

If you are in the database-selection process, MySQL is an ideal candidate for evaluation. You can try it with no risk or financial commitment. Time for installation and setup is less than for many other systems. If you get stuck, you can use the mailing lists to get help.

Perhaps you're currently running another database system but feel constrained by it: Performance of your current system is a concern; it's proprietary and you don't like being locked into it; you'd like to run on hardware that's not supported by your current system; your software is provided in binary-only format but you want to have the source available; or maybe it just costs too much! All of these are reasons to look into MySQL. Use this book to familiarize yourself with MySQL's capabilities, contact the MySQL sales crew, ask questions on the mailing lists, and you'll find the answers you need to make a decision.

What You Can Expect from This Book

You'll learn how to use MySQL effectively so that you can get your work done more productively. You'll be able to figure out how to get your information into a database, and you'll learn how to get it back out by formulating queries that answer the questions you want to ask of that data.

You need not be a programmer to understand or use SQL. This book shows you how it works. But there's more to understanding how to use a database system properly than knowing SQL syntax. This book emphasizes MySQL's unique capabilities and shows how to use them.

You'll also see how MySQL integrates with other tools. The book shows how to write your own programs that access MySQL databases, and you'll learn to use MySQL with Perl and PHP to generate dynamic Web pages created from the result of database queries.

If you'll be responsible for administering a MySQL installation, this book will tell you what your duties are and how to carry them out. You'll learn how to create user accounts, perform database backups, set up replication, and make sure your site is secure.

Road Map to This Book

This book has four parts. The first concentrates on general concepts of database use. The second focuses on writing your own programs that use MySQL. The third is for readers who have administrative duties. The fourth provides a set of reference appendixes.

Part I: General MySQL Use

- Chapter 1, "Getting Started with MySQL." Discusses how MySQL can be useful to you, provides a tutorial that introduces the interactive `mysql` client program, covers the basics of SQL, and demonstrates MySQL's general capabilities.

- Chapter 2, "Using SQL to Manage Data." Every major RDBMS now available understands SQL, but every database engine implements a slightly different SQL dialect. This chapter discusses SQL with particular emphasis on those features that make MySQL distinctive.

- Chapter 3, "Data Types." Discusses the data types that MySQL provides for storing your information, properties and limitations of each type, when and how to use them, expression evaluation, and type conversion.

- Chapter 4, "Views and Stored Programs." How to write and use SQL objects that are stored on the server side. These include views (virtual tables) and stored programs (functions and procedures, triggers, and events).

- Chapter 5, "Query Optimization." How to make your queries run faster.

Part II: Using MySQL Programming Interfaces

- Chapter 6, "Introduction to MySQL Programming." Discusses some of the application programming interfaces (APIs) for MySQL and provides a general comparison of the APIs that the book covers in detail.

- Chapter 7, "Writing MySQL Programs Using C." How to write C programs using the API provided by the MySQL C client library.

- Chapter 8, "Writing MySQL Programs Using Perl DBI." How to write Perl scripts using the DBI module. Covers standalone command-line scripts and scripts for Web site programming.

- Chapter 9, "Writing MySQL Programs Using PHP." How to use the PHP scripting language and the PHP Data Objects (PDO) database-access extension to write dynamic Web pages that access MySQL databases.

Part III: MySQL Administration

- Chapter 10, "Introduction to MySQL Administration." An overview of the database administrator's duties and what you should know to run a MySQL site successfully.

- Chapter 11, "The MySQL Data Directory." An in-depth look at the organization and contents of the data directory, the area under which MySQL stores databases, logs, and status files.

- Chapter 12, "General MySQL Administration." How to make sure your operating system starts and stops the MySQL server properly when your system comes up and shuts down. Also discusses configuring storage engines, tuning the server, log maintenance, and running multiple servers.

- Chapter 13, "Security and Access Control." What you need to know to make your MySQL installation safe from intrusion, both from other users on the server host and from clients connecting over the network. Discusses how to set up MySQL user accounts, explains the structure of the grant tables that control client access to the MySQL server, and describes how to set up your server to support secure connections over SSL.

- Chapter 14, "Database Maintenance, Backups, and Replication." Discusses how to reduce the likelihood of disaster through preventive maintenance, how to back up your databases, how to perform crash recovery if disaster strikes in spite of your preventive measures, and how to set up replication servers.

Part IV: Appendixes

- Appendix A, "Software Required to Use This Book." Where to get the major tools and sample database files described in the book.

- Appendix B, "Data Type Reference." The characteristics of MySQL's data types.

- Appendix C, "Operator and Function Reference." The operators and functions that are used to write expressions in SQL statements.

- Appendix D, "System, Status, and User Variable Reference." Describes each variable maintained by the MySQL server, and how to use your own variables in SQL statements.

- Appendix E, "SQL Syntax Reference." Describes each SQL statement supported by MySQL.

- Appendix F, "MySQL Program Reference." The programs provided in MySQL distributions.

- Appendix G, "C API Reference." The data types and functions in the MySQL C client library.

- Appendix H, "Perl DBI API Reference." The methods and attributes provided by the Perl DBI module.

- Appendix I, "PHP API Reference." The methods provided for MySQL support in PHP by the PDO extension.

How to Read This Book

Whatever part of the book you happen to be reading, it's best to try the examples as you go along. That means you should do two things:

- If MySQL isn't installed on your system, install it or ask someone to do so for you.

- Get the files needed to set up the sampdb sample database used throughout the book.

Appendix A, "Software Required to Use This Book," indicates where to obtain all the necessary components.

If you're new to MySQL or SQL, begin with Chapter 1, "Getting Started with MySQL." It provides you with a tutorial introduction that grounds you in basic MySQL and SQL concepts and brings you up to speed for the rest of the book. Then proceed to Chapter 2, "Using SQL to Manage Data," Chapter 3, "Data Types," and Chapter 4, "Views and Stored Programs," to find out how to describe and manipulate your own data so that you can exploit MySQL's capabilities for your own applications.

If you already know some SQL, you should still read Chapter 2, "Using SQL to Manage Data," and Chapter 3, "Data Types." SQL implementations vary, and you'll want to find out what makes MySQL's implementation distinctive in comparison to others with which you may be familiar. If you have experience with MySQL but need more background on performing particular tasks, use the book as a reference, looking up topics on a need-to-know basis. You'll find the reference appendixes especially useful.

If you're interested in writing your own programs to access MySQL databases, read the API chapters, beginning with Chapter 6, "Introduction to MySQL Programming." To produce a Web-based front end to your databases for easier access to them, or, conversely, to provide a database back end for your Web site to enhance your site with dynamic content, check out Chapter 8, "Writing MySQL Programs Using Perl DBI," and Chapter 9, "Writing MySQL Programs Using PHP."

If your responsibilities include administering a MySQL installation, read the chapters beginning with Chapter 10, "Introduction to MySQL Administration."

If you're evaluating MySQL to find out how it compares to your current RDBMS, several parts of the book are useful. Read the SQL syntax and data type chapters in Part I to compare MySQL to the version of SQL that you're used to, the programming chapters in Part II if you need to write custom applications, and the administrative chapters in Part III to assess the level of administrative support a MySQL installation requires. This information is also useful if you're not currently using a database but are performing a comparative analysis of MySQL along with other database systems for the purpose of choosing one of them.

Versions of Software Covered in This Book

The first edition of this book covered MySQL 3.22 and the beginnings of MySQL 3.23. The second edition expanded that range to include MySQL 4.0 and the first release of MySQL 4.1. The third edition covered MySQL 4.1 and the initial releases of MySQL 5.0. The fourth edition covered MySQL 5.0 and the initial releases of MySQL 5.1.

For this fifth edition, the baseline is MySQL 5.5. That is, the book covers MySQL 5.5 and the early releases of MySQL 5.6. Most of this book still applies if you have a version older than 5.5, but differences specific to older versions usually are not explicitly noted.

The MySQL 5.5 series has reached General Availability (GA) status, which means that it is suitable for production environments. There have been many changes compared to earlier pre-production 5.5 releases, so use the most recent version if possible (5.5.30 as I write). The MySQL 5.6 series currently is a development series (not intended for production use yet) but will reach GA status soon, and may have done so by the time you read this.

For information about older versions, check the MySQL Web site at http://dev.mysql.com/doc, where you can access the Reference Manual for each version.

When updating each edition with new material, it's always a challenge to keep the length down. In the interest of space, I have removed some information present in previous editions. The most pervasive change is that InnoDB is now the default storage engine (not MyISAM), so in keeping with the greater emphasis on InnoDB, there is less on MyISAM. Other more minor storage engines such as FEDERATED and BLACKHOLE are mentioned only in passing. I have removed information about `libmysqld` (the embedded server), `mysqlhotcopy`, `myisampack`, spatial data types and functions, and replaced detailed installation material with more general instructions. For information about any of those topics, I recommend the MySQL Reference Manual.

I also draw your attention to some other topics not covered in this book:

- The MySQL Connectors, which provide client access for Java, ODBC, and .NET programs.
- The NDB storage engine and MySQL Cluster, which provide in-memory storage, high availability, and redundancy. See the MySQL Reference Manual for details.
- The graphical user interface (GUI) tool, MySQL Workbench, which helps you use MySQL in a windowing environment.
- MySQL Enterprise, the commercial version of MySQL that includes features such as MySQL Enterprise Monitor that provides server monitoring and diagnostic capabilities, and MySQL Enterprise Backup for hot backups.

To acquire any of these products or see their documentation, visit `http://www.mysql.com/products` or `http://dev.mysql.com/doc`.

For the other major software packages discussed in the book, any recent versions should be sufficient for the examples shown. The following table shows the current versions at the time of writing.

Package	Version
Perl DBI module	1.623
Perl DBD::mysql module	4.020
PHP	5.4.10
Apache	2.4.3
CGI.pm	3.63

All software discussed in this book is available on the Internet. Appendix A, "Software Required to Use This Book," provides assistance for getting MySQL, Perl DBI, PHP and PDO, Apache, and CGI.pm onto your system. The appendix also contains instructions for obtaining the `sampdb` sample database that is used in examples throughout the book and contains the programs developed in the programming chapters.

If you are using Windows, I assume that you have Windows 2000 or newer. Some features covered in this book, such as named pipes and Windows services, are not available in older versions.

Conventions Used in This Book

This book uses the following typographical conventions:

- `Monospaced font` indicates hostnames, filenames, directory names, commands, options, and Web sites.

- **`Bold monospaced font`** is used in command examples to indicate input that you type.

- *`Italic monospaced font`* is used in commands to indicate where you should substitute a value of your own choosing.

Interactive examples assume that you enter commands by typing them into a terminal window or console window. To provide context, the prompt in command examples indicates the program from which you run the command. For example, SQL statements that are issued from within the `mysql` client program are shown preceded by the `mysql>` prompt. For commands that you issue from your command interpreter, the `%` prompt usually is used. In general, this prompt indicates commands that can be run either on Unix or Windows, although the particular prompt you see will depend on your command interpreter. (The command interpreter is your login shell on Unix, or `cmd.exe` on Windows.) More specialized command-line prompts are `#`, which indicates a command run on Unix as the `root` user with `su` or `sudo`, and `C:\>` to indicate a command intended specifically for Windows.

The following example shows a command that should be entered from your command interpreter. The `%` indicates the prompt (which you do not type). To issue the command, you'd enter the boldface characters as shown, and substitute your own username for the italic word:

```
% mysql --user=user_name sampdb
```

In SQL statements, SQL keywords and function names are written in uppercase. Database, table, and column names generally appear in lowercase.

In syntax descriptions, square brackets (`[]`) indicate optional information. In lists of alternatives, vertical bar (`|`) is used as a separator between items. A list enclosed within `[]` is optional and indicates that an item may be chosen from the list. A list enclosed within `{}` is mandatory and indicates that an item must be chosen from the list.

Additional Resources

If you have a question that this book doesn't answer, where should you turn? Useful documentation resources include the Web sites for the software you need help with, shown in the following table.

Package	Primary Web Site
MySQL	`http://dev.mysql.com/doc`
Perl DBI	`http://dbi.perl.org`
PHP	`http://www.php.net`
Apache	`http://httpd.apache.org`
CGI.pm	`http://search.cpan.org/dist/CGI.pm`

Those sites provide information such as reference manuals, frequently asked-question (FAQ) lists, and mailing lists:

- **Reference manuals.** The primary documentation included with MySQL itself is the Reference Manual. It's available in several formats, including online and downloadable versions.

- **Manual pages.** Documentation for the DBI module and its MySQL-specific driver, DBD::mysql, can be read from the command line with the `perldoc` command. Try `perldoc DBI` and `perldoc DBD::mysql`. The DBI document provides general concepts, and the MySQL driver document discusses capabilities specific to MySQL.

- **FAQs.** There are frequently-asked-question lists for DBI, PHP, and Apache.

- **Mailing lists.** Several mailing lists centering around the software discussed in this book are available. It's a good idea to subscribe to the ones that deal with the tools you want to use. It's also a good idea to use the archives for those lists that have them. When you're new to a tool, you will have many of the same questions that have been asked (and answered) many times, and there is no reason to ask again when you can find the answer with a quick search of the archives.

    Instructions for subscribing to the mailing lists vary. The following table indicates where you can find the necessary information.

Package	Mailing List Instructions
MySQL	`http://lists.mysql.com`
Perl DBI	`http://dbi.perl.org/support`
PHP	`http://www.php.net/mailing-lists.php`
Apache	`http://httpd.apache.org/lists.html`

- **Ancillary Web sites.** Besides the official Web sites, some of the tools discussed here have ancillary sites that provide more information, such as sample source code or topical articles. Check for a "Links" area on the official site you're visiting.

1

Getting Started with MySQL

This chapter provides an introduction to the MySQL relational database management system (RDBMS), and to the Structured Query Language (SQL) MySQL understands. It lays out basic terms and concepts you should understand, describes the `sampdb` sample database we'll use for examples, and provides a tutorial showing how to use MySQL to create a database and interact with it.

Begin here if you are new to database systems and perhaps uncertain whether you need one or can use one. Also read the chapter if you don't know anything about MySQL or SQL and need an introductory guide to get started. Readers who have experience with MySQL or other database systems might want to skim through the material. However, to become familiar with the purpose and contents of the `sampdb` database used throughout the book, everybody should read Section 1.2, "A Sample Database."

1.1 How MySQL Can Help You

This section describes situations in which the MySQL database system is useful. It will give you an idea of the kinds of things MySQL can do and how it can help you. If you need not be convinced about the usefulness of a database system—perhaps because you've already got a problem in mind and just want to find out how to put MySQL to work helping you solve it—you can proceed to Section 1.2, "A Sample Database."

A database system is essentially a high-powered way to manage lists of information. The information can come from many sources. It might be research data, business records, customer requests, sports statistics, sales reports, personal information, personnel records, bug reports, or student grades.

The power of a database system comes into play when the information you want to organize and manage is so voluminous or complex that your records become more burdensome than you care to deal with by hand. For large corporations processing millions of transactions a day, a database is a necessity. But even small-scale operations comprising a single person might maintain enough information that a database is required to manage it. Consider the following situations:

- You work in a dentist's office in which it's necessary to maintain patient records that track who visited when, what was done, upcoming appointments, insurance information, and so forth.

- That pile of research data you've been collecting over the course of many years needs to be analyzed for publication. You want to boil down large amounts of raw data to generate summary information, and to pull out selected subsets of observations for more detailed statistical analysis.

- You're a teacher who needs to keep track of grades and attendance. Each time you give a quiz or a test, you record every student's grade. It's easy enough to write down scores in a gradebook, but using the scores later is a tedious chore. You'd rather avoid sorting the scores for each test to determine the grading curve, and you'd really rather not add up each student's scores when you determine final grades at the end of the grading period. Counting each student's absences is no fun, either.

- The organization for which you serve as the secretary maintains a directory of members. (The organization could be anything—a professional society, a club, a symphony orchestra, or an athletic booster club.) You generate a printed directory each year for the members, based on a word processor document that you edit as membership information changes. You're tired of maintaining the directory that way because it limits what you can do with it. It's difficult to sort the entries different ways. You can't easily select just certain parts of each entry, such as a list consisting only of names and phone numbers. Nor can you easily find a subset of members, such as those who need to renew their memberships soon. If you could, it would eliminate the job of looking through the entries each month to find those members who need to be sent renewal notices. You've heard about the "paperless office" that's supposed to result from electronic record-keeping, but you haven't seen any benefit from it. The membership records are electronic, but, ironically, aren't in a form that can be used easily for anything *except* generating paper by printing the directory!

These scenarios range from situations involving small to large amounts of information. Their common characteristic is that they involve tasks that could be performed manually but are more efficiently managed using a database system.

What specific benefits should you expect to see from using a database system such as MySQL? It depends on your particular needs and requirements, and as illustrated by the preceding examples, those can vary quite a bit. However, it's commonly the case that database management systems are employed to handle tasks for which people otherwise use filing cabinets. Indeed, a database is like a big filing cabinet with a sophisticated built-in filing system. There are some important advantages of electronically maintained records over records maintained by hand. Consider the dentist's office scenario described earlier. Here are some of the ways MySQL can help you in its filing system capacity to manage patient records:

Reduced record filing time. You need not look through drawers in cabinets to figure out where to add a new record. You hand it to MySQL and it puts the record in the right place for you.

Reduced record retrieval time. When you're looking for records, you need not search each one yourself to find the ones you want. To send out reminders to all patients who haven't come in for their checkup in a while, you ask MySQL to find the appropriate records for you. Of course, you do this differently than if you were talking to another person, with whom you'd say, "Please determine which patients haven't visited within the last six months." Instead, you invoke a strange incantation:

```
SELECT last_name, first_name, last_visit FROM patient
WHERE last_visit < DATE_SUB(CURDATE(), INTERVAL 6 MONTH);
```

That can be pretty intimidating if you've never seen anything like it before, but the prospect of getting results in a second or two rather than spending an hour shuffling through your records should be attractive. In any case, that odd-looking bit of gobbledygook won't look strange for long. You'll understand exactly what it means by the time you've finished this chapter.

Flexible retrieval order. You needn't retrieve records in the order you stored them (by patient's last name, for example). MySQL pulls out records sorted in any order you like: by last name, insurance company name, date of last visit, and so forth.

Flexible output format. After you've found the records in which you're interested, there's no need to copy the information manually. MySQL generates a list for you. Sometimes you might just print the information. Other times you might want to use it in another program. For example, after you generate the list of patients who are overdue on their dental visits, you might feed this information into a word processor that prints out notices that you can send to those patients. Or you might be interested only in summary information, such as a count of the selected records. You need not count them yourself; MySQL generates the summary for you.

Simultaneous multiple-user access to records. With paper records, if two people want to look up a record at the same time, the second person must wait for the first one to put the record back. MySQL gives you multiple-user capability so that both can access the record simultaneously.

Remote access to and electronic transmission of records. Paper records require you to be where the records are located, or for someone to make copies and send them to you. Electronic records open up the potential for remote access to the records or electronic transmission of them. If your dental group has associates in branch offices, those associates can access your records from their own locations. You don't need to send copies by courier. If someone who needs records doesn't have the same kind of database software you do, you can select the desired records and send their contents over the network.

If you've used database management systems before, you already know about the benefits just described, and you may be thinking about how to go beyond the usual "replace the filing cabinet" applications. The way many organizations use a database in conjunction with a Web site is a good example. Suppose that your company has an inventory database used by the service desk staff when customers call to find out whether you have an item in stock and how much it costs. That's a relatively traditional use for a database. However, if your company puts up a Web site for customers to visit, you can provide an additional service: a search page that enables customers to check an item determine pricing, availability, and which stores have it in stock. If you support online ordering, customers need not even leave home to purchase your products. This gives customers the information they want, and the database provides it by searching the inventory information for the items in question—automatically. The customer gets the information immediately, without being put on hold listening to annoying canned music or being limited by the hours your service desk is open. And for every customer who uses your Web site, that's one less phone call that needs to be handled by a person on the service desk payroll. Perhaps the Web site can pay for itself this way.

But you can put the database to even better use than that. Web-based inventory search requests can provide information not only to your customers, but to your company as well. The queries tell you what customers are looking for, and the query results tell you whether you're able to satisfy their requests. To the extent you don't have what they want, you're probably losing business. So it makes sense to record information about inventory searches: what customers were looking for, and whether you had it in stock. Then you can use this information to adjust your inventory and provide better service to your customers.

So how does MySQL work? The best way to find out is to try it for yourself, and for that we'll need a database to work with.

1.2   A Sample Database

This section describes the sample database used in this book. It provides a source of examples for you to try as you learn to put MySQL to work, using two of the situations described earlier:

- The organizational secretary scenario. Our organization has these characteristics: Its members have an affinity for United States history (called, for lack of a better name, the U.S. Historical League). Members renew their membership periodically on a dues-paying basis. Dues go toward League expenses such as publication of a newsletter, "Chronicles of U.S. Past." The League also operates a small Web site; it hasn't been developed very much, but you'd like to change that.

- The grade-keeping scenario. You are a teacher who administers quizzes and tests during the grading period, records scores, and assigns grades. Afterward, you determine final grades and turn them in to the school office along with an attendance summary.

Now let's examine these situations more closely in terms of two requirements:

- You must decide what you want to get out of the database—that is, the goals you want to accomplish.

- You must figure out what you're going to put into the database—that is, what data you will keep track of.

Perhaps it seems backward to think about what comes out of the database before considering what goes in. After all, you must enter your data before you can retrieve it. But the way you use a database is driven by your goals, and those are more closely associated with what you want to get from your database than with what you put into it. You're not going to waste time and effort putting information into a database unless you plan to use it for something later.

1.2.1   The U.S. Historical League Project

The scenario here is that you as League secretary currently maintain the membership list using a word processing document. That works reasonably well for generating a printed directory but limits what else you can do with the information. You have several objectives in mind:

- You want to produce output from the directory in different formats, using information appropriate to the application. One goal is to generate the printed directory each year—a requirement the League has had in the past that you plan to continue to carry out. You can think of other uses for the information in the directory, too—for example, to provide the current-member list for the printed program distributed to attendees of the League's annual meeting. These applications involve different sets of information. The printed directory uses the entire contents of each member's entry. For the meeting program, you need to pull out only member names (something that hasn't been easy using a word processor).

- You want to search the directory for members who satisfy various criteria. For example, you want to know which members must renew their memberships soon. Another search-related application arises from the list of keywords you maintain for each member. These keywords describe areas of U.S. history in which each member is particularly interested (for example, the Civil War, the Depression, civil rights, or the life of Thomas Jefferson). Members sometimes ask you for a list of other members with interests similar to their own, and you'd like to be able to satisfy these requests.

- You want to put the directory online at the League's Web site. This would benefit both the members and yourself. If you can convert the directory to Web pages by some reasonably automated process, an online version of the directory would be always up to date, something not true of the printed version. And if the online directory were searchable, members could easily look for information themselves. For example, a member who wants to know which other members are interested in the Civil War could find that out without waiting for you to perform the search, and you wouldn't need to find the time to do it yourself.

Databases are not the most exciting things in the world, so I'm not about to make any wild claims that using one stimulates creative thinking. Nevertheless, when you stop thinking of information as something you must wrestle with (as you do when using your word processing document) and begin thinking of it as something you can manipulate relatively easily (as you hope to do with MySQL), it has a certain liberating effect on your ability to come up with new ways to use that information:

- If the information in the database can be moved to the Web site in the form of an online directory, you might also be able to make information flow the other way. Suppose that members could edit their own entries online to provide updates for the database. Then you wouldn't have to do all the editing yourself, and it would make the information in the directory more accurate.

- If you store email addresses in the database, you could use them to send email to members that haven't updated their entries in a while. The messages could show members the current contents of their entry, ask them to review it, and indicate how to make any needed modifications using the facilities provided on the Web site.

- A database might help make the Web site more useful in ways not even related to the membership list. The League's newsletter, "Chronicles of U.S. Past," has a children's section containing a history-based quiz in each issue. Some of the recent issues have focused on biographical facts about U.S. presidents. The Web site could have a children's section, too, where the quizzes are put online. Perhaps this section could even be made interactive, by putting the information from which quizzes are drawn in the database and having the Web server query the database for questions to present to visitors.

Well! At this point the number of uses for the database that you're coming up with make you realize you might be getting a little carried away. After pausing to come back down to earth, you start asking some practical questions:

- Isn't this a little ambitious? Won't it be a lot of work to set this up?

  Anything's easier when you're just thinking about it and not doing it, of course, and these ideas are not trivial to implement. Nevertheless, by the end of this book you'll have done everything we've just outlined. Just keep in mind that it's not necessary to do everything all at once. Break the job into pieces and tackle it a piece at a time.

- Can MySQL be used to accomplish all these goals?

  No, it can't, at least not by itself. For example, MySQL has no built-in Web-programming facilities. But you can combine MySQL with other tools that work with it to complement and extend its capabilities.

  We'll use the Perl scripting language and the Perl DBI (database interface) module to write scripts that access MySQL databases. Perl has excellent text-processing capabilities, which enables manipulation of query results in a highly flexible manner to produce output in a variety of formats. For example, we can use Perl to generate the directory in Rich Text Format (RTF), which can be read by all kinds of word processors, and in HTML format for Web browsers.

  We'll also use PHP, another scripting language. PHP is particularly adapted to writing Web applications, and it interfaces easily with databases. This enables you to initiate MySQL queries from Web pages and to generate new pages that include the results of database queries. PHP can be used with several Web servers (including Apache, the most popular server in the world), making it easy to do things such as presenting a search form and displaying the results of the search.

MySQL integrates well with these tools and gives you the flexibility to choose how to combine them to achieve the ends you have in mind. You're not locked into some all-in-one suite's components that have highly touted "integration" capabilities but that actually work well only with each other.

- And, finally, the big question: How much will all this cost? The League has a limited budget, after all.

  This might surprise you, but it probably won't cost anything. If you're familiar at all with database systems, you know that they're generally pretty pricey. By contrast, MySQL often can be used for free. Even in enterprise settings where you need guaranteed support and maintenance arrangements, MySQL is relatively inexpensive as database systems go. (Visit www.mysql.com for details.) The other tools we'll use (Perl, DBI, PHP, Apache) are free, so, all things considered, you can put together a useful system quite inexpensively.

The choice of operating system for developing the database is up to you. Virtually all the software we'll discuss runs under both Unix (which I use as an umbrella term that includes BSD Unix, Linux, Mac OS X, and so forth) and Windows. The few exceptions tend to be shell or batch scripts that are specific to either Unix or Windows.

1.2.2   The Grade-Keeping Project

Now let's consider the other situation for which we'll use the sample database. The scenario here is that you are a teacher, with grade-keeping responsibilities. You want to convert the grading process from a manual operation using a gradebook to an electronic representation using MySQL. In this case, the information you want to get from a database is implicit in the way you already use your gradebook now:

- For each quiz or test, you record the scores. For tests, you order the scores so that you can look at them and determine the cutoffs for each letter grade (A, B, C, D, and F).

- At the end of the grading period, you calculate each student's total score, sort the totals, and determine grades based on them. The totals might involve weighted calculations because you probably want to count tests more heavily than quizzes.

- You provide attendance information to the school office at the end of the grading period.

The objectives are to avoid manually sorting and summarizing scores and attendance records. In other words, you want MySQL to sort the scores and perform the calculations necessary to compute each student's total score and number of absences when the grading period ends. To accomplish these goals, you'll need the list of students in the class, the scores for each quiz and test, and the dates on which students are absent.

1.2.3   How the Sample Database Applies to You

If you're not particularly interested in the Historical League or in grade-keeping, you might be wondering what either scenario has to do with you. The answer is that they aren't an end in themselves. Rather, they illustrate what you can do with MySQL and tools that are related to it.

With a little imagination, you'll see how example database queries apply to the particular problems you want to solve. Suppose that you're working in that dentist's office I mentioned earlier. You won't see many dentistry-related queries in this book, but you will see that many of the queries you find here apply to patient record maintenance, office bookkeeping, and so forth. For example, determining which Historical League members need to renew their memberships soon is similar to determining which patients haven't visited the dentist for a while. Both are date-based queries, so once you learn to write the membership-renewal query, you can apply that skill to writing the delinquent-patient query in which you have a more immediate interest.

1.3   Basic Database Terminology

You may have noticed that, although this is a database book, you still haven't seen a whole bunch of jargon and technical terminology. In fact, I still haven't said anything at all about what "a database" actually looks like, even though we have a rough specification of how our sample database will be used. However, we're about to design that database, and then we'll begin implementing it, so we can't avoid terminology any longer. That's what this section is about. It describes some terms that come up throughout the book so you'll be familiar with them. Fortunately, many relational database concepts are really quite simple. Much of the appeal of relational databases stems precisely from the simplicity of their foundational concepts.

1.3.1   Structural Terminology

Within the database world, MySQL is classified as a relational database management system, or RDBMS. Let's break that down:

The database (the "DB" in RDBMS) is the repository for the information you store, structured in a simple, regular fashion:

- The collection of data in a database is organized into tables.
- Each table is organized into rows and columns.
- Each row in a table is a record.
- Records can contain several pieces of information; each column in a table corresponds to one of those pieces.

The management system (the "MS") is the software that lets you use your data by enabling you to insert, retrieve, modify, or delete records.

The word "relational" (the "R") indicates a particular kind of DBMS, one that is very good at relating (that is, matching) information stored in one table to information stored in another by looking for elements common to each of them. The power of a relational DBMS lies in its capability to pull data from those tables conveniently and to join information from related tables to produce answers to questions that can't be answered from individual tables alone. (Actually, "relational" has a formal definition that differs from the way I am using it. However, with apologies to purists, I find that my definition is more helpful for conveying the usefulness of an RDBMS.)

Here's an example that shows how a relational database organizes data into tables and relates the information from one table to another. Suppose that you run a Web site that includes a banner-advertisement service. You contract with companies that want their ads displayed when people visit the pages on your site. Each time a visitor hits one of your pages, you serve an ad embedded in the page that is sent to the visitor's browser and assess the company a small fee. This is a "hit" for the ad. To represent this information, you maintain three tables (see Figure 1.1). One table, company, has columns for company name, number, address, and telephone number. Another table, ad, lists ad numbers, the number for the company that "owns" the ad, and the amount you charge per hit. The third table, hit, logs each ad hit by ad number and the date on which the ad was served.

Some questions can be answered using the information in a single table. To determine the number of companies you have contracts with, you need count only the rows in the company table. Similarly, to determine the number of hits during a given time period, only the hit table need be examined. Other questions are more complex, and it's necessary to consult multiple tables to determine the answers. For example, to determine how many times each of the ads for Pickles, Inc. was served on July 14, you'd use all three tables as follows:

1. Look up the company name (Pickles, Inc.) in the company table to find the company number (14).

2. Use the company number to find matching rows in the ad table so you can determine the associated ad numbers. There are two such ads: 48 and 101.

3. For each of the matched rows in the ad table, use the ad number in the row to find matching rows in the hit table that fall within the desired date range; then count the number of matches. There are three matches for ad 48 and two matches for ad 101.

Sounds complicated! But that's just the kind of thing at which relational database systems excel. The complexity actually is somewhat illusory because each of the steps just described amounts to little more than a simple matching operation: Relate one table to another by matching values from one table's rows to values in another table's rows. This same simple operation can be exploited in various ways to answer all kinds of questions: How many different ads does each company have? Which company's ads are most popular? How much revenue does each ad generate? What is the total fee for each company for the current billing period?

Now you know enough relational database theory to understand the rest of this book, and we don't have to go into Third Normal Form, Entity-Relationship Diagrams, and all that kind of stuff. (If you want to read about such things, I suggest you begin with the works of C.J. Date or E.F. Codd.)

company table

company_name	company_num	address	phone
Big deal, Ltd.	13	14 Grand Blvd.	875-2934
Pickles, Inc.	14	59 Cucumber Dr.	884-2472
Real Roofing Co.	17	928 Shingles Rd.	882-4173
GigaFred & Son	23	2572 Family Ave.	847-4738

ad table

company_num	ad_num	hit_fee
14	48	0.01
23	49	0.02
17	52	0.01
13	55	0.03
23	62	0.02
23	63	0.01
23	64	0.02
13	77	0.03
23	99	0.03
14	101	0.01
13	102	0.01
17	119	0.02

hit table

ad_num	date
49	July 13
55	July 13
48	July 14
63	July 14
101	July 14
62	July 14
119	July 14
102	July 14
52	July 14
48	July 14
64	July 14
119	July 14
48	July 14
101	July 14
63	July 15
49	July 15
77	July 15
99	July 15

Figure 1.1   Banner advertisement tables.

1.3.2   Query Language Terminology

Communication with MySQL takes place using SQL (Structured Query Language). All major database systems understand SQL, although each implementation has vendor-specific aspects. SQL supports many different statements, which makes it possible to interact with your database in interesting and useful ways.

As with any language, SQL can seem strange while you're first learning it. For example, to create a table, you tell MySQL what the table's structure should be. You and I might think of the table in terms of a diagram or picture. MySQL doesn't, so you create the table by telling MySQL something like this:

```
CREATE TABLE company
(
  company_name  VARCHAR(30),
  company_num   INT,
  address       VARCHAR(30),
  phone         VARCHAR(12)
);
```

Statements like that can be somewhat imposing when you're new to SQL, but you need not be a programmer to learn how to use SQL effectively. As you gain familiarity with the language, you'll look at CREATE TABLE in a different light—as a powerful ally that helps you describe your information, not as a weird bit of gibberish.

1.3.3 MySQL Architectural Terminology

When you use MySQL, you're actually using at least two programs, because MySQL operates using a client/server architecture. One program is the MySQL server, mysqld. The server runs on the machine where your databases are stored. It listens for client requests coming in over the network and accesses database contents according to those requests to provide clients with the information they ask for. The other programs are client programs; they connect to the database server and issue queries to tell it what information they want.

Most MySQL distributions include the database server and several client programs. (If you use RPM packages on Linux, there are separate server and client RPM packages, so you should install both.) Use the client programs according to the purposes you want to achieve. The one most commonly used is mysql, an interactive program that lets you issue queries and see the results. Two administrative clients are mysqldump, a backup program that dumps table contents into a file, and mysqladmin, which enables you to check on the status of the server and performs other administrative tasks such as telling the server to shut down. MySQL distributions include other clients as well. If you have application requirements for which none of the standard clients is suited, MySQL also provides a client-programming library so that you can write your own programs. The library is usable directly from C programs. If you prefer a language other than C, interfaces are available for several other languages—Perl, PHP, Python, Java, and Ruby, to name some.

The client programs I discuss in this book all are used from the command line. If you'd like to try MySQL Workbench, a tool that provides a graphical user interface (GUI) and point-and-click capabilities, visit http://www.mysql.com/products/tools.

MySQL's client/server architecture has certain benefits:

- The server enforces concurrency control to prevent two users from modifying the same record at the same time. All client requests go through the server, so the server sorts out who gets to do what, and when. If multiple clients want to access the same table at the same time, they need not find and negotiate with each other. They send their requests to the server and it determines the order in which it performs them.

- You need not be logged in on the machine where your database is located. MySQL works in a networked environment, so you can run a client program from wherever you happen to be, and the client can connect to the server over the network. Distance isn't a factor; you can access the server from anywhere in the world. If the server is located on a computer in Australia, you can take your laptop computer on a trip to Iceland and still access your database. Does that mean anyone can get at your data, just by connecting to the Internet? No. MySQL includes a flexible security system, so you can permit access only to people who should have it. And you can make sure that those people are able to do only what they should. Perhaps Sally in the billing office should be able to read and update (modify) records, but Phil at the service desk should be able only to look at them. You can set each person's privileges accordingly. If you do want to run a self-contained system, set the access privileges so that clients can connect only from the host on which the server is running.

The Difference Between "MySQL" and "mysql"

To avoid confusion, I should point out that "MySQL" refers to the entire MySQL RDBMS, and "mysql" is the name of a particular client program. They sound the same if you pronounce them, but they're distinguished here by capitalization and typeface differences.

Speaking of pronunciation, MySQL is pronounced "my-ess-queue-ell." We know this because the MySQL Reference Manual says so. On the other hand, depending on who you ask, SQL is pronounced "ess-queue-ell" or "sequel." This book assumes the pronunciation "ess-queue-ell," which is why it uses constructs such as "an SQL query" rather than "a SQL query."

1.4   A MySQL Tutorial

You have all the background you need now. It's time to put MySQL to work!

This section helps you familiarize yourself with MySQL by providing a tutorial with examples. You'll create a sample database and some tables, then interact with the database by adding, retrieving, deleting, and modifying information in the tables. During this process, you'll learn the following things:

- The basics of the SQL language that MySQL understands. (If you already know SQL from having used some other RDBMS, it is a good idea to skim through this tutorial to see whether MySQL's dialect of SQL differs from the version with which you are familiar.)

- How to communicate with a MySQL server using a few of the standard MySQL client programs. As noted in the previous section, MySQL operates using a client/server architecture in which the server runs on the machine containing the databases and clients connect to the server over a network. This tutorial is based largely on the mysql client program, which reads SQL queries from you, sends them to the server to be executed, and displays the results so that you can see what happened. `mysql` runs on all platforms supported by MySQL and provides the most direct means of interacting with the server, so it's the logical client to begin with. Some examples use `mysqlimport` or `mysqlshow` instead.

This book uses `sampdb` as the sample database name. You might need to use a different name if someone else on your system is already using that name for their own database, or your MySQL administrator assigns you a different database name. In either case, substitute the actual name of your database whenever you see `sampdb` in examples.

Table names can be used exactly as shown in the examples, even if multiple users on your system have their own sample databases. In MySQL, it doesn't matter if other people use the same table names, as long as each of you uses your own database. MySQL prevents you from interfering with each other by keeping the tables in each database separate.

1.4.1 Obtaining the Sample Database Distribution

This tutorial refers at several points to files from the "sample database distribution" (also known as the `sampdb` distribution, after the name of the `sampdb` database). These files contain queries and data that enable you to set up the sample database. For instructions on getting the distribution, see Appendix A, "Software Required to Use This Book." When you unpack the distribution, it creates a directory named `sampdb` containing the files you'll need. I recommend that you change location into that directory whenever you're working through examples pertaining to the sample database.

To make it easier to invoke MySQL programs no matter which directory is your current location, you should add the MySQL `bin` directory that contains those programs to your command interpreter's search path. To do this, add the directory pathname to your `PATH` environment variable setting using the instructions in Section A.3.3, "Setting Your `PATH` Environment Variable."

1.4.2 Preliminary Requirements

In addition to obtaining the sample database distribution, you must satisfy a few other preliminary requirements to try the examples in this tutorial:

- You must have the MySQL software installed.
- You need a MySQL account so you can connect to the server.
- You need a database to work with.

The required software includes the MySQL clients and a MySQL server. The client programs must be located on the machine where you'll be working. The server can be located on your machine, although that is not required. As long as you have permission to connect to it, the server can be located anywhere. If your Internet service provider offers MySQL as a service, you can use MySQL that way. If you want to get MySQL and install it yourself, see Appendix A, "Software Required to Use This Book."

In addition to the MySQL software, you'll need a MySQL account so the server will permit you to connect and create your sample database and its tables. (If you already have a MySQL account with the server, you can use that, but you might want to set up a separate account for use with the material in this book.)

At this point, we run into something of a chicken-and-egg problem: To set up a MySQL account to use for connecting to the server, it's necessary to connect to the server. Typically, you do this by connecting as the MySQL root user on the host where the server is running and issuing CREATE USER and GRANT statements to create a new MySQL account and give it database privileges. If you've installed MySQL on your own machine and the server is running, you can connect to it as root and set up a new sample database administrator account with a username of sampadm and a password of secret as follows. Change the name and password to those you want to use, here and throughout the book.

```
% mysql -p -u root
Enter password: ******
mysql> CREATE USER 'sampadm'@'localhost' IDENTIFIED BY 'secret';
Query OK, 0 rows affected (0.04 sec)
mysql> GRANT ALL ON sampdb.* TO 'sampadm'@'localhost';
Query OK, 0 rows affected (0.01 sec)
```

The mysql command includes a -p option to cause mysql to prompt for the root user's MySQL password. Enter the password where you see ****** in the example. I assume that you have already set up a password for the MySQL root user and that you know what it is. If you haven't yet assigned a password, just press Enter at the Enter password: prompt. However, having no root password is insecure and you should assign one as soon as possible. For more information on the CREATE USER and GRANT statements, setting up MySQL user accounts, and changing passwords, see Chapter 13, "Security and Access Control."

After creating the sampadm account, type quit and press Enter to exit the mysql program.

The statements just shown are appropriate for connecting to MySQL from the same machine where the server is running. They enable you to connect to the server with the username sampadm and the password secret, and give you complete access to the sampdb database. However, GRANT doesn't create the database (you can grant privileges for a database before it exists). We'll get to database creation a bit later.

If you plan to connect to the MySQL server from a host different from the one where the server is running, change localhost to the name of the machine where you'll be working. For example, if you will connect to the server from the host boa.example.com, the statements should look like this:

```
mysql> CREATE USER 'sampadm'@'boa.example.com' IDENTIFIED BY 'secret';
mysql> GRANT ALL ON sampdb.* TO 'sampadm'@'boa.example.com';
```

If you don't have control over the server and cannot create an account, ask your MySQL administrator to set up an account for you. Then substitute the MySQL username, password, and database name that the administrator assigns you for sampadm, secret, and sampdb throughout the examples in this book.

1.4.3 Establishing and Terminating Connections to the MySQL Server

To connect to your server, invoke the `mysql` program from your command prompt (that is, from your Unix shell prompt, or from a console window prompt under Windows). The command looks like this:

```
% mysql options
```

Throughout this book, I use % to indicate the command prompt. That's one of the standard Unix prompts; another is $. Under Windows, you will see a prompt that looks something like `C:\>`. When you enter commands shown in examples, don't type the prompt itself.

The *options* part of the `mysql` command line might be empty, but more likely you'll have to issue a command that looks something like this:

```
% mysql -h host_name -p -u user_name
```

You might not need to supply all those options when you invoke `mysql`, but you'll probably have to specify at least a name and password. Here's what the options mean:

- `-h` *host_name* (alternative form: `--host=host_name`)

  The host where the MySQL server is running. If this is the same as the machine where you are running `mysql`, this option typically can be omitted.

- `-u` *user_name* (alternative form: `--user=user_name`)

  Your MySQL username. If you're using Unix and your MySQL username is the same as your login name, you can omit this option; `mysql` will use your login name as your MySQL username.

  Under Windows, the default username is ODBC, which is unlikely to be useful. Either specify a `-u` option on the command line, or add a default to your environment by setting the USER variable. For example, you can use the following `set` command to specify a username of `sampadm`:

  ```
  C:\> set USER=sampadm
  ```

  If you set the USER environment variable by using the System item in the Control Panel, it takes effect for each console window and you won't have to issue it at the prompt.

- `-p` (alternative form: `--password`)

  This option tells `mysql` to ask for your MySQL password by displaying an `Enter password:` prompt. For example:

  ```
  % mysql -h host_name -p -u user_name
  Enter password:
  ```

  When you see the `Enter password:` prompt, type in your password. (The password won't be echoed to the screen, in case someone's looking over your shoulder.) Note that your MySQL password is not necessarily the same password that you use to log in to Unix or Windows.

If you omit the -p option, mysql. assumes that you don't need one and doesn't prompt for it.

Another way to specify this option is to indicate the password value directly on the command line by typing the option as -p*your_pass* (alternative form: --password=*your_pass*). However, for security reasons, it's best to avoid that. The password is visible as you type it to others who can see your screen. Also, on Unix systems, other users might be able to use system tools to see the command line.

If you do decide to specify the password on the command line, there is *no space* between the -p option and the following password value. This behavior of -p is a common point of confusion, because it differs from the -h and -u options, which are associated with the word that follows them regardless of whether there is a space between the option and the word.

Suppose that your MySQL username and password are sampadm and secret. If the MySQL server is running on the same host where you are going to run mysql, you can leave out the -h option, and the mysql command to connect to the server looks like this:

```
% mysql -p -u sampadm
Enter password: ******
```

After you enter the command, mysql prints Enter password: to prompt for your password, and you type it in (the ****** indicates where you type secret).

If all goes well, mysql prints a greeting and a mysql> prompt indicating that it is waiting for you to issue queries. The full startup sequence looks something like this:

```
% mysql -p -u sampadm
Enter password: ******
Welcome to the MySQL monitor.  Commands end with ; or \g.
Your MySQL connection id is 13762
Server version: 5.5.30-log

Type 'help;' or '\h' for help. Type '\c' to clear the current input statement.

mysql>
```

To connect to a server running on some other machine, it's necessary to specify the hostname using an -h option. If that host is cobra.example.com, the command looks like this:

```
% mysql -h cobra.example.com -p -u sampadm
```

In most of the examples that follow that show a mysql command line, I'll omit out the -h, -u, and -p options for brevity and assume that you'll supply whatever options are necessary. You'll also need to use those options when you run other MySQL programs, such as mysqlshow.

After you've established a connection to the server, you can terminate your session any time by typing quit:

```
mysql> quit
Bye
```

You can also quit by typing `exit` or `\q`. On Unix, Control-D also quits.

When you're just starting to learn MySQL, you'll probably consider its security system to be an annoyance because it makes it harder to do what you want. (You must have permission to create and access a database, and you must specify your name and password whenever you connect to the server.) However, after you've moved beyond the sample database used in this book to entering and using your own records, your perspective will change radically. Then you'll appreciate the way that MySQL keeps other people from snooping through (or worse, destroying!) your information.

To find out how to set up your working environment so you need not specify connection parameters on the command line each time you run `mysql`, see Section 1.5, "Tips for Interacting with `mysql`." The most common way to simplify the connection process is to store your connection parameters in an option file. You might want to check that section right now to see how to set up such a file.

1.4.4 Executing SQL Statements

After you connect to the server, you can issue SQL statements for it to execute. This section describes some useful general principles about interacting with `mysql`.

To enter a statement in `mysql`, just type it in. At the end of the statement, type a semicolon character ('`;`') and press Enter. The semicolon tells `mysql` that the statement is complete. After you enter a statement, `mysql` sends it to the server to be executed. The server processes it and sends the result back to `mysql`, which displays the result to you.

The following example shows a simple statement that asks for the current date and time:

```
mysql> SELECT NOW();
+---------------------+
| NOW()               |
+---------------------+
| 2013-01-08 17:42:33 |
+---------------------+
1 row in set (0.00 sec)
```

Another way to terminate a statement is to use `\g` ("go") rather than a semicolon:

```
mysql> SELECT NOW()\g
+---------------------+
| NOW()               |
+---------------------+
| 2013-01-08 17:42:40 |
+---------------------+
1 row in set (0.00 sec)
```

Or you can use `\G`, which displays the results in "vertical" format, one value per line:

```
mysql> SELECT NOW(), USER(), VERSION()\G
*************************** 1. row ***************************
    NOW(): 2013-01-08 17:54:24
   USER(): sampadm@localhost
VERSION(): 5.5.30-log
1 row in set (0.00 sec)
```

For a statement that generates short output lines, \G is not so useful, but if the lines are so long that they wrap around on your screen, \G can make the output much easier to read.

mysql displays the statement result and a line that shows the number of rows the result consists of and the time elapsed during statement processing. In subsequent examples, I usually will not show the row-count line.

Because mysql waits for the statement terminator, you need not enter a statement all on a single line. You can spread it over several lines if you want:

```
mysql> SELECT NOW(),
    -> USER(),
    -> VERSION()
    -> ;
+---------------------+-------------------+------------+
| NOW()               | USER()            | VERSION()  |
+---------------------+-------------------+------------+
| 2013-01-08 17:54:56 | sampadm@localhost | 5.5.30-log |
+---------------------+-------------------+------------+
```

Observe how the prompt changes from mysql> to -> after you enter the first line of the statement. That tells you that mysql thinks you're still entering the statement, which is important feedback: If you forget the semicolon at the end of a statement, the changed prompt helps you realize that mysql is still waiting patiently for you to finish entering your statement. Otherwise, you'll be waiting impatiently, wondering why it's taking MySQL so long to execute your statement! mysql has several other prompts as well; they're all discussed in Appendix F, "MySQL Program Reference."

If you've begun entering a multiple-line statement and decide that you don't want to execute it, type \c to clear (cancel) it:

```
mysql> SELECT NOW(),
    -> VERSION(),
    -> \c
mysql>
```

Notice how the prompt changes back to mysql> to indicate that mysql is ready for a new statement.

The converse of entering a statement over several lines is to enter multiple statements on a single line, separated by terminators:

```
mysql> SELECT NOW();SELECT USER();SELECT VERSION();
+---------------------+
| NOW()               |
+---------------------+
| 2013-01-08 17:55:20 |
+---------------------+
+-------------------+
| USER()            |
+-------------------+
| sampadm@localhost |
+-------------------+
+------------+
| VERSION()  |
+------------+
| 5.5.30-log |
+------------+
```

For the most part, it doesn't matter whether you enter statements using uppercase, lowercase, or mixed case. These statements all retrieve the same information (although the column headings displayed for the results will differ in lettercase):

```
SELECT USER();
select user();
SeLeCt UsEr();
```

Examples in this book use uppercase for SQL keywords and function names, and lowercase for database, table, and column names.

When you invoke a function in a statement, write it with no space between the function name and the following parenthesis. A space may cause a syntax error to occur.

You can store statements in a file to create an SQL script, then tell `mysql` to read statements from the file rather than from the keyboard. Use your shell's input redirection facilities for this. For example, if I have statements stored in a file named `myscript.sql`, I can execute its contents with this command (remember to specify any required connection parameter options):

```
% mysql < myscript.sql
```

You can call the file whatever you want. I use the `.sql` suffix to indicate that the file contains SQL statements.

Invoking `mysql` this way to execute statements in a file is something that comes up again in Section 1.4.7, "Adding New Rows," when we enter data into the `sampdb` database. It's a lot more convenient to load a table by having `mysql` read `INSERT` statements from a file than to type in each statement manually.

The remainder of this tutorial shows many SQL statements you can try for yourself. These are indicated by the `mysql>` prompt before the statement, and such examples usually are accompanied by the output of the statement. You should be able to type in these statements as shown, and the resulting output should be the same. Statements that are shown without a prompt are intended simply to illustrate a point. You need not execute them, although of course you can if you like. Remember to include a terminator such as a semicolon at the end of each statement.

1.4.5   Creating a Database

Using a database involves several steps:

1. Creating the database
2. Creating the tables within the database
3. Manipulating the tables by inserting, retrieving, modifying, or deleting data

To create a new database, connect to the server using `mysql`. Then issue a CREATE DATABASE statement that specifies the database name:

```
mysql> CREATE DATABASE sampdb;
```

You must create the `sampdb` database before you can create any of the tables that will go in it or do anything with the contents of those tables.

You might expect that creating the database would also make it the default (or current) database, but that is not true. You can see this by executing the following statement to check what the default database is:

```
mysql> SELECT DATABASE();
+------------+
| DATABASE() |
+------------+
| NULL       |
+------------+
```

`NULL` means "no database is selected." To select `sampdb` as the default database, issue a USE statement:

```
mysql> USE sampdb;
mysql> SELECT DATABASE();
+------------+
| DATABASE() |
+------------+
| sampdb     |
+------------+
```

Another way to select a default database is to name it on the command line when you invoke `mysql`:

```
% mysql sampdb
```

That is, in fact, the usual way to select the database you want to use. If you need any connection parameters, specify them on the command line. For example, the following command enables the `sampadm` user to connect to the `sampdb` database on the local host (the default when no host is named):

```
% mysql -p -u sampadm sampdb
```

To connect to a MySQL server running on a remote host, specify that host on the command line:

```
% mysql -h cobra.example.com -p -u sampadm sampdb
```

Unless otherwise indicated, all the following examples assume that when you invoke `mysql`, you name the `sampdb` database on the command line to make it the default database. If you invoke `mysql` but forget to name the database on the command line, just issue a `USE sampdb` statement at the `mysql>` prompt.

1.4.6   Creating Tables

In this section, we'll build the tables needed for the `sampdb` sample database. First, we'll consider the tables needed for the Historical League, then those for the grade-keeping project. This is the part where some database books start talking about Analysis and Design, Entity-Relationship Diagrams, Normalization Procedures, and other such stuff. There's a place for all that, but I prefer just to say we need to think a bit about what our database will look like: what tables it should contain, what the contents of each table should be, and issues involved in deciding how to represent the data.

The choices made here about data representation are not absolute. In other situations, you might well elect to represent similar data in a different way, depending on the requirements of your applications and the uses to which you intend to put your data.

1.4.6.1   Tables for the U.S. Historical League

Table layout for the Historical League is pretty straightforward:

- A `president` table. This contains a descriptive record for each U.S. president. We'll need this for the online quiz on the League Web site (the interactive analog to the printed quiz that appears in the children's section of the League's newsletter).

- A `member` table. This is used to maintain current information about each member of the League. It'll be used for creating printed and online versions of the member directory, sending automated membership renewal reminders, and so forth.

1.4.6.1.1   The `president` Table

The `president` table will contain some basic biographical information about each United States president:

- **Name.** Names can be represented in a table several ways, such as a single column containing the entire name, or separate columns for the first and last name. It's simpler to use a single column, but that limits your flexibility:

    - If you enter the names with the first name first, you can't sort on last name.

    - If you enter the names with the last name first, you can't display them with the first name first.

    - It's harder to search for names. For example, to search for a particular last name, you must use a pattern and look for names that match the pattern. This is less efficient and slower than looking for an exact last name.

    To avoid these limitations, our `president` table will use separate columns for the first and last names.

    The first name column will also hold the middle name or initial. This shouldn't break any sorting we might do because it's not likely we'll want to sort on middle name (or even first name). Name display should work properly, too, because the middle name immediately follows the first name regardless of whether a name is printed in "Bush, George W." or in "George W. Bush" format.

    There is another slight complication. One president (Jimmy Carter) has a "Jr." at the end of his name. Where does that go? Depending on the format in which names are printed, this president's name is displayed as "James E. Carter, Jr.," or "Carter, James E., Jr." The "Jr." doesn't associate with either first or last name, so we'll create another column to hold a name suffix. This illustrates how even a single value can cause problems when you're trying to determine how to represent your data. It also shows why it's a good idea to know as much as possible about the data values you'll be working with before you put them in a database. If you have incomplete knowledge of what your values look like, you might have to change your table structure after you've already begun to use it. That's not necessarily a disaster, but in general it's something you want to avoid.

- **Birthplace (city and state).** Like the name, this too can be represented using a single column or multiple columns. It's simpler to use a single column, but as with the name, separate columns enable some operations not easily done otherwise. For example, it's easier to find rows for presidents born in a particular state if city and state are listed separately. We'll use separate columns for the two values.

- **Birth date and death date.** The only special problem here is that we can't require the death date to be filled in because some presidents are still living. The special value `NULL` means "no value," so we can use that in the death date column to signify "still alive."

1.4.6.1.2 The `member` Table

The `member` table for the Historical League membership list is similar to the `president` table in the sense that each row contains basic descriptive information for a single person. But each `member` row contains more columns:

- **Name.** We'll use the same three-column representation as for the `president` table: last name, first name, and suffix.

- **ID number.** This is a unique value assigned to each member when membership first begins. The League hasn't ever used ID numbers before, but now that the records are being made more systematic, it's a good time to start. (I am anticipating that you'll find MySQL beneficial and that you'll think of other ways to apply it to the League's records. When that happens, it'll be easier to associate rows in the `member` table with other member-related tables that you create if you use numbers rather than names.)

- **Expiration date.** Members must renew their memberships periodically to avoid having them lapse. For some applications, you might store the start date of the most recent renewal, but this is not suitable for the League's purposes. Memberships can be renewed for a variable number of years (typically one, two, three, or five years), and a date for the most recent renewal wouldn't tell you when the next renewal must take place. Therefore, we will store the end date of the membership. In addition, the League offers lifetime memberships. We could represent these with a date far in the future, but NULL seems more appropriate because "no value" logically corresponds to "never expires."

- **Email address.** Publishing email addresses will make it easier for those members that have them to communicate with each other more easily. For your purposes as League secretary, these addresses will enable you to send out membership renewal notices electronically rather than by postal mail. This should be easier than going to the post office, and less expensive as well. You'll also be able to use email to send members the current contents of their directory entries and ask them to update the information as necessary.

- **Postal address.** This is needed for contacting members who don't have email (or who don't respond to it). We'll use columns for street address, city, state, and ZIP code.

  I'm assuming that all League members live in the United States. For organizations with a membership that is international in scope, that assumption is an oversimplification. If you want to deal with addresses from multiple countries, you'll run into some sticky issues having to do with the different address formats used for different countries. For example, ZIP code is not an international standard, and some countries have provinces rather than states.

- **Phone number.** Like the address columns, this is useful for contacting members.

- **Special interest keywords.** Every member is assumed to have a general interest in U.S. history, but members probably also have some special areas of interest. This column records those interests. Members can use it to find other members with similar interests. (Strictly speaking, it would be better to have a separate table for keywords where each row consists of one keyword and the ID of the associated member. That is a complication we won't deal with.)

1.4.6.1.3   Creating the Historical League Tables

Now we're ready to create the Historical League tables. To do this, use the CREATE TABLE statement, which has the following general form:

```
CREATE TABLE tbl_name (column_specs);
```

`tbl_name` indicates the name you want to give the table, and `column_specs` provides the specifications for its columns. The statement also includes definitions for indexes, if there are any. Indexes make lookups faster; we'll discuss them further in Chapter 5, "Query Optimization."

For the `president` table, write the CREATE TABLE statement as follows:

```
CREATE TABLE president
(
  last_name   VARCHAR(15) NOT NULL,
  first_name  VARCHAR(15) NOT NULL,
  suffix      VARCHAR(5) NULL,
  city        VARCHAR(20) NOT NULL,
  state       VARCHAR(2) NOT NULL,
  birth       DATE NOT NULL,
  death       DATE NULL
);
```

You can execute this statement a couple of ways. Either enter it manually by typing it in, or use the prewritten statement that is contained in the create_president.sql file of the sampdb distribution.

To type in the statement yourself, invoke `mysql`, making `sampdb` the default database:

```
% mysql sampdb
```

Then enter the CREATE TABLE statement as just shown, including the trailing semicolon so `mysql` can tell where the statement ends. Indentation doesn't matter, and you need not put the line breaks in the same places. You can even enter the statement as one long line if you like.

To create the `president` table from a prewritten description, use the create_president.sql file from the `sampdb` distribution. This file is located in the `sampdb` directory created when you unpacked the distribution. Change location into that directory, then run this command:

```
% mysql sampdb < create_president.sql
```

Whichever way you invoke `mysql`, specify any connection parameters you might need (hostname, username, or password) on the command line following the command name.

Now let's look more closely at the CREATE TABLE statement. Each column specification in the statement consists of a column name, a data type (the kind of values the column will hold), and possibly some column attributes.

The two data types used in the `president` table are VARCHAR and DATE. VARCHAR(n) means the column contains variable-length character values, with a maximum length of n characters each. That is, they contain strings that might vary in size, but with an upper bound on their length. The value of n indicates how long you expect your values to be. state is defined as VARCHAR(2); that's all we need for entering states by their two-character abbreviations. The other string-valued columns must be longer to accommodate longer values.

The other data type we've used is DATE. This type indicates, not surprisingly, that the column holds date values. However, what might surprise you is the format in which dates are represented. MySQL expects dates to be written in 'CCYY-MM-DD' format, where CC, YY, MM, and DD represent the century, year within the century, month, and day of the month. This is the SQL standard for date representation (also known as "ISO 8601 format"). For example, to specify a date of "July 18, 2013" in MySQL, you use '2013-07-18', not '07-18-2013' or '18-07-2013'.

The only attributes we're using for the columns in the president table are NULL (values can be missing) and NOT NULL (values must be filled in). Most columns are NOT NULL, because we'll always require a value for them. The two columns that can have NULL values are suffix (most names don't have one), and death (for living presidents, there is no date of death).

For the member table, the CREATE TABLE statement looks like this:

```
CREATE TABLE member
(
  member_id   INT UNSIGNED NOT NULL AUTO_INCREMENT,
  PRIMARY KEY (member_id),
  last_name   VARCHAR(20) NOT NULL,
  first_name  VARCHAR(20) NOT NULL,
  suffix      VARCHAR(5) NULL,
  expiration  DATE NULL,
  email       VARCHAR(100) NULL,
  street      VARCHAR(50) NULL,
  city        VARCHAR(50) NULL,
  state       VARCHAR(2) NULL,
  zip         VARCHAR(10) NULL,
  phone       VARCHAR(20) NULL,
  interests   VARCHAR(255) NULL
);
```

As before, you can either type that statement manually into mysql or you can use a prewritten file. The file from the sampdb distribution that contains the CREATE TABLE statement for the member table is create_member.sql. To use it, execute this command:

```
% mysql sampdb < create_member.sql
```

In terms of data types, most columns of the member table except two are not very interesting because they are created as variable-length strings. The exceptions are member_id and expiration, which exist to hold sequence numbers and dates, respectively.

The main consideration for the member_id membership number column is that each of its values should be unique to avoid confusion between members. An AUTO_INCREMENT column is useful here because then we can let MySQL generate unique numbers for us automatically

when we add new members. Even though it just contains numbers, the definition for
member_id has several parts:

- INT signifies that the column holds integers (numeric values with no fractional part).

- UNSIGNED prohibits negative values.

- NOT NULL requires that the column value must be filled in. This prevents members from
  being created with no ID number.

- AUTO_INCREMENT is a special attribute in MySQL. It indicates that the column holds
  sequence numbers. The AUTO_INCREMENT mechanism works like this: If you provide
  no value for the member_id column when you create a new member table row, MySQL
  automatically generates the next sequence number and assigns it to the column. This
  special behavior also occurs if you explicitly assign the value NULL to the column. The
  AUTO_INCREMENT feature makes it easy to give each member a unique ID, because MySQL
  generates the values for us.

The PRIMARY KEY clause indicates that the member_id column is indexed to enable fast
lookups. It also sets up the constraint that each value in the column must be unique. The latter
property is desirable for member ID values, because it prevents us from using the same ID twice
by mistake. Besides, MySQL requires every AUTO_INCREMENT column to have some kind of
index, so the table definition would be illegal without one. (Any PRIMARY KEY column must
also be NOT NULL, so if we omitted NOT NULL from the member_id definition, MySQL would
add it automatically.)

If you don't understand that stuff about AUTO_INCREMENT and PRIMARY KEY, just think of
them as providing a magic way of generating indexed ID numbers. It doesn't particularly
matter what the values are, as long as they're unique for each member. (When you're ready for
more details about using AUTO_INCREMENT columns, see Chapter 3, "Data Types.")

The expiration column is a DATE. It permits NULL values, and it has a default value of NULL
as well, which means no date has been entered. As mentioned earlier, we'll use the convention
that an expiration value of NULL indicates that a member has a lifetime membership.

Now that you've told MySQL to create a couple of tables, make sure that it did so as you
expect. In mysql, issue the following statement to see the structure of the president table:

```
mysql> DESCRIBE president;
+------------+-------------+------+-----+---------+-------+
| Field      | Type        | Null | Key | Default | Extra |
+------------+-------------+------+-----+---------+-------+
| last_name  | varchar(15) | NO   |     | NULL    |       |
| first_name | varchar(15) | NO   |     | NULL    |       |
| suffix     | varchar(5)  | YES  |     | NULL    |       |
| city       | varchar(20) | NO   |     | NULL    |       |
| state      | varchar(2)  | NO   |     | NULL    |       |
| birth      | date        | NO   |     | NULL    |       |
| death      | date        | YES  |     | NULL    |       |
+------------+-------------+------+-----+---------+-------+
```

To see similar information for the `member` table, issue a `DESCRIBE member` statement. (If you're wondering why the `Default` column shows `NULL` for columns not defined to permit `NULL`, that's because `NULL` also indicates a column has no explicit `DEFAULT` clause.)

`DESCRIBE` is useful when you forget the name of a column in a table, or need to know its data type or how wide it is, and so forth. It's also useful for finding out the order in which MySQL stores columns in table rows. That order is important when you issue `INSERT` or `LOAD DATA` statements that expect column values to be listed in the default column order.

The information produced by `DESCRIBE` can be obtained in different ways. It may be abbreviated as `DESC`, or written as an `EXPLAIN` or `SHOW` statement. The following statements are synonymous:

```
DESCRIBE president;
DESC president;
EXPLAIN president;
SHOW COLUMNS FROM president;
SHOW FIELDS FROM president;
```

These statements also enable you to restrict the output to particular columns. For example, you can add a `LIKE` clause at the end of a `SHOW` statement to display information only for column names that match a given pattern:

```
mysql> SHOW COLUMNS FROM president LIKE '%name';
+------------+-------------+------+-----+---------+-------+
| Field      | Type        | Null | Key | Default | Extra |
+------------+-------------+------+-----+---------+-------+
| last_name  | varchar(15) | NO   |     |         |       |
| first_name | varchar(15) | NO   |     |         |       |
+------------+-------------+------+-----+---------+-------+
```

`DESCRIBE president '%name'` is equivalent. The '%' character used here is a special wildcard character that is described later in Section 1.4.9.7, "Pattern Matching."

`SHOW FULL COLUMNS` is like `SHOW COLUMNS` but displays additional column information. Try it now and see.

The `SHOW` statement has other forms that are useful for obtaining different types of information from MySQL. `SHOW TABLES` lists the tables in the default database, so with the two tables we've created so far in the `sampdb` database, the output looks like this:

```
mysql> SHOW TABLES;
+------------------+
| Tables_in_sampdb |
+------------------+
| member           |
| president        |
+------------------+
```

SHOW DATABASES lists the databases that are managed by the server to which you're connected:

```
mysql> SHOW DATABASES;
+--------------------+
| Database           |
+--------------------+
| information_schema |
| mysql              |
| sampdb             |
| test               |
+--------------------+
```

The list of databases varies from server to server, but you should see at least information_ schema and sampdb. information_schema is a special database that always exists, and you created sampdb yourself. You'll likely also see a database named test, which is created during the MySQL installation procedure. Depending on your access rights, you might see the database named mysql, which holds the grant tables that control who can do what.

The mysqlshow client program provides a command-line interface to the same kinds of information that the SHOW statement displays. Remember that when you run mysqlshow, you might need to provide appropriate command-line options for username, password, and hostname. These options are the same as when you run mysql.

With no arguments, mysqlshow displays a list of databases:

```
% mysqlshow
+--------------------+
|     Databases      |
+--------------------+
| information_schema |
| mysql              |
| sampdb             |
| test               |
+--------------------+
```

With a database name, mysqlshow displays the tables in the given database:

```
% mysqlshow sampdb
Database: sampdb
+-----------+
| Tables    |
+-----------+
| member    |
| president |
+-----------+
```

With a database and table name, mysqlshow displays information about the columns in the table, much like the SHOW FULL COLUMNS statement.

1.4.6.2 Tables for the Grade-Keeping Project

To determine what tables are required for the grade-keeping project, consider how you might write down scores when you use a paper-based gradebook. Figure 1.2 shows a page from your gradebook. The main body of this page is a matrix for recording scores. There is also other information needed for making sense of the scores. Student names and ID numbers are listed down the side of the matrix. (For simplicity, only four students are shown.) Along the top of the matrix, you write the dates when you give quizzes and tests. The figure shows that you've given quizzes on September 3, 6, 16, and 23, and tests on September 9 and October 1.

students		scores						
		Q	Q	T	Q	Q	T	
ID	name	9/3	9/6	9/9	9/16	9/23	10/1	...
1	Billy	14	10	73	14	15	67	...
2	Missy	17	10	68	17	14	73	...
3	Johnny	15	10	78	12	17	82	...
4	Jenny	14	13	85	13	19	79	...
...	...	...	...	...	...	...	...	...

Figure 1.2   Example gradebook.

To keep track of this kind of information using a database, we need a score table. What should rows in this table contain? That's easy. For each row, we need the student name, the date of the quiz or test, and the score. Figure 1.3 shows how some of the scores from the gradebook look represented in a table like this. (Dates are written the way MySQL represents them, in 'CCYY-MM-DD' format.)

score table

name	date	score
Billy	2012-09-23	15
Missy	2012-09-23	14
Johnny	2012-09-23	17
Jenny	2012-09-23	19
Billy	2012-10-01	67
Missy	2012-10-01	73
Johnny	2012-10-01	82
Jenny	2012-10-01	79

Figure 1.3   Initial score table layout.

Unfortunately, setting up the table in this way leaves out some information. For example, looking at the rows in Figure 1.3, it's unclear whether scores are for a quiz or a test. If quizzes and tests are weighted differently, it could be important to know score categories when determining final grades. We might infer the category from the range of scores on a given date (quizzes usually are worth fewer points than a test), but that's problematic because it relies on something not explicit in the data.

It's possible to distinguish scores if we record the category in each row by adding a column to the `score` table that contains 'T' or 'Q' to indicate "test" or "quiz," as in Figure 1.4. This has the advantage of making the score category explicit in the data. The disadvantage is redundancy. Observe that for all rows with a given date, the score category column always has the same value. The scores for September 23 all have a category of 'Q', and those for October 1 all have a category of 'T'. This is unappealing. If we record a set of scores for a quiz or test this way, not only will we enter the same date for each new record in the set, we enter the same score category over and over again. Ugh. Who wants to enter all that redundant information?

score table

name	date	score	category
Billy	2012-09-23	15	Q
Missy	2012-09-23	14	Q
Johnny	2012-09-23	17	Q
Jenny	2012-09-23	19	Q
Billy	2012-10-01	67	T
Missy	2012-10-01	73	T
Johnny	2012-10-01	82	T
Jenny	2012-10-01	79	T

Figure 1.4   `score` table layout, revised to include score type.

Let's try an alternative representation. Instead of recording score categories in the `score` table, we'll figure them out from the dates. We can keep a list of dates and use it to keep track of what kind of "grade event" (quiz or test) occurred on each date. Then we can determine whether any given score was from a quiz or a test by combining it with the information in our event list: Match the date in the `score` table row with the date in the `grade_event` table to get the event category. Figure 1.5 shows this table layout and demonstrates how the association works for a `score` table row with a date of September 23. By matching the row with the corresponding row in the `grade_event` table, we see that the score is for a quiz.

score table

name	date	score
Billy	2012-09-23	15
Missy	2012-09-23	14
Johnny	2012-09-23	17
Jenny	2012-09-23	19
Billy	2012-10-01	67
Missy	2012-10-01	73
Johnny	2012-10-01	82
Jenny	2012-10-01	79

grade_event table

date	category
2012-09-03	Q
2012-09-06	Q
2012-09-09	T
2012-09-16	Q
2012-09-23	Q
2012-10-01	T

Figure 1.5   `score` and `grade_event` tables, linked on date.

This is much better than trying to infer the score category based on some guess. Instead, we're deriving the category directly from data recorded explicitly in the database. It's also preferable to recording score categories in the `score` table; now we need to record each category only one time, rather than once per score row.

However, now we're combining information from multiple tables. If you're like me, when you first hear about this kind of thing, you think, "Yeah, that's a cute idea, but isn't it a lot of work to do all that looking up all the time; doesn't it just make things more complicated?"

In a way, that's correct; it is more work. Keeping two lists of records is more complicated than keeping one list. But take another look at your gradebook (see Figure 1.2). Aren't you already keeping two sets of records? Consider these facts:

- You keep track of scores using the cells in the score matrix, where each cell is indexed by student name and date (down the side and along the top of the matrix). This represents one set of records; it's analogous to the contents of the `score` table.

- How do you know what kind of event each date represents? You've written a little 'T' or 'Q' above the date! Thus, you're also keeping track of the association between date and score category along the top of the matrix. This represents a second set of records; it's analogous to the `grade_event` table contents.

In other words, even though you may not think about it as such, you're really not doing anything with the gradebook different from what I'm proposing to do by keeping information in two tables. The only real difference is that the two kinds of information aren't so explicitly separated in the paper-based gradebook.

The page in the gradebook illustrates something about the way we think of information, and also something about the difficulty of figuring out how to put information in a database: Our minds tend to integrate different kinds of information and interpret them as a whole. Databases don't work like that, which is why they sometimes seem artificial and unnatural. Our natural tendency to unify information makes it quite difficult sometimes even to realize when we have multiple types of data instead of just one. Because of this, it can be a challenge to "think as a database system thinks" about how best to represent your data.

One requirement imposed on the `grade_event` table by the layout shown in Figure 1.5 is that the dates must be unique because each date links rows from the `score` and `grade_event` tables. In other words, you cannot give two quizzes on the same day, or a quiz and a test. If you do, you'll have two sets of records in the `score` table and two records in the `grade_event` table, all with the same date, and you won't be able to tell how to match `score` rows with `grade_event` rows.

That problem will never come up if there is never more than one grade event per day. But is it valid to assume that will never happen? It might seem so; after all, you don't consider yourself sadistic enough to give a quiz and a test on the same day. But I've often heard people claim about their data, "That odd case will never occur." Then it turns out the odd case does occur on occasion, and usually you must redesign your tables to fix problems that the odd case causes.

It's better to think about the possible problems in advance and anticipate how to handle them. So, let's suppose that you might need to record two sets of scores for the same day sometimes.

How can we handle that? As it turns out, this problem isn't so difficult to solve. With a minor change to the way we lay out our data, multiple events on a given date won't cause trouble:

1. Add a column to the `grade_event` table and use it to assign a unique number to each row in the table. In effect, this gives each event its own ID number, so we'll call this the `event_id` column. If this seems like an odd thing to do, consider that your gradebook in Figure 1.2 already has this property implicitly: The event ID is just like the column number in your gradebook score matrix. The number might not be written down explicitly there and labeled "event ID," but that's what it is.

2. When you put scores in the `score` table, record event ID rather than date.

The result of these changes is shown in Figure 1.6. Now you link the `score` and `grade_event` tables using the event ID rather than the date, and you use the `grade_event` table to determine not just the category of each score, but also the date on which it occurred. Also, it's no longer the date that must be unique in the `grade_event` table, it's the event ID. This means you can have multiple tests and quizzes on the same day (your students will be thrilled to know this), and you'll be able to keep them straight in your records.

score table

name	event_id	score
Billy	5	15
Missy	5	14
Johnny	5	17
Jenny	5	19
Billy	6	67
Missy	6	73
Johnny	6	82
Jenny	6	79

grade_event table

event_id	date	category
1	2012-09-03	Q
2	2012-09-06	Q
3	2012-09-09	T
4	2012-09-16	Q
5	2012-09-23	Q
6	2012-10-01	T

Figure 1.6   `score` and `grade_event` tables, linked on event ID.

Unfortunately, from a human standpoint, the table layout in Figure 1.6 seems less satisfactory than the previous ones. The `score` table is more abstract because it contains fewer columns that have a readily apparent meaning. The table layout shown earlier in Figure 1.4 was easy to look at it and understand because the `score` table had columns for both dates and score categories. The current `score` table shown in Figure 1.6 has columns for neither. This seems highly removed from anything we can think about easily. Who wants to look at a `score` table that has "event IDs" in it? That's just not meaningful.

At this point, you reach a crossroads. You're intrigued by the possibility of performing grade-keeping electronically and not having to do all kinds of tedious manual calculations when assigning grades. But after considering how you actually would represent score information in a database, you're put off by how abstract and disconnected the representation seems to make that information.

This leads naturally to a question: "Maybe MySQL isn't for me. Would it be better not to use a database at all?" As you might guess, I will answer that question in the negative, because otherwise this book comes to a quick end. But when you're thinking about how to do a job, it's not a bad idea to consider alternatives and to ask whether you're better off using a database system such as MySQL, or something else such as a spreadsheet program:

- The gradebook has rows and columns, and so does a spreadsheet. This makes the gradebook and a spreadsheet conceptually and visually very similar.

- A spreadsheet program can perform calculations, so you could total up each student's scores using a calculation field. It might be a little tricky to weight quizzes and tests differently, but you could do it.

On the other hand, if you want to look at just part of your data (quizzes only or tests only, for example), perform comparisons such as boys versus girls, or display summary information in a flexible way, it's a different story. A spreadsheet doesn't work so well, whereas relational database systems perform those operations easily.

Another point to consider is that the abstract and disconnected nature of your data as represented in a relational database is not really a big deal, anyway. It's necessary to think about that representation when setting up the database so that you don't lay out your data in a way that doesn't make sense for what you want to do with it. However, after you determine the representation, you'll rely on the database engine to gather your data and present it in a way that is meaningful to you. You're not going to look at it as a bunch of disconnected pieces.

For example, when you retrieve scores from the score table, you want to see dates, not event IDs. That's not a problem. The database can look up dates from the grade_event table based on the event ID and show them to you. You may also want to see whether the scores are for tests or quizzes. That's not a problem, either. The database can look up score categories the same way—using event ID. Remember, that's what a database system like MySQL is good at: relating one thing to another to pull out information from multiple sources to present you with what you really want to see. In the case of our grade-keeping data, MySQL does the thinking about pulling information together using event IDs so you don't have to.

Now, just to provide a little advance preview of how you'd tell MySQL to do this relating of one thing to another, suppose that you want to see the scores for September 23, 2012. The query to pull out scores for an event given on a particular date looks like this:

```
SELECT score.name, grade_event.date, score.score, grade_event.category
FROM score INNER JOIN grade_event
ON score.event_id = grade_event.event_id
WHERE grade_event.date = '2012-09-23';
```

Pretty scary, huh? This query retrieves the student name, the date, score, and the score category by joining (relating) score table rows to grade_event table rows. The result looks like this:

```
+--------+------------+-------+----------+
| name   | date       | score | category |
+--------+----------- +-------+----------+
```

```
| Billy   | 2012-09-23 |    15 | Q         |
| Missy   | 2012-09-23 |    14 | Q         |
| Johnny  | 2012-09-23 |    17 | Q         |
| Jenny   | 2012-09-23 |    19 | Q         |
+---------+------------+-------+-----------+
```

Notice anything familiar about the format of that information? You should; it's the same as the table layout shown in Figure 1.4! And you need not know the event ID to get this result. You specify the date you're interested in and let MySQL figure out which score rows go with that date. So, if you've been wondering whether all the abstraction and disconnectedness loses us anything when it comes to getting information out of the database in a form that's meaningful to us, it doesn't.

Of course, after looking at that query, you might be wondering something else, too. Namely, it looks long and complicated; isn't writing something like that a lot of work to go to just to find the scores for a given date? Yes, it is. However, there are ways to avoid typing several lines of SQL each time you want to issue a query. Generally, you figure out once how to perform a query such as that one and then you store it so you can repeat it easily as necessary. We'll see how to do this in Section 1.5, "Tips for Interacting with mysql."

I've actually jumped the gun a little bit in showing you that query. It is, believe it or not, a little simpler than the one we're ultimately going to use to pull out scores. We need to make one more change to our table layout. Instead of recording student name in the score table, we'll use a unique student ID. (That is, we'll use the value from the "ID" column of your grade-book rather than from the "Name" column.) Then we create another table called student that contains name and student_id columns (see Figure 1.7).

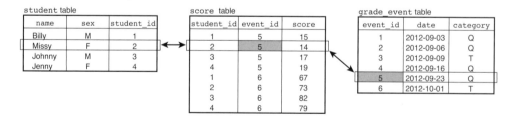

Figure 1.7   score, student, and grade_event tables, linked on student ID and event ID.

Why make this modification? For one thing, there might be two students with the same name. Using a unique student ID number helps you tell their scores apart. (This is exactly analogous to the way you can tell scores apart for a test and quiz given on the same day by using a unique event ID rather than the date.) After making this change to the table layout, the query we'll use to retrieve scores for a given date becomes a little more complex:

```
SELECT student.name, grade_event.date, score.score, grade_event.category
FROM grade_event INNER JOIN score INNER JOIN student
ON grade_event.event_id = score.event_id
AND score.student_id = student.student_id
WHERE grade_event.date = '2012-09-23';
```

If you're concerned because you don't find the meaning of that query immediately obvious, don't be. Most people wouldn't. We'll see the query again after we get further along into this tutorial, but the difference between now and later is that later it will make perfect sense to you. No, I'm not kidding.

You'll note from Figure 1.7 that I added something to the student table that wasn't in your gradebook: It contains a column for recording sex. This will permit simple things such as counting the number of boys and girls in the class or more complex things like comparing scores for boys and girls.

We're almost done designing the tables for the grade-keeping project. We need just one more table to record absences for attendance purposes. Its contents are relatively straightforward: a student ID number and a date (see Figure 1.8). Each row in the table indicates that the given student was absent on the given date. At the end of the grading period, we'll call on MySQL's counting abilities to summarize the table's contents to tell us how many days each student was absent.

absence table

student_id	date
2	2012-09-02
4	2012-09-15
2	2012-09-20

Figure 1.8   absence table.

1.4.6.2.1 The student Table

Now we know what our grade-keeping tables should look like, so let's create them. The CREATE TABLE statement for the student table looks like this:

```
CREATE TABLE student
(
  name       VARCHAR(20) NOT NULL,
  sex        ENUM('F','M') NOT NULL,
  student_id INT UNSIGNED NOT NULL AUTO_INCREMENT,
  PRIMARY KEY (student_id)
) ENGINE=InnoDB;
```

Observe that I've added something new to the CREATE TABLE statement (the ENGINE clause at the end). I'll explain its purpose shortly.

Type the CREATE TABLE statement into mysql or execute the following command:

```
% mysql sampdb < create_student.sql
```

The CREATE TABLE statement creates a table named student with three columns: name, sex, and student_id.

name is a variable-length string column that can hold up to 20 characters. This name representation is simpler than the one used for the Historical League tables; it uses a single column rather than separate first name and last name columns. That's because I know in advance that no grade-keeping query examples will need to do anything that would work better with separate columns. (Yes, that's cheating. I admit it. In practice, you would use multiple columns.)

sex indicates whether a student is a boy or a girl. It's an ENUM (enumeration) column, which means it can take only one of the values listed in the column specification: 'F' for female or 'M' for male. ENUM is useful when you have a restricted set of values that a column can hold. We could have used CHAR(1) instead, but ENUM makes the permitted column values more explicit. If you forget what the possible values are, issue a DESCRIBE statement. For an ENUM column, MySQL displays the list of legal enumeration values:

```
mysql> DESCRIBE student 'sex';
+-------+---------------+------+-----+---------+-------+
| Field | Type          | Null | Key | Default | Extra |
+-------+---------------+------+-----+---------+-------+
| sex   | enum('F','M') | NO   |     |         |       |
+-------+---------------+------+-----+---------+-------+
```

Values in an ENUM column need not be just a single character. The sex column could have been defined as something like ENUM('female','male') instead.

student_id is an integer column that will contain unique student ID numbers. Normally, you'd probably get ID numbers for your students from a central source, such as the school office. We'll just make them up, using an AUTO_INCREMENT column that is defined in much the same way as the member_id column that is part of the member table created earlier.

If you really were going to get student ID numbers from the office rather than generating them automatically, you would define the student_id column without the AUTO_INCREMENT attribute, but leave in the PRIMARY KEY clause, to prohibit duplicate or NULL ID values.

Now, what about the ENGINE clause at the end of the CREATE TABLE statement? This clause, if present, names the storage engine that MySQL should use for creating the table. A "storage engine" is a handler that manages a certain kind of table. MySQL has several storage engines, each with its own properties. The two most commonly used engines in MySQL are InnoDB (the default engine as of MySQL 5.5) and MyISAM (the default before 5.5).

I'll defer most discussion of differences between engines to Section 2.6.1, "Storage Engine Characteristics." For now, it is enough to say that the grade-keeping project table definitions explicitly specify InnoDB because we need it for something InnoDB offers called "referential integrity" through the use of foreign keys. That means we can use MySQL to enforce certain constraints on the interrelationships *between* tables, something that is important for the grade-keeping project tables:

- Score rows are tied to grade events and to students: We don't want to permit entry of rows into the `score` table unless the student ID and grade event ID are known in the `student` and `grade_event` tables.

- Similarly, absence rows are tied to students: We don't want to permit entry of rows into the `absence` table unless the student ID is known in the `student` table.

To enforce these constraints, we'll set up foreign key relationships. "Foreign" means "in another table," and "foreign key" indicates a key value that must match a key value in that other table. These concepts will become clearer as we create the rest of the grade-keeping project tables.

Earlier, we included no `ENGINE` clause when creating the Historical League tables (`president` and `member`), so they'll be created using whatever storage engine your server uses by default. As mentioned previously, that is InnoDB (unless the server has been reconfigured). The `student` table definition includes `ENGINE = InnoDB` explicitly in case the server is configured to use a different default.

1.4.6.2.2 The `grade_event` Table

The `grade_event` table has this definition:

```
CREATE TABLE grade_event
(
    date     DATE NOT NULL,
    category ENUM('T','Q') NOT NULL,
    event_id INT UNSIGNED NOT NULL AUTO_INCREMENT,
    PRIMARY KEY (event_id)
) ENGINE=InnoDB;
```

To create the `grade_event` table, type that `CREATE TABLE` statement into `mysql` or execute the following command:

```
% mysql sampdb < create_grade_event.sql
```

The `date` column holds a standard MySQL `DATE` value, in `'CCYY-MM-DD'` (year-first) format.

`category` represents score category. Like `sex` in the `student` table, `category` is an enumeration column. The permitted values are `'T'` and `'Q'`, representing "test" and "quiz."

`event_id` is an `AUTO_INCREMENT` column that is defined as a `PRIMARY KEY`, similar to `student_id` in the `student` table. Using `AUTO_INCREMENT` enables us to generate unique event ID values easily. As with the `student_id` column in the `student` table, the particular values are less important than that they be unique.

All the columns are defined as `NOT NULL` because none of them can be missing.

1.4.6.2.3   The `score` Table

The `score` table looks like this:

```
CREATE TABLE score
(
    student_id INT UNSIGNED NOT NULL,
    event_id   INT UNSIGNED NOT NULL,
    score      INT NOT NULL,
    PRIMARY KEY (event_id, student_id),
    INDEX (student_id),
    FOREIGN KEY (event_id) REFERENCES grade_event (event_id),
    FOREIGN KEY (student_id) REFERENCES student (student_id)
) ENGINE=InnoDB;
```

Here again the table definition contains something new: the FOREIGN KEY construct. We'll get to this in just a bit.

Create the table by typing the statement into `mysql` or by executing the following command:

```
% mysql sampdb < create_score.sql
```

The `score` column is an INT to hold integer score values. To permit scores such as 58.5 that have a fractional part, you'd use a data type that can represent them, such as DECIMAL.

The `student_id` and `event_id` columns are integer columns that indicate the student and event to which each score applies. By using them to link to the corresponding ID value columns in the `student` and `grade_event` tables, we'll be able to look up the student name and event date. There are a couple important points to note about the `student_id` and `event_id` columns:

- We've made the combination of the two columns a PRIMARY KEY. This ensures that we won't have duplicate scores for a student for a given quiz or test. Note that it's the combination of `event_id` and `student_id` that is unique. In the `score` table, neither value is unique by itself. There will be multiple score rows for each `event_id` value (one per student), and multiple rows for each `student_id` value (one for each quiz and test) taken by the student.

- For each ID column, a FOREIGN KEY clause defines a constraint. The REFERENCES part of the clause indicates which table and column the ID column refers to. The constraint on `event_id` is that each value in the column must match some `event_id` value in the `grade_event` table. Similarly, each `student_id` value in the `score` table must match some `student_id` value in the `student` table.

The PRIMARY KEY definition ensures that we won't create duplicate score rows. The FOREIGN KEY definitions ensure that we won't have rows with bogus ID values that don't exist in the `grade_event` or `student` tables.

Why is there an index on `student_id`? The reason is that, for any columns in a FOREIGN KEY definition, there should be an index on them or they should be the columns that are listed first in a multiple-column index, to enable faster lookups. For the FOREIGN KEY on event_id, that column is listed first in the PRIMARY KEY. For the FOREIGN KEY on student_id, the PRIMARY KEY cannot be used because student_id is not listed first. So, instead, we create a separate index on student_id.

InnoDB automatically creates an index if necessary on columns in a foreign key definition, but it might not use the same index definition you would (as discussed further in Section 2.13, "Foreign Keys and Referential Integrity"). Defining the index explicitly avoids this issue.

1.4.6.2.4   The absence Table

The absence table for recording lapses in attendance looks like this:

```
CREATE TABLE absence
(
    student_id INT UNSIGNED NOT NULL,
    date       DATE NOT NULL,
    PRIMARY KEY (student_id, date),
    FOREIGN KEY (student_id) REFERENCES student (student_id)
) ENGINE=InnoDB;
```

Type that statement into mysql or execute the following command:

```
% mysql sampdb < create_absence.sql
```

The student_id and date columns both are defined as NOT NULL to prohibit missing values. We make the combination of the two columns a primary key so we don't accidentally create duplicate rows. It wouldn't be fair to count a student absent twice on the same day, would it?

The absence table also includes a foreign key relationship, defined to ensure that each student_id value matches a student_id value in the student table.

The inclusion of foreign key relationships in the grade-keeping tables enacts constraints at data entry time: We want to insert only those rows that contain legal grade event and student ID values. However, the foreign key relationships have another effect. They set up dependencies that constrain the order in which you create and drop tables:

- The score table refers to the grade_event and student tables, so they must be created first before you can create the score table. Similarly, absence refers to student, so student must exist before you can create absence.

- If you drop (remove) tables, the reverse is true. You cannot drop the grade_event table if you have not dropped the score table first, and student cannot be dropped unless you have first dropped score and absence.

1.4.7   Adding New Rows

At this point, our database and its tables have been created. Now we need to put some rows into the tables. However, it's useful to know how to check what's in a table after you put something into it, so although retrieval is not covered in any detail until later in Section 1.4.9,

"Retrieving Information," you should know at least that the following statement will show you the complete contents of any table `tbl_name`:

```
SELECT * FROM tbl_name;
```

Example:

```
mysql> SELECT * FROM student;
Empty set (0.00 sec)
```

Right now, `mysql` indicates that the table is empty, but you'll see a different result after trying the examples in this section.

There are several ways to add data to a database. You can insert rows into a table manually by issuing `INSERT` statements. You can also add rows by reading them from a file, either in the form of prewritten `INSERT` statements that you feed to `mysql`, or as raw data values that you load using the `LOAD DATA` statement or the `mysqlimport` client program.

This section demonstrates each method of inserting rows into your tables. You should play with all of them to familiarize yourself with them and to see how they work. After you've tried each of the methods, go to Section 1.4.8, "Resetting the `sampdb` Database to a Known State," and run the commands you find there. Those commands drop the tables, re-create them, and load them with a known set of data. By executing them, you'll make sure that the tables contain the same rows that I worked with while writing the sections that follow, and you'll get the same results shown in those sections. (If you already know how to insert rows and just want to populate the tables, you can skip directly to that section.)

1.4.7.1   Adding Rows with `INSERT`

Let's start adding rows by using `INSERT`, an SQL statement for which you specify the table into which you want to insert a row of data and the values to put in the row. The `INSERT` statement has several formats.

Specify values for all the columns. The syntax looks like this:

```
INSERT INTO tbl_name VALUES(value1,value2,...);
```

Example:

```
mysql> INSERT INTO student VALUES('Kyle','M',NULL);
mysql> INSERT INTO grade_event VALUES('2012-09-03','Q',NULL);
```

With this syntax, the `VALUES` list must contain a value for each column in the table, in the order that the columns are stored in the table. (Normally, this is the order in which the columns are specified in the table's `CREATE TABLE` statement.) If you're not sure what the column order is, issue a `DESCRIBE tbl_name` statement to find out.

You can quote string and date values in MySQL using either single or double quotes, but single quotes are more standard. The `NULL` values are for the `AUTO_INCREMENT` columns in the `student` and `grade_event` tables. Inserting a "missing value" into an `AUTO_INCREMENT` column causes MySQL to generate the next sequence number for the column.

MySQL permits you to insert several rows into a table with a single INSERT statement by specifying multiple value lists:

```
INSERT INTO tbl_name VALUES(...),(...),... ;
```

Example:

```
mysql> INSERT INTO student VALUES('Avery','F',NULL),('Nathan','M',NULL);
```

This involves less typing than multiple INSERT statements, and also is more efficient for the server to execute. Note that a pair of parentheses is required around the column values for *each* row. The following statement is illegal because it parenthesizes column values incorrectly:

```
mysql> INSERT INTO student VALUES('Avery','F',NULL,'Nathan','M',NULL);
ERROR 1136 (21S01): Column count doesn't match value count at row 1
```

Name the columns to be assigned values and list the values. This is useful when you want to create a row for which only a few columns need to be set up initially.

```
INSERT INTO tbl_name (col_name1,col_name2,...) VALUES(value1,value2,...);
```

Example:

```
mysql> INSERT INTO member (last_name,first_name) VALUES('Stein','Waldo');
```

This form of INSERT supports multiple value lists, too:

```
mysql> INSERT INTO student (name,sex) VALUES('Abby','F'),('Joseph','M');
```

For any column not named in the column list, MySQL assigns its default value. For example, the preceding statements contain no values for the member_id or student_id columns, so MySQL assigns the default value of NULL. member_id and student_id are AUTO_INCREMENT columns, so the net effect in each case is to generate and assign the next sequence number, just as if you had assigned NULL explicitly.

Provide a list of column/value assignments. This syntax uses a SET clause containing col_name=value assignments rather than a VALUES() list:

```
INSERT INTO tbl_name SET col_name1=value1, col_name2=value2, ... ;
```

Example:

```
mysql> INSERT INTO member SET last_name='Stein',first_name='Waldo';
```

For any column not named in the SET clause, MySQL assigns its default value. This form of INSERT cannot be used to insert multiple rows with a single statement.

Now that you know how INSERT works, you can use it to see whether the foreign key relationships we set up really prevent entry of bad rows in the score and absence tables. Try inserting rows that contain ID values that are not present in the grade_event or student tables:

```
mysql> INSERT INTO score (event_id,student_id,score) VALUES(9999,9999,0);
ERROR 1452 (23000): Cannot add or update a child row: a foreign key
constraint fails (`sampdb`.`score`, CONSTRAINT `score_ibfk_1` FOREIGN
```

```
KEY (`event_id`) REFERENCES `grade_event` (`event_id`))
mysql> INSERT INTO absence SET student_id=9999, date='2012-09-16';
ERROR 1452 (23000): Cannot add or update a child row: a foreign key
constraint fails (`sampdb`.`absence`, CONSTRAINT `absence_ibfk_1`
FOREIGN KEY (`student_id`) REFERENCES `student` (`student_id`))
```

The error messages show that the constraints are working.

1.4.7.2   Adding New Rows from a File

Another method for loading rows into a table is to read them directly from a file. The file can contain INSERT statements or it can contain raw data. For example, the sampdb distribution contains a file named insert_president.sql that contains INSERT statements for adding new rows to the president table. Assuming that you are in the same directory where that file is located, you can execute those statements like this:

```
% mysql sampdb < insert_president.sql
```

If you're already running mysql, you can use a source command to read the file:

```
mysql> source insert_president.sql;
```

If you have the rows stored in a file as raw data values rather than as INSERT statements, you can load them with the LOAD DATA statement or with the mysqlimport client program.

The LOAD DATA statement is a bulk loader that reads data from a file. Use it from within mysql:

```
mysql> LOAD DATA LOCAL INFILE 'member.txt' INTO TABLE member;
```

Assuming that the member.txt data file is located in your current directory on the client host, this statement reads it and sends its contents to the server to be loaded into the member table. (The member.txt file can be found in the sampdb distribution.)

By default, the LOAD DATA statement assumes that column values are separated by tabs and that lines end with newlines (also known as "linefeeds"). It also assumes that the values are present in the order that columns are stored in the table (\N values in the file indicate NULL). It's possible to read files in other formats or to specify a different column order. For details, see the entry for LOAD DATA in Appendix E, "SQL Syntax Reference."

The keyword LOCAL in the LOAD DATA statement causes the data file to be read by the client program (in this case, mysql) and sent to the server to be loaded. It is possible to omit LOCAL, but then the file must be located on the server host, and you need the FILE server access privilege, which most MySQL users don't have. You should also specify the full pathname to the file so the server can find it.

If you get the following error with LOAD DATA LOCAL, the LOCAL capability might be disabled by default:

```
ERROR 1148 (42000): The used command is not allowed with this MySQL version
```

Try again after invoking `mysql` with the `--local-infile` option. For example:

```
% mysql --local-infile sampdb
mysql> LOAD DATA LOCAL INFILE 'member.txt' INTO TABLE member;
```

If that doesn't work, either, the server needs to be started with the `--local-infile` option.

Another way to load a data file is to use the `mysqlimport` client program from the command prompt. It generates a `LOAD DATA` statement for you:

```
% mysqlimport --local sampdb member.txt
```

As with the `mysql` program, if you need to specify connection parameters, indicate them on the command line preceding the database name.

For the command just shown, `mysqlimport` generates a `LOAD DATA` statement to load `member.txt` into the `member` table. That's because `mysqlimport` determines the table name from the name of the data file, using everything up to the first period of the filename as the table name. For example, `mysqlimport` would load files named `member.txt` and `president.txt` into the `member` and `president` tables. This means you should choose your filenames carefully or `mysqlimport` won't use the correct table name. If you tried to load files named `member1.txt` and `member2.txt`, `mysqlimport` would think it should load them into tables named `member1` and `member2`. If what you really want is to load both files into the `member` table, you could use names like `member.1.txt` and `member.2.txt`, or `member.txt1` and `member.txt2`.

1.4.8   Resetting the `sampdb` Database to a Known State

After you have tried the row-adding methods described in the preceding discussion, you should re-create and load the `sampdb` database tables to reset the database so that its contents are the same as what the next sections assume. Using the `mysql` program in the directory containing the `sampdb` distribution files, issue these statements:

```
% mysql sampdb
mysql> source create_member.sql;
mysql> source create_president.sql;
mysql> source insert_member.sql;
mysql> source insert_president.sql;
mysql> DROP TABLE IF EXISTS absence, score, grade_event, student;
mysql> source create_student.sql;
mysql> source create_grade_event.sql;
mysql> source create_score.sql;
mysql> source create_absence.sql;
mysql> source insert_student.sql;
mysql> source insert_grade_event.sql;
mysql> source insert_score.sql;
mysql> source insert_absence.sql;
```

If, as is likely, you don't want to type those statements individually, try this command on Unix:

```
% sh init_all_tables.sh sampdb
```

On Windows, use this command instead:

```
C:\> init_all_tables.bat sampdb
```

Whichever command you use, if you need to specify connection parameters, list them on the command line following the command name.

1.4.9   Retrieving Information

Our tables are created and loaded with data now, so let's see what we can do with that data. To retrieve and display information, use the SELECT statement. It enables you to retrieve information in as general or specific a manner as you like. You can display the entire contents of a table:

```
SELECT * FROM president;
```

Or you can select as little as a single column of a single row:

```
SELECT birth FROM president WHERE last_name = 'Eisenhower';
```

The SELECT statement has several clauses that you combine as necessary to retrieve the information in which you're interested. Each of these clauses can be simple or complex, so SELECT statements as a whole can be simple or complex. However, you won't find any page-long queries that take an hour to figure out in this book. When I see arm-length queries in something that I'm reading, I generally skip right over them, and I'm guessing that you do the same.

A simplified syntax of the SELECT statement is:

```
SELECT what to retrieve
FROM table or tables
WHERE conditions that data must satisfy;
```

To write a SELECT statement, specify what you want to retrieve and then some optional clauses. The clauses just shown (FROM and WHERE) are the most common ones, although others can be specified as well, such as GROUP BY, ORDER BY, and LIMIT. Remember that SQL is a free-format language, so when you write your own SELECT statements, you need not put line breaks in the same places I do.

The FROM clause usually is present, but you can omit it if you don't need to name any tables. For example, the following query simply displays the values of some expressions. These can be calculated without referring to the contents of any table, so no FROM clause is necessary:

```
mysql> SELECT 2+2, 'Hello, world', VERSION();
+-----+--------------+------------+
| 2+2 | Hello, world | VERSION()  |
+-----+--------------+------------+
|   4 | Hello, world | 5.5.30-log |
+-----+--------------+------------+
```

When you do use a FROM clause to specify a table from which to retrieve data, you'll also indicate which columns you want to see. The most "generic" form of SELECT uses * as a column specifier, which is shorthand for "all columns." The following query retrieves and displays all columns from the student table:

```
mysql> SELECT * FROM student;
+-----------+-----+------------+
| name      | sex | student_id |
+-----------+-----+------------+
| Megan     | F   |          1 |
| Joseph    | M   |          2 |
| Kyle      | M   |          3 |
| Katie     | F   |          4 |
...
```

The columns are displayed in the order that MySQL stores them in the table. This is the same order in which the columns are listed when you issue a DESCRIBE student statement. (The "…" shown at the end of the example indicates that the query returns more rows than are shown.)

You can explicitly name the column or columns you want to see. To select just student names, do this:

```
mysql> SELECT name FROM student;
+-----------+
| name      |
+-----------+
| Megan     |
| Joseph    |
| Kyle      |
| Katie     |
...
```

If you name more than one column, separate them by commas. The following statement is equivalent to SELECT * FROM student, but names each column explicitly:

```
mysql> SELECT name, sex, student_id FROM student;
+-----------+-----+------------+
| name      | sex | student_id |
+-----------+-----+------------+
| Megan     | F   |          1 |
| Joseph    | M   |          2 |
| Kyle      | M   |          3 |
| Katie     | F   |          4 |
...
```

You can name columns in any order:

```
SELECT name, student_id FROM student;
SELECT student_id, name FROM student;
```

You can even name a column more than once if you like, although generally that's kind of pointless.

It's also possible to select columns from more than one table at a time. This is called a "join" between tables. We'll get to joins in Section 1.4.9.10, "Retrieving Information from Multiple Tables."

Column names are not case sensitive in MySQL, so the following queries all retrieve the same information:

```
SELECT name, student_id FROM student;
SELECT NAME, STUDENT_ID FROM student;
SELECT nAmE, sTuDeNt_Id FROM student;
```

On the other hand, database and table names might be case sensitive. It depends on the filesystem used on the server host and on how MySQL is configured. Windows filenames are not case sensitive, so a server running on Windows does not treat database and table names as case sensitive. On Unix systems, filenames generally are case sensitive, so a server would treat database and table names as case sensitive. An exception to this occurs for Mac OS X Extended filesystems, which can be case insensitive.

If you want to have MySQL treat database and table names as not case sensitive, you can configure the server that way. See Section 11.2.6, "Operating System Constraints on Database Object Names."

1.4.9.1 Specifying Retrieval Criteria

To restrict the set of rows retrieved by the SELECT statement, use a WHERE clause that specifies the criteria that column values must satisfy. For example, you can search for a range of numeric values:

```
mysql> SELECT * FROM score WHERE score > 95;
+------------+----------+-------+
| student_id | event_id | score |
+------------+----------+-------+
|          5 |        3 |    97 |
|         18 |        3 |    96 |
|          1 |        6 |   100 |
|          5 |        6 |    97 |
|         11 |        6 |    98 |
|         16 |        6 |    98 |
+------------+----------+-------+
```

You can look for string values containing character data. For the default character set and collation (sort order), string comparisons are not case sensitive:

```
mysql> SELECT last_name, first_name FROM president
    -> WHERE last_name='ROOSEVELT';
```

```
+-----------+-------------+
| last_name | first_name  |
+-----------+-------------+
| Roosevelt | Theodore    |
| Roosevelt | Franklin D. |
+-----------+-------------+
mysql> SELECT last_name, first_name FROM president
    -> WHERE last_name='roosevelt';
+-----------+-------------+
| last_name | first_name  |
+-----------+-------------+
| Roosevelt | Theodore    |
| Roosevelt | Franklin D. |
+-----------+-------------+
```

You can look for dates:

```
mysql> SELECT last_name, first_name, birth FROM president
    -> WHERE birth < '1750-1-1';
+------------+------------+------------+
| last_name  | first_name | birth      |
+------------+------------+------------+
| Washington | George     | 1732-02-22 |
| Adams      | John       | 1735-10-30 |
| Jefferson  | Thomas     | 1743-04-13 |
+------------+------------+------------+
```

It's also possible to search for combinations of values:

```
mysql> SELECT last_name, first_name, birth, state FROM president
    -> WHERE birth < '1750-1-1' AND (state='VA' OR state='MA');
+------------+------------+------------+-------+
| last_name  | first_name | birth      | state |
+------------+------------+------------+-------+
| Washington | George     | 1732-02-22 | VA    |
| Adams      | John       | 1735-10-30 | MA    |
| Jefferson  | Thomas     | 1743-04-13 | VA    |
+------------+------------+------------+-------+
```

Expressions in WHERE clauses can use arithmetic operators (Table 1.1), comparison operators (Table 1.2), and logical operators (Table 1.3). You can also use parentheses to group parts of an expression. Operations can be performed using constants, table columns, and function calls. We will have occasion to use several of MySQL's functions in statements throughout this tutorial, but there are far too many to show here. See Appendix C, "Operator and Function Reference."

Table 1.1   **Arithmetic Operators**

Operator	Meaning
+	Addition
-	Subtraction
*	Multiplication
/	Division
DIV	Integer division
%	Modulo (remainder after division)

Table 1.2   **Comparison Operators**

Operator	Meaning
<	Less than
<=	Less than or equal to
=	Equal to
<=>	Equal to (works even for NULL values)
<> or !=	Not equal to
>=	Greater than or equal to
>	Greater than

Table 1.3   **Logical Operators**

Operator	Meaning
AND	Logical AND
OR	Logical OR
XOR	Logical exclusive-OR
NOT	Logical negation

When you're formulating a statement that requires logical operators, take care not to confuse the meaning of the logical AND operator with the way we use "and" in everyday speech. Suppose that you want to find "presidents born in Virginia and presidents born in

Massachusetts." That phrasing uses "and," which seems to imply that you'd write the statement as follows:

```
mysql> SELECT last_name, first_name, state FROM president
    -> WHERE state='VA' AND state='MA';
Empty set (0.01 sec)
```

It's clear from the empty result that the statement didn't work. Why not? Because the statement really means "Select presidents who were born both in Virginia and in Massachusetts," which makes no sense. In English, you might express the statement using "and," but in SQL, connect the two conditions with OR:

```
mysql> SELECT last_name, first_name, state FROM president
    -> WHERE state='VA' OR state='MA';
+------------+-------------+-------+
| last_name  | first_name  | state |
+------------+-------------+-------+
| Washington | George      | VA    |
| Adams      | John        | MA    |
| Jefferson  | Thomas      | VA    |
| Madison    | James       | VA    |
| Monroe     | James       | VA    |
| Adams      | John Quincy | MA    |
| Harrison   | William H.  | VA    |
| Tyler      | John        | VA    |
| Taylor     | Zachary     | VA    |
| Wilson     | Woodrow     | VA    |
| Kennedy    | John F.     | MA    |
| Bush       | George H.W. | MA    |
+------------+-------------+-------+
```

This disjunction between natural language and SQL is something to be aware of, not just when formulating your own queries, but also when you write queries for other people. It's best to listen carefully as they describe what they want to retrieve, but you don't necessarily want to transcribe their descriptions into SQL using the same logical operators. For the example just described, the proper English equivalent for the query is "Select presidents who were born either in Virginia or in Massachusetts."

To formulate queries where you're looking for any of several individual values, you might find it easier to use the IN() operator. The preceding query can be rewritten using IN() like this:

```
SELECT last_name, first_name, state FROM president
WHERE state IN('VA','MA');
```

IN() is especially convenient when you're comparing a column to a large number of values.

1.4.9.2 The NULL Value

The NULL value is special. It means "no value" or "unknown value" and cannot be compared to known values the way you compare two known values to each other. If you attempt to use NULL with the usual arithmetic comparison operators, the result is undefined:

```
mysql> SELECT NULL < 0, NULL = 0, NULL <> 0, NULL > 0;
+----------+----------+-----------+----------+
| NULL < 0 | NULL = 0 | NULL <> 0 | NULL > 0 |
+----------+----------+-----------+----------+
|     NULL |     NULL |      NULL |     NULL |
+----------+----------+-----------+----------+
```

In fact, you can't even compare NULL to itself because the result of comparing two unknown values cannot be determined:

```
mysql> SELECT NULL = NULL, NULL <> NULL;
+-------------+--------------+
| NULL = NULL | NULL <> NULL |
+-------------+--------------+
|        NULL |         NULL |
+-------------+--------------+
```

Instead of using =, <>, or != to test for equality or inequality with NULL values, use IS NULL or IS NOT NULL. For example, presidents who are still living have their death dates represented as NULL in the president table. To find them, use the following query:

```
mysql> SELECT last_name, first_name FROM president WHERE death IS NULL;
+-----------+-------------+
| last_name | first_name  |
+-----------+-------------+
| Carter    | James E.    |
| Bush      | George H.W. |
| Clinton   | William J.  |
| Bush      | George W.   |
| Obama     | Barack H.   |
+-----------+-------------+
```

To find non-NULL values, use IS NOT NULL. This query finds names that have a suffix part:

```
mysql> SELECT last_name, first_name, suffix
    -> FROM president WHERE suffix IS NOT NULL;
+-----------+------------+--------+
| last_name | first_name | suffix |
+-----------+------------+--------+
| Carter    | James E.   | Jr.    |
+-----------+------------+--------+
```

The MySQL-specific `<=>` comparison operator is true even for NULL-to-NULL comparisons. The preceding two queries can be rewritten to use this operator as follows:

```
SELECT last_name, first_name FROM president WHERE death <=> NULL;

SELECT last_name, first_name, suffix
FROM president WHERE NOT (suffix <=> NULL);
```

1.4.9.3   Sorting Query Results

Every MySQL user notices sooner or later that if you create a table, load some rows into it, and then issue a `SELECT * FROM tbl_name` statement, the rows tend to be retrieved in the same order in which they were inserted. That makes a certain intuitive sense, so it's natural to assume that rows are retrieved in insertion order by default. But that is not the case. After loading the table initially, deleting and inserting rows may change the order in which the server returns the table's rows.

Remember this about row retrieval order: There is *no guarantee* about the order in which the server returns rows unless you specify that order yourself. To do so, add an ORDER BY clause to the statement that defines the desired sort order. The following query returns president names, sorted lexically (alphabetically) by last name:

```
mysql> SELECT last_name, first_name FROM president
    -> ORDER BY last_name;
+------------+---------------+
| last_name  | first_name    |
+------------+---------------+
| Adams      | John Quincy   |
| Adams      | John          |
| Arthur     | Chester A.    |
| Buchanan   | James         |
...
```

By default, ORDER BY sorts columns in ascending order. Adding the ASC or DESC keyword following a column name specifies explicitly whether to sort it in ascending or descending order. For example, to sort president names in reverse (descending) name order, use DESC like this:

```
mysql> SELECT last_name, first_name FROM president
    -> ORDER BY last_name DESC;
+------------+---------------+
| last_name  | first_name    |
+------------+---------------+
| Wilson     | Woodrow       |
| Washington | George        |
| Van Buren  | Martin        |
| Tyler      | John          |
...
```

You can sort using multiple columns, and each column can be sorted independently in ascending or descending order. The following query retrieves rows from the `president` table, sorts them by reverse state of birth, and then sorts by ascending last name within each state:

```
mysql> SELECT last_name, first_name, state FROM president
    -> ORDER BY state DESC, last_name ASC;
+------------+---------------+-------+
| last_name  | first_name    | state |
+------------+---------------+-------+
| Arthur     | Chester A.    | VT    |
| Coolidge   | Calvin        | VT    |
| Harrison   | William H.    | VA    |
| Jefferson  | Thomas        | VA    |
| Madison    | James         | VA    |
| Monroe     | James         | VA    |
| Taylor     | Zachary       | VA    |
| Tyler      | John          | VA    |
| Washington | George        | VA    |
| Wilson     | Woodrow       | VA    |
| Eisenhower | Dwight D.     | TX    |
| Johnson    | Lyndon B.     | TX    |
...
```

NULL values in a column sort at the beginning for ascending sorts and at the end for descending sorts. To ensure that NULL values appear at a given end of the sort order, add an extra sort column that distinguishes NULL from non-NULL values. For example, if you sort presidents by reverse death date, living presidents (those with NULL death dates) appear at the end of the sort order. To put them at the beginning instead, use the following query. The IF() function evaluates the expression given by its first argument and returns the value of its second or third argument, depending on whether the expression is true or false. For the query shown, IF() evaluates to 0 for NULL values and 1 for non-NULL values. This places all NULL values ahead of all non-NULL values. Sorting on `last_name` as a secondary column orders rows with the same death value by last name.

```
mysql> SELECT last_name, first_name, death FROM president
    -> ORDER BY IF(death IS NULL,0,1), death DESC, last_name;
+------------+---------------+------------+
| last_name  | first_name    | death      |
+------------+---------------+------------+
| Bush       | George W.      | NULL       |
| Bush       | George H.W.    | NULL       |
| Carter     | James E.       | NULL       |
| Clinton    | William J.     | NULL       |
| Obama      | Barack H.      | NULL       |
| Ford       | Gerald R.      | 2006-12-26 |
| Reagan     | Ronald W.      | 2004-06-05 |
| Nixon      | Richard M.     | 1994-04-22 |
...
```

```
| Adams      | John    | 1826-07-04 |
| Jefferson  | Thomas  | 1826-07-04 |
| Washington | George  | 1799-12-14 |
+------------+---------------+------------+
```

1.4.9.4   Limiting Query Results

To see only a few rows when a query returns many, add a LIMIT clause. LIMIT is especially useful in conjunction with ORDER BY. MySQL enables you to limit the output of a query to the first *n* rows of the result. The following query selects the five presidents who were born first:

```
mysql> SELECT last_name, first_name, birth FROM president
    -> ORDER BY birth LIMIT 5;
+------------+------------+------------+
| last_name  | first_name | birth      |
+------------+------------+------------+
| Washington | George     | 1732-02-22 |
| Adams      | John       | 1735-10-30 |
| Jefferson  | Thomas     | 1743-04-13 |
| Madison    | James      | 1751-03-16 |
| Monroe     | James      | 1758-04-28 |
+------------+------------+------------+
```

Sorting in reverse order using DESC returns the five most recently born presidents instead:

```
mysql> SELECT last_name, first_name, birth FROM president
    -> ORDER BY birth DESC LIMIT 5;
+------------+-------------+------------+
| last_name  | first_name  | birth      |
+------------+-------------+------------+
| Obama      | Barack H.   | 1961-08-04 |
| Clinton    | William J.  | 1946-08-19 |
| Bush       | George W.   | 1946-07-06 |
| Carter     | James E.    | 1924-10-01 |
| Bush       | George H.W. | 1924-06-12 |
+------------+-------------+------------+
```

LIMIT also enables you to pull a section of rows from the middle of a result set. Specify two values: the number of rows to skip at the beginning of the result set, and the number of rows to return. The following query is similar to the previous one but returns 5 rows after skipping the first 10:

```
mysql> SELECT last_name, first_name, birth FROM president
    -> ORDER BY birth DESC LIMIT 10, 5;
+------------+------------+------------+
| last_name  | first_name | birth      |
+------------+------------+------------+
| Eisenhower | Dwight D.  | 1890-10-14 |
| Truman     | Harry S    | 1884-05-08 |
```

```
| Roosevelt | Franklin D. | 1882-01-30 |
| Hoover    | Herbert C.  | 1874-08-10 |
| Coolidge  | Calvin      | 1872-07-04 |
+-----------+-------------+------------+
```

To randomly select a row or set of rows from a table, use ORDER BY RAND() in conjunction with LIMIT:

```
mysql> SELECT last_name, first_name FROM president
    -> ORDER BY RAND() LIMIT 1;
+-----------+------------+
| last_name | first_name |
+-----------+------------+
| Johnson   | Lyndon B.  |
+-----------+------------+
mysql> SELECT last_name, first_name FROM president
    -> ORDER BY RAND() LIMIT 3;
+-----------+-------------+
| last_name | first_name  |
+-----------+-------------+
| Harding   | Warren G.   |
| Bush      | George H.W. |
| Jefferson | Thomas      |
+-----------+-------------+
```

1.4.9.5   Calculating and Naming Output Column Values

Most of the queries shown so far produce output by retrieving values from tables. It's also possible to calculate output values from the results of expressions, with or without reference to tables. The following query evaluates a simple expression (a constant), and a more complex expression that uses several arithmetic operations and a couple of function calls that produce the square root of an expression and format the result to three decimal places:

```
mysql> SELECT 17, FORMAT(SQRT(25+13),3);
+----+-----------------------+
| 17 | FORMAT(SQRT(25+13),3) |
+----+-----------------------+
| 17 | 6.164                 |
+----+-----------------------+
```

Expressions can also refer to table columns:

```
mysql> SELECT CONCAT(first_name,' ',last_name),CONCAT(city,', ',state)
    -> FROM president;
+----------------------------------+-------------------------+
| CONCAT(first_name,' ',last_name) | CONCAT(city,', ',state) |
+----------------------------------+-------------------------+
| George Washington                | Wakefield, VA           |
| John Adams                       | Braintree, MA           |
```

```
| Thomas Jefferson              | Albemarle County, VA   |
| James Madison                 | Port Conway, VA        |
...
```

That query formats president names as a single string by concatenating first and last names separated by a space. It also formats birthplaces as the birth cities and states separated by a comma and a space.

An expression that calculates a column value becomes the column's name and is used for its heading. That can lead to a very wide column if the expression is long, as the preceding query illustrates.   To make the output more meaningful and readable, assign the column a different name (an "alias") using the AS *name* construct:

```
mysql> SELECT CONCAT(first_name,' ',last_name) AS Name,
    -> CONCAT(city,', ',state) AS Birthplace
    -> FROM president;
+----------------------+------------------------+
| Name                 | Birthplace             |
+----------------------+------------------------+
| George Washington    | Wakefield, VA          |
| John Adams           | Braintree, MA          |
| Thomas Jefferson     | Albemarle County, VA   |
| James Madison        | Port Conway, VA        |
...
```

If the column alias contains spaces, put it in quotes:

```
mysql> SELECT CONCAT(first_name,' ',last_name) AS 'President Name',
    -> CONCAT(city,', ',state) AS 'Place of Birth'
    -> FROM president;
+----------------------+------------------------+
| President Name       | Place of Birth         |
+----------------------+------------------------+
| George Washington    | Wakefield, VA          |
| John Adams           | Braintree, MA          |
| Thomas Jefferson     | Albemarle County, VA   |
| James Madison        | Port Conway, VA        |
...
```

The keyword AS is optional when you provide a column alias:

```
mysql> SELECT 1 one, 2 two, 3 three;
+-----+-----+-------+
| one | two | three |
+-----+-----+-------+
|   1 |   2 |     3 |
+-----+-----+-------+
```

If a query result has a misnamed column and a missing column, check whether you forgot a comma between columns. If so, the second of them was treated as an alias for the first. For example, you might write a query to select president names as follows, forgetting the comma between the `first_name` and `last_name` columns. As a result, the `first_name` column is misnamed as `last_name` and the `last_name` column is missing:

```
mysql> SELECT first_name last_name FROM president;
+---------------+
| last_name     |
+---------------+
| George        |
| John          |
| Thomas        |
| James         |
...
```

1.4.9.6   Working with Dates

The principal thing to keep in mind when using dates in MySQL is that it always expects dates with the year first. To write July 27, 2012, use `'2012-07-27'`. Do not use `'07-27-2012'` or `'27-07-2012'`, as you might be more accustomed to writing. For input values in other formats, you might be able to convert them by using the `STR_TO_DATE()` function. For an example, see Section 3.2.6, "Temporal (Date and Time) Data Types."

MySQL supports many kinds of operations on dates:

- Sorting by date (we've done this several times already)
- Searching for particular dates or a range of dates
- Extracting parts of date values, such as the year, month, or day
- Calculating differences between dates
- Computing a date by adding an interval to or subtracting an interval from another date

Some examples of these operations follow.

To look for particular dates, either by exact value or in relation to another value, compare a `DATE` column to the value in which you're interested:

```
mysql> SELECT * FROM grade_event WHERE date = '2012-10-01';
+------------+----------+----------+
| date       | category | event_id |
+------------+----------+----------+
| 2012-10-01 | T        |        6 |
+------------+----------+----------+
mysql> SELECT last_name, first_name, death
    -> FROM president
    -> WHERE death >= '1970-01-01' AND death < '1980-01-01';
```

```
+-----------+------------+------------+
| last_name | first_name | death      |
+-----------+------------+------------+
| Truman    | Harry S    | 1972-12-26 |
| Johnson   | Lyndon B.  | 1973-01-22 |
+-----------+------------+------------+
```

To test or retrieve parts of dates, use functions such as YEAR(), MONTH(), or DAYOFMONTH(). For example, to find presidents born in March, look for dates with a month value of 3:

```
mysql> SELECT last_name, first_name, birth
    -> FROM president WHERE MONTH(birth) = 3;
+-----------+------------+------------+
| last_name | first_name | birth      |
+-----------+------------+------------+
| Madison   | James      | 1751-03-16 |
| Jackson   | Andrew     | 1767-03-15 |
| Tyler     | John       | 1790-03-29 |
| Cleveland | Grover     | 1837-03-18 |
+-----------+------------+------------+
```

The query also can be written in terms of the month name:

```
mysql> SELECT last_name, first_name, birth
    -> FROM president WHERE MONTHNAME(birth) = 'March';
+-----------+------------+------------+
| last_name | first_name | birth      |
+-----------+------------+------------+
| Madison   | James      | 1751-03-16 |
| Jackson   | Andrew     | 1767-03-15 |
| Tyler     | John       | 1790-03-29 |
| Cleveland | Grover     | 1837-03-18 |
+-----------+------------+------------+
```

To be more specific and find presidents born on a particular day in March, combine tests for MONTH() and DAYOFMONTH():

```
mysql> SELECT last_name, first_name, birth
    -> FROM president WHERE MONTH(birth) = 3 AND DAYOFMONTH(birth) = 29;
+-----------+------------+------------+
| last_name | first_name | birth      |
+-----------+------------+------------+
| Tyler     | John       | 1790-03-29 |
+-----------+------------+------------+
```

That is the kind of query you'd use for generating one of those "famous people who have birthdays today" lists that you see occasionally. However, for the special case of selecting rows that match month and day for "the current date," you need not plug in literal values the way the previous query did. To check for presidents born today, no matter what day of the year today is, compare their birthdays to the month and day parts of the CURDATE() function, which always returns the current date:

```
SELECT last_name, first_name, birth
FROM president WHERE MONTH(birth) = MONTH(CURDATE())
AND DAYOFMONTH(birth) = DAYOFMONTH(CURDATE());
```

To find the interval between dates, subtract one date from another. For example, to determine which presidents lived the longest, compute age at death by taking the difference from birth date. The TIMESTAMPDIFF() function is useful here because it takes an argument for specifying the unit in which to express the result (YEAR in this case):

```
mysql> SELECT last_name, first_name, birth, death,
    -> TIMESTAMPDIFF(YEAR, birth, death) AS age
    -> FROM president WHERE death IS NOT NULL
    -> ORDER BY age DESC LIMIT 5;
+-----------+------------+------------+------------+------+
| last_name | first_name | birth      | death      | age  |
+-----------+------------+------------+------------+------+
| Reagan    | Ronald W.  | 1911-02-06 | 2004-06-05 |   93 |
| Ford      | Gerald R.  | 1913-07-14 | 2006-12-26 |   93 |
| Adams     | John       | 1735-10-30 | 1826-07-04 |   90 |
| Hoover    | Herbert C. | 1874-08-10 | 1964-10-20 |   90 |
| Truman    | Harry S    | 1884-05-08 | 1972-12-26 |   88 |
+-----------+------------+------------+------------+------+
```

If you want the difference in days, an alternative way to compute a difference between dates is to use the TO_DAYS() function that converts a date to days. Determining how far dates are from some reference date is one application for this function. For example, to find Historical League members who need to renew their memberships soon, compute the difference between each member's expiration date and the current date. If it's less than some threshold value, a renewal will soon be needed. The following query finds memberships that have already expired or that will be due for renewal within 60 days:

```
SELECT last_name, first_name, expiration FROM member
WHERE (TO_DAYS(expiration) - TO_DAYS(CURDATE())) < 60;
```

The equivalent statement using TIMESTAMPDIFF() looks like this:

```
SELECT last_name, first_name, expiration FROM member
WHERE TIMESTAMPDIFF(DAY, CURDATE(), expiration) < 60;
```

To calculate one date from another, use DATE_ADD() or DATE_SUB(). These functions take a date and an interval and produce a new date. For example:

```
mysql> SELECT DATE_ADD('1970-1-1', INTERVAL 10 YEAR);
+----------------------------------------+
| DATE_ADD('1970-1-1', INTERVAL 10 YEAR) |
+----------------------------------------+
```

```
| 1980-01-01                              |
+-----------------------------------------+
mysql> SELECT DATE_SUB('1970-1-1', INTERVAL 10 YEAR);
+-----------------------------------------+
| DATE_SUB('1970-1-1', INTERVAL 10 YEAR) |
+-----------------------------------------+
| 1960-01-01                              |
+-----------------------------------------+
```

A query shown earlier in this section selected presidents who died during the 1970s, using literal dates for the endpoints of the selection range. That query can be rewritten to use a literal starting date and an ending date calculated from the starting date and an interval:

```
mysql> SELECT last_name, first_name, death
    -> FROM president
    -> WHERE death >= '1970-1-1'
    -> AND death < DATE_ADD('1970-1-1', INTERVAL 10 YEAR);
+-----------+------------+------------+
| last_name | first_name | death      |
+-----------+------------+------------+
| Truman    | Harry S    | 1972-12-26 |
| Johnson   | Lyndon B.  | 1973-01-22 |
+-----------+------------+------------+
```

For yet another way to write the membership-renewal query, use DATE_ADD():

```
SELECT last_name, first_name, expiration FROM member
WHERE expiration < DATE_ADD(CURDATE(), INTERVAL 60 DAY);
```

If the expiration column is indexed, this will be more efficient than the original query, for reasons discussed in Chapter 5, "Query Optimization."

Near the beginning of this chapter, you saw the following query for determining which of a dentist's patients haven't come in for their checkup in a while:

```
SELECT last_name, first_name, last_visit FROM patient
WHERE last_visit < DATE_SUB(CURDATE(), INTERVAL 6 MONTH);
```

That query may not have meant much to you then. Is it more meaningful now?

1.4.9.7   Pattern Matching

MySQL supports pattern matching operations that enable you to select rows without supplying an exact comparison value: Use the LIKE or NOT LIKE operator and specify a string containing wildcard characters. The character '_' matches any single character, and '%' matches any sequence of characters (including an empty sequence).

This pattern matches last names that begin with a 'W' or 'w' character:

```
mysql> SELECT last_name, first_name FROM president
    -> WHERE last_name LIKE 'W%';
+------------+------------+
| last_name  | first_name |
+------------+------------+
| Washington | George     |
| Wilson     | Woodrow    |
+------------+------------+
```

The following query demonstrates a common error. The "pattern match" returns nothing because it uses a pattern, not with LIKE, but with an arithmetic comparison operator:

```
mysql> SELECT last_name, first_name FROM president
    -> WHERE last_name = 'W%';
Empty set (0.00 sec)
```

The only way for such a comparison to succeed is for the column to contain exactly the string 'W%' or 'w%'.

This pattern matches last names that contain 'W' or 'w' anywhere in the name, not just at the beginning:

```
mysql> SELECT last_name, first_name FROM president
    -> WHERE last_name LIKE '%W%';
+------------+------------+
| last_name  | first_name |
+------------+------------+
| Washington | George     |
| Wilson     | Woodrow    |
| Eisenhower | Dwight D.  |
+------------+------------+
```

This pattern matches last names that contain exactly four characters:

```
mysql> SELECT last_name, first_name FROM president
    -> WHERE last_name LIKE '____';
+-----------+-------------+
| last_name | first_name  |
+-----------+-------------+
| Polk      | James K.    |
| Taft      | William H.  |
| Ford      | Gerald R.   |
| Bush      | George H.W. |
| Bush      | George W.   |
+-----------+-------------+
```

MySQL also provides another form of pattern matching based on regular expressions and the REXEXP operator. LIKE and REGEXP are discussed further in Section 3.5.1.1, "Operator Types," and Appendix C, "Operator and Function Reference."

1.4.9.8   Setting and Using User-Defined Variables

MySQL enables you to define your own variables. These can be set using query results, which provides a convenient way to save values for use in later queries. Suppose that you want to find out which presidents were born before Andrew Jackson. To determine that, you can retrieve his birth date into a variable, then select other presidents with a birth date earlier than the value of the variable:

```
mysql> SELECT @jackson_birth := birth FROM president
    -> WHERE last_name = 'Jackson' AND first_name = 'Andrew';
+-------------------------+
| @jackson_birth := birth |
+-------------------------+
| 1767-03-15              |
+-------------------------+
mysql> SELECT last_name, first_name, birth FROM president
    -> WHERE birth < @jackson_birth ORDER BY birth;
+------------+------------+------------+
| last_name  | first_name | birth      |
+------------+------------+------------+
| Washington | George     | 1732-02-22 |
| Adams      | John       | 1735-10-30 |
| Jefferson  | Thomas     | 1743-04-13 |
| Madison    | James      | 1751-03-16 |
| Monroe     | James      | 1758-04-28 |
+------------+------------+------------+
```

To write a user variable, use @var_name syntax. In a SELECT statement, assign the variable a value using an expression of the form @var_name := value. The first query therefore looks up the birth date for Andrew Jackson and assigns it to the @jackson_birth variable. (The result of the SELECT still is displayed; assigning a query result to a variable doesn't suppress the query output.) The second query refers to the variable and uses its value to find other president rows with a lesser birth value.

The preceding problem actually could be solved in a single query using a join or a subquery, but we're not to the point of writing those yet. And sometimes it's clearer to use a variable. (For the subquery solution, see Section 1.4.9.10, "Retrieving Information from Multiple Tables.")

Variables also can be assigned using a SET statement. In this case, either = or := are permitted as the assignment operator:

```
mysql> SET @today = CURDATE();
mysql> SET @one_week_ago := DATE_SUB(@today, INTERVAL 7 DAY);
mysql> SELECT @today, @one_week_ago;
+------------+---------------+
| @today     | @one_week_ago |
+------------+---------------+
| 2012-04-21 | 2012-04-14    |
+------------+---------------+
```

1.4.9.9   Generating Summaries

One of the most useful things MySQL can do for you is to boil down lots of raw data and summarize it. MySQL becomes a powerful ally when you learn to use it to generate summaries because that is an especially tedious, time-consuming, error-prone activity when done manually.

One simple type of summary shows the unique values present in a set of values. Use the DISTINCT keyword to remove duplicate rows from a result. For example, the different states in which presidents have been born can be found like this:

```
mysql> SELECT DISTINCT state FROM president ORDER BY state;
+--------+
| state  |
+--------+
| AR     |
| CA     |
| CT     |
| GA     |
| HI     |
| IA     |
| IL     |
| KY     |
| MA     |
| MO     |
...
```

Another form of summary involves counting, using the COUNT() function. If you use COUNT(*), it tells you the number of rows selected by your query. If a query has no WHERE clause, it selects all rows, so COUNT(*) tells you the number of rows in your table. The following query shows how many rows the Historical League member table contains:

```
mysql> SELECT COUNT(*) FROM member;
+----------+
| COUNT(*) |
+----------+
|      102 |
+----------+
```

If a query does have a WHERE clause, COUNT(*) tells you how many rows the clause matches. This query shows how many quizzes you have given your class so far:

```
mysql> SELECT COUNT(*) FROM grade_event WHERE category = 'Q';
+----------+
| COUNT(*) |
+----------+
|        4 |
+----------+
```

COUNT(*) counts every row selected. By contrast, COUNT(*col_name*) counts only non-NULL values. The following query demonstrates these differences:

```
mysql> SELECT COUNT(*), COUNT(email), COUNT(expiration) FROM member;
+----------+--------------+-------------------+
| COUNT(*) | COUNT(email) | COUNT(expiration) |
+----------+--------------+-------------------+
|      102 |           80 |                96 |
+----------+--------------+-------------------+
```

This shows that although the member table has 102 rows, only 80 of them have a value in the email column. It also shows that six members have a lifetime membership. (A NULL value in the expiration column indicates a lifetime membership, and since 96 out of 102 rows are not NULL, that leaves six.)

COUNT() combined with DISTINCT counts the number of distinct non-NULL values in a result. To count the number of different states in which presidents have been born, do this:

```
mysql> SELECT COUNT(DISTINCT state) FROM president;
+-----------------------+
| COUNT(DISTINCT state) |
+-----------------------+
|                    21 |
+-----------------------+
```

You can produce an overall count of values in a column, or break down the counts by categories. For example, you can determine the total number of students in your class by running this query:

```
mysql> SELECT COUNT(*) FROM student;
+----------+
| COUNT(*) |
+----------+
|       31 |
+----------+
```

But how many students are boys and how many are girls? One way to find out is by asking for a count for each sex separately:

```
mysql> SELECT COUNT(*) FROM student WHERE sex='f';
+----------+
| COUNT(*) |
+----------+
|       15 |
+----------+
mysql> SELECT COUNT(*) FROM student WHERE sex='m';
+----------+
| COUNT(*) |
+----------+
|       16 |
+----------+
```

However, that approach is tedious and not really very well suited for columns that might have several different values. Consider how you'd determine the number of presidents born in each state this way. You'd have to find out which states are represented so as not to miss any (SELECT DISTINCT state FROM president), and then run a SELECT COUNT(*) query for each state. That is clearly something you want to avoid.

Fortunately, it's possible to use a single query to count how many times each distinct value occurs in a column. For the student list, count boys and girls separately using a GROUP BY clause:

```
mysql> SELECT sex, COUNT(*) FROM student GROUP BY sex;
+-----+----------+
| sex | COUNT(*) |
+-----+----------+
| F   |       15 |
| M   |       16 |
+-----+----------+
```

The same form of query tells us how many presidents were born in each state:

```
mysql> SELECT state, COUNT(*) FROM president GROUP BY state;
+-------+----------+
| state | COUNT(*) |
+-------+----------+
| AR    |        1 |
| CA    |        1 |
| CT    |        1 |
| GA    |        1 |
| HI    |        1 |
| IA    |        1 |
| IL    |        1 |
| KY    |        1 |
| MA    |        4 |
| MO    |        1 |
...
```

When you count values in groups this way, the GROUP BY clause tells MySQL how to cluster values before counting them.

The use of COUNT(*) with GROUP BY to count values has a number of advantages over counting occurrences of each distinct column value individually:

- You need not know in advance what values are present in the column.
- You need only a single query, not several.
- You get all the results with a single query, so you can sort the output.

The first two advantages are important for expressing queries more easily. The third advantage is important because it affords more flexibility in displaying results. By default, MySQL uses the columns named in the GROUP BY clause to sort the results, but you can specify an ORDER BY clause to sort in a different order. For example, if you want number of presidents grouped by state of birth, but sorted with the most well-represented states first, you can use an ORDER BY clause as follows:

```
mysql> SELECT state, COUNT(*) AS count FROM president
    -> GROUP BY state ORDER BY count DESC;
+-------+-------+
| state | count |
+-------+-------+
| VA    |     8 |
| OH    |     7 |
| MA    |     4 |
| NY    |     4 |
| NC    |     2 |
| VT    |     2 |
| TX    |     2 |
| GA    |     1 |
| IL    |     1 |
| SC    |     1 |
...
```

When the column to use for sorting is produced by a summary function, you cannot refer to the function directly in the ORDER BY clause. Instead, give the column an alias and refer to it that way. The preceding query demonstrates this, where the COUNT(*) column is aliased as count.

To group results using GROUP BY with a calculated column, refer to it using an alias or column position, just as with ORDER BY. The following query determines how many presidents were born in each month of the year:

```
mysql> SELECT MONTH(birth) AS Month, MONTHNAME(birth) AS Name,
    -> COUNT(*) AS count
    -> FROM president GROUP BY Name ORDER BY Month;
+-------+-----------+-------+
| Month | Name      | count |
+-------+-----------+-------+
|     1 | January   |     4 |
|     2 | February  |     4 |
|     3 | March     |     4 |
|     4 | April     |     4 |
|     5 | May       |     2 |
|     6 | June      |     1 |
|     7 | July      |     4 |
|     8 | August    |     5 |
|     9 | September |     1 |
|    10 | October   |     6 |
|    11 | November  |     5 |
|    12 | December  |     3 |
+-------+-----------+-------+
```

`COUNT()` can be combined with `ORDER BY` and `LIMIT`. For example, to find the four most well-represented states in the `president` table, use this statement:

```
mysql> SELECT state, COUNT(*) AS count FROM president
    -> GROUP BY state ORDER BY count DESC LIMIT 4;
+-------+-------+
| state | count |
+-------+-------+
| VA    |     8 |
| OH    |     7 |
| MA    |     4 |
| NY    |     4 |
+-------+-------+
```

If you don't want to limit query output with a `LIMIT` clause, but rather by looking for particular values of `COUNT()`, use a `HAVING` clause. `HAVING` is similar to `WHERE` in that it specifies conditions that must be satisfied by output rows. It differs from `WHERE` in that it can refer to the results of summary functions like `COUNT()`. The following query tells you which states are represented by two or more presidents:

```
mysql> SELECT state, COUNT(*) AS count FROM president
    -> GROUP BY state HAVING count > 1 ORDER BY count DESC;
+-------+-------+
| state | count |
+-------+-------+
| VA    |     8 |
| OH    |     7 |
| MA    |     4 |
| NY    |     4 |
| NC    |     2 |
| VT    |     2 |
| TX    |     2 |
+-------+-------+
```

More generally, this is the type of query to run when you want to find duplicated values in a column. Or, to find nonduplicated values, use `HAVING count = 1`.

There are several summary functions other than `COUNT()`. The `MIN()`, `MAX()`, `SUM()`, and `AVG()` functions are useful for determining the minimum, maximum, total, and average values in a column. You can even use them all at the same time. The following query shows numeric characteristics for each quiz and test you've given. It also shows how many scores are used to compute each of the values. (Some students may have been absent and are not counted.)

```
mysql> SELECT
    -> event_id,
    -> MIN(score) AS minimum,
    -> MAX(score) AS maximum,
    -> MAX(score)-MIN(score)+1 AS span,
    -> SUM(score) AS total,
```

```
    -> AVG(score) AS average,
    -> COUNT(score) AS count
    -> FROM score
    -> GROUP BY event_id;
+----------+---------+---------+------+-------+---------+-------+
| event_id | minimum | maximum | span | total | average | count |
+----------+---------+---------+------+-------+---------+-------+
|        1 |       9 |      20 |   12 |   439 | 15.1379 |    29 |
|        2 |       8 |      19 |   12 |   425 | 14.1667 |    30 |
|        3 |      60 |      97 |   38 |  2425 | 78.2258 |    31 |
|        4 |       7 |      20 |   14 |   379 | 14.0370 |    27 |
|        5 |       8 |      20 |   13 |   383 | 14.1852 |    27 |
|        6 |      62 |     100 |   39 |  2325 | 80.1724 |    29 |
+----------+---------+---------+------+-------+---------+-------+
```

This information would be more meaningful if it was clear whether the `event_id` values represented quizzes or tests. However, to produce that information, we need to consult the `grade_event` table as well; we'll revisit this query in Section 1.4.9.10, "Retrieving Information from Multiple Tables."

To produce extra output lines that give you a "summary of summaries," add a `WITH ROLLUP` clause. This tells MySQL to calculate "super-aggregate" values for the grouped rows. Here's a simple example based on an earlier statement that counts the number of students of each sex. The `WITH ROLLUP` clause produces another line that summarizes the counts for both sexes:

```
mysql> SELECT sex, COUNT(*) FROM student GROUP BY sex WITH ROLLUP;
+------+----------+
| sex  | COUNT(*) |
+------+----------+
| F    |       15 |
| M    |       16 |
| NULL |       31 |
+------+----------+
```

The `NULL` in the grouped column indicates that corresponding count is the summary value for the preceding groups.

`WITH ROLLUP` can be used with the other aggregate functions as well. The following statement calculates grade summaries as just shown a few paragraphs earlier, but also produces an extra super-aggregate line:

```
mysql> SELECT
    -> event_id,
    -> MIN(score) AS minimum,
    -> MAX(score) AS maximum,
    -> MAX(score)-MIN(score)+1 AS span,
    -> SUM(score) AS total,
    -> AVG(score) AS average,
    -> COUNT(score) AS count
```

```
    -> FROM score
    -> GROUP BY event_id WITH ROLLUP;
+----------+---------+---------+------+-------+---------+-------+
| event_id | minimum | maximum | span | total | average | count |
+----------+---------+---------+------+-------+---------+-------+
|        1 |       9 |      20 |   12 |   439 | 15.1379 |    29 |
|        2 |       8 |      19 |   12 |   425 | 14.1667 |    30 |
|        3 |      60 |      97 |   38 |  2425 | 78.2258 |    31 |
|        4 |       7 |      20 |   14 |   379 | 14.0370 |    27 |
|        5 |       8 |      20 |   13 |   383 | 14.1852 |    27 |
|        6 |      62 |     100 |   39 |  2325 | 80.1724 |    29 |
|     NULL |       7 |     100 |   94 |  6376 | 36.8555 |   173 |
+----------+---------+---------+------+-------+---------+-------+
```

In this output, the final line displays aggregate values calculated based on all the preceding group summary values.

WITH ROLLUP is useful because it provides extra information that you would otherwise have to obtain by running another query. Using a single query is more efficient because the server need not examine the data twice. If the GROUP BY clause names more than one column, WITH ROLLUP produces additional super-aggregate lines that contain higher-level summary values.

1.4.9.10   Retrieving Information from Multiple Tables

The statements we've written so far have pulled data from a single table. But MySQL is capable of working much harder for you. I mentioned earlier that the power of a relational DBMS lies in its capability to combine information from multiple tables to answer questions that can't be answered from individual tables alone. This section describes how to write statements that do that.

One type of operation that selects information from multiple tables is called a "join" because you're producing a result by joining the information in one table to the information in another table. This is done by matching common values in the tables. Another type of multiple-table operation uses one SELECT nested within another SELECT. The nested SELECT is called a "subquery." This section describes both types of operations.

Let's work through a join example. Earlier, in Section 1.4.6.2, "Tables for the Grade-Keeping Project," a query to retrieve quiz or test scores for a given date was presented without explanation. Now it's time for the explanation. The query actually involves a three-way join, so we'll build up to it in two steps. In the first step, construct a query to select scores for a given date as follows:

```
mysql> SELECT student_id, date, score, category
    -> FROM grade_event INNER JOIN score
    -> ON grade_event.event_id = score.event_id
    -> WHERE date = '2012-09-23';
```

```
+------------+------------+-------+----------+
| student_id | date       | score | category |
+------------+------------+-------+----------+
|          1 | 2012-09-23 |    15 | Q        |
|          2 | 2012-09-23 |    12 | Q        |
|          3 | 2012-09-23 |    11 | Q        |
|          5 | 2012-09-23 |    13 | Q        |
|          6 | 2012-09-23 |    18 | Q        |
+------------+------------+-------+----------+
...
```

The query works by finding the `grade_event` row with the given date (`'2012-09-23'`), and using the event ID in that row to locate scores that have the same event ID. For each matching `grade_event` row and `score` row combination, it displays the student ID, score, date, and event category.

The query differs from others we have written in two important respects:

- The FROM clause names more than one table because we're retrieving data from more than one table:

  ```
  FROM grade_event INNER JOIN score
  ```

- The ON clause specifies that the `grade_event` and `score` tables are joined on the basis of matching the `event_id` values in each table:

  ```
  ON grade_event.event_id = score.event_id
  ```

Notice how we refer to the `event_id` columns as `grade_event.event_id` and `score.event_id` using *tbl_name.col_name* syntax so MySQL knows which tables we're referring to. This is because `event_id` occurs in both tables, so it's ambiguous if used without a table name to qualify it. The other columns in the query (`date`, `score`, and `category`) can be used without a table qualifier because they appear in only one of the tables and thus are unambiguous.

I generally prefer to qualify every column in a join to make it clearer (more explicit) which table each column is part of, and that's how I'll write joins from now on. In fully qualified form, the query looks like this:

```
SELECT score.student_id, grade_event.date, score.score, grade_event.category
FROM grade_event INNER JOIN score
ON grade_event.event_id = score.event_id
WHERE grade_event.date = '2012-09-23';
```

The first-stage query uses the `grade_event` table to map a date to an event ID, and uses the ID to find the matching scores in the `score` table. Output from the query contains `student_id` values, but names would be more meaningful. By using the `student` table, we can map student IDs onto names, which is the second step. To accomplish name display, use the fact that the `score` and `student` tables both have `student_id` columns enabling the rows in them to be linked. The resulting query follows:

```
mysql> SELECT
    -> student.name, grade_event.date, score.score, grade_event.category
    -> FROM grade_event INNER JOIN score INNER JOIN student
    -> ON grade_event.event_id = score.event_id
    -> AND score.student_id = student.student_id
    -> WHERE grade_event.date = '2012-09-23';
+-----------+------------+-------+----------+
| name      | date       | score | category |
+-----------+------------+-------+----------+
| Megan     | 2012-09-23 |    15 | Q        |
| Joseph    | 2012-09-23 |    12 | Q        |
| Kyle      | 2012-09-23 |    11 | Q        |
| Abby      | 2012-09-23 |    13 | Q        |
| Nathan    | 2012-09-23 |    18 | Q        |
...
```

This query differs in several ways from the previous one:

- The FROM clause now includes the student table because the statement uses it in addition to the grade_event and score tables.

- The student_id column was unambiguous before, so it was possible to refer to it in either unqualified (student_id) or qualified (score.student_id) form. Now it is ambiguous because it is present in both the score and student tables. Therefore, it *must* be qualified as score.student_id or student.student_id to make it clear which table to use.

- The ON clause has an additional term specifying that score table rows are matched against student table rows based on student ID:

  ```
  ON ... score.student_id = student.student_id
  ```

- The query displays the student name rather than the student ID. (To display both, just add student.student_id to the list of output columns.)

With this query, you can plug in any date and get back the scores for that date, complete with student names and the score category. You don't have to know anything about student IDs or event IDs. MySQL figures out the relevant ID values and uses them to match table rows.

Earlier, in Section 1.4.9.9, "Generating Summaries," we ran a query that produced a numeric characterization of the data in the score table. Output from that query listed event ID but did not include event dates or categories, because we didn't know then how to join the score table to the grade_event table to map the IDs onto dates and categories. Now we do. The following query is similar to one run earlier, but shows the dates and categories rather than simply the numeric event IDs:

```
mysql> SELECT
    -> grade_event.date,grade_event.category,
    -> MIN(score.score) AS minimum,
    -> MAX(score.score) AS maximum,
```

```
    -> MAX(score.score)-MIN(score.score)+1 AS span,
    -> SUM(score.score) AS total,
    -> AVG(score.score) AS average,
    -> COUNT(score.score) AS count
    -> FROM score INNER JOIN grade_event
    -> ON score.event_id = grade_event.event_id
    -> GROUP BY grade_event.date;
```

date	category	minimum	maximum	span	total	average	count
2012-09-03	Q	9	20	12	439	15.1379	29
2012-09-06	Q	8	19	12	425	14.1667	30
2012-09-09	T	60	97	38	2425	78.2258	31
2012-09-16	Q	7	20	14	379	14.0370	27
2012-09-23	Q	8	20	13	383	14.1852	27
2012-10-01	T	62	100	39	2325	80.1724	29

Although the GROUP BY column has a qualifier, it isn't strictly necessary for this query. GROUP BY refers to output columns, and there is only one such column named date, so MySQL knows which one you mean.

You can use functions such as COUNT() and AVG() to produce a summary over multiple columns, even if the columns come from different tables. The following query determines the number of scores and the average score for each combination of event date and student sex:

```
mysql> SELECT grade_event.date, student.sex,
    -> COUNT(score.score) AS count, AVG(score.score) AS average
    -> FROM grade_event INNER JOIN score INNER JOIN student
    -> ON grade_event.event_id = score.event_id
    -> AND score.student_id = student.student_id
    -> GROUP BY grade_event.date, student.sex;
```

date	sex	count	average
2012-09-03	F	14	14.6429
2012-09-03	M	15	15.6000
2012-09-06	F	14	14.7143
2012-09-06	M	16	13.6875
2012-09-09	F	15	77.4000
2012-09-09	M	16	79.0000
2012-09-16	F	13	15.3077
2012-09-16	M	14	12.8571
2012-09-23	F	12	14.0833
2012-09-23	M	15	14.2667
2012-10-01	F	14	77.7857
2012-10-01	M	15	82.4000

We can use a similar query to perform one of the grade-keeping project tasks, that of computing the total score per student at the end of the semester:

```
SELECT student.student_id, student.name,
SUM(score.score) AS total, COUNT(score.score) AS n
FROM grade_event INNER JOIN score INNER JOIN student
ON grade_event.event_id = score.event_id
AND score.student_id = student.student_id
GROUP BY score.student_id
ORDER BY total;
```

Another task the grade-keeping project involves is summarizing student absences. Absences are recorded in the absence table by student ID and date. To get student names (not just IDs), we must join the absence table to the student table, based on the student_id value. The following query lists student ID number and name along with a count of absences:

```
mysql> SELECT student.student_id, student.name,
    -> COUNT(absence.date) AS absences
    -> FROM student INNER JOIN absence
    -> ON student.student_id = absence.student_id
    -> GROUP BY student.student_id;
+------------+-------+----------+
| student_id | name  | absences |
+------------+-------+----------+
|          3 | Kyle  |        1 |
|          5 | Abby  |        1 |
|         10 | Peter |        2 |
|         17 | Will  |        1 |
|         20 | Avery |        1 |
+------------+-------+----------+
```

The output produced by the query is fine if you want to know only which students had absences. But if you turn in this list to the school office, they might say, "What about the other students? We want a value for every student." That's a slightly different question. It asks for the number of absences, even for students who had none. Because the question is different, the query that answers it is different as well.

To answer the question, we will use a LEFT JOIN rather than an inner join. LEFT JOIN tells MySQL to produce a row of output for each row selected from the table named first in the join (that is, the table named to the left of the LEFT JOIN keywords). By naming the student table first, we'll get output for every student, even those who are not represented in the absence table. To write this query, use LEFT JOIN between the tables named in the FROM clause (rather than separating them by a comma), and an ON clause that says how to match rows in the two tables. The query looks like this:

```
mysql> SELECT student.student_id, student.name,
    -> COUNT(absence.date) AS absences
    -> FROM student LEFT JOIN absence
    -> ON student.student_id = absence.student_id
```

```
    -> GROUP BY student.student_id;
+------------+-----------+-----------+
| student_id | name      | absences  |
+------------+-----------+-----------+
|          1 | Megan     |         0 |
|          2 | Joseph    |         0 |
|          3 | Kyle      |         1 |
|          4 | Katie     |         0 |
|          5 | Abby      |         1 |
|          6 | Nathan    |         0 |
|          7 | Liesl     |         0 |
...
```

There is no requirement that a join be performed between different tables. It might seem odd at first, but you can join a table to itself. For example, to determine whether any president was born in the same city as another, check each president's birthplace against every other president's birthplace:

```
mysql> SELECT p1.last_name, p1.first_name, p1.city, p1.state
    -> FROM president AS p1 INNER JOIN president AS p2
    -> ON p1.city = p2.city AND p1.state = p2.state
    -> WHERE (p1.last_name <> p2.last_name OR p1.first_name <> p2.first_name)
    -> ORDER BY state, city, last_name;
+-----------+--------------+-----------+-------+
| last_name | first_name   | city      | state |
+-----------+--------------+-----------+-------+
| Adams     | John Quincy  | Braintree | MA    |
| Adams     | John         | Braintree | MA    |
+-----------+--------------+-----------+-------+
```

There are two tricky things about this query:

- It's necessary to refer to two instances of the same table, so we create table aliases (p1, p2) and use them to disambiguate references to the table's columns. As with column aliases, the AS keyword is optional when naming table aliases.

- Each president's row matches itself, but we don't want to see that in the output. The WHERE clause prevents matching a row to itself by making sure that the rows being compared are for different president names.

A similar query finds presidents who were born on the same day of the year. However, birth dates cannot be compared directly because that would miss presidents who were born in different years. Instead, use MONTH() and DAYOFMONTH() to compare month and day of the birth date:

```
mysql> SELECT p1.last_name, p1.first_name, p1.birth
    -> FROM president AS p1 INNER JOIN president AS p2
    -> WHERE MONTH(p1.birth) = MONTH(p2.birth)
    -> AND DAYOFMONTH(p1.birth) = DAYOFMONTH(p2.birth)
```

```
    -> AND (p1.last_name <> p2.last_name OR p1.first_name <> p2.first_name)
    -> ORDER BY p1.last_name;
+-----------+------------+------------+
| last_name | first_name | birth      |
+-----------+------------+------------+
| Harding   | Warren G.  | 1865-11-02 |
| Polk      | James K.   | 1795-11-02 |
+-----------+------------+------------+
```

Using DAYOFYEAR() rather than the combination of MONTH() and DAYOFMONTH() would result in a simpler query, but it would produce incorrect results when comparing dates from leap years to dates from nonleap years.

Another kind of multiple-table retrieval uses a subquery, which is one SELECT nested within another. There are several types of subqueries, which are discussed further in Section 2.9, "Performing Multiple-Table Retrievals with Subqueries." A couple of examples will do for now. Suppose that you want to identify those students who have perfect attendance. That is equivalent to determining which students are not represented in the absence table, which can be done like this:

```
mysql> SELECT * FROM student
    -> WHERE student_id NOT IN (SELECT student_id FROM absence);
+-----------+-----+------------+
| name      | sex | student_id |
+-----------+-----+------------+
| Megan     | F   |          1 |
| Joseph    | M   |          2 |
| Katie     | F   |          4 |
| Nathan    | M   |          6 |
| Liesl     | F   |          7 |
...
```

The nested SELECT determines the set of student_id values that are present in the absence table, and the outer SELECT retrieves student rows that match none of those IDs.

A subquery also provides a single-statement solution to the question asked in Section 1.4.9.8, "Setting and Using User-Defined Variables," about which presidents were born before Andrew Jackson. The original solution used two statements and a user variable, but it can be done with a subquery as follows:

```
mysql> SELECT last_name, first_name, birth FROM president
    -> WHERE birth < (SELECT birth FROM president
    -> WHERE last_name = 'Jackson' AND first_name = 'Andrew');
+------------+------------+------------+
| last_name  | first_name | birth      |
+------------+------------+------------+
| Washington | George     | 1732-02-22 |
| Adams      | John       | 1735-10-30 |
| Jefferson  | Thomas     | 1743-04-13 |
```

```
| Madison    | James      | 1751-03-16 |
| Monroe     | James      | 1758-04-28 |
+------------+------------+------------+
```

The inner SELECT determines Andrew Jackson's birth date, and the outer SELECT retrieves presidents with a birth date earlier than his.

1.4.10 Deleting or Updating Existing Rows

Sometimes you want to get rid of rows or change their contents. The DELETE and UPDATE statements enable you to do this.

The DELETE statement has this form:

```
DELETE FROM tbl_name
WHERE which rows to delete;
```

The WHERE clause that specifies which rows should be deleted is optional, but if you leave it out the statement deletes all rows from the table. In other words, the simplest DELETE statement is also the most dangerous:

```
DELETE FROM tbl_name;
```

That statement wipes out the table's contents entirely, so be careful with it! To delete specific rows, use the WHERE clause to identify the rows in which you're interested. This is similar to using a WHERE clause in a SELECT statement to avoid selecting the entire table. For example, to specifically delete from the president table only those presidents born in Ohio, use this statement:

```
mysql> DELETE FROM president WHERE state='OH';
Query OK, 7 rows affected (0.01 sec)
```

If you're not really sure which rows a DELETE statement will remove, test the WHERE clause first in a SELECT statement to find out which rows it matches. This helps you ensure that you'll actually delete the rows you intend, and only those rows. Suppose that you want to delete the row for Teddy Roosevelt. Would the following statement do the job?

```
DELETE FROM president WHERE last_name='Roosevelt';
```

Yes, in the sense that it would delete the row you have in mind. No, in the sense that it also would delete the row for Franklin Roosevelt. It's safer to check the WHERE clause with a SELECT statement first, like this:

```
mysql> SELECT last_name, first_name FROM president
    -> WHERE last_name='Roosevelt';
+-----------+-------------+
| last_name | first_name  |
+-----------+-------------+
| Roosevelt | Theodore    |
| Roosevelt | Franklin D. |
+-----------+-------------+
```

From that, you can see the need to be more specific by adding a condition for the first name:

```
mysql> SELECT last_name, first_name FROM president
    -> WHERE last_name='Roosevelt' AND first_name='Theodore';
+-----------+------------+
| last_name | first_name |
+-----------+------------+
| Roosevelt | Theodore   |
+-----------+------------+
```

Now you know the WHERE clause that properly identifies only the desired row, and the DELETE statement can be constructed correctly:

```
mysql> DELETE FROM president
    -> WHERE last_name='Roosevelt' AND first_name='Theodore';
```

If that seems like a lot of typing to delete a row, well, better safe than sorry! Also, in situations such as this, you can minimize typing through the use of copy and paste or input line-editing techniques. For more information, see Section 1.5, "Tips for Interacting with mysql."

To modify existing rows, use UPDATE, which has this form:

```
UPDATE tbl_name
SET which columns to change
WHERE which rows to update;
```

The WHERE clause is just as for DELETE. It's optional, so if you don't specify one, every row in the table will be updated. For example, the following statement changes the name of each student to "George":

```
mysql> UPDATE student SET name='George';
```

Obviously, you must be careful with statements like that, so normally you add a WHERE clause to be more specific about which rows to update. Suppose that you recently added a new member to the Historical League but filled in only a few columns of his entry:

```
mysql> INSERT INTO member (last_name,first_name)
    -> VALUES('York','Jerome');
```

Then you realize you forgot to set his membership expiration date. You can fix that with an UPDATE statement that includes an appropriate WHERE clause to identify which row to change:

```
mysql> UPDATE member
    -> SET expiration='2013-7-20'
    -> WHERE last_name='York' AND first_name='Jerome';
```

You can update multiple columns with a single statement. The following UPDATE modifies Jerome's email and postal addresses:

```
mysql> UPDATE member
    -> SET email='jeromey@aol.com', street='123 Elm St',
    -> city='Anytown', state='NY', zip='01003'
    -> WHERE last_name='York' AND first_name='Jerome';
```

You can also "unset" a column by setting its value to NULL (if the column permits NULL values). If at some point in the future Jerome later decides to pay the big membership renewal fee that enables him to become a lifetime member, you can mark his row as "never expires" by setting his expiration date to NULL:

```
mysql> UPDATE member
    -> SET expiration=NULL
    -> WHERE last_name='York' AND first_name='Jerome';
```

With UPDATE, just as for DELETE, it's not a bad idea to test a WHERE clause using a SELECT statement to make sure that you're choosing the right rows to update. Otherwise, if your selection criteria are too narrow or too broad, you'll update too few or too many rows.

If you've tried the statements in this section, you'll have deleted and modified rows in the sampdb tables. Before proceeding to the next section, you should undo those changes. Do that by reloading the tables using the instructions given earlier, in Section 1.4.8, "Resetting the sampdb Database to a Known State."

1.5   Tips for Interacting with `mysql`

This section discusses how to interact with the `mysql` client program more efficiently and with less typing. It also describes how to connect to the server more easily and how to enter statements without typing each one by hand.

1.5.1   Simplifying the Connection Process

When you invoke `mysql`, it's likely that you need to specify connection parameters such as hostname, username, or password. That's a lot of typing just to run a program, and it quickly becomes tiresome. There are several ways to minimize the typing necessary to establish a connection to the MySQL server:

- Store connection parameters in an option file.
- Repeat commands by taking advantage of your shell's command history capabilities.
- Define a `mysql` command-line shortcut using a shell alias or script.

1.5.1.1   Using an Option File

MySQL enables you to store connection parameters in an option file. Then you need not type the parameters each time you run `mysql`; they're used just as if you had entered them on the command line. A big advantage of this technique is that the parameters can also be used by other MySQL clients such as `mysqlimport` or `mysqlshow`. In other words, an option file makes it easier to use not just `mysql` but many other programs as well. This section briefly describes how to set up an option file for use by client programs. For additional details, see Section F.2.2, "Option Files."

Under Unix, set up an option file by creating a file named `~/.my.cnf` (that is, a file named `.my.cnf` in your home directory). Under Windows, create an option file named `my.ini` in your MySQL installation directory, or in the root directory of the C drive (that is, `C:\my.ini`). An option file is a plain text file; create it using any text editor. The file's contents should look something like this:

```
[client]
host=server_host
user=your_name
password=your_pass
```

The `[client]` line signals the beginning of the `client` option group. MySQL client programs read the lines following it to obtain option values, until the end of the file or until a different option group begins. Replace *server_host*, *your_name*, and *your_pass* with the host-name, username, and password that you specify when you connect to the server. If the server is running on the host `cobra.example.com` and your MySQL username and password are `sampadm` and `secret`, put these lines in the `.my.cnf` file:

```
[client]
host=cobra.example.com
user=sampadm
password=secret
```

The `[client]` line is required, to define where the option group begins, but the lines that define parameter values are optional; you can specify just the ones you need. For example, if you're using Unix and your MySQL username is the same as your Unix login name, there is no need to include a `user` line. The default host is `localhost`, so if you connect to a server running on the local host, no `host` line is necessary.

Under Unix, an additional precaution you should take after creating the option file is to set its access mode to a restrictive value so no one else can read or modify it. Either of the following commands make the file accessible only to you:

```
% chmod 600 .my.cnf
% chmod u=rw,go-rwx .my.cnf
```

1.5.1.2   Using Your Shell's Command History

Shells such as `tcsh` and `bash` remember your commands in a history list and enable you to repeat commands from that list. If you use such a shell, your history list can help you avoid typing entire commands. For example, if you've recently invoked `mysql`, you can execute it again like this:

```
% !my
```

The '`!`' character tells your shell to search through your command history to find the most recent command that begins with "my" and reissue it as though you'd typed it again yourself. Some shells also enable you to move up and down through your history list using the up arrow and down arrow keys (or perhaps Control-P and Control-N). After selecting a command this way, press Enter to execute it. `tcsh` and `bash` have this facility, and other shells may as well. Check the documentation for your shell to find out more about using your history list.

1.5.1.3   Using Shell Aliases and Scripts

Your shell might provide an alias facility that enables a short command name to map to a long command. For example, in `csh` or `tcsh`, you can use the `alias` command to create an alias named `sampdb` like this:

```
alias sampdb 'mysql -h cobra.example.com -p -u sampadm sampdb'
```

The syntax for `bash` is slightly different:

```
alias sampdb='mysql -h cobra.example.com -p -u sampadm sampdb'
```

Defining the alias makes the following two commands equivalent:

```
% sampdb
% mysql -h cobra.example.com -p -u sampadm sampdb
```

Clearly, the first is easier to type than the second. To make the alias take effect each time you log in, put the `alias` command in one of your shell's startup files (for example, `.tcshrc` for `tcsh`, or `.bashrc` or `.bash_profile` for `bash`).

On Windows, a similar technique is to create a shortcut that points to the `mysql` program, then edit the shortcut's properties to include the appropriate connection parameters.

Another way to invoke commands with less typing is to create a script that executes `mysql` for you with the proper options. On Unix, a shell script that is equivalent to the `sampdb` alias just shown looks like this:

```
#!/bin/sh
exec mysql -h cobra.example.com -p -u sampadm sampdb
```

If you name the script `sampdb` and make it executable (with `chmod +x sampdb`), you can type `sampdb` at the command prompt to run `mysql` and connect to the `sampdb` database.

On Windows, use a batch file to do the same thing. Name the file `sampdb.bat` and put the following line in it:

```
mysql -h cobra.example.com -p -u sampadm sampdb
```

This batch file can be run either by typing `sampdb` at the prompt in a console window or by double-clicking its Windows icon.

If you need to access several databases or connect to several hosts, you can define multiple aliases, shortcuts, or scripts, each of which invokes `mysql` with different options.

1.5.2   Issuing Statements with Less Typing

`mysql` is an extremely useful program for interacting with your database, but its interface is most suitable for short, single-line queries. Although `mysql` itself doesn't care whether a query spreads across multiple lines, long queries aren't much fun to type. And it's annoying to enter a query, only to discover that you must retype it because it has a syntax error. These techniques help you avoid needless retyping:

- Use `mysql`'s input line-editing facility.

- Use copy and paste.

- Run `mysql` in batch mode.

1.5.2.1   Using the `mysql` Input Line Editor

`mysql` permits input line editing. You can manipulate the line you're currently entering, or recall previous input lines and re-enter them, either as is or after further modification. This is convenient when you're entering a line and spot a typo; you can back up within the line to correct the problem before pressing Enter. If you enter a query that has a mistake in it, you can recall the query, edit it to fix the problem, and then resubmit it. (This is easiest if you type the entire query on one line.)

Table 1.4 shows some key sequences you might find useful on Unix systems.

Table 1.4   **`mysql` Input Editing Commands**

Key Sequence	Meaning
Up arrow or Control-P	Recall previous line
Down arrow or Control-N	Recall next line
Left arrow or Control-B	Move cursor left (backward)
Right arrow or Control-F	Move cursor right (forward)
Escape b	Move backward one word
Escape f	Move forward one word
Control-A	Move cursor to beginning of line
Control-E	Move cursor to end of line
Control-D	Delete character under cursor
Delete	Delete character to left of cursor
Escape D	Delete word
Escape Backspace	Delete word to left of cursor
Control-K	Erase everything from cursor to end of line

On Windows, line-editing capabilities are not provided by `mysql`. However, Windows itself supports the commands shown in Table 1.5, so they become available to `mysql`.

Table 1.5 **Windows Input Editing Commands**

Key Sequence	Meaning
Up arrow	Recall previous line
Down arrow	Recall next line
Left arrow	Move cursor left (backward)
Right arrow	Move cursor right (forward)
Control-left arrow	Move backward one word
Control-right arrow	Move forward one word
Home	Move cursor to beginning of line
End	Move cursor to end of line
Delete	Delete character under cursor
Backspace	Delete character to left of cursor
Esc	Erase line
Page Up	Recall first command entered
Page Down	Recall last command entered
F3	Recall last command entered
F7	Display command pop-up; select with up arrow/down arrow
F9	Display command pop-up; select with command number
F8, F5	Cycle through command list

The following example describes a simple use for input editing. Suppose that you've entered this query while using `mysql`:

```
mysql> SHOW COLUMNS FROM persident;
```

If you notice that you've misspelled "president" as "persident" before pressing Enter, you can fix the query like this:

1. Press the left arrow a few times to move the cursor left until it's on the "`s`".
2. To erase the "`er`", press Delete or Backspace twice (whichever one erases the character to the left of the cursor on your system).
3. Type "`re`" to fix the error.
4. Press Enter to issue the query.

If you press Enter before you notice a misspelling, that's not a problem. After `mysql` displays its error message, press the up arrow to recall the line, then edit it as just described.

1.5.2.2   Using Copy and Paste to Issue Statements

If you use a windowing environment, the text of statements that you find useful can be saved in a file and recalled by copy and paste operations:

1. Invoke `mysql` in a terminal or console window.

2. Open the file containing your statements in a document window. (For example, I use `vi` on Unix and `gvim` on Windows.)

3. To execute a statement stored in your file, select it in the document and copy it. Then switch to your terminal window and paste the statement into `mysql`.

The procedure sounds cumbersome when written out like that, but when you're actually carrying it out, it provides a way to enter statements quickly and with no typing. With a little practice, it becomes second nature.

You can use copy and paste in the other direction, too (from your terminal window to your statement file). On Unix, when you enter statements in `mysql`, they are saved in a file named `.mysql_history` in your home directory. If you manually enter a statement that you want to save for further reference, quit `mysql`, open `.mysql_history` in an editor, and then copy and paste the statement from `.mysql_history` into your statement file.

1.5.2.3   Using `mysql` to Execute Script Files

It's not necessary to run `mysql` interactively. `mysql` can read input from a file in noninteractive (batch) mode. This is useful for statements that you run periodically because you need not retype them each time. Put the statements into a file once, then have `mysql` execute the contents of the file as needed.

Suppose that you have a query to find Historical League members who have an interest in a particular area of U.S. history by looking in the `interests` column of the `member` table. For example, to find members with an interest in the Great Depression, write the query like this:

```
SELECT last_name, first_name, email, interests FROM member
WHERE interests LIKE '%depression%'
ORDER BY last_name, first_name;
```

Put the query in a file `interests.sql`, and then execute it by feeding it to `mysql` like this:

```
% mysql sampdb < interests.sql
```

By default, `mysql` produces output in tab-delimited format when run in batch mode. If you want the same kind of table-format output you get when you run `mysql` interactively, use the `-t` option:

```
% mysql -t sampdb < interests.sql
```

To save the output, redirect it to a file:

```
% mysql -t sampdb < interests.sql > interests.out
```

If you are already running `mysql`, execute the contents of the file by using a `source` command:

```
mysql> source interests.sql
```

To use the query to find members with an interest in Thomas Jefferson, you could edit the query file to change `depression` to `Jefferson` and then run `mysql` again. That works okay as long as you don't use the query very often. If you do, a better method is needed. On Unix, one way to make the query more flexible is to put it in a shell script that takes an argument from the script command line and uses it to change the text of the query. That parameterizes the query so that you can specify the `interests` value when you run the script. To see how this works, write a little shell script, `interests.sh`:

```
#!/bin/sh
# interests.sh - find USHL members with particular interests
if [ $# -ne 1 ]; then echo 'Please specify one keyword'; exit; fi
mysql -t sampdb <<QUERY_INPUT
SELECT last_name, first_name, email, interests FROM member
WHERE interests LIKE '%$1%'
ORDER BY last_name, first_name;
QUERY_INPUT
```

The third line makes sure that there is one argument on the command line; it prints a short message and exits otherwise. Everything between `<<QUERY_INPUT` and the final `QUERY_INPUT` line becomes the input to `mysql`. Within the text of the query, the shell replaces the reference to `$1` with the argument from the command line. (In shell scripts, `$1`, `$2`, ... refer to the command arguments.) This causes the query to reflect whatever keyword you specify on the command line when you run the script.

Before you can run the script, you must make it executable:

```
% chmod +x interests.sh
```

Now you need not edit the script each time you run it. Just tell it what you're looking for on the command line:

```
% ./interests.sh depression
% ./interests.sh Jefferson
```

The `interests.sh` script is located in the `misc` directory of the `sampdb` distribution. An equivalent Windows batch file, `interests.bat`, is provided there as well.

> **Note**
>
> I suggest that you not install scripts like these publicly because they perform no safety checks on the arguments and thus are subject to SQL injection attacks. Suppose someone invokes the script like this:
>
> ```
> % ./interests.sh "Jefferson';DROP DATABASE sampdb;"
> ```
>
> The effect of this is to "inject" a `DROP DATABASE` statement into the statement to the `mysql` input in such a way that it actually executes.

1.6   Where to Now?

You know quite a bit about using MySQL now. You can set up a database and create tables. You can add rows to those tables, retrieve them in various ways, change them, or delete them. But the tutorial in this chapter only scratches the surface, and there's still a lot to know about MySQL. To see this, consider the current state of our `sampdb` database. We've created it and its tables and populated them with some initial data. During the process, we've seen how to write some of the queries needed for answering questions about the information in the database. But much remains to be done. For example, we have no convenient interactive way to enter new score rows for the grade-keeping project or new member entries for the Historical League directory. We have no convenient way to edit existing rows. And we still can't generate the printed or online forms of the League directory. We'll revisit those tasks and others in the upcoming chapters, particularly in Chapter 8, "Writing MySQL Programs Using Perl DBI," and Chapter 9, "Writing MySQL Programs Using PHP."

Where you go next in this book depends on what you're interested in. If you want to see how to finish the job we've started with our Historical League and grade-keeping projects, Part II covers how to write MySQL-based programs. If you're going to serve as the MySQL administrator for your site, Part III of this book deals with administrative tasks. However, I recommend acquiring additional general background in using MySQL first, by reading the remaining chapters in Part I. Those chapters provide further information on the syntax and use of SQL statements, discuss how MySQL handles data, and show how to make your queries run faster. A good grounding in these topics stands you in good stead no matter the context in which you use MySQL—whether you're running `mysql`, writing your own programs, or acting as a database administrator.

Using SQL to Manage Data

The MySQL server understands Structured Query Language (SQL). Therefore, SQL is the means by which you tell the server how to perform data management operations, and fluency with it is necessary for effective communication. When you use a program such as the mysql client, it functions primarily as a way for you to send SQL statements to the server to be executed. If you write programs in a language that has a MySQL interface, such as the Perl DBI module or PHP PDO extension, these interfaces enable you to communicate with the server by issuing SQL statements.

Chapter 1, "Getting Started with MySQL," presented a tutorial introducing many of MySQL's capabilities, including some basic use of SQL. We'll build on that material here to go into more detail on several topics:

- Changing the SQL mode to affect server behavior
- Referring to elements of databases
- Using multiple character sets
- Creating and destroying databases, tables, and indexes
- Obtaining information about databases and their contents
- Retrieving data using joins, subqueries, and unions
- Using multiple-table deletes and updates
- Performing transactions that enable statements to be grouped or canceled
- Setting up foreign key relationships
- Using the FULLTEXT search engine

The items just listed cover a broad range of topics of what you can do with SQL. Other chapters provide additional SQL-related information:

- Chapter 4, "Views and Stored Programs," discusses how to create and use views (virtual tables that provide alternative ways of looking at data) and stored programs (functions and procedures, triggers, and events).

- Chapter 12, "General MySQL Administration," describes how to use administrative statements such as GRANT and REVOKE to manage user accounts. It also discusses the privilege system that controls what operations accounts are permitted to perform.

- Appendix E, "SQL Syntax Reference," shows the syntax for SQL statements implemented by MySQL and the privileges required to use them. It also covers the syntax for using comments in your SQL statements.

See also the MySQL Reference Manual, especially for changes made in recent versions of MySQL.

2.1   The Server SQL Mode

The MySQL SQL mode affects several aspects of SQL statement execution, and the server has a system variable named sql_mode that enables you to configure this mode. The variable can be set globally to affect all clients, and each individual client can change the mode to affect its own session with (connection to) the server. This means that any client can change how the server treats it without impact on other clients.

The SQL mode affects behaviors such as handling of invalid values during data entry and identifier quoting. The following list describes a few of the possible mode values:

- STRICT_ALL_TABLES and STRICT_TRANS_TABLES enable "strict" mode. In strict mode, the server is more restrictive about accepting bad data values. (Specifically, it rejects bad values rather than changing them to the closest legal value.)

- TRADITIONAL is a composite mode. It is like strict mode, but enables other modes that impose additional constraints for even stricter data checking. Traditional mode causes the server to behave like more traditional SQL servers with regard to how it handles bad data values.

- ANSI_QUOTES tells the server to recognize double quote as an identifier quoting character.

- PIPES_AS_CONCAT causes || to be treated as the standard SQL string concatenation operator rather than as a synonym for the OR operator.

- ANSI is another composite mode. It turns on ANSI_QUOTES, PIPES_AS_CONCAT, and several other mode values that cause the server to conform more closely to standard SQL.

When you set the SQL mode, specify a value consisting of one or more mode values separated by commas, or an empty string to clear the value. Mode values are not case sensitive.

To set the SQL mode when you start the server, set the sql_mode system variable on the mysqld command line or in an option file. On the command line, you might use a setting like one of these:

```
--sql_mode="TRADITIONAL"
--sql_mode="ANSI_QUOTES,PIPES_AS_CONCAT"
```

To change the SQL mode at runtime, set the `sql_mode` system variable with a `SET` statement. Any client can set its own session-specific SQL mode:

```
SET sql_mode = 'TRADITIONAL';
```

To set the SQL mode globally, add the `GLOBAL` keyword:

```
SET GLOBAL sql_mode = 'TRADITIONAL';
```

Setting the global variable requires the `SUPER` administrative privilege. The global value becomes the default SQL mode for clients that connect afterward.

To determine the current value of the session or global SQL mode, use these statements:

```
SELECT @@SESSION.sql_mode;
SELECT @@GLOBAL.sql_mode;
```

The value returned consists of a comma-separated list of enabled modes, or an empty value if no modes are enabled.

Section 3.3, "How MySQL Handles Invalid Data Values," discusses the SQL mode values that affect handling of erroneous or missing values during data entry. Appendix D, "System, Status, and User Variable Reference," describes the full set of permitted mode values for the `sql_mode` variable. For additional information about using system variables, see Section 12.3.1, "Checking and Setting System Variable Values."

2.2   MySQL Identifier Syntax and Naming Rules

Almost every SQL statement uses identifiers in some way to refer to a database or its constituent elements such as tables, views, columns, indexes, stored routines, triggers, or events. When you refer to elements of databases, identifiers must conform to the following rules.

Legal characters in identifiers. Unquoted identifiers may consist of latin letters `a-z` in any lettercase, digits `0-9`, dollar, underscore, and Unicode extended characters in the range `U+0080` to `U+FFFF`. Identifiers can start with any character that is legal in an identifier, including a digit. However, an unquoted identifier cannot consist entirely of digits because that would make it indistinguishable from a number. MySQL's support for identifiers that begin with a number is somewhat unusual among database systems. If you use such an identifier, take particular care if it contains an 'E' or 'e' because those characters can lead to ambiguous expressions. For example, the expression `23e + 14` (with spaces surrounding the '+' sign) means column `23e` plus the number `14`, but what about `23e+14`? Does it mean the same thing, or is it a number in scientific notation?

Identifiers can be quoted (delimited) within backtick characters ('`'), which permits use of any character except a NUL byte or Unicode supplementary characters (`U+10000` and up):

```
CREATE TABLE `my table` (`my-int-column` INT);
```

Quoting is useful when an identifier is an SQL reserved word or contains spaces or other special characters. Quoting an identifier also enables it to be entirely numeric, something not true of unquoted identifiers. To include an identifier quote character within a quoted identifier, double it.

Your operating system might impose additional constraints on database and table identifiers. See Section 11.2.6, "Operating System Constraints on Database Object Names."

Aliases for column and table names can be fairly arbitrary. You should quote an alias within identifier quoting characters if it is an SQL reserved word, is entirely numeric, or contains spaces or other special characters. Column aliases also can be quoted with single quotes or double quotes.

Server SQL mode. If the ANSI_QUOTES SQL mode is enabled, you can quote identifiers with double quotes (although backticks still are permitted).

```
CREATE TABLE "my table" ("my-int-column" INT);
```

Enabling ANSI_QUOTES has the additional effect that string literals *must* be written using single quotes. If you use double quotes, the server interprets the value as an identifier, not as a string.

Names of built-in functions normally are not reserved and can be used as identifiers without quotes. However, if the IGNORE_SPACE SQL mode is enabled, function names become reserved and must be quoted if used as identifiers.

For instructions on setting the SQL mode, see Section 2.1, "The Server SQL Mode."

Identifier length. Most identifiers have a maximum length of 64 characters. The maximum length for aliases is 256 characters.

Identifier qualifiers. Depending on context, an identifier might need to be qualified to clarify what it refers to. To refer to a database, just specify its name:

```
USE db_name;
SHOW TABLES FROM db_name;
```

To refer to a table, you have two choices:

- A fully qualified table name consists of a database identifier and a table identifier:

    ```
    SHOW COLUMNS FROM db_name.tbl_name;
    SELECT * FROM db_name.tbl_name;
    ```

- A table identifier by itself refers to a table in the default (current) database. If sampdb is the default database, the following statements are equivalent:

    ```
    SELECT * FROM member;
    SELECT * FROM sampdb.member;
    ```

If no database is selected, it is an error to refer to a table without a database qualifier because the database to which the table belongs is unknown.

The same considerations about qualifying table names apply to names of views (which are "virtual" tables) and stored programs.

To refer to a table column, you have three choices:

- A name written as *db_name.tbl_name.col_name* is fully qualified.

- A partially qualified name written as *tbl_name.col_name* refers to a column in the named table in the default database.

- An unqualified name written simply as *col_name* refers to whatever table the surrounding context indicates. The following two queries use the same column names, but the context supplied by the FROM clause of each statement indicates the table from which to select the columns:

```
SELECT last_name, first_name FROM president;
SELECT last_name, first_name FROM member;
```

Usually, it's unnecessary to supply fully qualified names, although it's always legal to do so. If you select a database with a USE statement, it becomes the default database for subsequent statements and is implicit in every unqualified table reference. If you write a SELECT statement that refers to only one table, that table is implicit for every column reference in the statement. It's necessary to qualify identifiers only when a table or database cannot be determined from context. For example, if a statement refers to tables from multiple databases, you must reference any table not in the default database using *db_name.tbl_name* syntax to let MySQL know which database contains the table. Similarly, if a query uses multiple tables and refers to a column name that is used in more than one table, qualify the column identifier with a table identifier to make it clear which column you mean.

If you use quotes when referring to a qualified name, quote individual identifiers within the name separately. For example:

```
SELECT * FROM `sampdb`.`member` WHERE `sampdb`.`member`.`member_id` > 100;
```

Do not quote the name as a whole. This statement is incorrect:

```
SELECT * FROM `sampdb.member` WHERE `sampdb.member.member_id` > 100;
```

The requirement that a reserved word be quoted if used as an identifier is waived if the word follows a qualifier period because context then dictates that the reserved word is an identifier.

2.3   Case Sensitivity in SQL Statements

Case sensitivity rules in SQL statements vary for different statement elements, and also depend on what you are referring to and the operating system of the machine on which the server is running.

SQL keywords and function names. Keywords and function names are not case sensitive. They can be given in any lettercase. The following statements are equivalent:

```
SELECT NOW();
select now();
sElEcT nOw();
```

Database, table, and view names. MySQL represents databases and tables using directories and files in the underlying filesystem on the server host. As a result, the default case sensitivity of database and table names depends on how the operating system on that host treats filenames. Windows filenames are not case sensitive, so a MySQL server running on Windows does not treat database and table names as case sensitive. Servers running on Unix usually treat database and table names as case sensitive because Unix filenames are case sensitive. An exception is that names in Mac OS X Extended filesystems can be case insensitive.

MySQL represents each view using a file, so the preceding remarks about tables also apply to views.

Stored program names. Stored function and procedure names and event names are not case sensitive. Trigger names are case sensitive, which differs from standard SQL.

Column and index names. Column and index names are not case sensitive in MySQL. The following statements are equivalent:

```
SELECT name FROM student;
SELECT NAME FROM student;
SELECT nAmE FROM student;
```

Alias names. By default, table aliases are case sensitive. You can specify an alias in any letter-case (upper, lower, or mixed), but if you use it multiple times in a statement, you must use the same lettercase each time. If the `lower_case_table_names` system variable is nonzero, table aliases are not case sensitive.

String values. Case sensitivity of a string value depends on whether it is a binary or nonbinary string, and, for a nonbinary string, on the collation of its character set. This is true for literal strings and the contents of string columns. For further information, see Section 3.1.2, "String Values."

You should consider lettercase issues when you create databases and tables on a machine with case sensitive filenames if you might someday move them to a machine where filenames are not case sensitive. Suppose that you create two tables named abc and ABC on a Unix server where those names are considered distinct. You would have problems moving the tables to a Windows machine: abc and ABC are not distinguishable because names are not case sensitive. You would also have trouble replicating the tables from a Unix master server to a Windows slave server.

To avoid having case sensitivity become an issue, pick a given lettercase and always create databases and tables using names in that lettercase. Then case of names won't be a problem if you move a database to a different server. I recommend lowercase, particularly if you are using InnoDB tables, because InnoDB stores database and table names internally in lowercase.

To force creation of databases and tables with lowercase names even if not specified that way in CREATE statements, configure the server by setting the `lower_case_table_names` system variable. For more information, see Section 11.2.6, "Operating System Constraints on Database Object Names."

Regardless of whether a database or table name is case sensitive on your system, you must refer to it using the same lettercase throughout a given query. That is not true for SQL keywords, function names, or column and index names, all of which may be referred to in varying lettercase style throughout a query.

2.4 Character Set Support

MySQL supports multiple character sets, and character sets can be specified independently at the server, database, table, column, or string constant level. For example, if you want a table's columns to use `latin1` by default, but also to include a Hebrew column and a Greek column, you can do that. In addition, you can explicitly specify collations (sorting orders). It is possible to find out what character sets and collations are available, and to convert data from one character set to another.

This section provides general background on using character set support in MySQL. Chapter 3, "Data Types," provides more specific discussion of character sets, collations, binary versus nonbinary strings, and how to define and work with character-based table columns.

MySQL provides the following character set features:

- The server supports simultaneous use of multiple character sets.

- A given character set can have one or more collations. You can choose the collation most appropriate for your applications.

- Unicode support is provided by the `utf8` and `ucs2` character sets, which include Basic Multilingual Plane (BMP) characters, and the `utf16`, `utf32`, and `utf8mb4` character sets, which include BMP and supplementary characters. MySQL 5.6.1 adds `utf16le`, which is like `utf16` but uses little-endian rather than big-endian encoding.

- You can specify character sets at the server, database, table, column, and string constant level:
  - The server has a default character set.
  - `CREATE DATABASE` enables you to assign the database character set, and `ALTER DATABASE` enables you to change it.
  - `CREATE TABLE` and `ALTER TABLE` have clauses for table- and column-level character set assignment.
  - The character set for string constants is determined by context or can be specified explicitly.

- Several functions and operators are available for converting individual values from one character set to another, and the `CHARSET()` function returns the character set of a value. Similarly, the `COLLATE` operator can be used to alter the collation of a string and the `COLLATION()` function returns the collation of a string.

- `SHOW` statements and `INFORMATION_SCHEMA` tables provide information about the available character sets and collations.

- The server automatically reorders indexes when you change the collation of an indexed character column.

You cannot mix character sets within a string, or use different character sets for different rows of a given column. However, you can implement multi-lingual support by using a Unicode character set (which represents characters for many languages within a single encoding).

2.4.1   Specifying Character Sets

Character set and collation assignments can be made at several levels, from the default used by the server to the character set used for individual strings.

The server's default character set and collation are built in at compile time. You can override them at server startup or at runtime by setting the `character_set_server` and `collation_server` system variables, as described in Section 12.6.2, "Selecting the Default Character Set and Collation." If you specify only the character set, its default collation becomes the server's default collation. If you specify a collation, it must be compatible with the character set. A collation is compatible with a character set if its name begins with the character set name. For example, `utf8_danish_ci` is compatible with `utf8` but not with `latin1`.

In SQL statements that create databases and tables, two clauses specify database, table, and column character set and collation values:

```
CHARACTER SET charset
COLLATE collation
```

`CHARSET` can be used as a synonym for `CHARACTER SET`. `charset` is the name of a character set supported by the server, and `collation` is the name of one of that character set's collations. These clauses can be specified together or separately. If both are given, the collation name must be compatible with the character set. If only `CHARACTER SET` is given, its default collation is used. If only `COLLATE` is given, the character set is implicit in the first part of the character set name. These rules apply at several levels:

- To specify a default character set and collation for a database when you create it, use this statement:

  ```
  CREATE DATABASE db_name CHARACTER SET charset COLLATE collation;
  ```

  If no character set or collation is given, the database uses the server defaults.

- To specify a default character set and collation for a table, use `CHARACTER SET` and `COLLATE` table options at table creation time:

  ```
  CREATE TABLE tbl_name (...) CHARACTER SET charset COLLATE collation;
  ```

  If no character set or collation is given, the table uses the database defaults.

- Columns in a table can be assigned a character set and collation explicitly with CHARACTER SET and COLLATE attributes. For example:

  c CHAR(10) CHARACTER SET *charset* COLLATE *collation*

  If no character set or collation is given, the column uses the table defaults. These attributes apply to the CHAR, VARCHAR, TEXT, ENUM, and SET data types.

It's also possible to sort string values according to a specific collation by using the COLLATE operator. For example, if c is a latin1 column that has a collation of latin1_swedish_ci, but you want to order it using Spanish sorting rules, do this:

SELECT c FROM t ORDER BY c COLLATE latin1_spanish_ci;

2.4.2   Determining Character Set Availability and Current Settings

To find out which character sets and collations are available, use these statements:

SHOW CHARACTER SET;
SHOW COLLATION;

Each statement supports a LIKE clause that narrows the results to those character set or collation names matching a pattern. For example, the following statements list the Latin-based character sets and the collations available for the utf8 character set:

```
mysql> SHOW CHARACTER SET LIKE 'latin%';
+---------+--------------------------+--------------------+--------+
| Charset | Description              | Default collation  | Maxlen |
+---------+--------------------------+--------------------+--------+
| latin1  | cp1252 West European     | latin1_swedish_ci  |      1 |
| latin2  | ISO 8859-2 Central European | latin2_general_ci |      1 |
| latin5  | ISO 8859-9 Turkish       | latin5_turkish_ci  |      1 |
| latin7  | ISO 8859-13 Baltic       | latin7_general_ci  |      1 |
+---------+--------------------------+--------------------+--------+
mysql> SHOW COLLATION LIKE 'utf8%';
+--------------------+---------+-----+---------+----------+---------+
| Collation          | Charset | Id  | Default | Compiled | Sortlen |
+--------------------+---------+-----+---------+----------+---------+
| utf8_general_ci    | utf8    |  33 | Yes     | Yes      |       1 |
| utf8_bin           | utf8    |  83 |         | Yes      |       1 |
| utf8_unicode_ci    | utf8    | 192 |         | Yes      |       8 |
| utf8_icelandic_ci  | utf8    | 193 |         | Yes      |       8 |
| utf8_latvian_ci    | utf8    | 194 |         | Yes      |       8 |
| utf8_romanian_ci   | utf8    | 195 |         | Yes      |       8 |
| utf8_slovenian_ci  | utf8    | 196 |         | Yes      |       8 |
...
```

Collation names always begin with the character set name. Each character set has at least one collation, and one of them is its default collation.

Information about the available character sets or collations can also be obtained from the
`CHARACTER_SETS` or `COLLATIONS` table in the `INFORMATION_SCHEMA` database (see Section 2.7,
"Obtaining Database Metadata").

To display the server's current character set and collation settings, use `SHOW VARIABLES`:

```
mysql> SHOW VARIABLES LIKE 'character\_set\_%';
+--------------------------+--------+
| Variable_name            | Value  |
+--------------------------+--------+
| character_set_client     | utf8   |
| character_set_connection | utf8   |
| character_set_database   | latin1 |
| character_set_filesystem | binary |
| character_set_results    | utf8   |
| character_set_server     | latin1 |
| character_set_system     | utf8   |
+--------------------------+--------+
mysql> SHOW VARIABLES LIKE 'collation\_%';
+----------------------+-------------------+
| Variable_name        | Value             |
+----------------------+-------------------+
| collation_connection | utf8_general_ci   |
| collation_database   | latin1_swedish_ci |
| collation_server     | latin1_swedish_ci |
+----------------------+-------------------+
```

Several of these system variables affect how a client communicates with the server after
establishing a connection. For details, refer to Section 3.1.2.2, "Character Set-Related System
Variables."

2.4.3 Unicode Support

One of the reasons there are so many character sets is that different character encodings have
been developed for different languages. This presents several problems. For example, a given
character that is common to several languages might be represented by different numeric
values in different encodings. Also, different languages require different numbers of bytes to
represent characters. The latin1 character set is small enough that every character fits in a
single byte, but languages such as those used in Japan and China contain so many characters
that they require multiple bytes per character.

Unicode deals with these issues by providing a unified character-encoding system within which
character sets for all languages can be represented in a consistent manner.

The utf8 and ucs2 Unicode character sets include only characters in the Basic Multilingual
Plane (BMP), which is limited to 65,536 characters. They do not support supplementary characters outside the BMP.

- The `ucs2` character set corresponds to the Unicode UCS-2 encoding. It represents each character using 2 bytes, most significant byte first. UCS is an abbreviation for Universal Character Set.

- The `utf8` character set has a variable-length format that represents characters using from 1 to 3 bytes. It corresponds to the Unicode UTF-8 encoding. UTF is an abbreviation for Unicode Transformation Format.

Beginning with MySQL 5.5.3, other Unicode character sets are available that include supplementary characters in addition to BMP characters.

- The `utf16` and `utf32` character sets are like `ucs2` but with supplementary characters added. For `utf16`, BMP characters take 2 bytes (as for `ucs2`) and supplementary characters take 4 bytes. For `utf32`, all characters take 4 bytes.

- The `utf8mb4` character set contains all the `utf8` characters (which take 1 to 3 bytes each), but also supplementary characters that take 4 bytes each.

MySQL 5.6.1 adds `utf16le`, which is like `utf16` but uses little-endian rather than big-endian encoding.

2.5 Selecting, Creating, Dropping, and Altering Databases

MySQL provides several database-level statements: USE for selecting a default database, CREATE DATABASE for creating databases, DROP DATABASE for removing them, and ALTER DATABASE for modifying global database characteristics.

The keyword SCHEMA is a synonym for DATABASE in any statement where the latter occurs.

2.5.1 Selecting Databases

The USE statement selects a database to make it the default (current) database for a given session with the server:

```
USE db_name;
```

You must have some access privilege for the database or an error occurs.

It is not strictly necessary to select a database explicitly. You can refer to tables in a database without selecting it first by using qualified names that identify both the database and the table. For example, to retrieve the contents of the `president` table in the `sampdb` database without making it the default database, write the query like this:

```
SELECT * FROM sampdb.president;
```

Selecting a database doesn't mean that it must be the default for the duration of the session. You can issue USE statements as necessary to switch between databases. Nor does selecting a database limit you to using tables only from that database. While one database is the default, you can refer to tables in other databases by qualifying their names with the appropriate database identifier.

When you disconnect from the server, any notion by the server of which database was the default for the session disappears. If you connect to the server again, it doesn't remember what database you had selected previously.

2.5.2   Creating Databases

To create a database, use a CREATE DATABASE statement:

```
CREATE DATABASE db_name;
```

The database must not already exist, and you must have the CREATE privilege for it.

CREATE DATABASE supports several optional clauses. The full syntax is as follows:

```
CREATE DATABASE [IF NOT EXISTS] db_name
  [CHARACTER SET charset] [COLLATE collation];
```

By default, an error occurs if you try to create a database that already exists. To suppress this error and create a database only if it does not already exist, add an IF NOT EXISTS clause:

```
CREATE DATABASE IF NOT EXISTS db_name;
```

By default, the server character set and collation become the database default character set and collation. To set these database attributes explicitly, use the CHARACTER SET and COLLATE clauses. For example:

```
CREATE DATABASE mydb CHARACTER SET utf8 COLLATE utf8_icelandic_ci;
```

If CHARACTER SET is given without COLLATE, the character set default collation is used. If COLLATE is given without CHARACTER SET, the first part of the collation name determines the character set.

The character set must be one of those supported by the server, such as latin1 or sjis. The collation should be a legal collation for the character set. For further discussion of character sets and collations, see Section 2.4, "Character Set Support."

When you create a database, the MySQL server creates a directory under its data directory that has the same name as the database. The new directory is called the database directory. The server also creates a db.opt file in the database directory for storing attributes such as the database character set and collation. When you create a table in the database later, the database defaults become the table defaults if the table definition does not specify its own default character set and collation.

To see the definition for an existing database, use a SHOW CREATE DATABASE statement:

```
mysql> SHOW CREATE DATABASE mydb\G
*************************** 1. row ***************************
       Database: mydb
Create Database: CREATE DATABASE `mydb`
                /*!40100 DEFAULT CHARACTER SET utf8
                COLLATE utf8_icelandic_ci */
```

2.5.3 Dropping Databases

Dropping a database is as easy as creating one, assuming that you have the DROP privilege for it:

```
DROP DATABASE db_name;
```

The DROP DATABASE statement is not something to use with wild abandon. It removes the database and all its contents (tables, stored routines, and so forth), which are therefore gone forever unless you have been making regular backups.

A database is represented by a directory under the data directory, and the directory is intended for storage of objects such as tables, views, and triggers. If a DROP DATABASE statement fails, the reason most likely is that the database directory contains files not associated with database objects. DROP DATABASE will not delete such files, and as a result will not delete the directory, either. This means that the database directory continues to exist and will show up if you issue a SHOW DATABASES statement. To really drop the database if this occurs, manually remove any extraneous files and subdirectories from the database directory, then issue the DROP DATABASE statement again.

2.5.4 Altering Databases

The ALTER DATABASE statement changes a database's global attributes, if you have the ALTER privilege for it. Currently, the only such attributes are the default character set and collation:

```
ALTER DATABASE [db_name] [CHARACTER SET charset] [COLLATE collation];
```

The earlier discussion for CREATE DATABASE describes the effect of the CHARACTER SET and COLLATE clauses, at least one of which must be given.

If you omit the database name, ALTER DATABASE applies to the default database.

2.6 Creating, Dropping, Indexing, and Altering Tables

MySQL enables you to create tables, drop (remove) them, and change their structure with the CREATE TABLE, DROP TABLE, and ALTER TABLE statements. The CREATE INDEX and DROP INDEX statements enable you to add or remove indexes on existing tables. The following sections provide the details for these statements, but first it's necessary to discuss the storage engines that MySQL supports for managing different types of tables.

2.6.1   Storage Engine Characteristics

MySQL supports multiple storage engines (or "table handlers" as they used to be known). Each storage engine implements tables that have a specific set of properties or characteristics. Table 2.1 briefly describes these storage engines, and later discussion provides more detail about some of them (primarily InnoDB and MyISAM). Others are either less commonly used or, in the case of NDB, require extensive discussion beyond what can be given here. Consequently, the remainder of this book says little about them.

Table 2.1   **MySQL Storage Engines**

Storage Engine	Description
ARCHIVE	Archival storage (no modification of rows after insertion)
BLACKHOLE	Engine that discards writes and returns empty reads
CSV	Storage in comma-separated values format
FEDERATED	Engine for accessing remote tables
InnoDB	Transactional engine with foreign keys
MEMORY	In-memory tables
MERGE	Manages collections of MyISAM tables
MyISAM	The main nontransactional storage engine
NDB	The engine for MySQL Cluster

Some of the engine names have synonyms. MRG_MyISAM and NDBCLUSTER are synonyms for MERGE and NDB, respectively. The MEMORY and InnoDB storage engines originally were known as HEAP and Innobase, respectively. The latter names are still recognized but deprecated.

Originally, the MySQL server was built such that all storage engines to be made available were compiled in. Now the server uses a "pluggable" architecture that enables plugins to be loaded selectively, and many storage engines are built as plugins. This permits the DBA to treat those engines as optional and load only those needed. The plugin interface also permits storage engines from third-party developers to be integrated into the server. For information about this interface, see Section 12.4, "The Plugin Interface."

2.6.1.1   Checking Which Storage Engines Are Available

The engines actually available for a given server depend on your version of MySQL, how the server was configured at build time, and the startup options you use. For information about selecting storage engines, see Section 12.5, "Storage Engine Configuration."

To see which storage engines the server knows about, use the SHOW ENGINES statement:

```
mysql> SHOW ENGINES\G
*************************** 1. row ***************************
      Engine: InnoDB
     Support: DEFAULT
     Comment: Supports transactions, row-level locking, and foreign keys
Transactions: YES
          XA: YES
  Savepoints: YES
...
*************************** 8. row ***************************
      Engine: MyISAM
     Support: YES
     Comment: MyISAM storage engine
Transactions: NO
          XA: NO
  Savepoints: NO
...
```

The `Support` column value is YES or NO to indicate that the engine is or is not available, DISABLED if the engine is present but turned off, or DEFAULT for the storage engine that the server uses by default. The engine designated as DEFAULT should be considered available. The `Transactions` column indicates whether an engine supports transactions. XA and `Savepoints` indicate whether an engine supports distributed transactions (not covered in this book) and partial transaction rollback.

The `ENGINES` table in the `INFORMATION_SCHEMA` database provides the same information as `SHOW ENGINES`, but since you access it with SELECT, you can apply query conditions to select only the information in which you're interested. For example, this query uses the `ENGINES` table to check for available engines that support transactions:

```
mysql> SELECT ENGINE FROM INFORMATION_SCHEMA.ENGINES
    -> WHERE TRANSACTIONS = 'YES';
+--------+
| ENGINE |
+--------+
| InnoDB |
+--------+
```

2.6.1.2 Table Representation on Disk

Each time you create a table, MySQL creates a disk file that contains the table's format (that is, its definition). The format file has a basename that is the same as the table name and an .frm extension. For a table named t, the format file is named t.frm. The server creates the file in the database directory for the database that the table belongs to. The .frm file is an invariant because there is one for every table, no matter which storage engine manages the table. The name of a table as used in SQL statements might differ from the table-name part of the associated .frm file if the name contains characters that are problematic in filenames. See

Section 11.2.6, "Operating System Constraints on Database Object Names," for a description of the rules for mapping from SQL names to filenames.

Individual storage engines may also create other files that are unique to the table, to be used for storing the table's content. For a given table, any files specific to it are located in the database directory for the database that contains the table. Table 2.2 shows the filename extensions for table-specific files created by certain storage engines.

Table 2.2   **Table Files Created by Storage Engines**

Storage Engine	Files on Disk
InnoDB	`.ibd` (data and indexes)
MyISAM	`.MYD` (data), `.MYI` (indexes)
CSV	`.CSV` (data), `.CSM` (metadata)

For some storage engines, the format file is the only file specifically associated with a particular table. Other engines may store table content elsewhere than on disk, or may use one or more tablespaces (storage areas shared by multiple tables):

- The MEMORY storage engine stores table contents in memory, not on disk.

- By default, InnoDB stores table data and indexes in its system tablespace. That is, all InnoDB table contents are managed within a shared storage area, not within files specific to a particular table. Alternatively, InnoDB creates `.ibd` files if you configure it to use individual per-table tablespaces.

The following sections characterize the features and behavior of selected MySQL storage engines. For additional information about how engines represent tables physically, see Section 11.2.3, "Representation of Tables in the Filesystem."

2.6.1.3   The InnoDB Storage Engine

The InnoDB storage engine is the default engine in MySQL, unless you have configured your server otherwise. The following list describes some of its features:

- Transaction-safe tables with commit and rollback. Savepoints can be created to enable partial rollback.

- Automatic recovery after a crash.

- Foreign key and referential integrity support, including cascaded delete and update.

- Row-level locking and multi-versioning for good concurrency performance under query mix conditions that include both retrievals and updates.

- As of MySQL 5.6, InnoDB supports full-text searches and `FULLTEXT` indexes.

By default, InnoDB manages tables within a single system tablespace, rather than by using table-specific files like most other storage engines. The tablespace consists of one or more files and can include raw partitions. The InnoDB storage engine, in effect, treats the tablespace as a virtual filesystem within which it manages the contents of all InnoDB tables. Tables thus can exceed the size permitted by the filesystem for individual files. You can also configure InnoDB to use a separate tablespace file for each table. In this case, each table has an .ibd file in its database directory.

To configure individual tablespaces, enable the innodb_file_per_table system variable, either at server startup or at runtime. Enabling this variable also enables other InnoDB features, such as fast table truncation and row storage formats that offer more efficient table processing for some kinds of data. For more information, see Section 12.5.3.1.4, "Using Individual (Per-Table) InnoDB Tablespaces."

2.6.1.4   The MyISAM Storage Engine

The MyISAM storage engine offers these features:

- Key compression when storing runs of successive similar string index values. MyISAM also can compress runs of similar numeric index values because numeric values are stored with the high byte first. (Index values tend to vary faster in the low-order bytes, so high-order bytes are more subject to compression.) To enable numeric compression, use the PACK_KEYS=1 option when creating a MyISAM table.

- More features for AUTO_INCREMENT columns than provided by other storage engines. For more information, see Section 3.4, "Working with Sequences."

- Each MyISAM table has a flag that is set when a table-check operation is performed. MyISAM tables also have a flag indicating whether a table was closed properly when last used. If the server shuts down abnormally or the machine crashes, the flags can be used to detect tables that need to be checked. To do this automatically, start the server with the myisam_recover_options system variable set to a value that includes the FORCE option. This causes the server to check the table flags whenever it opens a MyISAM table and perform a table repair if necessary. See Section 14.3.1, "Using the Server's Auto-Recovery Capabilities."

- Full-text searches and FULLTEXT indexes.

- Spatial data types and SPATIAL indexes.

2.6.1.5   The MEMORY Storage Engine

The MEMORY storage engine uses tables that are stored in memory and that have fixed-length rows, two properties that make them very fast.

MEMORY tables are temporary in the sense that their contents disappear when the server terminates. That is, a MEMORY table still exists when the server restarts, but will be empty. However, in contrast to temporary tables created with CREATE TEMPORARY TABLE, MEMORY tables are visible to other clients.

MEMORY tables have characteristics that enable them to be handled more simply, and thus more quickly:

- By default, MEMORY tables use hashed indexes, which are very fast for equality comparisons but slow for range comparisons. Consequently, hashed indexes are used only for comparisons performed with the = and <=> equality operators, but not for comparison operators such as < or >. Hashed indexes also are not used in ORDER BY clauses for this reason.

- Rows are stored in MEMORY tables using fixed-length format for easier processing. A consequence is that you cannot use the BLOB and TEXT variable-length data types. VARCHAR is a variable-length type, but is permitted because it is treated internally as CHAR, a fixed-length type.

To use a MEMORY table for comparisons that look for a range of values using operators such as <, >, or BETWEEN, you can use BTREE indexes instead of hashed indexes. See Section 2.6.4.2, "Creating Indexes," and Section 5.1.3, "Choosing Indexes."

2.6.1.6   The NDB Storage Engine

NDB is MySQL's cluster storage engine. For this storage engine, the MySQL server actually acts as a client to a cluster of other processes that provide access to the NDB tables. Cluster node processes communicate with each other to manage tables in memory. The tables are replicated among cluster processes for redundancy. Memory storage provides high performance, and the cluster provides high availability because it survives failure of any given node.

NDB configuration and use is beyond the scope of this book and is not covered further here. See the MySQL Reference Manual for details.

2.6.1.7   Other Storage Engines

MySQL has several other storage engines that I group here under the "miscellaneous" category:

- The ARCHIVE engine provides archival storage. It's intended for storage of large numbers of rows that are written once and never modified thereafter. For this reason, it supports only a limited number of statements. INSERT and SELECT work, but REPLACE always acts like INSERT, and you cannot use DELETE or UPDATE. Rows are compressed during storage and decompressed during retrieval to save space. An ARCHIVE table can include an indexed AUTO_INCREMENT column; other columns cannot be indexed.

- The BLACKHOLE engine creates tables for which writes are ignored and reads return nothing. It is the database equivalent of the Unix /dev/null device.

- The CSV engine stores data in comma-separated values format. For each table, it creates a .csv file in the database directory. This is a plain text file in which each table row appears as a single line. The CSV engine does not support indexing.

- The FEDERATED engine provides access to tables that are managed by other MySQL servers. In other words, the contents of a FEDERATED table really are located remotely. For a FEDERATED table, you specify the host where the other server is running and provide the username and password of an account on that server. When you access the FEDERATED table, the local server connects to the remote server using this account.

- The MERGE engine provides a means of grouping a set of MyISAM tables into a single logical unit. Querying a MERGE table in effect queries all the constituent tables. One advantage of this is that you can exceed the maximum table size permitted by the filesystem for individual MyISAM tables. Partitioned tables provide an alternative to MERGE tables and are not limited to MyISAM tables. See Section 2.6.2.5, "Using Partitioned Tables."

2.6.2   Creating Tables

To create a table, use a CREATE TABLE statement. You must have the CREATE privilege for the table. The full syntax for this statement is complex because there are so many optional clauses, but it's usually fairly simple to use in practice. For example, most of the CREATE TABLE statements that we used in Chapter 1, "Getting Started with MySQL," are reasonably uncomplicated. If you start with the more basic forms and work up, you shouldn't have much trouble.

A CREATE TABLE statement specifies, at a minimum, the table name and a list of the columns in it. For example:

```
CREATE TABLE mytbl
(
  name    CHAR(20),
  birth   DATE NOT NULL,
  weight  INT,
  sex     ENUM('F','M')
);
```

In addition to the column definitions, you can specify how the table should be indexed when you create it. Another option is to leave the table unindexed when you create it and add the indexes later. For MyISAM tables, that's a good strategy if you plan to populate the table with a lot of data before you begin using it for queries. Updating indexes as you insert each row is much slower than loading the data into an unindexed MyISAM table and creating the indexes afterward.

We have already covered the basic syntax for CREATE TABLE in Chapter 1, "Getting Started with MySQL." Details on how to write column definitions are given in Chapter 3, "Data Types." Here, we deal more generally with some important extensions to CREATE TABLE that give you a lot of flexibility in how you construct tables:

- Table options that modify storage characteristics

- Creating a table only if it doesn't already exist

- Temporary tables that the server drops automatically when the client session ends

- Creating a table from another table or from the result of a SELECT query
- Using partitioned tables

2.6.2.1   Table Options

To modify a table's storage characteristics, add one or more table options following the closing parenthesis in the CREATE TABLE statement. For a complete list of options, see the description for CREATE TABLE in Appendix E, "SQL Syntax Reference."

One table option is ENGINE = *engine_name*, which specifies the storage engine to use for the table. For example, to create a MEMORY or MyISAM table, write the statement like this:

```
CREATE TABLE mytbl ( ... ) ENGINE=MEMORY;
CREATE TABLE mytbl ( ... ) ENGINE=MyISAM;
```

The engine name is not case sensitive. With no ENGINE option, the server creates the table using the default storage engine. The built-in default is InnoDB, but you can tell the server to use a different default using the instructions in Section 12.5.2, "Selecting a Default Storage Engine."

If you name a storage engine that is not enabled, two warnings occur:

```
mysql> CREATE TABLE t (i INT) ENGINE=ARCHIVE;
Query OK, 0 rows affected, 2 warnings (0.01 sec)
mysql> SHOW WARNINGS;
+---------+------+-----------------------------------------+
| Level   | Code | Message                                 |
+---------+------+-----------------------------------------+
| Warning | 1286 | Unknown storage engine 'ARCHIVE'        |
| Warning | 1266 | Using storage engine InnoDB for table 't' |
+---------+------+-----------------------------------------+
```

To make sure that a table uses a particular storage engine, be sure to include the ENGINE table option. Because the default engine can be changed, you might not get the default you expect if you omit ENGINE. In addition, verify that the CREATE TABLE statement produces no warnings, which often indicate that the specified engine was not available and that the default engine was used instead.

To tell MySQL to issue an error if the engine you specify is not available, (instead of substituting the default storage engine), enable the NO_ENGINE_SUBSTITUTION SQL mode.

To determine which storage engine a table uses, issue a SHOW CREATE TABLE statement and look for the ENGINE option in the output:

```
mysql> SHOW CREATE TABLE t\G
*************************** 1. row ***************************
       Table: t
Create Table: CREATE TABLE `t` (
  `i` int(11) DEFAULT NULL
) ENGINE=MyISAM DEFAULT CHARSET=latin1
```

The storage engine is also available in the output from the SHOW TABLE STATUS statement or the INFORMATION_SCHEMA.TABLES table.

The MAX_ROWS and AVG_ROW_LENGTH options can help you size a MyISAM table. By default, MyISAM creates tables with an internal row pointer size that permits table files to grow up to 256TB. If you specify the MAX_ROWS and AVG_ROW_LENGTH options, that gives MyISAM information that it should use a pointer size for a table that can hold at least MAX_ROWS rows.

To modify the storage characteristics of an existing table, table options can be used with an ALTER TABLE statement. For example, to change mytbl from its current storage engine to InnoDB, do this:

```
ALTER TABLE mytbl ENGINE=InnoDB;
```

For more information about changing storage engines, see Section 2.6.5, "Altering Table Structure."

2.6.2.2 Provisional Table Creation

To create a table only if it doesn't already exist, use CREATE TABLE IF NOT EXISTS. You can use this statement for an application that makes no assumptions about whether a table that it needs has been set up in advance. The application can go ahead and attempt to create the table as a matter of course. The IF NOT EXISTS modifier is particularly useful for scripts that you run as batch jobs with mysql. In this context, a regular CREATE TABLE statement doesn't work very well. The first time the job runs, it creates the table, but the second time, an error occurs because the table already exists. If you use IF NOT EXISTS, there is no problem. The first time the job runs, it creates the table, as before. For second and subsequent times, table creation attempts are silently ignored without error. This enables the job to continue processing as if the attempt had succeeded.

If you use IF NOT EXISTS, be aware that MySQL does not compare the table structure in the CREATE TABLE statement with the existing table. If a table exists with the given name but has a different structure, the statement does not fail. If that is a risk you wish not to take, it is better instead to precede your CREATE TABLE statement by DROP TABLE IF EXISTS.

2.6.2.3 TEMPORARY Tables

Adding the TEMPORARY keyword to a table-creation statement causes the server to create a temporary table that disappears automatically when your session with the server terminates:

```
CREATE TEMPORARY TABLE tbl_name ... ;
```

This is handy because you need not issue a DROP TABLE statement to get rid of the table, and the table doesn't persist if your session terminates abnormally. For example, if you have a complex query stored in a batch file that you run with mysql and you decide not to wait for it to finish, you can kill the script with impunity and the server will remove any TEMPORARY tables created by the script.

To create a temporary table using a particular storage engine, add an ENGINE table option to the CREATE TEMPORARY TABLE statement.

Although the server drops a TEMPORARY table automatically when your client session ends, you can drop it explicitly as soon as you're done with it to enable the server to free any resources associated with it. This is a good idea if your session with the server will not end for a while, particularly for temporary MEMORY tables.

A TEMPORARY table is visible only to the client that creates the table. Different clients can each create a TEMPORARY table with the same name and without conflict because each client sees only the table that it created.

The name of a TEMPORARY table can be the same as an existing permanent table. This is not an error, nor does the existing permanent table get clobbered. Instead, the permanent table becomes hidden (inaccessible) to the client that creates the TEMPORARY table while the TEMPORARY table exists. Suppose that you create a TEMPORARY table named member in the sampdb database. The original member table becomes hidden, and references to member refer to the TEMPORARY table. If you issue a DROP TABLE member statement, the TEMPORARY table is removed and the original member table "reappears." If you disconnect from the server without dropping the TEMPORARY table, the server automatically drops it for you. The next time you connect, the original member table is visible again. (The original table also reappears if you rename a TEMPORARY table that hides it to have a different name.)

The name-hiding mechanism works only to one level. That is, you cannot create two TEMPORARY tables with the same name.

Keep in mind the following caveats when considering whether to use a TEMPORARY table:

- If your client program automatically reconnects to the server if the connection is lost, any TEMPORARY tables will be gone when you reconnect. If you were using the TEMPORARY table to "hide" a permanent table with the same name, the permanent table now becomes the table that you use. For example, a DROP TABLE after an undetected reconnect will drop the permanent table. To avoid this problem, use DROP TEMPORARY TABLE instead.

- Because TEMPORARY tables are visible only within the session that created them, they are not useful with connection pooling mechanisms that do not guarantee the same connection for each statement that you issue.

- With connection pooling or persistent connections, your connection to the MySQL server will not necessarily close when your application terminates. Those mechanisms might hold the connection open for use by other clients, which means that you cannot assume that TEMPORARY tables will disappear automatically when your application terminates.

2.6.2.4 Creating Tables from Other Tables or Query Results

It's sometimes useful to create a copy of a table. For example, you might have a data file that you want to load into a table using LOAD DATA, but you're not quite sure about the options for specifying the data format. You can end up with malformed rows in the original table if you don't get the options right the first time. Using an empty copy of the original table enables you to experiment with the LOAD DATA options for specifying column and line delimiters until you're satisfied your input rows are being interpreted properly. Then you can load the file into the original table by rerunning the LOAD DATA statement with the original table name.

It's also sometimes desirable to save the result of a query into a table rather than displaying it on your screen. By saving the result, you can refer to it later without rerunning the original query, perhaps to perform further analysis on it.

MySQL provides two statements for creating new tables from other tables or from query results. These statements have differing advantages and disadvantages:

- CREATE TABLE ... LIKE creates a new table as an empty copy of the original one. It copies the original table structure exactly, so that each column is preserved with all of its attributes. The index structure is copied as well. However, the new table is empty, so to populate it a second statement is needed (such as INSERT INTO ... SELECT). Also, CREATE TABLE ... LIKE cannot create a new table from a subset of the original table's columns, and it cannot use columns from any other table but the original one.

- CREATE TABLE ... SELECT creates a new table from the result of an arbitrary SELECT statement. By default, this statement does not copy all column attributes such as AUTO_INCREMENT. Nor does creating a table by selecting data into it automatically copy any indexes from the original table, because result sets are not themselves indexed. On the other hand, CREATE TABLE ... SELECT can both create and populate the new table in a single statement. It also can create a new table using a subset of the original table and include columns from other tables or columns created as the result of expressions.

To use CREATE TABLE ... LIKE for creating an empty copy of an existing table, write a statement like this:

```
CREATE TABLE new_tbl_name LIKE tbl_name;
```

To create an empty copy of a table and then populate it from the original table, use CREATE TABLE ... LIKE followed by INSERT INTO ... SELECT:

```
CREATE TABLE new_tbl_name LIKE tbl_name;
INSERT INTO new_tbl_name SELECT * FROM tbl_name;
```

To create a table as a temporary copy of itself, include the TEMPORARY keyword:

```
CREATE TEMPORARY TABLE tbl_name LIKE tbl_name;
INSERT INTO tbl_name SELECT * FROM tbl_name;
```

Using a TEMPORARY table with the same name as the original can be useful when you want to try some statements that modify the contents of a table, without changing the original table. To use prewritten scripts that use the original table name, you need not edit them to refer to a different table. Just add the CREATE TEMPORARY TABLE and INSERT statements to the beginning of the script. The script will create a temporary copy and operate on the copy, which the server deletes when the script finishes. (However, bear in mind the auto-reconnect caveat noted in Section 2.6.2.3, "TEMPORARY Tables.")

To insert into the new table only some of the rows from the original table, add a WHERE clause that identifies which rows to select. The following statements create a new table named student_f that contains only the rows for female students from the student table:

```
CREATE TABLE student_f LIKE student;
INSERT INTO student_f SELECT * FROM student WHERE sex = 'f';
```

If you don't care about retaining the exact column definitions from the original table, CREATE TABLE … SELECT sometimes is easier to use than CREATE TABLE … LIKE because it can create and populate the new table in a single statement:

```
CREATE TABLE student_f SELECT * FROM student WHERE sex = 'f';
```

CREATE TABLE … SELECT also can create new tables that don't contain exactly the same set of columns in an existing table. You can use it to cause a new table to spring into existence on the fly to hold the result of an arbitrary SELECT query. This makes it exceptionally easy to create a table fully populated with the data in which you're interested, ready to be used in further statements. However, the new table can contain strange column names if you're not careful. When you create a table by selecting data into it, the column names are taken from the columns that you are selecting. If a column is calculated as the result of an expression, the name of the column is the text of the expression, which creates a table with an unusual column name:

```
mysql> CREATE TABLE mytbl SELECT PI() * 2;
mysql> SELECT * FROM mytbl;
+----------+
| PI() * 2 |
+----------+
| 6.283185 |
+----------+
```

That's unfortunate, because the column name can be referred to directly only as a quoted identifier:

```
mysql> SELECT `PI() * 2` FROM mytbl;
+----------+
| PI() * 2 |
+----------+
| 6.283185 |
+----------+
```

To avoid this problem, use a column alias to provide a name that is easier to work with:

```
mysql> DROP TABLE mytbl;
mysql> CREATE TABLE mytbl SELECT PI() * 2 AS mycol;
mysql> SELECT mycol FROM mytbl;
+----------+
| mycol    |
+----------+
| 6.283185 |
+----------+
```

A related difficulty occurs if you select from different tables columns that have the same name. Suppose that tables t1 and t2 both have a column c and you want to create a table from all combinations of rows in both tables. The following statement fails because it attempts to create a table with two columns named c:

```
mysql> CREATE TABLE t3 SELECT * FROM t1 INNER JOIN t2;
ERROR 1060 (42S21): Duplicate column name 'c'
```

To solve this problem, provide aliases as necessary to give each column a unique name in the new table:

```
mysql> CREATE TABLE t3 SELECT t1.c, t2.c AS c2
    -> FROM t1 INNER JOIN t2;
```

As mentioned previously, a shortcoming of CREATE TABLE ... SELECT is that it does not incorporate all characteristics of the original data into the structure of the new table. For example, creating a table by selecting data into it does not copy indexes from the original table, and it can lose column attributes. The retained attributes include whether the column is NULL or NOT NULL, the character set and collation, the default value, and the column comment.

In some cases, you can force specific attributes to be used in the new table by invoking the CAST() function in the SELECT part of the statement. The following CREATE TABLE ... SELECT statement forces the columns produced by the SELECT to be treated as INT UNSIGNED, TIME, and DECIMAL(10,5), as you can verify with DESCRIBE:

```
mysql> CREATE TABLE mytbl SELECT
    -> CAST(1 AS UNSIGNED) AS i,
    -> CAST(CURTIME() AS TIME) AS t,
    -> CAST(PI() AS DECIMAL(10,5)) AS d;
mysql> DESCRIBE mytbl;
+-------+----------------+------+-----+---------+-------+
| Field | Type           | Null | Key | Default | Extra |
+-------+----------------+------+-----+---------+-------+
| i     | int(1) unsigned | NO  |     | 0       |       |
| t     | time           | YES  |     | NULL    |       |
| d     | decimal(10,5)  | NO   |     | 0.00000 |       |
+-------+----------------+------+-----+---------+-------+
```

The permitted cast types are BINARY (binary string), CHAR, DATE, DATETIME, TIME, SIGNED, SIGNED INTEGER, UNSIGNED, UNSIGNED INTEGER, and DECIMAL.

It is also possible to provide explicit column definitions in the CREATE TABLE part, to be used for the columns retrieved by the SELECT part. Columns in the two parts are matched by name (not position), so provide aliases in the SELECT part as necessary to cause them to match properly:

```
mysql> CREATE TABLE mytbl (i INT UNSIGNED, t TIME, d DECIMAL(10,5))
    -> SELECT
    -> 1 AS i,
    -> CAST(CURTIME() AS TIME) AS t,
```

```
     -> CAST(PI() AS DECIMAL(10,5)) AS d;
mysql> DESCRIBE mytbl;
+-------+-----------------+------+-----+---------+-------+
| Field | Type            | Null | Key | Default | Extra |
+-------+-----------------+------+-----+---------+-------+
| i     | int(10) unsigned | YES |     | NULL    |       |
| t     | time            | YES  |     | NULL    |       |
| d     | decimal(10,5)   | YES  |     | NULL    |       |
+-------+-----------------+------+-----+---------+-------+
```

The technique of providing explicit definitions enables you to create numeric columns with specified precision and scale, character columns that have a different width than the longest value in the result set, and so forth. Also note that the `Null` and `Default` attributes for some of the columns differ in this example from those in the previous one. You can provide explicit definitions for those attributes in the CREATE TABLE part if necessary.

2.6.2.5   Using Partitioned Tables

MySQL supports table partitioning, which enables division of table contents into different physical storage locations. By sectioning table storage, partitioned tables offer benefits such as these:

- Table storage can be distributed over multiple devices, which may improve access time by virtue of I/O parallelism.

- The optimizer may be able to localize searches to specific partitions, or to search partitions in parallel.

To create a partitioned table, supply the list of columns and indexes in the CREATE TABLE statement, as usual. In addition, specify a PARTITION BY clause that defines a partitioning function to be used to assign rows to partitions, and possibly other partition-related options. A partitioning function assigns rows based on ranges or lists of values or hash values:

- Use range partitioning when rows contain a domain of values such as dates, income level, or weight that can be divided into discrete ranges.

- Use list partitioning when it makes sense to specify an explicit list of values for each partition, such as sets of postal codes, phone number prefixes, or IDs for entities that you group by geographical region.

- Use hash partitioning to distribute the rows among partitions according to hash values computed from row keys. You can either supply the hash function yourself or tell MySQL which columns to use and it computes values based on those columns using a built-in hash function.

The partitioning function must be deterministic so that the same input values consistently result in row assignment to the same partition. This rules out functions such as RAND() or NOW().

Suppose that you want to create a table for storing simple log entries consisting of a date and a descriptive string, and that you already have several years' worth of entries to be loaded into the table. For data entries that each contain a date, range partitioning is most natural. To assign rows for each year to a given partition, use the year part of the date value:

```
CREATE TABLE log_partition
(
  dt    DATETIME NOT NULL,
  info  VARCHAR(100) NOT NULL,
  INDEX (dt)
)
PARTITION BY RANGE(YEAR(dt))
(
  PARTITION p0 VALUES LESS THAN (2010),
  PARTITION p1 VALUES LESS THAN (2011),
  PARTITION p2 VALUES LESS THAN (2012),
  PARTITION p3 VALUES LESS THAN (2013),
  PARTITION pmax VALUES LESS THAN MAXVALUE
);
```

The MAXVALUE partition is assigned all rows that have dates from the year 2014 or later. When the year 2014 arrives, you can split that partition so that all year 2014 rows get their own partition and rows for 2015 and later go into the MAXVALUE partition:

```
ALTER TABLE log_partition REORGANIZE PARTITION pmax
INTO (
  PARTITION p4 VALUES LESS THAN (2014),
  PARTITION pmax VALUES LESS THAN MAXVALUE
);
```

By default, MySQL stores partitions under the directory for the database to which the partitioned table belongs. To distribute storage to other locations (for example, to place them on different physical devices), use the DATA_DIRECTORY and INDEX_DIRECTORY partition options. For more information about the syntax for these and other partitioning options, see the description for CREATE TABLE in Appendix E, "SQL Syntax Reference."

2.6.3   Dropping Tables

Dropping a table is much easier than creating it because you need not specify anything about the format of its contents. You just have to name it, assuming that you have the DROP privilege for it:

```
DROP TABLE tbl_name;
```

In MySQL, the DROP TABLE statement has several useful extensions. To drop multiple tables, specify them all in the same statement:

```
DROP TABLE tbl_name1, tbl_name2, ... ;
```

By default, an error occurs if you try to drop a table that does not exist. To suppress this error and generate a warning instead for nonexistent tables, include IF EXISTS in the statement:

```
DROP TABLE IF EXISTS tbl_name;
```

If the statement generates warnings, you can view them with SHOW WARNINGS.

IF EXISTS is particularly useful in scripts that you use with the mysql client. By default, mysql exits when an error occurs, and it is an error to try to remove a table that doesn't exist. For example, you might have a setup script that creates tables used as the basis for further processing in other scripts. In this situation, you want to make sure the setup script has a clean slate when it begins. If you use a regular DROP TABLE at the beginning of the script, it fails the first time because the tables have never been created. Using IF EXISTS makes the problem go away. If the tables exist, they are dropped. If they do not exist, no error occurs and the script continues to execute.

To drop a table only if it is a temporary table, include the TEMPORARY keyword:

```
DROP TEMPORARY TABLE tbl_name;
```

2.6.4   Indexing Tables

Indexes are the primary means of speeding up access to the contents of your tables, particularly for queries that involve joins on multiple tables. This is an important enough topic that most of an entire chapter discusses why you use indexes, how they work, and how best to take advantage of them to optimize your queries (see Chapter 5, "Query Optimization"). This section covers the characteristics of indexes for the various table types and the syntax for creating and dropping indexes.

2.6.4.1   Storage Engine Index Characteristics

MySQL provides quite a bit of flexibility for index construction:

- You can index single columns or multiple columns. Multiple-column indexes are also known as composite indexes.

- An index can be constrained to contain only unique values or permitted to contain duplicate values.

- You can have more than one index on a table to help optimize different types of queries on the table.

- For string data types other than ENUM or SET, you can elect to index a prefix of a column; that is, only the leftmost n characters, or n bytes for binary string types. (For BLOB and TEXT columns, you can set up an index only if you specify a prefix length.) If the column is mostly unique within the prefix length, you usually won't sacrifice performance, and may well improve it: Indexing a column prefix rather than the entire column can make an index much smaller and faster to access.

Not all storage engines offer all indexing features. Table 2.3 summarizes the index properties for some of MySQL's storage engines. The table does not include the MERGE storage engine, because MERGE tables are created from MyISAM tables and have similar index characteristics. Nor does it include the ARCHIVE, BLACKHOLE, or CSV engines, which support indexing either not at all or only in limited fashion.

Table 2.3 **Storage Engine Index Characteristics**

Index Characteristic	InnoDB	MyISAM	MEMORY
NULL values permitted	Yes	Yes	Yes
Columns per index	16	16	16
Indexes per table	64	64	64
Maximum index row size (bytes)	3072	1000	3072
Index column prefixes	Yes	Yes	Yes
Maximum prefix size (bytes)	767	1000	3072
BLOB/TEXT indexes	Yes	Yes	No
FULLTEXT indexes	As of 5.6.4	Yes	No
SPATIAL indexes	No	Yes	No
HASH indexes	No	No	Yes

One implication of the variations in index characteristics for different storage engines is that if you require an index to have certain properties, you may not be able to use certain types of tables. For example, to use a HASH index, you must use a MEMORY table. To index a TEXT column, you must use InnoDB or MyISAM.

To convert an existing table to use a different storage engine that has more suitable index characteristics, use ALTER TABLE. Suppose that you have an InnoDB table in MySQL 5.5 but need to perform searches using a FULLTEXT index. In MySQL 5.5, this is supported only by MyISAM. Convert the table using this statement:

```
ALTER TABLE tbl_name ENGINE=MyISAM;
```

2.6.4.2 Creating Indexes

MySQL can create several types of indexes:

- A unique index. This prohibits duplicate values for a single-column index, and duplicate combinations of values for a multiple-column (composite) index.

- A regular (nonunique) index. This gives you indexing benefits but permits duplicates.

- A FULLTEXT index, used for performing full-text searches. This index type is supported only for MyISAM tables (or, as of MySQL 5.6.4, InnoDB). For more information, see Section 2.14, "Using FULLTEXT Searches."

- A SPATIAL index. These can be used only with MyISAM tables containing spatial values, which are described briefly in Section 3.1.4, "Spatial Values."

- A HASH index. This is the default index type for MEMORY tables, although you can override the default to create BTREE indexes instead.

You can include index definitions for a new table when you use CREATE TABLE. For examples, see Section 1.4.6, "Creating Tables." To add indexes to existing tables, use ALTER TABLE or CREATE INDEX. (MySQL maps CREATE INDEX statements onto ALTER TABLE operations internally.)

ALTER TABLE is the more versatile than CREATE INDEX because it can create any kind of index supported by MySQL. For example:

```
ALTER TABLE tbl_name ADD INDEX index_name (index_columns);
ALTER TABLE tbl_name ADD UNIQUE index_name (index_columns);
ALTER TABLE tbl_name ADD PRIMARY KEY (index_columns);
ALTER TABLE tbl_name ADD FULLTEXT index_name (index_columns);
ALTER TABLE tbl_name ADD SPATIAL index_name (index_columns);
```

tbl_name is the name of the table to which the index should be added, and index_columns names the column or columns to index, separated by commas. The index name index_name is optional. If you leave it out, MySQL picks a name based on the name of the first indexed column.

An indexed column must be NOT NULL if indexed using a PRIMARY KEY or SPATIAL index. Other indexes permit indexed columns to contain NULL values.

A single ALTER TABLE statement can include multiple table alterations if you separate them by commas. This enables you to create several indexes at the same time, which is faster than adding them one at a time with individual ALTER TABLE statements.

To constrain an index to contain only unique values, create the index as a PRIMARY KEY or as a UNIQUE index. The two types of index are very similar, but have two differences:

- A table can contain only one PRIMARY KEY. This is because the name of a PRIMARY KEY is always PRIMARY and a table cannot have two indexes with the same name. You can place multiple UNIQUE indexes on a table.

- A PRIMARY KEY cannot contain NULL values. A UNIQUE index can. If a UNIQUE index can contain NULL values, it can contain multiple NULL values. (A NULL is not considered equal to any other value, even another NULL.)

CREATE INDEX can add most types of indexes, with the exception of PRIMARY KEY:

```
CREATE INDEX index_name ON tbl_name (index_columns);
CREATE UNIQUE INDEX index_name ON tbl_name (index_columns);
```

```
CREATE FULLTEXT INDEX index_name ON tbl_name (index_columns);
CREATE SPATIAL INDEX index_name ON tbl_name (index_columns);
```

tbl_name, *index_name*, and *index_columns* have the same meaning as for ALTER TABLE. Unlike ALTER TABLE, the index name is not optional with CREATE INDEX, and you cannot create multiple indexes with a single statement.

To create indexes for a new table with a CREATE TABLE statement, the syntax is similar to that used for ALTER TABLE, but you specify the index-creation clauses in addition to the column definitions:

```
CREATE TABLE tbl_name
(
  ... column definitions ...
  INDEX index_name (index_columns),
  UNIQUE index_name (index_columns),
  PRIMARY KEY (index_columns),
  FULLTEXT index_name (index_columns),
  SPATIAL index_name (index_columns),
  ...
);
```

As with ALTER TABLE, *index_name* is optional. MySQL picks an index name if you leave it out.

As a special case, you can create a single-column PRIMARY KEY or UNIQUE index by adding a PRIMARY KEY or UNIQUE clause to the end of a column definition. For example, the following CREATE TABLE statements are equivalent:

```
CREATE TABLE mytbl
(
  i INT NOT NULL PRIMARY KEY,
  j CHAR(10) NOT NULL UNIQUE
);

CREATE TABLE mytbl
(
  i INT NOT NULL,
  j CHAR(10) NOT NULL,
  PRIMARY KEY (i),
  UNIQUE (j)
);
```

The default index type for a MEMORY table is HASH. A hashed index is very fast for exact-value lookups, which is the typical way MEMORY tables are used. However, if you plan to use a MEMORY table for comparisons that can match a range of values (for example, id < 100), hashed indexes do not work well. You'll be better off creating a BTREE index instead, by adding a USING BTREE clause to the index definition:

```
CREATE TABLE namelist
(
  id   INT NOT NULL,
  name CHAR(100),
  INDEX (id) USING BTREE
) ENGINE=MEMORY;
```

To index a prefix of a string column, the syntax for naming the column in the index definition is *col_name*(n) rather than simply *col_name*. The prefix value, *n*, indicates that the index should include the first *n* bytes of column values for binary string types, or the first *n* characters for nonbinary string types. For example, the following statement creates a table with a CHAR column and a BINARY column. It indexes the first 10 characters of the CHAR column and the first 15 bytes of the BINARY column:

```
CREATE TABLE addresslist·
(
  name    CHAR(30) NOT NULL,
  address BINARY(60) NOT NULL,
  INDEX (name(10)),
  INDEX (address(15))
);
```

When you index a prefix of a string column, the prefix length, just like the column length, is specified in the same units as the column data type—that is, bytes for binary strings and characters for nonbinary strings. However, the maximum size of index entries are measured internally in bytes. The two measures are the same for single-byte character sets, but not for multi-byte character sets. For nonbinary strings that have multi-byte character sets, MySQL stores into index values as many complete characters as fit within the maximum permitted byte length.

In some circumstances, you may find it not only desirable but necessary to index a column prefix rather than the entire column:

- A prefix is required to index a BLOB or TEXT column.
- The length of index rows is equal to the sum of the length of the index parts of the columns that make up the index. If this length exceeds the maximum permitted number of bytes in index rows, you can make the index "narrower" by indexing a column prefix. Suppose that a MyISAM table that uses the latin1 single-byte character set contains four CHAR(255) columns named c1 through c4. An index value for each full column value takes 255 bytes, so an index on all four columns would require 1,020 bytes. However, the maximum length of a MyISAM index row is 1,000 bytes, so you cannot create a composite index that includes the entire contents of all four columns. However, you can create the index by indexing a shorter part of some or all of them. For example, you could index the first 250 characters from each column.

Columns in FULLTEXT indexes are indexed in full and do not have prefixes. If you specify a prefix length for a column in a FULLTEXT index, MySQL ignores it.

2.6.4.3 Dropping Indexes

To drop an index, use either a `DROP INDEX` or an `ALTER TABLE` statement. To use `DROP INDEX`, you must name the index to be dropped:

```
DROP INDEX index_name ON tbl_name;
```

To drop a `PRIMARY KEY` with `DROP INDEX`, specify the name `PRIMARY` as a quoted identifier:

```
DROP INDEX `PRIMARY` ON tbl_name;
```

That statement is unambiguous because a table is permitted only one `PRIMARY KEY` and its name is always `PRIMARY`.

Like the `CREATE INDEX` statement, `DROP INDEX` is handled internally as an `ALTER TABLE` statement. The preceding `DROP INDEX` statements correspond to the following `ALTER TABLE` statements:

```
ALTER TABLE tbl_name DROP INDEX index_name;
ALTER TABLE tbl_name DROP PRIMARY KEY;
```

If you don't know the names of a table's indexes, use `SHOW CREATE TABLE` or `SHOW INDEX` to find out.

When you drop columns from a table, indexes may be affected implicitly. Dropping a column that is a part of an index removes the column from the index as well. If you drop all columns in an index, MySQL drops the entire index.

2.6.5 Altering Table Structure

`ALTER TABLE` is a versatile statement and has many uses. We've already seen a few of its capabilities earlier in this chapter (for changing storage engines and for creating and dropping indexes). `ALTER TABLE` can also rename tables, add or drop columns, change column data types, and more. This section covers some of its features. For its complete syntax, see Appendix E, "SQL Syntax Reference."

`ALTER TABLE` is useful when you find that the structure of a table no longer reflects its intended use. Perhaps you want to record additional information, or the table contains information that has become superfluous. Maybe existing columns are too small, or it turns out that you've defined columns larger than you need and you'd like to make them smaller to save space and improve query performance. Here are some situations for which `ALTER TABLE` is valuable:

- You assign case numbers to records for a research project using an `AUTO_INCREMENT` column. You didn't expect your funding to last long enough to generate more than about 50,000 records, so you made the data type `SMALLINT UNSIGNED`, which holds a maximum of 65,535 unique values. However, the funding for the project was renewed, and it looks like you might generate another 50,000 records. You need a bigger type to accommodate more case numbers.

- Size changes can go the other way, too. Maybe you created a CHAR(255) column but now recognize that no value in the table is more than 100 characters long. You can shorten the column or convert it to VARCHAR(255) to save space.

- You want to convert a table to use a different storage engine to take advantage of features offered by that engine. For example, MyISAM tables are not transaction-safe, but you have an application that needs transactional capabilities. You can convert the affected tables to use InnoDB, which supports transactions. Or you might be using MyISAM in MySQL 5.5 because it supports FULLTEXT capabilities, but now you have upgraded to MySQL 5.6, which expands FULLTEXT support to InnoDB.

The syntax for ALTER TABLE looks like this:

```
ALTER TABLE tbl_name action [, action] ... ;
```

Each action specifies a modification to make to the table. Some database systems permit only a single action in an ALTER TABLE statement, but MySQL supports multiple actions, separated by commas.

> **Tip**
>
> If you need to remind yourself about a table's current definition before using ALTER TABLE, issue a SHOW CREATE TABLE statement. This statement is also useful after ALTER TABLE to verify that the alteration affected the table definition as you expect.

The following examples discuss some of the capabilities of ALTER TABLE.

Changing a column's data type. To change a data type, use either a CHANGE or MODIFY clause. Suppose that the column i in a table mytbl is SMALLINT UNSIGNED. To change it to MEDIUMINT UNSIGNED, use either of the following statements:

```
ALTER TABLE mytbl MODIFY i MEDIUMINT UNSIGNED;
ALTER TABLE mytbl CHANGE i i MEDIUMINT UNSIGNED;
```

Why is the column named twice in the statement that uses CHANGE? Because one thing that CHANGE can do that MODIFY cannot is to rename the column in addition to changing the type. If you had wanted to rename i to k at the same time you changed the type, you'd do so like this:

```
ALTER TABLE mytbl CHANGE i k MEDIUMINT UNSIGNED;
```

Remember that with CHANGE, you name the column you want to change and then specify its new name and definition. To retain the same column name, you must specify the name twice.

To rename a column without changing its data type, use CHANGE old_name new_name followed by the column's current definition.

To change a column's character set, use the CHARACTER SET attribute in the column definition:

```
ALTER TABLE t MODIFY c CHAR(20) CHARACTER SET ucs2;
```

An important reason for changing data types is to improve query efficiency for joins that compare columns from two tables. Indexes often can be used for comparisons in joins between similar column types, but comparisons are quicker when both columns are exactly the same type. Suppose that you're running a query like this:

```
SELECT ... FROM t1 INNER JOIN t2 WHERE t1.name = t2.name;
```

If `t1.name` is `CHAR(10)` and `t2.name` is `CHAR(15)`, the query won't run as quickly as if they were both `CHAR(15)`. You can make them the same by changing `t1.name` using either of these statements:

```
ALTER TABLE t1 MODIFY name CHAR(15);
ALTER TABLE t1 CHANGE name name CHAR(15);
```

Converting a table to a different storage engine. To convert a table from one storage engine to another, use an `ENGINE` clause that specifies the new engine name:

```
ALTER TABLE tbl_name ENGINE=engine_name;
```

`engine_name` is a name such as `InnoDB`, `MyISAM`, or `MEMORY`. Lettercase does not matter.

One reason to change a storage engine is to make it transaction-safe. Suppose that you have a MyISAM table and discover that an application that uses it needs to perform transactional operations, including rollback in case failures occur. MyISAM tables do not support transactions, but you can make the table transaction-safe by converting it to use InnoDB:

```
ALTER TABLE tbl_name ENGINE=InnoDB;
```

When you convert a table to a different engine, the permitted or sensible conversions may depend on the feature compatibility of the old and new engines. For example, if you have a table that includes a `BLOB` column, you cannot convert the table to use the MEMORY engine because MEMORY tables do not support `BLOB` columns.

There are circumstances under which you should not use `ALTER TABLE` to convert a table to use a different storage engine. For example:

- An InnoDB table can be converted to use another storage engine. However, if the table has foreign key constraints, they will be lost because only InnoDB supports foreign keys.
- MEMORY tables are held in memory and disappear when the server exits. If you require a table's contents to persist across server restarts, do not convert it to use the MEMORY engine.

Renaming a table. Use a `RENAME` clause that specifies the new table name:

```
ALTER TABLE tbl_name RENAME TO new_tbl_name;
```

Another way to rename tables is with `RENAME TABLE`. The syntax looks like this:

```
RENAME TABLE tbl_name TO new_tbl_name;
```

One thing that `RENAME TABLE` can do that `ALTER TABLE` cannot is rename multiple tables in the same statement. For example, you can swap the names of two tables like this:

```
RENAME TABLE t1 TO tmp, t2 TO t1, tmp TO t2;
```

If you qualify a table name with a database name, you can move a table from one database to another by renaming it. Either of the following statements move the table t from the `sampdb` database to the `test` database:

```
ALTER TABLE sampdb.t RENAME TO test.t;
RENAME TABLE sampdb.t TO test.t;
```

You cannot rename a table to a name that already exists.

2.7   Obtaining Database Metadata

MySQL provides several ways to obtain database metadata—that is, information about databases and the objects in them:

- `SHOW` statements such as `SHOW DATABASES` or `SHOW TABLES`
- Tables in the `INFORMATION_SCHEMA` database
- Command-line programs such as `mysqlshow` or `mysqldump`

The following sections describe how to use each of these information sources to access metadata.

2.7.1   Obtaining Metadata with `SHOW`

MySQL provides a `SHOW` statement that displays many types of database metadata. `SHOW` is helpful for keeping track of the contents of your databases and reminding yourself about the structure of your tables. The following examples demonstrate a few uses for `SHOW` statements.

List the databases you can access:

```
SHOW DATABASES;
```

Display the `CREATE DATABASE` statement for a database:

```
SHOW CREATE DATABASE db_name;
```

List the tables in the default database or a given database:

```
SHOW TABLES;
SHOW TABLES FROM db_name;
```

`SHOW TABLES` doesn't show `TEMPORARY` tables.

Display the `CREATE TABLE` statement for a table:

```
SHOW CREATE TABLE tbl_name;
```

Display information about columns or indexes in a table:

```
SHOW COLUMNS FROM tbl_name;
SHOW INDEX FROM tbl_name;
```

The DESCRIBE tbl_name and EXPLAIN tbl_name statements are synonymous with SHOW COLUMNS FROM tbl_name.

Display descriptive information about tables in the default database or in a given database:

```
SHOW TABLE STATUS;
SHOW TABLE STATUS FROM db_name;
```

Several forms of the SHOW statement take a LIKE 'pattern' clause permitting a pattern to be given that limits the scope of the output. MySQL interprets 'pattern' as an SQL pattern that may include the '%' and '_' wildcard characters. For example, this statement displays the names of columns in the student table that begin with 's':

```
mysql> SHOW COLUMNS FROM student LIKE 's%';
+------------+------------------+------+-----+---------+----------------+
| Field      | Type             | Null | Key | Default | Extra          |
+------------+------------------+------+-----+---------+----------------+
| sex        | enum('F','M')    | NO   |     | NULL    |                |
| student_id | int(10) unsigned | NO   | PRI | NULL    | auto_increment |
+------------+------------------+------+-----+---------+----------------+
```

To match a literal instance of a wildcard character in a LIKE pattern, precede it with a backslash. This is commonly done to match a literal '_', which occurs frequently in database, table, and column names.

Any SHOW statement that supports a LIKE clause can also be written to use a WHERE clause. The statement displays the same columns, but WHERE provides more flexibility about specifying which rows to return. The WHERE clause should refer to the SHOW statement column names. If the column name is a reserved word such as KEY, specify it as a quoted identifier. This statement determines which column in the student table is the primary key:

```
mysql> SHOW COLUMNS FROM student WHERE `Key` = `PRI`;
+------------+------------------+------+-----+---------+----------------+
| Field      | Type             | Null | Key | Default | Extra          |
+------------+------------------+------+-----+---------+----------------+
| student_id | int(10) unsigned | NO   | PRI | NULL    | auto_increment |
+------------+------------------+------+-----+---------+----------------+
```

It's sometimes useful to be able to tell from within an application whether a given table exists. You can use SHOW TABLES to find out (unless the table is a TEMPORARY table):

```
SHOW TABLES LIKE 'tbl_name';
SHOW TABLES FROM db_name LIKE 'tbl_name';
```

If the SHOW TABLES statement lists information for the table, it exists. It's also possible to determine table existence, even for TEMPORARY tables, with either of the following statements:

```
SELECT COUNT(*) FROM tbl_name;
SELECT * FROM tbl_name WHERE FALSE;
```

Each statement succeeds if the table exists, and fails if it doesn't. The first statement is most appropriate for MyISAM tables, for which COUNT(*) with no WHERE clause is highly optimized. It's not so good for InnoDB tables, which require a full scan to count the rows. The second statement is more general because it runs quickly for any storage engine. These statements are most suitable for use within application programming languages such as Perl or PHP because you can test the success or failure of the query and take action accordingly. They're not especially useful in a batch script that you run from mysql because you can't do anything if an error occurs except terminate (or ignore the error, but then there's obviously no point in running the query at all). Another strategy, which works in any context without failure, is to query the INFORMATION_SCHEMA database. See Section 2.7.2, "Obtaining Metadata with INFORMATION_SCHEMA."

To determine the storage engine for individual tables, you can use SHOW TABLE STATUS or SHOW CREATE TABLE. The output from either statement includes a storage engine indicator.

2.7.2 Obtaining Metadata with INFORMATION_SCHEMA

Another way to obtain information about databases is to access the INFORMATION_SCHEMA database. INFORMATION_SCHEMA is based on the SQL standard. That is, the access mechanism is standard, even though some of the content is MySQL-specific. This makes INFORMATION_SCHEMA more portable than the various SHOW statements, which are entirely MySQL-specific.

INFORMATION_SCHEMA is accessed through SELECT statements and can be used in a flexible manner. SHOW statements always display a fixed set of columns and you cannot capture the output in a table. With INFORMATION_SCHEMA, the SELECT statement can name specific output columns and a WHERE clause can specify any expression required to select the information that you want. Also, you can use joins or subqueries, and you can use CREATE TABLE ... SELECT or INSERT INTO ... SELECT to save the result of the retrieval in another table for further processing.

You can think of INFORMATION_SCHEMA as a virtual database in which the tables are views for different kinds of database metadata. To see what tables INFORMATION_SCHEMA contains, use SHOW TABLES:

```
mysql> SHOW TABLES IN INFORMATION_SCHEMA;
+---------------------------------------+
| Tables_in_information_schema          |
+---------------------------------------+
| CHARACTER_SETS                        |
| COLLATIONS                            |
| COLLATION_CHARACTER_SET_APPLICABILITY |
| COLUMNS                               |
| COLUMN_PRIVILEGES                     |
| ENGINES                               |
| EVENTS                                |
```

```
| FILES                                 |
| GLOBAL_STATUS                         |
| GLOBAL_VARIABLES                      |
| KEY_COLUMN_USAGE                      |
| PARAMETERS                            |
| PARTITIONS                            |
| PLUGINS                               |
| PROCESSLIST                           |
| PROFILING                             |
| REFERENTIAL_CONSTRAINTS               |
| ROUTINES                              |
| SCHEMATA                              |
| SCHEMA_PRIVILEGES                     |
| SESSION_STATUS                        |
| SESSION_VARIABLES                     |
| STATISTICS                            |
| TABLES                                |
| TABLESPACES                           |
| TABLE_CONSTRAINTS                     |
| TABLE_PRIVILEGES                      |
| TRIGGERS                              |
| USER_PRIVILEGES                       |
| VIEWS                                 |
+---------------------------------------+
```

The following list briefly describes some of the INFORMATION_SCHEMA tables just shown:

- SCHEMATA, TABLES, VIEWS, ROUTINES, TRIGGERS, EVENTS, PARAMETERS, PARTITIONS, COLUMNS

  Information about databases; tables, views, stored routines, triggers, and events within databases; routine parameters; table partitions; and columns within tables

- FILES

  Information about the files used to store tablespace data

- TABLE_CONSTRAINTS, KEY_COLUMN_USAGE

  Information about tables and columns that have constraints such as unique-valued indexes or foreign keys

- STATISTICS

  Information about table index characteristics

- REFERENTIAL_CONSTRAINTS

  Information about foreign keys

- CHARACTER_SETS, COLLATIONS, COLLATION_CHARACTER_SET_APPLICABILITY

  Information about supported character sets, collations for each character set, and mapping from each collation to its character set

- ENGINES, PLUGINS

  Information about storage engines and server plugins

- USER_PRIVILEGES, SCHEMA_PRIVILEGES, TABLE_PRIVILEGES, COLUMN_PRIVILEGES

  Global, database, table, and column privilege information from the user, db, tables_priv, and columns_priv tables in the mysql database

- GLOBAL_VARIABLES, SESSION_VARIABLES, GLOBAL_STATUS, SESSION_STATUS

  Global and session values of system and status variables

- PROCESSLIST

  Information about the threads executing within the server

Individual storage engines may add their own tables to INFORMATION_SCHEMA. For example, InnoDB does this.

To determine the columns contained in a given INFORMATION_SCHEMA table, use SHOW COLUMNS or DESCRIBE:

```
mysql> DESCRIBE INFORMATION_SCHEMA.CHARACTER_SETS;
+----------------------+-------------+------+-----+---------+-------+
| Field                | Type        | Null | Key | Default | Extra |
+----------------------+-------------+------+-----+---------+-------+
| CHARACTER_SET_NAME   | varchar(32) | NO   |     |         |       |
| DEFAULT_COLLATE_NAME | varchar(32) | NO   |     |         |       |
| DESCRIPTION          | varchar(60) | NO   |     |         |       |
| MAXLEN               | bigint(3)   | NO   |     | 0       |       |
+----------------------+-------------+------+-----+---------+-------+
```

To display information from a table, use a SELECT statement. (Neither INFORMATION_SCHEMA nor any of its table or column names are case sensitive.) The general query to see all the columns in any given INFORMATION_SCHEMA table is as follows:

```
SELECT * FROM INFORMATION_SCHEMA.tbl_name;
```

Include a WHERE clause to be specific about what you want to see.

The preceding section described the use of SHOW statements to determine whether a table exists or which storage engine it uses. INFORMATION_SCHEMA tables can provide the same information. This query uses INFORMATION_SCHEMA to test for the existence of a particular table, returning 1 or 0 to indicate that the table does or does not exist, respectively:

```
mysql> SELECT COUNT(*) FROM INFORMATION_SCHEMA.TABLES
    -> WHERE TABLE_SCHEMA='sampdb' AND TABLE_NAME='member';
+----------+
| COUNT(*) |
+----------+
|        1 |
+----------+
```

Use this query to check which storage engine a table uses:

```
mysql> SELECT ENGINE FROM INFORMATION_SCHEMA.TABLES
    -> WHERE TABLE_SCHEMA='sampdb' AND TABLE_NAME='student';
+--------+
| ENGINE |
+--------+
| InnoDB |
+--------+
```

2.7.3   Obtaining Metadata from the Command Line

The mysqlshow command provides some of the same information as certain SHOW statements, which enables you to get database and table information at your command prompt.

List databases managed by the server:

```
% mysqlshow
```

List tables in a database:

```
% mysqlshow db_name
```

Display information about columns in a table:

```
% mysqlshow db_name tbl_name
```

Display information about indexes in a table:

```
% mysqlshow --keys db_name tbl_name
```

Display descriptive information about tables in a database:

```
% mysqlshow --status db_name
```

The mysqldump client program enables you to see the structure of your tables in the form of a CREATE TABLE statement (much like SHOW CREATE TABLE). If you use mysqldump to review table structure, invoke it with the --no-data option so that you don't get swamped with your table's data!

```
% mysqldump --no-data db_name [tbl_name] ...
```

If you specify only the database name with no table names, mysqldump displays the structure for all tables in the database. Otherwise, it shows information only for the named tables.

For both mysqlshow and mysqldump, specify the usual connection parameter options as necessary, such as --host, --user, or --password.

2.8   Performing Multiple-Table Retrievals with Joins

It does no good to put records in a database unless you retrieve them eventually and do something with them. That's the purpose of the SELECT statement: to help you get at your data. SELECT probably is used more often than any other statement in the SQL language, but it can also be the trickiest; the conditions you use for choosing rows can be arbitrarily complex and can involve comparisons between columns in many tables.

The basic syntax of the SELECT statement looks like this:

```
SELECT select_list          # the columns to select
FROM table_list             # the tables from which to select rows
WHERE row_constraint        # the conditions rows must satisfy
GROUP BY grouping_columns   # how to group results
ORDER BY sorting_columns    # how to sort results
HAVING group_constraint     # the conditions groups must satisfy
LIMIT count;                # row count limit on results
```

Everything in this syntax is optional except the word SELECT and the *select_list* part that specifies what you want to produce as output. Some databases require the FROM clause as well. MySQL does not, which enables you to evaluate expressions without referring to any tables:

```
SELECT SQRT(POW(3,2)+POW(4,2));
```

In Chapter 1, "Getting Started with MySQL," we devoted quite a bit of attention to single-table SELECT statements, concentrating primarily on the output column list and the WHERE, GROUP BY, ORDER BY, HAVING, and LIMIT clauses. This section covers an aspect of SELECT that is often confusing: writing joins; that is, SELECT statements that retrieve rows from multiple tables. We'll discuss the types of join MySQL supports, what they mean, and how to specify them. This should help you employ MySQL more effectively because, in many cases, the real problem of figuring out how to write a query is determining the proper way to join tables.

One problem with using SELECT is that when you first encounter a new type of problem, it's not always easy to see how to write a SELECT query to solve it. However, after you figure it out, you can use that experience when you run across similar problems in the future. SELECT is probably the statement for which past experience plays the largest role in being able to use it effectively, simply because of the sheer variety of problems to which it applies. As you gain experience, you'll be able to adapt joins more easily to new problems, and you'll find yourself thinking things like, "Oh, yes, that's one of those LEFT JOIN things," or, "Aha, that's a three-way join restricted by the common pairs of key columns." (You may find it encouraging to hear that experience helps you. Or you may find it alarming to consider that you could wind up thinking in terms like that.)

Many of the examples that demonstrate how to use the forms of join operations that MySQL supports use the following two tables, t1 and t2:

```
Table t1:     Table t2:
+----+----+    +----+----+
| i1 | c1 |    | i2 | c2 |
```

```
+----+----+        +----+----+
| 1  | a  |        | 2  | c  |
| 2  | b  |        | 3  | b  |
| 3  | c  |        | 4  | a  |
+----+----+        +----+----+
```

The tables are deliberately small so the effect of each type of join can be readily seen.

Other types of multiple-table SELECT statement are subqueries (one SELECT nested within another) and UNION statements. These are covered in Section 2.9, "Performing Multiple-Table Retrievals with Subqueries," and Section 2.10, "Performing Multiple-Table Retrievals with UNION."

A related multiple-table feature that MySQL supports is the capability of deleting or updating rows in one table based on the contents of another. For example, you might want to remove rows in one table that aren't matched by any row in another, or copy values from columns in one table to columns in another. Section 2.11, "Multiple-Table Deletes and Updates," discusses these types of operations.

2.8.1 Inner Joins

If a SELECT statement names multiple tables in the FROM clause with the names separated by INNER JOIN, MySQL performs an inner join, which produces results by matching rows in one table with rows in another table. For example, if you join t1 and t2 as follows, each row in t1 is combined with each row in t2:

```
mysql> SELECT * FROM t1 INNER JOIN t2;
+----+----+----+----+
| i1 | c1 | i2 | c2 |
+----+----+----+----+
| 1  | a  | 2  | c  |
| 2  | b  | 2  | c  |
| 3  | c  | 2  | c  |
| 1  | a  | 3  | b  |
| 2  | b  | 3  | b  |
| 3  | c  | 3  | b  |
| 1  | a  | 4  | a  |
| 2  | b  | 4  | a  |
| 3  | c  | 4  | a  |
+----+----+----+----+
```

In this statement, SELECT * means "select every column from every table named in the FROM clause." You could also write this as SELECT t1.*, t2.*:

```
SELECT t1.*, t2.* FROM t1 INNER JOIN t2;
```

If you don't want to select all columns or you want to display them in a different left-to-right order, name each desired column, separated by commas.

A join that combines each row of each table with each row in every other table to produce all possible combinations is known as the "cartesian product." Joining tables this way has the potential to produce a very large number of rows because the possible row count is the product of the number of rows in each table. A join between three tables that contain 100, 200, and 300 rows, respectively, could return 100 × 200 × 300 = 6 million rows. That's a lot of rows, even though the individual tables are small. In cases like this, normally a WHERE clause is useful for reducing the result set to a more manageable size.

If you add a WHERE clause causing tables to be matched on the values of certain columns, the join selects only rows with equal values in those columns:

```
mysql> SELECT t1.*, t2.* FROM t1 INNER JOIN t2 WHERE t1.i1 = t2.i2;
+----+----+----+----+
| i1 | c1 | i2 | c2 |
+----+----+----+----+
|  2 | b  |  2 | c  |
|  3 | c  |  3 | b  |
+----+----+----+----+
```

The CROSS JOIN and JOIN join types are the same as INNER JOIN, so these statements are equivalent:

```
SELECT t1.*, t2.* FROM t1 INNER JOIN t2 WHERE t1.i1 = t2.i2;
SELECT t1.*, t2.* FROM t1 CROSS JOIN t2 WHERE t1.i1 = t2.i2;
SELECT t1.*, t2.* FROM t1 JOIN t2 WHERE t1.i1 = t2.i2;
```

The ',' (comma) join operator is similar as well:

```
SELECT t1.*, t2.* FROM t1, t2 WHERE t1.i1 = t2.i2;
```

However, the comma operator has a different precedence from the other join types, and it can sometimes produce syntax errors when the other types will not. I recommend that you avoid the comma operator.

INNER JOIN, CROSS JOIN, and JOIN (but not the comma operator) support alternative syntaxes for specifying how to match table columns:

- One syntax uses an ON clause rather than a WHERE clause. The following example shows this using INNER JOIN:

  ```
  SELECT t1.*, t2.* FROM t1 INNER JOIN t2 ON t1.i1 = t2.i2;
  ```

  ON can be used regardless of whether the joined columns have the same name.

- The other syntax involves a USING() clause; this is similar in concept to ON, but the name of the joined column or columns must be the same in each table. For example, the following query joins mytbl1.b to mytbl2.b:

  ```
  SELECT mytbl1.*, mytbl2.* FROM mytbl1 INNER JOIN mytbl2 USING (b);
  ```

2.8.2 Qualifying References to Columns from Joined Tables

References to each table column throughout a SELECT statement must resolve unambiguously to a single table named in the FROM clause. If only one table is named, there is no ambiguity; all columns must be columns of that table. If multiple tables are named, any column name that appears in only one table is similarly unambiguous. However, if a column name appears in multiple tables, references to the column must be qualified with a table identifier using *tbl_name.col_name* syntax to specify which table you mean. Suppose that a table mytbl1 contains columns a and b, and a table mytbl2 contains columns b and c. References to columns a or c are unambiguous, but references to b must be qualified as either mytbl1.b or mytbl2.b:

```
SELECT a, mytbl1.b, mytbl2.b, c FROM mytbl1 INNER JOIN mytbl2 ... ;
```

Sometimes a table name qualifier is not sufficient to resolve a column reference. For example, if you're performing a self-join (that is, joining a table to itself), you're using the table multiple times within the query and it doesn't help to qualify a column name with the table name. In this case, table aliases are useful for communicating your intent. You can assign an alias to any instance of the table and refer to columns from that instance as *alias_name.col_name*. The following query joins a table to itself, but assigns an alias to one instance of the table to enable column references to be specified unambiguously:

```
SELECT mytbl.col1, m.col2 FROM mytbl INNER JOIN mytbl AS m
WHERE mytbl.col1 > m.col1;
```

2.8.3 Left and Right (Outer) Joins

An inner join shows only rows where a match can be found in both tables. An outer join shows matches, too, but can also show rows in one table that have no match in the other table. Two kinds of outer joins are left and right joins. Most of the examples in this section use LEFT JOIN, which identifies rows in the left table that are not matched by the right table. RIGHT JOIN is the same except that the roles of the tables are reversed.

A LEFT JOIN works like this: You specify the columns to be used for matching rows in the two tables. When a row from the left table matches a row from the right table, the contents of the rows are selected as an output row. When a row in the left table has no match, it is still selected for output, but joined with a "fake" row from the right table that contains NULL in each column.

In other words, a LEFT JOIN forces the result set to contain a row for every row selected from the left table, whether or not there is a match for it in the right table. The left-table rows with no match can be identified by the fact that all columns from the right table are NULL. These result rows tell you which rows are missing from the right table. That is an interesting and important property, because this kind of problem comes up in many different contexts. Which customers have not been assigned an account representative? For which inventory items have no sales been recorded? Or, closer to home with our sampdb database: Which students have not taken a particular exam? Which students have no rows in the absence table (that is, which students have perfect attendance)?

Consider once again our two tables, t1 and t2:

```
Table t1:      Table t2:
+----+----+    +----+----+
| i1 | c1 |    | i2 | c2 |
+----+----+    +----+----+
| 1  | a  |    | 2  | c  |
| 2  | b  |    | 3  | b  |
| 3  | c  |    | 4  | a  |
+----+----+    +----+----+
```

If we use an inner join to match these tables on t1.i1 and t2.i2, we'll get output only for the values 2 and 3, because those are the values that appear in both tables:

```
mysql> SELECT t1.*, t2.* FROM t1 INNER JOIN t2 ON t1.i1 = t2.i2;
+----+----+----+----+
| i1 | c1 | i2 | c2 |
+----+----+----+----+
| 2  | b  | 2  | c  |
| 3  | c  | 3  | b  |
+----+----+----+----+
```

A left join produces output for every row in t1, whether or not t2 matches it. To write a left join, name the tables with LEFT JOIN in between rather than INNER JOIN:

```
mysql> SELECT t1.*, t2.* FROM t1 LEFT JOIN t2 ON t1.i1 = t2.i2;
+----+----+------+------+
| i1 | c1 | i2   | c2   |
+----+----+------+------+
| 1  | a  | NULL | NULL |
| 2  | b  | 2    | c    |
| 3  | c  | 3    | b    |
+----+----+------+------+
```

Now there is an output row even for the t1.i1 value of 1, which has no match in t2. All the columns in this row that correspond to t2 columns have a value of NULL.

One thing to watch out for with LEFT JOIN is that unless right-table columns are defined as NOT NULL, you may get problematic rows in the result. For example, if the right table contains columns with NULL values, you won't be able to distinguish those NULL values from NULL values that identify unmatched rows.

As mentioned earlier, a RIGHT JOIN is like a LEFT JOIN with the roles of the tables reversed. These two statements are equivalent:

```
SELECT t1.*, t2.* FROM t1 LEFT JOIN t2 ON t1.i1 = t2.i2;
SELECT t1.*, t2.* FROM t2 RIGHT JOIN t1 ON t1.i1 = t2.i2;
```

The following discussion is phrased in terms of LEFT JOIN. To adjust it for RIGHT JOIN, reverse the table roles.

LEFT JOIN is especially useful when you want to find *only* those left table rows that are unmatched by the right table. Do this by adding a WHERE clause that selects only the rows that have NULL values in a right table column—in other words, the rows in one table that are missing from the other:

```
mysql> SELECT t1.*, t2.* FROM t1 LEFT JOIN t2 ON t1.i1 = t2.i2
    -> WHERE t2.i2 IS NULL;
+----+----+------+------+
| i1 | c1 | i2   | c2   |
+----+----+------+------+
|  1 | a  | NULL | NULL |
+----+----+------+------+
```

Normally, when you write a query like this, your real interest is in the unmatched values in the left table. The NULL columns from the right table are of no interest for display purposes, so you would omit them from the output column list:

```
mysql> SELECT t1.* FROM t1 LEFT JOIN t2 ON t1.i1 = t2.i2
    -> WHERE t2.i2 IS NULL;
+----+----+
| i1 | c1 |
+----+----+
|  1 | a  |
+----+----+
```

Like INNER JOIN, a LEFT JOIN can be written using an ON clause or a USING() clause to specify the matching conditions. As with INNER JOIN, ON can be used whether or not the joined columns from each table have the same name, but USING() requires that they have the same names.

NATURAL LEFT JOIN is similar to LEFT JOIN; it performs a LEFT JOIN, matching all columns that have the same name in the left and right tables. (Thus, no ON or USING clause is given.)

As already mentioned, LEFT JOIN is useful for answering "Which values are missing?" questions. Let's apply this principle to the tables in the sampdb database and consider a more complex example than those shown earlier using t1 and t2.

For the grade-keeping project, first mentioned in Chapter 1, "Getting Started with MySQL," we have a student table listing students, a grade_event table listing the grade events that have occurred, and a score table listing scores for each student for each grade event. However, if a student was ill on the day of some quiz or test, the score table wouldn't contain any score for the student for that event. A makeup quiz or test should be given in such cases, but how do we find these missing rows?

The problem is to determine which students have no score for a given grade event, and to do this for each grade event. That is, we want to find which combinations of student and grade event are not present in the score table. This "which values are not present" wording is a tip-off that we want a LEFT JOIN. The join isn't as simple as in the previous examples, though:

We aren't just looking for values that are not present in a single column, we're looking for a two-column combination. The combinations we want are all the student/event combinations. These are produced by joining the `student` table to the `grade_event` table:

```
FROM student INNER JOIN grade_event
```

Then we take the result of that join and perform a LEFT JOIN with the `score` table to find the matches for student ID/event ID pairs:

```
FROM student INNER JOIN grade_event
    LEFT JOIN score ON student.student_id = score.student.id
                    AND grade_event.event_id = score.event_id
```

Note that the ON clause causes the rows in the `score` table to be joined according to matches in different tables named earlier in the join. That's the key for solving this problem. The LEFT JOIN forces a row to be generated for each row produced by the join of the `student` and `grade_event` tables, even when there is no corresponding `score` table row. The result set rows for these missing score rows can be identified by the fact that the columns from the `score` table will all be NULL. We can identify these rows by adding a condition in the WHERE clause. Any column from the `score` table will do, but because we're looking for missing scores, it's probably conceptually clearest to test the `score` column:

```
WHERE score.score IS NULL
```

We can also sort the results using an ORDER BY clause. The two most logical orderings are by event per student and by student per event. I'll choose the first:

```
ORDER BY student.student_id, grade_event.event_id
```

Now all we need to do is name the columns we want to see in the output, and we're done. Here is the final statement:

```
SELECT
  student.name, student.student_id,
  grade_event.date, grade_event.event_id, grade_event.category
FROM
  student INNER JOIN grade_event
  LEFT JOIN score ON student.student_id = score.student_id
                  AND grade_event.event_id = score.event_id
WHERE
  score.score IS NULL
ORDER BY
  student.student_id, grade_event.event_id;
```

Running the query produces these results:

```
+------------+------------+------------+----------+----------+
| name       | student_id | date       | event_id | category |
+------------+------------+------------+----------+----------+
| Megan      |          1 | 2012-09-16 |        4 | Q        |
| Joseph     |          2 | 2012-09-03 |        1 | Q        |
```

```
| Katie     |          4 | 2012-09-23 |        5 | Q        |          |
| Devri     |         13 | 2012-09-03 |        1 | Q        |          |
| Devri     |         13 | 2012-10-01 |        6 | T        |          |
| Will      |         17 | 2012-09-16 |        4 | Q        |          |
| Avery     |         20 | 2012-09-06 |        2 | Q        |          |
| Gregory   |         23 | 2012-10-01 |        6 | T        |          |
| Sarah     |         24 | 2012-09-23 |        5 | Q        |          |
| Carter    |         27 | 2012-09-16 |        4 | Q        |          |
| Carter    |         27 | 2012-09-23 |        5 | Q        |          |
| Gabrielle |         29 | 2012-09-16 |        4 | Q        |          |
| Grace     |         30 | 2012-09-23 |        5 | Q        |          |
+-----------+------------+------------+----------+----------+
```

Here's a subtle point. The output displays the student IDs and the event IDs. The `student_id` column appears in both the `student` and `score` tables, so at first you might think that the output column list could name either `student.student_id` or `score.student_id`. That's not the case, because the entire basis for being able to find the rows we're interested in is that all the `score` table columns are returned by the LEFT JOIN as NULL. Selecting `score.student_id` would produce only a column of NULL values in the output. The same principle applies to deciding which `event_id` column to display. It appears in both the `grade_event` and `score` tables, but the query selects `grade_event.event_id` because the `score.event_id` values will always be NULL.

2.9 Performing Multiple-Table Retrievals with Subqueries

A subquery is a SELECT statement written within parentheses and nested inside another statement. Here's an example that looks up the IDs for grade event rows that correspond to tests ('T') and uses them to select scores for those tests:

```
SELECT * FROM score
WHERE event_id IN (SELECT event_id FROM grade_event WHERE category = 'T');
```

Subqueries can return different types of information:

- A scalar subquery returns a single value.
- A column subquery returns a single column of one or more values.
- A row subquery returns a single row of one or more values.
- A table subquery returns a table of one or more rows of one or more columns.

Subquery results can be tested in different ways:

- Scalar subquery results can be evaluated using relative comparison operators such as = or <.

- IN and NOT IN test whether a value is present in a set of values returned by a subquery.

- ALL, ANY, and SOME compare a value to the set of values returned by a subquery.

- EXISTS and NOT EXISTS test whether a subquery result is empty.

A scalar subquery is the most restrictive because it produces only a single value. But as a consequence, scalar subqueries can be used in the widest variety of contexts. They are applicable essentially anywhere that you can use a scalar operand, such as a term of an expression, as a function argument, or in the output column list. Column, row, and table subqueries that return more information cannot be used in contexts that require a single value.

Subqueries can be correlated or uncorrelated. This is a function of whether a subquery refers to and is dependent on values in the outer query.

You can use subqueries with statements other than SELECT. However, for statements that modify tables (DELETE, INSERT, REPLACE, UPDATE, LOAD DATA), MySQL enforces the restriction that the subquery cannot select from the table being modified.

In some cases, subqueries can be rewritten as joins. You might find subquery rewriting techniques useful to see whether the MySQL optimizer does a better job with a join than the equivalent subquery.

The following sections discuss the kinds of operations you can use to test subquery results, how to write correlated subqueries, and how to rewrite subqueries as joins.

2.9.1   Subqueries with Relative Comparison Operators

The =, <>, >, >=, <, and <= operators perform relative-value comparisons. When used with a scalar subquery, they find all rows in the outer query that stand in particular relationship to the value returned by the subquery. For example, to identify the scores for the quiz that took place on '2012-09-23', use a scalar subquery to determine the quiz event ID and then match score table rows against that ID in the outer SELECT:

```
SELECT * FROM score
WHERE event_id =
(SELECT event_id FROM grade_event
   WHERE date = '2012-09-23' AND category = 'Q');
```

With this form of statement, where the subquery is preceded by a value and a relative comparison operator, the subquery must produce a only single value. That is, it must be a scalar subquery; if it produces multiple values, the statement will fail. In some cases, it may be appropriate to satisfy the single-value requirement by limiting the subquery result with LIMIT 1.

Use of scalar subqueries with relative comparison operators is handy for solving problems for which you'd be tempted to use an aggregate function in a WHERE clause. For example, to determine which of the presidents in the president table was born first, you might try this statement:

```
SELECT * FROM president WHERE birth = MIN(birth);
```

That doesn't work because you can't use aggregates in WHERE clauses. (The WHERE clause determines which rows to select, but the value of MIN() isn't known until *after* the rows have already been selected.) However, you can use a subquery to produce the minimum birth date like this:

```
SELECT * FROM president
WHERE birth = (SELECT MIN(birth) FROM president);
```

Other aggregate functions can be used to solve similar problems. The following statement uses a subquery to select the above-average scores from a given grade event:

```
SELECT * FROM score WHERE event_id = 5
AND score > (SELECT AVG(score) FROM score WHERE event_id = 5);
```

If a subquery returns a single row, you can use a row constructor to compare a set of values (that is, a tuple) to the subquery result. This statement returns rows for presidents who were born in the same city and state as John Adams:

```
mysql> SELECT last_name, first_name, city, state FROM president
    -> WHERE (city, state) =
    -> (SELECT city, state FROM president
    -> WHERE last_name = 'Adams' AND first_name = 'John');
+-----------+-------------+-----------+-------+
| last_name | first_name  | city      | state |
+-----------+-------------+-----------+-------+
| Adams     | John        | Braintree | MA    |
| Adams     | John Quincy | Braintree | MA    |
+-----------+-------------+-----------+-------+
```

You can also use ROW(city, state) notation, which is equivalent to (city, state). Both act as row constructors.

2.9.2 IN and NOT IN Subqueries

The IN and NOT IN operators can be used when a subquery returns multiple rows to be evaluated in comparison to the outer query. They test whether a comparison value is present in a set of values. IN is true for rows in the outer query that match any row returned by the subquery. NOT IN is true for rows in the outer query that match no rows returned by the subquery. The following statements use IN and NOT IN to find those students who have absences listed in the absence table, and those who have perfect attendance (no absences):

```
mysql> SELECT * FROM student
    -> WHERE student_id IN (SELECT student_id FROM absence);
+-------+-----+------------+
| name  | sex | student_id |
+-------+-----+------------+
| Kyle  | M   |          3 |
| Abby  | F   |          5 |
```

```
| Peter  | M   |          10 |
| Will   | M   |          17 |
| Avery  | F   |          20 |
+--------+-----+-------------+
mysql> SELECT * FROM student
    -> WHERE student_id NOT IN (SELECT student_id FROM absence);
+------------+-----+-------------+
| name       | sex | student_id  |
+------------+-----+-------------+
| Megan      | F   |           1 |
| Joseph     | M   |           2 |
| Katie      | F   |           4 |
| Nathan     | M   |           6 |
| Liesl      | F   |           7 |
...
```

IN and NOT IN also work for subqueries that return multiple columns. In other words, you can use them with table subqueries. In this case, use a row constructor to specify the comparison values to test against each column:

```
mysql> SELECT last_name, first_name, city, state FROM president
    -> WHERE (city, state) IN
    -> (SELECT city, state FROM president
    -> WHERE last_name = 'Roosevelt');
+------------+-------------+------------+-------+
| last_name  | first_name  | city       | state |
+------------+-------------+------------+-------+
| Roosevelt  | Theodore    | New York   | NY    |
| Roosevelt  | Franklin D. | Hyde Park  | NY    |
+------------+-------------+------------+-------+
```

IN and NOT IN actually are synonyms for = ANY and <> ALL, which are covered in the next section.

2.9.3   ALL, ANY, and SOME Subqueries

The ALL and ANY operators are used in conjunction with a relative comparison operator to test the result of a column subquery. They test whether the comparison value stands in particular relationship to all or some of the values returned by the subquery. For example, <= ALL is true if the comparison value is less than or equal to every value that the subquery returns, whereas <= ANY is true if the comparison value is less than or equal to any value that the subquery returns. SOME is a synonym for ANY.

This statement determines which president was born first by selecting the row with a birth date less than or equal to all the birth dates in the president table (only the earliest date satisfies this condition):

```
mysql> SELECT last_name, first_name, birth FROM president
    -> WHERE birth <= ALL (SELECT birth FROM president);
+------------+------------+------------+
| last_name  | first_name | birth      |
+------------+------------+------------+
| Washington | George     | 1732-02-22 |
+------------+------------+------------+
```

Less usefully, the following statement returns all rows because every date is less than or equal to at least one other date (itself):

```
mysql> SELECT last_name, first_name, birth FROM president
    -> WHERE birth <= ANY (SELECT birth FROM president);
+------------+--------------+------------+
| last_name  | first_name   | birth      |
+------------+--------------+------------+
| Washington | George       | 1732-02-22 |
| Adams      | John         | 1735-10-30 |
| Jefferson  | Thomas       | 1743-04-13 |
| Madison    | James        | 1751-03-16 |
| Monroe     | James        | 1758-04-28 |
...
```

When ALL, ANY, or SOME are used with the = comparison operator, the subquery can be a table subquery. In this case, you test return rows using a row constructor to provide the comparison values.

```
mysql> SELECT last_name, first_name, city, state FROM president
    -> WHERE (city, state) = ANY
    -> (SELECT city, state FROM president
    -> WHERE last_name = 'Roosevelt');
+-----------+-------------+-----------+-------+
| last_name | first_name  | city      | state |
+-----------+-------------+-----------+-------+
| Roosevelt | Theodore    | New York  | NY    |
| Roosevelt | Franklin D. | Hyde Park | NY    |
+-----------+-------------+-----------+-------+
```

As mentioned in the previous section, IN and NOT IN are shorthand for = ANY and <> ALL. That is, IN means "equal to any of the rows returned by the subquery" and NOT IN means "unequal to all rows returned by the subquery."

2.9.4   EXISTS and NOT EXISTS Subqueries

The EXISTS and NOT EXISTS operators merely test whether a subquery returns any rows. If it does, EXISTS is true and NOT EXISTS is false. The following statements show some trivial examples of these subqueries. The first returns 0 if the absence table is empty, the second returns 1:

```
SELECT EXISTS (SELECT * FROM absence);
SELECT NOT EXISTS (SELECT * FROM absence);
```

EXISTS and NOT EXISTS actually are much more commonly used in correlated subqueries. For examples, see Section 2.9.5, "Correlated Subqueries."

With EXISTS and NOT EXISTS, the subquery uses * as the output column list. There's no need to name columns explicitly, because the subquery is assessed as true or false based on whether it returns any rows, not based on the particular values that the rows might contain. You can actually write pretty much anything for the subquery column selection list, but if you want to make it explicit that you're returning a true value when the subquery succeeds, you might write it as SELECT 1 rather than SELECT *.

2.9.5   Correlated Subqueries

Subqueries can be uncorrelated or correlated:

- An uncorrelated subquery contains no references to values from the outer query, so it could be executed by itself as a separate statement. For example, the subquery in the following statement is uncorrelated because it refers only to the table t1 and not to t2:

  ```
  SELECT j FROM t2 WHERE j IN (SELECT i FROM t1);
  ```

- A correlated subquery does contain references to values from the outer query, and thus is dependent on it. Due to this linkage, a correlated subquery cannot be executed by itself as a separate statement. For example, the subquery in the following statement is true for each value of column j in t2 that matches a column i value in t1:

  ```
  SELECT j FROM t2 WHERE (SELECT i FROM t1 WHERE i = j);
  ```

Correlated subqueries commonly are used for EXISTS and NOT EXISTS subqueries, which are useful for finding rows in one table that match or don't match rows in another. Correlated subqueries work by passing values from the outer query to the subquery to see whether they match the conditions specified in the subquery. For this reason, it's necessary to qualify column names with table names if they are ambiguous (appear in more than one table).

The following EXISTS subquery identifies matches between the tables—that is, values that are present in both. The statement selects students who have at least one absence listed in the absence table:

```
SELECT student_id, name FROM student WHERE EXISTS
(SELECT * FROM absence WHERE absence.student_id = student.student_id);
```

NOT EXISTS identifies nonmatches—values in one table that are not present in the other. This statement selects students who have no absences:

```
SELECT student_id, name FROM student WHERE NOT EXISTS
(SELECT * FROM absence WHERE absence.student_id = student.student_id);
```

2.9.6   Subqueries in the FROM Clause

Subqueries can be used in the FROM clause to generate values. In this case, the result of the subquery acts like a table. A subquery in the FROM clause can participate in joins, its values can be tested in the WHERE clause, and so forth. With this type of subquery, you must provide a table alias to give the subquery result a name:

```
mysql> SELECT * FROM (SELECT 1, 2) AS t1 INNER JOIN (SELECT 3, 4) AS t2;
+---+---+---+---+
| 1 | 2 | 3 | 4 |
+---+---+---+---+
| 1 | 2 | 3 | 4 |
+---+---+---+---+
```

2.9.7   Rewriting Subqueries as Joins

It's often possible to rephrase a query that uses a subquery in terms of a join, and it's not a bad idea to examine queries that you might be inclined to write in terms of subqueries. A join is sometimes more efficient than a subquery, so if a SELECT written as a subquery takes a long time to execute, try writing it as a join to see whether it performs better. The following discussion shows how to do that.

2.9.7.1   Rewriting Subqueries That Select Matching Values

Here's an example statement containing a subquery; it selects scores from the score table only for tests (that is, it ignores quiz scores):

```
SELECT * FROM score
WHERE event_id IN (SELECT event_id FROM grade_event WHERE category = 'T');
```

The same statement can be written without a subquery by converting it to a simple join:

```
SELECT score.* FROM score INNER JOIN grade_event
ON score.event_id = grade_event.event_id WHERE grade_event.category = 'T';
```

As another example, the following query selects scores for female students:

```
SELECT * from score
WHERE student_id IN (SELECT student_id FROM student WHERE sex = 'F');
```

This can be converted to a join as follows:

```
SELECT score.* FROM score INNER JOIN student
ON score.student_id = student.student_id WHERE student.sex = 'F';
```

There is a pattern here. The subquery statements follow this form:

```
SELECT * FROM table1
WHERE column1 IN (SELECT column2a FROM table2 WHERE column2b = value);
```

Such queries can be converted to a join using this form:

```
SELECT table1.* FROM table1 INNER JOIN table2
ON table1.column1 = table2.column2a WHERE table2.column2b = value;
```

In some cases, the subquery and the join might return different results. This occurs when *table2* contains multiple instances of *column2a*. The subquery form produces only one instance of each *column2a* value, but the join produces them all and its output includes duplicate rows. To suppress these duplicates, begin the join with SELECT DISTINCT rather than SELECT.

2.9.7.2   Rewriting Subqueries That Select Nonmatching (Missing) Values

Another common type of subquery statement searches for values in one table that are not present in another table. As we've seen before, the "which values are not present" type of problem is a clue that a LEFT JOIN may be helpful. Here's the statement with a subquery seen earlier that tests for students who are *not* listed in the absence table (it finds those students with perfect attendance):

```
SELECT * FROM student
WHERE student_id NOT IN (SELECT student_id FROM absence);
```

This query can be rewritten using a LEFT JOIN as follows:

```
SELECT student.*
FROM student LEFT JOIN absence ON student.student_id = absence.student_id
WHERE absence.student_id IS NULL;
```

In general terms, the subquery statement form is as follows:

```
SELECT * FROM table1
WHERE column1 NOT IN (SELECT column2 FROM table2);
```

A query having that form can be rewritten like this:

```
SELECT table1.*
FROM table1 LEFT JOIN table2 ON table1.column1 = table2.column2
WHERE table2.column2 IS NULL;
```

This assumes that *table2.column2* is defined as NOT NULL.

The subquery does have the advantage of being more intuitive than the LEFT JOIN. "Not in" is a concept that most people understand without difficulty, because it occurs outside the context of database programming. The same cannot be said for the concept of "left join," for which there is no such basis for natural understanding.

2.10   Performing Multiple-Table Retrievals with UNION

To create a result set that combines the results from several queries, use a UNION statement. For the examples in this section, assume that you have three tables, t1, t2, and t3, that look like this:

```
mysql> SELECT * FROM t1;
+------+-------+
| i    | c     |
+------+-------+
|    1 | red   |
|    2 | blue  |
|    3 | green |
+------+-------+
mysql> SELECT * FROM t2;
+------+------+
| j    | c    |
+------+------+
|   -1 | tan  |
|    1 | red  |
+------+------+
mysql> SELECT * FROM t3;
+------------+------+
| d          | k    |
+------------+------+
| 1904-01-01 |  100 |
| 2004-01-01 |  200 |
| 2004-01-01 |  200 |
+------------+------+
```

Tables t1 and t2 have integer and character columns, and t3 has date and integer columns. To write a UNION statement that combines multiple retrievals, write multiple SELECT statements and put the keyword UNION between them. Each SELECT must retrieve the same number of columns. For example, to select the integer column from each table, do this:

```
mysql> SELECT i FROM t1 UNION SELECT j FROM t2 UNION SELECT k FROM t3;
+------+
| i    |
+------+
|    1 |
|    2 |
|    3 |
|   -1 |
|  100 |
|  200 |
+------+
```

UNION has the following properties.

Column name and data types. The column names for the UNION result come from the names of the columns in the first SELECT. The second and subsequent SELECT statements in the UNION must select the same number of columns, but corresponding columns need not have the same names or data types. (Normally, you write a UNION such that corresponding columns do have the same types, but MySQL performs type conversion as necessary if they do not.) Column matching occurs by position rather than by name, which is why the following two statements return different results, even though they select the same values from the two tables:

```
mysql> SELECT i, c FROM t1 UNION SELECT k, d FROM t3;
+------+------------+
| i    | c          |
+------+------------+
|    1 | red        |
|    2 | blue       |
|    3 | green      |
|  100 | 1904-01-01 |
|  200 | 2004-01-01 |
+------+------------+
mysql> SELECT i, c FROM t1 UNION SELECT d, k FROM t3;
+------------+-------+
| i          | c     |
+------------+-------+
| 1          | red   |
| 2          | blue  |
| 3          | green |
| 1904-01-01 | 100   |
| 2004-01-01 | 200   |
+------------+-------+
```

In each statement, the data type for each column of the result is determined from the selected values. In the first statement, strings and dates are selected for the second column. The result is a string column. In the second statement, integers and dates are selected for the first column, strings and integers for the second column. In both cases, the result is a string column.

Duplicate-row handling. By default, UNION eliminates duplicate rows from the result set:

```
mysql> SELECT * FROM t1 UNION SELECT * FROM t2 UNION SELECT * FROM t3;
+------------+-------+
| i          | c     |
+------------+-------+
| 1          | red   |
| 2          | blue  |
| 3          | green |
| -1         | tan   |
| 1904-01-01 | 100   |
| 2004-01-01 | 200   |
+------------+-------+
```

t1 and t2 both have a row containing values of 1 and 'red', but only one such row appears in the output. Also, t3 has two rows containing '2004-01-01' and 200, one of which has been eliminated.

UNION DISTINCT is synonymous with UNION; both retain only distinct rows.

To preserve duplicates, change each UNION to UNION ALL:

```
mysql> SELECT * FROM t1 UNION ALL SELECT * FROM t2 UNION ALL SELECT * FROM t3;
+------------+-------+
| i          | c     |
+------------+-------+
| 1          | red   |
| 2          | blue  |
| 3          | green |
| -1         | tan   |
| 1          | red   |
| 1904-01-01 | 100   |
| 2004-01-01 | 200   |
| 2004-01-01 | 200   |
+------------+-------+
```

If you mix UNION or UNION DISTINCT with UNION ALL, any distinct union operation takes precedence over any UNION ALL operations to its left.

ORDER BY and LIMIT handling. To sort a UNION result as a whole, place each SELECT within parentheses and add an ORDER BY clause following the last one. Because the UNION uses column names from the first SELECT, the ORDER BY should refer to those names, not the column names from the last SELECT:

```
mysql> (SELECT i, c FROM t1) UNION (SELECT k, d FROM t3)
    -> ORDER BY c;
+------+------------+
| i    | c          |
+------+------------+
|  100 | 1904-01-01 |
|  200 | 2004-01-01 |
|    2 | blue       |
|    3 | green      |
|    1 | red        |
+------+------------+
```

If a sort column is aliased, an ORDER BY at the end of the UNION must refer to the alias. Also, the ORDER BY cannot refer to table names. If you need to sort by a column specified as *tbl_name*.*col_name* in the first SELECT, alias the column and refer to the alias in the ORDER BY clause.

Similarly, to limit the number of rows returned by a UNION, add LIMIT to the end of the statement:

```
mysql> (SELECT * FROM t1) UNION (SELECT * FROM t2) UNION (SELECT * FROM t3)
    -> LIMIT 2;
+------+------+
| i    | c    |
+------+------+
| 1    | red  |
| 2    | blue |
+------+------+
```

ORDER BY and LIMIT also can be used within a parenthesized individual SELECT to apply only to that SELECT:

```
mysql> (SELECT * FROM t1 ORDER BY i LIMIT 2)
    -> UNION (SELECT * FROM t2 ORDER BY j LIMIT 1)
    -> UNION (SELECT * FROM t3 ORDER BY d LIMIT 2);
+------------+------+
| i          | c    |
+------------+------+
| 1          | red  |
| 2          | blue |
| -1         | tan  |
| 1904-01-01 | 100  |
| 2004-01-01 | 200  |
+------------+------+
```

ORDER BY within an individual SELECT is used only if LIMIT is also present, to determine which rows the LIMIT applies to. It does not affect the order in which rows appear in the final UNION result.

2.11 Multiple-Table Deletes and Updates

Sometimes it's useful to delete rows based on whether they match or don't match rows in another table. Similarly, it's often useful to update rows in one table using the contents of rows in another table. This section describes how to perform multiple-table DELETE and UPDATE operations. These types of statements draw heavily on the concepts used for joins, so be sure you're familiar with the material discussed earlier in Section 2.8, "Performing Multiple-Table Retrievals with Joins."

To perform a single-table DELETE or UPDATE, you refer only to the columns of one table and thus need not qualify the column names with the table name. For example, this statement deletes all rows in a table t that have id values greater than 100:

```
DELETE FROM t WHERE id > 100;
```

But what if you want to delete rows based not on properties inherent in the rows themselves, but rather on their relationship to rows in another table? Suppose that you want to delete from t those rows with id values that are present in or missing from another table t2?

To write a multiple-table DELETE, name all the tables in a FROM clause and specify the conditions used to match rows in the tables in the WHERE clause. The following statement deletes rows from table t1 where there is a matching id value in table t2:

```
DELETE t1 FROM t1 INNER JOIN t2 ON t1.id = t2.id;
```

Notice that if a column name appears in more than one of the tables, it is ambiguous and must be qualified with a table name.

The syntax also supports deleting rows from multiple tables at once. To delete rows from *both* tables where there are matching id values, name them both after the DELETE keyword:

```
DELETE t1, t2 FROM t1 INNER JOIN t2 ON t1.id = t2.id;
```

What if you want to delete nonmatching rows? A multiple-table DELETE can use any kind of join that you can write in a SELECT, so employ the same strategy that you'd use when writing a SELECT that identifies the nonmatching rows. That is, use a LEFT JOIN or RIGHT JOIN. For example, to identify rows in t1 that have no match in t2, write a SELECT like this:

```
SELECT t1.* FROM t1 LEFT JOIN t2 ON t1.id = t2.id WHERE t2.id IS NULL;
```

The analogous DELETE statement to find and remove those rows from t1 uses a LEFT JOIN as well:

```
DELETE t1 FROM t1 LEFT JOIN t2 ON t1.id = t2.id WHERE t2.id IS NULL;
```

MySQL supports a second multiple-table DELETE syntax. This syntax uses a FROM clause to list the tables from which rows are to be deleted and a USING clause to join the tables that determine which rows to delete. The preceding multiple-table DELETE statements can be rewritten using this syntax as follows:

```
DELETE FROM t1 USING t1 INNER JOIN t2 ON t1.id = t2.id;
DELETE FROM t1, t2 USING t1 INNER JOIN t2 ON t1.id = t2.id;
DELETE FROM t1 USING t1 LEFT JOIN t2 ON t1.id = t2.id WHERE t2.id IS NULL;
```

The principles involved in writing multiple-table UPDATE statements are quite similar to those used for DELETE: Name all the tables that participate in the operation and qualify column references as necessary. Suppose that the quiz you gave on September 23, 2012 contained a question that everyone got wrong, and then you discover that the reason for this is that your answer key was incorrect. As a result, you want to add a point to everyone's score. With a multiple-table UPDATE, you can do this as follows:

```
UPDATE score, grade_event SET score.score = score.score + 1
WHERE score.event_id = grade_event.event_id
AND grade_event.date = '2012-09-23' AND grade_event.category = 'Q';
```

In this case, you could accomplish the same objective using a single-table update and a subquery:

```
UPDATE score SET score = score + 1
WHERE event_id = (SELECT event_id FROM grade_event
WHERE date = '2012-09-23' AND category = 'Q');
```

But other updates cannot be written using subqueries. For example, you might want to not only identify rows to update based on the contents of another table, but to copy column values from one table to another. The following statement copies `t1.a` to `t2.a` for rows that have a matching `id` column value:

```
UPDATE t1, t2 SET t2.a = t1.a WHERE t2.id = t1.id;
```

To perform multiple-table deletes or updates for InnoDB tables, you need not use the syntax just described. Instead, set up a foreign key relationship between tables that includes an `ON DELETE CASCADE` or `ON UPDATE CASCADE` constraint. For details, see Section 2.13, "Foreign Keys and Referential Integrity."

2.12   Performing Transactions

A transaction is a set of SQL statements that execute as a unit and can be canceled if necessary. Either all the statements execute successfully, or none of them have any effect. This is achieved through the use of commit and rollback capabilities. If all of the statements in the transaction succeed, you commit it to record their effects permanently in the database. If an error occurs during the transaction, you roll it back to cancel it. Any statements executed up to that point within the transaction are undone, leaving the database in the state it was in prior to the point at which the transaction began.

Commit and rollback provide the means to ensure that halfway-done operations don't make their way into your database and leave it in a partially updated (inconsistent) state. The canonical example involves a financial transfer where money from one account is placed into another account. Suppose that Bill writes a check to Bob for $100.00 and Bob cashes the check. Bill's account should be decremented by $100.00 and Bob's account incremented by the same amount:

```
UPDATE account SET balance = balance - 100 WHERE name = 'Bill';
UPDATE account SET balance = balance + 100 WHERE name = 'Bob';
```

If a crash occurs between the two statements, the operation is incomplete. Depending on which statement executes first, Bill is $100 short without Bob having been credited, or Bob is given $100 without Bill having been debited. Neither outcome is correct. If transactional capabilities are not available, you must figure out the state of ongoing operations at crash time by examining your logs manually to determine how to undo them or complete them. The rollback capabilities of transaction support enable you to handle this situation properly by undoing the effect of the statements that executed before the error occurred. (You may still have to determine which transactions weren't entered and re-issue them, but at least you don't have to worry about half-transactions making your database inconsistent.)

Another use for transactions is to make sure that the rows involved in an operation are not modified by other clients while you're working with them. MySQL automatically performs locking for single SQL statements to keep clients from interfering with each other, but this is not always sufficient to guarantee that a database operation achieves its intended result, because some operations are performed over the course of several statements. In this case, different clients might interfere with each other. A transaction groups statements into a single execution unit to prevent concurrency problems that could otherwise occur in a multiple-client environment.

Transactional systems typically are characterized as providing ACID properties. ACID is an acronym for Atomic, Consistent, Isolated, and Durable, referring to four properties transactions should have:

- **Atomicity:** The statements comprising a transaction form a logical unit. You can't have just some of them execute.

- **Consistency:** The database is consistent before and after the transaction executes. For example, if rows in one table cannot have an ID that is not listed in another table, a transaction that attempts to insert a row with an invalid ID will fail and roll back.

- **Isolation:** One transaction has no effect on another, so that transactions executed concurrently have the same effect as if done one after the other.

- **Durability:** When a transaction executes successfully to completion, its effects are recorded permanently in the database.

Transactional processing provides stronger guarantees about the outcome of database operations, but also requires more overhead in CPU cycles, memory, and disk space. MySQL offers storage engines that are transaction-safe (such as InnoDB), and that are not transaction-safe (such as MyISAM and MEMORY). Transactional properties are essential for some applications and not for others, and you can choose which ones make the most sense for your applications. Financial operations typically need transactions, and the guarantees of data integrity outweigh the cost of additional overhead. On the other hand, for an application that logs web page accesses to a database table, a loss of a few rows if the server host crashes might be tolerable. In this case, using a nontransactional storage engine avoids the overhead required for transactional processing.

2.12.1   Using Transactions to Ensure Safe Statement Execution

Use of transactions requires a transactional storage engine such as InnoDB. Engines such as MyISAM and MEMORY will not work. If you're not sure whether your MySQL server supports transactional storage engines, see Section 2.6.1.1, "Checking Which Storage Engines Are Available."

By default, MySQL runs in autocommit mode, which means that changes made by individual statements are committed to the database immediately to make them permanent. In effect, each statement is its own transaction implicitly. To perform transactions explicitly, disable autocommit mode and then tell MySQL when to commit or roll back changes.

One way to perform a transaction is to issue a `START TRANSACTION` (or `BEGIN`) statement to suspend autocommit mode, execute the statements that make up the transaction, and end the transaction with a `COMMIT` statement to make the changes permanent. If an error occurs during the transaction, cancel it by issuing a `ROLLBACK` statement instead to undo the changes.

START TRANSACTION suspends the current autocommit mode, so after the transaction has been committed or rolled back, the mode reverts to its state prior to the START TRANSACTION. If autocommit was enabled beforehand, ending the transaction puts you back in autocommit mode. If it was disabled, ending the current transaction causes you to begin the next one.

The following example illustrates this approach. First, create a table to use:

```
mysql> CREATE TABLE t (name CHAR(20), UNIQUE (name)) ENGINE=InnoDB;
```

Next, initiate a transaction with START TRANSACTION, add a couple of rows to the table, commit the transaction, and then see what the table looks like:

```
mysql> START TRANSACTION;
mysql> INSERT INTO t SET name = 'William';
mysql> INSERT INTO t SET name = 'Wallace';
mysql> COMMIT;
mysql> SELECT * FROM t;
+---------+
| name    |
+---------+
| Wallace |
| William |
+---------+
```

You can see that the rows have been recorded in the table. If you had started up a second instance of mysql and selected the contents of t after the inserts but before the commit, the rows would not show up. They would not become visible to the second mysql process until the COMMIT statement had been issued by the first one.

If an error occurs during a transaction, you can cancel it with ROLLBACK. Using the t table again, you can see this by issuing the following statements:

```
mysql> START TRANSACTION;
mysql> INSERT INTO t SET name = 'Gromit';
mysql> INSERT INTO t SET name = 'Wallace';
ERROR 1062 (23000): Duplicate entry 'Wallace' for key 'name'
mysql> ROLLBACK;
mysql> SELECT * FROM t;
+---------+
| name    |
+---------+
| Wallace |
| William |
+---------+
```

The second INSERT attempts to place a row into the table that duplicates an existing name value, but fails because name has a UNIQUE index. After issuing the ROLLBACK, the table has only the two rows that it contained prior to the failed transaction. In particular, the successful INSERT that was performed before the failed one has been undone and its effect is not recorded in the table.

Issuing a START TRANSACTION statement while a transaction is in process commits the current transaction implicitly before beginning a new one.

Another way to perform transactions is to manipulate the autocommit mode directly using SET statements:

```
SET autocommit = 0;
SET autocommit = 1;
```

Setting the autocommit variable to zero disables autocommit, The effects of any statements that follow become part of the current transaction, which you end by issuing a COMMIT or ROLLBACK statement to commit or cancel it. With this method, autocommit remains off until you turn it back on, so ending one transaction also begins the next one. You can also commit a transaction by re-enabling autocommit.

To see how this approach works, begin with the same table as for the previous examples:

```
mysql> DROP TABLE t;
mysql> CREATE TABLE t (name CHAR(20), UNIQUE (name)) ENGINE=InnoDB;
```

Then disable autocommit mode, insert some rows, and commit the transaction:

```
mysql> SET autocommit = 0;
mysql> INSERT INTO t SET name = 'William';
mysql> INSERT INTO t SET name = 'Wallace';
mysql> COMMIT;
mysql> SELECT * FROM t;
+---------+
| name    |
+---------+
| Wallace |
| William |
+---------+
```

At this point, the two rows have been committed to the table, but autocommit mode remains disabled. If you issue further statements, they become part of a new transaction, which may be committed or rolled back independently of the first transaction. To verify that autocommit is still off and that ROLLBACK will cancel uncommitted statements, issue the following statements:

```
mysql> INSERT INTO t SET name = 'Gromit';
mysql> INSERT INTO t SET name = 'Wallace';
ERROR 1062 (23000): Duplicate entry 'Wallace' for key 'name'
mysql> ROLLBACK;
mysql> SELECT * FROM t;
+---------+
| name    |
+---------+
| Wallace |
| William |
+---------+
```

To re-enable autocommit mode, use this statement:

```
mysql> SET autocommit = 1;
```

As just described, a transaction ends when you issue a COMMIT or ROLLBACK statement, or when you re-enable autocommit while it is disabled. Transactions also end under other circumstances. In addition to the SET autocommit, START TRANSACTION, BEGIN, COMMIT, and ROLLBACK statements that affect transactions explicitly, certain other statements do so implicitly because they cannot be part of a transaction. In general, these tend to be DDL (data definition language) statements that create, alter, or drop databases or objects in them, or statements that are lock-related. For example, if you issue any of the following statements while a transaction is in progress, the server commits the transaction first before executing the statement:

```
ALTER TABLE
CREATE INDEX
DROP DATABASE
DROP INDEX
DROP TABLE
LOCK TABLES
RENAME TABLE
SET autocommit = 1 (if not already set to 1)
TRUNCATE TABLE
UNLOCK TABLES (if tables currently are locked)
```

For a complete list of statements that cause implicit commits in your version of MySQL, see the MySQL Reference Manual.

A transaction also ends if a client's session ends or is broken before a commit occurs. In this case, the server automatically rolls back any transaction the client had in progress.

If a client program automatically reconnects after its session with the server is lost, the connection is reset to its default state of having autocommit enabled.

Transactions are useful in all kinds of situations. Suppose that you're working with the score table that is part of the grade-keeping project and you discover that the grades for two students have gotten mixed up and need to be switched. The incorrectly entered grades are as follows:

```
mysql> SELECT * FROM score WHERE event_id = 5 AND student_id IN (8,9);
+------------+----------+-------+
| student_id | event_id | score |
+------------+----------+-------+
|          8 |        5 |    18 |
|          9 |        5 |    13 |
+------------+----------+-------+
```

To fix this, student 8 should be given a score of 13 and student 9 a score of 18. That can be done easily with two statements:

```
UPDATE score SET score = 13 WHERE event_id = 5 AND student_id = 8;
UPDATE score SET score = 18 WHERE event_id = 5 AND student_id = 9;
```

However, it's necessary to ensure that both statements succeed as a unit. This is a problem to which transactional methods may be applied. To use START TRANSACTION, do this:

```
mysql> START TRANSACTION;
mysql> UPDATE score SET score = 13 WHERE event_id = 5 AND student_id = 8;
mysql> UPDATE score SET score = 18 WHERE event_id = 5 AND student_id = 9;
mysql> COMMIT;
```

To accomplish the same thing by manipulating the autocommit mode explicitly instead, do this:

```
mysql> SET autocommit = 0;
mysql> UPDATE score SET score = 13 WHERE event_id = 5 AND student_id = 8;
mysql> UPDATE score SET score = 18 WHERE event_id = 5 AND student_id = 9;
mysql> COMMIT;
mysql> SET autocommit = 1;
```

Either way, the result is that the scores are swapped properly:

```
mysql> SELECT * FROM score WHERE event_id = 5 AND student_id IN (8,9);
+------------+----------+-------+
| student_id | event_id | score |
+------------+----------+-------+
|          8 |        5 |    13 |
|          9 |        5 |    18 |
+------------+----------+-------+
```

2.12.2   Using Transaction Savepoints

MySQL enables you to perform a partial rollback of a transaction. To do this, issue a SAVEPOINT statement within the transaction to set a named marker. To roll back to just that point in the transaction later, use a ROLLBACK statement that names the savepoint. The following statements illustrate how this works:

```
mysql> CREATE TABLE t (i INT) ENGINE=InnoDB;
mysql> START TRANSACTION;
mysql> INSERT INTO t VALUES(1);
mysql> SAVEPOINT my_savepoint;
mysql> INSERT INTO t VALUES(2);
mysql> ROLLBACK TO SAVEPOINT my_savepoint;
mysql> INSERT INTO t VALUES(3);
mysql> COMMIT;
mysql> SELECT * FROM t;
+------+
| i    |
+------+
|    1 |
|    3 |
+------+
```

After executing these statements, the first and third rows have been inserted, but the second one has been canceled by the partial rollback to the `my_savepoint` savepoint.

2.12.3   Transaction Isolation

Because MySQL is a multiple-user database system, different clients can attempt to use any given table at the same time. Storage engines such as MyISAM use table locking to keep clients from modifying a table at the same time, but this does not provide good concurrency performance when there are many updates. The InnoDB storage engine takes a different approach. It uses row-level locking for finer-grained control over table access by clients. One client can modify a row at the same time that another client reads or modifies a different row in the same table. If both clients want to modify a row at the same time, whichever of them acquires a lock on the row gets to modify it first. This provides better concurrency than table locking. However, there is the question of whether one client's transaction should be able to see the changes made by another client's transaction.

InnoDB implements transaction isolation levels to give clients control over what kind of changes made by other transactions they want to see. Different isolation levels permit or prevent problems that can occur when different transactions run simultaneously:

- Dirty reads. A dirty read occurs when a change made by one transaction can be seen by other transactions before the transaction has been committed. Another transaction thus might think the row has been changed, even though that will not really be true if the transaction that changed the row later is rolled back.

- Nonrepeatable reads. A nonrepeatable read refers to failure by a transaction to get the same result for a given SELECT statement each time it executes it. This might happen if one transaction performs a SELECT twice but another transaction changes some of the rows in between the two executions.

- Phantom rows. A phantom is a row that becomes visible to a transaction when it was not previously. Suppose that a transaction performs a SELECT and then another transaction inserts a row. If the first transaction runs the same SELECT again and sees the new row, that is a phantom.

To deal with these problems, InnoDB supports four transaction isolation levels. These levels determine which modifications made by one transaction can be seen by other transactions that execute at the same time:

- READ UNCOMMITTED: A transaction can see row modifications made by other transactions even before they have been committed.

- READ COMMITTED: A transaction can see row modifications made by other transactions only if they have been committed.

- REPEATABLE READ: If a transaction performs a given SELECT twice, the result is repeatable. That is, it gets the same result each time, even if other transactions have changed or inserted rows in the meantime.

- SERIALIZABLE: This isolation level is similar to REPEATABLE READ but isolates transactions more completely: Rows examined by one transaction cannot be modified by other transactions until the first transaction completes. This enables one transaction to read rows and at the same time prevent them from being modified by other transactions until it is done with them.

Table 2.4 shows for each isolation level whether it permits dirty reads, nonrepeatable reads, or phantom rows. The table is InnoDB-specific in that REPEATABLE READ does not permit phantom rows to occur. Some database systems do permit phantoms at the REPEATABLE READ isolation level.

Table 2.4   **Problems Permitted by Isolation Levels**

Isolation Level	Dirty Reads	Nonrepeatable Reads	Phantom Rows
READ UNCOMMITTED	Yes	Yes	Yes
READ COMMITTED	No	Yes	Yes
REPEATABLE READ	No	No	No
SERIALIZABLE	No	No	No

The default InnoDB isolation level is REPEATABLE READ. This can be changed at server startup with the --transaction-isolation option, or at runtime with the SET TRANSACTION statement. The statement has three forms:

```
SET GLOBAL TRANSACTION ISOLATION LEVEL level;
SET SESSION TRANSACTION ISOLATION LEVEL level;
SET TRANSACTION ISOLATION LEVEL level;
```

A client that has the SUPER privilege can use SET TRANSACTION to change the global isolation level, which then applies to any clients that connect thereafter. In addition, any client can change its own transaction isolation level, either for all subsequent transactions within its session with the server (if SESSION is specified) or for its next transaction only (if SESSION is omitted). No special privileges are required for the client-specific levels.

Can You Mix Transactional and Nontransactional Tables?

It is possible to use both transactional and nontransactional tables during the course of a transaction, but the result might not be what you expect. Statements for nontransactional tables always take effect immediately, even when autocommit is disabled. In effect, nontransactional tables are always in autocommit mode and each statement commits immediately. As a result, if you change a nontransactional table within a transaction and then attempt a rollback, the nontransactional table changes cannot be undone.

2.13   Foreign Keys and Referential Integrity

A foreign key relationship enables you to declare that an index in one table is related to an index in another. It also enables you to place constraints on what may be done to the tables in the relationship. The database enforces the rules of this relationship to maintain referential integrity. For example, the score table in the sampdb sample database contains a student_id column, which we use to relate score rows to students in the student table. When we created these tables in Chapter 1, "Getting Started with MySQL," we set up some explicit relationships between them. For example, we declared score.student_id to be a foreign key for the student.student_id column. That prevents a row from being entered into the score table unless its student_id value exists in the student table. In other words, the foreign key prevents entry of scores for nonexistent students.

Foreign keys are not useful just for row entry, but for deletes and updates as well. For example, we could set up a constraint such that if a student is deleted from the student table, all corresponding rows for the student in the score table are deleted automatically as well. This is called "cascaded delete" because the effect of the delete cascades from one table to another. Cascaded update is possible as well. For example, with cascaded update, changing a student's student_id value in the student table also changes the value in the student's corresponding score table rows.

Foreign keys maintain the consistency of your data, and they provide a certain measure of convenience. Without foreign keys, you are responsible for keeping track of inter-table dependencies and maintaining their consistency from within your applications. In some cases, doing this might not be much more work than issuing a few extra DELETE statements to make sure that when you delete a row from one table, you also delete the corresponding rows in any related tables. But it *is* extra work, and if the database engine will perform consistency checks for you, why not let it? Automatic checking capability is especially useful if your tables have particularly complex relationships. You likely will not want to be responsible for implementing these dependencies in your applications.

In MySQL, the InnoDB storage engine provides foreign key support. This section describes how to set up InnoDB tables to define foreign keys, and how foreign keys affect the way you use tables. First, it's necessary to define some terms:

- The parent is the table that contains the original key values.
- The child is the related table that refers to key values in the parent.

Parent table key values are used to associate the two tables. Specifically, an index in the child table refers to an index in the parent. The child index values must match those in the parent or else be set to NULL to indicate that there is no associated parent table row. The index in the child table is known as the "foreign key"—that is, the key that is foreign (external) to the parent table but contains values that point to the parent. A foreign key relationship can be set up to reject NULL values, in which case all foreign key values must match a value in the parent table.

InnoDB enforces these rules to guarantee that the foreign key relationship stays intact with no mismatches. This is called "referential integrity."

The following syntax shows how to define a foreign key in a child table:

```
[CONSTRAINT constraint_name]
FOREIGN KEY [fk_name] (index_columns)
  REFERENCES tbl_name (index_columns)
  [ON DELETE action]
  [ON UPDATE action]
  [MATCH FULL | MATCH PARTIAL | MATCH SIMPLE]
```

Although all parts of this syntax are parsed, InnoDB does not implement the semantics for all the clauses: The MATCH clause is not supported and is ignored if you specify it. Also, some *action* values are recognized but have no effect. (For storage engines other than InnoDB, the entire FOREIGN KEY definition is parsed but ignored.)

InnoDB pays attention to the following parts of the definition:

- The CONSTRAINT clause, if given, supplies a name for the foreign key constraint. If you omit it, InnoDB creates a name.

- FOREIGN KEY indicates the indexed columns in the child table that must match index values in the parent table. *fk_name* is the foreign key ID. If given, it is ignored unless InnoDB automatically creates an index for the foreign key; in that case, *fk_name* becomes the index name.

- REFERENCES names the parent table and the index columns in that table to which the foreign key in the child table refers. The *index_columns* part of the REFERENCES clause must have the same number of columns as the *index_columns* that follows the FOREIGN KEY keywords.

- ON DELETE enables you to specify what happens to the child table when parent table rows are deleted. The default if no ON DELETE clause is present is to reject any attempt to delete rows in the parent table that have child rows pointing to them. To specify an *action* value explicitly, use one of the following clauses:

    - ON DELETE NO ACTION and ON DELETE RESTRICT are the same as omitting the ON DELETE clause. Some database systems have deferred checks, and NO ACTION is a deferred check. For InnoDB, foreign key constraints are checked immediately, so NO ACTION and RESTRICT are the same.

    - ON DELETE CASCADE causes matching child rows to be deleted when the corresponding parent row is deleted. In essence, the effect of the delete is cascaded from the parent to the child. This enables you to perform multiple-table deletes by deleting rows only from the parent table and letting InnoDB delete the corresponding rows from the child table.

    - ON DELETE SET NULL causes index columns in matching child rows to be set to NULL when the parent row is deleted. If you use this option, all the indexed child table columns named in the foreign key definition must be defined to permit NULL values. (One implication of using this action is that you cannot define the foreign key to be a PRIMARY KEY; primary keys do not permit NULL values.)

    - ON DELETE SET DEFAULT is recognized but unimplemented and InnoDB issues an error.

- ON UPDATE enables you to specify what happens to the child table when parent table rows are updated. The default if no ON UPDATE clause is present is to reject any inserts or updates in the child table that result in foreign key values that don't have any match in the parent table index, and to prevent updates to parent table index values to which child rows point. The possible *action* values are the same as for ON DELETE and have similar effects.

To set up a foreign key relationship, follow these guidelines:

- The child table must have an index where the foreign key columns are listed as its first columns. The parent table must also have an index in which the columns in the REFERENCES clause are listed as its first columns. (In other words, the key columns must be indexed in the tables on both ends of the foreign key relationship.) You must create the parent table index explicitly before defining the foreign key relationship. InnoDB automatically creates an index on foreign key columns (the referencing columns) in the child table if the CREATE TABLE statement does not include such an index. This makes it easier to write the CREATE TABLE statement in some cases. However, an automatically created index will be a nonunique index and will include only the foreign key columns. You should define the index in the child table explicitly if you want it to be a PRIMARY KEY or UNIQUE index, or if it should include other columns in addition to those in the foreign key.

- Corresponding columns in the parent and child indexes must have compatible types. For example, you cannot match an INT column with a CHAR column. Corresponding character columns must be the same length. Corresponding integer columns must have the same size and must both be signed or both be UNSIGNED.

- You cannot index prefixes of string columns in foreign key relationships. (That is, for string columns, you must index the entire column, not just a leading prefix of it.)

In Chapter 1, "Getting Started with MySQL," we created tables for the grade-keeping project that have simple foreign key relationships. Now let's work through an example that is more complex. Begin by creating tables named parent and child, such that the child table contains a foreign key that references the par_id column in the parent table:

```
CREATE TABLE parent
(
  par_id    INT NOT NULL,
  PRIMARY KEY (par_id)
) ENGINE = INNODB;

CREATE TABLE child
(
  par_id    INT NOT NULL,
  child_id  INT NOT NULL,
  PRIMARY KEY (par_id, child_id),
  FOREIGN KEY (par_id) REFERENCES parent (par_id)
```

```
    ON DELETE CASCADE
    ON UPDATE CASCADE
) ENGINE = INNODB;
```

The foreign key in this case uses ON DELETE CASCADE to specify that when a row is deleted from the parent table, MySQL also should remove child rows with a matching par_id value automatically. ON UPDATE CASCADE indicates that if a parent row par_id value is changed, MySQL also should change any matching par_id values in the child table to the new value.

Now insert a few rows into the parent table, and then add some rows to the child table that have related key values:

```
mysql> INSERT INTO parent (par_id) VALUES(1),(2),(3);
mysql> INSERT INTO child (par_id,child_id) VALUES(1,1),(1,2);
mysql> INSERT INTO child (par_id,child_id) VALUES(2,1),(2,2),(2,3);
mysql> INSERT INTO child (par_id,child_id) VALUES(3,1);
```

These statements result in the following table contents, where each par_id value in the child table matches a par_id value in the parent table:

```
mysql> SELECT * FROM parent;
+--------+
| par_id |
+--------+
|      1 |
|      2 |
|      3 |
+--------+
mysql> SELECT * FROM child;
+--------+----------+
| par_id | child_id |
+--------+----------+
|      1 |        1 |
|      1 |        2 |
|      2 |        1 |
|      2 |        2 |
|      2 |        3 |
|      3 |        1 |
+--------+----------+
```

To verify that InnoDB enforces the key relationship for insertion, try adding a row to the child table that has a par_id value not found in the parent table:

```
mysql> INSERT INTO child (par_id,child_id) VALUES(4,1);
ERROR 1452 (23000): Cannot add or update a child row: a foreign key
constraint fails (`sampdb`.`child`, CONSTRAINT `child_ibfk_1` FOREIGN
KEY (`par_id`) REFERENCES `parent` (`par_id`) ON DELETE CASCADE
ON UPDATE CASCADE)
```

To test cascaded delete, see what happens when you delete a parent row:

```
mysql> DELETE FROM parent WHERE par_id = 1;
```

MySQL deletes the row from the parent table:

```
mysql> SELECT * FROM parent;
+--------+
| par_id |
+--------+
|      2 |
|      3 |
+--------+
```

In addition, it cascades the effect of the DELETE statement to the child table:

```
mysql> SELECT * FROM child;
+--------+----------+
| par_id | child_id |
+--------+----------+
|      2 |        1 |
|      2 |        2 |
|      2 |        3 |
|      3 |        1 |
+--------+----------+
```

To test cascaded update, see what happens when you update a parent row:

```
mysql> UPDATE parent SET par_id = 100 WHERE par_id =2;
mysql> SELECT * FROM parent;
+--------+
| par_id |
+--------+
|      3 |
|    100 |
+--------+
mysql> SELECT * FROM child;
+--------+----------+
| par_id | child_id |
+--------+----------+
|      3 |        1 |
|    100 |        1 |
|    100 |        2 |
|    100 |        3 |
+--------+----------+
```

The preceding example shows how to arrange for deletes or updates of a parent row to cause cascaded deletes or updates of any corresponding child rows. The ON DELETE and ON UPDATE clauses permit other actions. For example, one possibility is to let the child rows remain in the table but have their foreign key columns set to NULL. To do this, it's necessary to make several changes to the definition of the child table:

- Use ON DELETE SET NULL rather than ON DELETE CASCADE. This tells InnoDB to set the foreign key column (par_id) to NULL instead of deleting the rows.

- Use ON UPDATE SET NULL rather than ON UPDATE CASCADE. This tells InnoDB to set the foreign key column (par_id) to NULL when matching parent rows are updated.

- The original definition of child defines par_id as NOT NULL. That won't work with ON DELETE SET NULL or ON UPDATE SET NULL, so the column definition must be changed to permit NULL.

- The original definition of child also defines par_id to be part of a PRIMARY KEY. However, a PRIMARY KEY cannot contain NULL values. Changing par_id to permit NULL therefore also requires that the PRIMARY KEY be changed to a UNIQUE index. UNIQUE indexes enforce uniqueness except for NULL values, which can occur multiple times in the index.

To see the effect of these changes, re-create the parent table using the original definition and load the same initial rows into it. Then create the child table using the new definition shown here:

```
CREATE TABLE child
(
  par_id    INT NULL,
  child_id  INT NOT NULL,
  UNIQUE (par_id, child_id),
  FOREIGN KEY (par_id) REFERENCES parent (par_id)
    ON DELETE SET NULL
    ON UPDATE SET NULL
) ENGINE = INNODB;
```

With respect to inserting new rows, the child table behaves similarly to the original definition. That is, it permits insertion of rows with par_id values found in the parent table, but prohibits entry of values that aren't listed there:

```
mysql> INSERT INTO child (par_id,child_id) VALUES(1,1),(1,2);
mysql> INSERT INTO child (par_id,child_id) VALUES(2,1),(2,2),(2,3);
mysql> INSERT INTO child (par_id,child_id) VALUES(3,1);
mysql> INSERT INTO child (par_id,child_id) VALUES(4,1);
ERROR 1452 (23000): Cannot add or update a child row: a foreign key
constraint fails (`sampdb`.`child`, CONSTRAINT `child_ibfk_1` FOREIGN
KEY (`par_id`) REFERENCES `parent` (`par_id`) ON DELETE SET NULL
ON UPDATE SET NULL)
```

There is one difference with respect to inserting rows. Because the par_id column now is defined as NULL, you can explicitly insert rows into the child table that contain NULL and no error occurs. A difference in behavior also occurs when you delete a parent row. Try removing a parent row and then check the contents of the child table to see what happens:

```
mysql> DELETE FROM parent WHERE par_id = 1;
mysql> SELECT * FROM child;
+--------+----------+
| par_id | child_id |
+--------+----------+
|   NULL |        1 |
|   NULL |        2 |
|      2 |        1 |
|      2 |        2 |
|      2 |        3 |
|      3 |        1 |
+--------+----------+
```

In this case, the child rows that had 1 in the par_id column are not deleted. Instead, the par_id column is set to NULL, as specified by the ON DELETE SET NULL constraint.

Updating a parent row has a similar effect:

```
mysql> UPDATE parent SET par_id = 100 WHERE par_id = 2;
mysql> SELECT * FROM child;
+--------+----------+
| par_id | child_id |
+--------+----------+
|   NULL |        1 |
|   NULL |        1 |
|   NULL |        2 |
|   NULL |        2 |
|   NULL |        3 |
|      3 |        1 |
+--------+----------+
```

To see what foreign key relationships an InnoDB table has, use the SHOW CREATE TABLE statement.

If an error occurs when you attempt to create a table that has a foreign key, use the SHOW ENGINE INNODB STATUS statement to get the full error message.

2.14 Using FULLTEXT Searches

MySQL is capable of performing full-text searches, which enables you to look for words or phrases without using pattern-matching operations. There are three kinds of full-text search:

- Natural language searching (the default). MySQL parses the search string into words and searches for rows containing these words.

- Boolean mode searching. Words in the search string can include modifier characters that indicate specific requirements, such as that a given word should be present or absent in matching rows, or that rows must contain an exact phrase.

- Query expansion searching. This kind of search occurs in two phases. The first phase is a natural language search. Then a second search is done using the original search string concatenated with the most highly relevant matching rows from the first search. This expands the search on the basis of the assumption that words related to the original search string will match relevant rows that the original string did not.

Full-text search capability is enabled for a given table by creating a special kind of index and has the following characteristics:

- Full-text searches are based on FULLTEXT indexes. In MySQL 5.5, these can be created only for MyISAM tables. MySQL 5.6 introduces full-text support for InnoDB, but we'll stick with MyISAM here because you might not have 5.6. Only CHAR, VARCHAR, and TEXT columns can be included in a FULLTEXT index.

- Common words are ignored for FULLTEXT searches, where "common" means "present in at least half the rows." It's especially important to remember this when you're setting up a test table to experiment with the FULLTEXT capability. Be sure to insert at least three rows into your test table. If the table has just one or two rows, every word in it will occur at least 50% of the time and you'll never get any results!

- There is a built-in list of common words such as "the," "after," and "other" that are called "stopwords" and that are always ignored.

- Words that are too short are ignored. By default, "too short" is defined as fewer than four characters, but you can reconfigure the server to set the minimum length to a different value. (See Section 2.14.4, "Configuring the FULLTEXT Search Engine".)

- Words are defined as sequences of characters that include letters, digits, apostrophes, and underscores. This means that a string like "full-blooded" is considered to contain two words, "full" and "blooded." Normally, a full-text search matches whole words, not partial words, and the FULLTEXT engine considers a row to match a search string if it includes any of the words in the search string. If you use a boolean full-text search, you can impose the additional constraint that all the words must be present (either in any order, or, to perform a phrase search, in exactly the order listed in the search string). With a boolean search, it's also possible to match rows that do *not* include certain words, or to add a wildcard modifier to match all words that begin with a given prefix.

- A FULLTEXT index can be created for a single column or multiple columns. If it spans multiple columns, searches based on the index look through all the columns simultaneously. The flip side of this is that when you perform a search, you must specify a column list that corresponds exactly to the set of columns that matches some FULLTEXT index. For example, if you want to search col1 sometimes, col2 sometimes, and both col1 and col2 sometimes, you must create three indexes: one for each of the columns separately, and one that includes both columns.

The following examples show how to use full-text searching by creating FULLTEXT indexes and then performing queries on them using the MATCH operator. A script to create the table and some sample data to load into it are available in the full-text directory of the sampdb distribution.

Create a FULLTEXT index much the same way as other indexes: Define it with CREATE TABLE when creating the table initially, or add it afterward with ALTER TABLE or CREATE INDEX. Because FULLTEXT indexes require you to use MyISAM tables, you can take advantage of one of the properties of the MyISAM storage engine if you're creating a new table to use for FULLTEXT searches: Table loading proceeds more quickly if you populate the table first and then add the indexes afterward, rather than loading data into an already indexed table. Suppose that you have a data file named apothegm.txt containing famous sayings and the people to whom they're attributed:

```
Aeschylus               Time as he grows old teaches many lessons
Alexander Graham Bell   Mr. Watson, come here. I want you!
Benjamin Franklin       It is hard for an empty bag to stand upright
Benjamin Franklin       Little strokes fell great oaks
Benjamin Franklin       Remember that time is money
Miguel de Cervantes     Bell, book, and candle
Proverbs 15:1           A soft answer turneth away wrath
Theodore Roosevelt      Speak softly and carry a big stick
William Shakespeare     But, soft! what light through yonder window breaks?
Robert Burton           I light my candle from their torches.
```

If you want to search by phrase and attribution separately or together, you need to index each column separately, and also create an index that includes both columns. You can create, populate, and index a table named apothegm as follows:

```
CREATE TABLE apothegm (attribution VARCHAR(40), phrase TEXT) ENGINE=MyISAM;
LOAD DATA LOCAL INFILE 'apothegm.txt' INTO TABLE apothegm;
ALTER TABLE apothegm
  ADD FULLTEXT (phrase),
  ADD FULLTEXT (attribution),
  ADD FULLTEXT (phrase, attribution);
```

2.14.1   Natural Language FULLTEXT Searches

After setting up the table, perform natural language full-text searches on it using MATCH to name the column or columns to search and AGAINST() to specify the search string. For example:

```
mysql> SELECT * FROM apothegm WHERE MATCH(attribution) AGAINST('roosevelt');
+--------------------+------------------------------------+
| attribution        | phrase                             |
+--------------------+------------------------------------+
| Theodore Roosevelt | Speak softly and carry a big stick |
+--------------------+------------------------------------+
mysql> SELECT * FROM apothegm WHERE MATCH(phrase) AGAINST('time');
+--------------------+-------------------------------------------+
| attribution        | phrase                                    |
+--------------------+-------------------------------------------+
```

```
| Benjamin Franklin | Remember that time is money               |
| Aeschylus         | Time as he grows old teaches many lessons |
+-------------------+-------------------------------------------+
mysql> SELECT * FROM apothegm WHERE MATCH(attribution, phrase)
    -> AGAINST('bell');
+-----------------------+-------------------------------------+
| attribution           | phrase                              |
+-----------------------+-------------------------------------+
| Alexander Graham Bell | Mr. Watson, come here. I want you!  |
| Miguel de Cervantes   | Bell, book, and candle              |
+-----------------------+-------------------------------------+
```

In the last example, note how the query finds rows that contain the search word in different
columns, which demonstrates the FULLTEXT capability of searching multiple columns at once.
Also note that the order of the columns as named in the query is attribution, phrase. That
differs from the order in which they were named when the index was created (phrase, attribution), which illustrates that order does not matter. What matters is that there must be some
FULLTEXT index that consists of exactly the columns named.

To see only how many rows a search matches, use COUNT(*):

```
mysql> SELECT COUNT(*) FROM apothegm WHERE MATCH(phrase) AGAINST('time');
+----------+
| COUNT(*) |
+----------+
|        2 |
+----------+
```

Output rows for natural language FULLTEXT searches are ordered by decreasing relevance when
you use a MATCH expression in the WHERE clause. Relevance values are nonnegative floating
point values, with zero indicating "no relevance." To see these values, use a MATCH expression
in the output column list:

```
mysql> SELECT phrase, MATCH(phrase) AGAINST('time') AS relevance
    -> FROM apothegm;
+-----------------------------------------------+--------------------+
| phrase                                        | relevance          |
+-----------------------------------------------+--------------------+
| Time as he grows old teaches many lessons     | 1.3253291845321655 |
| Mr. Watson, come here. I want you!            |                  0 |
| It is hard for an empty bag to stand upright  |                  0 |
| Little strokes fell great oaks                |                  0 |
| Remember that time is money                   |  1.340062141418457 |
| Bell, book, and candle                        |                  0 |
| A soft answer turneth away wrath              |                  0 |
| Speak softly and carry a big stick            |                  0 |
| But, soft! what light through yonder window breaks? |            0 |
| I light my candle from their torches.         |                  0 |
+-----------------------------------------------+--------------------+
```

A natural language search finds rows that contain any of the search words, so a query such as the following returns rows that contain either "hard" or "soft":

```
mysql> SELECT * FROM apothegm WHERE MATCH(phrase)
    -> AGAINST('hard soft');
+---------------------+------------------------------------------------------+
| attribution         | phrase                                               |
+---------------------+------------------------------------------------------+
| Benjamin Franklin   | It is hard for an empty bag to stand upright         |
| Proverbs 15:1       | A soft answer turneth away wrath                     |
| William Shakespeare | But, soft! what light through yonder window breaks?  |
+---------------------+------------------------------------------------------+
```

Natural language mode is the default full-text search mode. To specify this mode explicitly, add IN NATURAL LANGUAGE MODE after the search string. The following statement performs the same search as the preceding example:

```
SELECT * FROM apothegm WHERE MATCH(phrase)
AGAINST('hard soft' IN NATURAL LANGUAGE MODE);
```

2.14.2   Boolean Mode FULLTEXT Searches

Greater control over multiple-word matching can be obtained by using boolean mode FULLTEXT searches. This type of search is performed by adding IN BOOLEAN MODE after the search string in the AGAINST() function. Boolean searches have the following characteristics:

- The 50% rule is ignored. Searches find words even if they occur in more than half of the rows.

- No sorting by relevance occurs.

- A search can require all words in a phrase to be present in a particular order. To match a phrase, specify it within double quotes. Matches occur for rows that contain the same words together in the same order as listed in the phrase:

```
mysql> SELECT * FROM apothegm
    -> WHERE MATCH(attribution, phrase)
    -> AGAINST('"bell book and candle"' IN BOOLEAN MODE);
+---------------------+------------------------+
| attribution         | phrase                 |
+---------------------+------------------------+
| Miguel de Cervantes | Bell, book, and candle |
+---------------------+------------------------+
```

- It's possible to perform a boolean mode full-text search on columns that are not part of a FULLTEXT index, although this is much slower than using indexed columns.

For boolean searches, modifiers may be applied to words in the search string. A leading plus or minus sign requires a word to be present or not present in matching rows. For example, a search string of 'bell' matches rows that contain "bell," but a search string of '+bell

-candle' in boolean mode matches only rows that contain "bell" and do not contain "candle."

```
mysql> SELECT * FROM apothegm
    -> WHERE MATCH(attribution, phrase)
    -> AGAINST('bell');
+----------------------+-----------------------------------+
| attribution          | phrase                            |
+----------------------+-----------------------------------+
| Alexander Graham Bell | Mr. Watson, come here. I want you! |
| Miguel de Cervantes  | Bell, book, and candle            |
+----------------------+-----------------------------------+
mysql> SELECT * FROM apothegm
    -> WHERE MATCH(attribution, phrase)
    -> AGAINST('+bell -candle' IN BOOLEAN MODE);
+----------------------+-----------------------------------+
| attribution          | phrase                            |
+----------------------+-----------------------------------+
| Alexander Graham Bell | Mr. Watson, come here. I want you! |
+----------------------+-----------------------------------+
```

A trailing asterisk acts as a wildcard so that any row containing words beginning with the search word match. For example 'soft*' matches "soft," "softly," "softness," and so forth:

```
mysql> SELECT * FROM apothegm WHERE MATCH(phrase)
    -> AGAINST('soft*' IN BOOLEAN MODE);
+----------------------+----------------------------------------------------+
| attribution          | phrase                                             |
+----------------------+----------------------------------------------------+
| Proverbs 15:1        | A soft answer turneth away wrath                   |
| William Shakespeare  | But, soft! what light through yonder window breaks?|
| Theodore Roosevelt   | Speak softly and carry a big stick                 |
+----------------------+----------------------------------------------------+
```

However, the wildcard feature cannot be used to match words shorter than the minimum index word length.

The entry for MATCH in Appendix C, "Operator and Function Reference," lists the full set of boolean mode modifiers.

Stopwords are ignored just as for natural language searches, even if marked as required. A search for '+Alexander +the +great' finds rows containing "Alexander" and "great," but ignores "the" as a stopword.

2.14.3   Query Expansion FULLTEXT Searches

A full-text search with query expansion performs a two-phase search. The initial search is like a regular natural language search. Then the most highly relevant rows from this search are used for the second phase. The words in these rows are used along with the original search terms to perform a second search. Because the set of search terms is larger, the result generally includes rows that are not found in the first phase but are related to them.

To perform this kind of search, add `WITH QUERY EXPANSION` following the search terms. The following example provides an illustration. The first query shows a natural language search. The second query shows a query expansion search. Its result includes an extra row that contains none of the original search terms. This row is found because it contains the word "candle" that is present in one of the rows found by the natural language search.

```
mysql> SELECT * FROM apothegm
    -> WHERE MATCH(attribution, phrase)
    -> AGAINST('bell book');
+----------------------+------------------------------------+
| attribution          | phrase                             |
+----------------------+------------------------------------+
| Miguel de Cervantes  | Bell, book, and candle             |
| Alexander Graham Bell | Mr. Watson, come here. I want you! |
+----------------------+------------------------------------+
mysql> SELECT * FROM apothegm
    -> WHERE MATCH(attribution, phrase)
    -> AGAINST('bell book' WITH QUERY EXPANSION);
+----------------------+---------------------------------------+
| attribution          | phrase                                |
+----------------------+---------------------------------------+
| Miguel de Cervantes  | Bell, book, and candle                |
| Alexander Graham Bell | Mr. Watson, come here. I want you!    |
| Robert Burton        | I light my candle from their torches. |
+----------------------+---------------------------------------+
```

2.14.4   Configuring the `FULLTEXT` Search Engine

Several full-text parameters are configurable and can be modified by setting system variables. The `ft_min_word_len` and `ft_max_word_len` variables determine the shortest and longest words to index in `FULLTEXT` indexes. Words with lengths outside the range defined by these two variables are ignored when `FULLTEXT` indexes are built. The default minimum and maximum values are 4 and 84.

Suppose that you want to change the minimum word length from 4 to 3. Do so like this:

1. Start the server with the `ft_min_word_len` variable set to 3. To ensure that this happens whenever the server starts, it's best to place the setting in an option file such as `/etc/my.cnf`:

   ```
   [mysqld]
   ft_min_word_len=3
   ```

2. For any existing tables that already have FULLTEXT indexes, you must rebuild those indexes. You can drop and add the indexes, but it's easier and sufficient to perform a quick repair operation:

```
REPAIR TABLE tbl_name QUICK;
```

3. Any new FULLTEXT indexes that you create after changing the parameter will use the new value automatically.

For more information on setting system variables, see Appendix D, "System, Status, and User Variable Reference." For details on using option files, see Appendix F, "MySQL Program Reference."

Note

If you use myisamchk to rebuild indexes for a table that contains any FULLTEXT indexes, see the FULLTEXT-related notes in the myisamchk description in Appendix F, "MySQL Program Reference."

3

Data Types

Virtually everything you do in MySQL involves data in some way or another because, by definition, the purpose of a database management system is to manage data. Even a statement as simple as SELECT 1 involves evaluation of an expression to produce an integer data value.

Every data value in MySQL has a type. For example, 37.4 is a number and 'abc' is a string. Sometimes data types are explicit, such as when you issue a CREATE TABLE statement that specifies the type for each column you define as part of the table:

```
CREATE TABLE mytbl
(
  int_col  INT,       # integer-valued column
  str_col  CHAR(20),  # string-valued column
  date_col DATE       # date-valued column
);
```

Other times data types are implicit, such as when you refer to literal values in an expression, pass values to a function, or use the value returned from a function. The following INSERT statement does all of those things:

```
INSERT INTO mytbl (int_col,str_col,date_col)
VALUES(14,CONCAT('a','b'),20130815);
```

The statement performs the following operations, all of which involve data types:

- It assigns the integer value 14 to the integer column int_col.

- It passes the string values 'a' and 'b' to the CONCAT() string-concatenation function and assigns the returned string value 'ab', to the string column str_col.

- It assigns the integer value 20130815 to the date column date_col. The assignment involves a type mismatch, but the integer value can reasonably be interpreted as a date value, so MySQL performs an automatic type conversion that converts the integer 20130815 to the date '2013-08-15'.

To use MySQL effectively, it's essential to understand how MySQL handles data. This chapter describes the types of data values you can use:

- The general categories of data values that MySQL can represent, including the NULL value.

- The specific data types MySQL provides for table columns, and the properties that characterize each data type. Some of MySQL's data types are fairly generic, such as the BLOB string type. Others behave in special ways that you should understand to avoid being surprised. These include the TIMESTAMP data type and integer types that have the AUTO_INCREMENT attribute.

The chapter also discusses the issues involved in working with those types:

- How the server's SQL mode affects treatment of bad data values, and the use of "strict" mode to reject bad values.

- How to generate and work with sequences.

- MySQL's rules for expression evaluation. You can use a wide range of operators and functions in expressions to retrieve, display, and manipulate data. Expression evaluation includes rules governing type conversion that come into play when a value of one type is used in a context requiring a value of another type. It's important to understand when type conversion happens and how it works; some conversions don't make sense and result in meaningless values. Assigning the string '13' to an integer column results in the value 13. However, assigning the string 'abc' to that column results in the value 0 (or an error in strict SQL mode) because 'abc' doesn't look like a number. Worse, if you perform a comparison without knowing the conversion rules, you can do considerable damage, such as updating or deleting every row in a table when you intend to affect only a few specific rows.

- How to choose data types appropriately for your table columns. It's important to know how to pick the best type for your purposes when you create a table, and when to choose one type over another when several related types might be applicable to the kind of values you want to store.

To supplement the discussion in this chapter about MySQL's data types, operators, and functions, see Appendix B, "Data Type Reference," and Appendix C, "Operator and Function Reference."

The examples shown throughout this chapter use the CREATE TABLE and ALTER TABLE statements extensively to create and alter tables. Those statements were discussed in Chapter 1, "Getting Started with MySQL," and Chapter 2, "Using SQL to Manage Data." See also Appendix E, "SQL Syntax Reference."

Data handling depends in some cases on how default values are defined and on the current SQL mode. For general background on setting the SQL mode, see Section 2.1, "The Server SQL Mode." In the current chapter, Section 3.2.3, "Specifying Column Default Values," covers default value handing, and Section 3.3, "How MySQL Handles Invalid Data Values," covers strict mode and the rules for treatment of bad data.

3.1   Data Value Categories

MySQL supports several general categories of data values. These include numbers, string values, temporal values such as dates and times, spatial values, and the NULL value.

3.1.1   Numeric Values

Numbers are values such as 48, 193.62, or -2.378E12. MySQL understands numbers specified as integers (which have no fractional part), fixed-point or floating-point values (which may have a fractional part), and bit-field values.

When you specify a number, do not include commas as a separator. For example, 12345678.90 is legal, but 12,345,678.90 is not.

3.1.1.1   Exact-Value and Approximate-Value Numbers

MySQL supports precision math for exact-value numbers, and approximate math for approximate-value numbers.

Exact-value numbers are used exactly as specified when possible. Exact values include integers (0, 14, -382) and numbers that have a decimal point (0.0, 38.5, -18.247).

Integers can be specified in decimal or hexadecimal format. In decimal format, an integer consists of a sequence of digits with no decimal point. Hexadecimal values are treated as strings by default, but in numeric contexts, a hexadecimal constant is treated as a 64-bit integer. For example, 0x10 is 16 decimal. Section 3.1.2, "String Values," describes hexadecimal value syntax.

An exact-value number with a fractional part consists of a sequence of digits, a decimal point, and another sequence of digits. The sequence of digits before or after the decimal point may be empty, but not both.

Approximate values are represented as floating-point numbers in scientific notation with a mantissa and exponent. This is indicated by immediately following an integer or number with a fractional part by 'e' or 'E', an optional sign character ('+' or '-'), and an integer exponent. The mantissa and exponent may be signed in any combination: 1.58E5, -1.58E5, 1.58E-5, -1.58E-5.

Hexadecimal numbers cannot be used in scientific notation; the 'e' that begins the exponent part is also a legal hex digit and thus is ambiguous.

Any number can be preceded by a plus or minus sign character ('+' or '-') to indicate a positive or negative value.

Calculations with exact values are exact, with no loss of accuracy within the limits of the precision possible for such values. For example, you cannot insert 1.23456 without loss into a column that permits only two digits after the decimal point. Calculations with approximate values are approximate and subject to rounding error.

MySQL evaluates an expression using exact or approximate math according to the following rules:

- An expression that involves any approximate value is evaluated as a floating-point (approximate) expression.

- An expression that contains only integer exact values is evaluated using BIGINT (64-bit) precision.

- An expression that contains only exact values, some of which have a fractional part, use DECIMAL arithmetic with 65 digits of precision.

- If any string must be converted to a number to evaluate an expression, it is converted to a double-precision floating-point value. Consequently, the expression is approximate by the preceding rules.

3.1.1.2   Bit-Field Values

Bit-field values can be written as b'val' or 0bval, where val consists of one or more binary digits (0 or 1). For example, b'1001' and 0b1001 represent 9 decimal.

A BIT value in a result set displays as a binary string, which may not print well. To convert it to an integer, add zero or use CAST():

```
mysql> SELECT b'1001' + 0, CAST(b'1001' AS UNSIGNED);
+-------------+---------------------------+
| b'1001' + 0 | CAST(b'1001' AS UNSIGNED) |
+-------------+---------------------------+
|           9 |                         9 |
+-------------+---------------------------+
```

3.1.2   String Values

Strings are values such as 'Madison, Wisconsin', 'patient shows improvement', or even '12345' (which looks like a number, but isn't). Usually, you can use either single or double quotes to surround a string value, but there are two reasons to prefer single quotes:

- The SQL standard specifies single quotes, so statements that use single-quoted strings are more portable to other database engines.

- If the ANSI_QUOTES SQL mode is enabled, MySQL treats the double quote as an identifier-quoting character, not as a string-quoting character. This means that a double-quoted value must refer to something like a database or table name. Consider the following statement:

  ```
  SELECT "last_name" from president;
  ```

  With ANSI_QUOTES enabled, the statement selects the values of the last_name column from the table. With ANSI_QUOTES disabled, the statement selects the literal string "last_name" once for each row in the president table.

For the examples following that use double quote as a string quoting character, assume that ANSI_QUOTES mode is not enabled.

MySQL recognizes several escape sequences within strings that indicate special characters, as shown in Table 3.1. Each sequence begins with a backslash character ('\') to signify a temporary escape from the usual rules for character interpretation. Note that a NUL byte is not the same as the SQL NULL value; NUL is a zero-valued byte, whereas NULL in SQL signifies the absence of a value.

Table 3.1 **String Escape Sequences**

Sequence	Meaning
\0	NUL (zero-valued byte)
\'	Single quote
\"	Double quote
\b	Backspace
\n	Newline (linefeed)
\r	Carriage return
\t	Tab
\\	Single backslash
\z	Control-Z (Windows EOF character)

The escape sequences shown in the table are case sensitive, and any character not listed in the table is interpreted as itself if preceded by a backslash. For example, \t is a tab, but \T is an ordinary 'T' character.

Table 3.1 shows that you can escape single or double quotes using backslash sequences, but you actually have several options for including quote characters within string values:

- Double the quote character if the string itself is quoted using the same character:

```
'I can''t'
"He said, ""I told you so."""
```

- Quote the string with the other quote character. In this case, you do not double the quote characters within the string:

```
"I can't"
'He said, "I told you so."'
```

- Escape the quote character with a backslash; this works regardless of the quote characters used to quote the string:

```
'I can\'t'
"I can\'t"
```

```
"He said, \"I told you so.\""
'He said, \"I told you so.\"'
```

To turn off the special meaning of backslash and treat it as an ordinary character, enable the NO_BACKSLASH_ESCAPES SQL mode.

Two forms of hexadecimal notation provide alternatives to using quotes for writing string values. Values may be specified using the standard SQL notation X'val', where val consists of pairs of hexadecimal digits ('0' through '9' and 'a' through 'f'). For example, X'0a' is 10 decimal, and X'ffff' is 65535 decimal. The leading 'X' and the nondecimal hex digits ('a' through 'f') can be specified in uppercase or lowercase:

```
mysql> SELECT X'4A', x'4a';
+-------+-------+
| X'4A' | x'4a' |
+-------+-------+
| J     | J     |
+-------+-------+
```

In string contexts, pairs of hexadecimal digits are interpreted as 8-bit numeric byte values in the range from 0 to 255, and the result is used as a string. In numeric contexts, a hexadecimal constant is treated as a number. The following statement illustrates the interpretation of a hex constant in each context:

```
mysql> SELECT X'61626364', X'61626364'+0;
+-------------+---------------+
| X'61626364' | X'61626364'+0 |
+-------------+---------------+
| abcd        |    1633837924 |
+-------------+---------------+
```

Hexadecimal values also may be written using 0x followed by one or more hexadecimal digits. The leading 0x is case sensitive. 0x0a and 0x0A are legal hexadecimal values, but 0X0a and 0X0A are not.

As with X'val' notation, 0x values are interpreted as strings, but may be used as numbers in numeric contexts:

```
mysql> SELECT 0x61626364, 0x61626364+0;
+------------+--------------+
| 0x61626364 | 0x61626364+0 |
+------------+--------------+
| abcd       |   1633837924 |
+------------+--------------+
```

X'val' notation requires an even number of digits. A value such as X'a' is illegal. If a hexadecimal value written using 0x notation has an odd number of hex digits, MySQL treats it as though the value has a leading zero. For example, 0xa is treated as 0x0a.

3.1.2.1   Types of Strings and Character Set Support

String values fall into two general categories, binary and nonbinary:

- A binary string is a sequence of bytes. These bytes are interpreted without respect to any concept of character set. A binary string has no special comparison or sorting properties. Comparisons are done byte by byte based on numeric byte values; all bytes are significant, including trailing spaces.

- A nonbinary string is a sequence of characters. It is associated with a character set, which determines the characters that are permitted and how MySQL interprets the string contents. Character sets have one or more collating (sorting) orders. The particular collation used for a string determines the ordering of characters in the character set, which affects comparison operations. The default character set and collation are `latin1` and `latin1_swedish_ci`.

  Trailing spaces in nonbinary strings are not significant in comparisons, except that for the `TEXT` types, index-based comparisons are padded at the end with spaces and a duplicate-key error occurs if you attempt to insert into a unique-valued `TEXT` index a value that is different from an existing value only in the number of trailing spaces.

Character units vary in their storage requirements. A single-byte character set such as `latin1` uses 1 byte per character, but there also are multi-byte character sets in which some or all characters require more than 1 byte. For example, the Unicode character sets available in MySQL are multi-byte. `ucs2` is a double-byte character set in which each character requires 2 bytes. `utf8` is a variable-length multi-byte character set with characters that take from 1 to 3 bytes. Some Unicode character sets take up to 4 bytes per character. See Section 2.4.3, "Unicode Support."

To find out which character sets and collations are available in your server, use these two statements:

```
mysql> SHOW CHARACTER SET;
+----------+---------------------------+---------------------+---------+
| Charset  | Description               | Default collation   | Maxlen  |
+----------+---------------------------+---------------------+---------+
| big5     | Big5 Traditional Chinese  | big5_chinese_ci     |       2 |
| dec8     | DEC West European         | dec8_swedish_ci     |       1 |
| cp850    | DOS West European         | cp850_general_ci    |       1 |
| hp8      | HP West European          | hp8_english_ci      |       1 |
| koi8r    | KOI8-R Relcom Russian     | koi8r_general_ci    |       1 |
| latin1   | cp1252 West European      | latin1_swedish_ci   |       1 |
...
| utf8     | UTF-8 Unicode             | utf8_general_ci     |       3 |
| ucs2     | UCS-2 Unicode             | ucs2_general_ci     |       2 |
...
mysql> SHOW COLLATION;
+----------------------+----------+-----+---------+----------+---------+
| Collation            | Charset  | Id  | Default | Compiled | Sortlen |
+----------------------+----------+-----+---------+----------+---------+
```

| big5_chinese_ci | big5 | 1 | Yes | Yes | 1 |
| big5_bin | big5 | 84 | | Yes | 1 |

...

latin1_german1_ci	latin1	5		Yes	1
latin1_swedish_ci	latin1	8	Yes	Yes	1
latin1_danish_ci	latin1	15		Yes	1
latin1_german2_ci	latin1	31		Yes	2
latin1_bin	latin1	47		Yes	1
latin1_general_ci	latin1	48		Yes	1
latin1_general_cs	latin1	49		Yes	1
latin1_spanish_ci	latin1	94		Yes	1

...

As shown by the output from SHOW COLLATION, each collation is tied to a particular character set, and a given character set might have several collations. Collation names usually consist of a character set name, a language, and an additional suffix. For example, utf8_icelandic_ci is a collation for the utf8 Unicode character set in which comparisons follow Icelandic sorting rules and characters are compared in case-insensitive fashion. Collation suffixes have the following meanings:

- _ci indicates a case-insensitive collation.

- _cs indicates a case-sensitive collation.

- _bin indicates a binary collation. That is, comparisons are based on numeric character code values without reference to any language. For this reason, _bin collation names do not include any language name. Examples: latin1_bin and utf8_bin.

Binary and nonbinary strings have different sorting properties:

- Binary strings are processed byte by byte in comparisons based solely on the numeric value of each byte. As a result, binary strings may seem to be case sensitive ('abc' <> 'ABC'), but that is only because uppercase and lowercase versions of a letter have different numeric byte values. There isn't really any notion of lettercase for binary strings. Lettercase is a function of collation, which applies only to character (nonbinary) strings.

- Nonbinary strings are processed character by character in comparisons, with the relative value of each character determined by the collating sequence used for the character set. For many collations, uppercase and lowercase versions of a given letter have the same collating value, so nonbinary string comparisons typically are not case sensitive. However, that is not true for case-sensitive or binary collations.

Because collations are used for comparison and sorting, they affect many operations:

- Comparisons operators: <, <=, =, <>, >=, >, and LIKE.

- Sorting: ORDER BY, MIN(), and MAX().

- Grouping: GROUP BY and DISTINCT.

To determine the character set or collation of a string, use the CHARSET() or COLLATION() function.

Quoted string literals are interpreted according to the current server settings. The default character set and collation are latin1 and latin1_swedish_ci. However, mysql and other clients can detect and adjust accordingly when you have the LANG or LC_ALL environment variable set to specify a locale. See Section 3.1.2.2, "Character Set-Related System Variables."

MySQL treats hexadecimal constants as binary strings by default:

```
mysql> SELECT CHARSET(X'0123'), COLLATION(X'0123');
+------------------+--------------------+
| CHARSET(X'0123') | COLLATION(X'0123') |
+------------------+--------------------+
| binary           | binary             |
+------------------+--------------------+
```

Two notational conventions can be used to force a string literal to be interpreted with a given character set. First, a string constant can be designated for interpretation with a given character set using the following notation, where charset names a supported character set:

_charset str

The _charset notation is called a "character set introducer." The string following the introducer can be written as a quoted string or as a hexadecimal value. These examples show how to cause strings to be interpreted in the latin2 or utf8 character set:

```
_latin2 'abc'
_latin2 X'616263'
_latin2 0x616263
_utf8 'def'
_utf8 X'646566'
_utf8 0x646566
```

For quoted strings, whitespace is optional between the introducer and the following string. For hexadecimal values, whitespace is required.

Second, the notation N'str' is equivalent to _utf8'str'. N (not case sensitive) must be followed immediately by a quoted string literal with no intervening whitespace.

Introducer notation works for quoted string literals or hexadecimal constants, but not for string expressions or column values. However, any string value can be used to produce a string in a designated character set using the CONVERT() function:

CONVERT(str USING charset);

Introducers and CONVERT() are not the same. An introducer merely modifies how the string is interpreted. It does not change the string value (except that for multi-byte character sets, padding might be added if the string does not contain enough bytes). CONVERT() takes a string argument and produces a new string in the desired character set. To see the difference between introducers and `CONVERT()`, consider the following two statements that refer to the `ucs2` double-byte character set:

```
mysql> SET @s1 = _ucs2 'ABCD';
mysql> SET @s2 = CONVERT('ABCD' USING ucs2);
```

Assume that the current character set is `latin1` (a single-byte character set). The first statement interprets each pair of characters in the string `'ABCD'` as a single double-byte `ucs2` character, resulting in a two-character `ucs2` string. The second statement converts each character of the string `'ABCD'` to the corresponding `ucs2` character, resulting in a four-character `ucs2` string.

What is the "length" of a string? It depends. If you measure with `CHAR_LENGTH()`, you get the length in characters. If you measure with `LENGTH()`, you get the length in bytes. For strings that contain multi-byte characters, the two values differ:

```
mysql> SELECT CHAR_LENGTH(@s1), LENGTH(@s1), CHAR_LENGTH(@s2), LENGTH(@s2);
+------------------+-------------+------------------+-------------+
| CHAR_LENGTH(@s1) | LENGTH(@s1) | CHAR_LENGTH(@s2) | LENGTH(@s2) |
+------------------+-------------+------------------+-------------+
|                2 |           4 |                4 |           8 |
+------------------+-------------+------------------+-------------+
```

Here is a somewhat subtle point. A binary string is not the same thing as a nonbinary string that has a binary collation:

- The binary string has no character set. It is interpreted with byte semantics and comparisons use single-byte numeric codes.

- A nonbinary string with a binary collation has character semantics and comparisons use numeric character values that might be based on multiple bytes per character.

Here's a way to see the difference between binary and nonbinary strings with regard to letter-case. Create a binary string, a nonbinary string that has a binary collation, and pass each string to the `UPPER()` function:

```
mysql> SET @s1 = BINARY 'abcd';
mysql> SET @s2 = _latin1 'abcd' COLLATE latin1_bin;
mysql> SELECT UPPER(@s1), UPPER(@s2);
+------------+------------+
| UPPER(@s1) | UPPER(@s2) |
+------------+------------+
| abcd       | ABCD       |
+------------+------------+
```

Why doesn't `UPPER()` convert the binary string to uppercase? This happens because the string has no character set, so there is no way to know which byte values correspond to uppercase or lowercase characters. To use a binary string with functions such as `UPPER()` and `LOWER()`, first convert it to a nonbinary string:

```
mysql> SELECT @s1, UPPER(CONVERT(@s1 USING latin1));
+------+--------------------------------+
| @s1  | UPPER(CONVERT(@s1 USING latin1)) |
+------+--------------------------------+
| abcd | ABCD                           |
+------+--------------------------------+
```

3.1.2.2   Character Set-Related System Variables

The server maintains several system variables that are involved in various aspects of character set support. Most of these variables refer to character sets and the rest refer to collations. Each of the collation variables is linked to a corresponding character set variable.

Some of the character set variables indicate properties of the server or the current database:

- `character_set_system` indicates the character set used for storing identifiers. This is always `utf8`.
- `character_set_server` and `collation_server` indicate the server's default character set and collation.
- `character_set_database` and `collation_database` indicate the character set and collation of the default database. These are read-only variables and set automatically by the server whenever you select a default database. If there is no default database, they're set to the server's default character set and collation. These variables come into play when you create a table but specify no explicit character set or collation. In this case, the table defaults are taken from the database defaults.

Other character set variables influence how communication occurs between the client and the server:

- `character_set_client` indicates the character set in which the client sends SQL statements to the server.
- `character_set_results` indicates the character set in which the server returns results to the client. "Results" include data values and also metadata such as column names.
- `character_set_connection` is used by the server. When it receives a statement string from the client, it converts the string from `character_set_client` to `character_set_connection` and works with the statement in the latter character set. (There is an exception: Any literal string in the statement that is preceded by a character set introducer is interpreted using the character set indicated by the introducer.) `collation_connection` is used for comparisons between literal strings within statement strings.
- `character_set_filesystem` indicates the filesystem character set. MySQL uses it to interpret literal strings known to refer to filenames in SQL statements such as LOAD DATA. These filename strings are converted from `character_set_client` to `character_set_filesystem` before opening the file. The default is `binary` (no conversion).

Very likely you'll find that most character set and collation variables are set to the same value by default. For example, the following output indicates that client/server communication takes place using the `latin1` character set:

```
mysql> SHOW VARIABLES LIKE 'character\_set\_%';
+--------------------------+--------+
| Variable_name            | Value  |
+--------------------------+--------+
| character_set_client     | latin1 |
| character_set_connection | latin1 |
| character_set_database   | latin1 |
| character_set_filesystem | binary |
| character_set_results    | latin1 |
| character_set_server     | latin1 |
| character_set_system     | utf8   |
+--------------------------+--------+
mysql> SHOW VARIABLES LIKE 'collation\_%';
+----------------------+-------------------+
| Variable_name        | Value             |
+----------------------+-------------------+
| collation_connection | latin1_swedish_ci |
| collation_database   | latin1_swedish_ci |
| collation_server     | latin1_swedish_ci |
+----------------------+-------------------+
```

A client that wants to talk to the server using another character set can change the communication-related variables. For example, to use `utf8`, change three variables:

```
mysql> SET character_set_client = utf8;
mysql> SET character_set_results = utf8;
mysql> SET character_set_connection = utf8;
```

However, it's more convenient to use a `SET NAMES` statement for this purpose. The following statement is equivalent to the preceding three `SET` statements:

```
mysql> SET NAMES 'utf8';
```

One restriction on setting the communication character set is that you cannot use `ucs2`, `utf16`, `utf16le`, or `utf32`.

Many client programs support a `--default-character-set` option that produces the same effect as a `SET NAMES` statement by informing the server of the desired communication character set.

An even easier method applies for the standard MySQL client programs such as `mysql` and `mysqladmin`. Set the `LANG` or `LC_ALL` environment variable to specify a locale and these clients detect it and adjust accordingly. For example, if I have `LC_ALL` set to `en_US.UTF-8`, the default character set and collation for literals are affected like this:

```
mysql> SELECT CHARSET('abcd'), COLLATION('abcd');
+-----------------+-------------------+
| CHARSET('abcd') | COLLATION('abcd') |
+-----------------+-------------------+
| utf8            | utf8_general_ci   |
+-----------------+-------------------+
```

For variables that come in pairs (a character set variable and a collation variable), the members of the pair are linked in the following ways:

- Setting the character set variable also sets the associated collation variable to the character set default collation.

- Setting the collation variable also sets the associated character set variable to the character set implied by the first part of the collation name.

For example, setting `character_set_connection` to `utf8` sets `collation_connection` to `utf8_general_ci`. Setting `collation_connection` to `latin1_spanish_ci` sets `character_set_connection` to `latin1`.

3.1.3   Temporal (Date and Time) Values

Temporal values contain date or time values such as `'2012-06-17'` or `'12:30:43'`. MySQL also understands combined date/time values, such as `'2012-06-17 12:30:43'`. Take special note of the fact that MySQL displays dates in year-month-day order, and input values must be given in that order. This syntax often surprises newcomers to MySQL, although it is standard SQL format (also known as "ISO 8601" format). You can display date values any way you like using the `DATE_FORMAT()` function, but the default display format lists the year first. For input values in other formats, you might be able to convert them by using the `STR_TO_DATE()` function. For an example, see Section 3.2.6, "Temporal (Date and Time) Data Types."

For combined date and time values, it is permitted to specify a 'T' character rather than a space between the date and time; for example, `'2008-12-31T12:00:00'`.

The syntax for time or combined date and time values permits a fractional seconds part following the time, consisting of a decimal point and up to 6 digits (microseconds) precision; for example, `'12:30:15.000045'` or `'2008-06-15 10:30:12.5'`.

3.1.4   Spatial Values

MySQL supports spatial values, although only for the InnoDB, MyISAM, NDB, and ARCHIVE storage engines. This capability enables representation of values such as points, lines, and polygons. These types are implemented per the OpenGIS specification, which is available at the Open Geospatial Consortium Web site (http://www.opengeospatial.org). For example, the following statement uses the text representation of a point value with X and Y coordinates of (10, 20) to create a `POINT` and assigns the result to a user-defined variable:

```
SET @pt = POINTFROMTEXT('POINT(10 20)');
```

This book covers spatial values only minimally. For more information about these types, see the MySQL Reference Manual.

3.1.5   Boolean Values

In expressions, zero is considered false and any nonzero, non-NULL value is considered true.

The special constants TRUE and FALSE evaluate to 1 and 0, respectively. They are not case sensitive.

3.1.6   The NULL Value

NULL is something of a "typeless" value. Generally, it's used to mean "no value," "unknown value," "missing value," "out of range," "not applicable," "none of the above," and so forth. You can insert NULL values into tables, retrieve them from tables, and test whether a value is NULL. However, you cannot perform arithmetic on NULL values; if you try, the result is NULL. Also, many functions return NULL if you invoke them with a NULL or invalid argument.

The keyword NULL is written without quotes and is not case sensitive. MySQL also treats a standalone \N (case sensitive) as NULL:

```
mysql> SELECT \N, ISNULL(\N);
+------+------------+
| NULL | ISNULL(\N) |
+------+------------+
| NULL |          1 |
+------+------------+
```

3.2   MySQL Data Types

Each table in a database contains one or more columns, and you specify a data type for each column when you create a table using a CREATE TABLE statement. A column data type is more specific than a general category such as "number" or "string." It is the means by which you characterize precisely the kind of values the column may contain, such as SMALLINT or VARCHAR(32). This in turn determines how MySQL treats those values. For example, you could store numeric values using either a numeric or string column, but MySQL will treat the values somewhat differently in each case. Each data type has several characteristics:

- What kind of values it can represent

- How much storage space values require

- Whether values are fixed-length (all values of the type take the same amount of space) or variable-length (the amount of space depends on the particular value being stored)

- How MySQL compares and sorts values of the type

- Whether and how the type can be indexed

The following discussion surveys MySQL's data types briefly, and then describes in more detail the syntax for defining them and the properties that characterize them, such as their range and storage requirements. The type specifications are shown as you use them in CREATE TABLE statements. Square brackets ([]) indicate optional information. For example, the syntax MEDIUMINT[(M)] indicates that the maximum display width, specified as (M), is optional. On the other hand, for VARCHAR(M), the absence of brackets indicates that (M) is required.

3.2.1 Data Type Overview

MySQL has numeric data types for integer, fixed-point, floating-point, and bit values, as shown in Table 3.2. Numeric types can be signed or unsigned, except BIT. A special attribute enables automatic generation of sequential integer or floating-point column values, which is useful for applications that require a series of unique identification numbers.

Table 3.2 **Numeric Data Types**

Type Name	Meaning
TINYINT	A very small integer
SMALLINT	A small integer
MEDIUMINT	A medium-sized integer
INT	A standard integer
BIGINT	A large integer
DECIMAL	A fixed-point number
FLOAT	A single-precision floating-point number
DOUBLE	A double-precision floating-point number
BIT	A bit field

Table 3.3 shows the MySQL string data types. Strings can hold anything, even arbitrary binary data such as used to represent images or sounds. Strings can be compared according to whether they are case sensitive. In addition, you can perform pattern matching on strings. (You can actually perform pattern matching even on numeric types, but it's more common with string types.)

Table 3.3 **String Data Types**

Type Name	Meaning
CHAR	A fixed-length nonbinary (character) string
VARCHAR	A variable-length nonbinary string

Type Name	Meaning
BINARY	A fixed-length binary string
VARBINARY	A variable-length binary string
TINYBLOB	A very small BLOB (binary large object)
BLOB	A small BLOB
MEDIUMBLOB	A medium-sized BLOB
LONGBLOB	A large BLOB
TINYTEXT	A very small nonbinary string
TEXT	A small nonbinary string
MEDIUMTEXT	A medium-sized nonbinary string
LONGTEXT	A large nonbinary string
ENUM	An enumeration; each column value is assigned one enumeration member
SET	A set; each column value is assigned zero or more set members

Table 3.4 shows the MySQL temporal types, where CC, YY, MM, DD, hh, mm, and ss represent the century, year, month, day of the month, hour, minute, and second parts, respectively. For temporal values, MySQL provides types for dates and times (either combined or separate) and timestamps (a special type that enables you to track when changes were last made to a row). There is also a type for efficiently representing year values when you don't need an entire date.

Table 3.4 **Temporal Data Types**

Type Name	Meaning
DATE	A date value, in '$CCYY-MM-DD$' format
TIME	A time value, in '$hh:mm:ss$' format
DATETIME	A date and time value, in '$CCYY-MM-DD\ hh:mm:ss$' format
TIMESTAMP	A timestamp value, in '$CCYY-MM-DD\ hh:mm:ss$' format
YEAR	A year value, in $CCYY$ or YY format

3.2.2 Specifying Column Types in Table Definitions

To create a table, issue a CREATE TABLE statement that includes a list of the columns in the table. Here's an example that creates a table named mytbl with three columns named f, c, and i:

```
CREATE TABLE mytbl
(
  f FLOAT(10,4),
  c CHAR(15) NOT NULL DEFAULT 'none',
  i TINYINT UNSIGNED NULL
);
```

Each column has a name, a type, and possibly optional attributes. Column definitions have this syntax:

`col_name col_type [type_attrs] [general_attrs]`

The name of the column, `col_name`, is always first in the definition and must be a legal identifier. The precise rules for identifier syntax are given in Section 2.2, "MySQL Identifier Syntax and Naming Rules." Briefly summarized, column identifiers may be up to 64 characters long, and may consist of latin letters, digits, the underscore and dollar sign characters ('_' and '$'), and Unicode extended characters. Keywords such as SELECT, DELETE, and CREATE normally are reserved and cannot be used. It is *possible* to include other characters within an identifier or use a reserved word as an identifier, but you must be willing to put up with the bother of quoting it whenever you refer to it. To quote an identifier, enclose it within backtick ('`') characters. If the ANSI_QUOTES SQL mode is enabled, it is permitted to quote identifiers within double quote ('"') characters instead.

`col_type` indicates the column data type; that is, the specific kind of values the column can hold. Some type specifiers indicate the maximum length of the values you store in the column. For others, the length is implied by the type name. For example, CHAR(10) specifies an explicit length of 10 characters, whereas TINYTEXT values have an implicit maximum length of 255 bytes. Some of the type specifiers permit you to indicate a maximum display width (how many characters to use for displaying values). For fixed-point and floating-point types, you can specify the number of significant digits and number of decimal places.

Following the column's data type, you can specify optional type-specific attributes as well as more general attributes. These attributes function as type modifiers that cause MySQL to change how it treats column values in some way:

- The permitted type-specific attributes depend on the data type. For example, UNSIGNED and ZEROFILL are permitted only for numeric types, and CHARACTER SET and COLLATE are permitted only for nonbinary string types.

- The general attributes may be given for any data type, with a few exceptions. You may specify NULL or NOT NULL to indicate whether a column can hold NULL values. For most data types, you can specify a DEFAULT clause to define a default value for the column. Section 3.2.3, "Specifying Column Default Values," describes default value handling.

If multiple column attributes are present, there are some constraints on the order in which they may appear. In general, you should be safe if you specify data type-specific attributes such as UNSIGNED or ZEROFILL before general attributes such as NULL or NOT NULL.

3.2.3   Specifying Column Default Values

For all but `BLOB` and `TEXT` types, spatial types, or columns with the `AUTO_INCREMENT` attribute, you can specify a `DEFAULT default_value` clause to indicate that a column should be assigned the value `default_value` when a new row is created that does not explicitly specify the column's value. With some limited exceptions for `TIMESTAMP` and `DATETIME` columns, `default_value` must be a constant. It cannot be an expression or refer to other columns.

If a column definition includes no explicit `DEFAULT` clause and the column can take `NULL` values, its default value is `NULL`. Otherwise, the column is created with no `DEFAULT` clause. That is, it has no default value. This affects how MySQL handles the column for new rows inserted into the table that specify no value for the column:

- When strict SQL mode is not in effect, the column is set to the implicit default for its data type. (Implicit defaults are described shortly.)

- When strict SQL mode is in effect, an error occurs if the table is transactional. The statement aborts and rolls back. For nontransactional tables, an error occurs and the statement aborts if the row is the first row inserted by the statement. If it is not the first row, you can elect to have the statement abort or to have the column set to its implicit default with a warning. The choice depends on which strict mode setting is in effect. See Section 3.3, "How MySQL Handles Invalid Data Values," for details. For information about transactions, see Section 2.12 "Performing Transactions."

The implicit default for a column depends on its data type:

- For numeric columns, the default is 0, except for columns that have the `AUTO_INCREMENT` attribute. For `AUTO_INCREMENT`, the default is the next number in the column sequence.

- For most temporal types, the default is the "zero" value for the type (for example, `'0000-00-00'` for `DATE`). For `TIMESTAMP` (and `DATETIME` as of MySQL 5.6), special auto-initialization rules apply. See Section 3.2.6.6, "Automatic Properties for Temporal Types."

- For string types other than `ENUM`, the default is the empty string. For `ENUM`, the default is the first enumeration element. For `SET`, the default when the column cannot contain `NULL` is the empty set, but that is equivalent to the empty string.

To see which columns in a table have a `DEFAULT` clause and what the default value is for those columns that have one, use `SHOW CREATE TABLE tbl_name`.

3.2.4   Numeric Data Types

MySQL's numeric data types fall into three groups:

- Exact-value types, which include the integer types and `DECIMAL`. Integer types are for numbers that have no fractional part, such as 43, -3, 0, or -798432. You can use integer columns for data represented by whole numbers, such as weights to the nearest pound, number of people in households, or inventory quantities. The `DECIMAL` type stores exact values that may have a fractional part, such as `3.14159`, `-.00273`, or `-4.78`. This is a good data type for information such as currency values. Integer and `DECIMAL` values are stored exactly as specified without rounding when possible, and calculations are exact.

- The floating-point types are available in single precision (`FLOAT`) and double precision (`DOUBLE`). These types, like `DECIMAL`, are for numbers that may have a fractional part, but they hold approximate-value numbers such as `3.9E+4` or `-0.1E-100` that are subject to rounding. They can be used when exact precision is not required or for values that are so large that `DECIMAL` cannot represent them. Some types of data you might represent as floating-point values are average crop yield or stellar distances.

- The `BIT` type is for storing bit-field values.

Values with a fractional part can be assigned to integer columns, but are rounded using the "round half up" rule: If the fractional part is .5 or greater, the value is rounded away from zero to the next integer (up for positive values, down for negative values). Conversely, integer values may be assigned to types that permit a fractional part. They have a fractional part of zero.

Table 3.5 shows the name and range of each numeric type, and Table 3.6 shows the amount of storage required for values of each type. M represents the maximum display width for integer types, the precision (number of significant digits) for floating-point and decimal types, and the number of bits for `BIT`. D represents the scale (number of digits following the decimal point) for types that have a fractional part.

Table 3.5 Numeric Data Type Ranges

Type Name	Range
`TINYINT[(M)]`	Signed values: −128 to 127 (-2^7 to 2^7-1); Unsigned values: 0 to 255 (0 to 2^8-1)
`SMALLINT[(M)]`	Signed values: −32768 to 32767 (-2^{15} to $2^{15}-1$); Unsigned values: 0 to 65535 (0 to $2^{16}-1$)
`MEDIUMINT[(M)]`	Signed values: −8388608 to 8388607 (-2^{23} to $2^{23}-1$); Unsigned values: 0 to 16777215 (0 to $2^{24}-1$)
`INT[(M)]`	Signed values: −2147483648 to 2147483647 (-2^{31} to $2^{31}-1$); Unsigned values: 0 to 4294967295 (0 to $2^{32}-1$)
`BIGINT[(M)]`	Signed values: −9223372036854775808 to 9223372036854775807 (-2^{63} to $2^{63}-1$); Unsigned values: 0 to 18446744073709551615 (0 to $2^{64}-1$)
`DECIMAL([M[,D]])`	Depends on M and D
`FLOAT[(M,D)]`	Minimum nonzero values: ±1.175494351E−38; Maximum nonzero values: ±3.402823466E+38
`DOUBLE[(M,D)]`	Minimum nonzero values: ±2.2250738585072014E−308; Maximum nonzero values: ±1.7976931348623157E+308
`BIT[(M)]`	0 to 2^M-1, $1 \leq M \leq 64$

Table 3.6   **Numeric Data Type Storage Requirements**

Type Name	Storage Required
TINYINT[(M)]	1 byte
SMALLINT[(M)]	2 bytes
MEDIUMINT[(M)]	3 bytes
INT[(M)]	4 bytes
BIGINT[(M)]	8 bytes
DECIMAL([M[,D]])	Depends on M, D
FLOAT[(M,D)]	4 bytes
DOUBLE[(M,D)]	8 bytes
BIT[(M)]	Depends on M

Storage for DECIMAL values depends on the number of digits on the left and right sides of the decimal point. For each side, 4 bytes are required for each multiple of nine digits, plus 1 to 4 bytes if there are any remaining digits. Storage per value is the sum of the left and right side storage.

A BIT(M) value requires approximately (M+7)/8 bytes.

3.2.4.1   Exact-Value Numeric Data Types

The exact-value data types include the integer types and the fixed-point DECIMAL type.

The integer types in MySQL are TINYINT, SMALLINT, MEDIUMINT, INT, and BIGINT. INTEGER is a synonym for INT. These types vary in the range of values they can represent and in the amount of storage space they require. (The larger the range, the more storage is required.) Integer columns can be defined as UNSIGNED to prohibit negative values; this shifts the range for the column upward to begin at 0.

Integer column definitions can include an optional display size M, which should be an integer from 1 to 255. It represents the number of characters used to display values for the column. For example, MEDIUMINT(4) specifies a MEDIUMINT column with a display width of 4. For integer column definitions with no explicit width, a default width is assigned. The defaults are the lengths of the "longest" values for each type.

The display size M for an integer column relates only to the number of characters used to display column values. It has *nothing* to do with the number of bytes of storage space required. For example, BIGINT values require 8 bytes of storage regardless of the display width. It is not possible to magically cut the required storage space for a BIGINT column in half by defining it as BIGINT(4). Nor does M have anything to do with the permitted range of values. If you define a column as `INT(3)`, that doesn't restrict it to a maximum value of 999. Also, displayed values are not chopped to M characters. If the printable representation of a particular value requires more than M characters, MySQL displays the full value.

`DECIMAL` is a fixed-point type: Values have a fixed number of decimals. The significance of this fact is that `DECIMAL` values are not subject to roundoff error the way that floating-point values are—a property that makes `DECIMAL` especially applicable to storing currency values.

`NUMERIC` and `FIXED` are synonyms for `DECIMAL`.

`DECIMAL` columns can be defined as `UNSIGNED`. Unlike the integer types, defining a `DECIMAL` type as `UNSIGNED` doesn't shift the type's range upward, it merely eliminates the negative end.

`DECIMAL` column definitions can include a maximum number of significant digits M and a number of decimal places D (that is, precision and scale). The value of M should be from 1 to 65. The value of D should be from 0 to 30 and no greater than M.

M and D are optional. If D is omitted, it defaults to 0. If M is omitted as well, it defaults to 10. In other words, the following equivalences hold:

```
DECIMAL = DECIMAL(10) = DECIMAL(10,0)
DECIMAL(n) = DECIMAL(n,0)
```

The values of M and D determine the maximum possible range for `DECIMAL`. If you vary M and hold D fixed, the range becomes larger as M becomes larger (see Table 3.7). If you hold M fixed and vary D, the range becomes smaller as D becomes larger (see Table 3.8).

Table 3.7   **How M Affects the Range of `DECIMAL` (M, D)**

Type Specification	Range
`DECIMAL(4,1)`	−999.9 to 999.9
`DECIMAL(5,1)`	−9999.9 to 9999.9
`DECIMAL(6,1)`	−99999.9 to 99999.9

Table 3.8   **How D Affects the Range of `DECIMAL` (M, D)**

Type Specification	Range
`DECIMAL(4,0)`	−9999 to 9999
`DECIMAL(4,1)`	−999.9 to 999.9
`DECIMAL(4,2)`	−99.99 to 99.99

3.2.4.2   Approximate-Value Numeric Data Types

MySQL provides two floating-point types, FLOAT and DOUBLE, that store approximate-value numbers. DOUBLE PRECISION is a synonym for DOUBLE. The REAL type is a synonym for DOUBLE by default, or for FLOAT if the REAL_AS_DEFAULT SQL mode is enabled.

Floating-point types can be defined as UNSIGNED. This eliminates the negative end of the type's range.

Just as for DECIMAL, floating-point column definitions can include a maximum number of significant digits M and a number of decimal places D (that is, precision and scale). The value of M should be from 1 to 255. The value of D should be from 0 to 30 and no greater than M.

M and D are optional. If you omit both from a column definition, values are stored to the full precision supported by your hardware.

FLOAT(p) syntax also is permitted. However, whereas p stands for the required number of bits of precision in standard SQL, it is treated differently in MySQL. p may range from 0 to 53 and is used only to determine whether the column stores single-precision or double-precision values. For p values from 0 to 24, the column is treated as single precision. For values from 25 to 53, the column is treated as double precision. That is, the column is treated as a FLOAT or DOUBLE with no M or D values.

3.2.4.3   The BIT Data Type

The BIT data type holds bit-field values. BIT column definitions can include an optional maximum width M that indicates the "width" of the column in bits. M should be an integer from 1 to 64. If omitted, M defaults to 1.

Values retrieved from BIT columns are not displayed in printable form by default. To display a printable representation of bit-field values, add zero or use CAST():

```
mysql> CREATE TABLE t (b BIT(3));  # 3-bit column; holds values 0 to 7
mysql> INSERT INTO t (b) VALUES(0),(b'11'),(b'101'),(b'111');
mysql> SELECT b+0, CAST(b AS UNSIGNED) FROM t;
+------+---------------------+
| b+0  | CAST(b AS UNSIGNED)  |
+------+---------------------+
|    0 |                   0 |
|    3 |                   3 |
|    5 |                   5 |
|    7 |                   7 |
+------+---------------------+
```

The BIN() function is useful for displaying bit-field values or the result of computations on them in binary notation:

```
mysql> SELECT BIN(b), BIN(b & b'101'), BIN(b | b'101') FROM t;
+--------+-----------------+-----------------+
| BIN(b) | BIN(b & b'101') | BIN(b | b'101') |
```

```
+--------+----------------+-----------------+
| 0      | 0              | 101             |
| 11     | 1              | 111             |
| 101    | 101            | 101             |
| 111    | 101            | 111             |
+--------+----------------+-----------------+
```

For octal or hexadecimal display, use `OCT()` or `HEX()` instead.

3.2.4.4   Numeric Data Type Attributes

The UNSIGNED attribute prohibits negative values. It is permitted for all numeric types except BIT, but is most commonly used with integer types. Making an integer column UNSIGNED doesn't change the "size" of the underlying data type's range; it shifts the range upward. Consider this table definition:

```
CREATE TABLE mytbl
(
  itiny    TINYINT,
  itiny_u TINYINT UNSIGNED
);
```

`itiny` and `itiny_u` are TINYINT columns with a range of 256 values, but they differ in the set of permitted values. The range of `itiny` is –128 to 127, whereas the range of `itiny_u` is shifted up, resulting in a range of 0 to 255.

UNSIGNED is useful for columns into which you plan to store information that doesn't take on negative values, such as population counts or attendance figures. Were you to use a signed column for such values, you would use only half of the data type's range. Making the column UNSIGNED effectively doubles the usable range. For example, if you use the column for sequence numbers, it takes twice as long to run out of values if you make it UNSIGNED.

You can also specify UNSIGNED for DECIMAL or floating-point columns, although the effect is slightly different from that for integer columns. The range does not shift upward; instead, the upper end remains unchanged and the lower end becomes zero (effectively cutting the range in half).

The SIGNED attribute is permitted for all numeric types that permit UNSIGNED. Because such types are signed by default, SIGNED has no effect but to indicate explicitly that a column permits negative values.

The ZEROFILL attribute is permitted for all numeric types except BIT. It causes displayed values for the column to be padded with leading zeros to the display width. Use ZEROFILL when you want to make sure column values always display using a given number of digits. Actually, it's more accurate to say "a given *minimum* number of digits" because values wider than the display width are displayed in full without being chopped. You can see this by issuing the following statements. Note that the final value is displayed in full, even though it is wider than the column's display width.

```
mysql> DROP TABLE IF EXISTS mytbl;
mysql> CREATE TABLE mytbl (my_zerofill INT(5) ZEROFILL);
mysql> INSERT INTO mytbl VALUES(1),(100),(10000),(1000000);
mysql> SELECT my_zerofill FROM mytbl;
+-------------+
| my_zerofill |
+-------------+
|       00001 |
|       00100 |
|       10000 |
|     1000000 |
+-------------+
```

If you specify the ZEROFILL attribute for a column, it automatically becomes UNSIGNED as well.

One other attribute, AUTO_INCREMENT, is permitted for integer or floating-point data types (although use with floating-point types is rare). Specify the AUTO_INCREMENT attribute when you want to generate a series of unique identifier values. When you insert NULL into an AUTO_INCREMENT column, MySQL generates the next sequence value and stores it in the column. Normally, unless you take steps to cause otherwise, AUTO_INCREMENT values begin at 1 and increase by 1 for each new row. The sequence may be affected if you delete rows from the table. That is, sequence values might be reused; it is storage engine-dependent whether this occurs.

You can have at most one AUTO_INCREMENT column in a table. The column should have the NOT NULL constraint, and it must be indexed. Generally, an AUTO_INCREMENT column is indexed as a PRIMARY KEY or UNIQUE index. Also, because sequence values always are positive, you normally define the column UNSIGNED as well. For example, you can define an AUTO_INCREMENT column in any of the following ways:

```
CREATE TABLE ai (i INT UNSIGNED NOT NULL AUTO_INCREMENT PRIMARY KEY);
CREATE TABLE ai (i INT UNSIGNED NOT NULL AUTO_INCREMENT UNIQUE);
CREATE TABLE ai (i INT UNSIGNED NOT NULL AUTO_INCREMENT, PRIMARY KEY (i));
CREATE TABLE ai (i INT UNSIGNED NOT NULL AUTO_INCREMENT, UNIQUE (i));
```

The first two forms shown specify the index information as part of the column definition. The second two specify the index as a separate clause of the CREATE TABLE statement. Using a separate clause is optional if the index includes only the AUTO_INCREMENT column. To create a multiple-column index that includes the AUTO_INCREMENT column, you must use a separate clause. (For an example, see Section 3.4.2.1, "AUTO_INCREMENT for MyISAM Tables.")

It is always permitted to define an AUTO_INCREMENT column explicitly as NOT NULL, but if you omit NOT NULL, MySQL adds it automatically.

Section 3.4, "Working with Sequences," discusses the behavior of AUTO_INCREMENT columns further.

Following the attributes just described, which are specific to numeric columns, you can specify NULL or NOT NULL. If you do not specify NULL or NOT NULL for a numeric column, it permits NULL by default (usually; as just mentioned, AUTO_INCREMENT columns default to NOT NULL).

You can also specify a default value using the DEFAULT attribute. The following table contains three INT columns, having default values of -1, 1, and NULL:

```
CREATE TABLE t
(
  i1 INT DEFAULT -1,
  i2 INT DEFAULT 1,
  i3 INT DEFAULT NULL
);
```

Section 3.2.3, "Specifying Column Default Values," describes the rules that MySQL uses for assigning a default value if a column definition includes no DEFAULT clause.

3.2.4.5 Choosing Numeric Data Types

When you choose a type for a numeric column, consider the range of values to be represented and choose the smallest type that covers the range. Choosing a larger type wastes space, leading to tables that are unnecessarily large and that cannot be processed as efficiently as if you had chosen a smaller type. TINYINT is the best for integers if the range of values in your data is small, such as a person's age or number of siblings. MEDIUMINT can represent millions of values and can be used for many more types of information, at some additional cost in storage space. BIGINT has the largest range of all but requires twice as much storage as the next smallest integer type (INT) and should be used only when really necessary. For floating-point values, DOUBLE takes twice as much space as FLOAT. Unless you need exceptionally high precision or an extremely large range of values, you can represent your data at half the storage cost by using FLOAT instead of DOUBLE.

Every numeric column's type determines its range of values. If you attempt to insert a value that lies outside the column's range, the result depends on whether strict SQL mode is enabled. If it is, an out of range value results in an error. If strict mode is not enabled, truncation occurs: MySQL clips the value to the appropriate endpoint of the range, uses the result, and generates a warning.

Value truncation occurs according to the range of the data type, not the display width. For example, a SMALLINT(3) column has a display width of 3 and a range from −32768 to 32767. The value 12345 is wider than the display width but within the range of the column, so it is inserted without clipping and retrieved as 12345. The value 99999 is outside the range, so it is clipped to 32767 when inserted. Subsequent retrievals return the value 32767.

For fixed-point or floating-point columns, if values are stored that have more digits in the fractional part than permitted by the column specification, rounding occurs. If you store 1.23456 in a FLOAT(8,1) column, the result is 1.2. If you store the same value in a FLOAT(8,4) column, the result is 1.2346. This means you should define such columns with a sufficient number of decimals to store values as precise as you require. If you require accuracy to thousandths, don't define a type with only two decimal places.

3.2.5   String Data Types

MySQL provides several data types for storing string values. Strings are often used for text values like these:

```
'N. Bertram, et al.'
'Pencils (no. 2 lead)'
'123 Elm St.'
'Monograph Series IX'
```

But strings are actually "generic" types in the sense that you can use them to represent any value. For example, you can use binary string types to hold binary data, such as images, sounds, or compressed gzip output.

Table 3.9 shows all the types provided by MySQL for defining string-valued columns, and the maximum size and storage requirements of each type. M represents the maximum length of column values (in bytes for binary strings and characters for nonbinary strings), and L represents the actual length of a given value in bytes. w is the number of bytes required for the widest character in the column's character set. The BLOB and TEXT types each have several variants that are distinguished by the maximum size of values they can hold.

Table 3.9   **String Data Types**

Type Name	Maximum Size	Storage Required
BINARY[(M)]	M bytes	M bytes
VARBINARY(M)	M bytes	L + 1 or 2 bytes
CHAR[(M)]	M characters	$M \times w$ bytes
VARCHAR(M)	M characters	L + 1 or 2 bytes
TINYBLOB, TINYTEXT	2^8–1 bytes	L + 1 bytes
BLOB, TEXT	2^{16}–1 bytes	L + 2 bytes
MEDIUMBLOB, MEDIUMTEXT	2^{24}–1 bytes	L + 3 bytes
LONGBLOB, LONGTEXT	2^{32}–1 bytes	L + 4 bytes
ENUM('value1','value2',...)	65,535 members	1 or 2 bytes
SET('value1','value2',...)	64 members	1, 2, 3, 4, or 8 bytes

Some types hold binary (byte) strings and others hold nonbinary (character) strings. For example, BINARY(20) holds 20 bytes, whereas CHAR(20) holds 20 characters (which requires more than 20 bytes for multi-byte characters). Section 3.1.2, "String Values," characterizes the differences between byte and character semantics for binary and nonbinary strings. Each binary string type for byte strings has a corresponding nonbinary type for character strings, as shown in Table 3.10.

Table 3.10   **Corresponding Binary and Nonbinary String Types**

Binary String Type	Nonbinary String Type
BINARY	CHAR
VARBINARY	VARCHAR
BLOB	TEXT

Each nonbinary string type, as well as ENUM and SET, can be assigned a character set and collation. Different columns can be assigned different character sets. Section 3.2.5.5, "String Data Type Attributes," discusses character set assignment.

BINARY and CHAR are fixed-length string types. For columns of these types, MySQL allocates the same amount of storage for every value and pads those that are shorter than the column length. Padding uses 0x00 bytes for BINARY and spaces for CHAR. Because CHAR(M) must be able to represent the largest possible string in the column's character set, each column requires $M \times w$ bytes, where w is the number of bytes required for the widest character in the character set. For example, ujis characters take from 1 to 3 bytes, so CHAR(20) must be allocated 60 bytes in case a value requires 3 bytes for all 20 characters.

Other string types are variable length. The amount of storage taken by a value varies from row to row and depends on the maximum permitted length of values to be stored in the column. This length is represented by L in the table for variable-length types. The extra bytes required in addition to L are the number of bytes needed to store the length of the value. MySQL handles variable-length values by storing both the content of the value and a prefix that records its length. These extra prefix "length bytes" are treated as an unsigned integer. There is a correspondence between a variable-length type's maximum length, the number of length bytes required for that type, and the range of the unsigned integer type that uses the same number of bytes. For example, a MEDIUMBLOB value may be up to $2^{24}-1$ bytes long and requires 3 bytes to record the length. The 3-byte integer type MEDIUMINT has a maximum unsigned value of $2^{24}-1$. That's not a coincidence.

The length prefix for VARBINARY and VARCHAR requires 1 byte if the maximum length of column values in bytes is less than 256, 2 bytes otherwise.

MySQL stores values for all string types except ENUM and SET as a sequence of bytes and interprets them either as bytes or characters depending on whether the type holds binary or nonbinary strings. Values that are too long to store are chopped to fit. (In strict mode, an error occurs instead unless the chopped characters are spaces.) But string types range from very small to very large, with the largest type able to hold nearly 4GB of data, so you should be able to find something long enough to avoid truncation of your information. (The effective maximum column size actually is imposed by the maximum packet size of the client/server communication protocol, which is 1MB by default.)

For ENUM and SET, the column definition includes a list of legal string values, but ENUM and SET values are stored internally as numbers, as detailed later in Section 3.2.5.4, "The ENUM and SET

Data Types." Attempting to store a value not in the list causes the value to be converted to ' ' (the empty string) unless strict mode is enabled. In strict mode, an error occurs instead.

3.2.5.1 The CHAR and VARCHAR Data Types

The CHAR and VARCHAR string types hold nonbinary strings, and thus have a character set and collation.

The primary differences between CHAR and VARCHAR lie in whether they have a fixed or variable length, and in how trailing spaces are treated:

- CHAR is a fixed-length type, whereas VARCHAR is a variable-length type.
- Values retrieved from CHAR columns have trailing spaces removed. For a CHAR(M) column, values that are shorter than M characters are padded with spaces to a length of M when stored, but trailing spaces are stripped when the values are retrieved. Enabling the PAD_CHAR_TO_FULL_LENGTH SQL mode causes retrieved CHAR column values to retain trailing spaces.
- For VARCHAR, trailing spaces are retained both for storage and retrieval.

CHAR columns can be defined with a maximum length M from 0 to 255. M is optional for CHAR and defaults to 1 if missing. Note that CHAR(0) is legal. A CHAR(0) column can be used to represent on/off values if you permit it to be NULL. Values in such a column can have one of two values: NULL or the empty string. A CHAR(0) column takes very little storage space in the table—only a single bit.

The syntactically permitted range of M for VARCHAR(M) is 1 to 65,535, but the effective maximum number of characters is less than 65,535 because MySQL has a maximum row size of 65,535 bytes. That has certain implications:

- A long VARCHAR requires two length bytes, which count against the row size.
- Use of multi-byte characters reduces the number of characters that can fit within the maximum row size.
- Inclusion of other columns in the table reduces the amount of space for the VARCHAR column in the row.

Keep in mind two general principles when choosing between CHAR and VARCHAR data types:

- If your values all are M characters long, a VARCHAR(M) column actually will use more space than a CHAR(M) column due to the extra byte or bytes required to record the length of values. On the other hand, if your values vary in length, VARCHAR columns have the advantage of taking less space. A CHAR(M) column always takes M characters, even if it is empty or NULL.
- If you're using MyISAM tables and your values don't vary much in length, CHAR is a better choice than VARCHAR because the MyISAM storage engine can process fixed-length rows more efficiently than variable-length rows. See Section 5.4, "Choosing Table Storage Formats for Efficient Queries."

3.2.5.2 The `BINARY` and `VARBINARY` Data Types

The `BINARY` and `VARBINARY` types are similar to `CHAR` and `VARCHAR`, with the following differences:

- `CHAR` and `VARCHAR` are nonbinary types that store characters and have a character set and collation. Comparisons are based on the collating sequence.

- `BINARY` and `VARBINARY` are binary types that store bytes and have no character set or collation. Comparisons are based on numeric byte values.

For a `BINARY(M)` column, values that are shorter than M bytes are padded with `0x00` bytes to a length of M when stored. Nothing is stripped on retrieval. For `VARBINARY`, no padding occurs when values are stored and no stripping occurs for retrieval.

3.2.5.3 The `BLOB` and `TEXT` Data Types

A "blob" is a binary large object—basically, a container that can hold anything you want to toss into it, and that can be as big as you like, up to 4GB. In MySQL, the `BLOB` type is really a family of types (`TINYBLOB`, `BLOB`, `MEDIUMBLOB`, `LONGBLOB`). These types are identical except in the maximum amount of information they can hold (see Table 3.9). `BLOB` columns store binary strings. They are useful for storing data that may grow very large or that may vary widely in size from row to row. Some examples are compressed data, encrypted data, images, and sounds.

MySQL also has a family of `TEXT` types (`TINYTEXT`, `TEXT`, `MEDIUMTEXT`, `LONGTEXT`). These are similar to the corresponding `BLOB` types, except that `TEXT` types store nonbinary strings rather than binary strings. That is, they store characters rather than bytes, and are associated with a character set and collation. This results in the general differences between binary and nonbinary strings that were described earlier in Section 3.1.2, "String Values." For example, comparisons of `BLOB` values use byte units. Comparisons of `TEXT` values use character units and are based on the column collation.

However, the maximum size for the `TEXT` types is the same as for the `BLOB` types. That is, the maximum size is measured in bytes for both, rather than in bytes for `BLOB` types and in characters for `TEXT` types (see Table 3.9).

`BLOB` or `TEXT` columns sometimes can be indexed, depending on the storage engine you're using:

- The InnoDB and MyISAM storage engines support `BLOB` and `TEXT` indexing. However, you must specify a prefix size to be used for the index. This avoids creating index entries that might be huge and thereby defeat any benefits to be gained by that index. The exception is that prefixes are not used for `FULLTEXT` indexes on `TEXT` columns. `FULLTEXT` searches are based on the entire content of the indexed columns; any prefix you specify is ignored.

- MEMORY tables do not support `BLOB` and `TEXT` indexes because the MEMORY engine does not support `BLOB` or `TEXT` columns at all.

`BLOB` or `TEXT` columns may require special care:

- Due to the typical large variation in the size of `BLOB` and `TEXT` values, tables containing them are subject to high rates of fragmentation if many deletes and updates are done. If you're using a MyISAM table to store `BLOB` or `TEXT` values, a periodic `OPTIMIZE TABLE` reduces fragmentation and maintains good performance. For more information, see Chapter 5, "Query Optimization."

- The `max_sort_length` system variable influences `BLOB` and `TEXT` comparison and sorting operations. Only the first `max_sort_length` bytes of each value are used. (For `TEXT` columns that use a multi-byte character set, this means that comparisons might involve fewer than `max_sort_length` characters.) If this causes a problem with the default `max_sort_length` value of 1024, increase the value before performing comparisons.

- For very large values, you might need to configure the server to increase the value of the `max_allowed_packet` parameter. For more information, see Section 12.7.1, "General-Purpose System Variables for Server Tuning." You will also need to increase the packet size on the client side for any client that wants to use very large values. The `mysql` and `mysqldump` clients support setting this value directly using a startup option.

3.2.5.4   The `ENUM` and `SET` Data Types

`ENUM` and `SET` are special string data types that permit only values chosen from a fixed (predefined) list of permitted strings. The primary difference between them is that `ENUM` column values must consist of exactly one member of the list of values, whereas `SET` column values may contain any or all members of the list. In other words, `ENUM` is used for values that are mutually exclusive, whereas `SET` permits multiple choices from the list.

The `ENUM` data type defines an enumeration that can have up to 65,535 members. `ENUM` columns may be assigned values consisting of exactly one member chosen from the list of values specified at table-creation time. Enumerations are commonly used to represent category values. For example, values in a column defined as `ENUM('N','Y')` can be either `'N'` or `'Y'`. Or you can use `ENUM` for such things as available sizes or colors for a product or for answers to multiple-choice questions in a survey or questionnaire where a single response must be selected:

```
employees ENUM('less than 100','100-500','501-1500','more than 1500')
color ENUM('red','green','blue','black')
size ENUM('S','M','L','XL','XXL')
vote ENUM('Yes','No','Undecided')
```

If you are processing selections from a Web page that includes mutually exclusive radio buttons, you can use an `ENUM` to represent the options from which a visitor to your site chooses. For example, if you run an online pizza-ordering service, `ENUM` columns can be used to represent the type of crust and size of pizza a customer orders:

```
crust ENUM('thin','regular','pan style','deep dish')
size ENUM('small','medium','large')
```

The SET type is similar to ENUM in the sense that when you create a SET column, you specify a list of permitted set members. The set can have up to 64 members. Unlike ENUM, each column value can consist of any number of members from the set. One use for SET is when you have a fixed set of values that are not mutually exclusive as they are in an ENUM column. For example, the online pizza service might have a set of check boxes for ingredients that a customer wants as pizza toppings, several of which might be chosen. You could use a SET to represent these ingredients:

```
SET('pepperoni','sausage','mushrooms','onions','ripe olives')
```

Then particular SET values represent those toppings actually selected by customers:

```
'pepperoni,mushrooms'
'sausage,onions'
'sausage,mushrooms,ripe olives'
'onions'
''
```

The final value shown (the empty string) means that the customer ordered no toppings. This is a permitted value for any SET column.

A SET column *definition* is written as a list of individual strings separated by commas to indicate what the set members are. A SET column *value*, on the other hand, is written as a single string. If the value consists of multiple set members, the members are separated within the string by commas. This means you shouldn't use a string containing a comma as a SET member.

The way you define the permitted value list for an ENUM or SET column is significant several ways:

- The list determines the possible permitted values for the column, as has already been discussed.

- If an ENUM or SET column has a collation that is not case sensitive, you can insert permitted values in any lettercase and they will be recognized. However, the lettercase of the strings as specified in the column definition determines the lettercase of column values when they are retrieved later. For example, if you have an ENUM('Y','N') column and you store 'y' and 'n' in it, the values are displayed as 'Y' and 'N' when you retrieve them. If the column has a case sensitive or binary collation, you must insert values using exactly the lettercase used in the column definition or the values will treated as invalid. On the other hand, you can have distinct elements that differ only in lettercase, something not true when you use a collation that is not case sensitive.

- The order of values in an ENUM definition is the order used for sorting. The order of values in a SET definition also determines sort order, although the relationship is more complicated because column values may contain multiple set members.

- When MySQL displays a SET value that consists of multiple set members, the order in which it lists the members within the value is determined by the order in which they appear in the SET column definition.

ENUM and SET are classified as string types because enumeration and set members are specified as strings when you create columns of these types. However, the ENUM and SET types actually have a split personality: The members are stored internally as numbers and you can work with them as such. This means that ENUM and SET types are more efficient than other string types because they often can be handled using numeric operations rather than string operations. It also means that ENUM and SET values can be used in either string or numeric contexts. Finally, ENUM and SET columns can cause confusion if you use them in string context but expect them to behave as numbers, or vice versa.

MySQL sequentially numbers ENUM members in the column definition beginning with 1. (The value 0 is reserved for the error member, which is represented in string form by the empty string.) The number of enumeration values determines the storage size of an ENUM column. 1 byte can represent 256 values and 2 bytes can represent 65,536 values. (Compare this to the ranges of the 1-byte and 2-byte integer types TINYINT UNSIGNED and SMALLINT UNSIGNED.) Thus, counting the error member, the maximum number of enumeration members is 65,536 and the storage size depends on whether there are more than 256 members. You can specify a maximum of 65,535 (not 65,536) members in the ENUM definition because MySQL reserves a spot for the error member as an implicit member of every enumeration. When you assign an invalid value to an ENUM column, MySQL assigns the error member. (In strict mode, an error occurs instead.)

The following example demonstrates that you can retrieve ENUM values in either string or numeric form (which shows the numeric ordering of enumeration members and also that the NULL value has no number in the ordering):

```
mysql> CREATE TABLE e_table (e ENUM('jane','fred','will','marcia'));
mysql> INSERT INTO e_table
    -> VALUES('jane'),('fred'),('will'),('marcia'),(NULL);
mysql> SELECT e, e+0, e+1, e*3 FROM e_table;
+--------+------+------+------+
| e      | e+0  | e+1  | e*3  |
+--------+------+------+------+
| jane   |    1 |    2 |    3 |
| fred   |    2 |    3 |    6 |
| will   |    3 |    4 |    9 |
| marcia |    4 |    5 |   12 |
| NULL   | NULL | NULL | NULL |
+--------+------+------+------+
```

You can compare ENUM members either by name or number:

```
mysql> SELECT e FROM e_table WHERE e='will';
+------+
| e    |
+------+
| will |
+------+
```

```
mysql> SELECT e FROM e_table WHERE e=3;
+------+
| e    |
+------+
| will |
+------+
```

It is possible to define the empty string as a permitted enumeration member, but this will only cause confusion. The string is assigned a nonzero numeric value, just as any other member listed in the definition. However, an empty string also is used for the error member that has a numeric value of 0, so it would correspond to two internal numeric element values. In the following example, assigning the invalid enumeration value 'x' to the ENUM column causes the error member to be assigned. This is distinguishable from the empty string member listed in the column definition only when retrieved in numeric form:

```
mysql> CREATE TABLE t (e ENUM('a','','b'));
mysql> INSERT INTO t VALUES('a'),(''),('b'),('x');
mysql> SELECT e, e+0 FROM t;
+------+------+
| e    | e+0  |
+------+------+
| a    |    1 |
|      |    2 |
| b    |    3 |
|      |    0 |
+------+------+
```

In strict mode, assigning the invalid value 'x' causes an error and no value is stored.

The numeric representation of SET columns is a little different from that for ENUM columns. Set members are not numbered sequentially. Instead, members correspond to successive individual bits in the SET value. The first set member corresponds to bit 0, the second member corresponds to bit 1, and so on. In other words, the numeric values of SET members all are powers of two. The empty string corresponds to a numeric SET value of 0.

SET values are stored as bit values. Eight set members per byte can be stored this way, so the storage size for a SET column is determined by the number of set members, up to a maximum of 64 members. SET values take 1, 2, 3, 4, or 8 bytes for set sizes of 1 to 8, 9 to 16, 17 to 24, 25 to 32, and 33 to 64 members.

The representation of a SET as a set of bits is what enables a SET value to consist of multiple set members. Any combination of bits can be turned on in the value, so the value may consist of any combination of the strings in the SET definition that correspond to those bits.

The following example shows the relationship between the string and numeric forms of a SET column. It displays the numeric value in both decimal and binary form:

```
mysql> CREATE TABLE s_table (s SET('table','lamp','chair','stool'));
mysql> INSERT INTO s_table
```

```
    -> VALUES('table'),('lamp'),('chair'),('stool'),(''),(NULL);
mysql> SELECT s, s+0, BIN(s+0) FROM s_table;
+-------+------+----------+
| s     | s+0  | BIN(s+0) |
+-------+------+----------+
| table |    1 | 1        |
| lamp  |    2 | 10       |
| chair |    4 | 100      |
| stool |    8 | 1000     |
|       |    0 | 0        |
| NULL  | NULL | NULL     |
+-------+------+----------+
```

If you assign to the column s a value of 'lamp,stool', MySQL stores it internally as 10 (binary 1010) because 'lamp' has a value of 2 (bit 1) and 'stool' has a value of 8 (bit 3).

When you assign values to SET columns, the substrings need not be listed in the same order that you used to define the column. However, when you retrieve the value later, members are displayed within the value in definition order. Also, if you assign to a SET column a value containing substrings that are not listed as set members, those strings drop out and the column is assigned a value consisting of the remaining substrings. When you retrieve the value later, the invalid substrings will not be present.

If you assign a value of 'chair,couch,table' to the column s in s_table, two things happen:

- 'couch' drops out because it's not a member of the set. This occurs because MySQL determines which bits correspond to each substring of the value to be assigned and turns them on in the stored value. 'couch' corresponds to no bit and is ignored.

- When you retrieve the value later, it appears as 'table,chair'. On retrieval, MySQL constructs the string value from the numeric value by scanning the bits in order, which automatically reorders the substrings to the order used when the column was defined. This behavior also means that if you specify a set member more than once in a value, it will appear only once when you retrieve the value. If you assign 'lamp,lamp,lamp' to a SET column, it will be simply 'lamp' when retrieved.

In strict mode, use of an invalid SET member causes an error instead and the value is not stored. In the preceding example, assigning a value containing 'couch' would cause an error and the assignment would fail.

The fact that MySQL reorders members in a SET value means that if you search for values using a string, you must list members in the proper order. If you insert 'chair,table' and then search for 'chair,table' you won't find the row; you must look for it as 'table,chair'.

Sorting and indexing of ENUM and SET columns is done according to the internal (numeric) values of column values. The following example might appear to be incorrect because the values are not displayed in alphanumeric order:

```
mysql> SELECT e FROM e_table ORDER BY e;
+--------+
| e      |
+--------+
| NULL   |
| jane   |
| fred   |
| will   |
| marcia |
+--------+
```

To better see what's going on, retrieve both the string and numeric forms of the ENUM values:

```
mysql> SELECT e, e+0 FROM e_table ORDER BY e;
+--------+------+
| e      | e+0  |
+--------+------+
| NULL   | NULL |
| jane   |    1 |
| fred   |    2 |
| will   |    3 |
| marcia |    4 |
+--------+------+
```

If you have a fixed set of values that you want to sort in a particular order, you can exploit the ENUM sorting properties: Represent the values as an ENUM column in a table and list the enumeration values in the column definition in the order that you want them to be sorted. Suppose that you have a table representing personnel for a sports organization, such as a football team, and that you want to sort output by personnel position so that it comes out in a particular order, such as coaches, assistant coaches, quarterbacks, running backs, receivers, linemen, and so on. Define the column as an ENUM and list the enumeration elements in the order that you want to see them. Then column values automatically will come out in that order for sort operations.

For cases where you want an ENUM to sort in normal lexical order, you can convert the column to a non-ENUM string by using CAST() and sorting the result:

```
mysql> SELECT CAST(e AS CHAR) AS e_str FROM e_table ORDER BY e_str;
+--------+
| e_str  |
+--------+
| NULL   |
| fred   |
| jane   |
| marcia |
| will   |
+--------+
```

CAST() doesn't change the displayed values, but has the effect in this statement of performing an ENUM-to-string conversion that alters their sorting properties so they sort as strings.

3.2.5.5 String Data Type Attributes

The attributes unique to the string data types are CHARACTER SET (or CHARSET) and COLLATE for designating a character set and collating order. You can specify these as options for the table itself to set its defaults, or for individual columns to override the table defaults. (Actually, each database also has a default character set and collation, as does the server itself. These defaults sometimes come into play during table creation, as we'll see later.)

The CHARACTER SET and COLLATE attributes apply to the CHAR, VARCHAR, TEXT, ENUM, and SET data types. They do not apply to the binary string data types (BINARY, VARBINARY, and BLOB), because those types contain byte strings, not character strings.

When you specify the CHARACTER SET and COLLATE attributes, whether at the column, table, or database level, the following rules apply:

- The character set must be one that the server supports. To display the available character sets, use SHOW CHARACTER SET.

- For a definition that includes both CHARACTER SET and COLLATE, the character set and collation must be compatible. For example, with a character set of latin2, you could use a collation of latin2_croatian_ci, but not latin1_bin. To display the collations for each character set, use SHOW COLLATION.

- For a definition with CHARACTER SET but without COLLATE, the character set's default collation is used.

- For a definition with COLLATE but without CHARACTER SET, the character set is determined from the first part of the collation name.

To see how these rules apply, consider the following statement. It creates a table that uses several character sets:

```
CREATE TABLE mytbl
(
  c1   CHAR(10),
  c2   CHAR(40) CHARACTER SET latin2,
  c3   CHAR(10) COLLATE latin1_german1_ci,
  c4   BINARY(40)
) CHARACTER SET utf8;
```

The resulting table has utf8 as its default character set. No COLLATE table option is given, so the default table collation is the default utf8 collation (which is utf8_general_ci). The c1 column definition contains no CHARACTER SET or COLLATE attributes of its own, so the table defaults are used for it. The table-level character set and collation are not used for c2, c3, and c4: c2 and c3 have their own character set information, and c4 has a binary string type, so the character set attributes do not apply. For c2, the collation is latin2_general_ci, the default collation for latin2. For c3, the character set is latin1, as implied by the collation name latin1_german1_ci.

To see character set information for an existing table, use SHOW CREATE TABLE:

```
mysql> SHOW CREATE TABLE mytbl\G
*************************** 1. row ***************************
       Table: mytbl
Create Table: CREATE TABLE `mytbl` (
  `c1` char(10) DEFAULT NULL,
  `c2` char(40) CHARACTER SET latin2 DEFAULT NULL,
  `c3` char(10) CHARACTER SET latin1 COLLATE latin1_german1_ci DEFAULT NULL,
  `c4` binary(40) DEFAULT NULL
) ENGINE=InnoDB DEFAULT CHARSET=utf8
```

If SHOW CREATE TABLE does not display a column character set, it is the same as the table default character set. If it does not display a column collation, it is the character set default collation.

You can also add the FULL keyword to SHOW COLUMNS to cause it to display collation information (from which character sets can be derived):

```
mysql> SHOW FULL COLUMNS FROM mytbl;
+-------+------------+-------------------+------+-----+---------+...
| Field | Type       | Collation         | Null | Key | Default |...
+-------+------------+-------------------+------+-----+---------+...
| c1    | char(10)   | utf8_general_ci   | YES  |     | NULL    |...
| c2    | char(40)   | latin2_general_ci | YES  |     | NULL    |...
| c3    | char(10)   | latin1_german1_ci | YES  |     | NULL    |...
| c4    | binary(40) | NULL              | YES  |     | NULL    |...
+-------+------------+-------------------+------+-----+---------+...
```

The preceding discussion mentions column and table character set assignments, but character sets actually can be designated at the column, table, database, or server level. When MySQL processes a character column definition, it determines which character set to use for it by trying the following rules in order:

1. If the column definition includes a character set, use that set. This includes the case where only a COLLATE attribute is present, because that implies which character set to use.

2. Otherwise, if the table definition includes a table character set option, use that set.

3. Otherwise, use the database character set as the table default character set, which also becomes the column character set. If the database was never assigned a character set explicitly, the database character set is taken from the server character set.

In other words, MySQL searches up through the levels at which character sets may be specified until it finds a character set defined, and then uses that for the column. The database always has a default character set, so the search process is guaranteed to terminate at the database level even if no character set is specified explicitly at any of the lower levels.

The character set name `binary` is special. Assigning the `binary` character set to a nonbinary string column is equivalent to defining the column using the corresponding binary string type. The following pairs of column definitions each show two equivalent definitions:

```
c1 CHAR(10) CHARACTER SET binary
c1 BINARY(10)

c2 VARCHAR(10) CHARACTER SET binary
c2 VARBINARY(10)

c3 TEXT CHARACTER SET binary
c3 BLOB
```

If you specify `CHARACTER SET binary` for a binary string column, it is ignored because the type already is binary. If you specify `CHARACTER SET binary` for an `ENUM` or `SET`, it is used as is.

If you assign the `binary` character set as a table option, it applies to each string column that does not have any character set information specified in its own definition.

MySQL provides some shortcut attributes for defining character columns:

- The `ASCII` attribute is shorthand for `CHARACTER SET latin1`.
- The `UNICODE` attribute is shorthand for `CHARACTER SET ucs2`.
- Specifying the `BINARY` attribute for a nonbinary string column, `ENUM`, or `SET` is shorthand for specifying the binary collation of the column's character set. For example, assuming a table default character set of `latin1`, these definitions are equivalent:

  ```
  c1 CHAR(10) BINARY
  c2 CHAR(10) CHARACTER SET latin1 BINARY
  c3 CHAR(10) CHARACTER SET latin1 COLLATE latin1_bin
  ```

  If you specify the `BINARY` attribute for a binary string column, it is ignored because the type already is binary.

The general attributes `NULL` or `NOT NULL` can be specified for any of the string types. If you specify neither one, `NULL` is the default. However, defining a string column as `NOT NULL` does not prevent you from storing an empty string (that is, `''`) in the column. In MySQL, an empty value is different from a missing value, so don't make the mistake of thinking that you can force a string column to contain nonempty values by defining it `NOT NULL`. If you require string values to be nonempty, that is a constraint you must enforce from within your own applications.

You can also specify a default value using a `DEFAULT` clause for all string data types except the `BLOB` and `TEXT` types. Section 3.2.3, "Specifying Column Default Values," describes the rules that MySQL uses for assigning a default value if a column definition includes no `DEFAULT` clause.

3.2.5.6 Choosing String Data Types

When you choose a data type for a string column, consider the following questions:

Are values represented as character or binary data? For character data, nonbinary string types are most appropriate. For binary data, use a binary string type.

Do you want comparisons to be lettercase-aware? If so, use one of the nonbinary string types, because those store characters and are associated with a character set and collation.

The case sensitivity of nonbinary string values for comparison and sorting purposes is controlled by the collation that you assign to them. To treat string values as equal regardless of lettercase, use a case-insensitive collation. Otherwise, use either a binary or case-sensitive collation. A binary collation compares character units using the numeric character codes. A case-sensitive collation compares character units using a specific collating order, which need not correspond to character code order. In either case, the lowercase and uppercase versions of a given character are considered distinct for comparisons. Suppose that 'mysql', 'MySQL', and 'MYSQL' are strings in the latin1 character set. They are all considered the same if compared using a case-insensitive collation such as latin1_swedish_ci, but as three different strings if compared using the binary latin1_bin collation or case-sensitive latin1_general_cs collation.

To use a string column both for case-sensitive and not case-sensitive comparisons, use a collation that corresponds to the type of comparison you will perform most often. For comparisons of the other type, apply the COLLATE operator to change the collation. For example, if mycol is a CHAR column that uses the latin1 character set, you can assign it the latin1_swedish_ci collation to perform case-insensitive comparisons by default. The following comparison is not case sensitive:

```
mycol = 'ABC'
```

For those times when you need case-sensitive comparisons, use the latin1_general_cs or latin1_bin collation. The following comparisons are case sensitive (it doesn't matter whether you apply the COLLATE operator to the left-hand string or the right-hand string):

```
mycol COLLATE latin1_general_cs = 'ABC'
mycol COLLATE latin1_bin = 'ABC'
mycol = 'ABC' COLLATE latin1_general_cs
mycol = 'ABC' COLLATE latin1_bin
```

Do you want to minimize storage requirements? If so, use a variable-length type, not a fixed-length type.

Will the permitted column values always be chosen from a fixed set of permitted values? If so, ENUM or SET might be a good choice.

ENUM also can be useful if you have a limited set of string values that you want to sort in some nonlexical order. Sorting of ENUM values occurs according to the order in which you list the enumeration values in the column definition, so you can make the values sort in any order you want.

Are trailing pad values significant? If values must be retrieved exactly as they are stored without addition or removal of trailing spaces (or 0x00 bytes, for binary data types) during storage or retrieval, use a TEXT or VARCHAR column for nonbinary strings and a BLOB or VARBINARY column for binary strings. This factor is important also if you are storing compressed, hashed, or encrypted values computed in such a way that the encoding method might result in trailing spaces. Table 3.11 shows how MySQL handles trailing padding for storage and retrieval operations on string data types.

Table 3.11   **String Data Type Pad-Value Handling**

Data Type	Storage	Retrieval	Result
CHAR	Space-padded	Stripped	Retrieved values have no trailing padding
BINARY	0x00-padded	No action	Retrieved values retain trailing padding
VARCHAR, VARBINARY	No action	No action	Trailing padding is not changed
TEXT, BLOB	No action	No action	Trailing padding is not changed

Enabling the PAD_CHAR_TO_FULL_LENGTH SQL mode causes retrieved CHAR column values to retain trailing spaces.

3.2.6   Temporal (Date and Time) Data Types

MySQL provides DATE, TIME, DATETIME, TIMESTAMP, and YEAR data types for storing temporal (time-related) values, with several important developments occurring in MySQL 5.6:

- MySQL 5.6.4 introduced fractional seconds support for the TIME, DATETIME, and TIMESTAMP data types. They now permit an optional fractional part of up to 6 digits (microseconds) precision.

- MySQL 5.6.5 introduced expanded support for automatically using the current timestamp as an initial value and for updates. For older versions, these properties are available for at most a single TIMESTAMP column in a table. They now can be used with any TIMESTAMP column, and for DATETIME columns as well.

- MySQL 5.6.6 deprecated YEAR(2) and creates such columns as YEAR(4) instead.

Table 3.12 shows the temporal data types and the range of legal values for each type. The ranges reflect the addition in MySQL 5.6.4 of fractional seconds support. (For versions before 5.6.4, ignore the fractional parts.)

Table 3.12   **Temporal Data Type Ranges**

Type Name	Range
DATE	`'1000-01-01'` to `'9999-12-31'`
TIME	`'-838:59:59[.000000]'` to `'838:59:59[.000000]'`
DATETIME	`'1000-01-01 00:00:00[.000000]'` to `'9999-12-31 23:59:59[.999999]'`
TIMESTAMP	`'1970-01-01 00:00:01[.000000]'` to `'2038-01-19 03:14:07[.999999]'`
YEAR	1901 to 2155

To declare a temporal column that includes a fractional part, write the definition as `type_name(fsp)`, where `type_name` is TIME, DATETIME, or TIMESTAMP, and `fsp` is the fractional seconds precision. For example, these TIME columns permit 3 and 6 fractional digits, respectively:

```
t1 TIME(3)
t2 TIME(6)
```

The `fsp` value must range from 0 to 6. If not given, the default is 0. For more information, see Section 3.2.6.5, "Fractional Second Capabilities for Temporal Types."

Table 3.13 shows the storage requirements for each temporal data type. Table 3.14 shows the extra storage for types declared to have a fractional seconds part.

Table 3.13   **Temporal Data Type Storage Requirements**

Type Name	Storage Required (Before 5.6.4)	Storage Required (5.6.4 and Up)
DATE	3 bytes	3 bytes
TIME	3 bytes	3 bytes + `fsp` storage
DATETIME	8 bytes	5 bytes + `fsp` storage
TIMESTAMP	4 bytes	4 bytes + `fsp` storage
YEAR	1 byte	1 byte

Table 3.14   **Fractional Seconds Part Storage Requirements**

Fractional Seconds Precision	Storage Required
0	0 bytes
1, 2	1 byte
3, 4	2 bytes
5, 6	3 bytes

Table 3.15 shows the "zero" value that is stored for each date and time type when you insert a value that is illegal for the type. If you prefer to have illegal values treated as errors and rejected, set the SQL mode appropriately; see Section 3.3, "How MySQL Handles Invalid Data Values." The "zero" value is also the default value for date and time columns that are defined with the NOT NULL attribute.

Table 3.15   Temporal Type "Zero" Values

Type Name	Zero Value
DATE	'0000-00-00'
TIME	'00:00:00[.000000]'
DATETIME	'0000-00-00 00:00:00[.000000]'
TIMESTAMP	'0000-00-00 00:00:00[.000000]'
YEAR	0000

MySQL represents dates in year-month-day order, in accordance with the standard SQL and ISO 8601 specifications. For example, the representation for December 3, 2015 is '2015-12-03'. For retrieval, you can display date and time values in a variety of formats by using the DATE_FORMAT() and TIME_FORMAT() functions.

For input dates, MySQL does provide some leeway in how you specify them. For example, it converts two-digit year values to four digits, and you need not supply a leading zero digit for month and day values that are less than 10. However, values must be in year-month-day order. Formats that you may be more used to, such as '12-3-99' or '3-12-99', will not be interpreted as you might intend. In such cases, you might find the STR_TO_DATE() function useful for converting strings in non-ISO format to ISO-format dates. For example, if the table mytbl has a date-valued column date_col, you can insert values like this:

```
mysql> INSERT INTO mytbl (date_col)
    -> VALUES(STR_TO_DATE('12-3-99','%m-%d-%Y'));
mysql> SELECT * FROM mytbl;
+------------+
| date_col   |
+------------+
| 1999-12-03 |
+------------+
```

Section 3.2.6.7, "Working with Temporal Values," further discusses the date interpretation rules that MySQL uses.

3.2.6.1   The DATE, TIME, and DATETIME Data Types

The DATE, TIME, and DATETIME types hold date values, time values, and combined date and time values, respectively. The formats for the three types of values are 'CCYY-MM-DD', '*hh:mm:ss*[*.uuuuuu*]', and '*CCYY-MM-DD hh:mm:ss*[*.uuuuuu*]', where *CC*, *YY*, *MM*, *DD*, *hh*, *mm*, *ss*, and *uuuuuu* represent the century, year, month, day of the month, hour, minute, second, and microsecond parts, respectively. Before MySQL 5.6.4, the fractional part for TIME and DATETIME values is permitted but discarded when values are stored.

As of MySQL 5.6.5, DATETIME columns can automatically use the current timestamp as an initial value and for updates. For more information, see Section 3.2.6.6, "Automatic Properties for Temporal Types."

If you assign a DATE value to a DATETIME column, MySQL automatically adds a time part of '00:00:00'. Conversions work in the other direction as well. If you assign a DATETIME value to a DATE or TIME column, MySQL discards the part that is irrelevant:

```
mysql> CREATE TABLE t (dt DATETIME, d DATE, t TIME);
mysql> INSERT INTO t (dt, d, t) VALUES(NOW(), NOW(), NOW());
mysql> SELECT * FROM t;
+---------------------+------------+----------+
| dt                  | d          | t        |
+---------------------+------------+----------+
| 2013-01-09 15:33:24 | 2013-01-09 | 15:33:24 |
+---------------------+------------+----------+
```

Conversion of TIME to DATETIME is version dependent: As of MySQL 5.6.4, the time is added to the current date. For older versions, the conversion does not necessarily produce a useful result.

MySQL treats the time in DATETIME and TIME values slightly differently. For DATETIME, the time part represents a time of day and must be in the range from '00:00:00' to '23:59:59'. A TIME value, on the other hand, represents elapsed time. That's why the range shown in Table 3.12 for TIME columns includes negative values and values larger than '23:59:59'.

Watch out if you insert "short" (not fully qualified) TIME values into a table. They may not be interpreted as you expect. For example, you'll probably find that if you insert '30' and '12:30' into a TIME column, one value will be interpreted from right to left and the other from left to right, resulting in stored values of '00:00:30' and '12:30:00'. If you want '12:30' to be taken as "12 minutes, 30 seconds," specify it in fully qualified form as '00:12:30'.

3.2.6.2   The TIMESTAMP Data Type

TIMESTAMP is a temporal data type that stores combined date and time values. (The word "timestamp" might appear to connote time only, but that is not the case.) The TIMESTAMP data type has the special properties noted in the following discussion.

TIMESTAMP columns have a range of values from '1970-01-01 00:00:01[.000000]' to '2038-01-19 03:14:07[.999999]'. As with DATETIME, before MySQL 5.6.4 the fractional part for TIMESTAMP values is permitted but discarded when values are stored. The range is tied to Unix time, where the first day of 1970 is "day zero," also known as "the epoch." MySQL stores each TIMESTAMP as a 4-byte number of seconds since the epoch. The beginning of 1970 determines the lower end of the TIMESTAMP range. (But note that the TIMESTAMP range does not begin with `'1970-01-01 00:00:00'`. You might expect that could be represented inter-nally as 0 seconds since the epoch, but 0 is used to represent the "zero" timestamp, `'0000-00-00 00:00:00'`.) The upper end of the range corresponds to the maximum 4-byte value for Unix time.

MySQL stores `TIMESTAMP` values in Universal Coordinated Time (UTC). When you store such a value, the server converts it from the session time zone to UTC. When you retrieve the value later, the server converts it back from UTC to the session time zone, so you see the same value that you stored. However, if another client connects to the server using a different time zone and retrieves the value, it sees the value adjusted to its own time zone. You can see this effect even within a single session if you change your session time zone:

```
mysql> CREATE TABLE t (ts TIMESTAMP);
mysql> SET time_zone = '+00:00';   # set time zone to UTC
mysql> INSERT INTO t VALUES('2000-01-01 00:00:00');
mysql> SELECT ts FROM t;
+---------------------+
| ts                  |
+---------------------+
| 2000-01-01 00:00:00 |
+---------------------+
mysql> SET time_zone = '+03:00';    # advance time zone 3 hours
mysql> SELECT ts FROM t;
+---------------------+
| ts                  |
+---------------------+
| 2000-01-01 03:00:00 |
+---------------------+
```

These examples specify time zones using values given as a signed offset in hours and minutes relative to UTC. It is also possible to use named time zones such as `'Europe/Zurich'` if the server time zone tables have been set up as described in Section 12.6.1, "Configuring Time Zone Support."

`TIMESTAMP` columns can automatically use the current timestamp as an initial value and for updates. Also, storing `NULL` into a `TIMESTAMP` column sets it to the current timestamp unless the column is defined with the `NULL` attribute to permit `NULL` values. For more information, see Section 3.2.6.6, "Automatic Properties for Temporal Types."

3.2.6.3 The YEAR Data Type

`YEAR` is a 1-byte data type intended for efficient representation of year values. A `YEAR` column definition may include a specification for a display width M, which should be either 4 or 2. If you omit M from a `YEAR` definition, the default is 4. `YEAR` has a range from `1901` to `2155`. The `YEAR` type suffices to store date information for which you need only the year part of the date, such as year of birth, year of election to office, and so forth. If you do not require a full date value, `YEAR` is much more space-efficient than other date types.

For YEAR(2), only the last two digits are displayed, and this type really is intended to store only values ranging from 1970 to 2069. If you use YEAR(2) to store values outside that range, their displayed values will be ambiguous. For example, 1970 and 2070 stored in a YEAR(2) column both display as 70. The easiest way to avoid this kind of problem is to avoid YEAR(2) and use YEAR(4) instead. Because of issues like this, YEAR(2) is deprecated as of MySQL 5.6.6: In existing tables, treatment of YEAR(2) columns remains unchanged, but for new tables, such columns are created as YEAR(4) instead.

MySQL converts two-digit input YEAR values into four-digit values using MySQL's year-guessing rules (see Section 3.2.6.8, "Interpretation of Ambiguous Year Values"). For example, 97 and 14 become 1997 and 2014. However, be aware that inserting the numeric value 00 into a four-digit YEAR column results in the value 0000 being stored, not 2000. If you want a value of 00 to convert to 2000, specify it in string form as '0' or '00'.

TINYINT has the same storage size as YEAR (1 byte), but not the same range. To cover the same range of years as YEAR by using an integer type, you would need a SMALLINT, which takes twice as much space. If the range of years you need to represent coincides with the range of the YEAR type, YEAR is more space-efficient than SMALLINT.

3.2.6.4   Temporal Data Type Attributes

Temporal column definitions can include the general attribute NULL or NOT NULL. If you specify neither one, NULL is the default except for TIMESTAMP, for which the default is NOT NULL.

You can also specify a default value using a DEFAULT clause. Section 3.2.3, "Specifying Column Default Values," describes the rules that MySQL uses for assigning a default value if a column definition includes no DEFAULT clause.

In most cases, default values must be constants. Except for TIMESTAMP and (as of MySQL 5.6.5) DATETIME, you cannot use a function such as CURRENT_TIMESTAMP to supply a value of "the current date and time" as a column default. TIMESTAMP and DATETIME columns are special because the default can be the current date and time. (For the rules that govern default values for these types, see Section 3.2.6.6, "Automatic Properties for Temporal Types.)" To achieve that result for other types, set the column value explicitly to CURRENT_TIMESTAMP whenever you create a new row. Alternatively, consider using a TIMESTAMP or DATETIME column instead, or set up a trigger that initializes the column to the appropriate value; see Section 4.2.3, "Triggers."

3.2.6.5   Fractional Second Capabilities for Temporal Types

This section describes how MySQL handles fractional seconds in temporal values. It applies primarily to MySQL 5.6.4 and up.

The syntax for declaring TIME, DATETIME, and TIMESTAMP types permits an optional fractional seconds precision (*fsp*) of up to 6 digits. The *fsp* value must be from 0 to 6, where 0 indicates no fractional part and 6 indicates microseconds precision. The default is 0 if *fsp* is not specified. For example, `TIME` and `TIME(0)` are equivalent and have no fractional part. `DATETIME(1)` permits date and time values to a precision of tenths of a second. `TIMESTAMP(6)` permits timestamps up to full microseconds precision.

Functions that take temporal arguments or return temporal values accept or return values with a fractional part. In some cases, functions that took no argument before MySQL 5.6.4 now accept an *fsp* argument to permit control over the number of fractional digits you'd like the return value to have. For example, `CURTIME()` returns the current time with no fractional part, but `CURTIME(3)` includes a fractional part to thousands of a second:

```
mysql> SELECT CURTIME(), CURTIME(3);
+-----------+--------------+
| CURTIME() | CURTIME(3)   |
+-----------+--------------+
| 12:22:31  | 12:22:31.475 |
+-----------+--------------+
```

The descriptions for individual functions in Section C.2.5, "Date and Time Functions," indicate when an *fsp* argument is permitted.

Prior to MySQL 5.6.4, support for microsecond values is limited. Some temporal functions such as `DATE_ADD()` use them, but if you attempt to store a value that includes a microseconds part in a temporal column, MySQL discards the microseconds part.

3.2.6.6 Automatic Properties for Temporal Types

`TIMESTAMP` and `DATETIME` columns can have automatic initialization and update properties:

- "Automatic initialization" means that for new rows the column is set to the current timestamp if you omit it from the `INSERT` statement.
- "Automatic update" means that for existing rows the column is updated to the current timestamp when you change any other column to a different value. (Setting a column to its current value does not count; this can in fact be done to prevent automatic updates.)

Before MySQL 5.6.5, you can designate any single `TIMESTAMP` column in a table to have either or both of those properties. You cannot have automatic initialization for one `TIMESTAMP` column and automatic update for another. Nor can you have automatic initialization for multiple columns, or automatic update for multiple columns.

MySQL 5.6.5 expands and generalizes support for automatic properties: Any `TIMESTAMP` column can have either or both of them, as can any `DATETIME` column.

Another special property, which applies only to `TIMESTAMP` columns, is that if you set the column to `NULL`, its value is set to the current timestamp. To permit `NULL` values to be stored in a `TIMESTAMP` column, define it with the `NULL` attribute.

Use this syntax to specify a `TIMESTAMP` column:

```
col_name TIMESTAMP [DEFAULT default_value] [ON UPDATE CURRENT_TIMESTAMP]
```

The DEFAULT and ON UPDATE attributes can be given in any order if both are given. The default value can be CURRENT_TIMESTAMP or a constant value such as 0 or a value in '*CCYY-MM-DD hh:mm:ss*' format. Synonyms for CURRENT_TIMESTAMP such as NOW() are also permitted.

As of MySQL 5.6.5, DATETIME columns permit these same DEFAULT and ON UPDATE attributes. Before 5.6.5, DATETIME permits only a constant value for the DEFAULT attribute and does not permit ON UPDATE.

To have one or both of the automatic properties for the first TIMESTAMP column in a table, you can define it using combinations of the DEFAULT and ON UPDATE attributes:

- With DEFAULT CURRENT_TIMESTAMP, the column has automatic initialization. It also has automatic update if ON UPDATE CURRENT_TIMESTAMP is given.

- With neither attribute, MySQL defines the column with both DEFAULT CURRENT_TIMESTAMP and ON UPDATE CURRENT_TIMESTAMP.

- With a DEFAULT *constant_value* attribute that specifies a constant value, the column does not have automatic initialization. It does have automatic update if ON UPDATE CURRENT_TIMESTAMP is given.

- Without DEFAULT but with ON UPDATE CURRENT_TIMESTAMP, the default value is 0 and the column has automatic update.

To use automatic initialization or update for a TIMESTAMP column other than the first one before MySQL 5.6.5, you must explicitly define the first one with a DEFAULT *constant_value* attribute and without ON UPDATE CURRENT_TIMESTAMP. Then you can use DEFAULT CURRENT_TIMESTAMP or ON UPDATE CURRENT_TIMESTAMP (or both) with any other single TIMESTAMP column.

As of MySQL 5.6.5, you can freely use either or both attributes with any TIMESTAMP column. In addition, DATETIME columns are permitted to have those attributes.

To defeat automatic initialization or update properties for a TIMESTAMP or DATETIME column that has those properties, set the column explicitly to the desired value for insert or update operations. For example, to prevent an update from changing the column, set it to its current value.

TIMESTAMP and DATETIME column definitions also can include the NULL or NOT NULL attribute. The default attribute for TIMESTAMP is NOT NULL. This has the special effect that when you explicitly set the column to NULL, MySQL sets it to the current timestamp. (This is true both for inserts and updates.) If you specify NULL in the column definition, setting the column to NULL stores NULL rather than the current timestamp. The default attribute for DATETIME is NULL and no special effect occurs from setting a DATETIME column to NULL.

Here is a table that contains a column that is set to the current timestamp for new rows and that is not automatically updated thereafter:

```
CREATE TABLE t1
(
  ts_created TIMESTAMP DEFAULT CURRENT_TIMESTAMP,
```

```
  ... other columns ...
);
```

To create a new row, initialize the column to the current timestamp by setting it to NULL or by omitting it from the INSERT statement. The column retains its value for subsequent updates unless you change it explicitly.

Here is a table that contains columns for both a time-created value and a last-modified value, using two TIMESTAMP columns:

```
CREATE TABLE t2
(
  ts_created  TIMESTAMP DEFAULT 0,
  ts_modified TIMESTAMP DEFAULT CURRENT_TIMESTAMP
                        ON UPDATE CURRENT_TIMESTAMP,
  ... other columns ...
);
```

To insert a new row, set both TIMESTAMP columns to NULL to set them to the insertion timestamp. To update an existing row, leave both columns alone; ts_modified is updated automatically to the modification timestamp if any other columns change value.

3.2.6.7   Working with Temporal Values

MySQL interprets input values for date and time columns in a variety of formats, including both string and numeric forms. In addition, as of MySQL 5.6.4, an optional fractional seconds part of up to 6 digits (microseconds) precision is permitted for the TIME, DATETIME, and TIMESTAMP data types. For example, these formats are permitted for DATETIME and TIMESTAMP values:

```
'CCYY-MM-DD hh:mm:ss[.uuuuuu]'
'YY-MM-DD hh:mm:ss[.uuuuuu]'
'CCYYMMDDhhmmss[.uuuuuu]'
'YYMMDDhhmmss[.uuuuuu]'
CCYYMMDDhhmmss[.uuuuuu]
YYMMDDhhmmss[.uuuuuu]
```

For DATE, TIME, or YEAR values, analogous equivalences hold.

MySQL interprets formats that have no century part (*CC*) using the rules described in Section 3.2.6.8, "Interpretation of Ambiguous Year Values." For string formats that include delimiter characters, you need not use '-' for dates and ':' for times. Any punctuation character may be used as the delimiter. Interpretation of values depends on context, not on the delimiter. For example, although times typically are specified using a delimiter of ':', MySQL won't interpret a value containing ':' as a time in a context where a date is expected. In addition, for the string formats that include delimiters, you need not specify two digits for month, day, hour, minute, or second values that are less than 10. The following are all equivalent:

```
'2012-02-03 05:04:09'
'2012-02-03 05:04:9'
```

```
'2012-02-03 05:4:9'
'2012-02-03 5:4:9'
'2012-02-3 5:4:9'
'2012-2-3 5:4:9'
```

MySQL may interpret values with leading zeros in different ways depending on whether they are specified as strings or numbers. The string `'001231'` will be seen as a six-digit value and interpreted as `'2000-12-31'` for a DATE, and as `'2000-12-31 00:00:00'` for a DATETIME. On the other hand, the number `001231` will be seen as `1231` after the parser gets done with it and then the interpretation becomes problematic. This is a case where it's best to supply a string value `'001231'`, or else use a fully qualified value if you are using numbers (that is, `20001231` for DATE and `200012310000` for DATETIME).

In general, you can freely assign values between the DATE, DATETIME, and TIMESTAMP types, but keep certain restrictions in mind:

- If you assign a DATETIME or TIMESTAMP value to a DATE, the time part is discarded.

- If you assign a DATE value to a DATETIME or TIMESTAMP, the time part of the resulting value is set to zero (`'00:00:00'`).

- The types have different ranges. In particular, TIMESTAMP has a more limited range (1970 to 2038). You cannot assign a pre-1970 DATETIME value to a TIMESTAMP and expect reasonable results. Nor can you assign values that are far in the future to a TIMESTAMP.

MySQL provides many functions for working with date and time values. For more information, see Appendix C, "Operator and Function Reference."

3.2.6.8   Interpretation of Ambiguous Year Values

For all date and time types that include a year part (DATE, DATETIME, TIMESTAMP, YEAR), MySQL handles values that contain two-digit years by converting them to four-digit years:

- Year values from 00 to 69 become 2000 to 2069
- Year values from 70 to 99 become 1970 to 1999

You can see the effect of these rules most easily by storing different two-digit values into a YEAR(4) column and retrieving the results:

```
mysql> CREATE TABLE y_table (y YEAR(4));
mysql> INSERT INTO y_table VALUES(68),(69),(99),(00),('00');
mysql> SELECT * FROM y_table;
+------+
| y    |
+------+
| 2068 |
| 2069 |
| 1999 |
```

```
| 0000 |
| 2000 |
+------+
```

The preceding example also demonstrates something you should note: Observe that `00` is converted to `0000`, not to `2000`. If you insert a numeric zero into `YEAR(4)`, that's what you get. To get `2000` using a value that does not contain the century, insert the string `'0'` or `'00'`. To ensure that MySQL sees a string and not a number, insert `YEAR` values using `CAST(value AS CHAR)` to produce a string result uniformly regardless of whether `value` is a string or a number.

Keep in mind that the rules for converting two-digit to four-digit year values provide only a reasonable guess. There is no way for MySQL to be certain about the meaning of a two-digit year when the century is unspecified. MySQL's conversion rules are adequate for many situations, but if they don't produce the values that you want, it is necessary to provide unambiguous data with four-digit years. For example, to enter birth and death dates into the `president` table, which lists U.S. presidents back into the 1700s, four-digit year values are in order. Values in these columns span several centuries, so letting MySQL guess the century from a two-digit year is the wrong thing to do.

3.3   How MySQL Handles Invalid Data Values

Historically, the dominant principle for data handling in MySQL has been, "Garbage in, garbage out." In other words, MySQL attempts to store any data value you give it, but if you don't verify the value first before storing it, you may not like what you get back out. However, several SQL modes enable you to reject bad values and cause an error to occur instead, which is more likely the behavior you expect if you are familiar with other database systems. The following discussion first discusses how MySQL handles improper data by default, then covers the changes that occur when you enable the SQL modes that affect data handling.

By default, MySQL handles of out-of-range or otherwise improper values as follows:

- For numeric or `TIME` columns, values outside the legal range are clipped to the nearest endpoint of the range and the resulting value is stored.

- For temporal columns other than `TIME`, illegal values are converted to the appropriate "zero" value for the type (see Table 3.15).

- For string columns other than `ENUM` or `SET`, strings that are too long are truncated to fit the maximum length of the column.

- Assignments to an `ENUM` or `SET` column depend on the values that are listed as legal in the column definition. If you assign to an `ENUM` column a value that is not listed as an enumeration member, the error member is assigned instead (that is, the empty string that corresponds to the zero-valued member). If you assign to a `SET` column a value containing substrings that are not listed as set members, those strings drop out and the column is assigned a value consisting of the remaining members.

MySQL reports these conversions as warnings for statements such as INSERT, REPLACE, UPDATE, LOAD DATA, and ALTER TABLE. To see the warning messages after executing one of those statements, use SHOW WARNINGS.

To turn on stricter checking of inserted or updated data values, enable one of the following SQL modes:

```
mysql> SET sql_mode = 'STRICT_ALL_TABLES';
mysql> SET sql_mode = 'STRICT_TRANS_TABLES';
```

For transactional tables, both modes are identical: If an invalid or missing value is found, an error occurs, the statement aborts and rolls back, and has no effect. For nontransactional tables, the modes have the following effects:

- For both modes, if an invalid or missing value is found in the first row of a statement that inserts or updates rows, an error occurs. The statement aborts and has no effect, similar to what happens for transactional tables.

- If an error occurs after the first row in a statement that inserts or updates multiple rows, some rows have already been modified. The two strict modes control whether the statement aborts at that point or continues to execute:

  - With STRICT_ALL_TABLES, an error occurs and the statement aborts. Because rows affected earlier by the statement were already modified, the result is a partial update.

  - With STRICT_TRANS_TABLES, MySQL aborts the statement for nontransactional tables only if doing so would have the same effect as for a transactional table. That is true only if the error occurs in the first row; an error in a later row leaves the earlier rows already changed. Those changes cannot be undone for a nontransactional table, so MySQL continues to execute the statement to avoid a partial update. It converts each invalid value to the closest legal value, as defined earlier in this section. For a missing value, MySQL sets the column to the implicit default for its data type, as described in Section 3.2.3, "Specifying Column Default Values."

Strict mode actually does not enable the strictest checking that MySQL can perform. You can enable any or all of the following modes to impose additional constraints on input data:

- ERROR_FOR_DIVISION_BY_ZERO prevents entry of values if division by zero occurs in strict mode. (Without strict mode, a warning occurs and NULL is inserted.)

- NO_ZERO_DATE prevents entry of the "zero" date value in strict mode.

- NO_ZERO_IN_DATE prevents entry of incomplete date values that have a month or day part of zero in strict mode.

For example, to enable strict mode for all storage engines and also check for divide-by-zero errors, set the SQL mode like this:

```
mysql> SET sql_mode = 'STRICT_ALL_TABLES,ERROR_FOR_DIVISION_BY_ZERO';
```

To turn on strict mode and all of the additional restrictions, you can simply enable TRADITIONAL mode:

```
mysql> SET sql_mode = 'TRADITIONAL';
```

TRADITIONAL is shorthand for "both strict modes, plus a bunch of other restrictions." This is more like the way that other "traditional" SQL DBMSs act with regard to data checking.

It is also possible to selectively weaken strict mode in some respects. If you enable the ALLOW_INVALID_DATES SQL mode, MySQL doesn't perform full checking of date parts. Instead, it requires only that months be in the range from 1 to 12 and days be in the range from 1 to 31 (which permits invalid values such as '2000-02-30' or '2000-06-31'). Another way to suppress errors is to use the IGNORE keyword with INSERT or UPDATE statements. With IGNORE, statements that would result in an error due to invalid values result only in a warning.

The options available give you the flexibility to choose the appropriate level of validity checking for your applications.

3.4   Working with Sequences

Many applications must generate unique numbers for identification purposes: membership numbers, sample or lot numbering, customer IDs, bug report or trouble ticket tags, and so forth.

MySQL's mechanism for providing unique numbers is the AUTO_INCREMENT column attribute, which enables you to generate sequential numbers automatically. However, AUTO_INCREMENT columns are handled somewhat differently by the storage engines that MySQL supports. The following discussion describes how AUTO_INCREMENT columns work in general and for specific storage engines so that you can use them effectively without running into the traps that sometimes surprise people. It also describes how to generate a sequence without using an AUTO_INCREMENT column. For additional information about the available engines in MySQL, see Section 2.6.1, "Storage Engine Characteristics."

3.4.1   General AUTO_INCREMENT Properties

AUTO_INCREMENT columns must be defined according to the following conditions:

- There can be only one column per table with the AUTO_INCREMENT attribute and it should have an integer data type. (AUTO_INCREMENT is permitted for floating-point types, but rarely used that way.)

- The column must be indexed. It is most common to use a PRIMARY KEY or UNIQUE index, but it is permitted to use a nonunique index.

- The column must have a NOT NULL constraint. MySQL makes the column NOT NULL even if you don't explicitly declare it that way.

Once created, an AUTO_INCREMENT column behaves like this:

- Inserting NULL into an AUTO_INCREMENT column causes MySQL to generate the next sequence number and insert it into the column. AUTO_INCREMENT sequences normally begin at 1 and increase monotonically, so successive rows inserted into a table get sequence values of 1, 2, 3, and so forth. Depending on the storage engine, it may be possible to set or reset the next sequence number explicitly or to reuse values deleted from the top end of the sequence.

- To obtain the value of the most recently generated sequence number, call the LAST_INSERT_ID() function. This enables you to reference the AUTO_INCREMENT value in subsequent statements even without knowing what the value is. LAST_INSERT_ID() returns 0 if no AUTO_INCREMENT value has been generated during the current session.

  LAST_INSERT_ID() is tied only to AUTO_INCREMENT values generated during the *current* session with the server. You can generate a sequence number, and then call LAST_INSERT_ID() to retrieve it later in the same session, even if other clients have generated their own sequence values in the meantime.

  For a multiple-row INSERT that generates several AUTO_INCREMENT values, LAST_INSERT_ID() returns the first one.

  If you use INSERT DELAYED, the AUTO_INCREMENT value is not generated until the row actually is inserted, so LAST_INSERT_ID() cannot be relied on to return the sequence value.

- Inserting a row without specifying a value for the AUTO_INCREMENT column is the same as inserting NULL into the column. If ai_col is an AUTO_INCREMENT column, these statements are equivalent:

```
INSERT INTO t (ai_col,name) VALUES(NULL,'abc');
INSERT INTO t (name) VALUES('abc');
```

- By default, inserting 0 into an AUTO_INCREMENT column has the same effect as inserting NULL. If you enable the NO_AUTO_VALUE_ON_ZERO SQL mode, inserting a 0 results in a 0 being stored, not the next sequence value.

- If you insert a row and specify a non-NULL, nonzero value for an AUTO_INCREMENT column that has a unique index, one of two things will happen. If a row already exists with that value, a duplicate-key error occurs. Otherwise, the row is inserted with the AUTO_INCREMENT column set to the given value. If this value is larger than the current next sequence number, the sequence is reset to continue with the next value after that for subsequent rows. In other words, you can "bump up" the counter by inserting a row with a sequence value greater than the current counter value.

- For some storage engines, values deleted from the top of a sequence are subject to reuse. If you delete the row containing the largest value in an AUTO_INCREMENT column, that value is reused the next time you generate a new value. If you delete all the rows in the table, all values are reused and the sequence starts over beginning at 1.

- If you use UPDATE to set an AUTO_INCREMENT column to a value that already exists in another row, a duplicate-key error occurs if the column has a unique index. If you update the column to a value larger than any existing column value, the sequence continues with the next number after that for subsequent rows. If you update the column by assigning 0 to it, it is set to 0 (regardless of whether NO_AUTO_VALUE_ON_ZERO is enabled).

- If you use REPLACE to update a row based on the value of the AUTO_INCREMENT column, the AUTO_INCREMENT value does not change. If you use REPLACE to update a row based on the value of some other column that has a primary key or unique index, the AUTO_INCREMENT column is updated with a new sequence number if you set it to NULL, or if you set it to 0 and NO_AUTO_VALUE_ON_ZERO is not enabled.

3.4.2 Storage Engine-Specific AUTO_INCREMENT Properties

The general AUTO_INCREMENT characteristics just described form the basis for understanding sequence behavior specific to particular storage engines. Most engines implement behavior that for the most part is similar to that just described, so keep the preceding discussion in mind as you read on. MyISAM offers the most flexibility for sequence handling, so the discussion begins with that storage engine.

3.4.2.1 AUTO_INCREMENT for MyISAM Tables

The MyISAM storage engine has the following AUTO_INCREMENT characteristics:

- MyISAM sequences normally are monotonic. The values in an automatically generated series are strictly increasing and are not reused if you delete rows. If the maximum value is 143 and you delete the row containing that value, MySQL still generates the next value as 144. There are two exceptions to this behavior:
  - If you empty a table with TRUNCATE TABLE, the counter resets to begin at 1.
  - Values deleted from the top of a sequence are reused if you use a composite index to generate multiple sequences within a table. (This technique is discussed shortly.)

- MyISAM sequences begin at 1 by default, but you can specify the initial value explicitly by using an AUTO_INCREMENT = n option in the CREATE TABLE statement. The following example creates a MyISAM table with an AUTO_INCREMENT column named seq that begins at 1,000,000:

```
CREATE TABLE mytbl
(
  seq INT UNSIGNED NOT NULL AUTO_INCREMENT,
  PRIMARY KEY (seq)
) ENGINE=MYISAM AUTO_INCREMENT=1000000;
```

A table can have only one AUTO_INCREMENT column, so there is never any ambiguity about the column to which the terminating AUTO_INCREMENT = n option applies.

- You can change the current sequence counter for an existing MyISAM table with ALTER TABLE. If the sequence currently stands at 1000, the following statement causes the next number generated to be 2000:

```
ALTER TABLE mytbl AUTO_INCREMENT=2000;
```

If you want to reuse values that have been deleted from the top of the sequence, you can do that, too. The following statement sets the counter as low as possible, causing the next number to be one larger than the current maximum sequence value:

```
ALTER TABLE mytbl AUTO_INCREMENT=1;
```

You cannot use the AUTO_INCREMENT option to set the current counter lower than the current maximum value in the table. If an AUTO_INCREMENT column contains the values 1 and 10, using AUTO_INCREMENT = 5 sets the counter so that the next automatic value is 11, not 5.

The MyISAM storage engine supports the use of composite (multiple-column) indexes for creating multiple independent sequences within the same table. To use this feature, create a multiple-column PRIMARY KEY or UNIQUE index that includes an AUTO_INCREMENT column as its final column. For each distinct key in the leftmost column or columns of the index, the AUTO_INCREMENT column generates a separate sequence of values. For example, you might use a table named bugs for tracking bug reports of several software projects, where the table is defined as follows:

```
CREATE TABLE bugs
(
  proj_name    VARCHAR(20) NOT NULL,
  bug_id       INT UNSIGNED NOT NULL AUTO_INCREMENT,
  description VARCHAR(100),
  PRIMARY KEY (proj_name, bug_id)
) ENGINE = MYISAM;
```

Here, the proj_name column identifies the project name and the description column contains the bug description. The bug_id column is an AUTO_INCREMENT column; by creating an index that ties it to the proj_name column, you can generate an independent series of sequence numbers for each project. Suppose that you enter the following rows into the table to register three bugs for SuperBrowser and two for SpamSquisher:

```
mysql> INSERT INTO bugs (proj_name,description)
    -> VALUES('SuperBrowser','crashes when displaying complex tables');
mysql> INSERT INTO bugs (proj_name,description)
    -> VALUES('SuperBrowser','image scaling does not work');
mysql> INSERT INTO bugs (proj_name,description)
    -> VALUES('SpamSquisher','fails to block known blacklisted domains');
mysql> INSERT INTO bugs (proj_name,description)
    -> VALUES('SpamSquisher','fails to respect whitelist addresses');
mysql> INSERT INTO bugs (proj_name,description)
    -> VALUES('SuperBrowser','background patterns not displayed');
```

The resulting table contents are as follows:

```
mysql> SELECT * FROM bugs ORDER BY proj_name, bug_id;
+--------------+--------+------------------------------------------+
| proj_name    | bug_id | description                              |
+--------------+--------+------------------------------------------+
| SpamSquisher |      1 | fails to block known blacklisted domains |
| SpamSquisher |      2 | fails to respect whitelist addresses     |
| SuperBrowser |      1 | crashes when displaying complex tables   |
| SuperBrowser |      2 | image scaling does not work              |
| SuperBrowser |      3 | background patterns not displayed        |
+--------------+--------+------------------------------------------+
```

The table numbers the `bug_id` values for each project separately, regardless of the order in which rows are entered for projects. You need not enter all rows for one project before you enter rows for another.

If you use a composite index to create multiple sequences, values deleted from the top of each individual sequence *are* reused. This differs from the usual MyISAM behavior of not reusing values.

3.4.2.2 AUTO_INCREMENT for InnoDB Tables

The InnoDB storage engine has the following AUTO_INCREMENT characteristics:

- The initial sequence value can be set with an AUTO_INCREMENT = n table option in the CREATE TABLE statement, and can be modified after table creation time using that option with ALTER TABLE.

- Values deleted from the top of the sequence normally are not reused. However, if you empty the table with TRUNCATE TABLE, the sequence is reset to begin at 1. Reuse can occur under the following conditions as well. The first time you generate a sequence value for an AUTO_INCREMENT column, InnoDB uses one greater than the current maximum value in the column (or 1 if the table is empty). InnoDB maintains this counter in memory for use in generating subsequent values; it is not stored in the table itself. This means that if you delete values from the top of the sequence and then restart the server, the deleted values are reused. Restarting the server also cancels the effect of using an AUTO_INCREMENT table option in a CREATE TABLE or ALTER TABLE statement.

- Gaps in a sequence can occur if transactions that generate AUTO_INCREMENT values are rolled back.

- Composite indexes cannot be used to generate multiple independent sequences within a table.

3.4.2.3 AUTO_INCREMENT for MEMORY Tables

The MEMORY storage engine has the following AUTO_INCREMENT characteristics:

- The initial sequence value can be set with an AUTO_INCREMENT = n table option in the CREATE TABLE statement, and can be modified after table creation time using that option with ALTER TABLE.

- Values deleted from the top of the sequence normally are not reused. However, if you empty the table with TRUNCATE TABLE, the sequence is reset to begin at 1.

- Composite indexes cannot be used to generate multiple independent sequences within a table.

3.4.3 Issues to Consider with AUTO_INCREMENT Columns

Keep the following points in mind to avoid being surprised by AUTO_INCREMENT column behavior:

- The primary purpose of the AUTO_INCREMENT mechanism is to enable you to generate a sequence of positive integers. The use of nonpositive numbers in an AUTO_INCREMENT column is unsupported. Consequently, you may as well define AUTO_INCREMENT columns to be UNSIGNED. With integer columns, using UNSIGNED also has the advantage of giving you twice as many sequence numbers before you hit the upper end of the data type's range.

- Adding AUTO_INCREMENT to a column definition is not a magic way of getting an unlimited sequence of numbers. AUTO_INCREMENT sequences are always bound by the range of the underlying data type. For example, if you use a TINYINT column, the maximum sequence number is 127. When you reach that limit, your application begins to fail with duplicate-key errors. If you use TINYINT UNSIGNED instead, the limit is extended to 255, but there is still a limit.

- Clearing a table's contents entirely with TRUNCATE TABLE may reset a sequence to begin again at 1, even for storage engines that normally do not reuse AUTO_INCREMENT values. The sequence reset occurs due to the way that MySQL attempts to optimize a complete table erasure operation: When possible, it tosses the data rows and indexes and re-creates the table from scratch rather than deleting rows one at a time. This causes sequence number information to be lost. To delete all rows but preserve the sequence information, suppress this optimization by using DELETE with a WHERE clause that is always true, to force MySQL to evaluate the condition for each row and thus to delete every row individually:

```
DELETE FROM tbl_name WHERE TRUE;
```

3.4.4 Tips for Working with AUTO_INCREMENT Columns

This section describes some useful techniques for working with AUTO_INCREMENT columns.

3.4.4.1 Adding a Sequence Number Column to a Table

Suppose that you create and populate a table:

```
mysql> CREATE TABLE t (c CHAR(10));
mysql> INSERT INTO t VALUES('a'),('b'),('c');
mysql> SELECT * FROM t;
```

```
+------+
| c    |
+------+
| a    |
| b    |
| c    |
+------+
```

Then you decide that you want to include a sequence number column in the table. To do this, issue an ALTER TABLE statement to add an AUTO_INCREMENT column, using the same kind of type definition that you'd use with CREATE TABLE. MySQL assigns sequence values to the AUTO_INCREMENT column automatically:

```
mysql> ALTER TABLE t ADD i INT UNSIGNED NOT NULL AUTO_INCREMENT PRIMARY KEY;
mysql> SELECT * FROM t;
+------+---+
| c    | i |
+------+---+
| a    | 1 |
| b    | 2 |
| c    | 3 |
+------+---+
```

3.4.4.2   Resequencing an Existing Column

If a table already has an AUTO_INCREMENT column, but you want to renumber it to eliminate gaps in the sequence that may have resulted from row deletions, the easiest way to do it is to drop the column and then add it again. When MySQL adds the column, it assigns new sequence numbers automatically.

Suppose that a table t looks like this, where i is the AUTO_INCREMENT column:

```
mysql> CREATE TABLE t (c CHAR(10), i INT UNSIGNED AUTO_INCREMENT
    -> NOT NULL PRIMARY KEY);
mysql> INSERT INTO t (c)
    -> VALUES('a'),('b'),('c'),('d'),('e'),('f'),('g'),('h'),('i'),('j'),
('k');
mysql> DELETE FROM t WHERE c IN('a','d','f','g','j');
mysql> SELECT * FROM t;
+------+----+
| c    | i  |
+------+----+
| b    | 2  |
| c    | 3  |
| e    | 5  |
| h    | 8  |
| i    | 9  |
| k    | 11 |
+------+----+
```

The following `ALTER TABLE` statement drops the column and then adds it again, renumbering the column in the process:

```
mysql> ALTER TABLE t
    -> DROP PRIMARY KEY,
    -> DROP i,
    -> ADD i INT UNSIGNED NOT NULL AUTO_INCREMENT PRIMARY KEY,
    -> AUTO_INCREMENT=1;
mysql> SELECT * FROM t;
+------+---+
| c    | i |
+------+---+
| b    | 1 |
| c    | 2 |
| e    | 3 |
| h    | 4 |
| i    | 5 |
| k    | 6 |
+------+---+
```

The `AUTO_INCREMENT = 1` clause resets the sequence to begin again at 1. For a MyISAM, InnoDB, or MEMORY table, you can use a value other than 1 to begin the sequence at a different value. For other storage engines, omit the `AUTO_INCREMENT` clause, because they do not permit the initial value to be specified this way. The sequence will begin at 1.

Although it's easy to resequence a column, and the question, "How do you do it?" is a common one, there usually is very little need to do so. MySQL doesn't care whether a sequence has holes in it, nor do you gain any performance efficiencies by resequencing. In addition, if you have rows in another table that refer to the values in the `AUTO_INCREMENT` column, resequencing the column destroys the correspondence between tables.

3.4.5 Generating Sequences Without `AUTO_INCREMENT`

MySQL supports a method for generating sequence numbers that doesn't use an `AUTO_INCREMENT` column at all. Instead, it uses an alternative form of the `LAST_INSERT_ID()` function that takes an argument. If you insert or update a column using `LAST_INSERT_ID(expr)`, the next call to `LAST_INSERT_ID()` with no argument returns the value of `expr`. In other words, MySQL treats `expr` as though it was generated as an `AUTO_INCREMENT` value. This enables you to create a sequence number and then retrieve it later in your session, confident that the value will not have been affected by the activity of other clients.

One way to use this strategy is to create a single-row table containing a value that you update each time you want the next value in the sequence. For example, you can create and initialize the table like this:

```
CREATE TABLE seq_table (seq INT UNSIGNED NOT NULL);
INSERT INTO seq_table VALUES(0);
```

Those statements set up seq_table with a single row containing a seq value of 0. To generate the next sequence number and retrieve it, do this:

```
UPDATE seq_table SET seq = LAST_INSERT_ID(seq+1);
SELECT LAST_INSERT_ID();
```

The UPDATE statement retrieves the current value of the seq column and increments it by 1 to produce the next value in the sequence. Generating the new value using LAST_INSERT_ID(seq+1) causes it to be treated like an AUTO_INCREMENT value, which enables it to be retrieved by calling LAST_INSERT_ID() with no argument. LAST_INSERT_ID() is client-specific, so you get the correct value even if other clients generate sequence numbers during the interval between the UPDATE and the SELECT.

This method can generate sequence values that increment by a value other than 1, or that are negative. For example, this statement can be executed repeatedly to generate a sequence of numbers that increase by 100 each time:

```
UPDATE seq_table SET seq = LAST_INSERT_ID(seq+100);
```

Repeating the following statement generates a sequence of decreasing numbers:

```
UPDATE seq_table SET seq = LAST_INSERT_ID(seq-1);
```

You can also generate a sequence that begins at an arbitrary value by setting the seq column to an appropriate initial value.

The preceding discussion describes how to set up a counter using a table with a single row. If you want multiple counters, add another column to the table to serve as a counter identifier, and use a different row in the table for each counter. Suppose that you have a Web site and you want to implement "this page has been accessed *n* times" page counters. Create a table with two columns. One column holds a name that uniquely identifies each counter. The other holds the current counter value. You can still use the LAST_INSERT_ID() function, but you determine which row it applies to by using the counter name. For example, create such a table with the following statement:

```
CREATE TABLE counter
(
  name  VARCHAR(255) CHARACTER SET latin1 COLLATE latin1_general_cs NOT NULL,
  value INT UNSIGNED,
  PRIMARY KEY (name)
);
```

The name column is a string so that you can name a counter whatever you want, and it's defined as a PRIMARY KEY to prevent duplicate names. This assumes that applications using the table agree on the names they'll be using. For Web counters, uniqueness of counter names is ensured simply by using the pathname of each page within the document tree as its counter name. The name column collation is case sensitive to cause pathname values to be treated as case sensitive. If your system has pathnames that are not case sensitive, use a collation that is not case sensitive.

To use the `counter` table, the `INSERT ... ON DUPLICATE KEY UPDATE` statement is useful, because it can insert a new row for a page that has not yet been counted, or update the count for an existing page. Also, by using `LAST_INSERT_ID(expr)` to generate the counter value, you can easily retrieve the current counter after updating it. For example, to initialize or increment the counter for the site's home page, and then retrieve the counter for display, do this:

```
INSERT INTO counter (name, value)
  VALUES('index.html', LAST_INSERT_ID(1))
  ON DUPLICATE KEY UPDATE value = LAST_INSERT_ID(value+1);
SELECT LAST_INSERT_ID();
```

An alternative approach for incrementing counters of existing pages without using `LAST_INSERT_ID()` is to do this:

```
UPDATE counter SET value = value+1 WHERE name = 'index.html';
SELECT value FROM counter WHERE name = 'index.html';
```

However, that doesn't work correctly if another client increments the counter after you issue the `UPDATE` and before you issue the `SELECT`. You could solve that problem by putting `LOCK TABLES` and `UNLOCK TABLES` around the two statements. Or you could create the table using a transactional storage engine and update the table within a transaction. Either method blocks other clients while you're using the counter, but the `LAST_INSERT_ID()` method accomplishes the same thing more easily. Because its value is client-specific, you always get the value you inserted, not the one from some other client, and you need not complicate the code with locks or transactions to keep other clients out.

3.5 Expression Evaluation and Type Conversion

Expressions contain terms and operators and are evaluated to produce values. Terms can include values such as constants, function calls, references to table columns, and scalar subqueries. These values can be combined using different kinds of operators, such as arithmetic or comparison operators, and terms of an expression can be grouped with parentheses. Expressions occur most commonly in the output column list and `WHERE` clause of `SELECT` statements. For example, here is a query that is similar to one used for age calculations in Section 1.4.9.6, "Working with Dates":

```
SELECT
  CONCAT(last_name, ', ', first_name),
  TIMESTAMPDIFF(YEAR, birth, death)
FROM president
WHERE
  birth > '1900-1-1' AND DEATH IS NOT NULL;
```

Each selected value represents an expression, as does the content of the `WHERE` clause. Expressions also occur in the `WHERE` clause of `DELETE` and `UPDATE` statements, the `VALUES()` clause of `INSERT` statements, and so forth.

When MySQL encounters an expression, it evaluates the expression to produce a result. For example, `(4*3) DIV (4-2)` evaluates to the value 6. Expression evaluation may involve type conversion, such as when MySQL converts the number `960821` into a date `'1996-08-21'` if the number is used in a context requiring a `DATE` value.

This section discusses how to write expressions in MySQL and the rules that govern the kinds of type conversions that occur during expression evaluation. Each of MySQL's operators is listed here, but MySQL has so many functions that only a few are touched on. For more information, see Appendix C, "Operator and Function Reference."

3.5.1   Writing Expressions

An expression can be as simple as a single constant, such as the numeric value 0 or string value `'abc'`.

Expressions can use function calls. Some functions take arguments (values inside the parentheses), and some do not. Multiple arguments should be separated by commas. When you invoke a built-in function, there can be spaces around arguments, but if there is a space between the function name and the opening parenthesis, the MySQL parser might misinterpret the function name. The usual result is a syntax error. You can tell MySQL to permit spaces after names of built-in functions by enabling the `IGNORE_SPACE` SQL mode, but that also causes function names to be treated as reserved words.

Expressions can include references to table columns. In the simplest case, when the table to which a column belongs is clear from context, a column reference may be given simply as the column name. Only one table is named in each of the following `SELECT` statements, so the column references are unambiguous, even though the same column names are used in each statement:

```
SELECT last_name, first_name FROM president;
SELECT last_name, first_name FROM member;
```

If it's not clear which table should be used, qualify the column name by preceding it with the proper table name. If it's not even clear which database should be used, precede the table name by a qualifying database name. You can also use the more-specific qualified forms in unambiguous contexts simply to be more explicit:

```
SELECT
  president.last_name, president.first_name,
  member.last_name, member.first_name
FROM president INNER JOIN member
WHERE president.last_name = member.last_name;

SELECT sampdb.student.name FROM sampdb.student;
```

For additional information about qualifiers, see Section 2.2, "MySQL Identifier Syntax and Naming Rules."

Scalar subqueries can be used to provide a single value in an expression. The subquery requires surrounding parentheses:

```
SELECT * FROM president WHERE birth = (SELECT MAX(birth) FROM president);
```

Finally, you can combine all these kinds of values (constants, function calls, column references, and subqueries) to form more complex expressions.

3.5.1.1 Operator Types

Terms of expressions can be combined using several kinds of operators. This section describes what they do, and Section 3.5.1.2, "Operator Precedence," discusses the order in which they are evaluated.

Arithmetic operators, listed in Table 3.16, include the usual addition, subtraction, multiplication, and division operators, as well as the modulo operator. Arithmetic is performed using BIGINT (64-bit) integer values for +, -, and * when both operands are integers. If both operands are integers, the result is unsigned if either operand is unsigned. For each operator other than DIV, if any operand is an approximate value, double-precision floating-point arithmetic is used. This is also true for strings converted to numbers, because strings are converted to double-precision numbers. Be aware that if an integer operation involves large values such that the result exceeds 64-bit range, you will get unpredictable results. (Actually, you should try to avoid exceeding 63-bit values; one bit is needed to represent the sign.)

Table 3.16 **Arithmetic Operators**

Operator	Syntax	Meaning
+	a + b	Addition; sum of operands
-	a - b	Subtraction; difference of operands
-	-a	Unary minus; negation of operand
*	a * b	Multiplication; product of operands
/	a / b	Division; quotient of operands
DIV	a DIV b	Division; integer quotient of operands
%	a % b	Modulo; remainder after division of operands

Logical operators, shown in Table 3.17, evaluate expressions to determine whether they are true (nonzero) or false (zero). It is also possible for a logical expression to evaluate to NULL if its value cannot be ascertained. For example, 1 AND NULL is of indeterminate value.

Table 3.17 **Logical Operators**

Operator	Syntax	Meaning
AND, &&	a AND b, a && b	Logical intersection; true if both operands are true
OR, ||	a OR b, a || b	Logical union; true if either operand is true
XOR	a XOR b	Logical exclusive-OR; true if exactly one operand is true
NOT, !	NOT a, !a	Logical negation; true if operand is false

As alternative forms of AND, OR, and NOT, MySQL supports the &&, ||, and ! operators, respectively, as used in the C programming language. Note in particular the || operator. Standard SQL specifies || as the string concatenation operator, but in MySQL it signifies a logical OR operation. If you use the following expression, expecting it to perform string concatenation, you may be surprised to discover that it returns the number 0:

```
'abc' || 'def'                                    → 0
```

This happens because 'abc' and 'def' are converted to integers for the operation, and both turn into 0. In MySQL, use CONCAT('abc','def') or proximity to concatenate strings:

```
CONCAT('abc','def')                               → 'abcdef'
'abc' 'def'                                       → 'abcdef'
```

To obtain standard SQL behavior for ||, enable the PIPES_AS_CONCAT SQL mode.

Bit operators, shown in Table 3.18, perform bitwise intersection, union, and exclusive-OR, where each bit of the result is evaluated as the logical AND, OR, or exclusive-OR of the corresponding bits of the operands. You can also perform bit shifts left or right. Bit operations are performed using BIGINT (64-bit) integer values.

Table 3.18 **Bit Operators**

Operator	Syntax	Meaning
&	a & b	Bitwise AND (intersection); each bit of result is set if corresponding bits of both operands are set
|	a | b	Bitwise OR (union); each bit of result is set if corresponding bit of either operand is set
^	a ^ b	Bitwise exclusive-OR; each bit of result is set only if exactly one corresponding bit of the operands is set
<<	a << b	Left shift of a by b bit positions
>>	a >> b	Right shift of a by b bit positions

Comparison operators, shown in Table 3.19, include operators for testing relative magnitude or lexical ordering of numbers and strings, as well as operators for performing pattern matching and for testing NULL values. The <=> operator is MySQL-specific. For a discussion of the comparison properties of strings, see Section 3.1.2, "String Values."

Table 3.19   **Comparison Operators**

Operator	Syntax	Meaning
=	a = b	True if operands are equal
<=>	a <=> b	True if operands are equal (even if NULL)
<>, !=	a <> b, a != b	True if operands are not equal
<	a < b	True if a is less than b
<=	a <= b	True if a is less than or equal to b
>=	a >= b	True if a is greater than or equal to b
>	a > b	True if a is greater than b
IN	a IN (b1, b2, ...)	True if a is equal to any of b1, b2, ...
BETWEEN	a BETWEEN b AND C	True if b <= a <= c
NOT BETWEEN	a NOT BETWEEN b AND C	True unless b <= a <= c
LIKE	a LIKE b	SQL pattern match; true if a matches b
NOT LIKE	a NOT LIKE b	SQL pattern match; true if a does not match b
REGEXP	a REGEXP b	Regular expression match; true if a matches b
NOT REGEXP	a NOT REGEXP b	Regular expression match; true if a does not match b
IS NULL	a IS NULL	True if operand is NULL
IS NOT NULL	a IS NOT NULL	True if operand is not NULL

Pattern matching enables you to look for values without having to specify an exact literal value. MySQL provides SQL pattern matching using the LIKE operator and the wildcard characters '%' (match any sequence of characters) and '_' (match any single character). MySQL also provides pattern matching based on the REGEXP operator and regular expressions that are similar to those used in Unix programs such as grep, sed, and vi. You must use one of these pattern-matching operators to perform a pattern match; you cannot use the = operator. To reverse the sense of a pattern match, use NOT LIKE or NOT REGEXP.

The two types of pattern matching differ in important respects besides the use of different operators and pattern characters:

- A LIKE SQL pattern matches only if it matches the entire string. A REGEXP regular expression matches if it is found anywhere in the string.

- LIKE is multi-byte safe. REGEXP works correctly only for single-byte character sets and does not take collation into account.

Patterns used with the LIKE operator may include the '%' and '_' wildcard characters. For example, the pattern 'Frank%' matches any string that begins with 'Frank':

```
'Franklin' LIKE 'Frank%'                        → 1
'Frankfurter' LIKE 'Frank%'                     → 1
```

The wildcard character '%' matches any sequence of characters, including the empty sequence, so 'Frank%' matches 'Frank':

```
'Frank' LIKE 'Frank%'                           → 1
```

This also means the pattern '%' matches any string, including the empty string. However, '%' does not match NULL. In fact, any pattern match where either operand is NULL fails:

```
'Frank' LIKE NULL                               → NULL
NULL LIKE '%'                                    → NULL
```

MySQL's LIKE operator compares its operands as binary strings if either operand is a binary string. If the operands are nonbinary strings, LIKE compares them according to their collation:

```
'Frankly' LIKE 'Frank%'                         → 1
'frankly' LIKE 'Frank%'                         → 1
BINARY 'Frankly' LIKE 'Frank%'                  → 1
BINARY 'frankly' LIKE 'Frank%'                  → 0
'Frankly' COLLATE latin1_general_cs LIKE 'Frank%' → 1
'frankly' COLLATE latin1_general_cs LIKE 'Frank%' → 0
```

This behavior differs from the standard SQL LIKE operator, which is case sensitive.

The other wildcard character permitted with LIKE is '_', which matches any single character. The pattern '___' matches any string of exactly three characters. 'c_t' matches 'cat', 'cot', 'cut', and even 'c_t' (because '_' matches itself).

Wildcard characters may be specified anywhere in a pattern. '%bert' matches 'Englebert', 'Bert', and 'Albert'. '%bert%' matches all of those strings, and also strings like 'Berthold', 'Bertram', and 'Alberta'. 'b%t' matches 'Bert', 'bent', and 'burnt'.

To match a literal instance of the '%' or '_' character, turn off its special meaning by preceding it with a backslash ('\%' or '_'):

```
'abc' LIKE 'a%c'                                → 1
'abc' LIKE 'a\%c'                               → 0
'a%c' LIKE 'a\%c'                               → 1
'abc' LIKE 'a_c'                                → 1
'abc' LIKE 'a\_c'                               → 0
'a_c' LIKE 'a\_c'                               → 1
```

MySQL's other form of pattern matching uses regular expressions. The operator is REGEXP rather than LIKE. The following examples demonstrate several common regular expression pattern characters.

The '.' character is a wildcard that matches any single character:

```
'abc' REGEXP 'a.c'                              → 1
```

The [...] construction matches any character listed between the square brackets:

```
'e' REGEXP '[aeiou]'                            → 1
'f' REGEXP '[aeiou]'                            → 0
```

To specify a range of characters, list the endpoints of the range separated by a dash ('-'). To negate the sense of the class (to match any character not listed), specify '^' as the first character of the class:

```
'abc' REGEXP '[a-z]'                            → 1
'abc' REGEXP '[^a-z]'                           → 0
```

'*' means "match any number of the preceding thing," so that, for example, the pattern 'x*' matches any number of 'x' characters:

```
'abcdef' REGEXP 'a.*f'                          → 1
'abc' REGEXP '[0-9]*abc'                        → 1
'abc' REGEXP '[0-9][0-9]*'                      → 0
```

"Any number" includes zero instances, which is why the second expression succeeds. To match one or more instances of the preceding thing, use '+' instead of '*':

```
'abc' REGEXP 'cd*'                              → 1
'abc' REGEXP 'cd+'                              → 0
'abcd' REGEXP 'cd+'                             → 1
```

'^pattern' and 'pattern$' anchor a pattern match so that the pattern *pattern* matches only when it occurs at the beginning or end of a string, and '^pattern$' matches only if *pattern* matches the entire string:

```
'abc' REGEXP 'b'                                → 1
'abc' REGEXP '^b'                               → 0
'abc' REGEXP 'b$'                               → 0
'abc' REGEXP '^abc$'                            → 1
'abcd' REGEXP '^abc$'                           → 0
```

MySQL's regular expression matching has other special pattern elements as well. For more information, see Appendix C, "Operator and Function Reference."

A LIKE or REGEXP pattern can be taken from a table column, although this is slower than a constant pattern if the column contains several different values. The pattern must be examined and converted to internal form each time the column value changes.

3.5.1.2   Operator Precedence

When MySQL evaluates an expression, the operators determine the order in which to group the terms of the expression. Some operators have higher precedence; that is, they are "stronger" than others in the sense that they are evaluated earlier than others. For example, multiplication and division have higher precedence than addition and subtraction. The following two expressions are equivalent because * and DIV are evaluated before + and -:

```
3 + 4 * 2 - 10 DIV 2                          → 6
3 + 8 - 5                                     → 6
```

The following list shows operator precedence, from highest precedence to lowest. Operators on the same line have the same precedence. Evaluation of operators at a higher precedence level within an expression occurs before operators at a lower precedence level. Evaluation of operators at the same precedence level occurs left to right within an expression, except that assignments evaluate right to left.

```
INTERVAL
BINARY   COLLATE
!
- (unary minus)   ~ (unary bit negation)
^
*   /   DIV   %   MOD
+   -
<<   >>
&
|
<   <=   =   <=>   <>   !=   >=   >   IN   IS   LIKE   REGEXP   RLIKE
BETWEEN   CASE   WHEN   THEN   ELSE
NOT
AND   &&
XOR
OR   ||
:=
```

Some operators have a different precedence depending on the SQL mode or MySQL version. For details, see Appendix C, "Operator and Function Reference."

To override the precedence of operators and change the evaluation order of expression terms, use parentheses to group terms:

```
1 + 2 * 3 - 4 / 5                            → 6.2000
(1 + 2) * (3 - 4) / 5                        → -0.6000
```

3.5.1.3 NULL Values in Expressions

Take care when using NULL values in expressions, because the result may not always be what you expect. The following guidelines will help you avoid surprises.

NULL as an operand to any arithmetic or bit operator produces a NULL result:

```
1 + NULL                                     → NULL
1 | NULL                                     → NULL
```

With logical operators, the result is NULL unless the result can be determined with certainty:

```
1 AND NULL                              → NULL
1 OR NULL                               → 1
0 AND NULL                              → 0
0 OR NULL                               → NULL
```

NULL as an operand to any comparison or pattern-matching operator produces a NULL result, except for the <=>, IS NULL, and IS NOT NULL operators, which are intended specifically for dealing with NULL values:

```
1 = NULL                                → NULL
NULL = NULL                             → NULL
1 <=> NULL                              → 0
NULL LIKE '%'                           → NULL
NULL REGEXP '.*'                        → NULL
NULL <=> NULL                           → 1
1 IS NULL                               → 0
NULL IS NULL                            → 1
```

Functions generally return NULL if given NULL arguments, except for those functions designed to deal with NULL arguments. For example, IFNULL() is able to handle NULL arguments and returns true or false appropriately. On the other hand, STRCMP() expects non-NULL arguments; if you pass it a NULL argument, it returns NULL rather than true or false.

In sorting operations, NULL values sort together. They appear first in ascending sorts and last in descending sorts.

3.5.2 Type Conversion

Whenever a value of one type appears in a context that requires a value of another type, MySQL performs type conversion automatically according to the kind of operation. Conversions occur for any of the following reasons:

- Operand conversion to a type appropriate for operator evaluation

- Function argument conversion to a type expected by the function

- Conversion of a value for storage in a table column of a different type

You can also perform explicit type conversion using a cast operator or function.

Numbers are converted to strings or temporal values using the character set and collation given by the character_set_connection and collation_connection system variables. The result is a nonbinary string unless character_set_connection is binary, in which case it is a binary string. (Before MySQL 5.5.3, a number to string conversion always produces a binary string.)

The following expression involves implicit type conversion. It consists of the addition operator + and two operands, 1 and '2':

```
1 + '2'                                 → 3
```

The operands are of different types (number and string), so MySQL converts one of them to make them the same type. But which one should it change? In this case, + is a numeric operator, so MySQL wants the operands to be numbers thus and converts the string '2' to the number 2. Then it evaluates the expression to produce the result 3.

Here's another example. The CONCAT() function concatenates strings to produce a longer string as a result. To do this, it interprets its arguments as strings, no matter their type. If you pass it a bunch of numbers, CONCAT() converts them to strings and returns their concatenation:

```
CONCAT(1,23,456)                                → '123456'
```

If the call to CONCAT() is part of a larger expression, further type conversion may take place. Consider the following expression and its result:

```
REPEAT('X',CONCAT(1,2,3)/10)                    → 'XXXXXXXXXXXX'
```

CONCAT(1,2,3) produces the string '123'. The expression '123'/10 is converted to 123/10 because division is an arithmetic operator. The result of this expression is 12.3, but REPEAT() expects an integer repeat count, so it rounds the count to produce 12. Then REPEAT('X',12) produces a string result of 12 'X' characters.

If all arguments to CONCAT() are nonbinary strings, the result is a nonbinary string. If any argument is a binary string, the result is a binary string. Numeric arguments are converted to strings as discussed earlier, and then the preceding rules apply.

Keep in mind that, by default, MySQL attempts to convert values to the type required by an expression rather than generating an error. Depending on the context, it converts values of each of the three general categories (numbers, strings, or dates and times) to values in any of the other categories. However, values can't always be converted from one type to another. If a value to be converted to a given type doesn't look like a legal value for that type, the conversion fails. Conversion to numbers of things like 'abc' that don't look like numbers results in a value of 0. Conversion to date or time types of things that don't look like a date or time result in the "zero" value for the type. For example, converting the string 'abc' to a date results in the "zero" date '0000-00-00'. On the other hand, any value can be treated as a string, so generally it's not a problem to convert a value to a string.

To prevent conversion of illegal values to the closest legal values during data input operations, you can enable strict mode to cause errors to occur instead. See Section 3.3, "How MySQL Handles Invalid Data Values."

MySQL also performs more minor type conversions. If you use a floating-point value in an integer context, the value is converted (with rounding). Conversion in the other direction works as well; an integer can be used without problem as a floating-point number.

Hexadecimal constants are treated as binary strings unless the context clearly indicates a number. In string contexts, each pair of hexadecimal digits is converted to a character and the result is used as a string, as the following examples illustrate:

```
0x61                                            → 'a'
0x61 + 0                                        → 97
```

```
X'61'                                                 → 'a'
X'61' + 0                                             → 97
CONCAT(0x61)                                          → 'a'
CONCAT(0x61 + 0)                                      → '97'
CONCAT(X'61')                                         → 'a'
CONCAT(X'61' + 0)                                     → '97'
```

For comparisons, context determines whether to treat a hexadecimal constant as a binary string or a number:

- This expression treats the operands as binary strings and performs a byte-by-byte comparison.

  ```
  0x0d0a = '\r\n'                                       → 1
  ```

- This expression compares a hexadecimal constant to a number, so it is converted to a number for the comparison.

  ```
  0x0a = 10                                             → 1
  ```

- This expression performs a binary string comparison. The first byte of the left operand has a lesser value than the first byte of the right operand, so the result is false.

  ```
  0xee00 > 0xff                                         → 0
  ```

- In this expression, the right operand hex constant is converted to a number because of the arithmetic operator. Then for the comparison, the left operand is converted to a number. The result is true because 0xee00 (60928) is numerically greater than 0xff (255).

  ```
  0xee00 > 0xff+0                                       → 1
  ```

It's possible to force a hexadecimal constant to be treated as a nonbinary string by using a character set introducer or CONVERT():

```
0x61                                                 → 'a'
0x61 = 'A'                                            → 0
_latin1 0x61 = 'A'                                    → 1
CONVERT(0x61 USING latin1) = 'A'                      → 1
```

Some operators force conversion of the operands to the type expected by the operator, no matter the types of the operands. Arithmetic operators are an example. They expect numbers, and the operands are converted accordingly:

```
3 + 4                                                → 7
'3' + 4                                              → 7
'3' + '4'                                            → 7
```

In a string-to-number conversion, it's not enough for a string simply to contain a number somewhere. MySQL doesn't look through the entire string hoping to find a number, it looks only at the beginning; if the string has no leading numeric part, the conversion result is 0:

```
'1973-2-4' + 0                                  → 1973
'12:14:01' + 0                                  → 12
'23-skidoo' + 0                                 → 23
'-23-skidoo' + 0                                → -23
'carbon-14' + 0                                 → 0
```

MySQL's string-to-number conversion rule converts numeric-looking strings to numeric values:

```
'-428.9' + 0                                    → -428.9
'3E-4' + 0                                      → 0.0003
```

This conversion does not work for hexadecimal-looking constants, though. Only the leading zero is used:

```
'0xff' + 0                                      → 0
```

The bit operators are even stricter than the arithmetic operators. They want the operators to be not just numeric, but integers, and type conversion occurs accordingly. This means that a fractional number such as 0.3 is not considered true, even though it's nonzero; when converted to an integer, the result is 0. In the following expressions, the operands are not considered true until they have a value of at least 1:

```
0.3 | .04                                       → 0
1.3 | .04                                       → 1
0.3 & .04                                       → 0
1.3 & .04                                       → 0
1.3 & 1.04                                      → 1
```

Pattern matching operators expect to operate on strings. This means you can use MySQL's pattern matching operators on numbers because it converts them to strings in the attempt to find a match!

```
12345 LIKE '1%'                                 → 1
12345 REGEXP '1.*5'                             → 1
```

The magnitude comparison operators (<, <=, =, and so on) are context sensitive; that is, they are evaluated according to the types of their operands. The following expression compares the operands numerically because they both are numbers:

```
2 < 11                                          → 1
```

This expression involves string operands and thus results in a lexical comparison:

```
'2' < '11'                                      → 0
```

In the following comparisons, the types are mixed, so MySQL compares them as numbers. As a result, both expressions are true:

```
'2' < 11                                        → 1
2 < '11'                                        → 1
```

When evaluating comparisons, MySQL converts operands as necessary according to the following rules:

- Other than for the `<=>` operator, comparisons involving NULL values evaluate as NULL. (`<=>` is like `=`, except that `NULL <=> NULL` is true, whereas `NULL = NULL` is NULL.)

- If both operands are strings, they are compared lexically as strings. Binary strings are compared byte by byte using the numeric value of each byte. Comparisons for nonbinary strings are performed character by character using the collating sequence of the character set in which the strings are expressed. If the strings have different character sets, the comparison may result in an error or fail to yield meaningful results. A comparison between a binary and a nonbinary string is treated as a comparison of binary strings.

- If both operands are integers, they are compared numerically as integers.

- Hexadecimal constants that are not compared to a number are compared as binary strings.

- Other than for IN(), if either operand is a TIMESTAMP or DATETIME value and the other is a constant, the operands are compared as TIMESTAMP values. This is done to make comparisons work better for ODBC applications.

- If one operand is a decimal value, the operands are compared as decimals if the other operand is a decimal or integer value, or as double-precision floating-point values otherwise.

- In other cases, the operands are compared numerically as double-precision floating-point values. Note that this includes the case of comparing a string and a number. The string is converted to a double-precision number, which results in a value of 0 if the string doesn't look like a number. For example, `'14.3'` converts to 14.3, but `'L4.3'` converts to 0.

3.5.2.1 Temporal Value Interpretation Rules

MySQL freely converts strings and numbers to date and time values as demanded by context in an expression, and vice versa. Date and time values are converted to numbers in numeric context; numbers are converted to dates or times in date or time contexts. This conversion to a date or time value happens when you assign a value to a date or time column or when a function requires a date or time value. In comparisons, the general rule is that date and time values compare as strings.

If the table `mytbl` contains a DATE column `date_col`, the following statements are equivalent:

```
INSERT INTO mytbl SET date_col = '2025-04-13';
INSERT INTO mytbl SET date_col = '20250413';
INSERT INTO mytbl SET date_col = 20250413;
```

In the following examples, the argument to the TO_DAYS() function is interpreted as the same value for all three expressions:

```
TO_DAYS('2025-04-13')                    → 739719
TO_DAYS('20250413')                      → 739719
TO_DAYS(20250413)                        → 739719
```

3.5.2.2   Testing or Forcing Type Conversion

To see how type conversion will be handled in an expression, issue a SELECT query that evaluates the expression so that you can examine the result:

```
mysql> SELECT X'41', X'41' + 0;
+-------+-----------+
| X'41' | X'41' + 0 |
+-------+-----------+
| A     |        65 |
+-------+-----------+
```

If you cannot tell from inspection the type of an expression, select it into a new table and check the table definition:

```
mysql> CREATE TABLE t SELECT X'41' AS col1, X'41' + 0 AS col2;
mysql> DESCRIBE t;
+-------+--------------+------+-----+---------+-------+
| Field | Type         | Null | Key | Default | Extra |
+-------+--------------+------+-----+---------+-------+
| col1  | varbinary(1) | NO   |     |         |       |
| col2  | double(17,0) | NO   |     | 0       |       |
+-------+--------------+------+-----+---------+-------+
```

Testing expression evaluation is especially useful for statements such as DELETE or UPDATE that modify rows, because you want to be sure you're affecting only the intended rows. One way to check an expression is to run a preliminary SELECT statement with the same WHERE clause that you're going to use with the DELETE or UPDATE statement to verify that the clause selects the proper rows. Suppose that the table mytbl has a CHAR column char_col containing these values:

```
'abc'
'00'
'def'
'00'
'ghi'
```

Given these values, what is the effect of the following statement?

```
DELETE FROM mytbl WHERE char_col = 00;
```

The intended effect is probably to delete the two rows containing the value '00'. The actual effect would be to delete all the rows—an unpleasant surprise. This is a consequence of MySQL's comparison rules. char_col is a string column, but 00 in the statement is not quoted, so it is treated as a number. By MySQL's comparison rules, a comparison involving a string and a number evaluates as a comparison of two numbers. As MySQL executes the DELETE statement, it converts each value of char_col to a number and compares it to 0. Unfortunately, although '00' converts to 0, so do all the strings that don't look like numbers. As a result, the WHERE clause is true for every row, and the DELETE statement empties the table. This is a case where it would have been prudent to test the WHERE clause with a SELECT statement prior to executing the DELETE, because that would have shown you that the expression selects too many rows:

```
mysql> SELECT char_col FROM mytbl WHERE char_col = 00;
+----------+
| char_col |
+----------+
| abc      |
| 00       |
| def      |
| 00       |
| ghi      |
+----------+
```

When you're uncertain about the way a value will be used, you may want to exploit MySQL's type conversion to force an expression to a value of a particular type, or to call a function that performs the desired conversion. The following list demonstrates several useful conversion techniques.

Add +0 or +0.0 to a term to force conversion to a numeric value:

```
0x65                                    → 'e'
0x65 + 0                                → 101
0x65 + 0.0                              → 101.0
```

To chop off the fractional part of a number, use FLOOR() or CAST(). To add a fractional part to an integer, add an exact-value zero with the required number of decimal digits:

```
FLOOR(13.3)                             → 13
CAST(13.3 AS SIGNED)                    → 13
13 + 0.0                                → 13.0
13 + 0.0000                             → 13.0000
```

To round instead, use ROUND() rather than CAST().

Use CAST() or CONCAT() to turn a value into a string:

```
14                                      → 14
CAST(14 AS CHAR)                        → '14'
CONCAT(14)                              → '14'
```

Use HEX() to convert a number to a hexadecimal string:

```
HEX(255)                                → 'FF'
HEX(65535)                              → 'FFFF'
```

You can also use HEX() with a string value to convert it to a string of hex digit pairs representing successive bytes in the string:

```
HEX('abcd');                            → '61626364'
```

Use ASCII() to convert a single-byte character to its ASCII value:

```
'A'                                          → 'A'
ASCII('A')                                   → 65
```

To go in the other direction from ASCII code to character, use CHAR():

```
CHAR(65)                                     → 'A'
```

Use DATE_ADD() or INTERVAL arithmetic to force a string or number to be treated as a date:

```
DATE_ADD(20130101, INTERVAL 0 DAY)          → '2013-01-01'
20130101 + INTERVAL 0 DAY                    → '2013-01-01'
DATE_ADD('20130101', INTERVAL 0 DAY)        → '2013-01-01'
'20130101' + INTERVAL 0 DAY                  → '2013-01-01'
```

Generally, you can convert a date value to numeric form by adding zero:

```
CURDATE()                                    → '2013-01-09'
CURDATE()+0                                  → 20130109
```

Temporal values with a time part convert to a value with a microseconds part:

```
NOW()                                        → '2012-06-25 09:35:17'
NOW()+0                                      → 20120625093517.000000
CURTIME()                                    → '09:35:17'
CURTIME()+0                                  → 93517.000000
```

To chop off the fractional part, cast the value to an integer:

```
CAST(NOW() AS UNSIGNED)                      → 20130109153603
CAST(CURTIME() AS UNSIGNED)                  → 153603
```

To convert a string from one character set to another, use CONVERT(). To check whether the result has the desired character set, use the CHARSET() function:

```
'abcd'                                       → 'abcd'
CONVERT('abcd' USING ucs2)                   → 'abcd'
CHARSET('abcd')                              → 'latin1'
CHARSET(CONVERT('abcd' USING ucs2))          → 'ucs2'
```

Preceding a string with a character set introducer does not cause conversion of the string, but MySQL interprets it as though it has the character set indicated by the introducer:

```
CHARSET(_ucs2 'abcd')                        → 'ucs2'
```

To determine the hexadecimal value of the UTF-8 character that corresponds to a given hexadecimal UCS-2 character, combine CONVERT() with HEX(). The following expression determines the UTF-8 value of the trademark symbol:

```
HEX(CONVERT(_ucs2 0x2122 USING utf8))        → 'E284A2'
```

To change the collation of a string, use the COLLATE operator. To check whether the result has the desired collation, use the COLLATION() function:

```
COLLATION('abcd')                              → 'latin1_swedish_ci'
COLLATION('abcd' COLLATE latin1_bin)           → 'latin1_bin'
```

The character set and collation must be compatible. If they are not, use a combination of CONVERT() to convert the character set first and COLLATE to change the collation:

```
CONVERT('abcd' USING latin2) COLLATE latin2_bin
```

To convert a binary string to a nonbinary string that has a given character set, use CONVERT():

```
0x61626364                                     → 'abcd'
0x61626364 = 'ABCD'                            → 0
CONVERT(0x61626364 USING latin1) = 'ABCD'      → 1
```

Alternatively, for binary quoted strings or hexadecimal values, use an introducer to change the interpretation of the binary string:

```
_latin1 0x61626364 = 'ABCD'                    → 1
```

To cast a nonbinary string to a binary string, use the BINARY keyword:

```
'abcd' = 'ABCD'                                → 1
BINARY 'abcd' = 'ABCD'                         → 0
'abcd' = BINARY 'ABCD'                         → 0
```

3.6 Choosing Data Types

Section 3.2, "MySQL Data Types," describes the data types from which you can choose and the general properties of those types, such as the kind of values they may contain, how much storage space they take, and so on. But how do you actually decide which types to use when you create a table? This section discusses factors to consider that help you choose.

The most "generic" data types are the string types. You can store anything in them because numbers and dates can be represented in string form. So should you just define all your columns as strings and be done with it? No. Let's consider a simple example. Suppose that you have values that look like numbers. You could represent these as strings, but should you? What happens if you do?

For one thing, you'll probably use more space, because numbers can be stored more efficiently using numeric columns than string columns. You'll also notice some differences in query results due to the different ways that numbers and strings are handled. For example, the sort order for numbers is not the same as for strings. The number 2 is less than the number 11, but the string '2' is lexically greater than the string '11'. You can work around this by using the column in a numeric context like this:

```
SELECT col_name + 0 as num ... ORDER BY num;
```

Adding zero to the column forces a numeric sort, but is that a reasonable thing to do? It's a useful technique sometimes, but you don't want to have to use it every time you want a numeric sort. Causing MySQL to treat a string column as a number has a couple of significant implications. It forces a string-to-number conversion for each column value, which is inefficient. Also, using the column in a calculation prevents MySQL from using any index on the column, which slows down the query further. Neither performance degradation occurs if you store the values as numbers in the first place.

The preceding example illustrates that several issues come into play when you choose data types. The simple choice of using one representation rather than another has implications for storage requirements, query handling, and processing performance. The following list gives a quick rundown of factors to think about when picking a type for a column.

What kind of values will the column hold? Numbers? Strings? Dates? You can represent any type of value as a string, but as we've just seen, if another type is more appropriate, it's likely that you'll get better performance if you use that type. However, assessing the kind of values you're working with isn't necessarily trivial, particularly for other people's data. It's especially important to ask what kind of values the column will hold if you're setting up a table for someone else. Be sure to ask questions and get the information required to make a good decision.

Do your values lie within some particular range? If they are integers, will they always be nonnegative? If so, you can use UNSIGNED. If they are strings, will they always be chosen from among a fixed, limited set of values? If so, you may find ENUM or SET a useful type.

There is a tradeoff between the range of a type and the amount of storage it uses. How "big" a type do you need? For numbers, you can choose small types with a limited range of values, or large types with a much larger range. For strings, you can make them short or long, so you wouldn't choose CHAR(255) if all the values you want to store contain fewer than 10 characters.

What are the performance and efficiency issues? Some types can be processed more efficiently than others. Numeric operations generally can be performed more quickly than string operations. Short strings can be compared more quickly than long strings, and also involve less disk overhead. For MyISAM tables, performance is better for fixed-length rows than for variable-length rows.

The following sections consider these issues in more detail, except for the performance issues, which are covered in Section 5.3, "Choosing Data Types for Efficient Queries."

Although you want to make the best data type choices you can when you create a table, it's not the end of the world if you make a choice that turns out to be nonoptimal. You can use ALTER TABLE to change the type to a better one. This might be as simple as changing a SMALLINT to MEDIUMINT after finding out your data set contains values larger than you originally thought. Or it can be more complex, such as changing a CHAR to an ENUM with a specific set of permitted values.

3.6.1   What Kind of Values Will the Column Hold?

The first thing you think of when trying to decide on a data type is the kind of values the column will store because that has the most evident implications for the type you choose. In general, you do the obvious thing: You store numbers in numeric columns, strings in string columns, and dates and times in temporal columns. If your numbers have a fractional part, you use a DECIMAL or floating-point type rather than an integer type. But sometimes there are exceptions. The principle here is that you need to understand the nature of your data to be able to choose the type in an informed manner. If you're going to store your own data, you probably have a good idea of how to characterize it. If others ask you to set up a table for them, it's sometimes a different story. It may not be so easy to know just what you're working with. Be sure to ask enough questions to find out what kind of values the table really should contain.

Suppose that you're told that a table needs a column to record "amount of precipitation." Is that a number? Or is it "mostly" numeric—that is, typically but not always coded as a number? For example, when you watch the news on television, the weather report generally includes a measure of precipitation. Sometimes this is a number (as in "0.25 inches of rain"), but sometimes it's a "trace" of precipitation, meaning "not much at all." That's fine for the weather report, but what does it mean for storage in a database? You either need to quantify "trace" as a number so that you can use a numeric data type to record precipitation amounts, or you need to use a string so that you can record the word "trace." Or you could come up with some more complicated arrangement, using a number column and a string column where you fill in one column and leave the other one NULL. Avoid that option, if possible; it makes the table harder to understand and writing queries for it more difficult.

I would probably try to store all rows in numeric form, and then convert them as necessary for display purposes. For example, if any nonzero amount of precipitation less than .01 inches is considered a trace amount, you could display values from the column like this:

```
SELECT IF(precip>0 AND precip<.01,'trace',precip) FROM ... ;
```

Some values are obviously numeric but you must determine whether to use an integer or noninteger type. You should ask what your units are and what accuracy you require. Is whole-unit accuracy sufficient or do you need to represent fractional units? This may help you distinguish between integer and fixed-point or floating-point data types. For example, if you're recording weights to the nearest pound, you can use an integer column. To record fractional units, you'd use a fixed-point or floating-point column. In some cases, you might even use multiple columns—for example, to record weight in terms of pounds and ounces.

Height is a numeric type of information for which there are several representational possibilities:

- Use a string such as '6-2' for a value like "6 feet, 2 inches." This has the advantage of having a form that's easy to look at and understand (certainly more so than "74 inches"), but it's difficult to use this kind of value for mathematical operations such as summation or averaging.

- Use one numeric column for feet and another for inches. This would be a little easier to work with for numerical operations, but two columns are more difficult to use than one.

- Use one numeric column representing inches. This is easiest for a database to work with, and least meaningful for humans. But remember that you don't have to present values in the same format that you use to work with them. You can reformat values for meaningful display using MySQL's many functions. That means this might be the best way to represent height.

Another type of numeric information is currency, such as U.S. dollars. Calculations use values that have dollars and cents parts. These look like floating-point values, but FLOAT and DOUBLE are subject to rounding error and are not suitable except for rows in which you need only approximate accuracy. Because people are touchy about their money, it's more likely you need a type that affords perfect accuracy. You have a couple of choices:

- Represent money as a DECIMAL(M,2) type, choosing M as the maximum width appropriate for the range of values you need. This gives you values with two decimal places of accuracy. The advantage of DECIMAL is that values are not subject to roundoff error and calculations are exact.

- Represent all currency values internally as cents using an integer type. The advantage is that calculations are done internally using integers, which is very fast. The disadvantage is that you will need to convert values on input or output by multiplying or dividing by 100.

Some kinds of "numbers" aren't. Telephone numbers, credit card numbers, and Social Security numbers all can be written using nondigit characters such as spaces or dashes and cannot be stored directly in a numeric column unless you strip the nondigits. But even with nondigits stripped, you may want to store values as strings rather than as numbers to avoid loss of leading zeros.

If you need to store date information, do the values include a time? That is, will they *ever* need to include a time? MySQL doesn't provide a date type that has an optional time part: DATE never has a time, and DATETIME must have a time. If the time really is optional, use a DATE column to record the date, and a separate TIME column to record the time. Then permit the TIME column to be NULL and interpret that as "no time":

```
CREATE TABLE mytbl
(
  date DATE NOT NULL,    # date is required
  time TIME NULL         # time is optional (may be NULL)
);
```

One type of situation in which it's especially important to determine whether you need a time value occurs when you're joining two tables with a master-detail relationship that are "linked" based on date information. Suppose that you're conducting research involving test subjects. Following a standard initial battery of tests, you might run several additional tests, with the choice of tests varying according to the results of the initial tests. You can represent this information using a master-detail relationship, in which the subject identification information and the standard initial tests are stored in a master row and any additional tests are stored as rows in a secondary detail table. Then link the two tables based on subject ID and the date on which the tests are given.

The question to answer in this situation is whether you can use just the date or whether you need both date and time. This depends on whether a subject might go through the testing procedure more than once during the same day. If so, record the time (for example, the time that the procedure begins), using either a DATETIME column or separate DATE and TIME columns that both must be filled in. Without the time value, you will not be able to associate a subject's detail rows with the proper master rows if the subject is tested twice in a day.

I've heard people claim "I don't need a time; I will never test a subject twice on the same day." Sometimes they're correct, but I have also seen some of these same people turn up later wondering how to prevent detail rows from being mixed up with the wrong master row after entering data for subjects who were tested multiple times in a day. Sorry, by then it's too late!

Sometimes you can deal with this problem by retrofitting a TIME column into the tables. Unfortunately, it's difficult to fix existing rows unless you have some independent data source, such as the original paper records. Otherwise, you have no way to disambiguate detail rows to associate them with the proper master row. Even if you have an independent source of information, this is very messy and likely to cause problems for applications that you've already written to use the tables. It's best to explain the issues to the table owners and make sure that you've gotten a good characterization of the data values before creating their tables.

Sometimes you have incomplete data, and this will influence your choice of data types. You may be collecting birth and death dates for genealogical research, and sometimes all you can find out is the year or year and month someone was born or died, but not the exact date. If you use a DATE column, you can't enter a date unless you have the full date. To be able to record whatever information you have, even if it's incomplete, you may have to keep separate year, month, and day columns. Then you can enter such parts of the date as you have and leave the rest NULL. Another possibility is to use DATE values in which the day or month and day parts are set to 0. Such "fuzzy" dates can be used to represent incomplete date values.

3.6.2   Do Your Values Lie Within Some Particular Range?

If you've decided on the general category from which to pick a data type for a column, thinking about the range of values you want to represent will help you narrow down your choices to a particular type within that category. Suppose that you want to store integer values. The range of your values determines the types you can use. If you need values in the range from 0 to 1000, you can use anything from a SMALLINT up to a BIGINT. If your values range up to 2 million, you can't use SMALLINT, so your choices range from MEDIUMINT to BIGINT.

You could, of course, simply use the largest type for the kind of value you want to store (BIGINT for the examples in the previous paragraph). But if you use the smallest type that is large enough for your purposes, you'll minimize the amount of storage used by your tables. Also, they will give you better performance because smaller columns usually can be processed more quickly than larger ones. Reading smaller values requires less disk activity, and more key values fit into in-memory index buffers, enabling indexed searches to be performed faster.

If you don't know the range of possible values, you must either guess or use BIGINT to accommodate the worst possible case. If you guess and the type you choose turns out later to be too small, all is not lost. Use ALTER TABLE later to make the column bigger.

Sometimes you discover that you can make a column smaller. In Section 1.4.6.2.3, "The score Table," we created a score table for the grade-keeping project that had a score column for recording quiz and test scores. The column was created using INT to keep the discussion simpler, but you can see now that if scores are in the range from 0 to 100, a better choice would be TINYINT UNSIGNED, because that would use less storage.

The range of values in your data also affects the attributes you can use with your data type. If values never are negative, you can use UNSIGNED; otherwise, you can't.

String types don't have a "range" in the same way numeric columns do, but they have a length, and the maximum length you need affects the column types you can use. If you're storing character strings that are shorter than 256 characters, you can use CHAR, VARCHAR, or TINYTEXT. If you want longer strings, you can use VARCHAR or a longer TEXT type.

For a string column used to represent a fixed set of values, consider using an ENUM or SET data type. These can be good choices because they are represented internally as numbers. Operations on them are performed numerically, which makes them more efficient than other string types. They also can be more compact than other string types, which saves space. In addition, you can prevent entry of values not present in the list of permitted values by enabling strict SQL mode. See Section 3.3, "How MySQL Handles Invalid Data Values."

When characterizing the range of values you have to deal with, the best terms are "always" and "never" (as in "always less than 1000" or "never negative"), because they enable you to constrain your data type choices more tightly. But be wary of using these terms when they're not really justified. Be especially wary if you're consulting with other people about their data and they start throwing around those two terms. When people say "always" or "never," be sure they really mean it. Sometimes people say their data always have a particular characteristic when they really mean "almost always."

Suppose that you're designing a table for a group of investigators who tell you, "Our test scores are always 0 to 100." Based on that statement, you choose TINYINT and you make it UNSIGNED because the values are always nonnegative. Then you find out that the people who code the data for entry into the database sometimes use −1 to mean "student was absent due to illness." Oops. They didn't tell you that. It might be acceptable to use NULL to represent such values, but if not, you'll have to record a −1, and then you can't use an UNSIGNED column. (This is an instance where ALTER TABLE comes to your rescue.)

Sometimes decisions for such cases can be made more easily by asking a simple question: Are there ever exceptions? If an exceptional case ever occurs, even just once, you must allow for it. You will find that people who talk to you about designing a database invariably think that if exceptions don't occur very often, they don't matter. When you're creating a table, you can't think that way. The question you need to ask isn't "how often do exceptions occur?" It's "do exceptions *ever* occur?" If they do, you must take them into account.

4

Views and Stored Programs

MySQL supports several types of server-side objects. These are objects that you create and the server stores for later execution.

Views are one type of stored object. A view is a virtual table. That is, it acts like a table but actually contains no data. Instead, it is defined in terms of tables or other views and provides alternative ways to look at table data. Views can make application development easier by providing a simple way to run complex queries.

Stored programs are another type of stored object. These come in several forms. Some can be invoked on demand. Others execute automatically when table modifications occur or when a scheduled time is reached:

- A stored function returns a result from a calculation for use in expressions.

- A stored procedure does not return a result directly but is used to perform general computations or produce result sets that are passed back to the client.

- A trigger is associated with a table and executes when the table is modified with INSERT, DELETE, or UPDATE statements.

- An event executes on a time-activated basis according to a schedule.

Stored programs provide several benefits and capabilities:

- The executable part of the object can use compound statements that extend SQL syntax to include blocks, loops, and conditional statements.

- All the code needed to define a stored program is sent over the network only once at program-creation time, not each time you want to execute it. This reduces overhead at execution time.

- A stored program enables encapsulation of complex calculations into a program unit that can be easily invoked by name.

- A stored program provides a means to standardize computational operations because all applications that use it perform those operations the same way.

- They provide a mechanism for handling errors.

- Database security is improved because you can enable controlled access to sensitive data by appropriate selection of the privileges a stored program has when it executes.

This chapter uses the following terminology:

- "Stored programs" refers collectively to stored functions and procedures, triggers, and events.

- "Stored routines" is a more limited term that refers only to stored functions and procedures. Both types of objects are defined using very similar syntax, so it is often natural to discuss them together. In fact, much database literature uses the term "stored procedures" to refer both to functions and procedures. I find this unhelpfully ambiguous and will not use the term that way.

This chapter shows how to create and use views and stored programs. It also covers the DEFINER clause that views and stored programs have in common and that is used for security purposes to control access to data.

The syntax descriptions for the CREATE statements discussed here show only the most important clauses. For the full syntax, see Appendix E, "SQL Syntax Reference."

4.1   Using Views

A view is a virtual table that is defined using a SELECT statement on tables or other views. Selecting from the view is equivalent to selecting from the statement it is defined as, but the view hides the details. The definition can include operations such as expression calculation and joins, so selecting from the view makes it easier to write a simple query to get the information you want.

A basic view can be nothing more than a way to select a subset of a table's columns. Suppose that you often want to select only the last_name, first_name, city, and state columns from the president table, but you don't want to write out all the columns like this:

```
SELECT last_name, first_name, city, state FROM president;
```

Nor do you want to use SELECT *. That's easier to write, but * retrieves columns you don't want. The solution is to define a view that retrieves only the desired columns:

```
CREATE VIEW vpres AS
SELECT last_name, first_name, city, state FROM president;
```

Now the view acts as a "window" into just those columns that you want to see. This means that you can use SELECT * with the view and get back only the columns named in the view definition:

```
mysql> SELECT * FROM vpres;
+------------+------------+--------------------+-------+
```

```
| last_name  | first_name  | city                | state |
+------------+-------------+---------------------+-------+
| Washington | George      | Wakefield           | VA    |
| Adams      | John        | Braintree           | MA    |
| Jefferson  | Thomas      | Albemarle County    | VA    |
| Madison    | James       | Port Conway         | VA    |
| Monroe     | James       | Westmoreland County | VA    |
...
```

To create a view, you must have the CREATE VIEW privilege for it, some privilege for every column selected by the SELECT statement, and the SELECT privilege for every column referred to elsewhere in that statement.

If you include a WHERE clause, MySQL adds it to the view definition when executing the statement to further restrict the result:

```
mysql> SELECT * FROM vpres WHERE last_name = 'Adams';
+-----------+-------------+-----------+-------+
| last_name | first_name  | city      | state |
+-----------+-------------+-----------+-------+
| Adams     | John        | Braintree | MA    |
| Adams     | John Quincy | Braintree | MA    |
+-----------+-------------+-----------+-------+
```

The same is true if you add ORDER BY, LIMIT, and so forth.

When you use a view, you can refer only to those columns named in the view definition. That is, you cannot refer to a column that is not part of the view, even if the column is part of the base table:

```
mysql> SELECT * FROM vpres WHERE suffix <> '';
ERROR 1054 (42S22): Unknown column 'suffix' in 'where clause'
```

The column names for a view by default are the output column names of its SELECT statement. To provide column names explicitly, add a list of names in parentheses following the view name in the view definition:

```
mysql> CREATE VIEW vpres2 (ln, fn) AS
    -> SELECT last_name, first_name FROM president;
```

To refer to this view, use the given column names rather than the names in the SELECT part of the view definition:

```
mysql> SELECT last_name, first_name FROM vpres2;
ERROR 1054 (42S22): Unknown column 'last_name' in 'field list'
mysql> SELECT ln, fn FROM vpres2;
+------------+----------------+
| ln         | fn             |
+------------+----------------+
| Washington | George         |
```

```
| Adams     | John    |         |
| Jefferson | Thomas  |         |
| Madison   | James   |         |
| Monroe    | James   |         |
...
```

The preceding view definitions were relatively simple, but the SELECT statement for a view can be quite elaborate. This enables you to hide the complexity and easily select information that is nontrivial to produce. In Section 1.4.9.10, "Retrieving Information from Multiple Tables," we developed a query for the grade-keeping project to retrieve test and quiz statistics. We can use that same query as the definition for a view that permits the same information to be retrieved much more easily:

```
CREATE VIEW grade_stats AS
SELECT
grade_event.date,grade_event.category,
MIN(score.score) AS minimum,
MAX(score.score) AS maximum,
MAX(score.score)-MIN(score.score)+1 AS span,
SUM(score.score) AS total,
AVG(score.score) AS average,
COUNT(score.score) AS count
FROM score INNER JOIN grade_event
ON score.event_id = grade_event.event_id
GROUP BY grade_event.date;
```

Selecting from the view performs the join and retrieves the results of the calculations:

```
mysql> SELECT * FROM grade_stats;
+------------+----------+---------+---------+------+-------+---------+-------+
| date       | category | minimum | maximum | span | total | average | count |
+------------+----------+---------+---------+------+-------+---------+-------+
| 2012-09-03 | Q        |       9 |      20 |   12 |   439 | 15.1379 |    29 |
| 2012-09-06 | Q        |       8 |      19 |   12 |   425 | 14.1667 |    30 |
| 2012-09-09 | T        |      60 |      97 |   38 |  2425 | 78.2258 |    31 |
| 2012-09-16 | Q        |       7 |      20 |   14 |   379 | 14.0370 |    27 |
| 2012-09-23 | Q        |       8 |      20 |   13 |   383 | 14.1852 |    27 |
| 2012-10-01 | T        |      62 |     100 |   39 |  2325 | 80.1724 |    29 |
+------------+----------+---------+---------+------+-------+---------+-------+
```

To see only certain columns, name them. To see only the information for a particular event, just specify the date and MySQL adds the WHERE clause to the view definition when executing it. The view makes it simple to select the desired information:

```
mysql> SELECT date, category, count, average
    -> FROM grade_stats WHERE date = '2012-09-16';
+------------+----------+-------+---------+
| date       | category | count | average |
+------------+----------+-------+---------+
```

```
| 2012-09-16 | Q         |    27 | 14.0370 |
+------------+---------+-------+---------+
```

Some views are updatable, which means that you can insert, update, and delete rows in the underlying table by means of operations on the view. Here is an example:

```
mysql> CREATE TABLE t (i INT);
mysql> INSERT INTO t (i) VALUES(1),(2),(3);
mysql> CREATE VIEW v AS SELECT i FROM t;
mysql> SELECT i FROM v;
+------+
| i    |
+------+
|    1 |
|    2 |
|    3 |
+------+
mysql> INSERT INTO v (i) VALUES(4);
mysql> DELETE FROM v WHERE i < 3;
mysql> SELECT i FROM v;
+------+
| i    |
+------+
|    3 |
|    4 |
+------+
mysql> UPDATE v SET i = i + 1;
mysql> SELECT i FROM v;
+------+
| i    |
+------+
|    4 |
|    5 |
+------+
```

For a view to be updatable, it must map directly onto a single table, it must select only columns that are simple references to table columns (not arbitrary expressions), and any operation on a view row must correspond to an operation on a single row in the underlying table. For example, if a view involves a summary calculated using an aggregate function, each view row can be based on multiple underlying table rows. In this case, the view is not updatable because there is no way to tell which underlying table row should be updated.

4.2 Using Stored Programs

This section describes how to write and use each type of stored program: stored functions and procedures, triggers, and events. But before getting into the details of any particular type of program, we'll begin with a discussion of a topic common to all of them: how to write compound statements.

4.2.1   Compound Statements and Statement Delimiters

A stored program that has a body consisting of a single SQL statement can be written with no special treatment. The following procedure uses a SELECT statement that displays the names of the tables in the sampdb database:

```
CREATE PROCEDURE sampdb_tables ()
  SELECT TABLE_NAME FROM INFORMATION_SCHEMA.TABLES
  WHERE TABLE_SCHEMA = 'sampdb' ORDER BY TABLE_NAME;
```

However, a stored program need not be limited to a single simple statement. The code can contain multiple SQL statements, and it can use constructs such as local variables, conditional statements, loops, and nested blocks. (See Section E.2, "SQL Statement Syntax (Compound Statements).")

To write a stored program that uses these features, use a compound statement, which consists of BEGIN and END to form a block within which an arbitrary number of statements can be written. The following procedure displays a message that greets you by name (or as "earthling" if you are an anonymous user):

```
CREATE PROCEDURE greetings ()
BEGIN
  # 77 = 16 for username + 60 for hostname + 1 for '@'
  DECLARE user CHAR(77) CHARACTER SET utf8;
  SET user = (SELECT CURRENT_USER());
  IF INSTR(user,'@') > 0 THEN
    SET user = SUBSTRING_INDEX(user,'@',1);
  END IF;
  IF user = '' THEN          # anonymous user
    SET user = 'earthling';
  END IF;
  SELECT CONCAT('Greetings, ',user, '!') AS greeting;
END;
```

With compound statements, the statements within a block must be separated by semicolon (';') characters as delimiters. That also is the default statement delimiter for the mysql program, so there is a conflict if you try to define stored programs using mysql. To deal with this, use the delimiter command to redefine mysql's default statement delimiter to one that does not appear in the routine definition. That causes mysql not to interpret semicolons as terminators and to pass the entire object definition to the server as a single statement. You can redefine the terminator to semicolon again after defining the stored program. The following example shows how to temporarily change the mysql delimiter to $ while a stored procedure is being defined, then execute the procedure after restoring the default delimiter:

```
mysql> delimiter $
mysql> CREATE PROCEDURE show_times()
    -> BEGIN
    ->    SELECT CURRENT_TIMESTAMP AS 'Local Time';
    ->    SELECT UTC_TIMESTAMP AS 'UTC Time';
    -> END$
mysql> delimiter ;
mysql> CALL show_times();
+---------------------+
| Local Time          |
+---------------------+
| 2012-05-03 18:18:19 |
+---------------------+

+---------------------+
| UTC Time            |
+---------------------+
| 2012-05-03 23:18:19 |
+---------------------+
```

The delimiter need not be $, and it need not be a single character:

```
mysql> delimiter EOF
mysql> CREATE PROCEDURE show_times()
    -> BEGIN
    ->    SELECT CURRENT_TIMESTAMP AS 'Local Time';
    ->    SELECT UTC_TIMESTAMP AS 'UTC Time';
    -> END EOF
mysql> delimiter ;
```

The principle to follow is that if a stored program's body contains any internal semicolons, you should redefine the delimiter while defining the program.

A compound statement need not be used only for complex stored programs. You can use one even if a program body consists of a single statement, or even no statements:

```
CREATE PROCEDURE do_little ()
BEGIN
  DO SLEEP(1);
END;

CREATE PROCEDURE do_nothing ()
BEGIN
END;
```

For stylistic consistency, you might prefer to use the BEGIN and END keywords around the body of every stored program definition, even when they are not strictly required.

4.2.2   Stored Functions and Procedures

Stored functions calculate and return a value for use in expressions, just like built-in functions such as COS() or HEX(). Stored procedures execute as standalone operations using the CALL statement rather than in expressions. Use a procedure if you need only to perform a computation to produce an effect or action without returning a value, or if the computation produces result sets (which a function cannot do).

To create a stored function or procedure, use a CREATE FUNCTION or CREATE PROCEDURE statement. Their basic syntax looks like this:

```
CREATE FUNCTION func_name ([param_list])
  RETURNS type
  routine_stmt

CREATE PROCEDURE proc_name ([param_list])
  routine_stmt
```

The following example creates a function that takes an integer-valued parameter representing a year. (I use p_ as a prefix to distinguish parameter names from other names such as those of tables or columns.) The function uses a subquery to determine how many presidents were born in that year and returns the count:

```
mysql> delimiter $
mysql> CREATE FUNCTION count_born_in_year(p_year INT)
    -> RETURNS INT
    -> READS SQL DATA
    -> BEGIN
    ->   RETURN (SELECT COUNT(*) FROM president WHERE YEAR(birth) = p_year);
    -> END$
mysql> delimiter ;
```

The function has a RETURNS clause to indicate the data type of its return value and a body that computes that value. The function body must include at least one RETURN statement to return a value to the caller. By defining a calculation as a function, you have a simple way to execute it without specifying all the logic each time, and it can be invoked just like a built-in function:

```
mysql> SELECT count_born_in_year(1908);
+--------------------------+
| count_born_in_year(1908) |
+--------------------------+
|                        1 |
+--------------------------+
mysql> SELECT count_born_in_year(1913);
+--------------------------+
| count_born_in_year(1913) |
+--------------------------+
|                        2 |
+--------------------------+
```

These statements invoke the function by itself, but stored functions can be used within arbitrarily complex expressions.

A function cannot return multiple values. You could write multiple functions and invoke them all from within a single statement, but another approach is to use a stored procedure that "returns" values through OUT parameters. The procedure should compute the desired values and assign them to the parameters, which then are accessible by the caller after the procedure returns. For details, see Section 4.2.2.2, "Stored Procedure Parameter Types."

If you define a stored function with the same name as a built-in function, qualify the function name with the database name when you invoke it. For example, if you define a stored function named PI() in the sampdb database, invoke it as sampdb.PI() to make clear that you do not mean the built-in function. Better yet, avoid this ambiguity by not using built-in function names for stored functions.

A stored procedure is similar to a stored function, but it doesn't return a value. Therefore, it does not have a RETURNS clause or any RETURN statements. The following simple stored procedure is similar to the count_born_in_year() function, but instead of calculating a count as a return value, it displays a result set containing a row of information for each president born in the given year:

```
mysql> delimiter $
mysql> CREATE PROCEDURE show_born_in_year(p_year INT)
    -> BEGIN
    ->   SELECT first_name, last_name, birth, death
    ->   FROM president
    ->   WHERE YEAR(birth) = p_year;
    -> END$
mysql> delimiter ;
```

Unlike a stored function, a stored procedure is not used in expressions. Instead, invoke it with the CALL statement:

```
mysql> CALL show_born_in_year(1908);
+------------+-----------+------------+------------+
| first_name | last_name | birth      | death      |
+------------+-----------+------------+------------+
| Lyndon B.  | Johnson   | 1908-08-27 | 1973-01-22 |
+------------+-----------+------------+------------+
mysql> CALL show_born_in_year(1913);
+------------+-----------+------------+------------+
| first_name | last_name | birth      | death      |
+------------+-----------+------------+------------+
| Richard M. | Nixon     | 1913-01-09 | 1994-04-22 |
| Gerald R.  | Ford      | 1913-07-14 | 2006-12-26 |
+------------+-----------+------------+------------+
```

The procedure body in this case executes a SELECT statement. As the example illustrates, the result set from this statement is not returned as the procedure value, but instead is sent to the client. A procedure can generate multiple result sets, each of which is sent in turn to the client.

The examples thus far have only selected information, but stored routines also can modify tables. The next routine, `update_expiration()`, takes the ID of a Historical League member and updates the appropriate membership row with the given expiration date:

```
CREATE PROCEDURE update_expiration (p_id INT UNSIGNED, p_date DATE)
BEGIN
  UPDATE member SET expiration = p_date WHERE member_id = p_id;
END;
```

The following calls of `update_expiration()` set member expirations to one year from the current date and to "lifetime membership" (NULL means "no expiration"):

```
mysql> CALL update_expiration(61, CURDATE() + INTERVAL 1 YEAR);
mysql> CALL update_expiration(87, NULL);
```

Stored functions are subject to the restriction that they cannot modify a table that is being read or written by the statement that invoked the function. Stored procedures normally do not have this restriction, but do become subject to it if they are invoked from within a stored function. For example, you cannot call `update_expiration()` from within a stored function that is invoked in a statement that selects from the `member` table.

4.2.2.1 Privileges for Stored Functions and Procedures

Stored functions and procedures belong to a database. To create a stored function or procedure, you must have the CREATE ROUTINE privilege for that database. By default, when you create a stored routine, the server automatically grants you the EXECUTE and ALTER ROUTINE privileges if you do not already have them, so that you can execute the routine or drop it. If you do drop the routine, the server also automatically revokes those privileges. To disable automatic privilege granting and revocation, set the `automatic_sp_privileges` system variable to 0.

If the server has binary logging enabled, stored functions are subject to additional conditions that are intended to make the binary log safe for backups and replication by restricting creation of functions that are nondeterministic or modify data. (If a function produces different results for given input values, restoring data by re-executing the binary log can fail to restore the original data, and the function can replicate differently on master and slave servers.) These conditions also apply to trigger creation. They are:

- If the `log_bin_trust_function_creators` system variable is not enabled, you must have the SUPER privilege to be able to create stored functions. Also, each function that you create should be deterministic and should not modify data. To signal this, declare it with one of the DETERMINISTIC, NO SQL, or READS SQL DATA characteristics. For example:

  ```
  CREATE FUNCTION half (p_value DOUBLE)
  RETURNS DOUBLE
  DETERMINISTIC
  BEGIN
    RETURN p_value / 2;
  END;
  ```

- If the `log_bin_trust_function_creators` system variable is enabled, no restrictions are enforced. This is most appropriate in situations where you can trust all users of the MySQL server not to define unsafe stored functions.

4.2.2.2 Stored Procedure Parameter Types

Each stored procedure parameter can have one of three types. For an IN parameter, the caller passes a value into the procedure. The value can be modified within the procedure, but changes are not visible to the caller after the procedure returns. An OUT parameter is the opposite. The procedure assigns a value to the parameter, which can be accessed by the caller after the procedure returns. An INOUT parameter enables the caller to pass in a value and get back a value.

To specify a parameter type explicitly, use IN, OUT, or INOUT immediately preceding the parameter name in the parameter list. Parameters are IN by default if no type is given.

To use an OUT or INOUT parameter, specify a variable name when you call the procedure. The procedure can set the parameter value, and the corresponding variable will have that value when the procedure returns. The OUT and INOUT parameter types can be especially useful when you require a computation that produces multiple result values. (A stored function returns only a single value, so it cannot be used to such situations.)

The following procedure demonstrates use of OUT parameters. It counts the number of male and female students in the `student` table and returns the counts in its parameters so the caller can access them:

```
CREATE PROCEDURE count_students_by_sex (OUT p_male INT, OUT p_female INT)
BEGIN
  SET p_male = (SELECT COUNT(*) FROM student WHERE sex = 'M');
  SET p_female = (SELECT COUNT(*) FROM student WHERE sex = 'F');
END;
```

To invoke the procedure, supply user-defined variables for the parameters. The procedure puts the counts into these parameters. After it returns, the variables contain the counts:

```
mysql> CALL count_students_by_sex(@male_count, @female_count);
mysql> SELECT @male_count, @female_count;
+-------------+---------------+
| @male_count | @female_count |
+-------------+---------------+
|          16 |            15 |
+-------------+---------------+
```

Are you limited to passing only user-defined variables as parameters? No. If you invoke `count_students_by_sex()` from within another stored program, local variables or parameters defined within that program can be passed as the parameters to `count_students_by_sex()`.

More involved examples might require additional parameters. For example, you might write a procedure that has an IN parameter that indicates the ID for a test or quiz in the `score` table.

The procedure could compute descriptive statistics from the relevant scores (mean, standard deviation, range, and so forth), then pass back all those values to the caller by means of OUT parameters.

The IN, OUT, and INOUT keywords do not apply to stored functions, triggers, or events. For stored functions, all parameters are like IN parameters. Triggers and events do not have parameters at all.

4.2.3   Triggers

A trigger is a stored program that is associated with a particular table and defined to activate for INSERT, DELETE, or UPDATE statements for that table. A trigger can be set to activate either before or after each row processed by the statement. The trigger definition includes a statement that executes when the trigger activates.

Triggers provide these benefits:

- A trigger can examine or change new data values to be inserted or used to update a row. This enables you to enforce data integrity constraints, such as verifying that a percentage is a value from 0 to 100. It is also possible to perform input data filtering.

- A trigger can supply default values for a column based on an expression, even for column types that can be defined only with a constant default value.

- A trigger can examine the current contents of a row before it is deleted or updated. This capability can be exploited to perform logging of changes to existing rows, for example.

To create a trigger, use the CREATE TRIGGER statement. The definition indicates the particular type of statement for which the trigger activates (INSERT, UPDATE, or DELETE), and whether it activates before or after rows are modified. The basic syntax for trigger creation looks like this:

```
CREATE TRIGGER trigger_name       # the trigger name
  {BEFORE | AFTER}                 # when the trigger activates
  {INSERT | UPDATE | DELETE}       # what statement activates it
  ON tbl_name                      # the associated table
  FOR EACH ROW trigger_stmt        # what the trigger does
```

trigger_name is the name of the trigger and tbl_name is the table with which the trigger is associated. For trigger naming, I like to adopt a convention that helps make the trigger purpose and table association clear, such as bi_tbl_name or ai_tbl_name for a BEFORE INSERT or AFTER INSERT trigger on tbl_name.

trigger_stmt is the trigger body; that is, the statement that executes when the trigger activates. In a trigger body, the syntax NEW.col_name can be used to refer to columns in the new row to be inserted or updated in an INSERT or UPDATE trigger. Similarly, OLD.col_name can be used to refer to columns in the old row to be deleted or updated in a DELETE or UPDATE trigger. To change a column value within a BEFORE trigger before the value is stored in the table, use SET NEW.col_name = value.

The following example shows a trigger bi_t for INSERT statements for a table t that has an integer percent column for storing percentage values (0 to 100) and a DATETIME column. The trigger uses BEFORE so that it can examine and possibly modify data values to be inserted into the table.

```
mysql> CREATE TABLE t (percent INT, dt DATETIME);
mysql> delimiter $
mysql> CREATE TRIGGER bi_t BEFORE INSERT ON t
    ->   FOR EACH ROW BEGIN
    ->     IF NEW.percent < 0 THEN
    ->       SET NEW.percent = 0;
    ->     ELSEIF NEW.percent > 100 THEN
    ->       SET NEW.percent = 100;
    ->     END IF;
    ->     SET NEW.dt = CURRENT_TIMESTAMP;
    ->   END$
mysql> delimiter ;
```

The trigger performs two actions:

- For attempts to insert a percentage value that lies outside the range from 0 to 100, the trigger converts the value to the nearest endpoint.

- The trigger automatically provides a value of CURRENT_TIMESTAMP for the DATETIME column. In effect, this works around the limitation that a column's default value must be a constant, and implements TIMESTAMP-like automatic initialization for a DATETIME column. (As of MySQL 5.6.5, DATETIME columns can be initialized to the current timestamp, so this part of the trigger is not needed. However, it does work as designed in 5.6 and for any earlier version as well, thus giving you a capability in version-independent fashion that is otherwise version dependent.)

To see how the trigger works, insert some rows into the table, then retrieve its contents:

```
mysql> INSERT INTO t (percent) VALUES(-2); DO SLEEP(2);
mysql> INSERT INTO t (percent) VALUES(30); DO SLEEP(2);
mysql> INSERT INTO t (percent) VALUES(120);
mysql> SELECT * FROM t;
+---------+---------------------+
| percent | dt                  |
+---------+---------------------+
|       0 | 2012-05-19 11:14:54 |
|      30 | 2012-05-19 11:14:56 |
|     100 | 2012-05-19 11:14:58 |
+---------+---------------------+
```

A trigger belongs to a table, so you must have the TRIGGER privilege for that table to create or drop triggers for it. (If you drop a table, MySQL drops any triggers associated with it.)

Trigger creation has some of the same constraints as stored function creation. See Section 4.2.2.1, "Privileges for Stored Functions and Procedures."

4.2.4 Events

MySQL has an event scheduler that enables you to perform time-activated database operations. An event is a stored program that is associated with a schedule. The schedule defines the time or times at which the event executes, and optionally when the event ceases to exist. Events are especially useful for performing unattended administrative operations such as periodic updates to summary reports, expiration of old data, or log table rotation. This section demonstrates row expiration. For an example that shows how to perform event-based log table rotation, see Section 12.8.7.4, "Expiring or Rotating Log Tables."

The event scheduler does not run by default, so you must enable it to use events. Put the following lines in an option file that the server reads at startup:

```
[mysqld]
event_scheduler=ON
```

To check the status of the event scheduler at runtime, use this statement:

```
SHOW VARIABLES LIKE 'event_scheduler';
```

To stop or start the scheduler at runtime, change the value of the event_scheduler system variable (it is a GLOBAL variable, so you must have the SUPER privilege):

```
SET GLOBAL event_scheduler = OFF;     # or 0
SET GLOBAL event_scheduler = ON;      # or 1
```

If you stop the scheduler, no events run. It is also possible to leave the scheduler running but disable individual events, as discussed later.

> **Note**
>
> If you set event_scheduler to DISABLED at startup, you can check but not change its status at runtime. You can create events, but they will not execute.

The event scheduler writes to the server's error log, which you can check for information about what the scheduler is doing. It logs events as it runs them, as well as errors that occur during event execution. If the event scheduler is not running when you expect it to be, check the error log for messages that indicate why.

To create an event, use the CREATE EVENT statement, which has this basic syntax:

```
CREATE EVENT event_name
  ON SCHEDULE
    {AT datetime | EVERY expr interval [STARTS datetime] [ENDS datetime]}
  DO event_stmt
```

An event belongs to a database, so you must have the EVENT privilege for that database to create or drop events for it.

The following example shows how to create a simple event that deletes old rows from a table. Suppose that you have a table named web_session that holds state information for sessions associated with users who visit your Web site, and that this table has a DATETIME column named last_visit that indicates the time of each user's most recent visit. To keep this table from accumulating stale rows, set up an event that periodically purges them. To execute the event every four hours and have it expire rows more than a day old, write the event definition like this:

```
CREATE EVENT expire_web_session
  ON SCHEDULE EVERY 4 HOUR
  DO
    DELETE FROM web_session
    WHERE last_visit < CURRENT_TIMESTAMP - INTERVAL 1 DAY;
```

The EVERY *n* *interval* clauses specifies periodic execution at fixed intervals. The *interval* values are like those used for the DATE_ADD() function, such as HOUR, DAY, or MONTH. Following EVERY, you can also include optional STARTS *datetime* and ENDS *datetime* clauses to specify the initial and final execution time. By default, an EVERY event runs for the first time immediately after it is created and has no final time.

The DO clause defines the event body, which is an SQL statement that executes when the event runs. As for other stored program types, this can be a simple statement or a compound statement written using BEGIN and END.

To create an event that runs only one time, use the AT scheduling type rather than EVERY. A definition such as the following creates an event that executes once, an hour in the future:

```
CREATE EVENT one_shot
  ON SCHEDULE AT CURRENT_TIMESTAMP + INTERVAL 1 HOUR
  DO ... ;
```

To disable an event to stop it from executing, or to re-enable a disabled event, use ALTER EVENT:

```
ALTER EVENT event_name DISABLE;
ALTER EVENT event_name ENABLE;
```

4.3   Security for Views and Stored Programs

Defining a view sets up a SELECT statement intended for later invocation. The same is true when you define a stored program: It creates an object to be executed later. This "execute later" aspect of such objects means that the user who executes the object might not be the user who originally defined it, which raises an important question: What security context should the server use for checking access privileges at execution time? That is, which account's privileges should apply?

By default, the server uses the account of the user who defined the object. Suppose that I define a stored procedure p() that accesses tables belonging to me. If I give you the EXECUTE privilege for p(), you can use CALL p() to invoke the procedure and it will access my tables on your behalf because it runs with my privileges. This type of security context can be good or bad:

- It's good in the sense that it enables carefully written stored programs to be set up that provide controlled access to tables for users who are not able to access them directly.

- It's bad if a user defines a stored program that accesses sensitive data but forgets that other people who can invoke the object have the same access to that data as its definer.

To explicitly specify the definer for a view or stored program, include a DEFINER = account clause in the CREATE statement for the object. This causes the named account to be treated as the definer for purposes of access checking at execution time. For example:

```
CREATE DEFINER = 'sampadm'@'localhost' PROCEDURE count_students()
  SELECT COUNT(*) FROM student;
```

In a DEFINER clause, the definer value can be an account name in 'user_name'@'host_name' format as used in account-management statements such as CREATE USER. (See Section 13.2.1.1, "Specifying Account Names.") For this format, user_name and host_name must both be given. Alternatively, the value can be CURRENT_USER or CURRENT_USER() to indicate the account of the user who executes the CREATE statement; this is the same account that is used by default if no DEFINER clause is present.

If you have the SUPER privilege, you can give any syntactically legal account name as the DEFINER value; a warning occurs if the account does not exist at the time. If you do not have the SUPER privilege, you can set the definer only to your own account, using either the literal account name or CURRENT_USER.

For views and stored routines (stored functions and procedures), the SQL SECURITY character-istic can be given for additional control over execution-time access checking. SQL SECURITY takes a value of DEFINER (execute with the definer's privileges) or INVOKER (execute with the privileges of the user who invoked the object).

SQL SECURITY INVOKER is preferable for situations when you don't want a view or stored routine to execute with any more privileges than a user already has. The following view accesses a table in the mysql database, but runs with invoker privileges. That way, if the invoker has no access to mysql.user, the view won't subvert that restriction.

```
CREATE SQL SECURITY INVOKER VIEW v
  AS SELECT CONCAT(User,'@',Host) AS Account, Password FROM mysql.user;
```

Triggers and events are invoked automatically by the server, so the concept of "invoking user" does not apply. Thus, they have no SQL SECURITY characteristic and always execute with definer privileges.

If a view or stored program runs with definer privileges at execution time and the definer account does not exist, an error occurs.

Within a view or stored program, the CURRENT_USER() function returns the account corre-sponding to the object's DEFINER attribute by default. For views and stored routines defined with the SQL SECURITY INVOKER characteristic, CURRENT_USER() returns the account for the invoking user.

5

Query Optimization

The world of relational database theory is a world dominated by tables and sets, and operations on tables and sets. A database is a set of tables, and a table is a set of rows and columns. When you issue a SELECT statement to retrieve rows from a table, you get back another set of rows and columns—that is, another table. These are abstract notions that make no reference to the underlying representation a database system uses to operate on the data in your tables. Another abstraction in set theory is that operations on tables happen all at once; queries are conceptualized as set operations for which there is no concept of time.

The real world is quite different. Database management systems implement abstract concepts but do so on real hardware bound by real physical constraints. As a result, queries take time— sometimes an annoyingly long time. And we, being impatient creatures, don't like to wait, so we leave the abstract world of instantaneous mathematical operations on sets and look for ways to speed up our queries. Fortunately, there are several techniques for doing so:

- Create indexes on tables to enable the database server to look up rows more quickly.

- Consider how to write queries to take advantage of those indexes to the fullest extent, and use the EXPLAIN statement to check whether the MySQL server really is doing so.

- Choose data types and table storage formats that the server can process efficiently.

This chapter focuses on those kinds of issues, with the goal of helping you optimize the performance of your database system so that it processes your queries as quickly as possible. MySQL is already quite fast, but even the fastest database can run queries more quickly if you help it do so.

5.1   Using Indexing

Of the many techniques for speeding up queries, indexing is the most important. That is, in general, the one thing that makes the most difference is the proper use of indexes. It's often true that when a query runs slowly, adding indexes solves the problem immediately. But it doesn't always work like that, because optimization isn't always simple. Nevertheless, if you don't use indexes, in many cases you're just wasting your time trying to improve performance by other means. Use indexing first to get the biggest performance boost; then see what other techniques might be helpful.

This section describes what indexes are and how they improve query performance. It also discusses the circumstances under which indexes might degrade performance and provides guidelines for choosing indexes for your tables wisely. In the next section, we'll discuss MySQL's query optimizer that attempts to find the most efficient way to execute queries. It's good to have some understanding of the optimizer in addition to knowing how to create indexes because then you'll be better able to take advantage of the indexes you create. Certain ways of writing queries actually prevent your indexes from being useful, and you want to avoid that.

5.1.1   Benefits of Indexing

Let's consider how an index works, beginning with a table that has no indexes. An unindexed table is simply an unordered collection of rows. Figure 5.1 shows the `ad` table that was discussed in Chapter 1, "Getting Started with MySQL." Because there are no indexes on this table, finding the rows for a particular company requires examining each row in the table to see whether it matches the desired value. This involves a full table scan, which is slow, as well as tremendously inefficient if the table is large but contains only a few rows that match the search criteria.

ad table

company_num	ad_num	hit_fee
14	48	0.01
23	49	0.02
17	52	0.01
13	55	0.03
23	62	0.02
23	63	0.01
23	64	0.02
13	77	0.03
23	99	0.03
14	101	0.01
13	102	0.01
17	119	0.02

Figure 5.1   Unindexed `ad` table.

Figure 5.2 shows the same table with the addition of an index on the `company_num` column in the `ad` table. The index contains an entry for each row in the `ad` table, but the index entries are sorted by `company_num` value. Now, instead of searching the table row by row looking for items that match, we can use the index. Suppose that we're looking for all rows for company 13. We begin scanning the index and find three values for that company. Then we reach the index value for company 14, which is higher than the one we're looking for. Index values are sorted, so when we read the index row containing 14, we know we won't find any more matches and can quit looking. Thus, one efficiency gained by using the index is that we can tell where the matching rows end and can skip the rest. Another efficiency comes about through the use of positioning algorithms for finding the first matching entry without doing a linear scan from the start of the index (for example, a binary search is much quicker than a scan). That way, we can quickly position to the first matching value and save a lot of time in the search. Databases use various techniques for positioning to index values quickly, but it's not so important here what those techniques are. What's important is that they work and that indexing is a good thing because it enables their use.

ad table

index
13
13
13
14
14
17
17
23
23
23
23
23

company_num	ad_num	hit_fee
14	48	0.01
23	49	0.02
17	52	0.01
13	55	0.03
23	62	0.02
23	63	0.01
23	64	0.02
13	77	0.03
23	99	0.03
14	101	0.01
13	102	0.01
17	119	0.02

Figure 5.2   Indexed ad table.

Why not just sort the data rows and dispense with the index? Wouldn't that produce the same type of improvement in search speed? Yes, it would—if the table had a single index. But you might want to add a second index, and you can't sort the data rows two different ways at once. For example, you might want one index on customer names and another on customer ID numbers or phone numbers. Using indexes as entities separate from the data rows solves the problem and enables multiple indexes to be created. In addition, rows in the index are generally shorter than data rows. When you insert or delete new values, it's easier to move around shorter index values to maintain the sort order than to move around the longer data rows.

The particular details of index implementations vary for different MySQL storage engines. For example, for a MyISAM table, the table's data rows are kept in a data file, and index values are kept in an index file. You can have more than one index on a table, but they're all stored in the same index file. Each index in the index file consists of a sorted array of key rows that are used for fast access into the data file.

By contrast, the InnoDB storage engine does not separate data rows and index values in the same way, although it does maintain indexes as sets of sorted values. By default, the InnoDB engine uses a single tablespace within which it manages data and index storage for all InnoDB tables. InnoDB can be configured to create each table with its own tablespace, but even so, a given table's data and indexes are stored in the same tablespace file.

The preceding discussion describes the benefit of an index in the context of single-table queries, where the use of an index speeds searches significantly by eliminating the need for full table scans. Indexes are even more valuable when you're running queries that perform joins on multiple tables. In a single-table full-scan query, the number of rows you must examine is the number of rows in the table. If the query involves multiple tables, the number of possible combinations skyrockets because it's the product of the number of rows in the tables.

Suppose that you have three unindexed tables, t1, t2, and t3, each containing a column i1, i2, and i3, respectively, and each consisting of 1,000 rows that contain the numbers 1 through 1000. A query to find all combinations of table rows in which the values are equal looks like this:

```
SELECT t1.i1, t2.i2, t3.i3
FROM t1 INNER JOIN t2 INNER JOIN t3
WHERE t1.i1 = t2.i2 AND t2.i2 = t3.i3;
```

The result of this query should be 1,000 rows, each containing three equal values. If we process the query in the absence of indexes, we have no idea which rows contain which values. Consequently, we must try all combinations to find the ones that match the WHERE clause. The number of possible combinations is 1,000 × 1,000 × 1,000 (one billion!), which is a million times more than the number of matches. That's a lot of wasted effort. To make things worse, as the tables grow, the time to process joins on those tables grows even more if no indexes are used, leading to very poor performance. We can speed things up considerably by indexing the tables, because the indexes enable the query to be processed like this:

1. Select the first row from table t1 and see what value the row contains.

2. Using the index on table t2, go directly to the row that matches the value from t1. Similarly, using the index on table t3, go directly to the row that matches the value from t2.

3. Proceed to the next row of table t1 and repeat the preceding procedure. Do this until all rows in t1 have been examined.

In this case, we still perform a full scan of table t1, but we can do indexed lookups on t2 and t3 to pull out rows from those tables directly. The query runs about a million times faster this way—literally. This example is contrived for the purpose of making a point, but the problems it illustrates are real, and adding indexes to tables that have none often results in dramatic performance gains.

MySQL uses indexes several ways:

- As just described, indexes are used to speed up searches for rows matching terms of a WHERE clause or rows that match rows in other tables when performing joins.

- For queries that use the MIN() or MAX() functions, MySQL can find the smallest or largest value in an indexed column quickly without examining every row.

- MySQL can often use indexes to efficiently perform sorting and grouping operations for ORDER BY and GROUP BY clauses.

- Sometimes MySQL can use an index to read all the information required for a query. Suppose that you're selecting values from an indexed numeric column in an InnoDB or MyISAM table, and you're selecting no other columns from the table. In this case, when MySQL reads an index value, it obtains the same value that it would get by reading the data row. There's no reason to read values twice, so the data row need not be accessed at all.

5.1.2 Costs of Indexing

In general, if MySQL can figure out how to use an index to process a query more quickly, it will. This means that, for the most part, if you don't index your tables, you're hurting yourself. You can see that I'm painting a rosy picture of the benefits of indexing. Are there disadvantages? Yes, there are costs both in time and in space. In practice, these drawbacks tend to be outweighed by the advantages, but you should know what they are.

First, indexes speed up retrievals but slow down inserts and deletes, as well as updates of values in indexed columns. That is, indexes slow down most operations that involve writing. This occurs because writing a row requires writing not only the data row; it requires changes to any indexes as well. The more indexes a table has, the more changes must be made, and the greater the average performance degradation. Most tables receive many reads and few writes, but for a workload with a high percentage of writes, the cost of index updating might be significant. Section 5.5, "Loading Data Efficiently," discusses what you can do to reduce this cost.

Second, an index takes up disk space, and multiple indexes take up correspondingly more space. This might cause you to reach a table size limit more quickly than if there are no indexes:

- For a MyISAM table, indexing it heavily may cause the index file to reach its maximum size more quickly than the data file.

- All InnoDB tables that are located within the InnoDB system tablespace compete for the same common pool of space, and adding indexes depletes storage within this tablespace more quickly. However, unlike the files used for MyISAM tables, the InnoDB system tablespace is not bound by your operating system's file-size limit, because it can be configured to use multiple files. As long as you have additional disk space, you can expand the tablespace by adding new components to it.

  InnoDB tables that use individual tablespaces store data and index values together in the same file, so adding indexes causes the table to reach the maximum file size more quickly.

The practical implication of these factors? If you don't need a particular index to help queries perform better, don't create it.

5.1.3 Choosing Indexes

The syntax for creating indexes is covered in Section 2.6.4.2, "Creating Indexes." I assume here that you've read that section. But knowing syntax doesn't in itself help you determine which indexes to create. That requires some thought about how you use your tables. This section gives some guidelines for identifying candidate columns to index.

Index columns used for searching, sorting, or grouping, not columns you select for output. In other words, the best candidate columns for indexing are the columns that appear in WHERE clauses, columns named in join clauses, or columns that appear in ORDER BY or GROUP BY clauses. Columns that appear only in the output column list following the SELECT keyword are not good candidates:

```
SELECT
    col_a                       ← not a candidate
FROM
    tbl1 LEFT JOIN tbl2
    ON tbl1.col_b = tbl2.col_c  ← candidates
WHERE
    col_d = expr;               ← a candidate
```

The columns that you display and the columns you use in the WHERE clause might be the same, of course. The point is that appearance of a column in the output column list is not in itself a good indicator that it should be indexed.

Columns that appear in join clauses or in expressions of the form *col1 = col2* in WHERE clauses are especially good candidates for indexing. col_b and col_c in the query just shown are examples of this. If MySQL can optimize a query using joined columns, it cuts down the potential table-row combinations quite a bit by eliminating full table scans.

Consider column cardinality. The cardinality of a column is the number of distinct values that it contains. For example, a column that contains the values 1, 3, 7, 4, 7, and 3 has a cardinality of four. Indexes work best for columns that have a high cardinality relative to the number of rows in the table (that is, columns that have many unique values and few duplicates). For a column that contains many different age values, an index readily differentiates rows. For a column that is used to record sex and contains only the two values 'M' and 'F', an index will not help. If the values occur about equally, you'll get about half of the rows whichever value you search for. Under these circumstances, the index might never be used at all, because the query optimizer generally skips an index in favor of a full table scan if it determines that a value occurs in a large percentage of a table's rows.

To determine the number of unique values in a column relative to the number of table rows, use a query like this:

```
mysql> SELECT COUNT(*), COUNT(DISTINCT state) FROM member;
+----------+-----------------------+
| COUNT(*) | COUNT(DISTINCT state) |
+----------+-----------------------+
|      102 |                    46 |
+----------+-----------------------+
```

Index short values. Use smaller data types when possible. For example, don't use a BIGINT column if a MEDIUMINT is large enough to hold the values you need to store, and don't use

`CHAR(100)` if none of your values are longer than 25 characters. Smaller values improve index processing several ways:

- Shorter values can be compared more quickly, so index lookups are faster.

- Smaller values result in smaller indexes that require less disk I/O.

- With shorter key values, index blocks in the key cache hold more key values. MySQL can hold more keys in memory at once, which improves the likelihood of locating key values without reading additional index blocks from disk.

For the InnoDB storage engine, which uses clustered indexes, it's especially beneficial to keep the primary key short. A clustered index stores the data rows together with (that is, clustered with) the primary key values. Other indexes are secondary indexes; these store the primary key value with the secondary index values. A lookup in a secondary index yields a primary key value, which then is used to locate the data row. The implication is that primary key values are duplicated into each secondary index, so if primary key values are longer, the extra storage is required for each secondary index as well.

Index prefixes of string values. To index a string column, specify a prefix length whenever it's reasonable to do so. For example, if you have a `CHAR(200)` column, don't index the entire column if most values are unique within the first 10 or 20 characters. Indexing the first 10 or 20 characters will save a lot of space in the index, and probably will make your queries faster as well. (Indexing shorter values gains you the advantages described in the previous item relating to comparison speed and disk I/O reduction.) You want to use some common sense, of course. Indexing just the first character from a column isn't likely to be helpful because the resulting index won't have very many distinct values.

You can index prefixes of `CHAR`, `VARCHAR`, `BINARY`, `VARBINARY`, `TEXT`, and `BLOB` columns, using the syntax described in Section 2.6.4.2, "Creating Indexes."

Take advantage of leftmost prefixes. When you create an n-column composite index, you actually create n indexes that MySQL can use. A composite index serves as several indexes because any leftmost set of columns in the index can be used to match rows. Such a set is called a "leftmost prefix." (This is different from indexing a prefix of a column, which creates an index using the first n characters or bytes of column values.)

Suppose that you have a table with a composite index on columns named `country`, `state`, and `city`. Rows in the index are sorted in `country/state/city` order, so they're automatically sorted in `country/state` order and in `country` order as well. This means that MySQL can take advantage of the index even if you specify only `country` values in a query, or only `country` and `state` values. Thus, the index can be used to search the following combinations of columns:

```
country, state, city
country, state
country
```

MySQL cannot use the index for searches that don't involve a leftmost prefix; for example, if you search by `state` or by `city`. If you search for a given country and a particular city (columns 1 and 3 of the index), the index can't be used for the combination of values, although MySQL can narrow the search using the index to find rows that match the country.

Don't over-index. Don't index everything in sight based on the assumption "the more, the better." Every additional index takes extra disk space and hurts performance of write operations, as has already been mentioned. Indexes must be updated and possibly reorganized when you modify a table, and the more indexes it has, the longer this takes. An index that is rarely or never used slows down table modifications unnecessarily. In addition, MySQL considers indexes when generating an execution plan for retrievals. Creating extra indexes creates more work for the query optimizer. It's also possible (if unlikely) that MySQL will fail to use the best index when the table has too many of them. To help avoid leading the optimizer astray, maintain only the indexes you need.

If you're thinking about adding an index to a table that is already indexed, consider whether the prospective index is a leftmost prefix of an existing index. If so, don't bother adding the index because, in effect, you already have it. For example, if you already have an index on `country`, `state`, and `city`, there is no point in adding an index on `country`. The exception is that for `FULLTEXT` indexes, you must have a separate index for each distinct set of columns that you want to search.

Match index types to the comparisons you perform. When you create an index, most storage engines choose the index implementation they will use. For example, InnoDB always uses B-tree indexes. MyISAM also uses B-tree indexes, except that it uses R-tree indexes for spatial data types. The MEMORY storage engine uses hash indexes by default, but also supports B-tree indexes and enables you to select which one you want. To choose an index type, consider what kind of comparison operations you plan to perform on the indexed column:

- For a hash index, a hash function is applied to each column value. The resulting hash values are stored in the index and used to perform lookups. (A hash function implements an algorithm that is likely to produce distinct hash values for distinct input values. The advantage of using hash values is that they can be compared more efficiently than the original values.) Hash indexes are very fast for exact-match comparisons performed with the `=` or `<=>` operators. But they are poor for comparisons that look for a range of values, as in these expressions:

  ```
  id < 30
  weight BETWEEN 100 AND 150
  ```

- B-tree indexes can be used effectively for comparisons involving exact or range-based comparisons that use the `<`, `<=`, `=`, `>=`, `>`, `<>`, `!=`, and `BETWEEN` operators. B-tree indexes can also be used for `LIKE` pattern matches if the pattern begins with a literal string rather than a wildcard character.

If you use a MEMORY table only for exact-value lookups, a hash index is a good choice. This is the default index type for MEMORY tables, so you need do nothing special. If you usually perform range-based comparisons, use a B-tree index instead. To specify this type of index, add `USING BTREE` to your index definition. For example:

```
CREATE TABLE lookup
(
    id      INT NOT NULL,
    name    CHAR(20),
    PRIMARY KEY (id) USING BTREE
) ENGINE=MEMORY;
```

If the types of searches you perform warrant it, a single MEMORY table can have both hash indexes and B-tree indexes, even on the same column.

Some types of comparisons cannot use indexes. If you perform comparisons only by passing column values to a function such as `STRCMP()`, there is no value in indexing the column. The server must evaluate the function value for each row, which precludes use of an index on the column.

Use the slow query log to identify queries that may be performing badly. This log can help you find queries that might benefit from indexing. (For general discussion of MySQL's logs, See Section 12.8, "Server Logs.") The slow query log is written as text, so it is viewable with any file-display program, or you can use the `mysqldumpslow` utility to summarize its contents. If a given query shows up repeatedly in this log, it might be suboptimal and subject to rewriting that will make it run more quickly. Keep in mind when assessing your slow query log that "slow" is measured in real time, so the server writes more queries to the slow query log when heavily loaded than when not.

5.2 The MySQL Query Optimizer

When you issue a statement, MySQL analyzes it to see which optimizations can be used to process it more quickly. In this section, we'll look at how the query optimizer works. For additional information about optimization measures that MySQL takes, consult the optimization chapter in the MySQL Reference Manual.

The MySQL query optimizer takes advantage of indexes, of course, but it also uses other information. For example, if you issue the following query, MySQL executes it very quickly, no matter how large the table is:

```
SELECT * FROM tbl_name WHERE FALSE;
```

In this case, MySQL looks at the `WHERE` clause, discovers that no rows can possibly satisfy the query, and doesn't bother to search the table. You can see this by issuing an `EXPLAIN` statement, which tells MySQL to display information about how it would execute a `SELECT` query, without actually executing it. (As of MySQL 5.6.3, you can also use `EXPLAIN` with `DELETE`, `INSERT`, `REPLACE`, and `UPDATE` statements.)

To use EXPLAIN, just put the word EXPLAIN in front of the SELECT statement:

```
mysql> EXPLAIN SELECT * FROM tbl_name WHERE FALSE\G
*************************** 1. row ***************************
           id: 1
  select_type: SIMPLE
        table: NULL
         type: NULL
possible_keys: NULL
          key: NULL
      key_len: NULL
          ref: NULL
         rows: NULL
        Extra: Impossible WHERE
```

Normally, EXPLAIN returns more information than that, including values more informative than NULL about the indexes that will be used to scan tables, the types of joins that will be used, and estimates of the number of rows that must be examined from each table. For examples, see Section 5.2.2, "Using EXPLAIN to Check Optimizer Operation."

In some cases, EXPLAIN actually does execute part of a query, if it contains subqueries in the FROM clause: EXPLAIN must execute the subqueries to find out what they return before analyzing the main SELECT statement. (As of MySQL 5.6.3, this behavior no longer occurs.)

5.2.1   How the Optimizer Works

The MySQL query optimizer has several goals, but its primary aims are to use indexes whenever possible and to use the most restrictive index in order to eliminate from consideration as many rows as possible as soon as possible. That last part might sound backward and unintuitive. After all, your goal in issuing a SELECT statement is to *find* rows, not to reject them. The optimizer, by contrast, tries to *reject* rows because the faster it can eliminate rows, the more quickly it can find the rows that do match your criteria. Queries can be processed more quickly if the most restrictive tests can be done first. Suppose that a query tests two columns, each of which has an index on it:

```
SELECT col3 FROM mytable
WHERE col1 = 'some value' AND col2 = 'some other value';
```

Suppose also that the test on col1 matches 900 rows, the test on col2 matches 300 rows, and that both tests together succeed on 30 rows. Testing col1 first results in 900 rows that must be examined to find the 30 that also match the col2 value. That's 870 failed tests. Testing col2 first results in 300 rows that must be examined to find the 30 that also match the col1 value. That's only 270 failed tests, so less computation and disk I/O is required. As a result, the optimizer will test col2 first because doing so results in less work overall.

To help the optimizer take advantage of indexes, use the guidelines described here.

Analyze your tables. This generates key value distribution statistics that help the optimizer make better estimates about index effectiveness. By default, when you compare values in indexed columns to a constant, the optimizer assumes that key values are distributed evenly within the index. The optimizer also does a quick check of the index to estimate how many entries will be used when determining whether the index should be used for constant comparisons. For InnoDB and MyISAM tables, you can tell the server to perform an analysis of key values by using `ANALYZE TABLE`.

A table that is populated and then remains static need be analyzed only once after being loaded. A table that undergoes updates should be reanalyzed occasionally (at a frequency corresponding to how often updates occur).

Use `EXPLAIN` to verify optimizer operation. The `EXPLAIN` statement can tell you whether indexes are being used. This information is helpful when you're trying different ways of writing a statement or checking whether adding indexes actually will make a difference in query execution efficiency.

Give the optimizer hints or override it when necessary. You can use `FORCE INDEX`, `USE INDEX`, or `IGNORE INDEX` after a table name in the table list of a join to give the server guidance about which indexes to prefer. See the description for `SELECT` in Appendix E, "SQL Syntax Reference."

You can also use `STRAIGHT_JOIN` to force the optimizer to use tables in a particular order. Normally, the MySQL optimizer considers itself free to determine the order in which to scan tables to retrieve rows most quickly. On occasion, the optimizer makes a suboptimal choice. If you find this happening, you can override the optimizer's choice using the `STRAIGHT_JOIN` keyword. A join performed with `STRAIGHT_JOIN` forces the tables to be joined in the order named in the `FROM` clause.

If you do this, try to order the tables to cause the most restrictive selection to come first. That is, order the tables to put first the one from which the smallest number of rows will be chosen. Queries perform better the earlier you can narrow the possible candidate rows.

`STRAIGHT_JOIN` can be specified at two points in a `SELECT` statement. You can specify it between the `SELECT` keyword and the selection list to have a global effect on all joins in the statement, or you can specify it in the `FROM` clause. The following two statements are equivalent:

```
SELECT STRAIGHT_JOIN ... FROM t1 INNER JOIN t2 INNER JOIN t3 ... ;
SELECT ... FROM t1 STRAIGHT_JOIN t2 STRAIGHT_JOIN t3 ... ;
```

Be sure to try the query with and without `STRAIGHT_JOIN`. MySQL might have some good reason not to use indexes in the order you think is best, and perhaps `STRAIGHT_JOIN` does not actually help. Check the execution plans with `EXPLAIN` to see how MySQL handles each statement.

Compare columns that have the same data type. When you compare indexed columns, identical data types give you better performance than dissimilar types. For example, `INT` differs from `BIGINT`, so an `INT`/`INT` or `BIGINT`/`BIGINT` comparison is faster than an `INT`/`BIGINT` comparison. CHAR(10) is considered the same as CHAR(10) or VARCHAR(10) but different from CHAR(12) or VARCHAR(12). If columns that you compare frequently have different types, consider using ALTER TABLE to modify one of them so the types match.

Make indexed columns stand alone in comparison expressions. If you use a column in a function call or as part of a more complex term in an arithmetic expression, MySQL can't use the index because it must compute the value of the expression for every row. Sometimes this is unavoidable, but sometimes you can rewrite a query to isolate the indexed column by itself.

The following WHERE clauses illustrate how this works. They are equivalent arithmetically, but quite different for optimization purposes:

```
WHERE mycol * 2 < 4
WHERE mycol < 4 / 2
```

For the first line, MySQL must retrieve the value of mycol for each row, multiply by 2, and then compare the result to 4. In this case, no index can be used. Each value in the column must be retrieved so that the expression on the left side of the comparison can be evaluated. For the second line, the optimizer simplifies the expression 4/2 to the value 2, and then uses an index on mycol to quickly find values less than 2. Therefore, the second line is better than the first.

Let's consider another example. Suppose that you have an indexed DATE column date_col. If you issue a query such as the one following, the index isn't used:

```
SELECT * FROM mytbl WHERE YEAR(date_col) < 1990;
```

The expression doesn't compare 1990 to an indexed column; it compares 1990 to a value calculated from the column, and that value must be computed for each row. As a result, the index on date_col is not used and query execution requires a full table scan. What's the fix? Use a literal date. Then the optimizer can use the index on date_col to find matching column values:

```
WHERE date_col < '1990-01-01'
```

But suppose that you don't have a specific date. You might be interested instead in finding rows that have a date that lies within a certain number of days from today. There are several ways to express a comparison of this type—not all of which are equally efficient. Here are three possibilities:

```
WHERE TO_DAYS(date_col) - TO_DAYS(CURDATE()) < cutoff
WHERE TO_DAYS(date_col) < cutoff + TO_DAYS(CURDATE())
WHERE date_col < DATE_ADD(CURDATE(), INTERVAL cutoff DAY)
```

For the first line, no index is used because the column must be retrieved for each row so the value of TO_DAYS(date_col) can be computed. The second line is better. Both cutoff and TO_DAYS(CURDATE()) are constants, so the right-hand side of the comparison can be calculated by the optimizer once before processing the query, rather than once per row. But the date_col column still appears in a function call, preventing use of the index. The third line is best of all. Again, the right-hand side of the comparison can be computed once as a constant before executing the query, but now the value is a date. That value can be compared directly to `date_col` values, which no longer need to be converted to days. In this case, the index can be used.

Don't use wildcards at the beginning of a `LIKE` pattern. Some string searches use a `WHERE` clause of the following form:

```
WHERE col_name LIKE '%string%'
```

That's the correct thing to do if you want to find the string no matter where it occurs in the column. But don't put '`%`' on both sides of the string simply out of habit. If you're really looking for the string only when it occurs at the beginning of the column, leave out the first '`%`'. Suppose that you're looking in a column containing last names for names like MacGregor or MacDougall that begin with '`Mac`'. In that case, write the `WHERE` clause like this:

```
WHERE last_name LIKE 'Mac%'
```

The optimizer looks at the literal initial part of the pattern and uses the index to find rows that match as though you'd written the following expression, which is in a form that enables an index on `last_name` to be used:

```
WHERE last_name >= 'Mac' AND last_name < 'Mad'
```

This optimization does not apply to pattern matches that use the `REGEXP` operator. `REGEXP` expressions are never optimized.

Take advantage of areas in which the optimizer is more mature. MySQL can do joins and subqueries, but subquery support is more recent. Consequently, the optimizer has been better tuned for joins than for subqueries in some cases. This has a practical implication when you have a subquery that runs slowly. As discussed in Section 2.9.7, "Rewriting Subqueries as Joins." some subqueries can be reformulated as logically equivalent joins. If your slow subquery is one of these, try writing it as a join to see whether it performs better. (This strategy is likely to be most advantageous before MySQL 5.6 because considerable work has gone into improving subquery performance in 5.6.)

Test alternative forms of queries, but run them more than once. When testing alternative forms of a query (for example, a subquery versus an equivalent join), run it several times each way. If you run a query only once each of two different ways, you'll often find that the second query is faster just because information from the first query is still cached and need not actually be read from the disk. You should also try to run queries when the system load is relatively stable to avoid effects due to other activities on your system.

Avoid overuse of automatic type conversion. MySQL performs automatic type conversion, but if you can avoid conversions, you may get better performance. For example, if `num_col` is an integer column, each of these queries returns the same result:

```
SELECT * FROM mytbl WHERE num_col = 4;
SELECT * FROM mytbl WHERE num_col = '4';
```

But the second query involves a type conversion. The conversion operation itself involves a small performance penalty for converting the integer and string to double to perform the comparison. A more serious problem is that if `num_col` is indexed, a comparison that involves type conversion may prevent the index from being used.

The opposite kind of comparison (comparing a string column to a numeric value) also can prevent use of an index. Suppose that you write a query like this:

```
SELECT * FROM mytbl WHERE str_col = 4;
```

In this case, an index on `str_col` cannot be used because there can be many different string values in `str_col` that are equal to 4 when converted to a number (for example, `'4'`, `'4.0'`, and `'4th'`). The only way to know which values qualify is to read each one, convert it, and perform the comparison. To avoid this problem if you are looking for a particular value such as `'4'`, specify it that way in the query:

```
SELECT * FROM mytbl WHERE str_col = '4';
```

5.2.2   Using `EXPLAIN` to Check Optimizer Operation

You can use the `EXPLAIN` statement to gain insight into the execution plans that the optimizer generates for processing statements. This section shows two uses for `EXPLAIN`:

- To determine whether writing a query different ways affects whether an index can be used.

- To investigate the effect of adding indexes on the optimizer's ability to generate efficient execution plans.

The discussion describes only those `EXPLAIN` output fields that are relevant for the examples. `EXPLAIN` output is discussed further in Appendix E, "SQL Syntax Reference." The output shown is what I see on my system. Depending on your server version and configuration, you might see somewhat different results.

Earlier, in Section 5.2.1, "How the Optimizer Works," the point was made that the way you write an expression can determine whether the optimizer can use available indexes. Specifically, the discussion there used the example that of the three following logically equivalent WHERE clauses, only the third enables use of an index:

```
WHERE TO_DAYS(date_col) - TO_DAYS(CURDATE()) < cutoff
WHERE TO_DAYS(date_col) < cutoff + TO_DAYS(CURDATE())
WHERE date_col < DATE_ADD(CURDATE(), INTERVAL cutoff DAY)
```

`EXPLAIN` enables you to check whether one way of writing an expression is better than another. To see this, let's try using each of the WHERE clauses to search for `expiration` column values in the `member` table, using a `cutoff` value of 30 days. However, as originally created, the `member` table has no index on the `expiration` column. To enable the relationship to be seen between index use and how an expression is written, first index the `expiration` column:

```
mysql> ALTER TABLE member ADD INDEX (expiration);
```

Then try EXPLAIN with each form of the expression to see what execution plans the optimizer comes up with:

```
mysql> EXPLAIN SELECT * FROM member
    -> WHERE TO_DAYS(expiration) - TO_DAYS(CURDATE()) < 30\G
*************************** 1. row ***************************
           id: 1
  select_type: SIMPLE
        table: member
         type: ALL
possible_keys: NULL
          key: NULL
      key_len: NULL
          ref: NULL
         rows: 102
        Extra: Using where

mysql> EXPLAIN SELECT * FROM member
    -> WHERE TO_DAYS(expiration) < 30 + TO_DAYS(CURDATE())\G
*************************** 1. row ***************************
           id: 1
  select_type: SIMPLE
        table: member
         type: ALL
possible_keys: NULL
          key: NULL
      key_len: NULL
          ref: NULL
         rows: 102
        Extra: Using where

mysql> EXPLAIN SELECT * FROM member
    -> WHERE expiration < DATE_ADD(CURDATE(), INTERVAL 30 DAY)\G
*************************** 1. row ***************************
           id: 1
  select_type: SIMPLE
        table: member
         type: range
possible_keys: expiration
          key: expiration
      key_len: 4
          ref: NULL
         rows: 6
        Extra: Using where
```

The results for the first two statements show that the index is not used. The type value indicates how values will be read from a table. ALL means "all rows will be examined." That is, a full table scan will be performed, without benefit of an index. The NULL in each of the key-related columns also indicates that no index is used.

By contrast, the result for the third statement shows that the WHERE clause is written such that the optimizer can use the index on the expiration column:

- The type value indicates that the optimizer can use the index to search for a specific range of values (those less than the date given on the right side of the expression).

- The possible_keys and key values show that the optimizer considers the index on expiration a candidate index and also the index it actually would use.

- The rows value shows that the optimizer estimates that it would need to examine six rows to process the query. That's better than the value of 102 for the first two execution plans.

A second use for EXPLAIN is to discover whether adding indexes would help the optimizer execute a statement more efficiently. For this example, I use just two tables that initially are unindexed. This suffices to show the effect of creating indexes on simple joins. The same principles apply to more complex joins that involve many tables.

The example output is derived from MyISAM tables, which result in clearer row count estimates of 1,000 when full table scans are involved, and thus a simpler narrative. For InnoDB tables, the results are broadly similar except that the full scan estimates vary from 1,000 because InnoDB uses a different estimation mechanism.

Suppose that we have two tables t1 and t2, each with 1,000 rows containing the values 1 to 1000. The query that we'll examine looks for those rows where corresponding values from the two tables are the same:

```
mysql> SELECT t1.i1, t2.i2 FROM t1 INNER JOIN t2
    -> WHERE t1.i1 = t2.i2;
+------+------+
| i1   | i2   |
+------+------+
|    1 |    1 |
|    2 |    2 |
|    3 |    3 |
|    4 |    4 |
|    5 |    5 |
...
```

With no indexes on either table, EXPLAIN produces this result:

```
mysql> EXPLAIN SELECT t1.i1, t2.i2 FROM t1 INNER JOIN t2
    -> WHERE t1.i1 = t2.i2\G
*************************** 1. row ***************************
           id: 1
  select_type: SIMPLE
        table: t1
         type: ALL
```

```
possible_keys: NULL
          key: NULL
      key_len: NULL
          ref: NULL
         rows: 1000
        Extra:
*************************** 2. row ***************************
           id: 1
  select_type: SIMPLE
        table: t2
         type: ALL
possible_keys: NULL
          key: NULL
      key_len: NULL
          ref: NULL
         rows: 1000
        Extra: Using where; Using join buffer
```

Here, `ALL` in the `type` column indicates a full table scan that examines all rows. `NULL` in the `possible_keys` column indicates that no candidate indexes were found for speeding up the query. Due to the lack of a suitable index, the `key`, `key_len`, and `ref` columns all are `NULL` as well. `Using where` indicates that information in the `WHERE` clause is used to identify qualifying rows.

Those pieces of information tell us that the optimizer finds no useful information for executing the query more efficiently and will proceed as follows:

- It will perform a full scan of `t1`.
- For each row from `t1`, it will perform a full scan of `t2`, using the information in the `WHERE` clause to identify qualifying rows.

The `rows` values show the optimizer's estimates about how many rows it will need to examine at each stage of the query. The estimate is 1,000 for `t1` because a full scan will be done. Similarly, the estimate is 1,000 for `t2`, but this is *for each row* in `t1`. In other words, the number of row combinations that the optimizer estimates it will examine to process the query is 1,000 × 1,000, or one million. That is highly wasteful of effort, because only 1,000 combinations actually satisfy the conditions in the `WHERE` clause.

To make this query more efficient, add an index on one of the joined columns and try the `EXPLAIN` statement again:

```
mysql> ALTER TABLE t2 ADD INDEX (i2);
mysql> EXPLAIN SELECT t1.i1, t2.i2 FROM t1 INNER JOIN t2
    -> WHERE t1.i1 = t2.i2\G
*************************** 1. row ***************************
           id: 1
  select_type: SIMPLE
        table: t1
```

```
         type: ALL
possible_keys: NULL
          key: NULL
      key_len: NULL
          ref: NULL
         rows: 1000
        Extra:
*************************** 2. row ***************************
           id: 1
  select_type: SIMPLE
        table: t2
         type: ref
possible_keys: i2
          key: i2
      key_len: 5
          ref: sampdb.t1.i1
         rows: 10
        Extra: Using where; Using index
```

This is an improvement. The output for t1 still indicates a full scan, but the optimizer can process t2 differently:

- type has changed from ALL to ref, meaning that a reference value (the value from t1) can be used to perform an index lookup to locate qualifying rows in t2.

- The reference value is given in the ref field: sampdb.t1.i1.

- The rows value drops from 1000 to 10, which shows that the optimizer believes that it will need to examine only 10 rows in t2 for each row in t1. (That is a somewhat pessimistic estimate. In fact, only one row in t2 will match each row from t1. We'll see a bit later how to help the optimizer improve this estimate.) The total estimated number of row combinations is 1,000 × 10 = 10,000. That's much better than the previous estimate of one million in the absence of any indexing.

Is there any value in indexing t1? After all, for this particular join, it's necessary to scan one of the tables, and no index is needed to do that. To see whether there's any effect, index t1.i1 and run EXPLAIN again:

```
mysql> ALTER TABLE t1 ADD INDEX (i1);
mysql> EXPLAIN SELECT t1.i1, t2.i2 FROM t1 INNER JOIN t2
    -> WHERE t1.i1 = t2.i2\G
*************************** 1. row ***************************
           id: 1
  select_type: SIMPLE
        table: t1
         type: index
possible_keys: i1
          key: i1
      key_len: 5
```

```
               ref: NULL
              rows: 1000
             Extra: Using index
*************************** 2. row ***************************
                id: 1
       select_type: SIMPLE
             table: t2
              type: ref
     possible_keys: i2
               key: i2
           key_len: 5
               ref: sampdb.t1.i1
              rows: 10
             Extra: Using where; Using index
```

This output is similar to that for the previous EXPLAIN, but adding the index did make some difference in the output for t1. type has changed from NULL to index and Extra has changed from blank to Using index. These changes indicate that, although a full scan of the indexed values still would be done, the optimizer now can read them directly from the index without touching the data file at all. You will see this kind of result for a MyISAM table when the optimizer knows that it can get all the information it needs by consulting only the index file. You'll also see it for InnoDB tables when the optimizer can use information solely from the index without another seek to get the data row.

One further step that helps the optimizer make better cost estimates is to run ANALYZE TABLE. This causes the server to generate key value distribution statistics. Analyzing the tables and running EXPLAIN again yields a better rows estimate:

```
mysql> ANALYZE TABLE t1, t2;
mysql> EXPLAIN SELECT t1.i1, t2.i2 FROM t1 INNER JOIN t2
    -> WHERE t1.i1 = t2.i2\G
*************************** 1. row ***************************
                id: 1
       select_type: SIMPLE
             table: t1
              type: index
     possible_keys: i1
               key: i1
           key_len: 5
               ref: NULL
              rows: 1000
             Extra: Using index
*************************** 2. row ***************************
                id: 1
       select_type: SIMPLE
             table: t2
              type: ref
```

```
possible_keys: i2
          key: i2
      key_len: 5
          ref: sampdb.t1.i1
         rows: 1
        Extra: Using where; Using index
```

In this case, the optimizer now estimates that each value from `t1` will match only one row in `t2`.

5.3   Choosing Data Types for Efficient Queries

Your choice of data type can influence query performance several ways. This section provides guidelines for choosing data types that can help queries run more quickly.

Use numeric rather than string operations. Calculations involving numbers generally are faster than those involving strings. Consider comparison operations. Numbers can be compared in a single operation. String comparisons may involve several byte-by-byte or character-by-character comparisons, more so as the strings become longer.

If a string column has a limited number of values, you can use an `ENUM` or `SET` type to get the advantages of numeric operations. These types are represented internally as numbers and can be processed more efficiently.

Consider alternative representations for strings. Sometimes you can improve performance by representing string values as numbers. For example, to represent IP addresses in dotted-quad notation, such as 192.168.0.4, you might use a string. Or you could instead convert the IP addresses to integer form by storing each part of the dotted-quad form in 1 byte of a 4-byte `INT` `UNSIGNED` type. Storing integers would both save space and speed lookups. On the other hand, representing IP addresses as `INT` values might make it difficult to perform pattern matches such as you might do if you wanted to look for numbers in a given subnet. Perhaps you can do the same thing by using bitmask operations. These kinds of issues illustrate that you cannot consider only space issues; you must decide which representation is most appropriate based on what you want to do with the values. (Whatever choice you make, the `INET_ATON()` and `INET_NTOA()` functions can help convert between the two representations.)

Don't use larger types when smaller ones will do. MySQL processes smaller types more quickly than larger types. For strings in particular, processing time is in direct relationship to string length. Also, with smaller types, your tables will be smaller and require less overhead for disk activity. For an indexed column, shorter values provide even more of a performance boost. Not only does the index speed up queries, shorter key values can be processed more quickly than longer values.

For columns that use fixed-size data types, choose the smallest type that holds the required range of values. Don't use `BIGINT` if `MEDIUMINT` will do. Don't use `DOUBLE` if you need only `FLOAT` precision. If you use fixed-length `CHAR` columns, don't make them unnecessarily long. If the longest value you store in a column is 40 characters long, define it as CHAR(40) rather than as CHAR(255).

For variable-size types, you may still be able to save space with smaller types. A BLOB uses 2 bytes to record the length of the value, a LONGBLOB uses 4 bytes. If you store values that are never as long as 64KB, using BLOB saves you 2 bytes per value. (Similar considerations apply for TEXT types.)

Define columns to be NOT NULL. If a column is NOT NULL, MySQL can handle it more quickly because column values need not be checked during query processing to see whether they are NULL. This may also enable you to write simpler queries because you need not check for NULL as a special case, and simpler queries generally can be processed more quickly.

Consider using ENUM **columns.** If you have a string column that has low cardinality (contains only a limited number of distinct values), consider converting it to an ENUM column. ENUM values can be processed quickly because they are represented internally as numeric values.

Use PROCEDURE ANALYSE(). Run PROCEDURE ANALYSE() to see what it tells you about the columns in your table:

```
SELECT * FROM tbl_name PROCEDURE ANALYSE();
SELECT * FROM tbl_name PROCEDURE ANALYSE(16,256);
```

One column of the output suggests the optimal data type for each of the columns in your table. The second example tells PROCEDURE ANALYSE() not to suggest ENUM types that contain more than 16 values or that take more than 256 bytes (you can change the values as you like). Without such restrictions, the output may be very long; ENUM definitions are often difficult to read.

Based on the output from PROCEDURE ANALYSE(), you may find that your table can be modified to take advantage of a more efficient type. To change a column's type, use ALTER TABLE.

Defragment tables that are subject to fragmentation. Tables that are modified a great deal, particularly those that contain variable-length columns, are subject to fragmentation. Fragmentation is bad because it leads to wasted space in the disk blocks used to store your table. Over time, you must read more blocks to get the valid rows, and performance is reduced. This is true for any table with variable-length rows, but is particularly acute for BLOB or TEXT columns because they can vary so much in size.

Used on a regular basis, OPTIMIZE TABLE eliminates or reduces wasted space in fragmented MyISAM or InnoDB tables and helps keep table performance from degrading. A defragmentation method that works for any storage engine is to dump the table with mysqldump, and then drop and re-create it using the dump file:

```
% mysqldump db_name tbl_name > dump.sql
% mysql db_name < dump.sql
```

Pack data into a BLOB **or** TEXT **column.** Using a BLOB or TEXT column to store data that you pack and unpack in your application may enable you to get everything with a single retrieval operation rather than with several. This can also be helpful for data values that are not easy to represent in a standard table structure or that change over time. In the discussion of the ALTER TABLE statement in Chapter 2, "Using SQL to Manage Data," one of the examples dealt with a table being used to hold results from the fields in a Web-based questionnaire. That example discussed how you could use ALTER TABLE to add columns to the table whenever you add questions to the questionnaire.

Another way to approach this problem is to have the application program that processes the Web form pack the data into some kind of data structure, and then insert it into a single BLOB or TEXT column. For example, you could represent the questionnaire responses using XML and store the XML string in a TEXT column. This adds application overhead on the client side for encoding the data (and decoding it later when you retrieve rows from the table), but simplifies the table structure, and eliminates the need to change the table structure when you change your questionnaire.

On the other hand, BLOB and TEXT values can cause their own problems, especially if you do a lot of DELETE or UPDATE operations. Deleting such values can leave large holes in the table that will be filled in later with a row or rows of probably different sizes. The preceding discussion of defragmentation suggests how you might deal with this.

Use a synthetic index. Synthetic index columns can sometimes be helpful. One method is to create a hash value based on other columns and store it in a separate column. Then you can find rows by searching for hash values. However, this technique is good only for exact-match queries. (Hash values are useless for range searches with operators such as < or >=.) Hash values can be generated by using the MD5() function. Other options are to use SHA2() or CRC32(). Or you can compute your own hash values using logic within your application. Remember that a numeric hash value can be stored very efficiently. If the hash algorithm might produce string values that have trailing spaces, do not store them using a data type that is subject to trailing-space removal.

A synthetic hash index can be particularly useful with BLOB and TEXT columns. It can be much quicker to find these kinds of values using a hash as an identifier value than by searching the BLOB or TEXT column itself.

Avoid retrieving large BLOB or TEXT values unless you must. For example, a SELECT * query that retrieves entire rows isn't a good idea unless you're sure the WHERE clause is going to restrict the results to just the rows you want. Otherwise, you may be pulling potentially very large values over the network for no purpose. This is another case where BLOB or TEXT identifier information stored in a synthetic index column can be useful. You can search that column to determine the row or rows you want and then retrieve the BLOB or TEXT values from the qualifying rows.

Segregate BLOB or TEXT columns into a separate table. Under some circumstances, it may make sense to move these columns out of a table into a secondary table, if that enables you to convert the table to fixed-length row format for the remaining columns. This reduces fragmentation in the primary table and enables you to take advantage of the performance benefits of having fixed-length rows. It also enables you to run SELECT * queries on the primary table without pulling large BLOB or TEXT values over the network.

5.4 Choosing Table Storage Formats for Efficient Queries

Some storage engines implement multiple storage formats, each of which has its own performance characteristics. The following suggestions provide general guidelines about choosing a format, but it's best to perform testing to verify that one format really excels another for a given application.

The MyISAM storage engine by default uses fixed-length rows if all columns have a fixed length, and variable-length rows if any column has a variable length. You can influence this by whether you choose CHAR versus VARCHAR (or BINARY versus VARBINARY) for string columns. Consider the tradeoff of space versus time. For columns of maximum length n, CHAR takes n characters for every row. VARCHAR takes on average half that, so if space is at a premium, use VARCHAR columns. If speed is your primary concern and you can afford the space, use CHAR (fixed-length) columns because MyISAM processes fixed-length rows more quickly than variable-length rows. This is especially true for tables that are modified often and therefore more subject to fragmentation:

- With variable-length rows, more fragmentation occurs for a table on which you perform many deletes or updates due to the differing sizes of the rows. You'll need to run OPTIMIZE TABLE periodically to maintain performance. This is not an issue with fixed-length rows.

- Tables with fixed-length rows are easier to reconstruct in the event of a table crash. The beginning of each row can be determined because they all have positions that are multiples of the fixed row size, something not true with variable-length rows. This is not a performance issue with respect to query processing, but it speeds up the table-repair process.

MEMORY tables use fixed-length rows that treat both CHAR and VARCHAR columns implicitly as CHAR, so it doesn't matter which you choose.

InnoDB does not treat fixed-length and variable-length columns differently (all rows use a header containing pointers to the column values), so using CHAR columns is not in itself intrinsically simpler than using VARCHAR columns. Consequently, the primary performance factor is the amount of storage used for rows. For columns of maximum length n, VARCHAR takes less space than CHAR on average and minimizes the amount of storage and disk I/O to process rows. CHAR takes n characters even for NULL, so the advantage for VARCHAR is even more pronounced for columns with many NULL values.

When you create an InnoDB table, choose the row storage format with characteristics that best match the data stored in the table:

- By default, InnoDB uses COMPACT row format, which is a reasonable general-purpose choice.

- For a table that contains repetitive data, COMPRESSED row format is often beneficial. The table will use less space (reducing the number of I/O operations to read it), and the time saved reading data likely will more than compensate the CPU time required to uncompress it. Compressed format is not useful for a table that stores random or already compressed values.

- For a table with long BLOB or TEXT values, DYNAMIC row format is most efficient.

To specify the row format for a new InnoDB table, use the ROW_FORMAT table option. For example:

```
CREATE TABLE t1 ( ... ) ENGINE=InnoDB ROW_FORMAT=COMPRESSED;
```

To check the row storage format of an existing table, use SHOW TABLE STATUS. To change the format of a table, use ALTER TABLE:

```
ALTER TABLE t1 ROW_FORMAT=DYNAMIC;
```

The COMPRESSED and DYNAMIC row formats require the Barracuda file format, which in turn requires that the innodb_file_per_table and innodb_file_format system variables be set properly. See Section 12.5.3.1.4, "Using Individual (Per-Table) InnoDB Tablespaces."

5.5   Loading Data Efficiently

Most of the time you'll probably be concerned about optimizing SELECT statements because they are the most common type of statement and because it's not always straightforward to figure out how to optimize them. By comparison, loading data into your database is straightforward. Nevertheless, there are strategies you can use to improve the efficiency of data-loading operations. The basic principles are these:

- The more you can reduce flushing to disk, the faster data loading will be. Therefore, bulk loading is more efficient than single-row loading because inserted rows can be cached, then flushed at the end of the load operation. Flushing once at the end rather than after each row can significantly reduce disk I/O.

- Loading is faster the fewer indexes a table has. If there are indexes, not only must the row's contents be added to the table, each index must also be modified to reflect the addition of the new row. For this reason, do not create unnecessary indexes, or drop them if they already exist.

- Shorter SQL statements are faster than longer statements because they involve less parsing on the part of the server and because they can be sent over the network from the client to the server more quickly.

Some of these factors may seem minor (the last one in particular), but if you're loading a lot of data, even small efficiencies make a difference. From the preceding general principles, several practical conclusions can be drawn about how to load data most quickly.

LOAD DATA (all forms) is more efficient than INSERT because it loads rows in bulk. The server must parse and interpret only one statement, not several. Also, the index needs flushing only after all rows have been processed, rather than after each row.

LOAD DATA is more efficient without LOCAL than with it. Without LOCAL, the file must be located on the server and you must have the FILE privilege, but the server can read the file directly from disk. With LOAD DATA LOCAL, the client reads the file and sends it over the network to the server, which is slower.

If you must use INSERT, try to use syntax that permits multiple rows to be inserted in a single statement:

```
INSERT INTO tbl_name VALUES(...),(...),... ;
```

The more rows you can specify in the statement, the better. This reduces the total number of statements required and minimizes the amount of index flushing. This principle might seem to contradict the earlier one that shorter statements can be processed faster than longer statements. But there is no contradiction. The issues here are that a single INSERT statement that inserts multiple rows is shorter overall than an equivalent set of individual single-row INSERT statements, and the multiple-row statement can be processed on the server with much less index flushing.

If you use mysqldump to generate database backup files, it generates multiple-row INSERT statements by default: The --opt (optimize) option is enabled, which turns on the --extended-insert option that produces multiple-row INSERT statements, as well as some other options that enable the dump file to be processed more efficiently when it is reloaded.

Avoid using the --complete-insert option with mysqldump. The resulting INSERT statements will be for single rows and will be longer and require more parsing than will multiple-row statements.

If you must use multiple INSERT statements, group them if possible to reduce index flushing. For transactional storage engines, do this by issuing the INSERT statements within a single transaction rather than in autocommit mode:

```
START TRANSACTION;
INSERT INTO tbl_name ... ;
INSERT INTO tbl_name ... ;
INSERT INTO tbl_name ... ;
COMMIT;
```

For nontransactional storage engines, obtain a write lock on the table and issue the INSERT statements while the table is locked:

```
LOCK TABLES tbl_name WRITE;
INSERT INTO tbl_name ... ;
INSERT INTO tbl_name ... ;
INSERT INTO tbl_name ... ;
UNLOCK TABLES;
```

Either way, you obtain the same benefit: MySQL flushes the index once after all the statements have been executed rather than once per INSERT statement. The latter is what happens in autocommit mode or if the table has not been locked.

For MyISAM tables, another strategy for reducing index flushing is to use the
DELAY_KEY_WRITE table option. With this option, data rows are written to the data file immediately as usual, but the key cache is flushed only occasionally rather than after each insert.
To use delayed index flushing on a server-wide basis, start mysqld with the delay_key_write
system variable set to ALL. In this case, the server delays index block writes for a table until
blocks must be flushed to make room for other index values, until a FLUSH TABLES statement
has been executed, or until the table is closed.

If you use delayed key writes for MyISAM tables, abnormal server shutdowns can cause
loss of index values. This is not a fatal problem because MyISAM indexes can be repaired
based on the data rows. To make sure that the repairs do happen, start the server with the
myisam_recover_options system variable set to a value that includes the FORCE option. This
option causes the server to check MyISAM tables when it opens them and repair them automatically as necessary.

For a replication slave server, you might want to set delay_key_write to ALL to delay index
flushing for all MyISAM tables, regardless of how they were created originally on the master
server.

Use the compressed client/server protocol to reduce the amount of data going over the
network. For most MySQL clients, this can be specified using the --compress command-line
option. Generally, this should only be used on slow networks because compression requires
quite a bit of processor time.

Let MySQL insert default values for you. That is, don't specify columns in INSERT statements
that will be assigned the default value anyway. On average, your statements will be shorter,
reducing the number of characters sent over the network to the server. In addition, because the
statements contain fewer values, the server does less parsing and value conversion.

For MyISAM tables, if you need to load a lot of data into a new table to populate it, create
the table without indexes, load the data, and then create the indexes. It's faster to create the
indexes all at once rather than to modify them for each row. For a table that already has
indexes, data loading may be faster if you drop or deactivate the indexes beforehand, then
rebuild or reactivate them afterward.

To drop and rebuild indexes, use DROP INDEX and CREATE INDEX, or the index-related forms
of ALTER TABLE. To deactivate and reactivate indexes, use the DISABLE KEYS and ENABLE
KEYS forms of ALTER TABLE, which turn off and on updating of any nonunique indexes in the
table:

```
ALTER TABLE tbl_name DISABLE KEYS;
... statements to load table contents ...
ALTER TABLE tbl_name ENABLE KEYS;
```

If you use a LOAD DATA statement to load data into an empty MyISAM table, the server
performs the index deactivation and activation automatically. Also, mysqldump adds the ALTER
TABLE statements by default.

For InnoDB tables, it is fast to drop and add secondary indexes, so consider doing that before a large data loading operation. This does not apply to the primary (clustered) index, so do not drop or add that index.

If you're considering using the strategy of dropping or deactivating indexes for loading data into a table, think about the overall circumstances of your situation in assessing whether any benefit is likely to be obtained. If you're loading a small amount of data into a large table, rebuilding the indexes probably will take longer than just loading the data without any special preparation.

The preceding data-loading principles also apply to mixed-query environments involving clients performing different kinds of operations. For example, generally you should avoid long-running SELECT queries on tables that are changed (written to) frequently. That causes a lot of contention and poor performance for the writers. A possible way around this, if your writes are mostly INSERT operations, is to add new rows to an auxiliary table and then add those rows to the main table periodically. This is not a viable strategy if you need to be able to access new rows immediately, but if you can afford to leave them inaccessible for a short time, use of the auxiliary table helps you in two ways. First, it reduces contention with SELECT queries that are taking place on the main table, so they execute more quickly. Second, it takes less time overall to load a batch of rows from the auxiliary table into the main table than to load the rows individually because bulk load operations are faster.

One application for this strategy is when you're logging Web page accesses from your Web server into a MySQL database. In this case, it may not be a high priority to make sure that the entries get into the main table right away.

5.6   Scheduling, Locking, and Concurrency

The previous sections focus primarily on making individual queries faster. This section looks at MySQL's scheduling policy and the general effect that storage engine locking levels have on concurrency among clients. Use this information when you choose storage engines for applications. The type of queries that predominate for a given application may be better handled by one engine than another. For the purposes of this discussion, a client performing a retrieval (a SELECT) is a reader. A client performing an operation that modifies a table (DELETE, INSERT, REPLACE, UPDATE) is a writer.

MySQL's scheduling policy can be summarized like this:

- Writes have higher priority than reads.
- Writes to a table must occur one at a time, and write requests are processed in the order in which they arrive.
- Multiple reads from a table can be processed simultaneously.

The InnoDB storage engine implements this scheduling policy using locking at the row level, but InnoDB locks rows only as necessary. In many cases, such as when only reads are done, InnoDB may use no locks at all.

The MyISAM, MERGE, and MEMORY storage engines implement locking at a different level, using table locks. They thus have differing performance characteristics in terms of contention management. Whenever a client accesses a table, a lock for it must be acquired first. When the client is finished with a table, the lock on it can be released. It's possible to acquire and release locks explicitly by issuing LOCK TABLES and UNLOCK TABLES statements, but normally the server's lock manager automatically acquires locks as necessary and releases them when they are no longer needed. The type of lock required depends on whether a client is writing or reading:

- To write to a table, a client must have a lock for exclusive table access. The table is in an inconsistent state while the operation is in progress because the data row is being deleted, added, or changed, and any indexes on the table may need to be updated to match. Permitting other clients to access the table while the table is in flux would cause problems. It's clearly a bad thing to permit two clients to write to the table at the same time because that would quickly corrupt the table into an unusable mess. But it's not good to permit a client to read from an in-flux table, either, because the table might be changing at the location being read, and the results would be inaccurate.

- To read from a table, a client must have a lock to prevent other clients from writing to the table and changing it during the read. The lock need not be for exclusive access, however. Reading doesn't change the table, so there is no reason one reader should prevent another from accessing the table. Therefore, a read lock enables other clients to read the table at the same time.

The locking level used by a storage engine has a significant effect on concurrency among clients. Suppose that two clients each want to update a row in a given table. To perform the update, each client requires a write lock. Greater concurrency can be achieved for an InnoDB table than for a MyISAM table. For InnoDB, both updates can proceed simultaneously as long as both clients aren't updating the same row. For MyISAM, the engine acquires a table lock for the first client, which causes the second client to block until the first one has finished.

In general, locking at a finer level enables better concurrency, because more clients can be using a table at the same time if they use different parts of it. The practical implication is that different storage engines will be better suited for different statement mixes:

- InnoDB tables can provide better performance when there are many updates. Because locking is done at the row level rather than at the table level, the extent of the table that is locked is smaller. This reduces lock contention and improves concurrency.

- MyISAM is extremely fast for retrievals. However, the use of table-level locks can be a problem in environments with mixed retrievals and updates, especially if the retrievals tend to be long-running. Under these conditions, updates may need to wait a long time before they can proceed.

Table locking does have an advantage over finer levels of locking in terms of deadlock prevention. With table locks, deadlock never occurs. The server can determine which tables are needed by looking at the statement and locking them all ahead of time. With InnoDB tables, deadlock can occur because the storage engine does not acquire all necessary locks at the beginning of a transaction. Instead, locks are acquired as necessary during the course of transaction processing. It's possible for two statements to acquire locks and then try to acquire further locks that each depend on already-held locks being released. As a result, each client holds a lock that the other needs before it can continue. This results in deadlock, and the server must abort one of the transactions.

6

Introduction to MySQL Programming

This chapter describes reasons for writing your own MySQL-based programs rather than using the standard client programs included in MySQL distributions. It also gives a conceptual overview of the interfaces we use for the three languages covered in the following chapters (C, Perl, and PHP), and discusses factors to consider when choosing a language for a program.

6.1 Why Write Your Own MySQL Programs?

MySQL distributions include a set of client programs that communicate with the server. For example, `mysqldump` exports table definitions and contents, `mysqladmin` performs administrative operations, and `mysql` lets you execute arbitrary SQL statements.

The standard client programs handle many of the most common tasks that MySQL users perform, but applications sometimes have requirements that are outside their capabilities. To deal with this, MySQL has a client application programming interface (API) that enables you to satisfy whatever specialized requirements your applications might have. The client API provides access to the MySQL server and opens up possibilities limited only by your own imagination.

In this part of the book, we discuss how to write MySQL-based programs that access your databases. To understand what you gain in doing so, consider what you can accomplish by writing your own programs in comparison to using the capabilities of the `mysql` client and its no-frills interface to the MySQL server:

- **Customized input handling.** With `mysql`, you enter raw SQL statements. With your own programs, you can provide input methods for the user that are more intuitive and easier to use. Your program can eliminate the need for its users to know SQL, or even to be aware of the role of the database in the task being performed. Input collection can be something as rudimentary as a command-line interface that prompts the user and reads a value, or a more sophisticated screen-based entry form. For example, most people find it much easier to specify search parameters by filling in a form than by issuing a SELECT statement.

- **User input validation.** You can require certain fields to be filled in a certain way. This enhances the safety and security of your applications.

- **Customized output.** `mysql` output is essentially unformatted; you have a choice of tab-delimited or tabular style. For nicer-looking output, you must format it yourself. This might be from something as simple as printing "Missing" rather than NULL. Or it might involve more complex requirements, such as invoice production, where you need to associate each invoice header with information about the customer and about each item ordered. This kind of report can easily exceed `mysql`'s formatting capabilities.

- **Freedom from constraints imposed by the nature of SQL itself.** For the most part, SQL scripts consist of a set of statements executed one at a time from beginning to end, with minimal error checking. If you execute a file of SQL queries using `mysql` in batch mode, `mysql` either quits after the first error, or, if you specify the `--force` option, executes all the queries indiscriminately, no matter how many errors occur. By writing your own program, it's possible to selectively adapt to the success or failure of queries by providing flow control around statement-execution operations. You can make execution of one query contingent on the success or failure of another, or make decisions about what to do next based on the result of a previous query.

  MySQL supports stored programs, which provide additional flexibility at the SQL level by means of flow-control and error-handling constructs. However, these constructs are not as flexible as those provided by general-purpose programming languages.

  In general, a tool other than `mysql` is needed for tasks that involve master-detail relationships and have complex output-formatting requirements. A program provides the "glue" that links queries together and enables you to use the output from one query as the input to another.

- **Integration of MySQL into any application.** Many programs stand to benefit by exploiting the capability of a database to provide information. The client-programming interface gives you the means to do this. An application that must verify a customer number or check whether an item is present in inventory can do so by issuing a quick query. A Web application that enables a client to ask for all books by a certain author can look them up in a database and send the results to the client's browser.

Chapter 1, "Getting Started with MySQL," enumerated several goals with respect to our `sampdb` sample database that require us to write programs to interact with the MySQL server. Some of these goals are shown in the following list:

- Format the Historical League member directory for printing

- Enable online presentation and searching of the member directory

- Send membership renewal notices by email

- Easily enter student scores into the gradebook using a Web browser

One issue that we consider in some detail is how to integrate MySQL's capabilities into a Web environment. MySQL does not support Web applications directly, but by combining MySQL with appropriate tools, you can issue queries from your Web server on behalf of a client user and send the results to the user's browser. This enables your databases to be accessed easily over the Web.

There are two complementary perspectives on the marriage of MySQL and the Web:

- **Use a Web server to provide enhanced access to MySQL.** In this case, your main interest is your database, and you want to use the Web as a tool to gain easier access to your data. This is the point of view that a MySQL administrator would take. The place of a database in such a scenario is explicit and obvious because it's the focus of your interest. For example, you can write Web pages that enable you to see a list of the tables in your database, and to examine the structure or contents of each one.

- **Use MySQL to enhance the capabilities of your Web server.** In this case, your primary interest is your Web site, and you may want to use MySQL as a tool for making your site's content more valuable to the people who visit it. This is the point of view a Web developer would take. For example, if you run a message board or discussion list at the site, you can use a database to keep track of the messages. The role of MySQL in this case is more subtle; users of the site might not even be aware that a database plays a part in the services the site offers.

These perspectives need not be mutually exclusive. For example, in the Historical League scenario, we'll use the Web as a means for members to gain easy access to the contents of the membership directory by making entries available online. That is a use of the Web to provide access to the database. At the same time, adding directory content to the League's Web site increases the site's value to members. That is a use of the database to enhance the services provided at the site.

No matter how you view the integration of MySQL with the Web, the implementation is similar. You connect your Web site front end to your MySQL back end, using the Web server as an intermediary. The Web server collects information from a client user, sends it to the MySQL server in the form of a query, and then retrieves the result and returns it to the client's browser for viewing.

You need not put your data online, of course, but often there are benefits to doing so in comparison with access through the standard MySQL client programs:

- People accessing your data through the Web can use whichever browser they prefer, on whatever platform they prefer. They're not limited to systems on which the standard MySQL client programs run. No matter how widespread the MySQL clients are, Web browsers are more so.

- The interface for a Web application can be made simpler than that of a standalone command-line MySQL client.

- A Web interface can be customized to the requirements of a particular application. The MySQL clients are general-purpose tools with a fixed interface.

- Dynamic Web pages extend MySQL's capabilities to do things that are difficult or impossible to do using only the standard MySQL clients. For example, you can't really use those clients to put together an application that incorporates a shopping cart.

Any programming language can be used to write Web-based applications, but some are more suitable than others. We consider this issue in Section 6.3, "Choosing an API."

6.2   APIs Available for MySQL

To facilitate application development, MySQL provides a client library written in the C programming language that enables you to access MySQL databases from within any C program. The client library implements an application programming interface (API) consisting of a set of data structures and functions.

MySQL interfaces for other languages can link the C client library into the language processor. The client library thus provides the means whereby MySQL bindings for other languages can be built on top of the C API. This type of interface exists for Perl, PHP, Python, Ruby, C++, Tcl, and others.

Each language binding defines its own interface that specifies the rules for accessing MySQL. There are many APIs available for MySQL. We concentrate on three of the most popular:

- **The C client library API.** This is the primary programming interface to MySQL. It's used to implement the standard clients in the MySQL distribution, such as `mysql`, `mysqladmin`, and `mysqldump`.

- **The DBI (Database Interface) API for Perl.** DBI is implemented as a Perl module that interfaces with other modules at the DBD (Database Driver) level, each of which provides access to a specific database server. The DBD module used here is the one that provides MySQL support. We use MySQL with DBI to create standalone scripts to be invoked from the command line, as well as scripts to be invoked through a Web server that provide Web access to MySQL.

- **The PHP API.** PHP is a scripting language that provides a convenient way of embedding programming constructs in Web pages. Such a page is processed by PHP on the server host before being sent to the client, which enables the script to generate dynamic content, such as including the result of a MySQL query into the page. Like DBI, PHP supports access to several database servers in addition to MySQL. It has server-specific interfaces, and interfaces that are more server independent. This book uses one of the latter, known as PHP Data Objects (PDO).

The remainder of this chapter provides a comparative overview of these three APIs, first to describe their general characteristics, and then to give you an idea why you might choose one over another for particular applications. The following three chapters discuss each of them in detail.

There's no reason to consider yourself locked into a single API, of course. Get to know several APIs and arm yourself with the knowledge that enables you to choose between them wisely. For a large project with several components, you might use multiple APIs and write some parts in one language and other parts in another language, depending on which one is most appropriate for each piece of the job.

If you need the software required to use any of the APIs, see Appendix A, "Software Required to Use This Book."

6.2.1 The C API

The C API is used within the context of compiled C programs. It's a client library that provides an interface for talking to the MySQL server, giving you the capabilities you need for establishing a connection to and conversing with the server.

The C clients provided in the MySQL distribution are based on this API. The C client library also serves as the basis for most of the MySQL bindings for other languages. For example, the MySQL-specific driver for the Perl DBI module is made MySQL-aware by linking in the code for the MySQL C client library.

6.2.2 The Perl DBI API

The DBI API is used to write database applications in the Perl scripting language. This API tries to work with multiple database servers, while at the same time hiding server-specific details from the script writer. DBI does this using Perl modules that work together in a two-level architecture (see Figure 6.1):

- The DBI (database interface) level provides the general-purpose interface for client scripts. This level provides an abstraction that does not refer to specific database servers.

- The DBD (database driver) level provides support for various database servers by means of drivers that are server specific. For MySQL, the DBD-level module is named DBD::mysql.

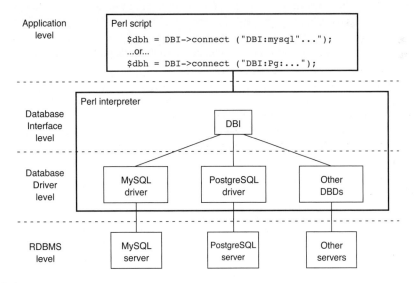

Figure 6.1   DBI architecture.

The DBI architecture enables you to write applications in relatively generic fashion. When you write a DBI script, you use a standard set of database-access calls. The DBI layer invokes the proper driver at the DBD level to handle your requests, and the driver handles the specific issues involved in communicating with the particular database server you're using. The DBD level passes data returned from the server back up to the DBI layer, which presents the data to your application. The form of the data is consistent no matter the database system from which it originated.

From the application writer's point of view, the result is an interface that hides differences between database servers, yet works with a wide variety of servers—as many as there are drivers for. DBI provides a consistent client interface that increases portability because you can access each database server in a uniform fashion.

The one aspect of script writing that is necessarily server-specific occurs when you connect to a database server, because you must indicate which driver to use to establish the connection. For example, to use a MySQL database, connect like this:

```
$dbh = DBI->connect ("DBI:mysql:...");
```

To use PostgreSQL or Oracle instead, connect like this:

```
$dbh = DBI->connect ("DBI:Pg:...");
$dbh = DBI->connect ("DBI:Oracle:...");
```

After establishing the connection, you need not make any specific reference to the driver. DBI and the driver itself work out the server-specific details. That's the theory, anyway. However, you should be aware of two factors that work against DBI script portability:

- SQL implementations differ between database systems, and it's perfectly possible to write SQL statements for one server that another does not understand. If your SQL is reasonably generic, your scripts are correspondingly reasonably portable between servers. But if your SQL is server dependent, your scripts are, too. For example, if a script uses the MySQL-specific SHOW VARIABLES statement, it won't work with other database servers.

- DBD modules often provide server-specific information to enable script writers to use features particular to a given database system. For example, the DBD for MySQL provides access to properties of columns in a query result such as the maximum length of values, whether columns are numeric, and so forth. Other database servers don't necessarily make analogous types of information available. DBD-specific features are antithetical to portability; by using them, you make it more difficult to use a script written for MySQL with other database systems.

Despite the potential of these two factors for making your scripts database specific, the DBI mechanism for providing database access in an abstract fashion is a reasonable means of achieving portability. It's up to you to decide how much to use nonportable features. As you will discover in Chapter 8, "Writing MySQL Programs Using Perl DBI," I make little effort to avoid MySQL-specific constructs provided by the MySQL DBD. That's because you should know what those constructs are so that you can decide for yourself whether to use them. For further information, see Appendix H, "Perl DBI API Reference," which lists all the MySQL-specific constructs.

6.2.3   The PHP API

Like Perl, PHP is a scripting language. Unlike Perl, PHP is designed less as a general-purpose language than as a language for writing Web applications. The PHP API is used primarily to embed executable scripts into Web pages. This makes it easy for Web developers to write pages with dynamically generated content. When a client browser sends a request for a PHP page to a Web server, PHP executes any script it finds in the page and replaces it with the script's output. The result is sent to the browser. This enables the page that actually appears in the browser to change according to the circumstances under which the page request occurs. For example, when the following short PHP script is embedded in a Web page, it displays the IP address of the client host that requested the page:

```
<?php echo $_SERVER["REMOTE_ADDR"]; ?>
```

As a less trivial and more interesting application, you can use a script to provide up-to-the-minute information to visitors based on the contents of your database. The following example shows a simple script such as might be used at the Historical League Web site. The script issues a query to determine the current League membership count and reports it to the person visiting the site:

```
<html>
<head>
<title>U.S. Historical League</title>
</head>
<body bgcolor="white">
<h2>U.S. Historical League</h2>
<p>Welcome to the U.S. Historical League Web Site.</p>
<?php
# USHL home page

try
{
  $dbh = new PDO("mysql:host=localhost;dbname=sampdb", "sampadm", "secret");
  $dbh->setAttribute (PDO::ATTR_ERRMODE, PDO::ERRMODE_EXCEPTION);
  $sth = $dbh->query ("SELECT COUNT(*) FROM member");
  $count = $sth->fetchColumn (0);
  print ("<p>The League currently has $count members.</p>");
  $dbh = NULL;  # close connection
}
catch (PDOException $e) { } # empty handler (catch but ignore errors)
?>
</body>
</html>
```

PHP scripts typically look like HTML pages with executable code embedded within `<?php` and `?>` tags. A page can contain any number of code fragments. This provides an extremely flexible approach to script development. For example, you can write a PHP script as a normal HTML page initially to set up the general page framework, then add code later to generate the dynamic parts of the page.

PHP actually has multiple types of database interfaces. Among these is a set of low-level librar-ies, each of which works with a single database server and which make no effort to unify the interface to different servers the way DBI does. Instead, the interface to each server looks much like the interface for the corresponding C library that implements the low-level API for that server. For example, the names of the low-level functions to access MySQL from within PHP scripts are very similar to the names of the functions in the MySQL C client library.

A more DBI-like approach for PHP is provided by the PHP Data Objects (PDO) extension. This extension has a more abstract interface to database systems using a two-level architecture similar to that of DBI. The PHP scripts in Chapter 9, "Writing MySQL Programs Using PHP," employ the PDO extension for database access.

6.3   Choosing an API

This section provides general guidelines to help you choose an API for various types of applica-tions. It compares the capabilities of the C, DBI, and PHP APIs to give you some idea of their relative strengths and weaknesses, and to indicate when you might choose one over another.

I am not advocating any one of these languages over the others, although I do have my prefer-ences. You will have your own preferences, too, as have the technical reviewers for this book. One reviewer felt I should emphasize the importance of C for MySQL programming to a much greater extent, whereas another thought I should discourage its use. Weigh the factors discussed in this section and come to your own conclusions.

A number of considerations enter into assessing which API is most suitable for a particular task:

- **Intended execution environment.** The context in which you expect the application to be used.

- **Performance.** How efficiently applications perform when written in the API language.

- **Ease of development.** How convenient the API and its language make application writing.

- **Portability.** Whether the application will be used for database systems other than MySQL.

Be aware that some of the factors interact. For example, you want an application that performs well, but it might be just as important to use a language that lets you develop the application quickly even if it doesn't perform quite as efficiently.

6.3.1   Execution Environment

When you write an application, consider the environment in which it will be used. For example, it might be a report generator program that you invoke from the shell, or an accounts payable summary program that runs as a `cron` job at the end of each month. Commands run from the shell or from `cron` generally stand on their own and require little information from the execution environment. On the other hand, you might be writing an application intended to be invoked by a Web server. Such a program might expect to be able to extract very specific types of information from its execution environment: What browser is the client using? What parameters were entered into a mailing list subscription request form? Did the client supply the correct password for accessing personnel information?

Each API language varies in its suitability for writing applications in these differing environments:

- C is a general-purpose language, so in principle you can use it for anything. In practice, C tends to be used more often for standalone programs rather than for Web programming. One reason might be that it's not as easy to perform text processing and memory management in C as it is in Perl or in PHP, and those capabilities tend to be heavily used in Web applications.

- Perl, like C, is suitable for writing standalone programs. However, it also happens that Perl is quite useful for Web site development—for example, by using the CGI.pm module. This makes Perl a handy language for writing applications that link MySQL with the Web. Such an application can interface to the Web using the CGI.pm module and interface to MySQL using DBI.

- PHP is intended by design for writing Web applications, so that's obviously the environment to which it is best suited. Furthermore, database access is one of PHP's biggest strengths, so it's a natural choice for Web applications that perform MySQL-related tasks. It's possible to write command-line scripts in PHP, but that's not very common.

Given these considerations, C and Perl are the most likely candidate languages if you're writing a standalone application. For Web applications, Perl and PHP are most suitable. If you need to write both types of applications, but don't know any of these languages and want to learn as few as possible, Perl might be your best option.

6.3.2 Performance

All other things being equal, we prefer to have applications run as quickly as possible. However, the actual importance of performance tends to be related to how frequently a program is used. For a program that you run once a month as a `cron` job during the night, performance might not matter that much. On the other hand, for a program run many times a second on a heavily used Web site, every bit of efficiency you gain can make a big difference. In the latter case, performance plays a significant role in the usefulness and appeal of your site. A slow site is annoying for visitors, no matter what the site is about, and if you depend on the site as a source of income, decreased performance translates directly into reduced revenue. You cannot service as many connections at a time, and visitors who tire of waiting give up and go elsewhere.

Performance assessment is a complex issue. The best indicator of how well your application will perform when written for a particular API is to write it under that API and try it. And the best comparative test is to implement multiple versions under different APIs to see how they stack up against each other. Of course, that's not how development usually works. More often, you just want to get your program written. After it's working, you can think about tuning it to see whether it can run faster or use less memory, or whether it has some other aspect that you can improve. But there are at least two general factors that you can count on as affecting performance in a relatively consistent way:

- Compiled programs execute more quickly than interpreted scripts. They are more efficient, use less memory, and execute more quickly than an equivalent version of the program written in a scripting language. This is because they execute directly and without the overhead of an intermediary language interpreter that executes the scripts. C is compiled and Perl and PHP are interpreted, so C programs generally run faster than Perl or PHP scripts. Thus, C might be the best choice for a heavily used program. However, it is still necessary to consider what the program is doing. The difference between compiled and interpreted programs is lessened if a scripted application spends most of its time executing compiled MySQL client library routines that are linked into the interpreter engine.

- For interpreted languages used in a Web context, performance is better when the interpreter is invoked as a Web server module rather than as a separate process. For example, if you use Apache, you can arrange for it to invoke the script interpreter as a separate process. In this mode of operation, when Apache needs to run a Perl or PHP script, it starts the corresponding interpreter and tells it to execute the script. In this case, Apache uses the interpreters as CGI programs—that is, it communicates with them using the Common Gateway Interface (CGI) protocol. In contrast, the interpreter can be used as a module that is linked in directly to the Apache binary and that runs as part of the Apache process itself. In Apache terms, the Perl and PHP interpreters take the form of the `mod_perl` and `mod_php` modules.

6.3.3 Development Time

The factors just described affect the performance of your applications, but raw execution efficiency may not be your only goal. Your own time is important, too, as is ease of programming, so another factor to consider in choosing an API for MySQL programming is how quickly you can develop your applications. If you can write a Perl or PHP script in half the time it takes to develop the equivalent C program, you might elect not to use the C API, even if the resulting application doesn't run quite as fast. It's often reasonable to be less concerned about a program's execution time than about the time you spend writing it, particularly for applications that aren't executed frequently. An hour of your time is worth a lot more than an hour of machine time!

Generally, scripting languages enable you to get a program going more quickly, especially for prototyping. application. At least two factors contribute to this. First, scripting languages tend to provide higher-level constructs than compiled languages. This enables you to think at a higher level of abstraction, so you can think about what you want to do rather than about the details involved in doing it. For example, PHP associative arrays and Perl hashes are great time savers for maintaining data involving key/value relationships (such as student ID/student name pairs). C has no such construct. To implement it in C, you must write code to handle many low-level details involving issues such as memory management, and you would need to debug it. This takes time. Another advantage of Perl and PHP is their capability for pattern matching and text manipulation. C is very rudimentary in these areas.

Second, the development cycle has fewer steps for scripting languages than for compiled languages. With C, you engage in an edit-compile-test cycle during application development. Every time you modify a program, you must recompile it before testing. With Perl and PHP, the development cycle is simply edit-test because you can run a script immediately after each modification with no compiling. On the other hand, the C compiler enforces more constraints on your program in the form of stricter type checking. The greater discipline imposed by the compiler can help you avoid bugs that you would not catch as easily in looser languages, such as Perl and PHP. If you misspell a variable name in C, the compiler warns you. PHP and Perl don't unless you ask them to. These tighter constraints can be especially valuable as your applications become larger and more difficult to maintain.

In general, the tradeoff is the usual one between compiled and interpreted languages for development time versus performance: Do you want to develop the program using a compiled language so that it executes more quickly when it runs, but spend more time writing it? Or do you want to write the program as a script so that you can get it running in the least amount of time, even at the cost of some execution speed?

6.3.4 Portability

Portability is a matter of how easily a program written to use MySQL can be modified to use a different database system. This may be something you don't care about. However, unless you can predict the future, it is a little risky to say, "I'll never use this program with any database system other than MySQL." Suppose that you get a different job and want to use your old programs, but your new employer uses a different database system? What then? If portability is a priority, consider these clear differences between APIs:

- The C API is not portable at all. By its very nature, it is designed specifically for MySQL.
- The Perl DBI API is very portable because database independence is an explicit DBI design goal.
- PHP script portability is similar to DBI if you use the PDO database-access extension mentioned earlier.

Portability in the form of database independence is especially important when you must access multiple database systems within the same application. For example, you might need to export data from one database system and import it into another, or generate a report using information combined from a number of database systems.

Writing MySQL Programs Using C

MySQL provides a client library written in the C programming language that you can use to write client programs that access MySQL databases. This library defines an application programming interface that includes the following facilities:

- Connection management routines that open and close a session with a server
- Routines that construct SQL statements, send them to the server, and process the results
- Status-checking and error-reporting functions that determine the reason for an error when an API call fails
- Routines that process options given in option files or on the command line

This chapter shows how to use the C client library to write your own programs, using conventions that are reasonably consistent with those used by the client programs included in the MySQL distribution.

The first part of this chapter develops a series of short programs. The series culminates in a simple program that serves as the framework for a client skeleton that does nothing but connect to and disconnect from the server. The reason for this is that although MySQL client programs are written for different purposes, one thing all have in common is that they must establish a connection to the server.

The resulting skeleton program is generic, but it also includes code to process options and handle errors, so it is usable as the basis for any number of other client programs. After developing it, we'll pause to consider how to execute various kinds of SQL statements. Initially, we'll discuss how to handle specific hardcoded statements, and then develop code that can be used to process arbitrary statements. After that, we'll add some statement-processing code to the skeleton to develop another program that's similar to the mysql client and that can be used to issue statements interactively.

The chapter then demonstrates several other activities that the client library supports:

- Writing client programs that communicate with the server over secure connections using the Secure Sockets Layer (SSL) protocol

- Sending multiple statements to the server at once and processing the result sets that come back

- Using server-side prepared statements

This chapter discusses only those functions and data types from the client library needed for the example programs. For a comprehensive listing of functions and types, see Appendix G, "C API Reference." You can use that appendix as a reference for further background on any part of the client library you're trying to use.

The example programs are available so that you can try them directly without typing them in yourself. For instructions on obtaining the sampdb distribution that contains these programs, see Appendix A, "Software Required to Use This Book." You'll find the programs under the capi directory of that distribution.

Where to Find Example Programs

A common question on the MySQL mailing list is "Where can I find some examples of clients written in C?" The answer, of course, is "right here in this book." In addition, a MySQL source distribution includes several client programs that happen to be written in C (mysql, mysqladmin, and mysqldump, for example). Because the distribution is readily available, it provides you with quite a bit of example client code. If you haven't already done so, grab a source distribution sometime and take a look at the programs in its client and tests directories.

7.1   Compiling and Linking Client Programs

This section describes how to compile and link a program that uses the MySQL client library. The commands to build clients vary somewhat from system to system, and you might need to modify the commands shown here a bit. However, the description is general, and you should be able to apply it to most client programs you write.

When you write a MySQL client program in C, you'll need a C compiler, obviously. The examples shown here use gcc, the most common compiler used on Unix. You'll also need the MySQL header files and client library.

The header files and client library constitute the basis of MySQL client programming support. If MySQL was installed on your system from a source or binary distribution, client programming support should have been installed as part of that process. If RPM packages were used, this support won't be present unless you installed the developer RPM. Should you need to obtain the MySQL header files and library, see Appendix A, "Software Required to Use This Book."

To compile and link a client program, you must specify where the MySQL header files and client library are located, if they are not installed in locations that the compiler and linker search by default. For the following examples, suppose that the header file and client library locations are /usr/local/include/mysql and /usr/local/lib/mysql. Modify the pathnames as appropriate for your own system.

To tell the compiler how to find the MySQL header files when you compile a source file into an object file, pass it an -I option that names the appropriate directory. For example, to compile myclient.c to produce myclient.o, use a command like this:

```
% gcc -c -I/usr/local/include/mysql myclient.c
```

To tell the linker where to find the client library and what its name is, pass -L/usr/local/lib/mysql and -lmysqlclient arguments when you link the object file to produce an executable binary, as follows:

```
% gcc -o myclient myclient.o -L/usr/local/lib/mysql -lmysqlclient
```

If your client consists of multiple files, name all the object files on the link command.

The link step may result in error messages having to do with functions that cannot be found. In such cases, you'll need to supply additional -l options to name the libraries containing the functions. If you see a message about compress() or uncompress(), try adding -lz or -lgz to tell the linker to search the zlib compression library:

```
% gcc -o myclient myclient.o -L/usr/local/lib/mysql -lmysqlclient -lz
```

If the message names the floor() function, add -lm to link in the math library. You might need to add other libraries as well.

As an alternative to figuring out the proper flags for compiling and linking MySQL programs yourself, you can use the mysql_config utility to do it for you. For example, the utility might indicate that the following options are needed:

```
% mysql_config --include
-I'/usr/local/mysql/include'
% mysql_config --libs
-L'/usr/local/mysql/lib' -lmysqlclient -lpthread -lz -lm -lrt -ldl
```

To use mysql_config directly within your compile or link commands, invoke it within backticks:

```
% gcc -c `mysql_config --include` myclient.c
% gcc -o myclient myclient.o `mysql_config --libs`
```

The shell executes mysql_config and substitutes its output into the surrounding command, which automatically provides the appropriate flags for gcc.

If you don't use make to build programs, I suggest you learn how so that you won't have to type a lot of program-building commands manually. Suppose that you have a client program, myclient, that comprises two source files, main.c and lib.c, and a header file, myclient.h.

A simple `Makefile` to build this program follows. Indented lines are indented with tabs; spaces will not work.

```
CC = gcc
INCLUDES = -I/usr/local/include/mysql
LIBS = -L/usr/local/lib/mysql -lmysqlclient


all: myclient

main.o: main.c myclient.h
        $(CC) -c $(INCLUDES) main.c
lib.o: lib.c myclient.h
        $(CC) -c $(INCLUDES) lib.c

myclient: main.o lib.o
        $(CC) -o myclient main.o lib.o $(LIBS)

clean:
        rm -f myclient main.o lib.o
```

Using the `Makefile`, you can rebuild your program whenever you modify any of the source files simply by running `make`, which displays and executes the necessary commands:

```
% make
gcc -c -I/usr/local/mysql/include/mysql myclient.c
gcc -o myclient myclient.o -L/usr/local/mysql/lib/mysql -lmysqlclient
```

That's easier and less error prone than typing long `gcc` commands. A `Makefile` also makes it easier to modify the build process. For example, if your system is one for which you need to link in additional libraries such as the math and compression libraries, edit the `LIBS` line in the `Makefile` to add `-lm` and `-lz`:

```
LIBS = -L/usr/local/lib/mysql -lmysqlclient -lm -lz
```

If you need other libraries, add them to the `LIBS` line as well. Thereafter when you run `make`, it will use the updated value of `LIBS` automatically.

Another way to change `make` variables other than editing the `Makefile` is to specify them on the command line. For example, if your C compiler is named `cc` rather than `gcc`, you can say so like this:

```
% make CC=cc
```

If `mysql_config` is available, you can use it to avoid writing literal include file and library directory pathnames in the `Makefile`. Write the `INCLUDES` and `LIBS` lines as follows:

```
INCLUDES = ${shell mysql_config --include}
LIBS = ${shell mysql_config --libs}
```

When `make` runs, it executes each `mysql_config` command and uses its output to set the corresponding variable value. The `${shell}` construct shown here is supported by GNU `make`;

you might need to use a somewhat different syntax if your version of make isn't based on GNU make.

If you're using an integrated development environment (IDE), you might not use a Makefile at all. The details depend on your particular IDE.

7.2   Connecting to the Server

Our first MySQL client program is about as simple as can be: It connects to a MySQL server, disconnects, and exits. That's not very useful in itself, but you have to know how to do it because you must be connected to a server before you can do anything with a MySQL database. Connecting to a server is such a common operation that code you develop to establish the connection is code you'll use in every client program you write. Besides, this task gives us something simple to start with. The code can be fleshed out later to do something more useful.

Our first client program, connect1, consists of a single source file, connect1.c:

```
/*
 * connect1.c - connect to and disconnect from MySQL server
 */

#include <my_global.h>
#include <my_sys.h>
#include <mysql.h>

static char *opt_host_name = NULL;      /* server host (default=localhost) */
static char *opt_user_name = NULL;      /* username (default=login name) */
static char *opt_password = NULL;       /* password (default=none) */
static unsigned int opt_port_num = 0;   /* port number (use built-in value) */
static char *opt_socket_name = NULL;    /* socket name (use built-in value) */
static char *opt_db_name = NULL;        /* database name (default=none) */
static unsigned int opt_flags = 0;      /* connection flags (none) */

static MYSQL *conn;                     /* pointer to connection handler */

int
main (int argc, char *argv[])
{
  MY_INIT (argv[0]);
  /* initialize client library */
  if (mysql_library_init (0, NULL, NULL))
  {
    fprintf (stderr, "mysql_library_init() failed\n");
    exit (1);
  }
  /* initialize connection handler */
  conn = mysql_init (NULL);
  if (conn == NULL)
```

```
  {
    fprintf (stderr, "mysql_init() failed (probably out of memory)\n");
    exit (1);
  }
  /* connect to server */
  if (mysql_real_connect (conn, opt_host_name, opt_user_name, opt_password,
      opt_db_name, opt_port_num, opt_socket_name, opt_flags) == NULL)
  {
    fprintf (stderr, "mysql_real_connect() failed\n");
    mysql_close (conn);
    exit (1);
  }
  /* disconnect from server, terminate client library */
  mysql_close (conn);
  mysql_library_end ();
  exit (0);
}
```

The source file begins by including the header files `my_global.h`, `my_sys.h`, and `mysql.h`. Depending on what a MySQL client program does, it might need to include other header files as well, but these three usually are the bare minimum:

- `my_global.h` includes several other header files that are likely to be generally useful, such as `stdio.h`. It also includes Windows compatibility information if you're compiling the program on Windows. (You might not intend to use Windows yourself, but if you plan to distribute your code, using `my_global.h` will help anyone else who does compile under Windows.)

- `my_sys.h` contains portability macros and definitions for structures and functions used by the client library.

- `mysql.h` defines the primary MySQL-related constants and data structures.

The order of inclusion is important; `my_global.h` is intended to be included before any other MySQL-specific header files.

Next, the program declares a set of variables corresponding to the parameters that need to be specified when connecting to the server. For this client, the parameters are hardwired to have default values. Later, we develop a more flexible approach that enables the defaults to be over-ridden using values specified either in option files or on the command line. (That's why the names all begin with `opt_`; the intent is that eventually those variables will become settable through command options.) The program also declares a pointer to a `MYSQL` structure that will serve as a connection handler.

The `main()` function of the program establishes and terminates the connection to the server. Making a connection is a two-step process:

1. Call `mysql_init()` to obtain a connection handler.

2. Call `mysql_real_connect()` to establish a connection to the server.

When you pass NULL to mysql_init(), it automatically allocates a MYSQL structure, initializes it, and returns a pointer to it. The MYSQL data type is a structure containing information about a connection. Variables of this type are called "connection handlers."

Another approach is to pass a pointer to an existing MYSQL structure. In this case, mysql_init() initializes that structure and returns a pointer to it without allocating the structure itself.

mysql_real_connect() takes about a zillion parameters:

- A pointer to the connection handler. This should be the value returned by mysql_init().

- The server host. This value is interpreted in a platform-specific way. On Unix, if you specify a string containing a hostname or IP address, the client connects to the given host by using a TCP/IP connection. If you specify NULL or the host "localhost", the client connects to the server running on the local host by using a Unix socket file.

  On Windows, the behavior is similar, except that for "localhost", a shared-memory or TCP/IP connection is used rather than a Unix socket file connection. On Windows, the connection is attempted to the local server using a named pipe if the host is "." or NULL and the server supports named-pipe connections.

- The username and password for the MySQL account to be used. If the name is NULL, the client library sends your login name to the server (or ODBC, for Windows). If the password is NULL, no password is sent.

- The name of the database to select as the default database after the connection has been established. If this value is NULL, no database is selected.

- The port number. This is used for TCP/IP connections. A value of 0 tells the client library to use the default port number.

- The socket filename. On Unix, the name is used for Unix socket file connections. On Windows, the name is interpreted as the name to use for a pipe connection. A value of NULL tells the client library to use the default socket (or pipe) name.

- A flags value. The connect1 program passes a value of 0 because it uses no special connection options.

For more information about mysql_real_connect(), see Appendix G, "C API Reference." The description there discusses in more detail issues such as how the hostname parameter interacts with the port number and socket filename parameters, and lists the options that can be specified in the flags parameter. The appendix also describes mysql_options(), which you can use to specify other connection-related options prior to calling mysql_real_connect().

To terminate the connection, invoke mysql_close() and pass it a pointer to the connection handler. If you allocated the handler automatically by passing NULL to mysql_init(), mysql_close() automatically deallocates the handler when you terminate the connection. After calling mysql_close(), the handler cannot be used for further communication with the server.

In addition to the connection-establishment code, `connect1.c` uses three other calls:

- `MY_INIT()` is an initialization macro. It sets a global variable to point to the name of your program (which you pass as its argument), for use by MySQL libraries in error messages. It also calls `my_init()` to perform some setup operations.

- `mysql_library_init()` initializes the MySQL client library. Call it before invoking any other `mysql_xxx()` functions.

- `mysql_library_end()` terminates use of the client library and performs any necessary cleanup. Call it when you are done using the client library.

To try `connect1`, compile and link it using the instructions given earlier in the chapter for building client programs, and then run it. Under Unix, run the program like this:

```
% ./connect1
```

The leading "`./`" might be necessary on Unix if your shell does not have the current directory ("`.`") in its search path. If the current directory is in your search path, or you are using Windows, you can omit the "`./`" from the command name:

```
% connect1
```

If `connect1` produces no output, it connected successfully. On the other hand, you might see something like this:

```
% ./connect1
mysql_real_connect() failed
```

This output indicates that no connection was established, but it doesn't tell you why. Very likely the reason for the failure is that the default connection parameters (hostname, username, and so on) are unsuitable. Assuming that is so, one way to fix the problem is to recompile the program after editing the initializers for the parameter variables and changing them to values that enable you to access your server. That might be beneficial in the sense that at least you'd be able to make a connection. But the program still would contain hardcoded values, which isn't very flexible if other people are to use it. It's also insecure because it exposes your password. You might think that the password becomes hidden when you compile your program into binary executable form, but it's not hidden at all if someone can run the `strings` utility on the binary. Also, anyone with read access to the source file can get the password with no work at all.

The preceding paragraph highlights two significant shortcomings of `connect1`:

- The error output isn't very informative about specific causes of problems.

- There is no flexible way for the user who runs the program to specify connection parameters. They are hardwired into the source code. It would be better to enable the user to override the parameters on the command line or in an option file.

The next section addresses these problems.

7.3 Handling Errors and Processing Command Options

Our next client, connect2, is similar to connect1 in the sense that it connects to the MySQL server, disconnects, and exits. However, connect2 has two important improvements:

- It does a better job of error reporting, using MySQL client library functions that return specific information about the causes of errors.

- It provides default connection parameters but enables the user to override them with options on the command line or in an option file.

7.3.1 Checking for Errors

Let's consider the topic of error-handling first. To start off, I want to emphasize that it's important to check for errors whenever you invoke a MySQL function that can fail. It seems to be fairly common in programming texts to say "Error checking is left as an exercise for the reader." I suppose that this is because checking for errors is—let's face it—such a bore. Nevertheless, it is necessary to test for error conditions and respond to them appropriately. The client library functions that return status values do so for a reason, and you ignore them at your peril. For example, if a function returns a pointer to a data structure or NULL to indicate an error, you'd better check the return value. Attempts to use NULL later in the program when a pointer to a valid data structure is expected will lead to strange results or crash your program.

Failure to check return values is an unnecessary cause of programming difficulties and is a phenomenon that plays itself out frequently on the MySQL mailing lists. Typical questions are "Why does my program crash when it issues this statement?" or "How come my query doesn't return anything?" In many cases, the program in question didn't check whether the connection was established successfully before issuing the statement or didn't check to make sure the server successfully executed the statement before trying to retrieve the results.

Don't make the mistake of assuming that every client library call succeeds. If you don't check return values, you'll end up trying to track down obscure problems that occur in your programs, or users of your programs will wonder why those programs behave erratically, or both.

Routines in the MySQL client library that return a value generally indicate success or failure in one of two ways, depending on whether the return value is a pointer or an integer.

Pointer-valued functions return a non-NULL pointer for success and NULL for failure. (NULL in this context means "a C NULL pointer," not "a MySQL NULL column value.")

Of the client library routines we've used so far, mysql_init() and mysql_real_connect() both return a pointer to the connection handler to indicate success and NULL to indicate failure.

Integer-valued functions generally return 0 for success and nonzero for failure. It's important not to test for specific nonzero values, such as −1. There is no guarantee that a client library function returns any particular value when it fails. On occasion, you may see code that tests a return value from a C API function `mysql_XXX()` incorrectly like this:

```
if (mysql_XXX () == -1)      /* this test is incorrect */
  fprintf (stderr, "something bad happened\n");
```

This test might work, and it might not. The MySQL API doesn't specify that any nonzero error return will be a particular value, other than that it (obviously) isn't zero. Write the test like this:

```
if (mysql_XXX () != 0)       /* this test is correct */
  fprintf (stderr, "something bad happened\n");
```

Alternatively, write the test like this, which is equivalent and slightly simpler to write:

```
if (mysql_XXX ())            /* this test is correct */
  fprintf (stderr, "something bad happened\n");
```

If you look through the source code for MySQL itself, you'll find that generally it uses the second form of the test.

Not every API call returns a value. The other client routine we've used, `mysql_close()`, is one that does not. (How could it fail? And if it did, so what? You were done with the connection, anyway.)

When a client library call does fail, three calls in the API tell you why:

- `mysql_error()` returns a string containing an error message.
- `mysql_errno()` returns a MySQL-specific numeric error code.
- `mysql_sqlstate()` returns an SQLSTATE code. The SQLSTATE value is more vendor neutral because it is based on the ANSI SQL and ODBC standards.

The argument to each function is a pointer to the connection handler. Call them immediately after an error occurs. If you issue another API call that returns a status, any error information you get from `mysql_error()`, `mysql_errno()`, or `mysql_sqlstate()` apply to the later call instead.

Generally, the user of a program will find an error message more enlightening than either error code, so if you report only one value, I suggest that it be the message. The examples in this chapter report all three values for completeness. However, it's tedious to write three function invocations every place an error might occur. Instead, let's write a utility function, `print_error()`, that prints an error message supplied by us as well as the error values provided by the MySQL client library routines. In other words, we won't write out the calls to the `mysql_errno()` `mysql_error()`, and `mysql_sqlstate()` functions like this each time an error test occurs:

```
if (...some MySQL function fails...)
{
  fprintf (stderr, "...some error message...:\nError %u (%s): %s\n",
           mysql_errno (conn), mysql_sqlstate (conn), mysql_error (conn));
}
```

It's easier to report errors by using a utility function that can be called like this instead:

```
if (...some MySQL function fails...)
{
  print_error (conn, "...some error message...");
}
```

`print_error()` prints the error message and calls the MySQL error functions. The `print_error()` call is simpler than the `fprintf()` call, so it's easier to write and it makes the program easier to read. Also, if `print_error()` is written to do something sensible even when `conn` is NULL, we can use it under circumstances such as when `mysql_init()` call fails. Then we won't have a mix of error-reporting calls—some to `fprintf()` and some to `print_error()`.

I can hear someone in the back row objecting: "Well, you don't really have to call every error function each time you want to report an error. You're deliberately overstating the drudgery of reporting errors that way so your utility function looks more useful. And you wouldn't really write all that error-printing code a bunch of times anyway; you'd write it once, and then use copy and paste when you need it again." Those are reasonable objections, but I respond to them as follows:

- Even if you use copy and paste, it's easier to do so with shorter sections of code.

- If it's easy to report errors, you're more likely to be consistent about checking for them when you should.

- Whether or not you prefer to invoke all error functions each time you report an error, writing out all the error-reporting code the long way leads to the temptation to take shortcuts and be inconsistent when you do report errors. Wrapping the error-reporting code in a utility function that's easy to invoke lessens this temptation and improves coding consistency.

- If you ever do decide to modify the format of your error messages, it's a lot easier if you need to make the change only one place, rather than throughout your program. Or, if you decide to write error messages to a log file instead of (or in addition to) writing them to `stderr`, it's easier if you only have to change `print_error()`. This approach is less error prone and, again, lessens the temptation to do the job halfway and be inconsistent.

- If you use a debugger when testing your programs, putting a breakpoint in the error-reporting function is a convenient way to have the program break to the debugger when it detects an error condition.

For these reasons, programs in the rest of this chapter that check for MySQL-related errors use `print_error()` to report problems.

The following listing shows the definition of `print_error()`, which provides the benefits just discussed:

```
static void
print_error (MYSQL *conn, char *message)
{
```

```
    fprintf (stderr, "%s\n", message);
    if (conn != NULL)
    {
      fprintf (stderr, "Error %u (%s): %s\n",
               mysql_errno (conn), mysql_sqlstate (conn), mysql_error (conn));
    }
}
```

The part of `connect2.c` that needs to check for errors is similar to the corresponding code in `connect1.c`, and looks like this when we use `print_error()`:

```
/* initialize connection handler */
conn = mysql_init (NULL);
if (conn == NULL)
{
  print_error (NULL, "mysql_init() failed (probably out of memory)");
  exit (1);
}


/* connect to server */
if (mysql_real_connect (conn, opt_host_name, opt_user_name, opt_password,
    opt_db_name, opt_port_num, opt_socket_name, opt_flags) == NULL)
{
  print_error (conn, "mysql_real_connect() failed");
  mysql_close (conn);
  exit (1);
}
```

The error-checking logic is based on the fact that both `mysql_init()` and `mysql_real_connect()` return NULL if they fail. Note that if `mysql_init()` fails, we pass NULL as the first argument to `print_error()`. That causes it not to invoke the MySQL error-reporting functions, because the connection handler passed to those functions cannot be assumed to contain any meaningful information. By contrast, if `mysql_real_connect()` fails, we do pass the connection handler to `print_error()`. The handler won't contain information that corresponds to a valid connection, but it *will* contain diagnostic information that can be extracted by the error-reporting functions. The handler also can be passed to `mysql_close()` to release any memory that may have been allocated automatically for it by `mysql_init()`. (Don't pass the handler to any other client routines, though! Because most of them assume a valid connection, your program may crash.)

The rest of the programs in this chapter perform error checking, and your own programs should, too. It's less work in the long run because you spend less time tracking down subtle problems.

7.3.2   Getting Connection Parameters at Runtime

Now we're ready to tackle the task of enabling users to specify connection parameters at runtime rather than using hardwired default parameters. The `connect1` program had a significant shortcoming in that the connection parameters were written literally into the source code. To change any of those values, you'd have to edit the source file and recompile it. That's not very convenient, especially if you intend to make your program available for other people to use. One common way to specify connection parameters at runtime is by using command-line options. For example, the programs in the MySQL distribution accept parameters in either of two forms, as shown in the following table.

Parameter	Long Option Form	Short Option Form
Hostname	`--host=host_name`	`-h host_name`
Username	`--user=user_name`	`-u user_name`
Password	`--password` or	`-p` or
	`--password=your_pass`	`-pyour_pass`
Port number	`--port=port_num`	`-P port_num`
Socket name	`--socket=socket_name`	`-S socket_name`

To be consistent with the standard MySQL clients, our `connect2` client program accepts those same formats. It's easy to do this because the client library supports option processing. In addition, `connect2` has the capability to extract information from option files. This enables you to put connection parameters in `~/.my.cnf` (that is, the `.my.cnf` file in your home directory) or in any global option file. Then you need not specify the options on the command line each time you invoke the program. The client library makes it easy to check for MySQL option files and pull any relevant values from them. By adding only a few lines of code to your programs, you can make them option file-aware, with no need to reinvent the wheel by writing your own code to do it. (For a description of option file syntax, see Section F.2.2, "Option Files.")

Before showing how option processing works in `connect2` itself, we develop two of programs that illustrate the general principles involved. These show how option handling works fairly simply and without the added complication of connecting to the MySQL server and processing statements.

> **Note**
>
> MySQL provides two other options that relate to connection establishment. `--protocol` speci-fies the connection protocol (TCP/IP, Unix socket file, and so on), and `--shared-memory-base-name` specifies the name of the shared memory to use for shared-memory connections on Windows. This chapter doesn't cover either option, but if you are interested, the `sampdb` distribution contains the source code for a program, `protocol`, that shows how to use them.

7.3.2.1 Accessing Option File Contents

To read option files for connection parameter values, invoke `load_defaults()`. This function looks for option files, parses their contents for any option groups in which you're interested, and rewrites your program's argument vector (the `argv[]` array). It puts information from those option groups in the form of command-line options at the beginning of `argv[]`. That way, the options appear to have been specified on the command line. When you parse the command options, you see the connection parameters in your normal option-processing code. The options are added to `argv[]` immediately after the command name and before any other arguments (rather than at the end), so that any connection parameters specified on the command line occur later than and thus override any options added by `load_defaults()`.

Here's a little program, `show_argv`, that demonstrates how to use `load_defaults()` and illustrates how it modifies your argument vector:

```
/*
 * show_argv.c - show effect of load_defaults() on argument vector
 */

#include <my_global.h>
#include <my_sys.h>
#include <mysql.h>

static const char *client_groups[] = { "client", NULL };

int
main (int argc, char *argv[])
{
int i;

  printf ("Original argument vector:\n");
  for (i = 0; i < argc; i++)
    printf ("arg %d: %s\n", i, argv[i]);

  MY_INIT (argv[0]);
  load_defaults ("my", client_groups, &argc, &argv);

  printf ("Modified argument vector:\n");
  for (i = 0; i < argc; i++)
    printf ("arg %d: %s\n", i, argv[i]);

  exit (0);
}
```

The option file-processing code involves several components:

- `client_groups[]` is an array of character strings indicating the names of the option file groups from which you want to obtain options. Client programs normally include at least `"client"` in the list (which represents the `[client]` group), but you can list as many groups as you like. The last element of the array must be `NULL` to indicate where the list ends.

- `MY_INIT()` is an initialization macro that we have used before. The important point here is that `MY_INIT()` calls `my_init()` to perform some setup operations required by `load_defaults()`.

- `load_defaults()` reads the option files. It takes four arguments: the prefix used in the names of your option files (this should always be `"my"`), the array listing the names of the option groups in which you're interested, and the addresses of your program's argument count and vector. Don't pass the values of the count and vector. Pass their addresses instead because `load_defaults()` needs to change their values. In particular, even though `argv` is already a pointer, you still pass `&argv`, that pointer's address.

`show_argv` prints its arguments twice to show the effect that `load_defaults()` has on the argument array. First it prints the arguments as they were specified on the command line. Then it calls `load_defaults()` and prints the argument array again.

To see how `load_defaults()` works, make sure that you have a `.my.cnf` file in your home directory with some settings specified for the `[client]` group. (On Windows, you can use the `C:\my.ini` file instead.) Suppose that the file looks like this:

```
[client]
user=sampadm
password=secret
host=some_host
```

If that is the case, executing `show_argv` should produce output like this:

```
% ./show_argv a b
Original argument vector:
arg 0: ./show_argv
arg 1: a
arg 2: b
Modified argument vector:
arg 0: ./show_argv
arg 1: --user=sampadm
arg 2: --password=secret
arg 3: --host=some_host
arg 4: a
arg 5: b
```

When `show_argv` prints the argument vector the second time, the values in the option file show up as part of the argument list. It's also possible that you'll see some options that were not specified on the command line or in your `~/.my.cnf` file. If this occurs, you will likely find that options for the `[client]` group are listed in a system-wide option file. This can happen because `load_defaults()` actually looks for option files in several locations. (For a list of these locations, see Section F.2.2, "Option Files.")

Client programs that use `load_defaults()` generally include `"client"` in the list of option group names (so that they get any general client settings from option files), but you can set up your option file-processing code to obtain options from other groups as well. Suppose that you want `show_argv` to read options in the `[client]` and `[show_argv]` groups. To accomplish this, find the following line in `show_argv.c`:

```
const char *client_groups[] = { "client", NULL };
```

Change the line to this:

```
const char *client_groups[] = { "show_argv", "client", NULL };
```

Then recompile `show_argv`, and the modified program will read options from both groups. To verify this, add a `[show_argv]` group to your `~/.my.cnf` file:

```
[client]
user=sampadm
password=secret
host=some_host

[show_argv]
host=other_host
```

With these changes, invoking `show_argv` again produces a result different from before:

```
% ./show_argv a b
Original argument vector:
arg 0: ./show_argv
arg 1: a
arg 2: b
Modified argument vector:
arg 0: ./show_argv
arg 1: --user=sampadm
arg 2: --password=secret
arg 3: --host=some_host
arg 4: --host=other_host
arg 5: a
arg 6: b
```

The order of option values in the argument array is determined by the order in which they are listed in your option file, not the order in which option groups are named in the `client_groups[]` array. This means you'll probably want to specify program-specific groups after the `[client]` group in your option file. That way, if you specify an option in both groups, the program-specific value takes precedence over the more general `[client]` group value. You can see this in the example just shown: The `host` option is specified in both the `[client]` and `[show_argv]` groups, but because the `[show_argv]` group appears last in the option file, its `host` setting appears later in the argument vector and takes precedence.

`load_defaults()` does not pick up values from your environment settings. To use the values of environment variables such as `MYSQL_TCP_PORT` or `MYSQL_UNIX_PORT`, you must arrange for that yourself by using `getenv()`. I'm not going to add that capability to our clients, but here's a short code fragment that shows how to check the values of two MySQL-related environment variables:

```
extern char *getenv ();
char *p;
int port_num = 0;
char *socket_name = NULL;

if ((p = getenv ("MYSQL_TCP_PORT")) != NULL)
  port_num = atoi (p);
if ((p = getenv ("MYSQL_UNIX_PORT")) != NULL)
  socket_name = p;
```

In the standard MySQL clients, environment variable values have lower precedence than values specified in option files or on the command line. To check environment variables in your own programs and be consistent with that convention, check the environment before (not after) calling `load_defaults()` or processing command-line options.

> ### `load_defaults()` and Security
>
> On multiple-user systems, utilities such as the `ps` program can display argument lists from arbitrary processes, including those being run by other users. Because of this, you might be wondering if there are any process-snooping implications of `load_defaults()` taking passwords that it finds in option files and putting them in your argument list. This actually is not a problem because `ps` displays the original `argv[]` contents. Any password argument created by `load_defaults()` points to an area of memory that it allocates for itself. That area is not part of the original vector, so `ps` never sees it.
>
> On the other hand, a password that is given on the command line *does* show up in `ps`, so it's not a good idea to specify passwords that way. One precaution a program can take to help reduce the risk is to remove the password from the argument list as soon as it starts executing. Section 7.3.2.2, "Processing Command-Line Arguments," shows how to do that.

7.3.2.2 Processing Command-Line Arguments

Using `load_defaults()`, we can get all the connection parameters into the argument vector, but we need a way to process the vector. The `handle_options()` function is designed for this. `handle_options()` is part of the MySQL client library, so you have access to it whenever you link in that library.

Some of the characteristics of the client library option-processing routines are as follows:

- Precise specification of the option type and range of legal values. For example, you can indicate not only that an option must have integer values, but that it must be positive and a multiple of 1024.

- Integration of help text to make it easy to print a help message by calling a standard library function. There is no need to write your own special code to produce a help message.

- Built-in support for the standard `--no-defaults`, `--print-defaults`, `--defaults-file`, and `--defaults-extra-file` options. (These options are described in Section F.2.2, "Option Files.")

- Support for a standard set of option prefixes, such as `--disable-`, `--enable-`, and `--loose-`, to make it easier to implement boolean (on/off) and ignorable options. (This capability is not used in this chapter, but is described in Section F.2, "Specifying Program Options.")

To demonstrate how to use MySQL's option-handling facilities, this section describes a `show_opt` program that invokes `load_defaults()` to read option files and set up the argument vector, then processes the result using `handle_options()`.

`show_opt` enables you to experiment with various ways of specifying connection parameters (whether in option files or on the command line), and to see the result by showing you what values would be used to make a connection to the MySQL server. `show_opt` is useful for getting a feel for what will happen in our next client program, `connect2`, which hooks up this option-processing code with code that actually does connect to the server.

To illustrate what happens at each phase of argument processing, `show_opt` performs the following actions:

1. Sets up default values for the hostname, username, password, and other connection parameters.

2. Prints the original connection parameter and argument vector values.

3. Calls `load_defaults()` to rewrite the argument vector to reflect option file contents, then prints the resulting vector.

4. Calls the option processing routine `handle_options()` to process the argument vector, then prints the resulting connection parameter values and whatever is left in the argument vector.

The following discussion explains how `show_opt` works, but first take a look at its source file, `show_opt.c`:

```
/*
 * show_opt.c - demonstrate option processing with load_defaults()
 * and handle_options()
 */

#include <my_global.h>
#include <my_sys.h>
#include <mysql.h>
#include <my_getopt.h>

static char *opt_host_name = NULL;    /* server host (default=localhost) */
static char *opt_user_name = NULL;    /* username (default=login name) */
static char *opt_password = NULL;     /* password (default=none) */
```

```c
static unsigned int opt_port_num = 0; /* port number (use built-in value) */
static char *opt_socket_name = NULL;  /* socket name (use built-in value) */

static const char *client_groups[] = { "client", NULL };

static struct my_option my_opts[] =   /* option information structures */
{
  {"help", '?', "Display this help and exit",
  NULL, NULL, NULL,
  GET_NO_ARG, NO_ARG, 0, 0, 0, 0, 0, 0},
  {"host", 'h', "Host to connect to",
  (uchar **) &opt_host_name, NULL, NULL,
  GET_STR, REQUIRED_ARG, 0, 0, 0, 0, 0, 0},
  {"password", 'p', "Password",
  (uchar **) &opt_password, NULL, NULL,
  GET_STR, OPT_ARG, 0, 0, 0, 0, 0, 0},
  {"port", 'P', "Port number",
  (uchar **) &opt_port_num, NULL, NULL,
  GET_UINT, REQUIRED_ARG, 0, 0, 0, 0, 0, 0},
  {"socket", 'S', "Socket path",
  (uchar **) &opt_socket_name, NULL, NULL,
  GET_STR, REQUIRED_ARG, 0, 0, 0, 0, 0, 0},
  {"user", 'u', "User name",
  (uchar **) &opt_user_name, NULL, NULL,
  GET_STR, REQUIRED_ARG, 0, 0, 0, 0, 0, 0},
  { NULL, 0, NULL, NULL, NULL, NULL, GET_NO_ARG, NO_ARG, 0, 0, 0, 0, 0, 0 }
};

static my_bool
get_one_option (int optid, const struct my_option *opt, char *argument)
{
  switch (optid)
  {
  case '?':
    my_print_help (my_opts);  /* print help message */
    exit (0);
  }
  return (0);
}

int
main (int argc, char *argv[])
{
int i;
int opt_err;
```

```
    printf ("Original connection parameters:\n");
    printf ("hostname: %s\n", opt_host_name ? opt_host_name : "(null)");
    printf ("username: %s\n", opt_user_name ? opt_user_name : "(null)");
    printf ("password: %s\n", opt_password ? opt_password : "(null)");
    printf ("port number: %u\n", opt_port_num);
    printf ("socket filename: %s\n",
            opt_socket_name ? opt_socket_name : "(null)");

    printf ("Original argument vector:\n");
    for (i = 0; i < argc; i++)
      printf ("arg %d: %s\n", i, argv[i]);

    MY_INIT (argv[0]);
    load_defaults ("my", client_groups, &argc, &argv);

    printf ("Argument vector after calling load_defaults():\n");
    for (i = 0; i < argc; i++)
      printf ("arg %d: %s\n", i, argv[i]);

    if ((opt_err = handle_options (&argc, &argv, my_opts, get_one_option)))
      exit (opt_err);

    printf ("Connection parameters after calling handle_options():\n");
    printf ("hostname: %s\n", opt_host_name ? opt_host_name : "(null)");
    printf ("username: %s\n", opt_user_name ? opt_user_name : "(null)");
    printf ("password: %s\n", opt_password ? opt_password : "(null)");
    printf ("port number: %u\n", opt_port_num);
    printf ("socket filename: %s\n",
            opt_socket_name ? opt_socket_name : "(null)");

    printf ("Argument vector after calling handle_options():\n");
    for (i = 0; i < argc; i++)
      printf ("arg %d: %s\n", i, argv[i]);

  exit (0);
}
```

The option-processing approach illustrated by show_opt.c involves several aspects that are common to any program that uses the MySQL client library to handle command options. In your own programs, you should do the same things:

1. In addition to the other files that we already have been including, include my_getopt.h as well. my_getopt.h defines the interface to MySQL's option-processing facilities.

2. Define an array of my_option structures. In show_opt.c, this array is named my_opts. The array should have one structure per option that the program understands. Each structure provides information such as an option's short and long names, its default value, whether the value is a number or string, and so forth.

3. After invoking `load_defaults()` to read the option files and set up the argument vector, call `handle_options()` to process the options. The first two arguments to `handle_options()` are the addresses of your program's argument count and vector. (Just as with `load_options()`, you pass the addresses of these variables, not their values.) The third argument points to the array of `my_option` structures. The fourth argument is a pointer to a helper function. The `handle_options()` routine and the `my_options` structures are designed to make it possible for most option-processing actions to be performed automatically for you by the client library. However, to permit special actions that the library does not handle, your program should also define a helper function for `handle_options()` to call. In `show_opt.c`, this function is named `get_one_option()`.

The `my_option` structure defines the types of information that must be specified for each option that the program understands:

```
struct my_option
{
  const char *name;               /* option's long name */
  int        id;                  /* option's short name or code */
  const char *comment;            /* option description for help message */
  void       *value;              /* pointer to variable to store value in */
  void       *u_max_value;        /* The user defined max variable value */
  struct st_typelib *typelib;     /* pointer to possible values (unused) */
  ulong      var_type;            /* option value's type */
  enum get_opt_arg_type arg_type; /* whether option value is required */
  longlong   def_value;           /* option's default value */
  longlong   min_value;           /* option's minimum allowable value */
  longlong   max_value;           /* option's maximum allowable value */
  longlong   sub_size;            /* amount to shift value by */
  long       block_size;          /* option value multiplier */
  void       *app_type;           /* reserved for application-specific use */
};
```

The members of the `my_option` structure are used as follows:

- `name` is the long option name. This is the `--name` form of the option, without the leading dashes. For example, if the long option is `--user`, list it as `"user"` in the `my_option` structure.

- `id` is the short (single-letter) option name, or a code value associated with the option if it has no single-letter name. For example, if the short option is `-u`, list it as `'u'` in the `my_option` structure. For options that have only a long name and no corresponding single-character name, you should make up a set of option code values to be used internally for the short names. The values must be unique and different from all the single-character names. (To satisfy the latter constraint, make the codes greater than 255, the largest possible single-character value. For an example, see Section 7.6, "Writing Clients That Include SSL Support.")

- `comment` is an explanatory string that describes the purpose of the option. This is the text to be displayed in a help message.

- `value` is the address of a generic pointer, declared as a `uchar **` value. If the option takes an argument, `value` points to the variable where you want the argument to be stored. After the options have been processed, you can check that variable to see what the option has been set to. The data type of the variable that's pointed to must be consistent with the value of the `var_type` member. If the option takes no argument, `value` is NULL.

- `u_max_value` is another address of a generic pointer, but it's used only by the server. For client programs, set `u_max_value` to NULL.

- `typelib` currently is unused. In future MySQL releases, it may be used to enable a list of legal values to be specified, in which case any option value given will be required to match one of these values.

- `var_type` indicates what kind of value must follow the option name on the command line. The following table shows these types, their meanings, and the corresponding C type.

`var_type` Value	Meaning	C Type
GET_NO_ARG	No value	
GET_BOOL	Boolean value	`my_bool`
GET_INT	Integer value	`int`
GET_UINT	Unsigned integer value	`unsigned int`
GET_LONG	Long integer value	`long`
GET_ULONG	Unsigned long integer value	`unsigned long`
GET_LL	Long long integer value	`long long`
GET_ULL	Unsigned long long integer value	`unsigned long long`
GET_STR	String value	`char *`
GET_STR_ALLOC	String value	`char *`
GET_DISABLED	Option is disabled	
GET_ENUM	Enumeration value (currently unused)	
GET_SET	Set value (currently unused)	
GET_DOUBLE	Double-precision (floating-point) value	`double`

The difference between GET_STR and GET_STR_ALLOC is that for GET_STR, the client library sets the option variable to point directly at the value in the argument vector, whereas for GET_STR_ALLOC, it makes a copy of the argument and sets the option variable to point to the copy.

The GET_DISABLED type can be used to indicate that an option is no longer available, or that it is available only when the program is built a certain way (for example, with debugging support enabled). To see an example, take a look at the mysql.cc file in a MySQL source distribution.

- arg_type indicates whether a value follows the option name, and may be any of the values shown in the following table. If arg_type is NO_ARG, var_type should be GET_NO_ARG.

arg_type Value	Meaning
NO_ARG	Option takes no following argument
OPT_ARG	Option may take a following argument
REQUIRED_ARG	Option requires a following argument

- def_value is for numeric-valued options. It is the default value to assign to the option if no explicit value is specified in the argument vector.

- min_value is for numeric-valued options. It is the smallest permitted value. Smaller values are bumped up to this value automatically. Use 0 to indicate "no minimum."

- max_value is for numeric-valued options. It is the largest permitted value. Larger values are bumped down to this value automatically. Use 0 to indicate "no maximum."

- sub_size is for numeric-valued options. It is an offset that is used to convert values from the range as given in the argument vector to the range that is used internally. For example, if values are given on the command line in the range from 1 to 256, but the program wants to use an internal range of 0 to 255, set sub_size to 1.

- block_size is for numeric-valued options. This value indicates a block size if it is nonzero. Option values given by the user are rounded down to the nearest multiple of this size if necessary. For example, if values must be even, set the block size to 2; handle_options() rounds odd values down to the nearest even number.

- app_type is reserved for application-specific use.

The my_opts array should have a my_option structure for each valid option, followed by a terminating structure that is set up as follows to indicate the end of the array:

```
{ NULL, 0, NULL, NULL, NULL, NULL, GET_NO_ARG, NO_ARG, 0, 0, 0, 0, 0, 0 }
```

When you invoke handle_options() to process the argument vector, it skips over the first argument (the program name), and then processes option arguments—that is, arguments that begin with a dash. This continues until it reaches the end of the vector or encounters the special two-dash "end of options" argument ('--'). As handle_options() moves through the argument vector, it calls the helper function once per option to enable that function to perform any special processing. handle_options() passes three arguments to the helper function: the short option value, a pointer to the option's my_option structure, and a pointer to the argument that follows the option in the argument vector (which will be NULL if the option is specified without a following value).

When handle_options() returns, the argument count and vector are reset appropriately to represent an argument list containing only the nonoption arguments.

Here is a sample invocation of show_opt and the resulting output (assuming that ~/.my.cnf still has the same contents as for the final show_argv example in Section 7.3.2.1, "Accessing Option File Contents"):

```
% ./show_opt -h yet_another_host --user=bill x
Original connection parameters:
hostname: (null)
username: (null)
password: (null)
port number: 0
socket filename: (null)
Original argument vector:
arg 0: ./show_opt
arg 1: -h
arg 3: yet_another_host
arg 3: --user=bill
arg 4: x
Argument vector after calling load_defaults():
arg 0: ./show_opt
arg 1: --user=sampadm
arg 2: --password=secret
arg 3: --host=some_host
arg 4: -h
arg 5: yet_another_host
arg 6: --user=bill
arg 7: x
Connection parameters after calling handle_options():
hostname: yet_another_host
username: bill
password: secret
port number: 0
socket filename: (null)
Argument vector after calling handle_options():
arg 0: x
```

The output shows that the hostname is picked up from the command line (overriding the value in the option file), and that the username and password come from the option file. handle_options() correctly parses options whether specified in short-option form (such as -h yet_another_host) or in long-option form (such as --user=bill).

The get_one_option() helper function is used in conjunction with handle_options(). For show_opt, it is fairly minimal and takes no action except for the --help or -? option (for which handle_options() passes an optid value of '?'):

```
static my_bool
get_one_option (int optid, const struct my_option *opt, char *argument)
{
  switch (optid)
  {
  case '?':
    my_print_help (my_opts);  /* print help message */
    exit (0);
  }
  return (0);
}
```

my_print_help() is a client library routine that automatically produces a help message for you, based on the option names and comment strings in the my_opts array. To see how it works, try the following command:

```
% ./show_opt --help
```

You can add other cases to the switch() statement in get_one_option() as necessary (and we do so in connect2 shortly). For example, get_one_option() is useful for handling password options. When you specify such an option, the password value may or may not be given, as indicated by OPT_ARG in the option information structure. That is, you can specify the option as --password or --password=*your_pass* if you use the long-option form, or as -p or -p*your_pass* if you use the short-option form. MySQL clients typically permit you to omit the password value on the command line, and then prompt you for it. This enables you to avoid giving the password on the command line, which keeps people from seeing your password. In later programs, we use get_one_option() to check whether a password value was given. We save the value if so, and otherwise set a flag to indicate that the program should prompt the user for a password before attempting to connect to the server.

You might find it instructive to modify the option structures in show_opt.c to see how your changes affect the program's behavior. For example, if you set the minimum, maximum, and block size values for the --port option to 100, 1000, and 25, you'll find after recompiling the program that you cannot set the port number to a value outside the range from 100 to 1000, and that values are rounded down to the nearest multiple of 25.

The option processing routines also handle the --no-defaults, --print-defaults, --defaults-file, and --defaults-extra-file options automatically. Try invoking show_opt with each of these options to see what happens.

7.3.3 Incorporating Option Processing into a Client Program

Now we're ready to write `connect2.c`. It has the following characteristics:

- It connects to the MySQL server, disconnects, and exits. This is similar to `connect1.c`, but uses the `print_error()` function developed earlier for reporting errors.

- It processes options on the command line or in option files. This is done using code similar to that from `show_opt.c`, modified to prompt the user for a password if necessary.

The resulting source file, `connect2.c`, looks like this:

```c
/*
 * connect2.c - connect to MySQL server, using connection parameters
 * specified in an option file or on the command line
 */

#include <my_global.h>
#include <my_sys.h>
#include <m_string.h>   /* for strdup() */
#include <mysql.h>
#include <my_getopt.h>

static char *opt_host_name = NULL;   /* server host (default=localhost) */
static char *opt_user_name = NULL;   /* username (default=login name) */
static char *opt_password = NULL;    /* password (default=none) */
static unsigned int opt_port_num = 0; /* port number (use built-in value) */
static char *opt_socket_name = NULL; /* socket name (use built-in value) */
static char *opt_db_name = NULL;     /* database name (default=none) */
static unsigned int opt_flags = 0;   /* connection flags (none) */

static int ask_password = 0;         /* whether to solicit password */

static MYSQL *conn;                  /* pointer to connection handler */

static const char *client_groups[] = { "client", NULL };

static struct my_option my_opts[] =  /* option information structures */
{
  {"help", '?', "Display this help and exit",
  NULL, NULL, NULL,
  GET_NO_ARG, NO_ARG, 0, 0, 0, 0, 0, 0},
  {"host", 'h', "Host to connect to",
  (uchar **) &opt_host_name, NULL, NULL,
  GET_STR, REQUIRED_ARG, 0, 0, 0, 0, 0, 0},
  {"password", 'p', "Password",
  (uchar **) &opt_password, NULL, NULL,
```

```
  GET_STR, OPT_ARG, 0, 0, 0, 0, 0, 0},
  {"port", 'P', "Port number",
  (uchar **) &opt_port_num, NULL, NULL,
  GET_UINT, REQUIRED_ARG, 0, 0, 0, 0, 0, 0},
  {"socket", 'S', "Socket path",
  (uchar **) &opt_socket_name, NULL, NULL,
  GET_STR, REQUIRED_ARG, 0, 0, 0, 0, 0, 0},
  {"user", 'u', "User name",
  (uchar **) &opt_user_name, NULL, NULL,
  GET_STR, REQUIRED_ARG, 0, 0, 0, 0, 0, 0},
  { NULL, 0, NULL, NULL, NULL, NULL, GET_NO_ARG, NO_ARG, 0, 0, 0, 0, 0, 0 }
};

static void
print_error (MYSQL *conn, char *message)
{
  fprintf (stderr, "%s\n", message);
  if (conn != NULL)
  {
    fprintf (stderr, "Error %u (%s): %s\n",
             mysql_errno (conn), mysql_sqlstate (conn), mysql_error (conn));
  }
}

static my_bool
get_one_option (int optid, const struct my_option *opt, char *argument)
{
  switch (optid)
  {
  case '?':
    my_print_help (my_opts);  /* print help message */
    exit (0);
  case 'p':                    /* password */
    if (!argument)             /* no value given; solicit it later */
      ask_password = 1;
    else                       /* copy password, overwrite original */
    {
      opt_password = strdup (argument);
      if (opt_password == NULL)
      {
        print_error (NULL, "could not allocate password buffer");
        exit (1);
      }
      while (*argument)
        *argument++ = 'x';
      ask_password = 0;
    }
```

```
      break;
    }
  return (0);
}


int
main (int argc, char *argv[])
{
int opt_err;

  MY_INIT (argv[0]);
  load_defaults ("my", client_groups, &argc, &argv);

  if ((opt_err = handle_options (&argc, &argv, my_opts, get_one_option)))
    exit (opt_err);

  /* solicit password if necessary */
  if (ask_password)
    opt_password = get_tty_password (NULL);

  /* get database name if present on command line */
  if (argc > 0)
  {
    opt_db_name = argv[0];
    --argc; ++argv;
  }

  /* initialize client library */
  if (mysql_library_init (0, NULL, NULL))
  {
    print_error (NULL, "mysql_library_init() failed");
    exit (1);
  }

  /* initialize connection handler */
  conn = mysql_init (NULL);
  if (conn == NULL)
  {
    print_error (NULL, "mysql_init() failed (probably out of memory)");
    exit (1);
  }

  /* connect to server */
  if (mysql_real_connect (conn, opt_host_name, opt_user_name, opt_password,
      opt_db_name, opt_port_num, opt_socket_name, opt_flags) == NULL)
  {
    print_error (conn, "mysql_real_connect() failed");
```

```
    mysql_close (conn);
    exit (1);
}

/* ... issue statements and process results here ... */

/* disconnect from server, terminate client library */
mysql_close (conn);
mysql_library_end ();
exit (0);
}
```

Compared to the connect1 and show_opt programs developed earlier, connect2 does a few new things:

- It permits a default database to be specified as a command-line argument. This is consistent with the behavior of the standard clients in MySQL distributions.

- If a password value is present in the argument vector, get_one_option() makes a copy of it and overwrites the original. This minimizes the time window during which a password specified on the command line is visible to ps or to other system status programs. (The window is only *minimized*, not eliminated. Specifying passwords on the command line still is a security risk.)

- If a password option is given with no value, get_one_option() sets a flag to indicate that the program should prompt the user for a password. That's done in main() after all options have been processed, using the get_tty_password() function. This is a utility routine in the client library that prompts for a password without echoing it on the screen. You may ask, "Why not just call getpass()?" The answer is that not all systems have that function (for example, Windows does not). get_tty_password() is portable across systems because it's configured to adjust to system idiosyncrasies.

Compile and link connect2, then try running it:

```
% ./connect2
```

If connect2 produces no output (as just shown), it connected successfully. On the other hand, you might see something like this:

```
% ./connect2
mysql_real_connect() failed:
Error 1045 (28000): Access denied for user 'sampadm'@'localhost'
(using password: NO)
```

This output indicates no connection was established, and it says why. In this case, Access denied means that you need to supply appropriate connection parameters. With connect1, there was no way to do so short of editing and recompiling. connect2 connects to the MySQL server according to the options you specify. Assume that there is no option file to complicate matters. If you invoke connect2 with no arguments, it connects to localhost and passes your

Unix login name and no password to the server. If instead you invoke `connect2` as shown in the following command, it prompts for a password (because there is no password value immediately following `-p`), connects to `some_host`, and passes the username `some_user` to the server as well as the password you enter when prompted:

```
% ./connect2 -h some_host -p -u some_user some_db
```

`connect2` also passes the database name `some_db` to `mysql_real_connect()` to make that the default database. If there is an option file, `connect2` processes its contents and modifies the connection parameters accordingly.

Let's step back for a moment and consider what's been achieved so far. The work that has gone into producing `connect2` accomplishes something that's necessary for every MySQL client: connecting to the server using appropriate parameters. It also does a good job of reporting errors if the connection attempt fails. What we have now serves as a framework that can be used as the basis for many different client programs. To write a new client, do this:

1. Make a copy of `connect2.c`.

2. If the program accepts additional options other than the standard ones that `connect2.c` knows about, add them to the `my_opts` array and modify the option-processing loop.

3. Add your own application-specific code between the connect and disconnect calls.

And you're done.

All the real action for your application will take place between the `mysql_real_connect()` and `mysql_close()` calls, but having a reusable skeleton means that you can concentrate more on what you're really interested in—accessing the content of your databases.

7.4   Processing SQL Statements

The purpose of connecting to the server is to conduct a conversation with it by executing statements while the connection is open. This section shows how to do that. Each statement execution involves these steps:

1. Construct the statement. The way you do this depends on the contents of the statement—in particular, whether it contains binary data.

2. Issue the statement by sending it to the server. The server will execute the statement and generate a result.

3. Process the statement result. This depends on what type of statement you issued. For example, a `SELECT` statement returns rows of data for you to process. An `INSERT` statement does not.

The MySQL client library includes two sets of routines for statement execution. The first set sends each statement to the server as a string and returns the results for all columns in string format. The second set uses a binary protocol that enables nonstring data values to be sent and returned in native format without conversion to and from string format.

This section discusses the original method for processing SQL statements. Section 7.8, "Using Server-Side Prepared Statements," covers the binary protocol.

One factor to consider in constructing statements is which function to use for sending them to the server. The more general statement-issuing routine is `mysql_real_query()`. With this routine, you provide the statement as a counted string (a string plus a length). You must keep track of the length of your statement string and pass that to `mysql_real_query()`, along with the string itself. Because the statement is treated as a counted string rather than as a null-terminated string, it may contain anything, including binary data or null bytes.

The other statement-issuing function, `mysql_query()`, is more restrictive in what it permits in the statement string but often is easier to use. Any statement passed to `mysql_query()` should be a null-terminated string. This means the statement text cannot contain null bytes because those would cause it to be interpreted erroneously as shorter than it really is. Generally speaking, if your statement can contain arbitrary binary data, it might contain null bytes, so you shouldn't use `mysql_query()`. On the other hand, when you are working with null-terminated strings, you have the luxury of constructing statements using standard C library string functions that you're probably already familiar with, such as `strcpy()` and `sprintf()`.

Another factor to consider in constructing statements is whether you need to perform any character-escaping operations. This is necessary if you want to construct statements using values that contain binary data or other troublesome characters, such as quotes or backslashes. This is discussed in Section 7.4.7.1, "Working with Strings That Contain Special Characters."

A simple outline of statement handling looks like this:

```
if (mysql_query (conn, stmt_str) != 0)
{
  /* failure; report error */
}
else
{
  /* success; find out what effect the statement had */
}
```

`mysql_query()` and `mysql_real_query()` both return zero for statements that succeed and nonzero for failure. To say that a statement "succeeded" means the server accepted it as legal and was able to execute it. It does not indicate anything about the effect of the statement. For example, it does not indicate that a SELECT statement selected any rows or that a DELETE statement deleted any rows. Checking what effect the statement actually had involves additional processing.

A statement may fail for many reasons. Common causes of failure include the following:

- It contains a syntax error.
- It's semantically illegal—for example, a statement that refers to a nonexistent table.
- You don't have sufficient privileges to access a table referred to by the statement.

Statements may be grouped into two broad categories: those that modify rows and those that return a result set (a set of rows). Statements such as INSERT, DELETE, and UPDATE modify rows and return a count to indicate the number of affected rows.

Statements such as SELECT and SHOW return a result set. In the MySQL C API, the result set returned by such statements is represented by the MYSQL_RES data type. This is a structure that contains the data values for the rows, and also metadata about the values (such as the column names and data value lengths). It is permitted for a result set to be empty (that is, to contain zero rows).

7.4.1   Handling Statements That Modify Rows

To process a statement that modifies rows, issue it with mysql_query() or mysql_real_query(). If the statement succeeds, you can find out how many rows were inserted, deleted, or updated by calling mysql_affected_rows().

The following example shows how to handle a statement that modifies rows:

```
if (mysql_query (conn, "INSERT INTO my_tbl SET name = 'My Name'") != 0)
{
  print_error (conn, "INSERT statement failed");
}
else
{
  printf ("INSERT statement succeeded; number of rows affected: %lu\n",
          (unsigned long) mysql_affected_rows (conn));
}
```

Note how the result of mysql_affected_rows() is cast to unsigned long for printing. This function returns a value of type my_ulonglong, but attempting to print a value of that type directly may not work on all systems. Casting the value to unsigned long and using a print format of %lu solves the problem. The same principle applies to any other functions that return my_ulonglong values, such as mysql_num_rows() and mysql_insert_id(). If you want your client programs to be portable across different systems, keep this in mind.

mysql_affected_rows() returns the number of rows affected by the statement, but the meaning of "rows affected" depends on the type of statement. For INSERT, REPLACE, or DELETE, it is the number of rows inserted, replaced, or deleted. For UPDATE, it is the number of rows updated, which means the number of rows that MySQL actually modified. MySQL does not update a row if its contents are the same as what you're updating it to. This means that although a row might be selected for updating (by the WHERE clause of the UPDATE statement), it might not actually be changed.

This meaning of "rows affected" for UPDATE actually is something of a controversial point because some people want it to mean "rows matched"—that is, the number of rows selected for updating, even if the update operation doesn't actually change their values. If your application requires such a meaning, request that behavior when you connect to the server by passing a value of CLIENT_FOUND_ROWS in the flags parameter to mysql_real_connect().

7.4.2 Handling Statements That Return a Result Set

Statements that return data do so in the form of a result set that you retrieve after issuing the statement by calling `mysql_query()` or `mysql_real_query()`. It's important to realize that in MySQL, SELECT is not the only statement that returns rows. Statements such as SHOW, DESCRIBE, EXPLAIN, and CHECK TABLE do so as well. For all these statements, you must perform additional row-handling processing after issuing the statement:

1. Generate the result set by calling `mysql_store_result()` or `mysql_use_result()`. These functions return a MYSQL_RES pointer for success or NULL for failure. Later, we cover the differences between `mysql_store_result()` and `mysql_use_result()`, as well as the conditions under which you choose one over the other. For now, our examples use `mysql_store_result()`, which retrieves the rows from the server immediately and buffers them in memory on the client side.

2. Call `mysql_fetch_row()` for each row of the result set. This function returns a MYSQL_ROW value, or NULL when there are no more rows. A MYSQL_ROW value is a pointer to an array of strings representing the values for each column in the row. What you do with the row depends on your application. For example, you might print the column values or perform some statistical calculation on them.

3. When you are done with the result set, call `mysql_free_result()` to deallocate the memory it uses. If you neglect to do this, your application leaks memory. It's especially important to dispose of result sets properly for long-running applications. Otherwise, you will notice your system slowly being taken over by processes that consume ever-increasing amounts of system resources.

The following example outlines how to process a statement that returns a result set:

```
MYSQL_RES *res_set;

if (mysql_query (conn, "SHOW TABLES FROM sampdb") != 0)
  print_error (conn, "mysql_query() failed");
else
{
  res_set = mysql_store_result (conn);  /* generate result set */
  if (res_set == NULL)
    print_error (conn, "mysql_store_result() failed");
  else
  {
    /* process result set, then deallocate it */
    process_result_set (conn, res_set);
    mysql_free_result (res_set);
  }
}
```

The example hides the details of result set processing within another function, `process_result_set()`, which we have not yet defined. Generally, operations that handle a result set are based on a loop that looks something like this:

```
MYSQL_ROW row;

while ((row = mysql_fetch_row (res_set)) != NULL)
{
  /* do something with row contents */
}
```

`mysql_fetch_row()` returns a `MYSQL_ROW` value, which is a pointer to an array of values. If the return value is assigned to a variable named `row`, each value within the row may be accessed as `row[i]`, where `i` ranges from 0 to one less than the number of columns in the row. There are several important points about the `MYSQL_ROW` data type to note:

- `MYSQL_ROW` is a pointer type, so declare a variable of that type as `MYSQL_ROW row`, not as `MYSQL_ROW *row`.

- Values for all data types, even numeric types, are returned in the `MYSQL_ROW` array as strings. To treat a value as a number, you must convert the string yourself.

- The strings in a `MYSQL_ROW` array are null-terminated. However, if a column can contain binary data, it might contain null bytes, so do not treat the value as a null-terminated string. Get the column length to find out how long the column value is. (Section 7.4.6, "Using Result Set Metadata," discusses how to determine column lengths.)

- SQL `NULL` values are represented by C `NULL` pointers in the `MYSQL_ROW` array. Unless you know that a column is declared `NOT NULL`, you should always check whether values for the column are `NULL`, or your program may crash as a result of attempting to dereference a `NULL` pointer.

What you do with each row depends on the purpose of your application. For purposes of illustration, let's just print each row as a set of column values separated by tabs. To do that, it's necessary to know how many columns values rows contain. That information is returned by another client library function, `mysql_num_fields()`.

Here's the code for `process_result_set()`:

```
void
process_result_set (MYSQL *conn, MYSQL_RES *res_set)
{
MYSQL_ROW    row;
unsigned int i;

  while ((row = mysql_fetch_row (res_set)) != NULL)
  {
    for (i = 0; i < mysql_num_fields (res_set); i++)
    {
      if (i > 0)
        fputc ('\t', stdout);
```

```
    printf ("%s", row[i] != NULL ? row[i] : "NULL");
  }
  fputc ('\n', stdout);
}
if (mysql_errno (conn) != 0)
  print_error (conn, "mysql_fetch_row() failed");
else
  printf ("Number of rows returned: %lu\n",
          (unsigned long) mysql_num_rows (res_set));
}
```

`process_result_set()` displays the contents of each row in tab-delimited format (displaying NULL values as the word "NULL") and prints a count of the number of rows retrieved. That count is available by calling `mysql_num_rows()`. Like `mysql_affected_rows()`, `mysql_num_rows()` returns a `my_ulonglong` value, so cast its value to `unsigned long` and use a `%lu` format to print it. But unlike `mysql_affected_rows()`, which takes a connection handler argument, `mysql_num_rows()` takes a result set pointer as its argument.

The code following the loop includes an error test as a precautionary measure. If you create the result set with `mysql_store_result()`, a NULL return value from `mysql_fetch_row()` always means "no more rows." However, if you create the result set with `mysql_use_result()`, a NULL return value from `mysql_fetch_row()` can mean "no more rows" or that an error occurred. Because `process_result_set()` has no idea whether its caller used `mysql_store_result()` or `mysql_use_result()` to generate the result set, the test enables it to detect errors properly either way.

The version of `process_result_set()` just shown takes a rather minimalist approach to printing column values—one that has certain shortcomings. Suppose that you execute this query:

```
SELECT last_name, first_name, city, state FROM president
ORDER BY last_name, first_name
```

You will receive the following output, which is not so easy to read:

```
Adams    John      Braintree    MA
Adams    John Quincy Braintree    MA
Arthur   Chester A. Fairfield    VT
Buchanan  James    Mercersburg PA
Bush     George H.W. Milton    MA
Bush     George W.  New Haven    CT
Carter   James E.   Plains   GA
...
```

We can make the output prettier by providing information such as column labels and making the values line up vertically. To do that, we need the labels, and we must know the widest value in each column. That information is available, but not as part of the column data values—it's part of the result set's metadata (data about the data). After we generalize our statement handler a bit, we'll write a nicer display formatter in Section 7.4.6, "Using Result Set Metadata."

Printing Binary Data

Columns containing binary values that include null bytes will not print properly using the `%s` `printf()` format specifier. `printf()` expects a null-terminated string and prints the column value only up to the first null byte. For binary data, it's best to use a function that accepts a column length argument so that you can print the full value. For example, you could use `fwrite()`.

7.4.3   A General-Purpose Statement Handler

The preceding statement-handling examples use knowledge of whether the statement should return any data. That was possible because the statements were hardwired into the code: We used an INSERT statement, which does not return a result set, and a SHOW TABLES statement, which does.

However, you might not always know what kind of statement a given statement represents. For example, if you execute a statement that you read from the keyboard or from a file, it might be anything. You won't know ahead of time whether to expect it to return rows, or even whether it's legal. What then? You certainly don't want to try to parse the statement to determine what kind of statement it is. That's the server's job, anyway.

Fortunately, you need not know the statement type in advance to be able to handle it properly. The MySQL C API makes it possible to write a general-purpose statement handler that correctly processes any kind of statement, whether or not it returns a result set, and whether it executes successfully or fails. Before writing the code for this handler, let's outline the procedure that it implements:

1. Issue the statement. If it fails, we're done.

2. If the statement succeeds, call `mysql_store_result()` to retrieve the rows from the server and create a result set.

3. If `mysql_store_result()` succeeds, the statement returned a result set. Process the rows by calling `mysql_fetch_row()` until it returns NULL, and then free the result set.

4. If `mysql_store_result()` fails, it could be that the statement does not return a result set, or that it should have but an error occurred while trying to retrieve the set. You can distinguish between these outcomes by passing the connection handler to `mysql_field_count()` and checking its return value.

   If `mysql_field_count()` returns 0, it means the statement returned no columns, and thus no result set. (This indicates that it was a statement such as INSERT, DELETE, or UPDATE.)

   If `mysql_field_count()` returns a nonzero value, it means that an error occurred, because the statement should have returned a result set but didn't. This can happen for various reasons. For example, the result set may have been so large that memory allocation failed, or a network outage between the client and the server may have occurred while fetching rows.

The following listing shows a function that processes any statement, given a connection handler and a null-terminated statement string:

```
void
process_statement (MYSQL *conn, char *stmt_str)
{
MYSQL_RES *res_set;

  if (mysql_query (conn, stmt_str) != 0)   /* the statement failed */
  {
    print_error (conn, "Could not execute statement");
    return;
  }

  /* the statement succeeded; determine whether it returned data */
  res_set = mysql_store_result (conn);
  if (res_set)       /* a result set was returned */
  {
    /* process rows and free the result set */
    process_result_set (conn, res_set);
    mysql_free_result (res_set);
  }
  else              /* no result set was returned */
  {
    /*
     * does the lack of a result set mean that the statement didn't
     * return one, or that it should have but an error occurred?
     */
    if (mysql_field_count (conn) == 0)
    {
      /*
       * statement generated no result set (it was not a SELECT,
       * SHOW, DESCRIBE, etc.); just report rows-affected value.
       */
      printf ("Number of rows affected: %lu\n",
              (unsigned long) mysql_affected_rows (conn));
    }
    else  /* an error occurred */
    {
      print_error (conn, "Could not retrieve result set");
    }
  }
}
```

7.4.4 Alternative Approaches to Statement Processing

The version of `process_statement()` just shown has these three properties:

- It uses `mysql_query()` to issue the statement.

- It uses `mysql_store_query()` to retrieve the result set.

- When no result set is obtained, it uses `mysql_field_count()` to distinguish occurrence of an error from a result set not being expected.

Alternative approaches are possible for all three of those aspects of statement handling:

- You can execute the statement using a counted string and `mysql_real_query()` rather than a null-terminated string and `mysql_query()`.

- You can create the result set by calling `mysql_use_result()` rather than `mysql_store_result()`.

- You can call `mysql_error()` or `mysql_errno()` rather than `mysql_field_count()` to determine whether result set retrieval failed or whether there was simply no set to retrieve.

Any or all of these approaches can be used instead of those used in `process_statement()`. Here is a `process_real_statement()` function analogous to `process_statement()` that uses all three alternatives:

```
void
process_real_statement (MYSQL *conn, char *stmt_str, unsigned int len)
{
MYSQL_RES *res_set;

  if (mysql_real_query (conn, stmt_str, len) != 0) /* the statement failed */
  {
    print_error (conn, "Could not execute statement");
    return;
  }

  /* the statement succeeded; determine whether it returned data */
  res_set = mysql_use_result (conn);
  if (res_set)       /* a result set was returned */
  {
    /* process rows and free the result set */
    process_result_set (conn, res_set);
    mysql_free_result (res_set);
  }
  else               /* no result set was returned */
  {
    /*
     * does the lack of a result set mean that the statement didn't
     * return one, or that it should have but an error occurred?
```

```
  */
  if (mysql_errno (conn) == 0)
  {
    /*
     * statement generated no result set (it was not a SELECT,
     * SHOW, DESCRIBE, etc.); just report rows-affected value.
     */
    printf ("Number of rows affected: %lu\n",
            (unsigned long) mysql_affected_rows (conn));
  }
  else  /* an error occurred */
  {
    print_error (conn, "Could not retrieve result set");
  }
 }
}
```

7.4.5 `mysql_store_result()` **Versus** `mysql_use_result()`

The `mysql_store_result()` and `mysql_use_result()` functions are similar in that both take
a connection handler argument and return a result set. However, the differences between them
actually are quite extensive. The primary difference between the two functions lies in the way
rows of the result set are retrieved from the server. `mysql_store_result()` retrieves all the
rows immediately when you call it. `mysql_use_result()` initiates the retrieval but doesn't
actually get any of the rows. These differing approaches to row retrieval give rise to all other
differences between the two functions. This section compares them so you'll know how to
choose the one most appropriate for a given application.

When `mysql_store_result()` retrieves a result set from the server, it fetches the rows,
allocates memory for them, and buffers them on the client side. Subsequent calls to
`mysql_fetch_row()` never return an error because they simply pull a row out of a data structure that already holds the result set. Consequently, a NULL return from `mysql_fetch_row()`
always means you've reached the end of the result set.

By contrast, `mysql_use_result()` retrieves no rows itself. Instead, it simply initiates a row-by-
row retrieval, which you must complete yourself by calling `mysql_fetch_row()` for each row.
In this case, although a NULL return from `mysql_fetch_row()` normally still means the end
of the result set has been reached, it may mean instead that an error occurred while communicating with the server. You can distinguish the two outcomes by calling `mysql_errno()` or
`mysql_error()`.

`mysql_store_result()` has greater memory and processing requirements than `mysql_use_`
`result()` because the entire result set is maintained in the client. The overhead for memory
allocation and data structure setup is greater, and a client that retrieves large result sets runs
the risk of running out of memory. If you're going to retrieve a lot of rows in a single result set,
you might want to use `mysql_use_result()` instead.

`mysql_use_result()` has lower memory requirements because only enough space to handle a single row at a time need be allocated. This can be faster because you're not setting up as complex a data structure for the result set. On the other hand, `mysql_use_result()` places a greater burden on the server, which must hold rows of the result set until the client sees fit to retrieve all of them. This makes `mysql_use_result()` a poor choice for certain types of clients:

- Interactive clients that advance from row to row at the request of the user. (You don't want the server waiting to send the next row just because the user decides to take a coffee break.)

- Clients that do a lot of processing between row retrievals.

In both of these types of situations, the client fails to retrieve all rows in the result set quickly. This ties up the server and can have a negative impact on other clients, particularly if you are using a storage engine like MyISAM that uses table locks: Tables from which you retrieve data are read-locked for the duration of the query. Other clients that are trying to update those tables will be blocked.

Offsetting the additional memory requirements incurred by `mysql_store_result()` are certain benefits of having access to the entire result set at once. All rows of the set are available, so you have random access into them: The `mysql_data_seek()`, `mysql_row_seek()`, and `mysql_row_tell()` functions enable you to access rows in any order you want. With `mysql_use_result()`, you can access rows only in the order in which they are retrieved by `mysql_fetch_row()`. If you intend to process rows in any order other than sequentially as they are returned from the server, you must use `mysql_store_result()` instead. For example, if you have an application that enables the user to browse back and forth among the rows selected by a query, you'd be best served by using `mysql_store_result()`.

With `mysql_store_result()`, you can access certain types of column information that are unavailable when you use `mysql_use_result()`. The number of rows in the result set is obtained by calling `mysql_num_rows()`. The maximum widths of the values in each column are stored in the `max_width` member of the `MYSQL_FIELD` column information structures. With `mysql_use_result()`, `mysql_num_rows()` doesn't return the correct value until you've fetched all the rows; similarly, `max_width` is unavailable because it can be calculated only after every row's data have been seen.

Because `mysql_use_result()` does less work than `mysql_store_result()`, it imposes a requirement that `mysql_store_result()` does not: The client must call `mysql_fetch_row()` for every row in the result set. If you fail to do this before issuing another statement, any remaining rows in the current result set become part of the next statement's result set and an "out of sync" error occurs. (To avoid this, call `mysql_free_result()` to fetch and discard any pending rows before issuing the second statement.) One implication of this processing model is that with `mysql_use_result()`, you can work only with a single result set at a time.

Sync errors do not happen with `mysql_store_result()` because when that function returns, there are no rows remaining to be fetched from the server. In fact, with `mysql_store_result()`, you need not call `mysql_fetch_row()` explicitly at all. This can sometimes be useful if all that you're interested in is whether you got a nonempty result, rather than what the result contains. For example, to find out whether a table `mytbl` exists, you can execute this statement:

```
SHOW TABLES LIKE 'mytbl'
```

If, after calling `mysql_store_result()`, the value of `mysql_num_rows()` is nonzero, the table exists. `mysql_fetch_row()` need not be called.

Result sets generated with `mysql_store_result()` should be freed with `mysql_free_result()` at some point, but this need not necessarily be done before issuing another statement. This means that you can generate multiple result sets and work with them simultaneously, in contrast to the "one result set at a time" constraint imposed when you're working with `mysql_use_result()`.

To provide maximum flexibility, give users the option of selecting either result set processing method. `mysql` and `mysqldump` are two programs that do this. They use `mysql_store_result()` by default but switch to `mysql_use_result()` if the `--quick` option is given.

7.4.6 Using Result Set Metadata

Result sets contain not only the column values for data rows but also information about the data. This information is called the result set "metadata," which includes the following:

- The number of rows and columns in the result set, available by calling `mysql_num_rows()` and `mysql_num_fields()`.
- The length of each column value in the current row, available by calling `mysql_fetch_lengths()`.
- Information about each column, such as the column name and type, the maximum width of each column's values, and the table containing the column. This information is stored in `MYSQL_FIELD` structures, which typically are obtained by calling `mysql_fetch_field()`. Appendix G, "C API Reference," describes the `MYSQL_FIELD` structure in detail and discusses all functions that provide access to column information.

Metadata availability depends partially on your result set processing method. As indicated in Section 7.4.5, "`mysql_store_result()` Versus `mysql_use_result()`," if you want to use the row count or maximum column length values, you must create the result set with `mysql_store_result()`, not with `mysql_use_result()`.

Result set metadata is helpful for making decisions about how to process result set data:

- Column names and widths are useful for producing nicely formatted output that lines up vertically and has column titles.
- The column count indicates how many times to iterate through a loop that processes successive column values for data rows.
- The row and column counts help you allocate data structures that depend on the dimensions of the result set.
- The data type of a column enables you to tell whether a column represents a number, whether it might contain binary data, and so forth.

Earlier, in Section 7.4.2, "Handling Statements That Return a Result Set," we wrote a version of `process_result_set()` that printed columns from result set rows in tab-delimited format. That's good for certain purposes (such as when you want to import the data into a spreadsheet), but it's not a nice display format for visual inspection or for printouts. Recall that our earlier version of `process_result_set()` produced this output:

```
Adams      John      Braintree    MA
Adams      John Quincy Braintree      MA
Arthur     Chester A.  Fairfield     VT
Buchanan      James      Mercersburg PA
Bush       George H.W. Milton   MA
Bush       George W.   New Haven    CT
Carter     James E.    Plains   GA
...
```

Let's write a different version of `process_result_set()` that produces tabular output instead by titling and "boxing" each column. This version displays those same results in a format that's easier to interpret:

```
+------------+---------------+--------------------+-------+
| last_name  | first_name    | city               | state |
+------------+---------------+--------------------+-------+
| Adams      | John          | Braintree          | MA    |
| Adams      | John Quincy   | Braintree          | MA    |
| Arthur     | Chester A.    | Fairfield          | VT    |
| Buchanan   | James         | Mercersburg        | PA    |
| Bush       | George H.W.   | Milton             | MA    |
| Bush       | George W.     | New Haven          | CT    |
| Carter     | James E.      | Plains             | GA    |
...

+------------+---------------+--------------------+-------+
```

The display algorithm performs these steps:

1. Determine the display width of each column.

2. Print a row of boxed column labels (delimited by vertical bars and preceded and followed by rows of dashes).

3. Print the values in each row of the result set, with each column boxed (delimited by vertical bars) and lined up vertically. Print numbers right justified and the word "NULL" for NULL values.

4. At the end, print a count of the rows retrieved.

This exercise provides a good demonstration showing how to use result set metadata because it requires knowledge of quite a number of things about the result set other than just the values of the data contained in its rows.

You may be thinking to yourself, "Hmm, that description sounds suspiciously similar to the way `mysql` displays its output." Yes, it does, and you're welcome to compare the source for `mysql` to the code we end up with for `process_result_set()`. They're not the same, and you might find it instructive to compare the two approaches to the same problem.

First, it's necessary to determine the display width of each column. The following listing shows how to do this. Observe that the calculations are based entirely on the result set metadata, and make no reference whatsoever to the row values:

```
MYSQL_FIELD    *field;
unsigned long col_len;
unsigned int  i;

/* determine column display widths; requires result set to be */
/* generated with mysql_store_result(), not mysql_use_result() */
mysql_field_seek (res_set, 0);
for (i = 0; i < mysql_num_fields (res_set); i++)
{
  field = mysql_fetch_field (res_set);
  col_len = strlen (field->name);
  if (col_len < field->max_length)
    col_len = field->max_length;
  if (col_len < 4 && !IS_NOT_NULL (field->flags))
    col_len = 4;  /* 4 = length of the word "NULL" */
  field->max_length = col_len;  /* reset column info */
}
```

This code calculates column widths by iterating through the MYSQL_FIELD structures for the columns in the result set. We position to the first structure by calling `mysql_field_seek()`. Subsequent calls to `mysql_fetch_field()` return pointers to the structures for successive columns. The width of a column for display purposes is the maximum of three values, each of which depends on metadata in the column information structure:

- The length of `field->name`, the column title.

- `field->max_length`, the length of the longest data value in the column.

- The length of the string "NULL", if `field->flags` indicates that the column can contain NULL values.

Notice that after the display width for a column is known, we assign that value to `max_length`, which is a member of a structure that we obtain from the client library. Is that permitted, or should the contents of the MYSQL_FIELD structure be considered read only? Normally, I would say "read only," but some of the client programs in the MySQL distribution change the `max_length` value in a similar way, so I assume that it's okay. (If you prefer an alternative approach that doesn't modify `max_length`, allocate an array of `unsigned long` values and store the calculated widths in that array.)

The display width calculations involve one caveat. Recall that max_length has no meaning when you create a result set using mysql_use_result(). Because we need max_length to determine the display width of the column values, proper operation of the algorithm requires that the result set be generated using mysql_store_result(). In programs that use mysql_use_result() rather than mysql_store_result(), one possible workaround is to use the length member of the MYSQL_FIELD structure, which tells you the maximum length that column values can be.

When we know the column widths, we're ready to print. Titles are easy to handle. For a given column, use the column information structure pointed to by field and print the name member, using the width calculated earlier:

```
printf (" %-*s |", (int) field->max_length, field->name);
```

For the data, loop through the rows in the result set, printing column values for the current row during each iteration. Printing column values from the row is a bit tricky because a value might be NULL, or it might represent a number (in which case we print it right justified). Column values are printed as follows, where row[i] holds the data value and field points to the column information:

```
if (row[i] == NULL)       /* print the word "NULL" */
  printf (" %-*s |", (int) field->max_length, "NULL");
else if (IS_NUM (field->type))  /* print value right-justified */
  printf (" %*s |", (int) field->max_length, row[i]);
else                      /* print value left-justified */
  printf (" %-*s |", (int) field->max_length, row[i]);
```

The value of the IS_NUM() macro is true if the column data type indicated by field->type is one of the numeric types, such as INT, FLOAT, or DECIMAL.

The final code to display the result set follows. Because we're printing lines of dashes multiple times, it's easier to write a print_dashes() function to do so rather than to repeat the dash-generation code several places:

```
void
print_dashes (MYSQL_RES *res_set)
{
MYSQL_FIELD   *field;
unsigned int  i, j;

  mysql_field_seek (res_set, 0);
  fputc ('+', stdout);
  for (i = 0; i < mysql_num_fields (res_set); i++)
  {
    field = mysql_fetch_field (res_set);
    for (j = 0; j < field->max_length + 2; j++)
      fputc ('-', stdout);
    fputc ('+', stdout);
  }
```

```
    fputc ('\n', stdout);
}

void
process_result_set (MYSQL *conn, MYSQL_RES *res_set)
{
MYSQL_ROW      row;
MYSQL_FIELD    *field;
unsigned long col_len;
unsigned int  i;

  /* determine column display widths; requires result set to be */
  /* generated with mysql_store_result(), not mysql_use_result() */
  mysql_field_seek (res_set, 0);
  for (i = 0; i < mysql_num_fields (res_set); i++)
  {
    field = mysql_fetch_field (res_set);
    col_len = strlen (field->name);
    if (col_len < field->max_length)
      col_len = field->max_length;
    if (col_len < 4 && !IS_NOT_NULL (field->flags))
      col_len = 4;  /* 4 = length of the word "NULL" */
    field->max_length = col_len;  /* reset column info */
  }

  print_dashes (res_set);
  fputc ('|', stdout);
  mysql_field_seek (res_set, 0);
  for (i = 0; i < mysql_num_fields (res_set); i++)
  {
    field = mysql_fetch_field (res_set);
    printf (" %-*s |", (int) field->max_length, field->name);
  }
  fputc ('\n', stdout);
  print_dashes (res_set);

  while ((row = mysql_fetch_row (res_set)) != NULL)
  {
    mysql_field_seek (res_set, 0);
    fputc ('|', stdout);
    for (i = 0; i < mysql_num_fields (res_set); i++)
    {
      field = mysql_fetch_field (res_set);
      if (row[i] == NULL)        /* print the word "NULL" */
        printf (" %-*s |", (int) field->max_length, "NULL");
      else if (IS_NUM (field->type))  /* print value right-justified */
        printf (" %*s |", (int) field->max_length, row[i]);
```

```
      else              /* print value left-justified */
        printf (" %-*s |", (int) field->max_length, row[i]);
    }
    fputc ('\n', stdout);
  }
  print_dashes (res_set);
  printf ("Number of rows returned: %lu\n",
          (unsigned long) mysql_num_rows (res_set));
}
```

The MySQL client library provides several ways to access the column information structures. For example, the code in the preceding example accesses these structures several times using loops of the following general form:

```
mysql_field_seek (res_set, 0);
for (i = 0; i < mysql_num_fields (res_set); i++)
{
  field = mysql_fetch_field (res_set);
  ...
}
```

However, the combination of `mysql_field_seek()` and `mysql_fetch_field()` is only one way of getting `MYSQL_FIELD` structures. For other ways, see the descriptions of the `mysql_fetch_fields()` and `mysql_fetch_field_direct()` functions in Appendix G, "C API Reference."

> **Use the `metadata` Program to Display Result Set Metadata**
>
> The `sampdb` distribution contains the source for a program named `metadata` that you can compile and run to see what metadata different kinds of statements produce. It prompts for and executes SQL statements, but displays result set metadata rather than result set contents. For comparison, invoke `mysql` with the `--column-type-info` option and execute the same statements.

7.4.7   Encoding Special Characters and Binary Data

Programs that execute statements must take care with certain characters. For example, to include a quote character within a quoted string, either double the quote or precede it by a backslash:

```
'O''Malley'
'O\'Malley'
```

This section describes how to handle quoting issues in string values and how to work with binary data.

7.4.7.1 Working with Strings That Contain Special Characters

If inserted literally into a statement, data values containing quotes, null bytes, or backslashes can cause problems when you try to execute the statement. The following discussion describes the nature of the difficulty and how to solve it.

Suppose that you want to construct a `SELECT` statement based on the contents of the null-terminated string pointed to by the `name_val` variable:

```
char stmt_buf[1024];

sprintf (stmt_buf, "SELECT * FROM mytbl WHERE name='%s'", name_val);
```

If the value of `name_val` is something like `O'Malley, Brian`, the resulting statement is illegal because a quote appears inside a quoted string:

```
SELECT * FROM mytbl WHERE name='O'Malley, Brian'
```

You must treat the inner quote specially so that the server doesn't interpret it as the end of the name. The standard SQL convention for doing this is to double the quote within the string. MySQL understands that convention, and also permits the quote to be preceded by a backslash, so you can write the statement using either of the following formats:

```
SELECT * FROM mytbl WHERE name='O''Malley, Brian'
SELECT * FROM mytbl WHERE name='O\'Malley, Brian'
```

To deal with this problem, use `mysql_real_escape_string()`, which encodes special characters to make them usable in quoted strings. Characters that `mysql_real_escape_string()` considers special are the null byte, single quote, double quote, backslash, newline, carriage return, and Control-Z. (The last one is special on Windows, where it sometimes signifies end-of-file.)

When should you use `mysql_real_escape_string()`? The safest answer is "always." However, if you're sure of the format of your data and know that it's okay—perhaps because you have performed some prior validation check on it—you need not encode it. For example, if you are working with strings that you know represent legal phone numbers consisting entirely of digits and dashes, you need not call `mysql_real_escape_string()`. Otherwise, you probably should.

`mysql_real_escape_string()` encodes problematic characters by turning them into two-character sequences that begin with a backslash. For example, a null byte becomes '\0', where the '0' is a printable ASCII zero, not a null. Backslash, single quote, and double quote become '\\', '\'', and '\"'.

To use `mysql_real_escape_string()`, invoke it like this:

```
to_len = mysql_real_escape_string (conn, to_str, from_str, from_len);
```

`mysql_real_escape_string()` encodes `from_str` and writes the result into `to_str`. It also adds a terminating null, which is convenient because you can use the resulting string with functions such as `strcpy()`, `strlen()`, or `printf()`.

`from_str` points to a `char` buffer containing the string to be encoded. This string may contain anything, including binary data. `to_str` points to an existing `char` buffer where you want the encoded string to be written; do not pass an uninitialized or NULL pointer, expecting `mysql_real_escape_string()` to allocate space for you. The length of the buffer pointed to by `to_str` must be at least `(from_len*2)+1` bytes long. (It's possible that every character in `from_str` needs encoding with two characters; the extra byte is for the terminating null.)

`from_len` and `to_len` are `unsigned long` values. `from_len` indicates the length of the data in `from_str`; it's necessary to provide the length because `from_str` may contain null bytes and cannot be treated as a null-terminated string. `to_len`, the return value from `mysql_real_escape_string()`, is the actual length of the resulting encoded string, not counting the terminating null.

When `mysql_real_escape_string()` returns, the encoded result in `to_str` can be treated as a null-terminated string because any null bytes in `from_str` are encoded as the printable '\0' sequence.

To rewrite the SELECT-constructing code so that it works even for name values that contain quotes, we could do something like this:

```
char stmt_buf[1024], *p;

p = strcpy (stmt_buf, "SELECT * FROM mytbl WHERE name='");
p += strlen (p);
p += mysql_real_escape_string (conn, p, name_val, strlen (name_val));
*p++ = '\'';
*p = '\0';
```

Yes, that's ugly. To simplify the code a bit, at the cost of using a second buffer, do this instead:

```
char stmt_buf[1024], buf[1024];

(void) mysql_real_escape_string (conn, buf, name_val, strlen (name_val));
sprintf (stmt_buf, "SELECT * FROM mytbl WHERE name='%s'", buf);
```

It's important to make sure that the buffers you pass to `mysql_real_escape_string()` really exist. Consider the following example, which violates that principle:

```
char *from_str = "some string";
char *to_str;
unsigned long len;

len = mysql_real_escape_string (conn, to_str, from_str, strlen (from_str));
```

What's the problem? `to_str` must point to an existing buffer, and it doesn't—it's not initialized and may point to some random location. Don't pass an uninitialized pointer as the `to_str` argument to `mysql_real_escape_string()` unless you want it to stomp merrily all over some random piece of memory.

7.4.7.2 Working with Binary Data

Another problematic situation involves the use of arbitrary binary data in a statement. This happens, for example, in applications that store images in a database. Because a binary value may contain any character (including null bytes, quotes, or backslashes), it cannot be considered safe to embed into a statement as is.

`mysql_real_escape_string()` is essential for working with binary data. This section shows how to do so, using image data read from a file. The discussion applies to any other form of binary data as well.

Suppose that you want to read images from files and store them in a table named `picture`, along with a unique identifier. The MEDIUMBLOB type is a good choice for binary values less than 16MB in size, so you could use a table specification like this:

```
CREATE TABLE picture
(
  pict_id   INT NOT NULL PRIMARY KEY,
  pict_data MEDIUMBLOB
);
```

To actually get an image from a file into the `picture` table, the following function, `load_image()`, does the job, given an identifier number and a pointer to an open file containing the image data:

```
int
load_image (MYSQL *conn, int id, FILE *f)
{
char        stmt_buf[1024*1024], buf[1024*10], *p;
unsigned long from_len;
int         status;

  /* begin creating an INSERT statement, adding the id value */
  sprintf (stmt_buf,
           "INSERT INTO picture (pict_id,pict_data) VALUES (%d,'",
           id);
  p = stmt_buf + strlen (stmt_buf);
  /* read data from file in chunks, encode each */
  /* chunk, and add to end of statement */
  while ((from_len = fread (buf, 1, sizeof (buf), f)) > 0)
  {
    /* don't overrun end of statement buffer! */
    if (p + (2*from_len) + 3 > stmt_buf + sizeof (stmt_buf))
    {
      print_error (NULL, "image is too big");
      return (1);
    }
    p += mysql_real_escape_string (conn, p, buf, from_len);
  }
```

```
  *p++ = '\'';
  *p++ = ')';
  status = mysql_real_query (conn, stmt_buf, (unsigned long) (p - stmt_buf));
  return (status);
}
```

load_image() doesn't allocate a very large statement buffer (1MB), so it works only for relatively small images. In a real-world application, you might allocate the buffer dynamically based on the size of the image file.

Getting an image value (or any binary value) back out of a database isn't nearly as much of a problem as putting it in to begin with. The data value is available in raw form in the MYSQL_ROW variable, and the length is available by calling mysql_fetch_lengths(). Just be sure to treat the value as a counted string, not as a null-terminated string.

7.5   An Interactive Statement-Execution Program

We are now in a position to put together much of what we've developed so far to write a simple interactive statement-execution client, exec_stmt. This program lets you enter statements, executes them using our general-purpose statement handler process_statement(), and displays the results using the process_result_set() display formatter developed earlier.

exec_stmt is similar in some ways to mysql, although of course with not as many features. There are several restrictions on what exec_stmt permits as input:

- Each input line must contain a single complete statement.
- Statements should not be terminated by a semicolon or by \g.
- The only non-SQL commands that are recognized are quit and \q, which terminate the program. You can also use Control-D to quit.

It turns out that exec_stmt is almost completely trivial to write (about a dozen lines of new code). Almost everything we need is provided by our client program skeleton (connect2.c) and by other functions that we have written already. The only thing we need to add is a loop that collects input lines and executes them.

To construct exec_stmt, begin by copying the client skeleton connect2.c to exec_stmt.c. Then add to that the code for the process_statement(), process_result_set(), and print_dashes() functions. Finally, in exec_stmt.c, look for the line in main() that says this:

```
/* ... issue statements and process results here ... */
```

Replace that line with this while loop:

```
while (1)
{
  char  buf[10000];

  fprintf (stderr, "query> ");                    /* print prompt */
```

```
  if (fgets (buf, sizeof (buf), stdin) == NULL) /* read statement */
    break;
  if (strcmp (buf, "quit\n") == 0 || strcmp (buf, "\\q\n") == 0)
    break;
  process_statement (conn, buf);                /* execute it */
}
```

Compile `exec_stmt.c` to produce `exec_stmt.o`, link `exec_stmt.o` with the client library to produce `exec_stmt`, and you're done. You have an interactive MySQL client program that can execute any statement and display the results. The following example shows how the program works, both for SELECT and non-SELECT statements, as well as for statements that are erroneous:

```
% ./exec_stmt
query> USE sampdb
Number of rows affected: 0
query> SELECT DATABASE(), USER()
+------------+-------------------+
| DATABASE() | USER()            |
+------------+-------------------+
| sampdb     | sampadm@localhost |
+------------+-------------------+
Number of rows returned: 1
query> SELECT COUNT(*) FROM president
+----------+
| COUNT(*) |
+----------+
|       43 |
+----------+
Number of rows returned: 1
query> SELECT last_name, first_name FROM president ORDER BY last_name LIMIT 3
+-----------+-------------+
| last_name | first_name  |
+-----------+-------------+
| Adams     | John        |
| Adams     | John Quincy |
| Arthur    | Chester A.  |
+-----------+-------------+
Number of rows returned: 3
query> CREATE TABLE t (i INT)
Number of rows affected: 0
query> SELECT j FROM t
Could not execute statement
Error 1054 (42S22): Unknown column 'j' in 'field list'
query> USE mysql
Could not execute statement
Error 1044 (42000): Access denied for user 'sampadm'@'localhost' to
database 'mysql'
```

7.6 Writing Clients That Include SSL Support

MySQL includes SSL support, and you can use it to write your own programs that access the server over secure connections. To show how this is done, this section describes the process of modifying `exec_stmt` to produce a similar client named `exec_stmt_ssl` that outwardly is much the same but enables encrypted connections to be established. For `exec_stmt_ssl` to work properly, MySQL must have been built with SSL support, and the server must be started with the proper options that identify its certificate and key files. You'll also need certificate and key files on the client end. For more information, see Section 13.5, "Setting Up Secure Connections Using SSL."

The `sampdb` distribution contains a source file, `exec_stmt_ssl.c`, from which the client program `exec_stmt_ssl` can be built. The following procedure describes how `exec_stmt_ssl.c` is created, beginning with `exec_stmt.c`:

1. Copy `exec_stmt.c` to `exec_stmt_ssl.c`. The remaining steps apply to `exec_stmt_ssl.c`.

2. To enable the compiler to detect whether SSL support is available, the MySQL header file `my_config.h` defines the symbol `HAVE_OPENSSL` appropriately. This means that when writing SSL-related code, you use the following construct so that the code is ignored if SSL cannot be used:

   ```
   #ifdef HAVE_OPENSSL
     ...SSL-related code here...
   #endif
   ```

   You need not include `my_config.h` explicitly because it is included by `my_global.h`, and `exec_stmt_ssl.c` already includes the latter file.

3. Modify the `my_opts` array that contains option information structures so that it includes entries for the standard SSL-related options (`--ssl-ca`, `--ssl-key`, and so forth). The easiest way to do this is to include the contents of the `sslopt-longopts.h` file into the `my_opts` array with an `#include` directive. After making the change, `my_opts` looks like this:

   ```
   static struct my_option my_opts[] =   /* option information structures */
   {
     {"help", '?', "Display this help and exit",
     NULL, NULL, NULL,
     GET_NO_ARG, NO_ARG, 0, 0, 0, 0, 0, 0},
     {"host", 'h', "Host to connect to",
     (uchar **) &opt_host_name, NULL, NULL,
     GET_STR, REQUIRED_ARG, 0, 0, 0, 0, 0, 0},
     {"password", 'p', "Password",
     (uchar **) &opt_password, NULL, NULL,
     GET_STR, OPT_ARG, 0, 0, 0, 0, 0, 0},
     {"port", 'P', "Port number",
     (uchar **) &opt_port_num, NULL, NULL,
   ```

```
    GET_UINT, REQUIRED_ARG, 0, 0, 0, 0, 0, 0},
    {"socket", 'S', "Socket path",
    (uchar **) &opt_socket_name, NULL, NULL,
    GET_STR, REQUIRED_ARG, 0, 0, 0, 0, 0, 0},
    {"user", 'u', "User name",
    (uchar **) &opt_user_name, NULL, NULL,
    GET_STR, REQUIRED_ARG, 0, 0, 0, 0, 0, 0},

#include <sslopt-longopts.h>

    { NULL, 0, NULL, NULL, NULL, NULL, GET_NO_ARG, NO_ARG, 0, 0, 0, 0, 0, 0 }
};
```

`sslopt-longopts.h` is a public MySQL header file. Its contents look like this
(reformatted slightly):

```
#ifdef HAVE_OPENSSL
    {"ssl", OPT_SSL_SSL,
    "Enable SSL for connection (automatically enabled with other flags).
    Disable with --skip-ssl.",
    (uchar **) &opt_use_ssl, (uchar **) &opt_use_ssl, 0,
    GET_BOOL, NO_ARG, 0, 0, 0, 0, 0, 0},
    {"ssl-ca", OPT_SSL_CA,
    "CA file in PEM format (check OpenSSL docs, implies --ssl).",
    (uchar **) &opt_ssl_ca, (uchar **) &opt_ssl_ca, 0,
    GET_STR, REQUIRED_ARG, 0, 0, 0, 0, 0, 0},
    {"ssl-capath", OPT_SSL_CAPATH,
    "CA directory (check OpenSSL docs, implies --ssl).",
    (uchar **) &opt_ssl_capath, (uchar **) &opt_ssl_capath, 0,
    GET_STR, REQUIRED_ARG, 0, 0, 0, 0, 0, 0},
    {"ssl-cert", OPT_SSL_CERT, "X509 cert in PEM format (implies --ssl).",
    (uchar **) &opt_ssl_cert, (uchar **) &opt_ssl_cert, 0,
    GET_STR, REQUIRED_ARG, 0, 0, 0, 0, 0, 0},
    {"ssl-cipher", OPT_SSL_CIPHER, "SSL cipher to use (implies --ssl).",
    (uchar **) &opt_ssl_cipher, (uchar **) &opt_ssl_cipher, 0,
    GET_STR, REQUIRED_ARG, 0, 0, 0, 0, 0, 0},
    {"ssl-key", OPT_SSL_KEY, "X509 key in PEM format (implies --ssl).",
    (uchar **) &opt_ssl_key, (uchar **) &opt_ssl_key, 0,
    GET_STR, REQUIRED_ARG, 0, 0, 0, 0, 0, 0},
#ifdef MYSQL_CLIENT
    {"ssl-verify-server-cert", OPT_SSL_VERIFY_SERVER_CERT,
    "Verify server's \"Common Name\" in its cert against hostname used
    when connecting. This option is disabled by default.",
    (uchar **) &opt_ssl_verify_server_cert,
    (uchar **) &opt_ssl_verify_server_cert, 0,
    GET_BOOL, NO_ARG, 0, 0, 0, 0, 0, 0},
#endif
#endif /* HAVE_OPENSSL */
```

4. The option structures defined by sslopt-longopts.h refer to the values OPT_SSL_SSL, OPT_SSL_KEY, and so forth. These are used for the short option codes and must be defined by your program, which can be done by adding the following lines preceding the definition of the my_opts array:

```
#ifdef HAVE_OPENSSL
enum options_client
{
  OPT_SSL_SSL=256,
  OPT_SSL_KEY,
  OPT_SSL_CERT,
  OPT_SSL_CA,
  OPT_SSL_CAPATH,
  OPT_SSL_CIPHER,
  OPT_SSL_VERIFY_SERVER_CERT
};
#endif
```

When writing your own applications that define codes for other options, make sure that those codes have values different from the OPT_SSL_XXX symbols.

5. The SSL-related option structures in sslopt-longopts.h refer to a set of variables that are used to hold the option values. To declare these, use an #include directive to include the contents of the sslopt-vars.h file into your program preceding the definition of the my_opts array. sslopt-vars.h looks like this:

```
#ifdef HAVE_OPENSSL
static my_bool opt_use_ssl   = 0;
static char *opt_ssl_ca      = 0;
static char *opt_ssl_capath  = 0;
static char *opt_ssl_cert    = 0;
static char *opt_ssl_cipher  = 0;
static char *opt_ssl_key     = 0;
#ifdef MYSQL_CLIENT
static my_bool opt_ssl_verify_server_cert= 0;
#endif
#endif
```

6. In the get_one_option() routine, add a line near the end that includes the sslopt-case.h file:

```
static my_bool
get_one_option (int optid, const struct my_option *opt, char *argument)
{
  switch (optid)
  {
  case '?':
    my_print_help (my_opts);  /* print help message */
```

```
      exit (0);
    case 'p':                    /* password */
      if (!argument)             /* no value given; solicit it later */
        ask_password = 1;
      else                       /* copy password, overwrite original */
      {
        opt_password = strdup (argument);
        if (opt_password == NULL)
        {
          print_error (NULL, "could not allocate password buffer");
          exit (1);
        }
        while (*argument)
          *argument++ = 'x';
        ask_password = 0;
      }
      break;
#include <sslopt-case.h>
  }
  return (0);
}
```

`sslopt-case.h` includes additional cases for the `switch()` statement that detect when any of the SSL options were given and sets the `opt_use_ssl` variable if so. It looks like this:

```
#ifdef HAVE_OPENSSL
  case OPT_SSL_KEY:
  case OPT_SSL_CERT:
  case OPT_SSL_CA:
  case OPT_SSL_CAPATH:
  case OPT_SSL_CIPHER:
  /*
     Enable use of SSL if we are using any ssl option
     One can disable SSL later by using --skip-ssl or --ssl=0
  */
    opt_use_ssl= 1;
    break;
#endif
```

The effect of this is that after option processing has been done, it is possible to determine whether the user wants a secure connection by checking the value of `opt_use_ssl`.

If you use the preceding procedure, the usual `load_defaults()` and `handle_options()` routines take care of parsing the SSL-related options and setting their values for you automatically. The only other thing you need to do is pass SSL option information to the client library before connecting to the server if the options indicate that the user wants an SSL connection.

Do this by invoking `mysql_ssl_set()` after calling `mysql_init()` and before calling `mysql_real_connect()`. The sequence looks like this:

```
/* initialize connection handler */
conn = mysql_init (NULL);
if (conn == NULL)
{
  print_error (NULL, "mysql_init() failed (probably out of memory)");
  exit (1);
}


#ifdef HAVE_OPENSSL
  /* pass SSL information to client library */
  if (opt_use_ssl)
    mysql_ssl_set (conn, opt_ssl_key, opt_ssl_cert, opt_ssl_ca,
                   opt_ssl_capath, opt_ssl_cipher);
  mysql_options (conn,MYSQL_OPT_SSL_VERIFY_SERVER_CERT,
                 (char*)&opt_ssl_verify_server_cert);
#endif


  /* connect to server */
  if (mysql_real_connect (conn, opt_host_name, opt_user_name, opt_password,
      opt_db_name, opt_port_num, opt_socket_name, opt_flags) == NULL)
  {
    print_error (conn, "mysql_real_connect() failed");
    mysql_close (conn);
    exit (1);
  }
```

This code doesn't test `mysql_ssl_set()` to see whether it returns an error. Any problems with the information you supply to that function results in an error when you call `mysql_real_connect()`.

Compile `exec_stmt_ssl.c` to produce the `exec_stmt_ssl` program and then run it. Assuming that the `mysql_real_connect()` call succeeds, you can proceed to issue statements. If you invoke `exec_stmt_ssl` with the appropriate SSL options, communication with the server should occur over an encrypted connection. To determine whether that is so, issue the following statement:

`SHOW STATUS LIKE 'Ssl_cipher'`

The value of `Ssl_cipher` will be nonblank if an encryption cipher is in use. (To make this easier, the version of `exec_stmt_ssl` included in the `sampdb` distribution issues the statement for you and reports the result.)

7.7 Using Multiple-Statement Execution

The MySQL client library supports multiple-statement execution capability. This enables you to send a string to the server consisting of multiple statements separated by semicolons, then retrieve the result sets one after the other.

Multiple-statement execution is not enabled by default, so you must tell the server when you want to use it. There are two ways to do this. The first is to add the `CLIENT_MULTI_STATEMENTS` option in the flags argument to `mysql_real_connect()` at connect time:

```
opt_flags |= CLIENT_MULTI_STATEMENTS;
if (mysql_real_connect (conn, opt_host_name, opt_user_name, opt_password,
    opt_db_name, opt_port_num, opt_socket_name, opt_flags) == NULL)
{
  print_error (conn, "mysql_real_connect() failed");
  mysql_close (conn);
  exit (1);
}
```

The other is to use `mysql_set_server_option()` to enable the capability for an existing connection. For example:

```
if (mysql_set_server_option (conn, MYSQL_OPTION_MULTI_STATEMENTS_ON) != 0)
  print_error (conn, "Could not enable multiple-statement execution");
```

Which method is preferable? If the program does not use stored procedures, either one is suitable. If the program does use stored procedures and invokes a CALL statement that returns a result set, use the first method. That's because `CLIENT_MULTI_STATEMENTS` also turns on the `CLIENT_MULTI_RESULTS` option, which must be enabled or an error occurs if a stored procedure attempts to return a result. (More preferable yet might be to add `CLIENT_MULTI_RESULTS` to the flags argument to `mysql_real_connect()`, because that makes it explicit that you're enabling the option.)

Two functions form the basis for checking the current status of result retrieval when you're processing multiple result sets:

- `mysql_more_results()` returns nonzero if more results are available and zero otherwise.
- `mysql_next_result()` returns a status and also initiates retrieval of the next set if more results are available. The status is zero if more results are available, –1 if not, and a value greater than zero if an error occurred.

You can use these functions by putting your result-retrieval code inside a loop. After retrieving a result with your usual code, check whether there are any results yet to be retrieved. If so, perform another iteration of the loop. If not, exit the loop. Depending on how you structure your loop, you may not need to call `mysql_more_results()` at all because you can also tell from the return value of `mysql_next_result()` whether more results are available.

In Section 7.4.3, "A General-Purpose Statement Handler," we wrote a function, `process_statement()`, that executes a statement and retrieves the result or displays the number of rows affected. By placing the result-retrieval code into a loop and incorporating `mysql_next_result()`, we can write a similar function, `process_multi_statement()`, that can retrieve multiple result sets:

```
void
process_multi_statement (MYSQL *conn, char *stmt_str)
{
MYSQL_RES *res_set;
int       status;
int       keep_going = 1;

  if (mysql_query (conn, stmt_str) != 0)  /* the statement(s) failed */
  {
    print_error (conn, "Could not execute statement(s)");
    return;
  }

  /* the statement(s) succeeded; enter result-retrieval loop */
  do {
    /* determine whether current statement returned data */
    res_set = mysql_store_result (conn);
    if (res_set)      /* a result set was returned */
    {
      /* process rows and free the result set */
      process_result_set (conn, res_set);
      mysql_free_result (res_set);
    }
    else              /* no result set was returned */
    {
      /*
       * does the lack of a result set mean that the statement didn't
       * return one, or that it should have but an error occurred?
       */
      if (mysql_field_count (conn) == 0)
      {
        /*
         * statement generated no result set (it was not a SELECT,
         * SHOW, DESCRIBE, etc.); just report rows-affected value.
         */
        printf ("Number of rows affected: %lu\n",
                (unsigned long) mysql_affected_rows (conn));
      }
      else  /* an error occurred */
      {
```

```
      print_error (conn, "Could not retrieve result set");
      keep_going = 0;
    }
  }
  /* determine whether more results exist */
  /* 0 = yes, -1 = no, >0 = error */
  status = mysql_next_result (conn);
  if (status != 0)     /* no more results, or an error occurred */
  {
    keep_going = 0;
    if (status > 0)    /* error */
      print_error (conn, "Could not execute statement");
  }
} while (keep_going);
}
```

If you like, just test whether the result of `mysql_next_result()` is zero, and exit the loop if not. The disadvantage of this simpler strategy is that if there are no more results, you don't know whether you've reached the end normally or an error occurred. In other words, you don't know whether to print an error message.

7.8 Using Server-Side Prepared Statements

In the earlier parts of this chapter, the code for SQL statement processing is based on the set of functions provided by the MySQL client library that send and retrieve all information in string form. This section discusses how to use the binary client/server protocol. The binary protocol supports server-side prepared statements and enables transmission of data values in native format.

Not all statements can be prepared. The initial implementation of prepared statements supported only the following statements: CREATE TABLE, DELETE, DO, INSERT, REPLACE, SELECT, SET, UPDATE, and most variations of SHOW. The list of supported statements has expanded since. See the MySQL Reference Manual for the current list.

To use the binary protocol, you must create a statement handler. With this handler, send a statement to the server to be "prepared," or preprocessed. The server analyzes the statement, remembers it, and sends back information about it that the client library stores in the statement handler. Further processing for the statement uses this handler.

A statement to be prepared can be parameterized by including '?' characters to indicate where data values appear that you will supply later when you execute the statement. For example, you might prepare a statement that looks like this:

```
INSERT INTO score (event_id, student_id, score) VALUES(?,?,?)
```

This statement includes three '?' characters that act as parameter markers or placeholders. Later, you can supply data values to be bound to the placeholders. These complete the statement when you execute it. By parameterizing a statement, you make it reusable: The same statement can be executed multiple times, each time with a new set of data values. This means that you send the text of the statement only once, and that each time you execute the statement, you send only the data values. For repeated statement execution, this provides a performance boost:

- The server needs to analyze the statement only once, not each time it is executed.

- Network overhead is reduced, because you send only the data values for each execution, not an entire statement.

- Data values are sent without conversion to string form, which reduces execution overhead. For example, the three columns named in the preceding INSERT statement all are INT columns. Were you to use mysql_query() or mysql_real_query() to execute a similar INSERT statement, it would be necessary to convert the data values to strings for inclusion in the text of the statement. With the prepared statement interface, you send the data values separately in binary format.

- No conversion is needed for retrieving results, either. In result sets returned by prepared statements, nonstring values are returned in binary format without conversion to string form.

The binary protocol does have some disadvantages, compared to the original nonbinary protocol:

- It is more difficult to use because more setup is necessary for transmitting and receiving data values.

- The binary protocol does not support all statements. For example, USE statements don't work.

- For interactive programs, you may as well use the original protocol. In that case, each statement received from the user is executed only once. There is little benefit to using prepared statements, which provide the greatest efficiency gain for statements that you execute repeatedly.

The general procedure for using a prepared statement involves these steps:

1. Allocate a statement handler by calling mysql_stmt_init(). This function returns a pointer to the handler, which you use for the following steps.

2. Call mysql_stmt_prepare() to send a statement to the server to be prepared and associated with the statement handler. The server determines certain characteristics of the statement, such as what kind of statement it is, how many parameter markers it contains, and whether it produces a result set when executed.

3. If the statement contains any placeholders, you must provide data for each of them before you can execute it. To do this, set up a MYSQL_BIND structure for each parameter. Each structure indicates one parameter's data type, its value, whether it is NULL, and so on. Then bind these structures to the statement by calling mysql_stmt_bind_param().

4. Invoke mysql_stmt_execute() to execute the statement.

5. If the statement modifies data rather than producing a result set (for example, if it is an INSERT or UPDATE), call `mysql_stmt_affected_rows()` to determine the number of rows affected by the statement.

6. If the statement produces a result set, call `mysql_stmt_result_metadata()` if you want to obtain metadata about the result set. To fetch the rows, you use MYSQL_BIND structures again, but this time they serve as receptacles for data returned from the server rather than a source of data to send to the server. You must set up one MYSQL_BIND structure for each column in the result set. They contain information about the values you expect to receive from the server in each row. Bind the structures to the statement handler by calling `mysql_stmt_bind_result()`, then invoke `mysql_stmt_fetch()` repeatedly to get each row. After each fetch, you can access the column values for the current row.

   Before calling `mysql_stmt_fetch()`, an optional action is to call `mysql_stmt_store_result()`. If you do this, the result set rows are fetched all at once from the server and buffered in memory on the client side. Also, the number of rows in the result set can be determined by calling `mysql_stmt_num_rows()`, which otherwise returns zero.

   After fetching the result set, call `mysql_stmt_free_result()` to release memory associated with it.

7. To re-execute the statement, return to step 3 to specify new parameter values.

8. To prepare a different statement using the handler, return to step 2.

9. When you're done with the statement handler, dispose of it by calling `mysql_stmt_close()`. If the client connection closes while the server still has prepared statements associated with the connection, the server disposes of them automatically.

A client application can prepare multiple statements, then execute each in the order appropriate to the application.

The following discussion describes how to write a simple program that inserts rows into a table and then retrieves them. The part of the program that processes an INSERT statement illustrates how to use placeholders in a statement and transmit data values to the server to be bound to the prepared statement when it is executed. The part that processes a SELECT statement shows how to retrieve a result set produced by a prepared statement. You can find the source for this program in the `prepared.c` and `process_prepared_statement.c` files in the `capi` directory of the `sampdb` distribution. I won't show the code for setting up the connection because it is similar to that for earlier programs.

The main part of the program that sets up to use prepared statements looks like this:

```
void
process_prepared_statements (MYSQL *conn)
{
MYSQL_STMT *stmt;
char       *use_stmt = "USE sampdb";
char       *drop_stmt = "DROP TABLE IF EXISTS t";
char       *create_stmt =
```

```
     "CREATE TABLE t (i INT, f FLOAT, c CHAR(24), dt DATETIME)";

     /* select database and create test table */

     if (mysql_query (conn, use_stmt) != 0
       || mysql_query (conn, drop_stmt) != 0
       || mysql_query (conn, create_stmt) != 0)
     {
       print_error (conn, "Could not set up test table");
       return;
     }

     stmt = mysql_stmt_init (conn);  /* allocate statement handler */
     if (stmt == NULL)
     {
       print_error (conn, "Could not initialize statement handler");
       return;
     }

     /* insert and retrieve some records */
     insert_rows (stmt);
     select_rows (stmt);

     mysql_stmt_close (stmt);       /* deallocate statement handler */
}
```

First, we select a database and create a test table. The table contains four columns of varying data types: INT, FLOAT, CHAR, and DATETIME. These different data types must be handled in slightly different ways, as will become evident.

After creating the table, we invoke mysql_stmt_init() to allocate a prepared statement handler, insert and retrieve some rows, and deallocate the handler. All the real work takes place in the insert_rows() and select_rows() functions, which we will get to shortly. For error handling, the program also uses a function, print_stmt_error(), that is similar to the print_error() function used in earlier programs but invokes the error functions that are specific to prepared statements:

```
static void
print_stmt_error (MYSQL_STMT *stmt, char *message)
{
  fprintf (stderr, "%s\n", message);
  if (stmt != NULL)
  {
    fprintf (stderr, "Error %u (%s): %s\n",
             mysql_stmt_errno (stmt),
             mysql_stmt_sqlstate (stmt),
             mysql_stmt_error (stmt));
  }
}
```

The `insert_rows()` function takes care of adding new rows to the test table:

```
static void
insert_rows (MYSQL_STMT *stmt)
{
char          *stmt_str = "INSERT INTO t (i,f,c,dt) VALUES(?,?,?,?)";
MYSQL_BIND    param[4];
int           my_int;
float         my_float;
char          my_str[26]; /* ctime() returns 26-character string */
MYSQL_TIME    my_datetime;
unsigned long my_str_length;
time_t        clock;
struct tm     *cur_time;
int           i;

  printf ("Inserting records...\n");

  if (mysql_stmt_prepare (stmt, stmt_str, strlen (stmt_str)) != 0)
  {
    print_stmt_error (stmt, "Could not prepare INSERT statement");
    return;
  }

  /*
   * zero the parameter structures, then perform all parameter
   * initialization that is constant and does not change for each row
   */

  memset ((void *) param, 0, sizeof (param));

  /* set up INT parameter */

  param[0].buffer_type = MYSQL_TYPE_LONG;
  param[0].buffer = (void *) &my_int;
  param[0].is_unsigned = 0;
  param[0].is_null = 0;
  /* buffer_length, length need not be set */

  /* set up FLOAT parameter */

  param[1].buffer_type = MYSQL_TYPE_FLOAT;
  param[1].buffer = (void *) &my_float;
  param[1].is_null = 0;
  /* is_unsigned, buffer_length, length need not be set */

  /* set up CHAR parameter */
```

```
param[2].buffer_type = MYSQL_TYPE_STRING;
param[2].buffer = (void *) my_str;
param[2].buffer_length = sizeof (my_str);
param[2].is_null = 0;
/* is_unsigned need not be set, length is set later */

/* set up DATETIME parameter */

param[3].buffer_type = MYSQL_TYPE_DATETIME;
param[3].buffer = (void *) &my_datetime;
param[3].is_null = 0;
/* is_unsigned, buffer_length, length need not be set */

if (mysql_stmt_bind_param (stmt, param) != 0)
{
  print_stmt_error (stmt, "Could not bind parameters for INSERT");
  return;
}

for (i = 1; i <= 5; i++)
{
  printf ("Inserting record %d...\n", i);

  (void) time (&clock); /* get current time */

  /* set the variables that are associated with each parameter */

  /* param[0]: set my_int value */
  my_int = i;

  /* param[1]: set my_float value */
  my_float = (float) i;

  /* param[2]: set my_str to current ctime() string value */
  /* and set length to point to var that indicates my_str length */
  (void) strcpy (my_str, ctime (&clock));
  my_str[24] = '\0';  /* chop off trailing newline */
  my_str_length = strlen (my_str);
  param[2].length = &my_str_length;

  /* param[3]: set my_datetime to current date and time components */
  cur_time = localtime (&clock);
  my_datetime.year = cur_time->tm_year + 1900;
  my_datetime.month = cur_time->tm_mon + 1;
  my_datetime.day = cur_time->tm_mday;
  my_datetime.hour = cur_time->tm_hour;
  my_datetime.minute = cur_time->tm_min;
```

```
    my_datetime.second = cur_time->tm_sec;
    my_datetime.second_part = 0;
    my_datetime.neg = 0;

    if (mysql_stmt_execute (stmt) != 0)
    {
      print_stmt_error (stmt, "Could not execute statement");
      return;
    }

    sleep (1);  /* pause briefly (to let the time change) */
  }
}
```

The overall purpose of insert_rows() is to insert into the test table five rows that contain these values:

- An INT value from 1 to 5.

- A FLOAT value from 1.0 to 5.0.

- A CHAR value. To generate these values, we call the ctime() system function to get the value of "now" as a string. ctime() returns values that have this format:

  Sun Sep 19 16:47:23 CDT 2004

- A DATETIME value. This also has the value of "now," but stored in a MYSQL_TIME structure. The binary protocol uses MYSQL_TIME structures to transmit DATETIME, TIMESTAMP, DATE, and TIME values.

The first thing we do in insert_rows() is prepare an INSERT statement by passing it to mysql_stmt_prepare(). The statement looks like this:

```
INSERT INTO t (i,f,c,dt) VALUES(?,?,?,?)
```

The statement contains four placeholders, so it's necessary to supply four data values each time the statement is executed. Placeholders typically represent data values in VALUES() lists or in WHERE clauses. But there are places in which they cannot be used:

- As identifiers such as table or column names. This statement is illegal:

  ```
  SELECT * FROM ?
  ```

- You can use placeholders on one side of an operator, but not on both sides. This statement is legal:

  ```
  SELECT * FROM student WHERE student_id = ?
  ```

  However, this statement is illegal:

  ```
  SELECT * FROM student WHERE ? = ?
  ```

  This restriction is necessary so that the server can determine parameter data types.

The next step is to set up an array of MYSQL_BIND structures, one for each placeholder. As demonstrated in insert_rows(), setting these up involves two stages:

1. Initialize all parts of the structures that will be the same for each row inserted.

2. Perform a row-insertion loop that, for each row, initializes the parts of the structures that vary for each row.

You could actually perform all initialization within the loop, but that would be less efficient.

The first initialization stage begins by zeroing the contents of the param array containing the MYSQL_BIND structures. The program uses memset(), but you can use bzero() if your system doesn't have memset(). These two statements are equivalent:

```
memset ((void *) param, 0, sizeof (param));
bzero ((void *) param, sizeof (param));
```

Clearing the param array implicitly sets all structure members to zero. Code that follows sets some members to zero to make it explicit what's going on, but that is not strictly necessary. In practice, you need not assign zero to any structure members after clearing the structures.

The next step is to assign the proper information to each parameter in the MYSQL_BIND array. For each parameter, the structure members that need to be set depend on the type of value you're transmitting:

- The buffer_type member always must be set; it indicates the data type of the value. Appendix G, "C API Reference," contains a table that lists each of the permitted type codes and shows the SQL and C types that correspond to each code.

- The buffer member should be set to the address of the variable that contains the data value. insert_rows() declares four variables to hold row values: my_int, my_float, my_str, and my_datetime. Each param[i].buffer value is set to point to the appropriate variable. When it comes time to insert a row, we set these four variables to the table column values and they are used to create the new row.

- The is_unsigned member applies only to integer data types. It should be set to true (nonzero) or false (zero) to indicate whether the parameter corresponds to an UNSIGNED integer type. Our table contains a signed INT column, so we set is_unsigned to zero. Were the column an INT UNSIGNED, we would set is_unsigned to 1, and would also declare my_int as unsigned int rather than as int.

- The is_null member indicates whether you're transmitting a NULL value. In the general case, you set this member to the address of a my_bool variable. Then, before inserting any given row, you set the variable true or false to specify whether the value to be inserted is NULL. If no NULL values are to be sent (as is the case here), you can set is_null to zero and no my_bool variable is needed.

- For character string values or binary data (BLOB values), two more MYSQL_BIND members come into play. These indicate the size of the buffer in which the value is stored and the actual size of the current value being transmitted. In many cases these might be the same, but they will differ if you're using a fixed-size buffer and sending values that vary in length from row to row. `buffer_length` indicates the size of the buffer. `length` is a pointer; it should be set to the address of an `unsigned long` variable that contains the actual length of the value to be sent.

For numeric and temporal data types, `buffer_length` and `length` need not be set. The size of each of these types is fixed and can be determined from the `buffer_type` value. For example, `MYSQL_TYPE_LONG` and `MYSQL_TYPE_FLOAT` indicate 4-byte and 8-byte values.

After the initial setup of the `MYSQL_BIND` array has been done, we bind the array to the prepared statement by passing the array to `mysql_stmt_bind_param()`. Then it's time to assign values to the variables that the `MYSQL_BIND` structures point to and execute the statement. This takes place in a loop that executes five times. Each iteration of the loop assigns values to the statement parameters:

- For the integer and floating-point parameters, it's necessary only to assign values to the associated `int` and `float` variables.

- For the string parameter, we assign the current time in string format to the associated `char` buffer. This value is obtained by calling `ctime()`, and then chopping off the newline character.

- The datetime parameter also is assigned the current time, but this is done by assigning the component parts of the time to the individual members of the associated `MYSQL_TIME` structure.

With the parameter values set, we execute the statement by invoking `mysql_stmt_execute()`. This function transmits the current values to the server, which incorporates them into the prepared statement and executes it.

When `insert_rows()` returns, the test table has been populated and `select_rows()` can be called to retrieve them:

```
static void
select_rows (MYSQL_STMT *stmt)
{
char          *stmt_str = "SELECT i, f, c, dt FROM t";
MYSQL_BIND    param[4];
int           my_int;
float         my_float;
char          my_str[24];
unsigned long my_str_length;
MYSQL_TIME    my_datetime;
my_bool       is_null[4];

  printf ("Retrieving records...\n");

  if (mysql_stmt_prepare (stmt, stmt_str, strlen (stmt_str)) != 0)
  {
```

```
    print_stmt_error (stmt, "Could not prepare SELECT statement");
    return;
  }

  if (mysql_stmt_field_count (stmt) != 4)
  {
    print_stmt_error (stmt, "Unexpected column count from SELECT");
    return;
  }

  /*
   * initialize the result column structures
   */

  memset ((void *) param, 0, sizeof (param)); /* zero the structures */

  /* set up INT parameter */

  param[0].buffer_type = MYSQL_TYPE_LONG;
  param[0].buffer = (void *) &my_int;
  param[0].is_unsigned = 0;
  param[0].is_null = &is_null[0];
  /* buffer_length, length need not be set */

  /* set up FLOAT parameter */

  param[1].buffer_type = MYSQL_TYPE_FLOAT;
  param[1].buffer = (void *) &my_float;
  param[1].is_null = &is_null[1];
  /* is_unsigned, buffer_length, length need not be set */

  /* set up CHAR parameter */

  param[2].buffer_type = MYSQL_TYPE_STRING;
  param[2].buffer = (void *) my_str;
  param[2].buffer_length = sizeof (my_str);
  param[2].length = &my_str_length;
  param[2].is_null = &is_null[2];
  /* is_unsigned need not be set */

  /* set up DATETIME parameter */

  param[3].buffer_type = MYSQL_TYPE_DATETIME;
  param[3].buffer = (void *) &my_datetime;
  param[3].is_null = &is_null[3];
  /* is_unsigned, buffer_length, length need not be set */
```

```c
if (mysql_stmt_bind_result (stmt, param) != 0)
{
  print_stmt_error (stmt, "Could not bind parameters for SELECT");
  return;
}

if (mysql_stmt_execute (stmt) != 0)
{
  print_stmt_error (stmt, "Could not execute SELECT");
  return;
}

/*
 * fetch result set into client memory; this is optional, but it
 * enables mysql_stmt_num_rows() to be called to determine the
 * number of rows in the result set.
 */

if (mysql_stmt_store_result (stmt) != 0)
{
  print_stmt_error (stmt, "Could not buffer result set");
  return;
}
else
{
  /* mysql_stmt_store_result() makes row count available */
  printf ("Number of rows retrieved: %lu\n",
          (unsigned long) mysql_stmt_num_rows (stmt));
}

while (mysql_stmt_fetch (stmt) == 0)  /* fetch each row */
{
  /* display row values */
  printf ("%d  ", my_int);
  printf ("%.2f  ", my_float);
  printf ("%*.*s  ", (int) my_str_length, (int) my_str_length, my_str);
  printf ("%04d-%02d-%02d %02d:%02d:%02d\n",
          my_datetime.year,
          my_datetime.month,
          my_datetime.day,
          my_datetime.hour,
          my_datetime.minute,
          my_datetime.second);
}

mysql_stmt_free_result (stmt);      /* deallocate result set */
}
```

`select_rows()` prepares a `SELECT` statement, executes it, and retrieves the result. In this case, the statement contains no placeholders:

```
SELECT i, f, c, dt FROM t
```

That means it's unnecessary to set up any `MYSQL_BIND` structures before executing the statement. But we're not off the hook. The bulk of the work in `select_rows()`, just as in `insert_rows()`, is setting up an array of `MYSQL_BIND` structures. The difference is that they're used to receive data values from the server *after* executing the statement rather than to set up data values to be sent to the server *before* executing the statement.

Nevertheless, the procedure for setting up the `MYSQL_BIND` array is somewhat similar to the corresponding code in `insert_rows()`:

1. Zero the array.

2. Set the `buffer_type` member of each parameter to the appropriate type code.

3. Point the `buffer` member of each parameter to the variable where the corresponding column value should be stored when rows are fetched.

4. Set the `is_unsigned` member for the integer parameter to zero.

5. For the string parameter, set the `buffer_length` value to the maximum number of bytes that should be fetched, and set `length` to the address of an `unsigned long` variable. At fetch time, this variable is set to the actual number of bytes fetched.

6. For every parameter, set the `is_null` member to the address of a `my_bool` variable. At fetch time, these variables are set to indicate whether the fetched values are `NULL`. (Our program ignores these variables after fetching rows because we know that the test table contains no `NULL` values. In the general case, you should check them.)

After setting up the parameters, we bind the array to the statement by calling `mysql_stmt_bind_result()`, then execute the statement.

At this point, you can immediately begin fetching rows by calling `mysql_stmt_fetch()`. Our program demonstrates an optional step that you can do first: It calls `mysql_stmt_store_result()`, which fetches the entire result set and buffers it in client memory. The advantage of doing this is that you can call `mysql_stmt_num_rows()` to find out how many rows are in the result set. The disadvantage is that it uses more memory on the client side.

The row-fetching loop involves calling `mysql_stmt_fetch()` until it returns a nonzero value. After each fetch, the variables associated with the parameter structures contain the column values for the current row.

Once all the rows have been fetched, a call to `mysql_stmt_free_result()` releases any memory associated with the result set.

At this point, `select_rows()` returns to the caller, which invokes `mysql_stmt_close()` to dispose of the prepared statement handler.

The preceding discussion provides a broad overview of the prepared statement interface and some of its key functions. The client library includes several other related functions; for more information, consult Appendix G, "C API Reference."

7.9 Using Prepared CALL Support

Prepared statement support got a boost in MySQL 5.5 with improved handling of prepared CALL statements to invoke stored procedures, including the capability of accessing the returned values of OUT and INOUT procedure parameters. Previously, prepared CALL statements could not produce multiple result sets and callers could not access returned parameter values.

For demonstration purposes, assume that the following stored procedure exists:

```
CREATE PROCEDURE grade_event_stats
  (IN p_event_id INT, OUT p_min INT, OUT p_max INT)
BEGIN
  -- display scores for event
  SELECT student_id, score
    FROM score
    WHERE event_id = p_event_id
    ORDER BY student_id;
  -- store min/max event scores in OUT parameters
  SELECT MIN(score), MAX(score)
    FROM score
    WHERE event_id = p_event_id
    INTO p_min, p_max;
END;
```

The procedure takes one IN parameter and two OUT parameters. Given a grade event ID as the its parameter, the procedure displays the scores for that event, and returns the minimum and maximum scores for the event in its two OUT parameters. If we were to call grade_event_stats() from the mysql client, the statements might look like this:

```
mysql> SET @p_min = NULL, @p_max = NULL;
mysql> CALL grade_event_stats(4, @p_min, @p_max);
+------------+-------+
| student_id | score |
+------------+-------+
|          2 |     7 |
|          3 |    17 |
|          4 |    16 |
|          5 |    20 |
...
mysql> SELECT @p_min, @p_max;
+--------+--------+
| @p_min | @p_max |
+--------+--------+
```

```
|     7 |    20 |
+--------+--------+
```

The following discussion shows how to use the C API to do the same thing. The source for this program is the `prepared_call.c` file in the `capi` directory of the `sampdb` distribution. To create the procedure, use `prepared_call_setup.sql` in that same directory:

```
% mysql sampdb < prepared_call_setup.sql
```

Prepared CALL support requires MySQL 5.5.3 or higher. To verify after connecting to a server that it has this capability, `prepared_call` checks the server version:

```
if (mysql_get_server_version (conn) < 50503)
{
  print_error (NULL, "Prepared CALL requires MySQL 5.5.3 or higher");
  mysql_close (conn);
  exit (1);
}
```

The next part of the program initializes a prepared statement handler and uses it to execute a prepared CALL statement. If that succeeds, it processes the procedure result:

```
stmt = mysql_stmt_init (conn);
if (!stmt)
  print_error (NULL, "Could not initialize statement handler");
else
{
  if (exec_prepared_call (stmt) == 0)
    process_call_result (conn, stmt);
  mysql_stmt_close (stmt);
}
```

Preparing a CALL statement is much like preparing other statements. Pass the statement string to `mysql_stmt_prepare()`, with data values represented by '?' placeholder characters. For CALL, the placeholders represent parameter values passed to the procedure. Parameter setup is necessarily specific to the number and types of parameters a procedure takes. For simplicity, all `grade_event_stats()` parameters are integers.

```
static int exec_prepared_call (MYSQL_STMT *stmt)
{
MYSQL_BIND params[3];   /* parameter buffers */
int        int_data[3]; /* parameter values */
int        i;

  /* prepare CALL statement */
  if (mysql_stmt_prepare (stmt, "CALL grade_event_stats(?, ?, ?)", 31))
  {
    print_stmt_error (stmt, "Cannot prepare statement");
    return (1);
```

```
  }

  /* initialize parameter structures and bind to statement */
  memset (params, 0, sizeof (params));

  for (i = 0; i < 3; ++i)
  {
    params[i].buffer_type = MYSQL_TYPE_LONG;
    params[i].buffer = (char *) &int_data[i];
    params[i].length = 0;
    params[i].is_null = 0;
  }

  if (mysql_stmt_bind_param (stmt, params))
  {
    print_stmt_error (stmt, "Cannot bind parameters");
    return (1);
  }

  /* assign parameter values and execute statement */
  int_data[0]= 4;   /* p_event_id */
  int_data[1]= 0;   /* p_min (OUT param; initial value ignored by procedure */
  int_data[2]= 0;   /* p_min (OUT param; initial value ignored by procedure */

  if (mysql_stmt_execute (stmt))
  {
    print_stmt_error (stmt, "Cannot execute statement");
    return (1);
  }
  return (0);
}
```

After executing the CALL statement, process its results, which can have several parts:

1. Statements executed within the procedure can each produce a result set. This includes statements such as SELECT, SHOW, and so forth.

2. If the procedure has any OUT or INOUT parameters, there is an additional single-row result set containing the final parameter values, in the order they appear in the procedure definition.

3. A final status packet. There is no result set associated with this, so you can distinguish it from the statement or parameter result sets because it has a result column count of zero.

All parts of the CALL result that are present must be processed. The statement and parameter result sets are optional, depending on how the procedure is written. The procedure always returns the final status packet, regardless of whether there are any preceding result sets.

The process_call_result() function shows a general-purpose loop that retrieves procedure results. The code makes no assumptions about whether the procedure produces any statement or parameter result sets. The retrieval loop has this logic:

1. Get the column count of the next result to determine whether it contains a result set or is the final status packet. A count of zero signifies the status packet, which requires no further processing.

2. A positive column count signifies a result set with that many columns. The result set could either be produced by a statement or contain the returned procedure parameter values. The connection handler has a status member containing a flag you can use to distinguish the two cases. (process_call_result() uses the flag only for information purposes, to announce for each result set how it was produced.) In either case, fetch the result set.

3. Check whether there are more results by calling mysql_stmt_next_result(). This function returns zero if more results are available, −1 if not, and a value greater than zero if an error occurred. Therefore, if the result is zero, return to step 1 to get the next result.

```
static void process_call_result (MYSQL *conn, MYSQL_STMT *stmt)
{
int status;
int num_cols;

  /*
   * For each result, check number of columns.  If none, the result is
   * the final status packet and there is nothing to do. Otherwise,
   * fetch the result set.
   */
  do {
    if ((num_cols = mysql_stmt_field_count (stmt)) > 0)
    {
      /* announce whether result set contains parameters or data set */
      if (conn->server_status & SERVER_PS_OUT_PARAMS)
        printf ("OUT/INOUT parameter values:\n");
      else
        printf ("Statement result set values:\n");

      if (process_result_set (stmt, num_cols))
        break; /* some error occurred */
    }

    /* status is -1 = done, 0 = more results, >0 = error */
    status = mysql_stmt_next_result (stmt);
    if (status > 0)
      print_stmt_error (stmt, "Error checking for next result");
  } while (status == 0);
}
```

To fetch the statement and parameter result sets, the loop calls `process_result_set()`, not shown. Check the `prepared_call.c` source to see what it does. For simplicity, it assumes that any retrieved values are integers. You'd modify that to be more general for programs that handle other data types.

Here is the output from running the `prepared_call` program:

```
% ./prepared_call sampdb
Statement result set values:
 val[1] = 2; val[2] = 7;
 val[1] = 3; val[2] = 17;
 val[1] = 4; val[2] = 16;
 val[1] = 5; val[2] = 20;
...
OUT/INOUT parameter values:
 val[1] = 7; val[2] = 20;
```

Take care to account for any differences between the positions of parameters in the procedure definition and their positions in the parameter result set. Observe that the preceding output says the returned parameter values have positions 1 and 2, although they are actually parameters 2 and 3 to procedure `grade_event_stats()`. Why is this? Because the final result set that returns the parameter values includes only OUT and INOUT parameters, not IN parameters. Any changes to IN parameters within the procedure are not seen by the caller. Therefore, they have the same values after the call as before and need not be returned in the procedure results.

Writing MySQL Programs Using Perl DBI

This chapter describes how to use the Perl DBI interface for MySQL. It does not discuss DBI philosophy or architecture. For information about those aspects of DBI (particularly in comparison with the C and PHP APIs), see Chapter 6, "Introduction to MySQL Programming."

The examples discussed here draw on our sample database, sampdb, using the tables created for the grade-keeping project and for the Historical League in Chapter 1, "Getting Started with MySQL."

I assume here a minimum version of DBI 1.50, although most of the material applies to earlier versions as well. DBI 1.50 requires at least Perl 5.6.0 (with 5.6.1 preferred). As of DBI 1.611, the minimum Perl version is 5.8.1. You must also have the DBD::mysql Perl module installed, as well as the MySQL C client library and header files. If you plan to write Web-based DBI scripts in the manner discussed here, you also need the CGI.pm module. In this chapter, CGI.pm is used in conjunction with the Apache Web server. If you need to obtain any of these packages, see Appendix A, "Software Required to Use This Book," which also has instructions for obtaining the sampdb distribution that contains the example scripts developed in this chapter. You'll find the scripts under the perlapi directory of that distribution.

For the most part, this chapter describes Perl DBI methods and variables only as they are needed for the discussion here. For a more comprehensive listing of methods and variables, see Appendix H, "Perl DBI API Reference." You can use that appendix as a reference for further background on any part of DBI that you're trying to use. Documentation is also available at http://dbi.perl.org or by running the following commands:

```
% perldoc DBI
% perldoc DBI::FAQ
% perldoc DBD::mysql
```

At the database driver (DBD) level, the driver for MySQL is built on top of the MySQL C client library, and therefore shares some of its characteristics. See Chapter 7, "Writing MySQL Programs Using C," for more information about that library.

8.1   Perl Script Characteristics

Perl scripts are text files, so you can create them using any text editor. All Perl scripts in this chapter follow the Unix convention that they begin with a `#!` (shebang) line that specifies the pathname of the program to use for executing the script. I use this line:

```
#!/usr/bin/perl
```

On Unix, you'll need to modify the `#!` line if the pathname to Perl is different on your system, such as `/opt/bin/perl`. Otherwise, Perl scripts won't run properly on your system.

You can invoke a Perl script `myscript.pl` as follows on any system to run it:

```
% perl myscript.pl
```

You may also be able to execute the script without naming the `perl` program explicitly. On Unix, do this by changing the file mode with `chmod` to make the script executable:

```
% chmod +x myscript.pl
```

Then to run the script, just type its name:

```
% ./myscript.pl
```

That is the script invocation style used for examples shown in this chapter. Include the leading "`./`" if the script is located in your current directory ("`.`") and your shell does not have the current directory in its search path. Otherwise, you can omit the "`./`" from the command name:

```
% myscript.pl
```

Under Windows, you can set up a filename association between Perl and filenames ending in `.pl`. For example, if you install ActiveState Perl, its installation program enables you to set up an association so that filenames ending with `.pl` are run by Perl. In that case, you can run a Perl script just by naming it on the command line:

```
C:\> myscript.pl
```

8.2   Perl DBI Overview

This section provides background information for DBI that you'll need for writing your own scripts and for understanding scripts written by others. If you're already familiar with DBI, you may want to skip directly to Section 8.3, "Putting DBI to Work."

8.2.1   DBI Data Types

In some ways, the Perl DBI API is similar to the C client library described in Chapter 7, "Writing MySQL Programs Using C." To use the C client library, you call functions and access MySQL-related data primarily by means of pointers to structures or to arrays. To use the DBI

API, you also call functions and use pointers to structures, except that functions are called "methods," pointers are called "references," pointer variables are called "handles," and the structures to which handles point are called "objects."

DBI uses several kinds of handles. These tend to be referred to in DBI documentation by the conventional names shown in Table 8.1. The way you use these handles will become clear as we go along. Several conventional names for nonhandle variables are used as well (see Table 8.2). This chapter doesn't actually use every one of these variable names, but it's useful to know them when you read DBI scripts written by other people.

Table 8.1   **Conventional Perl DBI Handle Variable Names**

Name	Meaning
$dbh	A handle to a database object
$sth	A handle to a statement (query) object
$fh	A handle to an open file
$h	A "generic" handle; the meaning depends on context

Table 8.2   **Conventional Perl DBI Nonhandle Variable Names**

Name	Meaning
$rc	The return code from operations that return true or false
$rv	The return value from operations that return an integer
$rows	The return value from operations that return a row count
@ary	An array (list) representing a row of values returned by a query

8.2.2   A Simple DBI Script

Let's start with a simple script, dump_members.pl, that illustrates several standard concepts in DBI programming, such as connecting to and disconnecting from the MySQL server, issuing SQL statements, and retrieving data. This script produces output consisting of the Historical League member list in tab-delimited format. The format is not so interesting in itself. It's more important at this point to see how to use DBI than to produce pretty output. dump_members.pl looks like this:

```
#!/usr/bin/perl
# dump_members.pl - dump Historical League membership list

use strict;
```

```
use warnings;
use DBI;

# data source name, username, password, connection attributes
my $dsn = "DBI:mysql:sampdb:localhost";
my $user_name = "sampadm";
my $password = "secret";
my %conn_attrs = (RaiseError => 1, PrintError => 0, AutoCommit => 1);

# connect to database
my $dbh = DBI->connect ($dsn, $user_name, $password, \%conn_attrs);

# issue query
my $sth = $dbh->prepare ("SELECT last_name, first_name, suffix, email,"
        . " street, city, state, zip, phone FROM member ORDER BY last_name");
$sth->execute ();

# read and display query result
while (my @ary = $sth->fetchrow_array ())
{
  print join ("\t", @ary), "\n";
}
$sth->finish ();

$dbh->disconnect ();
```

To try the script for yourself, either use the copy that's included in the sampdb distribution or create it using a text editor. If you use a word processor, be sure to save the script as plain text. Don't save it in the word processor's native format. You'll probably need to change at least some of the connection parameters, such as the hostname, database name, username, or password. (That will also be true for other scripts in this chapter that name the connection parameters as well.) Later, in Section 8.2.9, "Specifying Connection Parameters," we'll see how to get parameters from an option file instead of putting them directly in the script.

Now let's go through the script a piece at a time. The first line contains the standard where-to-find-Perl indicator:

```
#!/usr/bin/perl
```

This line is part of every script discussed in this chapter; I won't mention it further.

It's a good idea to include in a script at least a minimal description of its purpose, so the next line is a comment to give anyone who looks at the script a clue about what it does:

```
# dump_members.pl - dump Historical League membership list
```

Text from a '#' character to the end of a line is considered a comment. It's a useful practice to sprinkle comments throughout your scripts to explain how they work.

Next, we have several `use` statements:

```
use strict;
use warnings;
use DBI;
```

`use strict` tells Perl to require you to declare variables before using them. You can write scripts without this line, but it's useful for catching mistakes, so I recommend you always include it. For example, if you declare a variable `$my_var` but then later erroneously refer to it as `$mv_var`, the following message appears when you run the script in strict mode:

```
Global symbol "$mv_var" requires explicit package name at line n
```

When you see that, you think, "Huh? I never used any variable named `$mv_var`!" Then you look at line *n* of your script, see that you misspelled `$my_var` as `$mv_var`, and fix it. Without strict mode, Perl won't squawk about `$mv_var`; it simply creates a new variable by that name with a value of `undef` (undefined) and uses it without complaint. And you're left to wonder why your script doesn't work.

`use warnings` tells Perl to issue a warning if it finds that you use questionable language constructs or perform operations such as printing uninitialized variables. This is useful because it can alert you to code that should be written more carefully.

`use DBI` tells the Perl interpreter that it needs to pull in the DBI module. Without this line, an error occurs as soon as you try to do anything DBI-related in the script. It's unnecessary to indicate which DBD-level driver module to use; DBI activates the right one for you when you connect to your database server.

Because we're operating in strict mode, we must declare the variables the script uses, by means of the `my` keyword. Think of it as though the script is saying "I am explicitly indicating that these are my variables." The next section of the script sets up the variables that specify connection parameters, then uses them to connect to the database:

```
# data source name, username, password, connection attributes
my $dsn = "DBI:mysql:sampdb:localhost";
my $user_name = "sampadm";
my $password = "secret";
my %conn_attrs = (RaiseError => 1, PrintError => 0, AutoCommit => 1);

# connect to database
my $dbh = DBI->connect ($dsn, $user_name, $password, \%conn_attrs);
```

The `connect()` call is invoked as `DBI->connect()` because it's a method of the DBI class. (You don't really have to know what that means; it's just a little object-oriented jargon to make your head hurt. If you do want to know, it means that `connect()` is a function that "belongs" to DBI.) `connect()` takes several arguments:

- The data source, also known as the "data source name," or "DSN." The DSN indicates which DBD module to use and possibly other parameters.

- The username and password for your MySQL account.

- An optional argument indicating additional connection attributes. If given, this argument should be a reference to a hash that specifies connection attribute names and values.

Data source formats are determined by the requirements of the particular DBD module you use. For the MySQL driver, permitted DSN formats include either of the following:

```
DBI:mysql:db_name
DBI:mysql:db_name:host_name
```

The capitalization of DBI doesn't matter, but mysql must be lowercase. db_name represents the name of the database you want to use and host_name indicates the host where the server is running. If you omit the hostname, it defaults to localhost. (Section 8.2.9, "Specifying Connection Parameters," discusses other permitted data source formats.)

The connection-attribute hash that we specified as the value for %conn_attrs enables the RaiseError attribute and disables PrintError. These settings cause DBI to check for database-related errors and exit with an error message if it detects one. (That's why you see no error-checking code anywhere in the dump_members.pl script; DBI handles it all.) Section 8.2.3, "Handling Errors," covers alternative methods of responding to errors.

The attribute hash also enables the AutoCommit attribute. Currently, this is not strictly necessary (it's on by default), but the setting does make explicit that the script enables autocommit mode for transaction handling. The script doesn't include any explicit transactions, but there is some possibility that DBI will in the future require scripts to specify the AutoCommit attribute explicitly. Doing so in scripts now ensures that they are ready if such a change does occur.

To specify the connection attributes, you could instead provide the hash reference directly in the call to connect():

```
my $dbh = DBI->connect ($dsn, $user_name, $password,
                        { RaiseError => 1, PrintError => 0, AutoCommit => 1 });
```

Different people find one style or the other easier to read or edit, but operationally both approaches are the same.

If the connect() call succeeds, it returns a database handle, which we assign to $dbh. By default, connect() returns undef if it fails. However, because the script enables RaiseError, DBI exits after displaying an error message if something goes wrong in the connect() call. (This is true for other DBI methods, too. I'll describe what they return to indicate an error, but they don't return at all if RaiseError is enabled.)

After connecting to the database, dump_members.pl issues a SELECT statement to retrieve the membership list, then executes a loop to process each of the rows returned. These rows constitute the result set. To perform a SELECT, prepare the statement and execute it:

```
# issue query
my $sth = $dbh->prepare ("SELECT last_name, first_name, suffix, email,"
        . " street, city, state, zip, phone FROM member ORDER BY last_name");
$sth->execute ();
```

prepare() is invoked using the database handle; it passes the SQL statement to the driver for preprocessing before execution. Some drivers actually do something with the statement at this point. Others just remember it until you invoke execute() to cause the statement to be performed. The return value from prepare() is a statement handle, here assigned to $sth. The statement handle is used for all further processing related to the statement.

Notice that the statement string itself has no terminating semicolon. You no doubt have the habit of terminating SQL statements with a ';' character (developed through long hours of interaction with the mysql program). However, it's best to break yourself of that habit when using DBI, because semicolons often cause statements to fail with syntax errors. The same applies to adding \g or \G to statement strings, so don't. Those statement terminators are conventions of mysql and are not used when issuing statements in DBI scripts. The end of the statement string implicitly terminates the statement and no explicit terminator is necessary.

If you invoke a method without passing it any arguments, you can leave off the parentheses. These two calls are equivalent:

```
$sth->execute ();
$sth->execute;
```

I prefer to include the parentheses because they make the call look less like a variable reference to me. Your preference may differ.

After you call execute(), the rows of the membership list are available for processing. In the dump_members.pl script, the row-fetching loop simply prints the contents of each row as a tab-delimited set of values:

```
# read and display query result
while (my @ary = $sth->fetchrow_array ())
{
  print join ("\t", @ary), "\n";
}
$sth->finish ();
```

fetchrow_array() returns an array containing the column values of the current row, or an empty array when there are no more rows. Thus, the loop fetches successive rows returned by the SELECT statement and prints each one with tabs between column values.

NULL values in the database are returned as undef values to the Perl script, but these print as empty strings, not as the word "NULL". undef column values also have another effect when you run the script; they result in warnings like this from the Perl interpreter:

```
Use of uninitialized value in join at dump_members.pl line n.
```

These warnings are triggered by the inclusion of the use warnings statement. If you remove that statement and run the script again, the warnings go away. However, warnings mode is useful for discovering problems (such as printing uninitialized variables!). A better way to eliminate the warnings is to detect and deal with undef values. Section 8.2.5, "Handling Statements That Return a Result Set," discusses some techniques for doing so.

In the `print` statement, note that the tab and newline characters (represented as the `\t` and `\n` sequences, respectively) are enclosed in double quotes. In Perl, escape sequences are interpreted only when they occur within double quotes, not within single quotes. If single quotes had been used, the output would be full of literal instances of `\t` and `\n`.

After the row-fetching loop terminates, the call to `finish()` indicates that the statement handle is no longer needed and that any temporary resources allocated to it can be freed. In this script, the call to `finish()` is for illustrative purposes only. It need not actually be invoked here, because the row-fetching call will do so automatically when it encounters the end of the result set. `finish()` is more useful in situations where you fetch only part of the result set and do not reach its end (for example, if you fetch only the first row). Examples from this point on do not use `finish()` unless it's necessary.

Having printed the membership list, we're done, so we disconnect from the server before exiting:

```
$dbh->disconnect ();
```

`dump_members.pl` illustrates a number of concepts that are common to most DBI programs, and at this point you could probably start writing your own DBI programs without knowing anything more. For example, to write out the contents of some other table, all you need to do is change the text of the `SELECT` statement that is passed to the `prepare()` method. And in fact, if you want to see some applications of this technique, you can skip ahead immediately to the part of Section 8.3, "Putting DBI to Work," that discusses how to generate the member list for the Historical League's annual meeting program and the League's printed directory. However, DBI provides many other useful capabilities. The next sections cover some of these in more detail so that you can see how to do more than run simple `SELECT` statements in your Perl scripts.

8.2.3   Handling Errors

`dump_members.pl` turns on the `RaiseError` error-handling attribute when it invokes the `connect()` method so that errors would automatically terminate the script with an error message rather than just returning error codes. It's possible to handle errors in other ways. For example, you can check for errors yourself rather than having DBI do it.

To see how to control DBI's error-handling behavior, take a closer look at the connection attribute hash passed as the final argument to `connect()`:

```
# data source name, username, password, connection attributes
my $dsn = "DBI:mysql:sampdb:localhost";
my $user_name = "sampadm";
my $password = "secret";
my %conn_attrs = (RaiseError => 1, PrintError => 0, AutoCommit => 1);

# connect to database
my $dbh = DBI->connect ($dsn, $user_name, $password, \%conn_attrs);
```

The two attributes relevant for error handling are `RaiseError` and `PrintError`:

- If `RaiseError` is enabled (set to a nonzero value), DBI raises an exception when an error occurs in a DBI method. By default, this results in a call to `die()` to print a message and exit the script.

- If `PrintError` is enabled, DBI calls `warn()` to print a message when a DBI error occurs, but the script continues executing.

By default, `RaiseError` is disabled and `PrintError` is enabled. In this case, if the `connect()` call fails, DBI prints a message but continues executing. Thus, with the default error-handling behavior that you get if you omit the fourth argument to `connect()`, you might check for errors like this:

```
my $dbh = DBI->connect ($dsn, $user_name, $password)
            or exit (1);
```

In this case, if an error occurs, `connect()` returns `undef` to indicate failure, and that triggers the call to `exit()`. You need not print an error message because DBI already will have printed one.

If you were to explicitly specify the default values for the error-checking attributes, the settings passed to `connect()` would look like this:

```
my %conn_attrs = (RaiseError => 0, PrintError => 1, AutoCommit => 1);
my $dbh = DBI->connect ($dsn, $user_name, $password, \%conn_attrs)
            or exit (1);
```

That's more work to write, but the error-handling behavior is more obvious to the casual reader.

To check for errors and print your own messages, disable both `RaiseError` and `PrintError`:

```
my %conn_attrs = (RaiseError => 0, PrintError => 0, AutoCommit => 1);
my $dbh = DBI->connect ($dsn, $user_name, $password, \%conn_attrs)
            or die "Could not connect to server: $DBI::err ($DBI::errstr)\n";
```

The `$DBI::err` and `$DBI::errstr`, variables used in the code just shown are useful for constructing error messages. They contain the MySQL error code and error string, much like the `mysql_errno()` and `mysql_error()` C API functions. If no error occurred, `$DBI::err` will be 0 or `undef`, and `$DBI::errstr` will be the empty string or `undef`. (In other words, both variables will be false.)

To have DBI handle errors for you so that you need not check for them yourself, enable `RaiseError` and disable `PrintError`:

```
my %conn_attrs = (RaiseError => 1, PrintError => 0, AutoCommit => 1);
my $dbh = DBI->connect ($dsn, $user_name, $password, \%conn_attrs);
```

This is by far the easiest approach, and it is how almost all scripts presented in this chapter are written. The reason for disabling `PrintError` when enabling `RaiseError` is to prevent the possibility of having error messages being printed twice. (If both attributes are enabled, the DBI handlers for both might be called under some circumstances.)

Enabling `RaiseError` may not be appropriate if you want to execute some sort of cleanup code of your own when the script exits, although in this case you might be able to do what you want by redefining the `$SIG{__DIE__}` signal handler. Another reason to avoid enabling `RaiseError` is that DBI prints technical information in its messages, like this:

```
disconnect(DBI::db=HASH(0x197aae4)) invalidates 1 active statement. Either
destroy statement handles or call finish on them before disconnecting.
```

That's useful information for a programmer, but it could be the kind of thing you want to avoid presenting to the everyday user. In that case, it can be better to check for errors yourself and display messages that are more meaningful to the people you expect to be using the script. Or you might consider redefining the `$SIG{__DIE__}` handler here, too. That could be useful because you can enable `RaiseError` to simplify error handling, but replace the default error messages that DBI presents with your own messages. To provide your own __DIE__ handler, do something like this before executing any DBI calls:

```
$SIG{__DIE__} = sub { die "Sorry, an error occurred\n"; };
```

You can also define a subroutine in the usual fashion and set the signal handler value using a reference to the subroutine:

```
sub die_handler
{
  die "Sorry, an error occurred\n";
}

$SIG{__DIE__} = \&die_handler;
```

The following script, `dump_members2.pl`, illustrates how to write a script that checks for errors and print its own messages. `dump_members2.pl` processes the same statement as `dump_members.pl`, but explicitly disables `PrintError` and `RaiseError` and tests the result of every DBI call. When an error occurs, the script invokes the subroutine `bail_out()` to print a message and the contents of `$DBI::err` and `$DBI::errstr` before exiting:

```
#!/usr/bin/perl
# dump_members2.pl - dump Historical League membership list

use strict;
use warnings;
use DBI;

# data source name, username, password, connection attributes
my $dsn = "DBI:mysql:sampdb:localhost";
my $user_name = "sampadm";
my $password = "secret";
my %conn_attrs = (RaiseError => 0, PrintError => 0, AutoCommit => 1);
```

```perl
# connect to database
my $dbh = DBI->connect ($dsn, $user_name, $password, \%conn_attrs)
            or bail_out ("Cannot connect to database");

# issue query
my $sth = $dbh->prepare ("SELECT last_name, first_name, suffix, email,"
        . " street, city, state, zip, phone FROM member ORDER BY last_name")
            or bail_out ("Cannot prepare query");
$sth->execute ()
  or bail_out ("Cannot execute query");

# read and display query result
while (my @ary = $sth->fetchrow_array ())
{
  print join ("\t", @ary), "\n";
}
!$DBI::err
  or bail_out ("Error during retrieval");

$dbh->disconnect ()
  or bail_out ("Cannot disconnect from database");

# bail_out() subroutine - print error code and string, then exit

sub bail_out
{
my $message = shift;

  die "$message\nError $DBI::err ($DBI::errstr)\n";
}
```

bail_out() is similar to the print_error() function that we used for writing C programs in Chapter 7, "Writing MySQL Programs Using C," except that bail_out() exits rather than returning to the caller. bail_out() saves you the trouble of writing code to display the values of $DBI::err and $DBI::errstr every time you want to print an error message. Also, by encapsulating error message printing into a subroutine, you can change the format of your error messages uniformly throughout your script simply by making a change to the subroutine.

The dump_members2.pl script has a test following the row-fetching loop. Because the script doesn't automatically exit if an error occurs in fetchrow_array(), it's prudent to determine whether the loop terminated because the result set was read completely (normal termination) or because an error occurred. The loop terminates either way, of course, but if an error occurs, output from the script is truncated. Without an error check, the person running the script has no idea that something went wrong! If you're checking for errors yourself, be sure to test the result of your fetch loops.

8.2.4   Handling Statements That Modify Rows

Statements that modify rows, such as DELETE, INSERT, and UPDATE, are relatively easy to process compared to statements that return rows, such as SELECT, DESCRIBE, and SHOW. To process a non-SELECT statement, pass it to do() using the database handle. The do() method prepares and executes the statement in one step. For example, to create a new member entry for Marcia Brown with an expiration date of June 3, 2012, you can do the following:

```
$rows = $dbh->do ("INSERT INTO member (last_name,first_name,expiration)"
                . " VALUES('Brown','Marcia','2012-06-03')");
```

The do() method returns a count of the number of rows affected, undef if something goes wrong, and –1 if the number of rows is unknown. Errors can occur for various reasons. (For example, the statement might be malformed or you might not have permission to access the table.) For a non-undef return value, watch out for the case in which no rows are affected. When this happens, do() doesn't return the number 0; instead, it returns the string "0E0" (Perl's scientific notation form of zero). "0E0" evaluates to 0 in a numeric context but is considered true in conditional tests so that it can be distinguished easily from undef. If do() returned 0, it would be more difficult to distinguish between the occurrence of an error (undef) and the "no rows affected" case. You can check for an error using either of the following tests:

```
if (!defined ($rows))
{
  print "An error occurred\n";
}
if (!$rows)
{
  print "An error occurred\n";
}
```

In numeric contexts, "0E0" evaluates as 0, so the following code correctly prints the number of rows for any non-undef value of $rows:

```
if (!$rows)
{
  print "An error occurred\n";
}
else
{
  $rows += 0; # force conversion to number if value is "0E0"
  print "Number of rows affected: $rows\n";
}
```

You could also print $rows using a %d format specifier with printf() to force an implicit conversion to a number:

```
if (!$rows)
{
  print "An error occurred\n";
```

```
}
else
{
  printf "Number of rows affected: %d\n", $rows;
}
```

The `do()` method is equivalent to using `prepare()` followed by `execute()`. This means that the preceding `INSERT` statement can be issued as follows rather than by invoking `do()`:

```
$sth = $dbh->prepare ("INSERT INTO member (last_name,first_name,expiration)"
                     . " VALUES('Brown','Marcia','2012-06-03')");
$rows = $sth->execute ();
```

8.2.5 Handling Statements That Return a Result Set

This section provides more information about your options for executing row-fetching loops for `SELECT` statements (or for other `SELECT`-like statements that return rows, such as `DESCRIBE`, `EXPLAIN`, and `SHOW`). It also discusses how to get a count of the number of rows in a result, how to handle result sets for which no loop is necessary, and how to retrieve an entire result set all at once.

8.2.5.1 Writing Row-Fetching Loops

The `dump_members.pl` script retrieved data using a sequence of DBI methods: `prepare()` lets the driver preprocess the statement, `execute()` begins executing the statement, and `fetchrow_array()` fetches each row of the result set.

`prepare()` and `execute()` are fairly standard parts of processing any statement that returns rows. However, for fetching the rows, `fetchrow_array()` is actually only one choice from among several available methods (see Table 8.3).

Table 8.3 **DBI Row-Fetching Methods**

Method Name	Return Value
`fetchrow_array()`	Array of row values
`fetchrow_arrayref()`	Reference to array of row values
`fetch()`	Same as `fetchrow_arrayref()`
`fetchrow_hashref()`	Reference to hash of row values, keyed by column name

The following examples show how to use each row-fetching method. The examples loop through the rows of a result set, and for each row, print the column values separated by commas. There are more efficient ways to write the code in some cases, but the examples are written for illustrative purposes (to show the syntax for accessing individual column values), not for efficiency.

Use `fetchrow_array()` as follows:

```perl
while (my @ary = $sth->fetchrow_array ())
{
  my $delim = "";
  for (my $i = 0; $i < @ary; $i++)
  {
    $ary[$i] = "" if !defined ($ary[$i]); # NULL value?
    print $delim, $ary[$i];
    $delim = ",";
  }
  print "\n";
}
```

Each call to `fetchrow_array()` returns an array of row values, or an empty array when there are no more rows. The inner loop tests each column value to see whether it's defined, and sets it to the empty string if not. This converts NULL values (which are represented by DBI as `undef`) to empty strings. It might seem that this is an entirely superfluous action; after all, Perl prints nothing for both `undef` and the empty string. However, if the script is run with warnings enabled, Perl issues a "Use of uninitialized value" warning message if you attempt to print an `undef` value. Converting `undef` to the empty string eliminates the warnings. You'll see a similar construct used elsewhere throughout this chapter.

If you prefer to print a different value for `undef` values, such as the string "NULL", just change the `if`-test a little:

```perl
while (my @ary = $sth->fetchrow_array ())
{
  my $delim = "";
  for (my $i = 0; $i < @ary; $i++)
  {
    $ary[$i] = "NULL" if !defined ($ary[$i]); # NULL value?
    print $delim, $ary[$i];
    $delim = ",";
  }
  print "\n";
}
```

When working with an array of values, you can shorten the code a bit by using `map` to convert all the `undef` array elements at once:

```perl
while (my @ary = $sth->fetchrow_array ())
{
  @ary = map { defined ($_) ? $_ : "NULL" } @ary;
  print join (",", @ary), "\n";
}
```

`map` processes each element of the array using the expression within the braces and returns an array containing the resulting values.

An alternative to assigning the return value of `fetchrow_array()` to an array variable is to fetch column values into a set of scalar variables. This enables you to work with variable names that are more meaningful than `$ary[0]`, `$ary[1]`, and so forth. Suppose that you want to retrieve member name and email values into variables. Using `fetchrow_array()`, you could select and fetch rows like this:

```
my $sth = $dbh->prepare ("SELECT last_name, first_name, suffix, email"
                            . " FROM member ORDER BY last_name");
$sth->execute ();
while (my ($last_name, $first_name, $suffix, $email)
                        = $sth->fetchrow_array ())
{
  # do something with variables
}
```

To use a list of variables this way, make sure that the order of the columns selected by the statement matches the order of the variables into which you fetch the values. DBI has no idea of the order in which columns are named by your SELECT statement, so it's up to you to assign variables correctly. You can also cause column values to be assigned to individual variables automatically when you fetch a row, using a technique known as "parameter binding" (see Section 8.2.7, "Placeholders and Prepared Statements").

If you fetch a single value into a variable, be careful how you write the assignment. If you write the beginning of your loop like this, it will work correctly:

```
while (my ($val) = $sth->fetchrow->array ()) ...
```

The value is fetched in list context, so the test will fail only when there are no more rows. But if you write the test like this instead, it will fail in mysterious ways:

```
while (my $val = $sth->fetchrow->array ()) ...
```

Here, the value is fetched in scalar context, so if `$val` happens to be zero, `undef`, or the empty string, the test evaluates as false and terminates the loop, even though you have not yet reached the end of the result set.

The second row-fetching method, `fetchrow_arrayref()`, is similar to `fetchrow_array()`, but instead of returning an array containing the column values for the current row, it returns a reference to the array, or `undef` when there are no more rows. Use it like this:

```
while (my $ary_ref = $sth->fetchrow_arrayref ())
{
  my $delim = "";
  for (my $i = 0; $i < @{$ary_ref}; $i++)
  {
    $ary_ref->[$i] = "" if !defined ($ary_ref->[$i]); # NULL value?
    print $delim, $ary_ref->[$i];
    $delim = ",";
  }
  print "\n";
}
```

You access array elements through the array reference, $ary_ref. This is something like deref-erencing a pointer, so you use $ary_ref->[$i] rather than $ary[$i]. To convert the refer-ence to an array, use the @{$ary_ref} construct.

fetchrow_arrayref() is unsuitable for fetching variables into a list. For example, the follow-ing loop does not work:

```
while (my ($var1, $var2, $var3, $var4) = @{$sth->fetchrow_arrayref ()})
{
  # do something with variables
}
```

As long as fetchrow_arrayref() actually fetches a row, the loop functions properly. But when there are no more rows, fetchrow_arrayref() returns undef, and @{undef} isn't legal. (It's like trying to de-reference a NULL pointer in a C program.)

The third row-fetching method, fetchrow_hashref(), is used like this:

```
while (my $hash_ref = $sth->fetchrow_hashref ())
{
  my $delim = "";
  foreach my $key (keys (%{$hash_ref}))
  {
    $hash_ref->{$key} = "" if !defined ($hash_ref->{$key}); # NULL value?
    print $delim, $hash_ref->{$key};
    $delim = ",";
  }
  print "\n";
}
```

Each call to fetchrow_hashref() returns a reference to a hash of row values keyed on column names, or undef when there are no more rows. In this case, column values don't come out in any particular order, because members of Perl hashes are unordered. However, DBI keys the hash elements using the column names, so $hash_ref gives you a single variable through which you can access any column value by name. This means you can pull out the values (or any subset of them) in any order you want, and you need not know the order in which the columns were retrieved by the SELECT statement. For example, to access the name-related and email columns, you can do this:

```
while (my $hash_ref = $sth->fetchrow_hashref ())
{
  my $delim = "";
  foreach my $key ("last_name", "first_name", "suffix", "email")
  {
    $hash_ref->{$key} = "" if !defined ($hash_ref->{$key}); # NULL value?
    print $delim, $hash_ref->{$key};
    $delim = ",";
  }
  print "\n";
}
```

`fetchrow_hashref()` is especially useful when you want to pass a row of values to a function without requiring the function to know the order in which columns are named in the SELECT statement. In this case, you call `fetchrow_hashref()` to retrieve rows and write a function that accesses values from the row hash using column names.

Keep in mind the following caveats when you use `fetchrow_hashref()`:

- If you need every bit of performance, `fetchrow_hashref()` is not the best choice. It's less efficient than `fetchrow_array()` or `fetchrow_arrayref()`.

- By default, the column names are used as key values with the same lettercase as the column names written in the SELECT statement. In MySQL, column names are not case sensitive, so the statement will work the same way no matter what lettercase you use to write column names. But Perl hash key names *are* case sensitive, which may cause you problems. To avoid potential lettercase mismatch problems, tell `fetchrow_hashref()` to force column names into a particular lettercase by passing it a NAME_lc or NAME_uc attribute:

```
$hash_ref = $sth->fetchrow_hashref ("NAME_lc"); # use lowercase names
$hash_ref = $sth->fetchrow_hashref ("NAME_uc"); # use uppercase names
```

- The hash contains one element per unique column name. If you perform a join that returns columns from multiple tables with overlapping names, you won't be able to access all the column values. If you issue the following statement, `fetchrow_hashref()` returns a hash having only one element, name:

```
SELECT a.name, b.name FROM a INNER JOIN b WHERE a.name = b.name
```

To avoid this problem, use aliases to ensure that each column has a distinct name. If you rewrite the statement as follows, `fetchrow_hashref()` returns a reference to a hash with two elements, name and name2:

```
SELECT a.name, b.name AS name2 FROM a INNER JOIN b WHERE a.name = b.name
```

8.2.5.2 Determining the Number of Rows Returned by a Statement

How can you tell the number of rows returned by a SELECT or SELECT-like statement? One way is to count the rows as you fetch them. In fact, that is the *only* portable way in DBI to know how many rows a SELECT statement returned. The MySQL driver provides a `rows()` method that you can call after invoking `execute()`. But this is not portable to other database systems, and the DBI documentation explicitly discourages using `rows()` for SELECT statements. Even for MySQL, if you've set the `mysql_use_result` attribute, `rows()` doesn't return the correct result until you've fetched all the rows. So, you might as well just count the rows as you fetch them. (For more information about `mysql_use_result`, see Appendix H, "Perl DBI API Reference.")

8.2.5.3 Fetching Single-Row Results

It's not necessary to run a loop to get your results if the result set consists of a single row. Suppose that you want to write a script, `count_members.pl`, that tells you the current number of Historical League members. The code to perform the statement looks like this:

```
# issue query
my $sth = $dbh->prepare ("SELECT COUNT(*) FROM member");
$sth->execute ();

# read and display query result
my $count = $sth->fetchrow_array ();
$sth->finish ();
$count = "can't tell" if !defined ($count);
print "$count\n";
```

The SELECT statement returns only one row, so no loop is required; we call fetchrow_array()
just once. In addition, because we're selecting only one column, it's not even necessary to
assign the return value to an array. When fetchrow_array() is called in a scalar context
(where a single value rather than a list is expected), it returns one column of the row, or undef
if no row is available. DBI does not define which element of the row fetchrow_array()
returns in scalar context, but that's all right for the statement just shown. It retrieves only a
single value, so there is no ambiguity about what value is returned.

This code invokes finish() to free the result set, even though the set consists of just one row.
(fetchrow_array() frees a result set implicitly when it notices that you have reached the end
of the set, but that would happen here only if you called it a second time.)

Another type of query for which you expect at most a single row is one that contains LIMIT
1 to restrict the number of rows returned. A common use for this is to return the row that
contains the maximum or minimum value for a particular column. For example, the following
query prints the name and birth date of the president who was born most recently:

```
my $stmt = "SELECT last_name, first_name, birth FROM president"
         . " WHERE birth = (SELECT MAX(birth) FROM president)";
my $sth = $dbh->prepare ($stmt);
$sth->execute ();

my ($last_name, $first_name, $birth) = $sth->fetchrow_array ();
$sth->finish ();
if (!defined ($last_name))
{
  print "Query returned no result\n";
}
else
{
  print "Most recently born president: $first_name $last_name ($birth)\n";
}
```

Other types of statements for which no fetch loop is necessary are those that use MAX() or
MIN() to select a single row. But in all these cases, an even easier way to get a single-row result
is to use the database handle method selectrow_array(), which combines prepare(),
execute(), and row fetching into a single call. It returns an array (not a reference), or an

empty array if the query returned no row or an error occurred. The previous example can be rewritten like this using `selectrow_array()`:

```
my $stmt = "SELECT last_name, first_name, birth FROM president"
          . " WHERE birth = (SELECT MAX(birth) FROM president)";
my ($last_name, $first_name, $birth) = $dbh->selectrow_array ($stmt);
if (!defined ($last_name))
{
  print "Query returned no result\n";
}
else
{
  print "Most recently born president: $first_name $last_name ($birth)\n";
}
```

8.2.5.4 Working with Complete Result Sets

When you use a fetch loop, DBI provides no way to process the rows in any order other than that in which they are returned by the loop. Also, after you fetch a row, the previous row is lost unless you take steps to maintain it in memory. These behaviors aren't always desirable. For example, they're unsuitable if you need to make multiple passes through the rows to perform a statistical calculation. (Perhaps you want to go through the result set once to assess some general numeric characteristics of your data, and then step through the rows again performing a more specific analysis.)

It's possible to access your result set as a whole in a couple different ways. You can perform the usual fetch loop and save each row as you fetch it, or you can use a method that returns an entire result set all at once. Either way, you end up with a matrix containing one row per row in the result set, and as many columns as you selected. Then you can process elements of the matrix in any order you want, as many times as you want. The following discussion describes both approaches.

One way to use a fetch loop to capture the result set is to call `fetchrow_array()` and save an array of references to the rows. The following code does the same thing as the fetch-and-print loop in `dump_members.pl`, except that it saves all the rows, then prints the matrix. It illustrates how to determine the number of rows and columns in the matrix and how to access individual members of the matrix:

```
my @matrix = (); # array of array references

while (my @ary = $sth->fetchrow_array ()) # fetch each row
{
  push (@matrix, [ @ary ]); # save reference to just-fetched row
}

# determine dimensions of matrix
my $rows = scalar (@matrix);
my $cols = ($rows == 0 ? 0 : scalar (@{$matrix[0]}));
```

```
for (my $i = 0; $i < $rows; $i++)      # print each row
{
  my $delim = "";
  for (my $j = 0; $j < $cols; $j++)
  {
    $matrix[$i][$j] = "" if !defined ($matrix[$i][$j]); # NULL value?
    print $delim, $matrix[$i][$j];
    $delim = ",";
  }
  print "\n";
}
```

When you check the dimensions of the matrix, the number of rows must be determined first because calculation of the number of columns is contingent on whether the matrix is empty. If $rows is 0, the matrix is empty and $cols becomes 0 as well. Otherwise, calculate the number of columns as the number of elements in the first row, using the syntax @{$matrix[0]} to access the row as a whole.

The preceding example fetches each row as an array, then saves a reference to it. You might suppose that it would be more efficient to call fetchrow_arrayref() instead to retrieve row references directly:

```
my @matrix = (); # array of array references

while (my $ary_ref = $sth->fetchrow_arrayref ())
{
  push (@matrix, $ary_ref); # save reference to just-fetched row
}
```

That doesn't work, because fetchrow_arrayref() reuses the array to which the reference points. The resulting matrix is an array of references, each of which points to the same row—the final row retrieved. Therefore, if you want to construct a matrix by fetching a row at a time, use fetchrow_array() rather than fetchrow_arrayref().

As an alternative to using a fetch loop, invoke one of the DBI methods that return the entire result set. For example, fetchall_arrayref() returns a reference to an array of references, each of which points to the contents of one row of the result set. (That's a mouthful; it means that the return value is a reference to a matrix.) To use fetchall_arrayref(), call prepare() and execute(), then retrieve the result like this:

```
# fetch all rows as a reference to an array of references
my $matrix_ref = $sth->fetchall_arrayref ();
```

Determine the dimensions of the array and access its elements as follows:

```
# determine dimensions of matrix
my $rows = (!defined ($matrix_ref) ? 0 : scalar (@{$matrix_ref}));
my $cols = ($rows == 0 ? 0 : scalar (@{$matrix_ref->[0]}));

for (my $i = 0; $i < $rows; $i++)      # print each row
```

```
{
  my $delim = "";
  for (my $j = 0; $j < $cols; $j++)
  {
    $matrix_ref->[$i][$j] = "" if !defined ($matrix_ref->[$i][$j]); # NULL?
    print $delim, $matrix_ref->[$i][$j];
    $delim = ",";
  }
  print "\n";
}
```

fetchall_arrayref() returns a reference to an empty array if the result set is empty. The result is undef if an error occurs, so if you don't have RaiseError enabled, you must check the return value before you start using it.

The number of rows and columns is determined by whether the matrix is empty. To access an entire row $i of the matrix as an array, use the syntax @{$matrix_ref->[$i]}.

It's certainly simpler to use fetchall_arrayref() to retrieve a result set than to write a row-fetching loop, although the syntax for accessing array elements is a little trickier. A method that's similar to fetchall_arrayref() but that does even more work for you is selectall_arrayref(). This method performs the entire prepare(), execute(), fetch loop sequence for you. To use selectall_arrayref(), pass your statement directly to it using the database handle:

```
# fetch all rows as a reference to an array of references
my $matrix_ref = $dbh->selectall_arrayref ($stmt);

# determine dimensions of matrix
my $rows = (!defined ($matrix_ref) ? 0 : scalar (@{$matrix_ref}));
my $cols = ($rows == 0 ? 0 : scalar (@{$matrix_ref->[0]}));

for (my $i = 0; $i < $rows; $i++)        # print each row
{
  my $delim = "";
  for (my $j = 0; $j < $cols; $j++)
  {
    $matrix_ref->[$i][$j] = "" if !defined ($matrix_ref->[$i][$j]); # NULL?
    print $delim, $matrix_ref->[$i][$j];
    $delim = ",";
  }
  print "\n";
}
```

8.2.5.5 Checking for NULL Values

When you retrieve information from a database, you might need to distinguish between column values that are NULL from those that are zero or the empty string. This is easy to do because DBI returns NULL column values as undef. However, you must be sure to use the correct test. If you execute the following code fragment, it prints "false!" all three times:

```
$col_val = undef; if (!$col_val) { print "false!\n"; }
$col_val = 0;     if (!$col_val) { print "false!\n"; }
$col_val = "";    if (!$col_val) { print "false!\n"; }
```

What that demonstrates is that the form of the test is unable to distinguish between undef, 0, and the empty string. The next fragment prints "false!" for both tests, which shows that the test cannot distinguish undef from the empty string:

```
$col_val = undef; if ($col_val eq "") { print "false!\n"; }
$col_val = "";    if ($col_val eq "") { print "false!\n"; }
```

This fragment prints the same output, showing that the second test fails to distinguish 0 from the empty string:

```
$col_val = "";
if ($col_val eq "") { print "false!\n"; }
if ($col_val == 0)  { print "false!\n"; }
```

To distinguish between undef (NULL) column values and non-undef values, use defined(). After you know a value doesn't represent NULL, you can distinguish between other types of values using appropriate tests. For example:

```
if (!defined ($col_val)) { print "NULL\n"; }
elsif ($col_val eq "")   { print "empty string\n"; }
elsif ($col_val == 0)    { print "zero\n"; }
else                     { print "other\n"; }
```

It's important to perform the tests in the proper order because both the second and third comparisons are true if $col_val is an empty string. If you reverse the order of those comparisons, you'll incorrectly interpret empty strings as zero.

8.2.6   Quoting Special Characters in Statement Strings

Thus far, we have constructed statements in the most basic way possible, using simple quoted strings. That causes a problem at the Perl lexical level when your quoted strings contain quoted values. You can also have problems at the SQL level when you want to insert or select values that contain quotes, backslashes, or binary data. If you specify a statement as a Perl quoted string, you must escape any occurrences of the quoting character that occur within the statement string itself:

```
$stmt = 'INSERT INTO absence VALUES(14,\'2012-09-16\')';
$stmt = "INSERT INTO absence VALUES(14,\"2012-09-16\")";
```

Both Perl and MySQL permit you to quote strings using either single or double quotes, so you can sometimes avoid escaping by mixing quote characters:

```
$stmt = 'INSERT INTO absence VALUES(14,"2012-09-16")';
$stmt = "INSERT INTO absence VALUES(14,'2012-09-16')";
```

However, you must take care that the strings will be interpreted as you want. Consider these factors:

- The two types of quotes are not equivalent in Perl. Variable references are interpreted only within double quotes. Therefore, single quotes are not very useful when you want to construct statements by embedding variable references in the statement string. For example, if the value of $var is 14, the following two strings are not equivalent:

```
"SELECT * FROM member WHERE member_id = $var"
'SELECT * FROM member WHERE member_id = $var'
```

The resulting strings as Perl interprets them are as follows:

```
"SELECT * FROM member WHERE member_id = 14"
'SELECT * FROM member WHERE member_id = $var'
```

Clearly, the first string is more like something you'd want to pass to the MySQL server. For the second, the server will interpret $var as the literal name of a column in the member table.

- Single quotes and double quotes are not always equivalent in MySQL. If the server is running with the ANSI_QUOTES SQL mode disabled, you can indeed use either type of quote to quote a string. But with ANSI_QUOTES enabled, strings must be quoted with single quotes; double quotes can be used only for quoting identifiers such as database or table names. Consequently, it's safest to quote strings with single quotes, because that works regardless of the ANSI_QUOTES setting.

At the Perl level, an alternative to quoting strings with double quotes is to use the qq{} construct, which tells Perl to treat everything between qq{ and } as a double-quoted string. (Think of double-q as meaning "double-quote.") For example, these two lines are equivalent:

```
$date = "2012-09-16";
$date = qq{2012-09-16};
```

Using qq{}, you can construct statements without thinking so much about quoting issues because you can use quote characters (single or double) freely within the statement string without having to escape them. In addition, variable references are interpreted. Both properties of qq{} are illustrated by the following INSERT statement:

```
$id = 14;
$date = "2012-09-16";
$stmt = qq{INSERT INTO absence VALUES($id,'$date')};
```

You need not use '{' and '}' as the qq delimiters. Other forms, such as qq() and qq//, will work, too, as long as the closing delimiter doesn't occur within the string. I prefer qq{} because the '}' character is less likely than ')' or '/' to occur within the text of the statement and be mistaken for the end of the statement string. For example, ')' occurs within the INSERT statement just shown, so qq() would not be a useful construct for quoting the statement string.

The qq{} construct can cross line boundaries, which is useful if you want to make the statement string stand out from the surrounding Perl code:

```
$id = 14;
$date = "2012-09-16";
$stmt = qq{
  INSERT INTO absence VALUES($id,'$date')
};
```

This is also useful if you simply want to format your statement on multiple lines to make it more readable. For example, the SELECT statement in the dump_members.pl script looks like this:

```
$sth = $dbh->prepare ("SELECT last_name, first_name, suffix, email,"
    . " street, city, state, zip, phone FROM member ORDER BY last_name");
```

With qq{}, it could be written like this instead:

```
$sth = $dbh->prepare (qq{
        SELECT
          last_name, first_name, suffix, email,
          street, city, state, zip, phone
        FROM member
        ORDER BY last_name
      });
```

It's true that double-quoted strings can cross line boundaries, too. But I find that qq{ and } stand out better than two lone '"' characters and make the statement easier to read. This book uses both forms; see which you prefer.

The qq{} construct handles quoting issues at the Perl lexical level so that you can use quotes in a string easily without having Perl complain about them. However, you must also think about SQL-level syntax. Consider this attempt to insert a row into the member table:

```
$last = "O'Malley";
$first = "Brian";
$expiration = "2013-09-01";
$rows = $dbh->do (qq{
  INSERT INTO member (last_name,first_name,expiration)
  VALUES('$last','$first','$expiration')
});
```

The resulting string that do() sends to MySQL looks like this:

```
INSERT INTO member (last_name,first_name,expiration)
VALUES('O'Malley','Brian','2013-09-01')
```

That is not legal SQL because for 'O'Malley', a single quote occurs within a single-quoted string. We encountered this quoting problem earlier in Chapter 7, "Writing MySQL Programs Using C." There we dealt with the issue by using the mysql_real_escape_string() function. DBI provides a similar mechanism: For each quoted value that you want to use literally in a statement, call the quote() method and use its return value instead. The preceding example is more properly written as follows:

```
$last = $dbh->quote ("O'Malley");
$first = $dbh->quote ("Brian");
$expiration = $dbh->quote ("2013-09-01");
$rows = $dbh->do (qq{
  INSERT INTO member (last_name,first_name,expiration)
  VALUES($last,$first,$expiration)
});
```

Now the string that do() sends to MySQL looks like this, with the quote that occurs within the quoted string properly escaped:

```
INSERT INTO member (last_name,first_name,expiration)
VALUES('O\'Malley','Brian','2013-09-01')
```

Note that when you refer to $last and $first in the statement string, you do not add any surrounding quotes; the quote() method supplies them for you. If you add quotes yourself, your statement will have too many of them, as shown by the following example:

```
$value = "paul";
$quoted_value = $dbh->quote ($value);

print "The quoted value is: $quoted_value\n";
print "The quoted value is: '$quoted_value'\n";
```

These statements produce the following output:

```
The quoted value is: 'paul'
The quoted value is: ''paul''
```

In the second case, the string contains too many quotes.

8.2.7   Placeholders and Prepared Statements

In the preceding sections, we constructed statements by putting data values to be inserted or used as selection criteria directly into the statement string. It's not necessary to do this. DBI enables you to use special markers called "placeholders" within a statement string and supply the values to be used in place of those markers when the statement is executed. This is called "binding the values to the statement." By doing this, you get the character-quoting benefits of the quote() method without having to invoke quote() explicitly. In addition, if you're executing a statement over and over within a loop, you can prepare it first, then execute it multiple times. This avoids the overhead of preparing the statement before each execution.

As an illustration of how placeholders work, suppose that you're beginning a new semester at school and you want to clear out the student table for your gradebook and initialize it with new students by using a list of student names contained in a file. Without placeholders, you could delete the existing table contents and load the new names like this:

```
$dbh->do (qq{ DELETE FROM student } );   # delete existing rows
while (<>)                               # read each input line,
```

```
{                                         # use it to add a new row
  chomp;
  $_ = $dbh->quote ($_);
  $dbh->do (qq{ INSERT INTO student SET name = $_ });
}
```

This approach requires that you handle special characters in the data values yourself by calling quote(). It's also inefficient, because the basic form of the INSERT statement is the same each time, and do() calls prepare() and execute() each time through the loop. It's more efficient to call prepare() a single time to set up the INSERT before entering the loop and invoke only execute() within the loop. That avoids all invocations of prepare() but one. DBI enables this to be done as follows:

```
$dbh->do (qq{ DELETE FROM student } );  # delete existing rows
my $sth = $dbh->prepare (qq{ INSERT INTO student SET name = ? });
while (<>)                               # read each input line,
{                                        # use it to add a new row
  chomp;
  $sth->execute ($_);
}
```

In general, if you find yourself calling do() inside a loop, it's better to invoke prepare() prior to the loop and execute() inside it. Note the '?' character in the INSERT statement. That's the placeholder. When you invoke execute(), pass the value to be substituted for the placeholder when the statement is sent to the server. DBI automatically quotes special characters in the value, so there is no need to call quote().

Some things to note about placeholders:

- Do not enclose the placeholder character in quotes within the statement string. If you do, DBI will not recognize it as a placeholder.

- Do not use the quote() method to specify placeholder values, or you will get extra quotes in the values you're inserting.

- You can have more than one placeholder in a statement string, but be sure to pass as many values to execute() as there are placeholder markers.

- Each placeholder must specify a single value, not a list of values. For example, to specify multiple data values, you cannot prepare and execute a statement like this:

```
my $sth = $dbh->prepare (qq{
  INSERT INTO member last_name, first_name VALUES(?)
});
$sth->execute ("Adams,Bill,2014-07-19");
```

  You must specify the values separately and provide one placeholder for each:

```
my $sth = $dbh->prepare (qq{
  INSERT INTO member last_name, first_name VALUES(?,?,?)
});
$sth->execute ("Adams","Bill","2014-07-19");
```

- To specify NULL as a placeholder value, use undef.

- Placeholders and quote() are intended only for data values. Do not try to use a placeholder for keywords such as SELECT or for identifiers such as database, table, or column names. It won't work because the keyword or identifier will be placed into the statement surrounded by quotes, and the statement will fail with a syntax error.

For some database servers, you get another performance benefit from using placeholders, in addition to improved efficiency in loops. Certain servers cache prepared statements and possibly the statement execution plan. That way, if the same statement is received by the server later, it can be reused and processed more quickly without the initial preparation overhead. Statement caching is especially helpful for complex SELECT statements because it may take some time to prepare the statement and generate a good execution plan. Placeholders give you a better chance at making the statement cacheable because they make statements more generic than statements constructed by embedding specific data values directly in the statement string.

MySQL does not cache execution plans. MySQL has a query cache, but it operates by caching result sets for query strings, not execution plans. For more information, see Section 12.7.3, "Using the Query Cache."

By default, MySQL does not cache prepared statements, either. Parameter binding to placeholders takes place on the client side within the DBD::mysql module. However, the binary protocol implemented in the C client library does permit statements to be prepared on the server side and parameter binding to be handled by the server.

DBD::mysql can take advantage of this capability. To turn on server-side prepared statements and parameter binding, all you need to do is enable the mysql_server_prepare option. For example, given a database handle $dbh, this can be done as follows:

```
$dbh->{mysql_server_prepare} = 1;
```

To disable server-side prepared statements, set the option to 0.

Even if you don't use MySQL's server-side capabilities for prepared statements, it still can be beneficial to write your statements using placeholders: When you port a script for use with a database server that supports execution plan caching, it executes statements with placeholders more efficiently than those without.

The Mystery undef

Some DBI methods like do() and selectrow_array() that execute a statement string enable you to provide placeholder values to be bound to any '?' characters in the statement. For example, you can update a row like this:

```
my $rows = $dbh->do (
          "UPDATE member SET expiration = ? WHERE member_id = ?",
          undef, "2007-01-01", 14);
```

Or fetch a row like this:

```
my $ref = $dbh->selectrow_arrayref (
            "SELECT * FROM member WHERE member_id = ?",
            undef, 14);
```

Observe that, in both cases, the placeholder values are preceded by a mysterious `undef` argument that appears to do nothing. The reason it's there is that, for statement-execution methods that support placeholder arguments, those arguments are preceded by another argument that can be used to specify statement-processing attributes. Such attributes are rarely (if ever) used, but the argument still must be present, so just specify it as `undef`.

8.2.8 Binding Query Results to Script Variables

Placeholders enable you to substitute values into a statement string at statement execution time. In other words, you can parameterize the "input" to the statement. DBI also provides a corresponding output operation called "parameter binding" that enables you to parameterize the "output" by retrieving column values into variables automatically when you fetch a row without having to assign values to the variables yourself.

Suppose that you have a query to retrieve names from the `member` table. You can tell DBI to assign the values of the selected columns to Perl variables. When you fetch a row, the variables are automatically updated with the corresponding column values, which makes the retrieval very efficient. Here's an example that shows how to bind the columns to variables and access them in the fetch loop:

```
my ($last_name, $first_name, $suffix);
my $sth = $dbh->prepare (qq{
            SELECT last_name, first_name, suffix
            FROM member ORDER BY last_name, first_name
            });
$sth->execute ();
$sth->bind_col (1, \$last_name);
$sth->bind_col (2, \$first_name);
$sth->bind_col (3, \$suffix);
print "$last_name, $first_name, $suffix\n" while $sth->fetch ();
```

Call `bind_col()` after `execute()` and before fetching rows. Each call should specify a column number and a reference to the variable to be associated with the column. Column numbers begin with 1.

As an alternative to individual calls to `bind_col()`, you can pass all the variable references in a single call to `bind_columns()`:

```
my ($last_name, $first_name, $suffix);
my $sth = $dbh->prepare (qq{
            SELECT last_name, first_name, suffix
            FROM member ORDER BY last_name, first_name
```

```
        });
$sth->execute ();
$sth->bind_columns (\$last_name, \$first_name, \$suffix);
print "$last_name, $first_name, $suffix\n" while $sth->fetch ();
```

Call `bind_columns()` after `execute()` and before fetching rows.

8.2.9   Specifying Connection Parameters

The most direct way to establish a server connection is to specify all connection parameters as arguments to the `connect()` method:

```
my $dsn = "DBI:mysql:db_name:host_name";
my $dbh = DBI->connect ($dsn, user_name, password);
```

If you leave out connection parameters, DBI attempts to determine what values to use as follows:

- The `DBI_DSN` environment variable is used if defined and the data source name (DSN) is undefined or is the empty string. The `DBI_USER` and `DBI_PASS` environment variables are used if defined and the username and password are undefined (but not if they are the empty string). Under Windows, the `USER` variable is used if the username is undefined.
- If you leave out the hostname, DBI attempts to connect to the local host.
- If you specify `undef` or an empty string for the username, it defaults to your login name under Unix and `ODBC` under Windows.
- If you specify `undef` or an empty string for the password, no password is sent.

You can specify certain options in the DSN by appending them to the initial part of the string, each preceded by a semicolon. For example, the `mysql_read_default_file` option specifies an option file pathname:

```
my $dsn = "DBI:mysql:sampdb;mysql_read_default_file=/home/paul/.my.cnf";
```

When the script executes, it reads the named file for connection parameters. Suppose that `/home/paul/.my.cnf` has the following contents:

```
[client]
host=localhost
user=sampadm
password=secret
```

In this case, the `connect()` call attempts to connect to the MySQL server on `localhost` as user `sampadm` with password `secret`. Under Unix, you can tell your script to use the option file that belongs to whichever user happens to be running it by parameterizing the filename like this:

```
my $dsn = "DBI:mysql:sampdb;mysql_read_default_file=$ENV{HOME}/.my.cnf";
```

$ENV{HOME} contains the pathname to the home directory of the user running the script, so the connection parameters that it uses are pulled from that user's own option file. By writing a script in this way, you need not embed connection parameters literally in the script.

Using mysql_read_default_file causes the script to read only the named option file, which may be undesirable if you want it to look for parameters in system-wide option files as well (such as /etc/my.cnf under Unix or C:\my.ini under Windows). To have the script read all the standard option files for connection parameters, use mysql_read_default_group instead. This option causes parameters in the [client] group to be used, as well as in the group that you specify in the option's value. For example, if you have options that are specific to your sampdb-related scripts, you can list them in a [sampdb] group, then use a data source value like this:

```
my $dsn = "DBI:mysql:sampdb;mysql_read_default_group=sampdb";
```

To read only the [client] group from the standard option files, specify the option like this:

```
my $dsn = "DBI:mysql:sampdb;mysql_read_default_group=client";
```

For more details on options for specifying the data source string, see Appendix H, "Perl DBI API Reference." For more information on the format of MySQL option files, see Appendix F, "MySQL Program Reference."

One difficulty with using mysql_read_default_file on Windows is that file pathnames typically begin with a drive letter and a colon. That's a problem, because DBI interprets colon as the character that separates parts of the DSN string. It's possible to work around this, although the method is ugly:

1. Use chdir() to change location to the root directory of the drive where the option file is located, so that pathnames specified without a drive letter are interpreted relative to that drive.

2. Specify the filename as the value of the mysql_read_default_file option in the DSN, but without the leading drive letter or colon.

3. If it's necessary to leave the current directory undisturbed by the connect operation, save the current directory pathname before calling connect(), then chdir() back to it after connecting.

The following code fragment shows how to do this if you want to use the option file C:\my.ini. (Note that backslashes in Windows pathnames are specified as slashes in Perl strings.)

```
# save current directory pathname
use Cwd;
my $orig_dir = cwd ();
# change location to root dir of drive where file is located
chdir ("C:/") or die "Cannot chdir: $!\n";
# connect using parameters in C:\my.ini
my $dsn = "DBI:mysql:sampdb:localhost;mysql_read_default_file=/my.ini";
```

```
my %conn_attrs = (RaiseError => 1, PrintError => 0, AutoCommit => 1);
my $dbh = DBI->connect ($dsn, undef, undef, \%conn_attrs);
# change location back to original directory
chdir ($orig_dir) or die "Cannot chdir: $!\n";
```

Using an option file doesn't prevent you from specifying connection parameters in the connect() call (for example, if you want the script to connect as a particular user). Any explicit hostname, username, and password values specified in the connect() call override connection parameters found in the option file. For example, you might want your script to parse options such as --host and --user from the command line and use those values, if they are given, in preference to any found in an option file. That would be useful because it's the way the standard MySQL clients behave. Your DBI scripts would therefore be consistent with that behavior.

For the remaining command-line scripts that we develop in this chapter, I'll use some standard connection setup and teardown code. I'll just show it once here so that we can concentrate on the main body of each script as we write it:

```
#!/usr/bin/perl

use strict;
use warnings;
use DBI;

# parse connection parameters from command line if given

use Getopt::Long;
$Getopt::Long::ignorecase = 0; # options are case sensitive
$Getopt::Long::bundling = 1;   # -uname = -u name, not -u -n -a -m -e

# default parameters - all undefined initially
my ($host_name, $password, $port_num, $socket_name, $user_name);

GetOptions (
   # =i means an integer value is required after option
   # =s means a string value is required after option
   "host|h=s"     => \$host_name,
   "password|p=s" => \$password,
   "port|P=i"     => \$port_num,
   "socket|S=s"   => \$socket_name,
   "user|u=s"     => \$user_name
) or exit (1);

# construct data source
my $dsn = "DBI:mysql:sampdb";
$dsn .= ";host=$host_name" if $host_name;
$dsn .= ";port=$port_num" if $port_num;
$dsn .= ";mysql_socket=$socket_name" if $socket_name;
```

```
$dsn .= ";mysql_read_default_group=client";

# connect to server
my %conn_attrs = (RaiseError => 1, PrintError => 0, AutoCommit => 1);
my $dbh = DBI->connect ($dsn, $user_name, $password, \%conn_attrs);
```

This code initializes DBI, looks for connection parameters on the command line, and makes the connection to the MySQL server using parameters from the command line or found in the [client] group in the standard option files. If your connection parameters are listed in your option file, you won't have to enter them when you run a script that uses this code.

The final part of each script will be similar, too; it simply terminates the connection before exiting:

```
$dbh->disconnect ();
```

When we get to Web programming, Section 8.4, "Using DBI in Web Applications," we'll modify the connection setup code a bit, but the basic idea will be similar.

There is one unfortunate difference between the way the standard MySQL clients and the Getopt module handle command-line options. The standard clients have special option-processing code that permits a password option (--password or -p) to be specified with or without an immediately following password value, and to prompt for a password if the value is not given.

With Getopt, if you try to make the password value optional for --password and -p, you cannot unambiguously specify the option with no value unless it is either the last argument on the command line or is immediately followed by another option. Suppose that you have a script that expects a table name argument to follow the options. If the script is invoked as follows, Getopt interprets mytbl as the password value rather than prompting for a password:

```
% ./myscript.pl -u paul -p mytbl
```

To avoid this kind of problem, the code in the Perl framework just shown requires a password option, if given, to be specified with a value.

8.2.10   Debugging

To debug a malfunctioning DBI script, two techniques are commonly used, either alone or in tandem. First, sprinkle print statements throughout your script. This enables you to tailor your debugging output the way you want it, but you must add the statements manually. Second, use DBI's built-in tracing capabilities. This is more general and more systematic, and it occurs automatically after you turn it on. DBI tracing also shows you information about the operation of the driver that you cannot get otherwise.

8.2.10.1   Debugging Using Print Statements

Here's a common question: "I have a statement that works fine when I execute it using the mysql program, but it doesn't work from my DBI script. How come?" It's not unusual to find that the DBI script is issuing a different statement than you think. If you print a statement

before executing it, you might be surprised to see what you're actually sending to the server.
Suppose that a statement as you type it into `mysql` looks like this:

```
mysql> INSERT INTO member (last_name,first_name,expiration)
    -> VALUES('Brown','Marcia','2012-06-03');
```

Then you try the same thing in a DBI script (leaving out the statement-terminating semicolon,
of course):

```
$last = "Brown";
$first = "Marcia";
$expiration = "2012-06-03";
$stmt = qq{
  INSERT INTO member (last_name,first_name,expiration)
  VALUES($last,$first,$expiration)
};
$rows = $dbh->do ($stmt);
```

That doesn't work, even though it's the same statement. Or is it? Try printing it:

```
print "$stmt\n";
```

Here is the result:

```
INSERT INTO member (last_name,first_name,expiration)
VALUES(Brown,Marcia,2012-06-03)
```

From this output, you can see that the statement is not the same at all. There are no quotes
around the values in the `VALUES()` list. One way to specify the statement properly is like this,
using `quote()`:

```
$last = $dbh->quote ("Brown");
$first = $dbh->quote ("Marcia");
$expiration = $dbh->quote ("2012-06-03");
$stmt = qq{
  INSERT INTO member (last_name,first_name,expiration)
  VALUES($last,$first,$expiration)
};
$rows = $dbh->do ($stmt);
```

Alternatively, specify the statement using placeholders and pass the values to be inserted into it
as arguments to the `do()` method:

```
$last = "Brown";
$first = "Marcia";
$expiration = "2012-06-03";
$stmt = qq{
  INSERT INTO member (last_name,first_name,expiration)
  VALUES(?,?,?)
};
$rows = $dbh->do ($stmt, undef, $last, $first, $expiration);
```

Unfortunately, when you use the latter approach, you cannot see what the complete statement looks like by printing it because the placeholder values aren't evaluated until you invoke `do()`. When you use placeholders, tracing may be a more helpful debugging method.

8.2.10.2   Debugging Using Tracing

DBI offers a tracing mechanism that generates debugging information to help you figure out why a script doesn't work properly. Trace levels range from 0 (off) to 15 (maximum information). Generally, trace levels 1 through 4 are the most useful. For example, a level 2 trace shows you the text of statements that you're executing (including the result of placeholder substitutions), the result of calls to `quote()`, and so forth. This can be of immense help in tracking down a problem.

You can control tracing from within individual scripts using the `trace()` method, or by setting the `DBI_TRACE` environment variable to affect tracing for all DBI scripts you run.

To use the `trace()` call, pass a trace level argument and optionally a filename. If you specify no filename, all trace output goes to `STDERR`; otherwise, it goes to the named file. The following call sets up a level 1 trace to `STDERR`:

```
DBI->trace (1);
```

This call sets up a level 2 trace to a file named `trace.out`:

```
DBI->trace (2, "trace.out");
```

To disable tracing, specify a trace level of zero:

```
DBI->trace (0);
```

With `DBI->trace()`, all DBI operations are traced. For a more fine-grained approach, enable tracing at the individual handle level. This is useful when you have a good idea where a problem in your script lies and you don't want to wade through the trace output for everything that occurs up to that point. For example, if you're having problems with a particular `SELECT` query, trace the statement handle associated with the query:

```
$sth = $dbh->prepare (qq{ SELECT ... }); # create the statement handle
$sth->trace (1);                         # enable tracing on the statement
$sth->execute ();
```

If you specify a filename argument to any `trace()` call, whether for DBI as a whole or for an individual handle, all trace output goes to that file.

The `TraceLevel` attribute is an alternative to the `trace()` method. This attribute enables you to set or get the trace level for a given handle:

```
$dbh->{TraceLevel} = 3;                   # set database handle trace level
my $cur_level = $sth->{TraceLevel};       # get statement handle trace level
```

To turn on tracing globally so that it takes effect for all DBI scripts you run, set the `DBI_TRACE` environment variable from your shell. The syntax for this depends on your shell:

- For `csh` or `tcsh`:

  `% setenv DBI_TRACE value`

- For `sh`, `bash`, or `ksh`:

  `$ export DBI_TRACE=value`

- For Windows:

  `C:\> set DBI_TRACE=value`

The format of `value` is the same for all shells: a number `n` to turn on tracing at level `n` to `STDERR`, a filename to turn on level 2 tracing to the named file, or `n=file_name` to turn on level `n` tracing to the named file. Here are some examples, using `tcsh` syntax:

- A level 1 trace to `STDERR`:

  `% setenv DBI_TRACE 1`

- A level 1 trace to the file `trace.out`:

  `% setenv DBI_TRACE 1=trace.out`

- A level 2 trace to the file `trace.out`:

  `% setenv DBI_TRACE trace.out`

Using `DBI_TRACE` is advantageous in that you can enable DBI script tracing without making any changes to your scripts. But if you enable tracing to a file from your shell, be sure to disable it after you resolve the problem. Debugging output is appended to the trace file without overwriting it, so the file can become quite large if you're not careful. It's a particularly bad idea to define `DBI_TRACE` in a shell startup file such as `.cshrc`, `.tcshrc`, `.login`, or `.profile`!

To turn off `DBI_TRACE` for various command interpreters, use any of the commands shown:

- For `csh` or `tcsh`:

  `% setenv DBI_TRACE 0`
  `% unsetenv DBI_TRACE`

- For `sh`, `bash`, or `ksh`:

  `$ unset DBI_TRACE`
  `$ export DBI_TRACE=0`

- For Windows:

  `C:\> unset DBI_TRACE`
  `C:\> set DBI_TRACE=0`

8.2.11   Using Result Set Metadata

DBI provides access to result set metadata—that is, descriptive information about the rows selected by a query. To get this information, access the attributes of the statement handle associated with the query that generated the result set. Some of these are standard DBI attributes that are available across all database drivers (such as NUM_OF_FIELDS, the number of columns in the result set). Others, which are MySQL-specific, are provided by DBD::mysql, the MySQL driver for DBI. These attributes, such as mysql_max_length, which tells you the maximum width of the values in each column, are not applicable to other database systems. To the extent that you use any of the MySQL-specific attributes, you risk making your scripts nonportable to other databases. On the other hand, they can make it easier to get the information you want.

You must ask for metadata at the right time. Generally, result set attributes are not available for a SELECT statement until after you've invoked prepare() and execute(). In addition, attributes may become invalid after you reach the end of the result set with a row-fetching function or after you invoke finish().

The following example shows how to use one of the MySQL-specific metadata attributes, mysql_max_length, in conjunction with the more general attributes NUM_OF_FIELDS, which indicates the number of columns in the result set, and NAME, which holds their names. We can combine the information provided by these attributes to write a script, tabular.pl, that produces output from SELECT queries in the same tabular (boxed) style that you get when you run the mysql client program in interactive mode. The main body of tabular.pl follows. You can replace the SELECT statement with any other; the output-writing routines are independent of the particular statement.

```
my $sth = $dbh->prepare (qq{
        SELECT last_name, first_name, suffix, city, state
        FROM president ORDER BY last_name, first_name
    });
$sth->execute (); # attributes should be available after this call

# actual maximum widths of column values in result set
my @wid = @{$sth->{mysql_max_length}};
# number of columns in result set
my $ncols = $sth->{NUM_OF_FIELDS};

# adjust column widths if data values are narrower than column headings,
# or than the word "NULL" for columns that can be NULL
for (my $i = 0; $i < $ncols; $i++)
{
  my $name_wid = length ($sth->{NAME}->[$i]);
  $wid[$i] = $name_wid if $wid[$i] < $name_wid;
  $wid[$i] = 4 if $sth->{NULLABLE}->[$i] && $wid[$i] < 4;
}

# print tabular-format output
print_dashes (\@wid, $ncols);             # row of dashes
print_row ($sth->{NAME}, \@wid, $ncols);  # column headings
```

```
print_dashes (\@wid, $ncols);              # row of dashes
while (my $ary_ref = $sth->fetchrow_arrayref ())
{
  print_row ($ary_ref, \@wid, $ncols);     # row data values
}
print_dashes (\@wid, $ncols);              # row of dashes
```

After the statement has been initiated with `execute()`, we can grab the metadata we need. `$sth->{NUM_OF_FIELDS}` is a scalar value indicating how many columns are in the result set. `$sth->{NAME}` and `$sth->{mysql_max_length}` give us the column names and maximum width of each column's values. The value of each of these two attributes is a reference to an array that contains an element for each column of the result set, in the order that columns are named in the statement.

The remaining calculations are very much like those used for the `exec_stmt` program developed in Chapter 7, "Writing MySQL Programs Using C." For example, to avoid misaligned output, we adjust the column width values upward if the name of a column is wider than any of the data values in the column.

The output functions, `print_dashes()` and `print_row()`, also are similar to the corresponding code in `exec_stmt`:

```
sub print_dashes
{
my $wid_ary_ref = shift;  # reference to array of column widths
my $cols = shift;         # number of columns

  for (my $i = 0; $i < $cols; $i++)
  {
    print "+", "-" x ($wid_ary_ref->[$i]+2);
  }
  print "+\n";
}


# print row of data.  (doesn't right-align numeric columns)

sub print_row
{
my $val_ary_ref = shift;  # reference to array of column values
my $wid_ary_ref = shift;  # reference to array of column widths
my $cols = shift;         # number of columns

  for (my $i = 0; $i < $cols; $i++)
  {
    printf "| %-*s ", $wid_ary_ref->[$i],
           defined ($val_ary_ref->[$i]) ? $val_ary_ref->[$i] : "NULL";
  }
  print "|\n";
}
```

The output from `tabular.pl` looks like this:

```
+------------+---------------+--------+--------------------+-------+
| last_name  | first_name    | suffix | city               | state |
+------------+---------------+--------+--------------------+-------+
| Adams      | John          | NULL   | Braintree          | MA    |
| Adams      | John Quincy   | NULL   | Braintree          | MA    |
| Arthur     | Chester A.    | NULL   | Fairfield          | VT    |
| Buchanan   | James         | NULL   | Mercersburg        | PA    |
| Bush       | George H.W.   | NULL   | Milton             | MA    |
| Bush       | George W.     | NULL   | New Haven          | CT    |
| Carter     | James E.      | Jr.    | Plains             | GA    |
...
```

Our next script uses column metadata to produce output in a different format. This script, `show_member.pl`, enables you to take a quick look at Historical League member entries without entering any queries. Given a member's last name, it displays the selected entry like this:

```
% ./show_member.pl artel
member_id:  63
last_name:  Artel
first_name: Mike
suffix:
expiration: 2016-04-16
email:      mike_artel@venus.org
street:     4264 Lovering Rd.
city:       Miami
state:      FL
zip:        12777
phone:      075-961-0712
interests:  Civil Rights,Education,Revolutionary War
```

You can also invoke `show_member.pl` using a membership number, or using a SQL pattern to match several last names. The following commands show the entry for member 23 or the entries for members with last names that start with "C":

```
% ./show_member.pl 23
% ./show_member.pl C%
```

The main body of the `show_member.pl` script follows. It uses the NAME attribute to determine the labels to use for each row of output, and the NUM_OF_FIELDS attribute to find out how many columns the result set contains:

```
my $count = 0;   # number of entries printed so far
my @label = ();  # column label array
my $label_wid = 0;

while (@ARGV)    # run query for each argument on command line
{
```

```perl
my $arg = shift (@ARGV);

# default is a pattern search by last name...
my $clause = "last_name LIKE " . $dbh->quote ($arg);
# ...but do an ID search instead if argument is numeric
$clause = "member_id = " . $dbh->quote ($arg) if $arg =~ /^\d+$/;

# issue query
my $sth = $dbh->prepare (qq{
            SELECT * FROM member
            WHERE $clause
            ORDER BY last_name, first_name
          });
$sth->execute ();

# get column names to use for labels and
# determine max column name width for formatting
# (but do this only the first time through the loop)
if ($label_wid == 0)
{
  @label = @{$sth->{NAME}};
  foreach my $label (@label)
  {
    $label_wid = length ($label) if $label_wid < length ($label);
  }
}

# read and display query result
my $matches = 0;
while (my @ary = $sth->fetchrow_array ())
{
  # print newline before 2nd and subsequent entries
  print "\n" if ++$count > 1;
  foreach (my $i = 0; $i < $sth->{NUM_OF_FIELDS}; $i++)
  {
    # print label
    printf "%-*s", $label_wid+1, $label[$i] . ":";
    # print value, if there is one
    print " ", $ary[$i] if defined ($ary[$i]);
    print "\n";
  }
  ++$matches;
}
print "\nNo match was found for \"$arg\"\n" if $matches == 0;
}
```

The purpose of `show_member.pl` is to show the entire contents of an entry, no matter what the fields are. By using `SELECT *` to retrieve all the columns and the `NAME` attribute to find out what they are, this script works without modification even if columns are added to or dropped from the `member` table.

If you just want to know what columns a table contains without retrieving any rows, you can issue this statement:

```
SELECT * FROM tbl_name WHERE FALSE
```

The `WHERE FALSE` clause is false for all rows, so executing the statement has the effect of generating column metadata but returning no rows. After invoking `prepare()` and `execute()` in the usual way for the statement, you can get the column names from `@{$sth->{NAME}}`. Be aware that although this little trick of using an "empty" query works for MySQL, it's not portable and may not work for other database systems.

For more information on the attributes provided by DBI and by DBD::mysql, see Appendix H, "Perl DBI API Reference." It's up to you to determine whether you want to strive for portability by avoiding MySQL-specific attributes, or take advantage of them at the cost of portability.

8.2.12   Performing Transactions

One way to perform transactions in a DBI script is to issue explicit `SET autocommit`, `START TRANSACTION`, `COMMIT`, and `ROLLBACK` statements. (Section 2.12, "Performing Transactions," describes these statements.) However, DBI provides a transactional abstraction (expressed in terms of DBI methods and attributes) that issues the proper transaction-related SQL statements for you automatically. It's also portable to other database systems that support transactions, whereas the SQL statements may not be.

To use the DBI transaction mechanism, your application must use tables that are of a transaction-safe type. If they are not, use `ALTER TABLE` to change them. For example, to change a given table *tbl_name* to be an InnoDB table, use this statement:

```
ALTER TABLE tbl_name ENGINE=InnoDB;
```

Transactional processing in DBI follows this general procedure:

1. Disable (or temporarily suspend) autocommit mode so that SQL statements aren't committed until you commit them yourself.

2. Issue the statements that are part of a transaction, but do so within an `eval` block that executes with `RaiseError` enabled and `PrintError` disabled so that any errors terminate the block without printing errors. If the block executes successfully, the last operation within it should be to invoke `commit()` to commit the transaction.

3. When the `eval` block finishes, check its termination status. If an error occurred, invoke `rollback()` to cancel the transaction (and report the error if that's appropriate).

4. Restore the autocommit mode and error-handling attributes as necessary.

The following example implements this approach. It's based on a scenario from Chapter 2, "Using SQL to Manage Data," that showed how to issue transaction-related statements manually from the `mysql` client. The scenario is one in which you discover that you've mistakenly mixed up two scores for students in the `score` table and need to switch them: Student 8 has been given a score of 18, student 9 has been given a score of 13, and the scores should be the other way around. The two UPDATE statements needed to correct this problem are as follows:

```
UPDATE score SET score = 13 WHERE event_id = 5 AND student_id = 8;
UPDATE score SET score = 18 WHERE event_id = 5 AND student_id = 9;
```

You want to update both rows with the correct scores, but both updates must succeed as a unit. The example in the earlier chapter surrounded the updates by explicit SQL statements for setting the autocommit mode, committing, and rolling back. Within a Perl script that uses the DBI transaction mechanism, perform the updates as follows:

```perl
my $orig_re = $dbh->{RaiseError}; # save error-handling attributes
my $orig_pe = $dbh->{PrintError};
my $orig_ac = $dbh->{AutoCommit}; # save auto-commit mode

$dbh->{RaiseError} = 1;           # cause errors to raise exceptions
$dbh->{PrintError} = 0;           # but suppress error messages
$dbh->{AutoCommit} = 0;           # don't commit until we say so

eval
{
  # issue the statements that are part of the transaction
  my $sth = $dbh->prepare (qq{
            UPDATE score SET score = ?
            WHERE event_id = ? AND student_id = ?
          });
  $sth->execute (13, 5, 8);
  $sth->execute (18, 5, 9);
  $dbh->commit ();                # commit the transaction
};
if ($@)                           # did the transaction fail?
{
  print "A transaction error occurred: $@\n";
  # roll back, but use eval to trap rollback failure
  eval { $dbh->rollback (); }
}

$dbh->{AutoCommit} = $orig_ac;    # restore auto-commit mode
$dbh->{RaiseError} = $orig_re;    # restore error-handling attributes
$dbh->{PrintError} = $orig_pe;
```

The `eval` block does the work of performing the transaction, and its termination status is available in the `$@` variable. If the UPDATE statements and the `commit()` method execute without error, `$@` is empty. Otherwise, the eval block fails and `$@` holds the error message. In that case, the code following the `eval` prints the message and invokes `rollback()` to cancel the transaction. (The rollback operation occurs within its own `eval` block to prevent it from terminating the script if it fails.)

In this chapter, DBI scripts generally use an error-handling mode of `RaiseError` enabled and `PrintError` disabled. This means that they already have the values required for performing transactions, and thus it really wouldn't have been necessary to save, set, and restore those two attributes as shown in the example. However, doing so is a general-purpose approach that works even when you're not sure what the error-handling attribute settings are.

8.3   Putting DBI to Work

At this point you've seen a number of the concepts involved in DBI programming, so let's move on to some of the things we wanted to be able to do with our sample database. Of the goals outlined initially in Chapter 1, "Getting Started with MySQL," we'll tackle those following by writing DBI scripts:

- For the grade-keeping project, be able to retrieve scores for any given quiz or test.
- For the Historical League, be able to do the following:
  - Produce the member directory in different formats. We want a names-only list for use in the program distributed at the League's annual meeting, and in a format we can use for generating the printed directory.
  - Find League members whose memberships expire soon and send them email to let them know they need to renew.
  - Edit member entries. (When they renew their memberships, we'll need to update their expiration dates.)
  - Find members that share a common interest.
  - Put the directory online.

For some of these tasks, we'll write scripts that run from the command line. For the others, we'll create scripts in Section 8.4, "Using DBI in Web Applications," for use in conjunction with a Web server. This leaves us with a few goals to accomplish at the end of the chapter. We'll finish up those in Chapter 9, "Writing MySQL Programs Using PHP."

8.3.1   Generating the Historical League Directory

One of our goals is to produce information from the Historical League directory in different formats. The simplest format to be generated is a list of member names for the printed program distributed to attendees at the League's annual meeting. The format can be a simple plain text listing that will become part of the larger document used to create the meeting program. We need only something that can be pasted into that document.

For the printed member directory, we want something nicely formatted, so a better representation than plain text is needed. A reasonable choice here is RTF (Rich Text Format), a format developed by Microsoft that many word processors understand. Word is one such program, of course, but many others such as OpenOffice understand it as well. Different word processors support RTF to varying degrees, but we'll use a subset of the full RTF specification that should be understandable by any RTF-aware program. For example, on Mac OS X, the TextEdit editor and the Safari Web browser can read the RTF output that we'll generate.

The procedures for generating the annual meeting list (plain text) and RTF directory formats are essentially the same: Issue a query to retrieve the entries, then run a loop that fetches and formats each entry. Given that basic similarity, it would be nice to avoid writing separate scripts for each format. To that end, let's write a single script, gen_dir.pl, that can generate different types of output. We'll structure the script as follows:

1. Before writing out member entries, perform any initialization required for the output format. No initialization is needed for the plain text member list, but we must write some initial control language for the RTF version.

2. Fetch each entry and print it appropriately for the output format.

3. After the entries have been processed, perform any required cleanup and termination. Again, plain text format needs no special handling, but the RTF version requires some closing control language.

To anticipate that in the future we'll want to use this script to write output in other formats, let's make it extensible by setting up a "switchbox," that is, a hash with an element for each output format. Each element specifies which functions to invoke to carry out each output generation phase for a given format: an initialization function, an entry-writing function, and a cleanup function:

```
# switchbox containing formatting functions for each output format
my %switchbox =
(
  "text" =>                     # functions for plain text format
  {
    "init"    => undef,     # no initialization needed
    "entry"   => \&text_format_entry,
    "cleanup" => undef      # no cleanup needed
  },
  "rtf" =>                       # functions for RTF format
  {
    "init"    => \&rtf_init,
    "entry"   => \&rtf_format_entry,
    "cleanup" => \&rtf_cleanup
  }
);
```

Each element of the switchbox is keyed by a format name ("text" or "rtf"). We'll write the script so that a command-line argument indicates the desired format:

```
% ./gen_dir.pl text
% ./gen_dir.pl rtf
```

By setting up a switchbox this way, the capability for a new format can be added easily, if necessary:

1. Write three formatting functions for the output generation phases.

2. Add a new element to the switchbox that defines a format name and points to the output functions.

3. To produce output in the new format, invoke gen_dir.pl and specify the format name on the command line.

The code for selecting the proper switchbox entry according to the first argument on the command line follows. If no valid format name is present on the command line, the script produces an error message and displays a list of the permitted names. Otherwise, $func_ hashref is set to the appropriate switchbox entry:

```
my $formats = join (" ", sort (keys (%switchbox)));
# make sure one argument was specified on the command line
@ARGV == 1
    or die "Usage: gen_dir.pl format_type\nPermitted formats: $formats\n";

# determine proper switchbox entry from argument on command line;
# if no entry is found, the format type is invalid
my $func_hashref = $switchbox{$ARGV[0]};

defined ($func_hashref)
    or die "Unknown format: $ARGV[0]\nPermitted formats: $formats\n";
```

The format selection code is based on the fact that the output format names are the keys in the %switchbox hash. For each valid format name, the corresponding switchbox entry points to the output functions. For an invalid name, no entry exists. This makes it unnecessary to hard-wire any names into the format selection code, so if you add a new entry to the switchbox, the code detects it automatically with no change.

If a valid format name is specified on the command line, the preceding code sets $func_ hashref. Its value is a reference to the hash that points to the output-writing functions for the selected format. The following code uses it to invoke the initialization function, fetch and print the entries, and invoke the cleanup function:

```
# invoke the initialization function if there is one
&{$func_hashref->{init}} if defined ($func_hashref->{init});

# fetch and print entries if there is an entry formatting function
```

```
if (defined ($func_hashref->{entry}))
{
  my $sth = $dbh->prepare (qq{
             SELECT * FROM member ORDER BY last_name, first_name
           });
  $sth->execute ();
  while (my $entry_ref = $sth->fetchrow_hashref ("NAME_lc"))
  {
    # pass entry by reference to the formatting function
    &{$func_hashref->{entry}} ($entry_ref);
  }
}

# invoke the cleanup function if there is one
&{$func_hashref->{cleanup}} if defined ($func_hashref->{cleanup});
```

The entry-fetching loop uses `fetchrow_hashref()` for a reason. If the loop fetched an array, each formatting function would have to know the order of the columns. It's possible to figure that out by accessing the `$sth->{NAME}` attribute (which contains column names in the order in which they are returned), but why bother? By using a hash reference, each formatting function can refer to the column values it wants just by naming them using `$entry_ref->{col_name}` syntax.

All that remains is to write the functions named by the switchbox entries for each output format.

8.3.1.1 Generating the Plain Text Member List

The text output format requires no initialization or cleanup calls. We need only an entry-formatting function, `text_format_entry()`, that takes a reference to a member entry and prints the member's name. The tricky part of printing names is dealing with the suffix part. A suffix such as "Jr." or "Sr." is preceded by a comma and a space, whereas a suffix such as "II" or "III" is preceded only by a space:

```
Michael Alvis IV
Clarence Elgar, Jr.
Bill Matthews, Sr.
Mark York II
```

'I', 'V', and 'X' are the only letters used in the roman numerals for the 1st to the 39th generation. It's unlikely that we'll need any numerals beyond that range, so we can determine whether to add a comma by checking the suffix against this pattern:

```
/^[IVX]+$/
```

The code in `text_format_entry()` that puts the parts of the name together in the proper order is something we'll need for the RTF version of the directory as well. So instead of duplicating that code in `rtf_format_entry()`, let's enclose it within a helper function:

```
sub format_name
{
my $entry_ref = shift;

  my $name = $entry_ref->{first_name} . " " . $entry_ref->{last_name};
  if (defined ($entry_ref->{suffix}))      # there is a name suffix
  {
    # no comma for suffixes of I, II, III, etc.
    $name .= "," unless $entry_ref->{suffix} =~ /^[IVX]+$/;
    $name .= " " . $entry_ref->{suffix}
  }
  return ($name);
}
```

With `format_name()` in place, the implementation of the `text_format_entry()` function that prints an entry becomes almost completely trivial:

```
sub text_format_entry
{
  printf "%s\n", format_name ($_[0]);
}
```

8.3.1.2   Generating the Rich Text Format Directory

Generating the RTF version of the directory is a little more involved than generating the member list for the annual meeting program. For one thing, we must print more information from each entry. For another, we need to put out some RTF control language with each entry to achieve the formatting effects, and some control language at the beginning and end of the document. A minimal RTF document framework looks like this:

```
{\rtf0
{\fonttbl {\f0 Times;}}
\plain \f0 \fs24
  ...document content goes here...
}
```

The document begins and ends with curly braces '{' and '}'. RTF keywords begin with a backslash, and the first keyword of the document must be \rtf$n$, where n is the version number of the RTF specification that the document uses. Version 0 is fine for our purposes.

Within the document, we specify a font table to indicate the font to use for the entries. Font table information is listed in a group consisting of curly braces containing a leading \fonttbl keyword and some font information. The font table in the framework just shown defines font number 0 to be in Times. (We need only one font, but you could use more if you wanted to be fancier.)

The next few directives set up the default formatting style: \plain selects plain format, \f0 selects font 0 (defined as Times in the font table), and \fs24 sets the font size to 12 points (the number following `\fs` indicates the size in half-points). It's unnecessary to set up margins because most word processors supply reasonable defaults.

The initialization and cleanup functions produce the document framework. They look like this (note the doubled backslashes to get single backslashes in the output):

```
sub rtf_init
{
  print "{\\rtf0\n";
  print "{\\fonttbl {\\f0 Times;}}\n";
  print "\\plain \\f0 \\fs24\n";
}


sub rtf_cleanup
{
  print "}\n";
}
```

The entry-formatting function produces the document content. We take a very simple approach, printing each entry as a series of lines, with a label on each line. If the information corresponding to a particular output line is missing, the line is omitted. For example, the "Email:" line is not printed for members that have no email address. Some lines, such as the "Address:" line, are composed from the information in multiple columns (`street`, `city`, `state`, `zip`), so the script must deal with various combinations of missing values. Here's a sample of the output format:

```
Name: Mike Artel
Address: 4264 Lovering Rd., Miami, FL 12777
Telephone: 075-961-0712
Email: mike_artel@venus.org
Interests: Civil Rights,Education,Revolutionary War
```

For that entry, the RTF representation looks like this:

```
\b Name: Mike Artel\b0\par
Address: 4264 Lovering Rd., Miami, FL 12777\par
Telephone: 075-961-0712\par
Email: mike_artel@venus.org\par
Interests: Civil Rights,Education,Revolutionary War\par
```

To make the "Name:" line bold, it begins with `\b` followed by a space to turn boldface on, and ends with `\b0` to turn boldface off. The member name is formatted by the `format_name()` function shown earlier in Section 8.3.1.1, "Generating the Plain Text Member List." Each line has a paragraph marker (`\par`) at the end to tell the word processor to move to the next line—nothing too complicated. The primary difficulties lie in formatting the address string and determining which output lines to print:

```
sub rtf_format_entry
{
```

```
my $entry_ref = shift;

  printf "\\b Name: %s\\b0\\par\n", format_name ($entry_ref);
  my $address = "";
  $address .= $entry_ref->{street}
              if defined ($entry_ref->{street});
  $address .= ", " . $entry_ref->{city}
              if defined ($entry_ref->{city});
  $address .= ", " . $entry_ref->{state}
              if defined ($entry_ref->{state});
  $address .= " " . $entry_ref->{zip}
              if defined ($entry_ref->{zip});
  print "Address: $address\\par\n"
              if $address ne "";
  print "Telephone: $entry_ref->{phone}\\par\n"
              if defined ($entry_ref->{phone});
  print "Email: $entry_ref->{email}\\par\n"
              if defined ($entry_ref->{email});
  print "Interests: $entry_ref->{interests}\\par\n"
              if defined ($entry_ref->{interests});
  print "\\par\n";
}
```

You're not locked into this particular formatting style, of course. To change the style of the printed directory, simply change rtf_format_entry(). When the directory was in its original form (a word processing document), that was something not so easily done.

The gen_dir.pl script now is complete, and you can generate the directory in either plain text or RTF output format by running these commands:

```
% ./gen_dir.pl text > names.txt
% ./gen_dir.pl rtf > directory.rtf
```

At this point, it's a simple step to paste the plain text name file into the annual meeting program document or to use the RTF file with any program that understands RTF.

DBI makes it easy to extract the information we want from MySQL, and Perl's text-processing capabilities make it easy to put that information into the format we want to see. MySQL doesn't provide any particularly fancy way of formatting output, but that doesn't matter because of the ease with which you can integrate MySQL's database handling abilities into a language such as Perl, which has excellent text manipulation capabilities.

8.3.2 Sending Membership Renewal Notices

With the Historical League directory maintained in its original form (as a word processing document), it's a time-consuming and error-prone activity to determine which members need to be notified that their membership should be renewed. Now that we have the information in a database, it's possible to automate the renewal-notification process a bit. We can identify members who need to renew, and send them a message by email so that we don't have to contact them by phone or surface mail.

What we need to do is determine which memberships have expired already or are due for renewal within a certain number of days. The query for this involves a relatively simple date calculation:

```
SELECT ... FROM member
WHERE expiration < DATE_ADD(CURDATE(), INTERVAL cutoff DAY)
```

cutoff signifies the number of days of leeway to grant. The query selects member entries that are due for renewal in fewer than that many days (or that have already expired). To find only memberships that have expired, a cutoff value of 0 identifies rows with expiration dates in the past.

After identifying the rows that qualify for notification, what should we do with them? One option is to send mail directly from the same script, but it might be useful to be able to review the list first before sending any messages. For this reason, we'll use a two-stage approach:

1. Run a need_renewal.pl script to produce a list of members that need to renew. You can examine this list to verify or edit it, then use it as input to the second stage that sends the renewal notices.

2. Run a renewal_notify.pl script that sends members a "please renew" notice by email. The script should warn you about members that have no email address so that you can contact them by other means.

For the first part of this task, the need_renewal.pl script must identify which members need to renew. The main part of the script looks like this:

```
# use default cutoff of 30 days...
my $cutoff = 30;
# ...but reset if a numeric argument is given on the command line
$cutoff = shift (@ARGV) if @ARGV && $ARGV[0] =~ /^\d+$/;

# inform user what cutoff the script is using
warn "Using cutoff of $cutoff days\n";

my $sth = $dbh->prepare (qq{
        SELECT
          member_id, email, last_name, first_name, expiration,
          TO_DAYS(expiration) - TO_DAYS(CURDATE()) AS days
        FROM member
        WHERE expiration < DATE_ADD(CURDATE(), INTERVAL ? DAY)
        ORDER BY expiration, last_name, first_name
      });
$sth->execute ($cutoff);   # pass cutoff as placeholder value
```

```perl
while (my $entry_ref = $sth->fetchrow_hashref ())
{
  # convert undef values to empty strings for printing
  foreach my $key (keys (%{$entry_ref}))
  {
    $entry_ref->{$key} = "" if !defined ($entry_ref->{$key});
  }
  print join ("\t",
                $entry_ref->{member_id},
                $entry_ref->{email},
                $entry_ref->{last_name},
                $entry_ref->{first_name},
                $entry_ref->{expiration},
                $entry_ref->{days} . " days"),
          "\n";
}
```

The output from the need_renewal.pl script looks something like the following (you'll get different output because the results are determined against a current date that is different for you while reading this chapter than for me while writing it):

```
89  g.steve@pluto.com       Garner   Steve   2012-08-03  -38 days
18  york_mark@earth.com     York     Mark    2012-08-24  -17 days
82  john_edwards@venus.org  Edwards  John    2012-09-12  2 days
```

Observe that some memberships need to be renewed in a negative number of days. That means they've already expired! (This happens when you maintain rows manually; people slip through the cracks. Now that we have the information in a database, we're finding out that we missed a few people before.)

The second part of the renewal notification task involves a script renewal_notify.pl that sends out the notices by email. To make renewal_notify.pl a little easier to use, we can make it understand three kinds of command-line arguments: membership ID numbers, email addresses, and filenames. Numeric arguments signify membership ID values, and arguments containing a '@' character signify email addresses. Anything else is treated as the name of a file to read to find ID numbers or email addresses. This method enables you to specify members by their ID number or email address, and you can do so either directly on the command line or by listing them in a file. (In particular, you can save the output of need_renewal.pl in a file, then use the file as input to renewal_notify.pl.)

For each member who is to be sent a notice, the script looks up the relevant member table entry, extracts the email address, and sends a message to that address. If there is no address in the entry, renewal_notify.pl generates a warning message that you need to contact this member some other way.

The main argument-processing loop follows. If no arguments were specified on the command line, we read the standard input for input. Otherwise, we process each argument by passing it to interpret_argument() for classification as an ID number, an email address, or a filename:

```
if (@ARGV == 0)   # no arguments, read STDIN for values
{
  read_file (\*STDIN);
}
else
{
  while (my $arg = shift (@ARGV))
  {
    # interpret argument, with filename recursion
    interpret_argument ($arg, 1);
  }
}
```

The function `read_file()` reads the contents of a file (assumed to be open already) and looks at the first field of each line. (If we feed the output of `need_renewal.pl` to `renewal_notify.pl`, each line has several fields, but we want to look only at the first one, which is a member ID number.)

```
sub read_file
{
my $fh = shift;   # handle to already-opened file
my $arg;

  while (defined ($arg = <$fh>))
  {
    # strip off everything past column 1, including newline
    $arg =~ s/\s.*//s;
    # interpret argument, without filename recursion
    interpret_argument ($arg, 0);
  }
}
```

The `interpret_argument()` function classifies each argument to determine whether it's an ID number, an email address, or a filename. For ID numbers and email addresses, it looks up the appropriate member entry and passes it to `notify_member()`. We have to be careful with members specified by email address. It's possible that two members have the same address (for example, a husband and wife), and we don't want to send a message to someone to whom it doesn't apply. To avoid this, we look up the member ID corresponding to an email address to make sure that there is exactly one. If the address matches more than one ID number, it's ambiguous and we ignore it after printing a warning.

If an argument doesn't look like an ID number or email address, it's taken to be the name of a file to read for further input. We have to be careful here, too—we don't want to read a file if we're already reading a file, to avoid the possibility of an infinite loop:

```
sub interpret_argument
{
my ($arg, $recurse) = @_;
```

```
  if ($arg =~ /^\d+$/)     # numeric membership ID
  {
    notify_member ($arg);
  }
  elsif ($arg =~ /@/)      # email address
  {
    # get member_id associated with address
    # (there should be exactly one)
    my $stmt = qq{ SELECT member_id FROM member WHERE email = ? };
    my $ary_ref = $dbh->selectcol_arrayref ($stmt, undef, $arg);
    if (scalar (@{$ary_ref}) == 0)
    {
      warn "Email address $arg matches no entry: ignored\n";
    }
    elsif (scalar (@{$ary_ref}) > 1)
    {
      warn "Email address $arg matches multiple entries: ignored\n";
    }
    else
    {
      notify_member ($ary_ref->[0]);
    }
  }
  else                     # filename
  {
    if (!$recurse)
    {
      warn "filename $arg inside file: ignored\n";
    }
    else
    {
      open (IN, $arg) or die "Cannot open $arg: $!\n";
      read_file (\*IN);
      close (IN);
    }
  }
}
```

The notify_member() function is responsible for actually sending the renewal notice. If it turns out that the member has no email address, notify_member() can't send any message, but it prints a warning so that you know you need to contact the member some other way. You can invoke show_member.pl with the membership ID number shown in the message to see the full entry—to find out what the member's phone number and address are, for example. (For a description of show_member.pl, see Section 8.2.11, "Using Result Set Metadata.")

`notify_member()` looks like this:

```perl
sub notify_member
{
my $member_id = shift;

  warn "Notifying $member_id...\n";
  my $stmt = qq{ SELECT * FROM member WHERE member_id = ? };
  my $sth = $dbh->prepare ($stmt);
  $sth->execute ($member_id);
  my @col_name = @{$sth->{NAME}};
  my $entry_ref = $sth->fetchrow_hashref ();
  $sth->finish ();
  if (!$entry_ref)                          # no member found!
  {
    warn "NO ENTRY found for member $member_id!\n";
    return;
  }
  if (!defined ($entry_ref->{email}))   # no email address in entry
  {
    warn "Member $member_id has no email address; no message was sent\n";
    return;
  }
  open (OUT, "| $sendmail") or die "Cannot open mailer\n";
  print OUT <<EOF;
To: $entry_ref->{email}
Subject: Your USHL membership is in need of renewal

Greetings.  Your membership in the U.S. Historical League is
due to expire soon.  We hope that you'll take a few minutes to
contact the League office to renew your membership.  The
contents of your member entry are shown following.  Please note
particularly the expiration date.

Thank you.

EOF
  foreach my $col_name (@col_name)
  {
    printf OUT "$col_name:";
    printf OUT " $entry_ref->{$col_name}"
            if defined ($entry_ref->{$col_name});
    printf OUT "\n";
  }
  close (OUT);
}
```

The `notify_member()` function sends mail by opening a pipe to the `sendmail` program and shoving the mail message into the pipe. The pathname to `sendmail` is set as a parameter near the beginning of the `renewal_notify.pl` script. You might need to change this path because the location of `sendmail` varies from system to system:

```
# change path to match your system
my $sendmail = "/usr/sbin/sendmail -t -oi";
```

If you don't have `sendmail`, the script will not work properly. (For example, Windows systems typically do not have `sendmail` installed.) To handle this case, the `sampdb` distribution contains a modified version of `renewal_notify.pl` named `renewal_notify2.pl` that uses the Mail::Sendmail module that works without the `sendmail` program. If you install that module, you can use `renewal_notify2.pl` instead.

You could get fancier with this script. For example, you could add a column to the `member` table to record when the most recent renewal reminder was sent out and modify `renewal_notify.pl` to update that column when it sends mail. Doing so would help you to not send out notices too frequently. As it is, we'll just assume that you won't run this program more than once a month or so.

The two scripts are done now. Use them as follows:

1. Run `need_renewal.pl` to generate a list of memberships that have expired or will soon do so:

   ```
   % ./need_renewal.pl > tmp
   ```

2. Take a look at `tmp` to see whether it looks reasonable.

3. If so, use it as input to `renewal_notify.pl` to send renewal messages:

   ```
   % ./renewal_notify.pl tmp
   ```

To notify individual members, you can specify them by ID number or email address. For example, the following command notifies member 18 and the member having the email address `g.steve@pluto.com`:

```
% ./renewal_notify.pl 18 g.steve@pluto.com
```

8.3.3   Historical League Member Entry Editing

After we start sending out renewal notices, it's safe to assume that some of those notified will renew their memberships. When that happens, we need a way to update their entries with new expiration dates. In the next chapter, we develop a way to edit member rows over the Web, but this section shows how to write a command-line script, `edit_member.pl`, that enables you to update entries using the simple approach of prompting for new values for each part of an entry. It works like this:

- If invoked with no argument on the command line, `edit_member.pl` assumes that you want to enter a new member. It prompts for the required information and creates a new entry.

- If invoked with a membership ID number on the command line, `edit_member.pl` looks up the existing contents of the entry, then prompts for updates to each column. If you enter a value for a column, it replaces the current value. Pressing Enter leaves the column unchanged. Entering the word "none" clears the column's current value. Entering the word "exit" quits without creating the entry. (If you don't know a member's ID number, run `show_member.pl` *last_name* to see which entries match the given last name and from that determine the proper ID.)

It's probably overkill to enable an entire entry to be edited this way if all you want to do is update a member's expiration date. On the other hand, a script like this also provides a simple general-purpose way for its user to update any part of an entry without knowing any SQL. (One exception: `edit_member.pl` won't permit you to change the `member_id` field because that's automatically assigned when an entry is created and shouldn't change thereafter.)

The first thing `edit_member.pl` must know is the names of the columns in the `member` table and whether they can be assigned NULL values. The latter property is needed when a column value is cleared (to assign NULL to the column if it can take NULL values and the empty string otherwise). The required information is available in the COLUMNS table of the INFORMATION_ SCHEMA database:

```perl
my @col_name = ();       # array of column names
my %nullable = ();       # column nullability, keyed on column name
# get member table column names
my $sth = $dbh->prepare (qq{
            SELECT COLUMN_NAME, UPPER(IS_NULLABLE)
            FROM INFORMATION_SCHEMA.COLUMNS
            WHERE TABLE_SCHEMA = ? AND TABLE_NAME = ?
        });
$sth->execute ("sampdb", "member");
while (my ($col_name, $is_nullable) = $sth->fetchrow_array ())
{
  push (@col_name, $col_name);
  $nullable{$col_name} = ($is_nullable eq "YES");
}
```

Using the column information, the script produces an array containing the column names in order, and a hash keyed by column name that indicates whether each column is nullable. Then `edit_member.pl` enters its main loop:

```perl
if (@ARGV == 0) # if no arguments were given, create a new entry
{
  # pass reference to array of column names
  new_member (\@col_name);
}
else            # otherwise edit entries using arguments as member IDs
{
  # save @ARGV, then empty it so that when the script reads from
  # STDIN, it doesn't interpret @ARGV contents as input filenames
```

```perl
my @id = @ARGV;
@ARGV = ();
# for each ID value, look up the entry, then edit it
while (my $id = shift (@id))
{
  $sth = $dbh->prepare (qq{
            SELECT * FROM member WHERE member_id = ?
        });
  $sth->execute ($id);
  my $entry_ref = $sth->fetchrow_hashref ();
  $sth->finish ();
  if (!$entry_ref)
  {
    warn "No member exists with member ID = $id\n";
    next;
  }
  # pass reference to array of column names and reference to entry
  edit_member (\@col_name, $entry_ref);
  }
}
```

The code for creating a new member entry solicits values for each `member` table column, then issues an `INSERT` statement to add a new row:

```perl
sub new_member
{
my $col_name_ref = shift; # reference to array of column names
my $entry_ref = { };    # create new entry as a hash

  return unless prompt ("Create new entry (y/n)? ") =~ /^y/i;
  # prompt for new values; user types in new value, or Enter
  # to leave value unchanged, "NONE" to clear the value, or
  # "EXIT" to exit without creating the record.
  foreach my $col_name (@{$col_name_ref})
  {
    next if $col_name eq "member_id";   # skip key field
    my $col_val = col_prompt ($col_name, undef);
    next if $col_val eq "";             # user pressed Enter
    return if uc ($col_val) eq "EXIT";  # early exit
    if (uc ($col_val) eq "NONE")
    {
      # enter NULL if column is nullable, empty string otherwise
      $col_val = ($nullable{$col_name} ? undef : "");
    }
    $entry_ref->{$col_name} = $col_val;
  }
  # show values, ask for confirmation before inserting
```

```
show_member ($col_name_ref, $entry_ref);
return unless prompt ("\nInsert this entry (y/n)? ") =~ /^y/i;

# construct an INSERT query, then issue it.
my $stmt = "INSERT INTO member";
my $delim = " SET "; # put "SET" before first column, "," before others
foreach my $col_name (@{$col_name_ref})
{
  # only specify values for columns that were given one
  next if !defined ($entry_ref->{$col_name});
  # quote() quotes undef as the word NULL (without quotes),
  # which is what we want.  Columns that are NOT NULL are
  # assigned their default values.
  $stmt .= sprintf ("%s %s=%s", $delim, $col_name,
                    $dbh->quote ($entry_ref->{$col_name}));
  $delim = ",";
}
$dbh->do ($stmt) or warn "Warning: new entry not created!\n"
}
```

edit_member.pl uses two routines to prompt the user for information. prompt() asks a question and returns the answer:

```
sub prompt
{
my $str = shift;

  print STDERR $str;
  chomp ($str = <STDIN>);
  return ($str);
}
```

col_prompt() takes a column name argument. It prints the name as a prompt to solicit a new column value, and returns the value entered by the user:

```
sub col_prompt
{
my ($col_name, $entry_ref) = @_;

  my $prompt = $col_name;
  if (defined ($entry_ref))
  {
    my $cur_val = $entry_ref->{$col_name};
    $cur_val = "NULL" if !defined ($cur_val);
    $prompt .= " [$cur_val]";
  }
  $prompt .= ": ";
  print STDERR $prompt;
```

```
    my $str = <STDIN>;
    chomp ($str);
    return ($str);
}
```

The second argument to col_prompt() is a reference to the hash that represents the member entry. For creating a new entry, this value is undef, but when editing existing rows, it points to the current entry contents. In the latter case, col_prompt() includes the current column value in the prompt string so that the user can see it. The user can accept the value simply by pressing Enter.

The code for editing an existing member is similar to that for creating a new member. However, we have an entry to work with, so the prompt routine displays the current entry values, and the edit_member() function issues an UPDATE statement rather than an INSERT:

```
sub edit_member
{
# references to an array of column names and to the entry hash
my ($col_name_ref, $entry_ref) = @_;

  # show initial values, ask for okay to go ahead and edit
  show_member ($col_name_ref, $entry_ref);
  return unless prompt ("\nEdit this entry (y/n)? ") =~ /^y/i;
  # prompt for new values; user types in new value, or Enter
  # to leave value unchanged, "NONE" to clear the value, or
  # "EXIT" to exit without changing the record.
  foreach my $col_name (@{$col_name_ref})
  {
    next if $col_name eq "member_id";    # skip key field
    my $col_val = col_prompt ($col_name, $entry_ref);
    next if $col_val eq "";              # user pressed Enter
    return if uc ($col_val) eq "EXIT";  # early exit
    if (uc ($col_val) eq "NONE")
    {
      # enter NULL if column is nullable, empty string otherwise
      $col_val = ($nullable{$col_name} ? undef : "");
    }

    $entry_ref->{$col_name} = $col_val;
  }
  # show new values, ask for confirmation before updating
  show_member ($col_name_ref, $entry_ref);
  return unless prompt ("\nUpdate this entry (y/n)? ") =~ /^y/i;

  # construct an UPDATE query, then issue it.
  my $stmt = "UPDATE member";
  my $delim = " SET "; # put "SET" before first column, "," before others
  foreach my $col_name (@{$col_name_ref})
```

```
{
  next if $col_name eq "member_id"; # skip key field
  # quote() quotes undef as the word NULL (without quotes),
  # which is what we want.
  $stmt .= sprintf ("%s %s=%s", $delim, $col_name,
                    $dbh->quote ($entry_ref->{$col_name}));
  $delim = ",";
}
$stmt .= " WHERE member_id = " . $dbh->quote ($entry_ref->{member_id});
$dbh->do ($stmt) or warn "Warning: entry not undated!\n"
}
```

A problem with `edit_member.pl` is that it does no input value validation. For most fields in the `member` table, there isn't much to validate—they're just string fields. But for the expiration column, input values really should be checked to make sure that they look like dates. In a general-purpose data entry application, you'd probably want to extract information about a table to determine the types of all its columns. Then you could base validation constraints on those types. That's more involved than I want to go into here, but a minimal date value check can be added to the `col_prompt()` function to check the format of the input if the column is `expiration`:

```
sub col_prompt
{
my ($col_name, $entry_ref) = @_;

loop:
  my $prompt = $col_name;
  if (defined ($entry_ref))
  {
    my $cur_val = $entry_ref->{$col_name};
    $cur_val = "NULL" if !defined ($cur_val);
    $prompt .= " [$cur_val]";
  }
  $prompt .= ": ";
  print STDERR $prompt;
  my $str = <STDIN>;
  chomp ($str);
  # perform rudimentary check on the expiration date
  if ($str && $col_name eq "expiration")  # check expiration date format
  {
    if ($str !~ /^\d+\D\d+\D\d+$/)
    {
      warn "$str is not a legal date, try again\n";
      goto loop;
    }
  }
  return ($str);
}
```

The pattern tests for three sequences of digits separated by nondigit characters. This is only a partial check because it doesn't detect values such as "1999-14-92" as being illegal. To make the script better, you could give it more stringent date checks or add other checks such as requiring the first and last name fields to be given nonempty values.

Other improvements are possible:

- Skip the update operation for an existing entry if the user made no changes. To do this, save the original values of the member entry columns, then write the UPDATE statement so that it updates only those columns that the user changed. If there were none, the statement need not even be issued.

- Notify the user if the row was already changed by someone else while the user was editing it. To do this, write the WHERE clause to include AND *col_name* = *col_val* for each original column value. This causes the UPDATE to fail if someone else had changed the row, which provides feedback that two people are trying to change the entry at the same time.

- Enable strict SQL mode and other input restrictions, which causes MySQL itself to reject bad values and return an error if the input cannot be used as given:

  ```
  $dbh->do ("SET sql_mode = 'TRADITIONAL'");
  ```

Here's another shortcoming of the edit_member.pl script that you might consider how to address: As written, the script opens a connection to the database before executing the prompt loop and doesn't close the connection until after writing out the row within the loop. If the user takes a long time to enter or update the row, or just happens to do something else for a while, the connection can remain open for a long time. How would you modify edit_member.pl to hold the connection open only as long as necessary?

8.3.4   Finding Historical League Members with Common Interests

One of the duties of the Historical League secretary is to process requests from members for a list of other members who share a particular interest within the field of U.S. history, such as the Great Depression or the life of Abraham Lincoln. It's easy enough to find such members when the directory is maintained in a word processor document by using the word processor's "Find" function. However, producing a list consisting *only* of the qualifying member entries is more difficult because it involves a lot of copy and paste. With MySQL, the job becomes much easier because we can just run a query like this:

```
SELECT * FROM member WHERE interests LIKE '%lincoln%'
ORDER BY last_name, first_name
```

Unfortunately, the results don't look very nice if we run this query from the mysql client. Let's put together a little DBI script, interests.pl, to perform the search and produce better-looking output. interests.pl first checks to make sure that there is at least one argument named on the command line, because there is nothing to search for otherwise. Then, for each argument, the script searches the interests column of the member table:

```
@ARGV or die "Usage: interests.pl keyword\n";
search_members (shift (@ARGV)) while @ARGV;
```

To search for the keyword string, put '%' wildcard characters on each side and perform a pattern match so that the string can be found anywhere in the `interests` column. Then print the matching entries:

```
sub search_members
{
my $interest = shift;

  print "Search results for keyword: $interest\n\n";
  my $sth = $dbh->prepare (qq{
            SELECT * FROM member WHERE interests LIKE ?
            ORDER BY last_name, first_name
          });
  # look for string anywhere in interest field
  $sth->execute ("%" . $interest . "%");
  my $count = 0;
  while (my $hash_ref = $sth->fetchrow_hashref ())
  {
    format_entry ($hash_ref);
    ++$count;
  }
  print "Number of matching entries: $count\n\n";
}
```

The `format_entry()` function turns an entry into its printable representation. I won't show it here, because it's essentially the same as the `rtf_format_entry()` function from the `gen_dir.pl` script, with the RTF control words stripped out. Take a look at the `interests.pl` script in the `sampdb` distribution to see the implementation.

8.3.5 Putting the Historical League Directory Online

In Section 8.4, "Using DBI in Web Applications," we'll start writing scripts that connect to the MySQL server to extract information and write that information in the form of Web pages that appear in a client's Web browser. Those scripts generate HTML dynamically according to what the client requested. Before we reach that point, let's begin thinking about HTML by writing a DBI script that generates a static HTML document that can be loaded into a Web server's document tree. A good candidate for this task is to produce the Historical League directory in HTML format (after all, one of our goals was to put the directory online).

A simple HTML document has a structure something like the following:

```
<html>                          ← beginning of document
<head>                          ← beginning of document head
<title>My Page Title</title>    ← title of document
</head>                         ← end of document head
```

```
<body bgcolor="white">              ← beginning of document body
                                      (white background)
<h1>My Level 1 Heading</h1>         ← a level 1 heading


... content of document body ...


</body>                             ← end of document body
</html>                             ← end of document
```

It's not necessary to write a completely new script to generate the directory in HTML format. Recall that when we wrote the gen_dir.pl script, we used an extensible framework so that we'd be able to plug in code for producing the directory in additional formats. Let's take advantage of that extensibility now by adding code for generating HTML output. To do this, we need to make the following modifications to gen_dir.pl:

- New document initialization and cleanup functions

- A new function to format individual member rows

- A new switchbox element that identifies the format name and associates it with the functions that produce output in that format

The HTML document outline just shown breaks down pretty easily into prolog and epilog sections that can be handled by the initialization and cleanup functions, as well as a middle part that can be generated by the entry-formatting function. The HTML initialization function generates everything up through the heading, and the cleanup function generates the closing </body> and </html> tags:

```
sub html_init
{
  print "<html>\n";
  print "<head>\n";
  print "<title>U.S. Historical League Member Directory</title>\n";
  print "</head>\n";
  print "<body bgcolor=\"white\">\n";
  print "<h1>U.S. Historical League Member Directory</h1>\n";
}


sub html_cleanup
{
  print "</body>\n";
  print "</html>\n";
}
```

The real work, as usual, lies in formatting the entries. But even this isn't very difficult. We can make a copy of the rtf_format_entry() function named html_format_entry(), and modify it to make sure that any special characters in the entry are encoded and to replace the RTF control words with HTML markup tags:

```perl
sub html_format_entry
{
my $entry_ref = shift;

  # Convert &, ", >, and < to the corresponding HTML entities
  # (&amp;, &quot;, &gt, &lt;)
  foreach my $key (keys (%{$entry_ref}))
  {
    next unless defined ($entry_ref->{$key});
    $entry_ref->{$key} =~ s/&/&amp;/g;
    $entry_ref->{$key} =~ s/\"/&quot;/g;
    $entry_ref->{$key} =~ s/>/&gt;/g;
    $entry_ref->{$key} =~ s/</&lt;/g;
  }
  printf "<strong>Name: %s</strong><br />\n", format_name ($entry_ref);
  my $address = "";
  $address .= $entry_ref->{street}
              if defined ($entry_ref->{street});
  $address .= ", " . $entry_ref->{city}
              if defined ($entry_ref->{city});
  $address .= ", " . $entry_ref->{state}
              if defined ($entry_ref->{state});
  $address .= " " . $entry_ref->{zip}
              if defined ($entry_ref->{zip});
  print "Address: $address<br />\n"
              if $address ne "";
  print "Telephone: $entry_ref->{phone}<br />\n"
              if defined ($entry_ref->{phone});
  print "Email: $entry_ref->{email}<br />\n"
              if defined ($entry_ref->{email});
  print "Interests: $entry_ref->{interests}<br />\n"
              if defined ($entry_ref->{interests});
  print "<br />\n";
}
```

The function produces output that looks like this:

```
<strong>Name: Mike Artel</strong><br />
Address: 4264 Lovering Rd., Miami, FL 12777<br />
Telephone: 075-961-0712<br />
Email: mike_artel@venus.org<br />
Interests: Civil Rights,Education,Revolutionary War<br />
<br />
```

The script writes <br /> rather than <br> to produce the document as well-formed XHTML, which is more strict than HTML. Section 8.4.2.2, "Producing Web Output," briefly discusses some distinctions between HTML and XHTML.

The last modification needed for `gen_dir.pl` is to add to the switchbox another element that points to the HTML-writing functions. The modified switchbox looks like this, where the final element defines a format named `html` that points to the functions that produce the parts of an HTML document:

```
# switchbox containing formatting functions for each output format
my %switchbox =
(
  "text" =>                    # functions for plain text format
  {
    "init"    => undef,      # no initialization needed
    "entry"   => \&text_format_entry,
    "cleanup" => undef       # no cleanup needed
  },
  "rtf" =>                     # functions for RTF format
  {
    "init"    => \&rtf_init,
    "entry"   => \&rtf_format_entry,
    "cleanup" => \&rtf_cleanup
  },
  "html" =>                    # functions for HTML format
  {
    "init"    => \&html_init,
    "entry"   => \&html_format_entry,
    "cleanup" => \&html_cleanup
  }
);
```

To make the directory available in HTML format, run the following command and install the resulting output file, `directory.html`, in your Web server's document tree:

```
% ./gen_dir.pl html > directory.html
```

Whenever you update the `member` table in the database, you can run the command again and use the output to update the online version. To avoid running the command manually, another strategy is to set up a job that executes periodically to update the online directory automatically. On Unix, you can use `cron` for this. Suppose that the `gen_dir.pl` script is installed in `/usr/local/bin` and the Historical League directory in the Web server document tree is `/usr/local/apache/htdocs/ushl`. Then a `crontab` entry like this one can be used to update the directory every day at 04:00 (enter the entire command on a single line):

```
0 4 * * * /usr/local/bin/gen_dir.pl
  > /usr/local/apache/htdocs/ushl/directory.html
```

The user who runs this `cron` job must have permission to write files into the document tree directory.

8.4 Using DBI in Web Applications

The DBI scripts developed thus far were designed for use in a command-line environment. DBI is useful in other contexts as well, such as in the development of Web-based applications. When you write DBI scripts that can be invoked by your Web server in response to requests sent by Web browsers, you open up new and interesting possibilities for users to interact with your databases. For example, if you write a script that displays data in tabular form, it can easily turn each column heading into a link that can be selected to re-sort the data on that column. This enables users to view data in a different way with a single click, without entering any queries. Or you can provide a form into which a user can enter criteria for a database search, then display a page containing the results of the search. Simple capabilities like this dramatically alter the level of interactivity you provide for accessing the contents of your databases. In addition, Web browser display capabilities typically are better than what you get with a terminal window, so you can create nicer-looking output as well.

In this section, we'll create the following Web-based scripts:

- A general browser for the tables in the `sampdb` database. This isn't related to any specific task we want to accomplish with the database, but it illustrates several Web programming concepts and provides a convenient means of seeing what information the tables contain.

- A score browser that enables us to see the scores for any given quiz or test. This is handy as a quick means of reviewing grade event results for the grade-keeping project, and it's useful when we need to establish the grading curve for a test so that we can mark papers with letter grades.

- A script that finds Historical League members who share a common interest. This is done by permitting the user to enter a search phrase, then searching the `interests` column of the `member` table for that phrase. We already wrote a command-line script, `interests.pl`, to do this earlier, in Section 8.3.4, "Finding Historical League Members with Common Interests." But the command-line version can be executed only by people who have login accounts on the machine where the script is installed. Providing a Web-based version opens up the directory to anyone who has a Web browser. Having another version also provides an instructive point of reference, permitting comparison of multiple approaches to the same task. (Actually, we'll develop two Web-based implementations. One is based on pattern matching, just like `interests.pl`. The other performs FULLTEXT searches.)

These scripts use the CGI.pm Perl module, which provides an easy way to link DBI to the Web. (For instructions on getting CGI.pm, see Appendix A, "Software Required to Use This Book.") The CGI.pm module is so called because it helps you write scripts that use the Common Gateway Interface protocol that defines how a Web server communicates with other programs. CGI.pm handles the details involved in a number of common housekeeping tasks, such as collecting the values of parameters passed as input to your script by the Web server. CGI.pm also provides convenient methods for generating HTML output, which reduces the chance of writing out malformed HTML compared to writing raw HTML tags yourself.

You'll learn enough about CGI.pm in this chapter to write your own Web applications, but not all of its capabilities are covered. To learn more about this module, see *Official Guide to Programming with CGI.pm*, by Lincoln Stein (John Wiley, 1998), or search for "CGI" at `http://cpan.perl.org` to read the online documentation.

Another text covering CGI.pm that's specifically targeted to MySQL and DBI is my book *MySQL and Perl for the Web* (New Riders, 2000).

To find the Web-based scripts described in the remainder of this chapter, look in the `perlapi/web` directory of the `sampdb` distribution.

8.4.1   Setting Up Apache for CGI Scripts

In addition to DBI and CGI.pm, there's one more component we need for writing Web-based scripts: a Web server. The instructions here are geared toward using scripts with the Apache server, but you may be able to use a different server by adapting the instructions a bit.

I assume here that the components of your Apache installation are located under `/usr/local/apache` for Unix and under `C:\Apache` for Windows. For our purposes, the most important subdirectories of the Apache top-level directory are `htdocs` (for the HTML document tree), `cgi-bin` (for executable scripts and programs to be invoked by the Web server), and `conf` (for configuration files). These directories might be located somewhere else on your system. If so, make the appropriate adjustments to the following notes.

You should verify that the `cgi-bin` directory is not located within the Apache document tree. This is a safety precaution that prevents clients from requesting the source code for your scripts as plain text. You don't want malicious clients to be able to examine your scripts for security holes by siphoning off the text of the scripts and studying them.

To install a CGI script for use with Apache, copy it to your `cgi-bin` directory. Under Unix, the script must begin with a `#!` line and have its mode set to be executable, just as for a command-line script. In addition, it's a good idea to set the script to be owned by the user that Apache runs as and to be accessible only to that user. For example, if Apache runs as a user named `www`, use the following commands to make a script named `myscript.pl` owned by and executable and readable only by that user:

```
# chown www myscript.pl
# chmod u=rx,go-rwx myscript.pl
```

You might need to run these commands as `root`. If you don't have permission to install scripts in the `cgi-bin` directory, ask your system administrator to do so on your behalf.

Under Windows, the `chown` and `chmod` commands are unnecessary, but the script should still begin with a `#!` line. The line can list the full pathname to your Perl program. For example, if Perl is installed as `C:\Perl\bin\perl.exe`, the `#!` line can be written like this:

```
#!C:/Perl/bin/perl
```

Alternatively, on Windows, you can write the line more simply as follows if your PATH environment variable is set to include the directory in which Perl is installed:

```
#!perl
```

The Perl scripts in the sampdb distribution specify the pathname of Perl on the #! line as /usr/bin/perl. Modify each script if necessary to provide a pathname that is appropriate for your own system.

After a script has been installed in the cgi-bin directory, you can request it from your browser by sending the appropriate URL to your Web server. For example, for a Web server running on the local host, you would request myscript.pl from it using a URL like this:

```
http://localhost/cgi-bin/myscript.pl
```

Remember to change the example URLs throughout this chapter to point to your own Web server host rather than to localhost.

Requesting a script with your browser causes it to be executed by the Web server. The script's output is sent back to you, and the result appears as a page in your browser.

When you run DBI scripts from the command line, warnings and error messages go to your terminal. In a Web environment, there is no terminal, so these messages go to the Apache error log. You should determine where this log is located because it can provide useful information to help debug your scripts. On my system, it's the error_log file in the logs directory under the Apache root, /usr/local/apache. It may be somewhere else on your system. The location of the log is determined by the ErrorLog directive in the httpd.conf configuration file, which is located in Apache's conf directory.

8.4.2 A Brief CGI.pm Primer

To write a Perl script that uses the CGI.pm module, put a use CGI statement near the beginning of the script that imports the module's function names. The standard set of the most commonly used functions can be imported like this:

```
use CGI qw(:standard);
```

Then invoke CGI.pm functions to produce various kinds of HTML structures. In general, the functions are named after the corresponding HTML elements. For example, to produce a level 1 header and a paragraph, invoke the h1() and p() functions:

```
print h1 ("This is a header");
print p ("This is a paragraph");
```

CGI.pm also supports an object-oriented style of use that enables you to invoke its functions without importing the names. To do this, include a use statement and create a CGI object:

```
use CGI;
my $cgi = new CGI;
```

The object gives you access to CGI.pm functions, which you invoke as methods of the object:

```
print $cgi->h1 ("This is a header");
print $cgi->p ("This is a paragraph");
```

The object-oriented interface requires that you write the `$cgi->` prefix all the time; in this book I'll use the simpler function call interface. However, one disadvantage of the function call interface is that if a CGI.pm function has the same name as a Perl built-in function, you must invoke it in a nonconflicting way. For example, CGI.pm has a function named `tr()` that produces the `<tr>` and `</tr>` tags that surround the cells in a row of an HTML table. That function's name conflicts with the name of the built-in Perl `tr` transliteration function. To work around this problem when using the CGI.pm function call interface, invoke `tr()` either as `Tr()` or as `TR()`. This problem does not occur with the object-oriented interface because you invoke `tr()` as a method of your `$cgi` object (that is, as `$cgi->tr()`), which makes it clear that you're not referring to the built-in Perl function.

8.4.2.1   Checking for Web Input Parameters

One of the things that CGI.pm does for you is to handle all the ugly details involved in collecting input information provided by the Web server to your script. All you need to do to get that information is invoke the `param()` function. To get an array of the names of all available parameters, do this:

```
my @param = param ();
```

To retrieve the value of a particular parameter, pass its name to `param()`. If the parameter is set, `param()` returns its value, or `undef` if it isn't set:

```
my $my_param = param ("my_param");
print "my_param value: ", (defined ($my_param) ? $my_param : "not set"), "\n";
```

8.4.2.2   Producing Web Output

Many CGI.pm functions generate output to be sent to the client browser. Consider the following HTML document:

```
<html>
<head>
<title>My Simple Page</title>
</head>
<body bgcolor="white">
<h1>Page Heading</h1>
<p>Paragraph 1.</p>
<p>Paragraph 2.</p>
</body>
</html>
```

The following script uses CGI.pm output functions to produce the equivalent document:

```
#!/usr/bin/perl
# simple_doc.pl - produce simple HTML page

use strict;
use warnings;
use CGI qw(:standard);

print header ();
print start_html (-title => "My Simple Page", -bgcolor => "white");
print h1 ("Page Heading");
print p ("Paragraph 1.");
print p ("Paragraph 2.");
print end_html ();
```

The `header()` function generates a `Content-Type:` header that precedes the page content. It's necessary to write this header when producing Web pages from scripts, to let the browser know what kind of document to expect. (This differs from the way you write static HTML pages. For those, it's not necessary to produce a header because the Web server sends one to the browser automatically.) By default, `header()` writes a header that looks like this:

```
Content-Type: text/html
```

Following the `header()` invocation are calls to functions that generate the page content. `start_html()` produces the tags from the opening `<html>` tag through the opening `<body>` tag, `h1()` and `p()` write the heading and paragraph elements, and `end_html()` adds the closing document tags.

As illustrated by the `start_html()` call, many CGI.pm functions permit you to specify named parameters, with each parameter given in `-name=>value` format. This is advantageous for functions that take many parameters that are optional, because you can specify just those parameters you need, and you can list them in any order.

Using CGI.pm output-generating functions doesn't preclude you from writing raw HTML yourself if you want. You can mix the two approaches, combining calls to CGI.pm functions with print statements that generate literal tags. However, one of the advantages of using CGI.pm to generate output is that you can think in logical units rather than in terms of individual markup tags, and your HTML is less likely to contain errors. (The reason I say "less likely" is that CGI.pm won't prevent you from doing bizarre things, such as including a list inside of a heading.)

CGI.pm also provides some portability advantages that you don't get by writing your own HTML. For example, as of version 2.69, CGI.pm automatically writes XHTML output. If you're using an older version of CGI.pm that writes plain HTML, all you need to do to upgrade your scripts to start writing XHTML instead is update CGI.pm itself.

XHTML is similar to HTML but has a more well-defined format. HTML is easy to learn and use, but one of its problems is that browser implementations tend to differ in how they interpret it.

For example, they are forgiving of malformed HTML in different ways. This means that a not-quite-correct page may display properly in one browser but incorrectly in another. XHTML's requirements are stricter, to help ensure that documents are well formed. Some of the differences between HTML and XHTML follow:

- Unlike HTML, every opening tag in XHTML must have a closing tag. For example, paragraphs are written using `<p>` and `</p>` tags, but the closing `</p>` tag often is omitted in HTML documents. In XHTML, the `</p>` tag is required. For HTML tags that don't have any body, such as `<br>` and `<hr>`, the XHTML requirement that all tags be closed in leads to ungainly constructs like `<br></br>` and `<hr></hr>`. To deal with this, XHTML permits single-tag shortcut forms (`<br/>`, `<hr/>`) that serve for both the opening and closing tags. However, older browsers that see tags like these will sometimes mistake the tag names as br/ and hr/. Inserting a space before the slash and writing the tags as `<br />` and `<hr />` helps to minimize the occurrence of such problems.

- In HTML, tag and attribute names are not case sensitive. For example, `<BODY BGCOLOR="white">` and `<body bgcolor="white">` are the same. In XHTML, tag and attribute names are lowercase, so only `<body bgcolor="white">` is permitted.

- HTML attribute values can be unquoted or even missing. For example, this table data cell construct is legal in HTML:

```
<td width=40 nowrap>Some text</td>
```

In XHTML, attributes must have values, and they must be quoted. A common convention for attributes that normally are used in HTML without a value is to use the attribute name as its value. The XHTML equivalent of the preceding `<tr>` element looks like this:

```
<td width="40" nowrap="nowrap">Some text</td>
```

All the Web scripts in this book generate output that conforms to XHTML rules. In this chapter, we'll rely on CGI.pm to generate properly formatted XHTML markup. The scripts discussed in Chapter 9, "Writing MySQL Programs Using PHP," also produce XHTML but generate the markup tags for themselves because PHP doesn't provide tag-generating functions the way CGI.pm does.

8.4.2.3   Escaping HTML and URL Text

If text that you write to a Web page contains special characters, you should make sure that they are escaped properly by processing the text with `escapeHTML()`. This is also true when you construct URLs that contain special characters, although in that case you use the `escape()` function instead. It's important to use the appropriate encoding function because each one recognizes a different set of special characters and encodes them differently. `escapeHTML()` escapes special characters as their equivalent HTML entities. For example, '<' becomes the `&lt;` entity. `escape()` escapes each special character as % followed by two hexadecimal digits representing the numeric character code, so '<' becomes %3C. Consider the following short Perl script, `escape_demo.pl`, which demonstrates both forms of escaping:

```perl
#!/usr/bin/perl
# escape_demo.pl - demonstrate CGI.pm output-encoding functions

use strict;
use warnings;
use CGI qw(escapeHTML escape);  # import escapeHTML() and escape()

# Assign default string value, but use command-line argument if present
my $s = "1<=2, right?";
$s = shift (@ARGV) if @ARGV;
print "Unencoded string:            ", $s, "\n";
print "Encoded for use as HTML text: ", escapeHTML ($s), "\n";
print "Encoded for use in a URL:    ", escape ($s), "\n";
```

The script encodes the string $s using each function and prints the result. When you run it, the script produces the following output, from which you can see that encoding conventions for HTML text are not the same as encoding for URLs:

```
unencoded string:          1<=2, right?
encoded for use as HTML text: 1&lt;=2, right?
encoded for use in a URL:    1%3C%3D2%2C%20right%3F
```

If you provide a command-line argument to escape_demo.pl, the script encodes that argument rather than the default string. This enables you to see the encoding for a string of your own choosing.

The escape_demo.pl script imports the names of the encoding functions in the use CGI statement. Depending on how current your version of CGI.pm is, they might not be included in the standard set of functions, so you'll need to import them even if you also import the standard set, like this:

```perl
use CGI qw (:standard escapeHTML escape);
```

8.4.2.4 Writing Multiple-Purpose Pages

One of the primary reasons to write Web-based scripts that generate HTML instead of writing static HTML documents is that a script can produce different kinds of pages depending on the way it's invoked. All the CGI scripts we're going to write have that property. Each one operates as follows:

- When you first request the script from your browser, it generates an initial page that enables you to select what kind of information you want.

- When you make a selection, your browser sends a request back to the Web server that causes the script to be re-invoked. The script then retrieves and displays in a second page the specific information you requested.

An issue that must be addressed here is that you want the selection that you make from the first page to determine the contents of the second page, but Web pages normally are independent of one another unless you make some sort of special arrangements. The solution is to have the script generate pages that set a parameter to a value that tells the next invocation of the script what you want. When you first invoke the script, the parameter has no value; this tells the script to present its initial page. When you indicate what information you'd like to see, the script is invoked again, but this time the parameter is set to a value that instructs the script what to do.

There are different ways for Web pages to pass instructions to a script. One is for the page to include a form that the user fills in. When the user submits the form, its contents are submitted to the Web server. The server passes the information along to the script, which can find out what was submitted by invoking the `param()` function. This is what we'll do to implement keyword searches of the Historical League directory: The search page includes a form in which the user enters the keyword to search for.

Another way of specifying instructions for a script is to add parameter values to the end of the URL sent to the Web server to request the script. This is the approach we'll use for our `sampdb` table browser and score browser scripts. The way this works is that the script generates a page containing hyperlinks. When you select a link, it invokes the script again, but the link includes a parameter value that instructs the script what to do. In effect, the script invokes itself in different ways to provide different kinds of results, depending on which link you select.

A script can enable itself to be invoked by sending to the browser a page containing a self-referential hyperlink—that is, a link to its own URL. For example, if a script `myscript.pl` is installed in the Web server's `cgi-bin` directory, it can produce a page that contains this link:

```
<a href="/cgi-bin/myscript.pl">Click Me!</a>
```

When the user clicks on the text "Click Me!" in the page, the user's browser sends a request for `myscript.pl` back to the Web server. Of course, in and of itself, all that will do is cause the script to send out the same page again because no other information is supplied in the URL. However, if you add a parameter to it, that parameter is sent back to the Web server when the user selects the link. The server invokes the script and the script can call `param()` to detect that the parameter was set and take action according to its value.

To attach a parameter to the end of the URL, add a '?' character followed by a *name=value* pair indicating the parameter name and its value. For example, to add a `size` parameter with a value of `large`, write the URL like this:

```
/cgi-bin/myscript.pl?size=large
```

To attach multiple parameters, separate them by ';' or '&' characters:

```
/cgi-bin/myscript.pl?size=large;color=blue
```

CGI.pm understands either ';' or '&' as a parameter separator character. Other language APIs for Web programming vary in their conventions, so you'll need to know whether they expect ';' or '&' and construct URLs accordingly. We use ';' here.

To construct a self-referencing URL with attached parameters, a script should begin by calling the CGI.pm `url()` function to obtain its own URL, then append parameters to it like this:

```
$url = url ();          # get URL for script
$url .= "?size=large";  # add first parameter
$url .= ";color=blue";  # add second parameter
```

Using url() to get the script path enables you to avoid hardwiring the path into the code.

To generate a hyperlink, pass the URL to CGI.pm's a() function:

```
print a ({-href => $url}, "Click Me!");
```

The print statement produces a hyperlink that looks like this:

```
<a href="/cgi-bin/url.pl?size=large;color=blue">Click Me!</a>
```

The preceding example constructs the value of $url in somewhat cavalier fashion, because it doesn't take into account the possibility that the parameter values or the link label might contain special characters. Unless you're certain that the values and the label don't require any encoding, it's best to use the CGI.pm encoding functions. The escape() function encodes values to be appended to a URL, and escapeHTML() encodes regular HTML text. For example, if the value of the hyperlink label is stored in $label, and the values for the size and color parameters are stored in the variables $size and $color, you can perform the proper encoding like this:

```
$url = sprintf ("%s?size=%s;color=%s",
                url (), escape ($size), escape ($color));
print a ({-href => $url}, escapeHTML ($label));
```

To see how self-referential URL construction works in the context of an application, consider the following short CGI script, flip_flop.pl. When first invoked, it presents a page called Page A that contains a single hyperlink. Selecting the link invokes the script again, but the link also includes a pageb parameter to tell flip_flop.pl to display Page B. (In this case, we don't care about the parameter's value, just whether it's set.) Page B also contains a link to the script, but without a pageb parameter. This means that selecting the link in Page B causes the original page to be redisplayed. In other words, subsequent invocations of the script flip the page back and forth between Page A and Page B:

```
#!/usr/bin/perl
# flip_flop.pl - simple multiple-output-page CGI.pm script

use strict;
use warnings;
use CGI qw(:standard);

my $url;
my $this_page;
my $next_page;

# determine which page to display based on absence or presence
# of the pageb parameter
```

```
if (!defined (param ("pageb")))  # display page A w/link to page B
{
  $this_page = "A";
  $next_page = "B";
  $url = url () . "?pageb=1";
}
else                            # display page B w/link to page A
{
  $this_page = "B";
  $next_page = "A";
  $url = url ();
}

print header ();
print start_html (-title => "Flip-Flop: Page $this_page",
                  -bgcolor => "white");
print p ("This is Page $this_page. To select Page $next_page, "
         . a ({-href => $url}, "click here"));
print end_html ();
```

Install the script in your `cgi-bin` directory, then request it from your browser using a URL like this one, but substituting the name of your own Web server for `localhost`:

`http://localhost/cgi-bin/flip_flop.pl`

Select the link in the page several times to see how the script alternates the pages that it generates.

Now, suppose that another client comes along and starts requesting `flip_flop.pl`. What happens? Will the two of you interfere with each other? No, because the initial request from each of you includes no `pageb` parameter, and the script responds with its initial page. Thereafter, the requests sent by each of you include or omit the parameter according to which page you currently happen to be viewing. `flip_flop.pl` generates an alternating series of pages properly for each client, independent of the actions of any other client.

8.4.3   Connecting to the MySQL Server from Web Scripts

The command-line scripts developed earlier in Section 8.3, "Putting DBI to Work," shared a common preamble for establishing a connection to the MySQL server. Most of our CGI scripts share some preamble code, too, but it's a little different:

```
#!/usr/bin/perl

use strict;
use warnings;
use DBI;
use CGI qw(:standard);
```

```
use Cwd;
# option file that should contain connection parameters for UNIX
my $option_file = "/usr/local/apache/conf/sampdb.cnf";
my $option_drive_root;
# override file location for Windows
if ($^O =~ /^MSWin/i || $^O =~ /^dos/)
{
  $option_drive_root = "C:/";
  $option_file = "/Apache/conf/sampdb.cnf";
}

# construct data source and connect to server (under Windows, save
# current working directory first, change location to option file
# drive, connect, and restore current directory)
my $orig_dir;
if (defined ($option_drive_root))
{
  $orig_dir = cwd ();
  chdir ($option_drive_root)
    or die "Cannot chdir to $option_drive_root: $!\n";
}
my $dsn = "DBI:mysql:sampdb;mysql_read_default_file=$option_file";
my %conn_attrs = (RaiseError => 1, PrintError => 0, AutoCommit => 1);
my $dbh = DBI->connect ($dsn, undef, undef, \%conn_attrs);
if (defined ($option_drive_root))
{
  chdir ($orig_dir)
    or die "Cannot chdir to $orig_dir: $!\n";
}
```

This preamble differs from the one we used for command-line scripts in the following respects:

- The first section now contains use CGI and use Cwd statements. The first is for the CGI.pm module. The second is for the module that returns the pathname of the current working directory; it's used in case the script is running under Windows, as described later.

- No connection parameters are parsed from the command-line arguments. Instead, the code assumes that they'll be listed in an option file.

- Instead of using mysql_read_default_group to read the standard option files, we use mysql_read_default_file to read a single file intended specifically for options to be used by Web scripts that access the sampdb database. As shown, the code looks for options stored in /usr/local/apache/conf/sampdb.cnf under Unix, or in C:\Apache\conf\sampdb.cnf under Windows. Note that, under Windows, the code changes location to the root directory of the drive where the option file is located before connecting, and back to the original directory afterward. The rationale for this ugly hack is described in Section 8.2.9, "Specifying Connection Parameters."

The `sampdb` distribution contains a `sampdb.cnf` file that you can install for use by your DBI-based Web scripts. It looks like this:

```
[client]
host=localhost
user=sampadm
password=secret
```

To use the Web-based scripts developed in this chapter on your own system, change the option file location in the preamble if you use a different location. You must also install the `sampdb.cnf` option file in the appropriate location and list in it option values for the MySQL server host and the MySQL account name and password that you want to use.

Under Unix, set the option file to be owned by the account used to run Apache and set the file's mode to 400 or 600 so that no other user can read it. This prevents one form of security exploit because it keeps other users who have login accounts on the Web server host from reading the option file directly.

Unfortunately, the option file still can be read by other users who can install a script for the Web server to execute. Scripts invoked by the Web server execute with the privileges of the login account used for running the Web server. This means that another user who can install a Web script can write the script so that it opens the option file and displays its contents in a Web page. Because that script runs as the Web server user, it will have full permission to read the file, which exposes the connection parameters necessary to connect to MySQL and access the `sampdb` database. If you are the only person with login access on your Web server host, this doesn't matter. But if other users that you don't trust have login access on the machine, you might find it prudent to create a MySQL account that has read-only (`SELECT`) privileges on the `sampdb` database. Then list that account's name and password in the `sampdb.cnf` file, rather than your own name and password. That way you don't risk permitting scripts to connect to your database through a MySQL account that has permission to modify its tables. Chapter 13, "Security and Access Control," discusses how to create a MySQL user account with restricted privileges. The downside of this strategy is that with a read-only MySQL account, you can write scripts only for data retrieval, not for data entry.

Alternatively, arrange to execute scripts under Apache's suEXEC mechanism. This enables you to execute a script as a specific trusted login user so that you can write the script to get the connection parameters from an option file that is readable only to that user.

Still another option for writing a script is to have it solicit a MySQL account username and password from the client and use those values to establish a connection to the MySQL server. This is more suitable for scripts that you create for administrative purposes than for scripts that you provide for general use. In any case, you should be aware that some methods of name and password solicitation are subject to attack by anyone who can put a sniffer on the network between the Web server and your browser, so you may want to set up a secure connection. That is beyond the scope of this book.

As you may gather from the preceding paragraphs, Web script security can be a tricky thing. It's definitely a topic about which you should read more for yourself, because it's a big subject which I really cannot do justice to here. The book *MySQL and Perl for the Web* mentioned earlier includes a chapter devoted specifically to Web security, including instructions for setting up secure connections using SSL. Other good sources of information are the security material in the Apache manual, and the WWW security FAQ available at `http://www.w3.org/Security/Faq`.

8.4.4   A Web-Based Database Browser

Our first Web-based MySQL application is a simple script, `db_browse.pl`, that enables you to see what tables exist in the `sampdb` database and to examine the contents of any of these tables interactively from your Web browser. The script works like this:

- When you first request `db_browse.pl` from your browser, it connects to the MySQL server, retrieves a list of tables in the `sampdb` database, and sends your browser a page that presents each table as a hyperlink. When you select a table name link from this page, your browser sends a request to the Web server asking `db_browse.pl` to display the contents of that table.

- If `db_browse.pl` finds when it's invoked that you've selected a table name, it retrieves the contents of the table and presents the information to your Web browser. The heading for each column of data is the name of the column in the table. Headings are presented as hyperlinks; if you select one of them, your browser sends a request to the Web server to redisplay the same table, sorted by the column you selected.

> **Warning**
>
> Before we go any further, be aware that although `db_browse.pl` is instructive in terms of illustrating several useful Web programming concepts, it also represents a security hole. The script displays any table in the `sampdb` database, which can be a problem: In Chapter 9, "Writing MySQL Programs Using PHP," we'll write a script that Historical League members can use to edit their membership entries over the Web. Access to the entries is controlled through passwords that are stored in a `member_pass` table. Having `db_browse.pl` enabled at that point would enable anyone to look through the password table, and thus gain access to the information necessary to edit any `member` table entry! Thus, it's a good idea to remove the script from your `cgi-bin` directory after you've tried it and understand how it works. (Alternatively, install it on a private Web server not accessible to untrusted users.)

Assuming that you haven't been spooked by the preceding dire warnings, let's see how `db_browse.pl` works. The main body of the script puts out the initial part of the Web page, then checks the `tbl_name` parameter to see whether it's supposed to display some particular table:

```
#!/usr/bin/perl
# db_browse.pl - Enable sampdb database browsing over the Web

use strict;
use warnings;
```

```
use DBI;
use CGI qw (:standard escapeHTML escape);

# ... set up connection to database (not shown) ...

my $db_name = "sampdb";

# put out initial part of page
my $title = "$db_name Database Browser";
print header ();
print start_html (-title => $title, -bgcolor => "white");
print h1 ($title);

# parameters to look for in URL
my $tbl_name = param ("tbl_name");
my $sort_col = param ("sort_col");

# If $tbl_name has no value, display a clickable list of tables.
# Otherwise, display contents of the given table.  $sort_col, if
# set, indicates which column to sort by.

if (!defined ($tbl_name))
{
  display table_names ($dbh, $db_name)
}
else
{
  display_table_contents ($dbh, $db_name, $tbl_name, $sort_col);
}

print end_html ();
```

It's easy to obtain a parameter value because CGI.pm does all the work of finding out what information the Web server passes to the script. We need only call `param()` with the name of the parameter in which we're interested. In the main body of `db_browse.pl`, that parameter is named `tbl_name`. If it's not set, this is the initial invocation of the script and it displays the table list. Otherwise, it displays the contents of the table named by the `tbl_name` parameter, sorted by the column named in the `sort_col` parameter.

The `display_table_names()` function generates the initial page. `display_table_names()` retrieves the table list and writes out a bullet list in which each item is the name of a table in the `sampdb` database:

```
sub display_table_names
{
my ($dbh, $db_name) = @_;

  print p ("Select a table by clicking on its name:");
```

```
  # retrieve reference to single-column array of table names
  my $sth = $dbh->prepare (qq{
              SELECT TABLE_NAME FROM INFORMATION_SCHEMA.TABLES
              WHERE TABLE_SCHEMA = ? ORDER BY TABLE_NAME
            });
  $sth->execute ($db_name);

  # Construct a bullet list using the ul() (unordered list) and
  # li() (list item) functions.  Each item is a hyperlink that
  # re-invokes the script to display a particular table.
  my @item;
  while (my ($tbl_name) = $sth->fetchrow_array ())
  {
    my $url = sprintf ("%s?tbl_name=%s", url (), escape ($tbl_name));
    my $link = a ({-href => $url}, escapeHTML ($tbl_name));
    push (@item, li ($link));
  }
  print ul (@item);
}
```

The li() function adds <li> and </li> tags around each list item and ul() adds the <ul> and </ul> tags around the set of items. Each table name in the list is a hyperlink that reinvokes the script to display the contents of the named table. The resulting list generated by display_table_names() looks like this:

```
<ul>
<li><a href="/cgi-bin/db_browse.pl?tbl_name=absence">absence</a></li>
<li><a href="/cgi-bin/db_browse.pl?tbl_name=grade_event">grade_event</a></li>
<li><a href="/cgi-bin/db_browse.pl?tbl_name=member">member</a></li>
...
</ul>
```

If the tbl_name parameter has a value when db_browse.pl is invoked, the script passes that value to display_table_contents(), along with the name of the column by which to sort the results if one was given:

```
sub display_table_contents
{
my ($dbh, $db_name, $tbl_name, $sort_col) = @_;
my $sort_clause = "";
my @rows;
my @cells;

  # if sort column is specified, use it to sort the results
  if (defined ($sort_col))
  {
    $sort_clause = " ORDER BY " . $dbh->quote_identifier ($sort_col);
  }
```

```perl
# present a link that returns user to table list page
print p (a ({-href => url ()}, "Show Table List"));

print p (strong ("Contents of $tbl_name table:"));

my $sth = $dbh->prepare (
            "SELECT * FROM "
          . $dbh->quote_identifier ($db_name, $tbl_name)
          . "$sort_clause LIMIT 200"
          );
$sth->execute ();

# Use the names of the columns in the database table as the
# headings in an HTML table.  Make each name a hyperlink that
# causes the script to be reinvoked to redisplay the table,
# sorted by the named column.

foreach my $col_name (@{$sth->{NAME}})
{
  my $url = sprintf ("%s?tbl_name=%s;sort_col=%s",
                     url (),
                     escape ($tbl_name),
                     escape ($col_name));
  my $link = a ({-href => $url}, escapeHTML ($col_name));
  push (@cells, th ($link));
}
push (@rows, Tr (@cells));

# display table rows
while (my @ary = $sth->fetchrow_array ())
{
  @cells = ();
  foreach my $val (@ary)
  {
    # display value if non-empty, else display non-breaking space
    if (defined ($val) && $val ne "")
    {
      $val = escapeHTML ($val);
    }
    else
    {
      $val = " ";
    }
    push (@cells, td ($val));
  }
  push (@rows, Tr (@cells));
}
```

```
  # display table with a border
  print table ({-border => "1"}, @rows);
}
```

The query also includes a `LIMIT 200` clause, as a simple precaution against the script sending huge amounts of data to your browser. (That's not likely to happen for the tables in the `sampdb` database, but it might occur if you adapt the script to display the contents of tables in other databases.) `display_table_contents()` shows the rows from the table as an HTML table, using the `th()` and `td()` functions to produce table header and data cells, `Tr()` to group cells into rows, and `table()` to produce the `<table>` tags that surround the rows.

The HTML table presents column headings as hyperlinks that redisplay the database table. These links include a `sort_col` parameter that explicitly specifies the column to use for sorting. For example, for a page that displays the contents of the `grade_event` table, the column heading links look like this:

```
<a href="/cgi-bin/db_browse.pl?tbl_name=grade_event&sort_col=date">
date</a>
<a href="/cgi-bin/db_browse.pl?tbl_name=grade_event&sort_col=category">
category</a>
<a href="/cgi-bin/db_browse.pl?tbl_name=grade_event&sort_col=event_id">
event_id</a>
```

`display_table_contents()` uses a little trick of turning empty values into a nonbreaking space (` `). In a bordered table, some browsers don't display borders for empty cells properly; putting a nonbreaking space in the cell fixes that problem.

To write a more general script, you could alter `db_browse.pl` to browse multiple databases. For example, you could have the script begin by displaying a list of databases on the server, rather than a list of tables within a particular database. Then you could pick a database to get a list of its tables and go from there.

8.4.5 A Grade-Keeping Project Score Browser

Our next Web script, `score_browse.pl`, is designed to display scores that have been recorded for the grade-keeping project. Strictly speaking, we should have a way of entering the scores before we create a way of retrieving them, but I'm saving the score entry script until the next chapter. In the meantime, we do have several sets of scores in the database already from the early part of the grading period. We can use the script to display those scores, even in the absence of a convenient score entry method. The script displays an ordered list of scores for any test or quiz, which is useful for determining the grading curve and assigning letter grades.

`score_browse.pl` has some similarities to `db_browse.pl` (both serve as information browsers), but is intended for the more specific purpose of examining scores for a given quiz or test. The initial page presents a list of the possible grade events from which to choose, and enables the user to select any of them to see the scores associated with the event. Scores for a given event are sorted with the highest scores first, so you can use the result to determine the grading curve.

The `score_browse.pl` script needs to examine only one parameter, `event_id`, to see whether a grade event was specified. If not, `score_browse.pl` displays the rows of the `grade_event` table so that the user can select one. Otherwise, it displays the scores associated with the chosen event:

```
# ... set up connection to database (not shown) ...

# put out initial part of page
my $title = "Grade-Keeping Project -- Score Browser";
print header ();
print start_html (-title => $title, -bgcolor => "white");
print h1 ($title);

# parameter that tells us which grade event to display scores for
my $event_id = param ("event_id");

# if $event_id has no value, display the event list.
# otherwise display the scores for the given event.
if (!defined ($event_id))
{
  display_events ($dbh)
}
else
{
  display_scores ($dbh, $event_id);
}

print end_html ();
```

The `display_events()` function pulls out information from the `grade_event` table and displays it as a table, using column names from the query for the table column headings. Within each row, the `event_id` value is a hyperlink that can be selected to trigger a query that retrieves the scores for the event. The URL for each event is simply the path to `score_browse.pl` with a parameter attached that specifies the event number:

```
/cgi-bin/score_browse.pl?event_id=n
```

`display_events()` looks like this:

```
sub display_events
{
my $dbh = shift;
my @rows;
my @cells;

  print p ("Select an event by clicking on its number:");

  # get list of events
```

```
my $sth = $dbh->prepare (qq{
            SELECT event_id, date, category
            FROM grade_event
            ORDER BY event_id
          });
$sth->execute ();

# use column names for table column headings
for (my $i = 0; $i < $sth->{NUM_OF_FIELDS}; $i++)
{
  push (@cells, th (escapeHTML ($sth->{NAME}->[$i])));
}
push (@rows, Tr (@cells));

# display information for each event as a row in a table
while (my ($event_id, $date, $category) = $sth->fetchrow_array ())
{
  @cells = ();
  # display event ID as a hyperlink that reinvokes the script
  # to show the event's scores
  my $url = sprintf ("%s?event_id=%d", url (), $event_id);
  my $link = a ({-href => $url}, escapeHTML ($event_id));
  push (@cells, td ($link));
  # display event date and category
  push (@cells, td (escapeHTML ($date)));
  push (@cells, td (escapeHTML ($category)));
  push (@rows, Tr (@cells));
}

  # display table with a border
  print table ({-border => "1"}, @rows);
}
```

When the user selects an event, the browser sends a request for `score_browse.pl` that has an event ID at the end. `score_browse.pl` finds the `event_id` parameter set and calls the `display_scores()` function to list all the scores for the specified event. This function also displays the text "Show Event List" as a hyperlink back to the initial page so that the user can easily return to the event list page and select a different event:

```
sub display_scores
{
my ($dbh, $event_id) = @_;
my @rows;
my @cells;

  # Generate a link to the script that does not include any event_id
  # parameter.  If the user selects this link, the script displays
```

```perl
# the event list.
print p (a ({-href => url ()}, "Show Event List"));

# select scores for the given event
my $sth = $dbh->prepare (qq{
           SELECT
             student.name,
             grade_event.date,
             score.score,
             grade_event.category
           FROM
             student INNER JOIN score INNER JOIN grade_event
           ON
             student.student_id = score.student_id
             AND score.event_id = grade_event.event_id
           WHERE
             grade_event.event_id = ?
           ORDER BY
             grade_event.date ASC,
             grade_event.category ASC,
             score.score DESC
});
$sth->execute ($event_id);  # bind event ID to placeholder in query

print p (strong ("Scores for grade event $event_id"));

# use column names for table column headings
for (my $i = 0; $i < $sth->{NUM_OF_FIELDS}; $i++)
{
  push (@cells, th (escapeHTML ($sth->{NAME}->[$i])));
}
push (@rows, Tr (@cells));

while (my @ary = $sth->fetchrow_array ())
{
  @cells = ();
  foreach my $val (@ary)
  {
    # display value if non-empty, else display non-breaking space
    if (defined ($val) && $val ne "")
    {
      $val = escapeHTML ($val);
    }
    else
    {
      $val = " ";
```

```
    }
    push (@cells, td ($val));
  }
  push (@rows, Tr (@cells));
}

# display table with a border
print table ({-border => "1"}, @rows);
}
```

The statement that `display_scores()` executes is quite similar to one that we developed in Section 1.4.9.10, "Retrieving Information from Multiple Tables," which describes how to write joins. In that section, we asked for scores for a given date because dates are more meaningful than event ID values. In contrast, when we use `score_browse.pl`, we know the exact event ID. That's not because we think in terms of event IDs (we don't), but because the script presents a list of them from which to choose, along with their dates and categories. You can see that this type of interface reduces the need to know particular details. You need not know an event ID; it's necessary only to be able to recognize the date of the event you want. The script associates it with the proper ID for you.

8.4.6   Historical League Common-Interest Searching

The `db_browse.pl` and `score_browse.pl` scripts enable the user to make a selection from a list of choices in an initial page, where the choices are presented as hyperlinks that re-invoke the script with particular parameter values. Another way to enable users to provide information is to present a form that the user fills in. This is more appropriate when the range of possible choices isn't constrained to some easily determined set of values. Our next script demonstrates this method of soliciting user input.

In Section 8.3, "Putting DBI to Work," we constructed a command-line script, `interests.pl`, for finding Historical League members who share a particular interest. However, that script isn't something that League members have access to; the League secretary must run the script from the command prompt and then mail the result to the member who requested the list. It'd be nice to make this search capability more widely available so that members could use it for themselves. Writing a Web-based script is one way to do that. The rest of this section discusses two approaches to table searching. The first is based on pattern matching, and the second uses MySQL FULLTEXT search capabilities.

8.4.6.1   Performing Searches Using Pattern Matching

The first search script, `ushl_browse.pl`, displays a form into which the user can enter a keyword. When the user submits the form, the script is re-invoked to search the `member` table for qualifying members and display the results. The search is done by adding the '%' wildcard character to both ends of the keyword and performing a LIKE pattern match, which finds rows that have the keyword anywhere in the `interests` column value.

The main part of the script displays the keyword form. It also checks to see whether a keyword was just submitted and performs a search if so:

```perl
my $title = "U.S. Historical League Interest Search";
print header ();
print start_html (-title => $title, -bgcolor => "white");
print h1 ($title);

# parameter to look for
my $keyword = param ("keyword");

# Display a keyword entry form.  In addition, if $keyword is defined,
# search for and display a list of members who have that interest.

print start_form (-method => "post");
print p ("Enter a keyword to search for:");
print textfield (-name => "keyword", -value => "", -size => 40);
print submit (-name => "button", -value => "Search");
print end_form ();

# connect to server and run a search if a keyword was specified
if (defined ($keyword) && $keyword !~ /^\s*$/)
{
  # ... set up connection to database (not shown) ...
  search_members ($dbh, $keyword);
  # ... disconnect (not shown) ...
}
```

The script communicates information to itself a little differently than db_browse.pl or score_browse.pl. It does not add a parameter to the end of a URL. Instead, the browser encodes the information in the form and sends it as part of a post request. However, CGI.pm makes it irrelevant how the information is sent, because param() returns the parameter value no matter how it was sent—just one more thing that CGI.pm does to make Web programming easier.

Keyword searches are performed by the search_members() function. It takes a database handle and the keyword as arguments, and then runs the search query and displays the list of matching member rows:

```perl
sub search_members
{
my ($dbh, $interest) = @_;

  print p ("Search results for keyword: " . escapeHTML ($interest));
  my $sth = $dbh->prepare (qq{
          SELECT * FROM member WHERE interests LIKE ?
          ORDER BY last_name, first_name
        });
```

```
  # look for string anywhere in interest field
  $sth->execute ("%" . $interest . "%");
  my $count = 0;
  while (my $ref = $sth->fetchrow_hashref ())
  {
    html_format_entry ($ref);
    ++$count;
  }
  print p ("Number of matching entries: $count");
}
```

When you run the ushl_browse.pl script, you'll notice that each time you submit a keyword value, it's redisplayed in the form on the next page, even though the script specifies an empty string as the value of the keyword field when it generates the form. This happens because CGI.pm automatically fills in form fields with values from the script execution environment if they are present. To defeat this behavior and make the field blank every time, include an override parameter in the textfield() call:

```
print textfield (-name => "keyword",
                 -value => "",
                 -override => 1,
                 -size => 40);
```

search_members() uses a helper function html_format_entry() to display individual entries. That function is much like the one of the same name that we wrote earlier for the gen_dir.pl script. (See Section 8.3.1, "Generating the Historical League Directory.") However, whereas the earlier version of the function generated HTML by printing markup tags directly, the version used by ushl_browse.pl uses CGI.pm functions to produce the tags:

```
sub html_format_entry
{
my $entry_ref = shift;

  # encode characters that are special in HTML
  foreach my $key (keys (%{$entry_ref}))
  {
    next unless defined ($entry_ref->{$key});
    $entry_ref->{$key} = escapeHTML ($entry_ref->{$key});
  }
  print strong ("Name: " . format_name ($entry_ref)), br ();
  my $address = "";
  $address .= $entry_ref->{street}
              if defined ($entry_ref->{street});
  $address .= ", " . $entry_ref->{city}
              if defined ($entry_ref->{city});
  $address .= ", " . $entry_ref->{state}
              if defined ($entry_ref->{state});
```

```
    $address .= " " . $entry_ref->{zip}
                if defined ($entry_ref->{zip});
    print "Address: $address", br ()
                if $address ne "";
    print "Telephone: $entry_ref->{phone}", br ()
                if defined ($entry_ref->{phone});
    print "Email: $entry_ref->{email}", br ()
                if defined ($entry_ref->{email});
    print "Interests: $entry_ref->{interests}", br ()
                if defined ($entry_ref->{interests});
    print br ();
}
```

html_format_entry() uses the format_name() function to glue the first_name, last_name, and suffix column values together. It's identical to the function of the same name in the gen_dir.pl script.

8.4.6.2   Performing Searches Using a FULLTEXT Index

Historical League members may have multiple interests. If so, they are separated by commas in the interests column of the member table. For example:

```
Revolutionary War,Spanish-American War,Colonial period,Gold rush,Lincoln
```

Can you use ushl_browse.pl, to search for rows that match any of several keywords? Sort of, but not really. You can enter several words into the search form, but rows won't match unless you construct a more complicated query that looks for a match on each word. A more flexible way to approach the interest-searching task is to use a FULLTEXT index. This section describes a script ushl_ft_browse.pl that does so. For more information about MySQL's FULLTEXT capabilities, see Section 2.14, "Using FULLTEXT Searches."

Before you can use the member table for FULLTEXT searching, it must be a MyISAM table. If you created member using some other storage engine, convert it to a MyISAM table with ALTER TABLE:

```
ALTER TABLE member ENGINE=MyISAM;
```

Next, it's necessary to index the member table properly. To do that, use the following statement:

```
ALTER TABLE member ADD FULLTEXT (interests);
```

That enables the interests column to be used for FULLTEXT searches. The ushl_ft_ browse.pl script in the sampdb distribution is based on ushl_browse.pl, and differs from it only in the search_members() function that constructs the search query. The modified version of the function looks like this:

```
sub search_members
{
my ($dbh, $interest) = @_;
```

```
  print p ("Search results for keyword: " . escapeHTML ($interest));
  my $sth = $dbh->prepare (qq{
              SELECT * FROM member WHERE MATCH(interests) AGAINST(?)
              ORDER BY last_name, first_name
          });
  # look for string anywhere in interest field
  $sth->execute ($interest);
  my $count = 0;
  while (my $ref = $sth->fetchrow_hashref ())
  {
    html_format_entry ($ref);
    ++$count;
  }
  print p ("Number of matching entries: $count");
}
```

This version of `search_members()` has the following changes relative to the earlier one:

- The query uses `MATCH()` ... `AGAINST()` rather than `LIKE`.
- No '`%`' wildcard characters are needed to convert the keyword string to a pattern.

With these changes, you can invoke `ush1_ft_browse.pl` from your Web browser and enter multiple keywords into the search form (with or without commas). The script finds member entries that match any of them.

You could get a lot fancier with this script. One possibility is to take advantage of the fact that `FULLTEXT` searches can search multiple columns at once by setting up the index to span several columns and modifying `ush1_ft_browse.pl` to search them all. For example, you could drop the original `FULLTEXT` index and add another that uses the `last_name` and `full_name` columns in addition to the `interests` column:

```
ALTER TABLE member DROP INDEX interests;
ALTER TABLE member ADD FULLTEXT (interests,last_name,first_name);
```

To use the new index, modify the `SELECT` statement in the `search_members()` function to change `MATCH(interests)` to `MATCH(interests,last_name,first_name)`.

Another change you might make to `ush1_ft_browse.pl` is to add a couple of radio buttons to the form to enable the user to choose between "match any keyword" and "match all keywords" modes. The "match any" mode is the one which the script uses currently. To implement a "match all" mode, change the statement to use an `IN BOOLEAN MODE` type of `FULLTEXT` search, and precede each keyword by a '`+`' character to require that it be present in matching rows. For information about boolean mode searching, see Section 2.14.2, "Boolean Mode `FULLTEXT` Searches."

9

Writing MySQL Programs Using PHP

PHP is a scripting language for writing Web pages containing embedded code that is executed whenever a page is accessed and that can generate dynamic content to be included as part of the output sent to a client's Web browser. This chapter describes how to write PHP-based Web applications that use MySQL. For a comparison of PHP with the C and Perl DBI APIs for MySQL programming, see Chapter 6, "Introduction to MySQL Programming."

This chapter was written under the assumption that you use PHP in conjunction with the Apache Web server, although you can probably substitute a different server. PHP can be used as an Apache module or as a standalone interpreter used as a traditional CGI program. Running PHP as a module is preferable for performance reasons.

The examples in this chapter draw on our sampdb sample database, using the tables created for the grade-keeping project and for the Historical League in Chapter 1, "Getting Started with MySQL." If you need to obtain any of the software used here, see Appendix A, "Software Required to Use This Book," which also has instructions for obtaining the sampdb distribution that contains the example scripts developed in this chapter. You'll find the scripts under the phpapi directory of that distribution.

PHP offers several database-access interfaces for MySQL:

- The mysql extension is the original interface to MySQL. It consists of functions with names of the form mysql_xxx(). For the most part, these map directly onto the C API functions with the same names. mysql provides no access to features developed in MySQL 4.1 and up and is now considered deprecated.

- The "MySQL improved" extension, mysqli. This extension provides two calling styles. You can use it as a set of functions with names of the form mysqli_xxx(), or through an object-oriented interface.

- The PHP Data Objects (PDO) extension is less tied to specific database engines. PDO provides an object-oriented database-independent interface similar in design to the Perl DBI module. It uses a two-level architecture in which the top level presents a uniform interface and the lower level consists of drivers for various database engines. To switch from one driver to another, you modify the arguments passed to the connection call so that they are appropriate for the driver that you want to use.

This chapter uses PDO for writing PHP scripts. PDO works with PHP 5.0 and up, but this chapter assumes a minimum of PHP 5.1 because that is when PDO was first bundled with PHP. See http://www.php.net/pdo for more information.

The PDO driver for MySQL was originally designed to be linked against the MySQL C client library (the `libmysqlclient` library described in Appendix G, "C API Reference"). This design makes PHP dependent on a part of the MySQL distribution when you use PHP to access MySQL databases. Alternatively, the newer `mysqlnd` library is a native driver that implements the same communication protocol as `libmysqlclient` and can be used as a replacement for it. `mysqlnd` makes it possible to access MySQL databases from PHP without having the MySQL client library installed. `mysqlnd` is included in PHP as of version 5.3 and is the default library as of 5.4. Thus, to use PDO with `mysqlnd`, you'll need at least PHP 5.3.

For the most part, this chapter describes only those PDO objects and methods that are needed for the discussion here. It also covers only the MySQL driver for PDO. Drivers for other database engines are available as well, but are not discussed here. For a more comprehensive listing of the PDO interface, see Appendix I, "PHP API Reference." You'll likely also want to consult the PHP manual, which describes all PHP capabilities. The manual is available from the PHP Web site: http://www.php.net

Filenames for PHP scripts generally end with a suffix that enables your Web server to recognize that they should be executed by invoking the PHP interpreter. If you use a suffix that the server doesn't recognize, it will serve your PHP scripts as plain text. Scripts in this chapter use the .php suffix. For instructions on configuring Apache to recognize the suffix you want to use, see Appendix A, "Software Required to Use This Book." (If you are not in control of the Apache installation on your machine, check with the system administrator to find out the proper suffix to use.) The appendix also describes how to set up Apache to treat any script named index.php as the default page for the directory in which it is located, similar to the way Apache treats files named index.html.

To use the scripts developed in this chapter, you must install them where your Web server can access them. The convention used here is that the U.S. Historical League and grade-keeping projects have their own directories called ushl and gp at the top level of the Apache document tree. To set up your Web server that way, you should create those directories now. For a server running on the local host, pages in those two directories will have URLs that begin like this:

```
http://localhost/ushl/...
http://localhost/gp/...
```

For example, the home pages in each directory can be called index.php and are accessed as follows:

```
http://localhost/ushl/index.php
http://localhost/gp/index.php
```

If you have Apache configured to use `index.php` as the default page for a directory, the following URLs are equivalent in practice to the preceding ones:

```
http://localhost/ushl/
http://localhost/gp/
```

Remember to change the example URLs throughout this chapter to point to your own Web server host rather than to `localhost`.

9.1 PHP Overview

The basic operation of PHP is to interpret a script to produce a Web page that is sent to a client. A PHP script typically contains a mix of HTML and executable code. The HTML is sent to the client without modification, whereas the PHP code is executed and replaced by whatever output it produces. Consequently, the client never sees the code; it sees only the resulting HTML page. (The PHP scripts developed in this chapter generate pages that are well formed as XHTML, not just as HTML. For a brief description of XHTML, see Section 8.4.2.2, "Producing Web Output.")

When the PHP interpreter begins reading a file, it simply copies whatever it finds there to the output, under the assumption that the contents of the file represent literal text, such as HTML content. When PHP encounters a special opening tag, it switches from text copy mode to PHP code mode and starts interpreting the file as PHP code to be executed. The interpreter switches from code mode back to text mode when it sees another special tag that signals the end of the code. This enables you to mix static text (the HTML part) with dynamically generated results (output from the PHP code part) to produce a page that varies depending on the circumstances under which it is called. For example, you might use a PHP script to process the result of a form into which a user has entered parameters for a database search. Depending on what the user types, the search parameters might differ each time the form is submitted, so when the script searches for and displays the information the user requested, each resulting page is different.

Let's see how PHP works, beginning with an extremely simple script:

```
<html>
<body>
<p>hello, world</p>
</body>
</html>
```

This script is in fact *so* simple that it contains no PHP code! "What good is that?," you ask. That's a reasonable question. The answer is that it's sometimes useful to set up a script containing just the HTML framework for the page you want to produce and then add the PHP code later. This is perfectly legal, and the PHP interpreter has no problem with it.

To include PHP code in a script, distinguish it from the surrounding text with the special opening and closing tags: `<?php` and `?>`. When the PHP interpreter encounters the opening `<?php` tag, it switches from text mode to PHP code mode and treats whatever it finds as

executable code until it sees the closing `?>` tag. The code between the tags is interpreted and replaced by its output. The previous example can be rewritten to include a small section of PHP code like this:

```
<html>
<body>
<p><?php print ("hello, world"); ?></p>
</body>
</html>
```

In this case, the code part is minimal, consisting of a single line. When the code executes, it produces the output `hello, world`, which becomes part of the output sent to the client's browser. Thus, the Web page produced by this script is equivalent to the one produced by the preceding example, where the script consisted entirely of HTML.

PHP code can generate any part of a Web page. We've already seen one extreme, in which the entire script consists of literal HTML and contains no PHP code. The other extreme is to produce the HTML completely from within code mode:

```
<?php
print ("<html>\n");
print ("<body>\n");
print ("<p>hello, world</p>\n");
print ("</body>\n");
print ("</html>\n");
?>
```

These three examples demonstrate that PHP gives you a lot of flexibility in how you produce output. PHP leaves it to you to decide whatever combination of HTML and PHP code is appropriate. PHP is also flexible in that you need not put all your code in one place. You can switch between text mode and PHP code mode throughout the script however you please, as often as you want.

PHP supports tag styles other than the `<?php` and `?>` style that is used for examples in this chapter. See Appendix I, "PHP API Reference," for a description of the tag styles that are available and instructions on enabling them.

Standalone PHP Scripts

The example scripts in this chapter are written with the expectation that they will be invoked by a Web server to generate a Web page. However, if you have a standalone version of PHP, you can use it to execute PHP scripts from the command line. Suppose that you have a script named `hello.php` that looks like this:

```
<?php print ("hello, world\n"); ?>
```

To execute the script from the command line yourself, use this command:

```
% php hello.php
hello, world
```

This is sometimes useful when you're working on a script, because you can see right away whether it has syntax errors or other problems without having to request the script from a browser each time you make a change.

9.1.1   A Simple PHP Script

If PHP provided only the capability of producing what is essentially static HTML by means of print statements, it wouldn't be very useful. PHP's power is that it generates dynamic pages: output that can vary from one invocation of a script to the next. The script described in this section shows a simple example of this capability. It's still relatively short, but a bit more substantial than the previous examples. It shows how easily you can access a MySQL database from PHP and use the results of a query in a Web page. The script forms a simple basis for a home page for the Historical League Web site. As we go on, we'll make the script a bit more elaborate, but for now all it does is display a short welcome message and a count of the current League membership:

```
<html>
<head>
<title>U.S. Historical League</title>
</head>
<body bgcolor="white">
<h2>U.S. Historical League</h2>
<p>Welcome to the U.S. Historical League Web Site.</p>
<?php
# USHL home page

try
{
  $dbh = new PDO("mysql:host=localhost;dbname=sampdb", "sampadm", "secret");
  $dbh->setAttribute (PDO::ATTR_ERRMODE, PDO::ERRMODE_EXCEPTION);
  $sth = $dbh->query ("SELECT COUNT(*) FROM member");
  $count = $sth->fetchColumn (0);
  print ("<p>The League currently has $count members.</p>");
  $dbh = NULL;  # close connection
}
catch (PDOException $e) { } # empty handler (catch but ignore errors)
?>
</body>
</html>
```

The welcome message is just static text, so it's easiest to write it as literal HTML. The membership count, on the other hand, is dynamic and changes over time, so it must be determined at execution time by querying the `member` table in the `sampdb` database. To perform that task, the code within the opening and closing script tags follows these steps:

1. Open a connection to the MySQL server and make the `sampdb` database the default database.

2. Enable exceptions for subsequent PDO calls so that errors can be caught easily without testing for them explicitly.

3. Send a query to the server to determine how many members the Historical League has at the moment (assessed as the number of rows in the `member` table).

4. Use the query result to construct a message containing the membership count.

5. Close the connection to the MySQL server.

The script just shown can be found as the file named `index.php` in the `phpapi/ushl` directory of the `sampdb` distribution. Change the connection parameters as necessary, install a copy of the script as `index.php` in the `ushl` directory of your Web server's document tree, and request it from your browser using either of these URLs (changing the hostname and pathname as appropriate for your own Web server):

```
http://localhost/ushl/
http://localhost/ushl/index.php
```

Let's break down the script into pieces to see how it works. The first step is to connect to the server:

```
$dbh = new PDO("mysql:host=localhost;dbname=sampdb", "sampadm", "secret");
```

`new PDO()` invokes the constructor for the PDO class. The constructor attempts to connect to the database server and raises an exception if it fails. Otherwise, it returns a PDO object that serves as a database handle.

The first argument to `new PDO()` is a string called a "data source name." The second and third arguments are the username and password to use for connecting to the server: `sampadm` and `secret`. The DSN string tells PDO which driver to use, followed by driver-specific parameters. For MySQL, the driver name is `mysql`, and the parameters are the host where the server is running and the database to select as the default database. The DSN shown indicates that the MySQL server host and default database are `localhost` and `sampdb`. Both parameters following the colon are optional. The default value for `host` is `localhost`, so this parameter actually could have been omitted. If you omit `dbname`, no default database is selected. (The DSN can take other forms, and other parameters are permitted. For details, see Appendix I, "PHP API Reference.")

Perhaps it makes you nervous that the username and password are embedded in the script for all to see. And, indeed, it should. It's true that the name and password don't appear in the resulting Web page that is sent to the client, because the script's contents are replaced by its output. Nevertheless, if the Web server becomes misconfigured somehow and fails to recognize that your script needs to be processed by PHP, it sends the script as plain text, which exposes the connection parameters. We'll deal with this problem in Section 9.1.2, "Using PHP Library Files for Code Encapsulation."

The database handle returned by `new PDO()` becomes the means for further interaction with the MySQL server, such as issuing SQL statements to be executed. After a successful connection, the default error mode for PDO calls is to fail silently, which requires that you check for errors explicitly. To make it easier to handle problems, the script enables exceptions for PDO errors:

```
$dbh->setAttribute (PDO::ATTR_ERRMODE, PDO::ERRMODE_EXCEPTION);
```

With exceptions enabled, a `try`/`catch` construct can be used to "route" errors to an exception handler without explicit tests. If you don't use `try`/`catch`, exceptions terminate your script.

The script next sends the member-counting query to the server by invoking the database handle's `query()` method, then extracts and displays the result:

```
$sth = $dbh->query ("SELECT COUNT(*) FROM member");
$count = $sth->fetchColumn (0);
print ("<p>The League currently has $count members.</p>");
```

The `query()` method sends the query to the server to be executed. Note that the query string contains no terminating semicolon character or `\g` or `\G` sequence, in contrast to the way you issue statements from within the `mysql` program. `query()` is used for statements that return rows. (Use a different method, `exec()`, for statements that modify rows.) `query()` returns a `PDOStatement` object that is a statement handle for manipulating the result set.

For the query shown, the result set consists of a single row with a single column value representing the membership count. The script invokes the `$sth` object's `fetchColumn()` method to fetch the row and extract the first column (column 0).

After printing the count, the script closes the connection to the server by setting the database handle to `NULL`. This is optional. If you don't close the connection, PHP closes it when the script terminates.

The code for interacting with MySQL occurs within a `try` block to permit any exception raised for an error to be caught and handled by the corresponding `catch` block. The connection attempt raises an exception automatically if it fails, and the `setAttribute()` call enables exceptions for any subsequent PDO calls that fail. The `catch` block in the example is empty, so its effect is to trap and ignore errors. The script writes no message for an error because printing the membership count is ancillary to the greeting presented by the home page. An error message in this context is likely simply to be confusing to people visiting the Web site. Section 9.1.8, "Handling Errors," discusses other ways to deal with errors.

Variables in PHP

In PHP, you can make variables spring into existence simply by using them. Our home page script uses three such variables, `$dbh`, `$sth`, and `$count`, none of which are declared anywhere. (There are contexts for which you do declare a variable, such as in an exception handler or when you reference a global variable inside a function.)

Variables are signified by an identifier preceded by a dollar sign ('$'). This is true no matter what kind of value the variable represents, although for arrays and objects you tack on some

extra stuff to access individual elements of the value. If a variable $x represents a single scalar value, such as a number or a string, access it as just $x. If $x represents an array with numeric indices, access its elements as $x[0], $x[1], and so on. If $x represents an array with associative indices such as "yellow" or "large", access its elements as $x["yellow"] or $x["large"]. PHP arrays can even have both numeric and associative elements. For example, $x[1] and $x["large"] both can be elements of the same array. If $x represents an object, it has properties that you access as $x->property_name. For example, $x->yellow and $x->large may be properties of $x. Numbers are not legal as property names unless you use curly braces, so $x->{1} is a valid construct in PHP, but $x->1 is not. Curly braces can also be used to refer to property names that contain spaces or other illegal characters.

9.1.2 Using PHP Library Files for Code Encapsulation

PHP scripts differ from DBI scripts in that PHP scripts are located within your Web server document tree, whereas DBI scripts typically are located in a cgi-bin directory that's located outside of the document tree. This brings up a security issue: A server configuration error can cause pages located within the document tree to be served as plain text to clients. This means that usernames and passwords for establishing connections to the MySQL server are at a higher risk of being exposed to the outside world in a PHP script than in a DBI script.

Our initial Historical League home page script is subject to this problem because it contains the literal values of the MySQL username and password. Let's move these connection parameters out of the script using two of PHP's capabilities: functions and include files. We'll write a function sampdb_connect() that establishes a connection and returns a database handle, and put that function in an include file—a library file that is not part of our main script but that can be referenced from it. This approach has several benefits:

- **It's easier to write connection establishment code.** We can write the connection parameters once in the sampdb_connect() helper function, not in every individual script that needs to connect. Moving details like this into a library and out of our scripts tends to make them more understandable because you can concentrate on the unique aspects of each script without being distracted by common connection setup code.

- **The include file can be used by multiple scripts.** This promotes code reusability and makes code more maintainable. It also enables global changes to be made easily to every script that accesses the file. For example, if we move the sampdb database from localhost to boa.example.com, we need not change a bunch of individual scripts. Instead, we change only the hostname parameter in the include file where the sampdb_connect() function is defined.

- **The include file can be moved outside of the Apache document tree.** This means that clients cannot request the include file directly from their browsers, so its contents cannot be exposed to them even if the Web server becomes misconfigured. Using an include file is a good strategy for hiding any kind of sensitive information that you don't want to be sent offsite by your Web server. However, although this is a security improvement, don't be lulled into thinking that it makes the username and password secure in all senses. Other users who have login accounts on the Web server host (and thus have access to its filesystem) might be able to read the include file directly unless you take certain precautions. Section 8.4.3, "Connecting to the MySQL Server from Web Scripts," has some notes that pertain to installing DBI configuration files so as to protect them from other users. Similar precautions apply to PHP include files.

To use include files, you need a place to put them, and you must tell PHP to look for them. If your system already has such a location, you can use that. If not, use the following procedure to establish an include file location:

1. Create a directory outside of the Web server document tree in which to store PHP include files. I use `/usr/local/apache/lib/php`, which is outside the location of my document tree, `/usr/local/apache/htdocs`.

2. Include files can be accessed from scripts by full pathname or, if you set up PHP's search path, by just their basename (the last component of the pathname). The latter approach is more convenient because PHP will find the file for us. The search path used by PHP when searching for include files is controlled by the value of the `include_path` configuration setting in the PHP initialization file, `php.ini`. Find this file on your system (common locations are `/etc/php` and `/usr/local/lib`), and locate the `include_path` line. If it has no value, set it to the full pathname of your new include directory:

   ```
   include_path = "/usr/local/apache/lib/php"
   ```

   If `include_path` already has a value, add the new directory to that value:

   ```
   include_path = "/usr/local/apache/lib/php:current_value"
   ```

   For Unix, use colon characters as shown to separate directories listed in `include_path`. For Windows, use semicolons instead.

   After modifying `php.ini`, restart Apache so that your changes take effect.

   Use of PHP include files is analogous to the use of C header files. For example, the way that PHP can look for include files in several directories is similar to the way the C preprocessor looks in multiple directories for C header files.

3. Create the include file that you want to use and put it into the include directory. The file should have some distinctive name; we'll use `sampdb_pdo.php`. This file eventually will contain several functions, but to start with, it need contain only the `sampdb_connect()` function:

   ```
   <?php
   # sampdb_pdo.php - common functions for sampdb PDO-based PHP scripts

   # Function that uses our top-secret username and password to connect
   # to the MySQL server to use the sampdb database. It also enables
   # exceptions for errors that occur for subsequent PDO calls.
   # Return value is the database handle produced by new PDO().
   ```

```
function sampdb_connect ()
{
  $dbh = new PDO("mysql:host=localhost;dbname=sampdb",
                 "sampadm", "secret");
  $dbh->setAttribute (PDO::ATTR_ERRMODE, PDO::ERRMODE_EXCEPTION);
  return ($dbh);
}
?>
```

The `sampdb_connect()` function connects to the database server by constructing a data source name and passing it to `new PDO()` along with the MySQL account username and password. Then it sets the error-handling mode to cause exceptions to be raised for PDO errors and returns the database handle to use for further interaction with the server. Use the function like this:

```
$dbh = sampdb_connect ();
```

The reason for enabling exceptions in `sampdb_connect()` is that it's more convenient to turn them on in the library file rather than individually in each script that uses the library file.

Observe that the PHP code in the `sampdb_pdo.php` file is bracketed within `<?php` and `?>` script tags. That's because PHP begins reading include files in text copy mode. If you omit the tags, PHP sends out the file as plain text rather than interpreting it as PHP code. That's just fine if you intend the file to produce literal HTML, but if you want its contents to be executed, you must enclose the PHP code within script tags.

4. To reference the include file from a script, use one of the following statements:

```
include "sampdb_pdo.php";
require "sampdb_pdo.php";
include_once "sampdb_pdo.php";
require_once "sampdb_pdo.php";
```

PHP handles the four statements as follows:

- `include` and `require` include and evaluate the contents of the named file. They differ in that if the file is missing, `include` produces a warning and execution continues, whereas `require` produces an error and execution terminates.

- The `include_once` and `require_once` statements are similar to `include` and `require`, except that if PHP already has read the named file, it doesn't read it again. This can be useful when include files include other files, to avoid the possibility of including a file multiple times and perhaps triggering function redefinition errors.

The scripts in this chapter use `require_once`. When PHP sees the file-inclusion statement, it searches for the file and reads its contents. Anything in the file becomes accessible to the following parts of the script.

The sampdb distribution includes the sampdb_pdo.php file in its phpapi directory. Modify
the connection parameters as necessary to reflect those that you use for connecting to MySQL.
Then copy the file to the include directory that you want to use, and set the file's mode and
ownership so that it's readable by your Web server (and not by other users).

Now we can modify the Historical League home page to reference the sampdb_pdo.php include
file and connect to the MySQL server by invoking sampdb_connect():

```
<html>
<head>
<title>U.S. Historical League</title>
</head>
<body bgcolor="white">
<h2>U.S. Historical League</h2>
<p>Welcome to the U.S. Historical League Web Site.</p>
<?php
# USHL home page - version 2

require_once "sampdb_pdo.php";

try
{
  $dbh = sampdb_connect ();
  $sth = $dbh->query ("SELECT COUNT(*) FROM member");
  $count = $sth->fetchColumn (0);
  print ("<p>The League currently has $count members.</p>");
  $dbh = NULL;  # close connection
}
catch (PDOException $e) { } # empty handler (catch but ignore errors)
?>
</body>
</html>
```

The script just shown can be found as index2.php in the phpapi/ushl directory of the
sampdb distribution. Copy it to the ushl directory in your Web server's document tree, naming
it index.php to replace the file of that name that is there now. This action replaces the less
secure version with a more secure one because the new file contains no literal MySQL username
or password.

You may be thinking that we haven't really saved all that much coding in the home page by
using an include file. But just wait. The sampdb_pdo.php file can be used for other functions
as well, and thus serves as a convenient repository for any routine that we expect to be useful
in multiple scripts. In fact, we can create two more such functions to put in that file right now.
Every Web script we write in the remainder of the chapter will generate a fairly stereotypical set
of HTML tags at the beginning of a page and another set at the end. Rather than writing out
those tags in each script, we can write functions html_begin() and html_end() to generate

them for us. The `html_begin()` function can take a couple of arguments that specify a page title and header. The code for the two functions looks like this:

```php
function html_begin ($title, $header)
{
  print ("<html>\n");
  print ("<head>\n");
  if ($title != "")
    print ("<title>$title</title>\n");
  print ("</head>\n");
  print ("<body bgcolor=\"white\">\n");
  if ($header != "")
    print ("<h2>$header</h2>\n");
}

function html_end ()
{
  print ("</body>\n");
  print ("</html>\n");
}
```

After putting `html_begin()` and `html_end()` in `sampdb_pdo.php`, the Historical League home page can be modified to use them. The resulting script (`index3.php`) looks like this:

```php
<?php
# USHL home page - version 3

require_once "sampdb_pdo.php";

$title = "U.S. Historical League";
html_begin ($title, $title);
?>

<p>Welcome to the U.S. Historical League Web Site.</p>

<?php
try
{
  $dbh = sampdb_connect ();
  $sth = $dbh->query ("SELECT COUNT(*) FROM member");
  $count = $sth->fetchColumn (0);
  print ("<p>The League currently has $count members.</p>");
  $dbh = NULL;  # close connection
}
catch (PDOException $e) { } # empty handler (catch but ignore errors)

html_end ();
?>
```

Notice that the PHP code has been split into two pieces, with the literal HTML text of the welcome message appearing between the pieces. Copy `index3.php` to the `ushl` directory in your Web server's document tree, naming it `index.php` to replace the file of that name that is there now.

The use of functions for generating the initial and final part of the page provides an important capability. To change the look of your page headers or footers, just modify the functions appropriately, and every script that uses them will be affected automatically. For instance, you might want to put a message "Copyright USHL" at the bottom of each Historical League page. Adding the message to a page-trailer function such as `html_end()` is an easy way to do that.

9.1.3   A Simple Data-Retrieval Page

The script that we've embedded in the Historical League home page runs a query that returns just a single row (the membership count). Our next script shows how to process a multiple-row result set (the full contents of the `member` table). This is the PHP equivalent of the DBI script `dump_members.pl` developed in Section 8.2.2, "A Simple DBI Script," so it is named `dump_members.php`. The PHP version differs from the DBI version in that it's intended to be used in a Web environment rather than from the command line. For this reason, it produces output as HTML rather than tab-delimited text. To make rows and columns line up nicely, `dump_members.php` writes the member rows as an HTML table. The script looks like this:

```php
<?php
# dump_members.php - dump U.S. Historical League membership as HTML table

require_once "sampdb_pdo.php";

$title = "U.S. Historical League Member List";
html_begin ($title, $title);

$dbh = sampdb_connect ();

# issue statement
$stmt = "SELECT last_name, first_name, suffix, email,"
      . " street, city, state, zip, phone FROM member ORDER BY last_name";
$sth = $dbh->query ($stmt);

print ("<table>\n");          # begin table
# read results of statement, then clean up
while ($row = $sth->fetch (PDO::FETCH_NUM))
{
  print ("<tr>\n");           # begin table row
  for ($i = 0; $i < $sth->columnCount (); $i++)
  {
    # escape any special characters and print table cell
    print ("<td>" . htmlspecialchars ($row[$i]) . "</td>\n");
  }
```

```
  print ("</tr>\n");          # end table row
}
print ("</table>\n");         # end table

$dbh = NULL;  # close connection

html_end ();
?>
```

sampdb_connect() enables exceptions for PDO errors, but dump_members.php contains no try/catch construct to handle exceptions. What happens if an error occurs? In this case, PHP's default behavior is to terminate the script and print a message that describes the problem. This contrasts with the Historical League home page, where we used an empty exception handler to cause errors to be ignored. For the home page, displaying the membership count was just a little addition to the script's main purpose of presenting a greeting to the visitor, so printing a message if the count could not be retrieved would have just been a distraction. For dump_members.php, displaying database content is the entire reason for the script's existence, so if a problem occurs that prevents the result from being displayed, it's reasonable to print an error message indicating what the problem was.

After issuing the query to select the member table rows, the script uses the fetch() method, which returns the next row of the result set, or FALSE if there are no more. The PDO::FETCH_NUM argument tells fetch() to return a row with numerically indexed columns.

To encode values for display in the Web page, dump_members.php uses the htmlspecialchars() function to escape characters that are special in HTML, such as '<', '>', or '&'. (To encode values for inclusion with URLs, use urlencode() instead.) These two PHP encoding functions are similar to the CGI.pm escapeHTML() and escape() methods for Perl that are discussed in Section 8.4.2.3, "Escaping HTML and URL Text."

To try the dump_members.php script, install it in the ushl directory of your Web server document tree and access it from your Web browser using this URL:

```
http://localhost/ushl/dump_members.php
```

To let people know about dump_members.php, place a link to it in the Historical League home page script. The modified script (index4.php) looks like this:

```
<?php
# USHL home page - version 4

require_once "sampdb_pdo.php";

$title = "U.S. Historical League";
html_begin ($title, $title);
?>

<p>Welcome to the U.S. Historical League Web Site.</p>
```

```php
<?php
try
{
  $dbh = sampdb_connect ();
  $sth = $dbh->query ("SELECT COUNT(*) FROM member");
  $count = $sth->fetchColumn (0);
  print ("<p>The League currently has $count members.</p>");
  $dbh = NULL;  # close connection
}
catch (PDOException $e) { } # empty handler (catch but ignore errors)
?>


<p>
You can view the directory of members <a href="dump_members.php">here</a>.
</p>

<?php
html_end ();
?>
```

As for earlier home page revisions, copy index4.php to the ush1 directory in your Web server's document tree, naming it index.php to replace the file of that name that is there now.

The dump_members.php script demonstrates how a PHP script can retrieve information from MySQL and convert it to Web page content. If you like, modify the script to produce more elaborate results. One such modification is to display the values from the email column as live hyperlinks rather than as static text, to make it easier for site visitors to send mail to League members. The sampdb distribution contains a dump_members2.php script that does this. It differs from dump_members.php only slightly, in the loop that fetches and displays member entries. The original loop looks like this:

```php
while ($row = $sth->fetch (PDO::FETCH_NUM))
{
  print ("<tr>\n");              # begin table row
  for ($i = 0; $i < $sth->columnCount (); $i++)
  {
    # escape any special characters and print table cell
    print ("<td>" . htmlspecialchars ($row[$i]) . "</td>\n");
  }
  print ("</tr>\n");             # end table row
}
```

The email addresses are in the fourth column of the query result, so dump_members2.php treats that column differently from the rest, printing a hyperlink if the value is not empty:

```php
while ($row = $sth->fetch (PDO::FETCH_NUM))
{
  print ("<tr>\n");              # begin table row
```

```
for ($i = 0; $i < $sth->columnCount (); $i++)
{
  print ("<td>");
  # escape any special characters and print table cell;
  # email is in column 4 (index 3) of result
  if ($i == 3 && $row[$i] != "")
  {
    printf ("<a href=\"mailto:%s\">%s</a>",
            $row[$i],
            htmlspecialchars ($row[$i]));
  }
  else
  {
    print (htmlspecialchars ($row[$i]));
  }
  print ("</td>\n");
}
print ("</tr>\n");              # end table row
}
```

9.1.4   Processing Statement Results

PDO provides several ways to execute SQL statements:

- A PDO object has exec() and query() methods that take an SQL statement argument,
  execute the statement immediately, and return the result:

  - For statements such as DELETE, INSERT, REPLACE, and UPDATE that modify rows,
    invoke exec(), which returns a count to indicate how many rows were changed
    (deleted, inserted, replaced, or updated, as the case may be).

  - For statements such as SELECT that produce a result set, invoke query(), which
    returns a PDOStatement statement-handle object. Use this object to access result
    set information. For example, you can retrieve the rows in the result by invoking
    its fetch() method, or find out how many columns the result set has by calling
    columnCount().

- PDO also supports two-stage statement execution by means of prepared statements. The
  PDO object has a prepare() method that takes an SQL statement argument, but instead
  of executing the statement immediately, prepare() performs some initial processing
  and returns a PDOStatement statement-handle object. The statement handle has an
  execute() method for executing the statement and other methods for processing
  the result.

  prepare() and execute() can be used for all statements. They are not specific to
  statements that modify rows or statements that return rows.

Prepared statements also offer the important capabilities of statement re-execution for improved performance and handling of special characters in data values. See Section 9.1.6, "Using Prepared Statements."

The following sections examine PDO statement-execution capabilities in more detail. *The examples assume that exceptions are enabled for errors.*

9.1.4.1 Handling Statements That Modify Rows

Use the database handle exec() method for statements that modify rows. exec() returns a count that indicates how many rows were affected. Suppose that you want to delete the row for member 149 in the member table and report the result. The following example shows how to determine whether the statement actually deleted any rows:

```
$count = $dbh->exec ("DELETE FROM member WHERE member_id = 149");
if ($count > 0)
  print ("Member 149 was deleted\n");
else
  print ("No record for member 149 was found\n");
```

9.1.4.2 Handling Statements That Return a Result Set

Use the database handle query() method for statements that produce a result set. query() returns a PDOStatement statement-handle object that gives you access to the result set. The statement handle has a number of useful methods, such as these:

- fetch() returns successive rows of the result, or FALSE when there are no more.
- fetchColumn() is similar but returns a single column of each row.
- columnCount() returns the number of columns in the result set. (There is no corresponding row count method. You must fetch the rows and count them.)

The earlier examples that discuss the USHL home page showed how to fetch a single-value result using a single call to fetchColumn(). For cases when you expect to get back multiple rows containing multiple columns, it's common to invoke the fetch() method in a loop to fetch the results. The following example illustrates one way to do this. It also counts the rows while fetching them to determine how many there are.

```
$sth = $dbh->query ("SELECT * FROM member");
# fetch each row in result set
$count = 0;
while ($row = $sth->fetch (PDO::FETCH_NUM))
{
  # print values in row, separated by commas
  for ($i = 0; $i < $sth->columnCount (); $i++)
    print ($row[$i] . ($i < $sth->columnCount () - 1 ? "," : "\n"));
  $count++;
}
printf ("Number of rows returned: %d\n", $count);
```

`fetch()` takes an argument that specifies what kind of value to return. Table 9.1 lists some of the common fetch modes.

Table 9.1   **Row-Fetching Mode Values**

Argument	Return Value
PDO::FETCH_ASSOC	An array; access the elements by associative index
PDO::FETCH_NUM	An array; access the elements by numeric index
PDO::FETCH_BOTH	An array; access the elements by associative or numeric index
PDO::FETCH_OBJ	An object; access the elements as properties

The `fetch()` argument is optional; without it, the default mode is used. Unless you reset the default, it is PDO::FETCH_BOTH, so `fetch()` returns each row as an array with elements that can be accessed by column name or numeric index.

To set the default fetch mode prior to fetching rows, pass an extra argument to `query()` or invoke the statement handle `setFetchMode()` method. Each of the following examples sets the fetch mode to PDO::FETCH_NUM to affect subsequent retrieval of the result set:

```
$sth = $dbh->query ($stmt, PDO::FETCH_NUM);
```

```
$sth = $dbh->query ($stmt);
$sth->setFetchMode (PDO::FETCH_NUM);
```

With a fetch mode of PDO::FETCH_ASSOC, `fetch()` returns the next row of the result set as an associative array. Element names are the names of the columns selected by the query. For example, if you retrieve the last_name and first_name values from the president table, access the columns as follows:

```
$stmt = "SELECT last_name, first_name FROM president";
$sth = $dbh->query ($stmt);
while ($row = $sth->fetch (PDO::FETCH_ASSOC))
  printf ("%s %s\n", $row["first_name"], $row["last_name"]);
```

With a fetch mode of PDO::FETCH_NUM, `fetch()` returns the next row of the result set as an array, with elements that are accessed by numeric index beginning with 0. To determine the number of columns in the result set, invoke the statement handle's `columnCount()` method. The following simple loop fetches and prints row values in tab-delimited format:

```
$stmt = "SELECT * FROM president";
$sth = $dbh->query ($stmt);
while ($row = $sth->fetch (PDO::FETCH_NUM))
{
  for ($i = 0; $i < $sth->columnCount (); $i++)
    print ($row[$i] . ($i < $sth->columnCount () - 1 ? "\t" : "\n"));
}
```

A fetch mode of `PDO::FETCH_BOTH` causes `fetch()` to return an array with elements that can be accessed either by numeric index or column name. This is like a combination of `PDO::FETCH_NUM` and `PDO::FETCH_ASSOC`.

With a fetch mode of `PDO::FETCH_OBJ`, `fetch()` returns the next row of the result set as an object with properties accessed using `$row->col_name` syntax:

```
while ($row = $sth->fetch (PDO::FETCH_OBJ))
  printf ("%s %s\n", $row->first_name, $row->last_name);
```

What if your query contains calculated columns? For example, you might issue a query that returns values that are calculated as the result of an expression:

```
SELECT CONCAT(first_name, ' ', last_name) FROM president
```

A query written like that is unsuitable when fetching rows as objects. The name of the selected column is the expression itself, which isn't a legal property name. However, you can supply a legal name by giving the column an alias. The following query aliases the column as `full_name`:

```
SELECT CONCAT(first_name, ' ', last_name) AS full_name FROM president
```

If you fetch each row from that query as an object, the alias permits the column to be accessed as `$row->full_name`.

The preceding examples use a row-fetching loop of this form that assigns each row to the `$row` variable:

```
while ($row = $sth->fetch ([fetch_mode]))
  ... handle row ...
```

However, there are other ways to fetch rows. One is to fetch an array and assign the result to a list of variables. For example, to assign the `last_name` and `first_name` columns to variables named `$ln` and `$fn` and print the names in first name, last name order, do this:

```
$stmt = "SELECT last_name, first_name FROM president";
$sth = $dbh->query ($stmt);
while (list ($ln, $fn) = $sth->fetch (PDO::FETCH_NUM))
  printf ("%s %s\n", $fn, $ln);
```

The variables can have any legal names you like, but their order in the `list()` must correspond to the order of the columns selected by the query.

It's also possible to retrieve individual column values directly into PHP variables. To do this, bind columns of the result set to variables using `bindColumn()`, and fetch rows using the `PDO::FETCH_BOUND` fetch mode. That causes `fetch()` to return TRUE while rows remain, and to assign column values to the bound variables for each row fetched:

```
$stmt = "SELECT last_name, first_name FROM president";
$sth = $dbh->query ($stmt);
$sth->bindColumn (1, $ln);
$sth->bindColumn (2, $fn);
```

```
while ($sth->fetch (PDO::FETCH_BOUND))
  printf ("%s %s\n", $fn, $ln);
```

To fetch all rows at once into an array, use `fetchAll()`:

```
$rows = $sth->fetchAll ();
```

Like `fetch()`, `fetchAll()` uses the default fetch mode, or accepts an explicit fetch-mode argument.

A statement handle can be used as an iterator without invoking `fetch()` explicitly:

```
foreach ($sth as $row)
  printf ("%s %s\n", $row["first_name"], $row["last_name"]);
```

The default fetch mode determines how the rows are returned.

9.1.5   Testing for NULL Values in Query Results

PHP represents the SQL NULL value in result sets using the PHP NULL value. One way to check for NULL in a column value returned from a SELECT query is to use the `is_null()` function. The following example selects and prints names and email addresses from the `member` table, printing "No email address available" if the address is NULL:

```
$stmt = "SELECT last_name, first_name, email FROM member";
$sth = $dbh->query ($stmt);
while (list ($last_name, $first_name, $email) = $sth->fetch (PDO::FETCH_NUM))
{
  printf ("Name: %s %s, Email: ", $first_name, $last_name);
  if (is_null ($email))
    print ("No email address available");
  else
    print ($email);
  print ("\n");
}
```

You can also test for SQL NULL values by comparing a value to the PHP NULL constant using the === identically-equal-to operator:

```
if ($email === NULL)
  print ("No email address available");
else
  print ($email);
```

PHP NULL is the same as an unset value, so `isset()` provides another way to test for NULL values:

```
if (!isset ($email))
  print ("No email address available");
else
  print ($email);
```

9.1.6 Using Prepared Statements

The `exec()` and `query()` methods described earlier execute SQL statements and return their results immediately. PDO can also prepare and execute statements in separate steps. Use the database handle with `prepare()` to obtain a statement handle, and use the statement handle to execute the statement:

```
$sth = $dbh->prepare ($stmt);
$sth->execute ();
```

After executing a statement that modifies rows, you can get the rows-affected count by invoking `rowCount()`:

```
$count = $sth->rowCount ();
```

If the statement returns rows, methods such as `fetch()` and `columnCount()` apply. To determine the number of rows, count them as you fetch them. (`rowCount()` applies only to statements that modify rows.)

Prepared statements provide some important capabilities:

- Statement strings can contain placeholders rather than literal data values. After preparing a statement, bind specific data values to the placeholders prior to each execution, and PDO takes care of any handling needed to escape or quote special characters or NULL values. There are several ways to bind values to placeholders, as described in Section 9.1.7, "Using Placeholders to Handle Data Quoting Issues."

- A prepared statement can be executed repeatedly. This avoids the preparation overhead for each execution, which is very useful for statements that you plan to execute multiple times because it can provide enhanced performance. For example, to insert multiple rows, you can `prepare()` an INSERT statement once. Then `execute()` it within a loop that supplies data values for individual rows each time through the loop, using placeholders to bind the values to the statement.

9.1.7 Using Placeholders to Handle Data Quoting Issues

It's necessary to be aware of quoting issues in SQL statement strings in PHP, just as it is in other languages such as C and Perl. Suppose that you're constructing a statement to insert a new row into a table. In the statement string, you might put quotes around each value to be inserted into a string column:

```
$last = "O'Malley";
$first = "Brian";
$expiration = "2013-09-01";
$stmt = "INSERT INTO member (last_name,first_name,expiration)"
    . " VALUES('$last','$first','$expiration')";
```

The problem here is that one of the quoted values itself contains a quote (`O'Malley`), which results in a syntax error if you send the statement to the MySQL server. To deal with this in C, we could call `mysql_real_escape_string()` or `mysql_escape_string()`. In a Perl DBI script, we could use `quote()`. PDO has a database handle `quote()` method that accomplishes much the same objective. For example, a call to `quote("O'Malley")` returns the value `'O\'Malley'`. To use `quote()` for statement construction, insert the value that it returns directly into the statement string, without adding any extra quotes yourself:

```
$last = $dbh->quote ("O'Malley");
$first = $dbh->quote ("Brian");
$expiration = $dbh->quote ("2013-09-01");
$stmt = "INSERT INTO member (last_name,first_name,expiration)"
      . " VALUES($last,$first,$expiration)";
```

Unfortunately, `quote()` has some shortcomings that reduce its usefulness in comparison to its DBI counterpart of the same name:

- It is not implemented for all drivers, in which case it returns FALSE rather than a quoted string.

- For a value of NULL, you'd want to insert the word "NULL" into the statement string with no surrounding quotes. But if you pass NULL to `quote()`, it returns the quoted empty string (`''`). To deal with this, you must test and handle a value differentially depending on whether it represents a NULL value.

Because of these deficiencies, I recommend avoiding `quote()` except perhaps when you know you'll be working only with non-NULL string-valued data. A better approach is to use prepared statements. Then you can specify placeholders in SQL statements and let PDO do all the quoting for you. When you prepare an SQL statement, indicate where data values should go using '?' characters as placeholder markers. When you execute the statement, supply the data values as an array of parameters:

```
$stmt = "INSERT INTO member (last_name,first_name,expiration) VALUES(?,?,?)";
$sth = $dbh->prepare ($stmt);
$sth->execute (array ("O'Malley", "Brian", "2013-09-01"));
```

PDO takes care of any handling required for special characters in strings, and correctly processes nonstring values such as numbers and NULL.

A different way to supply the data values is to bind them to the placeholders individually with `bindValue()` before calling `execute()`:

```
$stmt = "INSERT INTO member (last_name,first_name,expiration) VALUES(?,?,?)";
$sth = $dbh->prepare ($stmt);
$sth->bindValue (1, "O'Malley");
$sth->bindValue (2, "Brian");
$sth->bindValue (3, "2013-09-01");
$sth->execute ();
```

The preceding examples use positional placeholders: '?' markers that are all the same and distinguished only by their position within the statement string. PDO also supports named-placeholder style in which a placeholder consists of a name preceded by a colon. Prepare the statement to be executed; then pass to `execute()` an associative array of values that ties each value to the appropriate name:

```
$stmt = "INSERT INTO member (last_name,first_name,expiration)
        VALUES(:last_name,:first_name,:expiration)";
$sth = $dbh->prepare ($stmt);
$sth->execute (array (
                ":last_name" => "O'Malley",
                ":first_name" => "Brian",
                ":expiration" =>"2013-09-01"
              ));
```

Alternatively, bind each value to its placeholder name before calling `execute()`:

```
$stmt = "INSERT INTO member (last_name,first_name,expiration)
        VALUES(:last_name,:first_name,:expiration)";
$sth = $dbh->prepare ($stmt);
$sth->bindValue (":last_name", "O'Malley");
$sth->bindValue (":first_name", "Brian");
$sth->bindValue (":expiration", "2013-09-01");
$sth->execute ();
```

One advantage of named placeholders is that it is easier to keep track of the association between placeholders and data values when there are large numbers of parameters.

9.1.8 Handling Errors

It's essential to arrange to handle errors when you interact with MySQL. If you assume that every call will succeed, you'll have a much more difficult time figuring out why your script doesn't work when an error does occur.

When you attempt to connect to the database server by invoking `new PDO()`, an exception occurs if the attempt fails. Assuming that the attempt succeeds and you get back a valid database handle, PDO processes errors for subsequent operations that use the handle according to the PDO error mode. Set the error mode as follows:

```
$dbh->setAttribute (PDO::ATTR_ERRMODE, mode_value);
```

PDO supports three error mode values:

- `PDO::ERRMODE_SILENT`: PDO does nothing other than set error information for the object that caused the error. This is the default error mode.

- `PDO::ERRMODE_WARNING`: This is similar to silent mode, but PDO emits a warning message in addition to setting the error information.

- `PDO::ERRMODE_EXCEPTION`: PDO raises an exception after setting the error information.

In all cases, if you know the object for which the error occurred, you can invoke its
`errorCode()` or `errorInfo()` methods to obtain error information:

- `errorCode()` returns a five-character SQLSTATE value. A return value equal to
  `PDO::ERR_NONE ("00000")` means "no error."

- `errorInfo()` returns a three-element array containing the SQLSTATE value and a driver-
  specific code and message. For MySQL, the latter two values are a numeric error code and
  descriptive error message.

  If the handle operation succeeds, the return value may be a single-element array
  containing the SQLSTATE value `PDO::ERR_NONE ("00000")`.

In silent or warning mode, error handling involves checking the result of each PDO operation
that might fail. For example:

```
if (!($sth = $dbh->prepare ("SELECT * FROM non_existent_table")))
  die ("Cannot prepare statement: " . $dbh->errorCode () . "\n");
else if (!$sth->execute ())
  die ("Cannot execute statement: " . $sth->errorCode () . "\n");
```

Note that `errorCode()` is invoked using the handle for which the error occurred. The same is
true for `errorInfo()`.

If you enable exceptions, PHP raises a `PDOException` when an error occurs for a PDO operation. If no error occurs, the operation succeeded. Otherwise, the exception causes PHP to terminate your script unless you catch the error. To do so, put the code that might fail into a `try`
block and the error-processing code in the corresponding `catch` block:

```
try
{
  # ... perform a database operation ...
}
catch (PDOException $e)
{
  # ... handle the error ...
}
```

The exception object (`$e` in the example) has its own methods that provide error information:

- `getCode()` returns an error code.
- `getMessage()` returns a string containing an error message.

The following example enables exceptions and shows how to display error information when a
statement fails to execute:

```
$dbh->setAttribute (PDO::ATTR_ERRMODE, PDO::ERRMODE_EXCEPTION);
try
{
  $dbh->exec ("DELETE FROM non_existent_table");
```

```
}
catch (PDOException $e)
{
  # Print error information from exception object
  print ("getCode value: " . $e->getCode () . "\n");
  print ("getMessage value: " . $e->getMessage () . "\n");
  # Print error information from database handle
  print ("errorCode value: " . $dbh->errorCode () . "\n");
  print ("errorInfo value: " . join (",", $dbh->errorInfo ()) . "\n");
}
```

The example displays information from the exception object ($e), and also from the database-handle object ($dbh). That's possible here because the only PDO handle used in the try block is $dbh. Were you using multiple handles in the try block, you wouldn't know in the catch block which of them caused the error, so you'd need to rely only on the exception methods. Alternatively, you could restructure the code to isolate use of each PDO handle into its own try/catch construct.

Some PHP functions or operations produce an error message if an error occurs, in addition to returning a status value. In Web contexts, this message appears in the page sent to the client browser, which may not be what you want. To suppress the (possibly cryptic) error message that a function normally would produce, precede the function name by the @ operator: For example, to suppress the error message from a function named some_func() so that you can report failure in a more suitable manner, do something like this:

```
$status = @some_func ();
```

9.2 Putting PHP to Work

The remaining part of this chapter tackles the goals set out in Chapter 1, "Getting Started with MySQL," that we have yet to accomplish:

- For the grade-keeping project, we need to write a script that enables us to enter and edit test and quiz scores.

- For visitors to the Historical League Web site, we want to develop an online quiz about U.S. presidents, and to make it interactive so that the questions can be generated on the fly.

- We also want to make it possible for Historical League members to edit their directory entries online. This will keep the information up to date and reduce the amount of entry editing that must be done by the League secretary.

Each of these scripts generates multiple Web pages and communicates from one invocation of the script to the next by means of information embedded in the pages it creates. If you're not familiar with the concept of inter-page communication, see Section 8.4.2.4, "Writing Multiple-Purpose Pages."

9.2.1 An Online Score-Entry Application

In this section, we turn our attention to the grade-keeping project and write a `score_entry.php` script for managing test and quiz scores. The Web directory for the project is named gp under the Apache document tree root, which corresponds to this URL for our site:

`http://localhost/gp/`

The directory is thus far unpopulated, so visitors requesting that URL may receive only a "page not found" error or an empty directory listing page. To rectify that problem, create a short script named `index.php` and place it in the gp directory to serve as the project's home page. The following script suffices for now. It contains two links. One link is to the `score_browse.pl` script that we wrote in Section 8.4.5, "A Grade-Keeping Project Score Browser," because that script pertains to the grade-keeping project. The other link is to the `score_entry.php` script that we're about to write:

```php
<?php
# Grade-Keeping Project home page

require_once "sampdb_pdo.php";

$title = "Grade-Keeping Project";
html_begin ($title, $title);
?>


<p>
<a href="/cgi-bin/score_browse.pl">View</a> test and quiz scores
</p>
<p>
<a href="score_entry.php">Enter or edit</a> test and quiz scores
</p>

<?php
html_end ();
?>
```

You can find this `index.php` script in the `phpapi/gp` directory of the sampdb distribution. Copy it to the gp directory of your Web server document tree.

Let's consider how to design and implement the `score_entry.php` script that lets us enter a set of test or quiz scores or edit existing sets of scores. Entry capability is useful whenever we have a new set of scores to add to the database. Editing capability is necessary for changing scores later; for example, to handle scores of students who take a test or quiz later than the rest of the class due to absence for illness or other reason, or to correct errors for scores entered incorrectly. Conceptually, the score entry script operates like this:

- The initial page presents a list of known grade events and enables you to choose one, or to indicate that you want to create a new event.

- If you choose to create a new event, the script presents a page that enables you to specify the date and event category (test or quiz). After it adds the event to the database, the script redisplays the event list page, which at that point includes the new event.

- If you choose an existing event from the list, the script presents a score-entry page showing the event ID, date, and category, a table that lists each student in the class, and a Submit button. Each row in the table shows one student's name and current score for the event. For new events, all scores are blank. For existing events, the scores are those you entered at some earlier time. You can fill in or change the scores, then select the Submit button. At that point, the script enters the scores into the `score` table or revises existing scores. This operation must be done as a transaction to make sure that all score modifications succeed as a unit or are canceled if an error occurs.

9.2.1.1 Collecting Web Input in PHP

Before implementing the `score_entry.php` script, we must take a slight detour to discuss how input parameters work in PHP. The script performs several different actions, which means that it must pass a status value from page to page so that the script can tell what it's supposed to do each time it's invoked. One way to do this is to pass parameters at the end of the URL. For example, we can add a parameter named `action` to the script URL like this:

```
http://localhost/gp/score_entry.php?action=value
```

Parameter values may also come from the contents of a form submitted by the user. Each field from a form returned by the user's browser as part of a form submission will have a name and a value.

PHP makes input parameters available to scripts through special arrays. Parameters encoded at the end of a URL and sent as part of a `get` request are placed in the `$HTTP_GET_VARS` global array and `$_GET` superglobal array. For parameters received in a `post` request (such as the contents of a form that has a `method` attribute value of `post`), the parameters are placed in the `$HTTP_POST_VARS` global array and `$_POST` superglobal array.

The global arrays must be declared explicitly if you use them in contexts other than at the top level of your PHP scripts, such as within function definitions. The superglobal arrays are accessible in any scope with no special declaration. For simplicity, we'll use the `$_GET` and `$_POST` superglobal arrays. (`$HTTP_GET_VARS` and `$HTTP_POST_VARS` are deprecated.)

`$_GET` and `$_POST` are associative arrays, with elements keyed to the parameter names. For example, an `action` parameter sent in the URL becomes available to a PHP script as the value of `$_GET["action"]`. Suppose that a form contains fields called `name` and `address`. When a user submits the form, the Web server invokes a script to process the form's contents. If the form is submitted as a `get` request, the script can find out what values were entered into the form by checking the values of the `$_GET["name"]` and `$_GET["address"]` variables. If the form is submitted as a `post` request, the variables are in `$_POST["name"]` and `$_POST["address"]`.

For forms that contain a lot of fields, it can be inconvenient to give them all unique names. PHP makes it easy to pass arrays in and out of forms. If you use field names such as x[0], x[1], and so forth, PHP stores them in $_GET["x"] or $_POST["x"], the value of which is itself an array. If you assign the array value to a variable $x, the array elements are available as $x[0], $x[1], and so on.

In most cases, we won't care whether a parameter was submitted using get or post, so we can write a utility routine, script_param(), that takes a parameter name and checks both arrays to find the parameter value. If the parameter is not present, the routine returns NULL:

```
function script_param ($name)
{
  $val = NULL;
  if (isset ($_GET[$name]))
    $val = $_GET[$name];
  else if (isset ($_POST[$name]))
    $val = $_POST[$name];
  if (get_magic_quotes_gpc ())
    $val = remove_backslashes ($val);
  return ($val);
}
```

script_param() enables a script to easily access the values of input parameters by name, without being concerned which array they might be stored in. It also processes the parameter value after extracting it by passing the value to remove_backslashes(). The purpose of doing this is to adapt to configurations that have the magic_quotes_gpc setting enabled with a line like this in the PHP initialization file:

```
magic_quotes_gpc = On;
```

If that setting is turned on, PHP adds backslashes to parameter values to quote special characters such as quotes or backslashes. The extra backslashes make it more difficult to check parameter values to see whether they're valid, so remove_backslashes() strips them out. It's implemented using a recursive algorithm because in PHP it's possible to create parameters that take the form of nested arrays:

```
function remove_backslashes ($val)
{
  if (is_array ($val))
  {
    foreach ($val as $k => $v)
      $val[$k] = remove_backslashes ($v);
  }
  else if (!is_null ($val))
    $val = stripslashes ($val);
  return ($val);
}
```

> **Web Input Parameters and** `register_globals`
>
> You may be familiar with PHP's `register_globals`, a now-deprecated configuration setting that causes Web input parameters to be registered directly into script variables. For example, a form field or URL parameter named x would be stored directly into a variable named $x in your script. Unfortunately, enabling this capability means that clients can set variables in your scripts in ways you may not intend. This is a security risk, for which reason the PHP development team recommends that `register_globals` be disabled. The `script_param()` routine deliberately uses only the arrays provided specifically for input parameters, which is more secure and also works regardless of the `register_globals` setting.

9.2.1.2   Displaying and Entering Scores

Now that we have support in place for extracting Web input parameters conveniently, we can use it for writing `score_entry.php`. That script must communicate information from one invocation of itself to the next. To do this, we use a parameter called `action`, which can be obtained as follows when the script executes:

```php
$action = script_param ("action");
```

If the parameter isn't set, the script is being invoked for the first time. Otherwise, it can test the value of $action to find out what to do. The general framework for `script_entry.php` looks like this:

```php
<?php
# score_entry.php - Score Entry script for grade-keeping project

require_once "sampdb_pdo.php";

# define action constants
define ("SHOW_INITIAL_PAGE", 0);
define ("SOLICIT_EVENT", 1);
define ("ADD_EVENT", 2);
define ("DISPLAY_SCORES", 3);
define ("ENTER_SCORES", 4);

# ... put input-handling functions here ...

$title = "Grade-Keeping Project -- Score Entry";
html_begin ($title, $title);

$dbh = sampdb_connect ();

# Determine what action to perform (the default is to
# present the initial page if no action is specified)

$action = script_param ("action");
```

```
if (is_null ($action))
  $action = SHOW_INITIAL_PAGE;

switch ($action)
{
case SHOW_INITIAL_PAGE:   # present initial page
  display_events ($dbh);
  break;
case SOLICIT_EVENT:       # ask for new event information
  solicit_event_info ();
  break;
case ADD_EVENT:           # add new event to database
  add_new_event ($dbh);
  display_events ($dbh);
  break;
case DISPLAY_SCORES:      # display scores for selected event
  display_scores ($dbh);
  break;
case ENTER_SCORES:        # enter new or edited scores
  enter_scores ($dbh);
  display_events ($dbh);
  break;
default:
  die ("Unknown action code ($action)\n");
}

$dbh = NULL;  # close connection

html_end ();
?>
```

The $action variable can take on several values, which we test in the switch statement. In PHP, switch is much like its C counterpart; it's used here to determine which action to take and to call the functions that implement the action. To avoid having to use literal action values, the switch statement refers to symbolic action names that are initialized earlier in the script using PHP's define() construct.

Let's examine the functions that handle these actions one at a time. The first one, display_events(), presents a list of permitted events by retrieving rows of the grade_event table from MySQL and displaying them. Each row of the table lists the event ID, date, and event category (test or quiz). The event ID appears in the page as a hyperlink that you can select to edit the scores for that event. Following the event rows, the function adds one more row containing a link that enables a new event to be created:

```
function display_events ($dbh)
{
  print ("Select an event by clicking on its number, or select\n");
  print ("New Event to create a new grade event:<br /><br />\n");
```

```php
print ("<table border=\"1\">\n");

# Print a row of table column headers

print ("<tr>\n");
display_cell ("th", "Event ID");
display_cell ("th", "Date");
display_cell ("th", "Category");
print ("</tr>\n");

# Present list of events.  Associate each event ID
# with a link that shows the scores for the event.

$stmt = "SELECT event_id, date, category
        FROM grade_event ORDER BY event_id";
$sth = $dbh->query ($stmt);

while ($row = $sth->fetch ())
{
  print ("<tr>\n");
  $url = sprintf ("%s?action=%d&event_id=%d",
                  script_name (),
                  DISPLAY_SCORES,
                  $row["event_id"]);
  display_cell ("td",
                "<a href=\"$url\">"
                  . $row["event_id"]
                  . "</a>",
                FALSE);
  display_cell ("td", $row["date"]);
  display_cell ("td", $row["category"]);
  print ("</tr>\n");
}

# Add one more link for creating a new event

print ("<tr align=\"center\">\n");
$url = sprintf ("%s?action=%d",
                script_name (),
                SOLICIT_EVENT);
display_cell ("td colspan=\"3\"",
              "<a href=\"$url\">Create New Event</a>",
              FALSE);
print ("</tr>\n");

print ("</table>\n");
}
```

The URLs for the hyperlinks that re-invoke `score_entry.php` are constructed using `script_name()`, a function that figures out the script's own pathname. `script_name()` is useful because it enables you to avoid hardwiring the name of the script into the code. (If you write the name literally, the script will break if you rename it.) `script_name()` can be found in the `sampdb_pdo.php` file.

`script_name()` is somewhat similar to `script_param()` in that it accesses a PHP superglobal array. However, it uses a different array because the script name is part of the information supplied by the Web server, not as part of the input parameters:

```
function script_name ()
{
  return ($_SERVER["SCRIPT_NAME"]);
}
```

The `display_cell()` function used by `display_events()` generates cells in the event table:

```
# Display a cell of an HTML table.  $tag is the tag name ("th" or "td"
# for a header or data cell), $value is the value to display, and
# $encode should be true or false, indicating whether or not to perform
# HTML-encoding of the value before displaying it.  $encode is optional,
# and is true by default.

function display_cell ($tag, $value, $encode = TRUE)
{
  if (strlen ($value) == 0) # is the value empty/unset?
    $value = " ";
  else if ($encode) # perform HTML-encoding if requested
    $value = htmlspecialchars ($value);
  print ("<$tag>$value</$tag>\n");
}
```

If you select the "Create New Event" link in the table that `display_events()` presents, `score_entry.php` is re-invoked with an action of SOLICIT_EVENT. That triggers a call to `solicit_event_info()`, which displays a form that enables you to enter the date and category for the new event:

```
function solicit_event_info ()
{
  printf ("<form method=\"post\" action=\"%s?action=%d\">\n",
          script_name (),
          ADD_EVENT);
  print ("Enter information for new grade event:<br /><br />\n");
  print ("Date: ");
  print ("<input type=\"text\" name=\"date\" value=\"\" size=\"10\" />\n");
  print ("<br />\n");
  print ("Category: ");
  print ("<input type=\"radio\" name=\"category\" value=\"T\"");
  print (" checked=\"checked\" />Test\n");
```

```
print ("<input type=\"radio\" name=\"category\" value=\"Q\" />Quiz\n");
print ("<br /><br />\n");
print ("<input type=\"submit\" name=\"submit\" value=\"Submit\" />\n");
print ("</form>\n");
}
```

The form generated by `solicit_event_info()` contains an edit field for entering the date, a pair of radio buttons for specifying whether the new event is a test or a quiz, and a Submit button. The default event category is `'T'` (test). (The script writes out literal HTML to construct the form here. For later scripts in this chapter, we'll develop a set of helper functions that generate form elements.)

When you fill in this form and submit it, `score_entry.php` is invoked again, this time with an `action` value equal to `ADD_EVENT`. The `add_new_event()` function then is called to enter a new row into the `grade_event` table:

```
function add_new_event ($dbh)
{
  $date = script_param ("date");        # get date and event category
  $category = script_param ("category"); # entered by user

  if (empty ($date))  # make sure a date was entered, and in ISO 8601 format
    die ("No date specified\n");
  if (!preg_match ('/^\d{4}\D\d{1,2}\D\d{1,2}$/', $date))
    die ("Please enter the date in ISO 8601 format (CCYY-MM-DD)\n");
  if ($category != "T" && $category != "Q")
    die ("Bad event category\n");

  $stmt = "INSERT INTO grade_event (date,category) VALUES(?,?)";
  $sth = $dbh->prepare ($stmt);
  $sth->execute (array ($date, $category));
}
```

`add_new_event()` uses the `script_param()` library routine to access the parameter values that correspond to the `date` and `category` fields in the new-event entry form. Then it performs some minimal safety checks:

- The date should not be empty, and it should have been entered in ISO 8601 format. The `preg_match()` function performs a pattern match for ISO 8601 format:

  ```
  preg_match ('/^\d{4}\D\d{1,2}\D\d{1,2}$/', $date)
  ```

  Single quotes are used here to prevent interpretation of the dollar sign and the backslash as special characters. The test is true if the date consists of three sequences of digits separated by nondigit characters. That's not bullet-proof, but it's easy to add to the script, and it catches many common errors.

  For additional safety, you might want to enable input data restrictions by setting the SQL mode before inserting the data. For example:

  ```
  $dbh->exec ("SET sql_mode = 'TRADITIONAL'");
  ```

- The event category must be one of the values permitted in the `category` column of the `grade_event` table (`'T'` or `'Q'`).

If the parameter values look okay, `add_new_event()` enters a new row into the `grade_event` table. The statement-execution code uses placeholders to ensure proper quoting of data values inserted into the query string. After executing the statement, `add_new_event()` returns to the main part of the script (the `switch` statement), which displays the event list again so that you can select the new event and begin entering scores for it.

When you select an item from the event list shown by the `display_events()` function, the `score_entry.php` script invokes the `display_scores()` function. Each event link contains an event number encoded as an `event_id` parameter, so `display_scores()` gets the parameter value, checks it to make sure it's an integer, and uses it in a query to retrieve a row for each student and any current scores the students may have for the event:

```
function display_scores ($dbh)
{
  # Get event ID number, which must look like an integer
  $event_id = script_param ("event_id");
  if (!ctype_digit ($event_id))
    die ("Bad event ID\n");

  # Select scores for the given event
  $stmt = "
    SELECT
      student.student_id, student.name, grade_event.date,
      score.score AS score, grade_event.category
    FROM student
      INNER JOIN grade_event
      LEFT JOIN score ON student.student_id = score.student_id
                    AND grade_event.event_id = score.event_id
    WHERE grade_event.event_id = ?
    ORDER BY student.name";
  $sth = $dbh->prepare ($stmt);
  $sth->execute (array ($event_id));

  # Fetch the rows into an array so we know how many there are
  $rows = $sth->fetchAll ();
  if (count ($rows) == 0)
    die ("No information was found for the selected event\n");

  printf ("<form method=\"post\" action=\"%s?action=%d&event_id=%d\">\n",
          script_name (),
          ENTER_SCORES,
          $event_id);

  # Print scores as an HTML table
```

```
for ($row_num = 0; $row_num < count ($rows); $row_num++)
{
  $row = $rows[$row_num];
  # Print event info and table heading preceding the first row
  if ($row_num == 0)
  {
    printf ("Event ID: %d, Event date: %s, Event category: %s\n",
            $event_id,
            $row["date"],
            $row["category"]);
    print ("<br /><br />\n");
    print ("<table border=\"1\">\n");
    print ("<tr>\n");
    display_cell ("th", "Name");
    display_cell ("th", "Score");
    print "</tr>\n";
  }
  print ("<tr>\n");
  display_cell ("td", $row["name"]);
  $col_val = sprintf ("<input type=\"text\" name=\"score[%d]\"",
                      $row["student_id"]);
  $col_val .= sprintf (" value=\"%d\" size=\"5\" /><br />\n",
                       $row["score"]);
  display_cell ("td", $col_val, FALSE);
  print ("</tr>\n");
}

print ("</table>\n");
print ("<br />\n");
print ("<input type=\"submit\" name=\"submit\" value=\"Submit\" />\n");
print "</form>\n";
}
```

The query that display_scores() uses to retrieve score information for the selected event is not just a simple join between tables, because that wouldn't select a row for any student who has no score for the event. In particular, for a new event, the join would select no rows, and the entry form would be empty! Instead, use a LEFT JOIN to force a row to be retrieved for each student, regardless of whether the student already has a score in the score table. If the student has no score for the given event, the value retrieved by the query is NULL. (Background for a query similar to the one that display_scores() uses to retrieve score rows from MySQL is given in Section 2.8.3, "Left and Right (Outer) Joins.")

The script places scores retrieved by the query into the form as input fields having names like score[*n*], where *n* is a student_id value. You can enter or edit the scores, then submit the form to have them stored in the database. When your browser sends the form back to the Web server, PHP converts these fields into elements of an array associated with the name score that can be retrieved as follows:

```
$score = script_param ("score");
```

Elements of the array are keyed by student ID, so we can easily associate each student with the corresponding score submitted in the form. Form processing might involve execution of several statements (one per student) and we don't want the update to succeed only partially. In Chapter 1, "Getting Started with MySQL," we created the score table as an InnoDB table. That enables us to take advantage of InnoDB's transactional capabilities. In particular, we make sure that the entire data-entry operation takes place as an atomic unit by performing it within a transaction. That way, the changes either all succeed together, or no changes at all are made. Transaction processing in PDO has this general structure (assuming that exceptions are enabled for PDO errors):

```
try
{
  $dbh->beginTransaction ();          # start the transaction
  # ... perform database operation ...
  $dbh->commit ();                    # transaction succeeded
}
catch (PDOException $e)
{
  $dbh->rollback ();                  # transaction failed
}
```

score_entry.php uses that structure ensure integrity of the data-entry operation, additionally placing the rollback operation is placed within its own try/catch construct to prevent it from terminating the script if it fails.

The enter_scores() function processes the form contents to determine which scores need to be updated or deleted:

```
function enter_scores ($dbh)
{
  # Get event ID number and array of scores for the event

  $event_id = script_param ("event_id");
  $score = script_param ("score");

  if (!ctype_digit ($event_id)) # must look like integer
    die ("Bad event ID\n");

  # Prepare the statements that are executed repeatedly
  $sth_del = $dbh->prepare ("DELETE FROM score
                            WHERE event_id = ? AND student_id = ?");
  $sth_repl = $dbh->prepare ("REPLACE INTO score
                             (event_id, student_id, score)
                             VALUES (?,?,?)");

  # Enter scores within a transaction
  try
  {
```

```php
    $dbh->beginTransaction ();

    $blank_count = 0;
    $nonblank_count = 0;
    foreach ($score as $student_id => $new_score)
    {
      $new_score = trim ($new_score);
      if (empty ($new_score))
      {
        # If no score is provided for student in the form, delete any
        # score the student may have had in the database previously
        ++$blank_count;
        $sth = $sth_del;
        $params = array ($event_id, $student_id);
      }
      else if (ctype_digit ($new_score)) # must look like integer
      {
        # If a score is provided, replace any score that
        # might already be present in the database
        ++$nonblank_count;
        $sth = $sth_repl;
        $params = array ($event_id, $student_id, $new_score);
      }
      else
      {
        throw new PDOException ("invalid score: $new_score");
      }
      $sth->execute ($params);
    }
    # Transaction succeeded, commit it
    $dbh->commit ();
    printf ("Number of scores entered: %d<br />\n", $nonblank_count);
    printf ("Number of scores missing: %d<br />\n", $blank_count);
  }
  catch (PDOException $e)
  {
    printf ("Score entry failed: %s<br />\n",
            htmlspecialchars ($e->getMessage ()));
    # Roll back, but use empty exception handler to catch rollback failure
    try
    {
      $dbh->rollback ();
    }
    catch (PDOException $e) { }
  }
  print ("<br />\n");
}
```

The script obtains and processes student ID values and the scores associated with them by iterating through the $score array:

- If the score is blank after any whitespace is trimmed from its ends, there is nothing to be entered. But just in case there was a score previously, the script tries to delete it. (Perhaps we mistakenly entered a score earlier for a student who actually was absent, and now we need to remove it.) If the student had no score, the DELETE finds no row to remove, but that's harmless.

- If the score is not blank, the function performs some rudimentary validation of the value and accepts it if it looks like an integer. Note that integer testing is done using a pattern match rather than PHP's is_int() function. The latter is for testing whether a variable's type is integer, but form values are encoded as strings. is_int() returns FALSE for any string, even if it contains only digit characters. What we need here is a content check to verify the string. The following function returns TRUE if every character from the beginning to the end of the string $str is a digit:

```
ctype_digit ($str)
```

If the score looks okay, we add it to the score table. The statement is REPLACE rather than INSERT because we might be replacing an existing score rather than entering a new one. If the student had no score for the grade event, REPLACE adds a new row, just like INSERT. Otherwise, REPLACE replaces the old score with the new one.

Prior to the loop, the script invokes beginTransaction(), which disables autocommit mode. Following the loop, the script commits the transaction if no errors occurred. If something goes wrong, the script rolls back the transaction.

That takes care of the score_entry.php script. All score entry and editing can be done from your Web browser now. One obvious shortcoming is that the script provides no security; anyone who can connect to the Web server can edit scores. The script that we'll write later for Historical League member entry editing shows a simple authentication scheme that could be adapted for this script.

9.2.2   Creating an Interactive Online Quiz

One of the goals for the Historical League Web site is to provide an online version of a quiz, similar to some of the quizzes that the League publishes in the children's section of its newsletter, "Chronicles of U.S. Past." We created the president table, in fact, precisely so that we could use it as a source of questions for a history-based quiz. Let's do this now, using a script called pres_quiz.php.

The basic idea is to pick and ask a question about a president at random, then solicit an answer from the user and check whether the answer is correct. The types of questions the script might present could be based on any part of the president table rows, but for simplicity, we'll constrain it to asking only where presidents were born. Another simplifying measure is to present the questions in multiple-choice format. It's easier for the user to pick from among a set of choices than to type in a response. It's also easier for the script to perform a simple comparison of the user's choice and the correct answer than to do pattern matching to check whatever the user might have typed in.

The `pres_quiz.php` script must perform two functions:

- When initially invoked, it should generate and display a new question using information from the `president` table.

- If the user has submitted a response, the script must check it and provide feedback to indicate whether it was correct. If the response was incorrect, the script should redisplay the same question. Otherwise, it should generate and display a new question.

The outline for the script is quite simple. It presents the initial question page if the user isn't submitting a response, and checks the answer otherwise:

```php
<?php
# pres_quiz.php - script to quiz user on presidential birthplaces

require_once "sampdb_pdo.php";

# ... put quiz-handling functions here ...

$title = "U.S. President Quiz";
html_begin ($title, $title);

$dbh = sampdb_connect ();

$response = script_param ("response");
if (is_null ($response))    # invoked for first time
  present_question ($dbh);
else                        # user submitted response to form
  check_response ($dbh);

$dbh = NULL;  # close connection

html_end ();
?>
```

To create the questions, we use ORDER BY RAND() combined with LIMIT 1 select rows at random from the `president` table. For example, to pick a president name and birthplace randomly, this query does the job:

```
SELECT CONCAT(first_name, ' ', last_name) AS name,
CONCAT(city, ', ', state) AS place
FROM president ORDER BY RAND() LIMIT 1;
```

The name is the president about whom we ask the question, and the birthplace is the correct answer to the question, "Where was this president born?" We must also present some incorrect choices, which we can select using a similar query:

```
SELECT DISTINCT CONCAT(city, ', ', state) AS place
FROM president ORDER BY RAND();
```

From the result of that query, we'll select the first four values that differ from the correct response. The query uses LIMIT 5 rather than LIMIT 4 in case it happens to select the correct response among the incorrect ones. The query uses DISTINCT to avoid the possibility of select- ing the same birthplace for the choice list more than once. DISTINCT would be unnecessary if birthplaces were unique, but they are not, as you can discover by issuing the following statement:

```
mysql> SELECT city, state, COUNT(*) AS count FROM president
    -> GROUP BY city, state HAVING count > 1;
+-----------+-------+-------+
| city      | state | count |
+-----------+-------+-------+
| Braintree | MA    |     2 |
+-----------+-------+-------+
```

The function that generates the question and the set of possible responses looks like this:

```
function present_question ($dbh)
{
  # Issue statement to pick a president and get birthplace
  $stmt = "SELECT CONCAT(first_name, ' ', last_name) AS name,
           CONCAT(city, ', ', state) AS place
           FROM president ORDER BY RAND() LIMIT 1";
  $sth = $dbh->query ($stmt);
  $row = $sth->fetch ();
  $name = $row["name"];
  $place = $row["place"];

  # Construct the set of birthplace choices to present.
  # Set up the $choices array containing five birthplaces, one
  # of which is the correct response.
  $stmt = "SELECT DISTINCT CONCAT(city, ', ', state) AS place
           FROM president ORDER BY RAND() LIMIT 5";
  $sth = $dbh->query ($stmt);
  $choices[] = $place;  # initialize array with correct choice
  while (count ($choices) < 5 && $row = $sth->fetch ())
  {
    if ($row["place"] != $place)
      $choices[] = $row["place"]; # add another incorrect choice
  }
  # Randomize choices, display form
```

```
  shuffle ($choices);
  display_form ($name, $place, $choices);
}
```

The `display_form()` function called by `present_question()` generates the quiz question using a form that displays the name of the president, radio buttons that list the possible
choices, and a Submit button. This form serves the obvious purpose of presenting quiz information to the user, but it also needs to do something else: It must present the quiz information to
the client and arrange that when the user submits a response, the information sent back to the
Web server enables the script to check whether the response is correct and redisplay the question if not.

Presenting the quiz question is straightforward enough: Display the president's name and possible birthplace choices. Arranging to check the response and possibly redisplay the question is
a little trickier. It requires access to the correct answer and also to all the information needed
to regenerate the question. One way to do this is to use a set of hidden fields to include all the
necessary information in the form. These fields become part of the form and are not displayed
for the user to see, but are returned when the user submits a response.

We call the hidden fields `name`, `place`, and `choices` to represent the president's name, correct
birthplace, and the set of possible choices, respectively. The choices can be encoded as a single
string easily by using `implode()` to concatenate the values with a special delimiter character
in between. (The delimiter enables us to properly break apart the string later with `explode()`
if it becomes necessary to redisplay the question.) The `display_form()` function handles form
production:

```
function display_form ($name, $place, $choices)
{
  printf ("<form method=\"post\" action=\"%s\">\n", script_name ());
  hidden_field ("name", $name);
  hidden_field ("place", $place);
  hidden_field ("choices", implode ("#", $choices));
  printf ("Where was %s born?<br /><br />\n", htmlspecialchars ($name));
  for ($i = 0; $i < 5; $i++)
  {
    radio_button ("response", $choices[$i], $choices[$i], FALSE);
    print ("<br />\n");
  }
  print ("<br />\n");
  submit_button ("submit", "Submit");
  print ("</form>\n");
}
```

`display_form()` uses several helper functions to generate the form fields. The first
is `hidden_field()`, which generates the `<input>` tag for a hidden field:

```
function hidden_field ($name, $value)
{
```

```
    printf ("<input type=\"%s\" name=\"%s\" value=\"%s\" />\n",
            "hidden",
            htmlspecialchars ($name),
            htmlspecialchars ($value));
}
```

Because `hidden_field()` is a general-purpose routine likely to be useful in many scripts, the logical place to put it is in our library file, `sampdb_pdo.php`. Note that it uses `htmlspecialchars()` to encode `<input>` tag attributes, in case they contain special characters such as quotes.

Two other helper functions, `radio_button()` and `submit_button()`, are implemented as follows:

```
function radio_button ($name, $value, $label, $checked)
{
  printf ("<input type=\"%s\" name=\"%s\" value=\"%s\"%s />%s\n",
          "radio",
          htmlspecialchars ($name),
          htmlspecialchars ($value),
          ($checked ? " checked=\"checked\"" : ""),
          htmlspecialchars ($label));
}

function submit_button ($name, $value)
{
  printf ("<input type=\"%s\" name=\"%s\" value=\"%s\" />\n",
          "submit",
          htmlspecialchars ($name),
          htmlspecialchars ($value));
}
```

When the user chooses a birthplace from among the available options and submits the form, the response is returned to the Web server as the value of the `response` parameter. We can discover the value of `response` by calling `script_param()`. This also gives us a way to figure out whether the script is being called for the first time or whether the user is submitting a response to a previously displayed form. The parameter is not present if this is a first-time invocation, so the main body of the script can determine what it should do based on the parameter's presence or absence:

```
$response = script_param ("response");
if (is_null ($response))    # invoked for first time
  present_question ($dbh);
else                        # user submitted response to form
  check_response ($dbh);
```

We must still write the `check_response()` function that compares the user's response to the correct answer. For this, the values present in the `name`, `place`, and `choices` hidden fields are needed. We encoded the correct answer in the `place` field of the form, and the user's response is in the `response` field, so to check the answer, all we need to do is compare the two. Based on the result of the comparison, `check_response()` provides some feedback, then either generates and displays a new question, or redisplays the same question:

```
function check_response ($dbh)
{
  $name = script_param ("name");
  $place = script_param ("place");
  $choices = script_param ("choices");
  $response = script_param ("response");

  # Is the user's response the correct birthplace?

  if ($response == $place)
  {
    print ("That is correct!<br />\n");
    printf ("%s was born in %s.<br />\n",
            htmlspecialchars ($name),
            htmlspecialchars ($place));
    print ("Try the next question:<br /><br />\n");
    present_question($dbh);
  }
  else
  {
    printf ("\"%s\" is not correct.  Please try again.<br /><br />\n",
            htmlspecialchars ($response));
    $choices = explode ("#", $choices);
    display_form ($name, $place, $choices);
  }
}
```

We're done. Add a link for `pres_quiz.php` to the Historical League home page, and visitors can try the quiz to test their knowledge. (You can copy `index5.php` from the `phpapi/ushl` directory of the `sampdb` distribution to the `ushl` directory in your Web server's document tree, naming it `index.php` to replace the file of that name that is there now.)

Hidden Fields Are Insecure

`pres_quiz.php` relies on hidden fields as a means of transmitting information that is needed for the next invocation of the script but that the user should not see. That's fine for a script like this, which is intended only for fun. But hidden fields should *not* be used for any information that the user must not ever be permitted to examine directly, because they are not secure in any sense. To see why not, install `pres_quiz.php` in the `ushl` directory of your Web server document tree and request it from your browser. Then use the browser's View Source command to see the raw HTML for the quiz page. There you'll find the contents of the `place` hidden field that contains the correct answer for the current quiz question, exposed for anyone to see. This means it's very easy to cheat on the quiz. That's no big deal for this particular application, but the example does illustrate that hidden fields are not secure in the least. For information that really must be kept secure from the user, use some other method such as a session where information is stored on the server side.

9.2.3   Historical League Online Member Entry Editing

Our final PHP script, `edit_member.php`, is intended to enable the Historical League members to edit their own directory entries online. Using this script, members will be able to correct or update their membership information whenever they want without having to contact the League office to submit the changes. Providing this capability should help keep the member directory more up to date, and, not incidentally, reduce the workload of the League secretary.

One precaution we must take is to make sure each entry can be modified only by the member the entry is for, or by the League secretary. That means we need some form of security. As a demonstration of a simple form of authentication, we'll use MySQL to store passwords for each member and require that a member supply the correct password to gain access to the editing form that our script presents. The script works as follows:

- When initially invoked, `edit_script.php` presents a login form containing fields for the member ID and a password.

- When the login form is submitted, the script looks in a password table that associates member IDs and passwords. If the password matches, the script looks up the member entry from the `member` table and displays it for editing.

- When the edited form is submitted, the script updates the entry in the database using the contents of the form.

For any of this to work, we need to assign passwords. An easy way to do this is to generate them randomly. The following statements set up a table named `member_pass`, then create a password for each member by generating an MD5 checksum from a random number and using the first eight characters of the result. In a real situation, you might let members pick their own passwords, but this technique provides a quick and easy way to set something up initially:

```
CREATE TABLE member_pass
(
  member_id INT UNSIGNED NOT NULL PRIMARY KEY,
  password  CHAR(8)
);
INSERT INTO member_pass (member_id, password)
  SELECT member_id, LEFT(MD5(RAND()), 8) AS password FROM member;
```

In addition to a password for each person listed in the `member` table, add a special entry to the `member_pass` table for member 0, with a password of `bigshot` that will serve as the administrative (superuser) password. The League secretary can use this password to gain access to any entry:

```
INSERT INTO member_pass (member_id, password) VALUES(0, 'bigshot');
```

> **Note**
>
> Before creating the `member_pass` table, you might want to remove the `db_browse.pl` script from your Web server's script directory. That script, written in Section 8.4.4, "A Web-Based Database Browser," permits anyone to browse the contents of any table in the `sampdb` database—including the `member_pass` table. Thus, it could be used to see any League member's password or the administrative password.

After the `member_pass` table has been set up, we're ready to begin building `edit_member.php`. The framework for the script looks like this:

```php
<?php
# edit_member.php - Edit U.S. Historical League member entries over the Web

require_once "sampdb_pdo.php";

# Define action constants
define ("SHOW_INITIAL_PAGE", 0);
define ("DISPLAY_ENTRY", 1);
define ("UPDATE_ENTRY", 2);

# ... put input-handling functions here ...

$title = "U.S. Historical League -- Member Editing Form";
html_begin ($title, $title);

$dbh = sampdb_connect ();

# Determine what action to perform (the default if
# none is specified is to present the initial page)

$action = script_param ("action");
if (is_null ($action))
  $action = SHOW_INITIAL_PAGE;

switch ($action)
{
case SHOW_INITIAL_PAGE:    # present initial page
  display_login_page ();
  break;
case DISPLAY_ENTRY:        # display entry for editing
  display_entry ($dbh);
```

```
    break;
case UPDATE_ENTRY:          # store updated entry in database
  update_entry ($dbh);
  break;
default:
  die ("Unknown action code ($action)\n");
}

$dbh = NULL;  # close connection

html_end ();
?>
```

The `display_login_page()` function presents the initial page containing a form that asks for a member ID and password:

```
function display_login_page ()
{
  printf ("<form method=\"post\" action=\"%s?action=%d\">\n",
          script_name (),
          DISPLAY_ENTRY);
  print ("Enter your membership ID number and password,\n");
  print ("then select Submit.\n<br /><br />\n");
  print ("<table>\n");
  print ("<tr>");
  print ("<td>Member ID</td><td>");
  text_field ("member_id", "", 10);
  print ("</td></tr>");
  print ("<tr>");
  print ("<td>Password</td><td>");
  password_field ("password", "", 10);
  print ("</td></tr>");
  print ("</table>\n");
  submit_button ("button", "Submit");
  print "</form>\n";
}
```

The form presents the captions and the value entry fields within an HTML table so they line up nicely. With only two fields, this is a minor touch, but it's a generally useful technique, especially when you create forms with captions of very dissimilar lengths, because it eliminates vertical raggedness. Lining up the form components makes the form easier for the user to read and understand.

`display_login_form()` uses two more helper functions that can be found in the sampdb_pdo.php library file. `text_field()` presents an editable text input field:

```
function text_field ($name, $value, $size)
{
```

```
  printf ("<input type=\"%s\" name=\"%s\" value=\"%s\" size=\"%s\" />\n",
          "text",
          htmlspecialchars ($name),
          htmlspecialchars ($value),
          htmlspecialchars ($size));
}
```

`password_field()` is similar, except that the `type` attribute is `password`.

When the user enters a member ID and password and submits the form, the `action` parameter will be equal to `DISPLAY_ENTRY`, and the `switch` statement in the next invocation of `edit_member.php` invokes the `display_entry()` function to check the password and display the member entry if the password matches:

```
function display_entry ($dbh)
{
  # Get script parameters; trim whitespace from the ID, but not
  # from the password, because the password must match exactly.

  $member_id = trim (script_param ("member_id"));
  $password = script_param ("password");

  if (empty ($member_id))
    die ("No member ID was specified\n");
  if (!ctype_digit ($member_id))               # must look like integer
    die ("Invalid member ID was specified (must be an integer)\n");
  if (empty ($password))
    die ("No password was specified\n");
  if (check_pass ($dbh, $member_id, $password)) # regular member
    $admin = FALSE;
  else if (check_pass ($dbh, 0, $password))     # administrator
    $admin = TRUE;
  else
    die ("Invalid password\n");

  $stmt = "SELECT
             last_name, first_name, suffix, email, street, city,
             state, zip, phone, interests, member_id, expiration
           FROM member WHERE member_id = ?
           ORDER BY last_name";
  $sth = $dbh->prepare ($stmt);
  $sth->execute (array ($member_id));

  if (!($row = $sth->fetch ()))
    die ("No user with member_id = $member_id was found\n");

  printf ("<form method=\"post\" action=\"%s?action=%d\">\n",
          script_name (),
```

```
            UPDATE_ENTRY);

    # Add member ID and password as hidden values so that next invocation
    # of script can tell which record the form corresponds to and so that
    # the user need not re-enter the password.

    hidden_field ("member_id", $member_id);
    hidden_field ("password", $password);

    # Format results of statement for editing

    print ("<table>\n");

    # Display member ID as static text

    display_column ("Member ID", $row, "member_id", FALSE);

    # $admin is true if the user provided the administrative password,
    # false otherwise. Administrative users can edit the expiration
    # date, regular users cannot.

    display_column ("Expiration", $row, "expiration", $admin);

    # Display other values as editable text

    display_column ("Last name", $row, "last_name");
    display_column ("First name", $row, "first_name");
    display_column ("Suffix", $row, "suffix");
    display_column ("Email", $row, "email");
    display_column ("Street", $row, "street");
    display_column ("City", $row, "city");
    display_column ("State", $row, "state");
    display_column ("Zip", $row, "zip");
    display_column ("Phone", $row, "phone");
    display_column ("Interests", $row, "interests");

    print ("</table>\n");

    submit_button ("button", "Submit");
    print "</form>\n";

}
```

The first thing `display_entry()` does is verify the password. If the password supplied by the user matches the password stored in the `member_pass` table for the given member ID, or if it matches the administrative password (that is, the password for the special member ID 0), `edit_member.php` displays the entry in a form so its contents can be edited. The password-checking function `check_pass()` runs a simple query to select a row from the `member_pass` table, then compares its `password` column value to the password supplied by the user in the login form:

```
function check_pass ($dbh, $id, $pass)
{
  $stmt = "SELECT password FROM member_pass WHERE member_id = ?";
  $sth = $dbh->prepare ($stmt);
  $sth->execute (array ($id));
  # TRUE if a password was found and it matches
  return (($row = $sth->fetch ()) && $row["password"] == $pass);
}
```

Assuming that the password matches, `display_entry()` looks up the row from the `member` table corresponding to the given member ID, then generates an editing form initialized with the values from the row. Most of the fields are editable text so that the user can change them, but there are two exceptions. First, the `member_id` value is displayed as static text. This is the key value that uniquely identifies the row, so it should not be changed. Second, the expiration date is not something that we want League members to be able to change. (They'd be able to push the date farther into the future, in effect renewing their memberships without paying their dues.) On the other hand, if the administrative password was given at login time, the script does present the expiration date in an editable field. Assuming that the League secretary knows this password, this enables the secretary to update the expiration date for members who renew their memberships.

The `display_column()` function handles display of field labels and values. Its arguments are the label to display next to the field value, the array that contains the row to be edited, the name of the column within the row that contains the field value, and a boolean value that indicates whether to present the value in editable or static form. The last value is optional, with a default value of TRUE:

```
function display_column ($label, $row, $col_name, $editable = TRUE)
{
  print ("<tr>\n");
  print ("<td>" . htmlspecialchars ($label) . "</td>\n");
  print ("<td>");
  if ($editable)  # display as editable field
    text_field ("row[$col_name]", $row[$col_name], 80);
  else            # display as read-only text
    print (htmlspecialchars ($row[$col_name]));
  print ("</td>\n");
  print ("</tr>\n");
}
```

For editable values, `display_column()` generates text fields using names that have the format `row[col_name]`. That way, when the user submits the form, PHP will place all the field values into an array variable, with elements keyed by column name. This makes it easy to extract the form contents and to associate each field value with its corresponding member table column when we update the row in the database. For example, by fetching the array into a $row variable, we can access the telephone number as $row["phone"].

The display_entry() function also embeds the member_id and password values as hidden fields in the form so that they will carry over to the next invocation of edit_script.php when the user submits the edited entry. The ID enables the script to determine which member table row to update, and the password enables it to verify that the user logged in before. (Notice that this simple authentication method involves passing the password back and forth in clear text, which isn't generally such a great idea. But the Historical League is not a high-security organization, so this method suffices for our purposes. Were you performing operations such as financial transactions, you'd certainly use a more secure form of authentication.)

The function that updates the membership entry when the form is submitted looks like this:

```
function update_entry ($dbh)
{
  # Get script parameters; trim whitespace from the ID, but not
  # from the password, because the password must match exactly,
  # or from the row, because it is an array.

  $member_id = trim (script_param ("member_id"));
  $password = script_param ("password");
  $row = script_param ("row");

  if (empty ($member_id))
    die ("No member ID was specified\n");
  if (!ctype_digit ($member_id))             # must look like integer
    die ("Invalid member ID was specified (must be an integer)\n");
  if (!check_pass ($dbh, $member_id, $password)
      && !check_pass ($dbh, 0, $password))
    die ("Invalid password\n");

  # Examine the metadata for the member table to determine whether
  # each column permits NULL values. (Make sure nullability is
  # retrieved in uppercase.)

  $stmt = "SELECT COLUMN_NAME, UPPER(IS_NULLABLE)
           FROM INFORMATION_SCHEMA.COLUMNS
           WHERE TABLE_SCHEMA = ? AND TABLE_NAME = ?";
  $sth = $dbh->prepare ($stmt);
  $sth->execute (array ("sampdb", "member"));
  $nullable = array ();
  while ($info = $sth->fetch ())
    $nullable[$info[0]] = ($info[1] == "YES");
```

```
# Iterate through each field in the form, using the values to
# construct an UPDATE statement that contains placeholders, and
# the array of data values to bind to the placeholders.

$stmt = "UPDATE member ";
$delim = "SET";
$params = array ();
foreach ($row as $col_name => $val)
{
  $stmt .= "$delim $col_name=?";
  $delim = ",";
  # If a form value is empty, update the corresponding column value
  # with NULL if the column is nullable.  This prevents trying to
  # put an empty string into the expiration date column when it
  # should be NULL, for example.
  $val = trim ($val);
  if (empty ($val))
  {
    if ($nullable[$col_name])
      $params[] = NULL; # enter NULL
    else
      $params[] = "";   # enter empty string
  }
  else
    $params[] = $val;
}
$stmt .= " WHERE member_id = ?";
$params[] = $member_id;

$sth = $dbh->prepare ($stmt);
$sth->execute ($params);
printf ("<br /><a href=\"%s\">Edit another member record</a>\n",
        script_name ());
}
```

The script first re-verifies the password to make sure someone isn't attempting to send a faked form, then updates the entry. The update requires some care because if a field in the form is blank, it may need to be entered as NULL rather than as an empty string. The expiration column is an example of this. Suppose that the League secretary logs in with the administrative password (so that the expiration field is editable) and clears the field to indicate "lifetime membership." This should correspond to a NULL membership expiration date in the database, not an empty string (which isn't a legal date). Therefore, it's necessary to be able to tell which columns can take NULL values and insert NULL (rather than an empty string) when such a column is left blank in the form.

To handle this problem, update_entry() looks up the metadata for the member table and constructs an associative array keyed on column name that indicates whether each column can have NULL values. This information is available in the COLUMNS table of the INFORMATION_ SCHEMA database. The values that we need from the table are the column name and whether it permits NULL values (that is, the COLUMN_NAME and IS_NULLABLE values).

At this point, the edit_member.php script is finished. Install it in the ushl directory of the web document tree, let the members know their passwords, and they'll be able to update their own membership information over the Web.

Introduction to MySQL Administration

MySQL has grown in complexity over time as it has become more capable. But as database systems go, MySQL is relatively simple to use, and the effort required to bring up a MySQL installation and use it is modest as well. This simplicity accounts for much of MySQL's popularity, especially among people who aren't, and don't want to be, system administrators. It helps to be a trained computer professional, but that's certainly not a requirement for running MySQL successfully.

Nevertheless, a MySQL installation doesn't run itself, regardless of your level of expertise. Someone must watch over it to make sure it operates smoothly and efficiently, and someone must know what to do when problems occur. If the job falls on you to make sure MySQL is happy at your site, keep reading.

Part III of this book, "MySQL Administration," examines the duties of MySQL administrators. This chapter provides a brief overview of the responsibilities involved in administering a MySQL installation. The following chapters provide detailed instructions for carrying them out.

If you are a new or inexperienced MySQL administrator, don't let the long list of responsibilities presented in this chapter scare you. Each task listed in the following sections is important, but you need not learn them all at once. If you like, use the chapters in this part of the book as a reference, looking up topics as you discover that you need to know about them.

If you have experience administering other database systems, you will find that running a MySQL installation is similar in some ways and that your experience is a valuable resource. But MySQL administration also has its own unique requirements. This part of the book will help you become familiar with them.

10.1 MySQL Components

The MySQL database system consists of several components. You should be familiar with what these components are and the purpose of each, so that you understand both the nature of the system you're administering and the tools available to help you do your job. If you take the time to understand what you're overseeing, your work will be much easier. To that end, you should acquaint yourself with the following aspects of MySQL.

The MySQL server. The server, `mysqld`, is the hub of a MySQL installation; it performs all manipulation of databases and tables. On Unix, several related scripts are available to assist in server startup. `mysqld_safe` is a related program used to start the server, monitor it, and restart it in case it goes down. The `mysql.server` script is useful on versions of Unix that use run-level directories for starting system services. If you run multiple servers on a single host, `mysqld_multi` can help you manage them more easily. On Windows, you have the choice of running the server from the command line or as a Windows service.

The MySQL clients and utilities. Several MySQL programs are available to help you communicate with the server. For administrative tasks, some of the most important ones are listed here:

- `mysql`—An interactive program that enables you to send SQL statements to the server and to view the results. You can also use `mysql` to execute batch scripts (text files containing SQL statements).

- `mysqladmin`—An administrative program for performing tasks such as shutting down the server, checking its configuration, or monitoring its status if it appears not to be functioning properly.

- `mysqldump`—A tool for backing up your databases or copying databases to another server.

- `mysqlcheck` and `myisamchk`—Programs that help you perform table checking, analysis, and optimization, as well as repairs if tables become damaged. `mysqlcheck` works with MyISAM tables and to some extent with tables for other storage engines. `myisamchk` is for use only with MyISAM tables.

The server's language, SQL. You should be able to talk to the server in its own language. As a simple example, you might need to find out why a user's privileges aren't working the way you expect them to work. There is no substitute for being able to go in and communicate with the server directly, which you can do by using the `mysql` client program to issue SQL statements that let you examine the grant tables.

If you don't know any SQL, be sure to acquire at least a basic understanding of it. A lack of SQL fluency will only hinder you in your administrative tasks, whereas the time you take to learn will be repaid many times over. Real mastery of SQL takes some time, but the basic skills can be attained quickly. For instruction in SQL and the use of the `mysql` command-line client, see Chapter 1, "Getting Started with MySQL."

The MySQL data directory. The server stores its databases and status files in the data directory. It's important to understand the structure and contents of this directory so that you know how the server uses the filesystem to represent databases and tables, as well as where the server logs are located and what they contain. For storage-distribution and performance reasons, you should also know your options regarding disk allocation.

10.2   General MySQL Administration

General administration deals primarily with the operation of mysqld, the MySQL server, and with providing your users with access to the server. The following duties are most important in carrying out this responsibility.

Server startup and shutdown. You should know how to start and stop the server manually from the command line and how to arrange for automatic startup and shutdown when your system starts and stops. It's also important to know how to get the server going again if it crashes or will not start properly.

User account maintenance. You should understand the difference between MySQL user accounts and Unix or Windows login accounts. You should know how to set up MySQL accounts by specifying which users can connect to the server, where they can connect from, and what they are permitted to do. You'll also need to know how to reset forgotten passwords.

Log maintenance. You should understand what types of logs are available and which ones will be useful to you, as well as when and how to perform log maintenance. Log rotation and expiration are essential for preventing the logs from filling up your filesystem.

Server configuration and tuning. The MySQL server is highly configurable. Some of the operational characteristics that you can control include which storage engines the server supports, the default character set, and its default time zone.

Another configuration issue involves server tuning. Your users want the server to perform at its best. The quick-and-dirty method for improving how well your server runs is to buy more memory or to get faster disks. But those brute-force techniques are no substitute for understanding how the server works. You should know what parameters are available for tuning the server's operation and how they apply to your situation. At some sites, queries tend to be mostly retrievals. At others, inserts and updates dominate. The choice of which parameters to change will be influenced by the query mix that you observe at your own site.

Multiple server management. It's useful to run multiple servers on the same machine under some circumstances. You can test a new MySQL release while leaving your current production server in place, or provide better privacy for different groups of users by giving each group its own server. (The latter scenario is particularly relevant to Internet service providers.) For such situations, you should know how to set up multiple simultaneous installations.

Updating MySQL software. New MySQL releases appear from time to time. You should know how to keep up to date with these releases to take advantage of bug fixes and new features. Understand the circumstances under which it's more reasonable to hold off on upgrading, and know how to choose between the stable and development releases.

10.3 · Access Control and Security

When you maintain a MySQL installation, it's important to make sure that the information your users entrust to their databases is kept secure. The MySQL administrator is responsible for controlling access to the data directory and the server, and should understand the following issues.

Filesystem security. A machine may host several user accounts that have no MySQL-related administrative duties. It's important to ensure that these accounts have no access to the data directory. This prevents them from compromising data on a filesystem level by copying database tables or removing them, or by being able to read logs that may contain sensitive information. You should know how to set up a user account to be used for running the MySQL server, how to set up the data directory so that it is owned by that user, and how to start up the server to run with that user's privileges.

MySQL server security. You must understand how the MySQL security system works so that when you set up user accounts, you grant them the proper privileges for accessing the MySQL server. Users connecting to the server over the network should have permission to do only what they are supposed to be able to do. You don't want to inadvertently grant overly permissive access to accounts due to faulty understanding of the security system!

10.4   Database Maintenance, Backups, and Replication

Every MySQL administrator hopes to avoid having to deal with corrupted or destroyed database tables. But hope alone won't keep problems from occurring. You should take steps to minimize your risks and learn what to do if bad things do happen.

Preventive maintenance. A regular program of preventive maintenance should be put in place to minimize the likelihood of database corruption or damage. You should also be making backups, of course, but preventive maintenance reduces the chance that you'll need to use them.

Database backups. In the event of a severe system crash, database backups are of crucial importance. You want to be able to restore your databases to the state they were in at the time of the crash with as little data loss as possible. Note that backing up your databases is not the same thing as performing general system backups (as is done, for example, by using the Unix `dump` program). The files corresponding to your database tables might be in flux due to server activity when system backups take place, so restoring those files will not give you internally consistent tables. The `mysqldump` program generates backup files that are more useful for database restoration, and it enables you to create backups without taking down the server. You might also need the backup files for moving databases to a different location in the event of a full disk.

Crash recovery. Should disaster strike in spite of your best efforts, you should know how to repair or restore your tables. Crash recovery should be necessary only rarely, but when it is, it's an unpleasant, high-stress business (especially with the phone ringing and people knocking on the door while you're scrambling to fix things). Nevertheless, you must know how to do it because your users will be quite unhappy otherwise! Be familiar with MySQL's table-checking and repair programs. Know how to recover data using your backup files and how to use the binary log to recover changes that were made after your most recent backup.

Database migration. If you decide to run MySQL on a faster host, you'll need to copy your databases to a different machine. You should understand the procedure for doing this, should the need arise. Database file contents might be machine dependent; if so, you can't just copy them from one system to another.

Database replication. Making a backup or a copy of a database takes a snapshot of its state at one point in time. Another option is to use replication, which involves setting up two servers in cooperative fashion such that changes to databases managed by one server are propagated on a continuing basis to the corresponding databases managed by the other server.

To use replication, you should know how to set up a server as a master replication server, and how to set up slave servers that replicate the master. If trouble occurs and replication stops, you must know where to look to identify the problem and how to get replication started again.

The preceding outline summarizes the responsibilities you undertake by becoming a MySQL administrator. The next few chapters discuss them in more detail and describe procedures to follow so that you can carry out these responsibilities effectively. We'll discuss the MySQL data directory first; that's the primary resource you're maintaining, and you should understand its layout and contents. From there, we move on to general administrative duties, a discussion of MySQL's security system, and maintenance and backups.

The MySQL Data Directory

Conceptually, different relational database systems are broadly similar: They manage a set of databases, and each database includes a set of tables. But every system has its own way of organizing the data it manages, and MySQL is no exception. By default, the MySQL server `mysqld` stores all information it manages under a location called the MySQL data directory. It stores all databases here, as well as the status files and logs that provide information about the server's operation. If you have any administrative responsibilities for a MySQL installation, familiarity with the layout and use of the data directory is fundamental to carrying out your duties. Even if you don't perform any MySQL administration, you can benefit from reading this chapter because it never hurts to have a better idea of how the server operates.

This chapter covers the following topics:

- **The data directory location.** Because the data directory is so central to the operation of the MySQL server, you should know how to determine where it is located so that you can administer its contents effectively.

- **How the server organizes and provides access to the databases and tables it manages.** This is important for setting up preventive maintenance schedules, and for performing crash recovery should table corruption ever occur.

- **What status files and logs the server generates and what they contain.** Their contents provide useful information about how the server is running, which is useful if you encounter problems.

- **How to change the default location or organization of the data directory.** This can be important for managing the allocation of disk resources on your system—for example, by balancing disk activity across drives or by relocating data to filesystems with more free space. You can also use this knowledge in planning placement of new databases.

For Unix systems, the chapter assumes the existence of a login account that is used for performing MySQL administrative tasks and for running the server. In this book, the user and group names for that account both are `mysql`. Section 12.2.1.1, "Running the Server Using an Unprivileged Login Account," discusses the reasons for using a designated login account for MySQL administration.

11.1   The Data Directory Location

A default data directory location is compiled into the server. Under Unix, typical defaults are `/usr/local/mysql/data` if you install MySQL from a binary or source distribution, or `/var/lib/mysql` if you install from an RPM package. Under Windows, the default data directory location often is `C:\ProgramData\MySQL` or `C:\Documents and Settings\All Users\Application Data\MySQL`, depending on your version of Windows.

If you compile MySQL from source, you can designate the default data directory location by using the `-DMYSQL_DATADIR=`*`dir_name`* command-line option when you run CMake.

To specify the data directory location at server startup, use a `--datadir=`*`dir_name`* option. This is useful for naming a location different from the compiled-in default. Another way to name the location is to list it in an option file that the server reads at startup. Then you need not specify it on the command line each time you start the server.

As a MySQL administrator, you should know where your server's data directory is located, but if you don't know (perhaps you are taking over for a previous administrator who left poor notes), there are several ways to find out. The following notes describe one method for use when the server is not running, and another for use when it is.

Look in an option file that the server reads when it starts. For example, if you look in `/etc/my.cnf` under Unix, you may find a `datadir` line in the `[mysqld]` option group of the file:

```
[mysqld]
datadir=/path/to/data/directory
```

The pathname indicates the location of the data directory.

If you are not sure where the server looks for option files, invoke it as follows and check the help message, which lists option file locations near the beginning:

```
% mysqld --verbose --help
```

If the server is running, connect to it and ask it for the data directory location. The server maintains a number of system variables pertaining to its operation, and it can report any of their values. The data directory location is indicated by the `datadir` variable, which you can obtain using a `SHOW VARIABLES` statement or a `mysqladmin variables` command. If you use `SHOW VARIABLES` on a Unix system, the result might look like this:

```
mysql> SHOW VARIABLES LIKE 'datadir';
+---------------+-----------------------+
| Variable_name | Value                 |
+---------------+-----------------------+
| datadir       | /usr/local/mysql/data/ |
+---------------+-----------------------+
```

From the command line, use `mysqladmin`:

```
% mysqladmin variables
+---------------+-----------------------+
```

```
| Variable_name | Value                  |
+---------------+------------------------+
...
| datadir       | /usr/local/mysql/data/ |
...
```

On Windows, the location might be something like `C:\ProgramData\MySQL` instead.

If you have multiple servers running, they will be listening on different network interfaces (TCP/IP ports, Unix socket files, or Windows named pipes or shared memory). You can get data directory information by connecting to each server in turn using appropriate connection parameter options.

If the data directory already has been created at one location and you want to move it somewhere else, see Section 11.3, "Relocating Data Directory Contents," which discusses relocation techniques.

11.2   Structure of the Data Directory

The MySQL data directory contains all the databases managed by the server. In general, these form a tree structure implemented in straightforward fashion by taking advantage of the hierarchical structure of the Unix or Windows filesystem:

- Each database has a database directory located under the data directory.

- Tables, views, and triggers within a database correspond to files in the database directory.

A given storage engine might use a storage structure that varies from the general hierarchical implementation of databases using directories and files. For example, the InnoDB storage engine can store all InnoDB tables from all databases within a single common tablespace. This tablespace comprises one or more large files that are treated as a single unified data structure within which tables and indexes are represented. InnoDB stores tablespace files in the data directory by default.

The data directory also may contain other files:

- The server's process ID (PID) file. When it starts, the server writes its process ID to this file so that other programs can discover the value if they need to send signals to the server.

- Status and log files generated by the server. These files provide important information about the server's operation and are valuable for administrators, especially when something goes wrong and you're trying to determine the cause of the problem. If some particular statement crashes the server, for example, you may be able to identify the offending statement by examining the logs. (If you configure the server to log to database tables rather than to files, the log tables are in the `mysql` database.)

- Server-related files, such as the DES key file or the server's SSL certificate and key files. It's common for administrators to use the data directory as the location for these files.

11.2.1   How the MySQL Server Provides Access to Data

When MySQL is used in the usual client/server setup, all databases under the data directory are managed by a single entity, the MySQL server `mysqld`. Client programs do not manipulate data directly. Instead, the server provides the sole point of contact for database access, acting as the intermediary between client programs and the data they want to use. Figure 11.1 illustrates this architecture.

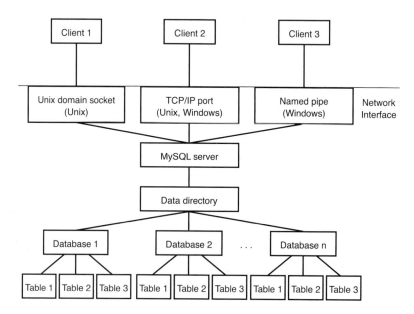

Figure 11.1   How the MySQL server controls access to the data directory.

When the server starts, it opens any logs that you request it to maintain, then presents a network interface to the data directory by listening for various types of network connections. (For the details on selecting network interfaces, see Section 12.2.4, "Controlling How the Server Listens for Connections.") To access data, a client program establishes a connection to the server, and then communicates requests as SQL statements to perform the desired operations such as creating a table, selecting rows, or updating rows. The server performs each operation and returns the result to the client. The server is multi-threaded and can service multiple simultaneous client connections. However, because update operations are performed one at a time, the server in effect serializes requests so that two clients can never change a given row at the same time.

Under normal conditions, having the server act as the sole arbiter of database access provides assurance against the kinds of corruption that can result from multiple processes accessing the database tables at the same time. Nevertheless, administrators should be aware that there are times when the server does not have exclusive control of the data directory. Direct-access maintenance utilities such as `myisamchk` are used for MyISAM table maintenance, troubleshooting, repair, and compression operations. These programs operate directly on the files that correspond to the tables. Because these utilities can change table contents, using them to operate on tables at the same time the server is doing so can cause table damage.

The surest way to avoid problems of this sort is to stop the server before running these table utilities. If that is not possible, it's very important to understand how to tell the server not to access a table while you're using a utility that operates directly on the table files. See Section 14.2, "Performing Database Maintenance with the Server Running," for instructions on how to cooperate with the server when using these programs. An alternative to myisamchk is to use statements such as CHECK TABLE and REPAIR TABLE (or the mysqlcheck program, which issues the statements for you). Those statements eliminate the problem of interaction with the server by instructing the server itself to perform the table maintenance operations.

11.2.2   Representation of Databases in the Filesystem

Each database managed by the MySQL server has its own database directory. Database directories exist as subdirectories of the data directory, each with the same name as the database it represents. For example, if *DATADIR* represents the location of the data directory for the server on your machine, a database named mydb corresponds to the database directory *DATADIR*/mydb on Unix, or *DATADIR*\mydb on Windows.

SHOW DATABASES produces essentially nothing more than a list of the names of the directories located within the data directory.

CREATE DATABASE db_name creates a directory named *db_name* under the data directory to act as the database directory. It also creates a db.opt file in the database directory that lists database attributes such as the default character set and collation. Under Unix, the database directory is owned by and accessible only to the login account that is used for running the server.

The DROP DATABASE statement is implemented nearly as simply. DROP DATABASE db_name removes the *db_name* directory in the data directory, along with any files contained within it for tables and other database objects such as views or triggers. This is almost the same as manually removing the database directory with a filesystem-level command such as rm on Unix or del on Windows. The DROP DATABASE statement and a filesystem command differ as follows:

- For DROP DATABASE, the server removes only files with extensions known to be used for tables and other database objects. If you've created other files or directories in the database directory, the server leaves them intact. In this case, the database directory cannot be removed and the DROP DATABASE statement returns an error. One implication of this is that the database name continues to be displayed by SHOW DATABASES. To deal with this, remove any extraneous files and subdirectories manually, and then issue the DROP DATABASE statement again.

- You cannot safely remove InnoDB tables in a database by removing the database directory. For each InnoDB table, InnoDB maintains a data dictionary entry in its system tablespace, and it might also store the table's contents there as well. If a database contains InnoDB tables, you must use DROP DATABASE so that the InnoDB storage engine can update its data dictionary and delete any table contents from the tablespace.

11.2.3   Representation of Tables in the Filesystem

MySQL supports several storage engines, such as InnoDB, MyISAM, and MEMORY. MySQL represents every table on disk by at least one file, which is the `.frm` format file that contains a description of the table's structure. The server creates the `.frm` file, and individual storage engines may create additional files that contain the data rows and index information. The names and structure of these files vary according to the storage engine.

The following discussion outlines the characteristics of some representative storage engines in terms of how they store files on disk. For additional information about how these engines differ in features and behavior, see Section 2.6.1, "Storage Engine Characteristics."

InnoDB is the default storage engine. Each InnoDB table has an `.frm` format file in the database directory that contains a definition of the table structure. For table contents, InnoDB has two ways to represent data, both based on tablespaces:

- **The system tablespace.** This tablespace consists of one or more large files in the data directory. These component files of the tablespace form a logically contiguous storage area equal in size to the sum of the sizes of the individual files. By default, InnoDB stores its tables in the system tablespace. For such tables, the only table-specific file is the `.frm` file.

- **Individual tablespaces.** You can configure InnoDB to use one tablespace file per table. In this case, each InnoDB table has two table-specific files in the database directory: the `.frm` file and an `.ibd` file that contains the table's data and indexes.

The system tablespace is used for another purpose, too. InnoDB maintains an internal data dictionary that contains information about each of its tables. This dictionary is stored in the system tablespace, which therefore is necessary even if you are using individual tablespaces to store table contents.

MySQL represents each MyISAM table by three files in the database directory of the database that contains the table. Each file has a basename that is the same as the table name, and an extension that indicates the purpose of the file. For example, a MyISAM table named `mytbl` has these three files:

- `mytbl.frm` is the format file that contains a description of the table structure.
- `mytbl.MYD` is the data file that stores the contents of the table's rows.
- `mytbl.MYI` contains index information for any indexes the table has.

MEMORY tables are in-memory tables. A MEMORY table has only an `.frm` file that describes its format in the database directory. The table is not otherwise represented in the filesystem at all because the server stores a MEMORY table's data and indexes in memory rather than on disk. When the server shuts down, the contents of a MEMORY table are lost. When the server restarts, the table still exists (because the `.frm` file still exists), but it is empty.

11.2.4   Representation of Views and Triggers in the Filesystem

View and trigger objects are associated with files in the database directory of the database containing the object.

A view consists of an .frm file that contains the view definition and other related attributes. The file basename corresponds to the view name, so a view named myview is represented by myview.frm.

A trigger is stored in a .TRG file that contains the trigger definition and other related attributes. The trigger file has a basename corresponding to the table to which the trigger belongs. For example, a trigger named mytrig associated with a table named mytbl is stored in mytbl.TRG, not mytrig.TRG. If a table has multiple triggers, the server stores the definitions for all of them in the same .TRG file. Each trigger also has a .TRN file named for the trigger that contains the name of the table with which the trigger is associated. For example, the trigger mytrig has a mytrig.TRN file that contains the table name mytbl.

11.2.5   How SQL Statements Map onto Table File Operations

Every storage engine uses an .frm file to store the table format (definition), so the output from SHOW TABLES FROM db_name is the same as a listing of the basenames of the .frm files in the database directory for db_name.

To create a table of any of the types supported by MySQL, issue a CREATE TABLE statement that defines the table's structure and that includes an ENGINE = engine_name clause to indicate which storage engine to use. If you omit the ENGINE clause, MySQL uses the default storage engine (InnoDB, unless you change it). The server creates an .frm file for the new table that contains the internal encoding of its definition and tells the appropriate storage engine to create any other files that are associated with the table. For example, InnoDB creates a data dictionary entry and initializes data and index information for the table within the appropriate InnoDB tablespace. MyISAM creates .MYD and .MYI data and index files, and CSV creates a .CSV data file. Under Unix, the ownership and mode of any files created to represent the table are set to enable access only to the account that is used to run the server.

When you issue an ALTER TABLE statement, the server re-encodes the table's .frm file to reflect the structural change indicated by the statement and modifies the table contents (data and indexes) likewise. This happens for CREATE INDEX and DROP INDEX as well because they are handled by the server as equivalent ALTER TABLE statements. If the ALTER TABLE statement changes the table's storage engine, the table contents are transferred to the new engine, which rewrites the contents using the appropriate type of files it uses to represent tables.

MySQL implements DROP TABLE by removing the files that represent the table. If you drop an InnoDB table, the InnoDB storage engine also updates its data dictionary and marks as free any space associated with the table within the InnoDB system tablespace.

For some storage engines, such as MyISAM, you can remove a table manually by removing the files in the database directory to which the table corresponds. For other storage engines, such as InnoDB or MEMORY, parts of the table might not be represented within the filesystem in table-specific files, so DROP TABLE does not have a filesystem command equivalent. For example, an InnoDB table stored in the system tablespace is always uniquely associated with an .frm file, but removing that file does not properly drop the table. The InnoDB data dictionary must be updated by InnoDB itself, and removing the .frm file leaves the table data and indexes "stranded" within the system tablespace.

If the InnoDB table has an individual tablespace, it is represented in the database directory by the .frm file and its own .ibd file. However, it is still not correct to "drop" the table by removing those files because that does not give InnoDB a chance to update the data dictionary. You must use DROP TABLE so that InnoDB can remove the files *and* update the data dictionary.

11.2.6   Operating System Constraints on Database Object Names

MySQL has general rules for identifiers that name databases and other objects such as tables. The rules are detailed in Section 2.2, "MySQL Identifier Syntax and Naming Rules," but may be summarized briefly as follows:

- Unquoted identifiers may consist of latin letters a-z in any lettercase, digits 0-9, dollar, underscore, and Unicode extended characters in the range U+0080 to U+FFFF.

- Quoting an identifier within backticks enables it to contain other characters (for example, `odd?name!`). Quoting is also often necessary if you use an SQL reserved word as an identifier. If the ANSI_QUOTES SQL mode is enabled, identifiers can be quoted within either backticks or double quotes.

- Identifiers can be up to 64 characters long.

In addition, the operating system on which a MySQL server runs may impose other constraints on identifiers. These stem from filesystem naming conventions because database and table names correspond to names of directories and files: Every database is represented in the filesystem by its database directory, and every table, no matter what storage engine is used, is represented in the filesystem by at least an .frm file. Therefore, these restrictions apply:

- MySQL permits database and table names to be up to 64 characters long, but the length of names is also bound by the length permitted by your operating system.

- Case sensitivity of the underlying filesystem affects how you name and refer to databases and tables. If the filesystem is case sensitive (as is typical for Unix), the two filenames abc and ABC refer to different files. If the filesystem is not case sensitive (as for Windows, or for Mac OS X Extended filesystems), abc and ABC refer to the same file. You should keep this issue in mind if you develop a database on a server that uses case-sensitive filenames and there is a possibility you might move or replicate the database to a server where filenames are not case sensitive.

The server encodes special characters in identifiers that may be problematic in filenames. This encoding enables use of characters such as '/' and '\' in names that appear in SQL statements: Any character outside the set of digits and Latin letters is mapped in the corresponding filename to '@' followed by an encoded character value. For example, '?' and '!' have encodings of 003f and 0021, so a table named odd?name! has an .frm file named odd@003fname@0021.frm. Other files associated with the table are named similarly.

As mentioned earlier, filesystem case sensitivity affects database and table naming. One way to deal with this issue is to always use names that have a given lettercase. Another is to run the server with the lower_case_table_names system variable set to 1, which has two effects:

- The server converts a table's name to lowercase before creating the corresponding disk files.

- When the table is referenced later in a statement, the server converts its name to lowercase before attempting to find the table on disk.

The result of these actions is that names uniformly are treated as not case sensitive, regardless of the filesystem case sensitivity. This makes it easier to move databases and tables between systems. However, if you plan to use this strategy, configure the server to set the lower_case_ table_names variable *before* you start creating databases or tables, not after. If you set the variable after having already created databases or tables that have names that include uppercase characters, the setting will not have the desired effect because you will already have names stored on disk that are not entirely lowercase. To avoid this problem, rename any tables that have names containing uppercase characters to names that are entirely lowercase before setting lower_case_table_names. (To rename a table, use ALTER TABLE or RENAME TABLE.) If you have a lot of tables that need to be renamed, or databases that have names containing uppercase characters, it is easier to dump the databases and then re-create them after setting lower_case_table_names:

1. Dump each database using mysqldump:

   ```
   % mysqldump --databases db_name > db_name.sql
   ```

2. Drop each database with DROP DATABASE.

3. Stop the server, reconfigure it to set lower_case_table_names to 1, and restart the server.

4. Reload each dump file using mysql:

   ```
   % mysql < db_name.sql
   ```

   With lower_case_table_names set, each database and table is re-created with a lowercase name on disk.

lower_case_table_names actually has several possible values, described in Appendix D, "System, Status, and User Variable Reference."

11.2.7 Factors That Affect Maximum Table Size

Table sizes in MySQL are bounded, but sizes are limited by a combination of factors, so it is not always a simple matter to determine precisely what the bounds are.

The operating system imposes a maximum file-size limit. This limit applies to files used to represent tables, such as the .MYD and .MYI files for a MyISAM table. It also applies to the files that make up any InnoDB tablespace. However, the overall InnoDB system tablespace size requirements can easily exceed the maximum file size. To work around this, configure the tablespace to consist of multiple files, each of which can be the maximum file size. Another way to circumvent the file-size limit is to use raw partitions in the InnoDB tablespace. Tablespace components that are on raw partitions can be as large as the partition itself. For configuration instructions, see Section 12.5.3.1, "Configuring the InnoDB Tablespace."

In addition to operating-system limits, MySQL has its own internal limits on table sizes. These vary by storage engine. For example:

- For InnoDB, the maximum size of the InnoDB system tablespace is 4 billion pages, where the page size is 16KB. The maximum tablespace size also is the bound on the size of any individual InnoDB table stored in the tablespace. If InnoDB is configured to use individual tablespaces, each table's contents are stored in its .ibd file. In this case, InnoDB table size is bound by operating system file-size limits.

- For MyISAM tables, the .MYD and .MYI files are limited to 256TB apiece by default. However, the files can be up to 65,536TB each if you use the AVG_ROW_LENGTH and MAX_ROWS options at table-creation time. (See the description of CREATE TABLE in Appendix E, "SQL Syntax Reference.") These options affect internal row pointer width, which determines the maximum number of rows the table can hold. If a MyISAM table has grown to its maximum size and you are getting error 135 or 136 for table operations, use ALTER TABLE to increase the option values. To change the default MyISAM pointer width directly, set the myisam_data_pointer_size system variable; the new setting applies to tables created thereafter.

For storage engines that represent data and indexes in separate files, a table's size limit is reached when any of its individual files hits the file-size limit. For a MyISAM table, the table's indexing characteristics affect which file this will be. For a table with no or few indexes, it is likely that the data file will reach its size limit first. For a heavily indexed table, the index file may reach the limit first.

The presence of an AUTO_INCREMENT column implicitly limits the number of rows a table may have. For example, if the column is TINYINT UNSIGNED, the maximum value it may hold is 255, so that also becomes the maximum number of rows the table may hold. Larger integer types permit more rows. More generally, including any PRIMARY KEY or UNIQUE index in a table limits its row count to the maximum number of unique values in the index.

To determine the actual table size you can achieve, consider all applicable factors. The effective maximum table size likely will be determined by the smallest of those factors. Suppose that you want to create a MyISAM table. MySQL permits the data and index files to reach 256TB each, using the default data pointer size. But if your operating system imposes a size limit on files of 2GB, that is the effective limit for the table files. On the other hand, if your system supports files that can be larger than 256TB, the determining factor on table size then will be a MySQL factor, namely the internal data pointer size. This is a factor that you can control.

With respect to InnoDB tables that are stored in the system tablespace, a single InnoDB table can grow as large as that tablespace and the tablespace can span multiple files to become quite large. But if, as is more likely, you have many InnoDB tables, they all share the same space and thus each is constrained in size not only by the size of the tablespace, but also by how much of the tablespace is allocated to other tables. Any individual InnoDB table can grow as long as the tablespace is not full. Conversely, when the tablespace fills up, no InnoDB table can grow any larger until you add another component to the tablespace to make it bigger. Alternatively, you can make the last tablespace component auto-extending, so that it will grow as long as it does not exceed the file-size limit of your system and disk space is available. For configuration instructions, see Section 12.5.3.1, "Configuring the InnoDB Tablespace."

11.2.8   Implications of Data Directory Structure for System Performance

The structure of the MySQL data directory is easy to understand because it uses the hierarchical structure of the filesystem in such a natural way. At the same time, this structure has certain performance implications, particularly regarding operations that open the files that represent database tables.

For storage engines that represent individual tables each with their own files, each open table can require a file descriptor. If a table is represented by multiple files, opening the table requires multiple file descriptors, not just one. The server caches descriptors intelligently, but a busy server can easily use up lots of them while servicing many simultaneous client connections or executing complex statements that reference several tables. This can be a problem, because file descriptors are a scarce resource on many systems, particularly those that set the default per-process descriptor limit fairly low. An operating system that imposes a low limit and makes no provision for increasing it is not a good choice for running a high-activity MySQL server.

Another effect of representing each table by its own files is that table-opening time increases with the number of tables. Operations that open tables map onto the file-opening operations provided by the operating system, and as such are bound by the efficiency of the system's directory-lookup routines. Normally this isn't much of an issue, but it is something to consider if you need large numbers of tables in a database. For example, a MyISAM table is represented by three files. If you require 10,000 MyISAM tables, your database directory will contain 30,000 files. With that many files, you may notice a slowdown due to the time taken by file-opening operations. If this is cause for concern, you might want to think about using a type of file-system that is highly efficient at dealing with large numbers of files. For example, XFS or JFS exhibit good performance even with large numbers of small files. If it is not possible to choose a different filesystem, it may be necessary to re-evaluate the structure of your tables in relation to the needs of your applications and reorganize your tables accordingly. Consider whether you really require so many tables; sometimes applications multiply tables needlessly. An application that creates a separate table per user results in many tables, all of which have identical structures. If you were to attempt combining the tables into a single table, it might be possible to do so by adding another column identifying the user to which each row applies. If this significantly reduces the number of tables, the application's performance improves.

As always in database design, you must consider whether this particular strategy is worthwhile for a given application. Reasons not to combine tables in the manner just described are as follows:

- Increased disk space requirements. Combining tables reduces the number of tables required (decreasing table-opening times), but adds another column (increasing disk space requirements). This is a typical time versus space tradeoff and you'd need to decide which factor is most important. If speed is paramount, you'd probably be willing to sacrifice a little extra disk space. If space is tight, it might be more acceptable to use multiple tables and live with a slight delay.

- Security considerations. These may constrain your ability or desire to combine tables. One reason to use a separate table per user is to enable access to each table for only a single MySQL account by means of table-level privileges. If you combine tables, data for all users will be in the same table.

  MySQL has no provision for restricting access to particular rows to a given user; thus, you might not be able to combine tables without compromising access control. One possibility is to use views that select rows only for the current user, and grant access through the views. Alternatively, if all access to the data is controlled by your application (users never connect directly to the database), you can combine the tables and use application logic to enforce row-level access to the combined result.

Another way to create many tables without requiring so many individual files is to use InnoDB tables and store them in the InnoDB system tablespace. In this case, the InnoDB storage engine associates only an `.frm` file uniquely with each table, and stores the data and index information for all InnoDB tables together. This minimizes the number of disk files needed to represent the tables, and it also substantially reduces the number of file descriptors required for open tables. InnoDB needs only one descriptor per component file of the tablespace (which is constant during the life of the server process), and briefly a descriptor for any table that it opens while it reads the table's `.frm` file.

11.2.9   MySQL Status and Log Files

In addition to database directories, the MySQL data directory contains a number of status and log files, as summarized in Table 11.1. The default location for each file is the server's data directory, and the default name for many of them is derived using the server host name, denoted as *HOSTNAME* in the table. The binary and relay logs are created as a numbered sequence of files, denoted by *nnnnnn*. The table lists only the server-level status and log files. Individual storage engines may create their own logs or other files. For example, InnoDB does so.

Table 11.1   **MySQL Status and Log Files**

File Type	Default Name	File Contents
Process ID file	`HOSTNAME.pid`	The server process ID
Error log	`HOSTNAME.err`	Startup and shutdown events and error conditions
General query log	`HOSTNAME.log`	Connect/disconnect events and statement information
Binary log	`HOSTNAME-bin.nnnnnn`	Binary representation of statements that modify data
Binary log index	`HOSTNAME-bin.index`	List of current binary log filenames
Relay log	`HOSTNAME-relay-bin.nnnnnn`	Data modifications received by slave server from master
Relay log index	`HOSTNAME-relay-bin.index`	List of current relay log filenames
Master info file	`master.info`	Parameters for connecting to master server
Relay info file	`relay-log.info`	Status of relay log processing
Slow query log	`HOSTNAME-slow.log`	Text of statements that take a long time to process

For the general query log and the slow query log, you can select whether the server writes to a log file, to a log table in the `mysql` database, or both. Section 12.8.6, "Using Log Tables," describes logging to tables in more detail.

11.2.9.1   The Process ID File

The MySQL server writes its process ID (PID) into the PID file when it starts, and removes the file when it shuts down. Other processes can use this file to determine whether the server is running and what its process ID is if so. For example, if the operating system runs the `mysql.server` script at system shutdown time to stop the MySQL server, that script examines the PID file to determine which process it needs to send a termination signal to.

If the server cannot create the PID file, it writes a message to the error log and continues.

11.2.9.2   The MySQL Logs

MySQL can maintain several types of log files. Most logging is optional; you use server startup options to enable just the logs you need and also to specify their names if you don't like the default names. Be aware that logs can grow quite large, so it's important to make sure they don't fill up your filesystem. You can expire the logs periodically to keep the amount of space that they use within bounds.

This section briefly describes a few of the log files. For more information about the logs, the options that control the server's logging behavior, and log expiration, see Section 12.8, "Server Logs."

The error log contains a record of diagnostic information produced by the server when exceptional conditions occur. If the server fails to start up or exits unexpectedly, this log is useful because it will often contain the reason why.

The general query log provides general information about server operation: who is connecting from where and what statements they are issuing. The binary log contains statement information, too, but only for statements that modify database contents. It also contains information such as timestamps needed to keep slave servers synchronized when the server is a master server in a replication setup. The contents of the binary log are written in binary format as "events" that can be executed by providing them as input to the `mysql` client. The accompanying binary log index file lists which binary log files the server currently is maintaining.

The binary log is useful if you have a crash and must revert to backup files, because you can repeat the updates performed after the backup was made by feeding the log files to the server. This enables you to bring your databases up to the state they were in when the crash occurred. The binary log is also used if you set up replication servers because it serves as a record of the updates that must be transmitted from a master server to slave servers. For more information, see Chapter 14, "Database Maintenance, Backups, and Replication."

It's a good idea to make sure that your log files are secure and not readable by arbitrary users, because they may contain the text of statements that include sensitive information such as passwords. For example, the following log entry displays the password for the `root` user; it's certainly not the kind of information you want just anyone to have access to:

```
080412 16:47:24      44 Query     SET PASSWORD FOR
                                   'root'@'localhost'=PASSWORD('secret')
```

The server writes log files to the data directory by default, so a good precaution for securing your logs is to secure the data directory against being accessed on the server host by login accounts other than the one used by the MySQL administrator. For details of this procedure, see Section 13.1.2, "Securing Your MySQL Installation."

11.3   Relocating Data Directory Contents

Earlier parts of this chapter discuss the data directory structure in its default configuration, which is that all databases, status files, and log files are located within it. However, you have some latitude in determining the placement of the data directory's contents. MySQL enables you to relocate the data directory itself or certain elements within it. There are several reasons you might want to do this:

- The filesystem that contains the data directory has become full and you need to move it to a filesystem with more capacity.

- If your data directory is on a busy disk drive, you can put it on a less active drive to balance disk activity across physical devices. You can put databases and log files on different drives or distribute databases across drives for the same reasons. Similarly, the InnoDB system tablespace is conceptually a single large block of storage, but you can put its individual component files on different drives to improve performance. If you use partitioned tables, you can do the same with individual table partitions.

- Putting databases on one disk and logs on another disk helps minimize the damage that can be caused by a failure of a single disk.

The rest of this section discusses which parts of the data directory can be moved and how you go about making such changes.

11.3.1   Relocation Methods

There are two ways to relocate the data directory or elements within it.

First, on any platform, you can specify an option at server startup, either on the command line or in an option file. For example, to specify the data directory location, start the server with a `--datadir=dir_name` option on the command line or put the following lines in an option file:

```
[mysqld]
datadir=dir_name
```

Typically, the option file group name for server options is `[mysqld]`, as shown in the example. However, depending on your circumstances, other option group names may be more appropriate. For example, if you're running multiple servers using `mysqld_multi`, the group names have the form `[mysqldn]`, where n is some integer associated with a particular server instance. Section 12.2.3, "Specifying Server Startup Options," discusses which option groups apply to different server startup methods, and also provides instructions for running multiple servers.

Second, on Unix, you can move the file or directory to be relocated, and then make a symlink (symbolic link) in the original location that points to the new location.

Neither method works universally for everything that is relocatable. Table 11.2 summarizes what can be relocated and which relocation methods can be used. If you use an option file, it is possible to specify options in a global option file such as `/etc/my.cnf` under Unix or `C:\my.ini` on Windows.

Table 11.2   **Relocation Method Summary**

Entity to Relocate	Applicable Relocation Methods
Entire data directory	Startup option or symlink
Individual database directories	Symlink
Individual database tables	Symlink
InnoDB tablespace files	Startup option
Server PID file	Startup option
Log files	Startup option

11.3.2   Relocation Precautions

Before you attempt to relocate anything, it is prudent to back up your data so that you can
restore it if you mess up the relocation operation. Also, you should stop the MySQL server
before relocating, then restart it afterward. For certain types of relocations, such as moving a
database directory, it is sometimes *possible* to keep the server running, but not recommended.
If you do that, you must make sure that the server is not accessing the database you're moving.
You should also issue a FLUSH TABLES statement before moving the database to make sure
that the server closes all open table files. Failure to observe these precautions can result in
damaged tables.

11.3.3   Assessing the Effect of Relocation

Before attempting to relocate anything, verify that the operation will have the desired effect.
For example, on Unix, you can use the du, df, and ls -l commands for obtaining disk space
information. However, you must correctly understand the layout of your filesystem for any of
these to be useful.

The following example illustrates a subtle trap to watch out for when assessing a data directory relocation. Suppose that your data directory is /usr/local/mysql/data and you want to
move it to /var/mysql because df indicates the /var filesystem has more free space:

```
% df -k /usr /var
Filesystem          1K-blocks      Used Available Use% Mounted on
/dev/sda5           28834716K 24078024K  3291968K  88% /usr
/dev/sda6           28834716K  9175456K 18194536K  34% /var
```

To find out how much space relocating the data directory should free up on the /usr filesystem, use du -s:

```
% du -s /usr/local/mysql/data
3264308K /usr/local/mysql/data
```

This result indicates that moving the data directory from /usr to var should free about 3GB
on /usr. But would it really? To find out, try df in the data directory. Suppose that you get
output like this:

```
% df -k /usr/local/mysql/data
Filesystem          1K-blocks      Used Available Use% Mounted on
/dev/sda6           28834716K  9175456K 18194536K  34% /var
```

That's odd. Why does df report the space on the /var filesystem? The following ls -l
command provides the answer:

```
% ls -l /usr/local/mysql/data
lrwxrwxr-x  1 mysql  mysql  10 Dec 11 23:46 data -> /var/mysql
```

This output shows that /usr/local/mysql/data is a symlink to /var/mysql. In other
words, the data directory *already* has been relocated to the /var filesystem and replaced with

a symlink that points there. So much for freeing up a lot of space on /usr by moving the data directory to /var!

If you want to move a database to another filesystem as an attempt to redistribute database storage, remember that if you are using InnoDB tables that are stored in the InnoDB system tablespace, the contents of those tables are *not* located in the database directory. For a database composed primarily of such InnoDB tables, relocating the database directory relocates only their .frm files, not their contents. This has little effect on storage distribution.

The lesson from these examples is that a few moments spent assessing the effect of relocation can keep you from wasting a lot of time moving things around, only to find that you've failed to achieve your objective.

11.3.4   Relocating the Entire Data Directory

To relocate the data directory, stop the MySQL server, then move the data directory to its new location. After the move, restart the server with a --datadir option that explicitly indicates the new location. On Unix, an alternative to using --datadir is to create a symbolic link in the original data directory location that points to the new location.

11.3.5   Relocating Individual Databases

The server always looks for database directories in the data directory, so the only way to relocate a database is by the symlink method. The procedure differs for Unix and Windows.

Under Unix, relocate a database as follows:

1. Stop the server if it is running.

2. Move the database directory to its new location, or copy it and remove the original.

3. Create a symlink in the data directory that has the name of the original database and that points to the new database location.

4. Restart the server.

The following example shows how to relocate a database bigdb from the /usr/local/mysql/data directory to /var/db:

```
% mysqladmin -p -u root shutdown
Enter password: ******
% cd /usr/local/mysql/data
% tar cf - bigdb | (cd /var/db; tar xf -)
% rm -rf bigdb
% ln -s /var/db/bigdb bigdb
% mysqld_safe &
```

Execute those commands while logged in as the MySQL administrator.

Under Windows, the database relocation procedure differs somewhat:

1. Stop the server if it is running.

2. Move the database directory to its new location, or copy it and remove the original.

3. Create a file in the MySQL data directory that acts as a symbolic link to let the MySQL server know where to find the relocated database directory. The file should have a `.sym` extension and a basename that is the database name. For example, if you move the `sampdb` database from `C:\mysql\data\sampdb` to `E:\mysql-book\sampdb`, create a file named `C:\mysql\data\sampdb.sym` that contains this line:

   ```
   E:\mysql-book\sampdb\
   ```

4. Make sure that symbolic link support is enabled when you restart the server. Windows servers should have this enabled by default, but you can enable it explicitly by using the `--symbolic-links` option on the command line or by placing these lines in an option file:

   ```
   [mysqld]
   symbolic-links
   ```

11.3.6   Relocating Individual Tables

Individual table relocation is supported only under limited circumstances:

- You must be using Unix and the table to be relocated must be a MyISAM table.

- Your operating system must have a working `realpath()` system call. If this is true, the result of the following query will be `YES`:

   ```
   mysql> SHOW VARIABLES LIKE 'have_symlink';
   +---------------+-------+
   | Variable_name | Value |
   +---------------+-------+
   | have_symlink  | YES   |
   +---------------+-------+
   ```

If both of those conditions are satisfied, you can move the table's `.MYD` data and `.MYI` index files to their new locations and then create symlinks to them in the database directory under the original data and index filenames. (Leave the `.frm` file in the database directory.) Before doing this, either stop the server while you move the files, or lock the table to prevent the server from using it, as described in Section 14.2, "Performing Database Maintenance with the Server Running."

11.3.7   Relocating the InnoDB System Tablespace

You configure the InnoDB system tablespace initially by listing the locations of its component files in an option file, using the `innodb_data_home_dir` and `innodb_data_file_path` system variables. (For details, see Section 12.5.3.1, "Configuring the InnoDB Tablespace.") If you have already created the tablespace, it's possible to relocate regular files that are part of it; for example, to distribute them across different filesystems. Because the file locations are specified using system variables, you can relocate some or all of the tablespace files like this:

1. Stop the server if it is running.

2. Move the tablespace file or files that you want to relocate.

3. Update the option file where the InnoDB configuration is defined, to reflect the new locations of any files that you moved.

4. Restart the server.

11.3.8   Relocating Status and Log Files

To relocate the PID file or a log file, stop the server, then restart it with the appropriate option to specify the file's new location. For example, to create the PID file as `/tmp/mysql.pid`, use `--pid_file=/tmp/mysql.pid` on the command line or include these lines in an option file:

```
[mysqld]
pid_file=/tmp/mysql.pid
```

If you specify the filename as an absolute pathname, the server creates the file using that pathname. If you use a relative name, the server creates the file under the data directory. For example, if you specify `--pid_file=mysqld.pid`, the PID file will be `mysqld.pid` in the data directory.

Some systems keep server PID files in a specific directory, such as `/var/run`. You might want to put the MySQL PID file there, too, for consistency of system operation. In similar fashion, if your system uses `/var/log` for log files, you can put the MySQL logs there, too. However, many systems permit only `root` to write to these directories. That means you'd need to run the server as `root`, which for security reasons is not a good idea. What you can do instead is create subdirectories `/var/run/mysql` and `/var/log/mysql` and set them to be owned by the account you use for running the server. For example, if that account has user and group names of `mysql`, execute the following commands as `root`:

```
# mkdir /var/run/mysql
# chown mysql /var/run/mysql
# chgrp mysql /var/run/mysql
# chmod u=rwx,go-rwx /var/run/mysql
# mkdir /var/log/mysql
# chown mysql /var/log/mysql
# chgrp mysql /var/log/mysql
# chmod u=rwx,go-rwx /var/log/mysql
```

Then the server won't have any problems writing files in those directories and you can start it with options that specify files there. For example:

```
[mysqld]
pid_file = /var/run/mysql/mysql.pid
log_error = /var/log/mysql/log.err
general_log = 1
general_log_file = /var/log/mysql/querylog
log-bin = /var/log/mysql/binlog
```

For more information about log file options and how to use them, see Section 12.8, "Server Logs."

General MySQL Administration

This chapter discusses the responsibilities that you must carry out to keep MySQL running smoothly if you administer MySQL at your site:

- Securing your MySQL setup after installing it
- Keeping the server running as much of the time as possible
- Monitoring and setting the server's operating parameters
- Selecting plugins to enable server features
- Maintaining server logs
- Tuning the server for better performance
- Analyzing what's going on with the underlying hardware and working around its physical constraints to improve performance
- Running multiple servers
- Determining whether and when to upgrade MySQL to a newer version

Other significant administrative concerns are discussed in Chapter 13, "Security and Access Control," and Chapter 14, "Database Maintenance, Backups, and Replication."

This chapter covers several programs that are essential for MySQL administrators to know about:

- The MySQL server, `mysqld`
- The `mysqld_safe`, `mysql.server`, and `mysqld_multi` server startup programs
- The `mysqladmin` administrative utility

Much of the information in this chapter is better appreciated with an understanding of MySQL's data directory, which is where the server stores databases, log files, and other information. For details, see Chapter 11, "The MySQL Data Directory." For additional information specific to the SQL statements and programs discussed here, see Appendix E, "SQL Syntax Reference," and Appendix F, "MySQL Program Reference."

12.1   Securing a New MySQL Installation

Let's begin with an administrative task that you should perform immediately after installing MySQL: Ensure that the server can be accessed only by authorized users. This is a matter of understanding what MySQL user accounts the installation procedure creates, setting up passwords for those accounts that you need, and removing accounts that you don't need.

The MySQL installation procedure populates the server's data directory with two databases:

- A `mysql` database containing the grant tables that control access by clients to the server

- A `test` database that can be used for testing purposes

If you've just installed MySQL for the first time, the grant tables in the `mysql` database contain accounts in their initial state that permits anyone to connect to the server without authenticating. This is insecure, so you should assign passwords to these accounts. If you're setting up another installation on a machine that already has MySQL installed in another location, you'll need to set up passwords for the new server. However, in this case, you might run into the complication that passwords might be picked up from option files created for the existing installation, as discussed in Section 12.1.2, "Setting Up Passwords for Additional Servers."

The following discussion assumes that you have not yet established any passwords. Some MySQL installers give you the option of creating passwords during the installation procedure. However, even if you use one of those installers, the information here will help you better understand the initial MySQL user accounts.

12.1.1   Establishing Passwords for the Initial MySQL Accounts

This section describes how to check which accounts are present in your grant tables and how to set their passwords. For concreteness, the examples here assume that you are running the MySQL server on a machine with a hostname of `cobra.example.com` and that you connect to the server from that same machine. Whenever you see that hostname in the instructions, substitute the name of your own server host. The examples also assume that your MySQL server has already been started, because you'll need to connect to it.

The MySQL installation procedure sets up the grant tables in the `mysql` database with two kinds of accounts:

- Accounts with a username of `root`. These are superuser accounts intended for administrative purposes. The `root` accounts have all privileges and can do anything, including deleting all your databases and shutting down the server. (The fact that the

MySQL and Unix superuser accounts both have the name `root` is coincidental. Each has exceptional privileges, but they have nothing to do with each other.)

- Accounts with a blank username. These are "anonymous" accounts; they enable people to connect to the server without having accounts explicitly set up for them in advance. Anonymous users usually are given very few privileges, to limit the scope of what they can do.

Every account known to a MySQL server is listed in the `user` table of its `mysql` database, so that's where you'll find the initial accounts. None of these accounts have passwords by default, because it's expected that you'll supply your own. Therefore, one of your first acts in administering a MySQL installation should be to establish passwords. Otherwise, unauthorized users can gain superuser access to your server by connecting as `root`.

After you secure the initial accounts, you can proceed to set up other accounts, to enable the members of your user community to connect to the server under names that you specify, and with privileges appropriate for what those users should be permitted to do. Section 13.2, "Managing MySQL User Accounts," provides instructions for creating new accounts and modifying existing ones.

Each row in the `user` table contains `Host` and `User` values that indicate the host from which a user can connect and the name the user must give when connecting from that host. Each row also has `Password` and `plugin` columns that indicate how the account authenticates: `Password` if nonempty is the account password (hashed so that it does not appear in plain text) and `plugin` if nonempty is the authentication plugin the server invokes to handle authentication for attempts to use the account. In addition, the `user` table row has a number of columns that indicate what superuser privileges the account has.

To see what accounts are present and whether they require authentication, connect to the server as `root` and query the `user` table. This should be possible without specifying a password because even `root` has no password initially:

```
% mysql -u root
mysql> SELECT Host, User, Password, plugin FROM mysql.user;
+-------------------+------+----------+--------+
| Host              | User | Password | plugin |
+-------------------+------+----------+--------+
| localhost         | root |          |        |
| cobra.example.com | root |          |        |
| 127.0.0.1         | root |          |        |
| ::1               | root |          |        |
| localhost         |      |          |        |
| cobra.example.com |      |          |        |
+-------------------+------+----------+--------+
```

The output that you see on your own server may not be exactly the same as shown here, but each account that you see where both `Password` and `plugin` are blank is one that is insecure and to which you should assign a password.

Where do the grant tables in the data directory come from? It depends on your platform:

- Under Unix, the data directory is initialized during the installation procedure by the `mysql_install_db` script. One purpose of `mysql_install_db` is to set up the grant tables in the `mysql` database. If you install MySQL on Linux from RPM packages on or Mac OS X using a DMG package, `mysql_install_db` is run for you automatically. Otherwise, you run it yourself. For more information, see Section F.7, "`mysql_install_db`."

- Under Windows, the data directory and the `mysql` database are included pre-initialized with the MySQL distribution.

Most of the initial accounts are the same on all platforms. A few are platform-specific. The following table shows those that are present on all platforms. None of the accounts have a password initially, although, as mentioned previously, an installer program might give you the option of establishing passwords.

Host	User	Superuser Privileges
localhost	root	All
127.0.0.1	root	All
::1	root	All
localhost		None

Those `user` table accounts permit connections by client programs as follows:

- The `root` accounts enable you to connect to the local MySQL server, using a hostname of `localhost`, the IPv4 address `127.0.0.1`, or the IPv6 address `::1`. For example, you can connect as `root` using either of these commands:

```
% mysql -h localhost -u root
% mysql -h 127.0.0.1 -u root
```

The account with `::1` as the `Host` value permits connections over IPv6 from the local host. If your system supports IPv6, you can connect using this account as follows:

```
% mysql -h ::1 -u root
```

As `root`, you have all privileges and can perform any operation.

- The account with a blank `User` value is an anonymous account. It permits connections to the local MySQL server, using a hostname of `localhost` and without specifying any username:

```
% mysql -h localhost
```

The anonymous user has no superuser privileges.

On Unix, where `mysql_install_db` is run to initialize the grant tables, you'll also a host-specific account for `root` and another for the anonymous user. If the server host is named `cobra.example.com`, the host-specific accounts are as shown in the following table.

Host	User	Superuser Privileges
cobra.example.com	root	All
cobra.example.com		None

You won't see those accounts on a Windows system because the grant tables are included pre-initialized with the MySQL distribution, and your hostname is unknown to the distribution packagers.

If you are logged in on `cobra.example.com`, the hostname-specific accounts permit you to connect to the local server by specifying the hostname, either as `root` or the anonymous user:

```
% mysql -h cobra.example.com -u root
% mysql -h cobra.example.com
```

On Windows, the installer program might give you the option of creating a `root` account that can connect from anywhere. This account has `Host` and `User` values of `%` (match any host) and `root`, and has all superuser privileges.

On all platforms, another grant table (the `db` table, not shown) contains privilege information that enables all users, even anonymous users, to use the `test` database or any database having a name that begins with `test_`.

The rest of this section describes how to set the `root` and anonymous-user passwords. The examples use a representative set of accounts, *but the particular set of SQL statements that you use depends on which accounts actually are present on your system.*

Depending on how you assign passwords, you may also need to tell the server to reload the grant tables so that it notices the change. The server performs access control using in-memory copies of the grant tables. For some methods of changing passwords in the `user` table, the server may not recognize that you've changed anything, so you must explicitly tell it to re-read the tables.

One password-assignment method is to connect to the server as `root`, determine which accounts are insecure because they have no authentication information specified, and use a `SET PASSWORD` statement for each one. Suppose that you connect to the server and find that the following accounts are insecure:

```
% mysql -u root
mysql> SELECT Host, User FROM mysql.user
    -> WHERE Password = '' AND plugin = '';
+--------------------+------+
| Host               | User |
+--------------------+------+
```

```
| localhost          | root |
| cobra.example.com  | root |
| 127.0.0.1          | root |
| ::1                | root |
| localhost          |      |
| cobra.example.com  |      |
+--------------------+------+
```

These accounts can be assigned passwords with SET PASSWORD statements. Each statement should specify an account name in 'user_name'@'host_name' format, using the User and Host values of the user table row that you want to modify. (If the User value is blank, the user_name value is '', the empty string.) To set the root and anonymous-user passwords for the accounts just shown, use the following statements:

```
mysql> SET PASSWORD FOR 'root'@'localhost' = PASSWORD('rootpass');
mysql> SET PASSWORD FOR 'root'@'cobra.example.com' = PASSWORD('rootpass');
mysql> SET PASSWORD FOR 'root'@'127.0.0.1' = PASSWORD('rootpass');
mysql> SET PASSWORD FOR 'root'@'::1' = PASSWORD('rootpass');
mysql> SET PASSWORD FOR ''@'localhost' = PASSWORD('anonpass');
mysql> SET PASSWORD FOR ''@'cobra.example.com' = PASSWORD('anonpass');
```

An alternative to SET PASSWORD is to modify the user table directly with UPDATE. This method can be used to specify a password for all accounts with a given User value, regardless of their Host value, and thus modify multiple accounts simultaneously. To set the password for all root accounts and all anonymous-user accounts, use these statements:

```
mysql> UPDATE mysql.user SET Password=PASSWORD('rootpass') WHERE User='root';
mysql> UPDATE mysql.user SET Password=PASSWORD('anonpass') WHERE User='';
mysql> FLUSH PRIVILEGES;
```

When you change passwords with SET PASSWORD, the server notices that you've modified the grant tables and automatically re-reads them to refresh its in-memory copy of the tables. If you use UPDATE to modify the user table directly, it's necessary to explicitly tell the server to reload the tables. That's the purpose of the FLUSH PRIVILEGES statement following the UPDATE statements.

Another option for dealing with anonymous-user accounts is to remove them entirely. I recommend this unless you have a specific reason to retain them. To remove the anonymous accounts, use DROP USER:

```
mysql> DROP USER ''@'localhost';
mysql> DROP USER ''@'cobra.example.com';
```

For DROP USER, the server automatically re-reads the grant tables and no FLUSH PRIVILEGES statement is needed.

One benefit of removing the anonymous-user accounts is that it improves security. Another is that it significantly simplifies the task of setting up nonanonymous accounts. If you leave the anonymous accounts in place, you may have to deal with the curious phenomenon described in Section 13.4.4, "A Privilege Puzzle." You can read that section for the details behind this phenomenon.

Now that you have established the account passwords (and reloaded the grant tables if necessary), the appropriate password is needed for each attempt to connect to the server. In particular, no one can connect as `root` without knowing the password:

```
% mysql -u root
ERROR 1045 (28000): Access denied for user 'root'@'localhost'
(using password: NO)
% mysql -p -u root
Enter password: rootpass
mysql>
```

The need to specify a password when connecting to the server from this point on is true not just for `mysql`, but also for other programs such as `mysqladmin` and `mysqldump`. For brevity, many of the examples in later sections of this chapter do not show the `-u` and `-p` options. I assume that you'll supply them as necessary whenever you connect to the server.

12.1.2 Setting Up Passwords for Additional Servers

The preceding instructions assume that you're establishing passwords on a system that hasn't had MySQL installed on it before. However, if MySQL is already installed in one location and you're setting the passwords for a new server installed in another location on the same machine, you may find when you attempt to connect to the new server without a password that it rejects the attempt with the following error:

```
% mysql -u root
ERROR 1045 (28000): Access denied for user 'root'@'localhost'
(using password: YES)
```

Hm! Why did the server say it received a password, when you didn't specify one? This usually indicates that you have an option file somewhere that contains the password for accessing a previously installed server. `mysql` finds the option file and automatically uses the password listed there. To override that and explicitly specify "no password," use a `--skip-password` option:

```
% mysql -u root --skip-password
```

This strategy also applies to other MySQL client programs, such as `mysqladmin`.

For additional discussion on using several servers, see Section 12.9, "Running Multiple Servers."

12.2   Arranging for MySQL Server Startup and Shutdown

One responsibility a MySQL administrator has is to make sure that the server, `mysqld`, is running as much of the time as possible so that your users can access it. Occasionally, however, it's necessary to stop the server. For example, if you're relocating the data directory, you can't have the server updating tables at the same time, so you must shut it down. The tension between the desire to keep the server running and the need to stop it occasionally is something this book can't resolve for you. But we will discuss how to get the server started and stopped so that you have the ability to perform either operation as you see fit. Many aspects of the procedures for this differ for Unix and Windows, so the following discussion covers them separately.

12.2.1   Running the MySQL Server On Unix

On Unix, the MySQL server can be started manually from the command line. It's also possible to arrange for the server to run automatically at system boot time as part of the standard startup procedure. (This is in fact probably how you'll start the server under normal operating conditions after you get everything set up the way you want.) But before discussing how to start the server, let's consider which login account should be used to start it. On a multi-user operating system such as Unix, you have a choice about which login account to use for running the server. If you start the server manually, it runs as the Unix user you happen to be logged in as. For example, if I log in as `paul` and start the server, it runs as `paul`. If instead I use the `su` command to switch user to `root` and then start the server, it runs as `root`.

Keep in mind two goals for your MySQL server startup procedures under Unix:

The server should run as some user other than `root`. To say the server runs "as" a given user means that the server process is associated with the user ID of that user's Unix login account, and that it has that user's privileges for reading and writing files in the filesystem. This has certain security implications, particularly for processes that run as the `root` user, because `root` is permitted to do anything, however dangerous. One way to avoid these dangers is to have the server relinquish its special privileges. Processes that start as `root` have the capability to change their user ID to another account and thus give up `root`'s privileges in exchange for those of a regular unprivileged user. This makes the process less dangerous. In general, you should limit the power of any process unless it really needs `root` access—and `mysqld` does not. It needs to access and manage the contents of the MySQL data directory, but little else. This means that if the server starts as `root`, you should tell it to change its user ID during startup to run as an unprivileged user.

The server should run as the same user every time it executes. It's inconsistent for the server to run with one user's privileges sometimes and with another user's privileges other times. That leads to files and directories being created under the data directory with varying ownerships, and results in the server not being able to access certain databases or tables depending on who it runs as. Consistently running the server as the same user avoids this problem.

12.2.1.1 Running the Server Using an Unprivileged Login Account

There are multiple benefits to using a separate, unprivileged account rather than `root` for MySQL-related activity:

- No one can exploit the server as a security hole to gain `root` access.

- Files that the server creates are owned by the unprivileged account rather than by `root`. For example, MySQL users who have the `FILE` privilege cannot cause the server to write `root`-owned files. The fewer such files on your system, the better.

- It's safer to perform MySQL administrative tasks while you are logged in as an unprivileged user than as `root`. If you make a mistake while performing a filesystem operation as `root`, the consequences can be devastating.

- It's cleaner conceptually and administratively to create a separate account devoted exclusively to MySQL activity. It's also easier to see what things on your system are MySQL related. For example, in the directory where `crontab` files are kept, you'll have a separate file for the MySQL user. Otherwise, the MySQL cron jobs will be listed in `root`'s `crontab` file, along with everything else done as `root` on a periodic basis.

To set up `mysqld` to run as an unprivileged non-`root` user, follow this procedure:

1. Stop the server if it's running:

```
% mysqladmin -p -u root shutdown
```

2. Choose which login account to use for running `mysqld`. You can also designate a group name specifically for use with MySQL. Here, we'll use `mysql` for both the user and group names. If you use different names, substitute them anywhere you see `mysql` as a user or group name elsewhere in this book. For example, you might install MySQL under your own account because you have no special administrative privileges on your system. In this case, you'll also run the server as yourself, so you should substitute your own login name and group name for `mysql`.

3. If necessary, create the login account for the username you've chosen, using your system's usual account-creation procedure. You'll need to do this as `root`.

   Should you elect to use the account named `mysql` for running the server, it might not be necessary to create it yourself. If you install MySQL on Linux using an RPM package, the installation procedure creates the account automatically. Mac OS X comes with a `mysql` account already set up. Other systems might do the same.

4. Modify the user and group ownership of the MySQL data directory and any subdirectories and files under it so that the `mysql` user owns them. For example, if the data directory is `/usr/local/mysql/data`, set up ownership for that directory and its contents as follows:

```
# chown -R mysql /usr/local/mysql/data
# chgrp -R mysql /usr/local/mysql/data
```

   Run those commands as `root`.

5. It's a good security precaution to set the access mode of the data directory to keep other people out. To do this, modify its permissions so that it can be accessed only by the `mysql` user. If the data directory is `/usr/local/mysql/data`, set up everything in and under it to be accessible only to `mysql` by turning off all the "group" and "other" permissions as follows:

```
# chmod -R go-rwx /usr/local/mysql/data
```

The last couple steps actually are part of the more comprehensive lockdown procedure detailed in Section 13.1.2, "Securing Your MySQL Installation." Check that section for additional instructions on making ownership and mode assignments, particularly if your MySQL installation has a nonstandard layout.

After completing the preceding procedure, make sure always to start the server with an option of `--user=mysql` so that it switches its user ID to `mysql` if it's invoked by `root`. This is true both for running the server manually as `root`, and for setting up the server to be invoked during your system's startup procedure. Unix systems perform startup operations as the Unix `root` user, so any processes initiated as part of that procedure execute by default with `root` privileges.

The best way to ensure that the user is specified consistently is to list it in an option file that the server reads. For example, put the following lines in `/etc/my.cnf`:

```
[mysqld]
user=mysql
```

For more information on option files, see Section 12.2.3, "Specifying Server Startup Options."

If you happen to start the server while logged in as `mysql`, the presence of the `user` line in your option file results in a warning that the option can be used only by `root`. This means that the server does not have the capability to change its user ID and will run as `mysql`. That's what you want anyway, so just ignore the warning.

12.2.1.2 Starting the Server on Unix

After deciding which login account to use for running MySQL, you have several choices about how to start the server. It's possible to start it manually from the command line or automatically during the system startup procedure. Methods for doing this include the following:

- **Invoke mysqld directly.** This is probably the least common method. I won't discuss it further, except to say that the following command is useful for finding out what startup options the server supports:

```
% mysqld --verbose --help
```

- **Invoke the mysqld_safe script.** `mysqld_safe` invokes the server for you and then monitors and restarts it if it terminates abnormally. `mysqld_safe` commonly is used on BSD-style versions of Unix, and it also is invoked by `mysql.server` on non-BSD systems and on Mac OS X.

`mysqld_safe` redirects error messages and other diagnostic output from the server to a file in the data directory to produce an error log or to `syslog`. If you send error output to a file, `mysqld_safe` sets the ownership of the file so that it is owned by the login account named by the `--user` option. This leads to trouble if you use different `--user` values at different times. The symptom is that `mysqld_safe`'s attempt to write to the error log file fails with a "permission denied" error. This is problematic because if you examine the error log to see what the difficulty is, it contains no useful information related to the cause! If this problem occurs, remove the error log file and invoke `mysqld_safe` again.

- **Invoke the `mysqld.server` script.** `mysql.server` starts the server by executing `mysqld_safe`. Invoke this script with an argument of `start` or `stop` to indicate whether you want the server to start or stop. It serves as a wrapper around `mysqld_safe` and commonly is used on systems that employ the System V method of arranging startup and shutdown scripts into several directories. Each directory corresponds to a particular run level and contains scripts to be invoked when the machine enters or exits that run level.

- **To coordinate several servers, use the `mysqld_multi` script.** This script reads an option file in which you list startup parameters for multiple servers. It enables you to start or stop each one, or check whether it is running. This startup script is more complicated than the others, so I'll defer discussion to Section 12.9, "Running Multiple Servers."

The `mysqld_safe` and `mysqld_multi` scripts are installed in the `bin` directory under the MySQL installation directory, and `mysql.server` can be found in the `support-files` directory. To use `mysql.server`, you might need to copy it to the proper run-level directory and make it executable. (Some installation methods install `mysql.server` for you. Linux RPM and Mac OS X DMG packages do so, for example.)

> **Note**
>
> Normally, you install `mysql.server` into the run-level directory under the name `mysql`, but I'll generally continue to discuss it using the name `mysql.server` to make it clear what I'm referring to. If you use a MySQL RPM obtained from another vendor, a similar startup script might be installed under a different name, such as `mysqld`.

The type of system you have determines the arrangements that you'll need to make to have a startup script execute at system boot time. Read through the following examples and use or adapt the instructions that most closely match the startup procedures for your system.

For BSD-style systems, it's common to have a few files in the `/etc` directory that initiate services at boot time. These files often have names that begin with `rc`, and it's likely that there will be a file named `rc.local` (or something similar) intended specifically for starting locally installed services. On an `rc`-based system, you might add lines such as the following to `rc.local` to start the server:

```
if [ -x /usr/local/bin/mysqld_safe ]; then
  /usr/local/bin/mysqld_safe &
fi
```

Modify the lines appropriately if the pathname to `mysqld_safe` is different on your system.

For System V-style systems, you can install `mysql.server`. Copy it to the appropriate run-level directory under `/etc`. This may have been done for you already if you run Linux and installed MySQL from an RPM package. Otherwise, install the script in the main startup script directory with the name you want to use, make sure the script is executable, and place links to it in the appropriate run-level directory.

The layout for run-level directories varies from system to system, so check to see how your system organizes them. For example, many Linux variants have a set of directories organized under `/etc/init.d` and `/etc/rc.d`. Such Linux systems typically have a `chkconfig` command that is intended for startup script management. You can use it to help you install the `mysql.server` script. The following instructions show how to install `mysql.server` into the startup directories using a name of `mysql`:

1. Copy the `mysql.server` script from wherever it's located into the `init.d` directory and make it executable:

   ```
   # cp mysql.server /etc/init.d/mysql
   # chmod +x /etc/init.d/mysql
   ```

2. Register the script and enable it:

   ```
   # chkconfig --add mysql
   # chkconfig mysql on
   ```

3. To verify that the script is properly enabled, run `chkconfig` with the `--list` option:

   ```
   # chkconfig --list mysql
   mysql           0:off   1:off   2:on    3:on    4:on    5:on    6:off
   ```

   The output indicates that the script executes automatically for run levels 2, 3, 4, and 5.

If you don't have `chkconfig`, you can use a manual procedure. To enable the script for run level 3, use these commands:

```
# cp mysql.server /etc/init.d/mysql
# cd /etc/init.d
# chmod +x mysql
# cd /etc/rc.d/rc3.d
# ln -s /etc/init.d/mysql S99mysql
```

Under Mac OS X, the `/Library/StartupItems` and `/System/Library/StartupItems` directories contain subdirectories for the services that are initiated at system boot time. The DMG package provided for Mac OS X at the MySQL Web site contains an installer that places a startup item for the MySQL server into one of these directories.

12.2.2   Running the MySQL Server On Windows

On Windows, you can start the MySQL server manually from the command line. It's also possible to create a Windows service for MySQL. You can set the service to run automatically when Windows starts and control it from the command line or by using the Windows Services Manager.

MySQL distributions for Windows include multiple servers, each built with different options. I'll use the server named `mysqld` in examples. Your distribution might also contain a server named `mysqld-debug`, which is like `mysqld` but with the addition of debugging support. Unless you need debugging capabilities, choose `mysqld` because `mysqld-debug` uses more memory and runs more slowly.

Windows servers provide two types of connections that Unix servers do not:

- Connections using named pipes, if the server is started with the `--named-pipe` option.

- Connections using shared memory, if the server is started with the `--shared-memory` option.

For more information about enabling these connection types, see Section 12.2.4, "Controlling How the Server Listens for Connections."

12.2.2.1   Running the Server Manually on Windows

To start the server manually from the command line, change location to the directory where it is installed and enter this command:

```
C:\> mysqld
```

You can specify other options on the command line or in an option file. See Section 12.2.3, "Specifying Server Startup Options."

To have error messages go to the console window rather than to the error log (the *HOSTNAME*. `err` file in the data directory by default), use the `--console` option:

```
C:\> mysqld --console
```

When you run the server in console mode, you can specify other options on the command line after the `--console` option or in an option file.

If you start the server from the command line, you may not see another command prompt until the server exits. That's okay. Just open another console window to use for running client programs.

To stop the server, use `mysqladmin`:

```
C:\> mysqladmin -p -u root shutdown
```

12.2.2.2   Running the Server as a Windows Service

On Windows, you can create a service for MySQL using this command:

```
C:\> "C:\Program Files\MySQL\MySQL Server 5.5\bin\mysqld" --install
```

The command uses the full pathname to the server. If your server is installed in a different location, modify the pathname accordingly.

The service-creation command does not actually start `mysqld`. Instead, it causes `mysqld` to run automatically whenever Windows starts. If you prefer to create a service that does not run automatically, install the server as a "manual" service:

```
C:\> "C:\Program Files\MySQL\MySQL Server 5.5\bin\mysqld" --install-manual
```

As a general rule, when you create a Windows service for MySQL, you give no other options on the command line and list them in an option file instead. (See Section 12.2.3, "Specifying Server Startup Options.") However, it is possible to specify a service name and option file as arguments, as described in the following discussion. This is especially useful when you create several MySQL services. (See also Section 12.9, "Running Multiple Servers.")

When you create a Windows service for MySQL, the default service name is `MySQL` (not case sensitive). It's possible to specify a service name explicitly following the `--install` option:

```
C:\> "C:\Program Files\MySQL\MySQL Server 5.5\bin\mysqld" --install
service_name
```

Each Windows service must have a unique name, so one reason for choosing a service name other than `MySQL` is that it enables you to run multiple MySQL servers as services. The service name affects which option groups the server reads from option files when it starts:

- With no `service_name` argument or a service name of `MySQL`, the server uses the default service name (`MySQL`) and reads the `[mysqld]` group from the standard option files.

- With a `service_name` argument different from `MySQL`, the server uses that name as the service name and reads the `[mysqld]` and `[service_name]` groups from the standard option files.

If you specify a service name, you can also specify a `--defaults-file` option as the final option on the command line when you create a MySQL service (enter the command on a single line):

```
C:\> "C:\Program Files\MySQL\MySQL Server 5.5\bin\mysqld"
      --install service_name --defaults-file=file_name
```

This gives you an alternative means of providing server-specific options. This syntax requires a service name to be given; to use the default service name, specify a `service_name` value of `MySQL`. The name of the file is remembered and used by the server whenever it starts, and it reads options only from that file. The groups read are `[mysqld]` and, if `service_name` is not `MySQL`, the `[service_name]` group.

A single option other than `--defaults-file` is permitted following the service name, but `--defaults-file` is more flexible because you can put as many options as you need in the file. For more information on option files, see Section 12.2.3, "Specifying Server Startup Options."

After the server has been installed as a service, you control it using the service name. This can be done from the command line, or from the Windows Services Manager if you prefer a graphical interface. The Services Manager location depends on your version of Windows.

To start or stop the service from the command line, use the following commands:

```
C:\> net start MySQL
C:\> net stop MySQL
```

If you use the Services Manager, it presents a window that displays a list of services, along with additional information such as whether each service is running and whether it is automatic or manual. To start or stop the MySQL server, select its entry in the services list and then choose the appropriate button or menu item.

You can also stop the server from the command line with `mysqladmin shutdown`.

> **Note**
>
> Although you can control services using either the Services Manager or commands issued from the command prompt, you should avoid interactions between the two approaches. Close the Services Manager before invoking service-related commands from the prompt.

To remove the MySQL server from the list of services, stop it if it is running, then issue this command:

```
C:\> mysqld --remove
```

The command removes the MySQL service having the default service name of `MySQL`. To indicate explicitly which service to remove, specify its name following the `--remove` option:

```
C:\> mysqld --remove service_name
```

12.2.3   Specifying Server Startup Options

On any platform, there are two primary methods for specifying startup options when you invoke the server:

- List the options on the command line. In this case, it's possible to use either the long or short forms of any option for which both forms are available. For example, you can use either `--user=mysql` or `-u mysql`.

- List the options in an option file. Options specified this way are given one per line. Only the long option form can be used, and it's written without the leading dashes:

  ```
  [mysqld]
  user=mysql
  ```

For a general discussion of the format and syntax of option files, and the locations in which the server looks for them, see Section F.2.2, "Option Files."

The two option-specification methods are not mutually exclusive. The server looks for options both in option files and on the command line, with options on the command line taking precedence.

It's generally easiest to use an option file because options specified that way take effect each time the server starts, whatever startup method you use. Listing options on the command line works only if you start the server manually or by using `mysqld_safe`. It does not work for `mysql.server`, which is intended to support only the `start` and `stop` arguments on the command line. Also, with limited exceptions, you cannot specify startup options on the command line if you use `--install`, `--install-manual`, or `--remove` to install or remove a Windows server as a service. (Section 12.2.2.2, "Running the Server as a Windows Service," discusses the exceptions.)

The locations in which the server looks for option files depends on your version of MySQL (see Section F.2.2, "Option Files"). However, `/etc/my.cnf` on Unix and `C:\my.ini` on Windows are pretty standard locations. To see the locations where the server looks for option files, run this command:

```
% mysqld --verbose --help
```

If the option file you want to use doesn't exist, create it as a plain text file.

Server startup options typically are placed in the `[mysqld]` option group. For example, to indicate that you want the server to run as `mysql` and to use a base directory location of `/usr/local/mysql`, put the following set of lines in the option file:

```
[mysqld]
user=mysql
basedir=/usr/local/mysql
```

That is equivalent to starting the server with options on the command line as follows:

```
% mysqld --user=mysql --basedir=/usr/local/mysql
```

Table 12.1 shows the standard list of option groups used by servers and the server startup programs. The line for `mysqld` also applies to servers with variant names such as `mysqld-debug` on Windows.

Table 12.1   **Option Groups Used by Server Programs**

Program	Option Groups Used By Program
mysqld	[mysqld], [server]
mysqld_safe	[mysqld], [server], [mysqld_safe]
mysql.server	[mysqld], [server], [mysql_server], [mysql.server]

When you place options in a group, choose the group that will be used in the context or contexts that you want. The `[mysqld]` and `[server]` groups are used for options that apply to `mysqld`. The `[mysqld_safe]`, `[mysql_server]`, and `[mysql.server]` groups enable you to specify options that apply only to one startup script or the other.

On Windows, if you create a Windows service for MySQL and do not use the default service name, that affects the option groups that the server reads. For details, see Section 12.2.2.2, "Running the Server as a Windows Service."

`mysql.server` reads option files to look only for `basedir`, `datadir`, `pid-file`, and `service-startup-timeout` option values.

12.2.4   Controlling How the Server Listens for Connections

The MySQL server listens for connections on several network interfaces, which you control as follows:

- On all platforms, the server listens for TCP/IP connections on an address and network port, unless started with the `--skip-networking` option. As of MySQL 5.6.6, the default is * (listen on all IPv4 and IPv6 interfaces). Before 5.6.6, the default is `0.0.0.0` (listen on all IPv4 interfaces). To specify an address, start the server with a `--bind-address=addr` option. The address can be an IPv4 or IPv6 address or a host name. In the latter case, the server resolves the host name to an IP address and uses that. The following list describes the effect of binding different address types on how the server accepts TCP/IP connections. Some `addr` values are special and permit connections on multiple network interfaces.

  - For `0.0.0.0`, the server accepts connections on all IPv4 interfaces.

  - For `::`, the server accepts connections on all IPv4 and IPv6 interfaces.

  - * is like `::` except that if IPv6 is not available, the server accepts connections only on all IPv4 interfaces.

  - For an IPv4-mapped address, the server accepts connections for both the IPv4 and IPv6 form of the address. For example, binding to `::ffff:192.168.0.3` permits clients to connect using a `--host` option value of `::ffff:192.168.0.3` or `192.168.0.3`.

  - For other IPv4 or IPv6 addresses, the server accepts connections for that single address. For example, binding to `192.168.0.3` permits connections only for that address.

  The default port number is 3306; to specify a different number, use the `--port` option.

- Under Unix, the server listens on a Unix domain socket file for connections from local clients that connect to the special hostname `localhost` or that specify the `--protocol=socket` option. Use of the socket file by the server cannot be turned off. The default socket file usually is `/tmp/mysql.sock`, although MySQL distributions from operating system vendors often use a different location. To specify a socket file pathname explicitly, use the `--socket` option.

- For Windows servers, named-pipe connections are disabled by default. To enable this capability, start the server with the `--named-pipe` option. This permits local clients to connect through the named pipe by specifying the `--protocol=pipe` option or by connecting to the special hostname "`.`" (period). By default, the pipe name is `MySQL` (not case sensitive). To specify a different name, use the `--socket` option.

- For Windows servers, shared-memory connections are disabled by default. To enable this capability, start the server with the `--shared-memory` option. When enabled, it becomes the default connection protocol for local clients. Local clients also can use the `--protocol=memory` option to specify use of shared memory explicitly. By default, the shared-memory name is `MYSQL` (case sensitive). To specify a different name, use the `--shared-memory-base-name` option.

On Windows, because the named-pipe and shared-memory connection types are disabled by default, it's common practice to enable them by adding the appropriate lines to the `[mysqld]` group in your option file:

```
[mysqld]
named-pipe
shared-memory
```

A client that wants to connect to a local server using TCP/IP even when some other protocol might be used by default should specify `127.0.0.1` as the server hostname. That's the address of the TCP/IP loopback interface. Another way to force a TCP/IP connection is to use the `--protocol=tcp` option.

If you run a single server, it's typical to let the server use its default network settings. If you run more than one server, it's necessary to make sure each one uses unique networking parameters. For more information, see Section 12.9, "Running Multiple Servers."

12.2.5   Stopping the Server

To stop the server manually, use `mysqladmin`:

```
% mysqladmin -p -u root shutdown
```

This works for both Unix and Windows. If you run the server as a service under Windows, it's also possible to use the graphical interface offered by the Services Manager to select and stop the server, or to stop the server manually from the command line like this:

```
C:\> net stop MySQL
```

If you have set up the server to start automatically when your system boots, you shouldn't need to do anything special to stop it automatically at system shutdown time. BSD Unix systems normally shut down processes by sending a TERM signal; programs respond to the signal appropriately (or are killed unceremoniously if they fail to do so). `mysqld` responds by terminating when it receives this signal.

For System V-style Unix systems that start the server with `mysql.server`, the shutdown process invokes that script with an argument of `stop` to tell the server to shut down. You can also invoke the script yourself to stop the server manually. For example, if you've installed the `mysql.server` script as `/etc/init.d/mysql`, invoke it as follows (you must be `root` to do this):

```
# /etc/init.d/mysql stop
```

If you run the MySQL server as a Windows service, the service manager automatically tells the server to stop when Windows shuts down. If you do not run the server as a service, stop the server manually with `mysqladmin shutdown` before shutting down Windows.

12.2.6 Regaining Control of the Server When You Cannot Connect to It

Under certain circumstances you might need to restart the server manually if you find that you no longer can connect to it. This presents a conundrum because typically you stop the server by connecting to it so that you can tell it to shut down (for example, by executing a `mysqladmin shutdown` command). How can this situation arise?

First, the MySQL `root` password might have gotten set to a value that you don't know. This can happen when you change the password—for example, if you accidentally type an invisible control character when you enter the new password value. Or you may simply have forgotten the password.

Second, under Unix, connections to `localhost` by default are made through a Unix domain socket file such as `/tmp/mysql.sock`. If the socket file gets removed, local clients can't use it to connect. This might happen if your system runs a `cron` job that removes temporary files in the `/tmp` directory now and then.

If the reason you cannot connect to the server is that the Unix socket file has been removed, you can get it back simply by restarting the server. (The server re-creates the socket file when it comes back up.) The trick here is that because the socket file is gone, you can't use it to establish a connection for telling the server to stop. You must establish a TCP/IP connection instead. To do this, connect to the local server by using the `--protocol=tcp` option or by specifying a host value of `127.0.0.1` rather than `localhost`:

```
% mysqladmin -p -u root --protocol=tcp shutdown
% mysqladmin -p -u root -h 127.0.0.1 shutdown
```

`127.0.0.1` is an IP address (it refers to the local host's loopback interface), so it explicitly forces a TCP/IP connection to be used rather than a socket connection.

If it is the case that the Unix socket file is being removed by a `cron` job, the missing-socket problem will recur until you change the `cron` job or use a socket file located somewhere else. You can specify a different socket by naming it in a global option file. For example, if the MySQL base directory is `/usr/local/mysql`, you can use a socket file in that directory by adding these lines to `/etc/my.cnf`:

```
[mysqld]
socket=/usr/local/mysql/mysql.sock

[client]
socket=/usr/local/mysql/mysql.sock
```

Restart the server after making the change so that it creates the socket file in the new location. It's necessary to specify the Unix socket file pathname both for the server and for client programs so that they all use the same file. If you set the pathname only for the server, client programs still expect to find the file at the old location. A limitation of this method is that it works only for clients that read the option file; some third-party programs might not. If you recompile MySQL from source, you can reconfigure the distribution to use a different pathname by default both for the server and clients. This automatically affects third-party programs that use the client library, unless they have been statically linked with the old library. In that case, you must recompile them to use the new library.

If you can't connect because you can't remember or don't know the `root` password, you must regain control of the server so that you can set the password again. To do this, use the following procedure:

1. Stop the server. Under Unix, if you can log in as `root` on the server host, you can terminate the server using the `kill` command. Find out the server's process ID by looking in the server's PID file (which usually is located in the data directory), or by using the `ps` command. Then try telling the server process to shut down normally by sending it a TERM signal:

   # **kill -TERM** *PID*

   That way, tables and logs will be flushed properly. If the server is hung and unresponsive to a normal termination signal, you can use `kill -9` to forcibly terminate it.

   # **kill -9** *PID*

   `kill -9` is a last resort because there might be unflushed modifications in memory, and you risk leaving tables in an inconsistent state.

   Under Linux, `ps` might show several `mysqld` "processes." These are really threads of the same process; you can kill any of them to kill them all.

   If you use `mysqld_safe` to start the server, it monitors the server for abnormal termination. Thus, if you kill the server with `kill -9`, `mysqld_safe` immediately restarts it. To avoid this, determine the PID of the `mysqld_safe` process and kill it first before killing `mysqld`.

   If you run the server as a service under Windows, you can stop it normally without knowing any passwords by using the Services Manager or by issuing this command:

   C:\> **net stop MySQL**

   To forcibly terminate the server on Windows, use the Task Manager (Alt-Control-Del). Like `kill -9` on Unix, this is a last resort.

2. Restart the server with the `--skip-grant-tables` option to disable use of the grant tables for verifying connections. That enables you to connect with no password and with all privileges. However, it also leaves your server wide open so that other people can connect the same way, so issue a `FLUSH PRIVILEGES` statement as soon as you connect:

```
% mysql
mysql> FLUSH PRIVILEGES;
```

The `FLUSH` statement causes the server to reread the grant tables and start using them again for access control. You will remain connected, but the server requires any subsequent connection attempts by other clients to be validated with the grant tables as usual. The `FLUSH` statement also re-enables the `SET PASSWORD` statement, which is disabled when the server is not using the grant tables. After reloading the tables, you can change the `root` password, as shown in Section 12.1, "Securing a New MySQL Installation." For example:

```
mysql> SET PASSWORD FOR 'root'@'localhost' = PASSWORD('rootpass');
```

Be sure to change the password for all `root` accounts if more than one exists.

3. After changing the `root` password, shut down the server and restart it using your normal startup procedure. You now should be able to connect to it as `root` using the new password.

Should you be forced to terminate the server with `kill -9` under Unix or with the Task Manager under Windows, the abrupt nature of the shutdown gives the server no chance to flush any unsaved changes to disk. To help deal with problems that may occur due to this kind of shutdown, it's a good idea to enable auto-recovery in the server. For details, see Section 14.3.1, "Using the Server's Auto-Recovery Capabilities."

12.3 Using System and Status Variables

The MySQL server has system variables that enable you to configure it, and status variables that enable you to monitor its performance. This section provides a general description of how to use them. For configuration parameters specific to individual storage engines, see Section 12.5, "Storage Engine Configuration." For additional server tuning discussion, see Section 12.7, "Server Tuning." For descriptions of individual variables, see Appendix D, "System, Status, and User Variable Reference."

System variables control the server's operational parameters. To display these variables, use the `SHOW VARIABLES` statement. If the default variable values are not appropriate, you can change them to configure the server with values that are better for the environment in which it runs. Some system variables are used for performance tuning, such as those that control the size of memory buffers. For example, if you have plenty of memory, you can tell the server to use larger buffers for disk and index operations. This holds more information in memory and decreases the number of disk accesses required. Other system variables affect how the server interacts with clients. These include variables that control the SQL mode, the default storage engine, and the current time zone.

The server also has a set of status variables that provide information about its performance as it runs. To display these variables, use the SHOW STATUS statement. Status variables are useful for monitoring the server and checking whether configuration changes made by modifying the system variables have the desired effect.

12.3.1   Checking and Setting System Variable Values

Most system variables can be set at server startup on the command line or in option files, using the same syntax as for program options described in Section F.2, "Specifying Program Options." System variables can be displayed at runtime with SHOW VARIABLES, and many can also be modified at runtime with SET. The ability to set variables at runtime gives you better control over server operation, and helps you avoid stopping the server to reconfigure it under circumstances when that might otherwise be necessary. For example, you can experiment with buffer sizes to see how that affects server performance, without having to stop and restart the server for each change. Changes made at runtime do not last beyond termination of the server process, but if you determine a better value for a system variable, you can set it in an option file to cause that value to be used for subsequent server restarts.

System variables exist at two levels: global and session-specific. Global variables affect the operation of the server as a whole. Session-specific variables affect only how the server treats a given client connection, or session. A client can change these locally within its own session, enabling it to customize the server to the behavior it requires without affecting other clients. For variables that have both values, the server uses the global values to initialize the corresponding session variables. This happens only when a new client session begins; changes to a global variable during a session do not affect the current value of the client's corresponding session variable.

A system variable can have both global and session values, only a global value, or only a session value. The following examples illustrate these possibilities:

- The sql_mode variable controls the SQL mode and affects several aspects of SQL statement processing by the server. It has both global and session values. Each client that connects gets its own session-specific sql_mode variable, which initially has the same value as the global variable. Any client can modify the session sql_mode value to change the server's behavior for its own session independent of other clients. A client that has the SUPER privilege also can change the global sql_mode value. The new global value becomes the session default for clients that connect after the change.

- The innodb_buffer_pool_size variable has only a global value. It controls the size of the cache that buffers InnoDB table data and indexes. This cache is shared among all clients, so there is no reason to have a session value for each client.

- The error_count variable has only a session value. It indicates the number of errors generated by the last statement in the current session that can generate errors.

Appendix D, "System, Status, and User Variable Reference," lists all system variables, indicates which of them can be set at startup time or runtime, and which have global or session values. The following discussion indicates how to get and set system variable values.

12.3.1.1   Checking System Variable Values

To see the current system variable values, use `SHOW VARIABLES`:

```
mysql> SHOW VARIABLES;
+----------------------------------+------------------+
| Variable_name                    | Value            |
+----------------------------------+------------------+
| auto_increment_increment         | 1                |
| auto_increment_offset            | 1                |
| autocommit                       | ON               |
| automatic_sp_privileges          | ON               |
| back_log                         | 50               |
| basedir                          | /usr/local/mysql |
| big_tables                       | OFF              |
...
```

With a `LIKE` clause, you can restrict output to rows for variables with names that match a given SQL pattern:

```
mysql> SHOW VARIABLES LIKE '%buffer%';
+------------------------------+-----------+
| Variable_name                | Value     |
+------------------------------+-----------+
| bulk_insert_buffer_size      | 8388608   |
| innodb_buffer_pool_instances | 1         |
| innodb_buffer_pool_size      | 134217728 |
| innodb_change_buffering      | all       |
| innodb_log_buffer_size       | 8388608   |
| join_buffer_size             | 131072    |
| key_buffer_size              | 8388608   |
...
```

To specify general conditions for selecting rows, use a `WHERE` clause. The following statement finds timeouts that are set to less than 60 seconds:

```
mysql> SHOW VARIABLES
    -> WHERE Variable_name LIKE '%timeout%' AND Value < 60;
+----------------------------+-------+
| Variable_name              | Value |
+----------------------------+-------+
| connect_timeout            | 10    |
| innodb_lock_wait_timeout   | 50    |
| innodb_rollback_on_timeout | OFF   |
| net_read_timeout           | 30    |
+----------------------------+-------+
```

By default, SHOW VARIABLES displays session variable values. To specifically request global or session variables, add a GLOBAL or SESSION qualifier to the statement:

```
SHOW GLOBAL VARIABLES;
SHOW SESSION VARIABLES;
```

LOCAL is a synonym for SESSION.

To select individual variable values, use @@GLOBAL.*var_name* syntax for a global variable, or @@SESSION.*var_name* or @@LOCAL.*var_name* for a session variable. If you use @@*var_name* syntax without a qualifier, the session variable is used if it exists and the global value if not.

Qualifier keywords and variable names are not case sensitive.

The @@-syntax is general purpose and can be used in SET, SELECT, or other SQL statements:

```
SELECT @@default_storage_engine AS 'Default storage engine';
```

You can also query the INFORMATION_SCHEMA tables named GLOBAL_VARIABLES and SESSION_VARIABLES to obtain system variable information. For example:

```
SELECT * FROM INFORMATION_SCHEMA.GLOBAL_VARIABLES
WHERE VARIABLE_NAME LIKE '%binlog%';
```

From the command line, mysqladmin variables displays global system variable values.

12.3.1.2   Setting System Variables at Server Startup

Most global system variables can be set when the server starts: Just treat a variable name as an option name and set it directly. For example, the max_connections variable controls the maximum number of simultaneous client connections. To set this variable to 200 on the mysqld command line, use this syntax:

```
% mysqld --max_connections=200
```

To set the variable in an option file, use this syntax:

```
[mysqld]
max_connections=200
```

Usually, it's more convenient to set system variables in an option file than on the command line because you need not remember to set them each time you start the server.

At server startup, dashes and underscores are interchangeable in system variable names, just as with option names. Thus, on the command line:

```
% mysqld --max-connections=200
```

Or, in an option file:

```
[mysqld]
max-connections=200
```

For variables that represent buffer sizes or lengths, values are in bytes if specified as a number with no suffix, or may be specified with a suffix of 'K', 'M', or 'G' (in any lettercase) to indicate kilobytes, megabytes, or gigabytes, respectively. These lines set the connection limit to 1024 and the InnoDB buffer pool size to 16MB:

```
[mysqld]
max_connections=1K
innodb_buffer_pool_size=16M
```

Some system variables cannot be set directly using a startup option and the server produces an error message if you try it. In such cases, there may be a related option. For example, you cannot directly set the `time_zone` variable at startup, but the `--default-time-zone` option can be used instead. Appendix D, "System, Status, and User Variable Reference," indicates which global system variables can be set directly. For those that cannot, the appendix lists the related option for setting the variable if there is one.

You should also check that appendix if you're looking for a description of a server option in Appendix F, "MySQL Program Reference," but don't find it. The option might actually be a system variable.

12.3.1.3 Setting System Variables at Runtime

The syntax for setting system variables at runtime depends on whether you're setting a global or session variable. To set a global variable named *var_name*, use a `SET` statement having one of these formats:

```
SET GLOBAL var_name = value;
SET @@GLOBAL.var_name = value;
```

To set a session variable, similar syntax applies:

```
SET SESSION var_name = value;
SET @@SESSION.var_name = value;
```

`LOCAL` is a synonym for `SESSION`.

If no qualifier is present, the `SET` statement modifies the session variable:

```
SET var_name = value;
SET @@var_name = value;
```

You must have the `SUPER` privilege to set a global variable. The setting persists until changed again or the server exits. No special privileges are needed to set a session variable. The setting persists until changed again or the current session terminates.

To set several variables in a single `SET` statement, separate the assignments with commas:

```
SET SESSION sql_warnings = 0, GLOBAL default_storage_engine = InnoDB;
```

In a statement that sets multiple variables, an explicit GLOBAL or SESSION qualifier applies to following variable settings that do not include a qualifier of their own. The following statement sets the global *v1* and *v2* variables, and the session *v3* and *v4* variables:

```
SET GLOBAL v1 = val1, v2 = val2, SESSION v3 = val3, v4 = val4;
```

Unlike variables that are set at startup, you cannot substitute dashes for underscores in the name at runtime, and you cannot specify the value using a suffix letter of 'K', 'M', or 'G'. However, you can use expressions, and expressions can refer to the values of other variables. The following statements set the global read_buffer_size value to 2MB, and the session value to twice that:

```
SET GLOBAL read_buffer_size = 2*1024*1024;
SET SESSION read_buffer_size = 2*@@GLOBAL.read_buffer_size;
```

System variables can be set to the special value DEFAULT. Assigning DEFAULT to a global variable sets it to the compiled-in default, even if a different value was specified at startup. Assigning DEFAULT to a session variable sets it to current value of the corresponding global variable.

MySQL supports the concept of a structured system variable, which consists of a set of related system variables that are grouped and accessed as components of the structured variable. This type of variable is used for configuring MyISAM key caches, as discussed in Section 12.7.2, "Storage Engine Tuning."

12.3.2   Checking Status Variable Values

The server maintains status variables that enable you to monitor its runtime operation. To display these variables, use the SHOW STATUS statement:

```
mysql> SHOW STATUS;
+------------------------------------+----------+
| Variable_name                      | Value    |
+------------------------------------+----------+
| Aborted_clients                    | 0        |
| Aborted_connects                   | 1        |
| Binlog_cache_disk_use              | 0        |
| Binlog_cache_use                   | 3        |
| Binlog_stmt_cache_disk_use         | 0        |
| Binlog_stmt_cache_use              | 0        |
| Bytes_received                     | 125      |
| Bytes_sent                         | 151      |
...
```

Status variables are set only by the server, so they are read only to users and cannot be modified with SET the way that system variables can.

Status variables, like system variables, have global and session-specific values, so the statement can take GLOBAL or SESSION qualifiers:

```
SHOW GLOBAL STATUS;
SHOW SESSION STATUS;
```

GLOBAL shows the status for the server as a whole (the aggregate value for all sessions since server startup). SESSION shows the status for the current session. The default is SESSION; LOCAL is a synonym for SESSION.

If a variable has only a global value, you get the same value for GLOBAL and SESSION.

With SHOW STATUS, as with SHOW VARIABLES, a LIKE or WHERE clause restricts output to those variables with names that match a given SQL pattern, or that satisfy general retrieval conditions. For example, to check the values of status variables associated with InnoDB logging activity, use this statement:

```
mysql> SHOW GLOBAL STATUS LIKE 'innodb%log%';
+------------------------------+----------+
| Variable_name                | Value    |
+------------------------------+----------+
| Innodb_log_waits             | 0        |
| Innodb_log_write_requests    | 45504    |
| Innodb_log_writes            | 1234     |
| Innodb_os_log_fsyncs         | 1384     |
| Innodb_os_log_pending_fsyncs | 0        |
| Innodb_os_log_pending_writes | 0        |
| Innodb_os_log_written        | 23465984 |
+------------------------------+----------+
```

You can also query the INFORMATION_SCHEMA tables named GLOBAL_STATUS and SESSION_STATUS to obtain status variable information. One advantage of this over SHOW STATUS is that you can use the values in calculations. For example:

```
SET @queries =
  (SELECT VARIABLE_VALUE FROM INFORMATION_SCHEMA.GLOBAL_STATUS
  WHERE VARIABLE_NAME LIKE 'Queries');
SET @uptime =
  (SELECT VARIABLE_VALUE FROM INFORMATION_SCHEMA.GLOBAL_STATUS
  WHERE VARIABLE_NAME LIKE 'Uptime');
SELECT @queries/@uptime/60 AS 'Queries per minute';
```

12.4 The Plugin Interface

Over time, the MySQL server architecture has become more "pluggable," such that code segments implementing aspects of server functionality can be compiled separately from the server, stored in external files, and loaded ("plugged in") on demand. In MySQL, plugins implement such features as storage engines, INFORMATION_SCHEMA tables, full-text search modifiers, replication mechanisms, auditing capabilities, and authentication methods.

The pluggable server architecture gives MySQL DBAs the freedom to customize server features by loading plugins selectively, and to reduce server footprint by not loading unneeded plugins. It also permits independent development of server features. For example, a third-party developer can create a storage engine as a plugin that ships separately from the server, without being tied to the server development cycle.

This section describes the general characteristics of the plugin interface. For information specifically about authentication plugins, see Section 13.2.7, "Pluggable Authentication and Proxy Users."

The plugin interface comprises these components:

- **Plugin files.** Server plugins are stored in object files, called plugin libraries because they can contain multiple plugins.

- **The plugin directory.** All plugin files must be installed in this location. The plugin directory often is `lib/plugin` under the MySQL installation directory, but you can determine the location from the value of the `plugin_dir` system variable. To use a different location, set the value of `plugin_dir` at server startup.

- **A "control language."** This enables the DBA to instruct the server which plugins to load; it takes the form of server options and SQL statements that enable plugin handling. For example, the `--plugin-load` option loads plugins at server startup, and the `INSTALL PLUGIN` statement loads them at runtime.

- **The plugin registry.** At startup, the server checks the `plugin` table in the `mysql` database and automatically loads plugins registered there, unless the `--skip-grant-tables` option is used. To register a plugin in this table, use `INSTALL PLUGIN`.

Plugin libraries have a platform-specific filename suffix. For example, a plugin file named `mylib.so` on Linux is named `mylib.dll` on Windows. The discussion here uses `.so` as the library suffix. Substitute the appropriate suffix for your own system.

For illustration, suppose that we have two plugin library object files installed in the server's plugin directory:

- A library named `my_engine.so` containing a single plugin that implements a storage engine named `MY_ENGINE`.

- A library named `info_tables.so` containing multiple plugins that implement `INFORMATION_SCHEMA` tables named `LOCKS` and `USERS` to display information about current locks and connected clients.

The plugin interface enables you to perform these operations:

- At server startup, load plugins from a file, individually or as a group

- At runtime, load or unload plugins individually

- At runtime, check which plugins are available

To load plugins at server startup, use the `--plugin-load` or `--plugin-load-add` option. For each, the option value is a list of one or more semicolon-separated *plugin_name=lib_name* or `lib_name` specifiers. Naming a plugin and library causes the server to load only that plugin from the library. Naming a library without a plugin name causes the server to load all plugins from the library. For example, to load all plugins in both libraries, put these lines in your server option file and restart the server:

```
[mysqld]
plugin-load=my_engine.so;info_tables.so
```

That is equivalent to more verbosely listing each plugin individually like this:

```
[mysqld]
plugin-load=my_engine=my_engine.so;locks=info_tables.so;users=info_tables.so
```

To load only the LOCKS plugin from `info_tables.so`, use these lines:

```
[mysqld]
plugin-load=locks=info_tables.so
```

Plugin lettercase does not matter. Filename lettercase matters if your filesystem is case sensitive.

`--plugin-load-add` is similar to `--plugin-load`. The difference between the two is that each instance of `--plugin-load` resets the list of plugins to be loaded and `--plugin-load-add` does not. If you specify `--plugin-load` multiple times, only the last one has any effect. Instances of `--plugin-load-add` add plugins to the set of plugins to be loaded. For example, to load all three plugins, naming them individually, you could do this:

```
[mysqld]
plugin-load-add=my_engine=my_engine.so
plugin-load-add=locks=info_tables.so
plugin-load-add=users=info_tables.so
```

`--plugin-load-add` is more convenient if you have a lot of plugins because you can list them over multiple easier-to-read lines and comment them out selectively as desired. With `--plugin-load`, you must use a single long option value and edit it to change the set of plugins to load.

The server has no memory across restarts for plugins loaded with `--plugin-load` or `--plugin-load-add`. If you restart the server without those options, it does not load the plugins.

To load plugins at runtime, use the INSTALL PLUGIN statement. Each instance of the statement names a plugin and the library object file that contains it. For example:

```
INSTALL PLUGIN my_engine SONAME 'my_engine.so';
INSTALL PLUGIN locks SONAME 'info_tables.so';
INSTALL PLUGIN users SONAME 'info_tables.so';
```

INSTALL PLUGIN performs a "sticky" install that need be done only once per plugin. That is, it not only loads a plugin but registers it in the `mysql.plugin` table so that the server automatically loads the plugin on subsequent restarts.

To uninstall a plugin at runtime, use UNINSTALL PLUGIN. For example:

```
UNINSTALL PLUGIN users;
```

UNINSTALL PLUGIN also unregisters the plugin from the mysql.plugin table (if it is listed there) so that it does not load on subsequent server restarts. If a plugin is not designed to permit unloading at runtime and can be deactivated only when the server shuts down, UNINSTALL PLUGIN results in an error.

Because INSTALL PLUGIN and UNINSTALL PLUGIN modify the mysql.plugin table, they require the INSERT and DELETE privileges for that table, respectively.

Regardless of whether you load plugins at server startup or at runtime, you can check which ones are present using the SHOW PLUGINS statement or the INFORMATION_SCHEMA PLUGINS table. For example:

```
mysql> SHOW PLUGINS;
+-----------+--------+--------------------+----------------+---------+
| Name      | Status | Type               | Library        | License |
+-----------+--------+--------------------+----------------+---------+
...
| my_engine | ACTIVE | STORAGE ENGINE     | my_engine.so   | GPL     |
...
| LOCKS     | ACTIVE | INFORMATION SCHEMA | info_tables.so | GPL     |
| USERS     | ACTIVE | INFORMATION SCHEMA | info_tables.so | GPL     |
...
```

If the server will load a plugin at startup because it was built in, registered in the mysql.plugin table, or specified using the --plugin-load or --plugin-load-add option, it is possible to control the plugin's activation state. To do this, use an option named after the plugin. For example, --my_engine=ON or --my_engine=OFF activate or deactivate the MY_ENGINE storage engine plugin. Following the plugin name, an optional value can be given:

- OFF: Do not activate the plugin. --disable-*plugin_name*, --skip-*plugin_name*, and --*plugin_name*=0 are equivalent.

- ON: Activate the plugin. This is the default action if no value follows the plugin name. --enable-*plugin_name* and --*plugin_name*=1 are equivalent. The server runs with the plugin disabled if loading fails.

- FORCE: Similar to ON, but the server does not start if loading fails.

- FORCE_PLUS_PERMANENT: Similar to FORCE, but the server also prevents the plugin from being unloaded at runtime with UNINSTALL PLUGIN. This option value was introduced in MySQL 5.5.7.

These option values are not case sensitive, nor is matching the option name to plugin names.

The LOAD_OPTION column of the INFORMATION_SCHEMA PLUGINS table indicates the activation state of loaded plugins.

12.5 Storage Engine Configuration

The MySQL server supports multiple storage engines and is highly configurable in terms of which engines to make available. For a general discussion about the role of storage engines in MySQL, see Section 2.6.1, "Storage Engine Characteristics." The following discussion describes how to configure which engines your server uses and provides general configuration information specifically for InnoDB. For InnoDB and MyISAM performance-related information, see Section 12.7.2, "Storage Engine Tuning."

12.5.1 Selecting Storage Engines

The MySQL server provides flexible control over which storage engines are available. The InnoDB engine is available by default (and is the default engine as well), but can be disabled. The MyISAM, MEMORY, MERGE, and CSV storage engines are always available by default and cannot be disabled. Other engines may be available, and you can selectively enable or disable them at startup as you like. For example, you might disable engines you don't need, to reduce server memory requirements. (However, if you disable an engine, you cannot access any tables that might already have been created by it.)

If a given storage engine is included in a MySQL installation, Table 12.2 shows its default status and the startup option to use to change its status. For more information about options to control the status of storage engine plugins at startup, see Section 12.4, "The Plugin Interface."

Table 12.2 **Storage Engine Configuration Control**

Engine	Default Status if Available	Option to Change Status
ARCHIVE	Enabled	`--archive=OFF` to disable
BLACKHOLE	Enabled	`--blackhole=OFF` to disable
CSV	Enabled	Cannot be disabled
FEDERATED	Disabled	`--federated` to enable
InnoDB	Enabled	`--innodb=OFF` to disable
MyISAM	Enabled	Cannot be disabled
MEMORY	Enabled	Cannot be disabled
MERGE	Enabled	Cannot be disabled

To see at runtime which storage engines are available and their status, use the `SHOW ENGINES` statement or query the `ENGINES` table of the `INFORMATION_SCHEMA` database. For example:

```
mysql> SELECT ENGINE, SUPPORT FROM INFORMATION_SCHEMA.ENGINES;
+--------------------+---------+
| ENGINE             | SUPPORT |
+--------------------+---------+
```

```
| CSV               | YES      |
| InnoDB            | DEFAULT  |
| MyISAM            | YES      |
| MRG_MYISAM        | YES      |
| MEMORY            | YES      |
+-------------------+----------+
```

For additional information, see Section 2.6.1.1, "Checking Which Storage Engines Are Available."

12.5.2   Selecting a Default Storage Engine

InnoDB is compiled in as the default engine, but you can select a different default engine at server startup or at runtime by setting the default_storage_engine system variable. For example, to make MyISAM the default engine, put the following lines in your server option file:

```
[mysqld]
default_storage_engine = myisam
```

To change the default storage engine at runtime, use one of the following statements:

```
SET GLOBAL default_storage_engine = engine_name;
SET SESSION default_storage_engine = engine_name;
```

The first statement requires the SUPER privilege and sets the default engine for all clients that connect thereafter. The second requires no special privilege, affects only the current client session, and can be used by any client to change its own default engine.

To check which storage engines are the global and session defaults, use this statement:

```
SELECT @@GLOBAL.default_storage_engine, @@SESSION.default_storage_engine;
```

Before MySQL 5.6.3, default_storage_engine applies to both permanent and TEMPORARY tables. As of 5.6.3, it applies only to permanent tables and a separate default_tmp_storage_engine variable specifies the default engine for TEMPORARY engines. A typical use for the latter is to avoid the transactional overhead of InnoDB for TEMPORARY tables by using MyISAM or MEMORY for them.

If you start the server with --innodb=OFF to disable InnoDB, set default_storage_engine (and default_tmp_storage_engine in MySQL 5.6) to some engine other than InnoDB or the server will not start.

12.5.3   Configuring the InnoDB Storage Engine

The default MySQL storage engine is InnoDB in MySQL 5.5. (Previously, it was MyISAM.) InnoDB manages a system tablespace for storing table contents and its data dictionary. You also have the option of configuring InnoDB to use one tablespace per table. InnoDB has its own log files and memory buffers as well.

12.5.3.1   Configuring the InnoDB Tablespace

By default, the InnoDB storage engine does not use separate files for each table. Instead, it manages all InnoDB tables within a single system tablespace, which is a logically unified block of storage that the engine treats as a giant data structure. (Think of the tablespace as something like a virtual filesystem.) For an InnoDB table stored in the system tablespace, the only file uniquely associated with the table is the `.frm` format file that is stored in the database directory of the database that the table belongs to. The system tablespace also contains the InnoDB data dictionary that stores information about table structure.

It is also possible to have InnoDB represent each table using its own tablespace file. To configure InnoDB to create tables using individual tablespaces, start the server with the `innodb_file_per_table` system variable enabled. In this case, the system tablespace is still needed because it contains the InnoDB data dictionary, although it need not be as large.

12.5.3.1.1   InnoDB System Tablespace Configuration Parameters

The InnoDB system tablespace, although logically a single storage area, comprises one or more files on disk. Each component can be a regular file or a raw partition, as configured by the options described here. It's possible to specify these options on the server command line, but in practice this is rarely done. Instead, configure the tablespace using an appropriate server group in an option file (for example, the `[mysqld]` or `[server]` group), so that the server uses the same configuration each time it starts.

Use the following system variables to control the number, size, and placement of the files in the system tablespace:

- `innodb_data_home_dir` defines the parent directory of the component files that make up the tablespace. The default is the server data directory.

- `innodb_data_file_path` defines the specifications for the component files of the tablespace under the InnoDB home directory. The value consists of one or more file specifications separated by semicolons. Each specification includes a filename, a size, and possibly other options, separated by colons. The combined size of the tablespace components must be at least 10MB. The default is a single 10MB auto-extending file named `ibdata1`.

Based on the default values, if you specify neither system variable, InnoDB creates the system tablespace as a single 10MB auto-extending file named `ibdata1` located in the server data directory.

Suppose that you want to create a tablespace consisting of two 4GB files named `innodata1` and `innodata2` in the data directory. No `innodb_data_home_dir` setting is required in this case because the data directory is the default. Configure the files as follows:

```
[mysqld]
innodb_data_file_path=innodata1:4G;innodata2:4G
```

The InnoDB storage engine combines the `innodb_data_home_dir` and `innodb_data_file_path` values to determine the tablespace file pathnames:

- If `innodb_data_home_dir` is not specified, its default is the pathname of the server data directory, and InnoDB interprets the filenames in `innodb_data_file_path` relative to the data directory.

- If `innodb_data_home_dir` is not empty, InnoDB interprets it as the directory under which all the file specifications in `innodb_data_file_path` are located, and interprets those filenames relative to the `innodb_data_home_dir` value.

- If `innodb_data_home_dir` is explicitly set to empty, InnoDB treats all file specifications in `innodb_data_file_path` as absolute pathnames.

Based on the preceding rules, the following three configurations each specify the same set of tablespace files, assuming that the data directory is `/var/mysql/data`:

```
[mysqld]
innodb_data_file_path=ibdata1:500M;ibdata2:500M
```

```
[mysqld]
innodb_data_home_dir=/var/mysql/data
innodb_data_file_path=ibdata1:500M;ibdata2:500M
```

```
[mysqld]
innodb_data_home_dir=
innodb_data_file_path=/var/mysql/data/ibdata1:500M;/var/mysql/data/ibdata2:500M
```

The `innodb_data_file_path` value consists of file specifications separated by semicolons, with the parts of each specification separated by colons. The simplest file specification syntax consists of a filename and a size, but other syntaxes are permitted:

```
path:size
path:size:autoextend
path:size:autoextend:max:maxsize
```

The first format specifies a file with a fixed size of *size*. The *size* value should be a positive integer followed by 'M' or 'G' to indicate units of megabytes or gigabytes, respectively. The second format specifies an auto-extending file; if the file fills up, InnoDB extends it incrementally. The third format is similar, but includes a value indicating the maximum size to which the auto-extending file is permitted to grow. Only the final component of the tablespace may be listed as auto-extending.

The default auto-extend increment is 8MB. To specify a different increment, set the `innodb_autoextend_increment` system variable.

12.5.3.1.2   Configuring the InnoDB System Tablespace

In the usual case, the system tablespace consists of regular files and does not include any raw partitions (device files). To perform the initial setup for a system tablespace that contains only regular files, use this procedure:

1. Add the appropriate lines to the option file.

2. Make sure that the directories exist in which the tablespace component files are to be created. InnoDB creates files, but not directories.

3. Make sure that none of the component files already exist.

4. Start the server. InnoDB notices that the files do not exist, and creates and initializes them.

If you've already started the server without configuring InnoDB explicitly, InnoDB will have created a system tablespace using the default configuration. To configure the tablespace explicitly, first stop the server and remove the InnoDB-related files (tablespace and log files). Then specify the configuration options to use and restart the server. (Do this *before* creating any InnoDB tables. Otherwise, dump the tables with `mysqldump` before reconfiguring, then reload them afterward.)

It is a little more complex to use raw partitions as components of the InnoDB system tablespace. Here are the reasons to consider doing so:

- You can easily create very large tablespaces. A partition component can span the entire extent of the partition. Regular file components are limited to the maximum file size permitted by your operating system.

- Each raw partition file is guaranteed to have entirely contiguous space on disk, whereas regular files are subject to filesystem fragmentation. When it initializes the tablespace, InnoDB tries to minimize fragmentation of regular files by writing enough zeros to the files to force space for them to be allocated all at once rather than incrementally. But this can only reduce fragmentation; it cannot guarantee that it will not occur.

- Raw partitions reduce overhead by eliminating the filesystem management layer. On some systems, this overhead may not be significant, but on others the difference might be enough to justify using partitions.

A factor that counts against using raw partitions in the InnoDB tablespace is that your system backup software might be oriented toward use with filesystems rather than partitions. In this case, using partitions would make it more difficult to perform system backups.

Including a raw partition in the tablespace involves and initial configuration and a subsequent reconfiguration. Suppose that you have a Unix system on which you want to use a 200GB partition that has a pathname of `/dev/rdsk8`. It's necessary to specify a value for `innodb_data_home_dir` because the partition doesn't lie under the data directory. If you set `innodb_data_home_dir` to an empty value, you can list the full pathname of the device file in `innodb_data_file_path` to configure the partition as follows:

1. Configure the partition initially with a size value that has a `newraw` suffix. This suffix
   tells InnoDB that the file is a raw partition that must be initialized:

   ```
   [mysqld]
   innodb_data_home_dir=
   innodb_data_file_path=/dev/rdsk8:200Gnewraw
   ```

2. Start the server. InnoDB sees the `newraw` suffix and initializes the partition. It also treats
   the tablespace as read only because it knows you have not performed the reconfiguration.

3. After InnoDB initializes the partition, stop the server.

4. Reconfigure the partition specification by changing the suffix from `newraw` to `raw`:

   ```
   [mysqld]
   innodb_data_home_dir=
   innodb_data_file_path=/dev/rdsk8:200Graw
   ```

5. Start the server again. InnoDB sees that the suffix is `raw` rather than `newraw` and assumes
   that the partition has been initialized and that it can use the tablespace in read/write
   fashion.

If you specify a raw partition as part of the InnoDB tablespace, make sure its permissions are set
so that the server has read/write access to it. Also, make sure the partition is being used for no
other purpose. Otherwise, you will have competing processes each thinking that they own the
partition and can use it as they please, with the result that they'll stomp all over each other's
data. For example, if you mistakenly specify a swap partition for use by InnoDB, your system
will behave quite erratically!

To configure the InnoDB system tablespace on Windows systems, specify backslashes in pathnames using either single forward slashes ('/') or doubled backslashes ('\\'). Also, you should
still separate the parts of each file specification with colons, even though colons may also
appear in filenames (full Windows pathnames begin with a drive letter and a colon). When
it encounters a colon, InnoDB resolves this ambiguity by looking at the following character.
InnoDB takes the next part of the specification as a size if the character is a digit, or as part of
a pathname otherwise. For example, the following configuration sets up a tablespace consisting
of files on the C and D drives with sizes of 500MB and 10GB:

```
[mysqld]
innodb_data_home_dir=
innodb_data_file_path=C:/ibdata1:500M;D:/ibdata2:10G
```

If startup fails when you're setting up the initial tablespace because InnoDB cannot create some
necessary file, check the error log to see what the problem was. Then remove all the files that
InnoDB created (excluding any raw partitions you may be using), correct the configuration
error, and start the server again. If you have raw partitions, remember to change the specification to say `newraw` when initializing the partitions and back to `raw` after starting and stopping
the server.

12.5.3.1.3   Reconfiguring the InnoDB System Tablespace

After you have initialized the InnoDB system tablespace and begun to use it, you cannot change the size of its component files. However, you can add another file at the end of the list of existing files, which may be necessary if the tablespace fills up. One symptom of a full tablespace is that InnoDB transactions consistently fail and roll back when they should succeed. To determine the amount of free space, check the `Data_free` value in the output from the following statement, where `tbl_name` is the name of any InnoDB table contained in the system tablespace:

```
mysql> SHOW TABLE STATUS LIKE 'tbl_name';
```

To make the system tablespace larger by adding another component, use this procedure:

1. Stop the server if it is running.

2. If the final component of the tablespace is an auto-extending file, you must change its specification to that of a fixed-size file before adding another file after it. To do this, determine the current actual size of the file. Then round the size down to the nearest multiple of 1MB (1,048,576 bytes, not 1,000,000 bytes) and use that size in the file's specification. Suppose that you have a file currently listed like this:

```
[mysqld]
innodb_data_file_path=ibdata1:100M:autoextend
```

If the file's actual size now is 121,634,816 bytes, use a size of 121,634,816 / 1,048,576 = 116MB and change the specification as follows:

```
[mysqld]
innodb_data_file_path=ibdata1:116M
```

3. Add the specification for the new component to the end of the current file list. If the new component is a regular file, make sure that it does not already exist. If the component is a raw partition, add it using the procedure described earlier for specifying a partition as part of the tablespace. (First with `newraw`, then with `raw` after starting and stopping the server.)

4. Restart the server.

12.5.3.1.4   Using Individual (Per-Table) InnoDB Tablespaces

To use one tablespace per InnoDB table, enable the `innodb_file_per_table` system variable:

```
[mysqld]
innodb_file_per_table=1
```

While this variable is enabled, each new InnoDB table is created with an `.frm` format file and an `.ibd` data file. Both are stored in the database directory for the database that contains the table. InnoDB automatically extends `.ibd` files as necessary.

Enabling or disabling use of individual tablespaces affects only how InnoDB creates *new* tables; it can access tables already created in the system tablespace or individual tablespaces regardless of changes to the `innodb_file_per_table` value.

For tables stored using their own `.ibd` files, InnoDB enables other features:

- For tables that are not referenced as foreign keys from other tables, TRUNCATE TABLE is much faster and reclaims disk space, two things not true for tables stored in the system tablespace.

- InnoDB supports multiple file formats, with the default format known as Antelope. With `innodb_file_per_table` enabled, it is possible to create tables that use Barracuda file format. To do this, you must also set the `innodb_file_format` system variable:

  ```
  [mysqld]
  innodb_file_per_table=1
  innodb_file_format=Barracuda
  ```

  Barracuda enables you to use COMPRESSED or DYNAMIC row storage format when you create new InnoDB tables. For information about the characteristics of these row formats, see Section 5.4, "Choosing Table Storage Formats for Efficient Queries."

Normally, you set the `innodb_file_per_table` and `innodb_file_format` system variables at server startup, but they can also be changed at runtime. This might be useful for settings that apply only to creating certain tables. For example:

```
SET GLOBAL innodb_file_per_table = 1;
SET GLOBAL innodb_file_format = 'Barracuda';
CREATE TABLE ... ENGINE=INNODB ROW_FORMAT=COMPRESSED;
SET GLOBAL innodb_file_format = 'Antelope';
SET GLOBAL innodb_file_per_table = 0;
```

12.5.3.2   InnoDB Storage Engine Variables

The preceding section discusses how to configure InnoDB's tablespace. InnoDB also has its own log files and memory buffers, and several other configuration parameters. The following list describes a few parameters commonly used to affect the general operation of the InnoDB storage engine.

- `innodb_buffer_pool_size`

  If you have the memory available, making the InnoDB buffer pool larger can reduce disk usage for accessing table data and indexes. For more information, see Section 12.7.2, "Storage Engine Tuning."

- `innodb_log_buffer_size`

  InnoDB tries to buffer information about each transaction in memory and flush it to disk in a single operation when the transaction finishes. If a transaction is large and exceeds the size of the buffer, more disk activity is required to flush the buffer multiple times before the transaction finishes. Increasing the size of the buffer enables larger transactions to be buffered in memory without early flushing. The default is 1MB. The maximum useful value is 8MB.

- `innodb_log_group_home_dir`

  InnoDB has its own log files, which it creates during server startup if they do not exist. These files have names that begin with `ib_`. By default, InnoDB creates them in the data directory. To explicitly specify the pathname to the directory where InnoDB should write its log files, use `innodb_log_group_home_dir`. (You might do this to distribute disk activity by putting these logs on a physical drive different from the data directory drive.) InnoDB creates only files, not directories, so make sure that the log file directory exists prior to starting the server.

- `innodb_log_file_size`, `innodb_log_files_in_group`

  When its logs fill up, InnoDB checkpoints the buffer pool by flushing it to disk. Using larger InnoDB log files reduces the frequency with which the logs fill up, and thus reduces the number of times this flushing occurs. (The tradeoff is that larger logs increase recovery time after a crash.) Modify `innodb_log_file_size` to change the size of the log files or `innodb_log_files_in_group` to change the number of files. The important characteristic is the total size of the logs, which is the product of the two values. The total size of the logs must not exceed 4GB.

  If the log files have already been created and you want to change their size, you must shut down the server cleanly so that InnoDB has a chance to fully process any ongoing transactions. Then remove the log files, reconfigure, and restart the server to let InnoDB create new files.

12.6 Globalization Issues

"Globalization" includes "internationalization" and "localization." Internationalization is the capability of software to be used according to local convention, for any of a variety of locations. Localization involves selecting a particular set of local conventions from among those that are supported. The following aspects of MySQL configuration relate to internationalization and localization:

- The server default time zone
- The default character set and collation
- The language for diagnostic and error messages
- The locale for day and month names

12.6.1 Configuring Time Zone Support

The MySQL server sets its default time zone by examining its environment. Most often, this is the local time zone of the server host, but you can specify the time zone explicitly at server startup. In addition, the server permits each client to override the default setting and set its own time zone. This enables applications to use time settings that depend on where the client program is running rather than where the server is running. The following discussion describes MySQL's capabilities for supporting multiple time zones.

Two system variables hold time zone information:

- `system_time_zone` is the time zone that the server determines at startup to be in effect on the server host. This variable exists only as a global system variable and cannot be reset at runtime. You can influence how the server sets `system_time_zone` at startup by setting the `TZ` environment variable to the desired time zone before starting the server. However, it may not be easy to guarantee that `TZ` will be set in some contexts, such as when the server is started during the system boot sequence. On Unix, another way to set the time zone is by specifying a `--timezone` option to the `mysqld_safe` startup script (not to `mysqld`, which does not understand the option). It's probably best to list this option in the `[mysqld_safe]` group of an option file, especially if you invoke `mysqld_safe` indirectly through `mysql.server`, which does not support command-line options. For example, to specify the U.S. Central time zone for `mysqld_safe`, add the following to your server option file:

```
[mysqld_safe]
timezone=US/Central
```

  The example shows one widely used syntax (it works on Linux and Mac OS X, for example). Another common syntax has this format:

```
[mysqld_safe]
timezone=CST6CDT
```

  Use whatever syntax applies on your system.

- `time_zone` is the MySQL server's default time zone. By default, its value is `SYSTEM`, which means "use the `system_time_zone` setting." To set `time_zone` at startup, use the `--default-time-zone` option for `mysqld`. As the server runs, it uses the global value of `time_zone` to set the session `time_zone` value for each client that connects, which becomes the client's default time zone. Any client can reset the time zone for its own session by setting the session `time_zone` variable. An administrative user who has the `SUPER` privilege can set the global `time_zone` variable to change the default for clients that connect thereafter.

To determine the current global and session time zone values, use this statement:

```
SELECT @@GLOBAL.time_zone, @@SESSION.time_zone;
```

The `time_zone` variable accepts three kinds of values, although one of them requires additional administrative action. The statements shown here set the session value. If you have the `SUPER` privilege, you can substitute `GLOBAL` to set the global value.

- To use the value of `system_time_zone`, set `time_zone` to `SYSTEM`:

```
SET SESSION time_zone = 'SYSTEM';
```

- To specify an offset from UTC, use a signed hour and minute:

```
SET SESSION time_zone = '+00:00';    # UTC
SET SESSION time_zone = '+03:00';    # 3 hours ahead of UTC
SET SESSION time_zone = '-11:00';    # 11 hours behind UTC
```

- To refer to a locale, use a named time zone:

```
SET SESSION time_zone = 'US/Central';
SET SESSION time_zone = 'CST6CDT';
SET SESSION time_zone = 'Asia/Jakarta';
```

To use the last method (setting the time zone by name), you must enable the server to under-stand time zone names by loading information from the operating system's time zone files into a set of tables in the `mysql` database. This does not happen automatically during the MySQL installation process, which creates but does not load the tables. To populate the time zone tables manually on a system that has time zone files, determine where the files are installed. Then use the `mysql_tzinfo_to_sql` program to read the files and construct SQL statements from their contents, and feed those statements to the `mysql` program to execute them. If the time zone file location is `/usr/share/zoneinfo`, the command to load the files into the `mysql` database looks like this:

```
% mysql_tzinfo_to_sql /usr/share/zoneinfo | mysql -p -u root mysql
```

After loading the tables, restart the server. That should suffice for most versions of Unix. For Windows or other systems that do not have a set of time zone files, you can obtain a package containing a set of pre-built MyISAM tables containing time zone information from this location:

```
http://dev.mysql.com/downloads/timezones.html
```

Download the package and unpack it. With the MySQL server stopped, copy the `.frm`, `.MYD`, and `.MYI` files into the `mysql` database directory under your data directory. Then restart the server.

12.6.2 Selecting the Default Character Set and Collation

A character set determines the characters permitted in string values. MySQL supports multiple character sets and you can select character sets at the server, database, table, column, and string constant levels. MySQL also supports multiple collating sequences per character set. Collations affect string comparison and sorting operations.

The default character set and collation are `latin1` and `latin1_swedish_ci`. To change these at server startup, set the `character_set_server` and `collation_server` system variables. The collation must be compatible with the character set. (That is, the beginning part of the collation name must be the same as the character set name.) Example:

```
% mysqld --character_set_server=utf8 \
    --collation_server=utf8_icelandic_ci
```

If you build the server from source, it's possible to change the defaults by using the DEFAULT_ CHARSET and DEFAULT_COLLATION options when you run CMake. Example:

```
% cmake -DDEFAULT_CHARSET=utf8 \
    -DDEFAULT_COLLATION=utf8_icelandic_ci
```

To indicate which character set a client program should use when you run it, use the --default-character-set option. If the character set files are not located where the program looks by default, tell the client program where they are by using the --character-sets-dir option.

For additional information on character set capabilities in MySQL, see Section 2.4, "Character Set Support." For details on creating character columns and using them, see Chapter 3, "Data Types."

12.6.3   Selecting the Language for Error Messages

The MySQL server is capable of producing diagnostic and error messages in several languages. The default is english. To see which languages are available, look under the share directory of your MySQL installation. Its subdirectories have names that correspond to the available languages.

To specify the error message language, set the lc_messages system variable to an appropriate locale, such as en_US for English or de_DE for German. The server finds the directory containing the error message file by translating the locale name to a language name and looking in the directory named by the lc_messages_dir variable for a subdirectory with the language name. If the default directory is not correct (share under the MySQL installation directory by default), set lc_messages_dir to the correct pathname. For example, to display error messages in German and indicate that error message information is located under /var/mysql/share, start the server like this:

```
% mysqld --lc_messages=de_DE --lc_messages_dir=/var/mysql/share
```

Both system variables can be set at server startup. Individual clients can set the session value of lc_messages at runtime to select a different language. This is useful when different clients of the same server need localized error messages in a language different from the default.

12.6.4   Selecting the Locale

The MySQL server determines how to display day and month names using the lc_time_names system variable. Its value affects the results from temporal functions such as DAYNAME(), MONTHNAME(), and DATE_FORMAT().

The default locale is en_US (English). To select a different locale, set lc_time_names at server startup or runtime. Individual clients can set the session value of lc_time_names at runtime to override the default. For example, starting the server with lc_time_names set to es_ES (Spanish) yields this result:

```
mysql> SELECT MONTHNAME('2000-07-01');
+-------------------------+
| MONTHNAME('2000-07-01') |
+-------------------------+
| julio                   |
+-------------------------+
```

A client that prefers Italian names instead can do this:

```
mysql> SET lc_time_names='it_IT';
mysql> SELECT MONTHNAME('2000-07-01');
+-------------------------+
| MONTHNAME('2000-07-01') |
+-------------------------+
| luglio                  |
+-------------------------+
```

12.7   Server Tuning

Administrators who have control of the MySQL server or the machine on which it runs can perform optimization or tuning operations. For example, some server parameters pertain to query processing and may be tuned, and certain hardware configuration factors have a direct effect on query processing speed. These optimizations improve the performance of the server as a whole, and thus have a beneficial effect for all MySQL users.

Keep the following principles in mind when performing administrative optimizations:

- Accessing data in memory is faster than accessing data from disk.

- Keeping data in memory as long as possible reduces disk activity.

- Retaining information from an index is more important than retaining contents of data rows.

The most important parameters you can change are the sizes of various caches, such as the table cache and storage engine caches that buffer information for indexing operations. If you have memory available, allocating it to the server's caches enables information to be held in memory longer and reduces disk activity. This is good because it's much faster to access information from memory than to read it from disk.

The following sections discuss several ways to optimize server operation:

- For information about several parameters that affect performance in general, see Section 12.7.1, "General-Purpose System Variables for Server Tuning."

- Individual storage engines provide their own parameters that enable you to configure how they perform. See Section 12.7.2, "Storage Engine Tuning."

- The MySQL server can cache query results to process repeated queries without re-executing them. See Section 12.7.3, "Using the Query Cache."

- Several hardware factors affect how MySQL performs. See Section 12.7.4, "Hardware Optimizations."

For general instructions on setting system variables, see Section 12.3.1, "Checking and Setting System Variable Values." When you change parameter values, follow these guidelines:

- Change one parameter at a time. Modifying multiple variables simultaneously makes it difficult to assess the effect of each change.

- Increase system variable values incrementally. If you increase a variable by a huge amount on the theory that more is always better, you may run your system out of resources, causing it to thrash or slow to a crawl because you've set the value too high.

- Rather than experimenting with parameter tuning on your production MySQL server, it might be prudent to set up a separate test server.

Other strategies that help the server operate more efficiently include the following:

- Disable unneeded storage engines. The server doesn't allocate memory for disabled engines, freeing you to devote it to other uses. Most storage engines can be excluded from the server binary at configuration time if you build MySQL from source. For those engines that are included in the server, many can be disabled at runtime with the appropriate startup options. For details, see Section 12.5.1, "Selecting Storage Engines."

- Keep access privileges simple. Although the server caches grant table contents in memory, if you have any rows in the `tables_priv`, `columns_priv`, or `procs_priv` tables of the `mysql` database, the server must check their contents when it does privilege checking for SQL statements. If those tables are empty, the server can optimize privilege checking by skipping those privilege levels. See Section 13.4.2, "Statement Access Verification."

12.7.1   General-Purpose System Variables for Server Tuning

The MySQL server has many modifiable system variables that enable you to affect its operation, such as those that control the size of memory buffers. If you have plenty of memory, you can tell the server to use larger buffers for disk and index operations. This holds more information in memory and decreases the number of disk accesses required. If your system is more modest, you can tell the server to use smaller buffers. This will likely make the server run more slowly but may improve overall system performance by preventing the MySQL server from hogging system resources to the detriment of other processes.

The following list describes some system variables that are useful for general performance tuning:

- `back_log`

  The maximum number of pending connection requests that can be queued while current connections are being processed. If you have a very busy site, increasing the `back_log` value can help if clients are slow to connect.

- `max_connections`

  The maximum number of simultaneous client connections the server supports. If your server is busy, you might need to increase this value. For example, if your MySQL server is used by an active Web server to process lots of statements generated by DBI or PHP scripts, visitors to your site might find requests being refused if this variable is set too low. (To determine the largest number of connections that have been open simultaneously, use `SHOW STATUS` to check the `Max_used_connections` status variable.)

- `table_open_cache`

  When the server opens table files, it tries to keep them open, to minimize the number of file open and close operations that must be done. To do this, it maintains information about open files in a table cache. If the server accesses lots of tables, the table cache fills up and the server closes tables that haven't been used for a while to make room for opening new tables.

  The default table cache size is 400, which may be too small on a busy server, or if you use features such as `innodb_file_per_table` or partitioned tables that increase the number of file descriptors required. If you have file descriptors available, making the table cache larger by increasing the `table_open_cache` system variable value enables `mysqld` to keep more tables open simultaneously.

  To assess table cache effectiveness, check the `Opened_tables` status indicator:

  ```
  SHOW STATUS LIKE 'Opened_tables';
  ```

  `Opened_tables` indicates the number of times a table had to be opened because it wasn't already open. (This value is also displayed as the `Opens` value in the output of the `mysqladmin status` command.) If the number remains stable or increases slowly, it's probably set to about the right value. If the number grows quickly, it means the cache is too small and that tables often must be closed to make room to open other tables. Closing a table is particularly expensive if its contents have been modified and must be flushed. A larger table cache lessens this drag on performance.

- `table_definition_cache`

  If you increase the `table_open_cache` value, consider also increasing `table_definition_cache`. This system variable controls the size of the cache used for storing table definitions (the information from `.frm` files), which are used when opening tables.

- `open_files_limit`

  If you increase the values of `max_connections` or `table_open_cache`, the server requires a larger number of file descriptors. That may cause problems with operating system limits on the per-process number of file descriptors, in which case you'll need to increase the limit or work around it. First, try setting the `open_files_limit` variable for `mysqld`. If you cannot set the open files limit high enough that way, you might need to configure your operating system to permit more file descriptors. Some systems can be configured simply by editing a system description file and restarting. For others, you must edit a kernel description file and rebuild the kernel. Consult the documentation for your system to see how to proceed.

A workaround for per-process file descriptor limits is to set up replication of your main MySQL server to one or more slave servers (see Section 14.8, "Setting Up Replication Servers"). All updates should be directed to the main server, but requests from clients that perform only retrievals can be distributed among all the servers. This reduces the client load and file descriptor requirements of the main server.

- `max_allowed_packet`

  The maximum size to which the buffer used for client communications can grow. The default buffer size is 1MB. The largest permitted value is 1GB. This variable is not so much a performance-related parameter, but larger values prevent errors from occurring for larger packets, and memory for the packet buffer is not allocated unless needed.

  The `mysql` and `mysqldump` clients have their own `max_allowed_packet` variable. If you have clients that send very long statements to the server (for example, statements that include large `BLOB` or `TEXT` values), this variable may need to be increased both on the server end and on the client end. For example, to start the server with a 16MB packet limit, add these lines to the server option file:

  ```
  [mysqld]
  max_allowed_packet=16M
  ```

  For occasions when you need to invoke `mysql` or `mysqldump` with a 16MB packet limit, do so like this:

  ```
  % mysql --max_allowed_packet=16M ...other options...
  % mysqldump --max_allowed_packet=16M ...other options...
  ```

  To use these client settings all the time, add these lines to your option file:

  ```
  [mysql]
  max_allowed_packet=16M

  [mysqldump]
  max_allowed_packet=16M
  ```

Some variables control resources that are allocated on a per-client basis. Increasing the global values of these variables has the potential to increase the server's resource requirements dramatically if many clients connect simultaneously. Two variables you might increase in hopes of improved performance are `read_buffer_size` and `sort_buffer_size`, which determine the size of the buffers that are used during read and sort operations. Be careful, though: These buffers are allocated for each session, so if you make the corresponding variable values quite large, performance may actually suffer due to exorbitant system resource consumption.

Instead of bumping up the sizes of per-session buffers by a large amount all at once, it's best to change the sizes incrementally and test your changes. This enables you to assess the effect of each change with less likelihood of serious performance degradation. Be sure to use realistic test conditions as well. The server allocates these buffers only as needed rather than as soon as a client connects. For example, the sort buffer is not allocated for a client unless it performs a query that requires a sort operation. The `join_buffer_size` variable controls the size of the buffer used for joins between tables, but a client that uses no joins needs no join buffer. (Conversely, a client that uses complex many-table joins needs multiple join buffers simultaneously.) Your test conditions should use clients that connect at the same time and run complex statements so you can assess the true effect on the server's memory requirements.

As an alternative to increasing the global values of variables that control the sizes of buffers allocated per client, leave the values unchanged and assume that individual clients will set the session values for such variables as need to be larger. For information about the distinctions between global and session system variables, see Section 12.3.1, "Checking and Setting System Variable Values."

12.7.2   Storage Engine Tuning

Some storage engines have tuning parameters you can exploit to get the best results for the workload your server handles. This section focuses on the most important performance-related resource for the InnoDB and MyISAM storage engines: Each engine's cache for buffering table information in memory. For general storage engine configuration information, see Section 12.5, "Storage Engine Configuration."

The storage engine table-information caches have different names (buffer pool for InnoDB, key buffer for MyISAM), but each operates using the same general principles:

- Initially, the cache is empty.

- When the server must examine information from a table during statement execution, it checks whether the information has already been read into the cache. If so, the server consults the in-memory values. Otherwise, the storage engine reads table contents from disk into the cache.

- If the cache is full when new values must be read, old information must be discarded (evicted) to make room for new. By default, each storage engine determines cache blocks to discard on the basis of a least recently used (LRU) algorithm. That is, the engine chooses blocks that have been unused for the longest time. This keeps the most actively used blocks in the cache and discards those least likely to be needed again soon.

- If a block chosen for eviction has not been modified, its contents are overwritten with newly read values. Otherwise, the block must be flushed back to the table from which it came before being overwritten.

Values not found in the cache when requested are "misses" and must be read from disk. Values that are found are "hits." The purpose of the cache is to reduce disk accesses (that is, to minimize the ratio of misses to requests). It boosts performance greatly because memory access is much faster than disk access. The cache enables disk I/O to be reduced for both reads and writes:

- There are fewer reads because information found in the cache need not be read from disk again.

- There are fewer writes because modifications to cached information need not be written to disk immediately. Multiple changes can be buffered and written in groups more efficiently than individual writes.

Even a small cache provides these benefits, but a larger cache accentuates them. Blocks containing frequently used index values tend to stay in the cache, and a larger cache increases the chance of a hit. This in turn decreases the need to discard blocks to make room for new ones and minimizes the number of disk accesses needed for index processing. If your server manages many tables for a given storage engine and the engine cache currently is small, increasing its size generally is one of the most useful configuration changes you can make.

However, setting cache size is something of a balancing act. You don't want to starve other processes running on the server host that require memory, and there are other memory needs within MySQL itself, such as connection buffers, sort and join buffers, temporary tables, and the query cache. Also, when you increase the size of a storage engine's cache, be careful not to make it so large that you use all available memory on your machine. That can lead to paging of the cache itself, which defeats the purpose of using a cache to retain information in memory.

The following sections provide engine-specific details on configuring the InnoDB and MyISAM table-information caches.

12.7.2.1   Configuring the InnoDB Buffer Pool

InnoDB treats its buffer pool as a list of blocks divided into new and old sublists containing blocks that have been accessed more recently and less recently. InnoDB uses a midpoint insertion strategy, adding new blocks to the pool at the head of the old sublist (where it meets the tail of the new sublist).

InnoDB inserts a block into the pool when a query needs it or when its readahead heuristics predict that it will be needed soon. Inserting a block differs from accessing it. "Access" occurs when a query actually examines the block contents.

By default, InnoDB inserts a block at the head of the old sublist, then moves it to the head of the new sublist the first time the block is accessed following insertion. The first access occurs immediately if the block was inserted because a query needs it, but might not occur for a while (if ever) for a block inserted due to readahead.

Accessing a block in the new sublist moves it to the head of the list only if it is not already close to the head. As time passes without access occurring for a block, it ages toward the end of the list. Blocks in the new sublist age past the boundary separating the new and old sublists. Blocks in the old sublist age off the end of the list and are discarded.

Two system variables control the size of the InnoDB buffer pool and whether it is divided into smaller pools:

- `innodb_buffer_pool_size`

  The total memory allocated to the buffer pool, in bytes. The default size is 128MB. You'll want to increase this value for systems that process InnoDB tables heavily and have memory available. A general guideline is to use 70-80% of your system's memory, but take into account memory needs of other MySQL resources and other processes on the server host.

- `innodb_buffer_pool_instances`

  By default, this variable is 1 and there is a single buffer pool. If `innodb_buffer_pool_size` is at least 1GB and you make `innodb_buffer_pool_instances` larger than 1, InnoDB treats the pool as that many smaller pool instances, each of which operates independently. InnoDB randomly assigns blocks read from disk to a given pool instance, which reduces contention because fewer sessions per instance attempt to access its shared data structures. (For example, even if one session has an exclusive lock on a pool, work that uses the other pools can proceed.) For best results, choose the values of `innodb_buffer_pool_size` and `innodb_buffer_pool_instances` so each instance is at least 1GB. Use of multiple pools normally is limited to large systems, such as 64-bit systems with lots of memory.

Two additional system variables affect the LRU algorithm of the InnoDB buffer pool (or each pool instance if you configure multiple instances):

- `innodb_old_blocks_pct`

  The percentage of the buffer pool devoted to the old sublist. This percentage is approximate because InnoDB manages some operations merely by moving back and forth the pointer that indicates the boundary between the new and old sublists (for example, when a block ages from the new sublist to the old). The default is 37 (3/8 of the pool). Permitted values range from 5 to 95. Smaller or larger values cause blocks in the new sublist to age into the old sublist more slowly or more quickly, respectively.

- `innodb_old_blocks_time`

  How many milliseconds a block must remain in the old sublist after the first access before the next access moves it to the new sublist. The default is 0: Blocks inserted into the old sublist move immediately to the new sublist when the first access occurs.

Table scans tend to access table blocks multiple times in quick succession and then not at all thereafter. To prevent such one-time accesses from filling the new sublist and evicting other blocks, set the value of `innodb_old_blocks_time` greater than 0. This is a good setting to use when you are performing backups, which involves lots of one-time scans. On the other hand, to preload the buffer pool with content from a table you expect to be accessed frequently, set the value of `innodb_old_blocks_time` to 0, scan the table to cause it to load into the cache, then revert the variable to its previous value.

12.7.2.2   Configuring the MyISAM Key Buffer

MyISAM stores tables using separate data and index files, which it handles differently:

- To cache data rows read from or written to data files, MyISAM relies on the operating system to use its own filesystem caching mechanism.

- To process index files, MyISAM maintains a key buffer that it uses for index-based retrievals and sorts, and for index creation and modification operations.

The most important parameter affecting MyISAM storage engine operation is the size of its key buffer. The default size is 8MB, which is a very conservative value. If you use MyISAM tables heavily and have memory available, making the key buffer larger should improve MyISAM performance considerably for index-related processing.

To configure the buffer, set the `key_buffer_size` system variable. For example, to set the size to 512MB, put these lines in an option file:

```
[mysqld]
key_buffer_size=512M
```

The MyISAM key buffer is shared among all MyISAM tables by default. If key values are not found in the cache and the cache is full, contention results: Values currently in the cache must be discarded and they must be read from disk again the next time they are needed.

If you have an especially heavily used MyISAM table, it would be beneficial to ensure that its keys remain in memory, but contention in the cache works against this. Contention can arise either when keys need to be read from the same table, or from other tables. You might avoid same-table contention by making the key cache large enough to hold all of a given table's indexes completely, but keys from other tables would still contend for space in the cache.

MyISAM offers a solution to this problem because it supports multiple key caches, which provides more control over cache operation through the following features:

- You can use the default single key cache or create multiple caches.

- You can control total cache size, cache block size, and buffer discard algorithm.

- You can assign tables to specific caches and preload table indexes into a cache.

These capabilities can be useful if you have a table that sees especially heavy use and you have sufficient memory to load its indexes into the cache. You can avoid both same-table and other-table contention: Create a cache that is large enough to hold a table's indexes completely and devote the cache exclusively to the use of that table. No disk I/O is necessary after the keys have been loaded into the cache. Also, key values will never need to be discarded from the cache and key lookups for the table can be done in memory.

Another common strategy is to assign a set of heavily used tables to a separate key cache so that index caching for them does not compete with all other tables, which are processed through the default cache.

To permit MyISAM key cache configuration, the server associates each cache with a set of system variables. Because these variables are related, they are grouped as components that form a structured system variable. Structured variables are an extension of simple system variables, so they are accessed using a syntax that combines a cache name and a variable name:

`cache_name.var_name`

Each key cache structured variable has these components:

- `key_buffer_size`

  The total size of the key cache, in bytes.

- `key_cache_block_size`

  The size of blocks in the key cache, in bytes. By default, blocks are 1024 bytes.

- `key_cache_limit`

  This variable influences the cache buffer reuse algorithm. If set to its default value of 100, the key cache uses a least recently used strategy for determining which cache buffers to reuse. If set lower than 100, the key cache uses a midpoint insertion strategy that splits the cache into warm and hot subchains. The value of `key_cache_limit` is the percentage of the key cache to use for the warm buffer subchain. The value can range from 1 to 100.

  With the midpoint insertion strategy that uses warm and hot subchains, the server attempts to keep the most frequently accessed buffer blocks in the hot subchain. Blocks can move between the hot or warm subchains as access to them increases or decreases. The server always chooses blocks to reuse and overwrite from the warm subchain. (The MyISAM key buffer hot and warm subchains are similar to the InnoDB buffer pool new and old sublists.)

- `key_cache_age_threshold`

  How long blocks stay unused in the hot subchain of the key cache before being moved to the warm subchain. Higher values permit blocks to remain in the hot subchain longer. The default is 300. The minimum value is 100.

One key cache is the default and has a name of `default`. References to a key cache component variable without a cache name apply to the default cache. Thus, `key_buffer_size` and `default.key_buffer_size` refer to the same variable. Key cache names must be legal identifiers and are not case sensitive. They can be quoted like any other identifier (see Section 2.2, "MySQL Identifier Syntax and Naming Rules").

To create a new key cache, assign a value to any component of the associated cache variable. For example, to create a cache named `my_cache` with a size of 24MB at server startup, add these lines to the server option file:

```
[mysqld]
my_cache.key_buffer_size=24M
```

To create the cache at runtime, use this statement:

```
SET GLOBAL my_cache.key_buffer_size = 24*1024*1024;
```

The GLOBAL keyword is necessary because key caches are global. No special privileges are required to access component values, but you must have the SUPER privilege to set them.

To assign MyISAM tables to a key cache after creating it, use CACHE INDEX. This statement names a key cache and one or more tables to be assigned to it. The following statement assigns the member and president tables to the cache named my_cache:

```
CACHE INDEX member, president IN my_cache;
```

It's possible to assign other tables to the same cache later. You can also preload table indexes into their assigned cache with LOAD INDEX INTO CACHE if you choose:

```
LOAD INDEX INTO CACHE member, president;
```

It is unnecessary to preload the indexes, but the server reads index blocks sequentially if you do. This is more efficient than waiting for them to be fetched as needed.

The CACHE INDEX and LOAD INDEX INTO CACHE statements require that you have the INDEX privilege for the named tables.

To destroy a key cache, set its size to zero. Any tables assigned to the cache are reassigned to the default cache. If you set the size of the default key cache to zero, indexes of tables assigned to it are processed using filesystem caching the same way as for MyISAM data files. This minimizes server memory use but slows performance.

Key cache assignments last only until the server exits. To make assignments each time the server starts, place the appropriate CACHE INDEX and LOAD INDEX INTO CACHE statements in a file and start the server with the init_file system variable set to the name of the file.

12.7.3   Using the Query Cache

The MySQL server can use a query cache to speed up processing of SELECT statements that are executed repeatedly. The resulting performance improvement often is dramatic. The query cache has these characteristics:

- The first time a given SELECT statement is executed, the server remembers the text of the query and the results that it returns.

- The next time the server sees that statement, it doesn't bother to execute it again. Instead, the server pulls the result directly from the query cache and returns it to the client.

- Query caching is based on the literal text of query strings as they are received by the server. Queries are considered the same if the text of the queries is exactly the same. Queries are considered different if they differ in lettercase or come from clients that are using different character sets or communication protocols. They also are considered different if they are otherwise identical but do not actually refer to the same tables (for example, if they refer to identically named tables in different databases).

- A query is not cached if the query returns nondeterministic results. For example, a query that uses NOW() returns different results over time and cannot be cached.

- When a table is modified, any cached queries that refer to it become invalid and are discarded. This prevents the server from returning out-of-date results.

To determine whether your server supports the query cache, check the have_query_cache system variable:

```
mysql> SHOW VARIABLES LIKE 'have_query_cache';
+------------------+-------+
| Variable_name    | Value |
+------------------+-------+
| have_query_cache | YES   |
+------------------+-------+
```

For a server that includes query cache support, cache operation is based on the values of three system variables:

- query_cache_type determines the operating mode of the query cache. The following table shows the possible mode values.

Mode	Meaning
0	Don't cache query results or retrieve cached results
1	Cache cacheable queries except those that begin with SELECT SQL_NO_CACHE
2	Cache on demand only cacheable queries that begin with SELECT SQL_CACHE

- query_cache_size determines the amount of memory to allocate for the cache, in bytes.

- query_cache_limit sets the maximum result set size that will be cached; query results larger than this value are never cached.

For example, to enable the query cache and allocate 16MB of memory for it, use the following settings in an option file:

```
[mysqld]
query_cache_type=1
query_cache_size=16M
```

The amount of memory indicated by query_cache_size is allocated even if query_cache_type is zero. To avoid wasting memory, set the size to zero unless you plan to enable the cache. Note that a size of zero effectively disables the cache even if query_cache_type is nonzero.

Enabling the query cache sounds like an easy way to increase performance, and it often is. There are, however, conditions under which you might find that it doesn't help or even hinders performance:

- Allocating a huge amount of memory to the query cache can result in the server spending excessive time comparing the current query to cached queries to determine whether the result is cached.

- On multi-processor systems, the MySQL server can execute queries for different connections on different processor cores. But checking the query cache involves a single thread, which can become a point of contention between connection threads running on different cores. One way to check this is to use `SHOW PROCESSLIST`. If you often see `Waiting for query cache lock` in the `State` column, that is a sign of contention for query cache access and it may be better to disable it.

Assuming that the query cache is enabled, individual clients begin with query caching behavior in the state indicated by the server's default caching mode. A client can change the default caching mode for its queries by using this statement:

```
SET query_cache_type = val;
```

`val` can be 0, 1, or 2, which have the same meanings as when setting the `query_cache_type` variable at server startup. In a `SET` statement, the symbolic values `OFF`, `ON`, and `DEMAND` are synonyms for 0, 1, and 2.

A client also can control caching of individual queries by adding a modifier following the `SELECT` keyword. `SELECT SQL_CACHE` for a cacheable query causes the result to be cached if the cache mode is `ON` or `DEMAND`. `SELECT SQL_NO_CACHE` causes the result not to be cached.

Suppression of caching can be useful for queries that retrieve information from a constantly changing table. In that case, the cache is unlikely to be of much use. Suppose that you're logging Web server requests to a table in MySQL, and also that you periodically run a set of summary queries on the table. For a reasonably busy Web server, new rows are inserted into the table frequently and thus any query results cached for the table become invalidated quickly. The implication is that although you might issue the summary queries repeatedly, it's likely that the query cache will be of no value for them. Under such circumstances, it makes sense to issue the queries using the `SQL_NO_CACHE` modifier to tell the server not to bother caching their results.

12.7.4   Hardware Optimizations

The earlier part of this chapter discusses techniques that help improve your server's performance regardless of your hardware configuration. You can, of course, get better hardware to make your server run faster. But not all hardware-related changes are equally valuable. When assessing what kinds of hardware improvements you might make, the most important principles are the same as those that apply to server parameter tuning: Put as much information in fast storage as possible, and keep it there as long as possible.

The following items describe several aspects of hardware configuration that can be modified to improve server performance:

Install more memory into your machine. This enables you to configure larger values for the server's cache and buffer sizes, which enables it to keep data in memory longer and with less need to fetch information from disk.

Use multi-processor hardware. For a multi-threaded application like the MySQL server, multi-processor hardware can execute multiple threads at the same time.

Reconfigure your system to remove all disk swap devices. This may be possible if you have enough RAM to do all swapping into a memory filesystem. Otherwise, some systems will continue to swap to disk even if you have sufficient RAM for swapping.

Add faster disks to improve I/O latency. For moving-head rotational disk drives, seek time typically is the primary determinant of performance. It's slow to move the heads laterally; after the heads have been positioned, reading blocks off the track is fast by comparison. However, if you have a choice between adding more memory and getting faster disks, add more memory. Memory is always faster than your disks, and adding memory enables you to use larger caches, which reduces disk activity.

To avoid seeks altogether, install a solid state drive (SSD) and configure MySQL to use it. SSDs have no seek time at all because there are no moving parts.

Take advantage of parallelism by distributing disk activity across physical devices. If you can split reading or writing across multiple physical devices, it will be quicker than reading and writing everything from the same device. For example, if you store databases on one device and logs on another, writing to both devices at once it will be faster than if databases and logs share the same device. Note that using different partitions on the same physical device doesn't count as parallelism. That won't help because they'll still contend for the same physical resource (disk heads). The procedure for moving logs and databases is described in Section 11.3, "Relocating Data Directory Contents."

Before you relocate data to a different device, make sure that you understand your system's load characteristics. If there's some other major activity already taking place on a particular physical device, putting a database there may actually make performance worse. For example, you may not realize any overall benefit if you process a lot of Web traffic and move a database onto the device where your Web server document tree is located.

Use of RAID devices can give you some advantages of parallelism as well.

12.8 Server Logs

The MySQL server can produce several kinds of logs. These are useful for diagnosing problems, improving server performance, enabling replication, and crash recovery. When the server begins executing, it examines its startup options to see whether it should perform logging and opens the appropriate logs if so. The following list describes each log briefly, and the next several sections provide more detail on each one:

- **The error log.** This log records server startups and shutdowns, as well as messages about problems or exceptional conditions. Look here if the server fails to start. It writes a message to the error log before terminating, to indicate what problem occurred.

- **The general query log.** This log records client connections, SQL statements received from clients, and other miscellaneous events. It is useful for monitoring server activity: who is connecting, from where, and what they are doing. It's the most convenient log to use when you want to find out what statements clients are sending to the server, which can be very useful for troubleshooting or debugging.

- **The slow query log.** This log helps you identify statements that may be in need of being rewritten for better performance. By default, if a query takes more than 10 seconds of real time, it is considered slow and the server writes it to the slow query log. Several system variables afford additional control over what is logged here.

- **The binary log and the binary log index file.** This log consists of one or more files that record modifications performed by UPDATE, DELETE, INSERT, CREATE TABLE, DROP TABLE, GRANT, and so forth. Binary log contents are written as data modification "events" encoded in binary format. The binary log files are accompanied by an index file that lists which binary log files exist at the moment.

  The binary log has two purposes:

  - It can be used in conjunction with your backups to restore tables after a crash: First, restore databases from your backup files. Then use mysqlbinlog to convert the binary log contents to text statements and use any statements that modified the databases subsequent to the backup as input to mysql to bring databases to the state they were in at the time of the crash.

  - It forms the basis for replication. The data modification events stored in the binary log are transmitted to replication slave servers.

- **The relay log and the relay log index file.** If the server is a replication slave, it maintains a relay log that contains a record of data-modification events received from the master that need to be executed. Relay log files have the same format as binary log files, and there is an index file that lists which relay log files exist on the slave.

Of all the logs, the general query log is most useful for monitoring the server, so when you first start using MySQL, I recommend that you enable the general log in addition to whatever other logs you want. After you have gained some experience with MySQL, you may want to turn off the general log to reduce the server's disk space usage.

By default, each enabled log is written as a file (or sequence of files) in the data directory. For some logs, you can choose to write them to alternative destinations:

- The error log can be sent to syslog.

- The general and slow query logs can be written to tables in the mysql database.

The server creates no log unless you ask for it, with these exceptions:

- On Unix, if you start the server with the `mysqld_safe` script, that script sets up the error log and tells the server to use it.

- On Windows, the server creates the error log *unless* you specify the `--console` option to send diagnostic information to the console window rather than to a file.

To enable server logging, use the options shown in the following table. If the log filename is optional (as indicated by square brackets) and you don't provide a name, the server uses a default name and writes the log file in the data directory. The server derives the default name for each of the log files from the name of your server host, represented by *HOSTNAME* in the following discussion. If you specify a log name as a relative pathname, the server interprets it relative to the data directory. To place a log in some other directory, specify a full pathname. The server creates any log file that does not exist. However, it does not create the directory where the file is to be written. Create the directory if necessary before starting the server or startup will fail.

Some of these options are actually system variables (as indicated by underscores in their names), but you can set them at server startup. These variables also can be changed at runtime.

Option	Purpose
`--general_log`	Enable general log
`--general_log_file=file_name`	General log filename
`--log-bin[=file_name]`	Enable binary log
`--log-bin-index=file_name`	Binary log index file
`--log_error[=file_name]`	Enable error log
`--log_output[=destination]`	General/slow query log destination
`--relay-log[=file_name]`	Enable relay log
`--relay-log-index=file_name`	Relay log index file
`--slow_query_log`	Enable slow query log
`--slow_query_log_file=file_name`	Slow query log filename

You can specify options for server logs on the command line for `mysqld` or `mysqld_safe`. However, because you usually specify log options the same way each time you start the server, it's most common to list them in an appropriate group of an option file. Typically, log options are listed in the `[mysqld]` group, but they need not always be. Section 12.2.3, "Specifying Server Startup Options," details the option groups applicable to the server and to the server startup programs. For example, the following lines enable an error log named `log.err` and a general query log named `qlog`, both in the server's data directory:

```
[mysqld]
log_error = log.err
general_log
general_log_file = qlog
```

Except for the binary and relay logs, these logs are written in text format and can be viewed directly. To display the contents of a binary or relay log file, use the `mysqlbinlog` utility.

In addition to the server logs just described, there may be other logs created by individual storage engines. For example, the InnoDB engine creates logs to be used for auto-recovery after a crash. You cannot control whether InnoDB generate its logs, but you can specify where it writes them by setting the `innodb_log_group_home_dir` system variable. The default location is the data directory. For more information, see Section 12.5.3, "Configuring the InnoDB Storage Engine."

12.8.1   The Error Log

The server uses the error log to record when it starts and stops, and for diagnostic and error information. The amount of information logged can be influenced by setting the `log_warnings` system variable, which takes values from 0 to 2 to select increasing levels of logging.

Some error log properties are handled differently on Unix and Windows, as described in the following discussion.

12.8.1.1   The Error Log on Unix

On Unix, `mysqld` creates no error log by default, but instead sends diagnostic output to the console. If you invoke `mysqld` directly, you can send error output to a file rather than to the console by setting the `log_error` system variable, either on the command line or in the `[mysqld]` group of an option file.

If you start the server by invoking `mysqld_safe`, an error log is created by default because `mysqld_safe` invokes `mysqld` with the server's output redirected to the error log. The default error log filename is *HOSTNAME*`.err`. To indicate a different error log name, set the `log_error` system variable, either on the command line or in the `[mysqld_safe]` or `[mysqld]` group of an option file. (`mysqld_safe` looks in `[mysqld]` option groups and uses the `log_error` value there if it finds one.)

If the error log file already exists but is not writable to the login account used for running the server, startup fails with no output being written to the error log. This can happen if you start the server with different `--user` values at different times. Use the same account consistently, as discussed in Section 12.2.1.1, "Running the Server Using an Unprivileged Login Account."

If you start the server with `mysqld_safe`, you can send error output to `syslog` rather than to a log file. To use `syslog` for diagnostic output, start `mysqld_safe` with the `--syslog` option rather than the `log_error` system variable. With logging to `syslog`, messages from `mysqld` and `mysqld_safe` are written with a tag (prefix) of `mysqld` and `mysqld_safe`, respectively. If you specify a `--syslog-tag=`*str* option, the tags are `mysqld-`*str* and `mysqld_safe-`*str* instead.

If you start the server using the `mysql.server` script, an error log is always created because `mysql.server` invokes `mysqld_safe`. However, `mysql.server` doesn't recognize any error-logging options on the command line or in its [mysql_server] option group. To specify any required options to `mysqld_safe` or `mysqld`, use the [mysqld_safe] or [mysqld] option file group, as described earlier in this section.

12.8.1.2   The Error Log on Windows

On Windows, the server writes diagnostic information to a file named *HOSTNAME*.err in the data directory by default. To indicate a different error log name, set the `log_error` system variable, either on the command line or in the [mysqld] group of an option file. If you start the server manually with the `--console` option, it writes diagnostic output to the console window rather than to the error log. (If the server runs as a Windows service, the `--console` option has no effect because there is no console to write to in that case.)

12.8.2   The General Query Log

The general query log records when clients connect to the server, each SQL statement sent to it by clients, and other events such as server startup and shutdown. The server writes statements to this log in the order that it receives them. This may differ from the order in which they finish executing, particularly for a mix of simple and complex statements.

To enable the general log, enable the `general_log` system variable. To specify a log filename, set the `general_log_file` system variable. The default name is *HOSTNAME*.log in the data directory. These variables can be set at server startup or changed at runtime.

You can write the general log to a file, a database table, or both. For details, see Section 12.8.6, "Using Log Tables."

12.8.3   The Slow Query Log

The slow query log records which queries took a long time to execute (10 seconds by default). Because the time a query takes is not known until it finishes, the server writes queries to the slow query log after they execute, not when it receives them. Slow queries also cause the server to increment its `Slow_queries` status variable.

The server writes the slow query log as text, so it is viewable with any file-display program, or you can use the `mysqldumpslow` utility to summarize its contents.

The slow query log can be useful for identifying queries that you might be able to improve if you rewrite them. However, when interpreting its contents, take the general system load into account. "Slowness" is measured in real time (not CPU time), so if your server is bogged down, it's more likely that a query will be assessed as slow, even if at some other time it runs under the limit.

To enable the slow query log, enable the `slow_query_log` system variable. To specify a log filename, set the `slow_query_log_file` system variable. The default name is *HOSTNAME*-slow.log in the data directory. These variables can be set at server startup or changed at runtime.

You can write the slow query log to a file, a database table, or both. For details, see Section 12.8.6, "Using Log Tables."

Several related options and system variables affect what the server writes to the slow query log:

- A query is "slow" as defined as the value of the `long_query_time` system variable in seconds (10 seconds by default). The minimum value is 0. The value can have a fractional part in microseconds. If slow queries are written to a log table, the fractional part of query execution time is discarded.

- Queries must also examine at least `min_examined_row_limit` rows or they are not logged. The default is 0.

- If started with the `--log-short-format` option, the server writes less information to the log.

- If started with the `--log-slow-admin-statements` option, the server logs slow administrative statements such as `ANALYZE TABLE` or `ALTER TABLE`.

- If the `log_queries_not_using_indexes` system variable is enabled, the server also logs queries that execute without using an index for row lookups. However, this might cause a lot of log output. As of MySQL 5.6.5, you can set the `log_throttle_queries_not_using_indexes` system variable to a nonzero value to indicate a per-minute limit on logging of queries that do not use indexes.

12.8.4 The Binary Log

The server uses the binary log to record data-modification "events" such as those resulting from `INSERT`, `DELETE`, or `UPDATE` statements. It does not write `SELECT` operations to this log. An `UPDATE` statement such as the following one does not appear in the binary log, either, because it doesn't actually change any values:

```
UPDATE t SET i = i;
```

Uses for the binary log include database backup and recovery, and to support replication. (To set up a server as a master server that is replicated to a slave server, you *must* enable the binary log.) Because the binary log is used for replication, it contains information that is useful for replication purposes, such as statement execution timestamps.

MySQL must execute a statement first to determine whether it modifies data, so it writes information to the binary log after statements finish executing, not when it receives them.

The server does not write information to the binary log as text, unlike other logs, but in a more efficient binary format. This means this log is not directly viewable. To display the contents of binary log files in readable text form, use the `mysqlbinlog` utility.

The fact that the server writes events to the binary log in the order they finish, not the order they are received, is an important property for making replication work properly. For statements that are part of a transaction, the server caches them until the transaction is committed.

Then the server logs all events in the transaction. If the transaction is rolled back, the transaction is not written to the binary log, because it results in no changes to the database.

Actually, it is more correct to say that rolled-back transactions *usually* are not written to the binary log. If a transaction makes changes to nontransactional tables such as MyISAM tables, those changes cannot be rolled back. In this case, even a rolled-back transaction is logged to the binary log, to ensure that changes to the nontransactional tables replicate properly.

To enable the binary log, specify the `--log-bin` option. If you give the option without a filename, the server generates binary log files in numbered sequence, using `HOSTNAME-bin` as the basename: `HOSTNAME-bin.000001`, `HOSTNAME-bin.000002`, and so forth. Otherwise, the server uses the name that you specify as the sequence basename (if the name includes an extension, the extension is ignored). The server generates the next file in the sequence each time you start it or flush the logs, or when the current log reaches its maximum size. This size is determined by the value of the `max_binlog_size` system variable.

If you enable binary logging, the server also creates an accompanying binary log index file that lists the names of the existing binary log files. The default index filename is the same as the basename of the binary log files, with an `.index` extension. To specify a name explicitly, use the `--log-bin-index` option. If the name includes no extension, the server adds `.index` to the name automatically. For example, if you specify `--log-bin-index=binlog`, the index filename becomes `binlog.index`.

If you use the `--log-short-format` option in conjunction with `--log-bin`, MySQL writes less information to the binary log.

The server can write events to the binary log using either statement-based or row-based format. For example, with statement-based logging, an `UPDATE` is written as an `UPDATE` statement, whereas with row-based logging, the `UPDATE` is written in terms of the changes to be made to individual rows that are updated. (See Section 14.8.3, "Binary Logging Formats.") The `binlog_format` system variable specifies which type of logging to use. Permitted values for this variable are `STATEMENT`, `ROW`, and `MIXED` (which uses row-based logging except in cases where statement-based logging must be used instead). The default is `STATEMENT`.

If you use the binary log for replication, do not delete any given binary log file until you are sure that its contents have been replicated to all applicable slave servers and it is no longer needed. Section 12.8.7.2, "Expiring Binary Log and Relay Log Files," describes how to verify this.

Binary Log Files and System Backups

Your binary (and relay) logs won't be any good for database recovery or replication if a disk crash causes you to lose them. Make sure you're performing regular filesystem backups. It's also a good idea to write these logs to a different disk from the one on which your databases are stored, which requires that you relocate them from the data directory where the server writes them by default. To do this, use the appropriate logging options to specify different log locations.

12.8.5   The Relay Log

The relay log is used with slave replication servers (see Section 14.8, "Setting Up Replication Servers"). A replication slave receives data modifications ("events") from the master server and writes them to its relay log as it receives them. The slave uses its relay log as a holding area where it stores these events until it can execute them.

Two slave server threads handle event reading and execution. The I/O thread reads events from the master and writes them to the relay logs. The SQL thead reads the relay log files, executes the events, and deletes each file when it has been completely processed. This decoupling of function enables the threads to run independently.

The relay log shares several characteristics with the binary log:

- The server creates relay log files in numbered sequence.

- An index file lists the current set of relay log files.

- Relay log files have the same format as binary log files, so you can display their contents with the `mysqlbinlog` program.

To enable the relay log, specify the `--relay-log` option. If you give the option without a filename, the server generates relay log files in numbered sequence, using `HOSTNAME-relay-bin` as the basename: `HOSTNAME-relay-bin.000001`, `HOSTNAME-relay-bin.000002`, and so forth. Otherwise, the server uses the name that you specify as the sequence basename (if the name includes an extension, the extension is ignored). The server generates the next file in the sequence each time you start it or flush the logs, or when the current log reaches its maximum size. This size is determined by the value of the `max_relay_log_size` system variable.

If you enable relay logging, the server also creates an accompanying relay log index file that lists the names of the existing relay log files. The default index filename is the same as the basename of the relay log files, with an `.index` extension. To specify a name explicitly, use the `--relay-log-index` option. If the name includes no extension, the server adds `.index` to the name automatically. For example, if you specify `--relay-log-index=relay-log`, the index filename becomes `relay-log.index`.

12.8.6   Using Log Tables

When the general query log or slow query log is enabled, you can write log output to a log file, a log table in the `mysql` database, or both.

To select log output destinations, set the `log_output` system variable when you start the server. Its value should list one or more comma-separated destination names: `FILE` (log to files), `TABLE` (log to tables), or `NONE` (produce no log). `NONE`, if present, overrides any other destinations. The default is `FILE` if `log_output` is not specified.

The `log_output` system variable determines which log destinations to use but does not enable logging. To enable the general query log or slow query log, enable the `general_log` or `slow_query_log` system variable.

To change logging destinations at runtime, set the global `log_output` system variable. For example, to temporarily disable logging, use this statement:

```
SET GLOBAL log_output='NONE';
```

To re-enable logging and use files as well as tables, do this:

```
SET GLOBAL log_output='FILE,TABLE';
```

If a log is enabled, the server writes startup messages to the log file, but writes no queries to the file thereafter unless the FILE destination has been selected.

With TABLE logging, the server writes to the `general_log` and `slow_log` tables in the `mysql` database.

With FILE logging, the global `general_log_file` and `slow_query_log_file` system variables determine the log filenames. The default names are *HOSTNAME*.log, and *HOSTNAME*-slow.log in the data directory, respectively. If logging to files is enabled, changing the value of either variable changes the name of the file to which the server writes the corresponding log.

The contents of the log tables are intended for viewing but cannot be modified except as done by the server itself. Consequently, you can use them with SELECT, but not INSERT, DELETE, or UPDATE. (You can empty a log table with TRUNCATE TABLE, however.)

12.8.7   Log Management

Logging is important, but has the potential to generate huge amounts of information, possibly filling up your disks. This is especially true if you have a busy server that processes lots of statements. To keep the last few logs available online while preventing logs from growing without bound, use log file expiration techniques. Several methods are available for keeping logs manageable:

- **Log rotation.** This applies to log files that have a fixed name, such as the error, general query, and slow query log files.

- **Age-based expiration.** This method removes log files older than a certain age. It applies to log files that are created in numbered sequence, such as the binary log. However, you should not use this technique if you use the binary log for replication.

- **Replication-related expiration.** If you use the binary log files for replication, do not expire them based on age. You should expire them only after you know they have been sent completely to each slave. This form of expiration therefore is based on determining which binary log files are still in use.

  A replication slave server creates the relay log files in numbered sequence and removes them automatically as it finishes processing them. To reduce the amount of relay log information stored on disk, lower the maximum permitted size by decreasing the value of the `max_relay_log_size` system variable.

- **Log table truncation or rotation.** If you log to tables in the `mysql` database, it's possible to truncate them or rename them and replace them with empty tables.

The following sections describe how to use these expiration methods. You can find the example log-expiration scripts discussed here in the `admin` directory of the `sampdb` distribution.

For any techniques that you put into practice, you should also consider how the log files fit into your database backup methods. It's a good idea to back up any log files that may be needed for recovery operations, so you shouldn't expire them before backing them up.

> ### Flushing the Logs
>
> Log flushing is often used as part of log expiration or rotation, to make sure that any buffered log information has been written to disk. Flushing the logs causes the server to close and reopen log files. To do this, execute a `mysqladmin flush-logs` command or a `FLUSH LOGS` statement. On Unix, sending a `SIGHUP` signal to the server also flushes the logs. `mysqladmin refresh` flushes the logs, but it does other things as well, such as flushing the table cache, so it's overkill if you just want to flush the logs.
>
> The server creates the binary and relay log files in numbered sequence, so flushing the logs causes the server to close the current log file and open a new one with the next number in the sequence.
>
> Log flushing does not affect storage engine-specific logs.

12.8.7.1   Rotating Fixed-Name Log Files

The MySQL server writes some types of log information to files that have fixed names, such as the error, general query, and slow query log files. To expire fixed-name log files, use log rotation. This enables you to maintain the last few logs online but limit the number to as many as you choose, to prevent them from overrunning your disk.

Log file rotation works like this: Suppose that your general query log file is named `qlog`. At the first rotation, rename `qlog` to `qlog.1` and tell the server to begin writing a new log file named `qlog`. (Rename the current log file while the server has it open, then flush the logs. This causes the server to close that file and open a new one, thereby creating a new log file with the original name.) At the second rotation, rename `qlog.1` to `qlog.2`, `qlog` to `qlog.1`, and tell the server to begin writing another new `qlog` file. In this way, each file rotates through the names `qlog.1`, `qlog.2`, and so forth. When the file reaches a certain point in the rotation, expire it by letting the previous file overwrite it. For example, to maintain a week's work of logs if you rotate the logs daily, you would keep `qlog.1` through `qlog.7`. At each rotation, expire `qlog.7` by letting `qlog.6` overwrite it to become the new `qlog.7`.

The frequency of log rotation and the number of old logs to keep depends on how busy your server is (active servers generate more log information) and how much disk space you're willing to allocate to old logs.

The following shell script, `rotate_fixed_logs.sh`, performs rotation of fixed-name log files on Unix:

```
#!/bin/sh
# rotate_fixed_logs.sh - rotate MySQL log file that has a fixed name
```

```
# Argument 1: log filename

if [ $# -ne 1 ]; then
  echo "Usage: $0 logname" 1>&2
  exit 1
fi

logname=$1

mv $logname.6 $logname.7
mv $logname.5 $logname.6
mv $logname.4 $logname.5
mv $logname.3 $logname.4
mv $logname.2 $logname.3
mv $logname.1 $logname.2
mv $logname $logname.1
mysqladmin flush-logs
```

The script takes the log filename as its argument. Either specify the full pathname of the file or change directory into the log directory and specify the file's name in that directory. For example, to rotate a log file named qlog in /usr/mysql/data, execute the script like this:

% **rotate_fixed_logs.sh /usr/mysql/data/qlog**

Or like this:

% **cd /usr/mysql/data**
% **rotate_fixed_logs.sh qlog**

> **Note**
> The first few times the log rotation script executes, you won't have a full set of log files in the rotation, so the script complains that it can't find all the files to be rotated. That's normal.

To make sure that you have permission to rename the log files, run the script while logged in under the same account that you use for running the server (in this book, that's the mysql account). Note that the mysqladmin command in the script includes no connection parameter arguments such as -u or -p. If the relevant parameters for invoking mysqladmin are stored in the .my.cnf option file in the mysql account home directory, you need not specify them on the mysqladmin command in the script. If you don't use an option file, the mysqladmin command must know how to connect to the server using a MySQL account that has sufficient privileges to flush the logs. To handle this, set up a limited-privilege MySQL account that can't do anything but issue flush commands (that is, the account should have only the RELOAD privilege). For example, to call the user flush and assign a password of flushpass, use the following statements:

```
CREATE USER 'flush'@'localhost' IDENTIFIED BY 'flushpass';
GRANT RELOAD ON *.* TO 'flush'@'localhost';
```

After creating this account, change the `mysqladmin` command in the `rotate_fixed_logs.sh` script to look like this:

```
mysqladmin -u flush -pflushpass flush-logs
```

Then protect the script against being read by other login accounts by making it accessible only to `mysql`. Execute the following command while logged in as `mysql`:

```
% chmod go-rwx rotate_fixed_logs.sh
```

To see how to use the `rotate_fixed_logs.sh` script to rotate and flush the logs automatically, consult Section 12.8.7.3, "Automating the Log-Expiration Procedure."

Under Linux, you may prefer to use the `logrotate` utility to install the `mysql-log-rotate` script that comes with the MySQL distribution, rather than using `rotate_fixed_logs.sh` or writing your own script. Look for `mysql-log-rotate` in `/usr/share/mysql` for RPM distributions, or in the `support-files` directory of your MySQL installation or source tree.

On Windows, you can perform log file renaming using the following batch script, `rotate_fixed_logs.bat`:

```
@echo off
REM rotate_fixed_logs.bat - rotate MySQL log file that has a fixed name

REM Argument 1: log filename

if not "%1" == "" goto ROTATE
@echo Usage: rotate_fixed_logs logname
goto DONE

:ROTATE
set logname=%1
erase %logname%.7
rename %logname%.6 %logname%.7
rename %logname%.5 %logname%.6
rename %logname%.4 %logname%.5
rename %logname%.3 %logname%.4
rename %logname%.2 %logname%.3
rename %logname%.1 %logname%.2
rename %logname% %logname%.1
mysqladmin flush-logs
:DONE
```

Invoke `rotate_fixed_logs.bat` much like the `rotate_fixed_logs.sh` shell script, with a single argument that names the log file to be rotated. For example, to rotate a log file named `qlog` in `C:\mysql\data`, execute the script like this:

```
C:\> rotate_fixed_logs C:\mysql\data\qlog
```

Or like this:

```
C:\> cd \mysql\data
C:\> rotate_fixed_logs qlog
```

12.8.7.2   Expiring Binary Log and Relay Log Files

Fixed-name log files can be expired using filename rotation, as just discussed. For logs such as the binary log and the relay log, the server generates logs in numbered sequence, so expiration needs to be handled a bit differently.

For the binary log, there are two approaches that you can take:

- Expire log files based on age (assessed as time of last modification). This applies if you are not using the binary log for replication.

- Expire log files based on whether they are still in use. This applies if you are using the binary log for replication.

To expire binary log files based on age, the easiest way is to set the `expire_logs_days` system variable. For example, to expire binary log files that have not been changed for a week, put these lines in an option file:

```
[mysqld]
expire_logs_days=7
```

When `expire_logs_days` has a value n greater than zero, the server automatically expires binary log files that are older than n days old and updates the binary log index file. The server checks whether to expire files when it starts and when it opens a new log file (for example, when the logs are flushed or the current file reaches the size indicated by the `max_binlog_size` system variable).

If you use the binary log for replication, don't use age-based expiration because age is not an indicator of whether a replicated log file can be removed. Suppose that a slave server is down and has not been sent the contents of a given binary log file. If the slave does not come back up by the time the file reaches its expiration age, the file would be discarded and replication would fail. To avoid this problem, you must consider a binary log file eligible for expiration only after its contents have replicated to all slave servers.

A difficulty here is that, due to the asynchronous nature of MySQL replication, the master server itself doesn't know how many slaves there are or which files have been propagated to them. The master won't purge binary log files that have not yet been sent to connected slaves, but there is no guarantee that a given slave is connected at any particular time. You must know which servers are acting as slaves and determine which master binary log file each is processing. To do this, connect to each slave, issue a SHOW SLAVE STATUS statement, and check the Master_Log_File column. Any binary log that is no longer used by any of the slaves can be removed.

To understand how this works, suppose that you have the following scenario:

- The local server is the master and it has two slaves, S1 and S2.

- On the master, its binary log files have names of `binlog.000038` through `binlog.000042`.

- SHOW SLAVE STATUS produces the following result on S1:

```
mysql> SHOW SLAVE STATUS\G
...
Master_Log_File: binlog.000041
...
```

  And this result on S2:

```
mysql> SHOW SLAVE STATUS\G
...
Master_Log_File: binlog.000040
...
```

In this case, the lowest-numbered binary log still required by the set of slave servers is `binlog.000040`, so any log with a lower number can be removed. To do that, connect to the master server and issue the following statement:

```
mysql> PURGE BINARY LOGS TO 'binlog.000040';
```

That causes the master to delete its binary log files up to but not including the named file, which for the situation just described includes `binlog.000038` and `binlog.000039`.

The SHOW SLAVE STATUS and PURGE BINARY LOGS statements require the SUPER privilege.

To expire relay log files, you need take no special action. A replication slave server creates the relay log files in numbered sequence. It generates a new relay log file when the current one reaches the maximum permitted size (or when the logs are flushed), and removes old files automatically as it finishes processing them. However, if the maximum relay log size is large, the current file also grows large. To use less disk space, set the `max_relay_log_size` system variable to a smaller value to lower the maximum permitted file size.

12.8.7.3   Automating the Log-Expiration Procedure

It's possible to invoke log expiration scripts manually, but you need not remember to do so if you can schedule the commands to run automatically. On Unix, one way to do this is to use the `cron` utility and set up a `crontab` file that defines the expiration schedule. (On Windows, try Scheduled Tasks instead.)

For information about `cron`, check the relevant Unix manual pages using these commands:

```
% man cron
% man crontab
% man 5 crontab
```

Suppose that you want to rotate a general query log named `qlog` by using the `rotate_fixed_logs.sh` script, that this script is installed in `/home/mysql/bin`, and that the log files are located in the `/var/mysql/data` directory. Log in as `mysql`, and then edit the `mysql` user's `crontab` file using this command:

```
% crontab -e
```

This command enables you to edit a copy of your current `crontab` file (which might be empty if no `cron` jobs have yet been set up). Add a line to the file that looks like this:

```
30 4 * * * /home/mysql/bin/rotate_fixed_logs.sh /var/mysql/data/qlog
```

This entry tells `cron` to run the script at 04:30 each day. Vary the scheduling as desired; check the `crontab` manual page for the format of the entries. For a busy server that generates lots of log information, you'll probably want to rotate the logs more frequently than for one that is less active.

To make sure that the logs are flushed regularly (for example, to generate the next numbered binary log), you can schedule a `mysqladmin flush-logs` command to execute periodically by adding another `crontab` entry. You might need to list the full pathname to `mysqladmin` to make sure that `cron` can find it.

12.8.7.4   Expiring or Rotating Log Tables

If the server writes the general query log or slow query log to tables in the `mysql` database, you can either truncate the tables or use a form of table rotation.

To truncate the tables, use these statements:

```
USE mysql;
TRUNCATE TABLE general_log;
TRUNCATE TABLE slow_log;
```

To rotate a log table, first create an empty copy. Then perform an atomic rename that "swaps out" the current table and replaces it with the empty one in a single statement:

```
USE mysql;
DROP TABLE IF EXISTS general_log_tmp, general_log_old;
CREATE TABLE general_log_tmp LIKE general_log;
RENAME TABLE general_log TO general_log_old, general_log_tmp TO general_log;
DROP TABLE IF EXISTS slow_log_tmp, slow_log_old;
CREATE TABLE slow_log_tmp LIKE slow_log;
RENAME TABLE slow_log TO slow_log_old, slow_log_tmp TO slow_log;
```

If you have the event scheduler is enabled, log table rotation can be done automatically by creating an event such as the one following. The event rotates the log tables each day. Change the `ON SCHEDULE` clause to vary the frequency.

```
CREATE EVENT mysql.rotate_log_tables
ON SCHEDULE EVERY 1 DAY
```

```
DO BEGIN
  DROP TABLE IF EXISTS general_log_tmp, general_log_old;
  CREATE TABLE general_log_tmp LIKE general_log;
  RENAME TABLE
    general_log TO general_log_old,
    general_log_tmp TO general_log;
  DROP TABLE IF EXISTS slow_log_tmp, slow_log_old;
  CREATE TABLE slow_log_tmp LIKE slow_log;
  RENAME TABLE
    slow_log TO slow_log_old,
    slow_log_tmp TO slow_log;
END;
```

12.9   Running Multiple Servers

Most people run a single MySQL server on a given machine, but sometimes multiple servers are useful or necessary:

- You want to test a new version of the server while leaving your production server undisturbed. In this case, you run different server binaries.

- You want to try replication to familiarize yourself with it, but you have only a single server host and must run the master and slave on the same machine.

- Operating systems typically impose per-process limits on the number of open file descriptors. If your system makes it difficult to raise the limit (for example, if doing so requires recompiling the kernel), running multiple instances of the server binary is one way to work around that limitation.

- Internet service providers often provide individual customers with their own MySQL installation, which necessarily requires multiple servers. This may involve running multiple instances of the same binary if all customers run the same version of MySQL, or different binaries if some customers run different versions than others.

12.9.1   General Multiple Server Issues

It's more complicated to run multiple servers than just one because you must keep them from interfering with each other. Some of the issues that arise occur at installation time. To install several different versions simultaneously, they must each be placed into a different location. For precompiled binary distributions, you can accomplish this by unpacking them into different directories. For source distributions that you compile yourself, you can set the CMAKE_INSTALL_ PREFIX option for CMake to specify a different installation location for each distribution.

Other issues occur at server start time. Every server process must have unique values for several parameters. For example, each server must listen to a different TCP/IP port for incoming connections to prevent conflicts. This is true whether you run different server binaries or multiple instances of a single binary. The same principle applies to other connection interfaces: Unix socket files, Windows named pipes, or shared memory. If you enable logging, each server must write to its own set of log files. Having different servers write to the same files is sure to cause problems.

You can specify a server's options at start time, typically in an option file. Alternatively, if you run several server binaries that you compile from source yourself, you can specify during the build process a different set of parameter values for each server to use. These become its built-in defaults, and you need not specify them explicitly at start time. However, if you compile from source, one reason to use option files is that parameters specified that way serve as explicit documentation of how each server is configured.

The following discussion enumerates several types of options that have the potential for causing conflicts if they're not set on a per-server basis. Some options influence others, so you may not need to set each one explicitly for every server. For example, each server must use a unique set of log files when it runs. But the data directory is the default location for all of them, so telling each server to use a different data directory implicitly results in different sets of log files.

Some of these options are actually system variables (as indicated by underscores in their names), but you can set them at server startup:

- If you're running different server versions, each distribution typically is installed under a different base directory. Each server also should have its own data directory. (This is mandatory on Windows and strongly recommended on Unix.) To specify these directories explicitly, use the options in the following table.

Option	Purpose
`--basedir=dir_name`	Pathname to root directory of MySQL installation
`--datadir=dir_name`	Pathname to data directory

  In many cases, the data directory is a subdirectory of the base directory, but not always. For example, an Internet service provider might provide a common set of MySQL server and client programs for its customers, but run for each customer an instance of the server that uses a customer-specific data directory. In this case, the base directory is the same for all servers, but individual data directories have different locations, perhaps under customer home directories.

- The network interface options in the following table must have different values for each server, to prevent multiple servers from listening on the same interfaces.

Option	Purpose
`--port=port_num`	Port number for TCP/IP connections
`--socket=file_name`	Unix domain socket-file pathname or Windows named-pipe name
`--shared-memory-base-name=name`	Name of shared memory to use for shared-memory connections (Windows only)

On Windows, the `--socket` and `--shared-memory-base-name` options need be given only for those servers that are run with the `--named-pipe` and `--shared-memory` options to enable named-pipe and shared-memory connections. In this case, one server can use the default named-pipe and shared-memory names (MySQL and MYSQL, respectively), but any others must specify different names.

- Each server must use different file names for status files such as the PID file, and for log files. Otherwise, multiple servers will contend to write to the same file. That is at best confusing, and at worst prevents things like replication from working correctly. The server creates status and log files named by the options in the following table under the data directory if you specify relative filenames. If each server uses a different data directory, you need not specify absolute pathnames to get each server to log to a distinct set of files. (See Section 12.8, "Server Logs," for more information about naming log files.)

Some of these options are actually system variables (as indicated by underscores in their names), but you can set them at server startup. These variables also can be changed at runtime.

Option	Purpose
`--general_log`	Enable general log
`--general_log_file=file_name`	General log filename
`--log-bin[=file_name]`	Enable binary log
`--log-bin-index=file_name`	Binary log index file
`--log_error[=file_name]`	Enable error log
`--log_output[=destination]`	General/slow query log destination
`--pid_file=file_name`	Process ID file
`--relay-log[=file_name]`	Enable relay log
`--relay-log-index=file_name`	Relay log index file
`--slow_query_log`	Enable slow query log
`--slow_query_log_file=file_name`	Slow query log filename

- Servers used as replication slaves each must have a unique set of master and relay log information files. These are created in the data directory by default and set explicitly with the `--master-info-file` and `--relay-log-info-file` options.

- Under Unix, if you use `mysqld_safe` to start your servers, it creates an error log file (in the data directory by default). To specify the error log name explicitly, set the `log_error` system variable. Alternatively, send error output to `syslog`. For details, see Section 12.8.1, "The Error Log."

- Each server that uses InnoDB must be configured to use its own system tablespace. Also, the directory in which the InnoDB storage engine writes its logs must be unique per server. By default, InnoDB writes its logs to the data directory. To change the location, set the `innodb_log_group_home_dir` system variable. For more information, see Section 12.5.3, "Configuring the InnoDB Storage Engine."

- Under Unix, it may be necessary to specify a `--user` option on a per-server basis to indicate the login account to use for running each server. This is very likely if you provide individual MySQL server instances for different users, each of whom "owns" a separate data directory.

- Under Windows, different servers that are installed as services each must use a unique service name.

12.9.2 Configuring and Compiling Different Servers

If you build different versions of the server from source, you must install them in different locations. The easiest way to keep them separate is to indicate a different installation base directory for each one by setting `CMAKE_INSTALL_PREFIX` when you run `CMake`. If you incorporate the version number into the base directory name, it's easy to tell which directory corresponds to which version of MySQL. This section illustrates one way to accomplish that goal. It describes the configuration conventions I use to keep my own MySQL installations separate.

I place all MySQL installations under a common directory, `/var/mysql`. To install a given distribution, I put it in a subdirectory of `/var/mysql` named using the distribution's version number. For example, I use `/var/mysql/50525` as the installation base directory for MySQL 5.5.25, which can be accomplished by running `CMake` with a `-DCMAKE_INSTALL_PREFIX=/var/mysql/50525` option. I also use other options for additional server-specific values, such as the TCP/IP port number and socket pathname. The configuration I use makes the TCP/IP port number equal to the version number, puts the socket file in the base directory, and names the data directory as `data` there.

To set up these configuration options, I use a shell script named `config-ver` that looks like this:

```
VERSION=50525
PREFIX="/var/mysql/$VERSION"
PORT="$VERSION"
ENGINES="
  -DWITH_INNOBASE_STORAGE_ENGINE=ON
  -DWITH_PARTITION_STORAGE_ENGINE=ON
  -DWITH_PERFSCHEMA_STORAGE_ENGINE=ON
"
OTHER="
  -DCPACK_MONOLITHIC_INSTALL=ON
  -DENABLED_LOCAL_INFILE=ON
  -DMYSQL_MAINTAINER_MODE=OFF
```

```
  -DWITH_SSL=bundled
"
OPTIONS="
  -DCMAKE_INSTALL_PREFIX=$PREFIX
  -DMYSQL_DATADIR=$PREFIX/data
  -DMYSQL_TCP_PORT=$PORT
  -DMYSQL_UNIX_ADDR=$PREFIX/mysql.sock
  $ENGINES $OTHER
"

cmake $OPTIONS .
```

I make sure the first line is set to the proper version number and modify the other values as necessary according to which of the optional storage engines to compile in, and so forth. That done, the following commands configure, build, and install the distribution:

```
% sh config-ver
% make
% make install
```

After installing a given version of MySQL, it's necessary to change location into its installation base directory and initialize the data directory and grant tables:

```
# cd /var/mysql/50525
# scripts/mysql_install_db --user=user_name
```

user_name is the name of the login account to be used for running the server (for example, the mysql account). Run these commands while logged in as root or as *user_name*.

At this point, I perform the lockdown procedure for the MySQL installation directory that is described briefly in Section 12.2.1.1, "Running the Server Using an Unprivileged Login Account," and in more detail in Section 13.1.2, "Securing Your MySQL Installation."

After that, all that remains is to set up any options that I want to use in option files and to arrange for starting the server. Section 12.9.4, "Using mysqld_multi for Server Management," discusses one way to do this.

12.9.3   Strategies for Specifying Startup Options

After you have your servers installed, how do you get them started with the proper set of options that each one needs? You have several choices:

- If you build the servers yourself, compile in a different set of defaults for each one and no options need to be given at start time. This has the disadvantage that it's not necessarily obvious what parameters any given server is using.

- Specify options at start time on the command line or in option files. If you specify lots of options, writing them on the command line is impractical. Putting them in option files is more convenient, although then the trick is to get each server to read the proper set of options. Strategies for accomplishing this include the following:

- Use a `--defaults-file` option to specify the file that the server should read to find all of its options, and specify a different file for each server. This way, you can put all the options needed by a given server into one file to fully specify its setup in a single place. (Note that when you use `--defaults-file`, none of the usual option files, such as `/etc/my.cnf`, are read.)

- Put any options that are common to all servers in a global option file such as `/etc/my.cnf` and use a `--defaults-extra-file` option on the command line to specify a file that contains additional options that are specific to a given server. For example, use the `[mysqld]` group in `/etc/my.cnf` for options that should apply to all servers. These need not be replicated in individual per-server option files.

  Be sure that any options placed into a common option group are understood by all servers that you run. For example, you can't use `--plugin-load-add` if any of your servers are older than version 5.6.3, which is when that option was introduced. Its presence in a common option group causes startup failure for older servers. Alternatively, you can use the `loose-opt_name` syntax to specify options that are not understood by all servers. Servers that do not understand an option given this way ignore it and continue to execute after logging a warning. For more information about "loose" options, see Section F.2, "Specifying Program Options."

- Use the `mysqld_multi` script to manage startup for multiple servers. This script enables you to list the options for all servers in a single file but associate each server with its own particular option group in the file.

- On Windows, you can run multiple services, using the special option file group naming conventions specific to this style of server setup. See Section 12.2.2.2, "Running the Server as a Windows Service."

The following sections show some ways to apply these strategies by demonstrating how to use `mysqld_multi` on Unix, and how to run multiple servers on Windows.

12.9.4 Using `mysqld_multi` for Server Management

On Unix, the `mysqld_safe` and `mysql.server` scripts that are commonly used to start the server both work best in a single-server setting. To make it easier to handle several servers, the `mysqld_multi` script can be used instead.

`mysqld_multi` works on the basis that you assign a specific number to each server setup, and then list that server's options in an option file `[mysqldn]` group, where n is the number. The option file can also contain a `[mysqld_multi]` group that lists options specifically for `mysqld_multi` itself. For example, if I have servers installed for MySQL 5.1.64, 5.5.25, and 5.6.6, I might designate their option groups as `[mysqld50164]`, `[mysqld50525]`, and `[mysqld50606]` and set up the options in the `/etc/my.cnf` file like this:

```
[mysqld50164]
basedir=/var/mysql/50164
datadir=/var/mysql/50164/data
mysqld=/var/mysql/50164/bin/mysqld_safe
socket=/var/mysql/50164/mysql.sock
port=50164
user=mysql
log_error=log.err
general_log
general_log_file=qlog
log-bin=binlog
skip-innodb

[mysqld50525]
basedir=/var/mysql/50525
datadir=/var/mysql/50525/data
mysqld=/var/mysql/50525/bin/mysqld_safe
socket=/var/mysql/50525/mysql.sock
port-50525
user=mysql
log_error=log.err
general_log
general_log_file=qlog
log-bin=binlog
innodb_data_file_path=ibdata1:50M:autoextend
event_scheduler=ON

[mysqld50606]
basedir=/var/mysql/50606
datadir=/var/mysql/50606/data
mysqld=/var/mysql/50606/bin/mysqld_safe
socket=/var/mysql/50606/mysql.sock
port=50606
user=mysql
log_error=log.err
general_log
general_log_file=qlog
log-bin=binlog
innodb_data_file_path=ibdata1:100M
lc_messages=fr_FR
character_set_server=utf8
```

The layout parameters that I've set up here for each server correspond to the directory configuration described in Section 12.9.2, "Configuring and Compiling Different Servers." I've also
specified additional server-specific parameters that correspond to variations in types of logs,
storage engines, and so forth.

To start a given server, invoke `mysqld_multi` with a command word of `start` and the server's option group number on the command line:

```
% mysqld_multi --no-log start 50525
```

The `--no-log` option causes status messages to be sent to the terminal rather than to a log file. This enables you to see what's going on more easily. You can specify more than one server by giving the group numbers as a comma-separated list. A range of server numbers can be specified by separating the numbers with a dash. There must be no whitespace in the server list. For example:

```
% mysqld_multi --no-log start 50164,50525-50606
```

To stop servers or obtain a status report indicating whether they are running, use a command word of `stop` or `report` followed by the server list. As of MySQL 5.6.3, you can also use `reload` (stop and restart). For these commands, `mysqld_multi` invokes `mysqladmin` to communicate with the servers, so you must also specify a username and password for an administrative account:

```
% mysqld_multi --nolog --user=root --password=rootpass stop 50164
% mysqld_multi --nolog --user=root --password=rootpass report 50164,50606
```

The user and password must be applicable to all servers that you want to control with a given command. `mysqld_multi` attempts to determine the location of `mysqladmin` automatically, or you can specify the path explicitly in the `[mysqld_multi]` group of an option file. You can also list a default administrative username and password in that option group to be used for the `stop` and `report` commands. For example:

```
[mysqld_multi]
mysqladmin=/usr/local/mysql/bin/mysqladmin
user=leeloo
password=multipass
```

From a security standpoint, it is preferable to list the administrative password in an option file rather than expose it on the command line. But if you put the password in an option file, make sure that the file isn't publicly readable! See Section 13.1.2.2, "Securing Option Files."

12.9.5 Running Multiple Servers on Windows

To run multiple servers on Windows, you can start the servers manually, or use multiple Windows services. It's also possible to mix the two approaches.

To start multiple servers manually, create an option file for each one that lists its parameters. For example, to run two servers that use the same program binaries but different data directories, you can create two option files. Suppose that MySQL is installed at `C:\mysql` with a data directory of `C:\mysql\data`, and you want to run a second instance of the server using a data directory at `C:\mysql\data2`. Your option files might look like this:

C:\my.ini1 file:

```
[mysqld]
basedir=C:/mysql
datadir=C:/mysql/data
port=3306
```

C:\my.ini2 file:

```
[mysqld]
basedir=C:/mysql
datadir=C:/mysql/data2
port=3307
```

The data directory must exist before you can start the second server. The easiest way to set up C:\mysql\data2 is to create it as a copy of C:\mysql\data. Use the following command (while no server is running):

```
C:\> xcopy C:\mysql\data C:\mysql\data2 /E
```

Then start the servers from the command line, using --defaults-file to tell each one to read a specific option file:

```
C:\> mysqld --defaults-file=C:\my.ini1
C:\> mysqld --defaults-file=C:\my.ini2
```

To create a Windows service for MySQL, use the --install option. For example, to install mysqld as a service, you might use one of these commands:

```
C:\> C:\mysql\bin\mysqld --install
C:\> C:\mysql\bin\mysqld --install service_name
```

The --install command uses the full pathname to the server. If your server is installed in a different location, modify the pathname in the command accordingly. With no service_name argument or a name of MySQL, the default service name (MySQL) is used; otherwise, the given name is used. (For the rules about which option groups the server reads in the two cases, see Section 12.2.2.2, "Running the Server as a Windows Service.")

Suppose that you want to run two instances of mysqld, using service names of MySQL and mysqlsvc2, shared-memory names of MYSQL and mysqlsvc2, and the same data directories shown in the previous example. Set up the options for each server in one of the standard option files (such as C:\my.ini) as follows:

```
# group for default ("MySQL") service
[mysqld]
basedir=C:/mysql
datadir=C:/mysql/data
port=3306
shared-memory
shared-memory-base-name=MYSQL
```

```
# group for "mysqlsvc2" service
[mysqlsvc2]
basedir=C:/mysql
datadir=C:/mysql/data2
port=3307
shared-memory
shared-memory-base-name=mysqlsvc2
```

The order of the groups is significant. The server installed under the default service name of MySQL reads only the [mysqld] option group. However, the server installed under the nondefault service name of mysqlsvc2 reads both the [mysqld] and [mysqlsvc2] groups. By placing the [mysqlsvc2] group second in the option file, it can be used to override all the options in the [mysqld] group with values that are appropriate for the server running as the mysqlsvc2 service.

To create and start the services, use these commands (again, modify the server pathname if its location differs from that shown):

```
C:\> C:\mysql\bin\mysqld --install
C:\> net start MySQL
C:\> C:\mysql\bin\mysqld --install mysqlsvc2
C:\> net start mysqlsvc2
```

If you provide a service name, you can also specify a --defaults-file option as the final option on the command line when you create the service:

```
C:\> C:\mysql\bin\mysqld --install service_name --defaults-file=file_name
```

This gives you an alternative means of providing server-specific options. The name of the file is remembered and used by the server whenever it starts, and it reads options only from the [mysqld] group of that file.

To shut down the servers, use mysqladmin shutdown, net stop, or the Services Manager. To uninstall the services, shut down the servers if they are running, and then remove each service by specifying --remove and the same service name that you used at server installation time. You can omit the service name if it is the default name (MySQL):

```
C:\> mysql --remove
C:\> mysql --remove mysqlsvc2
```

12.9.6   Running Clients of Multiple Servers

To use a client program when there are multiple servers running, connect to the desired server by specifying the appropriate connection parameters. This includes the use of mysqladmin for shutting down servers. For example, to connect to a server listening on port 50525:

```
% mysql --protocol=tcp --port=50525
```

To connect to a server on Windows using shared-memory name mysqlsvc2:

```
C:\> mysql --protocol=memory --shared-memory-base-name=mysqlsvc2
```

12.10   Updating MySQL

Because MySQL is actively developed, updates appear regularly. This raises the question for the administrator whether to upgrade a MySQL installation when new releases appear. Use the following guidelines to help you make this decision.

The first thing to do when a new release appears is to determine how it differs from previous releases. To make sure you're aware of new releases, subscribe to the MySQL announcements mailing list. (To find out how to subscribe to MySQL lists, visit `http://lists.mysql.com`.) Each announcement includes the new change notes, so this is a good way to remain apprised of new developments. (Alternatively, check the MySQL Release Notes to familiarize yourself with what's new.) Also, read the section on upgrading in the MySQL Reference Manual for the relevant release series. That section indicates any important issues you should consider and points out any special steps you must take when upgrading. This information is particularly important if the new release introduces behaviors that are incompatible with earlier releases.

After checking the release notes and the upgrading section in the manual, ask yourself these questions:

- Are you experiencing problems or security issues with your current version that the new version fixes?

- Does the new version have additional features that you want or need?

- Is performance improved for operations that you use?

If the answer to all these questions is no, you have no compelling reason to upgrade. If the answer to any question is yes, you might want to go ahead. However, it's often useful to wait a few days and watch the MySQL general-discussion mailing list to see what other people report about the release. Was the upgrade helpful? Were bugs or other problems found?

Here are some other factors to consider that may help you make your decision:

- Releases in a stable series are most often for bug fixes, not new features. There is generally less risk for upgrades within a stable series than within a development series.

- If you upgrade MySQL, you might need to upgrade other programs that are built with the MySQL C client library linked in. For example, after a MySQL upgrade, other libraries or applications that depend on the MySQL C client library might need to be rebuilt to link the new client library. (Examples include the Perl DBD::mysql module and PHP. An obvious symptom that you need to rebuild them is that all your MySQL-related DBI and PHP scripts start dumping core after you upgrade MySQL.) If you prefer to avoid these rebuilds, it might be better not to upgrade MySQL. If you use statically linked rather than dynamically linked programs, the likelihood of this problem is much reduced, but then your system memory requirements increase.

If you're still unsure whether to upgrade, you can test the new server independently of your current server, either by running it in parallel with your production server, or by installing it on a different machine. It's easier to maintain independence between servers if you use a different machine because you have greater freedom to configure it as you choose. If you elect to run the new server in parallel with an existing server on the same host, be sure to configure it with unique values for parameters such as the installation location, the data directory, and the network interfaces on which the server listens for connections. For details, see Section 12.9, "Running Multiple Servers."

In either case, you'll probably want to test the new server using a copy of the data in your existing databases. For instructions on copying databases, see Section 14.4, "Making Database Backups."

To generate an ongoing source of statements for execution by a test server, consider using a production server as a replication master and setting up the test server as a replication slave. That way, updates executed by the master server are sent to the slave server, providing it with a continual stream of input. The master will not send any retrievals to the slave, but you can point client programs at the slave and issue SELECT statements to see how it processes them.

Please Try Development Releases!

It's not a wise idea to use a development release for production purposes, such as managing your business assets. But I do encourage you to test new releases, perhaps with a copy of your production data. The more people that try new releases, the more thoroughly they are exercised. This improves the likelihood of finding bugs so they can be fixed. Bug reports are a significant factor in helping MySQL development move forward.

13

Security and Access Control

As a MySQL administrator, you are responsible for keeping databases secure so data can be accessed by only those who have the proper authorization. To accomplish this goal, you must maintain the security and integrity of your MySQL installation. Chapter 12, "General MySQL Administration," already touched on a security-related topic; namely, the importance of assigning passwords to MySQL accounts. That topic was dealt with as part of the process of getting your installation up and running. In this chapter, we'll look at security issues more closely:

- Why security is important and what kind of attacks you must guard against
- Internal security risks you face from other users with login accounts on the server host and what you can do about them by managing filesystem access
- External security risks you face from clients connecting to the server over the network and what you can do about them by managing MySQL user accounts

Internal security issues arise in relation to other users who have direct access to the MySQL server host—that is, other users who have login accounts on that host. Generally, internal security exploits involve filesystem access. To counter this, you need to protect the contents of your MySQL installation from being attacked by people who have accounts on the machine where the server runs. In particular, the server's data directory should be owned and controlled by the login account used for running the MySQL server. If you don't ensure this, your other security-related efforts may be compromised. For example, although you must make sure you've properly set up the MySQL accounts listed in the grant tables that control client connections over the network, the integrity of those tables depends on adequate filesystem protection. If the access mode for the data directory contents is too permissive, someone might be able to put in place an entirely different client access policy by replacing the files that correspond to the grant tables.

External security issues arise in relation to connections from over the network. It's necessary to protect the MySQL server from being attacked through network connections by clients requesting access to database contents. You should set up the MySQL grant tables so they don't permit access to the databases managed by the server unless a valid name and password are supplied. Another danger is that a third party might be able to monitor the network and capture traffic between the server and a client. To deal with such concerns, you can configure your MySQL installation to support connections that use the Secure Sockets Layer (SSL) protocol.

This chapter describes the security issues you should be aware of and shows how to prevent unauthorized access through the filesystem and over the network. The chapter often refers to the login account used for running the MySQL server and for performing other MySQL-related administrative tasks. The user and group names used here for this account both are `mysql`. Change the names in the examples if you use other user and group names (for example, if you run the MySQL server using your own login account).

13.1   Securing Filesystem Access to MySQL

This section shows how to lock down your MySQL installation to keep it from being tampered with by unauthorized users on the server host. The section applies only to Unix systems; I assume that if your server runs on Windows, you have complete control of the machine and there are no other local users.

The MySQL installation procedure creates several directories, some of which require protection different from others. For example, there is no need for the server program to be accessible to anyone other than the MySQL administrative login account. By contrast, the client programs normally should be publicly accessible so other users can run them—but not so accessible that they can be modified or replaced.

Other files to be protected are created after the initial installation, either by yourself as part of your post-installation configuration procedure, or by the server as it runs. Files created by you include option files or SSL-related files. Directories and files that the server creates for itself as it runs include database directories, the files under those directories that correspond to tables in the databases, log files, and the Unix socket file.

Clearly you want to maintain the privacy of the databases maintained by the server. Database owners usually, and rightly, consider database contents private. Even if they don't, it should be their choice to make the contents of a database public rather than having its contents exposed due to insufficient protection of the database directory.

Log files must be kept secure because they contain the text of statements sent by clients to the server. This is a general concern in that anyone with log file access can monitor changes to the contents of databases. A more specific security issue relating to log files is that they might contain the text of sensitive statements, including passwords. MySQL uses password encryption, but this applies to connection establishment after passwords already have been set up. The process of setting up a password involves a statement such as CREATE USER, GRANT, or SET PASSWORD, and these statements are logged in plain text form in some of the logs. An attacker who has read access to the logs may be able to discover sensitive information through an act as simple as running `grep` on the log files to look for words such as GRANT or PASSWORD.

Certain other files must be accessible to client programs, such as the Unix socket file. Normally you'll want to permit access to the file, but not full control of it. For example, users should be able to connect to the server through the socket file, but they should not be able to delete the file and compromise the ability of other users to connect to the server.

13.1.1   How to Steal Data

The following description provides a brief example that illustrates why security is important. It underscores the fact that you don't want other users to have direct access to the MySQL data directory.

The MySQL server provides a flexible privilege system implemented by means of the grant tables in the `mysql` database. You set up the contents of these tables to permit or deny database access to clients, which provides security against unauthorized network access to the data. However, setting up good security for network access to your databases is an exercise in futility if other users on the server host have direct access to the contents of the data directory. Unless you know that you are the only person who ever logs in on the MySQL server host, you must be concerned about the possibility of other people on that machine gaining access to the data directory.

Obviously you don't want other users on the server host to have direct write access to data directory files, because then they can stomp all over your status files or database tables. But direct read access is just as dangerous. If a table's files can be read, it is trivial to steal the files and to get MySQL itself to show you the contents of the table. How? Like this:

1. Install your own rogue MySQL server on the server host, but with a port, socket file, and data directory that differ from those used by the official server.

2. Run `mysql_install_db` to initialize your data directory. This action gives you full access to your server as the MySQL `root` user, and sets up a `test` database that can serve as a convenient repository for stolen tables.

3. Access the data directory of the server you want to attack, copying the files corresponding to the table or tables that you want to steal into the `test` directory under your own server's data directory. This action requires only read access to the targeted data directory.

4. Start your rogue server. Presto! Its `test` database now contains copies of the stolen tables, which you can access at will. `SHOW TABLES FROM test` shows which tables you have a copy of, and `SELECT *` shows the entire contents of any of them.

5. To be really nasty, open up the permissions on the anonymous user accounts for your server so anyone can connect to the server from any host to access your `test` database. That effectively publishes the stolen tables to the world.

Think about this scenario for a moment, then reverse the perspective. Do you want someone to do that to you? Of course not. So protect yourself using the instructions in the following discussion.

13.1.2   Securing Your MySQL Installation

The procedure described here shows how to set up ownerships and access modes for the directories and files that make up your MySQL installation. The instructions here use `mysql` for both the user and group names that are to be given ownership of the installation. (Whatever the user is, it should be something other than `root`, for reasons discussed in Section 12.2.1.1, "Running the Server Using an Unprivileged Login Account.") The instructions also assume that all parts of your MySQL installation are located under a single base directory, rather than scattered throughout your filesystem. In the examples, the installation base directory is `/usr/local/mysql` and the data directory is located under that with a pathname of `/usr/local/mysql/data`.

After going through the procedure, I'll describe how to handle some nonstandard types of installation layouts. Your system layout may vary from any of those described here, but you should be able to adapt the general principles appropriately. Change the names and pathnames as necessary for your own system. If you run multiple servers, you should perform the procedure for each one.

You can determine whether your data directory contains insecure files or directories by executing `ls -la`. Look for files or directories that have the "group" or "other" permissions turned on. Here's a listing of a data directory that is insecure, as are some of the database directories within it:

```
% ls -la /usr/local/mysql/data
total 10148
drwxrwxr-x   11 mysql   wheel     1024 May  8 12:20 .
drwxr-xr-x   22 root    wheel      512 May  8 13:31 ..
drwx------    2 mysql   mysql      512 Apr 16 15:57 menagerie
drwxrwxr-x    2 mysql   wheel      512 Jun 25  1998 mysql
drwx------    7 mysql   mysql     1024 May  7 10:45 sampdb
drwxrwxr-x    2 mysql   wheel     1536 Jun 25  1998 test
drwx------    2 mysql   mysql     1024 May  8 18:43 tmp
```

'`.`' represents the directory being listed; that is, `/usr/local/mysql/data`. '`..`' represents the parent directory, `/usr/local/mysql`. Some of the database directories have the proper permissions: `drwx------` enables read, write, and execute access to the owner, but no access to anyone else. But other directories have an overly permissive access mode: `drwxrwxr-x` enables read and execute access to all other users, even those outside of the `mysql` group. The situation shown in this example is one that resulted over time, starting with a (very) old MySQL installation that was progressively upgraded to successive newer versions. The less-restrictive permissions were created by older MySQL servers that were less stringent than more recent servers about setting permissions. (You can see that the more restrictive database directories, `menagerie`, `sampdb`, and `tmp`, all have more recent dates.) Current MySQL servers set the permissions on database directories that they create to be accessible only to the account they run as.

You can also use `ls -la` to check the base directory of the MySQL installation, `/usr/local/mysql`. For example, you might get a result something like this:

```
% ls -la /usr/local/mysql
total 44
drwxrwxr-x   13 mysql   mysql    1024 May  7 10:45 .
drwxr-xr-x   24 root    wheel    1024 May  1 12:54 ..
drwxr-xr-x    2 mysql   mysql    1024 Jul 16 20:58 bin
drwxrwxr-x   12 mysql   wheel    1024 May  8 12:20 data
drwxr-xr-x    3 mysql   mysql     512 May  7 10:45 etc
drwxr-xr-x    3 mysql   mysql     512 May  7 10:45 include
drwxr-xr-x    3 mysql   mysql     512 May  7 10:45 lib
drwxr-xr-x    3 mysql   mysql     512 May  7 10:45 man
drwxr-xr-x    6 mysql   mysql    1024 May  7 10:45 mysql-test
drwxr-xr-x    3 mysql   mysql     512 May  7 10:45 scripts
drwxr-xr-x    3 mysql   mysql     512 May  7 10:45 share
drwxr-xr-x    7 mysql   mysql    1024 May  7 10:45 support-files
```

Use the following procedure to lock down everything to be accessible only to the `mysql` account, except for those parts of the installation that other users have a legitimate need to access. For example, the `data` directory permissions and ownership need to be made more restrictive, as already indicated.

Note that some parts of this procedure *do not apply* if your installation is such that the MySQL server and client programs are installed in general system directories along with other non-MySQL programs. (This is typical if you install MySQL using RPM packages.) For example, the server might be located in /usr/sbin and the clients in /usr/bin. In that case, the ownership and mode of the MySQL programs should be set the same as other programs in those directories.

1. If the MySQL server is running, tell it to stop:

   ```
   % mysqladmin -p -u root shutdown
   ```

2. Set the owner and group name assignments of the entire MySQL installation to those of the MySQL administrative account using the following commands, which you must execute as `root`:

   ```
   # chown -R mysql /usr/local/mysql
   # chgrp -R mysql /usr/local/mysql
   ```

   Another popular approach is to make everything owned by `root` except the data directory, which you can accomplish like this:

   ```
   # chown -R root /usr/local/mysql
   # chgrp -R mysql /usr/local/mysql
   # chown -R mysql /usr/local/mysql/data
   # chgrp -R mysql /usr/local/mysql/data
   ```

   If you set the general ownership to `root`, you'll need to perform most of the following steps as `root`. Otherwise, you can perform them as `mysql`.

3. For the base directory and any of its subdirectories that clients should be able to access, change their mode so `mysql` has full access and everyone else has only read and execute permission. That may be how they are set already, but if not, change them. For example, the base directory can be set using either of the following commands:

```
% chmod 755 /usr/local/mysql
% chmod u=rwx,go=rx /usr/local/mysql
```

Similarly, the `bin` directory that contains the client programs can be set with either of these commands:

```
% chmod 755 /usr/local/mysql/bin
% chmod u=rwx,go=rx /usr/local/mysql/bin
```

4. Change the mode of your data directory and all files and directories under it so they are private to `mysql`:

```
% chmod -R go-rwx /usr/local/mysql/data
```

That prevents login accounts other than the one used for running the server from directly accessing the contents of your data directory.

After using the preceding instructions, your MySQL installation base directory has ownerships and permissions that look something like this:

```
% ls -la /usr/local/mysql
total 44
drwxr-xr-x   13 mysql   mysql      1024 May  7 10:45 .
drwxr-xr-x   24 root    wheel      1024 May  1 12:54 ..
drwxr-xr-x    2 mysql   mysql      1024 Jul 16 20:58 bin
drwx------   12 mysql   mysql      1024 May  8 12:20 data
drwxr-xr-x    3 mysql   mysql       512 May  7 10:45 include
drwxr-xr-x    3 mysql   mysql       512 May  7 10:45 lib
drwxr-xr-x    3 mysql   mysql       512 May  7 10:45 man
drwxr-xr-x    6 mysql   mysql      1024 May  7 10:45 mysql-test
drwxr-xr-x    3 mysql   mysql       512 May  7 10:45 scripts
drwxr-xr-x    3 mysql   mysql       512 May  7 10:45 share
drwxr-xr-x    7 mysql   mysql      1024 May  7 10:45 support-files
```

As shown, everything now is owned by `mysql`, with a group ownership of `mysql`. The exception is for '..', which refers to the parent directory of `/usr/local/mysql`. That directory is owned by and modifiable only by `root`, which is good. You don't want unprivileged users to be able to change things in the directory containing your installation.

The data directory under the base directory has even more restrictive permissions:

```
% ls -la /usr/local/mysql/data
total 10148
drwx------   11 mysql   mysql      1024 May  8 12:20 .
drwxr-xr-x   22 mysql   mysql       512 May  8 13:31 ..
```

```
drwx------    2 mysql  mysql      512 Apr 16 15:57 menagerie
drwx------    2 mysql  mysql      512 Jun 25  1998 mysql
drwx------    7 mysql  mysql     1024 May  7 10:45 sampdb
drwx------    2 mysql  mysql     1536 Jun 25  1998 test
drwx------    2 mysql  mysql     1024 May  8 18:43 tmp
```

Here, the '..' line refers to the parent of the data directory; that is, the MySQL base directory.

An exception to the mysql-only policy of access to the data directory may be necessary for particular files. For example, if you use the data directory as the location for the Unix socket file, it will be necessary to open up access to the directory a little. Otherwise, client programs won't be able to connect to the server through the socket. Alternatively, use a different location for the Unix socket file, such as the base directory. The same principle applies to other files that programs other than mysqld have a legitimate need to access, such as option files that contain global client parameters. (For information about implementing these approaches, see Section 13.1.2.1, "Securing the Unix Socket File.")

As stated earlier, the preceding procedure assumes that all MySQL-related files are located under a single base directory. If that's not true, you'll need to locate each MySQL-related directory and perform the appropriate operations on each of them. For example, if your data directory is located at /var/mysql/data rather than under /usr/local/mysql, you'll need to issue these commands to change the ownership of your installation properly:

```
# chown -R mysql /usr/local/mysql
# chgrp -R mysql /usr/local/mysql
# chown -R mysql /var/mysql/data
# chgrp -R mysql /var/mysql/data
```

Or, suppose that you create an innodb directory under the MySQL installation directory in which to keep InnoDB-related files. By default, these files are placed in the data directory. If you put them in your innodb directory instead, set that directory to have the same access mode as the data directory. This principle also applies if you relocate other files that normally would be placed in the data directory, such as log files.

Another complication occurs if some of the directories under the installation root are really symbolic links that point elsewhere. If your versions of chown and chgrp don't follow symlinks, track down the links and apply the ownership changes in the locations to which the links point. One way to do this is to use find:

```
# find /usr/local/mysql -follow -print | xargs chown mysql
# find /usr/local/mysql -follow -print | xargs chgrp mysql
```

Similar considerations apply to changing access modes. For example, if there are symbolic links under your data directory and chmod doesn't follow them, use this command instead:

```
# find /usr/local/mysql/data -follow -print | xargs chmod go-rwx
```

Because the ownership and permissions of the data directory contents at this point are set to enable access only for the mysql login user, you should make sure the server always runs as `mysql` from now on. An easy way to ensure this is to specify the user in the `[mysqld]` section of the `/etc/my.cnf` file or other `my.cnf` file that the server reads when it starts:

```
[mysqld]
user=mysql
```

That way, the server runs as `mysql` whether you start it while logged in as `root` or as `mysql`. For additional information on running the server using a specific login account, see Section 12.2.1.1, "Running the Server Using an Unprivileged Login Account."

After securing your MySQL installation, restart the server.

13.1.2.1 Securing the Unix Socket File

The server uses a Unix domain socket file for connections by clients to `localhost`. The socket file normally is publicly accessible so client programs can use it. However, it should not be located in a directory where arbitrary clients have delete permission. For example, it's common for the socket file to be created in the `/tmp` directory, but on some Unix systems, that directory has permissions that enable users to delete files other than their own. That means any user can remove the socket file and as a result prevent client programs from establishing `localhost` connections to the server until the server is restarted to re-create the socket file. It's better if the `/tmp` directory has its "sticky bit" set, so that even if anyone can create files in the directory, users can remove only their own files. You can set the sticky bit for the directory by executing the following command as `root`:

```
# chmod +t /tmp
```

Some installations place the socket file in the data directory, which leads to a problem if you make the data directory private to `mysql`: No client program can access the socket file, unless it is run by `root` or `mysql`. In this case, one option is to open up the data directory slightly. To enable client programs to access the socket file without providing full read access to the data directory, use this command:

```
% chmod go+x /usr/local/mysql/data
```

To avoid opening up the data directory this way, another approach is to change the location in which the server creates the socket file. For example, you might configure MySQL to create the file in the base directory by specifying a location of `/usr/local/mysql/mysql.sock`. Either specify the location in a global option file, or recompile from source to build in the location as the default. If you use an option file, be sure to specify the location both for the server and for clients:

```
[mysqld]
socket=/usr/local/mysql/mysql.sock

[client]
socket=/usr/local/mysql/mysql.sock
```

Recompiling is more work, but is a more complete solution because using an option file works only for client programs that check option files. (All the standard MySQL clients do, but third-party programs may not.) By recompiling, the new socket location becomes the default known by the client library; any program that uses the client library thus gets the new location as its own default, whether or not it uses option files.

13.1.2.2   Securing Option Files

Option files are a potential point of compromise to the extent that they contain options that should not be exposed:

- Don't make an option file publicly readable if it contains sensitive information such as MySQL account names or passwords.

- `/etc/my.cnf` normally is publicly readable because it's a common location in which to specify global client options. Do not use it for server options such as replication passwords.

- Each user-specific `.my.cnf` option file should be owned by and accessible only by the user in whose home directory the file appears. To do this for your own file, execute the following command in your home directory:

  ```
  % chmod u=rw,go-rwx .my.cnf
  ```

- Other option files need to have their access mode set depending on what you use them for.

One way to guard against user-specific option files having improper mode or ownership is to run a program that looks for a `.my.cnf` file in each user's home directory and corrects any problems. The following Perl script, `chk_mysql_opt_files.pl`, does this:

```perl
#!/usr/bin/perl
# chk_mysql_opt_files.pl - check user-specific .my.cnf files and make sure
# the ownership and mode is correct. Each file should be owned by the
# user in whose home directory the file is found. The mode should
# have the "group" and "other" permissions turned off.

# This script must be run as root.  Execute it with your password file as
# input.  If you have an /etc/passwd file, run it like this:
# chk_mysql_opt_file.pl /etc/passwd

use strict;
use warnings;

while (<>)
{
  next if /^#/ || /^\s*$/;           # skip comments, blank lines
  my ($uid, $home) = (split (/:/, $_))[2,5];
  my $cnf_file = "$home/.my.cnf";
  next unless -f $cnf_file;          # is there a .my.cnf file?
  if ((stat ($cnf_file))[4] != $uid) # test ownership
```

```
{
  warn "Changing ownership of $cnf_file to $uid\n";
  chown ($uid, (stat ($cnf_file))[5], $cnf_file);
}
my $mode = (stat ($cnf_file))[2];
if ($mode & 077)                        # test group/other access bits
{
  warn sprintf ("Changing mode of %s from %o to %o\n",
                $cnf_file, $mode, $mode & ~077);
  chmod ($mode & ~077, $cnf_file);
}
}
```

You can find `chk_mysql_opt_files.pl` in the `admin` directory of the `sampdb` distribution. You must run this script as `root` so it can change the mode and ownership of files owned by other users. To execute the script automatically, set it up as a nightly `cron` job run by `root`.

13.2   Managing MySQL User Accounts

A MySQL administrator must know how to set up accounts, by specifying which users can connect to the server, where they can connect from, and what they are permitted to do while connected. MySQL stores this information in the grant tables in the `mysql` database, which are manipulated by these account-management SQL statements:

- `CREATE USER`, `DROP USER`, and `RENAME USER` create, remove, and rename MySQL accounts.
- `GRANT` specifies account privileges (and creates accounts if they do not exist).
- `REVOKE` removes privileges from MySQL accounts.
- `SET PASSWORD` assigns passwords to accounts.
- `SHOW GRANTS` displays the privileges held by accounts.

Those statements affect the grant tables in the `mysql` database shown in Table 13.1.

Table 13.1   **MySQL Grant Tables**

Grant Table	Contents
user	Users who can connect to the server and their global privileges
db	Database privileges
tables_priv	Table privileges
columns_priv	Column privileges
procs_priv	Stored-routine privileges
proxies_priv	Proxy user privileges

Another grant table, `host`, is not affected by account-management statements, is obsolete, and is not discussed here.

When you issue a `CREATE USER` statement, you specify an account name and optionally authentication information (a password or authentication method), and the server creates a row for the account in the `user` table. This is also occurs for `GRANT` if the account does not already exist. For `GRANT`, if the statement specifies any global privileges (administrative privileges or privileges that apply to all databases), those are recorded in the `user` table, too. If `GRANT` specifies privileges that are specific to a given database, table, table column, or stored routine, they are recorded in the `db`, `tables_priv`, `columns_priv`, or `procs_priv` tables. Grants of the `PROXY` privilege are recorded in the `proxies_priv` table. `REVOKE` removes privileges from the grant tables, and `DROP USER` removes all rows associated with the account from the tables.

The following sections describe how to create and remove MySQL user accounts, how to grant and revoke privileges, and how to change passwords or reset lost passwords. It is also possible to manipulate the contents of the grant tables directly by issuing SQL statements like `INSERT` and `UPDATE`. However, account-management statements such as `CREATE USER` and `GRANT` are more convenient to work with conceptually because you describe the access modifications that you want to perform and the server maps your requests onto the proper grant table changes automatically. Nevertheless, although it's easier to use `CREATE USER` and `GRANT` than to modify the grant tables directly, I advise that you read the sections beginning with Section 13.3, "Grant Table Structure and Contents." The discussion there describes the grant tables in more detail, to help you understand how they work "underneath" the level of the account-management statements, and how the server uses their contents when clients attempt to connect or execute SQL statements.

> **Note**
>
> Some versions of MySQL introduce new grant tables or columns, which changes their structure. The first time you install MySQL on a machine, the installation procedure creates the grant tables with the structure that is current for the version that you install. If you upgrade MySQL to a newer version, run `mysql_upgrade` to update the grant tables with any modifications that have been made since your current version.
>
> By default, `mysql_upgrade` connects to the local server as the MySQL `root` user, so invoke it with the `root` password as follows, then restart the server:
>
> ```
> % mysql_upgrade --password=rootpass
> ```

13.2.1 High-Level MySQL Account Management

Three statements perform high-level operations on MySQL accounts:

- `CREATE USER` creates a new account and optionally assigns a password or authentication method:

  ```
  CREATE USER account [auth_info];
  ```

  `CREATE USER` grants no privileges; that is done with `GRANT`.

- DROP USER removes an existing account and any privileges associated with it:

  ```
  DROP USER account;
  ```

  DROP USER does not drop any databases or objects within databases that were accessible to the dropped account.

- RENAME USER changes the name of an existing account:

  ```
  RENAME USER from_account TO to_account;
  ```

All three statements can be used if you have the global CREATE USER privilege. Otherwise, you must have the INSERT, DELETE, or UPDATE privilege for the mysql database to use CREATE USER, DROP USER, or RENAME USER, respectively.

To set up a new account, it's generally possible to figure out the kind of CREATE USER statement to issue by asking these questions:

- What is the user's name?

- From which host or hosts should the user be able to connect?

- How does the user authenticate?

The answers to the first two questions determine the *account* value to use in the statement. Account names consist of a username and hostname. For the rules that govern their syntax, see Section 13.2.1.1, "Specifying Account Names."

The answer to the third question depends on whether you want to assign the account a password or specify that the server should use some other method to authenticate the user. For more information about authentication, see Section 13.2.1.3, "Specifying How an Account Authenticates."

13.2.1.1   Specifying Account Names

The *account* value in account-management statements such as CREATE USER consists of a username and hostname in 'user_name'@'host_name' format: In MySQL, you specify not only who can connect but from where. This enables you to set up separate accounts for two users who have the same name but that connect from different locations. MySQL lets you distinguish between them and assign privileges to each one independent of the other. The server stores the *user_name* and *host_name* values in the User and Host columns of the user table row for the account, and in any other grant table rows associated with the account.

An account name can also be specified as CURRENT_USER or CURRENT_USER(), which stands for the account you are using in your current session.

Your username in MySQL is just a name that you use to identify yourself when you connect to the server. The name has no necessary connection to your Unix or Windows login name. On Unix, client programs use your login name as your MySQL username by default if you don't specify a name explicitly, but that's just a convention. There also is nothing special about the name root that is used for the MySQL superuser that can do anything. You could just as well change this name to `superduper` in the grant tables, then connect as `superduper` to perform operations that require superuser privileges.

By choosing an *account* value appropriately, you can enable a user to connect from as specific or broad a set of hosts as you like. At one extreme, you can limit access to a single host if you know a user will connect only from that host:

```
CREATE USER 'boris'@'localhost' IDENTIFIED BY 'frost';
CREATE USER 'fred'@'ares.mars.net' IDENTIFIED BY 'steam';
```

Keep in mind that the hostname part is the host *from which* the client will be connecting. It is not the server host *to which* the client will connect (unless they happen to be the same).

Enabling a user to connect only from a single host is the strictest form of access you can allow. At the other extreme, you might have a user who travels a lot and must be able to connect from hosts all over the world. If the user's name is `max`, you can enable him to connect from anywhere like this:

```
CREATE USER 'max'@'%' IDENTIFIED BY 'mist';
```

The '`%`' character functions as a wildcard with the same meaning as in a `LIKE` pattern match. Thus, as a hostname specifier, `%` means "any host." This is the easiest way to set up a user, but it's also the least secure. (Using `%` also may result in occasional head scratching on your part, for reasons described in Section 13.4.4, "A Privilege Puzzle.")

The other `LIKE` wildcard character ('`_`') can be used in host values to match any single character. To specify a literal '`%`' or '`_`' wildcard character, precede it by a backslash.

To take a middle ground, you can enable a user to connect from a limited set of hosts. For example, to enable `mary` to connect from any host in the `example.com` domain, use a host specifier of `%.example.com`:

```
CREATE USER 'mary'@'%.example.com' IDENTIFIED BY 'fog';
```

The host part of the *account* value can be given using an IPv4 or IPv6 address rather than a hostname if you like. For an IPv4 host value, you can specify a literal IP address, an address that contains pattern characters, or an IP address with a netmask that indicates which bits to use for the network number:

```
CREATE USER 'joe'@'192.168.128.3' IDENTIFIED BY 'water';
CREATE USER 'ardis'@'192.168.128.%' IDENTIFIED BY 'snow';
CREATE USER 'rex'@'192.168.128.0/255.255.255.0' IDENTIFIED BY 'ice';
```

The first of these statements indicates a specific single address, `192.168.128.3`, from which the user can connect. The second specifies an IP pattern for the `192.168.128` Class C subnet. In the third statement, `192.168.128.0/255.255.255.0` specifies a netmask that has the first 24 bits turned on. It matches any host with `192.168.128` in the first 24 bits of its IP address. Netmask values must be `255.0.0.0`, `255.255.0.0`, `255.255.255.0`, or `255.255.255.255`.

Similar rules apply for IPv6 host values except that netmask notation is not supported.

Using a hostname of `localhost` in an account name enables a user to connect to the server from the local host in a number of ways:

- On Unix, the user can connect by specifying a host value of `localhost`, `127.0.0.1`, or `::1`. The `localhost` connection is made using the Unix socket file. `127.0.0.1` or `::1` cause a TCP/IP connection to be made using the local host's loopback IPv4 or IPv6 interface.

- On Windows, the user can connect by specifying a host value of `localhost`, `127.0.0.1`, or `::1`. These connections are made using TCP/IP, except that if the server supports shared-memory connections, a connection to `localhost` is made using shared memory by default. If the server supports named-pipe connections, the user can connect through the pipe by specifying a hostname of "`.`" (period).

If the username or hostname part of an *account* value can be used as an unquoted identifier, you need not quote it. If it contains any special characters such as '`-`' or '`%`', you must quote it. For example, in `boris@localhost`, both parts are legal without quotes. However, it is always safe to use quotes, and the examples in this book do so as a rule. Usernames and hostnames can be quoted either with string quoting characters or identifier quoting characters. Quote the username and hostname separately: Use `'boris'@'localhost'`, not `'boris@localhost'`.

If you give no hostname part at all in an account specifier, it's the same as using a host part of `%`. Thus, `'max'` and `'max'@'%'` are equivalent *account* values. This means that if you intend to specify an account of `'boris'@'localhost'` but mistakenly write `'boris@localhost'` instead, MySQL accepts it as legal. What happens is that MySQL interprets `'boris@localhost'` as containing only a user part and adds the default host part of `%` to it, resulting in an effective account name of `'boris@localhost'@'%'`. To avoid this, be sure to quote the user and host parts of account names separately.

13.2.1.2 Matching Host Values in Account Names to DNS

It's common to have problems connecting from the server host if you use the server's hostname rather than `localhost`. This can occur due to a mismatch between the way the name is specified in the grant tables and the way your DNS name resolver reports the name to programs. Suppose that the server host's fully qualified name is `cobra.example.com`. If the resolver reports an unqualified name, such as `cobra`, but the grant tables contain rows with the fully qualified name (or vice versa), this mismatch will occur.

To determine if this is happening on your system, try connecting to the local server using a `-h` option that specifies the name of your host:

```
% mysql -h cobra.example.com
```

Then look in the server's general log file. How does the server write the hostname there when it reports the connection attempt? Is the name in unqualified or fully qualified form? That tells you how you'll need to specify the hostname part when you use it in account names.

Similar matching problems can occur for an account specified using an IP value for the host part if DNS returns that value but in differing format. For example, if DNS returns an IP value of `192.168.10.14` for a given host, that matches accounts specified using a host part of `192.168.10.14` or `192.168.10.%`, but not accounts specified using `192.168.010.14` or `192.168.010.%`. If in doubt, run some DNS lookups to verify how your resolver returns values, and use the same format in account names.

13.2.1.3   Specifying How an Account Authenticates

`CREATE USER` syntax enables you to specify how an account authenticates by means of an optional *auth_info* clause:

```
CREATE USER account [auth_info]
```

The *auth_info* clause is also part of `GRANT` syntax; see Section 13.2.2, "Granting Privileges."

There are two forms the *auth_info* clause can take:

- To indicate that an account authenticates with a password, use this syntax:

  ```
  IDENTIFIED BY [PASSWORD] 'password'
  ```

  For example:

  ```
  CREATE USER 'pradeep'@'localhost' IDENTIFIED BY 'aurum';
  ```

  In this case, MySQL manages the password itself and stores it in the `Password` column of the `user` row for the account, using a hashed format identical to that produced by the `PASSWORD()` function. Normally, you omit the `PASSWORD` keyword and specify the literal password in plain text. MySQL converts the value as given to hashed format before storing it. In the special case that you want to specify the password in already hashed format, precede the value with the keyword `PASSWORD`. This might be the case if you are using the output of `SHOW GRANTS` to re-create an account. (`SHOW GRANTS` displays the hashed password value, not the literal password.)

- To specify a different authentication method, use the following syntax, naming an authentication plugin that implements the desired method and an optional string that provides extra information to the plugin:

  ```
  IDENTIFIED WITH auth_plugin [AS 'auth_string']
  ```

  For example:

  ```
  CREATE USER 'felipe'@'localhost' IDENTIFIED BY 'myplugin';
  ```

  In this case, MySQL does not manage a password directly but expects the plugin to report at connection time whether the user authenticates properly. For details, see Section 13.2.7, "Pluggable Authentication and Proxy Users." Currently, naming an authentication plugin is less common than specifying a password because authentication plugins were introduced relatively recently (in MySQL 5.5.7). Over time, authentication plugins should gain in popularity because they permit implementation of authentication methods that use credentials other than the type of passwords managed internally by MySQL itself. For example, an authentication plugin might access operating system passwords or interface with an external authentication server that implements a single sign-on mechanism.

When the server creates an account, clients can use it to connect to the server without authenticating if you don't specify an IDENTIFIED BY clause with a nonempty password or an IDENTIFIED WITH clause. This is insecure and should be avoided.

13.2.2   Granting Privileges

To give access privileges to an account, use the GRANT statement, which looks like this:

```
GRANT privileges [(columns)]
  ON what
  TO account [auth_info]
  [REQUIRE encryption requirements]
  [WITH grant or resource management options];
```

If the named account exists, GRANT modifies its privileges. If the account does not exist, GRANT creates it with the given privileges. To avoid the possibility of GRANT creating a new account for which no authentication is required (and thus is insecure), set the sql_mode system variable to enable the NO_AUTO_CREATE_USER SQL mode. This prevents GRANT from creating the account unless authentication information is provided.

Several of the clauses are optional and need not be specified at all. In general, you'll most commonly use the following parts:

- *privileges* indicates the privileges to assign to the account. For example, the SELECT privilege enables a user to issue SELECT statements and the SHUTDOWN privilege enables the user to shut down the server. Multiple privileges can be named, separated by commas.

- *columns* indicates the columns to which a privilege applies, separated by commas and listed within parentheses. This is optional, and used only to set up column-specific privileges. The column list must follow the name of *each* privilege to which it applies.

- *what* indicates the level at which the privileges apply. The most powerful level is the global level, for which any given privilege applies to all databases and all tables. Global privileges can be thought of as superuser privileges. Privileges also can be made database-specific, table-specific, column-specific (if you specify a *columns* clause), or routine-specific.

- *account* indicates which account is being granted the privileges. The *account* format is '*user_name*'@'*host_name*', as described in Section 13.2.1.1, "Specifying Account Names."

The *auth_info*, REQUIRE, and WITH clauses are optional:

- *auth_info* indicates the password or authentication method for the account. This is optional and is unnecessary if authentication information has already been specified for the account (for example, with CREATE USER). If present, the *auth_info* clause has the same syntax as for CREATE USER; see Section 13.2.1.3, "Specifying How an Account Authenticates." Any password specified for an existing account replaces its current password.

- Use a REQUIRE clause to set up accounts that must connect using secure SSL connections.

- Use a WITH clause to grant the GRANT OPTION privilege that enables the account to give its own privileges to other users. WITH also is used to specify resource management options that enable you to place limits on how many connections or statements an account can use per hour. These options help you prevent the account from hogging the server.

To specify what an account can do, it's generally possible to figure out the kind of GRANT statement to issue by asking these questions:

- What type of access should the account be given? That is, what level of privileges should the user have, and what should they apply to?

- Are secure connections required?

- Should the user be permitted to administer privileges?

- Should the user's resource consumption be limited?

The following sections show how to answer these questions and provide examples that illustrate how to use the clauses of the GRANT statement.

13.2.2.1   Defining the Privileges an Account Has

There are many privileges you can grant to an account. These can be grouped into two categories, administrative privileges and object privileges, described shortly. There are also two special privilege specifiers. ALL (or ALL PRIVILEGES) means "all privileges" (except GRANT OPTION). USAGE means "no privileges." It's used to change something about an account other than its privileges, such as its resource limits or whether it requires SSL. To supplement the descriptions here, see also Section 13.3, "Grant Table Structure and Contents," which discusses the privileges in terms of their relationship to the underlying grant tables.

The following privileges apply to administrative operations that control the operation of the server or a user's ability to grant privileges. Typically, you grant these sparingly because they enable users to affect server operation. For example, the SHUTDOWN privilege is one you should not hand out on an everyday basis.

- CREATE USER

    Enables you to use the CREATE USER, DROP USER, RENAME USER, and REVOKE ALL PRIVILEGES statements.

- FILE

Enables you to tell the server to read or write files on the server host. To keep the use of this privilege within certain bounds, the server takes certain precautions:

- You can access only files that are world-readable, and thus likely not to be considered protected in any way.

- Any file that you want to write must not already exist. This prevents you from coercing the server into overwriting important files, such as /etc/passwd, or database files in a database belonging to someone else. (Were this restriction not enforced, you could completely replace the contents of the grant tables in the mysql database, for example.)

Despite these precautions by the server, do not grant this privilege without just cause; it can be extremely dangerous, as discussed in Section 13.2.6, "Avoiding Access-Control Risks." If you do grant the FILE privilege, be sure not to run the server as the root login user on Unix, because root can create new files anywhere in the filesystem. Running the server from an ordinary login account ensures that it can create files only in directories accessible to that account. See also Section 12.2.1.1, "Running the Server Using an Unprivileged Login Account."

- GRANT OPTION

Enables you to grant other users the privileges you have yourself, including the GRANT OPTION privilege.

- PROCESS

The MySQL server is multi-threaded, which enables it to service multiple client connections simultaneously. These threads may be thought of as processes running within the server. The PROCESS privilege enables you to use the SHOW PROCESSLIST statement or the mysqladmin processlist command to view information about activities that are currently executing. This privilege gives you the ability to see all activities, even those associated with other users. You can always see your own activities, even without the PROCESS privilege.

- PROXY

Enables you to acquire the privileges of another user. In other words, you can act as a proxy for another user and do anything that user can do.

- RELOAD

Enables you to perform administrative server operations. With the RELOAD privilege, you have the ability to issue statements such as FLUSH and RESET. You can also perform the following mysqladmin commands: reload, refresh, flush-hosts, flush-logs, flush-privileges, flush-status, flush-tables, and flush-threads.

- REPLICATION CLIENT

Enables you to inquire about the location and status of master and slave servers using the SHOW MASTER STATUS and SHOW SLAVE STATUS statements.

- REPLICATION SLAVE

  Enables a client to connect to a master server and request slave server updates, and to use the SHOW SLAVE HOSTS and SHOW BINLOG EVENTS statements. This privilege must be granted to slave server accounts that are used to connect to the master.

- SHOW DATABASES

  Enables you to see all database names by issuing the SHOW DATABASES statement. If you don't have this privilege, you can see a given database name only if you have some privilege for it. However, this ability is conveyed by *any* global privilege that applies to databases, which includes the CREATE TEMPORARY TABLES and LOCK TABLES privileges that commonly are granted globally. To permit the SHOW DATABASES statement only to users who have the SHOW DATABASES privilege, start the server with the --skip-show-database option.

- SHUTDOWN

  Enables you to shut down the server, for example, with the mysqladmin shutdown command.

- SUPER

  Enables you to kill server processes with the KILL statement or the mysqladmin kill command. This privilege gives you the ability to kill any process, even those associated with other users. You can always kill your own processes, even without the SUPER privilege.

  Other statements enabled by this privilege are SET for modifying global system variables and global transaction characteristics, CHANGE MASTER, PURGE BINARY LOGS, SHOW MASTER STATUS, SHOW SLAVE STATUS, START SLAVE, and STOP SLAVE. SUPER also enables you to specify any account in the DEFINER clause of statements that define views or stored programs, and to perform DES decryption with the DES_DECRYPT() function based on the keys stored in the DES key file.

  The SUPER privilege enables the use of mysqladmin debug, and it overrides any max_connections setting when connecting to the server, so that you can access the connection slot that the server reserves for administrative connections even when all the regular slots are taken.

The following privileges apply to operations on objects such as databases, tables, and stored routines. They control access to data managed by the server.

- ALTER

  Enables you to use the ALTER TABLE statement, although you might also need additional privileges, depending on what you want to do with the table.

- ALTER ROUTINE

  Enables you to alter or drop stored functions and procedures.

- CREATE

  Enables you to create databases and tables. This privilege does not enable you to create indexes on a table, except those defined initially in its CREATE TABLE statement.

- CREATE ROUTINE

  Enables you to create stored functions and procedures.

- CREATE TABLESPACE

  Enables you to create, drop, or alter tablespaces.

- CREATE TEMPORARY TABLES

  Enables you to create temporary tables with the CREATE TEMPORARY TABLE statement.

- CREATE VIEW

  Enables you to create views.

- DELETE

  Enables you to remove rows from tables.

- DROP

  Enables you to drop databases and tables. This privilege does not enable you to drop indexes.

- EVENT

  Enables you to manipulate event scheduler events.

- EXECUTE

  Enables you to execute stored functions and procedures.

- INDEX

  Enables you to create or drop indexes from tables, assign indexes to key caches, and preload indexes into key caches.

- INSERT

  Enables you to insert rows into tables.

- LOCK TABLES

  Enables you to lock tables by issuing explicit LOCK TABLES statements. This privilege applies only to tables for which you also have the SELECT privilege, but enables you to place read or write locks, not just read locks. The privilege does not apply to locks that are acquired implicitly on your behalf by the server during the process of statement execution. Such locks are set and released automatically regardless of your LOCK TABLES privilege setting.

- REFERENCES

  This privilege is unused.

- SELECT

  Enables you to retrieve data from tables using SELECT statements. This privilege is unnecessary for SELECT statements such as SELECT NOW() or SELECT 4/2, which do nothing more than evaluate expressions and involve no tables.

- SHOW VIEW

  Enables use of the SHOW CREATE VIEW statement to see view definitions.

- TRIGGER

  Enables you to add and drop triggers.

- UPDATE

  Enables you to modify rows in tables.

Some operations require a combination of privileges. For example, REPLACE may implicitly cause a DELETE followed by an INSERT, so it requires both the DELETE and INSERT privileges. To grant a privilege, you must have that privilege yourself, and you must have the GRANT OPTION privilege.

You can grant privileges at different levels, from global to very specific. This is controlled by the ON clause specifier, as shown in Table 13.2. For the table-level specifiers, you can specify a (columns) clause following a privilege name to grant that privilege at the column level. A later example demonstrates this syntax.

Table 13.2   **Privilege-Level Specifiers**

Privilege Specifier	Level at Which Privileges Apply
ON *.*	Global privileges: all databases, all objects in databases
ON *	Database-level privileges for the default database; error if there is no default database
ON db_name.*	Database privileges: all objects in the named database
ON db_name.tbl_name	Table privileges: all columns in the named table
ON tbl_name	Table privileges: all columns in the named table in the default database
ON db_name.routine_name	Privileges for the named routine in the named database
ON account	Proxy privilege: account is the proxied user

To specify explicitly the type of object to which the privileges apply if there is an ambiguity, you can include a TABLE, FUNCTION, or PROCEDURE keyword (for example, ON TABLE mydb.mytbl or ON FUNCTION mydb.myfunc).

The USAGE privilege is specified only at the global level (that is, with ON *.*).

The ALL (or ALL PRIVILEGES) specifier grants all privileges that are available at a given level. For example, at the global level, ALL grants all privileges. At the table level, it grants only privileges that apply to tables. ALL can be used only when granting global, database, table, or routine privileges. For column privileges, you must name each privilege that you want to grant. "All privileges" actually means "all with one exception," the GRANT OPTION privilege that is required for GRANT and REVOKE operations.

Global privileges are the most powerful because they apply to any database. To create a super-user account that can do anything, including being able to grant privileges to other users, issue these statements:

```
CREATE USER 'ethel'@'localhost' IDENTIFIED BY 'coffee';
GRANT ALL ON *.* TO 'ethel'@'localhost' WITH GRANT OPTION;
```

The ON *.* clause means "all databases and all objects in them." As a safety precaution, the account created in the example can connect only from the local host. Limiting the hosts from which a superuser can connect is a good idea because it restricts the set of hosts from which password-cracking attempts can be mounted.

Administrative privileges tend to be global in nature, and thus, except for GRANT OPTION and PROXY, can be granted only using the ON *.* global-privilege specifier. For example, the RELOAD privilege enables use of FLUSH, so the following statements set up a user named flush that can do nothing but issue FLUSH statements:

```
CREATE USER 'flush'@'localhost' IDENTIFIED BY 'flushpass';
GRANT RELOAD ON *.* TO 'flush'@'localhost';
```

This type of MySQL account is useful for writing administrative scripts that perform operations such as flushing the logs during log file maintenance (see Section 12.8.7, "Log Management").

Database-level privileges apply to a particular database and all objects in it. To grant privileges at this level, use an ON db_name.* clause:

```
CREATE USER 'bill'@'mamba.example.com' IDENTIFIED BY 'rock';
GRANT ALL ON sampdb.* TO 'bill'@'mamba.example.com';

CREATE USER 'reader'@'%' IDENTIFIED BY 'dirt';
GRANT SELECT ON menagerie.* TO 'reader'@'%';
```

The first set of statements grants bill full privileges for any table in the sampdb database when he connects from mamba.example.com. The second creates a restricted-access user named reader that can connect from any host to access any table in the menagerie database, but only with SELECT statements. That is, reader is a "read-only" user.

You can list multiple privileges to be granted, separated by commas. For example, to give a user the ability to read and modify the contents of existing tables in the sampdb database, but not to create new tables or drop tables, do not grant the ALL privilege for the database. Instead, name only the specific privileges to be enabled:

```
CREATE USER 'jennie'@'%' IDENTIFIED BY 'boron';
GRANT SELECT,INSERT,DELETE,UPDATE ON sampdb.* TO 'jennie'@'%';
```

For more fine-grained access control below the database level, you can grant privileges for individual tables, or even for individual columns in tables. Column-specific privileges are useful
when there are parts of a table you want to hide from a user, or when a user should be able
to modify only particular columns. Suppose that someone volunteers to help you out at the
Historical League as an office assistant. You decide to grant your new assistant read-only access
to the member table that contains membership information, plus a column-specific UPDATE
privilege on the expiration and address-related columns of that table. That way, your assistant has write access only for the rather modest tasks of updating expiration dates as people
renew their memberships, and for making address changes. The statements needed to set up
this MySQL account follow:

```
CREATE USER 'assistant'@'localhost' IDENTIFIED BY 'officehelp';
GRANT SELECT, UPDATE (expiration,street,city,state,zip)
  ON sampdb.member TO 'assistant'@'localhost';
```

The GRANT statement grants read access to the entire member table (because no column list
follows SELECT), and grants update access only for the columns named in parentheses following the UPDATE privilege keyword.

To grant privileges at the column level for multiple privileges in a GRANT statement, the column
list in parentheses must follow each privilege name.

To enable an account to perform operations on stored routines (functions and procedures),
use the ALTER ROUTINE, and EXECUTE privileges at the global or database levels, or (except for
CREATE ROUTINE) for individual routines:

```
CREATE USER 'wilbur'@'localhost' IDENTIFIED BY 'sulfur';
GRANT CREATE ROUTINE ON sampdb.* TO 'wilbur'@'localhost';
GRANT EXECUTE ON PROCEDURE sampdb.count_students TO 'wilbur'@'localhost';
```

The PROXY privilege does not apply to a specific operation. Instead, it enables one user to
become a proxy for another. The proxy user has all the privileges of the proxied user. This
statement enables clint to have the privileges of bart:

```
GRANT PROXY ON 'bart'@'localhost' TO 'clint'@'localhost';
```

The syntax for granting PROXY is restricted: It must be named by itself, no REQUIRE clause is
permitted, and WITH is permitted only with GRANT OPTION. For more information, see Section
13.2.7, "Pluggable Authentication and Proxy Users."

To quote database, table, column, or routine names in a GRANT statement, quote them as identifiers, not as strings. For example:

```
GRANT SELECT, UPDATE (`expiration`,`street`,`city`,`state`,`zip`)
  ON `sampdb`.`member` TO 'assistant'@'localhost';
```

Rows in the grant tables do not "follow" database object renaming operations. For example,
privileges that name a given table or column are not updated if you rename the table or
column.

13.2.2.2   Using the "No Privileges" USAGE Privilege

The special USAGE privilege specifier means "no privileges." This may not seem very useful, but it is. It enables you to change characteristics of an account other than those that pertain to privileges, while leaving the existing privileges alone. To use it, "grant" the USAGE privilege at the global level, specify the account name, and provide the new nonprivilege characteristics of the account. For example, to change an account password, require that the user connect using SSL, or impose a connection limit on an account without affecting the privileges held by the account, use statements like these:

```
GRANT USAGE ON *.* TO account IDENTIFIED BY 'new_password';
GRANT USAGE ON *.* TO account REQUIRE SSL;
GRANT USAGE ON *.* TO account WITH MAX_CONNECTIONS_PER_HOUR 10;
```

13.2.2.3   Requiring an Account to Use Secure Connections

MySQL enables clients to establish secure connections using the SSL (Secure Sockets Layer) protocol, which encrypts the data stream between the client and the server so that it is not sent in the clear. In addition, X509 can be used as a means for the client to provide identification information over SSL connections. Secure connections provide an extra measure of protection, at the price of the extra CPU cycles required to perform encryption and decryption.

To specify requirements for secure connections, use a REQUIRE clause. To require only that a user connect using SSL without being more specific about the type of secure connection the user must make, use REQUIRE SSL:

```
CREATE USER 'eladio'@'%.example.com' IDENTIFIED BY 'flint';
GRANT ALL ON sampdb.* TO 'eladio'@'%.example.com' REQUIRE SSL;
```

To be more strict, you can require that the client present a valid X509 certificate:

```
GRANT ALL ON sampdb.* TO 'eladio'@'%.example.com' REQUIRE X509;
```

REQUIRE X509 imposes no constraints on the certificate's contents other than that it be valid. To be even more strict, REQUIRE enables you to indicate that the client's X509 certificate must have certain characteristics. These characteristics are given with ISSUER or SUBJECT options in the REQUIRE clause. ISSUER and SUBJECT refer to the certificate issuer and recipient. For example, the ssl directory of the sampdb distribution includes a client certificate file, client-cert.pem, that you can use for testing SSL connections. The issuer and subject values in the certificate can be displayed using the openssl command:

```
% openssl x509 -issuer -subject -noout -in client-cert.pem
issuer= /C=US/ST=WI/L=Madison/O=sampdb/OU=CA/CN=sampdb
subject= /C=US/ST=WI/L=Madison/O=sampdb/OU=client/CN=sampdb
```

The following GRANT statement indicates an account for which the client must present a certificate that matches both of those values:

```
GRANT ALL ON sampdb.* TO 'eladio'@'%.example.com'
  REQUIRE ISSUER '/C=US/ST=WI/L=Madison/O=sampdb/OU=CA/CN=sampdb'
  AND SUBJECT '/C=US/ST=WI/L=Madison/O=sampdb/OU=client/CN=sampdb';
```

You can also use `REQUIRE` to indicate that the connection must be encrypted using a particular cipher type:

```
GRANT ALL ON sampdb.* TO 'eladio'@'%.example.com'
  REQUIRE CIPHER 'DHE-RSA-AES256-SHA';
```

To indicate explicitly that secure connections are not required, use `REQUIRE NONE`. This is the default when you create a new account, but it can be used to remove the requirement for SSL from an account that currently has it.

Some additional points to be aware of when using a `REQUIRE` clause:

- Issuing a `GRANT` statement that requires an account to use secure connections only sets up a constraint on the account. It doesn't actually provide the means for a client program to connect securely with that account. For that to happen, MySQL must be configured to include SSL support, and you must start the server and clients in a particular way. Section 13.5, "Setting Up Secure Connections Using SSL," describes how to do this.

- If you specify that connections for an account must use SSL, but SSL is not supported by either the server or client programs, the account is effectively unusable.

- `REQUIRE` is used only to indicate whether an account *must* connect using secure connections. If the server and client programs are configured with SSL support, any user is still *permitted* to use secure connections, even if not required to do so.

- There is little point in using a `REQUIRE` clause for accounts that don't connect to the server over an external network. Such connections can't be snooped, so making them encrypted gains you nothing. Accounts like this include those that connect to the server only through a Unix socket file, a named pipe, shared memory, or to the network loopback interface IP address `127.0.0.1` or `::1`. These connections use interfaces that are handled internally to the host and for which no traffic crosses an external network.

13.2.2.4 Enabling an Account to Administer Privileges

To enable an account to grant its own privileges to other accounts, specify the `WITH GRANT OPTION` clause. To use this clause, you must have the `GRANT OPTION` privilege yourself.

One reason to give an account the `GRANT OPTION` privilege is to enable the owner of a database to control access to the database: Grant the owner all privileges on the database, including the `GRANT OPTION` privilege. For example, to permit `alicia` to connect from any host in the `big-corp.com` domain and administer privileges for all tables in the `sales` database, set up the account this way:

```
CREATE USER 'alicia'@'%.big-corp.com' IDENTIFIED BY 'shale';
GRANT ALL ON sales.* TO 'alicia'@'%.big-corp.com' WITH GRANT OPTION;
```

In effect, the `WITH GRANT OPTION` clause enables you to delegate access-granting rights to another user. But be aware that two users with the `GRANT OPTION` privilege can grant each other their own privileges. If you've given one user only the SELECT privilege but another user has GRANT OPTION plus other privileges in addition to SELECT, the second user can make the first one "stronger."

Another way to grant the GRANT OPTION privilege is simply to list it in the beginning part of the GRANT statement:

```
GRANT GRANT OPTION ON sales.* TO 'alicia'@'%.big-corp.com';
```

However, a statement such as this one will not work:

```
GRANT ALL,GRANT OPTION ON sales.* TO 'alicia'@'%.big-corp.com';
```

In a GRANT statement, ALL can be used only by itself, not in a list that names other privilege specifiers.

GRANT OPTION applies to all privileges at or below the level at which it is granted, not to individual privileges. If you give an account the GRANT OPTION privilege at a given level, the account can grant any privilege that it holds at that level. You cannot specify that the account can grant some of the privileges that it holds at that level but not others.

13.2.2.5   Limiting an Account's Resource Consumption

The MySQL grant system enables you to place limits on the number of times per hour that an account can connect to the server, and the number of statements or updates per hour the account can issue. A user cannot subvert the statement limits by using multiple connections to the server, because statements for all connections for a given account accrue to that account.

To specify any of these limits, use a WITH clause. The following statement sets up an account that has full access to the sampdb database, but can connect only ten times per hour and issue 200 statements per hour (of which at most 50 can be updates):

```
CREATE USER 'spike'@'localhost' IDENTIFIED BY 'pyrite';
GRANT ALL ON sampdb.* TO 'spike'@'localhost'
  WITH MAX_CONNECTIONS_PER_HOUR 10 MAX_QUERIES_PER_HOUR 200
  MAX_UPDATES_PER_HOUR 50;
```

The order of the resource management options within the WITH clause does not matter.

The default value for each option is zero, which means "no limit." Thus, if you have placed a resource limit on an account, you can remove the limit by changing the limit value to zero. For example, this statement removes the limit on how many times per hour spike can connect:

```
GRANT USAGE ON *.* TO 'spike'@'localhost'
  WITH MAX_CONNECTIONS_PER_HOUR 0;
```

The MAX_USER_CONNECTIONS resource limit controls the maximum number of simultaneous connections the account can have. If the limit is zero (the default), the limit is controlled by the value of the max_user_connections system variable. A nonzero value of that variable limits the account to that many simultaneous connections.

Any administrative user who has the RELOAD privilege can reset the current counter values by issuing a FLUSH USER_RESOURCES statement. FLUSH PRIVILEGES does this as well. After the counters have been reset, accounts that have reached their hourly limits once again can connect and issue statements. A reset also occurs for an individual account if you issue a GRANT statement that sets that account's limits.

13.2.3   Displaying Account Privileges

To see what privileges an account has, use the SHOW GRANTS statement:

```
SHOW GRANTS FOR 'sampadm'@'localhost';
```

To see your own privileges, use either of these statements:

```
SHOW GRANTS;
SHOW GRANTS FOR CURRENT_USER();
```

13.2.4   Revoking Privileges

To take away some or all of an account's privileges, use the REVOKE statement. The syntax for REVOKE is somewhat similar to that for the GRANT statement, except that TO is replaced by FROM, and there are no *auth_info*, REQUIRE, or WITH clauses:

```
REVOKE privileges [(columns)] ON what FROM account;
```

For example, the following GRANT statement grants all privileges on the sampdb database, and the REVOKE statement removes the account's privileges for making changes to existing rows:

```
GRANT ALL ON sampdb.* TO 'boris'@'localhost';
REVOKE DELETE,UPDATE ON sampdb.* FROM 'boris'@'localhost';
```

The GRANT OPTION privilege is not included in ALL. Revoke it from an account by naming it explicitly in the *privileges* part of a REVOKE statement:

```
REVOKE GRANT OPTION ON sales.* FROM 'alicia'@'%.big-corp.com';
```

To revoke a privilege, you must have that privilege yourself, and you must have the GRANT OPTION privilege.

To revoke all privileges held by an account at all levels, use this statement:

```
REVOKE ALL, GRANT OPTION FROM account;
```

Notice that there is no ON clause in this syntax. It requires the global CREATE USER privilege or the INSERT privilege for the mysql database.

If you revoke all of an account's privileges at the database, table, column, or routine level, or its proxy privileges, MySQL removes the corresponding account row from the db, tables_priv, columns_priv, procs_priv, or proxies_priv table. Revoking all of an account's global privileges sets the privilege columns to 'N' in its user table row, but does not delete the row. That is, REVOKE does not delete the account entirely, which means that the user can still connect to the server. To remove an account completely, use DROP USER instead of REVOKE (see Section 13.2.1, "High-Level MySQL Account Management").

Somewhat paradoxically, there are a few "revocation" operations that are done with GRANT. For example, if an account must connect using SSL, there is no REVOKE syntax for rescinding that requirement. Instead, issue a GRANT statement that grants the USAGE privilege at the global level (to leave existing privileges unchanged) and include a REQUIRE NONE clause to indicate that SSL is not required:

```
GRANT USAGE ON *.* TO account REQUIRE NONE;
```

Similarly, if you set up resource limits on a user, you don't remove those limits with REVOKE. Instead, use GRANT with USAGE to set the limit values to zero ("no limit"):

```
GRANT USAGE ON *.* TO account
  WITH MAX_CONNECTIONS_PER_HOUR 0 MAX_QUERIES_PER_HOUR 0
  MAX_UPDATES_PER_HOUR 0;
```

13.2.5   Changing Passwords or Resetting Lost Passwords

One way to change or reset an account's password is to use an UPDATE statement that identifies the User and Host values for the account's user table row, then flush the privileges:

```
mysql> USE mysql;
mysql> UPDATE user SET Password=PASSWORD('silicon')
    -> WHERE User='boris' AND Host='localhost';
mysql> FLUSH PRIVILEGES;
```

However, it's easier to use SET PASSWORD because you name the account using the same format as for other account-management statements, and it's unnecessary to flush the privileges explicitly:

```
mysql> SET PASSWORD FOR 'boris'@'localhost' = PASSWORD('silicon');
```

You can always change your own password with SET PASSWORD, unless you have connected as an anonymous user. To change the password for another account, you must have the UPDATE privilege for the mysql database.

Another, less common, way to change a password is to use GRANT USAGE with an IDENTIFIED BY clause, in which case you specify the password literally rather than by using the PASSWORD() function:

```
mysql> GRANT USAGE ON *.* TO 'boris'@'localhost' IDENTIFIED BY 'silicon';
```

If you need to reset the root password because you've forgotten it and can't connect to the server, you have something of a problem, because normally you must connect as root to change the root password. If you don't know the password, you'll need to force the server to stop and restart it without grant table validation. The procedure is described in Section 12.2.6, "Regaining Control of the Server When You Cannot Connect to It."

13.2.6 Avoiding Access-Control Risks

This section describes precautions to observe when you grant privileges, and the attendant risks of unwise choices.

Avoid creating anonymous-user accounts (accounts that have an empty username). Even if they don't have sufficient privileges to cause damage directly, permitting a user to connect still may provide access to that user to look around and gather information such as what databases and tables you have, or to monitor the server with SHOW STATUS and SHOW VARIABLES.

Find accounts with no authentication required and either remove them or require authentication. To find accounts that neither have a password nor use an authentication plugin, use this query:

```
SELECT Host, User FROM mysql.user WHERE Password = '' AND plugin = '';
```

To remove such accounts, use DROP USER. To require authentication, you can assign a password:

```
SET PASSWORD FOR account = PASSWORD('password');
```

Do not permit the use of passwords stored in the original (pre-MySQL 4.1) hash format; change them to the current more secure hash format. Values in the older format have a length of 16 and do not begin with the '*' character, so you can identify accounts that use them using either of these statements:

```
SELECT Host, User FROM mysql.user WHERE LENGTH(Password) = 16;
SELECT Host, User FROM mysql.user WHERE Password NOT LIKE '*%';
```

If these statements identify any accounts:

1. If the old_passwords system variable is set to 1 (ON), restart the server without enabling it.

2. For subsequent server restarts, always enable the secure_auth system variable. This prevents a client from resetting its password to the old format with OLD_PASSWORD() and connecting using that password. As of MySQL 5.6.5, this is unnecessary; secure_auth is enabled by default.

3. Use SET PASSWORD to reset the password for each account that has an old-format password.

Set the global sql_mode value to include the NO_AUTO_CREATE_USER mode to prevent GRANT statements from creating insecure new accounts. That is, if an account does not exist, GRANT fails and does not create the account unless the statement includes either an IDENTIFIED BY clause that specifies a nonempty password or an IDENTIFIED WITH clause that specifies an authentication plugin. Enabling NO_AUTO_CREATE_USER doesn't prevent a client from disabling that mode in its session, but helps prevent mistakes by nonmalicious users.

Unless you really need to use patterns in hostname specifiers, avoid doing so when setting up accounts. Broadening the range of hosts from which a given user can connect also broadens the range from which an imposter claiming to be that user can try to break in.

Grant superuser privileges sparingly. That is, don't enable privileges in user table rows. Those privileges are global and enable the user to affect the operation of your server or to access any database. For example, if you enable the DELETE privilege in a user table row, the account associated with the row can delete rows from any table in any database. Because of the super-user nature of privileges specified in the user table, it's generally best to grant no global privileges and grant privileges at a more specific level instead, to restrict user access to particular databases or database objects such as tables or stored routines. There are two exceptions to this principle:

- First, superusers such as root and other administrative accounts need global privileges to operate the server. These accounts tend to be few.

- Second, a few specific global privileges usually can be granted safely. These pertain to creating temporary tables, locking tables, and (perhaps) being able to use the SHOW DATABASES statement. Many installations grant these; others where tighter control is desired or necessary do not.

Don't grant privileges for the mysql database. It contains the grant tables, so a user with privileges for that database may be able to modify its tables to acquire privileges on any other database as well. In effect, granting privileges that enable a user to modify the mysql data-base tables gives that user all global privileges: If the user can modify the tables directly, that's equivalent to being able to issue any account-management statement you can think of.

Be careful with the GRANT OPTION privilege. Two users with different privileges that both have the GRANT OPTION privilege can make each other's access rights more powerful.

The FILE privilege is particularly dangerous; don't grant it lightly. Here's an example of something a user with the FILE privilege can do:

```
CREATE TABLE etc_passwd (pwd_entry TEXT);
LOAD DATA INFILE '/etc/passwd' INTO TABLE etc_passwd;
```

After executing those statements, the user has access to the contents of your server host's password file just by issuing a SELECT:

```
SELECT * FROM etc_passwd;
```

The name of any publicly readable file on the server host may be substituted for /etc/passwd in the LOAD DATA statement. If a user has connected from a remote host, the effect is that granting the FILE privilege enables network access for that user to a potentially large portion of your server host's filesystem.

The FILE privilege also can be exploited to compromise databases on systems that have insuf-ficiently restrictive data directory permissions. This is one reason you should set the data directory contents to be readable only by the server. If files corresponding to database tables are world-readable, not only can any user with an account on the server host read them, but any client user with the FILE privilege can connect over the network and read them, too! The following procedure demonstrates how:

1. Create a table containing a LONGBLOB column:

```
USE test;
CREATE TABLE tmp (b LONGBLOB);
```

2. Use the table to read the contents of each of the files that correspond to the table you want to steal. Suppose that a user has a MyISAM table named x in a database other_db. That table is represented by three files, x.frm, x.MYD, and x.MYI. Read those files and copy them into corresponding files in the test database like this:

```
LOAD DATA INFILE './other_db/x.frm' INTO TABLE tmp
    FIELDS ESCAPED BY '' LINES TERMINATED BY '';
SELECT * FROM tmp INTO OUTFILE 'x.frm'
    FIELDS ESCAPED BY '' LINES TERMINATED BY '';
DELETE FROM tmp;
LOAD DATA INFILE './other_db/x.MYD' INTO TABLE tmp
    FIELDS ESCAPED BY '' LINES TERMINATED BY '';
SELECT * FROM tmp INTO OUTFILE 'x.MYD'
    FIELDS ESCAPED BY '' LINES TERMINATED BY '';
DELETE FROM tmp;
LOAD DATA INFILE './other_db/x.MYI' INTO TABLE tmp
    FIELDS ESCAPED BY '' LINES TERMINATED BY '';
SELECT * FROM tmp INTO OUTFILE 'x.MYI'
    FIELDS ESCAPED BY '' LINES TERMINATED BY '';
```

3. After executing those statements, the test database directory also contains files named x.frm, x.MYD, and x.MYI. In other words, the test database contains a table x that is a stolen duplicate of the table in the other_db database.

To prevent this kind of attack, set the permissions on your data directory using the instructions in Section 13.1.2, "Securing Your MySQL Installation." As an additional measure, avoid granting the SHOW DATABASE privilege and run the server with the --skip-show-database option. This prevents users from using SHOW DATABASES and SHOW TABLES for databases to which they have no access, and helps to keep users from finding out about databases and tables they shouldn't be accessing.

The dangers of the FILE privilege are amplified if you run the MySQL server as root. That's inadvisable in the first place, and particularly when combined with FILE. Because root can create files anywhere in the filesystem, a user with the FILE privilege can cause the server to do so as well, even a user who has connected from a remote host. The server won't create a file that already exists, but it's sometimes possible to create new files that alters the operation of the server host or compromise its security. For example, if any of the files /etc/resolv.conf, /etc/hosts.equiv, /etc/hosts.lpd, or /etc/sudoers do not exist, a user who is able to cause the MySQL server to create them can drastically change the way your server host behaves.

To avoid these problems, don't run `mysqld` as `root`. (See Section 12.2.1.1, "Running the Server Using an Unprivileged Login Account.")

The `PROCESS` and `SUPER` privileges should be granted only to trusted MySQL accounts. With `PROCESS`, a user can use `SHOW PROCESSLIST` to see the text of statements being executed by the server. This enables a user to snoop on other users and possibly see information that should remain private. With `SUPER`, the user can kill other users' statements. `SUPER` also enables a user to purge log files and perform other actions that can compromise server operation.

Don't give the `RELOAD` privilege to people who don't need it. `RELOAD` enables a user to issue `FLUSH` and `RESET` statements, which can be abused several ways:

- Binary and relay log files have names that form a numbered sequence. If those logs are enabled, each `FLUSH LOGS` statement creates the next file in the sequence. A user with the `RELOAD` privilege can flush the logs repeatedly and cause the server to create large numbers of files.

- A user with the `RELOAD` privilege can defeat the resource management mechanism by reloading the grant tables with `FLUSH PRIVILEGES` or with `FLUSH USER_RESOURCES`. Both statements reset resource management counters to zero.

- `FLUSH TABLES` causes the server to flush its open-table cache. Used repeatedly, this degrades performance by preventing the server from taking advantage of the cache. Similarly, repeated use of `RESET QUERY CACHE` negates the benefits of the query cache.

- `RESET MASTER` causes a replication master server to delete all of its binary log files even if they still are in use, which prevents slaves from replicating correctly.

The `ALTER` privilege can be used in ways you may not intend. Suppose that you want one user to be able to access `table1` but not `table2`. Another user with the `ALTER` privilege may be able to subvert your intent by using `ALTER TABLE` to rename `table2` to `table1`.

13.2.7 Pluggable Authentication and Proxy Users

As explained in Section 13.2.1.3, "Specifying How an Account Authenticates," authentication information for the `CREATE USER` and `GRANT` statements is provided either with `IDENTIFIED BY` to specify a password or with `IDENTIFIED WITH` to specify an authentication plugin. This section provides further details on the use of authentication plugins. It also covers proxy users, an additional capability these plugins make possible that permits one user to gain the privileges of another.

13.2.7.1 Using Authentication Plugins

Syntax of the `IDENTIFIED WITH` clause for specifying an authentication plugin with `CREATE USER` is as follows (and is the same for `GRANT`):

```
CREATE USER account IDENTIFIED WITH auth_plugin [AS 'auth_string']
```

For an authentication plugin to be known by the server, it must be loaded first. (If that has not been done, load it using the instructions in Section 12.4, "The Plugin Interface.") Assuming that `auth_plugin` is loaded, the server creates a new row in the `user` grant table for the account, and stores the `auth_plugin` and `auth_string` values in the `plugin` and `authentication_string` columns of the row.

When a client attempts to connect to the server using this account, the server sees from the `plugin` value in the `user` table row that the client should be authenticated by the named plugin, invokes it, and passes the `authentication_string` value to it. The plugin communicates with the client program to receive the client's authentication credentials and indicates to the server whether the client authenticated properly. If not, the server rejects the connection.

Authentication plugins on the server side have corresponding plugins on the client side, and each server side plugin communicates to the client program which client-side plugin it should invoke to carry out the authentication process. Because of this, users need not specify which client plugin is required when they connect to the server. However, if the client-side plugin is not installed in the plugin directory on the client host, the connection fails. If the plugin is located somewhere other than where the client program looks by default, invoke the program using the `--plugin-dir` option to specify the location.

If you start the server with the `--skip-grant-tables` option, authentication plugins are not used because the server permits any client to connect without authenticating.

13.2.7.2 Creating Proxy Users

Authentication plugins in MySQL make possible the capability of user proxying. This permits one user A (the proxy user) to connect to the server and be treated as another user B (the proxied user). If A is a proxy for B and you connect to the server using the account for A, you have the privileges of B and can perform any operation permitted to B.

Not every authentication plugin supports proxying. To do so, a plugin must be written to return to the server not only whether a user A authenticated properly, but also the name of the proxied user B that A should be treated as for privilege checking. The way in which a plugin determines whether and how to map a proxy user onto a proxied user depends entirely on how the plugin is implemented; commonly, a plugin uses the `auth_string` value specified when the proxy user account was created. That is, when the proxy user connects, the plugin checks the authentication string and interprets its contents to determine how to map the user onto a proxied user. Suppose that you create an account like this:

```
CREATE USER ''@'localhost
  IDENTIFIED WITH auth_plugin
  AS 'user1=proxied_user1;user2=proxied_user2';
```

In this case, the account name uses the empty username and will match connection attempts from the localhost where the username does not match some more specific `localhost` account. For such attempts, if the client specified a `--user` value of `user1` or `user2`, the plugin might map the client onto `proxied_user1` or `proxied_user2`, respectively, and reject attempts from other client usernames.

Currently, only commercial MySQL distributions include proxy-supporting plugins. (See the MySQL Reference Manual for details.) Community MySQL distributions do not. For this reason, the following discussion describes how to create proxy users with a hypothetical plugin.

Suppose that we have an authentication plugin named `unix_auth` designed for Unix systems that works like this:

- The plugin enables users to connect to the MySQL server using their Unix account password. The plugin can be used without user proxying but does support that capability.

- To use the plugin without proxying, create an account without specifying an authentication string:

```
CREATE USER 'user1'@'localhost' IDENTIFIED WITH unix_auth;
```

  In this case, `user1` connects as follows, specifying the `user1` Unix password, and is authenticated for the MySQL account with the same username:

```
% mysql -p
Enter password: ...enter Unix user1 password here...
```

  The command line does not specify the username; we can suppose that the client-side plugin can examine the execution environment to determine the proper Unix login name to send to the server.

- To use the plugin with proxying, specify an authentication string that names the MySQL user to which the client should be proxied. For example:

```
CREATE USER 'user2'@'localhost' IDENTIFIED WITH unix_auth AS 'my_user';
```

  In this case, `user2` connects to the server using the `user2` Unix password, and is proxied to the `my_user` MySQL account.

The preceding discussion is somewhat incomplete. In addition to an authentication plugin that supports proxying and an account for the proxy user, proxying requires that the account for the proxied user exists, and that the proxy user has the PROXY privilege for the proxied account. Here is the general sequence of statements to permit proxying:

```
CREATE USER proxy_user auth_info;
CREATE USER proxied_user auth_info;
GRANT PROXY ON proxied_user TO proxy_user;
```

For the proxy user, the `auth_info` clause must name a plugin that supports user proxying. For the proxied user, the clause can name either a password or an authentication plugin.

A complete set of statements to create `user2` as a proxy for `my_user` looks like this:

```
CREATE USER 'user2'@'localhost' IDENTIFIED WITH unix_auth AS 'my_user';
CREATE USER 'my_user'@'localhost' IDENTIFIED BY 'my_user_password';
GRANT PROXY ON 'my_user'@'localhost' TO 'user2'@'localhost';
```

Now when `user2` connects to the MySQL server, statements issued during that user's session are evaluated in the context of whatever privileges `my_user` has. (Notice that we assign a password to the proxied account. This prevents clients from connecting directly to that account without authenticating.)

You might be asking why you would go to the trouble of mapping `user2` onto `my_user`. Why not just assign privileges directly to `user2`? Indeed, if you had a single user to proxy, you might not bother. But suppose that you wanted multiple Unix users to be treated as `my_user`. You could create accounts for each of them and map them all to `my_user`:

```
CREATE USER 'user3'@'localhost' IDENTIFIED WITH unix_auth AS 'my_user';
GRANT PROXY ON 'my_user'@'localhost' TO 'user3'@'localhost';
CREATE USER 'user4'@'localhost' IDENTIFIED WITH unix_auth AS 'my_user';
GRANT PROXY ON 'my_user'@'localhost' TO 'user4'@'localhost';
...
```

Or perhaps you'd like any Unix user who doesn't otherwise have a MySQL account to be mapped to the proxied user, `my_user`. In this case, you could set up a generic or default proxy user and simplify the mapping process:

```
CREATE USER ''@'localhost' IDENTIFIED WITH unixauth AS 'my_user';
GRANT PROXY ON 'my_user'@'localhost' TO ''@'localhost';
```

The approach of mapping multiple proxy users onto a single proxied user simplifies privilege management: You can update privileges for all of them simultaneously by updating the proxied account. Otherwise, you'd have to update privileges for each account individually.

13.3 Grant Table Structure and Contents

The MySQL access-control system is flexible, enabling you to set up user privileges in many different ways. Normally, you use account-management statements such as CREATE USER, GRANT, and REVOKE, which modify on your behalf the grant tables that control client access. However, you might find that user privileges don't seem to be working the way you want. For such situations, it's helpful to understand the structure of the MySQL grant tables and how the server uses them to determine access permissions. Such an understanding enables you to add, remove, or modify user privileges by modifying the grant tables directly. It also enables you to diagnose privilege problems when you examine the tables.

I assume that you've read Section 13.2.1, "High-Level MySQL Account Management," and that you understand how the account-management statements work. Those statements provide a convenient "front end" that enables you to set up MySQL accounts and associate privileges with them, but all the real action takes place in the MySQL grant tables.

The grant tables control access to MySQL databases by clients that connect to the server over the network. These tables are located in the `mysql` database and are initialized during the process of installing MySQL on a machine for the first time. These tables are named `user`, `db`, `tables_priv`, `columns_priv`, `procs_priv`, and `proxies_priv`. The server uses these tables as follows:

- The `user` table lists accounts for users that can connect to the server and which global (superuser) privileges each user has, if any. It's important to recognize that any privileges that are enabled in the `user` table are global privileges that apply to *all databases*. For guidelines on granting these safely, see Section 13.2.6, "Avoiding Access-Control Risks."

  The `user` table also has columns for authentication, for SSL options that pertain to the establishment of secure connections with SSL, and for resource management that can be used to prevent a given account from monopolizing the server.

- The `db` table lists which accounts have privileges for which databases. If you grant a privilege here, it applies to all objects in a database (tables, stored routines, and so forth).

- The `tables_priv` table lists table-level privileges. A privilege specified here applies to all columns in a table.

- The `columns_priv` table lists column-level privileges. A privilege specified here applies to a particular column in a table.

- The `procs_priv` table contains privileges for stored routines (functions and procedures). A privilege specified here applies to a particular routine in a database.

- The `proxies_priv` table indicates which accounts can be proxies for other accounts and acquire their privileges.

The `mysql` database also contains a grant table named `host` that is obsolete and discussed no further here.

The next several tables show the structure of each grant table, broken down by type of column. Each grant table contains two primary kinds of columns: scope-of-access columns that determine when a row applies, and privilege columns that determine which privileges a row grants. The privilege columns can be subdivided further into columns for administrative operations and those that are related to operations on particular kinds of objects. The `user` table has additional columns for authentication, SSL connections, and resource management; these are present only in the `user` table because they apply globally. Some of the grant tables contain other miscellaneous columns, but they don't concern us here because they have no bearing on account management.

Table 13.3   **Grant Table Scope-of-Access Columns**

`user` Table	`db` Table
Host	Host
User	User
	Db

tables_priv	columns_priv	procs_priv	proxies_priv
Table	Table	Table	Table
Host	Host	Host	Host
User	User	User	User
Db	Db	Db	Proxied_host
Table_name	Table_name	Routine_name	Proxied_user
	Column_name	Routine_type	

Table 13.4 **Grant Table Administrative Privilege Columns**

user **Table**	db **Table**	proxies_priv **Table**
Create_user_priv		
File_priv		
Grant_priv	Grant_priv	With_grant
Process_priv		
Reload_priv		
Repl_client_priv		
Repl_slave_priv		
Show_db_priv		
Shutdown_priv		
Super_priv		

Table 13.5 **Grant Table Object Privilege Columns**

user **Table**	db **Table**
Alter_priv	Alter_priv
Alter_routine_priv	Alter_routine_priv
Create_priv	Create_priv
Create_routine_priv	Create_routine_priv
Create_tablespace_priv	
Create_tmp_table_priv	Create_tmp_table_priv

Create_view_priv	Create_view_priv
Delete_priv	Delete_priv
Drop_priv	Drop_priv
Event_priv	Event_priv
Execute_priv	Execute_priv
Index_priv	Index_priv
Insert_priv	Insert_priv
Lock_tables_priv	Lock_tables_priv
References_priv	References_priv
Select_priv	Select_priv
Show_view_priv	Show_view_priv
Trigger_priv	Trigger_priv
Update_priv	Update_priv

tables_priv Table	columns_priv Table	procs_priv Table
Table_priv		Proc_priv
Column_priv	Column_priv	

Table 13.6   user Table Authentication, SSL, and Resource Management Columns

Authentication Columns	SSL Columns	Resource Management Columns
Password	ssl_type	max_connections
plugin	ssl_cipher	max_questions
authentication_string	x509_issuer	max_updates
	x509_subject	max_user_connections

The privilege system includes tables_priv, columns_priv, and procs_priv tables for defining privileges for specific tables, columns, and stored functions and procedures. There is no rows_priv table because MySQL provides no row-level privileges. For example, you cannot restrict a user's access to just those rows in a table that contain a particular value in some column. Applications that need this capability must implement it themselves. One way to achieve this is to create a view defined using WITH CHECK OPTION and grant the appropriate privileges on the view. Another way is to implement cooperative row-level locking using advisory locking functions such as GET_LOCK() and RELEASE_LOCK(). The procedure for this is described in Section C.2.8, "Advisory Locking Functions."

New releases of MySQL sometimes add new grant tables or columns. For example, the proxies_priv table was introduced in MySQL 5.5.7 to implement the PROXY privilege. When you upgrade an existing MySQL installation to such a version, it's necessary to update the grant tables before you can use the new privileges. Section 13.2, "Managing MySQL User Accounts," describes the procedure for doing this.

13.3.1   Grant Table Scope-of-Access Columns

The scope columns determine which grant table rows the server uses to determine privileges when an account attempts to perform a given operation. Each grant table row contains Host and User columns to indicate that the row applies to connections from a given host by a particular user. For example, a user table row with localhost and bill in the Host and User columns would be used for connections from the local host by bill, but not for connections by betty. The other tables contain additional scope columns. The db table contains a Db column to indicate which database the row applies to. Similarly, rows in the tables_priv and columns_priv tables contain scope columns that further narrow their scope to a particular table in a database or column in a table. The procs_priv scope columns specify which stored function or procedure a row applies to.

13.3.2   Grant Table Privilege Columns

The grant tables also contain privilege columns. For each row, these indicate which privileges are held by the user identified by the scope columns. For descriptions of the privileges supported by MySQL, see Section 13.2.2.1, "Defining the Privileges an Account Has." For the most part, privilege names bear an obvious resemblance to the names of privilege columns in the grant tables. For example, the SELECT privilege corresponds to the Select_priv column.

In the user and db tables, each privilege is specified as a separate column. These columns are all defined to have a type of ENUM('N','Y'), with a default value of 'N' (off). For example, the Select_priv column is defined like this:

```
Select_priv ENUM('N','Y') CHARACTER SET utf8 NOT NULL DEFAULT 'N'
```

Privileges in the tables_priv, columns_priv, and procs_priv, tables are represented by a SET, which enables any combination of privileges to be stored in a single column. The Table_priv column in the tables_priv table is defined like this:

```
SET('Select','Insert','Update','Delete','Create','Drop','Grant',
    'References','Index','Alter','Create_view','Show_view','Trigger')
CHARACTER SET utf8 NOT NULL DEFAULT ''
```

The Column_priv column in the columns_priv table is defined like this:

```
SET('Select','Insert','Update','References')
CHARACTER SET utf8 NOT NULL DEFAULT ''
```

There are fewer column privileges than table privileges because fewer operations make sense at the column level. For example, you can delete a row from a table to remove it, but you can't delete individual columns of a row.

Note that INSERT exists at the column level. If you have the INSERT privilege only for some columns in a table, you can specify values only for those columns when inserting new rows; the other columns are set to their default values.

The Proc_priv column in the procs_priv table is defined like this:

```
SET('Execute','Alter Routine','Grant')
CHARACTER SET utf8 NOT NULL DEFAULT ''
```

The tables_priv, columns_priv, and procs_priv tables are newer than the user and db tables, which is why they use the more efficient SET representation to list multiple privileges in a single column.

The user table contains some administrative privilege columns that are not present in any of the other grant tables, such as File_priv, Process_priv, Reload_priv, and Shutdown_priv. These privileges are present only in the user table because they are global privileges that are not associated with any particular database or table. It doesn't make sense to permit or not permit a user to shut down the server based on what the default database is, for example.

The proxies_priv table represents PROXY privilege relationships by indicating the proxy user account in the User and Host columns and the proxied user account in the Proxied_user and Proxied_host columns.

13.3.3   Grant Table Authentication Columns

The user table contains three columns that indicate how accounts authenticate: Password, plugin, and authentication_string. In the user row for a given account, if the plugin column is empty, clients authenticate for the account using the password in the Password column. Passwords are either blank (empty) or nonblank, and wildcards are not permitted. A blank password means not that any password matches but that the user must specify no password.

If the plugin column is not empty, clients authenticate according to the authentication method implemented by the named plugin, and the server passes the authentication_string value as information to the plugin. For more information, see Section 13.2.1.3, "Specifying How an Account Authenticates."

Passwords are stored as encrypted values, not literal text. If you store a literal password in the Password column, the user cannot connect! The CREATE USER and GRANT statements and the mysqladmin password command encrypt the password for you automatically. If you use statements such as INSERT, REPLACE, UPDATE, or SET PASSWORD to modify the grant tables, specify the password as PASSWORD('new_password'), not as 'new_password'.

13.3.4   Grant Table SSL-Related Columns

Several `user` table columns apply to authentication over SSL. (See Section 13.5, "Setting Up Secure Connections Using SSL.") The primary column is `ssl_type`, which indicates whether and what type of secure connection is required for an account. `ssl_type` is represented as an `ENUM` with four possible values:

```
ENUM('','ANY','X509','SPECIFIED') CHARACTER SET utf8 NOT NULL DEFAULT ''
```

The `ssl_type` enumeration values have the following meanings:

- `''` (the empty string) indicates that the account is not required to use secure connections. This is the default value; it's used when you set up an account but do not specify any `REQUIRE` clause or when you specify `REQUIRE NONE` explicitly.

- `'ANY'` indicates that the account must use a secure connection, but that it can be any kind of secure connection; it's a kind of "generic" requirement. The column is set to this value when you specify `REQUIRE SSL` in a `GRANT` statement.

- `'X509'` indicates that the account must use a secure connection and that the client must supply a valid X509 certificate. The contents of the certificate are not otherwise relevant. The column is set to this value when you specify `REQUIRE X509`.

- `'SPECIFIED'` indicates that the client must use a secure connection that meets specific requirements. The column is set to this value when you specify any combination of `ISSUER`, `SUBJECT`, or `CIPHER` values in the `REQUIRE` clause.

For all `ssl_type` values except `'SPECIFIED'`, the server ignores the values in the other SSL-related columns when validating client connection attempts. For `'SPECIFIED'`, the server checks the other columns, and for any that have nonempty values, the client must supply matching information:

- `ssl_cipher`, if nonempty, indicates the cipher method that the client must use when connecting. It can be used to prevent the client from using weak cipher methods.

- `x509_issuer`, if nonempty, indicates the issuer value that must be found in the X509 certificate presented by the client.

- `x509_subject`, if nonempty, indicates the subject value that must be found in the X509 certificate presented by the client.

`ssl_cipher`, `x509_issuer`, and `x509_subject` all are represented in the `user` table as `BLOB` columns.

13.3.5   Grant Table Resource Management Columns

The following columns in the `user` table enable you to limit the extent to which any given MySQL account can consume server resources:

- `max_connections` indicates the number of times per hour the account can connect to the server. A value of zero means "no limit." This column has the same name as the `max_connections` system variable, but the two are unrelated.

- `max_questions` indicates the number of statements per hour the account can issue. A value of zero means "no limit."

- `max_updates` is like `max_questions`, but applies more specifically to statements that modify data. A value of zero means "no limit."

- `max_user_connections` indicates the maximum permitted number of simultaneous client connections for the account. If the value is zero, the server assesses the simultaneous-connection limit using the global value of the `max_user_connections` system variable. A value greater than zero takes precedence over the `max_user_connections` system variable.

If the server restarts, the current counters are reset to zero. A reset also occurs, except for the `max_user_connections` value, if you reload the grant tables or issue a FLUSH USER_ RESOURCES statement.

For more information about setting account limits, see Section 13.2.2.5, "Limiting an Account's Resource Consumption."

13.4   How the Server Controls Client Access

The MySQL server enforces two stages of client access control. The first stage occurs when you attempt to connect to the server. The server looks at the `user` table to see whether it can find a row that matches the host you're connecting from, your name, and your authentication credentials (such as a password). If there is no match, you can't connect. If there is a match, the server also checks the `user` table SSL and resource management columns:

- If you've reached your connections-per-hour or simultaneous-connections limit, the server rejects the connection.

- If the `user` table row indicates that a secure connection is required, the server determines whether the credentials you supply match those required in the SSL-related columns. If not, the server rejects the connection.

If everything checks out okay, the server establishes the connection and you proceed to the second stage. If you are making a secure connection, your client program and the server encrypt the traffic between them.

In the second stage, the server checks two things for each statement you issue. First, it checks your statements-per-hour and updates-per-hour limits. Second, the server checks the grant tables to verify that you have sufficient access privileges to perform the statement. The limits are checked first because if you've reached them, there is little point in checking your privileges. The second stage continues until you disconnect from the server.

The following discussion describes in some detail the rules that the MySQL server uses to match grant table rows to incoming client connection requests and to statements. This includes the types of values that are legal in the grant table scope columns, how privilege values from different grant tables are combined, and the order in which the server searches rows from a given grant table.

13.4.1 Scope Column Contents

Each scope column is governed by rules that define what kinds of values are legal and how the server interprets those values. Some of the scope columns require literal values, but most of them permit wildcards or other special values.

- Host

  A `Host` column value can be a hostname or an IP address (either IPv4 or IPv6). The value `localhost` means the local host. It matches when a client connects from the local host to one of the server's local network interfaces, defined as follows:

  - The Unix socket file, on Unix systems.

  - A named pipe or shared memory, on Windows.

  - The TCP loopback interface, that is, the interface with an IP address of `127.0.0.1` or `::1`. This works on any system.

  `localhost` does not match if the client connects using the host's actual name or IP address. Suppose that the name of the local host is `cobra.example.com` and there are two rows for a user named `bob` in the `user` table, one with a `Host` value of `localhost` and the other with a value of `cobra.example.com`. The row with `localhost` matches if `bob` connects from the local host using either of the following commands, on either Unix or Windows:

  ```
  % mysql -p -u bob -h localhost
  % mysql -p -u bob -h 127.0.0.1
  % mysql -p -u bob -h ::1
  ```

  In addition, on Windows, the `localhost` row matches if `bob` connects like this:

  ```
  C:\> mysql -p -u bob -h .
  C:\> mysql -p -u bob --protocol=pipe
  C:\> mysql -p -u bob --protocol=memory
  ```

  The row with a `Host` value of `cobra.example.com` matches if `bob` connects from the local host using the server's hostname (`cobra.example.com`) or the IP address that corresponds to the hostname. The connection uses TCP/IP in both cases.

  You can specify `Host` values using wildcards. The '`%`' and '`_`' SQL pattern characters may be used and have the same meaning as when you use the `LIKE` operator in a statement. (Regular expressions of the type used with `REGEXP` are not permitted.) The SQL pattern characters work both for names and for IP addresses. For example, `%.example.com` matches any host in the `example.com` domain, and `%.edu` matches any host at any educational institution. Similarly, `10.0.%` matches any host in the 10.0 class B subnet, whereas `192.168.3.%` matches any host in the 192.168.3 class C subnet.

A `Host` value of `%` matches any host at all and may be used to enable a user to connect from anywhere. A blank `Host` value in a grant table is the same as `%`, with one exception: In the `db` table, a blank `Host` value means "check the `host` table for further information." However, the `host` table is obsolete, so you should not use a blank `db.Host` value.

For an IPv4 host value, you can also specify a network number with a netmask indicating which bits of the client IP address must match the network number. For example, `192.168.128.0/255.255.255.0` specifies a 24-bit network number and matches any client host for which the first 24 bits of its IP address have a value equal to `192.168.128`. You can think of this as another kind of wildcard. A netmask value must be `255.0.0.0`, `255.255.0.0`, `255.255.255.0`, or `255.255.255.255`. That is, it must begin with a multiple of eight bits set to 1, and have the remaining bits set to 0.

Netmasks are not supported for IPv6 addresses.

- `User`

  Usernames must be either literal values or blank (empty). A blank value matches any name and thus means "anonymous." Otherwise, the value matches exactly the name specified. In particular, `%` as a `User` value does not mean blank. It matches a user with a literal name of `%`, which is probably not what you want.

  When an incoming connection is verified against the `user` table, if the first matching row contains a blank `User` value, the client is considered to be an anonymous user.

- `Db`

  In the `db` table, `Db` values may be specified literally or by using the '`%`' or '`_`' SQL pattern characters to specify a wildcard. A value of `%` or blank matches any database. In the `columns_priv`, `tables_priv`, and `procs_priv` tables, `Db` values must be literal database names. They match exactly the name specified. Patterns and empty values are not permitted.

- `Table_name`, `Column_name`, `Routine_name`

  A value in these columns must be a literal table name, column name, or stored routine name, respectively. The value matches exactly the name specified. Patterns and empty values are not permitted.

- `Routine_type`

  A value in this column must be either `'FUNCTION'` or `'PROCEDURE'` and indicates whether the name in the row's `Routine_name` column applies to a stored function or procedure. The `Routine_name` and `Routine_type` values uniquely identify a stored routine in the database specified in the `Db` column.

- Proxied_host, Proxied_user

    These columns appear in the proxies_priv table, which also has Host and User columns that indicate the proxy user account. Proxied_host and Proxied_user indicate the proxied user account and have values like those specified earlier for Host and User.

The server treats scope columns as case sensitive or not as indicated in Table 13.7. Note in particular that Db and Table_name values are always case sensitive, even though treatment of database and table names in SQL statements depends on the filesystem case sensitivity of the host where the server runs (typically case sensitive under Unix, and not case sensitive under Windows).

Table 13.7 **Case Sensitivity in Grant Table Scope Columns**

Column	Case Sensitive
Host, Proxied_host	No
User, Proxied_user	Yes
Password	Yes
Db	Yes
Table_name	Yes
Column_name	No
Routine_name	No

13.4.2 Statement Access Verification

Each time you issue an SQL statement, the server determines whether you've reached your statement resource limits. These limits are given by the max_questions and max_updates values stored in the user table. If you have not reached your limits, the server also checks whether you have sufficient access privileges to execute the statement. It determines your privileges by checking the privileges from the user, db, tables_priv, columns_priv, and procs_priv tables, until the server either verifies that you have proper access or it has searched all the tables in vain. More specifically:

1. The server checks the user table row that matched when you connected initially, to see what global privileges you have. If you have any such privileges and they are sufficient for the statement, the server executes it.

2. If your global privileges are insufficient, the server looks for a row that matches you in the db table. If it finds one, it adds the privileges in that row to your global privileges. If the result is sufficient for the statement, the server executes it.

3. If the combination of your global and database-level privileges is insufficient, the server checks the tables_priv, columns_priv, and procs_privs tables to determine whether you have the necessary privileges to execute the statement.

4. If, after all the tables have been checked, you still don't have the privileges needed to execute the statement, the server rejects your attempt to do so.

In boolean terms, the server combines the privileges from the grant tables as follows:

```
user OR db OR tables_priv OR columns_priv or procs_priv
```

The preceding description no doubt makes access checking sound like a rather complicated process, especially when you consider that the server checks privileges for each statement from each client. However, the process is quite fast because the server doesn't actually look up information from the grant tables for every statement. Instead, it reads the contents of the tables into memory when it starts, then verifies statements using the in-memory copies. This gives a performance boost to access-checking operations. Furthermore, the simpler you keep privileges, the faster access checking will be. When the server reads the grant tables into memory, it notices whether any accounts have resource limits, and whether any have table-level, column-level, or routine-level privileges. If not, it knows that it need not check any of those types of information when checking privileges for statements issued by clients. This means the server can omit certain steps from the full access-checking procedure.

The use of in-memory copies of the grant tables for access checking has an important side effect: If you change the contents of the grant tables directly, the server won't notice the privilege change. For example, if you add a new MySQL user by using an INSERT statement to add a new row to the user table, that in itself does not enable the user named in the row to connect to the server. This is something that often confuses new administrators (and sometimes more-experienced ones!), but the solution is quite simple: Tell the server to reload the contents of the grant tables after you modify them directly. You can do this by issuing a FLUSH PRIVILEGES statement or by executing mysqladmin flush-privileges or mysqladmin reload.

It is unnecessary to tell the server to reload the grant tables when you use CREATE USER, DROP USER, RENAME USER, GRANT, REVOKE, or SET PASSWORD to set up or modify user accounts. The server maps those statements onto operations that modify the grant tables, then refreshes its in-memory copies of the tables automatically.

13.4.3   Scope Column Matching Order

The MySQL server sorts rows from the grant tables in a particular way, then tries to match incoming connections by looking through the rows in order. The first match found determines the row to use. It's important to understand the sort order, especially for the user table. This seems to trip up a lot of people in their attempts to understand MySQL security.

When the server reads the contents of the user table, it sorts rows according to the values in the Host and User columns. The Host column is dominant, so rows with the same Host value are sorted together, then ordered according to the User value. However, sorting is not lexical, or rather, it's only partially so. The principle to keep in mind is that the server prefers literal values over patterns, and more-specific patterns over less-specific patterns. This means that if you connect from boa.example.com and there are rows with Host values of boa.example.com and %.example.com, the server prefers the first row over the second. Similarly, %.example.com is preferred over %.net, which in turn is preferred over %. Matching for IP addresses works that way, too. For a client connecting from a host with an IP address of 192.168.3.14, rows with the following Host values all match, but are preferred in the order shown:

```
192.168.3.14
192.168.3.%
192.168.%
192.%
%
```

Another principle to remember is that when the server tries to match user table rows, it looks for a Host value match first and a User value match second, not the other way around.

13.4.4   A Privilege Puzzle

This section describes a particular scenario that demonstrates why it's useful to understand the order in which the server searches user table rows when validating connection attempts. It also shows how to solve a problem that seems to be fairly common with new MySQL installations, at least judged by the frequency with which it comes up on the MySQL mailing lists: A MySQL administrator sets up a new installation, including the default root and anonymous-user rows in the user table. A good administrator will assign passwords for the root accounts, but it's common (if inadvisable) to leave the anonymous users as is, with no passwords. Now, suppose that the administrator wants to set up a new account for a user who will connect from several different hosts. The easiest way to enable this is by creating the account with % as the host part of the account name in the GRANT statement so the user can connect from anywhere:

```
GRANT ALL ON sampdb.* TO 'fred'@'%' IDENTIFIED BY 'cocoa';
```

The intent here is to grant the user fred all privileges for the sampdb database and to enable him to connect from any host he likes. Unfortunately, the probable result is that fred can connect from any host, *except* the server host itself! Suppose that the server host is named cobra.example.com. If fred tries to connect remotely from the host boa.example.com, the attempt succeeds:

```
% mysql -p -u fred -h cobra.example.com sampdb
Enter password: cocoa
mysql>
```

But if fred tries to connect locally from the server host cobra.example.com, the attempt fails, even though fred supplies his password correctly:

```
% mysql -p -u fred -h localhost sampdb
Enter password: cocoa
ERROR 1045 (28000): Access denied for user 'fred'@'localhost'
(using password: YES)
```

This problem occurs if your user table contains any default anonymous-user rows that have blank usernames. Such rows are created by the mysql_install_db initialization script under Unix and are present in the pre-initialized user table included with Windows distributions. (Section 12.1, "Securing a New MySQL Installation," describes the initial user table rows.) The second connection attempt fails because when the server attempts to validate fred, one of the anonymous-user rows takes precedence over fred's row in the matching order. The anonymous-user row requires the user to connect with no password (rather than with the password cocoa), so a password mismatch results.

To understand why this happens, it's necessary to consider both how MySQL's grant tables are set up initially and how the server uses user table rows when it validates client connections. For example, under Unix, when you run the mysql_install_db script on cobra.example.com to initialize the grant tables, the resulting user table contains rows with Host and User values that look like this:

```
+-------------------+------+
| Host              | User |
+-------------------+------+
| localhost         | root |
| cobra.example.com | root |
| 127.0.0.1         | root |
| ::1               | root |
| localhost         |      |
| cobra.example.com |      |
+-------------------+------+
```

The first few rows enable users to connect as root from the local server. The last two rows enable users to connect anonymously from the local server. After the administrator sets up the account for fred with the GRANT statement shown earlier, the user table contains these rows:

```
+-------------------+------+
| Host              | User |
+-------------------+------+
| localhost         | root |
| cobra.example.com | root |
| 127.0.0.1         | root |
| ::1               | root |
| localhost         |      |
| cobra.example.com |      |
| %                 | fred |
+-------------------+------+
```

But the order of the rows as shown is not the order that the server uses when validating connection requests. Instead, it sorts rows by host first and then by user within host, putting more-specific values first and less-specific values last:

```
+-------------------+------+
| Host              | User |
```

```
+-------------------+------+
| localhost         | root |
| localhost         |      |
| 127.0.0.1         | root |
| ::1               | root |
| cobra.example.com | root |
| cobra.example.com |      |
| %                 | fred |
+-------------------+------+
```

The two rows with `localhost` in the `Host` column sort together, with the row for
`root` first because that's a more specific username than the blank value. The rows with
`cobra.example.com` sort together in a similar way. Furthermore, all of these rows have a literal
`Host` value with no wildcard characters, so they all sort ahead of the row for `fred`, which does
use a wildcard character in its `Host` value. In particular, both of the anonymous-user rows take
precedence over `fred`'s row in the sort order.

The result is that when `fred` attempts to connect from the local host, one of the rows with a
blank username matches before the row containing `%` in the `Host` column. The blank password
in the anonymous-user row doesn't match `fred`'s password of `cocoa`, so the connection fails.
One implication of this phenomenon is that it is possible for `fred` to connect from the local
host, *but only if he specifies no password.* Unfortunately, then he is validated as an anonymous
user and doesn't have the privileges associated with the `fred@%` account.

What all this means is that although it's very convenient to use wildcards when you set up an
account for a user who will connect from multiple hosts, the user may have problems connecting from the local host due to the anonymous rows in the `user` table.

There are two solutions to this problem. The first is to set up a second account for `fred` that
explicitly lists `localhost` as the host value:

```
GRANT ALL ON sampdb.* TO 'fred'@'localhost' IDENTIFIED BY 'cocoa';
```

If you do that, the server sorts the `user` table rows as follows:

```
+-------------------+------+
| Host              | User |
+-------------------+------+
| localhost         | fred |
| localhost         | root |
| localhost         |      |
| 127.0.0.1         | root |
| ::1               | root |
| cobra.example.com | root |
| cobra.example.com |      |
| %                 | fred |
+-------------------+------+
```

Now when `fred` connects from the local host, the row with `localhost` and `fred` matches ahead of the anonymous-user rows. When he connects from any other host, the row with `%` and `fred` matches. The downside of having two accounts for `fred` is that whenever you want to change his privileges or password, you must make the change twice.

The second solution is much easier; remove the anonymous accounts from the `user` table:

```
DROP USER ''@'localhost';
DROP USER ''@'cobra.example.com';
```

The remaining `user` table rows sort into this order:

```
+-------------------+------+
| Host              | User |
+-------------------+------+
| localhost         | root |
| 127.0.0.1         | root |
| ::1               | root |
| cobra.example.com | root |
| %                 | fred |
+-------------------+------+
```

Now when `fred` attempts to connect from the local host, he succeeds because there aren't any rows in the `user` table that match ahead of his.

To make MySQL administration easier, I recommend that you delete anonymous-user accounts from the grant tables. In my view, these accounts are not very useful and cause more problems than they're worth.

The puzzle presented in this section addresses a specific situation, but contains a more general lesson. If privileges for a given account don't work as you expect, check the grant tables to see whether there's some row containing `Host` values that are more specific than the row for the user in question and that match connection attempts by that user. If so, that may explain the problem. You might need to make the user's row more specific, or add another row to cover the more specific case.

13.5 Setting Up Secure Connections Using SSL

MySQL supports secure, encrypted connections using the Secure Sockets Layer (SSL) protocol. By default, an SSL-enabled MySQL installation enables a client to request secure connections on an optional basis. It's also possible for administrators to use GRANT to indicate that a given account is *required* to connect securely.

The benefit of SSL is primarily for connections to a remote server, to protect transmitted over a network that may be susceptible to snooping. There is little point in using SSL for connections to the local host that are made using a Unix socket file, a named pipe, shared memory, or to the network loopback interface IP address `127.0.0.1` or `::1`. The traffic for such connections never leaves the local host.

To take advantage of SSL encrypted connections between the server and client programs, use the following general procedure:

1. Make sure the server and client programs have been compiled with SSL support.

2. Start the server with options that tell it where to find its certificate and key files; these are necessary to set up secure connections.

3. To connect securely with a client program, invoke it with options that tell it where to find your own certificate and key files.

The following discussion describes this process in more detail.

Your MySQL distribution must be built with SSL support included. Either get a binary distribution that has SSL compiled in, or build MySQL from source. Binary distributions for most platforms support SSL. If you compile MySQL yourself, be sure to supply the necessary CMake options at configuration time (for example, -DWITH_SSL=bundled to use yaSSL or -DWITH_SSL=system to use OpenSSL). Verify that your server supports SSL by issuing the following statement:

```
mysql> SHOW VARIABLES LIKE 'have_ssl';
+---------------+----------+
| Variable_name | Value    |
+---------------+----------+
| have_ssl      | DISABLED |
+---------------+----------+
```

If you see DISABLED or YES, SSL support is available. DISABLED means that support is present but has not yet been enabled. That's okay; the files necessary to enable SSL are discussed next.

With a MySQL installation that includes SSL support, the server and its clients can communicate securely. Each end of a connection uses three files to set up secure communications:

- A Certificate Authority (CA) certificate. A CA is a trusted third party; its certificate can be used to verify the authenticity of the client and server certificates. It's common practice to purchase a CA certificate from a commercial entity, but you can generate your own.

- A certificate file that authenticates one side of the connection to the other. This is a public key.

- A key file, used to encrypt and decrypt traffic over the connection. This is a private key.

The server's certificate and key files must be installed first. If you have no files of your own, the ssl directory of the sampdb distribution contains some boilerplate files that you can use:

- ca-cert.pem, the Certificate Authority certificate

- server-cert.pem, the server's certificate

- server-key.pem, the server's public key

Copy these three files to your server's data directory, then add some lines to the `[mysqld]` group of an option file that the server reads when it starts, such as `/etc/my.cnf` on Unix or `C:\my.ini` on Windows. The options should indicate the pathnames to the certificate and key files. For example, if the data directory is `/usr/local/mysql/data`, list the options like this:

```
[mysqld]
ssl-ca=/usr/local/mysql/data/ca-cert.pem
ssl-cert=/usr/local/mysql/data/server-cert.pem
ssl-key=/usr/local/mysql/data/server-key.pem
```

You can put the certificate and key files elsewhere if you like, but the location should be one to which only the server has access. After you install the SSL files and modify the option file, restart the server.

At this point, you have enabled the server to permit encrypted connections, and `have_ssl` now should have a value of `YES`. However, client programs still can connect to the server only over unencrypted connections. To enable a client to use secure connections, specify certificate and key files for the client side as well. The `ssl` directory of the `sampdb` distribution contains files for this. You can use the same CA certificate file (`ca-cert.pem`). The client certificate and key files are named `client-cert.pem` and `client-key.pem`. Copy these three files to some directory under your own account. Then let the client program know where they are by adding some lines to an option file that the client reads when you execute it, such as the `.my.cnf` file in your home directory on Unix.

Suppose that I want to use encrypted connections for the `mysql` program. I can copy the SSL files to my home directory, `/home/paul`, then put the following lines in my `.my.cnf` file:

```
[mysql]
ssl-ca=/home/paul/ca-cert.pem
ssl-cert=/home/paul/client-cert.pem
ssl-key=/home/paul/client-key.pem
```

You can set up your own account similarly. It's also a good precaution to make sure your certificate and key files are accessible only to yourself. After modifying `.my.cnf` to indicate where the SSL files are located, invoke `mysql` and issue a `\s` or `status` command. The `SSL` line in the output should indicate that the connection is encrypted:

```
mysql> status;
--------------

mysql  Ver 14.14 Distrib 5.5.21, for Linux (i686)

Connection id:          5
Current database:
Current user:           sampadm@localhost
SSL:                    Cipher in use is DHE-RSA-AES256-SHA
...
```

You can also use the following statement to see what values the SSL-related server status variables have:

```
SHOW STATUS LIKE 'Ssl%';
```

The presence of the SSL-related options in the [mysql] option file group causes mysql to use SSL connections by default. If you comment out those lines or remove them from your option file, mysql uses a regular nonencrypted connection. It's also possible to ignore the SSL options by invoking mysql like this:

```
% mysql --skip-ssl
```

The SSL options in the [mysql] group can be copied to other program-specific groups to enable use of SSL for other programs. Should you put the options in the general [client] group? Perhaps not. That causes failure of any client program that doesn't understand how to use SSL. (To put the options there anyway, use the loose- prefix so that non-SSL-aware programs will ignore them.)

As an alternative to listing SSL options in the option file, you can specify them on the command line. For example, in the directory where the SSL files are located, I might invoke mysql like this (enter the command all on one line):

```
% mysql --ssl-ca=ca-cert.pem --ssl-cert=client-cert.pem
    --ssl-key=client-key.pem
```

However, doing all that typing often becomes burdensome.

The certificate and key files in the sampdb distribution suffice to enable you to establish encrypted connections. But they're publicly available (anyone can get the distribution), so connections thus established cannot truly be said to be secure. After you use these files to verify that SSL is working properly, you should replace them with ones that you generate yourself. For instructions on making your own certificate and key files, see the ssl/README.txt file in the sampdb distribution. You may also want to consider purchasing a commercial certificate.

The discussion thus far describes how any account can use SSL on an optional basis. You can also set up an account to prohibit unencrypted connections and require it to use SSL. To modify an existing account to require SSL connections, use a GRANT USAGE statement with a REQUIRE clause that specifies the constraints that connections must satisfy:

```
GRANT USAGE ON *.* TO 'account' REQUIRE require_options;
```

GRANT USAGE ON *.* leaves the account's privileges unchanged and modifies only SSL-related account attributes.

Suppose that there is an account for a user named laura who connects from the host viper.example.com. To require only that connections be encrypted, use this statement:

```
GRANT USAGE ON *.* TO 'laura'@'viper.example.com' REQUIRE SSL;
```

For more security, use REQUIRE X509 instead. In that case, laura must supply a valid X509 client certificate when connecting. (This will be the file named by the --ssl-cert option.) As long as the certificate is valid, its contents don't otherwise matter. To require specific certificate contents, use some combination of CIPHER, ISSUER, and SUBJECT in the REQUIRE clause. CIPHER indicates the type of encryption method you want the connection to use. ISSUER or SUBJECT indicate that the client certificate must have been issued by a particular source or for a particular recipient. These clauses narrow the scope of otherwise-valid certificates to include only those with specific content. The following GRANT statement requires a particular issuer in the client certificate and specifies the use of EXP1024-RC4-SHA encryption:

```
GRANT USAGE ON *.* TO 'laura'@'viper.example.com'
  REQUIRE ISSUER '/C=US/ST=WI/L=Madison/O=sampdb/OU=CA/CN=sampdb'
  CIPHER 'EXP1024-RC4-SHA';
```

If an account currently is set to require SSL and you want to rescind that requirement, use GRANT USAGE in conjunction with REQUIRE NONE:

```
GRANT USAGE ON *.* TO 'laura'@'viper.example.com' REQUIRE NONE;
```

For more information about the REQUIRE clause, see Section 13.2.2.3, "Requiring an Account to Use Secure Connections."

If you are using a MySQL API for a language such as Perl or PHP, SSL capabilities depend not only on the language API but on the MySQL client library that is linked into it. The client library must have been compiled with SSL support so that it can support SSL connections to the server. Also, the language API must be recent enough to use the SSL capabilities of the client library. For example, the PHP mysqlnd extension supports SSL connections but the older mysql extension does not.

Database Maintenance, Backups, and Replication

Ideally, MySQL runs smoothly from the time you first install it. But problems can occur for reasons ranging from power outages to hardware failure to improper shutdown of the MySQL server (such as when the server host crashes or you forcibly terminate it with `kill -9`). Events such as these, many of which are beyond your control, can result in database damage, typically caused by incomplete writes in the middle of table updates.

This chapter describes what you can do to minimize your risks and to be ready if disaster strikes anyway. The techniques covered here include making database backups, performing table checking and repair operations, and how to recover if you do lose data. The chapter also discusses database copying procedures for transferring a database from one server to another because these are often are quite similar to backup techniques. Another "copy" technique covered here is replication, in which you initialize a slave server with a duplicate of a master server's data and arrange for changes that occur thereafter on the master to propagate to the slave as well. The slave thus serves as a "continuous copy" of the master. Replication can be used for other purposes as well. To name two, client load can be split between servers to lessen the load on the master, and the slave can be more easily paused or stopped than the master for making backups.

14.1 Principles of Preventive Maintenance

This section summarizes general principles of preventive maintenance. Later sections provide implementation details.

To prepare against database problems, take the following actions:

- Enable the auto-recovery capabilities that the MySQL server provides.
- Set up scheduled preventive maintenance to perform table checking periodically. Routine table-checking procedures can help you detect and correct minor problems before they become worse.

- Set up a database backup schedule. Should the worst occur and you be faced with catastrophic system failure, you'll need the backups to perform recovery operations. Enable your binary log, too, so you have a record of updates that took place after the backup was made. (See Section 12.8.4, "The Binary Log.") Binary logging provides significant advantages for backup and replication and has negligible performance overhead, so there is little reason not to enable it.

If table damage or data loss does occur despite your efforts, exercise your options for dealing with these problems:

- Check your tables and fix any that are found to be corrupt if possible. Minor damage often can be corrected using MySQL's table repair capabilities.

- If table checking and repair does not get you up and running, perform data recovery using your backups and your binary log. Begin by using the backups to restore your tables to their state at the time of the backup. After that, re-apply any updates from the binary log that were made after the backup but before the crash occurred, to bring your tables fully up to date.

The tools at your disposal for carrying out these tasks include the capabilities of the MySQL server itself and also several other utilities included in the MySQL distribution:

- When the server starts, transactional storage engines can perform auto-recovery. You can also enable automatic table repair for the MyISAM storage engine. These capabilities are useful when the server restart follows a crash.

- Use the `mysqldump` program to make backups of your databases, should you need to recover them later.

- To tell the server to perform table maintenance operations on demand, use SQL statements such as CHECK TABLE and REPAIR TABLE. For a command-line interface to these statements, use the `mysqlcheck` program. The `myisamchk` utility also can check tables for problems and perform corrective actions.

Some of these programs, such as `mysqlcheck` and `mysqldump`, work in cooperation with the server. They connect as clients to the server and issue SQL statements that instruct the server what kind of table maintenance operation to perform. By contrast, `myisamchk` is an independent standalone program that operates directly on the files used to represent tables. Because the server also accesses those files while it runs, `myisamchk` acts in effect as a competitor to the server. This means that you must take steps to prevent `myisamchk` and the server from interfering with each other. For example, if you're repairing a table with `myisamchk`, it's necessary to keep the server from trying to write to the table at the same time. Failure to do so can result in much worse problems than those you're trying to correct!

The need to cooperate with the server arises in connection with several of the administrative tasks discussed in this chapter, from making backups to performing table repairs. Therefore, the next section begins by describing how to keep the server at bay when necessary, and sections following discuss how to prepare for problems, how to make backups, and how to use repair and recovery techniques if necessary.

Under Unix, operations that require you to directly work with table files or other files under the data directory should be performed while you're logged in as the MySQL administrator so you have permission to access the files. In this book, the name of that login account is `mysql`. It's also possible to access the files as `root`, but in that case, make sure when you're done that any files you work with have the same mode and ownership as when you began.

For a full listing of the options supported by the SQL statements and programs discussed in this chapter, see Appendix E, "SQL Syntax Reference," and Appendix F, "MySQL Program Reference."

14.2   Performing Database Maintenance with the Server Running

Some maintenance operations are performed by connecting to the server and telling it what to do. To perform consistency checks or table repairs on a MyISAM table, one way to do so is to issue a `CHECK TABLE` or `REPAIR TABLE` statement (or invoke the `mysqlcheck` program) and let the server do the work. In this case, the server will access the `.frm`, `.MYD`, and `.MYI` files that represent the table. This is the best approach to take if possible: When the server performs the requested maintenance operations, it handles any issues involved in coordinating access to the table so you need not think about them.

Other maintenance operations are performed by a program external to the server, in which case, you *must* think about issues of table access coordination. For example, another way to check or repair a MyISAM table is to invoke the `myisamchk` utility, which opens the table files directly without going through the server. While `myisamchk` accesses the table files, it's necessary to prevent the server from changing the table at the same time. If you don't do that, the competing efforts to access the table can damage it and make it unusable. It's obviously a bad thing for the server and `myisamchk` both to be writing to the table at the same time, but even having one of them reading while the other program is writing isn't good, either. The program doing the reading can become confused if the table is simultaneously changed by the other program.

The need to prevent the server from accessing tables comes up in other contexts as well:

- Compressing a MyISAM table with `myisampack`.
- Relocating a MyISAM table's data file or index file.
- Relocating a database.
- Using a backup technique that copies table files. To ensure consistent backup files, it's necessary to keep the server from changing the tables during the backup procedure.
- Using a recovery method that replaces damaged tables with good backup copies. While you are replacing the table, you must not permit the server to access it at all.

The most effective way to prevent the server from interfering with you is to shut it down. Clearly, if the server is not running, it can't access the tables you're working with. But administrators are understandably reluctant to take the server completely offline because that makes all databases and tables unavailable, not just those you want to check or repair.

To avoid stopping the server while at the same time preventing problems of interaction between a running server and operations that you're performing externally to it, coordinate with the server by using a locking protocol. The server has two kinds of locking:

- The server uses internal locking to keep requests from different clients from getting mixed up with each other—for example, to keep one client's SELECT query from being interrupted by another client's UPDATE statement. But you can also exploit internal locking to prevent clients from accessing a table while you are working with the table externally to the server.

- The server can use external locking to prevent other programs from modifying table files while it's using them. This is based on the locking capabilities available for your operating system at the filesystem level. Normally, the reason the server uses external locking is for cooperation with programs like myisamchk during table-checking operations. However, external locking doesn't work reliably on some systems. Another limitation is that external locking is useful only for operations that require read-only access to table files, such as table checking. External locking cannot be used for operations that require read/write access, such as table repair. External locking is based on file locking, but repair operations performed by myisamchk copy table files to new files as they work, and then use the new files to replace the originals. The server knows nothing of the new files, which renders useless any attempt at coordinating access by means of file locks.

The following discussion covers only the use of internal locking to coordinate with the server for table access. Because external locking is problematic, I advise you against using it and discuss it no further.

14.2.1   Locking Individual Tables for Read-Only or Read/Write Access

To use the server's internal locking mechanism to prevent it from accessing a table while you work on it, connect to the server with mysql and issue a LOCK TABLE statement for the table you want to use. Then, with mysql idle (that is, sitting there not doing anything with the table except keeping it locked), do whatever you need to with the table files. When you're done, switch back to your mysql session and release the lock to tell the server it's okay to use the table again.

> **Note**
>
> The internal-locking techniques described here for locking individual tables apply only when working with table files for storage engines such as MyISAM that represent each table with its own unique files. They *do not apply* to storage engines such as InnoDB that store information

about multiple tables in a given file. For example, InnoDB by default represents all InnoDB tables together within the files that make up its system tablespace. (Even when configured to use individual per-table tablespaces, InnoDB still stores some information about each table in its data dictionary, which is stored in the system tablespace.)

The locking protocol to use depends on whether you need read-only access or read/write access to the table's files. For operations that just check or copy the files, read-only access suffices. For operations that modify the files, such as table repair or replacing damaged files with good ones, you need read/write access.

The locking protocols use the LOCK TABLE and UNLOCK TABLE statements to acquire and release locks. They also use FLUSH TABLE to tell the server to flush any pending changes to disk and as a means of informing the server that it must reopen the table when next it accesses it. The examples use the FLUSH TABLE syntax that takes a table-name argument and flushes only that specific table.

You *must* perform all the LOCK, FLUSH, and UNLOCK statements from within a single session with the server. For example, you cannot connect to the server with the mysql program, lock a table, and then quit, intending to connect again later to unlock the table. That doesn't work because if you quit mysql, the server releases the lock automatically. At that point, the server considers itself free to use the table again, with the result that it is no longer safe for you to work with the table files.

One easy way to perform the locking procedures is to keep two windows open. This enables you to leave mysql running in one window while you work with the table files in the other. Or, in nonwindowing environment, use your shell's job control facilities to suspend and resume mysql processes while you work with the table.

14.2.1.1 Locking a Table for Read-Only Access

The read-only locking protocol is appropriate for operations that need only to read a table's files, such as copying files or checking them for inconsistencies. It's sufficient to acquire a read lock in this case; the server prevents other clients from modifying the table, but permits them to read it. This protocol is *not* for use when you need to modify a table.

1. In window A, invoke mysql and issue the following statements to obtain a read lock and flush the table:

   ```
   % mysql db_name
   mysql> LOCK TABLE tbl_name READ;
   mysql> FLUSH TABLE tbl_name;
   ```

   Acquiring a read lock prevents other clients from writing to the table and modifying it while you're checking it. The FLUSH statement causes the server to close the table files, which flushes any unwritten changes that might still be cached in memory.

2. With mysql sitting idle, switch to window B so you can work with the table files. For example, if tbl_name is a MyISAM table, you can make a backup by copying the files

that represent the table. If your current directory is the table's database directory, copy the files to a backup directory `/var/backup` like this:

```
% cp tbl_name.* /var/backup
```

This example is for illustration only. The commands you issue depend on the particular maintenance operation you perform.

3. When you're done working with the table, switch back to the `mysql` session in window A and release the table lock:

```
mysql> UNLOCK TABLE;
```

It's possible that your work with the table will indicate that further action is necessary. For example, a table-checking procedure might indicate that restoration or repairs are needed. These operations will require read/write access, which you can obtain safely using the protocol described in the next section.

14.2.1.2   Locking a Table for Read/Write Access

The read/write locking protocol discussed here is appropriate for operations such as table replacement or repair that modify a table's files. To do this, you must acquire a write lock to completely prevent all server access to the table while you work on it.

The locking procedure for read/write table access is similar to the procedure for read access, with two differences. First, you must obtain a write lock rather than a read lock. Because you'll be modifying the table, you can't let the server access it at all, not even to read it. Second, you must issue a second FLUSH TABLE statement after working with the table. If the maintenance operation rebuilds or repairs an index file, the server won't notice the new index unless you flush the table cache again.

To lock a table for read/write access, use this procedure:

1. Invoke `mysql` in window A and issue the following statements to obtain a write lock and flush the table:

```
% mysql db_name
mysql> LOCK TABLE tbl_name WRITE;
mysql> FLUSH TABLE tbl_name;
```

2. With `mysql` sitting idle, switch to window B so you can work directly with the table files. For example, if `tbl_name` is a MyISAM table, you can restore the table from a backup that was made by copying the files that represent the table. If your current directory is the table's database directory, copy the files from a backup directory `/var/backup` like this:

```
% cp /var/backup/tbl_name.* .
```

This example is for illustration only. The commands you issue depend on the particular maintenance operation you perform.

3. When you're done working with the table, switch back to the `mysql` session in window A, flush the table again and release the table lock:

```
mysql> FLUSH TABLE tbl_name;
mysql> UNLOCK TABLE;
```

14.2.2   Locking All Databases for Read-Only Access

A convenient way to prevent clients from making any changes to any table is to place a read lock on all tables in all databases at once. To do this, issue the following statements:

```
mysql> FLUSH TABLES WITH READ LOCK;
mysql> SET GLOBAL read_only = ON;
```

The FLUSH statement acquires a global read lock, and the SET statement blocks until all other clients release any table locks they have and finish any outstanding transactions. When the statement returns, it is safe for you to proceed and other clients will not interfere with you.

To permit changes to be made once again, use these statements:

```
mysql> SET GLOBAL read_only = OFF;
mysql> UNLOCK TABLES;
```

While the tables are locked this way, other clients can read but not change them. This is a good way to make the server quiescent for operations such as making backups using the `mysqldump` program. On the other hand, it's unfriendly to all clients that need to make updates, so you should hold the server lock no longer than necessary. It is also insufficient for operations such as making a binary backup of all tables managed by a transactional storage engine such as InnoDB because the engine might have outstanding transactions pending and only partly flushed to its log files. Operations like that require that you stop the server to make sure everything is flushed and all files are closed.

14.3   General Preventive Maintenance

This section outlines some general strategies to help you maintain the integrity of your databases:

- Enable the auto-recovery capabilities that the MySQL server provides.
- Schedule regular preventive maintenance to check your tables.
- Have a policy of making regular database backups, so you can recover if databases are damaged or lost.

The first two items are discussed here. For information about backup techniques, see Section 14.4, "Making Database Backups."

14.3.1   Using the Server's Auto-Recovery Capabilities

One of your first lines of defense in maintaining database integrity is the MySQL server's crash recovery capabilities. One of these (transactional storage engine recovery) is automatic and happens at server startup. Another (MyISAM recovery) is optional and must be enabled explicitly.

When the server starts, it can perform certain types of table checking to help deal with problems resulting from an earlier server or machine crash. MySQL is designed to recover from a variety of problems, so if you do nothing more than restart the server normally, it makes the necessary corrections for you in many cases. For example, the InnoDB storage engine checks for problems automatically. Committed transactions that are present in its redo log but not yet flushed to tables are rolled forward (redone). Uncommitted transactions in progress at the time of the crash are rolled back (discarded) using the undo log. The result is to leave your InnoDB tables in a consistent state, so their contents reflect all transactions that had been committed up to the point of the crash.

If InnoDB auto-recovery fails due to a nonrecoverable problem, the server exits after writing a message to the error log. To force the server to start up anyway so you can attempt a manual recovery procedure, see Section 14.7.4, "Coping with InnoDB Auto-Recovery Problems."

For MyISAM tables, the server supports an optional form of table recovery that you must enable explicitly. When you do so, the server performs a check each time it opens a MyISAM table. If the table was not closed properly after its most recent use or is marked as crashed, the server checks and repairs it. To enable MyISAM table recovery, start the server with the `myisam_recover_options` system variable set. The variable value is a comma-separated list of one or more of the following options: `BACKUP` (create a backup of the table if the repair will change it), `FORCE` (force recovery even if more than a row of data will be lost), `QUICK` (quick recovery), `DEFAULT` (recover with none of the other special handling), or `OFF` (no recovery). For example, to force recovery if problems are found, but create a backup first, put these lines in your server option file:

```
[mysqld]
myisam_recover_options=BACKUP,FORCE
```

Enabling MyISAM auto-recovery is useful as a general maintenance strategy because otherwise, a MyISAM table that the server finds to have problems becomes unavailable until you notice the problem and initiate repair manually. MyISAM recovery is especially important if you run the server with the `delay_key_write` system variable enabled or have individual MyISAM tables configured to use delayed key writes. Under those conditions, index changes are not flushed until tables close, which increases performance as the server runs, but also means that indexes will need repair for any delayed-key tables that are open at the time of a crash.

14.3.2   Scheduling Preventive Maintenance

In addition to enabling auto-recovery, consider setting up a preventive maintenance schedule. This helps detect problems automatically so you can take steps to correct them. By arranging to check your tables on a regular basis, you'll reduce the likelihood of having to resort to your backups. On Unix, this is most easily accomplished by using a `cron` job, typically invoked from the `crontab` file of the account used to run the server. (See Section 12.8.7.3, "Automating the Log-Expiration Procedure," for information about setting up `cron` jobs.)

The `mysqlcheck` program is useful for checking InnoDB and MyISAM tables while the server is online. Suppose that you want to set up a maintenance job that invokes `mysqlcheck`. If you run the server as the `mysql` user, you can set up periodic check from that user's `crontab` file. Add an entry to the file that looks something like this. Enter everything on a single line and use the path for `mysqlcheck` that is correct for your system:

```
45 3 * * 0 /usr/local/mysql/bin/mysqlcheck
    --all-databases --check-only-changed --silent
```

The entry tells `cron` to run `mysqlcheck` at 03:45 every Sunday. You can vary the time or scheduling as desired.

The `--all-databases` option tells `mysqlcheck` to check all tables in all databases. This gives you an easy way to use it for maximum effect. For the proper options to use to have `mysqlcheck` check only certain databases or tables, see the program description in Appendix F, "MySQL Program Reference."

The `--check-only-changed` option tells `mysqlcheck` to skip any table that hasn't been modified since it was last checked successfully, and `--silent` suppresses output unless there are errors in the tables. `cron` jobs typically generate a mail message if a job produces any output at all, and there's little reason to receive mail for table-checking jobs that find no problems. Note that even with `--silent`, you may get some diagnostic output if your databases have tables for storage engines that `mysqlcheck` doesn't know how to check.

Finally, remember to check mail for the `mysql` account or route it to your own account.

> **Note**
>
> While a table is being checked, it cannot be updated. Automatic-maintenance strategies might not be appropriate for large tables that need to be updated frequently if you cannot afford to block updates for the duration of the check operation.

14.4 Making Database Backups

It's important to back up your databases in case of damage of loss. If a serious system crash occurs, backups enable you to restore your tables with as little data loss as possible. Backups also enable you to help users who issue an unwise DROP DATABASE, DROP TABLE, or DELETE statement and request that you perform data recovery.

Database backups also are useful for certain nonrecovery operations, such as copying databases to another server. Most commonly, a database is transferred to a server running on another host, but you can also transfer data to a different server running on the same host. You might do this if you're testing a server for a new release of MySQL and want to use it with real data from your production server.

Another use for a backup is to set up a replication server: One first steps in setting up a slave server is to take a snapshot of the master server at a specific point in time. The backup serves as this snapshot, and loading it into the slave server brings it up to date with respect to the master server. Thereafter, updates made on the master server are replicated to the slave server through the standard replication protocol. See Section 14.8, "Setting Up Replication Servers."

Let's begin with some general principles that govern backup practices and help you decide which techniques to use. Then we'll cover the details of specific backup methods.

There are two general categories of database backups:

- Text-format backups made by using `mysqldump` to write table contents into dump files. These files consist of `CREATE TABLE` and `INSERT` SQL statements that can be reloaded into the server later to restore the tables.

- Binary backups made by directly copying the files containing table contents. This type of backup can be made in various ways. For example, you can use a program such as `cp`, `tar`, or `rsync`.

Each method has advantages and disadvantages. Some factors to consider are whether you can leave the server running, the time needed to make the backup, portability of the backup, and the scope of what is backed up.

- `mysqldump` cooperates with the MySQL server, so you can use it while the server is running. Binary-backup methods involve file copy operations that are done external to the server. Some of these methods require that you stop the server. For those that do not, you still must take steps to ensure that the server does not modify the tables while you copy them.

- `mysqldump` is slower than binary-backup techniques because the dump operation involves the server reading tables, converting their contents for transmission, and sending that information over the network connection to `mysqldump`. Binary-backup methods copy files at the filesystem level and require no conversion or network traffic.

- `mysqldump` generates text files containing SQL statements. These files are portable to other machines, even those with a different hardware architecture. They are therefore usable for copying databases from one server to another. Files generated by direct-copy binary backup methods may or may not be portable to other machines. It depends on whether your tables use a machine-independent storage format. InnoDB and MyISAM tables normally are machine independent. For those storage engines, directly copied files can be moved to a server running on a machine with a different hardware architecture. For information about portability of various storage engines, see Section 14.4.1, "Storage Engine Portability Characteristics."

- `mysqldump` output consists only of database contents (tables, views, stored routines, and so forth). It does not back up information not stored within a database, such as configuration files, log files, or replication status files. Binary backups can include any or all of these because you can copy any files you like as part of the backup.

Whichever backup method you choose, adherence to the following principles ensures the best results if you ever need to restore database contents:

- Perform backups regularly. Set a schedule and stick to it.

- Configure the server to perform binary logging (see Section 12.8, "Server Logs"). The binary log helps you restore databases after a crash: Use your backup files to restore the databases to the state they were in at the time of the backup, then re-apply the changes that occurred after the backup was made by re-executing the contents of the log files. This restores the tables in the databases to their state at the time the crash occurred.

- Use a consistent and meaningful naming scheme for your backup files. Names like `backup1`, `backup2`, and so forth are not particularly helpful. You'll waste time figuring out what's in the files when you need to perform a restore operation, You may find it useful to construct backup filenames using database names and dates. For example, if you dump the `sampdb` database on January 2, 2013, you might name the backup file `sampdb-2013-01-02`. If you run multiple servers, incorporate a server identifier into the name.

- Store your backup files on a filesystem different from the one you use for your databases. This reduces the likelihood of filling up the filesystem containing the data directory as a result of generating backups. Also, if the filesystem where you store the backups is on a different physical drive, you further reduce the extent of damage that can be caused by drive failure, because loss of any one drive cannot destroy both your data directory and your backups.

- Include your database backup files in your regular filesystem backups. If you have a complete crash that wipes out not only your data directory but also the disk drive containing your database backups, you'll be in real trouble. Back up your log files, too.

- To keep your backup files from filling your disk, expire them periodically. One technique for this is file rotation. Section 12.8.7, "Log Management," discusses expiration in relation to log files, but the same principles apply to backup files.

The following sections discuss storage engine portability and describe several specific backup methods. If you are using replication, Section 14.8.4, "Using a Replication Slave for Making Backups," describes a method that leaves your master server completely undisturbed.

14.4.1   Storage Engine Portability Characteristics

Any table managed by a given MySQL server is portable to another server in the sense that you can dump it into a text file with `mysqldump`, move the dump file to the machine where the other server runs, and load the file to re-create the table. Another kind of portability is "binary portability," which means that you can directly copy the disk files that represent the table to another machine, install them into the corresponding locations under the data directory, and expect the MySQL server there to be able to use the table.

A general condition for binary portability of tables is that the source and destination servers must be feature compatible. For example, the destination server must support the storage engine that manages the tables. If the server does not have the appropriate engine, it cannot access tables created by that engine on the source server.

Some storage engines create tables that are binary portable and some do not. The following remarks summarize binary portability for a few engines:

- InnoDB and MyISAM tables are stored in machine-independent format and are binary portable, assuming that your processor uses two's-complement integer arithmetic and IEEE floating-point format. Unless you have some kind of oddball machine, neither condition should present any real issues. ("Floating-point" means FLOAT and DOUBLE here. DECIMAL columns contain fixed-point values that use a portable storage format.)

  For InnoDB, an additional condition for binary portability is that database and table names should be lowercase. InnoDB stores these names in lowercase in its data dictionary, but the .frm file is created using the table name lettercase that you used in the CREATE TABLE statement. This can result in a case-sensitivity mismatch if you create databases or tables using names with uppercase characters and then try to move them to a platform with differing filename case sensitivity.

  For InnoDB, binary portability must be assessed for all InnoDB tables taken as a whole, not at the individual table level. By default, the InnoDB storage engine stores the contents of all its tables within a shared system tablespace rather than within table-specific files. Consequently, it's the InnoDB tablespace files that are or are not portable, not individual InnoDB tables. This means that the floating-point portability constraint applies if *any* InnoDB table uses floating-point columns. Even if you configure InnoDB to use individual (per-table) tablespaces, the data dictionary entries are stored in the system tablespace.

- CSV tables are binary portable because their .csv data files are plain text.

- MEMORY tables are not binary portable because their contents are stored in memory, not on disk.

Regardless of a storage engine's general portability characteristics, you should not attempt to copy table or tablespace files to another machine after you shut down the server unless the server shut down cleanly. If you perform a copy after an abnormal shutdown, you cannot assume the integrity of your tables. The tables may be in need of repair or there may be transaction information still stored in a storage engine's log files that needs to be applied or rolled back to bring tables up to date.

It is sometimes possible to tell a running server to leave tables alone while you copy their files. However, if the server is running and actively updating the tables or has changes still cached in memory, the table contents on disk will be in flux and the associated files will not yield usable table copies. For discussion of the conditions under which you can avoid stopping the server while copying tables, see Section 14.2, "Performing Database Maintenance with the Server Running."

14.4.2 Making Text Backups with `mysqldump`

The `mysqldump` program creates text dump files. By default, it writes a dump file in SQL format consisting of `CREATE TABLE` statements that create the tables being dumped and `INSERT` statements containing the data for the rows in the tables. To re-create the dumped tables later, reload the dump file into MySQL by using it as input to `mysql`. For example, to dump and reload a single table (`sampdb.member`), use these commands:

```
% mysqldump sampdb member > member.sql
% mysql sampdb < member.sql
```

Don't use `mysqlimport` to reload SQL-format `mysqldump` output. `mysqlimport` expects to read rows of data, not SQL statements.

To back up all tables from all databases into a single file, use a command like this:

```
% mysqldump --all-databases > /archive/mysql/dump-all.2013-01-02
```

However, the result is a rather large dump file if you have a lot of data. You can dump each single database into its own file, as follows:

```
% mysqldump mysql > /archive/mysql/mysql.2013-01-02
% mysqldump sampdb > /archive/mysql/sampdb.2013-01-02
% ...
```

Output from `mysqldump` looks something like this:

```
-- MySQL dump 10.13  Distrib 5.5.30, for Linux (i686)
--
-- Host: localhost    Database: sampdb
-- ------------------------------------------------------
-- Server version       5.5.30-log

 ... several SET statements ...


--
-- Table structure for table `absence`
--

DROP TABLE IF EXISTS `absence`;
/*!40101 SET @saved_cs_client     = @@character_set_client */;
/*!40101 SET character_set_client = utf8 */;
CREATE TABLE `absence` (
  `student_id` int(10) unsigned NOT NULL,
  `date` date NOT NULL,
  PRIMARY KEY (`student_id`,`date`),
  CONSTRAINT `absence_ibfk_1` FOREIGN KEY (`student_id`)
  REFERENCES `student` (`student_id`)
) ENGINE=InnoDB DEFAULT CHARSET=latin1;
```

```
/*!40101 SET character_set_client = @saved_cs_client */;


--
-- Dumping data for table `absence`
--

LOCK TABLES `absence` WRITE;
/*!40000 ALTER TABLE `absence` DISABLE KEYS */;
INSERT INTO `absence` VALUES (3,'2012-09-03'),(5,'2012-09-03'),
(10,'2012-09-06'),(10,'2012-09-09'),(17,'2012-09-07'),(20,'2012-09-07');
/*!40000 ALTER TABLE `absence` ENABLE KEYS */;
UNLOCK TABLES;

 ... rest of dump output ...
```

The rest of the file consists of more SQL statements, such as CREATE TABLE and INSERT.

Dump files often are large, so you may want to make them smaller. One way to reduce the size of a dump file is to compress it. On Windows, you can use WinZip or similar program to compress the dump and produce a file in Zip format. On Unix, you might use gzip or bzip2 instead. You can even compress the backup as you generate it by using a command pipeline:

```
% mysqldump sampdb | gzip > /archive/mysql/sampdb.2013-01-02.gz
% mysqldump sampdb | bzip2 > /archive/mysql/sampdb.2013-01-02.bz2
```

If large dump files are difficult to manage, it's possible to dump the contents of individual tables by naming them following the database name on the mysqldump command line. mysqldump dumps just the named tables rather than all the tables in the database, resulting in smaller, more manageable files. The following example shows how to dump subsets of the sampdb tables into separate files:

```
% mysqldump sampdb member president > hist-league.sql
% mysqldump sampdb student score grade_event absence > gradebook.sql
```

mysqldump has many options. The following list describes some that you may find useful. For others, see Appendix F, "MySQL Program Reference."

- Typically, you name a database on the mysqldump command line, optionally followed by specific table names. To dump several databases at once, use the --databases option. mysqldump then interprets all names as database names and dumps all tables in each of them. To dump all of a server's databases, use --all-databases. In this case, you supply no database or table name arguments. Both --databases and --all-databases cause the output for each database to be preceded by CREATE DATABASE IF NOT EXISTS and USE statements.

  Be careful with the --all-databases option if you intend to load the dump output into another server: The dump will include the grant tables in the mysql database, and you may not really want to replace the other server's grant tables.

- By default, `mysqldump` dumps both table structure (the `CREATE TABLE` statements) and table contents (the `INSERT` statements). To dump just one type of information or the other, use the `--no-create-info` or `--no-data` option.

- The `--opt` option optimizes the dump process. It enables several other options that have the effect of optimizing the dump process to generate smaller output. These options also optimize the restore process because the output can be processed more quickly when you reload the dump file later. For example, one effect of `--opt` is to cause `mysqldump` to write multiple-row `INSERT` statements. These take less space and can be reloaded more quickly than the equivalent set of single-row `INSERT` statements.

  The `--opt` option is enabled by default so you need not specify it explicitly. If you really want an unoptimized dump, use the `--skip-opt` option.

  Making backups using `--opt` is common because of the benefits for backup speed. Be warned, however, that the `--opt` option does have a price; what `--opt` optimizes is your backup procedure, not access by other clients to the database. The `--opt` option prevents anyone from updating any of the tables that you're dumping because it locks all the tables at once.

  `--opt` is useful for generating backup files that you intend to use for periodically refreshing the contents of another database (for example, a database on another server). That's because it automatically enables the `--add-drop-table` option, which tells `mysqldump` to precede each `CREATE TABLE` statement in the file with a `DROP TABLE IF NOT EXISTS` statement for the same table. When you take the backup file and load it into the second database later, you won't get an error if the tables already exist. If you run a second test server that's not a replication slave, you can use this technique to reload it periodically with a copy of the data from the databases on your production server.

  Another effect of `--opt` is to enable the `--extended-insert` option that causes `mysqldump` to write multiple-row `INSERT` statements. This saves space but is a disadvantage if you want a more readable dump file. To produce single-row `INSERT` statements, use the `--skip-extended-insert` option.

- The combination of `--flush-logs` and `--lock-all-tables` is helpful for checkpointing your database. `--lock-all-tables` acquires a global read lock, and `--flush-logs` closes and reopens the log files. If binary logging is enabled, flushing the logs creates a new binary log file that contains only those data modifications that occur subsequent to the checkpoint. This synchronizes your log to the time of the backup. (The downside is that locking all the tables is detrimental to other clients during the backup if they need to perform updates.)

  If you use `--flush-logs` to checkpoint the logs to the time of the backup, it's best to dump entire databases at a time. During restore operations, it's common to extract log contents on a per-database basis. If you dump individual tables, it's much more difficult to synchronize log checkpoints against your backup files. (There is no option for extracting updates for individual tables from the logs, so you'll have to extract them yourself.)

- To dump InnoDB tables, use the `--single-transaction` option to dump the tables within a transaction so you get a consistent backup.

- If your databases contain stored routines, triggers, and events, you can explicitly include them in dump output with the `--routines`, `--triggers`, and `--events` options. Each of these options has a `--skip` form as well (for example, `--skip-triggers`) to disable dumping of the corresponding objects. By default, triggers are included (because they are associated with tables), but stored routines and events are not.

- The `--master-data` option is useful when you are generating the dump file on a master server with the intent of setting up a replication slave. With this option, the dump file includes information about the master binary log coordinates at which the slave should begin replicating after you have initialized the slave with the contents of the file.

14.4.3   Making Binary Database Backups

A method for backing up databases or tables that doesn't involve `mysqldump` is to copy table files directly. Typically this is done using regular filesystem utilities (such as `cp`, `tar`, or `rsync`), or a special program developed for the task (such as MySQL Enterprise Backup, a commercial program). There are two key points to observe when you use a direct-copy backup method:

- Make sure the tables are not in use. If the server changes a table while you're copying it, the copy is worthless. The best way to ensure the integrity of your backups is to stop the server, copy the files, and restart the server. Some binary backup methods in fact require that you stop the server. If you don't want to stop the server (and the backup method doesn't require that you do so), use a read-only locking protocol to prevent the server from changing the tables while you're copying them. See Section 14.2, "Performing Database Maintenance with the Server Running."

- You must copy all files required to restore the tables that you're backing up. Direct-copy methods are easiest to use for storage engines such as MyISAM that represent a given table using a unique set of files in the database directory. To back up a MyISAM table, you need copy only its `.frm`, `.MYD`, and `.MYI` files. For a storage engine such as InnoDB, it's more complicated: You must copy the `.frm` files, plus all the tablespace files and the InnoDB log files.

If you make a binary backup, beware of symbolic links, such as symlinks in the data directory to database directories or symlinks to MyISAM data or index files. These present a problem because your file-copying technique might copy only the symlinks and not the data that they point to.

14.4.3.1   Making a Complete Binary Backup

A complete binary backup includes all files that store table contents and any log files used by specific storage engines. For good measure, you should also copy the binary log files. If the server is a replication slave, copy the relay log files and the `master.info` and `relay-log.info` files. Also, the slave may have created files with names of the form `SQL_LOAD-xxx` in its temporary file directory. You should back these up, too; they're needed for LOAD DATA statements. These files will be in the directory named by the slave_load_tmpdir system variable; if not given, it defaults to the value of the tmpdir system variable. To make it easier to identify these files for backup, create a directory devoted to use by the slave server, and start the slave with slave_load_tmpdir set to its pathname.

To properly copy all the files just discussed, you must stop the server and it must shut down cleanly, to permit storage engines to close their log files and the server to close any other logs it is writing.

All of that sounds like a lot of stuff to back up, but it is not necessarily complicated to do so. For example, all of your database directories are under the data directory, and logs and information files are created there by default as well. In this case, you can make a backup by stopping the server and copying the entire data directory. For example, to create a backup as a compressed tar file under the /archive/mysql directory, change location into the data directory and back up the whole thing. For example:

```
% cd /usr/local/mysql/data
% tar czf /archive/mysql/backup-all-2013-04-11.tar.gz .
```

14.4.3.2   Making a Partial Binary Backup

Making a partial binary backup by copying files is similar to making a complete backup, except that you copy only a subset of the full set of files. Suppose that you want to back up the mydb database located under the data directory /usr/local/mysql/data and store the backup under the archive directory /archive/mysql. Stop the server and then execute these commands:

```
% cd /usr/local/mysql/data
% cp -r mydb /archive/mysql
```

After executing these commands, the /archive/mysql/mydb directory contains a copy of the mydb database.

When you're done making the backup, restart the server.

In some cases, a partial backup can be made without stopping the server if you use a read-locking protocol to lock the tables that you want to copy. This is true if a database contains only MyISAM tables, for example. If the mydb database used in the preceding examples is such a database, you can read-lock and flush the tables prior to executing the backup commands, then release the table locks after the backup is complete.

14.4.4   Backing Up InnoDB Tables

Tables for the InnoDB transactional storage engine can be dumped using mysqldump, just like any other kind of tables. A useful option in this case is --single-transaction, which causes mysqldump to dump the tables within a transaction. For InnoDB, this ensures that the tables are not modified during the dump so you get a consistent backup.

To make a binary InnoDB backup, take care to observe the following special requirements:

- InnoDB has its own log files for transaction management that are active while the server is running. Therefore, to make a binary backup, you *must* stop the server. Furthermore, the server must shut down cleanly, not abnormally, to permit InnoDB to finish outstanding transactions and close its logs properly.

- To make a binary backup of your InnoDB tables, you must copy these files:

  - The system tablespace files.

  - The `.frm` file for each table.

  - The `.ibd` file for each table, if you have configured InnoDB to use individual tablespace files.

  - The InnoDB log files.

  - The option file in which the system tablespace configuration is specified. (Make a copy of the option file because you'll want it for reinitializing the system tablespace should you suffer loss of the current option file.)

You can also make a binary backup of InnoDB tables by using MySQL Enterprise Backup, a commercial program available from Oracle that enables you to make InnoDB backups with the server running. Visit `http://www.mysql.com` for details.

14.5   Copying Databases to Another Server

Database backups can be used to copy a database from one MySQL server to another. This section describes some methods for performing database transfers. For purpose of this discussion, I assume that the objective is to transfer a database from the server on the local host to a server on the remote host `boa.example.com`. However, the two servers could just as well be running on the same host. The following discussion describes how to copy entire databases, but you can adapt the techniques to copying individual tables.

The following discussion shows how to use two methods for copying a database to another server. The first makes a backup of the database that results in a file or set of files. You can copy the files to the second server host and load them into the second MySQL server. The second method dumps the database over the network from one server and loads it directly into the other server. This avoids the need for any intermediate files.

14.5.1   Copying Databases Using a Backup File

To copy a database using a text backup file, create the file using `mysqldump`, copy it to the second server host, and load it into the MySQL server there. The following example illustrates how to copy the `sampdb` database with this procedure:

1. Create a dump file:

```
% mysqldump --databases sampdb > sampdb.sql
```

The `--databases` option causes `mysqldump` to add `CREATE DATABASE IF EXISTS` and `USE` statements for the `sampdb` database. That way, when you load the dump file on the remote host, it automatically creates and selects the database so the dumped tables are loaded into that database.

2. Copy the dump file to the remote host. The following command uses `scp` to copy the file to the `/tmp` directory on `boa.example.com`:

```
% scp sampdb.sql boa.example.com:/tmp
```

3. Log in on the remote host and load the dump file into the MySQL server there:

```
% mysql < /tmp/sampdb.sql
```

Another approach is to use a binary backup: Copy database files (rather than a dump file) from one host to the other. Suppose that the `mydb` database has only MyISAM tables. In this case, table information is contained entirely in the files in the `mydb` database directory. If the local data directory is `/usr/local/mysql/data` and the remote data directory on `boa.example.com` is `/var/mysql/data`, the following commands copy the `mydb` database directory to that host:

```
% cd /usr/local/mysql/data
% scp -r mydb boa.example.com:/var/mysql/data
```

To copy database files to another host this way, certain requirements must be satisfied:

- Both machines must have the same hardware architecture, or the tables you're copying must all be for a binary-portable storage engine. The resulting tables on the second host may appear to have very strange contents otherwise.

- You must prevent the servers on *both* hosts from attempting to change the tables while you're copying them. The safest approach is to stop both servers while you're working with the tables.

14.5.2 Copying Databases from One Server to Another

The `mysqldump` technique shown in the previous section creates a dump file to be copied to the destination server host. Alternatively, you can write the output of `mysqldump` over the network directly to the other server so no intermediate file is needed. For example, to copy the `sampdb` database from the local host to the server on `boa.example.com`, do so like this:

```
% mysqldump --databases sampdb | mysql -h boa.example.com
```

`mysql` reads the dump output, connects to the server on `boa.example.com`, and loads the dump into that server.

If you cannot access the remote MySQL server from the local host, but you can access it by logging in there, use ssh to invoke mysql remotely:

```
% mysqldump --databases sampdb | ssh boa.example.com mysql
```

On a slow network, the --compress option can improve performance when copying a database to another machine because it reduces the amount of data traveling over the network:

```
% mysqldump --databases sampdb | mysql --compress -h boa.example.com sampdb
```

The --compress option is given for the program that communicates with the server on the remote host, not the one that communicates with the local server. Compression applies only to network traffic; it does not cause compressed tables to be created in the destination database.

14.6   Checking and Repairing Database Tables

Database damage occurs for a number of reasons and varies in extent. If you're lucky, you may simply have minor damage to a table or two (for example, if your machine goes down briefly due to a power outage). In this case, it's likely that the server can repair the damage when it comes back up. If you're not so lucky, you may have to recover your entire data directory (for example, if a disk dies and takes your data directory with it). Recovery also is needed under other circumstances, such as when users mistakenly drop databases or tables or delete a table's contents.

If you suspect that a table has become corrupted, check it for errors. If the table checks okay, you're done. If not, try to repair it using these guidelines:

- Begin with a faster but less extensive repair method.
- If you find that method is not sufficient, escalate to more extensive (but slower) repair methods, until either the damage has been repaired or you cannot escalate further.

In practice, most problems can be fixed without going to more extensive and slower repair methods.

This section describes table checking and repair procedures for dealing with more minor forms of damage. In the event of more major problems, such as tables or databases that are lost or irreparably damaged, you'll need to restore them from your database backups and the binary log. For instructions, see Section 14.7, "Using Backups for Data Recovery."

A general outline of the methods for checking and repairing InnoDB and MyISAM tables follows, with specific details given after that.

To check InnoDB tables, use CHECK TABLE statement, or use the mysqlcheck program, which connects to the server and issues the statement for you.

To repair an InnoDB table found to have problems, dump it with mysqldump. Then drop the table and reload the dump file to re-create it. The following sequence of commands shows how you might check, dump, and reload the absence table in the sampdb database:

```
% mysqlcheck sampdb absence
% mysqldump sampdb absence > absence.sql
% mysql sampdb < absence.sql
```

To check and repair MyISAM tables, you have a choice of approaches:

- Use the CHECK TABLE and REPAIR TABLE statements, or use the mysqlcheck program, which connects to the server and issues those statements for you.

- Use the myisamchk program, which operates on the table files directly.

As mentioned earlier in the chapter, if you have a choice when performing table maintenance between letting the server do the work or running an external utility, it's easier to let the server do the work. Then you need not be concerned about using any locking protocols to coordinate table access. That advantage applies with CHECK TABLE, REPAIR TABLE, and mysqlcheck, which the following sections describe how to use.

If you use myisamchk with the server running, you must use the locking protocols (see Section 14.2, "Performing Database Maintenance with the Server Running"). However, myisamchk does offer these advantages:

- You can use myisamchk when the server is stopped. CREATE TABLE and REPAIR TABLE require that the server be running.

- You can tell myisamchk to use larger buffers to make checking and repair operations run faster. This can be helpful if you have very large tables.

For information on using myisamchk for maintenance, see Section F.3, "myisamchk."

14.6.1 Checking Tables with CHECK TABLE

The CHECK TABLE statement provides an interface to the server's table checking capabilities. It works for InnoDB, MyISAM, ARCHIVE, and CSV tables, and for views.

To use CHECK TABLE, list one or more table names, optionally followed by modifiers that indicate what type of check to do. For example, the following statement performs a medium-level check on three tables, but only if they have not been properly closed:

```
CHECK TABLE tbl1, tbl2, tbl3 FAST MEDIUM;
```

The following list describes the available check options. They apply to MyISAM tables; other storage engines might ignore them. For more information, see Appendix E, "SQL Syntax Reference."

- CHANGED skips table checking if the table was properly closed and has not been changed since the last time it was checked.

- EXTENDED performs an extended check that attempts to ensure that the table is fully consistent.

- FAST checks a table only if it was not properly closed.

- MEDIUM checks the index, scans the data rows for problems, and performs a checksum verification. This is the default if no options are given.

- QUICK scans only the indexes and not the data rows.

- FOR UPGRADE determines whether the checked table is compatible with your current version of MySQL, so this option is useful after an upgrade.

14.6.2   Repairing Tables with REPAIR TABLE

The REPAIR TABLE statement provides an interface to the server's table repair capabilities. It works with MyISAM, ARCHIVE, and CSV tables.

To use REPAIR TABLE, list one or more table names, optionally followed by modifiers that indicate what type of repair to do. For example, the following statement tries to repair three tables in quick repair mode:

```
REPAIR TABLE tbl1, tbl2, tbl3 QUICK;
```

The following list describes the available repair options. These options apply to MyISAM tables; other storage engines might ignore them. For more information, see Appendix E, "SQL Syntax Reference."

- EXTENDED performs an extended repair that re-creates the indexes.

- QUICK attempts a quick repair of just the indexes; leaves the data file alone.

- USE_FRM uses the table's .frm file to reinitialize the index file and to determine how to interpret the contents of the data file so that the indexes can be rebuilt. This can be useful if the index has become lost or irrecoverably corrupted. However, it should be treated as a last resort and should be used *only* if your current version of MySQL is the same as that used to create the table; otherwise, you risk further damage to the table.

With no options, REPAIR TABLE performs a normal table repair that can fix most problems except the occurrence of duplicate values in an index that should contain only unique values.

14.6.3   Using mysqlcheck to Check and Repair Tables

The mysqlcheck program provides a command-line interface to the CHECK TABLE and REPAIR TABLE statements. It connects to the server and issues the appropriate statements for you based on the options you specify. Therefore, mysqlcheck can check or repair tables for the same storage engines as previously described for CHECK TABLE and REPAIR TABLE.

Typically, you invoke mysqlcheck with a database name, optionally followed by one or more table names. With just a database name, mysqlcheck checks all tables in the database:

```
% mysqlcheck sampdb
```

With table names following the database name, `mysqlcheck` checks only those tables:

```
% mysqlcheck sampdb president member
```

If you specify the `--databases` option, `mysqlcheck` interprets all nonoption arguments as database names and checks all tables in each database:

```
% mysqlcheck --databases sampdb test
```

If you specify `--all-databases`, `mysqlcheck` checks all tables in all databases. No database or table name arguments are needed:

```
% mysqlcheck --all-databases
```

`mysqlcheck` is more convenient than issuing the `CHECK TABLE` and `REPAIR TABLE` statements directly, because those statements require that you explicitly name each table to be checked or repaired. With `mysqlcheck`, it's much easier to check all tables in a database: It looks up the names of the tables in the database for you and issues statements that name the appropriate tables.

By default, `mysqlcheck` checks tables using a medium check, but supports options that enable explicit selection of the type of operation to perform. The following table shows some `mysqlcheck` options and the `CHECK TABLE` options to which they correspond. As with `CHECK TABLE`, these options apply to MyISAM tables; other storage engines might ignore them.

`mysqlcheck` Option	`CHECK TABLE` Option
`--check-only-changed`	CHANGED
`--extended`	EXTENDED
`--fast`	FAST
`--medium-check`	MEDIUM
`--quick`	QUICK

For MyISAM, ARCHIVE, and CSV tables, `mysqlcheck` can also perform table repair operations. The following table shows some `mysqlcheck` options and the `REPAIR TABLE` options to which they correspond. As with `REPAIR TABLE`, these options apply to MyISAM tables; other storage engines might ignore them.

`mysqlcheck` Options	`REPAIR TABLE` Option
`--repair`	No option (performs a standard repair operation)
`--repair --extended`	EXTENDED
`--repair --quick`	QUICK
`--repair --use-frm`	USE_FRM

14.7   Using Backups for Data Recovery

Recovery procedures involve two sources of information: backup files and the binary log. Backup files can be either dump files generated with a utility such as `mysqldump` or files copied using one of the binary backup methods.

The backup files restore tables to the state they were in at the time the backup was performed. The binary log files written after the backup operation contain the statements that have modified the tables since then. `mysqlbinlog` converts these log files back into text SQL statements so you can execute them with `mysql` to re-apply the changes made between the time of the backup and the time at which problems occurred.

The recovery procedure varies depending on how much information you must restore. In fact, it may be easier to restore an entire database than a single table, because it's easier to apply the binary log files for a database than for a table.

The discussion here assumes that you've been performing database backups and have binary logging enabled. If that's not true, you're living dangerously. You should enable the binary log right now and generate a new backup before reading further. You never want to be in the position of having irretrievably lost a table because you were lax about saving the information necessary to restore it. To find out how to enable the binary log, see Section 12.8.4, "The Binary Log." To make a backup, see the instructions in Section 14.4, "Making Database Backups."

14.7.1   Recovering Entire Databases

The general procedure for recovering one or more databases involves these steps:

1. Make a copy of the contents of the database directory or directories. You may want this later if you make a mistake or something goes wrong during recovery.

2. Reload the databases using your most recent backup files.

   If your backups are dump files generated by `mysqldump`, reload each file by using it as input to `mysql`.

   If the database or databases to be recovered include the `mysql` database that contains the grant tables and you are using dump files to recover the tables, reload them while running the server using the `--skip-grant-tables` option. Otherwise, the server may complain about not being able to find its grant tables. It's also a good idea to use `--skip-networking` to cause the server to reject all remote connection attempts while performing the restoration. After restoring the tables, stop the server and restart it normally so it uses the grant tables and listens to its network interfaces as usual.

   If you're using files from a binary backup (for example, a backup made with `tar` or `cp`), stop the server so it doesn't try to access the databases while they are being restored. Then copy the backup files back to their original locations (probably under the data directory), and restart the server.

3. Use the binary log to re-apply the data modifications that occurred subsequent to the time at which the backup was made. The procedure for this is given in Section 14.7.3, "Re-Executing Statements in Binary Log Files."

14.7.2 Recovering Individual Tables

Recovering an individual table can be more difficult than recovering a database. If you have a dump file generated by `mysqldump` that contains only that table, just reload the file. If you have a dump file that contains data for many tables, you can recover one of them by editing the file to delete the data for the other tables and then reloading the remainder. That's the easy part.

The more difficult part of recovery is extracting the parts of the binary logs that apply to the table. `mysqlbinlog` supports a `--database` option to limit its output to the statements for a single database, but there is no corresponding single-table option. A strategy that you might find useful in this situation is to restore more than you need (such as the entire database containing the table), then discard what you don't want. This procedure can actually be easier than trying to restore a single table by extracting the relevant parts from the binary log:

1. Restore the entire contents of the database that contains the table you want, but do so into a second, empty database. You can do this with your backups and by re-applying the binary log. However, there are two complications:

   - A dump file from `mysqldump` might contain a USE statement for the original database. You'll need to either change it or remove it before using the dump file as input to `mysql`.

   - Output from `mysqlbinlog` contains one or more USE statements for the original database. Save the output in a file so you can edit these statements to name the second database before using the file as input to `mysql`.

2. From the second database, use `mysqldump` to dump the table in which you are interested.

3. Drop the original table and load the dump file into the original database to re-create the table. If you run `mysqldump` with the `--opt` or `--add-drop-table` option, the dump file itself contains a DROP TABLE statement that removes the table before re-creating it.

For MyISAM tables, an alternative to using `mysqldump` is to directly copy the table files from the second database directory to the original database directory. To be safe, stop both servers while you perform the copy operation.

14.7.3 Re-Executing Statements in Binary Log Files

After you restore databases or tables from your backup files, re-apply the portions of your binary log files that contain the statements executed after the backup was made. This brings your tables up to date.

The `mysqlbinlog` program converts binary log files to statements in text form, making them easy to execute: Use the output from `mysqlbinlog` as input to `mysql`.

Depending on what you restored from backup, you might need to apply all statements in the binary log files, or just those for a particular database. You might also need to select only those statements that were executed within a particular time interval. `mysqlbinlog` can do these things. It can process multiple binary log files, and it can limit its output to statements for a given database or time interval.

The following instructions for applying the binary log files assume that the logs all have names of the form `binlog.nnnnnn`, where *nnnnnn* is the six-digit extension indicating the log sequence number. Adjust the instructions if your logs have a basename different from `binlog`. Also, I focus here on the use of local binary log files that exist on the same host where you execute `mysqlbinlog`. The program is capable of reading remote binary log files, but that is not covered here. For details on `mysqlbinlog` remote log processing options, see Appendix F, "MySQL Program Reference."

If the backup from which you restored your databases was made before all your current binary log files were written, you'll need to apply the contents of each file. To do so, use this command in the directory where the files are located:

```
% mysqlbinlog binlog.[0-9]* | mysql
```

The `binlog.[0-9]*` pattern in the `mysqlbinlog` command expands to the list of binary log files, normally in the same order in which they were generated by the server.

If you must edit the logs before re-executing them, convert them to text format and save the result in a file. Then edit the file and feed the result to `mysql`. Here is an example:

```
% mysqlbinlog binlog.[0-9]* > text_file
% vi text_file
% mysql < text_file
```

This strategy is necessary if the reason you're performing recovery and using the logs to restore information is that someone issued an ill-advised DROP DATABASE, DROP TABLE, or DELETE statement. You'll need to remove that statement from the logs before executing their contents.

Do not use `mysqlbinlog` and `mysql` to process binary log files one by one. There might be inter-file dependencies that will be broken unless you process the files as a group. For example, a TEMPORARY table created in one log file might be used in a later log file. If you process each log file separately, all TEMPORARY tables created by each log are dropped as the corresponding `mysql` invocation finishes and become unavailable to statements in the following logs.

To extract only those statements that pertain to a particular database, use the `--database` option to `mysqlbinlog`:

```
% mysqlbinlog --database=db_name binlog.[0-9]* | mysql
```

`mysqlbinlog` also supports several options for extracting statements that occur within a particular time interval (for example, statements written after a given backup was made). You may need to examine what's in the log files to see what option values to supply. Here is a sample of `mysqlbinlog` output (with some comment lines shortened to fit the page):

```
...
# at 1077
#121030 16:50:36 server id 1  end_log_pos 106   Query....
SET TIMESTAMP=1351633836;
```

```
INSERT INTO absence VALUES (3,'2012-09-03');
# at 1183
#121030 16:50:36 server id 1  end_log_pos 1210  Xid = 386
COMMIT;
# at 1210
#121030 16:50:36 server id 1  end_log_pos 106   Query....
SET TIMESTAMP=1351633836;
INSERT INTO absence VALUES (5,'2012-09-03');
# at 1316
#121030 16:50:36 server id 1  end_log_pos 1343   Xid = 387
COMMIT;
# at 1343
#121030 16:50:36 server id 1  end_log_pos 107   Query....
SET TIMESTAMP=1351633836;
INSERT INTO absence VALUES (10,'2012-09-06');
# at 1450
#121030 16:50:36 server id 1  end_log_pos 1477  Xid = 388
COMMIT;
...
```

Suppose that you want to re-apply the modifications in the binary log that were made beginning at `2012-10-30 16:50:36`. That value can be given to the `--start-datetime` option in either of these formats:

```
% mysqlbinlog --start-datetime="2012-10-30 16:50:36" binlog.[0-9]* | mysql
% mysqlbinlog --start-datetime=20121030165036 binlog.[0-9]* | mysql
```

There is a corresponding `--stop-datetime` option for giving the ending time. There are also position-based options that take position values shown in the log. For information, see the description of `mysqlbinlog` in Appendix F, "MySQL Program Reference."

14.7.4   Coping with InnoDB Auto-Recovery Problems

If the MySQL server or the server host crashes, the InnoDB storage engine performs auto-recovery when the MySQL server restarts. This section describes what to do in the rare instances that auto-recovery fails.

If InnoDB detects an unrecoverable problem during server startup, it writes a message to the error log and the server exits. In this case, set the `innodb_force_recovery` system variable to a nonzero value between 1 and 6 to cause the server to start up anyway. To set the variable, put a line in the `[mysqld]` group of your server's option file and restart the server:

```
[mysqld]
innodb_force_recovery=level
```

The InnoDB storage engine uses more conservative strategies for lower values of `level`. A typical recommended starting value is 4. With this variable enabled, InnoDB permits tables to be added or dropped, but their contents become read only. After the server starts, dump your

InnoDB tables with `mysqldump` to get back as much information as possible. Then remove the line that sets `innodb_force_recovery` from the option file and restart the server normally so that you can recreate the table contents: Drop the tables and restore them from the `mysqldump` output file. This procedure re-creates the tables in a form that is internally consistent, and may be sufficient to achieve a satisfactory recovery.

If you have MySQL 5.6.3 or later, another setting that might be helpful along with `innodb_force_recovery` is `innodb_force_load_corrupted`. This tells InnoDB to load tables even if they are marked corrupted. In some cases, this enables you to get a dump of tables that would be ignored normally.

If you need to restore all of your InnoDB tables, you must use your backups. The approach to take depends on what kind of backup you made:

- If you made a binary backup, you should have copies of the system and individual tablespace files, the InnoDB log files, the `.frm` file for each table, and the option file that defines your InnoDB configuration. After making sure the server is stopped, delete any existing InnoDB files and replace them with your backup copies. Then make sure your current server option file lists the InnoDB configuration the same way as your saved option file and restart the server.

- If you backed up your InnoDB tables by running `mysqldump` to generate a dump file, you should reinitialize the system tablespace and InnoDB logs and reload the dump file into InnoDB:

    1. Stop the server and remove any existing InnoDB-related files: the system and individual tablespace files (other than raw partitions), the InnoDB log files, and the `.frm` files for all InnoDB tables.

    2. Configure the system tablespace the same way you did initially and restart the server. InnoDB then re-creates its system tablespace and log files. For instructions, see Section 12.5.3.1, "Configuring the InnoDB Tablespace." Remember that initializing the tablespace is a two-step process if you're using any raw partitions.

    3. Reload your dump file or files by using them as input to `mysql`. This re-creates the InnoDB tables.

After restoring the InnoDB tables from the backups, re-apply any updates from your binary log that occurred after the backup was made. (See Section 14.7.3, "Re-Executing Statements in Binary Log Files.") This is easiest if you're restoring your InnoDB tables as part of restoring your entire set of databases, because in that case you can apply all the updates made subsequent to the backup. If you're restoring only your InnoDB tables, applying the logs is trickier because you should use the updates only for those tables.

14.8   Setting Up Replication Servers

One form of database "replication" involves simply copying a database to another server. But if the original database changes and you want to keep the copy up to date, you must repeat the operation later. To achieve continual updating of a secondary database as changes are made to the contents of a master database, use MySQL's live replication capabilities. This enables you to keep a copy of a database and make sure that changes to the original database propagate on a timely basis to the copy automatically.

14.8.1 How Replication Works

Database replication in MySQL works like this:

- In a replication relationship, one server is the master and another server is the slave. Each server must be assigned a unique replication ID.

- There can be multiple slaves per master. A slave can serve as a master to another slave, thus creating a chain of replication servers.

- Each slave must begin with its databases synchronized to those of its master. That is, any database to be replicated on the slave must be an identical copy of the master database when replication begins. After that, updates made on the master server propagate to the slave. Updates should not be made directly to the replicated databases on the slave.

- Communication of updates is based on the master server's binary logs, which is where updates are recorded that are to be sent to the slaves. Binary logging therefore must be enabled on the master server. Stored updates in the binary log are called "events."

- Each slave server must have permission to connect to the master and request updates. When a slave connects to its master, it tells the master how far into the master's binary log it had progressed when it last connected. This progress is expressed in replication coordinates: A binary log filename and position within that file. The master then begins sending to the slave those events in the binary log that occurred after the given coordinates. When the slave has read all available events, it pauses and waits for more.

- As new updates occur on the master server, it writes them to its binary log for later transmission to its slaves.

- The master server handles connected slaves much as it handles regular clients, and connected slaves count against the limit set by the `max_connections` system variable.

- On the slave side, the server uses two threads to handle replication duties. The I/O thread receives events to be processed from the master server and writes them to the slave's relay log. The SQL thread reads events from the relay log and executes them. The relay log serves as the means by which the I/O thread communicates changes to the SQL thread. As each relay log file is processed completely, the slave removes it automatically. The I/O and SQL threads operate independently, so each can be stopped or started separately from the other. This decoupling of function into different threads has important benefits. For example, the I/O thread can continue to read events from the master server while you stop the SQL thread so no updates occur in the slave's databases while you make a backup.

Replication support is an area of active development, so it's sometimes difficult to keep track of just which replication-related feature was added when. You should consider compatibility constraints between different server versions. In general, I recommend that you follow these guidelines:

- Within a given MySQL series (5.5, 5.6, and so forth), try to use the most recent version possible. This gives you the benefit of the richest feature set and the greatest number of restrictions removed and problems eliminated.

- Try to match binary log formats for your master and slave servers. For example, try to match 5.5 masters with 5.5 slaves, not 5.5 masters with 5.1 slaves or vice versa. If your master and slave versions must differ, replicate from older masters to newer slaves, not the other way around.

- The servers must be feature compatible. For example, if the master server uses tables that require a storage engine not enabled on the slave, you may encounter problems.

14.8.2   Establishing a Master-Slave Replication Relationship

The following procedure shows how to set up master-slave replication between two servers:

1. Determine what ID value you want to assign to each server and record it in an option file that the server reads when it starts. These IDs must differ and each should be a positive integer from 1 to $2^{32}-1$. The ID values will be needed for the server-id startup option used with each server. In addition, enable binary logging on the master if it is not already enabled. To accomplish this on the master and slave, respectively, use option groups with the following lines:

```
[mysqld]
server-id=master_server_id
log-bin=binlog_name
```

```
[mysqld]
server-id=slave_server_id
```

   Restart both servers so the changes take effect.

2. On the master server, set up an account that the slave server can use to connect to the master server and request updates:

```
CREATE USER 'slave_user'@'slave_host' IDENTIFIED BY 'slave_pass';
GRANT REPLICATION SLAVE ON *.* TO 'slave_user'@'slave_host';
```

   Remember the slave_user and slave_pass values for later when you tell the slave server how to connect to the master. No other privileges are needed if the account is used only for the single, limited purpose of replication. However, you may want to grant additional privileges to the account if you plan to use it connect to the master from the slave host "manually" with the mysql program for testing. Then you won't be so limited in what you can do. (For example, if REPLICATION SLAVE is the only privilege granted to the account, you might not even be able to see database names on the master server with SHOW DATABASES.)

3. Connect to the master server and determine its current replication coordinates by executing SHOW MASTER STATUS:

```
mysql> FLUSH TABLES; SHOW MASTER STATUS;
+---------------+----------+--------------+------------------+
| File          | Position | Binlog_Do_DB | Binlog_Ignore_DB |
+---------------+----------+--------------+------------------+
| binlog.000093 |   1707   |              |                  |
+---------------+----------+--------------+------------------+
```

Remember the File and Position values. You will need them later so you can tell the slave the point from which to start reading binary log events from the master.

Important: Make sure that no updates occur on the master from the time you determine its replication coordinates until after you make a snapshot of its data to be transferred to the slave.

4. The slave server must begin with an exact copy of the databases to be replicated. Perform the initial synchronization of the slave to the master server by copying the master's databases to the slave. One way to do this is to make a backup on the master host, and then move it to the slave host and load it into the slave server. Another method is to copy all the databases over the network from the master to the slave. Database backup and copying techniques are discussed earlier in this chapter.

If you haven't created any databases or tables on the master, you can skip this step because there is nothing to take a snapshot of.

5. Connect to the slave and use CHANGE MASTER to configure it with the parameters for connecting to the master server and the initial replication coordinates:

```
CHANGE MASTER TO
    MASTER_HOST = 'master_host',
    MASTER_USER = 'slave_user',
    MASTER_PASSWORD = 'slave_pass',
    MASTER_LOG_FILE = 'log_file_name',
    MASTER_LOG_POS = log_file_pos;
```

'master_host' is the name of the host where the master server is running. The 'slave_user' and 'slave_pass' values should be the name and password of the account that you set up on the master server earlier for the slave server to use when it connects to the master to request updates. 'log_file_name' and log_file_pos are the values you obtained from SHOW MASTER STATUS.

On Unix, MySQL uses a socket file for connections to localhost, but replication through a socket file is not supported. Therefore, if the master host is the same as the slave host, use 127.0.0.1 rather than localhost to make sure that the slave uses a TCP/IP connection.

If the master isn't listening on the default port, include a MASTER_PORT option in the CHANGE MASTER statement to indicate a port number.

6. Tell the slave to start replicating:

```
START SLAVE;
```

The slave should connect to the master and start replicating. You can check this with the `SHOW SLAVE STATUS` statement on the slave.

The slave stores the `CHANGE MASTER` parameters in a file named `master.info` in its data directory to record the initial replication status, and updates the file as replication proceeds. If you need to change replication parameters later, connect to the slave and use `CHANGE MASTER` again. The slave automatically updates the `master.info` file with these changes.

The information stored in the `master.info` file includes the username and password for connecting to the master server. This information should be confidential, so make sure that the file is accessible only to the MySQL administrator's login account on the slave server. For example, lock down the data directory contents as described in Section 13.1.2, "Securing Your MySQL Installation."

The procedure just described is based on the assumption that you want to replicate all databases from the master to the slave. However, it's very likely that you don't want to use the same user accounts on both servers. (For example, you might want to set up a private replication slave that people cannot connect to even if they have an account on the master.) To maintain accounts on the slave separately from those on the master, do two things:

1. When you transfer the initial data snapshot from the master to the slave, don't include the `mysql` database, or else back up the slave's `mysql` database before the transfer and restore it after.

2. Tell the slave to ignore any updates from the master for the `mysql` database. Do this as follows in the slave's option file:

```
[mysqld]
replicate-wild-ignore-table=mysql.%
```

That option can be given multiple times, once per database, if you want the slave to ignore tables in several databases.

It's possible to exclude databases on the master side rather than on the slave side by using the `binlog-ignore-db` option in the master's option file. This reduces traffic between the master and slave, but also unfortunately causes the binary log to contain no information for the ignored databases. That information is needed for performing recovery on the master after a crash, so database exclusion on the slave side is preferable.

After you have replication set up and running, there are several statements that you may find useful for monitoring or controlling the master and the slave. Details about these statements are available in Appendix E, "SQL Syntax Reference." A brief summary follows:

- `SHOW SLAVE STATUS` on a slave shows whether replication is running and the current replication coordinates. The coordinates can be used to determine which binary log files from the master are no longer needed.

- `PURGE BINARY LOGS` on the master expires binary log files. You can use this after issuing a `SHOW SLAVE STATUS` statement on each of the slaves to determine which log files no longer are needed.

- The `STOP SLAVE` and `START SLAVE` statements suspend and resume a slave server's replication-related activity. These statements can be useful for telling the slave to be quiescent while you're making a backup, for example. (See Section 14.8.4, "Using a Replication Slave for Making Backups.")

As mentioned earlier, a slave server uses two threads internally to manage replication. The I/O thread talks to the master server, receives updates from it, and writes updates to its relay log. The SQL thread reads the relay log and executes the updates it finds there. You can use `STOP SLAVE` and `START SLAVE` to suspend or resume each thread individually by adding `IO_THREAD` or `SQL_THREAD` to the end of the statement. For example, `STOP SLAVE SQL_THREAD` stops execution by the slave of the updates in the relay log, but enables the slave to continue to read updates from the master and record them in the relay log.

Relay log files are generated in numbered sequence, much like the binary log files. There also is a relay log index file analogous to the binary log index. The default relay log and index files are `HOSTNAME-relay-bin.nnnnnn` and `HOSTNAME-relay-bin.index` in the data directory. The defaults can be changed with the `--relay-log` and `--relay-log-index` server startup options. For more information, see Section 12.8.5, "The Relay Log."

14.8.3   Binary Logging Formats

By default, the server writes data-modification events to the binary log as SQL statements. This is known as statement-based binary logging (and replication based on it is statement-based replication). The server can also log changes to individual data rows. This is row-based logging. A third type of logging, mixed format, permits the server to switch between statement-based and row-based logging as it deems best.

In general, statement-based logging produces smaller log files with contents that are easier to understand. Row-based logging provides finer specification of updates to be made, which is advantageous for replication when the original statements might be nondeterministic and produce different effects on master and slave.

To specify the logging format, set the `binlog_format` system variable at startup or at runtime. Permitted values are `STATEMENT`, `ROW`, and `MIXED`.

14.8.4   Using a Replication Slave for Making Backups

If you have a replication slave server set up, it can help you resolve a conflict of interest that arises from your duties as a MySQL administrator:

- On the one hand, it's important to maximize the availability of your server to the members of your user community, which includes permitting them to make database updates.

- On the other hand, it's important to make backups, which is best done while you prevent anyone from making database changes. Also, for recovery purposes, backups are most useful if you make sure your backup file and log file checkpoints are synchronized, either by stopping the server or by locking all the tables at once.

The goal of maintaining accessibility conflicts with that of enforcing complete or partial loss of database access to clients while making backups. A replication slave provides a way out of this dilemma. Rather than making backups of the master server, use the slave server instead. Stop the slave or suspend replication on it before you make the backup. Then restart the slave or resume replication afterward, and the slave will catch up on any updates made by the master server during the backup period. This way you need not stop the master or otherwise make it unavailable to clients during the backup.

The following list describes some possible strategies for backing up the slave:

- For a binary backup of all slave data, stop the slave server, follow the instructions in Section 14.4.3.1, "Making a Complete Binary Backup," and restart the server.

- For a backup using a method such as `mysqldump` that does not require the slave to be stopped, you can back up the slave while the SQL thread is stopped, and then restart the thread after making the backup: Suspend replication on the slave with STOP SLAVE SQL_THREAD and flush its logs. Then make the backup and resume replication with START SLAVE. This way the slave won't make changes to databases while you're backing them up. The I/O thread can be left running; it continues to write events to the relay log that it receives from the master. When you restart the SQL thread after making the backup, it catches up with any accumulated updates.

  This approach assumes that clients do not make updates on the slave server. You should also not use this method if you intend to use a binary backup method that copies database files directly. Even though the SQL thread is stopped, there might be information cached in memory that has not been flushed to disk.

- Some backup methods do not require even that you suspend replication. For example, if you're backing up a single database containing only MyISAM tables, you can use `mysqldump` with the appropriate options to lock all the tables at once. In these cases, the slave server can continue to run, but it won't attempt any updates to the locked tables during the backup. When the backup program finishes and releases the locks, the slave resumes update processing automatically.

- Make a backup while the slave is in a read-only state.

The following procedure shows how to implement the final strategy in the preceding list:

1. Prevent updates on the slave by making it read only:

```
mysql> FLUSH TABLES WITH READ LOCK;
mysql> SET GLOBAL read_only = ON;
```

2. Perform the backup; for example, by using `mysqldump`. (This technique does not work for binary backups made by directly copying files and directories because transactional storage engines might still have transactions not yet flushed.)

3. Permit updates on the slave again:

```
mysql> SET GLOBAL read_only = OFF;
mysql> UNLOCK TABLES;
```

A

Software Required to Use This Book

This appendix describes how to obtain the `sampdb` distribution needed for setting up the sample database used for examples throughout this book. To use the distribution, you must also have MySQL running. To that end, the appendix additionally indicates where to obtain MySQL and related software such as the Perl DBI and CGI.pm modules, PHP, and Apache. It also provides brief installation notes for MySQL and the required Perl and PHP software, and instructions on configuring Apache for use with PHP.

For any software package you install, read carefully the instructions that come with the package and consult other sources as necessary. For example, the MySQL manual contains a chapter that deals extensively with installation procedures.

A.1 Obtaining the `sampdb` Sample Database Distribution

The `sampdb` distribution is available at `http://www.kitebird.com/mysql-book` and contains the files needed to set up and access the `sampdb` sample database. The distribution is available in compressed `tar` file and Zip archive formats. To unpack a distribution in `tar` format, use one of these commands (use the second command if your version of `tar` doesn't understand the `z` option):

```
% tar zxf sampdb.tar.gz
% gunzip < sampdb.tar.gz | tar xf -
```

To unpack a Zip-format distribution, use a utility such as WinZip, `pkunzip`, or `unzip`.

Unpacking the distribution creates a directory named `sampdb` that includes several files and subdirectories:

- The `README.txt` file contains instructions for using the distribution. This is the first file you should look at. Individual subdirectories of the distribution may also contain a `README.txt` file with additional information.

- There are files used for creating and loading the `sampdb` database in Chapter 1, "Getting Started with MySQL."

- The `capi` directory contains the C programs used in Chapter 7, "Writing MySQL Programs Using C."

- The `perlapi` directory contains the Perl DBI scripts used in Chapter 8, "Writing MySQL Programs Using Perl DBI."

- The `phpapi` directory contains the PHP scripts used in Chapter 9, "Writing MySQL Programs Using PHP."

- The `ssl` directory contains certificate and key files for setting up SSL connections between MySQL client programs and the server. See Section 13.5, "Setting Up Secure Connections Using SSL."

The `sampdb` directory also includes a few other directories containing files that are referenced from other points in this book. Check the `README.txt` file for further information.

A.2   Obtaining MySQL and Related Software

To use this book, you must install MySQL if you haven't already done so. Depending on how you plan to access MySQL, you may also need to install additional software:

- To write Perl scripts that access MySQL databases, you need the DBI and DBD::mysql modules. If you plan to write Web-based DBI scripts, the CGI.pm module is required as well, and you'll need a Web server.

- To write PHP scripts as described in this book, you must have PHP and the PHP Data Objects (PDO) database-access extension, and you'll need a Web server.

This book uses the Apache server for Web-based scripts, but others may work.

If you have an account with an Internet service provider that offers MySQL services, it's very likely that all these packages have been installed already. In that case, just go ahead and use them. Otherwise, check the following table to find the primary distribution point for each package.

Package	Location
MySQL	`http://dev.mysql.com`
Perl modules	`http://cpan.perl.org`
PHP	`http://www.php.net`
Apache	`http://httpd.apache.org`

The version of a package that you install depends on your needs:

- For maximum stability, be conservative and use the most recent stable version of a package. That gives you the benefit of the newest features and the greatest number of bug fixes without exposing you to experimental code in development versions.

- To be on the cutting edge, or if you require a feature that's available only in the newest version, use the latest development release.

The distribution sites for each package indicate which versions are stable releases and which are development releases. They also provide per-version feature change lists to help you decide which release is best for you.

MySQL stable releases are currently produced from the 5.5 series and development releases from the 5.6 series. This book uses MySQL 5.5 as its baseline but also covers some of the features available in early 5.6 releases available at the time of writing. For a production site, I recommend that you use a stable release and not a development release, so my recommendation for most readers is to use MySQL 5.5. To experiment with newer features, use MySQL 5.6.

Precompiled binaries are available for many of the installation packages. Binary distributions typically are available in the native packaging format for some platforms, such as RPM packages for Linux or DMG packages for Mac OS X. Other more generic formats also are available, such as compressed `tar` files for Unix systems and Zip archives for Windows. If you prefer to compile software from source, or if a binary distribution isn't available for your platform, you'll need a C compiler (C++ for MySQL).

Some platforms have their own packaging system. This is common on Unix, and Unix-like systems such as Linux. In such cases, it's very likely that you can use the packaging system to install all the software you need. For example, you might be able to use the FreeBSD port system, `emerge` on Gentoo Linux, `yum` on Red Hat Linux, or `apt-get` on Debian Linux.

The remainder of this appendix provides installation notes for MySQL and the required Perl and PHP software.

A.3   MySQL Installation Notes

Installing MySQL involves the following steps:

1. If you are going to install a server on a Unix system, decide which login account to use for running MySQL and create the account if necessary.

2. Obtain and unpack any distributions to be installed. If you are using a source distribution, compile it and install it.

3. Set your `PATH` environment variable to include the `bin` directory located under the MySQL installation directory. This makes it easier to invoke MySQL programs without typing their full pathnames.

4. If you are not going to run a server and intend to use only MySQL client programs to access a server maintained by someone else, you can skip the remaining steps.

5. Initialize the data directory and the grant tables in the `mysql` database. Some installation package types do this for you. This includes server RPM packages on Linux and DMG packages on Mac OS X. On Windows, it is not necessary to initialize the data directory or the grant tables because they are included pre-initialized in the distribution.

6. Start the server.

7. Initialize other system tables in the `mysql` database.

The following sections provide additional details for each of those steps.

After installing MySQL, there are other actions that you'll probably want to perform:

- Assign passwords to MySQL accounts for better security. The default installation permits connections to MySQL without a password.

- Arrange for the server to start and stop automatically as part of your system's normal startup and shutdown procedures, and put the `--user` option in an option file to avoid having to specify it each time you start the server.

- Enable logging, which is useful for monitoring the server, for replication, and for data recovery procedures.

- Configure the server further. For example, you can enable or disable storage engines, or specify tuning parameters for them.

Instructions for performing these and other administrative procedures are given in Chapter 12, "General MySQL Administration." In particular, you should read the sections on assigning passwords, server startup and shutdown, and running the server using an unprivileged user account.

A.3.1   Creating a Login Account for the MySQL User

This step is necessary only if you're going to run a MySQL server. You can skip it if you plan to use MySQL client software only.

On Unix, the MySQL server can be run using any account on your system, but for security and administrative reasons, do not run the server as `root`. I recommend that you create a separate account to use for MySQL administration and that you run the server as that user. That way, you can log in as that user and have full privileges in the data directory to perform maintenance and troubleshooting. For additional discussion on the benefits of using an account other than `root` for MySQL, see Section 12.2.1.1, "Running the Server Using an Unprivileged Login Account."

This book uses `mysql` for both the Unix user and group names of the MySQL administrative account. If you plan to install MySQL only for your own use, you can run it from your own account, in which case you'll use your own login and group names wherever you see `mysql` for a user or group name in this book.

Procedures for creating user accounts vary from system to system. Consult your local documentation for specific details. (If you use RPM packages on Linux, installing a server package automatically creates a login account as necessary for a user named `mysql`.)

Before you create an account to use for running MySQL, check first to see whether your system already has one. Many Unix systems include a `mysql` user and group among the set of standard accounts. For example, Mac OS X includes a `mysql` account (which satisfies the assumption made by Mac OS X DMG packages that a login account named `mysql` already exists).

A.3.2 Installing MySQL

To install MySQL on Windows, I recommand that you use the MySQL Installer. This installer walks you through the steps required to install MySQL.

On Unix, MySQL distributions contain one or more of the following components:

- The `mysqld` server
- Client programs (`mysql`, `mysqladmin`, and so forth)
- Client programming support (C libraries and header files)

Some packaging formats may split a full distribution into multiple components, so be sure to install the packages that give you everything you need. For example, RPM packages may divide the distribution into server, client, and development packages. If you plan to connect to a server that's running on another machine, you need not install a server. But you should always install client software so that you can connect to whichever server you use. If you plan to write your own programs, you'll need the development package.

It is also possible to build MySQL from a source distribution. This is more involved than installing from a binary (pre-built) distribution because you must compile the software, but you also get more control over configuration parameters. For example, you can compile the distribution to include only the storage engines that you want.

A.3.3 Setting Your `PATH` Environment Variable

Your shell (command interpreter) uses the `PATH` environment variable to determine where to look for programs when you enter commands at the command prompt. It's easier to invoke MySQL programs if you set your `PATH` variable to include the `bin` directory located under the MySQL installation directory. Then you can type command names without specifying their full pathnames.

On Unix, `PATH` usually is set in one of your shell's startup files, such as `.tcshrc` for `tcsh`, or `.bashrc` or `.bash_profile` for `bash`. For example, if you use `tcsh`, there might be a line in your `.tcshrc` file that looks like this:

```
setenv PATH /bin:/usr/bin:/usr/local/bin
```

If the MySQL programs are installed in `/usr/local/mysql/bin`, change the value of PATH as follows:

```
setenv PATH /usr/local/mysql/bin:/bin:/usr/bin:/usr/local/bin
```

If you use `bash`, one or more of your shell startup files might contain a line like this:

```
PATH=/bin:/usr/bin:/usr/local/bin
```

Change the setting to this:

```
PATH=/usr/local/mysql/bin:/bin:/usr/bin:/usr/local/bin
```

After you modify the shell startup file or files, the new setting takes effect each time you log in thereafter.

On Windows, set your PATH value like this:

1. Right-click My Computer on the desktop and select Properties.

2. Select the Advanced tab and click Environment Variables.

3. Select Path from the system variable list and click Edit.

4. Add the appropriate `bin` directory to the path, preceded by a semicolon to separate it from the last directory currently in the path. For example, if you install MySQL in `C:\mysql`, add `;C:\mysql\bin` to your path.

You might need to open a new console window (or perhaps restart Windows) to see the effect of the change.

A.3.4   Initializing the Data Directory and Grant Tables

Before you can use your MySQL installation, you must initialize the data directory and the grant tables in the `mysql` database. These tables control access to your server. This step is necessary only if you're going to run a MySQL server. You can skip it if you plan to use MySQL client software only. You can also skip it on Windows because the grant tables are included pre-initialized in Windows distributions.

In the following instructions, *DATADIR* represents the pathname to your data directory. It typically is located under your MySQL installation base directory and named `data` or `var`. Normally, you run the commands shown here as `root`. If you're logged in as the MySQL user (for example, `mysql`) or you've installed MySQL under your own account because you intend to run it for yourself, you can execute the commands without being `root` and should omit the `--user` option. You can also skip the `chown` and `chgrp` commands.

To initialize the data directory, the `mysql` database, and the default grant tables, change location into the MySQL installation directory and run the `mysql_install_db` script. (You need not do this if you are installing from RPM packages or a Mac OS X package because they run `mysql_install_db` for you.) For example, if you installed MySQL into `/usr/local/mysql`, the commands look like this:

```
# cd /usr/local/mysql
# scripts/mysql_install_db --user=mysql
```

After running `mysql_install_db`, change the user and group ownership and the access mode of all files under the data directory. Assuming that the user and group names both should be `mysql`, the commands look like this:

```
# chown -R mysql DATADIR
# chgrp -R mysql DATADIR
# chmod -R go-rwx DATADIR
```

The `chown` and `chgrp` commands change the ownership to the MySQL login account user and group, and `chmod` changes the access mode to keep everybody out of the data directory except that user.

The last few steps actually are part of the more comprehensive lockdown procedure detailed in Section 13.1.2, "Securing Your MySQL Installation." Check that section for additional instructions on making your installation secure.

If `mysql_install_db` fails, consult the installation chapter in the MySQL Reference Manual to see what it says about the problem you're encountering. If `mysql_install_db` doesn't run to completion successfully, any grant tables it may have created are likely incomplete. You should remove them because `mysql_install_db` does not try to re-create any tables that it finds already created. You can remove the entire `mysql` database like this:

```
# rm -rf DATADIR/mysql
```

A.3.5 Starting the Server

After MySQL has been installed, you can start the server. The procedure differs for Unix and Windows.

A.3.5.1 Starting the Server on Unix

Run the commands in this section from the MySQL installation directory. Normally, you run the commands as `root` and use the `--user` option to tell the server to run as `mysql`. However, if you're logged in as the MySQL user (for example, `mysql`) or you're running MySQL under your own account, omit the `--user` option.

Change location into the MySQL installation base directory (for example, `/usr/local/mysql`) and use `mysqld_safe` to start the server:

```
# cd /usr/local/mysql
# bin/mysqld_safe --user=mysql &
```

You can specify other options on the command line or specify options in an option file. See Section 12.2.3, "Specifying Server Startup Options."

A.3.5.2   Starting the Server on Windows

If you installed MySQL in a location other than the default selected by the installer, you must place a [mysqld] option group in an option file that the server reads when it starts, so that it can determine where the installation base directory and the data directory are located. Typical option files are the my.ini file in the MySQL installation directory or C:\my.ini. For example, if you install MySQL in C:\mysql, the option group should look like this (note the use of forward slashes in the pathnames rather than backslashes):

```
[mysqld]
basedir=C:/mysql
datadir=C:/mysql/data
```

If you chose a different installation directory, change the pathnames in the option file.

To start the server manually from the command line, change location to the directory where it is installed and enter this command:

```
C:\> mysqld
```

You can specify other options on the command line or in an option file. See Section 12.2.3, "Specifying Server Startup Options."

To run the server in console mode so that it displays error messages in a console window, invoke it with the --console option:

```
C:\> mysqld --console
```

When you run the server in console mode, you can specify other options on the command line after the --console option or in an option file.

If you start the server from the command line, you may not see another command prompt until the server exits. If this occurs, just open another console window in which to run MySQL client programs.

Another way to run the server on Windows is to create a service for MySQL that starts automatically whenever Windows starts. For details, see Section 12.2.2.2, "Running the Server as a Windows Service."

A.3.6   Initializing Other System Tables

After starting the server, there are other system tables in the mysql database you can optionally set up, such as the time zone tables and the server-side help tables.

The time zone tables permit named time zones to be used. To enable them, use the instructions in Section 12.6.1, "Configuring Time Zone Support."

The mysql command-line client can access server-side help via the help command. To enable this command, you must set up the help tables in the mysql database. Most installation methods do this automatically for a first-time install, and current distributions of MySQL for

Windows include preinitialized help tables. It should not be necessary to set up the help tables manually.

If you use an installation method that does not set up the help tables, you can load them manually. To do this, make sure that the server is running. Then locate the `fill_help_tables.sql` file, which contains SQL statements that create and load the tables. Likely locations are in `/usr/share/mysql`, the `share` directory under the MySQL base installation directory, or the `scripts` directory of a source distribution. After you find the file, execute the following command in the directory where the file is located:

```
% mysql -p -u root mysql < fill_help_tables.sql
```

The command will prompt you for the MySQL `root` account password. Omit the `-p` option if you have not yet set up a password.

A.4   Perl DBI Installation Notes

To write Perl scripts that access MySQL databases, the DBI software must be available. You must install any of the following that are not present on your system:

- The DBI module provides the general DBI driver, and the DBD::mysql module provides the MySQL-specific driver. DBI requires at least Perl 5.6.0 (with 5.6.1 preferred). As of DBI 1.611, the minimum Perl version is 5.8.1. (If you don't have Perl installed, visit `http://www.perl.com`, download a Perl distribution, and install it before you install DBI support.)

- The MySQL C client libraries and header files must be available because DBD::mysql uses them. (They should already have been installed as part of the MySQL installation procedure.)

- To write Web-based DBI scripts, you need the CGI.pm module.

To find out whether a given Perl module is installed already, use the `perldoc` command:

```
% perldoc DBI
% perldoc DBD::mysql
% perldoc CGI
```

If the module is installed, `perldoc` will display its documentation. Otherwise, obtain any Perl modules you need by visiting `http://cpan.perl.org`.

A.5   PHP and PDO Installation Notes

This book uses PHP with the PHP Data Objects (PDO) database-access extension for writing scripts used by means of a Web server. It's assumed that you'll use the Apache Web server, although you can probably substitute a different server. To use PDO, PHP must be installed. If PHP is not present on your system, visit `http://www.php.net` to obtain a distribution.

The PDO driver for MySQL can be linked against the MySQL C client library (the `libmysqlclient` library described in Appendix G, "C API Reference") or the `mysqlnd` library. `mysqlnd` is a native driver that implements the same communication protocol as `libmysqlclient` and can be used as a replacement for it. If you don't use `mysqlnd`, the MySQL client library must be installed in addition to PDO. (That library should already have been installed as part of the MySQL installation procedure.)

PDO works with PHP 5.0 and up, but this appendix assumes a minimum of PHP 5.1 because that is when PDO was first bundled with PHP. To use PDO with `mysqlnd`, you'll need at least PHP 5.3. See `http://www.php.net/pdo` for more information.

If you compile PHP from source, be sure to use the configuration options that include MySQL and PDO support. For Windows, PHP binary distributions are available in Zip archive and `.msi` installer formats. If you use a Zip archive, unpack it at the location where you want PHP installed. The `.msi` package is more convenient because it walks you through configuring Apache for PHP support and sets your PATH environment variable to include the PHP installation location. However, if you use the installer, be sure to select extension installation or PDO and MySQL support will not be installed.

If you encounter problems setting up PHP, check the "VERBOSE INSTALL" section of the INSTALL file included with the PHP distribution.

After PHP and PDO have been installed, check the Apache configuration file, `httpd.conf`. You'll need to instruct Apache to load the PHP module when it starts, and also how to recognize PHP scripts. (`httpd.conf` can include other files using Include directives. If you don't see in that file the information that is described in the following paragraphs, check any included files as well.)

To tell Apache to load the PHP module, `httpd.conf` must include LoadModule and AddModule directives in the appropriate sections (look for other similar directives). The directives might already have been added for you during PHP installation. If not, you must add them yourself. They should look something like this, although the pathname in the LoadModule directive might need adjustment for your system:

```
LoadModule php5_module libexec/libphp5.so
AddModule mod_php5.c
```

Next, edit `httpd.conf` to tell Apache how to recognize PHP scripts. PHP recognition is based on the filename extension that you use for PHP scripts. The most common extension is `.php`, which is the extension used for examples in this book. To enable `.php` as the PHP script extension, include the following line in the `httpd.conf` file:

```
AddType application/x-httpd-php .php
```

You can also tell Apache to recognize `index.php` as a permitted default file for a directory when no filename is specified at the end of a URL. You'll probably find a line in `httpd.conf` that looks like this:

```
DirectoryIndex index.html
```

Change it to this:

```
DirectoryIndex index.php index.html
```

After editing the Apache configuration file, stop the `httpd` server if it was already running; then restart it. On many systems, commands such as the following accomplish this (executed as `root`):

```
# /usr/local/apache/bin/apachectl stop
# /usr/local/apache/bin/apachectl start
```

You can also set up Apache to start and stop at system startup and shutdown time. See the Apache documentation for instructions. Normally, this involves running `apachectl start` at boot time and `apachectl stop` at shutdown time.

Data Type Reference

This appendix describes the data types provided by MySQL. For more information on the use of each type, see Chapter 3, "Data Types."

Type name specifications use the following conventions:

- Square brackets ([]) in syntax descriptions indicate optional information.

- *M* represents the maximum display width for integer types, the precision (number of significant digits) for floating-point and decimal types, the number of bits for BIT, and the maximum length for string types. In string column definitions, the length is specified in bytes for binary string types and in characters for nonbinary string types.

- *D* represents the scale (number of digits following the decimal point) for numeric types that have a fractional part. *D* must be less than or equal to *M* or an error occurs.

- *fsp* represents the fractional seconds precision for temporal types that permit fractional seconds.

Each type description includes one or more of the following kinds of information:

Meaning. A short description of the type.

Permitted attributes. Optional attribute keywords that may be associated with the data type in CREATE TABLE or ALTER TABLE statements. Attributes are listed in alphabetical order, but this does not necessarily correspond to the order imposed by the syntax of CREATE TABLE or ALTER TABLE (described in Appendix E, "SQL Syntax Reference"). The attributes listed for individual data type descriptions are in addition to global attributes that apply to all or almost all data types. The global attributes are listed here rather than in each type description:

- NULL or NOT NULL may be specified for any type.

- DEFAULT *default_value* may be specified in all column definitions except for integer columns that have the AUTO_INCREMENT attribute, BLOB and TEXT columns, and spatial columns. With the exception of the TIMESTAMP and (from MySQL 5.6.5 on) DATETIME types, default values must be constants. For example, you cannot specify DEFAULT CURDATE() for a DATE column.

Permitted length. For columns with string data types, this is the maximum permitted length of values that can be stored in the column.

Range. For numeric or temporal (date and time) types, the range of values that the type can represent. For integer numeric types, two ranges are given because integer columns can be signed or unsigned, and the ranges differ for each case.

Zero value. For temporal types, the "zero" value that is stored if an illegal value is inserted into the column. (The SQL mode must be set to permit this or an error occurs for illegal values.)

Default value. The default value if no explicit DEFAULT attribute is present in the type specification. This applies only when strict SQL mode is not enabled. If no DEFAULT clause is given in strict mode, the column is defined with a default of NULL if it can take NULL values, and with no default value otherwise. For further information, see Section 3.2.3, "Specifying Column Default Values."

Storage required. The number of bytes or characters required to store values of the type. For some types, this value is fixed. For other types, the number varies depending on the length of the value stored in the column.

Comparisons. For string types, this value specifies how comparisons are performed (which affects grouping, sorting, and indexing as well). Binary string types are compared byte by byte using the numeric value of each byte. Nonbinary string types are compared character by character based on the character set collating sequence.

Synonyms. Synonyms for the type name.

Note. Miscellaneous observations about the type.

If you're not sure how your version of MySQL will treat a given column definition, create a table that contains a column defined the way you're wondering about; then use SHOW CREATE TABLE or DESCRIBE to see how MySQL reports the definition. For example, if you can't remember the effect of the UNICODE character type attribute or SERIAL shorthand data type, create a table that uses them; then tell MySQL to display the resulting table definition:

```
mysql> CREATE TABLE t (c CHAR(10) UNICODE, s SERIAL);
mysql> SHOW CREATE TABLE t\G
*************************** 1. row ***************************
       Table: t
Create Table: CREATE TABLE `t` (
  `c` char(10) CHARACTER SET ucs2 DEFAULT NULL,
  `s` bigint(20) unsigned NOT NULL AUTO_INCREMENT,
  UNIQUE KEY `s` (`s`)
) ENGINE=InnoDB DEFAULT CHARSET=latin1
```

B.1 Numeric Types

MySQL provides exact-value and approximate-value numeric data types. Numeric types have different ranges, so choose them according to the range of values you need to represent. There is also a BIT type for representing bit-field values.

The integer and fixed-point (DECIMAL) types are exact-value data types. FLOAT and DOUBLE types are approximate-value data types. For the exact-value types, values are stored exactly as given and calculations are performed exactly with no rounding error if the values and calculations are within range of the types. For approximate-value types, calculations are subject to rounding error.

For integer types, a column must be indexed if the AUTO_INCREMENT attribute is specified. Inserting NULL into an AUTO_INCREMENT column causes the next sequence value to be inserted into the column. Typically, this is a value that is one greater than the column's current maximum value. Chapter 3, "Data Types," details the precise behavior of AUTO_INCREMENT columns. (AUTO_INCREMENT can be used with floating-point columns as well, but this is uncommon.)

The ZEROFILL and UNSIGNED attributes can be given for numeric types other than BIT:

- Values are padded with leading zeros to the column's display width if the ZEROFILL attribute is specified.

- If the UNSIGNED attribute is specified, negative values are not permitted. (SIGNED is also a permitted attribute, but has no effect because numeric types are signed by default.)

SERIAL DEFAULT VALUE as an attribute for integer or floating-point data types is shorthand for NOT NULL AUTO_INCREMENT UNIQUE.

In some cases, specifying one attribute causes another to be enabled as well. Specifying ZEROFILL for a numeric type automatically causes the column to be UNSIGNED. Specifying AUTO_INCREMENT automatically causes the column to be NOT NULL.

Note that the DESCRIBE and SHOW COLUMNS statements report the default value for an AUTO_INCREMENT column as NULL, although you cannot store a literal NULL into such a column. This indicates that you produce the default column value (the next sequence number) by setting the column to NULL when you create a new row.

B.1.1   Integer Types

- TINYINT[(M)]

  Meaning. A very small integer. M is the maximum display width, from 1 to 255. If omitted, M defaults to 4 (or 3 if the column is UNSIGNED).

  Permitted attributes. AUTO_INCREMENT, SERIAL DEFAULT VALUE, UNSIGNED, ZEROFILL.

  Range. −128 to 127 (-2^7 to 2^7-1), or 0 to 255 (0 to 2^8-1) if UNSIGNED.

  Default value. NULL if the column can be NULL; 0 if NOT NULL.

  Storage required. 1 byte.

  Synonyms. INT1[(M)]. BOOL and BOOLEAN are synonyms for TINYINT(1).

- SMALLINT[(*M*)]

  Meaning. A small integer. *M* is the maximum display width, from 1 to 255. If omitted, *M* defaults to 6 (or 5 if the column is UNSIGNED).

  Permitted attributes. AUTO_INCREMENT, SERIAL DEFAULT VALUE, UNSIGNED, ZEROFILL.

  Range. −32768 to 32767 (-2^{15} to $2^{15}-1$), or 0 to 65535 (0 to $2^{16}-1$) if UNSIGNED.

  Default value. NULL if the column can be NULL; 0 if NOT NULL.

  Storage required. 2 bytes.

  Synonyms. INT2[(*M*)].

- MEDIUMINT[(*M*)]

  Meaning. A medium-sized integer. *M* is the maximum display width, from 1 to 255. If omitted, *M* defaults to 9 (or 8 if the column is UNSIGNED).

  Permitted attributes. AUTO_INCREMENT, SERIAL DEFAULT VALUE, UNSIGNED, ZEROFILL.

  Range. −8388608 to 8388607 (-2^{23} to $2^{23}-1$), or 0 to 16777215 (0 to $2^{24}-1$) if UNSIGNED.

  Default value. NULL if the column can be NULL; 0 if NOT NULL.

  Storage required. 3 bytes.

  Synonyms. INT3[(*M*)] and MIDDLEINT[(*M*)].

- INT[(*M*)]

  Meaning. A normal-sized integer. *M* is the maximum display width, from 1 to 255. If omitted, *M* defaults to 11 (or 10 if the column is UNSIGNED).

  Permitted attributes. AUTO_INCREMENT, SERIAL DEFAULT VALUE, UNSIGNED, ZEROFILL.

  Range. −2147483648 to 2147483647 (-2^{31} to $2^{31}-1$), or 0 to 4294967295 (0 to $2^{32}-1$) if UNSIGNED.

  Default value. NULL if the column can be NULL; 0 if NOT NULL.

  Storage required. 4 bytes.

  Synonyms. INTEGER[(*M*)] and INT4[(*M*)].

- BIGINT[(*M*)]

  Meaning. A large integer. *M* is the maximum display width, from 1 to 255. If omitted, *M* defaults to 20.

  Permitted attributes. AUTO_INCREMENT, SERIAL DEFAULT VALUE, UNSIGNED, ZEROFILL.

  Range. −9223372036854775808 to 9223372036854775807 (-2^{63} to $2^{63}-1$), or 0 to 18446744073709551615 (0 to $2^{64}-1$) if UNSIGNED.

  Default value. NULL if the column can be NULL; 0 if NOT NULL.

  Storage required. 8 bytes.

Synonyms. `INT8[(M)]`.

Note. `SERIAL` as a data type name is shorthand for `BIGINT UNSIGNED NOT NULL AUTO_INCREMENT UNIQUE`.

B.1.2   Fixed-Point Types

- `DECIMAL[(M, [D])]`

  Meaning. A fixed-point number. M is the number of significant digits that values can have, from 1 to 65. D is the number of decimal places, from 0 to 30. If D is 0, column values have no decimal point or fractional part. If omitted, M and D default to 10 and 0, respectively.

  Permitted attributes. `UNSIGNED`, `ZEROFILL`.

  Range. The range for a given `DECIMAL` column is determined by M and D and whether the `UNSIGNED` attribute is given.

  Default value. `NULL` if the column can be `NULL`; 0 if `NOT NULL`.

  Storage required. Storage depends on the number of digits on the left and right sides of the decimal point. For each side, 4 bytes are required for each multiple of nine digits, plus 1 to 4 bytes if there are any remaining digits. Storage per value is the sum of the left and right side storage.

  Synonyms. `NUMERIC[(M, [D])]`, `DEC[(M, [D])]`, and `FIXED[(M, [D])]`.

B.1.3   Floating-Point Types

- `FLOAT(p)`

  Meaning. A floating-point number. In standard SQL, the precision p represents the minimum required bits of precision. In MySQL, p is used only to determine whether the data type is single-precision or double-precision:

  - For values of p from 0 to 24, the type is single-precision, equivalent to `FLOAT` with no M or D specifiers.

  - For values of p from 25 to 53, the type is double-precision, equivalent to `DOUBLE` with no M or D specifiers.

  Values of p outside the range from 0 to 53 are illegal.

  Permitted attributes. `UNSIGNED`, `ZEROFILL`.

  Range. See the `FLOAT` and `DOUBLE` type descriptions later in this section.

  Default value. `NULL` if the column can be `NULL`; 0 if `NOT NULL`.

  Storage required. 4 bytes for single-precision; 8 bytes for double-precision.

- FLOAT[(M,D)]

  Meaning. A small floating-point number; single-precision (less precise than DOUBLE). M is the number of significant digits that values can have, from 1 to 255. D is the number of decimal places, from 0 to 30. If D is 0, column values have no decimal point or fractional part. If M and D are omitted, the display size and number of decimals are undefined; values are stored to the full precision supported by your hardware.

  Permitted attributes. UNSIGNED, ZEROFILL.

  Range. Minimum nonzero values are ±1.175494351E–38; maximum nonzero values are ±3.402823466E+38. Negative values are prohibited if the column is UNSIGNED.

  Default value. NULL if the column can be NULL; 0 if NOT NULL.

  Storage required. 4 bytes.

  Synonyms. FLOAT4 is a synonym for FLOAT with no M or D specifiers. If the REAL_AS_FLOAT SQL mode is enabled, REAL[(M,D)] is a synonym for FLOAT[(M,D)].

- DOUBLE[(M,D)]

  Meaning. A large floating-point number; double-precision (more precise than FLOAT). M and D have the same meaning as for FLOAT.

  Permitted attributes. UNSIGNED, ZEROFILL.

  Range. Minimum nonzero values are ±2.2250738585072014E–308; maximum nonzero values are ±1.7976931348623157E+308. Negative values are prohibited if the column is UNSIGNED.

  Default value. NULL if the column can be NULL; 0 if NOT NULL.

  Storage required. 8 bytes.

  Synonyms. DOUBLE PRECISION[(M,D)] is a synonym for DOUBLE[(M,D)], as is REAL[(M,D)] if the REAL_AS_FLOAT SQL mode is not enabled. FLOAT8 is a synonym for DOUBLE with no M or D specifiers.

B.1.4 BIT Type

- BIT[(M)]

  Meaning. A bit-field value. M should be an integer from 1 to 64 indicating the number of bits per value. If omitted, M defaults to 1.

  Permitted attributes. None, other than the global attributes.

  Default value. NULL if the column can be NULL; 0 if NOT NULL.

  Storage required. Approximately $(M+7)/8$ bytes.

B.2 String Types

The MySQL string types are general-purpose types, commonly used to store binary or character (text) data. Types are available to hold values of varying maximum lengths and can be chosen according to whether you want values to be treated as binary or nonbinary strings.

BINARY, VARBINARY, and the BLOB types are binary string types. A binary string is a sequence of bytes, and its length is measured in bytes. Binary strings have no character set and values are compared based on their numeric byte values.

CHAR, VARCHAR, and the TEXT types are nonbinary string types. A nonbinary string is a sequence of characters. It has a character set and collation. The character set defines the permitted characters for the data type and the collation defines the character sort order. A length as specified in a nonbinary string column definition indicates the maximum number of characters the column should be able to hold.

Lengths of nonbinary string values normally are measured in characters but can be measured in bytes instead. To obtain the length of a nonbinary string in characters or bytes, use the CHAR_LENGTH() or LENGTH() function, respectively. A nonbinary string that is n characters long is also n bytes long if it contains single-byte characters, but more than n bytes long if it contains multi-byte characters. This affects the storage requirements for nonbinary string columns:

- Fixed-length columns such as CHAR(M) require enough space to store M instances of the widest character in the character set. For example, characters in the utf8 character set vary from 1 to 3 bytes each, so CHAR(M) requires $M \times 3$ bytes.

- Variable-length columns such as VARCHAR(M) require only enough space to store the actual characters in a given value, plus the prefix that store the value's length in bytes. A VARCHAR(10) column with the double-byte ucs2 character set requires 1 byte for the length prefix, plus anywhere from 0 bytes for an empty string to 20 bytes for a 10-character string.

You can specify a character set and collation for the nonbinary string types (CHAR, VARCHAR, TEXT), as well as for the ENUM and SET types:

- The syntax for specifying a character set is CHARACTER SET charset, where charset is a character set name such as latin1, greek, or utf8. CHARSET is a synonym for CHARACTER SET.

- The syntax for specifying a collation is COLLATE collation, where collation names a permitted collation for the character set.

- If no character set or collation are given, they are determined from the table defaults. For a character set given without a collation, the collation is the default collation for the character set. For a collation given without a character set, the character set is implied by the collation name. If a character set and collation both are given, the collation must be compatible with the character set. For example, the latin1_bin collation is compatible with latin1 but not with utf8.

- The binary character set and the BINARY column attribute are treated specially:

    - If you specify CHARACTER SET binary for a nonbinary string type, it causes conversion to the corresponding binary string type. That is, CHAR becomes BINARY, VARCHAR becomes VARBINARY, and the TEXT types become BLOB types. ENUM and SET have no corresponding binary types, so CHARACTER SET binary simply becomes a column attribute as is.

    - The BINARY attribute is equivalent to specifying the binary collation for the character set (the collation name that ends with _bin). For example, a column defined as CHAR(10) CHARACTER SET utf8 BINARY becomes CHAR(10) CHARACTER SET utf8 COLLATE utf8_bin.

- For nonbinary string types, the ASCII and UNICODE attributes are shorthand for CHARACTER SET latin1 and CHARACTER SET ucs2, respectively.

The permitted character sets and collations supported by the server can be determined with the SHOW CHARACTER SET and SHOW COLLATION statements. These statements show which collation is the default for each character set. You can also examine the CHARACTER_SETS and COLLATIONS tables in the INFORMATION_SCHEMA database, which contain equivalent information.

Handling of values that are too long to be stored in a string column depends on the SQL mode value. If strict mode is not enabled, values are chopped to fit. Also, a warning is generated unless the chopped characters are spaces. In strict mode, an error occurs and no value is inserted if nonspace characters must be chopped.

Handling of trailing pad values varies for different string types:

- For CHAR, values are padded with spaces if necessary to the column length when stored. Trailing spaces are removed when values are retrieved.

- For BINARY, values are padded with 0x00 bytes if necessary to the column length when stored. Nothing is removed when values are retrieved.

- For VARBINARY, VARCHAR, and the BLOB and TEXT types, no padding is added or removed when values are stored or retrieved.

- For ENUM and SET, any trailing spaces in member values listed in the column definition are ignored. Consequently, any trailing spaces are stripped from values stored in the column because MySQL converts each value to the corresponding internal numeric value of the column member. This affects comparisons as well, in that trailing spaces are not significant in values compared to ENUM or SET columns.

B.2.1   Binary String Types

- BINARY[(*M*)]

  Meaning. A fixed-length binary string 0 to *M* bytes long. *M* should be an integer from 0 to 255. If omitted, *M* defaults to 1.

  Permitted attributes. None, other than the global attributes.

  Permitted length. 0 to *M* bytes.

  Default value. NULL if the column can be NULL; ' ' (empty string) if NOT NULL.

  Storage required. *M* bytes.

  Comparisons. Byte by byte, based on numeric byte values.

- VARBINARY(*M*)

  Meaning. A variable-length binary string 0 to *M* bytes long. *M* should be an integer from 0 to 65535.

  Permitted attributes. None, other than the global attributes.

  Permitted length. 0 to *M* bytes (possibly less than *M* as indicated in the Note).

  Default value. NULL if the column can be NULL; ' ' (empty string) if NOT NULL.

  Storage required. Length of value (in bytes), plus a 1-byte or 2-byte prefix to record the length. The prefix requires 1 byte if the maximum length of column values in bytes is less than 256, and 2 bytes otherwise.

  Comparisons. Byte by byte, based on numeric byte values.

  Note. In practice, the maximum length of a VARBINARY column is limited to 65535 bytes, and possibly less, depending on storage engine internal row-size limits and the space required by other columns in the table.

- TINYBLOB

  Meaning. A small BLOB (binary string) value.

  Permitted attributes. None, other than the global attributes.

  Permitted length. 0 to 255 (0 to 2^8-1) bytes.

  Default value. NULL if the column can be NULL, ' ' (empty string) if NOT NULL.

  Storage required. Length of value (in bytes), plus 1 byte to record the length.

  Comparisons. Byte by byte, based on numeric byte values.

- BLOB[(*M*)]

  Meaning. A normal-sized BLOB (binary string) value.

  Permitted attributes. None, other than the global attributes.

Permitted length. 0 to 65535 (0 to $2^{16}-1$) bytes. If a length M is given, it is used to choose the appropriate data type and then discarded. For lengths of 1 to 65535, the data type becomes BLOB. For lengths of 65536 or greater, the data types becomes whichever of MEDIUMBLOB or LONGBLOB is required to accommodate values of the given length.

Default value. NULL if the column can be NULL, ' ' (empty string) if NOT NULL.

Storage required. Length of value (in bytes), plus 2 bytes to record the length.

Comparisons. Byte by byte, based on numeric byte values.

- MEDIUMBLOB

  Meaning. A medium-sized BLOB (binary string) value.

  Permitted attributes. None, other than the global attributes.

  Permitted length. 0 to 16777215 (0 to $2^{24}-1$) bytes.

  Default value. NULL if the column can be NULL, ' ' (empty string) if NOT NULL.

  Storage required. Length of value (in bytes), plus 3 bytes to record the length.

  Comparisons. Byte by byte, based on numeric byte values.

  Synonyms. LONG VARBINARY.

- LONGBLOB

  Meaning. A large BLOB (binary string) value.

  Permitted attributes. None, other than the global attributes.

  Permitted length. 0 to 4294967295 (0 to $2^{32}-1$) bytes.

  Default value. NULL if the column can be NULL, ' ' (empty string) if NOT NULL.

  Storage required. Length of value (in bytes), plus 4 bytes to record the length.

  Comparisons. Byte by byte, based on numeric byte values.

B.2.2   Nonbinary String Types

- CHAR[(*M*)]

  Meaning. A fixed-length nonbinary string 0 to *M* characters long. *M* should be an integer from 0 to 255. If omitted, *M* defaults to 1.

  Permitted attributes. BINARY, CHARACTER SET, COLLATE.

  Permitted length. 0 to *M* characters.

  Default value. NULL if the column can be NULL; ' ' (empty string) if NOT NULL.

  Storage required. *M* characters, which is *M* × *w* bytes, where *w* is the number of bytes required for the widest character in the column character set.

Comparisons. Character by character, based on the column collation.

Synonyms. NCHAR(*M*) and NATIONAL CHAR(*M*) are synonyms for CHAR(*M*) CHARACTER SET utf8.

- VARCHAR(*M*)

  Meaning. A variable-length nonbinary string 0 to *M* characters long. *M* should be an integer from 0 to 65535.

  Permitted attributes. BINARY, CHARACTER SET, COLLATE.

  Permitted length. 0 to *M* characters (possibly less than *M*, as indicated in the Note).

  Default value. NULL if the column can be NULL; ' ' (empty string) if NOT NULL.

  Storage required. Length of value (in bytes), plus a 1-byte or 2-byte prefix to record the length. The prefix requires 1 byte if the maximum length of column values in bytes is less than 256, and 2 bytes otherwise.

  Comparisons. Character by character, based on the column collation.

  Synonyms. CHAR VARYING(*M*). NVARCHAR(*M*), NCHAR VARYING(*M*), and NATIONAL CHAR VARYING(*M*) are synonyms for VARCHAR(*M*) CHARACTER SET utf8.

  Note. In practice, the maximum length of a VARCHAR column is limited to 65535 bytes, and possibly less depending on storage engine internal row-size limits, whether the column character set is single-byte or multi-byte, and the space required by other columns in the table.

- TINYTEXT

  Meaning. A small TEXT (nonbinary string) value.

  Permitted attributes. BINARY, CHARACTER SET, COLLATE.

  Permitted length. 0 to 255 (0 to 2^8-1) bytes; the number of characters is less if the value contains multi-byte characters.

  Default value. NULL if the column can be NULL, ' ' (empty string) if NOT NULL.

  Storage required. Length of value (in bytes), plus 1 byte to record the length.

  Comparisons. Character by character, based on the column collation.

- TEXT[(*M*)]

  Meaning. A normal-sized TEXT (nonbinary string) value.

  Permitted attributes. BINARY, CHARACTER SET, COLLATE.

  Permitted length. 0 to 65535 (0 to $2^{16}-1$) bytes; the number of characters is less if the value contains multi-byte characters. If a length *M* is given, it is used to choose the appropriate data type and then discarded. For lengths of 1 to 65535, the data type becomes TEXT. For lengths of 65536 or greater, the data types becomes whichever of MEDIUMTEXT or LONGTEXT is required to accommodate values of the given length.

Default value. NULL if the column can be NULL, ' ' (empty string) if NOT NULL.

Storage required. Length of value (in bytes), plus 2 bytes to record the length.

Comparisons. Character by character, based on the column collation.

- MEDIUMTEXT

Meaning. A medium-sized TEXT (nonbinary string) value.

Permitted attributes. BINARY, CHARACTER SET, COLLATE.

Permitted length. 0 to 16777215 (0 to $2^{24}-1$) bytes; the number of characters is less if the value contains multi-byte characters.

Default value. NULL if the column can be NULL, ' ' (empty string) if NOT NULL.

Storage required. Length of value (in bytes), plus 3 bytes to record the length.

Comparisons. Character by character, based on the column collation.

Synonyms. LONG VARCHAR.

- LONGTEXT

Meaning. A large TEXT (nonbinary string) value.

Permitted attributes. BINARY, CHARACTER SET, COLLATE.

Permitted length. 0 to 4294967295 (0 to $2^{32}-1$) bytes; the number of characters is less if the value contains multi-byte characters.

Default value. NULL if the column can be NULL, ' ' (empty string) if NOT NULL.

Storage required. Length of value (in bytes), plus 4 bytes to record the length.

Comparisons. Character by character, based on the column collation.

B.2.3 ENUM and SET Types

- ENUM('value1','value2',...)

Meaning. An enumeration; column values can be assigned exactly one member of the value list.

Permitted attributes. CHARACTER SET, COLLATE.

Default value. NULL if the column can be NULL; first enumeration value if NOT NULL.

Storage required. 1 byte for enumerations with 1 to 255 members; 2 bytes for enumerations with 256 to 65535 members.

Comparisons. Based on the numeric value of column values.

Note. In the data type definition, any trailing spaces present in member values are ignored.

- SET('*value1*','*value2*',...)

    Meaning. A set; column values can be assigned zero or more members of the value list.

    Permitted attributes. CHARACTER SET, COLLATE.

    Default value. NULL if the column can be NULL; '' (empty set) if NOT NULL.

    Storage required. 1 byte (for sets with 1 to 8 members), 2 bytes (9 to 16 members), 3 bytes (17 to 24 members), 4 bytes (25 to 32 members), or 8 bytes (33 to 64 members).

    Comparisons. Based on the numeric value of column values.

    Note. In the data type definition, any trailing spaces present in member values are ignored.

B.3   Temporal (Date and Time) Types

MySQL provides several types to represent temporal data. Types are available for dates and times, either separate or in combination, and a type for storing years when you don't need a complete date. Some types can be initialized automatically to the current date and time for new rows, and updated to the current date and time automatically when other columns in rows change.

The terms *CC*, *YY*, *MM*, and *DD* in date formats represent the century, year, month, and day of month parts, respectively. The terms *hh*, *mm*, and *ss* in time formats represent the hour, minute, and second parts, respectively. In addition, MySQL 5.6.4 introduced fractional seconds support for the TIME, DATETIME, and TIMESTAMP types and permits an optional fractional part of up to 6 digits (microseconds) precision for these types. The term *uuuuuu* in time formats indicates this fractional part. (For versions before 5.6.4, ignore this part.)

In type syntax descriptions, *fsp* represents the fractional seconds precision for types that permit a fractional part. The precision must have a value from 0 to 6, where 0 indicates no fractional part and 6 indicates microseconds precision. The default is 0 if *fsp* is not specified.

As of MySQL 5.6.4, storage requirements change for the types that permit a fractional part. Storage for the nonfractional part is as indicated in individual type descriptions. Storage for the fractional part is the same across types; the following table shows the number of bytes required.

Fractional Seconds Precision	Storage Required
0	0 bytes
1, 2	1 byte
3, 4	2 bytes
5, 6	3 bytes

MySQL 5.6.5 introduced expanded support for automatically using the current timestamp as an initial value and for updates. Whereas previously these properties were available for at most a single `TIMESTAMP` column in a table, they now can be used with any `TIMESTAMP` column, and for `DATETIME` columns as well.

- `DATE`

  Meaning. A date, in `'CCYY-MM-DD'` format.

  Permitted attributes. None, other than the global attributes.

  Range. `'1000-01-01'` to `'9999-12-31'`.

  Zero value. `'0000-00-00'`.

  Default value. `NULL` if the column can be `NULL`; `'0000-00-00'` if `NOT NULL`.

  Storage required. 3 bytes.

- `DATETIME[(fsp)]`

  Meaning. A date and time value, in `'CCYY-MM-DD hh:mm:ss[.uuuuuu]'` format. As of MySQL 5.6.4, `fsp` is permitted to specify a fractional seconds precision from 0 to 6. If omitted, `fsp` defaults to 0.

  Permitted attributes. Before MySQL 5.6.5, no attributes are permitted, other than the global attributes. As of 5.6.5, `DATETIME` columns also can include `DEFAULT CURRENT_TIMESTAMP` or `ON UPDATE CURRENT_TIMESTAMP`, or both. The meanings are as for `TIMESTAMP`. See also Section 3.2.6.6, "Automatic Properties for Temporal Types."

  Range. `'1000-01-01 00:00:00[.000000]'` to `'9999-12-31 23:59:59[.999999]'`.

  Zero value. `'0000-00-00 00:00:00[.000000]'`.

  Default value. `NULL` if the column can be `NULL`; `'0000-00-00 00:00:00[.000000]'` if `NOT NULL`.

  Storage required. Before MySQL 5.6.4, 8 bytes; thereafter, 5 bytes plus storage for fractional seconds.

- `TIME[(fsp)]`

  Meaning. A time, in `'hh:mm:ss[.uuuuuu]'` format (or `'-hh:mm:ss[.uuuuuu]'` for negative values). As of MySQL 5.6.4, `fsp` is permitted to specify a fractional seconds precision from 0 to 6. If omitted, `fsp` defaults to 0.

  Permitted attributes. None, other than the global attributes.

  Range. `'-838:59:59[.000000]'` to `'838:59:59[.000000]'`.

  Zero value. `'00:00:00[.000000]'`.

  Default value. `NULL` if the column can be `NULL`; `'00:00:00[.000000]'` if `NOT NULL`.

  Storage required. Before MySQL 5.6.4, 3 bytes; thereafter, 3 bytes plus storage for fractional seconds.

Note. Although `'00:00:00[.000000]'` is used as the zero value when illegal values are inserted into a TIME column, it is also a legal value that lies within the normal column range.

- TIMESTAMP[(*fsp*)]

  Meaning. A timestamp (date and time), in `'CCYY-MM-DD hh:mm:ss[.uuuuuu]'` format. As of MySQL 5.6.4, *fsp* is permitted to specify a fractional seconds precision from 0 to 6. If omitted, *fsp* defaults to 0. The TIMESTAMP type has several special behaviors:

  - Inserting a NULL into any TIMESTAMP column of a table inserts the current date and time, unless the column has been declared to permit NULL.

  - TIMESTAMP columns may have two auto-modification properties:

    - Automatic initialization: When a row is created, the default value for the column is the current timestamp.

    - Automatic updating: When a row is updated, changing the value of any other column in the row causes the TIMESTAMP column to be updated to the date and time at which the modification occurs.

  Before MySQL 5.6.5, at most one TIMESTAMP column per table can have these properties, and you can designate which one should be treated this way. As of MySQL 5.6.5, any TIMESTAMP column can have these properties, in any combination. For additional details, see Section 3.2.6.6, "Automatic Properties for Temporal Types."

  Permitted attributes. Before MySQL 5.6.5, at most one TIMESTAMP column in a table can have attributes of DEFAULT CURRENT_TIMESTAMP or ON UPDATE CURRENT_TIMESTAMP, or both. You cannot use one attribute with one TIMESTAMP column and the other attribute with another TIMESTAMP column, nor can you use either attribute with more than one TIMESTAMP column. As of MySQL 5.6.5, any TIMESTAMP column can have these attributes, in any combination.

  DEFAULT CURRENT_TIMESTAMP causes the column to be set to the current date and time at row creation time if no value is given for the column. ON UPDATE CURRENT_TIMESTAMP causes the column to be updated with the current date and time when any other column in the row is changed from its current value. CURRENT_TIMESTAMP() and NOW() are understood as synonyms for CURRENT_TIMESTAMP.

  If the initial TIMESTAMP keyword in the column definition includes an *fsp* value, the same value must be used in any DEFAULT or ON UPDATE clauses present that specify an automatic property.

  A constant DEFAULT value can be specified to assign a TIMESTAMP column a fixed date and time value or zero.

  The NULL attribute can be given to permit a TIMESTAMP column to store NULL values. Without this attribute, storing a NULL into a TIMESTAMP column sets it to the current date and time.

Range. `'1970-01-01 00:00:01[.000000]'` to partially through the year 2038.

Zero value. `'0000-00-00 00:00:00[.000000]'`.

Default value. `DESCRIBE` and `SHOW COLUMNS` display the default value as `CURRENT_TIMESTAMP` if the column is set automatically to the current date and time when rows are created. Otherwise, the constant date and time default value is displayed. See the discussion of the permitted attributes.

Storage required. Before MySQL 5.6.4, 4 bytes; thereafter, 4 bytes plus storage for fractional seconds.

- `YEAR[(M)]`

Meaning. A year value. If given, *M* must be 2 or 4 for formats of `YY` or `CCYY`. If omitted, *M* defaults to 4.

Permitted attributes. None, other than the global attributes.

Range. `1901` to `2155`, and `0000` for `YEAR(4)`. For `YEAR(2)`, the range is the same, but only the last two digits are displayed. To avoid ambiguity about the values stored in a `YEAR(2)`, restrict those values to the range from `1970` to `2069`; alternatively, use `YEAR(4)`.

Zero value. `0000` for `YEAR(4)`; `00` for `YEAR(2)`.

Default value. `NULL` if the column can be `NULL`; `0000` or `00` if `NOT NULL`.

Storage required. 1 byte.

Note. As of MySQL 5.6.6, `YEAR(2)` is deprecated. Such columns are created as `YEAR(4)` instead.

C

Operator and Function Reference

This appendix lists the operators and functions used to construct expressions in SQL statements. Unless otherwise indicated, each has been present in MySQL at least as early as MySQL 5.5.0. Changes since MySQL 5.5.0 are indicated in the descriptions for individual operators and functions.

Most operator and function examples use the following format:

```
expr                                    → result
```

The expression *expr* demonstrates how to use an operator or function, and *result* shows the value that results from evaluating the expression. For example:

```
RIGHT('my cat',3)                       → 'cat'
```

This means that the function call RIGHT('my cat',3) produces the string result 'cat'. To try an example shown in this appendix for yourself, invoke the mysql program, type in the expression with SELECT in front of it and a semicolon after it, and press Enter:

```
mysql> SELECT RIGHT('my cat',3);
+-------------------+
| RIGHT('my cat',3) |
+-------------------+
| cat               |
+-------------------+
```

MySQL does not require a SELECT statement to have a FROM clause, which makes it easy to experiment with operators and functions by entering expressions this way.

Examples in this appendix include complete SELECT statements for functions that cannot be demonstrated otherwise. Section C.2.6, "Summary Functions," is written that way because those functions make no sense except in reference to a particular table.

Function names, as well as operators that are words, such as BETWEEN, can be specified in any lettercase.

Operator and function syntax descriptions use the following conventions:

- *expr* represents an expression; depending on the context, this may be a numeric, string, or date or time expression, and may incorporate constants, references to table columns, or other expressions.

- *str* represents a string; it can be a literal string, a reference to a table column that has a string data type, or an expression that produces a string.

- *n* represents an integer (as do letters near to *n* in the alphabet).

- *x* represents a floating-point number (as do letters near to *x* in the alphabet).

- Other argument names are used less often and are defined where used.

- Square brackets ([]) indicate optional information.

- Vertical bars (|) separate alternative items in a list. If a list is enclosed in square brackets, one alternative may be chosen. If a list is enclosed in curly brackets ({}), one alternative must be chosen.

- An ellipsis (...) indicates that the term preceding the ellipsis can be repeated.

Expression evaluation often involves type conversion of the values in the expression. For details on the circumstances under which conversions occur and the rules that MySQL uses to convert values from one type to another, see Section 3.5.2, "Type Conversion."

C.1   Operators

Operators are used to combine terms in expressions to perform arithmetic, compare values, perform bitwise or logical operations, and match patterns.

C.1.1   Operator Precedence

Operators have differing precedence levels. The following list shows these levels, from highest to lowest. Operators on the same line have the same precedence. Evaluation of operators at a higher precedence level within an expression occurs before operators at a lower precedence level. Evaluation of operators at the same precedence level occurs left to right within an expression, except that assignments evaluate right to left.

```
INTERVAL
BINARY  COLLATE
!
-  (unary minus)  ~  (unary bit negation)
^
*  /  DIV  %  MOD
```

```
+   -
<<  >>
&
|
<   <=  =  <=>  <>  !=  >=  >  IN  IS  LIKE  REGEXP  RLIKE
BETWEEN  CASE  WHEN  THEN  ELSE
NOT
AND  &&
XOR
OR  ||
:=
```

The unary operators (unary minus, unary bit negation, NOT, BINARY, and COLLATE) bind more tightly than the binary operators. That is, they group with the immediately following term in an expression, not with the rest of the expression as a whole.

```
-2+3                                      → 1
-(2+3)                                     → -5
```

Some operator precedences vary depending on the server SQL mode or MySQL version:

- If the PIPES_AS_CONCAT SQL mode is enabled, || is a string concatenation operator rather than logical OR, and its precedence is elevated to a level between ^ and the unary operators.

- NOT has a lower precedence than the ! operator. To make NOT have the same precedence as !, enable the HIGH_NOT_PRECEDENCE SQL mode.

C.1.2   Grouping Operators

These operators enable you to group expression terms to control order of evaluation or to group values into tuples.

- (...)

  Parentheses group parts of an expression. They override the default operator precedence that otherwise determines the order in which terms of an expression are evaluated. (See Section C.1.1, "Operator Precedence.") Parentheses also may be used simply for visual clarity to make an expression more readable. Nested parenthesized expressions are evaluated from innermost to outermost.

  ```
  1 + 2 * 3 / 4                          → 2.5000
  (((1 + 2) * 3) / 4)                     → 2.2500
  ```

- (expr[,expr]...)
  ROW(expr[,expr]...)

  These row constructors can be used to express a comparison between two tuples (sets) of values. The tuples to be compared must contain the same number of values. The two syntaxes (with and without the ROW keyword) are equivalent. For example, if a subquery returns a row containing three values, you can compare the result to a given three-value tuple using either of the following constructs:

```
SELECT ... FROM t2 WHERE (0,1,2) = (SELECT col1, col2, col3 FROM ...);
SELECT ... FROM t2 WHERE ROW(0,1,2) = (SELECT col1, col2, col3 FROM ...);
```

Row constructors can be used in nonsubquery contexts as well. The following statement is legal:

```
SELECT * FROM president WHERE (first_name,last_name) = ('John','Adams');
```

C.1.3   Arithmetic Operators

These operators perform standard arithmetic. The arithmetic operators work on numbers, not strings (although MySQL automatically converts strings that look like numbers to the corresponding numeric value).

Arithmetic operators follow these rules:

- Strings are converted to double-precision numbers when used in numeric context.

- Calculations use 64-bit integer arithmetic for +, -, and * if both operands are integers. This means that expressions involving large values might exceed the range of 64-bit integer calculations. Overflow results in an error.

- If both operands are integers and at least one is unsigned, the result is unsigned.

- The operand with the greatest precision determines the precision of the result for +, -, /, *, and % if either operand is real.

- Division performed with / uses 64-bit integer arithmetic in contexts where the result is used as an integer.

- Division of two exact-value numbers performed with / has a scale equal to the scale of the dividend plus the value of the div_precision_increment system variable, which is 4 by default.

- Arithmetic involving NULL values produces a NULL result.

The following arithmetic operators are available:

- +

  Addition; evaluates to the sum of the operands.

  ```
  2 + 2                                    → 4
  3.2 + 4.7                                → 7.9
  '43bc' + '21d'                           → 64
  'abc' + 'def'                            → 0
  ```

The final example in this listing shows that + does not serve as the string concatenation operator the way it does in some languages. Instead, MySQL converts the strings to numbers before performing the arithmetic operation. Strings that don't look like numbers become 0. To concatenate strings, use the CONCAT() function.

- -

Subtraction or unary minus; evaluates to the difference of the operands when used between two terms of an expression, or to the negative of the operand when used in front of a single term (that is, it flips the sign of the term).

```
10 - 7                                      → 3
-(10 - 7)                                   → -3
```

- *

Multiplication; evaluates to the product of the operands.

```
2 * 3                                       → 6
2.3 * -4.5                                  → -10.35
```

- /

Division; evaluates to the quotient of the operands. Division by zero produces a NULL result.

```
3 / 1                                       → 3.0000
1 / 3                                       → 0.3333
1 / 0                                       → NULL
```

- DIV

Integer division; evaluates to the quotient of the operands with no fractional part. Division by zero produces a NULL result. If either operand is not an integer, both operands are treated as DECIMAL values and the result is converted to integer. If the result is larger than a BIGINT value, an error occurs.

```
3 DIV 1                                     → 3
1 DIV 3                                     → 0
1 DIV 0                                     → NULL
```

- %, MOD

The modulo operator; evaluates to the remainder of *m* divided by *n*. The *m* % *n* or *m* MOD *n* operator syntax is equivalent to the MOD(*m*, *n*) function syntax. As with division, the modulo operator with a divisor of zero returns NULL.

```
12 % 4                                      → 0
12 % 5                                      → 2
12 % 0                                      → NULL
```

For values with a fractional part, modulo returns the exact remainder after division.

```
14.4 % 3.2                                  → 1.6
```

C.1.4   Comparison Operators

Comparison operators return 1 if the comparison is true and 0 if the comparison is false. You can compare numbers or strings. Operands are converted as necessary according to the following rules:

- Other than for the `<=>` operator, comparisons involving NULL values evaluate as NULL. (`<=>` is like =, except that NULL `<=>` NULL is true, whereas NULL = NULL is NULL.)

- If both operands are strings, they are compared lexically as strings. Binary strings are compared byte by byte using the numeric value of each byte. Comparisons for nonbinary strings are performed character by character using the collating sequence of the character set in which the strings are expressed. If the strings have different character sets, the comparison may result in an error or fail to yield meaningful results. A comparison between a binary and a nonbinary string is treated as a comparison of binary strings.

- If both operands are integers, they are compared numerically as integers.

- Hexadecimal constants that are not compared to a number are compared as binary strings.

- Other than for `IN()`, if either operand is a TIMESTAMP or DATETIME value and the other is a constant, the operands are compared as TIMESTAMP values. This is done to make comparisons work better for ODBC applications.

- If one operand is a decimal value, the operands are compared as decimals if the other operand is a decimal or integer value, or as double-precision floating-point values otherwise.

- In other cases, the operands are compared numerically as double-precision floating-point values. Note that this includes the case of comparing a string and a number. The string is converted to a double-precision number, which results in a value of 0 if the string doesn't look like a number. For example, `'14.3'` converts to 14.3, but `'L4.3'` converts to 0.

The following comparisons illustrate these rules:

```
2 < 12                              → 1
'2' < '12'                          → 0
'2' < 12                            → 1
```

The first comparison involves two integers, which are compared numerically. The second comparison involves two strings, which are compared lexically. The third comparison involves a string and a number, so the string is converted to double precision and the operands are compared as double-precision values.

MySQL performs string comparisons as follows: Binary strings are compared byte by byte using the numeric value of each byte. Comparisons for nonbinary strings are performed character by character using the collating sequence of the character set in which the strings are expressed. If the strings have different character sets, the comparison may result in an error or fail to yield meaningful results. A comparison between a binary and a nonbinary string is treated as a comparison of binary strings.

- =

  Evaluates to 1 if the operands are equal, and 0 otherwise.

  ```
  1 = 1                                              → 1
  1 = 2                                              → 0
  'abc' = 'abc'                                      → 1
  'abc' = 'ABC'                                      → 1
  'abc' = 'def'                                      → 0
  'abc' = 0                                          → 1
  ```

  `'abc'` is equal to both `'abc'` and `'ABC'` for string comparisons that are not case sensitive. `'abc'` is equal to 0 because it's converted to a number in accordance with the comparison rules. Because `'abc'` doesn't look like a number, it's converted to 0 for purposes of the comparison.

  For nonbinary strings, the collation of the operands determines the comparison value of characters that are similar but differ in lettercase or in accent or diacritical marks.

  String comparisons are not case sensitive unless the comparison involves a binary string, or a nonbinary string with a binary or case-sensitive collation. For example, a case-sensitive comparison is performed if you use the BINARY keyword or are comparing values from BINARY, VARBINARY, or BLOB columns.

  ```
  'abc' = 'ABC'                                           → 1
  BINARY 'abc' = 'ABC'                                    → 0
  BINARY 'abc' = 'abc'                                    → 1
  _latin1 'abc' COLLATE latin1_bin = 'ABC'               → 0
  _latin1 'abc' COLLATE latin1_general_cs = 'ABC'   → 0
  ```

  Trailing spaces are significant for binary string comparisons, but not for nonbinary string comparisons.

  ```
  BINARY 'a' = 'a '                                  → 0
  'a' = 'a '                                         → 1
  ```

- <=>

  NULL-safe equality; this operator is similar to =, except that it evaluates to 1 when the operands are equal, even when they are NULL.

  ```
  1 <=> 1                                            → 1
  1 <=> 2                                            → 0
  NULL <=> NULL                                      → 1
  NULL = NULL                                        → NULL
  ```

  The final two examples show how <=> and = handle NULL comparisons differently.

- `<>, !=`

    Evaluates to 1 if the operands are unequal, and 0 otherwise.

    ```
    3.4 != 3.4                              → 0
    'abc' <> 'ABC'                          → 0
    BINARY 'abc' <> 'ABC'                   → 1
    'abc' != 'def'                          → 1
    ```

- `<`

    Evaluates to 1 if the left operand is less than the right operand, and 0 otherwise.

    ```
    3 < 10                                  → 1
    105.4 < 10e+1                           → 0
    'abc' < 'ABC'                           → 0
    'abc' < 'def'                           → 1
    ```

- `<=`

    Evaluates to 1 if the left operand is less than or equal to the right operand, and 0 otherwise.

    ```
    'abc' <= 'a'                            → 0
    'a' <= 'abc'                            → 1
    13.5 <= 14                              → 1
    (3 * 4) - (6 * 2) <= 0                  → 1
    ```

- `>`

    Evaluates to 1 if the left operand is greater than the right operand, and 0 otherwise.

    ```
    PI() > 3                                → 1
    'abc' > 'a'                             → 1
    SIN(0) > COS(0)                         → 0
    ```

- `>=`

    Evaluates to 1 if the left operand is greater than or equal to the right operand, and 0 otherwise.

    ```
    'abc' >= 'a'                            → 1
    'a' >= 'abc'                            → 0
    13.5 >= 14                              → 0
    (3 * 4) - (6 * 2) >= 0                  → 1
    ```

- *expr* BETWEEN *min* AND *max*
  expr NOT BETWEEN *min* AND *max*

    BETWEEN evaluates to 1 if *expr* lies within the range of values spanned by *min* and *max* (inclusive), and 0 otherwise. For NOT BETWEEN, the opposite is true. If the operands *expr*, *min*, and *max* are all of the same type, these expressions are equivalent:

    expr BETWEEN *min* AND *max*
    (*min* <= *expr* AND *expr* <= *max*)

If the operands are not of the same type, type conversion occurs and the two expressions may not be equivalent. In that case, comparison occurs using the rules given at the beginning of this section.

```
'def' BETWEEN 'abc' AND 'ghi'              → 1
'def' BETWEEN 'abc' AND 'def'              → 1
13.3 BETWEEN 10 AND 20                      → 1
13.3 BETWEEN 10 AND 13                      → 0
2 BETWEEN 2 AND 2                           → 1
'B' BETWEEN 'A' AND 'a'                     → 0
BINARY 'B' BETWEEN 'A' AND 'a'             → 1
```

For `BETWEEN` expressions that use mixed temporal types or mixed temporal types and strings, it is best to use `CAST()` to ensure that all operands have the same type.

- `CASE [expr] WHEN expr1 THEN result1 ... [ELSE default] END`

  When the initial expression, `expr`, is present, `CASE` compares it to the expression following each `WHEN`. For the first one that is equal, the corresponding `THEN` value becomes the result. This is useful for comparing a given value to a set of values.

  ```
  CASE 0 WHEN 1 THEN 'T' WHEN 0 THEN 'F' END    → 'F'
  CASE 'F' WHEN 'T' THEN 1 WHEN 'F' THEN 0 END  → 0
  ```

  When the initial expression, `expr`, is not present, `CASE` evaluates `WHEN` expressions. For the first one that is true (nonzero, non-`NULL`), the corresponding `THEN` value becomes the result. This is useful for performing nonequality tests or testing arbitrary conditions.

  ```
  CASE WHEN 1=0 THEN 'absurd' WHEN 1=1 THEN 'obvious' END
                                                → 'obvious'
  ```

  If no `WHEN` expression matches, the `ELSE` value is the result. If there is no `ELSE` clause, `CASE` evaluates to `NULL`.

  ```
  CASE 0 WHEN 1 THEN 'true' ELSE 'false' END    → 'false'
  CASE 0 WHEN 1 THEN 'true' END                 → NULL
  CASE WHEN 1=0 THEN 'true' ELSE 'false' END    → 'false'
  CASE WHEN 1/0 THEN 'true' END                 → NULL
  ```

  The return type for a `CASE` expression is determined from the aggregated types of the return values by default.

  ```
  CASE 1 WHEN 0 THEN 0 ELSE 1 END               → 1
  CASE 1 WHEN 0 THEN '0' ELSE '1' END           → '1'
  ```

  However, the default return type is also affected by surrounding context, which may cause conversion to string, number, and so forth.

  Note that the `CASE` expression differs from the `CASE` statement described in Section E.2.1, "Control Structure Statements."

- *expr* IN (*value1,value2,...*)
  expr NOT IN (*value1,value2,...*)

  IN() evaluates to 1 if *expr* is one of the values in the list, and 0 otherwise. For NOT IN(), the opposite is true. These expressions are equivalent:

  expr NOT IN (*value1,value2,...*)
  NOT (*expr* IN (*value1,value2,...*))

  If all values in the list are constants, MySQL sorts them and evaluates the IN() test using a binary search, which is very fast.

3 IN (1,2,3,4,5)	→ 1
'd' IN ('a','b','c','d','e')	→ 1
'f' IN ('a','b','c','d','e')	→ 0
3 NOT IN (1,2,3,4,5)	→ 0
'd' NOT IN ('a','b','c','d','e')	→ 0
'f' NOT IN ('a','b','c','d','e')	→ 1

- *expr* IS {FALSE | TRUE | UNKNOWN}

  These constructs test *expr* against logical false, true, or unknown, and return 0 (false) or 1 (true). A value of 0 is considered false, nonzero, non-NULL values are considered true, and NULL is unknown.

2 IS FALSE	→ 0
2 IS TRUE	→ 1
2 IS UNKNOWN	→ 0
NULL IS FALSE	→ 0
NULL IS TRUE	→ 0
NULL IS UNKNOWN	→ 1

- *expr* IS NULL
  expr IS NOT NULL

  IS NULL evaluates to 1 if the value of expr is NULL, and 0 otherwise. IS NOT NULL is the opposite. These expressions are equivalent:

  expr IS NOT NULL
  NOT (*expr* IS NULL)

  IS NULL and IS NOT NULL should be used to determine whether the value of *expr* is NULL. You cannot use the regular equality and inequality comparison operators (=, <>, !=) for this purpose. (However, you can use <=> to test for equality with NULL.)

NULL IS NULL	→ 1
0 IS NULL	→ 0
NULL IS NOT NULL	→ 0
0 IS NOT NULL	→ 1
NOT (0 IS NULL)	→ 1
NOT (NULL IS NULL)	→ 0

C.1.5 Bit Operators

This section describes operators that perform bitwise calculations. Bit operations are performed using BIGINT values (64-bit integers), which limits the maximum range of the operations. Bit operations produce 64-bit unsigned values, or NULL if any operand is NULL.

- &

  Evaluates to the bitwise AND (intersection) of the operands.

  ```
  1 & 1                                    → 1
  1 & 2                                    → 0
  7 & 5                                    → 5
  ```

- |

  Evaluates to the bitwise OR (union) of the operands.

  ```
  1 | 1                                    → 1
  1 | 2                                    → 3
  1 | 2 | 4 | 8                            → 15
  1 | 2 | 4 | 8 | 15                       → 15
  ```

- ^

  Evaluates to the bitwise XOR (exclusive-OR) of the operands.

  ```
  1 ^ 1                                    → 0
  1 ^ 0                                    → 1
  255 ^ 127                                → 128
  ```

- <<

  Shifts the leftmost operand left the number of bit positions indicated by the right operand. Shifting by a negative amount results in a value of zero.

  ```
  1 << 2                                   → 4
  2 << 2                                   → 8
  1 << 63                                  → 9223372036854775808
  1 << 64                                  → 0
  ```

  The last two examples demonstrate the limits of 64-bit calculations.

- >>

  Shifts the leftmost operand right the number of bit positions indicated by the right operand. Shifting by a negative amount results in a value of zero.

  ```
  16 >> 3                                  → 2
  16 >> 4                                  → 1
  16 >> 5                                  → 0
  ```

- ~

  Performs bitwise negation (inversion) of the following operand. That is, all 0 bits become 1 and vice versa.

~0	→ 18446744073709551615
~(-1)	→ 0
~~(-1)	→ 18446744073709551615

C.1.6   Logical Operators

Logical operators (also known as "boolean operators") test the truth or falsity of expressions. Logical operations return 1 for true, 0 for false, and NULL for unknown. Logical operators interpret nonzero, non-NULL operands as true, 0 as false, and NULL as unknown.

Logical operators expect operands to be numbers, so string operands are converted to numbers before the operator is evaluated.

In MySQL, !, ||, and && indicate logical operations, as they do in C. In particular, || does not perform string concatenation as it does in standard SQL. Use the CONCAT() function instead to concatenate strings. To treat || as the string concatenation operator, enable the PIPES_AS_CONCAT SQL mode.

- NOT, !

  Logical negation; evaluates to 1 if the following operand is false and 0 if the operand is true, except that NOT NULL is NULL.

NOT 0	→ 1
NOT 1	→ 0
NOT NULL	→ NULL
NOT 3	→ 0
NOT NOT 1	→ 1
NOT '1'	→ 0
NOT '0'	→ 1
NOT 'abc'	→ 1

  The last several examples demonstrate conversion of a string operand to a number before operator evaluation.

  The precedence of NOT can be modified as described in Section C.1.1, "Operator Precedence."

- AND, &&

  Logical AND; evaluates to 1 if both operands are true (nonzero, non-NULL), 0 if either operand is false, and NULL otherwise (the result cannot be determined).

4 AND 2	→ 1
0 AND 0	→ 0
0 AND 3	→ 0
1 AND NULL	→ NULL

```
0 AND NULL                                  → 0
NULL AND NULL                               → NULL
```

- OR, ||

  Logical OR; evaluates to 1 if either operand is true (nonzero, non-NULL), 0 if both operands are false, and NULL otherwise (the result cannot be determined).

  ```
  4 OR 2                                      → 1
  0 OR 3                                      → 1
  0 OR 0                                      → 0
  1 OR NULL                                   → 1
  0 OR NULL                                   → NULL
  NULL OR NULL                                → NULL
  ```

- XOR

  Logical exclusive-OR; evaluates to 1 if exactly one operand is true (nonzero, non-NULL), and 0 otherwise. Evaluates to NULL (unknown) if either operand is NULL.

  ```
  0 XOR 0                                     → 0
  0 XOR 9                                     → 1
  7 XOR 0                                     → 1
  5 XOR 2                                     → 0
  ```

C.1.7 Cast Operators

Cast operators change how a value is interpreted or convert values from one type to another.

- _charset str

  The _charset operator is called an "introducer." It causes the following string constant or column value to be interpreted using a given character set. charset must be the name of a character set supported by the server. For example, the following expressions interpret the string 'abcd' using a character set of latin2 or utf8:

  ```
  _latin2 'abcd'
  _utf8 'abcd'
  ```

  For introducers for multi-byte character sets, padding of the result may occur if the end of the operand does not have the proper number of bytes to create a complete character.

- BINARY str

  BINARY causes the following operand to be treated as a binary string. Comparisons involving the result are performed byte by byte using the numeric value of each byte. If the following operand is a number, it is converted to string form:

  ```
  'abc' = 'ABC'                               → 1
  'abc' = BINARY 'ABC'                        → 0
  BINARY 'abc' = 'ABC'                        → 0
  '2' < 12                                    → 1
  '2' < BINARY 12                             → 0
  ```

In the last example, BINARY causes a number-to-string conversion. The operands then are compared as binary strings.

- *str* COLLATE *collation*

    The COLLATE operator causes the given string *str* to have the given collation (which must be one of the legal collations for the character set of *str*). COLLATE affects operations such as comparisons, sorting, grouping, and DISTINCT.

    ```
    SELECT ... WHERE utf8_str COLLATE utf8_icelandic_ci > 'M';
    SELECT MAX(greek_str COLLATE greek_general_ci) FROM ... ;
    SELECT ... GROUP BY latin1_str COLLATE latin1_german2_ci;
    SELECT ... ORDER BY sjis_str COLLATE sjis_bin;
    SELECT DISTINCT latin2_str COLLATE latin2_croatian_ci FROM ...;
    ```

C.1.8   Pattern-Matching Operators

MySQL provides SQL pattern matching using LIKE and regular expression pattern matching using REGEXP. SQL pattern matching succeeds only if the pattern matches the entire string to be matched. Regular expression pattern matching succeeds if the pattern is found anywhere in the string.

Section 3.5.1.1, "Operator Types," provides additional discussion and examples of pattern matching.

- *str* LIKE *pattern* [ESCAPE '*c*']
  str NOT LIKE *pattern* [ESCAPE '*c*']

    LIKE performs an SQL pattern match and evaluates to 1 if the pattern string *pattern* matches the entire string expression *str*. If the pattern does not match, LIKE evaluates to 0. For NOT LIKE, the opposite is true. These expressions are equivalent:

    ```
    str NOT LIKE pattern [ESCAPE 'c']
    NOT (str LIKE pattern [ESCAPE 'c'])
    ```

    The result is NULL if either operand is NULL.

    Two characters have special meaning in SQL patterns and serve as wildcards:

    - '%' matches any sequence of characters (including an empty string) other than NULL.

    - '_' (underscore) matches any single character.

    Patterns may contain either or both wildcard characters.

    ```
    'catnip' LIKE 'cat%'                          → 1
    'dogwood' LIKE '%wood'                         → 1
    'bird' LIKE '____'                             → 1
    'bird' LIKE '___'                              → 0
    'dogwood' LIKE '%wo__'                         → 1
    ```

LIKE compares the strings as binary strings if either operand is a binary string, or using the operand collation if the operands are nonbinary strings.

```
'abc' LIKE 'ABC'                                → 1
BINARY 'abc' LIKE 'ABC'                         → 0
'abc' LIKE BINARY 'ABC'                         → 0
'abc' LIKE 'ABC' COLLATE latin1_general_ci      → 1
'abc' LIKE 'ABC' COLLATE latin1_general_cs      → 0
```

Because '%' matches any sequence of characters, it matches no characters.

```
'' LIKE '%'                                     → 1
'cat' LIKE 'cat%'                               → 1
```

In MySQL, you can use LIKE with numeric expressions.

```
50 + 50 LIKE '1%'                               → 1
200 LIKE '2__'                                  → 1
```

To match a wildcard character literally, turn off its special meaning in the pattern string by preceding it with the escape character, '\'.

```
'100% pure' LIKE '100%'                         → 1
'100% pure' LIKE '100\%'                        → 0
'100% pure' LIKE '100\% pure'                   → 1
```

To interpret '\' literally, enable the NO_BACKSLASH_ESCAPES SQL mode. Alternatively, to redefine the escape character, specify an ESCAPE clause.

```
'100% pure' LIKE '100^%' ESCAPE '^'             → 0
'100% pure' LIKE '100^% pure' ESCAPE '^'        → 1
```

If NO_BACKSLASH_ESCAPES is enabled, the ESCAPE clause cannot specify an empty string.

- *str* REGEXP *pattern*
  str NOT REGEXP *pattern*

REGEXP performs a regular expression pattern match. It evaluates to 1 if the pattern string *pattern* matches the string expression *str*, and 0 otherwise. For NOT REGEXP, the opposite is true. These expressions are equivalent:

```
str NOT REGEXP pattern
NOT (str REGEXP pattern)
```

The result is NULL if either operand is NULL.

REGEXP compares the strings as binary strings if either operand is a binary string, or using the operand collation if the operands are nonbinary strings.

```
'abc' REGEXP 'ABC'                              → 1
BINARY 'abc' REGEXP 'ABC'                       → 0
'abc' REGEXP BINARY 'ABC'                       → 0
'abc' REGEXP 'ABC' COLLATE latin1_bin           → 0
'abc' COLLATE latin1_bin REGEXP 'ABC'           → 0
```

REGEXP is not multi-byte safe and works only for single-byte character sets.

Regular expressions are similar to the patterns used by the Unix utilities grep and sed. The following table shows the permitted pattern sequences.

Element	Meaning
^	Match the beginning of the string
$	Match the end of the string
.	Match any single character, including newline
[...]	Match any character appearing between the brackets
[^...]	Match any character not appearing between the brackets
e*	Match zero or more instances of pattern element e
e+	Match one or more instances of pattern element e
e?	Match zero or one instances of pattern element e
e1|e2	Match pattern element e1 or e2
e{m}	Match m instances of pattern element e
e{m, }	Match m or more instances of pattern element e
e{,n}	Match zero to n instances of pattern element e
e{m,n}	Match m to n instances of pattern element e
(...)	Group pattern elements into a single element
other	Nonspecial characters match themselves

A regular expression pattern need not match the entire string; it need only be found somewhere in the string.

```
'cats and dogs' REGEXP 'dogs'                    → 1
'cats and dogs' REGEXP 'cats'                    → 1
'cats and dogs' REGEXP 'c.*a.*d'                 → 1
'cats and dogs' REGEXP 'o'                       → 1
'cats and dogs' REGEXP 'x'                       → 0
```

Use ^ or $ to force a pattern to match only at the beginning or end of the string.

```
'abcde' REGEXP 'b'                    → 1
'abcde' REGEXP '^b'                   → 0
'abcde' REGEXP 'b$'                   → 0
'abcde' REGEXP '^a'                   → 1
'abcde' REGEXP 'e$'                   → 1
'abcde' REGEXP '^a.*e$'              → 1
```

The [...] and [^...] constructs specify character classes. Within a class, a range of characters may be indicated using a dash between the first and last characters of the range. For example, [a-z] matches any lowercase letter from 'a' to 'z', and [0-9] matches any decimal digit.

```
'bin' REGEXP '^b[aeiou]n$'              → 1
'bxn' REGEXP '^b[aeiou]n$'              → 0
'oboeist' REGEXP '^ob[aeiou]+st$'       → 1
'wolf359' REGEXP '[a-z]+[0-9]+'         → 1
'wolf359' REGEXP '[0-9a-z]+'            → 1
'wolf359' REGEXP '[0-9]+[a-z]+'         → 0
```

To include a literal ']' within a class, it must be the first character of the class. To include a literal '-', it must be the first or last character of the class. To include a literal '^', it must not be the first character after the '['.

Several special regular expression POSIX character class constructions having to do with collating sequences and equivalence classes are available as well, as shown in the following table.

Class	Meaning
[:alnum:]	Alphabetic and numeric characters
[:alpha:]	Alphabetic characters
[:blank:]	Whitespace (space or tab characters)
[:cntrl:]	Control characters
[:digit:]	Decimal digits (0-9)
[:graph:]	Graphic (nonblank) characters
[:lower:]	Lowercase alphabetic characters
[:print:]	Graphic or space characters
[:punct:]	Punctuation characters
[:space:]	Space, tab, newline, or carriage return
[:upper:]	Uppercase alphabetic characters
[:xdigit:]	Hexadecimal digits (0-9, a-f, A-F)

The POSIX class constructors are used within a character class and the class names include the '[' and ']' square bracket characters in their names, so when you write a character class expression that refers to any of them, be sure to include enough brackets.

```
'abc' REGEXP '[[:space:]]'              → 0
'a c' REGEXP '[[:space:]]'              → 1
'abc' REGEXP '[[:digit:][:punct:]]'     → 0
'a0c' REGEXP '[[:digit:][:punct:]]'     → 1
'a,c' REGEXP '[[:digit:][:punct:]]'     → 1
```

Within a character class, the special markers `[:<:]` and `[:>:]` match the beginning and end of word boundaries, respectively. A word character is considered to be any character in the `alnum` class or underscore. A word consists of one or more word characters not preceded by or followed by word characters.

```
'a few words' REGEXP '[[:<:]]few[[:>:]]'          → 1
'a few words' REGEXP '[[:<:]]fe[[:>:]]'           → 0
```

MySQL uses syntax similar to C for escape sequences within regular expression strings. For example, '\n', '\t', and '\\' are interpreted as newline, tab, and backslash. To specify such characters in a pattern, double the backslashes ('\\n', '\\t', and '\\\\'). One backslash is stripped off during query parsing; interpretation of the remaining escape sequence occurs during the pattern match operation.

- *str* RLIKE *pattern*
  str NOT RLIKE *pattern*

  RLIKE and NOT RLIKE are synonyms for REGEXP and NOT REGEXP.

C.2   Functions

Functions are called to perform calculations and return values. By default, functions must be invoked with no space between the function name and the parenthesis following it or an error may occur:

```
mysql> SELECT NOW();
+---------------------+
| NOW()               |
+---------------------+
| 2013-01-08 15:34:46 |
+---------------------+
mysql> SELECT NOW ();
ERROR 1630 (42000): FUNCTION NOW does not exist
```

If the IGNORE_SPACE SQL mode is enabled, the server permits spaces after names of built-in functions, although a side effect is that all function names become reserved words. Certain programs may permit this behavior to be selected by other means. For example, you can start mysql with the `--ignore-space` option; in C programs, you can call `mysql_real_connect()` with the CLIENT_IGNORE_SPACE option.

In most cases, multiple arguments to a function are separated by commas. Spaces are permitted around function arguments. Both of the following lines are legal:

```
CONCAT('abc','def')
CONCAT( 'abc' , 'def' )
```

There are a few exceptions that use alternative syntax, such as `TRIM()` or `EXTRACT()`:

```
TRIM(' ' FROM ' x ')                        → 'x'
EXTRACT(YEAR FROM '2018-01-01')             → 2018
```

Each function entry describes its syntax.

C.2.1 Comparison Functions

These functions perform comparison of values.

- `ELT(n,str1,str2,...)`

  Returns the *n*-th element from the list of strings *str1*, *str2*, ... Returns `NULL` if *n* is `NULL`, the *n*-th string is `NULL`, or there is no *n*-th string. The index of the first string is 1. `ELT()` is complementary to `FIELD()`.

  ```
  ELT(3,'a','b','c','d','e')                  → 'c'
  ELT(0,'a','b','c','d','e')                  → NULL
  ELT(6,'a','b','c','d','e')                  → NULL
  ELT(FIELD('b','a','b','c'),'a','b','c')     → 'b'
  ```

- `FIELD(arg0,arg1,arg2,...)`

  Finds *arg0* in the list of arguments *arg1*, *arg2*, ... and returns the index of the matching argument (beginning with 1). Returns 0 if there is no match or if *arg0* is `NULL`. String comparison is used if all arguments are strings, numeric comparison if all arguments are numbers, and double-precision comparison otherwise. `FIELD()` is complementary to `ELT()`.

  ```
  FIELD('b','a','b','c')                      → 2
  FIELD('d','a','b','c')                      → 0
  FIELD(NULL,'a','b','c')                     → 0
  FIELD(ELT(2,'a','b','c'),'a','b','c')       → 2
  ```

- `GREATEST(expr1,expr2,...)`

  Returns the largest argument, where "largest" is defined according to the following rules:

  - The result is `NULL` if any argument is `NULL`.
  - If the function is called in an integer context or all its arguments are integers, the arguments are compared as integers.
  - If the function is called in a floating-point context or all its arguments are floating-point values, the arguments are compared as floating-point values.
  - If neither of the preceding two rules apply, the arguments are compared as strings, using the string comparison rules described at the beginning of Section C.1.4, "Comparison Operators."

```
GREATEST(2,3,1)                              → 3
GREATEST(38.5,94.2,-1)                       → 94.2
GREATEST('a','ab','abc')                     → 'abc'
GREATEST(1,3,5)                              → 5
GREATEST('A','b','C')                        → 'C'
GREATEST(BINARY 'A','b','C')                 → 'b'
```

- IF(*expr1*, *expr2*, *expr3*)

If *expr1* is true (nonzero, non-NULL), returns *expr2*; otherwise, it returns *expr3*. The return type for IF() is determined using the following tests, in order: A string, if *expr2* or *expr3* is a string; a floating-point value if either is a floating-point value; or an integer if either is an integer.

```
IF(1,'true','false')                         → 'true'
IF(0,'true','false')                         → 'false'
IF(NULL,'true','false')                      → 'false'
IF(1.3,'nonzero','zero')                     → 'nonzero'
IF(0.3 <> 0,'nonzero','zero')                → 'nonzero'
```

Note that the IF() function differs from the IF statement described in Section E.2.1, "Control Structure Statements."

- IFNULL(*expr1*, *expr2*)

Returns *expr2* if the value of the expression *expr1* is NULL; otherwise, it returns *expr1*. IFNULL() returns a number or string according to the context in which it occurs.

```
IFNULL(NULL,'null')                          → 'null'
IFNULL('not null','null')                    → 'not null'
```

- INTERVAL(*n*, *n1*, *n2*, ...)

Returns 0 if *n* < *n1*, 1 if *n* < *n2*, and so on, or –1 if *n* is NULL. That is, INTERVAL() finds the position of the first argument within the intervals defined by the remaining arguments. All arguments must be integers. The values *n1*, *n2*, ... must be in strictly increasing order (*n1* < *n2* < ...) because a fast binary search is used. INTERVAL() behaves unpredictably otherwise.

```
INTERVAL(2,0,1,3)                            → 2
INTERVAL(7,1,3,5,7,9)                        → 4
```

- ISNULL(*expr*)

Returns 1 if the value of the expression *expr* is NULL; otherwise, it returns 0.

```
ISNULL(NULL)                                 → 1
ISNULL(0)                                    → 0
ISNULL(1)                                    → 0
```

- LEAST(*expr1*,*expr2*,...)

  Returns the smallest argument, where "smallest" is defined using the same comparison rules as for the GREATEST() function.

LEAST(2,3,1)	→ 1
LEAST(38.5,94.2,-1)	→ -1
LEAST('a','ab','abc')	→ 'a'

- NULLIF(*expr1*,*expr2*)

  Returns *expr1* if the two expression values differ, NULL if they are the same.

NULLIF(3,4)	→ 3
NULLIF(3,3)	→ NULL

- STRCMP(*str1*,*str2*)

  This function returns 1, 0, or –1, depending on whether the first argument is lexically greater than, equal to, or less than the second argument. If either argument is NULL, the function returns NULL. STRCMP() compares the strings as binary strings if either operand is a binary string, or using the operand collation if the operands are nonbinary strings.

STRCMP('a','a')	→ 0
STRCMP('a','A')	→ 0
STRCMP(BINARY 'a','A')	→ 1
STRCMP('A' COLLATE latin1_general_ci,'a')	→ 0
STRCMP('A' COLLATE latin1_general_cs,'a')	→ -1

C.2.2 Cast Functions

These functions convert values from one type to another.

- CAST(*expr* AS *type*)

  Cast an expression value *expr* to a given type. The *type* value may be BINARY[(*n*)] (binary string), CHAR[(*n*)] (nonbinary string), DATE, DATETIME, TIME, SIGNED [INTEGER], UNSIGNED [INTEGER], or DECIMAL[(*M*[,*D*])].

CAST(304 AS BINARY)	→ '304'
CAST(-1 AS UNSIGNED)	→ 18446744073709551615
CAST(13 AS DECIMAL(5,2))	→ 13.00

  An optional length *n* may be specified for BINARY and CHAR, which causes the result to have no more than *n* bytes or characters, respectively. For BINARY, values with less than *n* bytes are padded to a length of *n* with 0x00 bytes.

  CAST() can be useful for forcing columns to have a particular type when creating a new table with CREATE TABLE ... SELECT.

  ```
  mysql> CREATE TABLE t SELECT CAST(20130101 AS DATE) AS date_val;
  mysql> SHOW COLUMNS FROM t;
  ```

```
+----------+------+------+-----+---------+-------+
| Field    | Type | Null | Key | Default | Extra |
+----------+------+------+-----+---------+-------+
| date_val | date | YES  |     | NULL    |       |
+----------+------+------+-----+---------+-------+
mysql> SELECT * FROM t;
+------------+
| date_val   |
+------------+
| 2013-01-01 |
+------------+
```

CONVERT() is similar to CAST(), but CONVERT() has ODBC syntax, whereas CAST() has standard SQL syntax.

- CONVERT(*expr*, *type*)
  CONVERT(*expr* USING *charset*)

  The first form of CONVERT() serves the same purpose as CAST(), but has slightly different syntax. The *expr* and *type* arguments have the same meaning. The second (USING) form converts the value to a string that has the given character set.

CONVERT(304,BINARY)	→ '304'
CONVERT(-1,UNSIGNED)	→ 18446744073709551615
CONVERT('abc' USING utf8);	→ 'abc'

C.2.3   Numeric Functions

Numeric functions return NULL if you pass arguments that are out of range or otherwise invalid.

- ABS(*x*)

  Returns the absolute value of *x*.

ABS(13.5)	→ 13.5
ABS(-13.5)	→ 13.5

- ACOS(*x*)

  Returns the arccosine of *x*, or NULL if *x* is not in the range from −1 to 1.

ACOS(1)	→ 0
ACOS(0)	→ 1.5707963267949
ACOS(-1)	→ 3.1415926535898

- ASIN(*x*)

  Returns the arcsine of *x*, or NULL if *x* is not in the range from −1 to 1.

ASIN(1)	→ 1.5707963267949
ASIN(0)	→ 0
ASIN(-1)	→ -1.5707963267949

- ATAN(*x*)
  ATAN(*y*, *x*)

  The one-argument form of ATAN() returns the arctangent of *x*. The two-argument form is a synonym for ATAN2().

ATAN(1)	→ 0.78539816339745
ATAN(0)	→ 0
ATAN(-1)	→ -0.78539816339745

- ATAN2(*y*, *x*)

  This is like ATAN(*y*/*x*), but it uses the signs of both arguments to determine the quadrant of the return value.

ATAN2(1,1)	→ 0.78539816339745
ATAN2(1,-1)	→ 2.3561944901923
ATAN2(-1,1)	→ -0.78539816339745
ATAN2(-1,-1)	→ -2.3561944901923

- CEILING(*x*)
  CEIL(*x*)

  Returns the smallest integer not less than *x*. If the argument has an exact-value numeric type, the result value does, too. Otherwise, the result has a floating-point (approximate-value) type. This is true even though the result has no fractional part.

CEILING(3.8)	→ 4
CEILING(-3.8)	→ -3

- COS(*x*)

  Returns the cosine of *x*, where *x* is measured in radians.

COS(0)	→ 1
COS(PI())	→ -1

- COT(*x*)

  Returns the cotangent of *x*, where *x* is measured in radians.

COT(PI()/4)	→ 1

- CRC32(*str*)

  Computes a cyclic redundancy check value from the argument, which is treated as a string. The result is a 32-bit unsigned value in the range from 0 to $2^{32}-1$, or NULL if the argument is NULL.

CRC32('xyz')	→ 3951999591
CRC32('0')	→ 4108050209
CRC32(0)	→ 4108050209
CRC32(NULL)	→ NULL

- DEGREES(*x*)

Returns the value of *x*, converted from radians to degrees.

```
DEGREES(PI())                               → 180
DEGREES(PI()*2)                             → 360
DEGREES(PI()/2)                             → 90
DEGREES(-PI())                              → -180
```

- EXP(*x*)

Returns e^x, where *e* is the natural logarithm base.

```
EXP(1)                                      → 2.718281828459
EXP(2)                                      → 7.3890560989307
EXP(-1)                                     → 0.36787944117144
1/EXP(1)                                    → 0.36787944117144
```

- FLOOR(*x*)

Returns the largest integer not greater than *x*. If the argument has an exact-value numeric type, the result value does, too. Otherwise, the result has a floating-point (approximate-value) type. This is true even though the result has no fractional part.

```
FLOOR(3.8)                                  → 3
FLOOR(-3.8)                                 → -4
```

- LN(*x*)

This is a synonym for LOG().

- LOG(*x*)
  LOG(*b*,*x*)

The one-argument form of LOG() returns the natural (base *e*) logarithm of *x*.

```
LOG(0)                                      → NULL
LOG(1)                                      → 0
LOG(2)                                      → 0.69314718055995
LOG(EXP(1))                                 → 1
```

The two-argument form returns the logarithm of *x* to the base *b*.

```
LOG(10,100)                                 → 2
LOG(2,256)                                  → 8
```

You can also compute the logarithm of *x* to the base *b* using LOG(*x*)/LOG(*b*).

```
LOG(100)/LOG(10)                            → 2
LOG10(100)                                  → 2
```

- `LOG10(x)`

Returns the logarithm of x to the base 10.

`LOG10(0)`	→ `NULL`
`LOG10(10)`	→ `1`
`LOG10(100)`	→ `2`

- `LOG2(x)`

Returns the logarithm of x to the base 2.

`LOG2(0)`	→ `NULL`
`LOG2(255)`	→ `7.9943534368589`
`LOG2(32767)`	→ `14.99995597177`

`LOG2()` tells you the "width" of a value in bits. One use for this is to assess the amount of storage required for the value.

- `MOD(m, n)`

`MOD()` performs a modulo operation. `MOD(m, n)` function syntax is equivalent to `m % n` or `m MOD n` operator syntax (see Section C.1.3, "Arithmetic Operators").

- `PI()`

Returns the value of π.

`PI()`	→ `3.141593`

- `POW(x, y)`
  `POWER(x, y)`

Returns x^y, that is, x raised to the power y.

`POW(2,3)`	→ `8`
`POW(2,-3)`	→ `0.125`
`POW(4,.5)`	→ `2`
`POW(16,.25)`	→ `2`

- `RADIANS(x)`

Returns the value of x, converted from degrees to radians.

`RADIANS(0)`	→ `0`
`RADIANS(360)`	→ `6.2831853071796`
`RADIANS(-360)`	→ `-6.2831853071796`

- `RAND()`
  `RAND(n)`

`RAND()` returns a random floating-point value in the range from 0.0 to 1.0. The argument n, if given, should be an integer. If the argument is a constant, `RAND()` uses it as the seed value for the randomizer. You can use a seed value when you need a repeatable sequence of numbers for the values in a column of a result set.

```
RAND()                                           → 0.1036697114852
RAND()                                           → 0.5725383884949
RAND(10)                                         → 0.65705152196535
RAND(10)                                         → 0.65705152196535
```

If the argument is not constant, it is used as the seed value each time RAND() is called. (For example, if you name a column, then for each row, the column value seeds the randomizer for that row.)

Seeding operations are client-specific. If one client invokes RAND(n) to seed the random number generator, that does not affect the numbers returned for other clients.

If RAND() appears in the WHERE clause, it is invoked once for each execution of the clause.

- ROUND(x)
  ROUND(x, d)

ROUND() returns the value of x, rounded to a number with d decimal places. If d is 0 or missing, the result has no decimal point or fractional part. The return value has the same numeric type as the first argument, so the result has no decimals if that argument is an integer. Numbers specified as strings undergo the usual conversion to double-precision and are handled as such.

```
ROUND(15.3)                                      → 15
ROUND(15.5)                                      → 16
ROUND(-33.27834,2)                               → -33.28
ROUND(1,4)                                       → 1
ROUND('1',4)                                     → 1.0000
```

If d is negative, ROUND() trims any fractional part and causes ABS(d) digits to the left of the decimal point to become zero.

```
ROUND(123456,-2)                                 → 123500
```

ROUND() handles rounding for x as follows:

- For approximate-value numbers, rounding depends on the underlying math library.

- Exact-value numbers with a fractional part of .5 or greater are rounded away from zero. Exact-value numbers with a fractional part less than .5 are rounded toward zero. For example, 1.5 and –1.5 round to 2 and –2, whereas 1.49 and –1.49 round to 1 and –1.

For information about what constitutes an exact or approximate number, see Section 3.1.1.1, "Exact-Value and Approximate-Value Numbers."

- SIGN(*x*)

  Returns –1, 0, or 1, depending on whether the value of *x* is negative, zero, or positive.

SIGN(15.803)	→ 1
SIGN(0)	→ 0
SIGN(-99)	→ -1

- SIN(*x*)

  Returns the sine of *x*, where *x* is measured in radians.

SIN(0)	→ 0
SIN(PI()/2)	→ 1

- SQRT(*x*)

  Returns the nonnegative square root of *x*.

SQRT(625)	→ 25
SQRT(2.25)	→ 1.5
SQRT(-1)	→ NULL

- TAN(*x*)

  Returns the tangent of *x*, where *x* is measured in radians.

TAN(0)	→ 0
TAN(PI()/4)	→ 1

- TRUNCATE(*x*, *d*)

  Returns the value *x*, with the fractional part truncated to *d* decimal places. If *d* is 0, the result has no decimal point or fractional part. If *d* is greater than the number of decimal places in *x*, the fractional part is right-padded with trailing zeros to the desired width.

TRUNCATE(1.23,1)	→ 1.2
TRUNCATE(1.23,0)	→ 1
TRUNCATE(1.23,4)	→ 1.2300

  If *d* is negative, TRUNCATE() trims any fractional part and zeros ABS(*d*) digits to the left of the decimal point.

TRUNCATE(123456.789,-3)	→ 123000

C.2.4 String Functions

Most of the functions in this section return a string result. Some of them, such as LENGTH(), take strings as arguments and return a number. For functions that operate on strings based on string positions, the position of the first (leftmost) character is 1, not 0.

Several string functions are multi-byte safe: CHAR_LENGTH(), INSERT(), INSTR(), LCASE(), LEFT(), LOCATE(), LOWER(), LTRIM(), MID(), POSITION(), REPLACE(), REVERSE(), RIGHT(), RPAD(), RTRIM(), SUBSTRING(), SUBSTRING_INDEX(), TRIM(), UCASE(), and UPPER().

- ASCII(*str*)

  Returns the integer value of the leftmost byte of the string *str*, in the range from 0 to 255. It returns 0 if *str* is empty or NULL if *str* is NULL. *str* should contain only 8-bit characters.

ASCII('abc')	→ 97
ASCII('')	→ 0
ASCII(NULL)	→ NULL

- BIN(*n*)

  Returns a string containing the binary-digit representation of the argument *n*. These expressions are equivalent; see the description of CONV() for more information.

BIN(65)	→ '1000001'
CONV(65,10,2)	→ '1000001'

- CHAR(*n1*,*n2*,... [USING *charset*])

  Interprets the *n1*, *n2*, ... arguments as numeric character codes and returns a string in the connection character set consisting of the concatenation of the corresponding character values. Character codes larger than 255 produce multiple result bytes. Without USING, the return value is a binary string. With USING, the return value has the named character set. If the result is not legal for the character set, a warning occurs (and in strict SQL mode, the result is NULL). NULL arguments are ignored.

CHAR(65)	→ 'A'
CHAR(97)	→ 'a'
CHAR(89,105,107,101,115,33)	→ 'Yikes!'

- CHAR_LENGTH(*str*)
  CHARACTER_LENGTH(*str*)

  These functions are similar to LENGTH(), except that the argument length is counted in characters, not bytes. (Each multi-byte character is counted as having a length of 1.)

- CHARSET(*str*)

  Returns the name of the character set of the given string, or NULL if the argument is NULL.

CHARSET('abc')	→ 'latin1'
CHARSET(CONVERT('abc' USING utf8))	→ 'utf8'
CHARSET(123)	→ 'binary'

- COALESCE(*expr1*,*expr2*,...)

  Returns the first non-NULL element in the list, or NULL if no argument is non-NULL.

COALESCE(NULL,1/0,2,'a',45+97)	→ '2'
COALESCE(NULL,1/0)	→ NULL

- COERCIBILITY(*str*)

  Returns the collation coercibility of a string, or NULL if the argument is illegal. Coercibility is the degree to which a string is subject to having its collation changed in expressions that involve other strings. The following table shows the return values, from lesser to greater coercibility.

Coercibility	Meaning
0	Collation is explicit, cannot be coerced
1	No collation specified
2	Collation is implicit
3	Collation of system values such as USER()
4	Collation is coercible
5	Collation is ignorable (as for NULL)

  ```
  COERCIBILITY(_utf8 'abc' COLLATE utf8_bin)    → 0
  COERCIBILITY('abc')                           → 4
  ```

- COLLATION(*str*)

  Returns the name of the collation of the given string, or NULL if the argument is illegal.

  ```
  COLLATION(_latin2 'abc')                              → 'latin2_general_ci'
  COLLATION(CONVERT('abc' USING utf8) COLLATE utf8_bin)
                                                        → 'utf8_bin'
  ```

- CONCAT(*str1*,*str2*,...)

  Returns a string consisting of the concatenation of its arguments, or NULL if any argument is NULL. The result is a binary string if any argument is a binary string, or a nonbinary string if each argument is a nonbinary string. Numeric arguments are converted to strings. This conversion produces a nonbinary string as of MySQL 5.5.3, and a binary string in earlier versions.

  ```
  CONCAT('abc','def')             → 'abcdef'
  CONCAT('abc')                   → 'abc'
  CONCAT('abc',NULL)              → NULL
  CONCAT('Hello',', ','goodbye')  → 'Hello, goodbye'
  ```

  Another way to concatenate strings is by proximity; specify them next to each other.

  ```
  'three' 'blind' 'mice'      → 'threeblindmice'
  'abc' 'def' = 'abcdef'      → 1
  ```

- CONCAT_WS(*delim,str1,str2,...*)

  Similar to CONCAT(), but returns a string consisting of the concatenation of its second and following arguments, with the *delim* string used as the separator between strings. Returns NULL if *delim* is NULL, but ignores NULL values in the list of strings to be concatenated.

CONCAT_WS(',','a','b','','d')	→ 'a,b,,d'
CONCAT_WS('*-*','lemon','lime',NULL,'grape')	→ 'lemon*-*lime*-*grape'

- CONV(*n,from_base,to_base*)

  Given a number *n* represented in base *from_base*, returns a string representation of *n* in base *to_base*. The result is NULL if any argument is NULL. *from_base* and *to_base* should be integers in the range from 2 to 36. *n* is treated as a BIGINT value (64-bit integer) but may be specified as a string because numbers in bases higher than 10 may contain nondecimal digits. (This also is why CONV() returns a string; the result may contain characters from 'A' to 'Z' for bases 11 to 36.) The result is 0 if *n* is not a legal number in base *from_base*. For example, if *from_base* is 16 and *n* is 'abcdefg', the result is 0 because 'g' is not a legal hexadecimal digit.

  Nondecimal characters in *n* may be specified in either uppercase or lowercase. Nondecimal characters in the result will be uppercase.

  Convert 14 specified as a hexadecimal number to binary:

CONV('e',16,2)	→ '1110'

  Convert 255 specified in binary to octal:

CONV(11111111,2,8)	→ '377'
CONV('11111111',2,8)	→ '377'

  n is treated as an unsigned number by default. If you specify *to_base* as a negative number, *n* is treated as a signed number.

CONV(-10,10,16)	→ 'FFFFFFFFFFFFFFF6'
CONV(-10,10,-16)	→ '-A'

- EXPORT_SET(*n,on,off*[,*delim*[,*bit_count*]])

  Returns a string consisting of the strings *on* and *off*, separated by the delimiter string *delim*. The default delimiter is a comma. *on* is used to represent each bit that is set in the value *n*, and *off* is used to represent each bit that is not set. The leftmost string in the result corresponds to the low-order bit in *n*. *bit_count* indicates the maximum number of bits in *n* to examine. The default *bit_count* value is 64, which also is its maximum value. Returns NULL if any argument is NULL.

EXPORT_SET(7,'+','-','',5)	→ '+++--'
EXPORT_SET(0xa,'1','0','',6)	→ '010100'
EXPORT_SET(97,'Y','N',',',8)	→ 'Y,N,N,N,N,Y,Y,N'

- FIND_IN_SET(*str*, *str_list*)

str_list is a string consisting of substrings separated by commas (that is, it is like a SET value). FIND_IN_SET() returns the index of *str* within *str_list*. Returns 0 if *str* is not present in *str_list*, or NULL if either argument is NULL. The index of the first substring is 1.

FIND_IN_SET('cow','moose,cow,pig')	→ 2
FIND_IN_SET('dog','moose,cow,pig')	→ 0

- FORMAT(*x*, *d*[, *locale*])

Formats the number *x* to *d* decimals using a format like '*nn,nnn.nnn*' and returns the result as a string. If *d* is 0, the result has no decimal point or fractional part.

FORMAT(1234.56789,3)	→ '1,234.568'
FORMAT(999999.99,2)	→ '999,999.99'
FORMAT(999999.99,0)	→ '1,000,000'

Note the rounding behavior exhibited by the final example.

The locale determines the decimal point, thousands separator, and grouping between separators. The default locale is 'en_US', which may be overridden using the optional *locale* argument. Permitted values are the same as for the lc_time_names system variable.

- FROM_BASE64(*str*)

Converts a base-64-encoded string and returns the original value, or NULL if the argument is not a base-64 string. This function is the inverse of TO_BASE64().

TO_BASE64('hello')	→ 'aGVsbG8='
FROM_BASE64(TO_BASE64('hello'))	→ 'hello'

FROM_BASE64() was introduced in MySQL 5.6.1.

- HEX(*n*)
  HEX(*str*)

With a numeric argument *n*, HEX() returns the hexadecimal-digit representation of the argument, as a string. These expressions are equivalent; see the description of CONV() for more information.

HEX(65)	→ '41'
CONV(65,10,16)	→ '41'

With a string argument, HEX() returns a string consisting of each character in the argument represented as two hex digits. This form of HEX() is the inverse of UNHEX().

HEX('255')	→ '323535'
HEX('abc')	→ '616263'
UNHEX(HEX('abc'))	→ 'abc'

- INSERT(*str*,*pos*,*len*,*ins_str*)

  Returns the string *str*, with the substring beginning at position *pos* and *len* characters long replaced by the string *ins_str*. Returns the original string if *pos* is out of range, or NULL if any argument is NULL.

INSERT('nighttime',6,4,'fall')	→ 'nightfall'
INSERT('sunshine',1,3,'rain or ')	→ 'rain or shine'
INSERT('sunshine',0,3,'rain or ')	→ 'sunshine'

- INSTR(*str*,*substr*)

  INSTR() is like the two-argument form of LOCATE(), but with the arguments reversed. These expressions are equivalent:

  INSTR(*str*,*substr*)
  LOCATE(*substr*,*str*)

- LCASE(*str*)

  This is a synonym for LOWER().

- LEFT(*str*,*len*)

  Returns the leftmost *len* characters from the string *str*, or the entire string if there aren't that many characters. Returns the empty string if *len* is NULL or less than 1. Returns NULL if either argument is NULL.

LEFT('my left foot',2)	→ 'my'
LEFT(NULL,10)	→ NULL
LEFT('abc',NULL)	→ NULL
LEFT('abc',0)	→ ''

- LENGTH(*str*)

  Returns the length of the string *str*, in bytes. Multi-byte characters are counted as having a length greater than 1. To measure the length in characters, use CHAR_LENGTH().

LENGTH('abc')	→ 3
LENGTH(CONVERT('abc' USING ucs2))	→ 6
LENGTH('')	→ 0
LENGTH(NULL)	→ NULL

- LOCATE(*substr*,*str*)
  LOCATE(*substr*,*str*,*pos*)

  The two-argument form of LOCATE() returns the position of the first occurrence of the string *substr* within the string *str*, or 0 if *substr* does not occur within *str*. Returns NULL if any argument is NULL. If the position argument *pos* is given, LOCATE() starts looking for *substr* at that position. LOCATE() compares the strings as binary strings if either operand is a binary string, or using the operand collation if the operands are nonbinary strings.

```
LOCATE('b','abc')                                → 2
LOCATE('b','ABC')                                → 2
LOCATE(BINARY 'b','ABC')                          → 0
LOCATE('b' COLLATE latin1_general_ci,'ABC')      → 2
LOCATE('b' COLLATE latin1_general_cs,'ABC')      → 0
```

- LOWER(*str*)

Returns the string *str* with all the characters converted to lowercase, or NULL if *str* is NULL.

```
LOWER('New York, NY')                            → 'new york, ny'
LOWER(NULL)                                       → NULL
```

Lettercase conversion is based on the collation of the argument's character set. If the argument is a binary string, there is no character set or collation and LOWER() returns the argument unchanged.

```
LOWER(BINARY 'New York, NY')                     → 'New York, NY'
LOWER(0x414243)                                  → 'ABC'
```

To deal with this, convert or cast the argument to a nonbinary string that has an appropriate collation.

```
LOWER(CONVERT(BINARY 'New York, NY' USING latin1))
                                                 → 'new york, ny'
LOWER(_latin1 0x414243)                          → 'abc'
```

- LPAD(*str*,*len*,*pad_str*)

Returns a string consisting of the value of the string *str*, left-padded with the string *pad_str* to a length of *len* characters. Returns NULL if any argument is NULL.

```
LPAD('abc',12,'def')                             → 'defdefdefabc'
LPAD('abc',10,'.')                               → '.......abc'
```

LPAD() shortens the result to *len* characters if *str* has a length greater than *len*.

```
LPAD('abc',2,'.')                                → 'ab'
```

- LTRIM(*str*)

Returns the string *str* with leftmost (leading) spaces removed, or NULL if *str* is NULL.

```
LTRIM('  abc  ')                                 → 'abc  '
```

- MAKE_SET(*n*,*bit0_str*,*bit1_str*,...)

Constructs a SET value (a string consisting of substrings separated by commas) based on the value of the integer *n* and the strings *bit0_str*, *bit1_str*, ... For each bit set in the value of *n*, the corresponding string is included in the result. (If bit 0 is set, the result includes *bit0_str*, and so on.) If *n* is 0, the result is the empty string. If *n* is NULL, the result is NULL. If any string in the list is NULL, it is ignored when constructing the result string.

```
MAKE_SET(8,'a','b','c','d','e')          → 'd'
MAKE_SET(1|2|4,'a','b','c','d','e')       → 'a,b,c'
MAKE_SET(2+16,'a','b','c','d','e')        → 'b,e'
MAKE_SET(-1,'a','b','c','d','e')          → 'a,b,c,d,e'
```

The final example selects every string because the value –1 has all bits turned on.

- MATCH(*col_list*) AGAINST(*str* [*search_mode*])

  MATCH performs a search operation using a FULLTEXT index. The MATCH list consists of one or more column names separated by commas. These must be the columns that make up a FULLTEXT index on the table you are searching. The *str* argument to AGAINST() indicates the word or words to search for in the given columns. Words are sequences of characters made up of letters, digits, apostrophes, or underscores. The parentheses are optional for MATCH, but not for AGAINST.

  By default, the search is performed in natural language mode. An explicit *search_mode* argument can have one of the following values:

  - IN NATURAL LANGUAGE MODE

  - IN BOOLEAN MODE

  - [IN NATURAL LANGUAGE MODE] WITH QUERY EXPANSION

  For a natural language search, MATCH() produces a relevance ranking for each row. Ranks are nonnegative floating-point numbers, with a rank of zero indicating that the search words were not found. Positive values indicate that at least one search word was found. Words present in the more than half the rows of the table are ignored (considered to have zero relevance because they are so common). In addition, MySQL has an internal list of stopwords that are never considered relevant (for example, "the" and "but").

  If the search mode is IN BOOLEAN MODE, search results are based purely on absence or presence of the search words without regard to how often they occur in the table. For boolean searches, words in the search string can be modified with the following operators to affect how the search is done:

  - A leading + or - indicates that the word must be present or absent.

  - A leading < or > decreases or increases a word's contribution to the relevance value calculation.

  - A leading ~ negates a word's contribution to the relevance value calculation, but does not exclude rows containing the word entirely as - would.

  - A trailing * acts as a wildcard operator. For example, act* matches act, acts, action, and so forth.

  - A phrase search may be performed by surrounding the phrase within double quotes (*"phrase"*). For a match to occur, each word must be present together in the order given in the phrase.

  - Parentheses group words into expressions. Parenthesized expressions can be nested.

Words with no modifiers are treated as optional in a boolean search, just as for natural language searches.

It's possible to perform a boolean-mode search in the absence of a FULLTEXT index, but this can be quite slow.

If the search mode is WITH QUERY EXPANSION or IN NATURAL LANGUAGE MODE WITH QUERY EXPANSION, a natural language search is done once using the search string, and then again using the search string and the information from the first few most highly relevant matches from the original search. This enables rows with content related to the original search string to be found.

For more information on FULLTEXT searching, see Section 2.14, "Using FULLTEXT Searches."

- MID(*str*,*pos*,*len*)
  MID(*str*,*pos*)

  The three-argument form of MID() returns a substring of the string *str* beginning at position *pos* and *len* characters long. The two-argument form returns the substring beginning at pos to the end of the string. Returns NULL if any argument is NULL.

MID('what a dull example',8,4)	→ 'dull'
MID('what a dull example',8)	→ 'dull example'

  MID() is actually a synonym for SUBSTRING() and can be used with any of the forms of syntax that SUBSTRING() permits.

- OCT(*n*)

  Returns a string containing the octal-digit representation of the argument *n*. These expressions are equivalent; see the description of CONV() for more information.

OCT(65)	→ '101'
CONV(65,10,8)	→ '101'

- OCTET_LENGTH(*str*)

  This is a synonym for LENGTH().

- ORD(*str*)

  Returns the ordinal value of the first character of the string *str*, or NULL if *str* is NULL. If the first character is a single-byte character, ORD() is the same as ASCII().

ORD('abc')	→ 97
ASCII('abc')	→ 97

  For a multi-byte character, ORD() returns a value determined from the numeric values of the character's individual bytes *b1* through *bn* (from right to left):

  $$b1 + (b2 \times 256) + (b3 \times 256 \times 256) + \ldots$$

- POSITION(*substr* IN *str*)

  This is like the two-argument form of LOCATE(). These expressions are equivalent:

  ```
  POSITION(substr IN str)
  LOCATE(substr,str)
  ```

- QUOTE(*str*)

  Processes its argument to return a string that is properly quoted for use in an SQL statement. This is useful for writing queries that produce other queries as their result. For non-NULL values, the return value has each single quote, backslash, Control-Z character, and NUL (zero-valued byte) escaped with a leading backslash, and the result is surrounded by single quotes. If *str* is NULL, the return value is the word "NULL" with no surrounding single quotes.

  ```
  QUOTE("Let's go!")                         → 'Let\'s go!'
  QUOTE(NULL)                                → NULL
  ```

- REPEAT(*str*,*n*)

  Returns a string consisting of *n* repetitions of the string *str*. Returns the empty string if *n* is nonpositive, or NULL if either argument is NULL.

  ```
  REPEAT('x',10)                             → 'xxxxxxxxxx'
  REPEAT('abc',3)                            → 'abcabcabc'
  ```

- REPLACE(*str*,*from_str*,*to_str*)

  Returns a string consisting of the string *str* with all occurrences of the string *from_str* replaced by the string *to_str*. If *to_str* is empty, the effect is to delete occurrences of *from_str*. If *from_str* is empty, REPLACE() returns *str* unchanged. Returns NULL if any argument is NULL.

  ```
  REPLACE('abracadabra','a','oh')            → 'ohbrohcohdohbroh'
  REPLACE('abracadabra','a','')              → 'brcdbr'
  REPLACE('abracadabra','','x')              → 'abracadabra'
  ```

- REVERSE(*str*)

  Returns a string consisting of the string *str* with the characters reversed. Returns NULL if *str* is NULL.

  ```
  REVERSE('abracadabra')                     → 'arbadacarba'
  REVERSE('tararA ta tar a raT')             → 'Tar a rat at Ararat'
  ```

- RIGHT(*str*,*len*)

  Returns the rightmost *len* characters from the string *str*, or the entire string if there aren't that many characters. Returns the empty string if *len* is NULL or less than 1. Returns NULL if either argument is NULL.

  ```
  RIGHT('rightmost',4)                       → 'most'
  ```

- RPAD(*str*,*len*,*pad_str*)

  Returns a string consisting of the value of the string *str*, right-padded with the string *pad_str* to a length of *len* characters. Returns NULL if any argument is NULL.

  RPAD('abc',12,'def')   → 'abcdefdefdef'
  RPAD('abc',10,'.')   → 'abc.......'

  RPAD() shortens the result to *len* characters if *str* has a length greater than *len*.

  RPAD('abc',2,'.')   → 'ab'

- RTRIM(*str*)

  Returns the string *str* with rightmost (trailing) spaces removed, or NULL if *str* is NULL.

  RTRIM(' abc ')   → ' abc'

- SOUNDEX(*str*)
  expr1 SOUNDS LIKE *expr2*

  SOUNDEX() returns a soundex string calculated from the string *str*, or NULL if *str* is NULL. Nonalphanumeric characters in *str* are ignored. International nonalphabetic characters outside the range from 'A' to 'Z' are treated as vowels. SOUNDEX() results may not be meaningful for strings with multi-byte characters or for languages other than English.

  SOUNDEX('Cow')   → 'C000'
  SOUNDEX('Cowl')   → 'C400'
  SOUNDEX('Howl')   → 'H400'
  SOUNDEX('Hello')   → 'H400'

  The SOUNDS LIKE operator is equivalent to the SOUNDEX() function.

- SPACE(*n*)

  Returns a string consisting of *n* spaces, the empty string if *n* is nonpositive, or NULL if *n* is NULL.

  SPACE(6)   → '   '
  SPACE(0)   → ''
  SPACE(NULL)   → NULL

- SUBSTR(*arguments*)

  SUBSTR() is a synonym for SUBSTRING(). The same argument formats apply.

- SUBSTRING(*str*,*pos*)
  SUBSTRING(*str*,*pos*,*len*)
  SUBSTRING(*str* FROM *pos*)
  SUBSTRING(*str* FROM *pos* FOR *len*)

Returns a substring from the string *str*, beginning at position *pos*, or NULL if any argument is NULL. If a *len* argument is given, returns a substring that many characters long; otherwise, it returns the entire rightmost part of *str*, beginning at position *pos*.

```
SUBSTRING('abcdef',3)                              → 'cdef'
SUBSTRING('abcdef',3,2)                            → 'cd'
```

These expressions are equivalent:

```
SUBSTRING(str,pos,len)
SUBSTRING(str FROM pos FOR len)
MID(str,pos,len)
```

- SUBSTRING_INDEX(*str*,*delim*,*n*)

Returns a substring from the string *str*. If *n* is positive, SUBSTRING_INDEX() finds the *n*-th occurrence of the delimiter string *delim*, and then returns everything to the left of that delimiter. If *n* is negative, SUBSTRING INDEX() finds the *n*-th occurrence of *delim*, counting back from the right end of *str*, and then returns everything to the right of that delimiter. If SUBSTRING_INDEX() does not find *delim* in *str*, it returns the entire string. Returns NULL if any argument is NULL.

```
SUBSTRING_INDEX('jar-jar','j',-2)                  → 'ar-jar'
SUBSTRING_INDEX('sampadm@localhost','@',1)         → 'sampadm'
SUBSTRING_INDEX('sampadm@localhost','@',-1)        → 'localhost'
```

- TO_BASE64(*str*)

Returns the base-64 encoding of the argument, or NULL if the argument is NULL. Numeric arguments are treated as strings. This function is the inverse of FROM_BASE64().

```
TO_BASE64('abc')                                   → 'YWJj'
TO_BASE64('123')                                   → 'MTIz'
TO_BASE64(123)                                     → 'MTIz'
```

TO_BASE64() was introduced in MySQL 5.6.1.

- TRIM([*trim_str* FROM] *str*)
  TRIM([{LEADING | TRAILING | BOTH} [*trim_str*] FROM] *str*)

The first form returns the string *str* with leading and trailing instances of the string *trim_str* trimmed off. In the second form, if LEADING is specified, TRIM() strips leading occurrences of *trim_str*. If TRAILING is specified, TRIM() strips trailing occurrences of *trim_str*. If BOTH is specified, TRIM() strips leading and trailing occurrences of *trim_str*. The default is BOTH if none of LEADING, TRAILING, or BOTH is specified. Spaces are trimmed if *trim_str* is not specified.

```
TRIM('^' FROM '^^^xyz^^')                          → 'xyz'
TRIM(LEADING '^' FROM '^^^xyz^^')                  → 'xyz^^'
TRIM(TRAILING '^' FROM '^^^xyz^^')                 → '^^^xyz'
TRIM(BOTH '^' FROM '^^^xyz^^')                     → 'xyz'
TRIM(BOTH FROM '   abc   ')                        → 'abc'
TRIM('   abc   ')                                  → 'abc'
```

- UCASE(*str*)

This is a synonym for UPPER().

- UNHEX(*expr*)

The argument is interpreted as a string containing pairs of hexadecimal digits. Each pair of digits is converted to a character and the return value is a binary string consisting of these characters. UNHEX() is the inverse of HEX().

UNHEX('414243')	→ 'ABC'
HEX(UNHEX('414243'))	→ '414243'
UNHEX(HEX('ABC'))	→ 'ABC'
UNHEX(414243)	→ 'ABC'
CHARSET(UNHEX('414243'))	→ 'binary'

- UPPER(*str*)

Returns the string *str* with all the characters converted to uppercase, or NULL if *str* is NULL.

UPPER('New York, NY')	→ 'NEW YORK, NY'
UPPER(NULL)	→ NULL

See the description of the LOWER() function for notes regarding lettercase conversion of binary strings.

- WEIGHT_STRING(*str* [AS *type*(*n*)] [LEVEL *levels*] [*flags*])

Returns the weight string for *str* as a binary string that indicates how *str* is handled for comparison and sorting operations. Two strings with equal weight strings compare as equal, otherwise they have the same relative ordering as their weight strings. The AS option causes *str* to have a given type and length, and the LEVEL option specifies which collation levels to return. Currently, no *flags* values are implemented.

If *str* is a binary string, the weight string is the same as *str*. If *str* is a nonbinary string, it has a collation and the result string contains collation weights. If *str* is NULL, the result is NULL. The examples here use HEX() to present the weight strings in printable format:

HEX(WEIGHT_STRING(BINARY 'Hello'))	→ '48656C6C6F'
HEX(WEIGHT_STRING('Hello'))	→ '48454C4C4F'
HEX(WEIGHT_STRING(_utf8'Hello'))	→ '00480045004C004C004F'

str can be cast to a given type and length using an AS clause. To treat *str* as a CHAR string *n* characters long, use AS CHAR(*n*). The string will be padded at the end with spaces as necessary. AS BINARY(*n*) treats the string as a binary string *n* bytes long and padding uses 0x00 bytes. *n* must be 1 or greater. *str* is truncated rather than padded if its length is greater than *n*.

A collation might have levels. By default, the result includes weights for all levels. To return weights only for particular levels, use a LEVEL clause. The *levels* value can be a list of one or more comma-separated integers, or a range of two dash-separated integers.

Levels in a list must be in increasing order. The second level in a range is treated as the first level if it is less than the first level. Individual level values are clipped to lie within 1 and the maximum level for the collation if they are outside that range.

Level values in a list can be followed by a modifier: ASC to return unmodified weights (the default), DESC to return bit-inverted weights, or REVERSE to return weights for the reversed value of *str*.

```
HEX(WEIGHT_STRING('abc' LEVEL 1 ASC))        → '414243'
HEX(WEIGHT_STRING('abc' LEVEL 1 DESC))       → 'BEBDBC'
HEX(WEIGHT_STRING('abc' LEVEL 1 REVERSE))    → '434241'
```

WEIGHT_STRING() was introduced in MySQL 5.6.0.

C.2.5   Date and Time Functions

The date and time functions take various types of arguments. In general, a function that expects a DATE argument also accepts a DATETIME or TIMESTAMP argument and ignores the time part of the value. Some functions that expect a TIME value accept DATETIME or TIMESTAMP arguments and ignore the date part.

Many of the functions in this section are able to interpret numeric arguments as temporal values.

```
MONTH('1906-04-18')        → 4
MONTH(19060418)            → 4
```

Similarly, for many functions that return a temporal value, MySQL converts the return value to a string or number, depending on context.

```
CURDATE()                          → '2012-08-26'
CONCAT('Today is ', CURDATE())     → 'Today is 2012-08-26'
CURDATE() + 0                      → 20120826
```

When conversion of a time or date and time value to number occurs, the numeric value has a microseconds part of .000000. To chop this off, cast the result to an integer.

```
NOW()+0                         → 20120806163317.000000
CAST(NOW() AS UNSIGNED)         → 20120806163317
CURTIME()+0                     → 163317.000000
CAST(CURTIME() AS UNSIGNED)     → 163317
```

Several functions that extract part of a date return 0 for "incomplete" dates. For example, MONTH() and DAYOFMONTH() return 0 for an argument of '2013-00-00'. The same is true for date-part format specifiers as used with DATE_FORMAT().

If you don't supply legal date or time values to date and time functions, you can't expect a reasonable result. Verify your arguments first.

- ADDDATE(*date*, INTERVAL *expr interval*)
  ADDDATE(*date*, *expr*)

  For the first syntax, ADDDATE() takes a date or date and time value *date*, adds a temporal interval to it, and returns the result. This is a synonym for DATE_ADD().

  ADDDATE('2004-12-01', INTERVAL 1 YEAR)   → '2005-12-01'

  For the second syntax, ADDDATE() takes a date or date and time value *date*, adds a temporal value representing number of days to it, and returns the result.

  ADDDATE('2004-12-01', 365)   → '2005-12-01'

  The second syntax can be rewritten in terms of the first syntax like this:

  ADDDATE(*date*, *expr*) = ADDDATE(*date*, INTERVAL *expr* DAY)

- ADDTIME(*expr1*, *expr2*)

  Adds the two expressions and returns the result. *expr1* should be a time or date and time value, and *expr2* should be a time value.

  ADDTIME('06:30:00.5', '12:30:00.4')   → '19:00:00.900000'
  ADDTIME('2004-01-01 00:00:00', '12:30:00')   → '2004-01-01 12:30:00'

- CONVERT_TZ(*date*, *from_zone*, *to_zone*)

  Given the date or date and time value *date*, CONVERT_TZ() treats it as a value in the time zone *from_zone*, converts it to a value in the time zone *to_zone*, and returns the result. Returns NULL if any argument is invalid. Time zones are specified as described in Section 12.6.1, "Configuring Time Zone Support." For CONVERT_TZ() to work properly, the resulting value must lie within the range of the TIMESTAMP data type.

  CONVERT_TZ('2019-02-11 00:00:00', 'US/Central', 'US/Eastern')
                                                           → '2019-02-11 01:00:00'
  CONVERT_TZ('2019-02-11', '+00:00', '-03:00')   → '2019-02-10 21:00:00'

- CURDATE()

  Returns the current date in the session time zone as a DATE value in '*CCYY-MM-DD*' format.

  CURDATE()   → '2012-08-26'

- CURRENT_DATE()

  This is a synonym for CURDATE(). The parentheses are optional.

- CURRENT_TIME([*fsp*])

  This is a synonym for CURTIME(). The parentheses are optional unless the *fsp* argument is given.

- `CURRENT_TIMESTAMP([fsp])`

  This is a synonym for `NOW()`. The parentheses are optional unless the `fsp` argument is given.

- `CURTIME([fsp])`

  Returns the current time of day in the session time zone as a `TIME` value in `'hh:mm:ss'` format. Beginning with MySQL 5.6.4, the optional `fsp` argument can be given to specify that the return value should have a fractional seconds precision of 0 to 6 digits. Before 5.6.4, any argument is ignored.

`CURTIME()`	→ `'15:01:02'`
`CURTIME(2)`	→ `'15:01:02.20'`

- `DATE(expr)`

  Returns the date part of `expr`, which should be a date or date and time expression.

`DATE('2008-03-12')`	→ `'2008-03-12'`
`DATE('2008-03-12 16:15:00')`	→ `'2008-03-12'`

- `DATE_ADD(date, INTERVAL expr interval)`

  Takes a date or date and time value `date`, adds a temporal interval to it, and returns the result. `expr` specifies the time value to be added to `date` (or subtracted, if `expr` is negative), and `interval` specifies how to interpret the interval. The result is a `DATE` value if `date` is a `DATE` value and no time-related values are involved in calculating the result. Otherwise, the result is a `DATETIME` value. The result is `NULL` if `date` is not a legal date.

`DATE_ADD('2009-12-01', INTERVAL 1 YEAR)`	→ `'2010-12-01'`
`DATE_ADD('2009-12-01', INTERVAL 60 DAY)`	→ `'2010-01-30'`
`DATE_ADD('2009-12-01', INTERVAL -3 MONTH)`	→ `'2009-09-01'`
`DATE_ADD('2009-12-01 08:30:00', INTERVAL 12 HOUR)`	→ `'2009-12-01 20:30:00'`

  The following table shows the permitted `interval` values, their meanings, and the format in which to specify values for each interval type. The keyword `INTERVAL` and the `interval` specifiers are not case sensitive.

Interval Type	Meaning	Value Format
`MICROSECOND`	Microseconds	`uuuuuu`
`SECOND`	Seconds	`ss`
`SECOND_MICROSECOND`	Seconds and microseconds	`'ss.uuuuuu'`
`MINUTE`	Minutes	`mm`
`MINUTE_SECOND`	Minutes and seconds	`'mm:ss'`
`MINUTE_MICROSECOND`	Minutes, seconds, and microseconds	`'mm:ss.uuuuuu'`
`HOUR`	Hours	`hh`

Interval Type	Meaning	Value Format
HOUR_MINUTE	Hours and minutes	`'hh:mm'`
HOUR_SECOND	Hours, minutes, and seconds	`'hh:mm:ss'`
HOUR_MICROSECOND	Hours, minutes, seconds, and microseconds	`'hh:mm:ss.uuuuuu'`
DAY	Days	`DD`
DAY_HOUR	Days and hours	`'DD hh'`
DAY_MINUTE	Days, hours, and minutes	`'DD hh:mm'`
DAY_SECOND	Days, hours, minutes, and seconds	`'DD hh:mm:ss'`
DAY_MICROSECOND	Days, hours, minutes, seconds, and microseconds	`'DD hh:mm:ss.uuuuuu'`
WEEK	Weeks	`WW`
MONTH	Months	`MM`
QUARTER	Quarters	`QQ`
YEAR	Years	`YY`
YEAR_MONTH	Years and months	`'YY-MM'`

The expression *expr* that is added to the date can be specified as a number or as a string, unless it contains nondigit characters, in which case it must be a string. The delimiter characters can be any punctuation character.

```
DATE_ADD('2005-12-01',INTERVAL '2:3' YEAR_MONTH)   → '2008-03-01'
DATE_ADD('2005-12-01',INTERVAL '2-3' YEAR_MONTH)   → '2008-03-01'
```

The parts of the value of *expr* are matched from right to left against the parts to be expected based on the *interval* specifier. For example, the expected format for HOUR_SECOND is `'hh:mm:ss'`. An *expr* value of `'15:21'` is interpreted as `'00:15:21'`, not as `'15:21:00'`.

```
DATE_ADD('2003-12-01 12:00:00',INTERVAL '15:21' HOUR_SECOND)
                                          → '2003-12-01 12:15:21'
```

If *interval* is YEAR, MONTH, or YEAR_MONTH and the day part of the result is larger than the number of days in the result month, the day is set to the maximum number of days in that month.

```
DATE_ADD('2003-12-31',INTERVAL 2 MONTH)      → '2004-02-29'
```

An alternative syntax can be used for date addition:

```
'2003-12-31' + INTERVAL 2 MONTH              → '2004-02-29'
INTERVAL 2 MONTH + '2003-12-31'              → '2004-02-29'
```

- DATE_FORMAT(*date*,*format*)

Formats a date or date and time value *date* according to the formatting string *format* and returns the resulting string. Use DATE_FORMAT() to reformat date or date and time values from the form MySQL uses to other desired formats.

```
DATE_FORMAT('2014-12-01','%M %e, %Y')        → 'December 1, 2014'
DATE_FORMAT('2014-12-01','The %D of %M')     → 'The 1st of December'
```

The following table shows the permitted specifiers in the formatting string. The ranges shown for the numeric month and day specifiers begin with zero because zero may be produced for dates that are incomplete, such as '2004-00-13' or '1998-12-00'. The lc_time_names system variable determines the month and day name language for specifiers that produce such names.

The '%' character preceding each format code is required. Characters present in the formatting string that are not listed in the table are copied to the result string literally.

If you refer to time specifiers for a DATE value, the time part of the value is treated as '00:00:00'.

```
DATE_FORMAT('2014-12-01','%i')               → '00'
```

Specifier	Meaning
%f	Microseconds in six-digit form (000000, 000001, …)
%S, %s	Second in two-digit form (00, 01, …, 59)
%i	Minute in two-digit form (00, 01, …, 59)
%H	Hour in two-digit form, 24-hour time (00, 01, …, 23)
%h, %I	Hour in two-digit form, 12-hour time (01, 02, …, 12)
%k	Hour in numeric form, 24-hour time (0, 1, …, 23)
%l	Hour in numeric form, 12-hour time (1, 2, …, 12)
%T	Time in 24-hour form (*hh:mm:ss*)
%r	Time in 12-hour form (*hh:mm:ss* AM or *hh:mm:ss* PM)
%p	AM or PM
%W	Weekday name (Sunday, Monday, …, Saturday)
%a	Weekday name in abbreviated form (Sun, Mon, …, Sat)
%d	Day of the month in two-digit form (00, 01, …, 31)
%e	Day of the month in numeric form (0, 1, …, 31)
%D	Day of the month with English suffix (0th, 1st, 2nd, 3rd, …)
%w	Day of the week in numeric form (0=Sunday, 1=Monday, …, 6=Saturday)
%j	Day of the year in three-digit form (001, 002, …, 366)

Specifier	Meaning
`%U`	Week (00, ..., 53), where Sunday is the first day of the week
`%u`	Week (00, ..., 53), where Monday is the first day of the week
`%V`	Week (01, ..., 53), where Sunday is the first day of the week
`%v`	Week (01, ..., 53), where Monday is the first day of the week
`%M`	Month name (January, February, ..., December)
`%b`	Month name in abbreviated form (Jan, Feb, ..., Dec)
`%m`	Month in two-digit form (00, 01, ..., 12)
`%c`	Month in numeric form (0, 1, ..., 12)
`%Y`	Year in four-digit form
`%y`	Year in two-digit form
`%X`	Year for the week in which Sunday is the first day, four-digit form
`%x`	Year for the week in which Monday is the first day, four-digit form
`%%`	A literal '%' character

- `DATE_SUB(date, INTERVAL expr interval)`

  DATE_SUB() performs date arithmetic in the same manner as DATE_ADD(), except that *expr* is subtracted from the date or date and time value *date*. See DATE_ADD() for more information.

  ```
  DATE_SUB('2009-12-01', INTERVAL 1 MONTH)                → '2009-11-01'
  DATE_SUB('2009-12-01', INTERVAL '13-2' YEAR_MONTH)      → '1996-10-01'
  DATE_SUB('2009-12-01 04:53:12', INTERVAL '13-2' MINUTE_SECOND)
                                                          → '2009-12-01 04:40:10'
  ```

  An alternative syntax can be used for date subtraction:

  ```
  '2009-12-01' - INTERVAL 1 MONTH                         → '2009-11-01'
  ```

  Using this syntax, the INTERVAL clause must be on the right side of the subtraction operator, because you cannot subtract a date from an interval.

- `DATEDIFF(expr1, expr2)`

  Returns the difference in number of days between the two expressions, which should be date or date and time values. The result is positive if the first argument is later than the second. Any time part in the values is ignored.

  ```
  DATEDIFF('1987-01-01', '1987-01-08')                    → -7
  DATEDIFF('1987-01-08', '1987-01-01')                    → 7
  DATEDIFF('1987-01-01 12:00:00', '1987-01-08')           → -7
  DATEDIFF('1987-01-08', '1987-01-01 12:00:00')           → 7
  ```

- DAY(*date*)

  This is a synonym for DAYOFMONTH().

- DAYNAME(*date*)

  Returns a string containing the weekday name for the date value *date*, or NULL if the name cannot be determined. The lc_time_names system variable determines the day name language.

DAYNAME('2004-12-01')	→ 'Wednesday'
DAYNAME('1900-12-01')	→ 'Saturday'
DAYNAME('1900-12-00')	→ NULL

- DAYOFMONTH(*date*)

  Returns the numeric value of the day of the month for the date value *date*, in the range from 0 to 31 (0 for partial dates with no day part).

DAYOFMONTH('2002-12-01')	→ 1
DAYOFMONTH('2002-12-25')	→ 25
DAYOFMONTH('2002-12-00')	→ 0

- DAYOFWEEK(*date*)

  Returns the numeric value of the weekday for the date value *date*. Weekday values are in the range from 1 for Sunday to 7 for Saturday, per the ODBC standard. See also the WEEKDAY() function.

DAYOFWEEK('2004-12-05')	→ 1
DAYNAME('2004-12-05')	→ 'Sunday'
DAYOFWEEK('2004-12-18')	→ 7
DAYNAME('2004-12-18')	→ 'Saturday'

- DAYOFYEAR(*date*)

  Returns the numeric value of the day of the year for the date value *date*, in the range from 1 to 366.

DAYOFYEAR('2002-12-01')	→ 335
DAYOFYEAR('2004-12-31')	→ 366

- EXTRACT(*interval* FROM *datetime*)

  Returns the part of the date and time value *datetime* indicated by *interval*, which can be any of the interval specifiers permitted for DATE_ADD().

EXTRACT(YEAR FROM '2002-12-01 13:42:19')	→ 2002
EXTRACT(MONTH FROM '2002-12-01 13:42:19')	→ 12
EXTRACT(DAY FROM '2002-12-01 13:42:19')	→ 1
EXTRACT(HOUR_MINUTE FROM '2002-12-01 13:42:19')	→ 1342
EXTRACT(SECOND FROM '2002-12-01 13:42:19')	→ 19

`EXTRACT()` can be used with dates that have "missing" parts.

`EXTRACT(YEAR FROM '2004-00-12')`	→ 2004
`EXTRACT(MONTH FROM '2004-00-12')`	→ 0
`EXTRACT(DAY FROM '2004-00-12')`	→ 12

- `FROM_DAYS(n)`

Given a numeric value n representing the number of days since the year 0 (typically obtained by calling `TO_DAYS()`), returns the corresponding date.

`TO_DAYS('2009-12-01')`	→ 734107
`FROM_DAYS(734107 + 3)`	→ '2009-12-04'

`FROM_DAYS()` is intended only for dates covered by the Gregorian calendar (1582 on).

- `FROM_UNIXTIME(unix_timestamp)`
  `FROM_UNIXTIME(unix_timestamp, format)`

Given a Unix timestamp value `unix_timestamp` such as is returned by `UNIX_TIMESTAMP()`, returns a date and time in the session time zone as a `DATETIME` value in `'CCYY-MM-DD hh:mm:ss'` format. If the `format` argument is given, the return value is formatted as a string just as it would be by the `DATE_FORMAT()` function.

`UNIX_TIMESTAMP()`	→ 1328381427
`FROM_UNIXTIME(1328381427)`	→ '2012-02-04 12:50:27'
`FROM_UNIXTIME(1328381427,'%Y')`	→ '2012'

- `GET_FORMAT(val_type, format_type)`

Returns a format string of the type that can be used with the `DATE_FORMAT()`, `TIME_FORMAT()`, and `STR_TO_DATE()` functions. The `val_type` argument indicates a data type and can be `DATE`, `TIME`, `DATETIME`, or `TIMESTAMP`. The `format_type` argument indicates which style of format string to return and can be `'EUR'` (European), `'INTERNAL'` (internal representation), `'ISO'` (ISO 9075, not ISO 8601), `'JIS'` (Japanese Industrial Standards), or `'USA'` (United States).

`GET_FORMAT()` returns format strings for each combination of `val_type` and `format_type`, as shown in the following table.

val_type	format_type	Format String
DATE	'EUR'	'%d.%m.%Y'
DATE	'INTERNAL'	'%Y%m%d'
DATE	'ISO'	'%Y-%m-%d'
DATE	'JIS'	'%Y-%m-%d'
DATE	'USA'	'%m.%d.%Y'
TIME	'EUR'	'%H.%i.%s'

val_type	format_type	Format String
TIME	'INTERNAL'	'%H%i%s'
TIME	'ISO'	'%H:%i:%s'
TIME	'JIS'	'%H:%i:%s'
TIME	'USA'	'%h:%i:%s %p'
DATETIME	'EUR'	'%Y-%m-%d %H.%i.%s'
DATETIME	'INTERNAL'	'%Y%m%d%H%i%s'
DATETIME	'ISO'	'%Y-%m-%d %H:%i:%s'
DATETIME	'JIS'	'%Y-%m-%d %H:%i:%s'
DATETIME	'USA'	'%Y-%m-%d %H.%i.%s'

Note that the date part of the 'EUR' and 'USA' format strings for DATETIME differs from the 'EUR' and 'USA' format strings for DATE.

- HOUR(*time*)

Returns the numeric value of the hour for the time value *time*, in the range from 0 to 23.

```
HOUR('12:31:58')                              → 12
HOUR(123158)                                  → 12
```

- LAST_DAY(*date*)

Returns the date for the last day of the month in which the argument falls. *date* should be a date or date and time value.

```
LAST_DAY('2003-07-01')                        → '2003-07-31'
LAST_DAY('2003-07-01 12:30:00')               → '2003-07-31'
```

- LOCALTIME([*fsp*])
  LOCALTIMESTAMP([*fsp*])

These functions are synonyms for NOW(). The parentheses are optional unless the *fsp* argument is given.

- MAKEDATE(*year*, *day_of_year*)

Given a year and a day of the year, returns a date value, or NULL if *day_of_year* is less than 1.

```
MAKEDATE(2010,365)                            → '2010-12-31'
MAKEDATE(2010,367)                            → '2011-01-02'
MAKEDATE(2010,0)                              → NULL
```

- MAKETIME(*hour*,*minute*,*second*)

Returns a time value constructed from the given hour, minute, and second, or NULL if the arguments are out of range. The minute and second values should be in the range from 0 to 59. The hour can be outside that range. If the hour is negative, the result is negative.

MAKETIME(0,0,0)	→ '00:00:00'
MAKETIME(12,59,59)	→ '12:59:59'
MAKETIME(12,59,60)	→ NULL
MAKETIME(-12,59,59)	→ '-12:59:59'

- MICROSECOND(*expr*)

Returns the microsecond part of the given time or date and time value. The return value has a range of 0 to 999999.

MICROSECOND('00:00:00.000001');	→ 1
MICROSECOND('2004-06-30: 23:59:59.5');	→ 500000

- MINUTE(*time*)

Returns the numeric value of the minute for the time value *time*, in the range from 0 to 59.

MINUTE('12:31:58')	→ 31
MINUTE(123158)	→ 31

- MONTH(*date*)

Returns the numeric value of the month of the year for the date value *date*, in the range from 0 to 12 (0 for partial dates with no month part).

MONTH('2002-12-01')	→ 12
MONTH(20021201)	→ 12
MONTH('2002-00-01')	→ 0

- MONTHNAME(*date*)

Returns a string containing the month name for the date value *date*, or NULL for partial dates with no month part. The lc_time_names system variable determines the month name language.

MONTHNAME('2002-12-01')	→ 'December'
MONTHNAME(20021201)	→ 'December'
MONTHNAME('2002-00-01')	→ NULL

- NOW([*fsp*])

Returns the current date and time in the session time zone as a DATETIME value in 'CCYY-MM-DD hh:mm:ss' format. Beginning with MySQL 5.6.4, the optional *fsp* argument can be given to specify that the return value should have a fractional seconds precision of 0 to 6 digits. Before 5.6.4, any argument is ignored.

NOW()	→ '2012-02-04 12:51:22'

NOW() returns the date and time when the statement in which it appears began to execute, regardless of how long the statement takes. If NOW() occurs within a stored function or trigger, it returns the time when the function or trigger began executing; compare this behavior with that of SYSDATE().

- PERIOD_ADD(*period*, *n*)

  Adds *n* months to the period value *period* and returns the result. The return value format is CCYYMM. The *period* argument format can be CCYYMM or YYMM (neither is a date value).

PERIOD_ADD(201002,12)	→ 201102
PERIOD_ADD(0802,-3)	→ 200711

- PERIOD_DIFF(*period1*, *period2*)

  Takes the difference of the period-valued arguments and returns the number of months between them. The arguments can be in the format CCYYMM or YYMM (neither is a date value).

PERIOD_DIFF(200302,200202)	→ 12
PERIOD_DIFF(200711,0802)	→ -3

- QUARTER(*date*)

  Returns the numeric value of the quarter of the year for the date value *date*, in the range from 1 to 4.

QUARTER('2008-12-01')	→ 4
QUARTER('2009-01-01')	→ 1

- SECOND(*time*)

  Returns the numeric value of the second for the time value *time*, in the range from 0 to 59.

SECOND('12:31:58')	→ 58
SECOND(123158)	→ 58

- SEC_TO_TIME(*seconds*)

  Given a number of seconds *seconds*, returns the corresponding time as a TIME value in 'hh:mm:ss' format.

SEC_TO_TIME(29834)	→ '08:17:14'

- STR_TO_DATE(*str*, *format_str*)

  Interprets the string argument *str* using the formatting argument *format_str* and returns a TIME, DATE, or DATETIME value, depending on the formatting specifiers present in *format_str*. You can use this function to interpret temporal values in non-ISO format. STR_TO_DATE() performs the inverse operation of DATE_FORMAT(), and the format specifiers listed in the description of DATE_FORMAT() also are legal for

`STR_TO_DATE()`. If *str* is illegal or cannot be interpreted using the given format string, the result is NULL.

```
STR_TO_DATE('3/16/1960','%m/%d/%Y')              → '1960-03-16'
STR_TO_DATE('12.20.32','%H.%i.%s')               → '12:20:32'
STR_TO_DATE('3/16/1960 12:20:32','%m/%d/%Y %H:%i:%s')
                                                 → '1960-03-16 12:20:32'
STR_TO_DATE('3/16/1960','%m-%d-%Y')              → NULL
```

- `SUBDATE(date,INTERVAL expr interval)`
  `SUBDATE(date,expr)`

  For the first syntax, `SUBDATE()` takes a date or date and time value *date*, subtracts a temporal interval from it, and returns the result. This is a synonym for `DATE_SUB()`.

  ```
  SUBDATE('2009-12-01',INTERVAL 1 MONTH)         → '2009-11-01'
  ```

  For the second syntax, `SUBDATE()` takes a date or date and time value *date*, subtracts a temporal value representing number of days from it, and returns the result. This is similar to the corresponding syntax for `ADDDATE()`.

  ```
  SUBDATE('2009-12-01',30)                       → '2009-11-01'
  ```

- `SUBTIME(expr1,expr2)`

  Subtracts the second expression from the first and returns the result. *expr1* should be a time or date and time value, and *expr2* should be a time value.

  ```
  SUBTIME('06:30:00.5','12:30:00.4')             → '-05:59:59.900000'
  SUBTIME('2009-01-01 00:00:00','12:30:00')      → '2008-12-31 11:30:00'
  ```

- `SYSDATE()`

  Returns the current date and time in the session time zone as a DATETIME value in `'CCYY-MM-DD hh:mm:ss'` format. This function is similar to NOW(), except that `SYSDATE()` returns the date and time when it executes, whereas NOW() returns the beginning execution time of the statement within which it occurs. (See the description of NOW() for more detail.) To make SYSDATE() behave like NOW(), start the server with the `--sysdate-is-now` option.

- `TIME(expr)`

  Returns the time part of *expr*, which should be a time or date and time expression.

  ```
  TIME('16:15:00')                               → '16:15:00'
  TIME('2005-03-12 16:15:00')                    → '16:15:00'
  ```

- `TIME_FORMAT(time,format)`

  Formats the time value *time* according to the formatting string format and returns the resulting string. This function also accepts DATETIME or TIMESTAMP arguments. The formatting string is like that used by DATE_FORMAT(), but only time-related specifiers are permitted. Other specifiers result in a NULL value or 0.

```
TIME_FORMAT('12:31:58','%H %i')                    → '12 31'
TIME_FORMAT(123158,'%H %i')                        → '12 31'
```

- TIME_TO_SEC(*time*)

  Given a value *time* representing elapsed time, returns a number representing the corresponding number of seconds. The return value can be passed to SEC_TO_TIME() to convert it back to a time.

```
TIME_TO_SEC('08:17:14')                            → 29834
SEC_TO_TIME(29834)                                 → '08:17:14'
```

  If given a DATETIME or TIMESTAMP value, TIME_TO_SEC() ignores the date part.

```
TIME_TO_SEC('2012-03-26 08:17:14')                 → 29834
```

- TIMEDIFF(*expr1*,*expr2*)

  Returns the time difference between *expr1* and *expr2*, which represent start and end times, respectively. They should both be time or date and time values; you cannot mix a time value with a date and time value.

```
TIMEDIFF('00:00:00','09:30:45')                    → '-09:30:45'
TIMEDIFF('09:30:45','00:00:00')                    → '09:30:45'
```

- TIMESTAMP(*expr1*[,*expr2*])

  The single-argument form takes a date or date and time value *expr1* and returns a DATETIME value. The two-argument form adds the time value *expr2* to *expr1* and returns the result as a DATETIME value.

```
TIMESTAMP('1985-12-14');                           → '1985-12-14 00:00:00'
TIMESTAMP('1985-12-14 09:00:00');                  → '1985-12-14 09:00:00'
TIMESTAMP('1985-12-14','18:00:00');                → '1985-12-14 18:00:00'
TIMESTAMP('1985-12-14 09:00:00','18:00:00');       → '1985-12-15 03:00:00'
TIMESTAMP('1985-12-14 09:00:00','-18:00:00');      → '1985-12-13 15:00:00'
```

- TIMESTAMPADD(*interval*,*expr1*,*expr2*)

  Interprets *expr1* as an integer number of units given by the *interval* argument, adds it to the date or date and time value *expr2*, and returns the result. The permitted *interval* values are MICROSECOND, SECOND, MINUTE, HOUR, DAY, WEEK, MONTH, QUARTER, and YEAR. Any of these values can be given with a prefix of SQL_TSI_.

```
TIMESTAMPADD(DAY,12,'1995-07-01')                  → '1995-07-13'
TIMESTAMPADD(MONTH,12,'1995-07-01')                → '1996-07-01'
TIMESTAMPADD(SQL_TSI_MONTH,12,'1995-07-01')        → '1996-07-01'
```

- TIMESTAMPDIFF(*interval*,*expr1*,*expr2*)

  Calculates the difference between the date or date and time expressions *expr1* and *expr2*, and returns the result in the units given by the *interval* argument. Permitted *interval* values are those given in the description for TIMESTAMPADD().

```
TIMESTAMPDIFF(DAY,'1995-07-01','1995-08-01')      → 31
TIMESTAMPDIFF(MONTH,'1995-07-01','1995-08-01')    → 1
```

- TO_DAYS(*date*)

  Returns a numeric value representing the date value *date* converted to the number of days since the year 0. The return value can be passed to FROM_DAYS() to convert it back to a date.

  ```
  TO_DAYS('2010-12-01')                             → 734472
  FROM_DAYS(734472)                                 → '2010-12-01'
  ```

  If given a DATETIME or TIMESTAMP value, TO_DAYS() ignores the time part.

  ```
  TO_DAYS('2010-12-01 12:14:37')                    → 734472
  ```

  TO_DAYS() is intended only for dates covered by the Gregorian calendar (1582 on).

- TO_SECONDS(*expr*)

  Returns the number of seconds since year 0 for the given date or date and time expression, or NULL if the argument is invalid.

  ```
  TO_SECONDS('1790-07-17')                          → 56504044800
  ```

- UNIX_TIMESTAMP()
  UNIX_TIMESTAMP(*date*)

  When called with no arguments, returns the number of seconds since the reference date '1970-01-01 00:00:00' UTC. When called with a date-valued argument *date*, returns the number of seconds between the reference date and the argument. *date* can be specified as a DATE, DATETIME, or TIMESTAMP value, or as a number in the format *CCYYMMDD* or *YYMMDD*. The server interprets *date* as a value in the session time zone and converts it to UTC, unless the value comes from a TIMESTAMP column (in which case, the stored value is already in UTC).

  ```
  UNIX_TIMESTAMP()                                  → 1328381580
  UNIX_TIMESTAMP('2007-12-01')                      → 1196488800
  UNIX_TIMESTAMP(20071201)                          → 1196488800
  ```

- UTC_DATE()

  Returns the current UTC date as a DATE value in '*CCYY:MM:DD*' format. The parentheses are optional.

  ```
  UTC_DATE()                                        → '2012-08-26'
  ```

- UTC_TIME([*fsp*])

  Returns the current UTC time as a TIME value in '*hh:mm:ss*' format. Beginning with MySQL 5.6.4, the optional *fsp* argument can be given to specify that the return value should have a fractional seconds precision of 0 to 6 digits. Before 5.6.4, any argument is ignored. The parentheses are optional unless the *fsp* argument is given.

```
UTC_TIME()                                              → '20:00:18'
UTC_TIME(3)                                             → '20:00:18.465'
```

- UTC_TIMESTAMP([fsp])

  Returns the current UTC date and time as a DATETIME value in 'CCYY-MM-DD hh:mm:ss' format. Beginning with MySQL 5.6.4, the optional fsp argument can be given to specify that the return value should have a fractional seconds precision of 0 to 6 digits. Before 5.6.4, any argument is ignored. The parentheses are optional unless the fsp argument is given.

  ```
  UTC_TIMESTAMP()                                       → '2012-08-26 20:48:23'
  ```

- WEEK(date[,mode])

  When called with a single argument, returns a number representing the week of the year for the date value date, in the range from 0 to 53. The week is assumed to start on Sunday. When called with two arguments, WEEK() returns the same kind of value, but the mode argument indicates the day on which the week starts and whether to return a value in the range from 0 to 53 or 1 to 53. The following table indicates the meaning of the possible mode values.

Mode	Starting Day	Return Range	Meaning
0	Sunday	0..53	Week 1 is first week containing a Sunday
1	Monday	0..53	Week 1 is first week with more than three days
2	Sunday	1..53	Week 1 is first week containing a Sunday
3	Monday	1..53	Week 1 is first week with more than three days
4	Sunday	0..53	Week 1 is first week with more than three days
5	Monday	0..53	Week 1 is first week containing a Monday
6	Sunday	1..53	Week 1 is first week with more than three days
7	Monday	1..53	Week 1 is first week containing a Monday

  If mode is missing, the default_week_format system variable applies.

  ```
  WEEK('2003-12-08')                                    → 49
  WEEK('2003-12-08',0)                                  → 49
  WEEK('2003-12-08',1)                                  → 50
  ```

  A WEEK() value of 0 indicates that the date occurs prior to the first instance of the week starting day (Sunday or Monday, depending on the mode value).

```
WEEK('2005-01-01')                      → 0
DAYNAME('2005-01-01')                   → 'Saturday'
WEEK('2006-01-01',1)                    → 0
DAYNAME('2006-01-01')                   → 'Sunday'
```

- WEEKDAY(*date*)

  Returns the numeric value of the weekday for the date value *date*, or NULL if the name cannot be determined. Weekday values are in the range from 0 for Monday to 6 for Sunday; see also the DAYOFWEEK() function.

```
WEEKDAY('2002-12-08')                   → 6
DAYNAME('2002-12-08')                   → 'Sunday'
WEEKDAY('2002-12-16')                   → 0
DAYNAME('2002-12-16')                   → 'Monday'
WEEKDAY('2002-12-00')                   → NULL
```

- WEEKOFYEAR(*date*)

  This is the same as WEEK(*date*,3).

- YEAR(*date*)

  Returns the numeric value of the year for the date value *date*.

```
YEAR('1974-12-01')                      → 1974
YEAR(19741201)                          → 1974
```

- YEARWEEK(*date*[,*mode*])

  Returns a number in the format *CCYYWW* representing the year and week of the year for the date value *date*. The *mode* argument, if given, is the same as for the WEEK() function.

```
YEARWEEK('2006-01-01')                  → 200601
YEARWEEK('2006-01-01',0)                → 200601
YEARWEEK('2006-01-01',1)                → 200552
```

  The year for the result may differ from the year in the argument for the first or last week of the year.

```
WEEK('2008-01-01')                      → 0
YEARWEEK('2008-01-01')                  → 200752
```

C.2.6   Summary Functions

Summary (or "aggregate") functions calculate a single value based on a group of values. The resulting value is based only on the non-NULL values from the group, with the exception that COUNT(*) counts all rows. Summary functions are useful for summarizing an entire set of values or producing summaries for each subgroup of a set of values when the query includes a GROUP BY clause. See Section 1.4.9.9, "Generating Summaries."

For the examples in this section, assume the existence of a table `mytbl` with an integer column `mycol` that contains eight rows with the values 1, 3, 5, 5, 7, 9, 9, and `NULL`.

```
mysql> SELECT mycol FROM mytbl;
+-------+
| mycol |
+-------+
|     1 |
|     3 |
|     5 |
|     5 |
|     7 |
|     9 |
|     9 |
|  NULL |
+-------+
```

- AVG([DISTINCT] *expr*)

  Returns the average value for all non-NULL values of *expr*, or NULL if there are no non-NULL values.

  ```
  SELECT AVG(mycol) FROM mytbl           → 5.5714
  SELECT AVG(mycol)*2 FROM mytbl         → 11.1429
  SELECT AVG(mycol*2) FROM mytbl         → 11.1429
  ```

  DISTINCT causes AVG() to return the average of the distinct *expr* values.

- BIT_AND(*expr*)

  Returns the bitwise AND value for all non-NULL values of *expr*, or ~0 if there are no non-NULL values.

  ```
  SELECT BIT_AND(mycol) FROM mytbl       → 1
  ```

- BIT_OR(*expr*)

  Returns the bitwise OR value for all non-NULL values of *expr*, or 0 if there are no non-NULL values.

  ```
  SELECT BIT_OR(mycol) FROM mytbl        → 15
  ```

- BIT_XOR(*expr*)

  Returns the bitwise exclusive-OR value for all non-NULL values of *expr*, or 0 if there are no non-NULL values.

  ```
  SELECT BIT_XOR(mycol) FROM mytbl       → 5
  ```

- COUNT(*expr*)
  COUNT(*)
  COUNT(DISTINCT *expr1*,*expr2*,...)

With an expression argument, returns a count of the number of non-NULL values or *expr*, 0 if there are no non-NULL values. With an argument of *, returns a count of all rows in the result set, regardless of their contents.

```
SELECT COUNT(mycol) FROM mytbl                    → 7
SELECT COUNT(*) FROM mytbl                         → 8
```

For MyISAM tables, COUNT(*) with no WHERE clause is optimized to return the number of rows in the table named in the FROM clause very quickly. When more than one table is named, COUNT(*) returns the product of the number of rows in the individual tables.

```
SELECT COUNT(*) FROM mytbl AS m1 INNER JOIN mytbl AS m2
                                                   → 64
```

With DISTINCT, COUNT() counts the number of distinct non-NULL values.

```
SELECT COUNT(DISTINCT mycol) FROM mytbl            → 5
SELECT COUNT(DISTINCT MOD(mycol,3)) FROM mytbl     → 3
```

If multiple expressions are given, COUNT(DISTINCT) counts the number of distinct combinations of non-NULL values.

- GROUP_CONCAT([DISTINCT] *var_list* [ORDER BY ...] [SEPARATOR *str*])

This function concatenates the non-NULL values in a group of strings and returns the result. It returns NULL if there are no non-NULL values. You can use DISTINCT to remove duplicates, ORDER BY to sort the results, and SEPARATOR to specify the delimiter between strings. By default, GROUP_CONCAT() does not perform duplicate removal or sorting, and separates values by commas.

```
mysql> CREATE TABLE t (name CHAR(10));
mysql> INSERT INTO t VALUES('dog'),('cat'),('rat'),('dog'),('rat');
mysql> SELECT GROUP_CONCAT(name) FROM t;
+---------------------+
| GROUP_CONCAT(name)  |
+---------------------+
| dog,cat,rat,dog,rat |
+---------------------+
mysql> SELECT GROUP_CONCAT(name SEPARATOR ':') FROM t;
+---------------------------------+
| GROUP_CONCAT(name SEPARATOR ':')|
+---------------------------------+
| dog:cat:rat:dog:rat             |
+---------------------------------+
mysql> SELECT GROUP_CONCAT(name ORDER BY name DESC) FROM t;
+---------------------------------------+
| GROUP_CONCAT(name ORDER BY name DESC)  |
+---------------------------------------+
| rat,rat,dog,dog,cat                    |
+---------------------------------------+
```

```
mysql> SELECT GROUP_CONCAT(DISTINCT name ORDER BY name) FROM t;
+------------------------------------------+
| GROUP_CONCAT(DISTINCT name ORDER BY name) |
+------------------------------------------+
| cat,dog,rat                              |
+------------------------------------------+
```

Values returned by GROUP_CONCAT() are limited in length to the value of the group_concat_max_len system variable. To permit longer values, increase the value of this variable.

- MAX([DISTINCT] expr)

  Returns the maximum non-NULL value of expr, or NULL if there are no non-NULL values. With strings or temporal values, MAX() returns the lexically or temporally greatest value.

  SELECT MAX(mycol) FROM mytbl   → 9

  With DISTINCT, MAX() returns the maximum distinct expr value (which does not change the result).

- MIN([DISTINCT] expr)

  Returns the minimum non-NULL value of expr, or NULL if there are no non-NULL values. With strings or temporal values, MIN() returns the lexically or temporally least value.

  SELECT MIN(mycol) FROM mytbl   → 1

  With DISTINCT, MIN() returns the minimum distinct expr value (which does not change the result).

- STD(expr)
  STDDEV(expr)
  STDDEV_POP(expr)

  Returns the population standard deviation for all non-NULL values of expr, or NULL if there are no non-NULL values.

  SELECT STDDEV_POP(mycol) FROM mytbl   → 2.7701

- STDDEV_SAMP(expr)

  Returns the sample standard deviation for all non-NULL values of expr, or NULL if there are no non-NULL values.

  SELECT STDDEV_SAMP(mycol) FROM mytbl   → 2.9921

- SUM([DISTINCT] expr)

  Returns the sum for all non-NULL values of expr, or NULL if there are no non-NULL values.

  SELECT SUM(mycol) FROM mytbl   → 39

  With DISTINCT, SUM() returns the sum of the distinct expr values.

- VARIANCE(*expr*)
  VAR_POP(*expr*)

  Returns the population variance for all non-NULL values of *expr*, or NULL if there are no non-NULL values.

  SELECT VAR_POP(mycol) FROM mytbl   → 7.6735

- VAR_SAMP(*expr*)

  Returns the sample variance for all non-NULL values of *expr*, or NULL if there are no non-NULL values.

  SELECT VAR_SAMP(mycol) FROM mytbl   → 8.9524

C.2.7 Security and Compression Functions

These functions perform security-related operations such as encrypting or compressing strings. Several of these functions come in pairs, with one function producing an encrypted value and the other performing decryption. Such pairs of functions typically use a string as a key or password value. To get back the original value, you must decrypt a value with the same key used to encrypt it. The decrypted result is meaningless otherwise.

To save the result in a database when using encryption functions that return a binary string, use a column that has a binary string data type (VARBINARY or one of the BLOB types). This prevents problems that might occur with a nonbinary string type, such as character set conversion or truncation of trailing spaces.

Certain encryption functions return ASCII strings and the return value is a nonbinary string in the connection character set: MD5(), OLD_PASSWORD(), PASSWORD(), SHA(), SHA1(), and SHA2(). These functions return binary strings prior to MySQL 5.5.3 (5.5.6 for SHA2()).

- AES_DECRYPT(*str*,*key_str*)

  Given an encrypted string *str* obtained as a result of a call to AES_ENCRYPT(), decrypts it using the key string *key_str* and returns the resulting string. Returns NULL if either argument is NULL.

  AES_DECRYPT(AES_ENCRYPT('secret','scramble'),'scramble')
                                          → 'secret'

- AES_ENCRYPT(*str*,*key_str*)

  Encrypts the string *str* with the key string *key_str* using the Advanced Encryption Standard (AES) and a 128-bit key length. Returns the result as a binary string, or NULL if either argument is NULL. The string can be decoded with AES_DECRYPT() using the same key string.

- COMPRESS(*str*)

  Returns a compressed version of the argument string as a binary string, or NULL if the server was not compiled with a compression library.

- DECODE(*str*,*key_str*)

  Given an encrypted string *str* obtained as a result of a call to ENCODE(), decrypts it using the key string *key_str*. Returns the resulting string, or NULL if *str* is NULL.

  DECODE(ENCODE('secret','scramble'),'scramble')   → 'secret'

- DES_DECRYPT(*str* [,*key_str*])

  Decrypts a string *str*, which should be an encrypted value produced by DES_ENCRYPT(). If SSL support is not enabled or decryption fails, DES_DECRYPT() returns NULL.

  If a *key_str* argument is given, it is used as the decryption key. Otherwise, DES_DECRYPT() uses a key from the server's DES key file to decrypt the string. The key number is determined from bits 0–6 of the first byte of the encrypted string. The location of the key file is specified at server startup using the --des-key-file option.

  If *str* does not look like an encrypted string, DES_DECRYPT() returns the string unchanged. (This occurs, for example, if the first byte does not have bit 7 set.)

  Use of the single-argument form of DES_DECRYPT() requires the SUPER privilege.

- DES_ENCRYPT(*str* [,{*key_num*|*key_str*}])

  Performs DES encryption on the string *str* and returns the encrypted result as a binary string. The encrypted string can be decrypted with DES_DECRYPT(). If SSL support is not enabled or encryption fails, DES_ENCRYPT() returns NULL.

  If a *key_str* argument is given, it is used as the encryption key. If a *key_num* argument is given, it should be a value from 0 to 9, indicating the key number of an entry in the server's DES key file. In this case, the encryption key is taken from that entry. If no *key_str* or *key_num* argument is given, the first key from the DES key file is used to perform encryption. (This is not necessarily the same as specifying a *key_num* value of 0.)

  The first byte of the resulting string indicates how the string was encrypted. This byte will have bit 7 set, and bits 0–6 indicate the key number. The number is 0 to 9 to specify which key in the DES key file was used to encrypt the string, or 127 if a *key_str* argument was used. For example, if you encrypt a string using key 3, the first byte of the result is 131 (that is, 128+3). If you encrypt a string with a *key_str* value, the first byte is 255 (that is, 128+127).

  For encryption performed on the basis of a key number, the server reads the DES key file to find the corresponding key string. The location of the key file is specified at server startup using the --des-key-file option. The key file contains lines of the following format:

  key_num key_str

  Each *key_num* value should be a number from 0 to 9 and the *key_str* value is the corresponding encryption key. *key_num* and *key_str* should be separated by at least one whitespace character. Lines in the key file can be arranged in any order.

Unlike DES_DECRYPT(), DES_ENCRYPT() does not require the SUPER privilege to use keys from the DES key file. (Anyone can encrypt information based on the key file; only privileged users are permitted to use it for decryption.)

- ENCODE(*str*, *key_str*)

Encrypts the string *str* using the key string *key_str* and returns the result as a binary string. The string can be decoded with DECODE() using the same key string.

- ENCRYPT(*str* [,*salt*])

Encrypts the string *str* and returns the resulting string, or NULL if either argument is NULL. This is a nonreversible encryption. The *salt* argument, if given, should be a string with two characters or more characters. By specifying a *salt* value, the encrypted result for *str* will be the same each time. With no *salt* argument, MySQL uses a random value, so identical calls to ENCRYPT() yield different results over time.

```
ENCRYPT('secret','AB')          → 'ABS5SGh1EL6bk'
ENCRYPT('secret','AB')          → 'ABS5SGh1EL6bk'
ENCRYPT('secret')               → 'ByUthKNv3.LsE'
ENCRYPT('secret')               → 'Hyx4rhb7Qdvpk'
```

ENCRYPT() uses the Unix crypt() system call and is subject to system-specific behavior. In particular, on some systems, crypt() looks at only the first eight characters of the string to be encrypted. If crypt() is unavailable on your system, ENCRYPT() always returns NULL.

str should not be a string in the ucs2, utf16, utf16le, or utf32 character set. crypt() interprets a NUL byte as terminating the argument, but those character sets permit NUL within the string value.

- MD5(*str*)

Calculates a 128-bit checksum from the string *str* based on the RSA Data Security, Inc. MD5 Message-Digest algorithm. The return value is a nonbinary string consisting of 32 hexadecimal digits, or NULL if the argument is NULL. See also the notes in the section introduction regarding the string return type.

```
MD5('secret')          → '5ebe2294ecd0e0f08eab7690d2a6ee69'
```

- OLD_PASSWORD(*str*)

This function returns the encrypted password value that PASSWORD() returned prior to MySQL 4.1. See the notes in the section introduction regarding the string return type.

- PASSWORD(*str*)

Given a string *str*, calculates and returns an encrypted password string of the form used in the MySQL grant tables. This is a nonreversible encryption. See the notes in the section introduction regarding the string return type.

```
PASSWORD('secret')          → '*14E65567ABDB5135D0CFD9A70B3032C179A49EE7'
```

PASSWORD() does *not* use the same algorithm as the one used on Unix to encrypt user account passwords. For that type of encryption, use ENCRYPT().

If the old_passwords system variable is 1, PASSWORD() encrypts the password with the hashing algorithm that was used prior to MySQL 4.1. In this case, PASSWORD() and OLD_PASSWORD() return the same value.

- SHA1(*str*)
  SHA(*str*)

  Calculates a 160-bit checksum from the string *str* using the Secure Hash Algorithm. The return value is a nonbinary string consisting of 40 hexadecimal digits, or NULL if the argument is NULL. See also the notes in the section introduction regarding the string return type.

  SHA1('secret')   → 'e5e9fa1ba31ecd1ae84f75caaa474f3a663f05f4'

  SHA1() is more secure than MD5() but less secure than SHA2().

- SHA2(*str, hash_length*)

  This function is similar to SHA1(), but is more secure. It hashes the first argument, producing a result with a bit length indicated by the second argument. The hash length must be 224, 256, 384, or 512. The result is a nonbinary string of the specified number of bits, represented as hexadecimal digits. The result is NULL if either argument is NULL or the hash length is invalid. See also the notes in the section introduction regarding the string return type.

  SHA2('secret',224)
              → '95c7fbca92ac5083afda62a564a3d014fc3b72c9140e3cb99ea6bf12'

  SHA2() was introduced in MySQL 5.5.5.

- UNCOMPRESS(*str*)

  Given a string that was compressed with the COMPRESS() function, UNCOMPRESS() returns the original string. Returns NULL if the argument is not a compressed string or if the server was not compiled with a compression library.

- UNCOMPRESSED_LENGTH(*str*)

  Given a string that was compressed with the COMPRESS() function, returns the length of the original uncompressed string. Returns NULL if the server was not compiled with a compression library.

C.2.8   Advisory Locking Functions

The functions in this section implement advisory (cooperative) locking. You can use them to write applications that cooperate based on the status of an agreed-upon lock name. The primary functions are GET_LOCK() and RELEASE_LOCK(), which acquire and release locks. Two other functions, IS_FREE_LOCK() and IS_USED_LOCK(), query the status of a lock and determine which client holds a lock.

The basis for advisory locking is that you lock a name, which is nothing more than a string. An advisory lock is private in the sense that only the client that holds the lock can release it, but global in the sense that any client can query the status of the lock name.

To acquire a lock, call GET_LOCK(*str*, *timeout*), where *str* indicates the lock name and *timeout* is a timeout value in seconds. GET_LOCK() returns 1 if the lock was obtained successfully within the timeout period, 0 if the lock attempt failed due to timing out, or NULL if an error occurred.

The *timeout* value indicates how long to wait while attempting to obtain the lock, not the duration of the lock. After the lock is obtained, it remains in force until released.

The following call acquires a lock named 'Nellie', waiting up to 10 seconds for it:

GET_LOCK('Nellie',10)

The lock applies only to the string name itself. It does not lock a database, a table, or rows or columns within a table. In other words, the lock does not prevent other clients from doing anything to database tables, which is why GET_LOCK() locking is advisory only—it simply enables other cooperating clients to determine whether the lock is in force.

A client that has a lock on a name blocks attempts by other clients to lock the name (or attempts by other threads within a multi-threaded client that maintains multiple sessions with the server). Suppose that client 1 locks the string 'Nellie'. If client 2 attempts to lock the same string, it blocks until client 1 releases the lock or until the timeout period expires. If client 1 releases the lock within the timeout period, client 2 will acquire the lock successfully. Otherwise, client 2 will fail.

Because two sessions cannot lock a given string at the same time, applications that agree on a name can use the lock status of that name as an indicator of when it is safe to perform operations related to the name. For example, you can construct a lock name based on a unique key value for a row in a table to enable cooperative locking of that row.

To release a lock explicitly, call RELEASE_LOCK() with the lock name:

RELEASE_LOCK('Nellie')

RELEASE_LOCK() returns 1 if the lock was released successfully, 0 if the lock belongs to another session, or NULL if no such lock exists.

Any lock held by a client is automatically released if the same client issues another GET_LOCK() call, because only one string at a time can be locked per client session. In this case, the lock being held is released before the new lock is obtained, even if the lock name is the same. Lock release also occurs when the client's session with the server terminates. Thus, if a very long-running client times out due to inactivity, the server releases any lock it holds.

To test the status of a lock name, you have two options:

- Invoke IS_FREE_LOCK(*str*), which returns 1 if the name is currently not locked, 0 if the name is locked, or NULL if an error occurred.

- Invoke IS_USED_LOCK(*str*), which returns the connection ID of the client that holds a lock on the name, or NULL if there is no such lock.

You can also use GETLOCK(str,0) as a simple poll to determine without waiting whether str is locked. However, this has the side effect of locking the string if it is not currently locked, so you must remember to call RELEASE_LOCK() as appropriate.

All advisory locking functions return NULL if the lock name argument is NULL.

- GET_LOCK(str,timeout)

  Attempt to acquire an advisory lock on the name indicated by the string str within a timeout value of timeout seconds. GET_LOCK() returns 1 if the lock was obtained successfully within the timeout period, 0 if the lock attempt failed due to timing out, or NULL if an error occurred.

- IS_FREE_LOCK(str)

  Checks the status of the advisory lock named by str. Returns 1 if the name is available for locking, 0 if the name is locked, or NULL if an error occurred.

- IS_USED_LOCK(str)

  Returns the connection ID of the client that holds a lock on str, or NULL if there is no such lock.

- RELEASE_LOCK(str)

  Releases the advisory lock named by str. Returns 1 if the lock was released successfully, 0 if the lock is held by another session, or NULL if no such lock exists.

C.2.9   IP Address Functions

The functions in this section perform manipulation and testing of IP addresses, both in the IPv4 family and (as of MySQL 5.6.3) the IPv6 family.

- INET_ATON(str)

  Given an IPv4 address as a string in dotted-quad notation, returns the corresponding integer representation in network byte order, or NULL if the argument is not a valid IPv4 address.

INET_ATON('64.28.67.70')	→ 1075594054
INET_ATON('255.255.255.255')	→ 4294967295
INET_ATON('256.255.255.255')	→ NULL
INET_ATON('www.mysql.com')	→ NULL

- INET_NTOA(n)

  Given an IPv4 address as an integer in network byte order, returns the corresponding dotted-quad string representation, or NULL if the argument is illegal.

INET_NTOA(1075594054)	→ '64.28.67.70'
INET_NTOA(2130706433)	→ '127.0.0.1'

- INET6_ATON(*expr*)

  Given an IPv6 or IPv4 address as a string, returns the corresponding numeric value in network byte order as a binary string, or NULL if the argument is illegal. For a non-NULL return value, its type is VARINARY(16) or VARINARY(4) for an IPv6 or IPv4 address, respectively. To convert the result to printable form, use HEX().

  ```
  HEX(INET6_ATON('::1'))                    → '00000000000000000000000000000001'
  HEX(INET6_ATON('192.168.10.14'))          → 'C0A80A0E'
  ```

  INET6_ATON() was introduced in MySQL 5.6.3.

- INET6_NTOA(*expr*)

  Given the numeric form of an IPv6 or IPv4 address as a binary string, returns the corresponding string representation, or NULL if the argument is illegal.

  ```
  INET6_NTOA(INET6_ATON('::1'))             → '::1'
  INET6_NTOA(INET6_ATON('192.168.10.14'))   → '192.168.10.14'
  ```

  INET6_NTOA() was introduced in MySQL 5.6.3.

- IS_IPV4(*expr*)

  If the argument is a valid string IPv4 address, returns 1, otherwise 0.

  ```
  IS_IPV4('::1')                            → 0
  IS_IPV4('192.168.10.14')                  → 1
  ```

  IS_IPV4() was introduced in MySQL 5.6.3.

- IS_IPV4_COMPAT(*expr*)
  IS_IPV4_MAPPED(*expr*)

  These functions interpret IPv6 addresses in the form returned by INET6_ATON(); that is, in numeric form as a binary string. They determine whether the argument represents a valid string IPv4-compatible or IPv4-mapped IPv6 address, respectively. If so, each function returns 1, otherwise 0. An IPv4-compatible or IPv4-mapped address has the format ::*ipv4_addr* or ::ffff:*ipv4_addr*, respectively.

  ```
  IS_IPV4_COMPAT(INET6_ATON('::1'))                      → 0
  IS_IPV4_COMPAT(INET6_ATON('::192.168.10.14'))          → 1
  IS_IPV4_COMPAT(INET6_ATON('::ffff:192.168.10.14'))
                                                         → 0
  IS_IPV4_MAPPED(INET6_ATON('::1'))                      → 0
  IS_IPV4_MAPPED(INET6_ATON('::192.168.10.14'))          → 0
  IS_IPV4_MAPPED(INET6_ATON('::ffff:192.168.10.14'))
                                                         → 1
  ```

  IS_IPV4_COMPAT() and IS_IPV4_MAPPED() were introduced in MySQL 5.6.3.

- IS_IPV6(*expr*)

    If the argument is a valid string IPv6 address, returns 1, otherwise 0. This function
    returns 0 for IPv4 addresses.

    ```
    IS_IPV6('::1')                              → 1
    IS_IPV6('192.168.10.14')                    → 0
    ```

    IS_IPV6() was introduced in MySQL 5.6.3.

C.2.10   XML Functions

The functions in this section enable a string representing an XML fragment to be processed
with an XPath expression, either to extract text from the fragment or return the fragment with
a matched element replaced by another string. The XML string arguments must contain tags
that are properly balanced and nested.

These functions use XPath 1.0. For general information about XPath, see the specification at
http://www.w3.org/TR/xpath. There are some limitations on XPath support. See the MySQL
Reference Manual for the current restrictions.

- EXTRACTVALUE(*xml_str*,*xpath_expr*)

    Applies the XPath expression to evaluate the XML string and returns the content of the
    first text node from the element matched by the expression. If the expression matches
    multiple elements, the result is the first text node from each of the matched elements
    concatenated with spaces between.

    ```
    EXTRACTVALUE('<a><b>B</b><c>C</c></a>','//b')     → 'B'
    EXTRACTVALUE('<a><b>B1</b><b>B2</b><b>B3</b></a>','//b')
                                                      → 'B1 B2 B3'
    ```

    If there is no match, the result is the empty string (the same as if there is a match for an
    element with no text content).

- UPDATEXML(*xml_str*,*xpath_expr*,*xml_new*)

    Applies the XPath expression to evaluate the XML string, replaces the matched element
    with *xml_new*, and returns the result. If the expression matches nothing or matches
    multiple elements, the XML string is returned without modification.

C.2.11   Spatial Functions

MySQL supports functions that operate on spatial values. These functions are numerous but
tend to fall into groups, the members of which are highly similar. For example, conversion
functions for points, lines, polygons, and other spatial types are all much the same. For this
reason and to save space, this appendix does not cover them, and I refer you to the MySQL
Reference Manual.

C.2.12 Miscellaneous Functions

The functions in this section do not fall into any of the categories in the preceding sections.

- BENCHMARK(n, $expr$)

  Evaluates the expression $expr$ repetitively n times. BENCHMARK() is unusual in that it is intended for use within the mysql client program. Its return value is always 0, and thus of no use. The value of interest is the elapsed time that mysql displays following the result of the query:

  ```
  mysql> SELECT BENCHMARK(1000000,PASSWORD('secret'));
  +---------------------------------------+
  | BENCHMARK(1000000,PASSWORD('secret')) |
  +---------------------------------------+
  |                                     0 |
  +---------------------------------------+
  1 row in set (2.35 sec)
  ```

  The time is only an approximate indicator of how quickly the server evaluates the expression because it represents wall-clock time on the client, not CPU time on the server. The time can be influenced by factors such as the load on the server, whether the server is in a runnable state or swapped out when the query arrives, and so forth. You may want to execute it several times to see what a representative value is.

- BIT_COUNT(n)

  Returns the number of bits set in the argument, which is treated as a BIGINT value (a 64-bit integer).

  ```
  BIT_COUNT(0)                              → 0
  BIT_COUNT(1)                              → 1
  BIT_COUNT(2)                              → 1
  BIT_COUNT(7)                              → 3
  BIT_COUNT(-1)                             → 64
  BIT_COUNT(NULL)                           → NULL
  ```

- BIT_LENGTH(str)

  Returns the length of the string str in bits, or NULL if the argument is NULL.

  ```
  BIT_LENGTH('abc')                         → 24
  BIT_LENGTH('a long string')               → 104
  BIT_LENGTH(CONVERT('abc' USING ucs2))     → 48
  ```

- CONNECTION_ID()

  Returns the connection identifier that the server associates with the current client session. Every client has an identifier that is unique among the set of currently connected clients.

  ```
  CONNECTION_ID()                           → 10146
  ```

- CURRENT_USER()

The MySQL server authenticates each client against some particular account row in the `mysql.user` table. The CURRENT_USER() function returns the values from the `User` and `Host` columns of that row for the current client session, as a `utf8` string in `'user_name@host_name'` format. The parentheses are optional.

```
CURRENT_USER()                                      → 'sampadm@localhost'
SUBSTRING_INDEX(CURRENT_USER(),'@',1)               → 'sampadm'
```

You can use CURRENT_USER() to determine who the server believes you to be. This might differ from the user that you specified when connecting if the server authenticates you as some other account. In particular, if the server authenticates you as an anonymous user, the username part of the return value is empty, whereas the username part of the value returned by USER() contains the username you specified when making the connection.

Within a view or stored program, the CURRENT_USER() function returns the account corresponding to the object's DEFINER attribute by default. For views and stored routines defined with the SQL SECURITY INVOKER characteristic, CURRENT_USER() returns the account for the invoking user.

- DATABASE()

Returns a `utf8` string containing the default database name, or NULL if there is no default database. If called within a stored routine, DATABASE() returns the database with which the routine is associated.

```
DATABASE()                                          → 'sampdb'
```

- FOUND_ROWS()

Returns the number of rows that a preceding SELECT statement would have returned without a LIMIT clause. For example, this statement returns a maximum of 10 rows:

```
mysql> SELECT * FROM mytbl LIMIT 10;
```

To determine how many rows the statement would have returned without the LIMIT clause, do this:

```
mysql> SELECT SQL_CALC_FOUND_ROWS * FROM mytbl LIMIT 10;
mysql> SELECT FOUND_ROWS();
```

- DEFAULT(col_name)

The INSERT statement permits you to specify the keyword DEFAULT to insert a column's default value into a new row. However, that keyword is not permitted in arbitrary expressions or in other contexts. For example, you cannot use it to reset a column to its default value in an UPDATE statement. Use the DEFAULT() function for this. Given a column name, it returns the column's default value, or produces an error if the column has no default.

```
UPDATE counts SET counter = DEFAULT(counter)
WHERE max_time > expire_time;
```

- LAST_INSERT_ID()
  LAST_INSERT_ID(*expr*)

  With no argument, returns the first AUTO_INCREMENT value generated successfully by the most recent INSERT statement, or 0 if no such value has been generated. If the statement inserts multiple rows, LAST_INSERT_ID() returns the value for the first of them. If an error occurs, the value of LAST_INSERT_ID() is undefined.

  With an argument, the LAST_INSERT_ID() result is the argument value, but the value is treated as if it was automatically generated, which is useful for generating sequences.

  For additional details, see Section 3.4, "Working with Sequences." For both forms of LAST_INSERT_ID(), the server maintains the value on a per-session basis. It cannot be changed by other clients, even by those that cause their own new automatically generated values to be created.

- LOAD_FILE(*file_name*)

  Reads the file *file_name* and returns its contents as a string. If the filename is a literal string, it is interpreted in the character set given by character_set_filesystem. The file must be located on the server host, must be specified as an absolute (full) pathname, and must be world-readable to ensure that you're not trying to read a protected file. If the secure_file_priv system variable is nonempty, its value should be a directory and the file must be located in that directory. Because the file must be on the server host, you must have the FILE privilege. If any of these conditions fail, LOAD_FILE() returns NULL.

- MASTER_POS_WAIT(*log_file*,*pos*[,*timeout*])

  This function is used for testing replication. When executed on a slave server, it blocks until the slave has read and processed events from the master server up to the replication coordinates specified by the *log_file* and *pos* arguments. The *timeout* value, if given, places a limit on the number of seconds MASTER_POS_WAIT() should wait. A value of 0 or less is equivalent to no timeout.

  MASTER_POS_WAIT() returns the number of events it had to wait for to reach the given replication coordinates. If the slave had already reached the coordinates, the function returns immediately with a value of 0. A return value of –1 indicates that the function timed out, an error occurred, or the master server information has not been initialized. A return value of NULL indicates that the slave SQL thread was not running or was stopped while the function was waiting.

- NAME_CONST(*name*,*value*)

  This function is used internally (for example, to write statements to the binary log). It returns *value*, with a column name of *name*. Both arguments must be constants.

- ROW_COUNT()

  This function is like the mysql_affected_rows() C API function. The return value depends on the type of the previous statement:

- For data manipulation statements other than SELECT: Returns the number of rows affected (inserted, deleted, or updated).

- For SELECT: Returns –1 if the statement returns a result set. Otherwise, returns the number of rows retrieved into a destination. For example, SELECT ... INTO var_name returns 1, and SELECT ... INTO file_name returns the number of rows written to the file.

- For data definition statements (such as CREATE TABLE): Returns 0.

If a statement produces an error, ROW_COUNT() returns –1.

- SCHEMA()

This is a synonym for DATABASE().

- SESSION_USER()

This is a synonym for USER().

- SLEEP(seconds)

Pauses for the given number of seconds and returns 0, or returns 1 if it is interrupted. The seconds argument can have a fractional part.

- SYSTEM_USER()

This is a synonym for USER().

- USER()

Returns a utf8 string representing the username that the client specified when connecting to the MySQL server, and the host from which the client connected. The return value is a string in 'user_name@host_name' format.

```
USER()                                → 'paul@localhost'
SUBSTRING_INDEX(USER(),'@',1)         → 'paul'
SUBSTRING_INDEX(USER(),'@',-1)        → 'localhost'
```

- UUID()

Returns a "universal unique identifier." The intent is that the return value from one call to UUID() should differ from the value from any other call. Uniqueness of the return value is not guaranteed, but duplicated values should be very unlikely.

```
UUID()                → '4550868e-3c1f-1027-9cc8-78fa7f8d46b6'
```

The return value is a five-part utf8 string of hexadecimal digits generated from a 128-bit number. The first four parts should be temporally unique, and the last part should be spatially unique. The first three parts of the value are derived from a timestamp. The fourth part ensures uniqueness for situations in which the sequence of timestamp might not be monotonic, as happens when time changes for daylight saving time. The fifth part is an IEEE 802 node number. This might be generated from a value assumed to unique to your server host, such as a network interface address. If no such unique value can be obtained, a 48-bit random number is used instead.

- UUID_SHORT()

Similar to UUID(), but the universal identifier is a 64-bit unsigned integer, not a string.

UUID_SHORT()   → 94344395712626688

For the value to be unique, these conditions must be true: The server_id system variable value must be unique among your replication servers and have a value between 0 and 255; you do not turn back the server system time between server restarts; the average rate of UUID_SHORT() invocation does not exceed 16 million times/second between server restarts.

- VALUES(col_name)

This function is for use with the INSERT ... ON DUPLICATE KEY UPDATE statement. In the UPDATE clause, VALUES(col_name) returns the value to be inserted into the named column had no duplicate key error occurred. Outside of that context, it returns NULL. The function can be used to construct the alternative insert value in relation to the original insert value.

- VERSION()

Returns a utf8 string describing the server version.

VERSION()   → '5.5.28-log'

The value consists of a version number, possibly followed by one or more suffixes, such as -log to indicate that logging is enabled or -debug to indicate that the server is running in debug mode.

D

System, Status, and User Variable Reference

This appendix describes several types of MySQL variables:

- System variables that you can set to configure the server or check to obtain the current configuration
- Status variables that provide information about the server's current operational state
- User variables that you can define, assign values to, and refer to in expressions

Values for variables that represent buffer sizes or lengths generally are given in bytes. Exceptions are noted as necessary.

Unless otherwise indicated, the variables listed here have been present in MySQL at least as early as MySQL 5.5.0. Variables that were introduced or that have changed in meaning since then are noted.

D.1   System Variables

System variables provide information about the server's configuration and capabilities. Most system variables can be set at server startup. At runtime, each system variable has a global or session value, or both. Many system variables are dynamic; that is, they can be modified while the server is running. These types of information are given in the description for each variable on the same line as the variable name:

- For variables that can be set at server startup, the word "startup" appears, followed either by "set directly" or an option. The words "set directly" mean that you can set the variable directly on the command line or in an option file by using an option with the same name as the variable name. (Section F.2.1.2, "Setting Program Variables," describes the syntax for doing so.) Otherwise, "startup" is followed by the option that you use to set the variable. For example, you set the `time_zone` variable by using the `--default-time-zone` option. When an option is given, its meaning is found in the description for the `mysqld` program in Appendix F, "MySQL Program Reference."

- To indicate a variable's scope, the word "scope" appears followed by either (or both) the words "global" or "session" to indicate whether the variable has a `GLOBAL` form or `SESSION` form, or both. A variable that is read only at runtime normally has only a global value.

- For variables that can be modified while the server is running, the word "dynamic" appears.

To display system variables, use the `SHOW VARIABLES` statement or execute the `mysqladmin variables` command. You can also examine the `INFORMATION_SCHEMA` tables named `GLOBAL_VARIABLES` and `SESSION_VARIABLES` to obtain system variable information. To display the value of individual variables, use `SELECT @@GLOBAL.var_name` for global variables, or `SELECT @@SESSION.var_name` or `SELECT @@var_name` for session variables.

To set system variables, use the `SET` statement. To set a global variable, you must have the `SUPER` privilege. Setting session variables normally requires no special privilege. The few exceptions are noted.

System variable names are not case sensitive.

For more information about setting system variables at runtime or examining their values, see Section 12.3.1, "Checking and Setting System Variable Values."

Some of the variables described here are present only under certain configurations or on certain platforms. For example, `debug` is available only if the server is compiled with debugging support. `named_pipe` is available only on Windows.

The following list describes the more general system variables. A separate section describes variables for the InnoDB storage engine.

- `auto_increment_increment` (startup: set directly; scope: global, session; dynamic)

  The amount by which `AUTO_INCREMENT` values increase each time the server generates a new sequence value. The range of values is 1 to 65,535; the default is 1.

- `auto_increment_offset` (startup: set directly; scope: global, session; dynamic)

  The starting value for `AUTO_INCREMENT` sequences. The range of values is 1 to 65,535; the default is 1.

- `autocommit` (startup: set directly; scope: global, session; dynamic)

  The autocommit mode for transaction processing. This is 1 by default, so autocommit is enabled and statements take effect immediately; essentially, each statement is its own transaction. Setting the value to 0 disables autocommit so that subsequent statements do not take effect until a commit is performed (either with a `COMMIT` statement, or by setting `autocommit` to 1). Statements in the transaction may be canceled with `ROLLBACK` if a commit has not occurred. Setting `autocommit` to 1 re-enables autocommit (and implicitly commits any pending transaction).

- `automatic_sp_privileges` (startup: set directly; scope: global; dynamic)

If this variable is 1 (the default), the server automatically grants you the `EXECUTE` and `ALTER ROUTINE` privileges if necessary when you create a stored routine, so that you can execute, change, or drop the routine later. The server also revokes those privileges when you drop the routine. If `automatic_sp_privileges` is 0, automatic privilege granting and revocation does not occur.

- `back_log` (startup: set directly; scope: global)

The maximum number of pending connection requests that can be queued while current connections are being processed.

- `basedir` (startup: set directly; scope: global)

The pathname of the MySQL installation root directory. Many other pathnames are resolved in relation to this directory if they are given as relative pathnames.

- `big_tables` (startup: set directly; scope: global, session; dynamic)

Setting this variable to 1 enables large result sets to be processed by saving all temporary results to disk rather than by holding them in memory. Performance is slower, but `SELECT` statements that require large temporary tables will not generate "table full" errors. The default is 0 (hold temporary tables in memory). Normally you need not set this variable because the server automatically saves results to disk as required.

- `bind_address` (startup: set directly; scope: global)

The IP address to which the server is bound to listen for TCP/IP client connections. The default is `*` as of MySQL 5.6.6 (listen on all IPv4 and IPv6 interfaces) and `0.0.0.0` in earlier versions (listen on all IPv4 interfaces). For more information, see Section 12.2.4, "Controlling How the Server Listens for Connections." This variable was introduced in MySQL 5.6.1.

- `binlog_cache_size` (startup: set directly; scope: global; dynamic)

The size of the cache used to store SQL statements that are part of a transaction before they are flushed to the binary log. (This occurs only if the transaction is committed or includes statements that update nontransactional tables. If a transaction that updates only transactional tables is rolled back, the statements are discarded.)

- `binlog_checksum` (startup: set directly; scope: global; dynamic)

Whether to include checksums with events written to the binary log. Permitted values are `NONE` (do not write checksums) and `CRC32`. This variable was introduced in MySQL 5.6.2. The default is `NONE` before MySQL 5.6.6, and `CRC32` thereafter.

- `binlog_direct_non_transactional_updates` (startup: set directly; scope: global, session; dynamic)

  A transaction that updates both transactional and nontransactional tables can result in updates on a master that differ on slaves because updates to nontransactional statements become visible to other sessions before they appear in the binary log. Enabling this variable (it is disabled by default) causes nontransactional upates to be written to the binary log immediately rather than being cached until transaction commit. Enabling this variable is effective only for statements replicated using statement-based logging.

- `binlog_format` (startup: set directly; scope: global, session; dynamic)

  The binary logging format. The value can be STATEMENT, ROW, or MIXED, for statement-based, row-based, or mixed logging format. With mixed format, the server switches between statement- and row-based logging automatically. The default is STATEMENT. At runtime, a client must have the SUPER privilege to change this variable, even to change the session value.

- `binlog_row_image` (startup: set directly; scope: global, session; dynamic)

  Row-based binary logging uses before and after "images" to describe the original and changed rows. `binlog_row_image` controls how many columns these images contain. FULL (the default) logs all columns. MINIMAL logs only columns needed to identify rows and changed columns. NOBLOB is like FULL, minus inessential BLOB and TEXT columns. This variable was introduced in MySQL 5.6.2.

- `binlog_rows_query_log_events` (startup: set directly; scope: global, session; dynamic)

  With row-based binary logging, enabling this variable causes information useful for debugging to be included in the binary log. This variable was introduced in MySQL 5.6.2.

- `binlog_stmt_cache_size` (startup: set directly; scope: global; dynamic)

  The size of the cache for nontransactional statement executed within a transaction. The default is 32K. This variable was introduced in MySQL 5.5.9.

- `bulk_insert_buffer_size` (startup: set directly; scope: global, session; dynamic)

  The size of the cache used to help optimize bulk inserts into MyISAM tables. This includes LOAD DATA statements, multiple-row INSERT statements, and INSERT INTO ... SELECT statements. A value of 0 disables the optimization.

- `character_set_client` (scope: global, session; dynamic)

  The character set of statements sent by the client to the server.

- `character_set_connection` (scope: global, session; dynamic)

  The character set of the client-server connection. This is used to interpret string literals (except those that begin with an introducer) and for the character set of strings that result from number-to-string conversions.

- `character_set_database` (scope: global, session; dynamic)

  The character set of the default database, if there is one. If there is no default database (for example, if the client connects without selecting a database), this variable is set to the value of `character_set_server`. The server sets the value of `character_set_database` each time you select a different database.

- `character_set_filesystem` (startup: set directly; scope: global, session; dynamic)

  The filesystem character set. This is used to evaluate string literals that indicate filenames, such as the data file in LOAD DATA statements. The server converts the filename from the character set named by `character_set_client` to that named by `character_set_filesystem` before accessing the file. The default is `binary` (no conversion).

- `character_set_results` (scope: global, session; dynamic)

  The character set of query results sent by the server to the client.

- `character_set_server` (startup: set directly; scope: global, session; dynamic)

  The server's default character set.

- `character_set_system` (scope: global)

  The system character set. Its value is always `utf8`. This is the character set used for metadata such as database, table, and column names. It is also used for functions such as DATABASE(), CURRENT_USER(), USER(), and VERSION().

- `character_sets_dir` (startup: set directly; scope: global)

  The directory where character set files are located.

- `collation_connection` (scope: global, session; dynamic)

  The connection character set collation.

- `collation_database` (scope: global, session; dynamic)

  The database character set collation, if there is one. If there is no default database (for example, if the client connects without selecting one), this variable is set to the value of `collation_server`. The server sets the value of `collation_database` each time you select a different database.

- `collation_server` (startup: set directly; scope: global, session; dynamic)

  The default collation for the server's default character set.

- `completion_type` (startup: set directly; scope: global, session; dynamic)

  The completion type for transactions. A value of 0 or NO_CHAIN (the default) leaves COMMIT and ROLLBACK unaffected. A value of 1 or CHAIN causes them to be equivalent to COMMIT AND CHAIN and ROLLBACK AND CHAIN. A value of 2 or RELEASE causes them to be equivalent to COMMIT RELEASE and ROLLBACK RELEASE. With AND CHAIN, when a transaction completes, the server starts a new one with the same isolation level. With AND RELEASE, when a transaction completes, the server terminates the session.

- `concurrent_insert` (startup: set directly; scope: global; dynamic)

  For a MyISAM table that has no holes in the middle of the data file, the server can permit concurrent inserts to add new rows at the end of the table while retrievals are being performed on the existing rows. This variable controls whether the server permits concurrent inserts. Values of 0 (or `NEVER`) or 1 (or `AUTO`) disable or enable this feature. A value of 2 (or `ALWAYS`) enables concurrent inserts even for MyISAM tables that have holes in the data file; new rows are added to the end of a table that is in use, or into the holes otherwise. The default is 1.

- `connect_timeout` (startup: set directly; scope: global; dynamic)

  The number of seconds that `mysqld` waits for packets during the initial connection handshake. The default is 10.

- `core_file` (startup: set directly; scope: global)

  Whether the server generates a core file before exiting when a fatal error occurs. This variable was introduced in MySQL 5.6.2.

- `datadir` (startup: set directly; scope: global)

  The pathname of the MySQL data directory.

- `date_format` (scope: global)

  This variable is unused.

- `datetime_format` (scope: global)

  This variable is unused.

- `debug` (scope: global, session; dynamic)

  The type of debugging output. See the description for `--debug` in Section F.2.1, "Standard MySQL Program Options." This variable is present only if the server is compiled with debugging support.

- `default_storage_engine` (startup: set directly; scope: global, session; dynamic)

  The default storage engine for tables that are created with no `ENGINE` = *engine_name* option or with an unsupported *engine_name* value. The engine name is not case sensitive. The default is InnoDB.

- `default_tmp_storage_engine` (startup: set directly; scope: global, session; dynamic)

  Like `default_storage_engine`, but for tables created with `CREATE TEMPORARY TABLE`. This variable was introduced in MySQL 5.6.3.

- `default_week_format` (startup: set directly; scope: global, session; dynamic)

  The default mode value when the `WEEK()` or `YEARWEEK()` function is invoked without the optional *mode* argument.

- `delay_key_write` (startup: set directly; scope: global; dynamic)

Whether the server respects delayed key writes for MyISAM tables that are created with the `DELAY_KEY_WRITE` option. This variable can have three values:

- `ON` (the default) tells the server to honor the `DELAY_KEY_WRITE` option for tables defined with that option: Key writes are delayed for tables defined with `DELAY_KEY_WRITE=1`, but not for tables defined with `DELAY_KEY_WRITE=0`.

- `OFF` means that key writes are never delayed for any table, no matter how it was defined.

- `ALL` forces key writes always to be delayed for every table, no matter how it was defined.

It's common to run replication slave servers with `delay_key_write` set to `ALL` to obtain increased performance for MyISAM tables by delaying key writes no matter how the tables were created originally.

- `delayed_insert_limit` (startup: set directly; scope: global; dynamic)

The number of rows from `INSERT DELAYED` statements that the delayed-row handler for a table inserts before checking whether any new `SELECT` statements for the table have arrived. If any have arrived, the handler suspends the insert operation to enable retrievals to execute.

- `delayed_insert_timeout` (startup: set directly; scope: global; dynamic)

When a handler for `INSERT DELAYED` operations finishes inserting queued rows, it waits this many seconds to see whether any new `INSERT DELAYED` rows arrive. If so, it handles them; otherwise, it terminates.

- `delayed_queue_size` (startup: set directly; scope: global; dynamic)

The number of rows that may be queued per table for `INSERT DELAYED` statements. If the queue is full, further `INSERT DELAYED` statements for the table block until there is room in the queue.

- `div_precision_increment` (startup: set directly; scope: global, session; dynamic)

For division of two exact-value numbers performed with the / operator, this variable indicates how many digits of scale to add. For example, `.1/.7` is `.14286` or `.1428571` when `div_precision_increment` has a value of 4 or 6, respectively. The value can range from 0 to 30; the default is 4.

- `eq_range_index_dive_limit` (startup: set directly; scope: global, session; dynamic)

For equality comparisons processed using nonunique indexes, the number of ranges above which the optimizer switches to making row estimates using index statistics instead of index dives. A value of 0 disables use of statistics. The default is 10. This variable was introduced in MySQL 5.6.5. Prior to 5.6.5, index dives were used regardless of the number of ranges.

- error_count (scope: session)

  This is a read-only session variable that indicates the number of errors generated by the last statement that can generate errors.

- event_scheduler (startup: set directly; scope: global; dynamic)

  The status of the event scheduler. The value can be OFF, ON, or DISABLED. If the event scheduler is set to DISABLED at startup, its status cannot be changed at runtime. If the scheduler is set to either OFF or ON at startup, its status can be changed between those two values at runtime. The default is OFF.

- expire_logs_days (startup: set directly; scope: global; dynamic)

  If the value is other than the default of 0, the server automatically removes binary log files older than that many days and updates the binary log index file. The server checks for expiration when it starts and when it opens a new binary log file.

- external_user (scope: session)

  This is a read-only session variable that can be set by the authentication plugin used to authenticate the current user. This variable was introduced in MySQL 5.5.7.

- flush (startup: set directly; scope: global; dynamic)

  Whether the server flushes MyISAM tables to disk after each update. This reduces the risk of table corruption in the event of a crash but seriously degrades performance. Thus, it is useful only if you have an unstable system. The default is OFF.

- flush_time (startup: set directly; scope: global; dynamic)

  If this variable is nonzero, the server closes tables to flush pending changes to disk every flush_time seconds. If your system is unreliable and tends to lock up or restart often, forcing out table changes this way degrades performance but can reduce the chance of table corruption or data loss. The default is 0 for Unix and 1800 (30 minutes) for Windows.

- foreign_key_checks (scope: global, session; dynamic)

  Setting this variable to 0 or 1 disables or enables foreign key checking for InnoDB tables. The default is to perform checking. Disabling key checks can be useful, for example, to restore a dump file that creates and loads tables in an order different from that required by their foreign key relationships. You can re-enable key checking after loading the tables.

- ft_boolean_syntax (startup: set directly; scope: global; dynamic)

  The list of operators that are supported for FULLTEXT searches that use IN BOOLEAN MODE.

- ft_max_word_len (startup: set directly; scope: global)

  The maximum length of words that can be included in FULLTEXT indexes. Longer words are ignored. If you change the value of this variable, you should rebuild the FULLTEXT indexes for any MyISAM tables that have them. The default is 84.

- ft_min_word_len (startup: set directly; scope: global)

  The minimum length of words that can be included in FULLTEXT indexes. Shorter words are ignored. If you change the value of this variable, you should rebuild the FULLTEXT indexes for any MyISAM tables that have them. The default is 4.

- ft_query_expansion_limit (startup: set directly; scope: global)

  This variable is used for full-text searches that are done using the WITH QUERY EXPANSION clause. It determines the number of "top matches" to use for the second phase of each search.

- ft_stopword_file (startup: set directly; scope: global)

  The stopword file for FULLTEXT indexes. The default is to use the built-in list of stopwords. To disable stopwords, set the value to the empty string. If you change the value of this variable or the contents of the stopword list, you should rebuild the FULLTEXT indexes for any MyISAM tables that have them.

- general_log (startup: set directly; scope: global; dynamic)

  Whether logging to the general query log is enabled. If so, log_output controls the log destinations.

- general_log_file (startup: set directly; scope: global; dynamic)

  The name of the general query log file, for use if the FILE logging destination is enabled. The default is HOSTNAME.log in the data directory, where HOSTNAME is the name of the server host. If the file name is given as a relative path, the server interprets it relative to the data directory.

- group_concat_max_len (startup: set directly; scope: global, session; dynamic)

  The upper limit on the length of values that the GROUP_CONCAT() function should return (1024 by default).

- have_compress (scope: global)

  Whether the zlib compression library is available that the server needs to implement the COMPRESS() and UNCOMPRESS() functions. If not, the functions cannot be used.

- have_crypt (scope: global)

  Whether the crypt() system call is available that the server needs to implement the CRYPT() function. If not, the function cannot be used.

- have_dynamic_loading (scope: global)

  Whether the server supports dynamic plugin loading.

- have_geometry (scope: global)

  Whether spatial data types can be used.

- have_openssl (scope: global)

  Whether the server supports encrypted client connections using SSL. have_openssl and have_ssl are synonymous.

- have_query_cache (scope: global)

  Whether the query cache is available.

- have_rtree_keys (scope: global)

  Whether RTREE indexes are available for SPATIAL indexes.

- have_ssl (scope: global)

  See the description for have_openssl.

- have_symlink (scope: global)

  This variable is DISABLED if the server was started with the --skip-symbolic-links option. Otherwise, it has a value of YES or NO, but the meaning is platform dependent. On Unix, it indicates whether table symbolic linking is supported for MyISAM tables. On Windows, it indicates whether database symlinking is supported. See Section 11.3, "Relocating Data Directory Contents."

- host_cache_size (startup: set directly; scope: global; dynamic)

  The size of the host cache used to hold information about client connection attempts and whether they succeed or fail. Hosts from which connections fail too often are blocked until the cache is flushed. Changing the variable value at run time flushes the cache (the same effect as FLUSH HOSTS). The default is 128. This variable was introduced in MySQL 5.6.5.

- hostname (scope: global)

  The server hostname. The MySQL server determines the value when it starts.

- identity (scope: session; dynamic)

  This is a synonym for the last_insert_id session variable.

- ignore_db_dirs (startup: set directly; scope: global)

  This variable is set by instances of the --ignore-db-dir option that indicate directories in the data directory not to be treated as database directories by SHOW DATABASES or INFORMATION_SCHEMA tables. The default is empty. This variable was introduced in MySQL 5.6.3.

- init_connect (startup: set directly; scope: global; dynamic)

  A nonempty value specifies one or more SQL statements separated by semicolons to be executed for each client that connects to the server. This variable can be used to modify the initial session environment in which clients begin. init_connect is ignored for users who have the SUPER privilege, to prevent an incorrect or unwise statement in the variable value from causing administrative users to be unable to connect to the server to correct the problem.

- `init_file` (startup: set directly; scope: global)

  A nonempty value specifies the name of a file containing SQL statements to be executed by the server when it starts. If the filename is given as a relative path, the server interprets it relative to the data directory. The file should contain one statement per line and statements should not end with ; or other terminator.

- `init_slave` (startup: set directly; scope: global; dynamic)

  For a master replication server, this variable, if nonempty, specifies statements to be executed for each slave replication server when the slave connects. The value should be one or more SQL statements, separated by semicolons.

- `innodb_xxx`

  See Section D.1.1, "InnoDB System Variables."

- `insert_id` (scope: session; dynamic)

  Setting this variable specifies the value to be used by the next INSERT statement when inserting an AUTO_INCREMENT column. This is used for binary log processing.

- `interactive_timeout` (startup: set directly; scope: global, session; dynamic)

  The number of seconds an interactive client session can remain idle before the server considers itself free to close it. For noninteractive clients, the value of the wait_timeout variable is used instead.

- `join_buffer_size` (startup: set directly; scope: global, session; dynamic)

  The minimum size of the buffer used for joins that are performed without use of indexes and require a table scan, and for certain types of indexed scans.

- `keep_files_on_create` (startup: set directly; scope: global, session; dynamic)

  If an explicit DATA DIRECTORY or INDEX DIRECTORY option is given for a CREATE TABLE statement for a MyISAM table and the server finds an existing data or index file, respectively, in the named directory, it returns an error. The keep_files_on_create variable controls how the server handles MyISAM table creation when no DATA DIRECTORY or INDEX DIRECTORY option specifies where to place the data or index file. If keep_files_on_create is OFF (the default), and the server finds an existing .MYD data file or .MYI index file, it overwrites it. If the variable is ON, the server returns an error.

- `key_buffer_size` (startup: set directly; scope: global; dynamic)

  The size of the buffer used for caching MyISAM table index blocks. This buffer is shared among sessions.

  This variable and the other key cache variables (key_cache_age_threshold, key_cache_block_size, and key_cache_limit) exist as a group and can be accessed as components of a structured system variable. Multiple key caches can be created for finer control over key cache use. For more information, see Section 12.7.2, "Storage Engine Tuning."

- `key_cache_age_threshold` (startup: set directly; scope: global; dynamic)

  How long buffers stay unused in the hot subchain of the MyISAM key cache before being moved to the warm subchain. Higher values enable blocks to remain in the hot subchain longer. The default is 300. The minimum value is 100.

- `key_cache_block_size` (startup: set directly; scope: global; dynamic)

  The block size for the MyISAM key cache. By default, a block is 1024 bytes.

- `key_cache_limit` (startup: set directly; scope: global; dynamic)

  If set to the default value of 100, the MyISAM key cache uses a least recently used strategy for cache buffer reuse. If set lower than 100, the key cache uses a midpoint insertion strategy and the variable value is the percentage of the key cache to use for the warm buffer subchain. The value should be from 1 to 100.

- `language` (startup: set directly; scope: global)

  This variable is obsolete. Use `lc_messages` and `lc_messages_dir` instead.

- `large_files_support` (scope: global)

  Whether the server was built to support handling large files.

- `large_page_size` (scope: global)

  The size of large memory pages, if large page support is enabled. Otherwise, the value is 0.

- `large_pages` (startup: set directly; scope: global)

  Whether to enable large memory page support. Large pages are supported only on Linux.

- `last_insert_id` (scope: session; dynamic)

  Setting this variable specifies the value to be returned by `LAST_INSERT_ID()`. This is used for binary log processing.

- `lc_messages` (startup: set directly; scope: global, session; dynamic)

  The locale for error messages. The server translates the locale name to a language name and looks in the directory named by the `lc_messages_dir` variable for a directory with the language name to find the location of the error message file. See Section 12.6.3, "Selecting the Language for Error Messages."

- `lc_messages_dir` (startup: set directly; scope: global)

  The directory in which error message files are located.

- `lc_time_names` (startup: set directly; scope: global, session; dynamic)

  The locale for the language used for display of day and month names by the `DATE_FORMAT()`, `DAYNAME()`, and `MONTHNAME()` functions. The default locale value is en_US but can be set to other POSIX-style names such as es_AR (Spanish/Argentina) or zh_HK (Chinese/Hong Kong). See Section 12.6.4, "Selecting the Locale."

- `license` (scope: global)

The server license type; for example, `GPL` if the server is running under the terms of the GNU General Public License.

- `local_infile` (startup: set directly; scope: global; dynamic)

Whether the server permits the `LOCAL` modifier for `LOAD DATA` statements.

- `lock_wait_timeout` (startup: set directly; scope: global, session; dynamic)

How long in seconds to wait for each metadata lock. If a statment blocks longer than this waiting for a lock, an error occurs. The permitted range of values is 1 to 31536000 (1 year, the default). This variable was introduced in MySQL 5.5.3.

- `locked_in_memory` (startup: use `--memlock`; scope: global)

Whether the server is locked in memory.

- `log` (scope: global)

This variable is obsolete and is removed in MySQL 5.6. Use `general_log` instead.

- `log_bin` (scope: global)

Whether the binary log is enabled. Note that the `--log-bin` option sets `log_bin_basename`, not `log_bin`.

- `log_bin_basename` (scope: global)

The complete pathname of the binary log file. This variable was introduced in MySQL 5.6.2.

- `log_bin_index` (scope: global)

The name of the binary log index file. This variable was introduced in MySQL 5.6.2.

- `log_bin_trust_function_creators` (startup: set directly; scope: global; dynamic)

To create or alter stored functions, you must have the `CREATE ROUTINE` or `ALTER ROUTINE` privilege, respectively. However, if binary logging is enabled and `log_bin_trust_function_creators` is 0 (the default), you must also have the `SUPER` privilege and declare that the function is deterministic or does not modify data. To disable these additional requirements, set `log_bin_trust_function_creators` to 1.

- `log_error` (startup: set directly; scope: global)

The name of the error log file. If you do not set this variable, the server writes error output to the terminal. If you specify this variable at server startup without a value, the log filename is `HOSTNAME.err` in the data directory, where `HOSTNAME` is the name of the server host. If the file name is given as a relative path, the server interprets it relative to the data directory. If the file name is given as a name that has no extension, `mysqld` adds an extension of `.err`.

- `log_output` (startup: set directly; scope: global; dynamic)

  The output destinations for the general query log and slow query log, if those logs are enabled. The value lists destination names separated by commas. Permitted destinations are `TABLE`, `FILE`, and `NONE`. If present, `NONE` disables logging and takes precedence over any other values. The default is `FILE`.

  Set the `general_log` or `slow_query_log` system variable to enable or disable the respective log. Set the `general_log_file` or `slow_query_log_file` system variable to specify the name of the respective log file.

- `log_queries_not_using_indexes` (startup: set directly; scope: global; dynamic)

  If the slow query log is enabled, this variable controls whether queries that do not use indexes to perform lookups should be logged. This can rapidly cause the log to become larger; see `log_throttle_queries_not_using_indexes`.

- `log_slave_updates` (startup: set directly; scope: global)

  For updates that a replication slave server receives from its master's binary log, this variable controls whether the slave logs the updates to its own binary log. By default, slave update logging is disabled but can be enabled to permit a slave to act as a master to another slave in a chained replication configuration.

- `log_throttle_queries_not_using_indexes` (startup: set directly; scope: global; dynamic)

  The maximum number of statements per minute that can be written to the slow query log, if `log_queries_not_using_indexes` is enabled. The default is 0, which mean "no limit." This variable was introduced in MySQL 5.6.5.

- `log_slow_queries` (startup: set directly; scope: global)

  This variable is obsolete and is removed in MySQL 5.6. Use `slow_query_log` instead.

- `log_warnings` (startup: set directly; scope: global, session; dynamic)

  The logging level for logging noncritical warnings to the error log. A value of 0 disables these warnings and 1 (the default) enables warnings. Values greater than 1 increase the logging level to include information about aborted connections and access-denied errors.

- `long_query_time` (startup: set directly; scope: global, session; dynamic)

  Any query taking longer than this value in seconds (and that examines at least `min_examined_row_limit` rows) is considered "slow" and causes the `Slow_queries` status variable to be incremented. In addition, the server writes the query to the slow query log if that log is enabled.

  The minimum and default values are 0 and 10. The value can include a fractional part in microseconds. However, a fractional part is logged only if the log destination is a file and not the `mysql.slow_log` table.

- `low_priority_updates` (startup: set directly; scope: global, session; dynamic)

  If this variable is enabled, updates have a lower priority than retrievals, for storage engines that use table-level locking. Statements that modify table contents (DELETE, INSERT, REPLACE, UPDATE) wait until no SELECT is active or pending for the table. SELECT statements that arrive while another is active begin executing immediately rather than waiting for low-priority modification statements. Enabling this variable has the same effect as specifying the LOW_PRIORITY option for statements that support it, such as INSERT and UPDATE. For individual INSERT statements, the HIGH_PRIORITY modifier can be given to cancel the effect of this variable and elevate the insert to normal priority.

- `lower_case_file_system` (scope: global)

  This variable indicates the case sensitivity of filenames for the filesystem that contains the data directory. ON means that names are not case sensitive. (Think of ON as meaning that lowercase and uppercase versions of a filename are considered the same.) OFF means that names are case sensitive.

- `lower_case_table_names` (startup: set directly; scope: global)

  This variable controls how the directory names and filenames corresponding to database and table names are treated for CREATE DATABASE and CREATE TABLE statements. It also controls how the server performs name comparisons when executing statements. The following table shows the permitted values.

Value	Meaning
0	Names are created on disk as given in CREATE DATABASE and CREATE TABLE statements. Name comparisons are case sensitive. This is the default on systems that have case-sensitive filenames.
1	Names are forced to lowercase when databases and tables are created. Name comparisons are not case sensitive.
2	Name lettercase is preserved, but name comparisons are not case sensitive. That is, names are created as given in CREATE statements, but not compared in case-sensitive fashion. Use this value only for filesystems that do not have case-sensitive filenames.

  If `lower_case_table_names` has not been set explicitly, the server sets `lower_case_table_names` to 2 automatically if filenames are not case sensitive on the filesystem that contains the data directory. Setting `lower_case_table_names` to a nonzero value also causes table aliases not to be case sensitive.

- `master_info_repository` (startup: set directly; scope: global; dynamic)

  Whether a slave server writes master log information to a file or table. If the value is FILE (the default), the slave logs to the file named by the `--master-info-file` option. If the value is TABLE, the server logs to the `mysql.slave_master_info` table. This variable was introduced in MySQL 5.6.2.

- `master_verify_checksum` (startup: set directly; scope: global; dynamic)

  Whether a master server verifies checksums of events read from the binary log before sending them to slaves. The default is OFF. This variable was introduced in MySQL 5.6.2.

- `max_allowed_packet` (startup: set directly; scope: global, session; dynamic)

  The maximum size of the buffer used for communication between the server and the client. The buffer is initially allocated to be `net_buffer_length` bytes long but may grow up to `max_allowed_packet` bytes as necessary. The value also constrains the maximum size of strings handled within the server, for example, by string SQL functions. The default and maximum values for `max_allowed_packet` are 1MB and 1GB, respectively. The session value is read only.

- `max_binlog_cache_size` (startup: set directly; scope: global; dynamic)

  The maximum binary log cache size. Statements that make up a transaction are stored in the binary log cache and then written to the binary log at commit time. If the transaction exceeds this size, it must be flushed to a temporary disk file. Statements that affect nontransactional statements are cached separately; see `max_binlog_stmt_cache_size`.

- `max_binlog_size` (startup: set directly; scope: global; dynamic)

  The maximum size of a binary log file. If the current binary log file reaches this size, the server closes it and begins the next one. The permitted range of values is 4KB to 1GB; the default is 1GB.

  If `max_relay_log_size` is 0, `max_binlog_size` also limits the size of slave server relay log files.

- `max_binlog_stmt_cache_size` (startup: set directly; scope: global; dynamic)

  This is like `max_binlog_cache_size` but for statements that affect nontransactional tables, which are cached separately. This variable was introduced in MySQL 5.5.9.

- `max_connect_errors` (startup: set directly; scope: global; dynamic)

  The number of failed connections from a host that can occur before the host is blocked from further connection attempts. This is done on the basis that someone may be attempting to break in from that host. To clear the host cache and re-enable blocked hosts, use the FLUSH HOSTS statement or `mysqladmin flush-hosts` command. See also the `Connect_errors_xxx` status variables.

- `max_connections` (startup: set directly; scope: global; dynamic)

  The maximum permitted number of simultaneous client connections. The default is 151.

- `max_delayed_threads` (startup: set directly; scope: global, session; dynamic)

  The maximum number of threads that will be created to handle INSERT DELAYED statements. Any such statements received while the maximum number of handlers are already in use are treated as non-DELAYED statements. A client can set the session variable value to 0 to disable DELAYED inserts for its own session.

- `max_error_count` (startup: set directly; scope: global, session; dynamic)

  The maximum number of error, warning, and note messages the server stores. (Such messages are always *counted*; this variable controls only how many of the associated messages are *stored* and available to SHOW ERRORS and SHOW WARNINGS.)

- `max_heap_table_size` (startup: set directly; scope: global, session; dynamic)

  The maximum permitted size of new MEMORY tables. Existing tables are unaffected by changes to this variable unless they are modified with ALTER TABLE or TRUNCATE TABLE. This variable can be used to prevent the server from using excessive amounts of memory. It also affects how the server treats internal memory tables; see the description for `tmp_table_size`.

- `max_insert_delayed_threads` (startup: use --max-delayed-threads; scope: global, session; dynamic)

  This variable is a synonym for `max_delayed_threads`.

- `max_join_size` (startup: set directly; scope: global, session; dynamic)

  When executing a join, the MySQL optimizer estimates how many row combinations it will need to examine. If the estimate exceeds `max_join_size` rows, an error occurs. This can be used if users tend to write indiscriminate SELECT statements that return an inordinate number of rows. The limit does not apply to query results stored in the query cache because cached results can be returned without re-executing the query.

  This variable is used in combination with `sql_big_selects`, as discussed in the description for that variable. Setting `max_join_size` to a value other than DEFAULT automatically sets `sql_big_selects` to 0.

- `max_length_for_sort_data` (startup: set directly; scope: global, session; dynamic)

  The query optimizer uses this variable to determine which type of `filesort` operation to perform for ORDER BY operations.

- `max_prepared_stmt_count` (startup: set directly; scope: global; dynamic)

  The maximum number of prepared statements that the server can maintain simultaneously. Lower values can be used to limit memory use by the server. The value can be from 0 to 1,000,000; the default is 16,382. Use a value of 0 to disable use of prepared statements entirely.

- `max_relay_log_size` (startup: set directly; scope: global; dynamic)

  The maximum size of a slave server relay log file. If the current relay log file reaches this size, the server closes it and begins the next one. If the value is 0, the server uses the value of `max_binlog_size` to limit relay log file sizes. The permitted range of nonzero values is 4KB to 1GB; the default is 0.

- `max_seeks_for_key` (startup: set directly; scope: global, session; dynamic)

  The query optimizer uses this variable when performing key-based lookups. If an index has low cardinality (few unique values), the optimizer may assume that key lookups will require many seeks and perform a table scan instead. Setting this variable to a low value tells the optimizer to assume that at most that many index seeks will be required, which causes it to favor use of the index over a table scan.

- max_sort_length (startup: set directly; scope: global, session; dynamic)

  Data values are sorted using the first max_sort_length bytes of each value. The default is 1024. Decreasing the variable value yields shorter comparison times without loss of accuracy if sorted values are unique within this many bytes. If sorted values are not unique within this many bytes, increasing this variable enables them to be better distinguished.

- max_sp_recursion_depth (startup: set directly; scope: global, session; dynamic)

  The maximum depth to which each stored procedure may recurse. The default is 0 (no recursion permitted) and the maximum is 255.

- max_tmp_tables (startup: set directly; scope: global, session; dynamic)

  This variable is unused.

- max_user_connections (startup: set directly; scope: global, session; dynamic)

  The maximum permitted number of simultaneous client connections per account. The default of 0 means "no limit." The number of connections is bound globally in any case by the value of max_connections.

  The session value for this variable is read only. The session value is the same as the global value unless the account row in the user table has a nonzero MAX_USER_CONNECTIONS value. In that case, the session value is taken from the account row.

  To specify connection limits for specific accounts, use the GRANT statement.

- max_write_lock_count (startup: set directly; scope: global; dynamic)

  After this many write locks to a table, the server begins to elevate the priority of statements that are waiting to acquire a read lock for the table.

- metadata_locks_cache_size (startup: set directly; scope: global)

  The size of the cache used by the server for metadata locks. This variable was introduced in MySQL 5.5.19.

- min_examined_row_limit (startup: set directly; scope: global, session; dynamic)

  The minimum number of rows that a query must examine to qualify for logging to the slow query log. The default is 0.

- myisam_data_pointer_size (startup: set directly; scope: global; dynamic)

  The size in bytes for row pointers in MyISAM index files. The value can range from 2 to 7; the default is 6.

  The pointer size can be influenced for individual tables by specifying the MAX_ROWS table option.

- `myisam_max_sort_file_size` (startup: set directly; scope: global; dynamic)

  MyISAM table index rebuilding for statements such as REPAIR TABLE, ALTER TABLE, or LOAD DATA can use a temporary file or the key cache. The value of this variable determines which method is used; if the temporary file would be larger than this value, the key cache is used instead.

- `myisam_mmap_size` (startup: set directly; scope: global)

  The maximum amount of memory to use for memory mapping of commpressed MyISAM table files. This variable was introduced in MySQL 5.5.1.

- `myisam_recover_options` (startup: set directly; scope: global)

  The mode to use for automatic MyISAM table repair. If enabled, when the server opens a MyISAM table, it does a repair if the table is marked as crashed or was not closed properly when last used. The value should be a comma-separated list of one or more of the following options: BACKUP (create a backup of the table if the repair will change it), FORCE (force recovery even if more than a row of data will be lost), QUICK (quick recovery), DEFAULT (recover with none of the other special handling), or OFF (no recovery; this is the default).

  It's a good idea to enable automatic repair if you run the server with the delay_key_write system variable enabled or have individual MyISAM tables configured to enable delayed index writes.

- `myisam_repair_threads` (startup: set directly; scope: global, session; dynamic)

  The number of threads to use for creating MyISAM table indexes during repair operations. The default is 1 for single-threaded repair. Setting the value higher than 1 for multi-threaded repair should be considered experimental.

- `myisam_sort_buffer_size` (startup: set directly; scope: global, session; dynamic)

  The size of the buffer allocated to sort an index for MyISAM tables during operations such as ALTER TABLE, CREATE INDEX, and REPAIR TABLE.

- `myisam_stats_method` (startup: set directly; scope: global, session; dynamic)

  Whether the server should consider NULL values equal or distinct when calculating index key value distribution statistics for MyISAM tables. The value can be nulls_equal (all NULL values are in the same group), nulls_unequal (each NULL value forms a distinct group), or nulls_ignored (NULL values are ignored).

- `myisam_use_mmap` (startup: set directly; scope: global; dynamic)

  Whether the server uses memory mapping to read and write MyISAM tables. The default is OFF.

- `named_pipe` (startup: set directly)

  Whether the server permits named-pipe connections by clients. Such connections are supported only on Windows. The default is OFF.

- `net_buffer_length` (startup: set directly; scope: global, session; dynamic)

  The initial size of the connection and result buffers used for communication between the server and the client. This buffer may be expanded up to `max_allowed_packet` bytes long. The value can range from 1KB to 1MB; the default is 16KB. The session value is read only.

- `net_read_timeout` (startup: set directly; scope: global, session; dynamic)

  The number of seconds to wait for data from a client before timing out.

- `net_retry_count` (startup: set directly; scope: global, session; dynamic)

  The number of times to retry an interrupted read.

- `net_write_timeout` (startup: set directly; scope: global, session; dynamic)

  The number of seconds to wait while writing data to a client before timing out.

- `new` (startup: set directly; scope: global, session; dynamic)

  This variable is unused.

- `old` (startup: set directly; scope: global)

  A compatibility variable that enables older behavior for some features. Currently, it causes index hints not to apply to `ORDER BY` or `GROUP BY` execution.

- `old_alter_table` (startup: set directly; scope: global, session; dynamic)

  For some `ALTER TABLE` operations that in MySQL 5.0 required a temporary copy of the table, current servers do not need the temporary copy. Enabling this variable causes the server to use the temporary copy.

- `old_passwords` (startup: set directly; scope: global, session; dynamic)

  As of MySQL 4.1, the server supports a more secure password hashing method than previously. Existing accounts that have passwords hashed the old way are still supported, but by default this variable is disabled and new passwords are hashed using the new method. Enable the variable to cause password hashing to use the older pre-4.1 method. This is possibly useful to downgrade the server or move the accounts to an older server.

- `open_files_limit` (startup: set directly; scope: global)

  The number of file descriptors the server attempts to reserve. If you set it to a nonzero value at startup, but the actual value displayed by the server is smaller than specified, the value indicates the maximum number of file descriptors permitted by the operating system. (If the server displays a value of 0, it means the operating system didn't permit `mysqld` to change the number of descriptors.) If you don't set the value at startup or set it to 0, the server uses the larger of `max_connections` × 5 and `max_connections` + `table_open_cache` × 2 as the number of descriptors to reserve. `open_files_limit` controls allocation of file descriptors separately from those controlled by `innodb_open_files`.

- `optimizer_prune_level` (startup: set directly; scope: global, session; dynamic)

  The query optimizer examines multiple execution plans to determine the best one. This variable determines how the optimizer handles intermediate plans. If `optimizer_prune_level` is 1 (the default), the optimizer discards intermediate plans based on the number of rows each one estimates must be examined. If the variable is 0, the optimizer performs an exhaustive search of all plans.

- `optimizer_search_depth` (startup: set directly; scope: global, session; dynamic)

  Controls the depth to which the optimizer searches for execution plans. A value of 0 causes the optimizer to pick a reasonable value automatically. The default is to do an exhaustive search.

- `optimizer_switch` (startup: set directly; scope: global, session; dynamic)

  This variable controls optimizer strategies that can be switched on or off. Its value is a comma-separated list of `flag=value` settings, where `value` can be on or off. You can also set a flag to `default` to return it to whatever its default value is, or set `optimizer_switch` itself to `default` to restore all flag defaults. For descriptions of the various strategies, see the MySQL Reference Manual.

- `optimizer_trace_`*`xxx`* (startup: set directly; scope: global, session)

  System variables that begin with `optimizer_trace` are used for tracing internal operation of the query optimizer. These variables were introduced in MySQL 5.6.3.

- `performance_schema_`*`xxx`*

  System variables that begin with `performance_schema` pertain to the Performance Schema used for collecting and analyzing server performance data. For details, see the MySQL Reference Manual.

- `pid_file` (startup: set directly; scope: global)

  `mysqld` starts, it writes its process ID (PID) into a file. This variable specifies the pathname of the PID file. The file may be used by other processes to determine the server's process number, typically for purposes of sending a signal to it. For example, `mysql.server` reads the file when it sends a signal to the server to shut down. If the file name is given as a relative path, the server interprets it relative to the data directory. The default is *`host_name`*`.pid`.

- `plugin_dir` (startup: set directly; scope: global)

  The pathname of the directory where plugins are located.

- `port` (startup: set directly; scope: global)

  The number of the TCP/IP port the server uses to listen for client connections.

- `preload_buffer_size` (startup: set directly; scope: global, session; dynamic)

  How large a buffer to allocate when preloading indexes with the `LOAD INDEX` statement.

- protocol_version (scope: global)

  The version number of the client/server protocol the server is using.

- proxy_user (scope: session)

  This is a read-only session variable that indicates the proxy user, if proxying is in effect, and NULL otherwise. This variable was introduced in MySQL 5.5.7.

- pseudo_thread_id (scope: session; dynamic)

  This variable is used internally by the server.

- query_alloc_block_size (startup: set directly; scope: global, session; dynamic)

  The block size for allocation of temporary memory while parsing and executing statements.

- query_cache_limit (startup: set directly; scope: global; dynamic)

  The maximum size of cached query results; larger results are not cached. The default is 1MB.

- query_cache_min_res_unit (startup: set directly; scope: global; dynamic)

  The block size for allocation of memory for storing results in the query cache. The default is 4KB.

- query_cache_size (startup: set directly; scope: global; dynamic)

  The amount of memory to use for query result caching. Setting this variable to 0 disables the query cache, even if query_cache_type is not OFF. Conversely, setting this variable to a nonzero value causes that much memory to be allocated, even if query_cache_type is OFF. The value should be a multiple of 1024.

- query_cache_type (startup: set directly; scope: global, session; dynamic)

  The mode of operation of the query cache, if query_cache_size is greater than 0. The following table shows the permitted values.

Mode	Meaning
0	Don't cache query results or retrieve cached results
1	Cache cacheable queries except those that begin with SELECT SQL_NO_CACHE
2	Cache on demand only cacheable queries that begin with SELECT SQL_CACHE

  If you set the query_cache_type variable in a SET statement, the symbolic values OFF, ON, and DEMAND are synonyms for 0, 1, and 2.

- query_cache_wlock_invalidate (startup: set directly; scope: global, session; dynamic)

  If this variable is 0 (the default), clients can retrieve cached query results for a table even if another client acquires a WRITE lock on the table. Setting this variable to 1 cause the cached results to be invalidated when a client acquires a WRITE lock, which forces other clients to wait for the lock to be released.

- `query_prealloc_size` (startup: set directly; scope: global, session; dynamic)

  The size of the buffer allocated for parsing and executing statements. This buffer is not freed between statements, unlike blocks allocated under the control of the `query_alloc_block_size` variable.

- `rand_seed1`, `rand_seed2` (scope: session; dynamic)

  These read-only session variables are used internally for replicating the `RAND()` function.

- `range_alloc_block_size` (startup: set directly; scope: global, session; dynamic)

  The block size for allocation of memory while performing range optimizations.

- `read_buffer_size` (startup: set directly; scope: global, session; dynamic)

  The size of the buffer used by threads that perform sequential table scans. A buffer is allocated as necessary per client.

- `read_only` (startup: set directly; scope: global; dynamic)

  This variable controls whether a server operates in read-only fashion for client connections. By default, `read_only` is `OFF`, updates by clients are accepted in the usual way (that is, they have privileges to do so). When set to `ON`, updates are permitted only for statements received from the master (for a slave server) or issued by clients that have the `SUPER` privilege, and `SET PASSWORD` requires `SUPER`. `read_only` does not apply to `TEMPORARY` tables.

  You cannot enable the variable while you hold explicit table locks or have an outstanding transaction. If you attempt to enable `read_only` while other clients hold table locks or have outstanding transactions, your request blocks until those locks are released and transactions have terminated. While the request is blocked, other clients block if they attempt to acquire new table locks or begin transactions. These conditions for blocking do not apply to `FLUSH TABLES WITH READ LOCK`, which acquires a global read lock, not a table lock.

- `read_rnd_buffer_size` (startup: set directly; scope: global, session; dynamic)

  The size of the buffer used for reading rows in order after a sort. A buffer is allocated as necessary per client.

- `relay_log` (startup: set directly; scope: global)

  The name of the relay log file.

- `relay_log_basename` (scope: global)

  The complete pathname of the relay log file. This variable was introduced in MySQL 5.6.2.

- `relay_log_index` (scope: global)

  The name of the relay log index file.

- `relay_log_info_file` (startup: set directly; scope: global)

  The name of the relay log info file, `relay-log.info` by default.

- relay_log_info_repository (startup: set directly; scope: global; dynamic)

  Whether a slave server writes relay log information to a file or table. If the value is FILE (the default), the slave logs to the file named by the --relay-log-info-file option. If the value is TABLE, the server logs to the mysql.slave_relay_log_info_file table. This variable was introduced in MySQL 5.6.2.

- relay_log_purge (startup: set directly; scope: global; dynamic)

  When set to 1 (the default), a slave server removes each relay log file as soon as it is no longer needed. If set to 0, the relay log files are not removed automatically.

- relay_log_recovery (startup: set directly; scope: global)

  This variable can be useful after a slave server crash. Enabling it at startup causes the slave to remove any relay logs it has not yet processed and fetch them again from the master. This variable is disabled by default.

- relay_log_space_limit (startup: set directly; scope: global)

  The maximum permitted combined size of the relay log files. When this limit is reached, the slave I/O thread waits for the SQL thread to process more events and free space by deleting log files.

- report_host, report_password, report_port, report_user (scope: global)

  On a slave replication server, these variables can be set to indicate values that the slave should report to the master when it connects. They need not correspond to the values actually used by the slave to establish the connection. These values show up in the output of SHOW SLAVE HOSTS when that statement is executed on the master. The report_user and report_password values are not reported unless the master is started with the --show-slave-auth-info option.

- secure_auth (startup: set directly; scope: global; dynamic)

  Whether the server permits connections only for accounts that have the password format introduced in MySQL 4.1. When set to OFF, the server also permits connections to accounts that have passwords in the older pre-4.1 format. The default is OFF before MySQL 5.6.5, ON thereafter.

- secure_file_priv (startup: set directly; scope: global)

  When set to a directory pathname, the server permits LOAD DATA and SELECT ... INTO OUTFILE statements and the LOAD_FILE() function only for operations in that directory. The value is empty by default (no such restriction).

- server_id (startup: set directly; scope: global; dynamic)

  The server's replication ID number. If 0, the server is not participating in replication. Otherwise, the value must be an integer from 1 to $2^{32}-1$ and unique among communicating replication servers.

- server_uuid (scope: global)

  The automatically generated UUID value for the server. This variable was introduced in MySQL 5.6.0.

- `shared_memory` (startup: set directly)

  Whether the server permits shared-memory connections by clients. Such connections are supported only on Windows. The default is OFF.

- `shared_memory_base_name` (startup: set directly)

  The shared-memory name for shared-memory connections. The default name is MYSQL (case sensitive)

- `skip_external_locking` (startup: set directly; scope: global)

  Whether use of external locking (filesystem locking) is suppressed.

- `skip_name_resolve` (startup: set directly; scope: global)

  This variable is disabled by default. Enabling it suppresses hostname resolution, and the grant tables must specify hosts by IP number or as localhost.

- `skip_networking` (startup: set directly; scope: global)

  If this variable is disabled (the default), the server permits TCP/IP connections. Enabling it disables TCP/IP connections. Clients can connect from the local host only, and must do so using a non-TCP/IP interface. Unix clients can connect using a Unix socket file. Windows clients can connect using shared memory or a named pipe if those connection types are enabled.

- `skip_show_database` (startup: set directly; scope: global)

  If this variable is disabled (the default), any user can issue the SHOW DATABASES statement. It displays all databases if the user has the SHOW DATABASES privilege, or those databases for which the user has some privilege otherwise. If the variable is enabled, the SHOW DATABASES statement can be used only by users who have the SHOW DATABASES privilege, and it displays all databases.

- `slave_allow_batching` (startup: set directly; scope: global; dynamic)

  Enable a slave server to batch requests; applies only to MySQL Cluster.

- `slave_checkpoint_group` (startup: set directly; scope: global; dynamic)

  If multi-threaded slave execution is enabled (see slave_parallel_threads), this variable controls the maximum number of transactions the slave executes before taking a checkpoint. The default is 512. Permitted values range from 32 to 512KB. This variable was introduced in MySQL 5.6.3. Checkpointing depends on both slave_checkpoint_group and slave_checkpoint_period; exceeding either limit causes the slave to checkpoint and reset the counters associated with both of them.

- `slave_checkpoint_period` (startup: set directly; scope: global; dynamic)

  If multi-threaded slave execution is enabled (see slave_parallel_threads), this variable controls the maximum time in milliseconds the slave executes before taking a checkpoint. The default is 300. Permitted values range from 1 to 4GB. This variable was introduced in MySQL 5.6.3. See also slave_checkpoint_group.

- `slave_compressed_protocol` (startup: set directly; scope: global; dynamic)

  Whether compression should be used to reduce the amount of traffic sent between a slave server and its master. This requires that both the master and slave support the compressed protocol.

- `slave_exec_mode` (startup: set directly; scope: global; dynamic)

  The slave execution mode, either STRICT (the default) or IDEMPOTENT. The latter setting might be useful for replication topologies involving loops or multiple masters, to suppress duplicate-key and key-not-found errors.

- `slave_load_tmpdir` (startup: set directly; scope: global)

  The pathname of the directory used for processing LOAD DATA statements if the server is a replication slave. The default is the value of the `tmpdir` system variable.

- `slave_max_allowed_packet` (startup: set directly; scope: global; dynamic)

  Like `max_allowed_packet`, but for slave SQL and I/O threads. The default is 1GB.

- `slave_net_timeout` (startup: set directly; scope: global; dynamic)

  The number of seconds to wait for data from a master server before timing out.

- `slave_parallel_workers` (startup: set directly; scope: global; dynamic)

  Setting the variable greater than 0 on a slave server enables multi-threaded replication. The SQL thread that normally executes all events received from the slave instead becomes a coordinator of `slave_parallel_workers` worker threads that execute events. The default is 0. Permitted values range from 0 to 1024. This variable was introduced in MySQL 5.6.3.

- `slave_pending_jobs_size_max` (startup: set directly; scope: global; dynamic)

  If multi-threaded slave execution is enabled (see `slave_parallel_threads`), this variable controls the maximum amount of memory to use to cache unprocessed events for worker threads. The default is 16MB. Permitted values range from 1KB to 18EB. This variable was introduced in MySQL 5.6.3.

- `slave_skip_errors` (startup: set directly; scope: global)

  The list of errors that a slave server should ignore rather than suspending replication if they occur. (However, it's usually better to determine what is causing problems so that you can resolve them rather than using this variable to ignore them.) A value of `all` means all errors should be ignored. Otherwise, the value should be a list of one or more error numbers separated by commas.

- `slave_sql_verify_checksum` (startup: set directly; scope: global; dynamic)

  Whether the slave SQL thread should verify checksums of events read from the relay log. If a checksum error occurs, replication stops. The default is OFF. This variable was introduced in MySQL 5.6.2.

- `slave_transaction_retries` (startup: set directly; scope: global; dynamic)

  The number of times that a slave should retry a transaction that fails due to deadlock or because a storage engine's timeout has been reached. The default is 10.

- `slave_type_conversions` (startup: set directly; scope: global; dynamic)

  This variable indicates the permitted type conversions on a slave server for row-based replication. The default is the empty string (disallow conversions). A nonempty value should be a comma-separated list of one or more of the values `ALL_LOSSY` (permit conversions that lose information) or `ALL_NON_LOSSY` (permit conversions that do not lose information). This variable was introduced in MySQL 5.5.3.

- `slow_launch_time` (startup: set directly; scope: global; dynamic)

  The number of seconds that defines "slow" thread creation. Any thread taking longer to create causes the `Slow_launch_threads` status variable to be incremented.

- `slow_query_log` (startup: set directly; scope: global; dynamic)

  Whether logging to the slow query log is enabled. If so, `log_output` controls the log destinations.

- `slow_query_log_file` (startup: set directly; scope: global; dynamic)

  The name of the slow query log file, for use if the `FILE` logging destination is enabled. The default is `HOSTNAME-slow.log` in the data directory, where `HOSTNAME` is the name of the server host. If the file name is given as a relative path, the server interprets it relative to the data directory.

- `socket` (startup: set directly; scope: global)

  The pathname of the Unix domain socket, or the name of the named pipe under Windows.

- `sort_buffer_size` (startup: set directly; scope: global, session; dynamic)

  The size of the buffer used by threads for performing sort operations (`GROUP BY` or `ORDER BY`). This buffer is allocated as necessary per client. Normally, if you may have many clients that do sorting at the same time, it is unwise to make this value very large (more than 1MB).

- `sql_auto_is_null` (scope: global, session; dynamic)

  If this is set to 1, the most recently generated `AUTO_INCREMENT` value can be selected using a clause of the form `WHERE col_name IS NULL`, where `col_name` is the name of the `AUTO_INCREMENT` column. Some ODBC programs use this feature. To disable it, set the variable to 0. The default is 0 (1 before MySQL 5.5.3).

- `sql_big_selects` (scope: global, session; dynamic)

  The server uses this variable in conjunction with the `max_join_size` system variable. If `sql_big_selects` is 1 (the default), the server accepts queries that return result sets of any size. If `sql_big_selects` is 0, the server rejects queries that are likely to return a large number of rows. In this case, the value of max_join_size is used when executing a join: The server makes an estimate of the number of row combinations it will need to examine, and if that value exceeds the value of max_join_size, the server returns an error rather than executing the query.

Setting max_join_size to a value other than DEFAULT automatically sets sql_big_selects to 0.

- sql_buffer_result (scope: global, session; dynamic)

Setting this variable to 1 causes the server to use internal temporary tables to hold results from SELECT statements. The effect is that the server can more quickly release locks held on the tables from which the results are produced. The default is 0.

- sql_log_bin (scope: global, session; dynamic)

Setting the session value of this variable to 0 or 1 disables or enables binary logging for the current client session. At runtime, a client must have the SUPER privilege to change this variable, even to change the session value. This variable has no effect unless the binary log is enabled.

- sql_log_off (scope: global, session; dynamic)

Setting the session value of this variable to 0 or 1 enables or disables statement logging to the general query log for the current client session. At runtime, a client must have the SUPER privilege to change this variable, even to change the session value. This variable has no effect unless the general log is enabled.

- sql_mode (startup: set directly; scope: global, session; dynamic)

The server SQL mode. This variable modifies certain aspects of the server's behavior to cause it to act according to standard SQL, or to be compatible with other database servers or older MySQL servers. The value should be an empty string to clear the mode, or a comma-separated list of one or more of the mode values described following. The default is NO_ENGINE_SUBSTITUTION as of MySQL 5.6.6, the empty string in earlier versions. Some mode values are simple and enable one behavior. Others are composite modes that serve as shorthand enabling a set of modes to be specified more easily. Mode values are not case sensitive.

The term "strict mode" refers to a sql_mode setting that has STRICT_TRANS_TABLES or STRICT_ALL_TABLES enabled to cause the server to be strict about data checking. Section 3.3, "How MySQL Handles Invalid Data Values," further discusses strict mode and other modes that affect input data handling.

The following list describes the simple SQL mode values:

- ALLOW_INVALID_DATES

In strict mode, suppresses full date validity checking for DATE and DATETIME values. The only requirements are that the month be in the range from 1 to 12 and the day in the range from 1 to 31. TIMESTAMP values must be valid regardless of whether this mode is enabled.

- `ANSI_QUOTES`

  Treats the double quote character as a quote character for identifiers such as database, table, and column names, and not as a string quote character. (Backticks are permitted for name quoting regardless of whether this mode is enabled.)

- `ERROR_FOR_DIVISION_BY_ZERO`

  For inserts or updates, division (or modulo) operations with a divisor of 0 normally produce a result of `NULL` and no warning, even in strict mode. Enabling `ERROR_FOR_DIVISION_BY_ZERO` changes this behavior. With strict mode not enabled, division by 0 still produces a result of `NULL` but a warning occurs. With strict mode enabled, division by 0 during `INSERT` and `UPDATE` statements causes an error and the statement fails. To suppress the error for inserts or updates and produce a result of `NULL` and a warning, use `INSERT IGNORE` or `UPDATE IGNORE`.

- `HIGH_NOT_PRECEDENCE`

  This mode changes the precedence of the `NOT` operator to be the same as the `!` operator.

- `IGNORE_SPACE`

  Causes the server to ignore spaces between names of built-in functions and the '(' character that introduces the argument list. Normally, function names should be followed immediately by the parenthesis with no intervening spaces. This mode causes function names to be treated as reserved words.

- `NO_AUTO_CREATE_USER`

  Prohibits `GRANT` statements from creating insecure new accounts. That is, if an account does not exist, `GRANT` fails and does not create the account unless the statement includes either an `IDENTIFIED BY` clause that specifies a nonempty password, or an `IDENTIFIED WITH` clause that specifies an authentication plugin.

- `NO_AUTO_VALUE_ON_ZERO`

  Normally, inserting 0 into an `AUTO_INCREMENT` column has the same result as inserting `NULL`: MySQL generates the next sequence number and stores it in the column. With this mode enabled, inserting 0 into an `AUTO_INCREMENT` column causes 0 to be stored.

- `NO_BACKSLASH_ESCAPES`

  Causes backslash ('\') not to be treated as an escape character within strings, but rather as an ordinary character with no special meaning.

- `NO_DIR_IN_CREATE`

  Ignores `DATA DIRECTORY` and `INDEX DIRECTORY` table options in `CREATE TABLE` and `ALTER TABLE` statements.

- NO_ENGINE_SUBSTITUTION

  This mode determines how the server handles CREATE TABLE or ALTER TABLE statements that include an ENGINE option that names a storage engine that is not available. If NO_ENGINE_SUBSTITUTION is enabled, an error occurs and the table is not created (or altered). If NO_ENGINE_SUBSTITUTION is disabled, substitution of the default storage engine is permitted.

- NO_FIELD_OPTIONS

  Makes the output of SHOW CREATE TABLE statements more portable by suppressing inclusion of MySQL-specific column-related options.

- NO_KEY_OPTIONS

  Makes the output of SHOW CREATE TABLE statements more portable by suppressing inclusion of MySQL-specific index-related options.

- NO_TABLE_OPTIONS

  Makes the output of SHOW CREATE TABLE statements more portable by suppressing inclusion of MySQL-specific table-related options.

- NO_UNSIGNED_SUBTRACTION

  By default, subtraction between integer operands results in an unsigned result if either operand is unsigned. This mode causes the result to be signed, which is compatible with the behavior of MySQL prior to version 4.0.

- NO_ZERO_DATE

  In strict mode, rejects '0000-00-00' as a valid date. Normally, MySQL permits "zero" date values to be stored. This mode can be overridden by using INSERT IGNORE rather than INSERT.

- NO_ZERO_IN_DATE

  In strict mode, rejects dates that have a month or day part of zero. (A zero year is permitted.) Normally, MySQL permits such date values to be stored. In nonstrict mode or if INSERT IGNORE is used, MySQL stores such dates as '0000-00-00'.

- ONLY_FULL_GROUP_BY

  Normally, MySQL permits SELECT statements with nonaggregate columns in the output column list or the HAVING clause that are not named in the GROUP BY clause. For example:

  ```
  SELECT a, b, COUNT(*) FROM t GROUP BY a;
  ```

  The ONLY_FULL_GROUP_BY flag requires nonaggregate output columns (or HAVING columns) to be named in the GROUP BY:

  ```
  SELECT a, b, COUNT(*) FROM t GROUP BY a, b;
  ```

- PAD_CHAR_TO_FULL_LENGTH

  Normally, the server removes trailing spaces from CHAR column values when it retrieves them. Enabling this mode suppresses CHAR column trailing-space removal so that retrieved values have the full column length.

- PIPES_AS_CONCAT

  Causes || to be treated as a string concatenation operator rather than as logical OR.

- REAL_AS_FLOAT

  The REAL data type becomes a synonym for FLOAT rather than for DOUBLE.

- STRICT_ALL_TABLES

  Enables strict checking of input data values for all storage engines to cause MySQL to reject most invalid values. Use TRADITIONAL to be even more strict.

- STRICT_TRANS_TABLES

  Enables strict checking of input data values for transactional storage engines to cause MySQL to reject most invalid values. In addition, enable strict checking for nontransactional storage engines when that is possible (such as for single-row INSERT statements). Use TRADITIONAL to be even more strict.

The following table lists the composite SQL modes and shows the set of modes each one comprises.

Composite Mode	Constituent Modes
ANSI	ANSI_QUOTES, IGNORE_SPACE, PIPES_AS_CONCAT, REAL_AS_FLOAT
DB2	ANSI_QUOTES, IGNORE_SPACE, NO_FIELD_OPTIONS, NO_KEY_OPTIONS, NO_TABLE_OPTIONS, PIPES_AS_CONCAT
MAXDB	ANSI_QUOTES, IGNORE_SPACE, NO_AUTO_CREATE_USER, NO_FIELD_OPTIONS, NO_KEY_OPTIONS, NO_TABLE_OPTIONS, PIPES_AS_CONCAT
MSSQL	ANSI_QUOTES, IGNORE_SPACE, NO_FIELD_OPTIONS, NO_KEY_OPTIONS, NO_TABLE_OPTIONS, PIPES_AS_CONCAT
MYSQL323	HIGH_NOT_PRECEDENCE, NO_FIELD_OPTIONS
MYSQL40	HIGH_NOT_PRECEDENCE, NO_FIELD_OPTIONS
ORACLE	ANSI_QUOTES, IGNORE_SPACE, NO_AUTO_CREATE_USER, NO_FIELD_OPTIONS, NO_KEY_OPTIONS, NO_TABLE_OPTIONS, PIPES_AS_CONCAT
POSTGRESQL	ANSI_QUOTES, IGNORE_SPACE, NO_FIELD_OPTIONS, NO_KEY_OPTIONS, NO_TABLE_OPTIONS, PIPES_AS_CONCAT
TRADITIONAL	ERROR_FOR_DIVISION_BY_ZERO, NO_AUTO_CREATE_USER, NO_ZERO_DATE, NO_ZERO_IN_DATE, STRICT_ALL_TABLES, STRICT_TRANS_TABLES

`TRADITIONAL` mode is so called because it enables the modes that cause handling of input values to be like traditional databases that reject invalid data. It's like strict mode but includes several additional constraints for even stricter checking.

- `sql_notes` (scope: global, session; dynamic)

Setting this variable to 0 or 1 (the default) controls whether the server suppresses or records `Note`-level warnings.

- `sql_quote_show_create` (scope: global, session; dynamic)

This variable controls whether to quote identifiers (database, table, column, and index names) in the output from `SHOW CREATE TABLE` and `SHOW CREATE DATABASE` statements. The default is 1 (use quoting). Turning quoting off by setting the variable to 0 may be useful when producing `CREATE TABLE` statements for use with other database servers. If you disable quoting, be sure that your tables do not use names that are reserved words or contain special characters.

Identifiers are quoted with backtick ('`') characters if the `ANSI_QUOTES` SQL mode is disabled, and with double quote ('"') characters if it is enabled.

- `sql_safe_updates` (scope: global, session; dynamic)

If this variable is 1, the server accepts `UPDATE` and `DELETE` statements only if the rows to be modified are identified by key values or if a `LIMIT` clause is used. The default of 0 enforces no such restriction.

- `sql_select_limit` (scope: global, session; dynamic)

Specifies the maximum number of rows to return from a `SELECT` statement. The presence of an explicit `LIMIT` clause in a statement takes precedence over this variable. The default is the maximum permitted number of rows per table. A value of `DEFAULT` restores this default if you have changed it.

This variable has no effect within stored routines, or for `SELECT` operations that do not return rows to the client (such as subqueries, `INSERT INTO ... SELECT`, and `CREATE TABLE ... SELECT`).

- `sql_slave_skip_counter` (scope: global; dynamic)

If you have the `SUPER` privilege, you can set this as a `GLOBAL` variable to a value of n to tell a slave replication server to skip the next n events received from its master server. If the resulting position lies in the middle of a group of events (such as those for a transaction), the slave then skips the remaining events in the group as well.

- `sql_warnings` (scope: global, session; dynamic)

If set to 1, MySQL reports warning counts even for single-row inserts. For the default of 0, warning counts are reported only for `INSERT` statements that insert multiple rows.

- `ssl_xxx`

  The `ssl_xxx` variables indicate the values of the corresponding `--ssl-xxx` options given to the server at startup. (For example, `ssl_ca` indicates the value of the `--ssl-ca` option.) The value of each variable is the empty string if the corresponding option was not given. The values are NULL if SSL support is not available.

- `storage_engine` (scope: global, session; dynamic)

  Deprecated as of MySQL 5.5.3. Use `default_storage_engine` instead.

- `stored_program_cache` (startup: set directly; scope: global; dynamic)

  How many stored routines the server caches per connection. The default is 256. This variable was introduced in MySQL 5.5.21.

- `sync_binlog` (startup: set directly; scope: global; dynamic)

  When set to 0 (the default), the server does not flush the binary log to disk. When set to a positive value n, the server flushes the log after every n writes to the binary log. In this case, lower values provide greater safety in the event of a crash, but also affect performance more adversely.

- `sync_frm` (startup: set directly; scope: global; dynamic)

  When this variable is enabled (the default), the server flushes the `.frm` file for each nontemporary table at table-creation time, to synchronize file contents to disk.

- `sync_master_info` (startup: set directly; scope: global; dynamic)

  For a slave server, if this variable is 0 (the default), the slave does not force its `master.info` file to be synchronized to disk. Instead, normal file system flushing occurs. If the value is greater than 0, the slave synchronizes the file to disk after each group of that many events.

- `sync_relay_log` (startup: set directly; scope: global; dynamic)

  For a slave server, if this variable is 0 (the default), the slave does not force its relay log to be synchronized to disk. Instead, normal file system flushing occurs. If the value is greater than 0, the slave synchronizes the relay log to disk after each group of that many writes. If autocommit is enabled, a write occurs once per statement, and once per transaction otherwise.

- `sync_relay_log_info` (startup: set directly; scope: global; dynamic)

  This variable is like `sync_master_info`, but for the `relay-log.info` file.

- `system_time_zone` (scope: global)

  The server's system time zone. The server tries to determine the variable value when it starts by consulting the system. To set the value explicitly, set the TZ environment variable or specify the `--timezone` option to `mysqld_safe`.

- `table_definition_cache` (startup: set directly; scope: global; dynamic)

  The number of table definitions (from `.frm` files) that the server can store in its definition cache.

- `table_open_cache` (startup: set directly; scope: global; dynamic)

  The maximum number of tables that can be open.

- `table_open_cache_instances` (startup: set directly; scope: global)

  How many instances to use for partitioning the open tables cache. The default is 1 (essentially, no partitioning). Dividing the cache might reduce intersession contention under high load. This variable was introduced in MySQL 5.6.6.

- `thread_cache_size` (startup: set directly; scope: global; dynamic)

  The maximum number of threads to maintain in the thread cache. Threads reclaimed from clients that disconnect are put in the cache if it's not already full. This enables new connections to be serviced by reusing cached threads rather than creating new threads, as long as threads remain in the cache. The thread cache is used when the server uses one thread per currently connected client.

- `thread_concurrency` (startup: set directly; scope: global)

  This variable is obsolete.

- `thread_handling` (startup: set directly; scope: global)

  The thread model that the server uses for handling client connections. The value can be `no-threads` (a single connection thread) or `one-thread-per-connection` (one thread per currently connected client). The default is `one-thread-per-connection`.

- `thread_stack` (startup: set directly; scope: global)

  The stack size for each thread.

- `time_format` (scope: global)

  This variable is unused.

- `time_zone` (startup: use `--default-time-zone`; scope: global, session; dynamic)

  The server's current time zone. A value of `SYSTEM` indicates that the server is using the value of the `system_time_zone` variable. A client can modify the session value of this variable to set the time zone for its own session.

- `timestamp` (scope: session; dynamic)

  Setting this variable specifies a `TIMESTAMP` value for the current session. This is used for binary log processing. The `timestamp` value affects the value returned by `NOW()`, but not the value returned by `SYSDATE()`.

- `tmp_table_size` (startup: set directly; scope: global, session; dynamic)

  The maximum permitted size for internal temporary tables (that is, tables that the server creates automatically while processing statements). If a temporary table exceeds the smaller of `max_heap_table_size` and `tmp_table_size`, the server converts it from an internal in-memory table to a MyISAM table on disk. If you have memory to spare, higher values of this variable enable the server to maintain larger temporary tables in memory without converting them to on-disk format.

- `tmpdir` (startup: set directly; scope: global)

The pathname of the directory where the server creates temporary files. The value can be given as a list of directories, to be used in round-robin fashion. Under Unix, separate directory names by colons; under Windows, separate them by semicolons.

- `transaction_alloc_block_size` (startup: set directly; scope: global, session; dynamic)

The block size for allocation of temporary memory needed for processing statements that are stored as part of a transaction prior to writing the transaction to the binary log at commit time.

- `transaction_prealloc_size` (startup: set directly; scope: global, session; dynamic)

The size of the buffer that is allocated for processing statements that are part of a transaction. This buffer is not freed between statements, unlike blocks allocated under the control of the `transaction_alloc_block_size` variable.

- `tx_isolation` (startup: use `--transaction-isolation`; scope: global, session; dynamic)

The default transaction isolation level.

- `tx_read_only` (startup: use `--transaction-read-only`; scope: global, session; dynamic)

Whether the default transaction access mode is read only. The default is `OFF` (read/write). This variable was introduced in MySQL 5.6.5.

- `unique_checks` (scope: global, session; dynamic)

Setting this variable to 0 or 1 disables or enables uniqueness checks for secondary indexes in InnoDB tables. Disabling these checks can increase performance when importing data into InnoDB tables, but this should not be done unless you know that data values do not violate uniqueness requirements.

- `updatable_views_with_limit` (startup: set directly; scope: global, session; dynamic)

When disabled, the server prohibits updates (`UPDATE` or `DELETE` statements) to views that do not use a primary key in the underlying table, even if the update contains a `LIMIT 1` clause to constrain the update to a single row. When enabled (the default), the update is permitted and the server produces only a warning.

- `version` (scope: global)

The server version. The value consists of a version number, possibly followed by one or more suffixes, such as `-log` to indicate that logging is enabled or `-debug` to indicate that the server is running in debug mode.

- `version_comment` (scope: global)

  The value of the `-DWITH_COMMENT` option specified to `CMake` at the time the server was configured. The default is `"Source distribution"` if no comment was specified at configuration time.

- `version_compile_machine` (scope: global)

  The compilation machine (hardware type). The value is determined during the configuration process when MySQL is built.

- `version_compile_os` (scope: global)

  The compilation operating system. The value is determined during the configuration process when MySQL is built.

- `wait_timeout` (startup: set directly; scope: global, session; dynamic)

  The number of seconds a noninteractive client session can remain idle before the server considers itself free to close it. For interactive clients, the value of the `interactive_timeout` variable is used instead.

- `warning_count` (scope: session)

  This is a read-only session variable that indicates the number of errors, warnings, and notes generated by the last statement that can generate such messages.

D.1.1   InnoDB System Variables

The following system variables pertain to the InnoDB storage engine.

- `ignore_builtin_innodb` (scope: global)

  This variable is unused.

- `innodb_adaptive_flushing` (startup: set directly; scope: global; dynamic)

  Whether InnoDB attempts to avoid I/O bursts by using the workload level to change the flush rate for dirty pages in the buffer pool. The default is `ON`.

- `innodb_adaptive_flushing_lwm` (startup: set directly; scope: global; dynamic)

  The low-water mark for percentage of redo log capacity at which InnoDB enables adaptive flushing. The default is 10. This variable was introduced in MySQL 5.6.6.

- `innodb_adaptive_hash_index` (startup: set directly; scope: global; dynamic)

  Whether InnoDB uses adaptive hash indexes; that is, whether it monitors index lookups and builds hash indexes on the fly if doing so is likely to improve performance. The default is `ON`.

- `innodb_adaptive_max_sleep_delay` (startup: set directly; scope: global; dynamic)

  Whether InnoDB uses the workload level to adjust `innodb_thread_sleep_delay`. A value of 0 disables adjustments. Nonzero values up to the maximum of 1,000,000 specify the limit in microseconds of how far up InnoDB will adjust `innodb_thread_sleep_delay`. The default is 150000. This variable was introduced in MySQL 5.6.3.

- `innodb_additional_mem_pool_size` (startup: set directly; scope: global)

  The size of the InnoDB memory pool for storing internal data structures.

- `innodb_autoextend_increment` (startup: set directly; scope: global; dynamic)

  If the InnoDB system tablespace is configured to be auto-extending when it becomes full, this variable controls the increment size for extending it. The value is specified in megabytes. The default is 8, with a maximum of 1000.

- `innodb_autoinc_lock_mode` (startup: set directly; scope: global)

  This variable controls the locking algorithm InnoDB uses for generating AUTO_INCREMENT values. The permitted values are 0, 1 (the default), and 2. In general, these values permit increasing levels of locking scalability, better concurrency, and less blocking when there are multiple transactions simultaneously generating auto-increment values. For a multiple-row INSERT that generates several such values, modes 0 and 1 guarantee consecutive values within the statement. Mode 2 does not: It permits value allocation to be interleaved between statements, so that although values generated for a given statement are monotonic, they are not necessarily consecutive. This also affects replication. Modes 0 and 1 are safe for statement-based replication, but allocation of values for mode 2 is nondeterministic, so this mode is not safe. (All modes are safe for row-based replication.)

- `innodb_buffer_pool_dump_at_shutdown` (startup: set directly; scope: global; dynamic)

  Whether InnoDB performs a buffer pool dump to disk at shutdown. The default is OFF. This variable was introduced in MySQL 5.6.3.

- `innodb_buffer_pool_dump_now` (startup: set directly; scope: global; dynamic)

  Setting this variable to ON causes InnoDB to perform an immediate buffer pool dump to disk. The default is OFF. This variable was introduced in MySQL 5.6.3.

- `innodb_buffer_pool_filename` (startup: set directly; scope: global; dynamic)

  The name of the file InnoDB uses for buffer pool dump and load operations. The default is ib_buffer_pool in the data directory. This variable was introduced in MySQL 5.6.3.

- `innodb_buffer_pool_instances` (startup: set directly; scope: global)

  How many areas to divide the InnoDB buffer pool into, if the value of innodb_buffer_pool_size is at least 1GB. The default is 1 (a single pool), with a maximum of 64. For best results, choose the values of innodb_buffer_pool_size and innodb_buffer_pool_instances so that each instance is at least 1GB. This variable was introduced in MySQL 5.5.4.

- `innodb_buffer_pool_load_abort` (startup: set directly; scope: global; dynamic)

  Setting this variable to ON causes InnoDB to abort any buffer pool load from disk currently in progress. The default is OFF. This variable was introduced in MySQL 5.6.3.

- `innodb_buffer_pool_load_at_startup` (startup: set directly; scope: global)

  Whether InnoDB performs a buffer pool load from disk at startup. The default is OFF. This variable was introduced in MySQL 5.6.3.

- `innodb_buffer_pool_load_now` (startup: set directly; scope: global; dynamic)

Setting this variable to `ON` causes InnoDB to perform an immediate buffer pool load from disk. The default is `OFF`. This variable was introduced in MySQL 5.6.3.

- `innodb_buffer_pool_size` (startup: set directly; scope: global)

The size of the InnoDB cache for buffering table data and indexes. The default is 128MB.

- `innodb_change_buffer_max_size` (startup: set directly; scope: global; dynamic)

The maximum percentage of the buffer pool InnoDB reserves for change buffering. The default is 25. Permitted values range from 0 to 50. This variable was introduced in MySQL 5.6.2.

- `innodb_change_buffering` (startup: set directly; scope: global; dynamic)

How InnoDB buffers table changes to delay write operations for secondary indexes. By buffering writes, InnoDB can sometimes group them and perform sequential rather than random I/O for better performance. The following table shows the permitted values.

Value	Meaning
all	Buffer all changes; this is the default
none	Buffer no changes
changes	Buffer inserts and deletes
deletes	Buffer changes that mark index records for deletion
inserts	Buffer inserts
purges	Buffer purges that garbage-collect marked deletions

- `innodb_checksum_algorithm` (startup: set directly; scope: global; dynamic)

InnoDB writes a checksum value in each block of its tablespaces. This variable controls the algorithm used to calculate checksums. The following table shows the permitted values. The `strict_xxx` values are like their counterparts except that InnoDB stops if it encounters multiple checksum types in a tablespace.

Value	Meaning
none, strict_none	Write a constant value as the checksum
crc32, strict_crc32	Use a CRC32 algorithm
innodb, strict_innodb	The default algorithm

This variable was introduced in MySQL 5.6.3.

- `innodb_checksums` (startup: set directly; scope: global)

  Whether InnoDB table checksum calculation is enabled. The default is ON. As of MySQL 5.6.3, this variable is deprecated in preference to `innodb_checksum_algorithm`.

- `innodb_commit_concurrency` (startup: set directly; scope: global; dynamic)

  How may threads can commit simultaneously. A value of 0 (default) means "no limit."

- `innodb_concurrency_tickets` (startup: set directly; scope: global; dynamic)

  When a thread wants to enter InnoDB, it can do so only if the number of threads is less than the limit set by `innodb_thread_concurrency`. Otherwise, the thread is queued until the number of threads drops below the limit. When the thread is permitted to enter, it can then leave and re-enter InnoDB without restriction as many times as the value of `innodb_concurrency_tickets`. The default is 500.

- `innodb_data_file_path` (startup: set directly; scope: global)

  The specifications for the InnoDB tablespace component files. Section 12.5.3.1, "Configuring the InnoDB Tablespace," discusses the format of the variable value.

- `innodb_data_home_dir` (startup: set directly; scope: global)

  The pathname of the directory relative to which the InnoDB tablespace component files are located. If the value is empty, component filenames are interpreted as absolute pathnames.

- `innodb_doublewrite` (startup: set directly; scope: global)

  Whether the InnoDB doublewrite buffer is enabled. The default is ON.

- `innodb_fast_shutdown` (startup: set directly; scope: global; dynamic)

  A value of 0 or 1 indicates whether InnoDB uses its quicker shutdown method that skips some of the operations that it performs normally. With a value of 2, InnoDB flushes its logs and stops.

- `innodb_file_format` (startup: set directly; scope: global; dynamic)

  The format to use for new InnoDB tables if `innodb_file_per_table` is enabled. The default format is `Antelope`, and the other permitted value is `Barracuda`. Use `Barracuda` to enable features not supported by `Antelope`, such as `COMPRESSED` row format.

- `innodb_file_format_check` (startup: set directly; scope: global)

  The InnoDB system tablespace contains a flag indicating the highest file format used in the tablespace. The setting of this variable at server startup controls whether InnoDB checks this flag to determine if the format is higher than this version of InnoDB supports. If the variable is enabled (the default) and the format is higher, startup fails with an error. If the format is not higher, InnoDB sets `innodb_file_format_max` to that format.

- innodb_file_format_max (startup: set directly; scope: global; dynamic)

  See the description of innodb_file_format_check.

- innodb_file_io_threads (startup: set directly)

  This variable is unused.

- innodb_file_per_table (startup: set directly; scope: global; dynamic)

  If this variable is 0 (the default), InnoDB creates each new table in its system tablespace. If the value is 1, InnoDB uses individual tablespaces: Each new table gets its own .ibd file in the database directory where the table contents are stored. In this case, the system tablespace is used only for the InnoDB data dictionary entry, not for data or index storage.

  This variable affects only how InnoDB creates *new* tables; it can access tables already created in the system tablespace or individual tablespaces regardless of changes to the innodb_file_per_table value.

- innodb_flush_log_at_trx_commit (startup: set directly; scope: global; dynamic)

  This variable controls how InnoDB log flushing occurs. The following table shows the permitted values.

Value	Meaning
0	Write to the log and flush to disk once per second
1	Write to the log and flush to disk at each commit
2	Write to the log at each commit, but flush to disk only once per second

  InnoDB guarantees ACID properties only if the value is 1 (the default). Otherwise, up to about a second's worth of the most recent transactions may be lost if a crash occurs. Setting the value to 0 reduces the amount of flushing to disk that InnoDB performs. However, this comes at a somewhat increased potential for losing the most recently committed transactions if a crash occurs.

- innodb_flush_method (startup: set directly; scope: global)

  The method that InnoDB uses for flushing files. It applies only on Unix. The permitted values are fdatasync (use fsync() to flush data and log files), O_DSYNC (use fsync() to flush data files and O_SYNC to open and flush log files), or O_DIRECT (use fsync() to flush data and log files and O_DIRECT or directio() as available to open data files). The default is fdatasync. On Windows, the value is always async_unbuffered.

- innodb_flush_neighbors (startup: set directly; scope: global; dynamic)

  Whether InnoDB flushes dirty pages from the buffer pool alone or along with neighboring pages located in the same extent (group of pages). Flushing neighbors can combine write operations and reduce overhead for seek time on rotational disk devices. This variable was introduced in MySQL 5.6.3 as a boolean with a default of ON. As of 5.6.6, this variable is tristate, with permitted values of 0 (do not flush neighbors), 1 (flush contiguous neighbors), and 2 (flush all neighbors in extent).

- `innodb_force_load_corrupted` (startup: set directly; scope: global)

  Whether InnoDB loads tables at startup that have been marked corrupted. The default is OFF, so normally such tables are ignored. Enabling the variable may permit recovery of data you cannot access with the value disabled; restart the server with the value disabled again after recovery. For more information, see Section 14.7.4, "Coping with InnoDB Auto-Recovery Problems." This variable was introduced in MySQL 5.5.18.

- `innodb_force_recovery` (startup: set directly; scope: global)

  Normally 0, but may be set to a value from 1 to 6 to cause the server to start up after a crash even if InnoDB recovery fails. For a description of how to use this variable, see Section 14.7.4, "Coping with InnoDB Auto-Recovery Problems."

- `innodb_ft_xxx`

  Before MySQL 5.6.4, full-text search support is limited to MyISAM tables. System variables that begin with `innodb_ft` pertain to full-text search support for InnoDB tables, which was introduced in MySQL 5.6.4. For details, see the MySQL Reference Manual.

- `innodb_io_capacity` (startup: set directly; scope: global; dynamic)

  An approximate limit on number of I/O operations per second performed by InnoDB for background tasks. The default is 200 and the minimum is 100. For slow rotational disks, you might decrease the value. For SSD disks, you might increase it. See also `innodb_io_capacity_max`.

- `innodb_io_capacity_max` (startup: set directly; scope: global; dynamic)

  If the value of `innodb_io_capacity` is not high enough during emergency situations, `innodb_io_capacity_max` is the maximum to which InnoDB can extend the limit. The default is two times the `innodb_io_capacity` default, subject to the constraints that the server uses a minimum of 2000. This variable was introduced in MySQL 5.6.6.

- `innodb_large_prefix` (startup: set directly; scope: global; dynamic)

  The usual maximum index prefix length for InnoDB indexes is 767 bytes. Enabling this variable permits prefixes up to 3072 bytes for tables that use COMPRESSED or DYNAMIC row format. The default is OFF. This variable was introduced in MySQL 5.5.14.

- `innodb_lock_wait_timeout` (startup: set directly; scope: global, session; dynamic)

  The number of seconds InnoDB waits for a lock for a transaction. If the lock cannot be acquired, InnoDB rolls back the transaction.

- `innodb_locks_unsafe_for_binlog` (startup: set directly; scope: global)

  This variable affects how InnoDB handles index row locking, but is deprecated as of MySQL 5.6.3 and should be considered obsolete. To obtain the same effect as this variable (less strict locking), but on a more flexible session- or transaction-specific basis, use SET TRANSACTION to set the transaction isolation level to READ COMMITTED. See Section 2.12.3, "Transaction Isolation."

- `innodb_log_buffer_size` (startup: set directly; scope: global)

  The size of the InnoDB transaction log buffer. Values usually range from 1MB to 8MB; the default is 1MB.

- `innodb_log_file_size` (startup: set directly; scope: global)

  The size of each InnoDB log file. The product of `innodb_log_file_size` and `innodb_log_files_in_group` determines the total InnoDB log size.

- `innodb_log_files_in_group` (startup: set directly; scope: global)

  The number of log files InnoDB maintains. The product of `innodb_log_file_size` and `innodb_log_files_in_group` determines the total InnoDB log size.

- `innodb_log_group_home_dir` (startup: set directly; scope: global)

  The pathname of the directory where InnoDB should write its log files.

- `innodb_lru_scan_depth` (startup: set directly; scope: global; dynamic)

  InnoDB uses a background operation to look for dirty pages to flush from its buffer pool. This variable controls how far into the page list (sorted in least recently used order) this operation looks. Reasonable changes from the default value of 1024 include decreasing the value for a server with a write-heavy workload and large buffer pool, or increasing the value for a server with I/O capacity to spare. This variable was introduced in MySQL 5.6.3.

- `innodb_max_dirty_pages_pct` (startup: set directly; scope: global; dynamic)

  The percentage of dirty pages that InnoDB permits in its buffer pool before it considers it necessary to flush the log to disk. The permitted range of values is 0 to 100; the default is 90.

- `innodb_max_dirty_pages_pct_lwm` (startup: set directly; scope: global; dynamic)

  The low-water mark for percentage of buffer pool dirty pages at which InnoDB enables preflushing to reduce the dirty page ratio. The default of 0 disables preflushing. Permitted values range from 0 to 99. This variable was introduced in MySQL 5.6.6.

- `innodb_max_purge_lag` (startup: set directly; scope: global; dynamic)

  InnoDB maintains a purge thread that purges rows to be deleted as a result of delete or update operations. In cases when small groups of rows are inserted and deleted at roughly the same rate, it is possible for the purge thread to fall behind in its operation, resulting in large numbers of to-be-deleted rows taking up space that otherwise would be freed. The `innodb_max_purge_lag` variable controls how much to delay INSERT, UPDATE, and DELETE statements, causing them to lag so that the purge thread can proceed more efficiently. The default is 0 (that is, no delay). For nonzero values, the delay is proportional to $((n\ /\ \texttt{innodb\_max\_purge\_lag}) \times 10) - 5$ milliseconds, where n is the number of transactions that have rows marked for deletion.

- `innodb_max_purge_lag_delay` (startup: set directly; scope: global; dynamic)

  A cap in milliseconds on the delay that can be produced by `innodb_max_purge_lag`. The default is 0 (no cap). This variable was introduced in MySQL 5.6.5.

- `innodb_mirrored_log_groups` (startup: set directly; scope: global)

  The number of InnoDB log file groups to maintain. The value should always be 1.

- `innodb_monitor_disable`, `innodb_monitor_enable`, `innodb_monitor_reset`, `innodb_monitor_reset_all` (startup: set directly; scope: global)

  These variables control the operation of the `INFORMATION_SCHEMA.innodb_metrics` table. For details, see the MySQL Reference Manual. These variables were introduced in MySQL 5.6.2.

- `innodb_old_blocks_pct` (startup: set directly; scope: global; dynamic)

  The percentage of the InnoDB buffer pool devoted to the old sublist. The default is 37 (3/8 of the pool). Permitted values range from 5 to 95. For additional detail, see Section 12.7.2.1, "Configuring the InnoDB Buffer Pool."

- `innodb_old_blocks_time` (startup: set directly; scope: global; dynamic)

  How many milliseconds a block must remain in the old sublist of the InnoDB buffer pool after the first access before the next access moves it to the new sublist. The default is 0: Blocks inserted into the old sublist move immediately to the new sublist when the first access occurs. For additional detail, see Section 12.7.2.1, "Configuring the InnoDB Buffer Pool."

- `innodb_open_files` (startup: set directly; scope: global)

  If `innodb_file_per_table` is set to 1 to enable individual tablespaces, `innodb_open_files` indicates how many file descriptors InnoDB can use to keep `.ibd` files open simultaneously. The minimum value is 10 and the default is 300. `innodb_file_per_table` controls allocation of file descriptors separate from those controlled by `open_files_limit`; descriptors used for `.ibd` files are not used by the table cache.

- `innodb_page_size` (startup: set directly; scope: global)

  The size of pages in InnoDB tablespaces. The default is 16KB. Permitted values are 4KB, 8KB, and 16KB. This setting takes effect only when InnoDB initializes tablespaces, so you should set it before initializing MySQL, or before removing and re-creating InnoDB tablespace files. This variable was introduced in MySQL 5.6.4.

- `innodb_print_all_deadlocks` (startup: set directly; scope: global; dynamic)

  Whether InnoDB writes diagnostic information to the error log about transaction deadlocks. The default is OFF. This variable was introduced in MySQL 5.6.2.

- `innodb_purge_batch_size` (startup: set directly; scope: global; dynamic)

  The number of redo log records that cause a purge operation to flush changed buffer pool blocks to disk. The default is 20. This variable was introduced in MySQL 5.5.4.

- `innodb_purge_threads` (startup: set directly; scope: global)

  How many background threads InnoDB uses for purge operations (removal of deleted rows no longer needed by any transaction). The default is 0. This variable was introduced in MySQL 5.5.4.

- `innodb_random_read_ahead` (startup: set directly; scope: global; dynamic)

  Whether InnoDB attempts to predict when pages located in an extent (group of pages) will be needed and perform an asynchronous readhead operation for them. The prediction is based on whether other pages from the extent have been read, regardless of the order they were read. The default is OFF.

- `innodb_read_ahead_threshold` (startup: set directly; scope: global; dynamic)

  If InnoDB detects a pattern sequential page access consisting of `innodb_read_ahead_threshold` or more pages from the same extent (group of pages), it performs an asychronous readahead operation for pages in the next extent. The default is 56. Permitted values range from 0 to 64.

- `innodb_read_io_threads` (startup: set directly; scope: global)

  How many threads InnoDB uses for read operations. The range of values is 1 to 64; the default is 4.

- `innodb_replication_delay` (startup: set directly; scope: global; dynamic)

  If the limit indicated by `innodb_thread_concurrency` has been reached on a slave server, this variable is the delay in milliseconds of the replication thread. The default is 0.

- `innodb_rollback_on_timeout` (startup: set directly; scope: global)

  This variable controls what InnoDB does when a transaction times out. With a value of OFF (the default), InnoDB rolls back only the last statement. With a value of ON, InnoDB rolls back the entire transaction.

- `innodb_rollback_segments` (startup: set directly; scope: global; dynamic)

  How many rollback segments InnoDB uses in the system tablespace within a transaction. The default is 128. This variable was introduced in MySQL 5.5.11. It was replaced in 5.6.3 by `innodb_undo_logs`.

- `innodb_sort_buffer_size` (startup: set directly; scope: global)

  The size in bytes of buffers InnoDB uses for merge sorts during index creation. The default is 1MB. The minimum is 512KB in MySQL 5.6.4, and 64KB in 5.6.5 and up. This variable was introduced in MySQL 5.6.4. Before 5.6.4, a fixed size of 1MB is used.

- `innodb_spin_wait_delay` (startup: set directly; scope: global; dynamic)

  The maximum wait between polls for a spin lock. This is a unitless value, but larger values mean longer waits. The default is 6; the minimum is 0.

- `innodb_stats_method` (startup: set directly; scope: global; dynamic)

  Whether the server should consider NULL values equal or distinct when calculating index key value distribution statistics for InnoDB tables. The value can be `nulls_equal` (all NULL values are in the same group), `nulls_unequal` (each NULL value forms a distinct group), or `nulls_ignored` (NULL values are ignored).

- `innodb_stats_on_metadata` (startup: set directly; scope: global; dynamic)

  Whether InnoDB updates statistics for statements that access table metadata, such as `SHOW INDEX` or `SHOW TABLE STATUS`, or for accesses to the `STATISTICS` and `TABLES INFORMATION_SCHEMA` tables. The effect is similar to running `ANALYZE TABLE`. The default is `ON`.

- `innodb_stats_persistent_sample_pages` (startup: set directly; scope: global; dynamic)

  How many index pages InnoDB samples to estimate statistics. The default is 20. This setting is ignored unless `innodb_analyze_is_persistent` is enabled. Otherwise, InnoDB uses the value of `innodb_stats_transient_sample_pages`. This variable was introduced in MySQL 5.6.2.

- `innodb_stats_sample_pages` (startup: set directly; scope: global; dynamic)

  In MySQL 5.5, how many index pages InnoDB samples to estimate statistics. The default is 8. As of MySQL 5.6.3, this variable is deprecated in preference to `innodb_stats_transient_sample_pages`.

- `innodb_stats_transient_sample_pages` (startup: set directly; scope: global; dynamic)

  How many index pages InnoDB samples to estimate statistics. The default is 8. This setting is ignored unless `innodb_analyze_is_persistent` is disabled. Otherwise, InnoDB uses the value of `innodb_stats_persistent_sample_pages`. This variable was introduced in MySQL 5.6.2.

- `innodb_strict_mode` (startup: set directly; scope: global, session; dynamic)

  Whether InnoDB is stricter about the syntax for table and index creation and alteration statements. If this variable is enabled, InnoDB treats as errors conflicting clauses that otherwise would be treated as warnings. This is similar to enabling strict SQL mode.

- `innodb_support_xa` (startup: set directly; scope: global, session; dynamic)

  Whether InnoDB supports two-phase commit in XA transactions. The default is `ON` but can be set to `OFF` for better performance if you don't use XA transactions.

- `innodb_sync_spin_loops` (startup: set directly; scope: global; dynamic)

  How many times a thread waits for InnoDB to free a mutex before being suspended.

- `innodb_table_locks` (startup: set directly; scope: global, session; dynamic)

  This variable controls how InnoDB handles a `LOCK TABLE` statement to acquire a write lock for an InnoDB table when autocommit is disabled. A value of `ON` (the default) causes InnoDB to acquire an internal table lock. A value of `OFF` causes InnoDB to wait until no other thread has a lock for the table. Disabling this variable can prevent some deadlocks for applications that use `LOCK TABLES` with autocommit mode disabled.

- `innodb_thread_concurrency` (startup: set directly; scope: global; dynamic)

  The limit on the number of threads that InnoDB tries to maintain. A value of 0 (the default) means "no limit." Permitted values range from 0 to 1000.

- `innodb_thread_sleep_delay` (startup: set directly; scope: global; dynamic)

  The time in microseconds that InnoDB threads sleep before being placed in the InnoDB queue. The default is 10,000 (10 seconds); a value of 0 means "don't sleep."

- `innodb_undo_directory` (startup: set directly; scope: global)

  The directory where InnoDB creates separate undo log tablespaces, if `innodb_undo_logs` and `innodb_undo_tablespaces` are nonzero. The default is '.', which indicates the default directory where InnoDB creates other log files. This variable was introduced in MySQL 5.6.3.

- `innodb_undo_logs` (startup: set directly; scope: global; dynamic)

  How many rollback segments InnoDB uses in the system tablespace within a transaction. The default is 128. This variable was introduced in MySQL 5.6.3. It replaces `innodb_rollback_segments`.

- `innodb_undo_tablespaces` (startup: set directly; scope: global)

  How many tablespace files InnoDB uses for separate undo logs. The default is 0. This variable was introduced in MySQL 5.6.3.

- `innodb_use_native_aio` (startup: set directly; scope: global)

  On Linux, whether to use the asynchronous I/O subsystem. The default is ON. This variable was introduced in MySQL 5.5.4.

- `innodb_use_sys_malloc` (startup: set directly; scope: global)

  Whether InnoDB uses the system memory allocator. The default is ON; disabling this variable causes InnoDB to use its own allocator.

- `innodb_version` (scope: global)

  The InnoDB storage engine version number.

- `innodb_write_io_threads` (startup: set directly; scope: global)

  How many threads InnoDB uses for write operations. The range of values is 1 to 64; the default is 4.

- `timed_mutexes` (startup: set directly; scope: global; dynamic)

  Whether to collect InnoDB mutex timing information. The default is OFF.

D.2   Status Variables

Status variables provide information about the server's current operational state. To display status variables, use the SHOW STATUS statement or execute the mysqladmin extended-status command. Status variables (like system variables) have global and session-specific values. These represent the sum over all clients and the value for the current client, respectively. If a variable has only a global value, the same value is returned for the global and session variables. You can also query the INFORMATION_SCHEMA tables named GLOBAL_STATUS and SESSION_STATUS to obtain status variable information.

For more information about examining status variables at runtime, see Section 12.3.2, "Checking Status Variable Values."

Status variable names are not case sensitive.

The following list describes the more general status variables. Separate sections after that describe sets of variables that are related to each other. These include variables for the InnoDB storage engine, the query cache, and SSL.

- Aborted_clients

  The number of client connections aborted due to clients not closing the connection properly.

- Aborted_connects

  The number of attempts to connect to the server that failed.

- Binlog_cache_disk_use

  The number of transactions that used a temporary disk file because their size exceeded the value of the binlog_cache_size system variable.

- Binlog_cache_use

  The number of transactions that could be held in the binary log cache because their size did not exceed the value of the binlog_cache_size system variable.

- Binlog_stmt_cache_disk_use

  The number of nontransactional statements stored in a temporary file because the statement cache was full. This variable was introduced in MySQL 5.5.9.

- Binlog_stmt_cache_use

  The number of nontransactional statements stored in the statement cache. This variable was introduced in MySQL 5.5.9.

- Bytes_received

  The number of bytes received from all clients (for the global value) or the current client (for the session value).

- `Bytes_sent`

  The number of bytes sent to all clients (for the global value) or the current client (for the session value).

- `Com_xxx`

  The server maintains a set of status variables that serve as counters to indicate the number of times particular types of statements (commands) have been executed. There are dozens of such variables, and they all have similar names, so they are not listed individually here. Each statement counter variable name begins with `Com_`, and has a suffix that indicates the type of statement to which the counter corresponds. For example, `Com_select` and `Com_drop_table` indicate, respectively, how many SELECT and DROP TABLE statements the server has executed.

- `Compression`

  Whether traffic sent using the client/server protocol uses compression.

- `Connection_errors_xxx`

  These variables track various kinds of errors that occur when clients attempt to connect. These variables were introduced in MySQL 5.6.5.

- `Connections`

  The number of attempts to connect to the server (both successful and unsuccessful).

- `Created_tmp_disk_tables`

  The number of on-disk internal temporary tables the server created while processing statements.

- `Created_tmp_files`

  The number of temporary files the server created.

- `Created_tmp_tables`

  The number of internal temporary tables the server created while processing statements.

- `Delayed_errors`

  The number of errors that have occurred while processing INSERT DELAYED rows.

- `Delayed_insert_threads`

  The number of INSERT DELAYED handlers.

- `Delayed_writes`

  The number of INSERT DELAYED rows that have been written.

- `Flush_commands`

  The number of table flush operations that have been executed.

- `Handler_commit`

  The number of requests to commit a transaction.

- `Handler_delete`

  The number of requests to delete a row from a table.

- `Handler_external_lock`

  This variable is related to the number of locking operations, both at the beginning and end of table access. Divide by two for the number of operations. This variable was introduced in MySQL 5.6.2.

- `Handler_mrr_init`

  Some storage engines provide their own implementation for the Multi-Range Read optimization strategy. This variable indicates how many times the server used this implementations. This variable was introduced in MySQL 5.6.1.

- `Handler_prepare`

  The number of prepares for two-phase commits.

- `Handler_read_first`

  The number of requests to read the first row from an index.

- `Handler_read_key`

  The number of requests to read a row based on an index value.

- `Handler_read_last`

  The number of requests to read the last row from an index. This variable was introduced in MySQL 5.5.7.

- `Handler_read_next`

  The number of requests to read the next row in index order.

- `Handler_read_prev`

  The number of requests to read the previous row in descending index order.

- `Handler_read_rnd`

  The number of requests to read a row based on its position.

- `Handler_read_rnd_next`

  The number of requests to read the next row. If this number is high, you are likely performing many statements that require full table scans or that are not using indexes properly.

- `Handler_rollback`

  The number of requests to roll back a transaction.

- `Handler_savepoint`

  The number of requests to create a transaction savepoint.

- Handler_savepoint_rollback

  The number of requests to roll back to a transaction savepoint.

- Handler_update

  The number of requests to update a row in a table.

- Handler_write

  The number of requests to insert a row in a table.

- Innodb_*xxx*

  See Section D.2.1, "InnoDB Status Variables."

- Key_blocks_not_flushed

  The number of blocks in the key cache that have been modified but not yet flushed to disk.

- Key_blocks_unused

  The number of unused blocks in the key cache.

- Key_blocks_used

  The largest number of blocks in the key cache that have been in use simultaneously.

- Key_read_requests

  The number of requests to read a block from the key cache.

- Key_reads

  The number of reads of index blocks from disk.

- Key_write_requests

  The number of requests to write a block to the key cache.

- Key_writes

  The number of writes of index blocks to disk.

- Last_query_cost

  The query optimizer's most recent query cost calculation. The value is useful only for queries that do not use UNION or subqueries. The value is 0 if no query cost has yet been calculated. The value is set for queries served using the query cache.

- Last_query_partial_plans

  For the most recently executed query, the number of iterations in preparing an execution plan by the optimizer. This variable was introduced in MySQL 5.6.5.

- Max_used_connections

  The largest number of connections that have been open simultaneously.

- `Not_flushed_delayed_rows`

  The number of rows waiting to be written for `INSERT DELAYED` statements.

- `Open_files`

  The number of open files.

- `Open_streams`

  The number of open streams. A stream is a file opened with `fopen()`; this applies only to log files.

- `Open_table_definitions`

  The number of cached `.frm` files.

- `Open_tables`

  The number of open tables, not counting `TEMPORARY` tables.

- `Opened_files`

  The number of times the server has opened a file. (Some storage engines might not increment this counter.)

- `Opened_files`

  The number of times the server opened a file using its internal `my_open()` library function.

- `Opened_table_definitions`

  The number of times the server has opened an `.frm` file.

- `Opened_tables`

  The number of times the server has opened a table. If this number is high, it may be a good idea to increase your table cache size.

- `Performance_schema_xxx`

  Status variables that begin with `Performance_schema` pertain to the Performance Schema used for collecting and analyzing server performance data. For details, see the MySQL Reference Manual.

- `Prepared_stmt_count`

  The number of prepared statements.

- `Qcache_xxx`

  See Section D.2.2, "Query Cache Status Variables."

- `Questions`

  The number of statements received by the server (this includes both successful and unsuccessful statements). The ratio of `Questions` to `Update` yields the number of statements per second.

- Select_full_join

  The number of "full" joins; that is, joins performed without using indexes.

- Select_full_range_join

  The number of joins performed using a range search on a reference table.

- Select_range

  The number of joins performed using a range on the first table.

- Select_range_check

  The number of joins for which a range search was used to fetch rows on a secondary table.

- Select_scan

  The number of joins that used a full scan of the first table.

- Slave_heartbeat_period

  The replication heartbeat interval in seconds.

- Slave_last_heartbeat

  A TIMESTAMP value indicating when the last heartbeat was received from the master. This variable was introduced in MySQL 5.6.1.

- Slave_open_temp_tables

  The number of temporary tables the slave SQL thread has open.

- Slave_received_heartbeats

  The number of heartbeats received from the master since the last CHANGE MASTER statement or since the slave was restarted or reset.

- Slave_retried_transactions

  The number of times the slave SQL thread has retried transactions.

- Slave_running

  Whether the slave I/O and SQL threads both are running.

- Slow_launch_threads

  The number of threads that took longer than slow_launch_time seconds to create.

- Slow_queries

  The number of queries that look longer than long_query_time seconds to execute.

- Sort_merge_passes

  The number of merge passes performed by the sort algorithm.

- `Sort_range`

  The number of sort operations that used a range.

- `Sort_rows`

  The number of rows sorted.

- `Sort_scan`

  The number of sort operations that used a full table scan.

- `Ssl_xxx`

  See Section D.2.3, "SSL Status Variables."

- `Table_locks_immediate`

  The number of table lock requests satisfied immediately with no waiting.

- `Table_locks_waited`

  The number of table lock requests satisfied only after waiting. If this value is high, it indicates that you have a lot of contention for table locks.

- `Table_open_cache_hits, Table_open_cache_misses, Table_open_cache_overflows`

  These variables provide statistics about the operation of the open tables cache. Hits and misses are lookups that find or do not find a table in the cache. Overflows are the number of times the cache has been extended past the size indicated by `table_open_cache`. These variables were introduced in MySQL 5.6.6.

- `Tc_log_max_pages_used`

  The maximum number of pages that have been used for the transaction coordinator recovery log file.

- `Tc_log_page_size`

  The page size for the transaction coordinator recovery log file.

- `Tc_log_page_waits`

  The number of times a two-phase commit had to wait for a free page in the transaction coordinator recovery log file.

- `Threads_cached`

  The number of threads in the thread cache.

- `Threads_connected`

  The number of open connections.

- `Threads_created`

  The number of times the server has created a thread to handle client connections.

- `Threads_running`

  The number of threads that are active (not sleeping).

- `Uptime`

  The number of seconds since the server started running.

- `Uptime_since_flush_status`

  The number of seconds since FLUSH STATUS was most recently executed.

D.2.1 InnoDB Status Variables

The following variables display information about the operation of the InnoDB storage engine. Many of them are available in the output of SHOW ENGINE INNODB STATUS, but are more easily parsed in the output from SHOW STATUS.

- `Innodb_available_undo_logs`

  How many InnoDB undo logs are available. (The `innodb_undo_logs` system variable indicates how many are active.) This variable was introduced in MySQL 5.6.5.

- `Innodb_buffer_pool_pages_data`

  The number of pages in the InnoDB buffer pool that contain data. This counts clean pages that have not been modified and dirty pages that contain modified data.

- `Innodb_buffer_pool_dump_status`

  The current status of a buffer pool dump operation. This variable was introduced in MySQL 5.6.3.

- `Innodb_buffer_pool_load_status`

  The current status of a buffer pool load operation. This variable was introduced in MySQL 5.6.3.

- `Innodb_buffer_pool_pages_dirty`

  The number of pages in the InnoDB buffer pool that contain modified data.

- `Innodb_buffer_pool_pages_flushed`

  The number of InnoDB buffer pool pages for which flush requests have been issued.

- `Innodb_buffer_pool_pages_free`

  The number of free pages in the InnoDB buffer pool.

- `Innodb_buffer_pool_pages_latched`

  The number of pages in the InnoDB buffer pool in the process of being read or written or that cannot be flushed and freed for reuse. Displayed only if MySQL is built with UNIV_DEBUG defined.

- `Innodb_buffer_pool_pages_misc`

  The number of pages allocated in the InnoDB buffer pool for internal operations.

- `Innodb_buffer_pool_pages_total`

  The total number of pages in the InnoDB buffer pool.

- `Innodb_buffer_pool_read_ahead`

  The number of pages the InnoDB read-ahead background thread read into the InnoDB buffer pool.

- `Innodb_buffer_pool_read_ahead_evicted`

  The number of pages read by the InnoDB read-ahead background thread that were then evicted without being used by queries.

- `Innodb_buffer_pool_read_requests`

  The number of logical read requests issued by InnoDB.

- `Innodb_buffer_pool_reads`

  The number of single-page reads done due to not being able to perform a logical read from the InnoDB buffer pool.

- `Innodb_buffer_pool_wait_free`

  The number of times InnoDB had to wait for writes to the buffer pool to be flushed. Writes usually are done in the background, but InnoDB must perform a wait if no pages are available when it needs to read a page or create a new one.

- `Innodb_buffer_pool_write_requests`

  The number writes to the InnoDB buffer pool.

- `Innodb_data_fsyncs`

  The number of sync-to-disk operations performed by InnoDB.

- `Innodb_data_pending_fsyncs`

  The number of pending InnoDB data sync-to-disk operations.

- `Innodb_data_pending_reads`

  The number of pending InnoDB data-read operations.

- `Innodb_data_pending_writes`

  The number of pending InnoDB data-write operations.

- `Innodb_data_read`

  The number of bytes read by InnoDB.

- `Innodb_data_reads`

  The number of InnoDB data-read operations.

- `Innodb_data_writes`

  The number of InnoDB data-write operations.

- `Innodb_data_written`

  The number of bytes written by InnoDB.

- `Innodb_dblwr_pages_written`

  The number of pages written to the InnoDB doublewrite buffer.

- `Innodb_dblwr_writes`

  The number of writes to the InnoDB doublewrite buffer.

- `Innodb_have_atomic_builtins`

  Indicates whether MySQL was built with atomic operations enabled.

- `Innodb_log_waits`

  The number of times InnoDB had to wait for writes to the log buffer pool to be flushed.

- `Innodb_log_write_requests`

  The number of requests to write to the InnoDB log file.

- `Innodb_log_writes`

  The number of writes to the InnoDB log file.

- `Innodb_num_open_files`

  How many files InnoDB has open. This variable was introduced in MySQL 5.6.2.

- `Innodb_os_log_fsyncs`

  The number of sync-to-disk operations for the InnoDB log file.

- `Innodb_os_log_pending_fsyncs`

  The number of pending sync-to-disk operations for the InnoDB log file.

- `Innodb_os_log_pending_writes`

  The number of pending write operations for the InnoDB log file.

- `Innodb_os_log_written`

  The number of bytes written to the InnoDB log file.

- `Innodb_page_size`

  The compiled-in page size used by InnoDB. This can be used to convert measurements that are counted in page units to byte units. The default is 16KB.

- `Innodb_pages_created`

  The number of pages created by InnoDB.

- `Innodb_pages_read`

  The number of pages read by InnoDB.

- `Innodb_pages_written`

  The number of pages written by InnoDB.

- `Innodb_row_lock_current_waits`

  The number of row locks InnoDB is waiting to acquire.

- `Innodb_row_lock_time`

  The total time in milliseconds spent acquiring InnoDB row locks.

- `Innodb_row_lock_time_avg`

  The average time in milliseconds required to acquire an InnoDB row lock.

- `Innodb_row_lock_time_max`

  The maximum time in milliseconds required to acquire an InnoDB row lock.

- `Innodb_row_lock_waits`

  The number of times InnoDB waited to acquire a row lock.

- `Innodb_rows_deleted`

  The number of rows deleted from InnoDB tables.

- `Innodb_rows_inserted`

  The number of rows inserted into InnoDB tables.

- `Innodb_rows_read`

  The number of rows read from InnoDB tables.

- `Innodb_rows_updated`

  The number of rows updated in InnoDB tables.

- `Innodb_truncated_status_writes`

  How many times the output from SHOW ENGINE INNODB STATUS was truncated. This variable was introduced in MySQL 5.5.7.

D.2.2 Query Cache Status Variables

The following variables display information about the operation of the query cache.

- `Qcache_free_blocks`

  The number of free memory blocks in the query cache.

- `Qcache_free_memory`

  The amount of free memory in the query cache.

- `Qcache_hits`

  The number of query requests satisfied by queries held in the cache.

- `Qcache_inserts`

  The number of queries that have ever been registered in the query cache.

- `Qcache_lowmem_prunes`

  The number of cached query results discarded from the query cache to make room for newer results.

- `Qcache_not_cached`

  The number of queries that were uncacheable or for which caching was suppressed with the `SQL_NO_CACHE` keyword.

- `Qcache_queries_in_cache`

  The number of queries registered in the cache.

- `Qcache_total_blocks`

  The total number of memory blocks in the query cache.

D.2.3   SSL Status Variables

The following variables provide information about the SSL management code. Many of them reflect the state of the current session, and will be blank unless the session actually is secure. These variables are unavailable unless the server has been built with SSL support.

- `Ssl_accept_renegotiates`

  The number of start renegotiations in server mode.

- `Ssl_accepts`

  The number of started SSL/TLS handshakes in server mode.

- `Ssl_callback_cache_hits`

  The number of sessions successfully retrieved from the external session cache in server mode.

- `Ssl_cipher`

  The SSL cipher (protocol) for the session (blank if no cipher is in effect). You can use this variable to determine whether the session is encrypted.

- `Ssl_cipher_list`

  The list of available SSL ciphers.

- `Ssl_client_connects`

  The number of started SSL/TLS handshakes in client mode.

- `Ssl_connect_renegotiates`

  The number of start renegotiations in client mode.

- `Ssl_ctx_verify_depth`

  The SSL context verification depth.

- `Ssl_ctx_verify_mode`

  The SSL context verification mode.

- `Ssl_default_timeout`

  The default SSL session timeout.

- `Ssl_finished_accepts`

  The number of successfully established SSL/TLS sessions in server mode.

- `Ssl_finished_connects`

  The number of successfully established SSL/TLS sessions in client mode.

- `Ssl_server_not_after`

  The last valid date for the SSL certificate. This variable was introduced in MySQL 5.6.3.

- `Ssl_server_not_before`

  The first valid date for the SSL certificate. This variable was introduced in MySQL 5.6.3.

- `Ssl_session_cache_hits`

  The number of SSL sessions found in the session cache.

- `Ssl_session_cache_misses`

  The number of SSL sessions not found in the session cache.

- `Ssl_session_cache_mode`

  The type of SSL caching used by the server.

- `Ssl_session_cache_overflows`

  The number of sessions removed from the cache because it was full.

- `Ssl_session_cache_size`

  The number of sessions that can be stored in the SSL session cache.

- `Ssl_session_cache_timeouts`

  The number of sessions that have timed out.

- `Ssl_sessions_reused`

  Whether the session was reused from an earlier session.

- `Ssl_used_session_cache_entries`

  The number of sessions in the session cache.

- Ssl_verify_depth

  The SSL verification depth.

- Ssl_verify_mode

  The SSL verification mode.

- Ssl_version

  The SSL protocol version of the session.

D.3   User-Defined Variables

User-defined variables (or, more simply, "user variables") can be assigned values, and you can refer to those variables in other statements later.

User-defined variable names consist of '@' followed by an identifier and follow rules similar to those for legal identifiers (see Section 2.2, "MySQL Identifier Syntax and Naming Rules"). However, a user variable name can contain '.' without needing to be quoted, unlike identifiers. User variable names are not case sensitive.

User variables can be assigned values with the = or := operators in SET statements or with the := operator in other statements such as SELECT. Multiple assignments can be performed in a single statement.

```
mysql> SET @x = 0, @y = 2;
mysql> SET @color := 'red', @size := 'large';
mysql> SELECT @x, @y, @color, @size;
+------+------+--------+-------+
| @x   | @y   | @color | @size |
+------+------+--------+-------+
| 0    | 2    | red    | large |
+------+------+--------+-------+
mysql> SELECT @count := COUNT(*) FROM member;
+--------------------+
| @count := COUNT(*) |
+--------------------+
|                102 |
+--------------------+
```

User variables can be assigned integer, decimal, floating-point, string, or NULL values, and can be assigned from arbitrary expressions, including those that refer to other variables. If you access a user variable that has not yet been assigned a value, its value is NULL.

User variable values do not persist across sessions with the server. That is, values are lost when a session terminates.

In SELECT statements that return multiple rows, variable assignment occurs for each row. The final value is the value assigned for the last row.

String-valued user variables have the same character set and collation as those of the value they are assigned:

```
mysql> SET @s = CONVERT('abc' USING latin2) COLLATE latin2_czech_cs;
mysql> SELECT CHARSET(@s), COLLATION(@s);
+-------------+-----------------+
| CHARSET(@s) | COLLATION(@s)   |
+-------------+-----------------+
| latin2      | latin2_czech_cs |
+-------------+-----------------+
```

E

SQL Syntax Reference

This appendix describes the syntax for SQL statements provided by MySQL. Unless otherwise indicated, the statements listed here have been present in MySQL at least as early as MySQL 5.5.0. Changes made since then are so noted.

This appendix has three parts:

- SQL statements other than those for compound statements.
- SQL statements used for compound statements, which are written using BEGIN and END and can be used for writing stored programs: functions, procedures, triggers, and events that are stored on the server side.
- The syntax for writing comments in SQL code. Comments are used to write descriptive text that is ignored by the server, and to hide MySQL-specific keywords that will be executed by MySQL but ignored by other database servers.

Statement syntax descriptions use the following conventions:

- Square brackets ([]) indicate optional information.
- Vertical bars (|) separate alternative items in a list. If a list is enclosed in square brackets, one alternative may be chosen. If a list is enclosed in curly brackets ({}), one alternative must be chosen.
- An ellipsis (...) indicates that the term preceding the ellipsis can be repeated.
- *n* indicates an integer.
- 'str' indicates a string value. A quoted value such as 'file_name' or 'pattern' indicates a more-specific kind of value such as a filename or pattern.

This appendix does not cover statements or statement clauses that relate to user-defined functions (UDFs), XA transactions, or that are specific to MySQL Cluster or less-used storage engines such as FEDERATED.

Some general synonyms always hold, so I list them here rather than every place in which they can be used:

- Any of the following formats specify a character set:

```
CHARACTER SET charset
CHARSET [=] charset
```

These synonymous forms can be used in table and column definitions, and in the CREATE DATABASE and ALTER DATABASE statements.

- SCHEMA and SCHEMAS are synonyms for DATABASE and DATABASES, respectively, and can freely be substituted in statements anywhere you might use the latter two keywords. For example, you can create a database with either CREATE DATABASE or CREATE SCHEMA.

- COLUMNS and FIELDS are synonymous.

E.1　SQL Statement Syntax (Noncompound Statements)

This section describes the syntax and meaning of each of MySQL's SQL statements, other than those for writing compound statements (for the latter, see Section E.2, "SQL Statement Syntax (Compound Statements)"). A statement fails if you do not have the necessary privileges to use it. For example, USE db_name fails if you have no permissions to access the database db_name.

ALTER DATABASE

```
ALTER DATABASE [db_name] db_attr ...
ALTER DATABASE db_name UPGRADE DATA DIRECTORY NAME
```

This statement changes database attributes or upgrades the database directory name encoding. It requires the ALTER privilege for the database.

For the first syntax, the permitted db_attr database attribute values are the same as those listed in the entry for CREATE DATABASE. The statement applies to the default database if the database name is omitted. If there is no default database, an error occurs.

The UPGRADE DATA DIRECTORY NAME syntax is for use when you upgrade from a version older than MySQL 5.1. It re-encodes the name of the database directory if necessary to the filesystem encoding currently used by MySQL if the name contains special characters.

ALTER EVENT

```
ALTER
  [DEFINER = definer_name]
  EVENT event_name
  [ON SCHEDULE schedule]
  [ON COMPLETION [NOT] PRESERVE]
  [RENAME TO new_event_name]
  [ENABLE | DISABLE [ON SLAVE]]
```

```
[COMMENT 'str']
[DO event_stmt]
```

Alters an existing event to have the given definition. The RENAME TO clause renames the event. The other clauses are described in the entry for CREATE EVENT. You must have the EVENT privilege for the database to which the event belongs.

ALTER FUNCTION, ALTER PROCEDURE

```
ALTER {FUNCTION | PROCEDURE} routine_name [characteristic] ...

characteristic:
    COMMENT 'str'
  | {CONTAINS SQL | NO SQL | READS SQL DATA | MODIFIES SQL DATA}
  | LANGUAGE SQL
  | SQL SECURITY {DEFINER | INVOKER}
```

These statements alter the characteristics of stored routines. They require the ALTER ROUTINE privilege for the given routine. The characteristics are as described in the entry that covers the CREATE FUNCTION and CREATE PROCEDURE statements.

ALTER TABLE

```
ALTER [IGNORE] TABLE tbl_name [action [, action] ...]
```

ALTER TABLE enables you to rename tables or modify their structure. To use it, specify the table name along with any actions to be performed on the table. The IGNORE keyword comes into play if the action could produce duplicate key values in a unique index in the altered table. Without IGNORE, the effect of the ALTER TABLE statement is canceled. With IGNORE, rows that duplicate values for unique key values are deleted.

During the ALTER TABLE operation, other clients can read from the original table. Clients that try to update the table are blocked until the operation completes, at which point the updates are applied to the new table.

action values specify alterations, each of which is performed in turn. Some actions cannot be combined with other actions, as indicated in the action descriptions. If no action is specified, ALTER TABLE has no effect.

For index-definition actions that include index_option clauses, some storage engines permit you to specify the indexing algorithm or other index definition modifiers. For details about which indexing values are supported in different versions of MySQL, see the entry for CREATE INDEX. For additional information about index creation, see Section 2.6.4, "Indexing Tables."

An action value may be any of the following:

- table_option

  Specifies a table option of the kind that may be given in the table_option part of a CREATE TABLE statement. The comma separating consecutive table options may be omitted.

```
ALTER TABLE score ENGINE=MyISAM CHECKSUM=1;
ALTER TABLE sayings CHARACTER SET utf8;
```

Any version-specific or storage engine-specific constraints on the availability of a given table option are as described in the entry for CREATE TABLE. If you attempt to alter a table to use a storage engine that is not available, the effect of the ALTER TABLE statement is subject to the setting of the NO_ENGINE_SUBSTITUTION SQL mode.

The [DEFAULT] CHARACTER SET table option changes the default table character set but does not convert existing the columns to that character set. To perform the latter operation, use a CONVERT TO CHARACTER SET action.

ALTER TABLE ignores the DATA DIRECTORY and INDEX DIRECTORY table options.

- ADD [COLUMN] col_name col_definition [FIRST | AFTER col_name]

  Adds a column to the table. col_name is the column name. col_definition is the column definition; it has the same format as for the CREATE TABLE statement. The column is placed first in the table if the FIRST keyword is given or is placed after the named column if AFTER col_name is given. If column placement is not specified, the column is placed last in the table.

  ```
  ALTER TABLE t ADD name CHAR(20);
  ALTER TABLE t ADD id INT UNSIGNED NOT NULL PRIMARY KEY FIRST;
  ALTER TABLE t ADD birth DATE AFTER name;
  ```

- ADD [COLUMN] (create_definition,...)

  Adds columns or indexes to the table. Each create_definition is a column or index definition, in the same format as for CREATE TABLE.

- ADD [CONSTRAINT [name]] FOREIGN KEY [fk_name]
    (index_columns) reference_definition

  Adds a foreign key definition to the table. This is supported only for InnoDB tables. The foreign key is based on the columns named in index_columns, which lists one or more columns in the table separated by commas. Any CONSTRAINT name, if given, is ignored. fk_name is the foreign key ID. If given, it is ignored unless InnoDB automatically creates an index for the foreign key; in that case, fk_name becomes the index name. reference_definition defines how the foreign key relates to the parent table. The syntax is described in the entry for CREATE TABLE.

  ```
  ALTER TABLE child
    ADD FOREIGN KEY (par_id) REFERENCES parent (par_id) ON DELETE CASCADE;
  ```

  ADD FOREIGN KEY and DROP FOREIGN KEY actions cannot appear in the same ALTER TABLE statement.

- ADD FULLTEXT [INDEX | KEY] [index_name]
    (index_columns) [index_option] ...

Adds a FULLTEXT index to a MyISAM or (as of MySQL 5.6.4) InnoDB table. The index is based on the columns named in *index_columns*, which lists one or more nonbinary string columns in the table separated by commas. *index_name* is specified as for the ADD INDEX action.

```
ALTER TABLE poetry ADD FULLTEXT (author,title,stanza);
```

- ADD {INDEX | KEY} [*index_name*]
  (*index_columns*) [*index_option*] ...

Adds an index to the table. The index is based on the columns named in *index_columns*, which lists one or more columns in the table separated by commas. If the index name *index_name* is omitted, MySQL chooses a name automatically based on the name of the first indexed column.

- ADD [CONSTRAINT [*name*]] PRIMARY KEY
  (*index_columns*) [*index_option*] ...

Adds a primary key on the given columns. The key is given the name PRIMARY. *index_columns* is specified as for the ADD INDEX action. Each column must be defined as NOT NULL. An error occurs if a primary key already exists.

```
ALTER TABLE president ADD PRIMARY KEY (last_name, first_name);
```

- ADD SPATIAL [INDEX | KEY] [*index_name*]
  (*index_columns*) [*index_option*] ...

Adds a SPATIAL index to a MyISAM table. The index is based on the columns named in *index_columns*, which lists one or more spatial columns in the table separated by commas. Each column must be defined as NOT NULL. *index_name* is specified as for the ADD INDEX action.

```
ALTER TABLE coordinates ADD SPATIAL (x,y);
```

- ADD [CONSTRAINT [*name*]] UNIQUE [INDEX | KEY]
  [*index_name*]
  (*index_columns*) [*index_option*] ...

Adds a unique-valued index to *tbl_name*. *index_name* and *index_columns* are specified as for the ADD INDEX action.

```
ALTER TABLE absence ADD UNIQUE id_date (student_id, date);
```

- ALTER [COLUMN] *col_name* {SET DEFAULT *value* | DROP DEFAULT}

Modifies the column's default value, either to the specified value, or by dropping the current default value. In the latter case, a new implicit default value might be assigned, as described in Section 3.2.3, "Specifying Column Default Values."

```
ALTER TABLE grade_event ALTER category SET DEFAULT 'Q';
ALTER TABLE grade_event ALTER category DROP DEFAULT;
```

- CHANGE [COLUMN] *old_col_name new_col_name col_definition*
  [FIRST | AFTER *col_name*]

  Changes a column's name and definition. *old_col_name* and *new_col_name* are the column's current and new names, and *col_definition* is the definition to which the column should be changed. *col_definition* is in the same format as for the CREATE TABLE statement, including any column attributes such as NULL, NOT NULL, and DEFAULT. Note that to change the definition but not the name, it's necessary to specify the same name twice. FIRST and AFTER have the same effect as for ADD COLUMN.

  ```
  ALTER TABLE student CHANGE name name VARCHAR(40);
  ALTER TABLE student CHANGE name student_name CHAR(30) NOT NULL;
  ```

- CONVERT TO CHARACTER SET *charset* [COLLATE *collation*]

  Converts the table default character set and all nonbinary character columns in the table to the given character set. A *charset* value of binary converts the columns to the corresponding binary string data types; DEFAULT converts the table to use the database character set. The COLLATE clause may be given to specify a collation as well. If COLLATE is omitted, the character set default collation is used.

- DISABLE KEYS

  For a MyISAM table, this action disables the updating of nonunique indexes that normally occurs when the table is changed. To re-enable index updating, use ENABLE KEYS.

  ```
  ALTER TABLE score DISABLE KEYS;
  ```

- DISCARD TABLESPACE

  This action applies to InnoDB tables that use individual tablespaces. It removes the *tbl_name*.ibd file that stores the table contents. This action cannot be used in conjunction with other actions.

- DROP [COLUMN] *col_name* [RESTRICT | CASCADE]

  Removes the column from the table, and from any indexes of which it is a part. If all columns from an index are removed, the index is removed as well.

  ```
  ALTER TABLE president DROP suffix;
  ```

  The RESTRICT and CASCADE keywords are parsed but ignored and have no effect.

- DROP FOREIGN KEY *fk_name*

  Drops the named foreign key definition. ADD FOREIGN KEY and DROP FOREIGN KEY actions cannot appear in the same ALTER TABLE statement.

- DROP {INDEX | KEY} *index_name*

  Removes the index from the table.

  ```
  ALTER TABLE member DROP INDEX name;
  ```

- `DROP PRIMARY KEY`

Removes the primary key from the table. An error occurs if there is no primary key.

```
ALTER TABLE president DROP PRIMARY KEY;
```

- `ENABLE KEYS`

For a MyISAM table, re-enables updating for nonunique indexes that were disabled with `DISABLE KEYS`.

```
ALTER TABLE score ENABLE KEYS;
```

- `FORCE`

Performs a "null" operation that rebuilds the table without changing its structure. This action has no effect before MySQL 5.5.11.

- `IMPORT TABLESPACE`

This action applies to InnoDB tables that use individual tablespaces. It associates the `tbl_name.ibd` file in the table's database directory with the table. The `.ibd` must have been created by the same server into which it is imported. (Presumably, the table's former `.ibd` file previously had been removed with `DISCARD TABLESPACE`.) This action cannot be used in conjunction with other actions.

- `MODIFY [COLUMN] col_name col_definition [FIRST | AFTER col_name]`

Changes the definition of a column. `col_name` names the column to be modified. The column definition `col_definition` is given using the same format for column definitions shown in the entry for the `CREATE TABLE` statement, including any column attributes such as `NULL`, `NOT NULL`, and `DEFAULT`. `FIRST` and `AFTER` have the same effect as for `ADD COLUMN`.

```
ALTER TABLE student MODIFY name VARCHAR(40) DEFAULT '' NOT NULL;
```

- `ORDER BY col_list`

Sorts the rows in the table according to the columns named in `col_list`, which lists the names of one or more columns in the table separated by commas. This clause should be last if multiple clauses are given. The default sort order is ascending. Follow a column name by `ASC` or `DESC` to specify ascending or descending order explicitly. Sorting a table this way may improve performance of subsequent queries that retrieve rows in the same order. This is mostly useful for a table that will not be modified afterward, because rows do not remain in order if the table is modified after performing the `ORDER BY` operation.

```
ALTER TABLE score ORDER BY event_id, student_id;
```

- `RENAME [TO | AS] new_tbl_name`

Renames the table to `new_tbl_name`. If you rename an InnoDB table on which other tables depend for foreign key relationships, InnoDB adjusts the dependencies to point to the renamed table.

```
ALTER TABLE president RENAME TO prez;
```

ALTER TABLE supports partitioning modifications. The entry for CREATE TABLE defines the meaning of the *partition_scheme* and *partition_definition* terms used in the following action descriptions. If any one of these partitioning options appears in an ALTER TABLE statement, you cannot use any of the others.

- *partition_scheme*

  Partitions the table according to the specified partitioning description. If the table is not partitioned, it becomes partitioned. Otherwise, the new partitioning replaces the old.

- ADD PARTITION (*partition_definition*)

  Adds a new partition to a partitioned table.

- {ANALYZE | CHECK | OPTIMIZE | REBUILD | REPAIR | TRUNCATE}
    PARTITION {*partition_name* [, *partition_name*] ... | ALL}

  Performs the specified action on the named partitions. Each of these actions permits ALL instead of a list of partition names, to affect all partitions. TRUNCATE does not work with subpartitions.

- COALESCE PARTITION *n*

  Causes a partitioned table to have *n* fewer partitions by merging data in the removed partitions into those remaining. This works only for HASH or KEY partitions. To remove LIST or RANGE partitions, use DROP PARTITION.

- DROP PARTITION *partition_name* [, *partition_name*] ...

  Drops the named partitions. DROP works only for LIST or RANGE partitions; data in the dropped partitions is lost. To reduce the number of HASH or KEY partitions, use COALESCE PARTITION.

- EXCHANGE PARTITION *partition_name* WITH TABLE *tbl_name2*

  Exchanges the named partition from the partitioned table *tbl_name* with the unpartitioned table *tbl_name2*. Aside from partitioning, the two tables must have identical structure. *tbl_name2* must not have rows that fall outside the partition definition, and must not participate in any foreign key references.

- REMOVE PARTITIONING

  Removes all partitioning, resulting in an unpartitioned table.

- REORGANIZE PARTITION *partition_name* [, *partition_name*] ...
    INTO (*partition_definition* [, *partition_definition*] ...)

  Repartitions the named partitions using the new partitioning definitions.

ALTER VIEW

```
ALTER
  [ALGORITHM = {MERGE | TEMPTABLE | UNDEFINED}]
  [DEFINER = definer_name]
  [SQL SECURITY = {DEFINER | INVOKER}]
  VIEW view_name [(col_list)] AS select_stmt
  [WITH [CASCADED | LOCAL] CHECK OPTION]
```

Alters an existing view to have the given definition. The clauses have the same meanings as described in the entry for CREATE VIEW.

ALTER VIEW requires the CREATE VIEW and DROP privileges for the view and some privilege for each column used in the SELECT statement that defines the view. ALTER VIEW can be used only by the definer or a user who has the SUPER privilege.

ANALYZE TABLE

```
ANALYZE
  [NO_WRITE_TO_BINLOG | LOCAL]
  {TABLE | TABLES} tbl_name [, tbl_name] ...
```

This statement causes MySQL to analyze each of the named tables, storing the distribution of key values present in each table's indexes. It works for InnoDB and MyISAM tables. ANALYZE TABLE requires the SELECT and INSERT privileges for each table.

If binary logging is enabled, MySQL writes the ANALYZE TABLE statement to the binary log unless the NO_WRITE_TO_BINLOG or LOCAL option is given.

After analysis, the Cardinality column of the output from SHOW INDEX indicates the approximate number of distinct values in the indexes. Information from the analysis can be used by the optimizer during subsequent queries to perform certain types of joins more quickly.

Analyzing a table requires a read lock, which prevents that table from being updated during the operation. ANALYZE TABLE does nothing if the table was previously analyzed and has not been changed since.

ANALYZE TABLE produces output in the format described in the entry for CHECK TABLE.

BEGIN

```
BEGIN [WORK]
```

This statement is a synonym for START TRANSACTION; see the entry for that statement.

BEGIN can also be used with END in stored programs to create a compound statement; see Section E.2, "SQL Statement Syntax (Compound Statements)."

BINLOG

```
BINLOG 'str'
```

`BINLOG` statements are generated by `mysqlbinlog`, such that `'str'` is the base-64 encoding of a binary log event in printable form. When re-executed, the server decodes the string to recover a data-change event. This statement requires the `SUPER` privilege.

CACHE INDEX

```
CACHE INDEX
  tbl_index_spec [, tbl_index_spec] ...
  IN cache_name

tbl_index_spec:
  tbl_name
    [PARTITION (partition_name [, partition_name] ... | ALL)]
    [[INDEX | KEY] (index_name [, index_name] ...)]
```

Sets up an association between one or more MyISAM tables and the named key cache, which must already exist. You must have the `INDEX` privilege for each table named in the statement. The default key cache is named `default`. The table indexes can be loaded into the cache later with `LOAD INDEX`. Although the syntax permits designating only certain indexes, the implementation associates all indexes in each table with the cache.

The following statement caches indexes for the `member` statement in the key cache named `member_cache`:

```
CACHE INDEX member IN member_cache;
```

For partitioned tables, the `PARTITION` clause permits cache assignments for specific partitions.

`CACHE INDEX` produces output in the format described in the entry for `CHECK TABLE`.

For more information about MyISAM key cache management, see Section 12.7.2, "Storage Engine Tuning."

CALL

```
CALL routine_name([proc_param [, proc_param] ...])

CALL routine_name[()]
```

Invokes the named stored procedure. The optional parameter list consists of one or more parameter values separated by commas. If any of these are `OUT` or `INOUT` parameters, the procedure can return values through them.

When the stored procedure returns, you can get the rows-affected value for the final statement executed within it by invoking the `ROW_COUNT()` function. From C, the same value can be obtained by calling `mysql_affected_rows()`.

If the procedure takes no arguments, the `()` following the procedure name is optional.

CHANGE MASTER

CHANGE MASTER TO *option* [, *option*] ...

Changes replication parameters for a slave server, to indicate which master host to use, how to connect to it, or which logs to use. The slave saves the parameters in its master.info and relay-log.info files and uses those files for subsequent restarts. Many of these parameters are also visible in the output of SHOW SLAVE STATUS.

Each *option* specifies a parameter definition in *param* = *value* format, chosen from the following list:

- IGNORE_SERVER_IDS = (*server_id_list*)

  Causes the slave to ignore events originally from any server with an ID named in *server_id_list*, which is given as a list of zero or more comma-separated server IDs. To clear the set of ignored servers, specify an empty list.

- MASTER_BIND = '*interface*'

  The IP address to bind to when connecting to the master. This option was introduced in MySQL 5.6.1.

- MASTER_CONNECT_RETRY = *n*

  The number of seconds to wait between attempts to connect to the master.

- MASTER_DELAY = *n*

  The number of seconds of replication delay. The slave waits to execute each event until at least *n* seconds after it was executed on the master. The default is 0. This option was introduced in MySQL 5.6.0.

- MASTER_HEARTBEAT_PERIOD = *interval*

  When the heartbeat interval passes on the master without any event being written to the binary log, the master sends a heartbeat to the slave. This option tells the master how long an interval to use in seconds. The value can contain a fractional part in milliseconds. A value of 0 disables heartbeats. The default is slave_net_timeout/2. The RESET SLAVE statement resets the heartbeat interval to the default.

- MASTER_HOST = '*host_name*'

  The host where the master server is running.

- MASTER_LOG_FILE = '*file_name*'

  The name of the master binary log file from which to begin or resume replication.

- MASTER_LOG_POS = *n*

  The position within the master binary log file from which to begin or resume replication.

- MASTER_PASSWORD = '*pass_val*'

  The password to use for connecting to the master server.

- `MASTER_PORT` = *n*

  The TCP/IP port number to use for connecting to the master server.

- `MASTER_RETRY_COUNT` = *n*

  The number of times to attempt a connection to a master server before giving up. This option was introduced in MySQL 5.6.1.

- `MASTER_SSL` = {0 | 1}

  `MASTER_SSL_CA` = '*file_name*'

  `MASTER_SSL_CAPATH` = '*dir_name*'

  `MASTER_SSL_CERT` = '*file_name*'

  `MASTER_SSL_CIPHER` = '*str*'

  `MASTER_SSL_CRL` = '*file_name*'

  `MASTER_SSL_CRLPATH` = '*dir_name*'

  `MASTER_SSL_KEY` = '*file_name*'

  `MASTER_SSL_VERIFY_SERVER_CERT` = {0 | 1}

  These options specify parameters for establishing an SSL connection to the master. They have the same meaning as the corresponding `--ssl-`*xxx* options described in Section F.2.1.1, "Standard SSL Options." The slave saves the values of these options to its `master.info` file but they have no effect unless the slave has SSL support enabled. The `MASTER_SSL_CRL` and `MASTER_CRLPATH` options were introduced in MySQL 5.6.3.

- `MASTER_USER` = '*user_name*'

  The username of the account to use for connecting to the master server. As of MySQL 5.6.4, it is an error to set this value to NULL or an empty string or to leave it unset when specifying `MASTER_PASSWORD`.

- `RELAY_LOG_FILE` = '*file_name*'

  The slave relay log filename.

- `RELAY_LOG_POS` = *n*

  The current position within the slave relay log.

Parameters not specified in the statement maintain their current values, with the following exception: Changes to `MASTER_HOST` or `MASTER_PORT` normally indicate that you're switching to a different master server, so if you specify either of those options, the `MASTER_LOG_FILE` and `MASTER_LOG_POS` values are set to the beginning of the master's first binary log file.

You should not mix the `MASTER_LOG_FILE` and `MASTER_LOG_POS` options with the `RELAY_LOG_FILE` and `RELAY_LOG_POS` options in the same statement.

The `CHANGE MASTER` statement deletes any existing relay log files and begins a new one unless the `RELAY_LOG_FILE` or `RELAY_LOG_POS` options are specified.

CHECK TABLE

CHECK {TABLE | TABLES} tbl_name [, tbl_name] ... [option] ...

This statement checks tables for errors. It works with InnoDB, MyISAM, ARCHIVE, and CSV tables. CHECK TABLE can also check view definitions for problems such as references to nonexistent tables. CHECK TABLE requires the SELECT privilege for each table or view to be checked.

For InnoDB tables, the server terminates after writing a message to the error log if it finds a problem, to prevent further errors from occurring. For MyISAM tables, CHECK TABLE also updates index statistics.

Each option value can be one of the following options. Unless otherwise specified, these options apply to MyISAM tables; other storage engines might ignore them.

- CHANGED skips table checking if the table was properly closed and has not been changed since the last time it was checked.

- EXTENDED performs an extended check that attempts to ensure that the table is fully consistent. This is the most thorough check available, and consequently the slowest. For example, it verifies that each key in each index points to a data row.

- FAST checks a table only if it was not properly closed.

- MEDIUM checks the index, scans the data rows for problems, and performs a checksum verification. This is the default if no options are given.

- QUICK scans only the indexes and not the data rows. This option applies to InnoDB and MyISAM tables.

- FOR UPGRADE determines whether the checked table is compatible with your current version of MySQL, so this option is useful after an upgrade. If there is an incompatibility, the server runs a full check. If the full check fails, you should attempt to repair the table. The server updates the table's .frm file with the current MySQL version unless there was an incompatibility and the full check failed. This option is not specific to MyISAM tables.

If you aren't checking a table with FOR UPGRADE and you don't specify one of QUICK, MEDIUM, or EXTENDED when checking a MyISAM table, CHECK TABLE defaults to MEDIUM if the table has variable-length rows. If it has fixed-length rows, the default is QUICK if you specify CHANGED or FAST, and MEDIUM otherwise.

It's possible for CHECK TABLE to modify a table in some cases, but the modification consists only of setting an internal flag. For example, if a table is marked as corrupt or as not having been closed properly, but the check finds no problems, CHECK TABLE marks the table as okay.

CHECK TABLE returns information about the result of the operation. For example:

```
mysql> CHECK TABLE t;
+--------+-------+----------+----------+
| Table  | Op    | Msg_type | Msg_text |
+--------+-------+----------+----------+
| test.t | check | status   | OK       |
+--------+-------+----------+----------+
```

ANALYZE TABLE, CACHE INDEX, LOAD INDEX INTO CACHE, OPTIMIZE TABLE, and REPAIR
TABLE also return information in this format. Table indicates the table on which the operation
was performed. Op indicates the type of operation carried out by the statement. The Msg_type
and Msg_text columns provide information about the result of the operation; if this value does
not indicate that the table is okay or already up to date, you should repair it.

CHECKSUM TABLE

```
CHECKSUM {TABLE | TABLES} tbl_name [, tbl_name] ...
    [QUICK | EXTENDED]
```

Reports a table checksum. For partitioned tables, this statement returns 0 before MySQL 5.6.4
unless you specify EXTENDED. CHECKSUM TABLE requires the SELECT privilege for each table.

```
mysql> CHECKSUM TABLE president;
+-------------------+------------+
| Table             | Checksum   |
+-------------------+------------+
| sampdb.president  | 3032762697 |
+-------------------+------------+
```

If a table does not exist, the Checksum value is NULL, and a warning is generated.

By default, the statement reports the live checksum if the storage engine supports it. (A live
checksum is one that is updated each time the table is modified.) For a MyISAM table, you can
enable live checksumming by using the CHECKSUM = 1 table option with CREATE TABLE or
ALTER TABLE.

With the QUICK option, the statement reports the live checksum if there is one and NULL otherwise. With the EXTENDED option, the reported checksum is calculated by reading the entire
table. This operation becomes slower as the table size increases.

COMMIT

```
COMMIT [WORK] [AND [NO] CHAIN] [[NO] RELEASE]
```

Commits changes made by statements in the current transaction, to record those changes
permanently in the database. COMMIT works only for transactional storage engines. (For
nontransactional storage engines, statements are committed as they are executed.)

The optional keyword WORK has no effect. The CHAIN and RELEASE clauses affect how the
server handles transaction completion. With AND CHAIN, when a transaction ends, another one
begins with the same isolation level. With RELEASE, when a transaction ends, the server terminates the current session. Adding NO to either CHAIN or RELEASE causes a new transaction not
to begin or the session not to terminate, respectively. The behavior of COMMIT in the absence of
these clauses is determined by the setting of the completion_type system variable. By default,
neither CHAIN nor RELEASE is applied.

COMMIT has no effect if autocommit has not been disabled with START TRANSACTION or by setting the autocommit variable to 0.

Some statements implicitly end any current transaction, as if a COMMIT had been performed, because they cannot be part of a transaction. In general, these tend to be DDL (data definition language) statements that create, alter, or drop databases or objects in them, or statements that are lock-related. For example, if you issue any of the following statements while a transaction is in progress, the server commits the transaction first before executing the statement:

```
ALTER TABLE
CREATE INDEX
DROP DATABASE
DROP INDEX
DROP TABLE
LOCK TABLES
RENAME TABLE
SET autocommit = 1 (if not already set to 1)
TRUNCATE TABLE
UNLOCK TABLES (if tables currently are locked)
```

For a complete list of statements that cause implicit commits, see the MySQL Reference Manual for your version of MySQL.

CREATE DATABASE

```
CREATE DATABASE [IF NOT EXISTS] db_name [db_attr] ...

db_attr:
    [DEFAULT] CHARACTER SET [=] charset
  | [DEFAULT] COLLATE [=] collation
```

Creates a database with the given name. You must have the CREATE privilege for the database. Attempts to create a database with a name that already exists normally result in an error; if the IF NOT EXISTS clause is specified, the database is not created but no error occurs.

The optional CHARACTER SET and COLLATE attributes may be given following the database name to specify a default character set and collation for the database. These attributes are used for tables for which no character set or collation is given explicitly. charset can be a character set name, or DEFAULT to use the current server character set. collation can be a collation name, or DEFAULT to use the current server collation.

If neither attribute is given, the server character set and collation are used. If CHARACTER SET is given without COLLATE, the character set default collation is used. If COLLATE is given without CHARACTER SET, the character set is determined from the collation. If both CHARACTER SET and COLLATE are given, the collation must be compatible with the character set.

MySQL stores database attributes in the db.opt file in the database directory.

CREATE EVENT

```
CREATE
  [DEFINER = definer_name]
  EVENT [IF NOT EXISTS] event_name
  ON SCHEDULE schedule
  [ON COMPLETION [NOT] PRESERVE]
  [ENABLE | DISABLE | DISABLE ON SLAVE]
  [COMMENT 'str']
  DO event_stmt

schedule:
    AT datetime
  | EVERY expr interval [STARTS datetime] [ENDS datetime]
```

Creates a new event named *event_name* for the event scheduler. You must have the EVENT privilege for the database to which the event belongs. By default, the event is created in the default database. To create the event in a specific database, give the name in *db_name.event_name* format.

The DEFINER clause determines the security context (the account to use for access checking) when the event executes, as described in Section 4.3, "Security for Views and Stored Programs." The default is to use the account for the user who executes the CREATE EVENT statement.

The ON SCHEDULE clause determines the execution schedule for the event (assuming that the event scheduler is running). In the formats for this clause, *datetime* is a date and time value. The CURRENT_TIMESTAMP function (or its synonyms) can be used to represent the current date and time. *datetime* expressions can use INTERVAL *expr interval* arithmetic to add or subtract temporal intervals. This syntax is described in the entry for the DATE_ADD() function in Section C.2.5, "Date and Time Functions." The *interval* value should not use any specifier that involves fractional seconds.

For ON SCHEDULE, the AT scheduling type sets up an event that executes once at the specified time. The EVERY scheduling type sets up a repeating event that executes at regular intervals. The repeat time consists of a quantity and an *interval* modifier that specifies how to interpret the interval (for example, 5 HOUR or '1:30' MINUTE_SECOND). By default, the first execution occurs as soon as the event is created and execution occurs every interval thereafter. The STARTS clause, if present, specifies the initial start time. The ENDS clause, if present, indicates the time at which the event no longer executes. In the ON SCHEDULE clause, do not use references to tables, stored functions, or user-defined functions.

The DO clause specifies the statement to be executed when the event runs. It should be a single SQL statement. To use multiple statements, enclose them within BEGIN and END to form a compound statement. (See Section E.2, "SQL Statement Syntax (Compound Statements).")

By default, the server drops an event after it completes its final execution. ON COMPLETION NOT PRESERVE specifies the same behavior explicitly. ON COMPLETION PRESERVE causes the event not to be dropped.

The ENABLE and DISABLE options specify that the event status when it is created should be enabled (run according to schedule) or disabled (do not run). DISABLE ON SLAVE indicates an event that is enabled on the server where it is created but is disabled on any slave to which it replicates.

At event creation time, the current value of the sql_mode system variable is saved for use when the event executes.

Events take no input and produce no output. That is, you cannot pass parameters to an event, and output is discarded for statements such as SELECT that produce a result set.

CREATE FUNCTION, CREATE PROCEDURE

```
CREATE
    [DEFINER = definer_name]
    FUNCTION routine_name ([func_param [, func_param] ...])
    RETURNS type
    [characteristic] ...
    routine_stmt

CREATE
    [DEFINER = definer_name]
    PROCEDURE routine_name ([proc_param [, proc_param] ...])
    [characteristic] ...
    routine_stmt

func_param:
    param_name type

proc_param:
    [IN | OUT | INOUT] param_name type

characteristic:
    COMMENT 'str'
    | {CONTAINS SQL | NO SQL | READS SQL DATA | MODIFIES SQL DATA}
    | [NOT] DETERMINISTIC
    | LANGUAGE SQL
    | SQL SECURITY {DEFINER | INVOKER}
```

These statements create new stored routines (functions and procedures). You must have the CREATE ROUTINE privilege for the given routine.

By default, the routine is created in the default database. To create the routine in a specific database, give the name in db_name.routine_name format. A function and a procedure can have the same name, but there cannot be two functions or two procedures with the same name in the same database.

Each function parameter is defined by giving the parameter name and its type. The type is any valid MySQL data type. Parameters supply values to a function when it is invoked, but changes to the parameters within the function are not visible to the caller when the function returns. (That is, they are treated as IN parameters.)

For a function, a RETURNS statement must follow the parameter list to indicate the data type for the return value.

Each procedure parameter also is defined with a name and type, but the name can be preceded by IN, OUT, or INOUT to indicate that the parameter is for input only, output only, or both input and output. The default is IN if none is present.

- An IN parameter supplies a value to the procedure. Changes to the parameter inside the procedure are not visible in the calling program after the procedure terminates.

- An OUT parameter does not supply a value to the procedure. Its initial value inside the procedure is NULL and it can be modified inside the procedure. Its final value is visible to the calling program after the procedure terminates.

- An INOUT parameter supplies a value to the procedure and any changes to its value within the procedure become visible to the caller.

One or more *characteristic* values can be given, separated by spaces:

- COMMENT

  A descriptive comment for the routine. The comment is displayed by the SHOW statements that display routine information.

- CONTAINS SQL, NO SQL, READS SQL DATA, MODIFIES SQL DATA

  These characteristics provide a hint about how the routine accesses data. In MySQL, they have no effect on what statements the server actually permits the routine to execute.

  - CONTAINS SQL: The routine contains SQL statements. This is the default if no data-access characteristic is specified.

  - NO SQL: The routine contains no SQL statements.

  - READS SQL DATA: The routine contains SQL statements that read but do not modify data.

  - MODIFIES SQL DATA: The routine contains statements that might modify data.

- DETERMINISTIC, NOT DETERMINISTIC

  DETERMINISTIC indicates that a function always produces the same result when called with the same parameter values. NOT DETERMINISTIC indicates that it might not. For example, a function that uses NOW() as its return value is likely not deterministic.

- LANGUAGE SQL

  Indicates the language of the routine. This is parsed and ignored; MySQL supports only SQL as a stored routine language.

- SQL SECURITY

  This characteristic, together with the DEFINER clause, determines the security context (the account to use for access checking) when the routine executes, as described in

Section 4.3, "Security for Views and Stored Programs." If `DEFINER` is omitted, the default is to use the account for the user who executes the `CREATE` statement. The account against which privileges are checked must have the `EXECUTE` privilege for the routine to be able to invoke it. By default, MySQL automatically grants the `EXECUTE` and `ALTER ROUTINE` privileges to the routine creator, and revokes them when the routine is dropped. To turn off this behavior, disable the `automatic_sp_privileges` system variable.

`routine_stmt` is the SQL statement that represents the body of the routine. It should be a single SQL statement. To use multiple statements, enclose them within `BEGIN` and `END` to form a compound statement. (See Section E.2, "SQL Statement Syntax (Compound Statements).")

Functions return a value to the caller and thus must have at least one `RETURN` statement in the body. However, functions cannot execute statements that produce a result set.

At routine creation time, the current value of the `sql_mode` system variable is saved for use when the routine executes.

CREATE INDEX

```
CREATE [UNIQUE | FULLTEXT | SPATIAL] INDEX index_name
  ON tbl_name (index_columns) [index_option] ...

index_option:
    index_type
  | COMMENT 'str'
  | KEY_BLOCK_SIZE [=] n
  | WITH PARSER parser_name

index_type: USING {BTREE | HASH | RTREE}
```

Adds an index named `index_name` to the table `tbl_name`. The index is based on the columns named in `index_columns`, which lists one or more columns in the table separated by commas. Internally, MySQL handles this statement as an `ALTER TABLE` statement. For details, see the entry for `ALTER TABLE`. To create several indexes on a table, it's preferable to use `ALTER TABLE`; you can add all the indexes with a single statement, which is faster than adding them individually.

By default, a nonunique index is created. The `UNIQUE`, `FULLTEXT`, or `SPATIAL` keyword, if given, indicates a specific kind of index. `CREATE INDEX` cannot be used to create a `PRIMARY KEY`; use `ALTER TABLE` instead.

`FULLTEXT` indexes are supported for MyISAM or (as of MySQL 5.6.4) InnoDB tables, but only for nonbinary string columns (`CHAR`, `VARCHAR`, `TEXT`). `SPATIAL` indexes are supported only for MyISAM tables, and only for `NOT NULL` spatial columns.

At the end of an index definition, these `index_option` values are permitted:

- `index_type` denotes an indexing algorithm, which is permitted for some storage engines. The algorithm value can be `BTREE` for InnoDB and MyISAM tables, either `HASH` or `BTREE` for MEMORY tables, and `RTREE` for `SPATIAL` indexes in MyISAM tables.

- COMMENT `'str'` provides a descriptive comment for the index (up to 1024 characters). This option was introduced in MySQL 5.5.3.

- KEY_BLOCK_SIZE `[=]` *n* suggests a size in bytes that the storage engine should use for key blocks in the index. A value of 0 means to use the default size.

- WITH PARSER *parser_name* is permitted only for FULLTEXT indexes. It names the full-text parser plugin to use for the index. See the MySQL Reference Manual for details on parser plugins.

For additional information about index creation, see Section 2.6.4, "Indexing Tables."

CREATE TABLE

```
CREATE [TEMPORARY] TABLE [IF NOT EXISTS] tbl_name
  {
      (create_definition,...) [table_option] ...
        [partition_scheme] [trailing_select]
  | [(create_definition,...) [table_option] ...
        [partition_scheme] trailing_select
  | LIKE tbl_name2
  | (LIKE tbl_name2)
  }

table_option: (see following discussion)

trailing_select:
  [IGNORE | REPLACE] [AS] select_stmt

create_definition:
    col_name col_definition [reference_definition]
  | [CONSTRAINT [name]] PRIMARY KEY
      [index_name]
      (index_columns) [index_option] ...
  | [CONSTRAINT [name]] UNIQUE [INDEX | KEY]
      [index_name]
      (index_columns) [index_option] ...
  | {INDEX | KEY} [index_name]
      (index_columns) [index_option] ...
  | {FULLTEXT | SPATIAL} [INDEX | KEY]
      [index_name] (index_columns) [index_option] ...
  | [CONSTRAINT [name]] FOREIGN KEY [fk_name]
      (index_columns) [reference_definition]
  | CHECK (expr)

col_definition:
  data_type
    [NOT NULL | NULL] [DEFAULT default_value]
    [AUTO_INCREMENT] [PRIMARY KEY] [UNIQUE [KEY]]
```

```
    [COMMENT 'str']
```

index_option: (see following discussion)

reference_definition:
```
  REFERENCES tbl_name (index_columns)
    [MATCH FULL | MATCH PARTIAL | MATCH SIMPLE]
    [ON DELETE reference_action]
    [ON UPDATE reference_action]
```

reference_action:
```
      RESTRICT | CASCADE | SET NULL | NO ACTION | SET DEFAULT
```

partition_scheme:
```
  PARTITION BY
    {
        RANGE (expr)
      | RANGE COLUMNS (col_list)
      | LIST (expr)
      | LIST COLUMNS (col_list)
      | [LINEAR] HASH (expr)
      | [LINEAR] KEY (col_list)
    }
    [PARTITIONS n]
    [SUBPARTITION BY
      {
          [LINEAR] HASH (expr)
        | [LINEAR] KEY (col_list)
      }
      [SUBPARTITIONS n]
    ]
    [(partition_definition [, partition_definition] ...)]
```

partition_definition:
```
  PARTITION partition_name
    [VALUES {LESS THAN {(expr) | MAXVALUE} | IN (value_list)}]
    [partition_option] ...
    [(subpartition_definition [, subpartition_definition] ...)]
```

subpartition_definition:
```
  SUBPARTITION subpartition_name
    [partition_option] ...
```

partition_option: (see following discussion)

The CREATE TABLE statement creates a new table named *tbl_name* in the default database. To create a table in a specific database, give the name in *db_name*.*tbl_name* format. You must have the CREATE privilege for the table.

Normally, attempts to create a table with a name that already exists result in an error. No error occurs under two conditions. First, if the IF NOT EXISTS clause is specified, the table is not created and no error occurs. Second, if TEMPORARY is specified and the original table is not a temporary table, the new temporary table is created, and the original table named `tbl_name` becomes hidden to the client while the temporary table exists. The original table remains visible to other clients because a temporary table is visible only to the client that created it. The original table becomes visible again to the current client if an explicit DROP TABLE is issued for the temporary table, or if the temporary table is renamed to some other name. You must have the CREATE TEMPORARY TABLE privilege to create temporary tables.

If the TEMPORARY keyword is given, the table exists only until the current client session ends or a DROP TABLE statement drops it.

The `create_definition` list names the columns and indexes to create. The list is optional if you create the table by means of a trailing SELECT statement. `table_option` values enable you to specify properties for the table. `partition_scheme` defines partitioning characteristics if table storage is to be partitioned. If a trailing `select_stmt` is specified (in the form of an arbitrary SELECT statement), the table is created using the result set that it returns. A trailing LIKE clause creates the new table as an empty copy of an existing table. Later sections describe these clauses more fully.

Column and index definitions. A `create_definition` may be a column or index definition, a FOREIGN KEY clause, or a CHECK clause. CHECK is parsed but ignored. FOREIGN KEY is treated similarly, except for InnoDB tables.

A column definition `col_definition` begins with a data type `data_type` and may be followed by several optional keywords. The type may be any of the data types listed in Appendix B, "Data Type Reference." See that appendix for type-specific attributes that apply to the columns you want to define. Other optional keywords may follow the data type:

- NULL, NOT NULL

  Specifies that the column may or may not contain NULL values. If neither is specified, NULL is the default.

- DEFAULT `default_value`

  Specifies the default value for the column. This cannot be used for BLOB or TEXT types, spatial types, or columns with the AUTO_INCREMENT attribute. Except for TIMESTAMP and (as of MySQL 5.6.5) DATETIME, a default value must be a constant, specified as a number, a string, or NULL. For the rules that MySQL uses for assigning a default value if you include no DEFAULT clause, see Section 3.2.3, "Specifying Column Default Values."

- AUTO_INCREMENT

  This keyword applies only to integer and floating-point data types. An AUTO_INCREMENT column is special in that when you insert NULL into it, the value actually inserted is the next value in the column sequence. Typically, this is one greater than the current maximum value in the column. AUTO_INCREMENT values start at 1 by default. (Some storage engines permit the initial value to be specified with an AUTO_INCREMENT table option. See the discussion of table options that follows.) The column must also be indexed and should be NOT NULL. There can be at most one AUTO_INCREMENT column per table.

- [PRIMARY] KEY

  Specifies that the column is a PRIMARY KEY. A PRIMARY KEY must be NOT NULL, so MySQL adds NOT NULL to the column definition if you omit it.

- UNIQUE [KEY]

  Specifies that the column is a UNIQUE index.

- COMMENT 'str'

  A descriptive comment for the column (up to 1024 characters). This attribute is displayed by SHOW CREATE TABLE and SHOW FULL COLUMNS.

The PRIMARY KEY, UNIQUE, INDEX, KEY, FULLTEXT, and SPATIAL clauses specify indexes. PRIMARY KEY and UNIQUE specify indexes that must contain unique values. INDEX and KEY are synonymous; they specify indexes that may contain duplicate values. The index is based on the columns named in index_columns, which lists one or more columns in the table separated by commas. If the index name index_name is omitted, MySQL chooses a name automatically based on the name of the first indexed column.

FULLTEXT indexes are supported for MyISAM or (as of MySQL 5.6.4) InnoDB tables, but only for nonbinary string columns (CHAR, VARCHAR, TEXT). SPATIAL indexes are supported only for MyISAM tables, and only for NOT NULL spatial columns.

At the end of an index definition, index_option values are permitted as described in the entry for CREATE INDEX. For additional information about index creation, see Section 2.6.4, "Indexing Tables."

Table options. Each table_option value specifies an additional characteristic of the table, chosen from the following list. Each option setting applies to all storage engines unless otherwise noted. Settings can be separated by whitespace or commas.

- AUTO_INCREMENT [=] n

  The first AUTO_INCREMENT value to generate for the table. This option is effective for InnoDB, MyISAM, and MEMORY tables. For InnoDB tables, the effect is canceled if you restart the server before generating any AUTO_INCREMENT values.

- AVG_ROW_LENGTH [=] n

  The approximate average row length of your table. For MyISAM tables, MySQL uses the product of the AVG_ROW_LENGTH and MAX_ROWS values to determine the maximum data file size. The MyISAM storage engine can use internal row pointers from 2 to 7 bytes wide. The default pointer width is wide enough to permit tables up to 256TB. If you require a larger table (and your operating system supports larger files), the MAX_ROWS and AVG_ROW_LENGTH table options provide information that advises MyISAM to adjust the internal pointer width. A large product of these values causes the engine to use wider pointers, enabling file sizes up to 65,536TB. Conversely, a small product advises the engine to use smaller pointers. This won't save you much space for a single small table, but the cumulative savings may be significant if you have many of them.

To size the data pointers directly, set the `myisam_data_pointer_size` system variable before creating the table.

- `[DEFAULT] CHARACTER SET [=] charset`

The table's default character set. `charset` may be a character set name, or `DEFAULT` to use the database character set. This option determines which character set to use for character columns that are defined with no explicit character set. In the following example, `c1` and `c2` are assigned the `sjis` and `ujis` character sets, respectively:

```
CREATE TABLE t
(
  c1 CHAR(50) CHARACTER SET sjis,
  c2 CHAR(50)
) CHARACTER SET ujis;
```

This table option also applies to subsequent table modifications made with `ALTER TABLE` for character column definition changes that do not name a character set explicitly.

- `CHECKSUM [=] {0 | 1}`

If this option is set to 1, MySQL maintains a live checksum for the table that is updated whenever the table is modified. There is a slight penalty for updates to the table, but the presence of checksums improves the table checking process. (MyISAM tables only.)

- `[DEFAULT] COLLATE [=] collation`

The table's default character set collation. `collation` may be a collation name, or `DEFAULT` to use the table character set default collation.

- `COMMENT [=] 'str'`

A descriptive comment for the table (up to 2048 characters). This comment is displayed by `SHOW CREATE TABLE` and `SHOW TABLE STATUS`.

- `DATA DIRECTORY [=] 'dir_name'`

This option is used only for MyISAM tables and only on Unix. It indicates the directory in which to write the data (`.MYD`) file. `'dir_name'` must be a full pathname. This option works only if the server is started without the `--skip-symbolic-links` option. On some Unix variants, symlinks are not thread-safe and are disabled by default. This option is ignored for partitioned tables. If the `keep_files_on_create` system variable is enabled, an error occurs if there is already a `.MYD` file for the table in the specified directory.

- `DELAY_KEY_WRITE [=] {0 | 1}`

If this is set to 1, the key cache is flushed only occasionally for the table, rather than after each insert operation. This improves performance but may require that the table be repaired if a crash occurs. (MyISAM tables only.)

- ENGINE [=] *engine_name*

The storage engine to use for the table. The default engine is InnoDB unless the server has been configured otherwise. To start the server with a different default engine, use the instructions in Section 12.5.2, "Selecting a Default Storage Engine." The known engine names can be displayed with the SHOW ENGINES statement. If you attempt to create a table using a storage engine that is not available, the effect of the statement is subject to the setting of the NO_ENGINE_SUBSTITUTION SQL mode. Storage engines are described in Section 2.6.1, "Storage Engine Characteristics."

- INDEX DIRECTORY [=] '*dir_name*'

This option is like DATA DIRECTORY (and has the same constraints) but indicates the directory in which to write the index (.MYI) file.

- INSERT_METHOD [=] {NO | FIRST | LAST}

This is used for MERGE tables to specify how to insert rows. A value of NO prohibits inserts entirely. Values of FIRST or LAST indicate that rows should be inserted into the first or last of the MyISAM tables that make up the MERGE table.

- KEY_BLOCK_SIZE [=] *n*

A suggested size in bytes that the storage engine should use for key blocks in indexes. A value of 0 means to use the default size. This table default can be overridden by index definitions that include their own KEY_BLOCK_SIZE option.

- MAX_ROWS [=] *n*

A hint to the storage engine about the maximum number of rows you plan to store in the table. The table will be created to permit at least this many rows. The description of the AVG_ROW_LENGTH option indicates how this value is used.

- MIN_ROWS [=] *n*

A hint to the storage engine about the minimum number of rows you plan to store in the table. This option can be used for MEMORY tables to give the MEMORY storage engine a hint about how to optimize memory usage.

- PACK_KEYS [=] {0 | 1 | DEFAULT}

This option controls index compression for MyISAM tables, which enables runs of similar index values to be compressed. The usual effect is an improvement in retrieval performance but an update penalty. A value of 0 specifies no index compression. A value of 1 specifies compression for string (CHAR, VARCHAR, BINARY, VARBINARY) and numeric index values. A value of DEFAULT specifies compression only for long string columns.

- ROW_FORMAT [=]
    {DEFAULT | COMPACT | COMPRESSED | DYNAMIC | FIXED | REDUNDANT}

The row storage format. DEFAULT permits the storage engine to choose its default format. A storage engine may ignore this option if the specified row format cannot be used. For example, FIXED cannot be used if the table contains BLOB or TEXT columns. Use SHOW TABLE STATUS and check the Row_format value to see what format the storage engine actually chose.

For InnoDB tables, the default format is COMPACT. The older original InnoDB format can be specified explicitly using REDUNDANT. If you enable the system variables that permit InnoDB to create tables in Barracuda file format, you have other row storage formats to choose from. To do this, set innodb_file_per_table=1 and innodb_file_format=Barracuda. (See Section 12.5.3.1.4, "Using Individual (Per-Table) InnoDB Tablespaces.") Then you can specify a ROW_FORMAT value of COMPRESSED or DYNAMIC. For information about the characteristics of these row formats, see Section 5.4, "Choosing Table Storage Formats for Efficient Queries."

For MyISAM tables, a value of DYNAMIC or FIXED specifies variable-length or fixed-length row format. If you use the myisampack program to compress a MyISAM table (which also makes it read only), myisampack sets the row format to COMPRESSED.

- UNION [=] (tbl_list)

  This option is used for MERGE tables. It specifies a comma-separated list of the MyISAM tables that make up the MERGE table.

Trailing SELECT statement. If a *select_stmt* clause is specified (as a trailing SELECT statement), the table is created using the contents of the result set returned by the statement. Rows that duplicate values in a unique index are either ignored or replace existing rows according to whether IGNORE or REPLACE is specified. If neither is specified, the statement aborts with an error.

Trailing LIKE clause. If a trailing LIKE *tbl_name2* clause is given, the table is created as an empty copy of *tbl_name2*. You must have the SELECT privilege for *tbl_name2*. The copy includes the same column definitions, index definitions, and table options, with these exceptions: The DATA DIRECTORY and INDEX DIRECTORY table options are not copied, nor are foreign key definitions.

Foreign key support. The InnoDB storage engine provides foreign key support. A foreign key in a child table is indicated by FOREIGN KEY, an optional foreign key ID, a list of the columns that make up the foreign key, and a REFERENCES definition. The ID, if given, is ignored unless InnoDB automatically creates an index for the foreign key; in that case, *fk_name* becomes the index name. The REFERENCES definition names the parent table and columns to which the foreign key refers, and indicates what to do when a parent table row is deleted. The default actions are to prevent deletes or updates to the parent or child tables that would compromise referential integrity. The RESTRICT and NO ACTION actions are the same as specifying no action. The ON DEFAULT and ON UPDATE clauses may be given to specify explicit actions. The actions that InnoDB implements are CASCADE (delete or update the corresponding child table rows) and SET NULL (set the foreign key columns in the corresponding child table rows to NULL). The SET DEFAULT action is not implemented and InnoDB issues an error.

MATCH clauses in REFERENCE definitions are parsed but not used. (However, MATCH should be avoided because it causes ON DELETE and ON UPDATE to be ignored.) If you specify a foreign key definition for a storage engine other than InnoDB, the entire definition is ignored.

For further discussion of foreign keys, see Section 2.13, "Foreign Keys and Referential Integrity."

Partitioning options. MySQL supports table partitioning, a feature that enables you to define tables for which storage is divided into different sections. The following discussion provides a brief summary of the syntax for defining table partitions. See Section 2.6.2.5, "Using Partitioned Tables," for other discussion and examples, and the MySQL Reference Manual for additional information.

A partitioning description begins with PARTITION BY and either a partitioning function that computes a value for each table row, or a list of column names. The function value or column values for the row determine the partition in which to store the row. The description optionally may also include these components:

- A PARTITIONS *n* clause to indicate how many partitions the table has. *n* should be a positive integer. If this clause is present and any *partition_definition* clauses are also present, there must be *n* such definitions. The maximum number of partitions is 1024, including subpartitions.

- A description of how to divide partitions into subpartitions.

- A list of *partition_definition* clauses for the partitions. Each *partition_definition* describes the characteristics of a single partition. It provides a name for the partition, and can include a VALUES clause describing which partitioning function values map into the partition, other partition options, and a list of subpartition definitions. Each *subpartition_definition* clause is similar but describes a subpartition and cannot contain a VALUES clause or subpartition definitions.

The following list describes the different ways of assigning table rows to partitions. In these descriptions, *expr* is an integer-valued expression that refers to one or more columns in the table, and *col_list* is a comma-separated list of from one to sixteen column names. Column names can refer only to the table being created, not to other tables.

- RANGE (*expr*) partitioning associates each partition with a subset of the range of possible values of *expr*. It must be used in conjunction with partition definitions that each include a VALUES LESS THAN clause specifying the integer-valued upper limit on values that map into the partition. (NULL is not permitted as a limit; NULL values map into the first partition.) The VALUES clauses for successive partitions should list increasing upper limit values. The final partition can use MAXVALUE, which applies to all values not accounted for by the preceding partitions.

```
CREATE TABLE t (income BIGINT, ...)
PARTITION BY RANGE (income)
(
    PARTITION p0 VALUES LESS THAN (10000),
```

```
    PARTITION p1 VALUES LESS THAN (30000),
    PARTITION p2 VALUES LESS THAN (75000),
    PARTITION p3 VALUES LESS THAN MAXVALUE
);
```

- RANGE COLUMNS (col_list) partitioning is similar to RANGE(expr), but instead of a single expression, it uses a list of column names for partitioning. The VALUES LESS THAN clause for each partition lists a non-NULL literal value for each column defining the upper limits on the values permitted in the partition. For example, if the partition specification begins with PARTITION BY RANGE COLUMNS (col1, col2, col3), each VALUES clause is of the form VALUES LESS THAN (val1, val2, val3) specifying the maximum value for each column. Each column in col_list must be an integer, string, or temporal column other than BIT, BLOB, TEXT, ENUM, or SET. Each literal value in the VALUES LESS THAN clauses must have the same data type as the corresponding column in col_list.

- LIST (expr) partitioning associates each partition with a list of values. It must be used in conjunction with partition definitions that each include a VALUES IN clause enumerating a list of integer values that map into the partition. NULL is permitted, but MAXVALUE is not. If expr can evaluate to NULL, include NULL in one of the VALUES lists.

```
CREATE TABLE t (id INT NULL, ...)
PARTITION BY LIST(id)
(
  PARTITION p0 VALUES IN (1, 2, 3),
  PARTITION p1 VALUES IN (4, 5, 6, NULL)
);
```

- LIST COLUMNS (col_list) partitioning is analogous to RANGE COLUMNS(col_list), but for lists. Similar conditions on the permitted column types apply. VALUES IN is used rather than VALUES LESS THAN, but similar conditions apply on the types of values specified. (Unlike LIST, which requires partitioning by integer values, the VALUES IN clauses of LIST COLUMNS can specify noninteger values.) Each VALUES IN clause provides one or more parenthesized lists of values. The values in each list must have the same number of columns, but the number of lists in each clause can vary. For example, if a table contains two INT columns named i1 and i2 that you want to use for partitioning, you could use LIST COLUMNS like this:

```
PARTITION BY LIST COLUMNS (i1, i2)
(
  PARTITION p1 VALUES IN ((NULL, NULL)),
  PARTITION p2 VALUES IN ((0, 0), (0, 1), (0, 2)),
  PARTITION p3 VALUES IN ((1, 0), (1, 1))
)
```

- HASH (expr) partitioning associates rows with partitions based on expr values computed from row content. Typically, HASH() partitioning is used with a PARTITIONS n clause that specifies how many partitions to create. Row assignment is based on the remainder of dividing expr by n.

```
CREATE TABLE t (d DATE, ...)
PARTITION BY HASH(TO_DAYS(d))
PARTITIONS 5;
```

The HASH() partitioning expression can be preceded by LINEAR, which changes the hashing algorithm. One advantage of LINEAR is that certain partition management operations become more efficient, such as adding or dropping partitions with ALTER TABLE. However, it is also likely that rows will be less evenly distributed among partitions than if LINEAR is not used.

- KEY (col_list) partitioning is similar to HASH() partitioning, but you name the table columns from which to compute the hash value and the server supplies the hashing function. KEY() can be preceded by LINEAR.

If you include a list of partition definitions for HASH() or KEY() partitioning, the definitions should not have VALUES clauses. VALUES is used only with RANGE() and LIST().

expr must be deterministic, such that it always produces the same result for a given input. For example, expr can use ABS(), but not RAND(). CREATE TABLE returns an error if you use a function that is not permitted.

For RANGE() or LIST() partitioning, expr must evaluate to an integer value or NULL. For HASH(), expr must evaluate to a non-NULL, nonnegative integer, so if the expression references any noninteger column, it must convert the column values to integer. For example, if d is a DATE column, you can use TO_DAYS(d) to convert dates to number of days so that HASH(TO_DAYS(d)) is a valid hash function.

For KEY(), the arguments are column names, but these columns need not have integer data types.

Each partition_option value specifies an additional characteristic for a partition, chosen from the following list. (The descriptions use the term "partition" but these options can also be used in subpartition definitions.)

- COMMENT [=] 'str'

  A descriptive comment for the partition.

- DATA DIRECTORY [=] 'dir_name', INDEX DIRECTORY [=] 'dir_name'

  These options are similar to the previously described table options of the same names. They indicate where to store data or indexes for the partition. The default location is the database directory for the database that contains the table.

- MAX_ROWS [=] n, MIN_ROWS [=] n

  These options are hints that indicate the maximum and minimum number of rows you plan to store in the partition. n should be a positive integer.

- [STORAGE] ENGINE [=] engine_name

  The storage engine to use for the partition. Mixed engines are not supported, so if you use this clause, you must name the same engine for all partitions.

The following statements demonstrate some ways to use CREATE TABLE:

- Create a table with three columns. The id column is a PRIMARY KEY, and the last_name and first_name columns are used in a multiple-column index:

```
CREATE TABLE customer
(
  id          SMALLINT UNSIGNED NOT NULL AUTO_INCREMENT,
  last_name   CHAR(30) NOT NULL,
  first_name  CHAR(20) NOT NULL,
  PRIMARY KEY (id),
  INDEX (last_name, first_name)
);
```

- Create a temporary table and make it a MEMORY table for greater speed:

```
CREATE TEMPORARY TABLE tmp_table
  (id MEDIUMINT NOT NULL UNIQUE, name CHAR(40))
  ENGINE=MEMORY;
```

- Create a table as an empty copy of another table:

```
CREATE TABLE prez_copy LIKE president;
```

- Create a table using the contents of another table:

```
CREATE TABLE prez_copy SELECT * FROM president;
```

- Create a table using only partial contents of another table:

```
CREATE TABLE prez_alive SELECT last_name, first_name, birth
  FROM president WHERE death IS NULL;
```

If column definitions are specified for a table that is created and populated by means of a trailing SELECT statement, the definitions are applied after the table contents have been inserted into the table. For example, you can define that a selected column should be indexed as a PRIMARY KEY:

```
CREATE TABLE new_tbl (PRIMARY KEY (a)) SELECT a, b, c FROM old_tbl;
```

You can specify definitions for the columns in the new table to override the definitions that would be used by default based on the characteristics of the result set:

```
CREATE TABLE new_tbl
(a INT UNSIGNED NOT NULL AUTO_INCREMENT, b DATE, PRIMARY KEY (a))
  SELECT a, b, c FROM old_tbl;
```

CREATE TRIGGER

```
CREATE
  [DEFINER = definer_name]
  TRIGGER trigger_name trigger_time trigger_event
  ON tbl_name
  FOR EACH ROW trigger_stmt
```

Associates a trigger with a table, such that when a given event occurs for the table, the trigger activates and executes the triggered statement. By default, `tbl_name` is assumed to be in the default database. To name a table in a specific database, give the name in `db_name.tbl_name` format. CREATE TRIGGER requires the TRIGGER privilege for the table with which the trigger is associated.

When the trigger activates, the DEFINER clause determines the security context (the account to use for access checking), as described in Section 4.3, "Security for Views and Stored Programs." The default is to use the account for the user who executes the CREATE TRIGGER statement. The relevant account must have the TRIGGER privilege for the table, the SELECT privilege for `tbl_name` if the trigger definition refers to any of its columns using NEW or OLD, and the UPDATE privilege for `tbl_name` if the trigger definition modifies any of its columns using SET NEW.`col_name`. The account must also have any privileges normally required for the statements within the trigger definition.

The `trigger_time` value is either BEFORE or AFTER, indicating that the triggered statement should be executed before or after each row processed by the statement that caused the trigger to be activated.

The `trigger_event` value should be INSERT, UPDATE, or DELETE to indicate what kind of statement causes trigger activation.

`trigger_stmt` is the SQL statement that represents the body of the trigger. It should be a single SQL statement. To use multiple statements, enclose them within BEGIN and END to form a compound statement. (See Section E.2, "SQL Statement Syntax (Compound Statements).")

The syntax OLD.`col_name` can be used to refer to columns in the old row to be deleted or updated in a DELETE or UPDATE trigger. Similarly, NEW.`col_name` can be used to refer to columns in the new row to be inserted or updated in an INSERT or UPDATE trigger. OLD and NEW are not case sensitive.

In a BEFORE trigger, you can change the values in the new row by using a SET statement:

```
SET NEW.col_name = value
```

At trigger creation time, the current value of the `sql_mode` system variable is saved for use when the trigger executes.

Triggers do not take parameters, and, like stored functions, cannot execute statements that produce a result set.

CREATE USER

```
CREATE USER account [auth_info]
  [, account [auth_info] ] ...

auth_info:
    IDENTIFIED BY [PASSWORD] 'password'
  | IDENTIFIED WITH auth_plugin [AS 'auth_string']
```

Creates one or more MySQL accounts. This statement requires the global CREATE USER privilege or the INSERT privilege for the mysql database.

For each account, a row is created in the mysql.user table with no privileges. It is an error if the account already exists. Name each account in 'user_name'@'host_name' format, as described in Section 13.2.1.1, "Specifying Account Names."

The auth_info clause, if present, specifies whether the account authenticates using a password or by means of an authentication plugin. For details, see Section 13.2.1.3, "Specifying How an Account Authenticates." Clients can use the account to connect to the server without authenticating if you don't you specify an IDENTIFIED BY clause with a nonempty password or an IDENTIFIED WITH clause. This is insecure and should be avoided.

```
CREATE USER 'myname'@'localhost' IDENTIFIED BY 'mypass';
```

CREATE VIEW

```
CREATE [OR REPLACE]
    [ALGORITHM = {MERGE | TEMPTABLE | UNDEFINED}]
    [DEFINER = definer_name]
    [SQL SECURITY = {DEFINER | INVOKER}]
    VIEW view_name [(col_list)] AS select_stmt
    [WITH [CASCADED | LOCAL] CHECK OPTION]
```

Creates a view. By default, an error occurs if a view with the same name already exists. If the OR REPLACE clause is given, the new view replaces the old one.

col_list, if present, provides names for the columns returned by the view. There must be a name for each column. If col_list is omitted, the view column names come from the columns selected by the SELECT statement in the view definition.

select_stmt is a SELECT statement that defines the view. It can refer to tables or other views.

To create the view, you must have the CREATE VIEW privilege for it, some privilege for every column selected by select_stmt, and the SELECT privilege for every column referred to elsewhere in select_stmt. You must also have the DROP privilege for the view if you use OR REPLACE.

When the view is invoked, the DEFINER and SQL SECURITY clauses determine the security context (the account to use for access checking), as described in Section 4.3, "Security for Views and Stored Programs." The default is to use the account for the user who executes the CREATE VIEW statement.

The ALGORITHM clause determines how the view is processed. For MERGE, when you issue a statement that references the view, the view definition is merged into the statement. The resulting statement is executed. For TEMPTABLE, temporary tables are used during the course of executing the view. For UNDEFINED, the server chooses which algorithm to use. The default is UNDEFINED.

The WITH CHECK OPTION clause applies to updatable views (views that can be used with UPDATE or other table-modifying statements to update the underlying table). It permits use of the view to insert or update only those rows in the underlying table for which the WHERE clause in the SELECT statement is true. The CASCADED and LOCAL keywords apply in the case that the view definition refers to other views. With CASCADED, checks cascade to underlying views. With LOCAL, checks are restricted to the current view. The default is CASCADED if neither is given.

DEALLOCATE PREPARE

```
{DEALLOCATE | DROP} PREPARE stmt_name
```

Deallocates a prepared statement named stmt_name that previously was prepared with PREPARE. After deallocation, the statement cannot be executed again.

DELETE

```
DELETE [LOW_PRIORITY] [QUICK] [IGNORE]
  FROM tbl_name
  [PARTITION (partition_name [, partition_name] ...)]
  [WHERE where_expr] [ORDER BY ...] [LIMIT n]

DELETE [LOW_PRIORITY] [QUICK] [IGNORE]
  tbl_list
  FROM tbl_refs
  [WHERE where_expr]

DELETE [LOW_PRIORITY] [QUICK] [IGNORE]
  FROM tbl_list
  USING tbl_refs
  [WHERE where_expr]

tbl_list:
  tbl_name[.*]
  [PARTITION (partition_name [, partition_name] ...)]
  [, tbl_name[.*]
    [PARTITION (partition_name [, partition_name] ...)]
  ] ...
```

DELETE removes rows from a table and returns a deleted-row count. As of MySQL 5.6.2, DELETE supports a PARTITION clause for partitioned tables to indicate the partitions or subpartitions from which to delete rows. In this case, if a row to be deleted is not in any named partition, it remains unchanged.

The first form of the DELETE statement deletes rows from the table tbl_name. The second and third forms can delete rows from multiple tables, or delete rows based on conditions that involve multiple tables. The syntax for tbl_refs is like that for SELECT, except that you cannot specify a subquery as a table.

The rows deleted are those that match the conditions specified in the WHERE clause:

```
DELETE FROM score WHERE event_id = 14;
DELETE FROM member WHERE expiration < CURDATE();
```

If the WHERE clause is omitted, *all rows in the table are deleted*. (Another way to empty a table, if you don't need a row count, is to use TRUNCATE TABLE.)

LOW_PRIORITY causes the statement to be deferred until no clients are reading from the table. This option is effective only for storage engines that use table-level locking, such as MyISAM or MEMORY.

For MyISAM tables, specifying QUICK may make the statement quicker; the MyISAM storage engine does not perform its usual index tree leaf merging.

With the IGNORE modifier, errors that occur while rows are being deleted are ignored. These errors generate warnings instead.

If the LIMIT clause is given, the value *n* specifies the maximum number of rows to delete.

With ORDER BY, rows are deleted in the resulting sort order. Combined with LIMIT, this provides more precise control over which rows are deleted. ORDER BY has the same syntax as for SELECT.

The second and third forms of DELETE enable rows to be deleted from multiple tables at once. They also enable you to identify the rows to delete based on joins between tables. Names in the list of tables from which rows are to be deleted may be given as *tbl_name* or *tbl_name.**; the latter form is supported for ODBC compatibility.

The *tbl_refs* clause specifies which tables to join for determination of the rows to delete. This clause may declare aliases for the tables named therein. Other parts of the statement may refer to but not declare table aliases.

To delete rows in t1 having id values that match those in t2, use the first multiple-table syntax like this:

```
DELETE t1 FROM t1 INNER JOIN t2 WHERE t1.id = t2.id;
```

Or the second syntax like this:

```
DELETE FROM t1 USING t1 INNER JOIN t2 WHERE t1.id = t2.id;
```

Multiple-table DELETE statements do not permit ORDER BY or LIMIT clauses. Also, the WHERE clause cannot include a subquery that selects rows from a table from which rows are deleted.

DESCRIBE

```
{DESCRIBE | DESC} tbl_name [col_name | 'pattern']
{DESCRIBE | DESC} stmt
```

DESCRIBE with a table or view name produces the same output as SHOW COLUMNS. For more information, see the entry for SHOW. With this syntax, a trailing column name restricts output to information for the given column. A trailing string is interpreted as a pattern, as for the LIKE operator, and restricts output to those columns having names that match the pattern.

- Display output for the last_name column of the president table:

  ```
  DESCRIBE president last_name;
  ```

- Display output for both the last_name and first_name columns of the president table:

  ```
  DESCRIBE president '%name';
  ```

DESCRIBE with a following statement is a synonym for EXPLAIN. Before MySQL 5.6.3, the statement must be a SELECT. As of 5.6.3, the statement can be SELECT, DELETE, INSERT, REPLACE, or UPDATE. For more information, see the entry for EXPLAIN.

DO

```
DO expr [, expr] ...
```

Evaluates the expressions without returning any results. This makes DO more convenient than SELECT for expression evaluation because you need not deal with a result set. For example, DO can be used for setting variables or for invoking functions that you are interested in primarily for their side effects rather than for their return values.

```
DO @sidea := 3, @sideb := 4, @sidec := SQRT(@sidea*@sidea+@sideb*@sideb);
DO RELEASE_LOCK('mylock');
```

DROP DATABASE

```
DROP DATABASE [IF EXISTS] db_name
```

Removes the given database and its contents. You must have the DROP privilege for the database.

The IF EXISTS clause may be specified to suppress the error that normally results if the database does not exist. In this case, a warning is generated instead.

A database is represented by a directory under the data directory. The server deletes only files and directories that it can identify as having been created by itself (for example, .frm files). It does not delete other files and directories. If you have put nontable files in that directory, those files are not deleted by the DROP DATABASE statement. This results in failure to remove the database directory and DROP DATABASE fails. In that case, the database will continue to be listed by SHOW DATABASES. To correct this problem, remove any extraneous files and subdirectories manually, and then issue the DROP DATABASE statement again.

A successful DROP DATABASE returns a row count that indicates the number of tables and views dropped. (This actually is the number of .frm files removed, which amounts to the same thing.)

DROP EVENT

```
DROP EVENT [IF EXISTS] event_name
```

Removes the given event. The IF EXISTS clause may be specified to suppress the error that normally results if an event does not exist. In this case, a warning is generated instead. You must have the EVENT privilege for the database to which the event belongs.

DROP FUNCTION, DROP PROCEDURE

```
DROP {FUNCTION | PROCEDURE} [IF EXISTS] routine_name
```

Removes the named stored function or stored procedure. These statements require the ALTER ROUTINE privilege for the given routine.

The IF EXISTS clause may be specified to suppress the error that normally results if the routine does not exist. In this case, a warning is generated instead.

DROP INDEX

```
DROP INDEX index_name ON tbl_name
```

Removes the index index_name from the table tbl_name. Internally, MySQL handles this statement as an ALTER TABLE DROP INDEX statement. For details, see the entry for ALTER TABLE. To use DROP INDEX to drop a PRIMARY KEY, the index name is PRIMARY, which must be quoted as an identifier:

```
DROP INDEX `PRIMARY` ON tbl_name;
```

DROP TABLE

```
DROP [TEMPORARY] {TABLE | TABLES} [IF EXISTS]
    tbl_name [, tbl_name] ...
    [RESTRICT | CASCADE]
```

Removes each named table from the database to which it belongs. With the TEMPORARY keyword, drops only TEMPORARY tables.

The IF EXISTS clause may be specified to suppress the error that normally results if a table does not exist. In this case, a warning is generated instead.

The RESTRICT and CASCADE keywords are parsed but ignored and have no effect.

DROP TRIGGER

```
DROP TRIGGER [IF EXISTS] trigger_name
```

Removes a trigger. By default, the trigger is dropped in the default database. To drop the trigger from a specific database, give the name in db_name.trigger_name format. DROP TRIGGER requires the TRIGGER privilege for the table with which the trigger is associated.

The IF EXISTS clause may be specified to suppress the error that normally results if the trigger does not exist. In this case, a warning is generated instead.

If a table has triggers, dropping the table also drops its triggers.

DROP USER

```
DROP USER account [, account] ...
```

DROP USER removes all grant table rows associated with each account. This statement requires the global CREATE USER privilege or the DELETE privilege for the mysql database.

DROP USER drops each account and any privileges held by it, but not any databases or other objects created by the dropped account. Name each account in 'user_name'@'host_name' format, as described in Section 13.2.1.1, "Specifying Account Names." It is an error if the account does not exist.

```
DROP USER 'myname'@'localhost';
```

DROP VIEW

```
DROP VIEW [IF EXISTS]
  view_name [, view_name] ...
  [RESTRICT | CASCADE]
```

Removes each named view from the database to which it belongs. You must have the DROP privilege for the view.

The IF EXISTS clause may be specified to suppress the error that normally results if a view does not exist. In this case, a warning is generated instead.

The RESTRICT and CASCADE keywords are parsed but ignored and have no effect.

EXECUTE

```
EXECUTE stmt_name [USING @var_name [, @var_name] ...]
```

Executes a prepared statement named stmt_name that was previously prepared with PREPARE. The USING clause must be given if the prepared statement contains any placeholder markers. The clause should provide a comma-separated list of user variables that provides values for each successive placeholder in the statement.

EXPLAIN

```
EXPLAIN tbl_name [col_name | 'pattern']
```

```
EXPLAIN
  [EXTENDED | PARTITIONS | FORMAT = {TRADITIONAL | JSON}]
  {SELECT ... | DELETE ... | INSERT ... | REPLACE ... | UPDATE ...}
```

The first form of this statement is equivalent to DESCRIBE tbl_name. For more information the entry for DESCRIBE.

The second form of the EXPLAIN statement provides information about the query execution plan that the MySQL optimizer would generate for processing the statement following the EXPLAIN keyword:

```
EXPLAIN SELECT score.* FROM score INNER JOIN grade_event
ON score.event_id = grade_event.event_id AND grade_event.event_id = 14;
```

Before MySQL 5.6.3, the statement must be a SELECT. As of 5.6.3, the statement can be SELECT, DELETE, INSERT, REPLACE, or UPDATE.

Following the EXPLAIN keyword, you can specify an optional indicator for the type of output to produce:

- EXTENDED causes EXPLAIN to produce additional execution plan information; use SHOW WARNINGS immediately after EXPLAIN to see this information.

- PARTITIONS produces an extra output column containing information about partitions.

- FORMAT indicates whether to produce output in "traditional" (default) format or JSON format. JSON output includes extended and partition information as applicable. This option was introduced in MySQL 5.6.5.

In the default output format, EXPLAIN produces one or more rows containing the following columns:

- id

  The ID number for the SELECT to which this output row applies. There can be more than one SELECT if the statement includes subqueries or is a UNION.

- select_type

  The type of the SELECT to which this output row applies, as shown in the following table.

Type	Meaning
SIMPLE	A SELECT with no UNION or subquery parts
PRIMARY	The outermost or leftmost SELECT
UNION	The second or later SELECT in a UNION
DEPENDENT UNION	Like UNION, but dependent on an outer query
UNION RESULT	The result of a UNION
SUBQUERY	The first SELECT in a subquery
DEPENDENT SUBQUERY	Like SUBQUERY, but dependent on an outer query
DERIVED	A subquery in the FROM clause
UNCACHEABLE SUBQUERY	A subquery result that cannot be cached
UNCACHEABLE UNION	The second or later select of an uncacheable subquery UNION

- `table`

The table to which the output row refers.

- `partitions`

The partitions that would be used. This column is displayed if the `PARTITIONS` option is present. For nonpartitioned tables, the value is `NULL`.

- `type`

The type of join that MySQL will perform. From best to worst, the possible types are `system`, `const`, `eq_ref`, `ref`, `ref_or_null`, `index_merge`, `unique_subquery`, `index_subquery`, `range`, `index`, and `ALL`. The better types are more restrictive, meaning that MySQL has to look at fewer rows from the table when performing the retrieval.

- `possible_keys`

The indexes that MySQL considers candidates for finding rows in the table named in the `table` column. A value of `NULL` means that no indexes were found.

- `key`

The index that MySQL actually will use for finding rows in the table. (There might be several keys listed here if MySQL uses an `index_merge` join type, because that optimization uses several indexes to process the query.) A value of `NULL` indicates that no index will be used.

- `key_len`

How much of the index will be used. This will be less than the full index row length if MySQL will use a leftmost prefix of the index.

- `ref`

The values to which MySQL will compare index values. The word `const` or '???' means the comparison is against a constant; a column name indicates a column-to-column comparison.

- `rows`

An estimate of the number of rows from the table that MySQL must examine to perform the query. The product of the values in this column is an estimate of the total number of row combinations that must be examined from all tables.

- `filtered`

An estimated percentage of the rows that will be joined with previous tables. This column is displayed if the `EXTENDED` option is present.

- `Extra`

Other information about the execution plan. The value can be blank or contain one or more values such as those following:

- Using `filesort`: Index values must be written to a file and sorted so that the associated rows can be retrieved in sorted order.

- Using `index`: MySQL can retrieve information for the table using only information in the index without examining data rows.

- Using `temporary`: A temporary table must be created.

- Using `where`: Information in the WHERE clause of the SELECT statement is used to select rows.

Other values might appear in this field that are not listed here; see the MySQL Reference Manual for the current set of `Extra` values.

FLUSH

```
FLUSH [NO_WRITE_TO_BINLOG | LOCAL] option [, option] ...
```

Flushes internal caches used by the server. You must have the RELOAD privilege, and possibly other privileges for certain operations, as noted later.

If binary logging is enabled, MySQL writes most FLUSH statements to the binary log unless the NO_WRITE_TO_BINLOG or LOCAL option is given. Exceptions that are not logged in any case are FLUSH LOGS, FLUSH MASTER, FLUSH SLAVE, and both forms of FLUSH TABLES WITH READ LOCK. These are not logged to avoid problems on replication slaves.

Each `option` value should be one of the items in the following list. For the TABLES options, TABLE is a synonym. None of the TABLES options can be combined with other options in the same FLUSH statement.

- DES_KEY_FILE

  Reloads the DES key file used by the DES_ENCRYPT() and DES_DECRYPT() functions.

- HOSTS

  Flushes the host cache. This may be necessary if connections from some client host result in more than `max_connect_errors` errors and the server starts blocking connections from that host.

- [`log_type`] LOGS

  Flushes the log files by closing and reopening them. If the binary log or relay log are enabled, this causes the next file in the numbered log file sequence to be opened. As of MySQL 5.5.3, the LOGS keyword can be preceded by a specifier indicating which particular log to flush. BINARY, ERROR, GENERAL, RELAY, or SLOW flushes the binary log, error log, general query log, slave relay log, or slow query log, respectively. ENGINE tells storage engines to flush any logs they maintain that they can flush. InnoDB flushes its logs and takes a checkpoint.

- PRIVILEGES

Reloads the grant tables. It is necessary to tell the server to reload these tables explicitly if you modify them directly using statements such as INSERT or UPDATE, If you modify the tables with GRANT or REVOKE, the server reloads its in-memory copies of the tables automatically. This option also affects account resource management limits; it has the same effect as the USER_RESOURCES option.

- QUERY CACHE

Flushes the query cache to defragment it, without removing statements from the cache. (To clear the cache, use RESET QUERY CACHE.)

- STATUS

Reinitializes the server status variables.

- TABLES [tbl_name [, tbl_name] ...]

Without any table names, closes all open tables in the table cache. With a comma-separated list of one or more table names, flushes those tables rather than the entire table cache. As of MySQL 5.5.3, this operation cannot be used while any LOCK TABLES is in effect for READ locks. Use the corresponding WITH READ LOCK syntax to read-lock and flush tables.

If the query cache is operational, FLUSH TABLES also flushes the query cache.

- TABLES WITH READ LOCK

Flushes all tables in all databases and then places a global read lock on them, which is held until you issue an UNLOCK TABLES statement. This statement permits clients to read tables, but prohibits any changes from being made, which is useful for getting a backup for your entire server with the guarantee that no tables will change during the backup period. The disadvantage of doing this, from the client point of view, is that the period during which updates are prohibited is greater.

- TABLES tbl_name [, tbl_name] ... WITH READ LOCK

Flushes the named tables and acquires read locks for them, which are held until you issue an UNLOCK TABLES, LOCK TABLES, or START TRANSACTION statement. In addition to RELOAD, you must have the LOCK TABLES privilege for each table. This operation applies only to base tables. It ignores TEMPORARY tables and produces an error for views. This syntax was introduced in MySQL 5.5.3.

- USER_RESOURCES

Resets the per-hour counters for account resource management limits (such as MAX_QUERIES_PER_HOUR). Accounts that have reached their limits can once again proceed in their activities. This option does not affect any MAX_USER_CONNECTIONS limit; it is not a per-hour restriction.

GRANT

```
GRANT priv_type [(col_list)] [, priv_type [(col_list)] ] ...
  ON [TABLE | FUNCTION | PROCEDURE]
    {*.* | * | db_name.* | db_name.tbl_name
      | tbl_name | db_name.routine_name}
  TO account [auth_info] [, account [auth_info] ] ...
  [REQUIRE security_options]
  [WITH grant_or_resource_options]

GRANT PROXY ON account
  TO account [auth_info] [, account [auth_info] ] ...
  [WITH GRANT OPTION]

auth_info:
    IDENTIFIED BY [PASSWORD] 'password'
  | IDENTIFIED WITH auth_plugin [AS 'auth_string']
```

The GRANT statement grants access privileges to one or more MySQL accounts. To use this statement, you must have the GRANT OPTION privilege as well as the privileges that you are trying to grant.

The syntax for granting the PROXY privilege is more restricted than for other privileges: The privilege must be named by itself, no REQUIRE clause is permitted, and WITH is permitted only with GRANT OPTION.

Each priv_type value specifies a privilege to be granted, chosen from the following table. ALL and PROXY are used by themselves. For the other privileges, you may specify one or more of them as a comma-separated list. ALL signifies the combination of all the other privileges available at a given level, except for GRANT OPTION, which must be granted separately or by adding a WITH GRANT OPTION clause. For example, at the table level, ALL grants only privileges that apply to tables.

Privilege Name	Operation Enabled by Privilege
ALTER	Alter tables and indexes
ALTER ROUTINE	Alter or drop stored functions and procedures
CREATE	Create databases and tables
CREATE ROUTINE	Create stored functions and procedures
CREATE TABLESPACE	Create, drop, or alter tablespaces
CREATE TEMPORARY TABLES	Create temporary tables using TEMPORARY keyword
CREATE USER	Use high-level account-management statements
CREATE VIEW	Create views
DELETE	Delete rows from tables
DROP	Remove databases, tables, and other objects

Privilege Name	Operation Enabled by Privilege
EVENT	Create, drop, or alter events for event scheduler
EXECUTE	Execute stored functions and procedures
FILE	Read and write files on the server host
GRANT OPTION	Grant privileges to other accounts
INDEX	Create or drop indexes
INSERT	Insert new rows into tables
LOCK TABLES	Explicitly lock tables with LOCK TABLES statements
PROCESS	View information about threads executing within the server
PROXY	User proxying
REFERENCES	Unused (reserved for future use)
RELOAD	Reload grant tables or flush logs or caches
REPLICATION CLIENT	Ask about master and slave server locations
REPLICATION SLAVE	Act as replication slave server
SELECT	Retrieve rows from tables
SHOW DATABASES	See all database names with SHOW DATABASES
SHOW VIEW	See view definitions with SHOW CREATE VIEW
SHUTDOWN	Shut down the server
SUPER	Kill threads and perform other supervisory operations
TRIGGER	Create or drop triggers
UPDATE	Modify table rows
ALL [PRIVILEGES]	All operations (except GRANT and REVOKE)
USAGE	A special "no privileges" privilege

The PROXY privilege was introduced in MySQL 5.5.7.

The LOCK TABLES privilege can be exercised only on tables for which you also have the SELECT privilege, but it enables you to place any kind of lock, not just read locks.

You can always view or kill your own threads. The PROCESS or SUPER privilege enables you to view or kill, respectively, threads that belong to any account, not just your own. ALTER ROUTINE and CREATE ROUTINE apply only to stored routines, not to user-defined functions (UDFs).

The ON clause specifies how widely to grant privileges, as shown in the following table.

Privilege Specifier	Level at Which Privileges Apply
ON *.*	Global privileges: all databases, all objects in databases
ON *	Database-level privileges for the default database; error if there is no default database
ON db_name.*	Database privileges: all objects in the named database
ON db_name.tbl_name	Table privileges: all columns in the named table
ON tbl_name	Table privileges: all columns in the named table in the default database
ON db_name.routine_name	Privileges for the named routine in the named database
ON account	Proxy privilege: account is the proxied user

To specify explicitly the type of object to which the privileges apply if there is an ambiguity, you can include a TABLE, FUNCTION, or PROCEDURE keyword (for example, ON TABLE mydb.mytbl or ON FUNCTION mydb.myfunc).

To grant table or column privileges, the table must already exist.

When you use ALL as a privilege name, it grants only those privileges that are available at the level for which you are granting privileges. For example, RELOAD is available only as a global privilege, so it is granted by GRANT ALL if you specify ON *.*, but not if you specify ON db_name.*. In the latter case, only those privileges that apply to databases are granted. ALL can be used only when granting global, database, table, or routine privileges.

USAGE means "no privileges." It applies only at the global level.

GRANT OPTION applies to all privileges granted at a given level. For example, if you grant SELECT and INSERT for a given database to an account, you cannot make just one of them grantable by that account.

When a table is named in the ON clause, a privilege may be made column-specific by following it with a list of one or more comma-separated column names in a (col_list) clause. (This applies only for the INSERT, REFERENCES, SELECT, and UPDATE privileges, which are the only ones that may be granted on a column-specific basis.)

The TO clause specifies one or more accounts to which the privileges should be granted. Name each account in 'user_name'@'host_name' format, as described in Section 13.2.1.1, "Specifying Account Names."

Each account name may be followed by an optional auth_info clause to specify whether the account authenticates using a password or by means of an authentication plugin. The syntax is the same as for CREATE USER; see the description of that statement. For additional details, see Section 13.2.1.3, "Specifying How an Account Authenticates." Any password specified for an existing account replaces its current password.

If the named account does not exist, GRANT creates it. In this case, clients can use the account to connect to the server without authenticating if you don't specify authentication information (an IDENTIFIED BY clause with a nonempty password or an IDENTIFIED WITH clause). To prevent GRANT from creating an account unless the statement includes authentication information, enable the NO_AUTO_CREATE_USER SQL mode.

Database, table, column, and routine names, if quoted, must be quoted using identifier quoting characters. Usernames and hostnames can be quoted using identifier or string quoting characters. For example:

```
GRANT INSERT (`mycol`) ON `test`.`t` TO 'myuser'@'localhost';
```

The REQUIRE clause, if given, enables you to specify that secure connections are to be used and what kinds of information the client is required to supply. The REQUIRE keyword may be followed by:

- NONE: Secure connections are not required.

- SSL: A generic connection type; it requires that connections for the account use SSL.

- X509: The user must supply a valid X509 certificate. In this case, the client can present any X509 certificate; it doesn't matter what its contents are other than that it is valid.

- One or more of the following options to require that the connection be established with certain characteristics:

  - CIPHER 'str': The connection must be established with 'str' as its encryption cipher.

  - ISSUER 'str': The client certificate must have 'str' as the certificate issuer value.

  - SUBJECT 'str': The client certificate must have 'str' as the certificate subject value.

  If you give more than one of these options, they may optionally be separated by AND. Order of the options doesn't matter.

The WITH clause, if given, is used to specify that the account is able to grant other accounts the privileges that it holds itself, and to place limits on the account's resource consumption. The permitted options are shown in the following list. You may specify more than one option; order does not matter.

- GRANT OPTION: This account can grant its own privileges to other accounts, including the right to grant privileges.

- MAX_CONNECTIONS_PER_HOUR *n*: The account can make *n* connections to the server per hour.

- MAX_QUERIES_PER_HOUR *n*: The account can issue *n* statements per hour.

- MAX_UPDATES_PER_HOUR *n*: The account can issue *n* statements that modify data per hour.

- MAX_USER_CONNECTIONS *n*: The account can make a maximum of *n* simultaneous connections to the server.

For MAX_CONNECTIONS_PER_HOUR, MAX_QUERIES_PER_HOUR, and MAX_UPDATES_PER_HOUR, a value of 0 means "no limit." For MAX_USER_CONNECTIONS, a value of 0 means that the value of the max_user_connections system variable applies.

The following statements demonstrate some ways to use the GRANT statement. For other examples, see Section 13.2.2, "Granting Privileges." For information on enabling SSL, see Section 13.5, "Setting Up Secure Connections Using SSL." In each case, no IDENTIFIED clause is given because it is assumed that the account has already been created and assigned a password with CREATE USER.

- Enable paul to access all tables in the sampdb database from any host. The following two statements are equivalent because omitting the hostname part of an account identifier is equivalent to specifying % as the hostname:

  ```
  GRANT ALL ON sampdb.* TO 'paul';
  GRANT ALL ON sampdb.* TO 'paul'@'%';
  ```

- Grant an account read-only privileges for the tables in the menagerie database. The lookonly user can connect from any host in the xyz.com domain:

  ```
  GRANT SELECT ON menagerie.* TO 'lookonly'@'%.xyz.com';
  ```

- Grant an account full privileges, but only for the member table in the sampdb database. The member_mgr user can connect from a single host:

  ```
  GRANT ALL ON sampdb.member TO 'member_mgr'@'boa.example.com';
  ```

- Grant an account superuser privileges, including the ability to grant privileges to other users. The user must connect from the local host:

  ```
  GRANT ALL ON *.* TO 'superduper'@'localhost' WITH GRANT OPTION;
  ```

- Grant an anonymous user full access to the menagerie database:

  ```
  GRANT ALL ON menagerie.* TO ''@'localhost';
  ```

- Grant to a report-generator account permission to execute stored routines in the admin database:

  ```
  GRANT EXECUTE ON admin.* TO 'report_generator'@'localhost';
  ```

- Grant an account full access to the privatedb database, but require that connections be made using SSL with a valid X509 certificate:

  ```
  GRANT ALL ON privatedb.* TO 'paranoid'@'%.mydomain.com' REQUIRE X509;
  ```

- Grant an account limited access such that it can issue only 100 statements per hour, of which at most 10 may be updates:

```
GRANT ALL ON test.* TO 'caleb'@'localhost'
  WITH MAX_QUERIES_PER_HOUR 100 MAX_UPDATES_PER_HOUR 10;
```

- Grant clint permission to be a proxy for bart:

```
GRANT PROXY ON 'bart'@'localhost' TO 'clint'@'localhost';
```

HANDLER

```
HANDLER tbl_name OPEN [[AS] alias_name]

HANDLER tbl_name READ
  {FIRST | NEXT}
  [where_clause] [limit_clause]

HANDLER tbl_name READ index_name
  {FIRST | NEXT | PREV | LAST }
  [where_clause] [limit_clause]

HANDLER tbl_name READ index_name
  {< | <= | = | => | >} (expr_list)
  [where_clause] [limit_clause]

HANDLER tbl_name CLOSE
```

HANDLER provides a low-level interface to the InnoDB and MyISAM storage engines that bypasses the optimizer and accesses table contents directly. To access a table through the HANDLER interface, first use HANDLER … OPEN to open it. The table remains available for use until you issue a HANDLER … CLOSE statement to close it explicitly or until or the session terminates. While the table is open, use HANDLER … READ to access the table's contents.

HANDLER provides no protection against concurrent updates. It does not lock the table, so it's possible for the table to be modified while HANDLER has it open, and there is no guarantee that the modifications will be reflected in the rows that you read from the table.

Be aware that some statements can reset an open handler and cause it to lose its position, such as statements within the handler session that use any table, or FLUSH TABLES in any session.

INSERT

```
INSERT [DELAYED | LOW_PRIORITY | HIGH_PRIORITY] [IGNORE]
  [INTO] tbl_name
  [PARTITION (partition_name [, partition_name] ...)]
  [(col_list)]
  {VALUES | VALUE} (expr [, expr] ...) [, (...)] ...
  [ON DUPLICATE KEY UPDATE col_name=expr [, col_name=expr] ...]
```

```
INSERT [DELAYED | LOW_PRIORITY | HIGH_PRIORITY] [IGNORE]
  [INTO] tbl_name
  [PARTITION (partition_name [, partition_name] ...)]
  SET col_name=expr [, col_name=expr] ...
  [ON DUPLICATE KEY UPDATE col_name=expr [, col_name=expr] ...]

INSERT [LOW_PRIORITY | HIGH_PRIORITY] [IGNORE]
  [INTO] tbl_name
  [PARTITION (partition_name [, partition_name] ...)]
  [(col_list)]
  {SELECT ... | (SELECT ...)}
  [ON DUPLICATE KEY UPDATE col_name=expr [, col_name=expr] ...]
```

Inserts rows into an existing table *tbl_name* and returns the number of rows inserted. As of MySQL 5.6.2, INSERT supports a PARTITION clause for partitioned tables to indicate the partitions or subpartitions into which to insert rows. In this case, if a row would not be inserted in any named partition, an error occurs.

Syntax for INSERT has three forms:

The first form of INSERT requires a VALUES() list that specifies all values to be inserted. If no *col_list* is given, the VALUES() list must specify one value for each column in the table. If a *col_list* is given consisting of one or more comma-separated column names, one value per column must be specified in the VALUES() list. Columns not named in the column list are set to their default values. Multiple value lists may be specified, enabling multiple rows to be inserted using a single INSERT statement.

```
INSERT INTO absence (student_id, date) VALUES(14,'2011-11-03'),(34,NOW());
```

The *col_list* and VALUES() list may be empty, which can be used as follows to create a row for which all columns are set to their default values:

```
INSERT INTO t () VALUES();
```

The second form of INSERT inserts columns named in the SET clause to the values given by the corresponding expressions. Columns not named are set to their default values.

```
INSERT INTO absence SET student_id = 14, date = '2011-11-03';
INSERT INTO absence SET student_id = 34, date = NOW();
```

The word DEFAULT may be used in a VALUES() list or SET clause to set a column to its default value explicitly without knowing what the default value is. More generally, to refer to a column's default value in expressions, you can use DEFAULT(*col_name*). The following statement sets the column i to 0 if its default value is NULL and to 1 otherwise:

```
INSERT INTO t SET i = IF(DEFAULT(i) IS NULL,1,0);
```

The third form of INSERT inserts into *tbl_name* the rows retrieved by the SELECT statement. The rows must contain as many columns as are in *tbl_name*, or as many columns as are named in *col_list* if a column list is specified. When a column list is specified, any columns not named in the list are set to their default values.

```
INSERT INTO score (student_id, score, event_id)
  SELECT student_id, 100 AS score, 15 AS event_id FROM student;
```

You cannot use a subquery to select rows from the same table into which you are inserting them.

If strict SQL mode is in effect when an INSERT executes, it is an error to omit a column that has no DEFAULT clause in its definition or to specify its value by using DEFAULT.

If inserting a row would result in a duplicate key value in a unique index, INSERT terminates in error and no more rows are inserted. Adding IGNORE causes such rows not to be inserted and no error occurs. In strict SQL mode, IGNORE also causes data conversion errors that otherwise would terminate the statement to be treated as nonfatal warnings. Columns are set to the nearest legal value in this case.

The ON DUPLICATE KEY UPDATE clause applies for rows that would result in a duplicate-key violation for a unique-valued index. With this clause, the INSERT is converted to an UPDATE that modifies the column of the existing row using the column assignments following the UPDATE keyword. If an update did occur, the rows-affected count returned by INSERT is 2 rather than 1.

The DELAYED, LOW_PRIORITY, and HIGH_PRIORITY options affect execution scheduling:

- DELAYED causes the rows to be placed into a queue for later insertion, and the statement returns immediately so that the client may continue on without waiting. However, in this case, LAST_INSERT_ID() will not return the AUTO_INCREMENT value for any AUTO_INCREMENT column in the table. DELAYED inserts work for MyISAM, MEMORY, and ARCHIVE tables. DELAYED is ignored for INSERT INTO ... SELECT and INSERT INTO ... ON DUPLICATE KEY UPDATE. DELAYED is ignored if mixed with stored functions or triggers such that an INSERT refers to stored functions that access tables or triggers or the INSERT is invoked within a stored function or trigger. DELAYED is not supported for views or partitioned tables.

  DELAYED is not supported for InnoDB, the default storage engine. Also, DELAYED is deprecated as of MySQL 5.6.6 and will disappear at some point, so it's probably best to avoid it.

- LOW_PRIORITY causes the statement to be deferred until no clients are reading from the table.

- HIGH_PRIORITY causes the effect of the --low-priority-updates server option to be canceled for a single statement. (If the server is started with this option, it lowers the priority of INSERT and other update statements, the same way LOW_PRIORITY does for a single statement.) HIGH_PRIORITY also prevents the INSERT from being performed concurrently with SELECT statements if it otherwise would be.

The LOW_PRIORITY and HIGH_PRIORITY options are effective only for storage engines that use table-level locking, such as MyISAM or MEMORY.

INSTALL PLUGIN

```
INSTALL PLUGIN plugin_name SONAME 'plugin_lib'
```

Installs a plugin from a plugin library object file, which must be present in the directory named by the plugin_dir system variable. This statement also registers the plugin in the mysql.plugin table so that the server loads it on subsequent restarts. INSTALL PLUGIN requires the INSERT privilege for the mysql.plugin table. For more information, see Section 12.4, "The Plugin Interface."

KILL

```
KILL [CONNECTION | QUERY] thread_id
```

Kills the server thread with the given thread_id. You must have the SUPER privilege to kill the thread, unless it is one of your own. The KILL statement permits only a single ID. The mysql-admin kill command performs the same operation, but permits multiple thread ID values to be specified on the command line.

The CONNECTION option has the same effect as no option: The thread with the given ID is terminated. QUERY terminates any statement that the thread is executing, but not the thread itself.

LOAD DATA

```
LOAD DATA [LOW_PRIORITY | CONCURRENT] [LOCAL] INFILE 'file_name'
  [IGNORE | REPLACE]
  INTO TABLE tbl_name
  [PARTITION (partition_name [, partition_name] ...)]
  [CHARACTER SET charset]
  [field_options] [line_options]
  [IGNORE n {LINES | ROWS}]
  [(col_or_user_var_name, ...)]
  [SET col_name = expr [, col_name = expr] ...]
```

LOAD DATA reads input records from the file file_name and loads them in bulk into the table tbl_name. This is faster than using a set of INSERT statements. As of MySQL 5.6.2, LOAD DATA supports a PARTITION clause for partitioned tables to indicate the partitions or subpartitions into which to insert rows. In this case, an error occurs if a row would not be inserted in any named partition.

LOAD DATA returns an information string in this format:

```
Records: n  Deleted: n  Skipped: n  Warnings: n
```

If the warning count is nonzero, use SHOW WARNINGS to see what the problems were.

`LOW_PRIORITY` causes the statement to be deferred until no clients are reading from the table. This option is effective only for storage engines that use table-level locking, such as MyISAM or MEMORY.

`CONCURRENT` applies only for MyISAM tables. If the table has no holes in the middle, new rows are loaded at the end of the table. In this case, other clients can retrieve from the table concurrently while rows are being loaded.

Without the `LOCAL` keyword, the file is read directly by the server on the server host. In this case, you must have the `FILE` privilege and the file must either be located in the database directory of the default database or be world-readable. If the `secure_file_priv` system variable is nonempty, its value should be a directory and the file must be located in that directory. If `LOCAL` is specified, the client reads the file on the client host and sends its contents over the network to the server. In this case, the `FILE` privilege is not required, but the file must be readable by the client user. `LOCAL` can be disabled or enabled selectively. If it is disabled on the server side, you cannot use it from the client side. If it is enabled on the server side, but disabled by default on the client side, you'll need to enable it explicitly. For example, with the `mysql` program, you can use the `--local-infile` flag to enable the `LOCAL` capability.

When `LOCAL` is omitted from the `LOAD DATA` statement, the server locates the file as follows:

- If `'file_name'` is an absolute pathname, the server looks for the file starting from the root directory.
- If `'file_name'` is a relative pathname, interpretation depends on whether the name contains a single component. If so, the server looks for the file in the database directory of the default database. If the filename contains multiple components, the server looks for the file beginning from the server's data directory.

If `LOCAL` is given, filename interpretation is as follows:

- If `'file_name'` is an absolute pathname, the client looks for the file starting from the root directory.
- If `'file_name'` is a relative pathname, the client looks for the file beginning from your current directory.

For Windows, backslashes in filenames may be written either as slashes ('/') or as doubled backslashes ('\\').

By default, the contents of the file are interpreted using the character set named by the `character_set_database` system variable. To indicate the file's character set explicitly, use the `CHARACTER SET` clause. (However, the character set cannot be `ucs2`, `utf16`, `utf16le`, or `utf32`, which also means that you cannot load files that use these character sets.)

Rows that duplicate values in a unique index are either ignored or replace existing rows according to whether `IGNORE` or `REPLACE` is specified. If neither is specified, an error occurs, and any remaining records are ignored. If `LOCAL` is specified, transmission of the file cannot be interrupted, so the default behavior is like `IGNORE` if neither duplicate-handling option is given.

The *field_options* and *line_options* clauses indicate the format of the data. (The options available in these clauses also apply to the corresponding clauses of the SELECT ... INTO OUTFILE statement.) The two clauses have this syntax:

```
field_options:
  [FIELDS
    [TERMINATED BY 'str']
    [[OPTIONALLY] ENCLOSED BY 'char']
    [ESCAPED BY 'char' ] ]

line_options:
  [LINES
    [STARTING BY 'str']
    [TERMINATED BY 'str'] ]
```

The 'str' and 'char' values may include the escape sequences in the following table to indicate special characters. The sequences should be given in the lettercase shown.

Sequence	Meaning
\0	NUL (zero-valued byte)
\b	Backspace
\n	Newline (linefeed)
\r	Carriage return
\s	Space
\t	Tab
\'	Single quote
\"	Double quote
\\	Backslash
\z	Control-Z (Windows EOF character)

You can also use hexadecimal constants to indicate arbitrary characters. For example, LINES TERMINATED BY 0x02 indicates that lines are terminated by Control-B (ASCII 2) characters.

If the FIELDS clause is given, at least one of the TERMINATED BY, ENCLOSED BY, or ESCAPED BY options must be given. If multiple options are present, they may appear in any order. Similarly, if the LINES clause is given, at least one of the STARTING BY or TERMINATED BY options must be given, but if both are present, they may appear in any order. FIELDS must precede LINES if both are given.

Options for the FIELDS clause are used as follows:

- TERMINATED BY specifies the character or characters that delimit values within a line.

- ENCLOSED BY specifies a quote character that is stripped from the ends of field values if it is present. This occurs regardless of whether OPTIONALLY is present. For output (SELECT ... INTO OUTFILE), the ENCLOSED BY character is used to enclose field values in output lines. If OPTIONALLY is given, values are quoted only for CHAR and VARCHAR columns.

  To include an instance of the ENCLOSED BY character within an input field value, it should either be doubled or preceded by the ESCAPED BY character. Otherwise, it is interpreted as signifying the end of the field. For output, instances of the ENCLOSED BY character within field values are preceded by the ESCAPED BY character.

- The ESCAPED BY character specifies how to escape special characters. In the following examples, assume that the escape character is backslash ('\'). For input, the unquoted sequence \N (backslash-N) is interpreted as NULL. The \0 sequence (backslash-ASCII '0') is interpreted as a zero-valued byte. For other escaped characters, the escape character is stripped off, and the following character is used literally. For example, \" is interpreted as a double quote, even if field values are enclosed within double quotes.

  For output, the escape character is used to encode NULL as an unquoted \N sequence, and zero-valued bytes as \0. In addition, instances of the ESCAPED BY and ENCLOSED BY characters are preceded by the escape character (if necessary), as are the first characters of the field and line termination strings. If the ESCAPED BY character is empty (ESCAPED BY ''), no escaping is done. (In this case, NULL is written as NULL, not \N.) To specify an escape character of '\', double it (ESCAPED BY '\\').

Options for the LINES clause are used as follows:

- The STARTING BY value specifies one or more characters that begin lines. This value *and everything preceding it* on the line is taken as the line beginning.

- The TERMINATED BY value specifies one or more characters that signify the ends of lines.

If neither FIELDS nor LINES is given, the defaults are as if you had specified them like this:

```
FIELDS TERMINATED BY '\t' ENCLOSED BY '' ESCAPED BY '\\'
LINES STARTING BY '' TERMINATED BY '\n'
```

In other words, fields within a line are tab-delimited without being quoted, backslash is treated as the escape character, and lines are terminated by newline characters.

If the TERMINATED BY and ENCLOSED BY values for the FIELDS clause are both empty, a fixed-width row format is used with no delimiters between fields. Column values are read (or written, for output) using a width large enough for all values in the column. For example, VARCHAR(15) and MEDIUMINT columns are read as 15-character and 8-character fields for input. For output, the columns are written using 15 characters and 8 characters. NULL values are written as strings of spaces.

NULL values in an input data file are indicated by the unquoted sequence \N. If the FIELDS ENCLOSED BY character is not empty, all non-NULL input values must be quoted with the enclosed-by character and the unquoted word NULL also is interpreted as a NULL value.

If the IGNORE _n_ LINES clause is given, the first _n_ lines of the input are discarded. (ROWS is a synonym for LINES.) For example, if your data file has a row of column headers that you don't want to read into the database table, use IGNORE 1 LINES:

```
LOAD DATA LOCAL INFILE 'mytbl.txt' INTO TABLE mytbl IGNORE 1 LINES;
```

By default, input lines are assumed to contain one value per column in the table. If a list consisting of one or more comma-separated column names is given, input lines should contain a value for each named column. Columns not named in the list are set to their default values. If an input line is short of the expected number of values, columns for which values are missing are set to their default values.

If strict SQL mode is in effect when LOAD DATA executes, it is an error for a value to be missing for a column that has no DEFAULT clause in its definition, or to assign NULL to a NOT NULL column.

The list can include column names or user variable names, and a SET clause can be given to perform additional processing of input values before they are loaded into the table. For example, the following statement loads the first input column into col1, ignores the second column, loads the sum of the third and fourth columns into col2, and uses UUID() to provide a generated value for col3:

```
LOAD DATA LOCAL INFILE 'mytbl.txt' INTO TABLE mytbl
  (col1,@skip,@addend1,@addend2)
  SET col2 = @addend1 + @addend2, col3 = UUID();
```

The SET clause consists of one ore more assignment expressions separated by commas. The left hand side of each assignment must name a table column. User variables are not permitted for fixed-width input format because no column width can be determined. Scalar subqueries can be used to provide column values except that you cannot select values from the same table into which you are loading data.

If you have a tab-delimited text file that you created on Windows, you can use the default column separator, but the lines are probably terminated by carriage return/newline pairs. To load the file, specify that lines are terminated by carriage-return/newline pairs:

```
LOAD DATA LOCAL INFILE 'mytbl.txt' INTO TABLE mytbl
  LINES TERMINATED BY '\r\n';
```

You may end up with a malformed row in the database if you load a data file that was created on Windows by a program that uses the odd MS-DOS convention of putting the Control-Z character at the end of the file to indicate end-of-file. Either create the file using a program that doesn't do this, or delete the row after loading the file.

Files in comma-separated values (CSV) format have commas between fields, and fields may be quoted with double quotes. Assuming lines have newlines at the end, the LOAD DATA statement to load such a file looks like this:

```
LOAD DATA LOCAL INFILE 'mytbl.txt' INTO TABLE mytbl
  FIELDS TERMINATED BY ',' ENCLOSED BY '"';
```

Hexadecimal notation is useful for specifying arbitrary control characters. The following statement reads a file for which fields are separated by Control-A (ASCII 1) characters, and lines are terminated by Control-B (ASCII 2) characters:

```
LOAD DATA LOCAL INFILE 'mytbl.txt' INTO TABLE mytbl
  FIELDS TERMINATED BY 0x01 LINES TERMINATED BY 0x02;
```

LOAD INDEX INTO CACHE

```
LOAD INDEX INTO CACHE
  tbl_index_spec [, tbl_index_spec] ...

tbl_index_spec:
  tbl_name
    [PARTITION (partition_name [, partition_name] ... | ALL)]
    [[INDEX | KEY] (index_name [, index_name] ...)]
    [IGNORE LEAVES]] ...
```

Loads indexes from each named MyISAM table into the key cache to which the table is assigned. This is the default key cache unless the table has been assigned to another cache with the CACHE INDEX statement. All index blocks are loaded by default, or only nonleaf blocks in the index tree if IGNORE LEAVES is specified.

For partitioned tables, the PARTITION clause permits cache loading of specific partitions.

As with the CACHE INDEX statement, the syntax for LOAD INDEX INTO CACHE permits individual indexes to be specified, but the implementation is such that all indexes for a table are loaded.

You must have the INDEX privilege for each table named in the statement.

LOAD INDEX INTO CACHE produces output in the format described in the entry for CHECK TABLE.

For more information about MyISAM key cache management, see Section 12.7.2, "Storage Engine Tuning."

LOAD XML

```
LOAD XML [LOW_PRIORITY | CONCURRENT] [LOCAL] INFILE 'file_name'
  [IGNORE | REPLACE]
  INTO TABLE tbl_name
  [PARTITION (partition_name [, partition_name] ...)]
  [CHARACTER SET charset]
  [ROWS IDENTIFIED BY '<tag_name>']
  [IGNORE n {LINES | ROWS}]
  [(col_or_user_var_name, ...)]
  [SET col_name = expr [, col_name = expr] ...]
```

This statement is similar to LOAD DATA but differs in these ways:

- The file to be loaded should be an XML file.

- The ROWS IDENTIFIED BY clause, if given, names the tag (including angle brackets) that identifies where rows in the file begin and end. The default is '<row>'.

Rows for the destination table can be specified in any of three formats in the input XML file. The file can use different formats for different rows.

- Within <row> elements, column names and values come from attribute names and values.

  ```
  <row col_name1="value1" col_name2="value2" ... />
  ```

- Within <row> elements, column names and values come from subelement tag names and contents.

  ```
  <row>
    <col_name1>value1</col_name1>
    <col_name2>value2</col_name2>
    ...
  </row>
  ```

- Within <row> elements, column names and values come from subelement attribute values and contents.

  ```
  <row>
    <field name="col_name1>value1</field>
    <field name="col_name2>value2</field>
    ...
  </row>
  ```

LOCK TABLE

```
LOCK {TABLE | TABLES}
  tbl_name [[AS] alias_name] lock_type
  [, tbl_name [[AS] alias_name] lock_type] ...
```

Obtains a lock on the named tables or views, waiting if necessary until all locks are acquired. If you lock a view, the statement locks the base tables used by the view. This statement requires the LOCK TABLES privilege and the SELECT privilege for each table or view to be locked.

Each lock_type value must be one of the following:

- READ [LOCAL]: Acquires a read lock. This blocks other clients from writing to the table, but permits reading.

  READ LOCAL is a variation on a READ lock, designed for concurrent insert situations. It applies only to MyISAM tables that do not have any holes in the middle resulting from deleted or updated rows. READ LOCAL enables you to lock a table explicitly but still permit other clients to perform concurrent inserts. (If the table does have holes in it, the lock is treated as a regular READ lock.)

- [LOW_PRIORITY] WRITE: Acquires a write lock. This blocks all clients from reading or writing the table. The LOW_PRIORITY modifier used to alter lock acquisition behavior, but does nothing as of MySQL 5.5.3.

LOCK TABLE releases any existing locks that you currently hold. Thus, to lock multiple tables, you must lock them all using a single LOCK TABLE statement. While you have acquired locks with LOCK TABLE, you cannot refer to any not-locked tables. When a session terminates, the server automatically releases any locks it holds.

LOCK TABLE permits an alias to be specified so that you can lock a table under an alias that you intend to use when referring to the table in a subsequent query. If you refer to a table multiple times in a query, you must obtain a lock for each instance of the table, locking aliases as necessary. You must request all the locks in the same statement.

```
LOCK TABLE student READ, score WRITE, grade_event READ;
LOCK TABLE member READ;
LOCK TABLE t AS t1 READ, t AS t2 READ;
```

If a transaction is in progress, LOCK TABLE causes an implicit commit. Table locks acquired with LOCK TABLE are released implicitly if you start a transaction with START TRANSACTION.

OPTIMIZE TABLE

```
OPTIMIZE [NO_WRITE_TO_BINLOG | LOCAL]
  {TABLE | TABLES} tbl_name [, tbl_name] ...
```

DELETE, REPLACE, and UPDATE statements may result in areas of unused space in a table. To counter this, OPTIMIZE TABLE performs table optimization operations. It works with InnoDB, MyISAM, and ARCHIVE tables. OPTIMIZE TABLE requires the SELECT and INSERT privileges on each table.

If binary logging is enabled, MySQL writes the OPTIMIZE TABLE statement to the binary log unless the NO_WRITE_TO_BINLOG or LOCAL option is given.

For an InnoDB table, OPTIMIZE TABLE is mapped to ALTER TABLE to update the table index statistics and free unused space in the clustered index.

For a MyISAM table, OPTIMIZE TABLE performs the following actions:

- Defragments the table to eliminate wasted space and reduce the table size
- Coalesces the contents of variable-length rows that have become fragmented into noncontiguous pieces, to store each row contiguously
- Sorts the index pages if necessary
- Updates the internal table statistics

Issuing an OPTIMIZE TABLE statement for a MyISAM table is like executing myisamchk with the `--check-only-changed`, `--quick`, `--sort-index`, and `--analyze` options. However, with myisamchk, you must arrange to prevent the server from accessing the table at the same time. With OPTIMIZE TABLE, the server does the work and makes sure that other clients do not modify the table while it's being optimized.

For an ARCHIVE table, OPTIMIZE TABLE performs table analysis and recompresses the table to reduce the storage required.

OPTIMIZE TABLE produces output in the format described in the entry for CHECK TABLE.

PREPARE

PREPARE stmt_name FROM {'str' | @var_name}

Prepares a statement and assigns it the name stmt_name. The statement can be executed later with EXECUTE and deallocated with DEALLOCATE PREPARE. If there was already a previously prepared statement with the given name, that statement is deallocated before the new statement is prepared. Statement names are not case sensitive.

Specify the statement to be prepared either as a string literal or a user variable. The set of permitted statements that can be used with PREPARE has expanded over time. The initial set included CREATE TABLE, DELETE, DO, INSERT, REPLACE, SELECT, SET, UPDATE, and most variations of SHOW. Other statements have been added; consult the MySQL Reference Manual for your version of MySQL to see which statements qualify. PREPARE, EXECUTE, and DEALLOCATE PREPARE *cannot* be prepared.

The prepared statement can contain '?' characters that serve as placeholder markers. When you execute the statement later, supply data values to be bound to these placeholders. Placeholders enable you to parameterize the statement so that you can use the same prepared statement with different data values per execution. Placeholders cannot be used for identifiers or SQL keywords.

PREPARE, EXECUTE, and DEALLOCATE provide an SQL-level interface to prepared statements. They are not the same as or as efficient as the binary API for prepared statements that is discussed in Chapter 7, "Writing MySQL Programs Using C," and Appendix G, "C API Reference."

PURGE BINARY LOGS

PURGE {BINARY | MASTER} LOGS {TO 'log_name' | BEFORE 'date'}

Deletes all the binary log files on the server that were generated earlier than the named file or before the given date (in 'CCYY-MM-DD hh:mm:ss' format), and resets the binary log index file to list only those log files that remain. Normally, you use this after running SHOW SLAVE STATUS on each of the master's slaves to determine which log files are still in use. This statement requires the SUPER privilege.

The following statement removes any of `binlog.000001` through `binlog.000009` that exist and causes `binlog.000010` to become the first of the remaining log files:

```
PURGE BINARY LOGS TO 'binlog.000010';
```

RELEASE SAVEPOINT

```
RELEASE SAVEPOINT savepoint_name
```

Releases the savepoint with the given name from the savepoints for the current transaction, or returns an error if the savepoint does not exist. No commit or rollback occurs.

RENAME TABLE

```
RENAME {TABLE | TABLES} tbl_name TO new_tbl_name
  [, tbl_name TO new_tbl_name] ...
```

Renames one or more tables. RENAME TABLE is similar to ALTER TABLE ... RENAME, except that it can rename multiple tables, and locks them all during the rename operation. This is advantageous if you need to perform an "atomic" rename that prevents any of the tables from being accessed during the operation.

If you rename an InnoDB table on which other tables depend for foreign key relationships, InnoDB adjusts the dependencies to point to the renamed table.

RENAME TABLE cannot be used for TEMPORARY tables.

An error occurs if you try to rename a table into another database if there are triggers for the table.

RENAME TABLE applies to views unless you try to rename the view into another database.

RENAME USER

```
RENAME USER from_account TO to_account
  [, from_account TO to_account] ...
```

Renames one or more MySQL accounts. This statement requires the global CREATE USER privilege or the UPDATE privilege for the `mysql` database.

Each `from_account` is renamed to the corresponding `to_account`. An error occurs if `from_account` does not exist or if `to_account` already exists. Name each account in `'user_name'@'host_name'` format, as described in Section 13.2.1.1, "Specifying Account Names."

```
RENAME USER 'myname'@'localhost' TO 'yourname'@'localhost';
```

RENAME USER updates privileges held by the original account to apply to the new account. However, it does not change any object definitions that refer to the original account. For example, each stored program with a DEFINER clause that refers to the original account must be updated to refer to the new account.

REPAIR TABLE

```
REPAIR [NO_WRITE_TO_BINLOG | LOCAL]
  {TABLE | TABLES} tbl_name [, tbl_name] ... [option] ...
```

This statement performs table repair operations. It works with MyISAM, ARCHIVE, and CSV tables. REPAIR TABLE requires the SELECT and INSERT privileges on each table.

If binary logging is enabled, MySQL writes the REPAIR TABLE statement to the binary log unless the NO_WRITE_TO_BINLOG or LOCAL option is given.

REPAIR TABLE with no options performs a normal table repair that can fix most problems except the occurrence of duplicate values in an index that should contain only unique values. The following list describes the permitted *option* values. These options apply to MyISAM tables; other storage engines might ignore them.

- EXTENDED performs an extended repair that re-creates the indexes.

- QUICK attempts a quick repair of just the indexes; leaves the data file alone.

- USE_FRM uses the table's .frm file to reinitialize the index file and to determine how to interpret the contents of the data file so the indexes can be rebuilt. This can be useful if the index has become lost or irrecoverably corrupted. However, it should be treated as a last resort and used *only* if your current version of MySQL is the same as that used to create the table. Otherwise, you risk further damage to the table. The USE_FRM option cannot be used with partitioned tables.

REPAIR TABLE produces output in the format described in the entry for CHECK TABLE.

REPLACE

```
REPLACE [DELAYED | LOW_PRIORITY]
  [INTO] tbl_name
  [PARTITION (partition_name [, partition_name] ...)]
  [(col_list)]
  {VALUES | VALUE} (expr [, expr] ...) [, (...)] ...

REPLACE [DELAYED | LOW_PRIORITY]
  [INTO] tbl_name
  [PARTITION (partition_name [, partition_name] ...)]
  [(col_list)]
  {SELECT ... | (SELECT ...)}

REPLACE [DELAYED | LOW_PRIORITY]
  [INTO] tbl_name
  [PARTITION (partition_name [, partition_name] ...)]
  SET col_name=expr [, col_name=expr] ...
```

The basic action of REPLACE statement is like INSERT, with the exception that if a row to be inserted has a value for a unique index that duplicates the value in a row already present in the table, the old row is deleted before the new one is inserted. For this reason, there is no IGNORE clause option in the syntax of REPLACE. Also, REPLACE has does not support ON DUPLICATE KEY UPDATE. For more information, see the entry for INSERT. REPLACE requires the INSERT and DELETE privileges for the table.

As of MySQL 5.6.2, REPLACE supports a PARTITION clause for partitioned tables to indicate the partitions or subpartitions into which to insert rows. In this case, if a row would not be inserted in any named partition, an error occurs.

It's possible for a REPLACE to delete more than one row if the table contains multiple unique indexes. This can happen if a new row matches values in several of the unique indexes, in which case all the matching rows are deleted before the new row is inserted.

RESET

```
RESET option [, option] ...
```

The RESET statement is similar to FLUSH in that it affects log or cache information. RESET requires the RELOAD privilege.

option values should be chosen from the following list:

- MASTER: Deletes the existing binary log files for a replication master server, creates a new file with the numbering sequence set to 000001, and resets the binary log index to name just the new file.

- QUERY CACHE: Clears the query cache and removes any queries currently registered in it. To defragment the cache without clearing it, use the FLUSH QUERY CACHE statement instead.

- SLAVE: Tells the server, if it is acting as a replication slave, to remove any existing relay log files and begin a new relay log, and to forget its replication coordinates (that is, its current replication binary log filename and position within that file).

REVOKE

```
REVOKE priv_type [(col_list)] [, priv_type [(col_list)] ...]
  ON [TABLE | FUNCTION | PROCEDURE]
    {*.* | * | db_name.* | db_name.tbl_name
    | tbl_name | db_name.routine_name}
    | tbl_name | db_name.routine_name}
  FROM account [, account ] ...

REVOKE ALL [PRIVILEGES], GRANT OPTION
  FROM account [, account ] ...

REVOKE PROXY ON account
  FROM account [, account ] ...
```

The REVOKE statement revokes privileges from the named account or accounts. Name each account in `'user_name'@'host_name'` format, as described in Section 13.2.1.1, "Specifying Account Names." An error occurs for nonexistent accounts.

In the first syntax, the `priv_type`, `col_list`, and ON clauses are specified the same way as for the GRANT statement. To use this statement, you must have the GRANT OPTION privilege and you must possess the privileges that you are trying to revoke.

The second syntax has a fixed privilege list and no ON clause. It revokes all privileges held by each of the named accounts. The second syntax requires the global CREATE USER privilege or the UPDATE privilege for the `mysql` database.

The third syntax revokes the PROXY privilege for the ON account for the accounts named in the FROM clause.

REVOKE does not remove an account's row from the `mysql.user` grant table. This means that the account still can be used to connect to the MySQL server even when all its privileges have been revoked. To remove the account entirely, use the DROP USER statement (or manually delete the account row from the `mysql.user` table).

- Revoke privileges that permit the `member_mgr` user to modify the `member` table in the `sampdb` database:

  ```
  REVOKE INSERT,DELETE,UPDATE ON sampdb.member
    FROM 'member_mgr'@'boa.example.com';
  ```

- Revoke all privileges for a single table in the menagerie database from the anonymous user on the local host:

  ```
  REVOKE ALL ON menagerie.pet FROM ''@'localhost';
  ```

- ALL revokes all but the GRANT OPTION privilege. To revoke that privilege as well, you must do so explicitly:

  ```
  REVOKE GRANT OPTION ON menagerie.pet FROM ''@'localhost';
  ```

- Revoke all privileges held at all levels by superduper@localhost:

  ```
  REVOKE ALL, GRANT OPTION FROM 'superduper'@'localhost';
  ```

- Revoke the PROXY privilege on proxied_user from proxy_user:

  ```
  REVOKE PROXY ON proxied_user FROM proxy_user;
  ```

ROLLBACK

```
ROLLBACK [WORK] [AND [NO] CHAIN] [[NO] RELEASE]
ROLLBACK [WORK] TO [SAVEPOINT] savepoint_name
```

Rolls back changes made by statements that are part of the current transaction so that those changes are forgotten. This works only for transactional storage engines. (For nontransactional storage engines, statements are committed as they are executed and thus cannot be rolled back.)

The optional keyword WORK has no effect. The CHAIN and RELEASE clauses have the same effect as described in the entry for COMMIT.

If the TO SAVEPOINT clause is given, the statement rolls back the current transaction only to the named savepoint.

ROLLBACK does nothing if autocommit mode has not been disabled with START TRANSACTION or by setting the autocommit variable to 0.

SAVEPOINT

```
SAVEPOINT savepoint_name
```

Creates a transaction savepoint with the given name. Any existing savepoint with the given name is deleted. Statements executed later within the current transaction can be rolled back to the savepoint with the ROLLBACK TO SAVEPOINT statement.

SELECT

```
SELECT
  [select_option] ...
  select_expr [, select_expr] ...
  [FROM tbl_refs
  [WHERE where_expr]
  [GROUP BY {col_name | expr | position}
    [ASC | DESC], ...  [WITH ROLLUP]]
  [HAVING where_expr]
  [ORDER BY {col_name | expr | position}
    [ASC | DESC], ...]
  [LIMIT {[skip_count,] show_count | show_count OFFSET skip_count}]
  [PROCEDURE procedure_name([param_list])]
  [
      INTO OUTFILE 'file_name'
        [CHARACTER SET charset]
        [field_options] [line_options]
    | INTO DUMPFILE 'file_name'
    | INTO var_name [, var_name ] ...
  ]
  [FOR UPDATE | LOCK IN SHARE MODE] ]
```

SELECT normally is used to retrieve rows from one or more tables. However, because everything in the statement is optional except the SELECT keyword and at least one select_expr, it's also possible to write statements that simply evaluate expressions:

```
SELECT 'one plus one =', 1+1;
```

For compatibility with database systems that require a FROM clause, MySQL recognizes the DUAL pseudo-table:

```
SELECT 'one plus one =', 1+1 FROM DUAL;
```

A subquery is one SELECT nested within another; for examples, see Section 2.9, "Performing Multiple-Table Retrievals with Subqueries." Subqueries also can be used in the WHERE clause of DELETE and UPDATE statements or with INSERT and REPLACE statements. However, you cannot use a subquery to select rows from a table that you are modifying.

Each *select_option* value can be one of the options in the following list:

- ALL, DISTINCT, DISTINCTROW: These keywords control whether duplicate rows are returned. ALL causes all rows to be returned, which is the default. DISTINCT and DISTINCTROW specify that duplicate rows should be eliminated from the result set.

- HIGH_PRIORITY: Specifying HIGH_PRIORITY gives the statement a higher priority if it normally would have to wait. If other statements, such as INSERT or UPDATE, are waiting to write to tables named in the SELECT because some other client is reading the tables, HIGH_PRIORITY causes a SELECT statement to be given priority over those write statements. This should be done only for SELECT statements that you know will execute quickly and that must be done immediately, because it slows down execution of the write statements. This option is effective only for storage engines that use table-level locking, such as MyISAM or MEMORY.

- SQL_BUFFER_RESULT: Tells the server to buffer the query result in a separate temporary table rather than keeping the table or tables named in the SELECT locked while waiting for the entire query result to be sent to the client. This helps the server release the locks sooner, which gives other clients access to the tables more quickly. However, using this option also requires more disk space and memory.

- SQL_CACHE, SQL_NO_CACHE: If the query result is cacheable and the query cache is operating in demand mode, SQL_CACHE causes the result to be cached. SQL_NO_CACHE suppresses any caching of the query result. These two options are mutually exclusive, and cannot appear in subqueries or other than in the first SELECT of a UNION.

- SQL_CALC_FOUND_ROWS: Normally, the row count from a query that includes a LIMIT clause is the number of rows actually returned. SQL_CALC_FOUND_ROWS tells the server to determine how large the query result would be without the LIMIT. To obtain the row count, issue a SELECT FOUND_ROWS() statement following the initial SELECT.

- SQL_BIG_RESULT, SQL_SMALL_RESULT: These keywords provide a hint that the result set will be large or small, which gives the optimizer information that it can use to process the query more effectively.

- STRAIGHT_JOIN: Forces tables to be joined in the order named in the FROM clause. This option may be useful if you believe that the optimizer is not making the best choice.

The *select_expr* expressions list the output columns to be returned, separated by commas. Columns may be references to table columns or expressions (including scalar subqueries). Any column may be assigned a column alias using AS *alias_name* syntax (the AS keyword is optional). The alias then becomes the column name in the output and may also be referred to in GROUP BY, ORDER BY, and HAVING clauses. However, you cannot refer to column aliases in a WHERE clause.

The special notation * means "all columns from the tables named in the FROM clause," and
`tbl_name.*` means "all columns from the named table."

The FROM clause names one or more tables from which rows should be selected. MySQL
supports the following join syntax:

```
tbl_refs:
  tbl_ref [, tbl_ref] ...

tbl_ref:
    tbl_factor
  | join_tbl

tbl_factor:
    tbl_name
  | (subquery) [AS] alias_name
  | (tbl_refs)
  | { OJ tbl_ref LEFT OUTER JOIN tbl_ref ON conditional_expr }

join_tbl:
    tbl_ref [INNER | CROSS] JOIN tbl_factor [join_condition]
  | tbl_ref STRAIGHT_JOIN tbl_factor [ON conditional_expr]
  | tbl_ref {LEFT | RIGHT} [OUTER] JOIN tbl_ref join_condition
  | tbl_ref NATURAL [{LEFT | RIGHT} [OUTER]] JOIN tbl_factor

join_condition:
    ON conditional_expr
  | USING (col_list)
```

Each `tbl_name` may be accompanied by an alias or index hints. In addition, as of MySQL 5.6.2,
SELECT supports a PARTITION clause for partitioned tables to indicate the partitions or subpartitions from which to select rows. That is, the full syntax for referring to a table actually looks
like this:

```
tbl_name
  [PARTITION (partition_name [, partition_name] ...)]
  [[AS] alias_name]
  [{USE | IGNORE | FORCE} {INDEX | KEY}
   [FOR {JOIN | ORDER BY | GROUP BY}]
   (index_list)]
```

Tables may be assigned aliases in the FROM clause using either `tbl_name alias_name` or
`tbl_name AS alias_name` syntax. An alias provides an alternative name by which to refer to
the table columns elsewhere in the query.

It is also permitted to specify a table in the FROM clause by means of a subquery within parentheses, as long as you provide an alias so that the table can be referred to elsewhere in the
statement:

```
SELECT * FROM (SELECT 1) AS t;
```

The USE INDEX, IGNORE INDEX, and FORCE INDEX clauses provide index hints to the optimizer. They may be helpful in cases where the optimizer doesn't make the correct choice about which index to use in a join. USE INDEX tells the optimizer to select an index only from those named in *index_list*. IGNORE INDEX tells the optimizer which indexes not to use. FORCE INDEX is like USE INDEX but tells the optimizer to consider table scans very expensive compared to using the listed indexes.

index_list should name one or more indexes separated by commas, except that the *index_list* for USE can be empty to indicate "use no indexes." Each index should be the name of an index from the table, or the keyword PRIMARY to indicate the table's PRIMARY KEY.

Index hints apply only to selecting rows and joining tables, not to processing ORDER BY or GROUP BY clauses. To apply a hint only to selecting and joining, use FOR JOIN.

Multiple index hints per *tbl_name* reference are permitted. However, you cannot use both USE INDEX and FORCE INDEX for the same reference.

For FULLTEXT indexes, index hints have no effect except for boolean-mode searches with FOR JOIN or no FOR modifier.

Joins select rows from the named tables as indicated in the following descriptions. The rows actually returned to the client may be limited by WHERE, HAVING, or LIMIT clauses.

- For a single table named by itself, SELECT retrieves rows from that table.

- If multiple tables are named and separated by commas, SELECT returns all possible combinations of rows from the tables. Using JOIN, CROSS JOIN, or INNER JOIN is similar to using a comma if there is no ON or USING clause. STRAIGHT_JOIN is similar, but forces the optimizer to join the tables in the order that the tables are named. It may be used if you believe that the optimizer is not making the best choice.

- Unlike the comma operator, joins performed with JOIN, CROSS JOIN, or INNER JOIN can be specified with an ON or USING() clause to constrain matches between tables. Matching rows are determined according to the condition specified in the ON *conditional_expr* clause or the USING (*col_list*) clause. *conditional_expr* is an expression of the form that may be used in the WHERE clause. *col_list* consists of one or more comma-separated column names, each of which must be a column that occurs in both of the joined tables.

- LEFT JOIN retrieves rows from the joined tables, but forces a row to be generated for every row in the left table, even if there is no matching row in the right table. When there is no match, columns from the right table are returned as NULL values. The ON or USING() clause following the table names is given as for JOIN, CROSS JOIN, or INNER JOIN. LEFT OUTER JOIN is equivalent to LEFT JOIN. So is the syntax that begins with OJ, which is included for ODBC compatibility. The curly braces shown for the OJ syntax are not metacharacters; they are literal characters that must be present in the statement.

- NATURAL LEFT JOIN is equivalent to LEFT JOIN USING (*col_list*), where *col_list* names all the columns that are common to both tables.

- The RIGHT JOIN types are like the corresponding LEFT JOIN types, but with the table roles reversed.

- The precedence of comma joins is less than other join types. Mixing comma joins with other types may result in "Unknown column" errors. Replacing comma with INNER JOIN often helps in such cases.

The WHERE clause specifies an expression that is applied to rows selected from the tables named in the FROM clause. Rows that do not satisfy the criteria given by the expression are rejected. The result set may be further limited by HAVING and LIMIT clauses. Column aliases may not be referred to in the WHERE clause.

The GROUP BY and ORDER BY clauses have similar syntax. GROUP BY col_list is used to group rows of the result set based on the columns named in the list. This clause is used when you specify summary functions such as COUNT() or MAX() in a select_expr. ORDER BY col_list indicates that the result set should be sorted based on the named columns. In either clause, columns may be referred to by column names or aliases, or by position within the list of select_expr expressions. Column positions are unsigned integers beginning with 1, but use of column positions is nonstandard and deprecated. You can also use expressions to group or sort by expression results. For example, ORDER BY RAND() sorts rows in random order.

In a GROUP BY or ORDER BY clause, you can follow any column in the column list with ASC or DESC to indicate that the column should be sorted in ascending or descending order. The default for each column is ascending if neither keyword is present. Sort order indicators are permitted in GROUP BY clauses because, in MySQL, GROUP BY not only groups rows, it sorts the results. The output order resulting from GROUP BY is overridden by any ORDER BY clause that is present. To prevent the implicit ordering that results from GROUP BY (and thus not incur the sorting overhead), use ORDER BY NULL.

WITH ROLLUP can be used at the end of a GROUP BY clause. It causes the output to include summary rows for higher-level combinations of the grouped columns, plus an overall summary at the end.

The HAVING clause specifies a secondary expression that is used to limit rows after they have satisfied the conditions named by the WHERE clause and after they have been grouped according to any GROUP BY clause. Rows that do not satisfy the HAVING condition are rejected. HAVING is useful for expressions involving summary functions that cannot be tested in the WHERE clause. However, if a condition is legal in either the WHERE clause or the HAVING clause, it is preferable to place it in the WHERE clause where it is subject to analysis by the optimizer.

The LIMIT clause can be used to select a section of rows from the result set. It takes either one or two arguments, which must be integer constants. LIMIT n returns the first n rows. LIMIT m, n skips the first m rows and returns the next n rows.

PROCEDURE names a procedure to which the data in the result set is sent before a result set is returned to the client. The optional parameter list, param_list, is a comma-separated list of values to pass to the procedure. You can use PROCEDURE ANALYSE() to obtain information about the characteristics of the data in the columns named in the column selection list. See Section 5.3, "Choosing Data Types for Efficient Queries."

The INTO formats specify a destination for the query result. An alternative placement for INTO is to specify it earlier in the statement, following the *select_expr* list. If you use an INTO clause, the statement cannot be used as a nested SELECT.

The result of a SELECT statement may be written into a file *file_name* using an INTO OUTFILE '*file_name*' clause. To specify the character set in which values should be written, include a CHARACTER SET clause. If this is omitted or the character set is binary, no conversion occurs. The syntax of the *field_options* and *line_options* clauses is the same as for the corresponding clauses of the LOAD DATA statement. For more information, see the entry for LOAD DATA.

INTO DUMPFILE '*file_name*' is similar to INTO OUTFILE but writes only a single row and writes the output entirely without interpretation. That is, it writes raw values without delimiters, quotes, or terminators. This can be useful if you want to write BLOB data such as an image or other binary data to a file.

For both INTO OUTFILE and INTO DUMPFILE, the location of the file is determined using the same rules that apply when reading non-LOCAL files with LOAD DATA. You must have the FILE privilege, the output file must not already exist, and the file is created by the server on the server host with a world-accessible mode. Its ownership is set to the account used to run the server.

INTO followed by a comma-separated list of variable names stores the results of the SELECT into the variables. Each variable can be either a user-defined variable of the form *@var_name*, or, within a stored program, a parameter or local variable. The query must select a single row of values and must name one variable per output column.

The FOR UPDATE and LOCK IN SHARE MODE clauses place locks on the rows that are examined during query execution. The locks remain in force until the current transaction is committed or rolled back. These locking clauses can be useful in multiple-statement transactions. If you use FOR UPDATE with a table for which the storage engine uses row-level locks (InnoDB), the examined rows are write-locked for exclusive use. Using LOCK IN SHARE MODE sets read locks on the rows, enabling other clients to read but not modify them. Note that if the query optimizer finds no index to use for examining rows, it must scan (and thus lock) all rows in the table.

The following statements demonstrate some ways to use the SELECT statement. For many other examples, see Chapter 1, "Getting Started with MySQL," and Chapter 2, "Using SQL to Manage Data."

- Select the entire contents of a table:
  ```
  SELECT * FROM president;
  ```

- Select entire contents, but sort by name:
  ```
  SELECT * FROM president ORDER BY last_name, first_name;
  ```

- Select rows for presidents born on or after '1900-01-01':
  ```
  SELECT * FROM president WHERE birth >= '1900-01-01';
  ```

- Do the same, but sort in birth order:

    SELECT * FROM president WHERE birth >= '1900-01-01' ORDER BY birth;

- Determine which states are represented by rows in the member table:

    SELECT DISTINCT state FROM member;

- Select rows from member table and write columns as comma-separated values into a file:

    SELECT * INTO OUTFILE '/tmp/member.txt'
      FIELDS TERMINATED BY ',' FROM member;

- Select the top five scores for a particular grade event:

    SELECT * FROM score WHERE event_id = 9 ORDER BY score DESC LIMIT 5;

SET

    SET assignment [, assignment] ...

    assignment: var_name {= | :=} expr

The SET statement assigns values to system variables, user-defined variables, and stored program paramters or local variables. Appendix D, "System, Status, and User Variable Reference," provides information about system and user-defined variables. Section E.2.2, "Declaration Statements," describes declaration syntax for stored program local variables. SET also is used for a few miscellaneous settings described later in this entry.

Other statements that begin with SET (SET PASSWORD and SET TRANSACTION) are described in separate entries later in this appendix.

When SET is used to assign values to variables, var_name in each assignment is the variable to be assigned a value and expr is the expression that indicates the value to assign to the variable. The assignment operator in a SET statement can be either = or :=.

SET can be used to assign values to user-defined variables, which are named using @var_name syntax:

    SET @day = CURDATE(), @time = CURTIME();

SET also can assign values to system variables, many of which are dynamic and can be changed while the server is running. Dynamic system variables exist at two levels. Global system variables are server-wide and affect all clients. Session system variables (also called local system variables) are specific to a given client session only. For variables that exist at both levels, a given client's session variables are initialized from the values of the corresponding global variables when the client connects. A client must have the SUPER privilege to modify a global variable, but needs no privileges to modify its own session variables.

The syntax for setting system variables has several forms. To set a global variable (for example, the global sql_mode value), use a statement having either of the following forms:

    SET GLOBAL sql_mode = 'ANSI_QUOTES';
    SET @@GLOBAL.sql_mode = 'ANSI_QUOTES';

To set a session variable, substitute the word SESSION for GLOBAL:

```
SET SESSION sql_mode = 'ANSI_QUOTES';
SET @@SESSION.sql_mode = 'ANSI_QUOTES';
```

You can also use LOCAL as a synonym for SESSION.

If none of GLOBAL, SESSION, or LOCAL is present, the SET statement modifies the session-level variable:

```
SET sql_mode = 'ANSI_QUOTES';
SET @@sql_mode = 'ANSI_QUOTES';
```

To check the value of system variables, use the SHOW VARIABLES statement. You can also examine the INFORMATION_SCHEMA tables named GLOBAL_VARIABLES and SESSION_VARIABLES. To display the value of individual variables, use SELECT:

```
SELECT @@GLOBAL.sql_mode, @@SESSION.sql_mode, @@LOCAL.sql_mode;
```

For more information on use of system variables, see Section 12.3.1, "Checking and Setting System Variable Values."

The following list describes miscellaneous settings that can be controlled with SET:

- SET CHARACTER SET {charset | DEFAULT}

  Sets the character_set_client and character_set_results session variables to the named character set, and sets the character_set_connection session variable to the value of character_set_database. These variables affect conversion of character data sent to and from the server. The charset value cannot be ucs2, utf16, utf16le, or utf32.

  SET CHARACTER SET DEFAULT restores the default character set mapping.

- SET NAMES {charset [COLLATE collation] | DEFAULT}

  Sets the character_set_client, character_set_connection, and character_set_results session variables to the named character set, and sets collation_connection to the default collation for character_set_connection. The COLLATE clause may be given to specify the collation explicitly. charset and collation may be quoted or unquoted strings. These variables affect conversion of character data sent to and from the server. The charset value cannot be ucs2, utf16, utf16le, or utf32.

  SET NAMES DEFAULT restores the default character set mapping.

SET PASSWORD

```
SET PASSWORD [FOR account] = PASSWORD('pass_val')
SET PASSWORD [FOR account] = OLD_PASSWORD('pass_val')
SET PASSWORD [FOR account] = 'encrypted_pass_val'
```

SET PASSWORD changes the password for a MySQL account. You can always change your own password, unless you have connected as an anonymous user. To change the password for another account, you must have the UPDATE privilege for the mysql database. If the read_only system variable is enabled, you must also have the SUPER privilege.

With no FOR clause, the statement sets the password for the current account. With a FOR clause, it sets the password for the named account, which should be given in 'user_name'@'host_name' format, as described in Section 13.2.1.1, "Specifying Account Names."

The password value, 'pass_val' should be encrypted using PASSWORD() for standard encryption or OLD_PASSWORD() for the older (pre-MySQL 4.1) encryption. If you use neither function, 'encrypted_pass_val' should be given as an already encrypted password string.

```
SET PASSWORD = PASSWORD('secret');
SET PASSWORD FOR 'paul' = PASSWORD('secret');
SET PASSWORD FOR 'paul'@'localhost' = PASSWORD('secret');
SET PASSWORD FOR 'bill'@'%.bigcorp.com' = PASSWORD('old-sneep');
```

SET TRANSACTION

```
SET [GLOBAL | SESSION] TRANSACTION
    trans_characteristic [, trans_characteristic ] ...

trans_characteristic:
    ISOLATION LEVEL level
  | READ WRITE
  | READ ONLY
```

This statement sets transaction processing characteristics. It takes an optional scope indicator specifying how the characteristics apply to transactions.

Set the statement scope as follows:

- The GLOBAL option sets the characteristics globally (server-wide), and they become the default level for all clients that connect thereafter.

- The SESSION option sets the session (client-specific) characteristics, and they apply for subsequent transactions within the current session.

- With neither option, the statement sets the characteristics only for the next transaction within the current session. This is not permitted while there is an active transaction.

The SUPER privilege is required to use the GLOBAL option. Any client can change its own session or next-transaction characteristics.

As of MySQL 5.6.3, the statement takes one or more characteristics separated by commas. Before 5.6.3, the statement permits only the ISOLATION LEVEL characteristic to be specified.

If the ISOLATION LEVEL characteristic is given, the transaction level indicated by level should be one of the following values:

- READ UNCOMMITTED: A transaction can see row modifications made by other transactions even if they have not been committed.

- `READ COMMITTED`: A transaction can see row modifications made by other transactions only if they have been committed.

- `REPEATABLE READ`: If a transaction performs a given `SELECT` twice, the result is repeatable. That is, it gets the same result each time, even if other transactions have changed or inserted rows in the meantime.

- `SERIALIZABLE`: This isolation level is similar to `REPEATABLE READ` but isolates transactions more completely: Rows selected by one transaction cannot be modified by other transactions until the first transaction completes.

The `ISOLATION LEVEL` characteristic applies to the InnoDB storage engine. The default isolation level is `REPEATABLE READ`. Nontransactional storage engines do not have isolation levels.

For further discussion of transaction isolation and isolation levels, see Section 2.12.3, "Transaction Isolation."

The `READ WRITE` and `READ ONLY` characteristics determine the transaction access mode; that is, whether a transaction permits table modifications. (`TEMPORARY` tables can be modified regardless of access mode.) These characteristics are mutually exclusive and cannot be used in the same statement. They were introduced in MySQL 5.6.5.

SHOW

```
SHOW {BINARY | MASTER} LOGS
SHOW BINLOG EVENTS
SHOW CHARACTER SET
SHOW COLLATION
SHOW COLUMNS
SHOW CREATE DATABASE
SHOW CREATE EVENT
SHOW CREATE {FUNCTION | PROCEDURE}
SHOW CREATE TABLE
SHOW CREATE TRIGGER
SHOW CREATE VIEW
SHOW DATABASES
SHOW ENGINE
SHOW ENGINES
SHOW ERRORS
SHOW EVENTS
SHOW {FUNCTION | PROCEDURE} STATUS
SHOW GRANTS
SHOW INDEX
SHOW MASTER STATUS
SHOW OPEN TABLES
SHOW PLUGINS
SHOW PRIVILEGES
SHOW PROCESSLIST
SHOW SLAVE HOSTS
```

```
SHOW SLAVE STATUS
SHOW STATUS
SHOW TABLE STATUS
SHOW TABLES
SHOW TRIGGERS
SHOW VARIABLES
SHOW WARNINGS
```

The SHOW statements provide information about databases and objects in them such as tables or stored programs, or information about server operation. Several of the statements take an optional FROM *db_name* clause, enabling you to specify the database for which information should be shown. If the clause is not present, the default database is used. In each of the statements that support FROM to specify a table or database name, IN can be used as a synonym.

Some forms permit an optional LIKE '*pattern*' clause to limit output to values that match the pattern. '*pattern*' is interpreted as an SQL pattern and may contain the '%' or '_' wildcard characters.

INFORMATION_SCHEMA provides another way to obtain database metadata, and many INFORMATION_SCHEMA tables contain information similar to that displayed by SHOW statements. In addition, those SHOW statements that support LIKE '*pattern*' can be written with a WHERE clause instead to specify which rows to display. For more information, see Section 2.7, "Obtaining Database Metadata."

SHOW BINARY LOGS

```
SHOW {BINARY | MASTER} LOGS
```

This statement displays the names and sizes of the current binary log files. On a master replication server, it can be useful before issuing a PURGE BINARY LOGS statement after running SHOW SLAVE STATUS on each of the slaves to determine the master binary log files to which they currently are positioned.

This statement requires the SUPER privilege, or, as of MySQL 5.5.25, either SUPER or REPLICATION CLIENT.

SHOW BINLOG EVENTS

```
SHOW BINLOG EVENTS [IN 'file_name'] [FROM position]
  [LIMIT [skip_count,] show_count]
```

This statement displays events from the binary log. This statement requires the REPLICATION SLAVE privilege. To display events from a slave relay log, use SHOW RELAYLOG EVENTS.

Events correspond roughly to SQL statements. If the filename is omitted, the first binary log file is used. If the position is omitted, the statement reads from the beginning of the file. The LIMIT clause, if given, restricts the number of rows displayed. Its syntax is the same as the LIMIT clause for SELECT.

The output from SHOW BINLOG EVENTS includes the following columns:

- Log_name: The binary log filename.

- Pos: The position of the event within the log file.

- Event_type: The type of event, such as Query for a statement that is to be executed.

- Server_id: The ID of the server that logged the event.

- End_log_pos: The position of the next byte after the event in the log file.

- Info: Event information, such as the statement text for a Query event.

SHOW CHARACTER SET

```
SHOW CHARACTER SET [LIKE 'pattern' | WHERE where_expr]
```

Displays a list of the character sets supported by the server. A LIKE clause restricts output to rows for character sets with names that match the given pattern. A WHERE clause restricts output to rows that satisfy the given expression.

The output from SHOW CHARACTER SET includes the following columns:

- Charset: The short character set name. This is the name as used in SQL statements.

- Description: A longer descriptive character set name.

- Default collation: The name of the character set default collation.

- Maxlen: The length of the "widest" character in the character set, in bytes. For multi-byte character sets, this value is greater than one. For non-multi-byte sets, all characters take a single byte, so the value is one.

SHOW COLLATION

```
SHOW COLLATION [LIKE 'pattern' | WHERE where_expr]
```

Displays a list of available collations for each character set. A LIKE clause restricts output to rows for collations with names that match the given pattern. A WHERE clause restricts output to rows that satisfy the given expression.

The output from SHOW COLLATION includes the following columns:

- Collation: The collation name.

- Charset: The name of the collation's character set.

- Id: The collation ID number.

- Default: Yes if the collation is the default collation for its character set, and blank otherwise.

- `Compiled:` `Yes` if the collation is compiled into the server, and blank otherwise.

- `Sortlen:` A cost factor relating to the amount of memory that must be allocated for internal string conversion operations when the collation is used to sort values.

SHOW COLUMNS

```
SHOW [FULL] COLUMNS {FROM | IN} tbl_name
 [{FROM | IN} db_name] [LIKE 'pattern' | WHERE where_expr]
```

Displays the columns for the given table or view. The output includes only those columns for which you have some privilege. `SHOW FIELDS` is a synonym for `SHOW COLUMNS`. With the `FULL` keyword, the statement displays the `Collation`, `Privilege`, and `Comment` output fields. A `LIKE` clause restricts output to rows for columns with names that match the given pattern. A `WHERE` clause restricts output to rows that satisfy the given expression.

To specify the database that contains the table, use a `FROM db_name` clause or write the table name in `db_name.tbl_name` format:

```
SHOW COLUMNS FROM president;
SHOW COLUMNS FROM president FROM sampdb;
SHOW COLUMNS FROM sampdb.president;
```

The output from `SHOW COLUMNS` provides the following information about each column in the table. The `Collation`, `Privileges`, and `Comment` values are displayed only if the `FULL` keyword is given.

- `Field:` The column name.

- `Type:` The column data type. This may include type attributes following the type name.

- `Collation:` The collation name for nonbinary string columns, `NULL` for other columns. The collation name implies the character set name.

- `Null:` `YES` if the column can contain `NULL` values, `NO` otherwise.

- `Key:` Whether the column is indexed: `PRI` for any column in a `PRIMARY KEY`, `UNI` for the first column of a `UNIQUE` index, `MUL` for the first column of a (nonunique) index that permits multiple instances of values in the column. If the value is blank, the column is not indexed or is indexed but does not qualify for one of the other designators.

- `Default:` The column's default value. A value of `NULL` indicates either an explicit `NULL` default or that the column definition includes no `DEFAULT` clause.

- `Extra:` Extra information about the column. The value is `auto_increment` for columns with the `AUTO_INCREMENT` attribute, `on update CURRENT_TIMESTAMP` for columns with the `ON UPDATE CURRENT_TIMESTAMP` attribute, and blank otherwise.

- `Privileges:` The privileges that you hold for the column.

- `Comment:` The value of any `COMMENT` attribute in the column definition.

SHOW CREATE

```
SHOW CREATE DATABASE [IF NOT EXISTS] db_name
SHOW CREATE EVENT event_name
SHOW CREATE FUNCTION func_name
SHOW CREATE PROCEDURE proc_name
SHOW CREATE TABLE tbl_name
SHOW CREATE TRIGGER trigger_name
SHOW CREATE VIEW view_name
```

The SHOW CREATE obj_type statements display the CREATE obj_type statement that creates the named object. You cannot display the CREATE statement for an object unless you have some privilege for it. Several of the statements also display other information about the object, such as the sql_mode value in effect when it was created.

For SHOW CREATE DATABASE, if the statement includes an IF NOT EXISTS clause, the output CREATE DATABASE statement does as well.

SHOW DATABASES

```
SHOW DATABASES [LIKE 'pattern' | WHERE where_expr]
```

Displays the databases available on the server host. A LIKE clause restricts output to rows for databases with names that match the given pattern. A WHERE clause restricts output to rows that satisfy the given expression.

If you don't have the SHOW DATABASES privilege, you'll see only the databases for which you have some kind of access privilege. If the server was started with the --skip-show-database option, you'll see all databases if you have the SHOW DATABASES privilege and none otherwise.

SHOW ENGINE

```
SHOW ENGINE engine_name info_type
```

This statement displays information about storage engines. It requires the PROCESS privilege.

- SHOW ENGINE INNODB MUTEX

  Displays information about InnoDB mutexes.

- SHOW ENGINE INNODB STATUS

  Displays information about internal operation of the InnoDB storage engine.

- SHOW ENGINE PERFORMANCE_SCHEMA STATUS

  Displays information about internal operation of the Performance Schema (which is implemented as a storage engine).

SHOW ENGINES

```
SHOW [STORAGE] ENGINES
```

Displays the storage engines that the server knows about. For each engine, the output includes the following columns to indicate the support level and provide a brief description of the engine characteristics:

- Engine: The storage engine name (InnoDB, MyISAM, and so forth).

- Support: The level of support for the engine: YES for supported, NO for not supported, DISABLED for supported but disabled at runtime, or DEFAULT to indicate that the storage engine is the default engine. The default engine is always enabled.

- Comment: Descriptive text about the storage engine.

- Transactions: Whether the engine supports transactions.

- XA: Whether the engine supports distributed transactions.

- Savepoints: Whether the engine supports partial transaction rollback.

SHOW ERRORS

```
SHOW ERRORS [LIMIT [skip_count,] show_count]
SHOW COUNT(*) ERRORS
```

SHOW ERRORS is like SHOW WARNINGS but displays only messages that have error severity. SHOW COUNT(*) ERRORS is like SHOW COUNT(*) WARNINGS but displays the value of the error_count system variable rather than the value of warning_count. For more information, see the description of SHOW WARNINGS.

SHOW EVENTS

```
SHOW EVENTS [{FROM | IN} db_name]
  [LIKE 'pattern' | WHERE where_expr]
```

This statement displays information about the events in the default database, or in the named database if the FROM clause is given. It requires the EVENT privilege for the database containing the events. A LIKE clause restricts output to rows for events with names that match the given pattern. A WHERE clause restricts output to rows that satisfy the given expression.

SHOW FUNCTION STATUS, SHOW PROCEDURE STATUS

```
SHOW {FUNCTION | PROCEDURE} STATUS
  [LIKE 'pattern' | WHERE where_expr]
```

These statements display descriptive information about the stored functions or procedures in the default database. A LIKE clause restricts output to rows for routines with names that match the given pattern. A WHERE clause restricts output to rows that satisfy the given expression.

SHOW GRANTS

```
SHOW GRANTS [FOR account]
```

Displays grant information about the specified account, which should be given in `'user_name'@'host_name'` format, as described in Section 13.2.1.1, "Specifying Account Names."

```
SHOW GRANTS FOR 'root'@'localhost';
SHOW GRANTS FOR ''@'cobra.example.com';
```

You can also use any of the following statements to display the privileges that are granted to the account that you are connected to the server as:

```
SHOW GRANTS FOR CURRENT_USER();
SHOW GRANTS FOR CURRENT_USER;
SHOW GRANTS;
```

For the SHOW GRANTS formats that display current-user privileges, the output within a stored procedure that executes with SQL SECURITY DEFINER context corresponds to the procedure definer rather than its invoker.

SHOW INDEX

```
SHOW {INDEX | INDEXES | KEYS} {FROM | IN} tbl_name
  [{FROM | IN} db_name] [WHERE where_expr]
```

Displays information about a table's indexes. You must have some privilege for some column in the table.

To specify the database that contains the table, use a FROM db_name clause or write the table name in db_name.tbl_name format:

```
SHOW INDEX FROM score;
SHOW INDEX FROM score FROM sampdb;
SHOW INDEX FROM sampdb.score;
```

A WHERE clause restricts output to rows that satisfy the given expression.

The output from SHOW INDEX includes the following columns:

- Table: The name of the table that contains the index.
- Non_unique: 1 if the index can contain duplicate values, 0 if it cannot.
- Key_name: The index name.
- Seq_in_index: The number of the column within the index. Index columns are numbered beginning with 1.
- Column_name: The name of the table column in the index to which the current output row apples.
- Collation: The column sort order within the index. The values may be A (ascending), D (descending), or NULL (not sorted). Currently, descending keys are not available.

- `Cardinality`: The approximate number of unique values in the index. `myisamchk` updates this value for MyISAM tables when run with the `--analyze` option. The `ANALYZE TABLE` statement updates this value for InnoDB and MyISAM tables. `OPTIMIZE TABLE` does so for MyISAM tables.

- `Sub_part`: The prefix length in bytes, if only a prefix of the column is indexed. This is `NULL` if the entire column is indexed.

- `Packed`: How the key is packed, or `NULL` if it is not packed.

- `Null`: `YES` if the column can contain `NULL` values, blank otherwise.

- `Index_type`: The algorithm used to index the column, such as `BTREE`, `FULLTEXT`, or `HASH`.

- `Comment`: Reserved for internal comments about the index.

- `Index_comment`: Any comment included in the index definition.

SHOW MASTER STATUS

```
SHOW MASTER STATUS
```

This statement is used on replication master servers. The output includes the following columns to display information about the status of the binary log:

- `File`: The binary log filename.

- `Position`: The current position at which the server is writing to the file.

- `Binlog_Do_DB`: A comma-separated list of databases that are explicitly replicated to the binary log with `--binlog-do-db` options; blank if there are none.

- `Binlog_Ignore_DB`: A comma-separated list of databases that are explicitly excluded from the binary log with `--binlog-ignore-db` options; blank if there are none.

SHOW OPEN TABLES

```
SHOW OPEN TABLES [{FROM | IN} db_name]
  [LIKE 'pattern' | WHERE where_expr]
```

Displays the list of open non-`TEMPORARY` tables registered in the table cache for which you have some privilege. A `LIKE` clause restricts output to rows for tables with names that match the given pattern. A `WHERE` clause restricts output to rows that satisfy the given expression.

The output from `SHOW OPEN TABLES` includes the following columns:

- `Database`: The database that contains the table.

- `Table`: The name of the table.

- `In_use`: The number of times the table currently is in use.

- `Name_locked`: Whether the table has a name lock such as is required to use the table without accessing its contents (for example, for `RENAME TABLE`).

SHOW PLUGINS

```
SHOW PLUGINS
```

Displays information about installed plugins.

The output from SHOW PLUGINS includes the following columns:

- Name: The plugin name.
- Status: The plugin status: ACTIVE, INACTIVE, DISABLED, DELETED.
- Type: The plugin type; for example, STORAGE ENGINE.
- Library: The plugin library object file, or NULL if the plugin is built in.
- License: The plugin license type.

SHOW PRIVILEGES

```
SHOW PRIVILEGES
```

Displays the privileges that can be granted and information about the purpose of each one.

SHOW PROCESSLIST

```
SHOW [FULL] PROCESSLIST
```

Displays information about the currently executing server activity. If you have the PROCESS privilege, the statement displays all information. Otherwise, it displays information only about your own activity.

The output from SHOW PROCESSLIST includes the following columns:

- Id: The client process ID number.
- User: The username for the account associated with the process.
- Host: The host from which the client is connected.
- db: The default database for the process, NULL if none.
- Command: The type of command being executed.
- Time: How long in seconds the process has been in its current state.
- State: Information about what MySQL is doing while processing an SQL statement.
- Info: The first 100 characters of the statement being executed, or the entire statement if the FULL keyword is given.

SHOW RELAYLOG EVENTS

```
SHOW RELAYLOG EVENTS [IN 'file_name'] [FROM position]
  [LIMIT [skip_count,] show_count]
```

This statement is similar to SHOW BINLOG EVENTS, but displays slave relay log contents.

SHOW SLAVE HOSTS

```
SHOW SLAVE HOSTS
```

This statement is used on replication master servers to display information about the slave servers currently registered with it. It requires the `REPLICATION SLAVE` privilege.

The output from `SHOW SLAVE HOSTS` includes the following columns:

- `Server_id`: The slave server ID.
- `Host`: The slave host.
- `User`: The username of the account that the slave used to connect to the master.
- `Password`: The password of the account that the slave used to connect to the master.
- `Port`: The port the slave listens on. The `Port` column value is 0 (3306 before MySQL 5.5.23) unless the slave is started with the `report_port` system variable set.
- `Master_id`: The master server ID.
- `Slave_UUID`: The slave UUID value. This column was introduced in MySQL 5.6.0.

SHOW SLAVE STATUS

```
SHOW SLAVE STATUS
```

This statement is used on slave servers and displays information about the replication status of the server. Many of these values reflect parameters specified using the `CHANGE MASTER` statement. The output from `SHOW SLAVE STATUS` includes the following columns:

- `Slave_IO_State`: The state of the slave I/O thread. This is the same as the `State` value that `SHOW PROCESSLIST` displays for the I/O thread.
- `Master_Host`: The master host to which the slave is connected.
- `Master_User`: The username of the account used for connecting to the master.
- `Master_Port`: The port number used for connecting to the master.
- `Connect_Retry`: The number of seconds to wait between attempts to connect to the master.
- `Master_Log_File`: The name of the current master binary log file.
- `Read_Master_Log_Pos`: The current position within the master binary log file where the slave I/O thread is reading.
- `Relay_Log_File`: The name of the current relay log file.
- `Relay_Log_Pos`: The current position of the slave SQL thread within the relay log file.
- `Relay_Master_Log_File`: The name of the master binary log file that contains the event most recently executed by the SQL thread.

- `Slave_IO_Running`: Whether the slave I/O thread is running and has connected to the master.

- `Slave_SQL_Running`: Whether the slave SQL thread is running.

- `Replicate_Do_DB, Replicate_Ignore_DB Replicate_Do_Table, Replicate_Ignore_Table, Replicate_Wild_Do_Table, Replicate_Wild_Ignore_Table`: A comma-separated list of databases or tables that are explicitly replicated or excluded from replication with the `--replicate-do-db`, `--replicate-ignore-db`, `--replicate-do-table`, `--replicate-ignore-table`, `--replicate-wild-do-table`, and `--replicate-wild-ignore-table` options; blank if there are none.

- `Last_Errno, Last_Error`: These columns are aliases for `Last_SQL_Errno` and `Last_SQL_Error`.

- `Skip_Counter`: The current number of events from the master that the slave should skip. (To cause the slave to skip events, set its global `sql_slave_skip_counter` system variable.)

- `Exec_Master_Log_Pos`: The current position within the master binary log file where the slave SQL thread is executing.

- `Relay_Log_Space`: The combined size of the relay log files.

- `Until_Condition`: The condition specified in an UNTIL clause of a START SLAVE statement to indicate when the SQL thread should stop reading and executing events:

    - `None`: No UNTIL clause was specified.

    - `Master`: The slave is reading until its SQL thread reaches a specific position in the master binary log.

    - `Relay`: The slave is reading until its SQL thread reaches a specific position in its relay log.

If the `Until_Condition` value is `Master` or `Relay`, the `Until_Log_File` and `Until_Log_Pos` column values indicate the filename and position at which the SQL thread will stop executing.

- `Until_Log_File, Until_Log_Pos`: See the description of `Until_Condition`.

- `Master_SSL_Allowed`: Whether SSL is used to connect to the master server: `Yes` if SSL connections can be used, `No` if they cannot, and `Ignored` if SSL connections are permitted, but the slave server was not built with SSL support enabled.

- `Master_SSL_CA_File, Master_SSL_CA_Path, Master_SSL_Cert, Master_SSL_Cipher, Master_SSL_Key, Master_SSL_Verify_Server_Cert, Master_SSL_Crl, Master_SSL_Crlpath`: The SSL parameters to use for connecting to the master. `Master_SSL_Crl` and `Master_SSL_Crlpath` were introduced in MySQL 5.6.3.

- `Seconds_Behind_Master`: The difference in seconds between the current time and the timestamp recorded in the master event most recently executed by the slave SQL thread. This value is zero if the SQL thread has caught up with the I/O thread and is idle, and

NULL if no event has been executed or the slave parameters have been changed with a CHANGE MASTER or RESET SLAVE statement.

- Last_IO_Errno, Last_IO_Error: The most recent error number and message for the IO thread. The values are 0 and the empty string if there was no error. The server also writes nonempty message values to its error log.

- Last_SQL_Errno, Last_SQL_Error: Like Last_IO_Errno and Last_IO_Error, but for the SQL thread.

- Replicate_Ignore_Server_Ids: The IDs of servers from which to ignore events.

- Master_Server_Id: The master's server_id value.

- Master_UUID: The master's server_uuid value. This column was introduced in MySQL 5.6.1.

- Master_Info_File: The name of the slave's master.info file. This column was introduced in MySQL 5.6.1.

- SQL_Delay: The replication delay in seconds. This column was introduced in MySQL 5.6.1.

- SQL_Remaining_Delay: The number of seconds of delay the slave is still waiting until executing the next event, NULL if it is not waiting. This column was introduced in MySQL 5.6.1.

- Slave_SQL_Running_State: The state of the slave SQL thread. This is the same as the State value that SHOW PROCESSLIST displays for the SQL thread. This column was introduced in MySQL 5.6.1.

- Master_Retry_Count: How many times the slave will attempt a connection to the master before giving up. This column was introduced in MySQL 5.6.1.

- Master_Bind: The network interface the slave is bound to. This column was introduced in MySQL 5.6.1.

- Last_IO_Error_Timestamp: When the most recent I/O thread error occurred. This column was introduced in MySQL 5.6.2. Before 5.6.2, the timestamp was part of the Last_IO_Error value.

- Last_SQL_Error_Timestamp: When the most recent SQL thread error occurred. This column was introduced in MySQL 5.6.2. Before 5.6.2, the timestamp was part of the Last_SQL_Error value.

SHOW STATUS

```
SHOW [GLOBAL | SESSION ] STATUS
  [LIKE 'pattern' | WHERE where_expr]
```

Displays the server's status variables and their values. These variables provide information about the server's operational state. A LIKE clause restricts output to rows for variables with names that match the given pattern. A WHERE clause restricts output to rows that satisfy the given expression.

The server can display the values of status variables at the global (server-wide) or session (client-specific) scope. These represent the sum over all clients and the value for the current client, respectively. By default, SHOW displays the session value for any given variable. To display global or session values explicitly, specify a scope indicator:

```
SHOW GLOBAL STATUS;
SHOW SESSION STATUS;
```

If a variable has only a global value, you get the same value for GLOBAL and SESSION. LOCAL is a synonym for SESSION.

You can also query the INFORMATION_SCHEMA tables named GLOBAL_STATUS and SESSION_STATUS to obtain status variable information.

For more information about the use of status variables, see Section 12.3.2, "Checking Status Variable Values." For descriptions of each one, see Appendix D, "System, Status, and User Variable Reference."

SHOW TABLE STATUS

```
SHOW TABLE STATUS [{FROM | IN} db_name]
  [LIKE 'pattern' | WHERE where_expr]
```

Displays descriptive information about the non-TEMPORARY tables in a database for which you have some privilege. This statement also displays the views in a database, but all columns are NULL except that Name is the view name and Comment is view. A LIKE clause restricts output to rows for tables with names that match the given pattern. A WHERE clause restricts output to rows that satisfy the given expression.

The output from SHOW TABLE STATUS includes the following columns:

- Name: The table name.
- Engine: The storage engine (InnoDB, MyISAM, and so forth).
- Version: The version number of the .frm file for the table.
- Row_format: The row storage format. This comes from the ROW_FORMAT table option specified for CREATE TABLE.
- Rows: The number of rows in the table. For some storage engines such as InnoDB, this is an approximate count.
- Avg_row_length: The average number of bytes used by table rows.
- Data_length: The actual size in bytes of the table data file.
- Max_data_length: The maximum size that the table data file can grow to.

- Index_length: The actual size in bytes of the index file.

- Data_free: The number of unused bytes in the data file. If this number is very high, it might be a good idea to issue an OPTIMIZE TABLE statement for the table to defragment it. For InnoDB tables, this column indicates the amount of free space in the InnoDB tablespace in which the table is stored. (The table might be in the system tablespace or have its own tablespace.)

- Auto_increment: The next value AUTO_INCREMENT value to be generated for the table.

- Create_time: The table creation time.

- Update_time: The most recent table modification time; NULL if the storage engine does not maintain this value.

- Check_time: The most recent table check or repair time; NULL if the storage engine does not maintain this value or if the table has never been checked or repaired.

- Collation: The table collation. The collation name implies the character set name.

- Checksum: The table checksum value; NULL if one has not been calculated.

- Create_options: Extra options that were specified as table_option values in the CREATE TABLE statement that created the table or subsequent ALTER TABLE statements.

- Comment: The text of any comment specified when the table was created.

SHOW TABLES

```
SHOW [FULL] TABLES [{FROM | IN} db_name]
   [LIKE 'pattern' | WHERE where_expr]
```

Displays the names of the non-TEMPORARY tables in a database for which you have some privilege. This statement also displays view names. The FULL keyword may be given to display a column that indicates for each row whether the name refers to a table (BASE_TABLE) or a view (VIEW). A LIKE clause restricts output to rows for tables with names that match the given pattern. A WHERE clause restricts output to rows that satisfy the given expression.

SHOW TRIGGERS

```
SHOW TRIGGERS [{FROM | IN} db_name]
   [LIKE 'pattern' | WHERE where_expr]
```

This statement displays information about the triggers in the default database, or in the named database if the FROM clause is given. The output includes results only for tables on which you have the TRIGGER privilege. A LIKE clause restricts output to rows for triggers from tables with names that match the given pattern. A WHERE clause restricts output to rows that satisfy the given expression.

SHOW VARIABLES

```
SHOW [GLOBAL | SESSION ] VARIABLES
  [LIKE 'pattern' | WHERE where_expr]
```

Displays a list of system variables and their values. These variables provide information about the server's configuration and capabilities. A LIKE clause restricts output to rows for variables with names that match the given pattern. A WHERE clause restricts output to rows that satisfy the given expression.

The server can display the values of system variables for the global (server-wide) or session (client-specific) scope. By default, SHOW VARIABLES displays session variable values. (Before MySQL 5.5.3, it displays the session value, or the global value if there is no session value.) To display global or session values explicitly, specify a scope indicator:

```
SHOW GLOBAL VARIABLES;
SHOW SESSION VARIABLES;
```

LOCAL is a synonym for SESSION. It is also possible to retrieve the values of individual dynamic variables with SELECT:

```
SELECT @@GLOBAL.sql_mode, @@SESSION.sql_mode, @@LOCAL.sql_mode;
```

Using SELECT has the advantage that you can more easily manipulate the query result in certain contexts.

You can also examine the INFORMATION_SCHEMA tables named GLOBAL_VARIABLES and SESSION_VARIABLES to obtain system variable information.

For more information about the use of system variables, see Section 12.3.1, "Checking and Setting System Variable Values." For descriptions of each one, see Appendix D, "System, Status, and User Variable Reference."

SHOW WARNINGS

```
SHOW WARNINGS [LIMIT [skip_count,] show_count]
SHOW COUNT(*) WARNINGS
```

SHOW WARNINGS displays error, warnings, and notes generated by the most recent statement that generates such messages. If that statement executed successfully, SHOW WARNINGS returns an empty set.

SHOW COUNT(*) WARNINGS displays the value of the warning_count system variable that counts the number of messages. (A related variable, error_count, counts only errors.) It is possible for the value of warning_count to be larger than the number of messages displayed by SHOW WARNINGS. The max_error_count system variable limits the number of messages that can be stored for display by SHOW WARNINGS, but warning_count counts all messages regardless of whether they are stored.

The LIMIT clause, if given, restricts the number of rows displayed. Its syntax is the same as the LIMIT clause for SELECT.

START SLAVE

```
START SLAVE [thread_option [, thread_option] ...]

START SLAVE [SQL_THREAD] UNTIL
  MASTER_LOG_FILE = 'file_name', MASTER_LOG_POS = position

START SLAVE [SQL_THREAD] UNTIL
  RELAY_LOG_FILE = 'file_name', RELAY_LOG_POS = position

START SLAVE [USER = 'user_name'] [PASSWORD = 'pass_val']
  [DEFAULT_AUTH = 'auth_plugin'] [PLUGIN_DIR = 'dir_name']
```

This statement, together with STOP SLAVE, controls the operation of replication threads on a slave server. With no options, START SLAVE initiates and STOP SLAVE terminates both the slave I/O and SQL threads. `thread_option` values may be specified to indicate which threads to start or stop:

- IO_THREAD: Start or stop the I/O thread that reads events from the master server and stores them in the relay log.

- SQL_THREAD: Start or stop the SQL thread that reads events from the relay log and executes them.

If no thread or SQL_THREAD is named, an UNTIL clause can be used. Depending on which pair of log file and position options are named in the clause, the slave runs until its SQL thread reaches the given position in the master binary log or slave relay log. If the SQL thread is already running, the server ignores the UNTIL clause and generates a warning. If the clause includes the SQL_THREAD option, the server starts only the SQL thread. Otherwise, it starts both threads.

As of MySQL 5.6.4, START SLAVE can specify parameters for using an authentication plugin. This syntax permits the following options; those present must be given in the order shown:

- USER: The username. This cannot be given as NULL or an empty string, and must be specified if the PASSWORD option is present.

- PASSWORD: The user password.

- DEFAULT_AUTH: The authentication plugin name. If omitted, the default is MySQL native password authentication.

- PLUGIN_DIR: The directory where the plugin is located.

START TRANSACTION

```
START TRANSACTION
    [trans_characteristic [, trans_characteristic ] ...]

trans_characteristic:
    WITH CONSISTENT SNAPSHOT
  | READ WRITE
  | READ ONLY
```

Begins a transaction by disabling autocommit mode until the next COMMIT or ROLLBACK statement. Statements executed while autocommit is disabled thus are committed or rolled back as a unit.

After the transaction has been committed or rolled back, autocommit mode is restored to the state it was in prior to START TRANSACTION. To manipulate autocommit mode explicitly, set the autocommit system variable as described in Section 2.12.1, "Using Transactions to Ensure Safe Statement Execution."

The WITH CONSISTENT SNAPSHOT characteristic, if given, causes the transaction to begin with a consistent read. For InnoDB, this clause does not change the current isolation level, so it is effective only if the level is REPEATABLE READ or SERIALIZABLE.

The READ WRITE and READ ONLY characteristics determine the transaction access mode; that is, whether a transaction permits table modifications. (TEMPORARY tables can be modified regardless of access mode.) These characteristics are mutually exclusive and cannot be used in the same statement. They were introduced in MySQL 5.6.5.

START TRANSACTION implicitly releases any table locks that the client has acquired with LOCK TABLE but has not yet released. Executing START TRANSACTION while a transaction is in progress causes that transaction to be committed implicitly.

STOP SLAVE

STOP SLAVE [thread_option [, thread_option] ...]

This statement, together with START SLAVE, controls the operation of replication threads on a slave server. For details about the permitted thread_option values, see the entry for START SLAVE.

TRUNCATE TABLE

TRUNCATE [TABLE] tbl_name

TRUNCATE TABLE performs a fast truncation of table contents by dropping and re-creating the table. This is much faster than deleting each row individually. You must have the DROP privilege for the table.

For InnoDB, this statement is not permitted and returns an error if any foreign keys reference the table.

This statement is not transaction-safe. An error occurs if you issue a TRUNCATE TABLE statement within a transaction or while you hold any explicit table locks.

UNINSTALL PLUGIN

UNINSTALL PLUGIN plugin_name

Uninstalls the named plugin and unregisters it from the mysql.plugin table (if it is listed there) so that it does not load on subsequent server restarts. INSTALL PLUGIN requires the DELETE privilege for the mysql.plugin table. For more information, see Section 12.4, "The Plugin Interface."

UNION

```
select_stmt
  UNION [DISTINCT | ALL] select_stmt
  [UNION [DISTINCT | ALL] select_stmt] ...
  [ORDER BY col_list] [LIMIT [skip_count,] show_count]
```

UNION combines the results of multiple SELECT statements. Each SELECT statement must produce the same number of columns in its result set. The column names from the first SELECT determine the column names of the final result. The data types of the columns are determined taking into account all values from the corresponding columns of the selected tables.

The UNION keyword can be followed by DISTINCT to eliminate duplicate rows or by ALL to preserve duplicates and return all selected rows. The implicit default is to eliminate duplicates if neither DISTINCT nor ALL is given. Any DISTINCT union operation (either explicit or implicit) takes precedence over any ALL union operations to its left:

```
mysql> SELECT 1 UNION ALL SELECT 2 UNION ALL SELECT 1;
+---+
| 1 |
+---+
| 1 |
| 2 |
| 1 |
+---+
mysql> SELECT 1 UNION ALL SELECT 2 UNION SELECT 1;
+---+
| 1 |
+---+
| 1 |
| 2 |
+---+
```

To use ORDER BY and LIMIT clauses with any individual SELECT, enclose each SELECT within parentheses. (ORDER BY within an individual SELECT is used only if LIMIT is also present, to determine which rows the LIMIT applies to. It does not affect the order in which rows appear in the final UNION result.) To apply ORDER BY or LIMIT to the UNION as a whole, enclose each SELECT within parentheses and add ORDER BY or LIMIT following the final closing parenthesis. In this case, any columns named in an ORDER BY should refer to the names of the columns in the first SELECT.

UNLOCK TABLE

```
UNLOCK {TABLE | TABLES}
```

This statement releases any table locks being held by the current client. The server automatically releases table locks held by a client if the client begins a transaction or the client session terminates.

UPDATE

```
UPDATE [LOW_PRIORITY] [IGNORE]
  tbl_name
  [PARTITION (partition_name [, partition_name] ...)]
  SET col_name=expr [, col_name=expr ] ...
  [WHERE where_expr] [ORDER BY ... ] [LIMIT n]

UPDATE [LOW_PRIORITY] [IGNORE] tbl_refs
  SET col_name=expr [, col_name=expr ] ...
  [WHERE where_expr] [ORDER BY ... ] [LIMIT n]
```

For the first syntax, UPDATE modifies the contents of existing rows in the table *tbl_name*. As of MySQL 5.6.2, UPDATE supports a PARTITION clause for partitioned tables to indicate the partitions or subpartitions into which to update rows. In this case, if a row to be updated is not in any named partition, it remains unchanged.

The second UPDATE syntax is like the first, but enables multiple tables to be named to perform a multiple-table update. The syntax for *tbl_refs* is like that for SELECT, (including support for a PARTITION clause following each table name), except that you cannot specify a subquery as a table.

The rows to be updated are those selected by the expression specified in the WHERE clause. For the selected rows, each column named in the SET clause is set to the value of the corresponding expression.

```
UPDATE member SET expiration = NULL, phone = '197-602-4832'
  WHERE member_id = 14;
```

The WHERE clause can include subqueries, but they cannot select rows from a table that is being updated.

If no WHERE clause is given, *all rows in the table are updated.*

By default, UPDATE returns the number of rows that were updated. However, a row is not considered as having been updated unless some column value actually changed. Setting a column to the value it already contains is not considered to affect the row. If your application really needs to have UPDATE return how many rows matched the WHERE clause regardless of whether the UPDATE actually changed any values, specify the CLIENT_FOUND_ROWS flag when you establish a connection to the server. See the entry for the mysql_real_connect() function in Appendix G, "C API Reference."

LOW_PRIORITY causes the statement to be deferred until no clients are reading from the table. This option is effective only for storage engines that use table-level locking, such as MyISAM or MEMORY.

If updating a row would result in a duplicate key value in a unique index, UPDATE terminates in error and no more rows are updated. Adding IGNORE causes such rows not to be updated and no error occurs. In strict mode, IGNORE also causes data conversion errors that otherwise would terminate the statement to be treated as nonfatal warnings. Columns are updated to the nearest legal value in this case.

ORDER BY causes rows to be updated according to the resulting sort order. This clause has the same syntax as for SELECT.

If the LIMIT clause is given, the value *n* specifies the maximum number of rows to update.

For a multiple-table UPDATE, the WHERE clause can specify conditions based on a join between tables, and the SET clause can update columns in multiple tables. For example, the following statement updates rows in t1 having id values that match those in t2, copying the quantity values from t2 to t1:

```
UPDATE t INNER JOIN t2 SET t.quantity = t2.quantity WHERE t.id = t2.id;
```

USE

```
USE db_name
```

Selects *db_name* to make it the default database (the database for table, view, and stored program references that include no explicit database name). After a successful USE statement, the server sets the session character_set_database and collation_database system variables to the database character set and collation.

The USE statement fails if the database doesn't exist or if you have no privileges for accessing it.

E.2   SQL Statement Syntax (Compound Statements)

This section describes the syntax for statements that are used within compound statements, which are written using BEGIN and END and can be used for writing stored programs: functions, procedures, triggers, and events that are stored on the server side.

Each statement within a program body must be terminated by a semicolon (';') character. If you use the mysql program to create a stored routine that has a multiple-statement body, you should temporarily redefine the mysql statement delimiter so that mysql itself does not interpret ';' characters. To do this, use the delimiter command. Be sure to choose as your delimiter something that does not occur within the statements that define the routine. For more information about defining stored programs, with examples, see Section 4.2.1, "Compound Statements and Statement Delimiters."

E.2.1   Control Structure Statements

The statements in this section group statements into blocks and provide flow-control constructs. Each occurrence of *stmt_list* in the syntax for these statements indicates a list of one or more statements, each terminated by a semicolon character (';').

Some of the constructs can be labeled (BEGIN, LOOP, REPEAT, and WHILE). Labels are not case sensitive but must follow these rules:

- If a label appears at the beginning of a construct, a label with the same name may also appear at the end.

- A label may not appear at the end without a matching label at the beginning.

BEGIN ... END

```
BEGIN [stmt_list] END

label: BEGIN [stmt_list] END [label]
```

The BEGIN ... END construct creates a block within which multiple statements can be grouped. If a stored program body contains more than one statement, they must be grouped within a BEGIN block. Also, if a BEGIN block contains any DECLARE statements, they must appear the beginning of the block.

CASE

```
CASE [expr]
  WHEN expr1 THEN stmt_list1
  [WHEN expr2 THEN stmt_list2] ...
  [ELSE stmt_list]
END IF
```

The CASE statement provides a branching flow-control construct. This statement differs from the CASE operator described in Section C.1.4, "Comparison Operators."

If the initial expression, expr, is present, CASE compares it to the expression following each WHEN. For the first one that is equal, the statement list for the corresponding THEN value is executed. This is useful for comparing a given value to a set of values.

When the initial expression, expr, is not present, CASE evaluates WHEN expressions. For the first one that is true, the statement list for the corresponding THEN value is executed. This is useful for performing nonequality tests or testing arbitrary conditions.

If no WHEN expression matches, the statement list for the ELSE clause is executed, if there is one.

IF

```
IF expr1 THEN stmt_list1
  [ELSEIF expr2 THEN stmt_list2] ...
  [ELSE stmt_list]
END IF
```

The IF statement provides a branching flow-control construct. This statement differs from the IF() function described in Section C.2.1, "Comparison Functions."

If the expression following the IF keyword is true, the statement list following the initial THEN is executed. Otherwise, expressions for any following ELSEIF clauses are evaluated. For the first one that is true, the corresponding statement list is executed. If no expression is true, the statement list for the ELSE clause is executed, if there is one.

ITERATE

```
ITERATE label
```

The ITERATE statement is used within looping constructs to begin the next iteration of the loop. It can appear within LOOP, REPEAT, and WHILE.

LEAVE

LEAVE *label*

The LEAVE statement is used to exit a labeled flow-control construct. The statement must appear within the construct that has the given label.

LOOP

LOOP *stmt_list* END LOOP

label: LOOP *stmt_list* END LOOP [*label*]

This statement sets up an execution loop. The statements within the loop execute repeatedly until control is transferred out of the loop.

REPEAT

REPEAT *stmt_list* UNTIL *expr* END REPEAT

label: REPEAT *stmt_list* UNTIL *expr* END REPEAT [*label*]

This statement sets up an execution loop. The statements within the loop execute repeatedly until the expression *expr* is true.

RETURN

RETURN *expr*

The RETURN statement is used only within stored functions (not stored procedures, triggers, or events). When executed, it terminates execution of the function, and the value of *expr* becomes the value returned to the statement that invoked the function. There must be at least one RETURN statement within a function.

WHILE

WHILE *expr* DO *stmt_list* END WHILE

label: WHILE *expr* DO *stmt_list* END WHILE [*label*]

This statement sets up an execution loop. The statements within the loop execute repeatedly as long as the expression *expr* is true.

E.2.2   Declaration Statements

DECLARE

DECLARE *var_name* [, *var_name*] ... *type* [DEFAULT *value*]

DECLARE *condition_name* CONDITION FOR *named_condition*

named_condition: {SQLSTATE [VALUE] *sqlstate_value* | *mysql_errno*}

```
DECLARE cursor_name CURSOR FOR select_stmt

DECLARE handler_type
  HANDLER FOR handler_condition [, handler_condition] ...
  statement

handler_type: {CONTINUE | EXIT}

handler_condition:
    SQLSTATE [VALUE] sqlstate_value
  | mysql_errno
  | condition_name
  | SQLWARNING
  | NOT FOUND
  | SQLEXCEPTION
```

Variants of the DECLARE statement declare local variables, conditions, cursors, and handlers. DECLARE can appear only at the beginning of a BEGIN block. If multiple declarations occur, they must appear in this order:

1. Variable and condition declarations

2. Cursor declarations

3. Handler declarations

DECLARE followed by a list of comma-separated variables declares local variables for use within the routine. A local variable is accessible within the BEGIN block where it is declared and any nested blocks, but not in any outer blocks.

A local variable can be initialized in the DECLARE statement with a DEFAULT clause. If there is no DEFAULT clause, the initial value is NULL. To assign a value to a local variable later in the routine, use a SET, SELECT ... INTO, or FETCH ... INTO statement.

DECLARE ... CONDITION creates a name for a condition. condition_name can be referred to in DECLARE ... HANDLER, SIGNAL, and RESIGNAL statements. named_condition can be either an SQLSTATE value represented as a five-character quoted string, or a numeric MySQL-specific error number.

DECLARE ... CURSOR declares a cursor and associates it with a given SELECT statement, which should not contain an INTO clause. The cursor can be opened with an OPEN statement, used with FETCH to retrieve rows, and closed with CLOSE.

DECLARE ... HANDLER associates one or more conditions with a statement to be executed when any of the conditions occur (the statement can be a BEGIN ... END compound statement). The handler_type value indicates what happens after the handler executes. With CONTINUE, execution continues. With EXIT, execution terminates for the BEGIN block in which the handler is declared.

handler_condition can be any of the following types of values:

- An SQLSTATE value represented as a five-character string. The value should not begin with '00' because that represents success, not an error.

- A numeric MySQL-specific error number. The value should not be zero because that represents success, not an error.

- A named condition previously declared with DECLARE ... CONDITION.

- SQLWARNING, which stands for any SQLSTATE value that begins with '01'.

- NOT FOUND, which stands for any SQLSTATE value that begins with '02'.

- SQLEXCEPTION, which stands for any SQLSTATE value that does not begin with '00', '01', or '02'.

For examples of each type of DECLARE, see Section E.2.3, "Cursor Statements."

E.2.3 Cursor Statements

The statements in this section enable you to open and close cursors, and to use them for fetching rows while open. Cursors in MySQL are read only and can be used only to move forward a row at a time within a result set (that is, they are not scrollable). The following example demonstrates how to use each of the cursor-related statements. It also shows each of the DECLARE variants, which are often used in conjunction with cursor loops.

```
CREATE PROCEDURE p ()
BEGIN
  DECLARE more_data INT DEFAULT TRUE;
  DECLARE id INT;
  DECLARE no_data CONDITION FOR SQLSTATE '02000';
  DECLARE curs CURSOR FOR SELECT member_id FROM sampdb.member;
  DECLARE CONTINUE HANDLER FOR no_data
    BEGIN
      SET more_data = FALSE;
    END;

  -- open cursor, fetch rows using cursor until No Data occurs
  OPEN curs;
  WHILE more_data DO
    FETCH curs INTO id;
  END WHILE;
  CLOSE curs;
END;
```

CLOSE

```
CLOSE cursor_name
```

Closes the given cursor, which must be open. An open cursor closes automatically when the BEGIN block within which the cursor was declared ends.

FETCH

```
FETCH [[NEXT] FROM] cursor_name INTO var_name [, var_name] ...
```

Fetches the next row from the given cursor into the named variable or variables. The cursor must be open. If no row is available, an error with an SQLSTATE value of 02000 (No Data) occurs.

OPEN

```
OPEN cursor_name
```

Opens the given cursor so that it can be used with FETCH.

E.2.4   Condition-Handling Statements

As SQL statements execute, they produce diagnostic information about conditions that occur. This information can be examined with GET DIAGNOSTICS. It is also possible to raise conditions explicitly with SIGNAL and RESIGNAL. This section describes these statements. See also Section E.2.2, "Declaration Statements," for the syntax for declaring named conditions and condition handlers.

GET DIAGNOSTICS

```
GET [CURRENT] DIAGNOSTICS
{
    var_name = stmt_info_type
    [, var_name = stmt_info_type] ...
  | CONDITION n
    var_name = condition_info_type
    [, var_name = condition_into_type] ...
}

stmt_info_type:
    NUMBER
  | ROW_COUNT

condition_info_type:
    CLASS_ORIGIN
  | SUBCLASS_ORIGIN
  | RETURNED_SQLSTATE
```

```
| MESSAGE_TEXT
| MYSQL_ERRNO
| CONSTRAINT_CATALOG
| CONSTRAINT_SCHEMA
| CONSTRAINT_NAME
| CATALOG_NAME
| SCHEMA_NAME
| TABLE_NAME
| COLUMN_NAME
| CURSOR_NAME
```

This statement enables you to examine the contents of the diagnostic area, which contains two types of information generated by statements: Information about the statement itself (such as the number of affected rows or number of conditions that occurred), and information about the conditions the statement generated (such as error messages and codes). The diagnostic area can contain information about multiple conditions. GET DIAGNOSTICS was introduced in MySQL 5.6.4.

The CURRENT keyword has no meaning in MySQL and may be omitted. Standard SQL has a stack of diagnostic areas. MySQL has just one, which is always current.

Each instance of GET DIAGNOSTICS returns either statement information, or, with a CONDITION clause, condition information. For example, to fetch the number of affected rows and conditions for a statement into user-defined variables, do this:

```
GET DIAGNOSTICS
    @affected_rows = ROW_COUNT, @condition_count = NUMBER;
```

To fetch the SQLSTATE value and error message for condition 2, do this:

```
GET DIAGNOSTICS CONDITION 2
    @sqlstate = RETURNED_SQLSTATE, @message = MESSAGE_TEXT;
```

The condition number for the CONDITION clause must be an integer from 1 to the number of conditions. It can be specified using a literal value, user-defined variable, system variable, stored program local variable, or stored function or procedure parameter. The max_error_count system variable controls how many conditions the diagnostic area can store. The warning_count variable indicates how many error, warning, and note conditions occurred. This can be more than NUMBER because it counts conditions whether or not there is room to store them. error_count is similar but counts only error conditions.

The remainder of the statement that indicates what information to fetch consists of one or more variable assignments separated by commas. Each variable var_name can be a user-defined variable, stored program local variable, or stored function or procedure parameter. Permitted names for the types of information to assign to variables are described following. Numeric items are integer valued; other values are strings.

For statement information in the diagnostic area, these items are available:

- NUMBER: The number of conditions in the diagnostic area. It is possible for there to be no conditions, in which case NUMBER is 0. To determine how many conditions there are, use a statement like this:

  ```
  GET DIAGNOSTICS @condition_count = NUMBER;
  ```

- ROW_COUNT: The number of rows affected by the statement.

For condition information in the diagnostic area, the following items are available. With the exception of RETURNED_SQLSTATE, these can also be named in the SET clause of SIGNAL and RESIGNAL. Those two statements set the value of RETURNED_SQLSTATE indirectly by means of the condition they name.

- CLASS_ORIGIN, SUBCLASS_ORIGIN: The class and subclass of the RETURNED_SQLSTATE value. If that value is defined in the ISO 9075-2 SQL standards document, the class is 'ISO 9075', otherwise 'MySQL'. If the class is 'ISO 9075' or RETURNED_SQLSTATE ends with '000', the subclass is 'ISO 9075', otherwise 'MySQL'.

- RETURNED_SQLSTATE: The SQLSTATE string.

- MESSAGE_TEXT: The error message.

- MYSQL_ERRNO: The MySQL error number.

- CONSTRAINT_CATALOG, CONSTRAINT_SCHEMA, CONSTRAINT_NAME: The catalog, schema, and name of a violated constraint. Always empty in MySQL.

- CATALOG_NAME, SCHEMA_NAME, TABLE_NAME, COLUMN_NAME, The relevant catalog, schema, table, and column for the condition. Always empty in MySQL.

- CURSOR_NAME: The relevant cursor name for the condition. Always empty in MySQL.

The "always empty" values are always empty for GET DIAGNOSTICS. They can be set nonempty by SIGNAL or RESIGNAL because those statements assign values to condition area members.

Statements that use tables clear the diagnostic area when they begin executing. Other statements clear the diagnostic area of conditions from previous statements if a condition occurs during execution. The exceptions are GET DIAGNOSTICS and RESIGNAL, which add their conditions to the diagnostic area rather than clearing it. You can use GET DIAGNOSTICS, SHOW WARNINGS, or SHOW ERRORS to retrieve or display condition information without clearing the diagnostic area.

RESIGNAL

```
RESIGNAL [condition_value]
  [SET condition_info_type = value
    [, condition_info_type = value] ...]

condition_value, condition_info_type, value:
  see SIGNAL description
```

The RESIGNAL statement is similar to SIGNAL but is used to pass along previously generated condition information, perhaps modifying or adding to it. This can be useful within a condition handler if you discover that a condition is one better handled in an outer context rather than the current context. Unlike SIGNAL, RESIGNAL can be used only if some condition handler is active.

See the description for SIGNAL for an explanation of the syntax terms used for RESIGNAL. The RESIGNAL statement is much the same, except that *condition_value* is optional:

- RESIGNAL with no *condition_value* passes along the existing condition information. If a SET clause is present, the assignments in the clause modify the named parts of the condition information.

- RESIGNAL with a *condition_value* adds a copy of the most recent condition to the end of the condition area and modifies it according to *condition_value* and any assignments present in the SET clause if one is present.

SIGNAL

```
SIGNAL condition_value
  [SET condition_info_type = value
    [, condition_info_type = value] ...]

condition_value:
    SQLSTATE [VALUE] sqlstate_value
  | condition_name

condition_info_type:
    CLASS_ORIGIN
  | SUBCLASS_ORIGIN
  | MESSAGE_TEXT
  | MYSQL_ERRNO
  | CONSTRAINT_CATALOG
  | CONSTRAINT_SCHEMA
  | CONSTRAINT_NAME
  | CATALOG_NAME
  | SCHEMA_NAME
  | TABLE_NAME
  | COLUMN_NAME
  | CURSOR_NAME
```

This statement enables you to signal errors, which can be helpful for dealing with problems during statement execution and providing information about what happened.

The *condition_value* following the SIGNAL keyword indicates the condition to signal, specified either as a five-character SQLSTATE literal string or a condition name that has been declared with a DECLARE ... CONDITION statement. For information about SQLSTATE values and the syntax for DECLARE statements, see Section E.2.2, "Declaration Statements."

The optional SET clause assigns values to condition information items; this enables you to "describe" the condition. The SET clause consists of one or more comma-separated assignments, each of which names a type of information and the value to assign to it. The following code tests the divisor of a division operation. If division by zero would occur, it signals an error, setting the MySQL error number and error message:

```
IF divisor <> 0 THEN
  SET ratio = numerator / divisor;
ELSE
  SIGNAL SQLSTATE '22012'
    SET MYSQL_ERRNO = 1365, MESSAGE_TEXT = 'Division by zero attempt';
END IF;
```

In each assignment, the *value* to be assigned cannot be a general expression. It can be specified using only a literal value, user-defined variable, system variable, stored program local variable, or stored function or procedure parameter.

For a list of permitted condition information type names and their meanings, see the description of GET DIAGNOSTICS.

E.3   Comment Syntax

MySQL permits you to intersperse comments with your SQL code, which can be useful for documenting statements that you store in files. The MySQL server understands three types of comments:

- Anything from '#' to the end of the line is treated as a comment. This syntax is the same as in most Unix shells and in many scripting languages, such as Perl, PHP, and Ruby.

  ```
  # this is a single line comment
  ```

- Anything between '/*' and '*/' is treated as a comment. This form of comment may span multiple lines. The syntax is the same as in the C programming language.

  ```
  /* this is a single line comment */
  /* this
     is a multiple line
     comment
  */
  ```

- You can begin a comment with two dashes and a space ('-- '), or two dashes and a control character such as a newline. Everything from the dashes to the end of the line is treated as a comment.

  ```
  --
  -- This is a comment
  --
  ```

The MySQL double-dash comment style is somewhat different from the comment style of standard SQL, which begins with just two dashes and does not require the space before any following text. MySQL requires a space after the dashes as an aid for disambiguation. Statements with expressions such as 5--7 might be taken as containing a comment starting sequence otherwise. It's not likely you'd write such an expression as 5-- 7, so this is a useful heuristic. Still, it is only a heuristic, and you should take care if you import SQL code that contains double-dash comments from other database systems into MySQL.

The server ignores comments when executing statements, with the exception that it gives C-style comments that begin with '/*!' special treatment. You can "hide" MySQL-specific keywords in C-style comments by beginning the comment with '/*!' rather than with '/*'. MySQL looks inside this special type of comment and interprets the keywords, but other database servers ignore them as part of the comment. This has a portability benefit, at least for other servers that understand C-style comments: It is possible to write code that takes advantage of MySQL-specific functions when executed by MySQL but that can be used with other database servers without modification. The following two statements are equivalent for database servers other than MySQL, but MySQL performs an INSERT LOW_PRIORITY operation for the second:

```
INSERT INTO mytbl (id,date) VALUES(13,'2013-09-28');
INSERT /*! LOW_PRIORITY */ INTO mytbl (id,date) VALUES(13,'2013-09-28');
```

C-style comments can be version-specific. Follow the opening '/*!' sequence with a five-digit version number and the server will ignore the comment unless it is at least as recent as the version named. The comment in the following DELETE statement is ignored unless the server is version 5.6.2 or higher (the server understands the PARTITION clause for DELETE only as of MySQL 5.6.2):

```
DELETE FROM mytbl /*!50602 PARTITION (p1) */ WHERE date < '2010-01-01';
```

F

MySQL Program Reference

This appendix provides general information about invoking MySQL programs and describes in some detail the programs named in the following list. Each program's section includes a description of its purpose, its invocation syntax, the options it supports, and a description of any internal variables it has. Unless otherwise indicated, the program options and variables listed here are present in MySQL as least as early as MySQL 5.5.0. Changes made since then are so noted.

- `myisamchk`

  Check and repair MyISAM tables, perform key distribution analysis, and disable and enable indexes.

- `mysql`

  Interact with the MySQL server or execute statements from a file in batch mode.

- `mysql.server`

  Start and stop the MySQL server.

- `mysql_config`

  Display the proper flags for compiling MySQL-based programs.

- `mysql_install_db`

  Initialize the server's data directory and grant tables.

- `mysql_upgrade`

  Upgrade databases after installing a newer MySQL version.

- `mysqladmin`

  Perform administrative operations.

- `mysqlbinlog`

  Display binary and relay log files in text format.

- mysqlcheck

  Check, repair, optimize, and analyze tables.

- mysqld

  The MySQL server; this program must be running so that clients have access to databases.

- mysqld_multi

  Start and stop multiple servers.

- mysqld_safe

  Start and monitor the MySQL server.

- mysqldump

  Dump database contents.

- mysqlimport

  Load bulk data into tables.

- mysqlshow

  Display information about databases or tables.

- perror

  Display error code meanings.

Square brackets ([]) in syntax descriptions indicate optional information.

F.1   Displaying a Program's Help Message

Each program description later in this appendix lists the options the program currently understands. If a program doesn't seem to recognize an option listed in its description, you may have an older version of the program that precedes the addition of the option, or a newer version in which the option has been deprecated and removed.

To get a list of supported options, check the program's help message, which provides a quick way to get information from the program itself. For the server (mysqld), invoke it with both --version and --help. For other programs, use just --help. For example, if you're not sure how to use mysqlimport, invoke it like this for instructions:

```
% mysqlimport --help
```

The -? option is the same as --help, although your shell (command interpreter) might treat the '?' character as a filename wildcard character:

```
% mysqlimport -?
mysqlimport: No match.
```

If that happens, try this instead:

```
% mysqlimport -\?
```

Some options show up in help messages only under certain circumstances. For example, the SSL-related options appear only if MySQL has been compiled with SSL support, and Windows-only options such as `--pipe` appear only on Windows systems.

The help message from a MySQL program also displays the locations where the program looks by default for option files and lists the variables it supports.

F.2 Specifying Program Options

Most MySQL programs understand several options that affect their operation. Options may be specified on the command line or in option files. In addition, some options may be specified by setting environment variables. Options specified on the command line take precedence over options specified any other way, and options in option files take precedence over environment variable values.

Most options have both a long (full-word) form and a short (single-letter) form. The `--help` and `-?` option pair described previously is an example of this. Long-form options that are followed by a value should be given in `--name=val` or `--name val` format, where `name` is the option name pair and `val` is its value. If a short-form option is followed by a value, in most cases the option and the value may be separated by whitespace. For example, when you specify a username, `-usampadm` is equivalent to `-u sampadm`. The `-p` (password) option is an exception; the password value is optional but if given *must* follow the `-p` with no intervening space.

Option names are case sensitive, but option values may or may not be case sensitive. For example, values such as usernames and passwords are case sensitive, but the value for the `--protocol` option is not case sensitive. To make a TCP/IP connection, `--protocol=tcp` and `--protocol=TCP` are equivalent.

Many options are "boolean" and have a value of on or off. Such options have a base form, and a standard set of related forms are recognized, as shown in the following table.

Option	Meaning
`--name`	Base option form; enables the option
`--enable-name`	`--enable-` prefix; enables the option
`--disable-name`	`--disable-` prefix; disables the option
`--skip-name`	`--skip-` prefix; disables the option
`--name=1`	`=1` suffix; enables the option
`--name=0`	`=0` suffix; disables the option

For example, many MySQL client programs enable you to specify the use of compression in the client/server protocol. For these programs, specify the --compress option to enable compression, or omit it to not use compression. However, there are other ways to achieve the same end: --enable-compress and --compress=1 also enable compression, and --disable-compress, --skip-compress, and --compress=0 cause compression not to be used.

The formats that explicitly disable an option are especially useful for options that are on by default. In the case of protocol compression, you can disable it simply by omitting the --compress option. But that does not work for options that are on by default. For example, the --quote-names option for mysqldump is enabled by default. You cannot disable name quoting by omitting the option, but you can do so by specifying any of --skip-quote-names, --disable-quote-names, or --quote-names=0.

The program descriptions in this appendix use the indicator "(*boolean*)" to signify which options are subject to the preceding interpretation—that is, options for which the prefixes and suffixes shown in the table are supported.   '

When in doubt, check a program's help message to find out which option forms it supports (see Section F.1, "Displaying a Program's Help Message").

MySQL programs have other standard option-processing features:

- Long options can be shortened to unambiguous prefixes, which can make it easier to specify options that have very long names. If you specify a prefix not long enough to be unambiguous, the program you invoke will tell you so and list those options that match the prefix:

```
% mysql --h
mysql: ambiguous option '--h' (help, html)
```

- You can set program variables from the command line or in option files by treating variable names as option names. Although variable names have underscores rather than dashes, you can use either dashes or underscores in option or variable names on the command line or in option files. (The initial double dash for long options on the command line cannot be given as dashes, however.) For more information, see Section F.2.1.2, "Setting Program Variables."

- MySQL supports a --loose- option prefix that makes it easier to use differing versions of a program that do not understand the same set of options. With --loose, an unrecognized option results only in a warning, not program termination with an error. For example, versions of mysql from 5.5.3 on accept --auto-vertical-output, but older versions do not. If you specify the option as --loose-auto-vertical-output, any version of mysql uses or ignores the option according to whether it understands it.

- The MySQL server, mysqld, supports a --maximum- prefix for specifying a maximum value to which user-modifiable variables may be set. For example, the server enables users to set their sort buffer size by changing the sort_buffer_size variable. To place a maximum limit of 64MB on the value of this variable, start the server with a --maximum-sort_buffer_size=64M option.

F.2.1 Standard MySQL Program Options

Several options have a standard meaning and most or all MySQL programs interpret them the same way. Rather than repeat their meanings in multiple program descriptions, I describe them here once, and the "Standard Options Supported" section for each program entry indicates which of these options a program understands. That section lists only long-format names, but programs understand the corresponding short-format options as well, unless otherwise specified.

The following list describes the standard options. The default values shown are those that apply unless MySQL has been reconfigured at compile time.

- `--bind-address=addr`

  For client programs, this option was introduced in MySQL 5.6.1 and indicates the IP address to bind to when connecting to the server. This can be useful on machines that have multiple network interfaces. For the server, this option has a more complex meaning. See Section F.12.2, "Options Specific to `mysqld`."

- `--character-sets-dir=dir_name`

  The directory where character set files are stored.

- `--compress, -C` (*boolean*)

  This option is used only by client programs, to request use of the compressed client/server communication protocol if the client and server both support it.

- `--debug=debug_options, -# debug_options`

  Turn on debugging output. This option has no effect unless MySQL was built with debugging support enabled. The `debug_options` string consists of colon-separated options. A typical value is `d:t:o,file_name`, which enables debugging, turns on function call entry and exit tracing, and sends output to the file `file_name`.

  If you expect to do much debugging, you should examine the DBUG library user manual for a description of all the options you can use. The manual is located in the `dbug` directory in MySQL source distributions.

- `--debug-check` (*boolean*)

  Check the use of memory and open files when the program exits.

- `--debug-info` (*boolean*)

  This is like `--debug-check` but also displays information about memory and CPU use.

- `--default-auth=plugin_name`

  For clients, the authentication plugin to use. It should be unnecessary to use this option because the server sends the plugin name based on the client username specified. This option was introduced in MySQL 5.5.7.

- `--default-character-set=charset`

  The character set to use as the default. The `charset` value cannot be `ucs2`, `utf16`, `utf16le`, or `utf32`.

- `--help, -?`

  Display a help message and exit. See also Section F.1, "Displaying a Program's Help Message."

- `--host=host_name, -h host_name`

  This option is used only by client programs. It indicates the host to connect to (that is, the host where the server is running). The default is `localhost`.

- `--password[=pass_val], -p[pass_val]`

  This option is used only by client programs, to indicate the password to use when connecting to the server. If you specify no `pass_val` after the option name, the program prompts you to enter a password. If you do specify `pass_val` after `-p`, it must immediately follow the option letter with no space in between. In other words, the short form must be given as `-ppass_val`, *not* as `-p pass_val`.

  To explicitly specify "no password," use `--skip-password`. This is useful when an option file contains a password that you want to ignore.

- `--pipe, -W`

  Specify use of a named pipe to connect to the server. This option is used only for client programs running under Windows, and only for connecting to Windows servers that have named-pipe support enabled.

- `--plugin-dir=dir_name`

  For the server, the directory where server-side plugins are located. For clients, the directory where client-side plugins are located. This option was introduced in MySQL 5.5.7.

- `--port=port_num, -P port_num`

  For `mysqld`, this option specifies the port on which to listen for TCP/IP connections. The default port number is 3306. For client programs, this is the port number to use when connecting to the server over TCP/IP.

- `--protocol=protocol_type`

  This option is used only by client programs, to indicate what type of connection to make to the server. The `protocol_type` value can be `tcp` (use TCP/IP), `socket` (use a Unix socket file), `pipe` (use a Windows named pipe), or `memory` (use shared memory). The value is not case sensitive.

  Some connection types are platform specific or usable only for connecting to a local server running on the same host as the client program:

  - Socket, named-pipe, and shared-memory connections can be used only for connecting to a local server.

  - Socket connections can be used only on Unix.

- Named-pipe and shared-memory connections can be used only on Windows.
- TCP/IP connections can be used on any platform and can be used to connect to local or remote servers.

The --protocol option can be used in conjunction with other options that provide information about connecting to the server:

- For TCP/IP connections, the --host and --port options specify the hostname and TCP/IP port number.
- For socket and named-pipe connections, the --socket option specifies the Unix socket filename on Unix or the named-pipe name on Windows.
- For shared-memory connections, the --shared-memory-base-name option specifies the shared-memory name.

- --shared-memory-base-name=*name*

The name of the shared memory to use for shared-memory connections. The default is MYSQL. The value is case sensitive.

- --silent, -s

Tell the program to run in silent mode. This doesn't necessarily mean the program is completely silent, simply that it produces less output than usual. Some programs permit this option to be specified multiple times to cause the program to become increasingly silent.

- --socket=*file_name*, -S *file_name*

For client programs on Unix, this is the full pathname of the Unix socket file to use when connecting to the server with a hostname of localhost. The default Unix socket filename is /tmp/mysql.sock. The pathname is case sensitive if filenames are case sensitive on the MySQL host. For client programs on Windows, this is the name of the pipe to use when connecting to the server using a named pipe. The default pipe name is MySQL. Pipe names are not case sensitive.

- --user=*user_name*, -u *user_name*

For mysqld, this option indicates the name or user ID of the Unix account to use for running the server. For this option to be effective, the server must be started as root so that it can change its user ID to the account that you specify. For client programs, this is the MySQL username to use when connecting to the server. The default is your login name under Unix and ODBC under Windows.

- --verbose, -v

Tell the program to run in verbose mode; the program produces more output than usual. Some programs permit this option to be specified multiple times to cause the program to be increasingly verbose.

- --version, -V

Tell the program to print its version information string and exit.

F.2.1.1   Standard SSL Options

The following options are used for establishing secure connections. They are available if MySQL is compiled with SSL support. See Section 13.5, "Setting Up Secure Connections Using SSL," for information on enabling secure connections.

- `--ssl` (*boolean*)

  Enable SSL connections. `--ssl` is implied by each of the other SSL options; the more common use of this option is as `--skip-ssl` to disable use of SSL.

- `--ssl-ca=`*file_name*

  The pathname to the certificate authority file.

- `--ssl-capath=`*dir_name*

  The pathname to a directory of trusted certificates for certificate verification.

- `--ssl-cert=`*file_name*

  The pathname to the certificate file.

- `--ssl-cipher=`*str*

  A string listing the SSL ciphers that can be used to encrypt traffic sent over the connection. The value should name one or more cipher types separated by commas.

- `--ssl-crl=`*file_name*

  The pathname to the certificate revocation list file. This option was introduced in MySQL 5.6.3.

- `--ssl-crlpath=`*dir_name*

  The pathname to a directory of certificate revocation list files. This option was introduced in MySQL 5.6.3.

- `--ssl-key=`*file_name*

  The pathname to the key file.

- `--ssl-verify-server-cert` (*boolean*)

  This option applies only to client programs, to tell the client to check the Common Name value in the certificate received from the server. If this value differs from the server host to which the client connected, the connection attempt is abandoned.

F.2.1.2   Setting Program Variables

Several MySQL programs have variables (operating parameters) that you can set. One way to set a variable is by treating its name as an option. For example, to invoke `mysql` with the `connect_timeout` variable set to 10, use this command:

```
% mysql --connect_timeout=10
```

This syntax also permits underscores in variable names to be given as dashes, which makes variable options look more like other options:

```
% mysql --connect-timeout=10
```

For variables that represent buffer sizes or lengths, values are in bytes if specified as a number with no suffix, or can be specified with a suffix of 'K', 'M', or 'G', to indicate kilobytes, megabytes, or gigabytes. Suffixes are not case sensitive; you can also use 'k', 'm', or 'g'.

Each program's variables are listed in the program's description in this appendix, and are also displayed in the program's help message (see Section F.1, "Displaying a Program's Help Message").

F.2.2 Option Files

Most MySQL programs support option files. These provide a means of storing program options so that you need not type them on the command line each time you invoke a program. Any option specified in an option file can be overridden by explicitly specifying the option on the command line with a different value. Exception: mysqld uses the *first* instance of the --user option, to prevent an instance in an option file from being overridden on the command line.

MySQL programs that support option files look for them in several locations, but it is normally not an error for an option file to be missing. This means you usually must create option files yourself. Option files must be text files, so if you create an option file in a word processor, be sure to save it in plain text format, not in the word processor's native document format.

Under Unix, the option files shown in the following table are read in order if they exist. In addition, if an option file is named with the --defaults-extra-file option, it is read just before ~/.my.cnf.

Filename	Contents
/etc/my.cnf	Global options
/etc/mysql/my.cnf	Global options
SYSCONFDIR/my.cnf	Global options
$MYSQL_HOME/my.cnf	Server-specific options
~/.my.cnf	User-specific options

~ represents the pathname to your home directory. SYSCONFDIR comes from the -DSYSCONFDIR option given to CMake at MySQL configuration time. Its default value is the etc directory under the installation directory compiled in to the distribution. $MYSQL_HOME is an environment variable that can be set for use by mysqld_safe to a directory containing a server-specific option file. If it is not set, mysqld_safe tries to set it automatically to find a my.cnf file in the MySQL installation directory.

Under Windows, the option files shown in the following table are read in order if they exist. In addition, if an option file is named with the `--defaults-extra-file` option, it is read after those in the table.

Filename	Contents
WINDIR\my.ini, *WINDIR*\my.ini	Global options
C:\my.ini, C:\my.cnf	Global options
INSTALLDIR\my.ini, *INSTALLDIR*\my.ini	Global options

WINDIR is the pathname to the Windows directory. *INSTALLDIR* is the pathname to the MySQL installation directory.

Global option files are used by all MySQL programs that are option file-aware. User-specific files on Unix are read by programs run by that user.

Windows users should be especially careful about the following issues when using option files:

- Windows pathname components are separated by backslash ('\') characters, which MySQL treats as escape characters. To handle this for options that take pathname values, write backslashes as slashes ('/') or as doubled backslashes ('\\').

- On Windows, filenames may be displayed with extensions hidden. If you create an option file named my.cnf, the name may display as just my. Should you notice that and attempt to change the name to my.cnf, you may find that the option file no longer works. This is because you actually will have renamed the file from my.cnf to my.cnf.cnf!

Several options related to option-file processing are standard across most MySQL programs and have the following meanings; if you use any of them, it must be the first option on the command line, except that it is permitted for `--print-defaults` to immediately follow `--defaults-file` or `--defaults-extra-file`.

- `--defaults-extra-file=file_name`

  Specify an option file to read in addition to the regular option files. The file is read after any global and server-specific option files and before the user-specific file. The file must exist and be readable or an error occurs.

- `--defaults-file=file_name`

  Specify the sole file from which to read options. Normally, programs search for option files in several locations (as described earlier), but if `--defaults-file` is specified, only the named file is read. The file must exist and be readable or an error occurs.

- `--defaults-group-suffix=suffix`

  Read the option groups with the usual names and also those with the concatenation of the usual names and the given suffix.

- `--no-defaults`

  Suppress the use of any option files. In addition, this option causes other option-file-related options such as `--defaults-file` to be unrecognized.

- `--print-defaults`

  Display the option values that will be used if you invoke the program with no options on the command line. This shows the values that will be read from option files (and environment variables). `--print-defaults` is useful for verifying proper setup of an option file. It's also useful if a MySQL program seems to use options that you never specified; try `--print-defaults` to determine whether options are being read from some option file.

A program's help message lists the locations where the program looks by default for option files (see Section F.1, "Displaying a Program's Help Message"). The default set of files to read is affected by use of `--defaults-file`, `--defaults-extra-file`, or `--no-defaults`.

Options in option files are specified in groups (or sections). Here's an example:

```
[client]
user=sampadm
password=secret

[mysql]
skip-auto-rehash

[mysqlshow]
status
```

Group names are written inside square brackets and are not case sensitive. The special `[client]` group enables you to specify options that apply to all client programs. Otherwise, a group name usually corresponds to a specific program name. In the preceding example, `[mysql]` indicates the option group for the `mysql` client and `[mysqlshow]` indicates the option group for `mysqlshow`. The standard MySQL client programs look at both the `[client]` group and the group with the same name as the client name. For example, `mysql` looks at the `[client]` and `[mysql]` groups, and `mysqlshow` looks at the `[client]` and `[mysqlshow]` groups.

Be careful about putting options in the `[client]` group that are understood only by a single client. For example, `skip-auto-rehash` is specific to `mysql`. If you put this option in the `[client]` group, you will find that other client programs such as `mysqlimport` no longer work. (They display an error message followed by a help message.) Place `skip-auto-rehash` in a `[mysql]` group instead.

Any options following a group name are associated with that group. An option file may contain any number of groups, and later groups take precedence over earlier groups. If a given option is found multiple times in the groups a program looks at, the value listed last is used. Exception:

mysqld uses the *first* instance of the --user option, to prevent an instance in an option file from being overridden on the command line.

Specify each option on a separate line. The first word on the line is the option name, in long-name format without the leading dashes. For example, to specify compression on the command line, you can use either -C or --compress, but in an option file, you can use only compress. Any long-format option supported by a program can be listed in an option file. If the option requires a value, separate the name and value by an '=' character.

Consider the following command line:

```
% mysql --compress --user=sampadm --max_allowed_packet=16M
```

To specify the same information in an option file using the [mysql] group, do so as follows:

```
[mysql]
compress
user=sampadm
max_allowed_packet=16M
```

You can quote an option value with either single quotes or double quotes. This is useful if the value contains spaces.

Leading spaces in option file lines are ignored, as are spaces around the '=' characters that separate option names and values. Lines that are empty or that begin with '#' or ';' are treated as comments and ignored. You can also begin a comment in the middle of a line with a '#' character (but not with a ';' character).

The escape sequences shown in the following table can be used in option file values to specify special characters.

Sequence	Meaning
\b	Backspace
\n	Newline (linefeed)
\r	Carriage return
\s	Space
\t	Tab
\\	Backslash

Option files can include directives that cause other option files to be read:

- !include *file_name*

  Reads the named option file.

- !includedir *dir_name*

  Reads all option files in the named directory. Option files are identified as those having an extension of .cnf on Unix, or either .ini or .cnf on Windows. The order in which the files are read is undefined.

Included files follow the usual option file syntax. Only options from the option group that is current at the point of inclusion are used.

F.2.2.1   Keeping User-Specific Option Files Private

Under Unix, your user-specific option file, .my.cnf in your home directory, should be owned by you and its mode should be set to 600 or 400 so that other users cannot read it. You don't want your MySQL username and password exposed to anyone other than yourself. To make your own option file private, issue either of the following commands in your home directory:

```
% chmod 600 .my.cnf
% chmod go-rwx .my.cnf
```

The same cautions apply to the history file written by the mysql client program, .mysql_history in your home directory. You should protect it the same way.

F.2.2.2   Using my_print_defaults to Check Options

The my_print_defaults utility is useful for determining what options a program reads from option files. It searches option files and shows which options are found there for one or more option groups. For example, the mysql program uses options from the [client] and [mysql] option groups. To find out which options in your option files apply to mysql, invoke my_print_defaults like this:

```
% my_print_defaults client mysql
```

Similarly, the server mysqld uses options in the [mysqld] and [server] groups. To determine what options are present in option files, use this command:

```
% my_print_defaults mysqld server
```

F.2.3   Environment Variables

MySQL programs look at the values of the several environment variables to obtain option settings. Environment variables have low precedence; option values specified using them can be overridden by options in an option file or on the command line.

MySQL programs check the following environment variables:

- LANG, LC_ALL

  If either of these environment variables is set to specify a locale, MySQL client programs use the value to set the default character set. This is like using the --default-character-set option.

- MYSQL_DEBUG

  The options to use when debugging. This variable has no effect unless MySQL was built with debugging support enabled. Setting MYSQL_DEBUG is like using the --debug option.

- MYSQL_PWD

  The password to use when establishing connections to the MySQL server. Setting MYSQL_PWD is like using the --password option.

  Using the MYSQL_PWD variable to store a password constitutes a security risk because other users on your system can easily discover its value. For example, on some systems, the ps utility shows environment variable settings for other users.

- MYSQL_TCP_PORT

  For mysqld, this is the port on which to listen for TCP/IP connections. For client programs, this is the port number to use when establishing a TCP/IP connection to the server. Setting MYSQL_TCP_PORT is like using the --port option.

- MYSQL_UNIX_PORT

  For mysqld, this is the socket file on which to listen for local connections. For client programs, this is the pathname of the Unix socket file to use when establishing socket file connections to the server running on localhost. Setting MYSQL_UNIX_PORT is like using the --socket option.

- TMPDIR

  The pathname of the directory in which to create temporary files. Setting this variable is like using the --tmpdir option, except that it should name only a single directory.

- USER

  The MySQL username to use when connecting to the server. This variable is used only by client programs running under Windows; setting it is like using the --user option.

The mysql client checks the value of three additional environment variables:

- MYSQL_HISTFILE

  On Unix, the name of the file to use for storing command-line history during interactive use. The default if this variable is not set is .mysql_history in your home directory,

- MYSQL_HOST

  The host to connect to when establishing a connection to the MySQL server. Setting this variable is like using the --host option.

- MYSQL_PS1

  The string to use instead of mysql> for the primary prompt. The string can contain the special sequences listed in Section F.4.5, "mysql Prompt Definition Sequences."

F.3 `myisamchk`

The `myisamchk` utility performs maintenance operations on MyISAM tables. (It does not work for partitioned tables; use `mysqlcheck` instead.) `myisamchk` checks and repairs damaged tables, displays table information, performs index key value distribution analysis, and disables or enables indexes.

Tables managed by the MyISAM storage engine have data and index filenames with suffixes of `.MYD` and `.MYI`, respectively. If you tell `myisamchk` to operate on a table of the wrong type, it prints a warning message and ignores the table.

Invoke `myisamchk` with the names of the tables to be checked:

```
myisamchk [options] tbl_name[.MYI] ...
```

With no options, `myisamchk` checks the named tables for errors. Otherwise, it processes the tables according to the meaning of the specified options. If you perform an operation that might modify a table, it's a good idea to make a copy of it first.

An argument that specifies a table can be either the name of a table, `tbl_name`, or the name of its index file, `tbl_name.MYI`. These commands are equivalent:

```
% myisamchk member
% myisamchk member.MYI
```

Using index filenames is convenient if your command interpreter expands filename patterns. To check all the MyISAM tables in the current directory, use a wildcard that specifies all index names:

```
% myisamchk *.MYI
```

`myisamchk` makes no assumptions about where table files are located. If they are not in the current directory, you must specify the pathname to them. Because table files are not assumed to be located under the server's data directory, you can copy them to another directory and operate on the copies rather than the originals.

Many `myisamchk` operations can also be performed by issuing SQL statements to the server. These statements include `ANALYZE TABLE`, `CHECK TABLE`, `OPTIMIZE TABLE`, and `REPAIR TABLE`. You can issue these statements directly, or you can use the `mysqlcheck` program, which provides a command-line interface to several SQL table-maintenance statements. In general, it is easier and safer to use these statements or `mysqlcheck` rather than `myisamchk`. For more information, see Section 14.6, "Checking and Repairing Database Tables."

One caution to observe when using `myisamchk` to perform maintenance on a table is that you must prevent the server from accessing the table concurrently. This is necessary because the server and `myisamchk` both access table files directly. If they are permitted to do so at the same time, you can destroy the table. Before using `myisamchk`, consult Section 14.2, "Performing Database Maintenance with the Server Running," which discusses how to prevent the server from using a table while `myisamchk` is working on it.

You must also take special care when using myisamchk for tables that contain FULLTEXT indexes if both of these conditions are true:

- You are using myisamchk to perform an operation that modifies indexes. These include analysis and repair operations.

- You are running the server using a nondefault value for any of these FULLTEXT-related system variables: ft_max_word_len, ft_min_word_len, or ft_stopword_file.

When both of these conditions hold, you must use appropriate options to tell myisamchk what FULLTEXT parameters to use, because it does not know what values the server is using. If you do not do this, myisamchk will build FULLTEXT indexes using different parameter values than the server expects and FULLTEXT searches will return incorrect results. Suppose that you run your server using the following nondefault option settings for the minimum word length and stopword file:

```
[mysqld]
ft_min_word_len=2
ft_stopword_file=/var/mysql/data/my-stopwords
```

In this case, you must indicate those same values to myisamchk for any index-changing operation that you perform on tables that contain FULLTEXT indexes. You can do this on the command line with --ft_min_word_len and --ft_stopword_list options, but it's better to record the values in an option file so that you don't forget to use them. Use an option group similar to the one used for the server:

```
[myisamchk]
ft_min_word_len=2
ft_stopword_file=/var/mysql/data/my-stopwords
```

To avoid the problem of FULLTEXT parameter mismatch entirely, use SQL statements such as REPAIR TABLE or ANALYZE TABLE for table maintenance. Then the server does the index modification, and, because it knows what FULLTEXT parameters it is using, applies them for maintenance operations on tables that contain FULLTEXT indexes.

F.3.1 Standard Options Supported by myisamchk

```
--character-sets-dir   --help          --verbose
--debug                --silent        --version
```

For general descriptions of these options, see Section F.2.1, "Standard MySQL Program Options."

The --silent option means that only error messages are printed. The --verbose option prints more information when given with the --check, --description, or --extend-check options. The --silent and --verbose options can be specified multiple times for increased effect.

The standard --help option prints the help message with options grouped by function. myisamchk also supports --HELP and -H options that display all options in a single alphabetical list.

F.3.2 Options Specific to myisamchk

Some of these options refer to index numbers. Indexes are numbered beginning with 1. To determine the index numbering for a particular table, issue a SHOW INDEX statement or use a mysqlshow --keys command. The Key_name column in the output lists indexes in the same order that myisamchk sees them.

- --analyze, -a

  Perform key distribution analysis. This can help the server perform index-based lookups and joins more quickly. To obtain information about key distribution after the analysis, run myisamchk again with the --description and --verbose options.

- --backup, -B

  For options that modify the data (.MYD) file, make a backup using a filename of the form tbl_name-time.BAK. time is a number representing a timestamp. myisamchk creates the backup file in the directory where the table files are located.

- --block-search=n, -b n

  Display the start of the table row that contains a block starting at block n. This is for debugging only.

- --check, -c

  Check tables for errors. This is the default action if no options are specified.

- --check-only-changed, -C

  Check tables only if they have not been changed since the last check.

- --correct-checksum

  For tables created with the CHECKSUM = 1 option, ensure that the checksum information in the table is correct.

- --data-file-length=n, -D n

  The maximum length in bytes to which the data file should be permitted to grow when rebuilding a data file that has become full. (This occurs when a file reaches the size limit imposed by MySQL or by the file-size constraints of your operating system. It also occurs when the number of rows reaches the limit imposed by internal table data structures.) This option is effective only when used with --recover or --safe-recover.

- --description, -d

  Display descriptive information about the table.

- `--extend-check, -e`

  Perform an extended table check. It should rarely be necessary to use this option because `myisamchk` normally finds any errors with one of the less extensive check modes.

- `--fast, -F`

  Check tables only if they have not been closed properly. This can occur, for example, if the server host machine crashes while `mysqld` has the tables open, so that `mysqld` has no opportunity to close them.

- `--force, -f`

  Force a table to be checked or repaired even if a temporary file for the table already exists. Normally, `myisamchk` simply exits after printing an error message if it finds a file named `tbl_name`.TMD, because that might indicate that another instance of the program is already running. However, the file might also exist because you killed a previous invocation of `myisamchk` while it was running, in which case the file can safely be removed. If you know that to be the case, use `--force` to tell `myisamchk` to run even if the temporary file exists. (Alternatively, remove the temporary file manually.)

  If you use `--force` when checking tables, `myisamchk` automatically restarts with `--recover` for any table found to have problems. In addition, `myisamchk` updates the table state in the same way that the `--update-state` option does.

- `--information, -i`

  Display statistical information about table contents.

- `--keys-used=n, -k n`

  Used with `--recover`. The option value n is a bitmask that indicates which indexes to use. The first index is bit zero. (For example, a value of 6 is binary 110 and indicates that the second and third indexes should be used.) A value of 0 turns off all indexes, which can be used to improve the performance of INSERT, DELETE, and UPDATE operations. Turning the indexes back on restores normal indexing behavior (specify a bitmask that includes an enabled bit for each index).

- `--max-record-length=n`

  Ignore rows that are larger than n bytes if memory cannot be allocated for them.

- `--medium-check, -m`

  Check tables using a method that is faster than `--extend-check`, but slightly less thorough. This check mode should suffice for most circumstances. Medium check mode works by calculating CRC values for the keys in the index and comparing them with the CRC values calculated from the indexed columns in the data file.

- `--parallel-recover, -p`

  Perform recovery the same way as for `--recover`, but rebuild indexes in parallel using multiple threads. This can be faster than a nonparallel rebuild, but this option should be considered experimental.

- `--quick, -q` (*boolean*)

This option is used in conjunction with `--recover` for faster repair than when `--recover` is used alone. The data file is not touched when both options are given. To force the program to modify the data file if duplicate key values are found, specify the `--quick` option twice.

- `--read-only, -T`

Cause tables not to be marked as having been checked.

- `--recover, -r`

Perform a normal recovery operation. This can fix most problems except the occurrence of duplicate values in an index that should contain only unique values.

- `--safe-recover, -o`

Perform recovery using a method that is slower than the one used for `--recover`, but that can fix a few problems that `--recover` cannot. `--safe-recover` also uses less disk space than `--recover`.

- `--set-auto-increment[=n], -A[n]`

Set the AUTO_INCREMENT counter so that subsequent sequence values start at n (or at a higher value if the table already contains rows with AUTO_INCREMENT values as large as n). If no value n is specified, this option sets the next AUTO_INCREMENT value to one greater than the current maximum value stored in the table.

If n is specified after `-A`, there must be no intervening space or the value will not be interpreted correctly.

To set the AUTO_INCREMENT value for a MyISAM table without using `myisamchk`, issue a statement of the following form:

```
ALTER TABLE tbl_name AUTO_INCREMENT = n;
```

- `--set-collation=collation`

The collation to use for rebuilding and sorting table index entries. The collation name implies the character set name.

- `--sort-index, -S`

Sort the index blocks to speed up sequential block reads for subsequent retrievals.

- `--sort-records=n, -R n`

Sort data rows according to the order in which rows are listed in index n. Subsequent retrievals based on the given index should be faster. The first time you perform this operation on a table, it may be very slow because your rows will be unordered. ALTER TABLE ... ORDER BY accomplishes the same thing as `--sort-records`, and normally will be faster.

- `--sort-recover, -n`

  Force sorted recovery even if the temporary file necessary to perform the operation would become quite large.

- `--start-check-pos=n`

  The position *n* at which to begin reading the data file. This option is used only for debugging.

- `--tmpdir=dir_name, -t dir_name`

  The pathname of the directory to use for temporary files. The default is the value of the TMPDIR environment variable, or /tmp if that variable is not set. The option value can be given as a list of directories, to be used in round-robin fashion. Under Unix, separate directory names by colons; under Windows, separate them by semicolons.

- `--unpack, -u`

  Unpack a table that was packed by myisampack. This option can be used to convert a compressed read-only table to modifiable form. It cannot be used with --quick or with --sort-records.

- `--update-state, -U`

  Update the internal flag that is stored in the table to indicate its state. Tables that are okay are marked as such, and tables for which an error occurs are marked as in need of repair. Using this option makes subsequent invocations of myisamchk with the --check-only-changed option more efficient for tables that are okay.

- `--wait, -w`

  If a table is locked, wait until it is available. Without --wait, myisamchk waits 10 seconds for a lock, then displays an error message if no lock can be obtained.

F.3.3   Variables for `myisamchk`

The following myisamchk variables can be set using the instructions given in Section F.2.1.2, "Setting Program Variables."

For tables that contain FULLTEXT indexes, note the caution described in the introductory myisamchk program description.

- `decode_bits`

  The number of bits to use when decoding compressed tables. Larger values may result in faster operation but will require more memory. The default of 9 generally is sufficient.

- `ft_max_word_len`

  The maximum length of words that can be included in FULLTEXT indexes. Longer words are ignored. The default is 84.

- ft_min_word_len

  The minimum length of words that can be included in FULLTEXT indexes. Shorter words are ignored. The default is 4.

- ft_stopword_file

  The stopword file for FULLTEXT indexes. The default is to use the built-in stopword list.

- key_buffer_size

  The size of the buffer used for index blocks. (This is used for --safe-recover, but not for --recover or --sort-recover.) The default is 512KB.

- key_cache_block_size

  The size of blocks in the key buffer. The default is 1MB.

- myisam_block_size

  The block size used for index blocks in the .MYI file. The default is 1MB.

- read_buffer_size

  The read buffer size. The default is 256KB.

- sort_buffer_size

  The size of the buffer used for key value sorting operations. (This is used for --recover or --sort-recover, but not for --safe-recover.) The default is 2MB.

- sort_key_blocks

  This variable is related to the depth of the B-tree structure used for the index. The default is 16; you should not need to change it.

- stats_method

  Whether to consider NULL values equal or distinct for calculating index key value distribution statistics. The value can be nulls_equal (all NULL values are in the same group), nulls_unequal (each NULL value forms a distinct group), or nulls_ignored (NULL values are ignored).

- write_buffer_size

  The write buffer size. The default is 256KB.

F.4 mysql

The mysql client program enables you to connect to the server, issue SQL statements, and view the results.

```
mysql [options] [db_name]
```

If you specify a *db_name* argument, that database becomes the default database for your session. If you specify no *db_name* argument, mysql starts with no default database and you must either qualify all table references with a database name or issue a USE db_name statement to specify a default database.

mysql can be run interactively. You can also use it in batch mode to execute statements stored in a file if you redirect the input of the command to read from that file. For example:

```
% mysql -u sampadm -p -h cobra.example.com sampdb < my_sql_file
```

When used interactively, mysql displays a mysql> prompt to indicate when it's waiting for input. To issue a statement, type it in (using multiple lines if necessary), then indicate the end of the statement by typing ';' (semicolon) or \g. mysql sends the statement to the server, displays the results, and then prints another prompt to indicate that it's ready for another statement. \G also terminates a statement, but causes statement results to be formatted "vertically" (that is, with one column value per output line).

mysql varies the prompt to indicate what it's waiting for as you enter input lines, as shown in the following table. The mysql> prompt is the primary prompt, displayed at the beginning of each statement. The other prompts are secondary prompts, displayed to obtain additional lines for the current statement.

Prompt	Meaning
mysql>	Waiting for the first line of a new statement
->	Waiting for the next line of the current statement
'>	Waiting for completion of a single-quoted string in the current statement
">	Waiting for completion of a double-quoted string in the current statement
`>	Waiting for completion of a quoted identifier in the current statement
/*>	Waiting for completion of /* ... */ comment

The '> and "> prompts indicate that you've begun a single-quoted or double-quoted string on a previous line and have not yet entered the terminating quote. Similarly, `> indicates an unterminated quoted identifier. /*> indicates that the beginning /* but not the ending */ of a /* ... */ comment has been seen. Usually, when you see these prompts, you've forgotten to terminate a string, identifier, or comment. If that's the case, to escape from string-collection mode, enter the appropriate matching quote or comment ending that is indicated by the prompt, followed by \c to cancel the current statement.

On Unix, when mysql is used in interactive mode, it saves statements in a history file. The name of this file is .mysql_history in your home directory by default, and it can be specified explicitly by setting the MYSQL_HISTFILE environment variable. This file should have a restricted access mode to prevent other users from seeing its contents; see Section F.2.2.1, "Keeping User-Specific Option Files Private." If you don't want to save a history file, remove .mysql_history and then either create a symbolic link named .mysql_history that points to /dev/null or set MYSQL_HISTFILE to /dev/null.

Some options suppress use of the history file. Generally, these are options that indicate noninteractive use of `mysql`, such as `--batch`, `--html`, and `--quick`.

On systems that support an input-editing library, statements can be recalled from the command history and re-issued, either with or without further editing. On Windows, line-editing capabilities are not provided by `mysql`. However, Windows itself supports several editing commands, so they become available to `mysql`. For information about editing commands, see Section 1.5.2.1, "Using the `mysql` Input Line Editor."

F.4.1 Standard Options Supported by `mysql`

`--bind-address`	`--help`	`--silent`
`--character-sets-dir`	`--host`	`--socket`
`--compress`	`--password`	`--user`
`--debug`	`--pipe`	`--verbose`
`--debug-check`	`--port`	`--version`
`--debug-info`	`--protocol`	
`--default-character-set`	`--shared-memory-base-name`	

For general descriptions of these options, see Section F.2.1, "Standard MySQL Program Options." `mysql` also supports the standard SSL options listed in Section F.2.1.1, "Standard SSL Options."

`--silent` and `--verbose` can be given multiple times for increased effect.

`-I` is a synonym for `--help`.

F.4.2 Options Specific to `mysql`

- `--auto-rehash` (*boolean*)

  When `mysql` starts, it can hash database, table, and column names to construct a data structure that enables fast completion of names: Type the initial part of a name when entering a statement, then press Tab. `mysql` completes the name unless it's ambiguous; press Tab again to see the possible completions.

  Name hashing is on by default, although it does not take effect until you have selected a default database. `--skip-auto-rehash` suppresses hash calculation, which enables `mysql` to start up more quickly, particularly if you have many tables.

  If hashing is disabled, to enable name completion after starting `mysql`, use the `rehash` command at the `mysql>` prompt.

- `--auto-vertical-output` (*boolean*)

  Use vertical output style automatically for query results that exceed the terminal width. See also `--vertical`. This option was introduced in MySQL 5.5.3.

- `--batch, -B`

  Run in batch mode. `mysql` displays query results in tab-delimited format (each row on a separate line with tabs between column values). This is especially convenient for generating output to be imported into another program, such as a spreadsheet application. Query results include an initial row of column headings by default. To suppress these headings, use the `--skip-column-names` option.

- `--binary-mode` (*boolean*)

  Disable translation of `\r\n` to `\n` and interpretation of `\0` as a statement terminator. This option is intended for situations in which you're using `mysql` to process output from `mysqlbinlog` that might contain arbitrary data values such as `BLOB` values. When `mysql` is used noninteractively, this option also disables commands except `charset` and `delimiter`. This option was introduced in MySQL 5.6.3.

- `--column-names` (*boolean*)

  Display column names as column headers in query results. Use `--skip-column-names` to suppress display of column names. You can also achieve that effect by specifying the `--silent` option twice.

- `--column-type-info` (*boolean*)

  Include result set metadata with query output.

- `--comments, -c` (*boolean*)

  For statements that contain comments, include these comments when sending the statements to the server. By default, comments are stripped (same as specifying `--skip-comments`).

- `--database=db_name, -D db_name`

  Use *db_name* as the default database.

- `--delimiter=str`

  Set the statement delimiter. The default delimiter is the semicolon (`';'`).

- `--execute=stmt, -e stmt`

  Execute the statement and quit. Enclose the statement in quotes to prevent your shell (command interpreter) from treating it as multiple command-line arguments. To specify multiple statements, separate them by semicolons in the *stmt* value.

- `--force, -f` (*boolean*)

  Normally when `mysql` reads statements from a file, it exits if an error occurs. This option causes `mysql` to continue processing statements, regardless of errors.

- `--html, -H` (*boolean*)

  Produce HTML output.

- `--i-am-a-dummy` (*boolean*)

  This option is a synonym for `--safe-updates`.

- `--ignore-spaces, -i`

  Cause the server to ignore spaces between names of built-in functions and the '(' character that introduces the argument list. Normally, function names should be followed immediately by the parenthesis with no intervening spaces. This option also causes function names to be treated as reserved words.

- `--init-command=stmt`

  Specify a statement to execute after connecting to the MySQL server, or after reconnecting if auto-reconnect is enabled. See the description of `--execute` for information about specifying the statement string.

- `--line-numbers` (*boolean*)

  Display line numbers in error messages. This is the default. To suppress line numbers, use `--skip-line-numbers`.

- `--local-infile` (*boolean*)

  Enable or disable LOAD DATA LOCAL. The LOCAL capability might be present but disabled by default. If LOAD DATA LOCAL results in an error, try again after invoking `mysql` with the `--local-infile` option. This option can also be used to disable LOCAL if it is enabled, for example, with `--disable-local-infile`.

  This option is ineffective if the server has been configured to prohibit use of LOCAL.

- `--named-commands, -G` (*boolean*)

  Enable long forms of `mysql`'s internal commands at the beginning of any input line. If this capability is disabled with `--skip-named-commands`, long commands are permitted only at the primary prompt and not at the secondary prompts. That is, they are not permitted on the second and subsequent lines of a multiple-line statement.

- `--no-auto-rehash, -A`

  This is the same as `--skip-auto-rehash`. See the description for `--auto-rehash`.

- `--no-beep, -b` (*boolean*)

  Suppress production of beeps when errors occur.

- `--one-database, -o`

  This option is used when updating databases from the contents of a binary log file. It tells `mysql` to update only the default database (the database named on the command line) and ignore updates to other databases. If no database is named on the command line, no updates are performed.

- `--pager[=program]`

  The name of a paging program to use for displaying long query results one page at a time (for example, /bin/more or /bin/less). If *program* is missing, `mysql` determines the paging program from the value of the PAGER environment variable. Output paging is unavailable in batch mode, and does not work under Windows. To disable paging, use `--skip-pager`.

- `--prompt=str`

  Change the primary prompt from `mysql>` to the string defined by `str`. The string can contain the special sequences listed in Section F.4.5, "`mysql` Prompt Definition Sequences."

- `--quick, -q`

  Normally `mysql` retrieves the entire result of a query from the server before displaying it. This option causes each row to be displayed as it is retrieved, which uses much less memory and may enable some large statements to be performed successfully that would fail otherwise. However, this option should not be specified for interactive use; if the user pauses the output or suspends `mysql`, the server continues to wait, which can interfere with other clients.

- `--raw, -r` (*boolean*)

  Write column values without escaping any special characters. This option is used in conjunction with `--batch`.

- `--reconnect` (*boolean*)

  Automatically reconnect to the server if the connection is lost. This option is enabled by default. To disable it, use `--skip-reconnect`.

  Automatic reconnection can cause problems in some circumstances. For example, any currently active transaction is rolled back and the values of session variables are lost with no indication that this has happened.

- `--safe-updates, -U` (*boolean*)

  This option places limits on some operations and can be beneficial for new MySQL users:

  - Updates (statements that modify data) are permitted only if the rows to be modified are identified by key values or if a `LIMIT` clause is used. This helps prevent statements that mistakenly change or wipe out all or large parts of a table.

  - Result sets produced by nonjoin retrievals are limited to one thousand rows unless a `LIMIT` clause is used. Retrievals that involve a join are rejected if the optimizer estimates that it will need to examine more than one million rows. This helps prevent inadvertent generation of very large query results.

  These limits can be changed by setting the `select_limit` and `max_join_size` variables.

- `--secure-auth` (*boolean*)

  Prevent connecting to the server unless it supports the password hashing algorithm introduced in MySQL 4.1. This option is enabled by default as of MySQL 5.6.7, disabled in earlier versions.

- `--show-warnings` (*boolean*)

  Automatically display any warnings, as though you issued `SHOW WARNINGS` after each statement.

- --sigint-ignore (*boolean*)

  Ignore SIGINT signals, typically sent by typing Control-C. Control-C tells mysql to kill the current statement. mysql exits if the statement could not be killed or you enter another Control-C before the statement is killed. Using --sigint-ignore prevents mysql from interpreting Control-C as just described.

- --skip-column-names, -N

  See the description for --column-names.

- --skip-line-numbers, -L

  See the description for --line-numbers.

- --table, -t (*boolean*)

  Produce output in tabular format, with values in each row delimited by bars and lined up vertically. This is the default output format when mysql is not run in batch mode.

- --tee=*file_name*

  Append a copy of all output to the named file. To disable output copying, use --skip-tee. This option does not work in batch mode.

- --unbuffered, -n (*boolean*)

  After each statement, flush the buffer used for communication with the server.

- --vertical, -E

  Display query results vertically—that is, with each row of a query result formatted as a set of output lines, one column per line. (Each line consists of a column name and value.) The display for each row is preceded by a line indicating the row number within the result set. Vertical display format may be useful when a query produces very long lines.

  If this option is not specified, you can enable vertical display format for individual queries by terminating them with \G rather than with ';' or \g. See also --auto-vertical-output.

- --wait, -w

  Wait and retry if a connection to the server cannot be established.

- --xml, -X (*boolean*)

  Produce XML output.

F.4.3 Variables for mysql

The following mysql variables can be set using the instructions given in Section F.2.1.2, "Setting Program Variables."

- connect_timeout

  The number of seconds to wait before timing out when attempting to connect to the server. The default is 0.

- `max_allowed_packet`

  The maximum size of the buffer used for communication between the server and the client. The default is 16MB and the maximum is 1GB.

- `max_join_size`

  The row limit on the execution of joins if the `--safe-updates` option is given. The server rejects joins for which it believes it will need to examine more than `max_join_size` rows. The default is 1,000,000.

- `net_buffer_length`

  The initial size of the buffer used for communication between the server and the client. This buffer can be expanded up to `max_allowed_packet` bytes long. The default is 16KB.

- `select_limit`

  The limit on the number of rows returned by SELECT statements if the `--safe-updates` option is given. The default is 1,000.

F.4.4   `mysql` Commands

In addition to enabling you to send SQL statements to the MySQL server, `mysql` implements several of its own commands. Each command must be given on a single line. Most of the commands have a long form consisting of a word, and a short form consisting of a backslash followed by a single letter. Commands in long form are not case sensitive. Commands in short form must be specified using the lettercase shown in the following list. A semicolon at the end of the line is unnecessary but permitted for long-form commands, but should be omitted for short-form commands.

If you have disabled named commands (for example, with the `--skip-named-commands` option), long command names are recognized only at the primary `mysql>` prompt. If `mysql` is used noninteractively and invoked with the `--binary-mode` option, all commands are disabled except `charset` and `delimiter`.

- `clear, \c`

  Clear (cancel) the current statement—that is, the one you are in the process of typing. This command does not cancel a statement that has already been sent to the server and for which `mysql` is displaying output.

- `charset [charset], \C [charset]`

  Change the default character set and send a SET NAMES statement to the server so the server uses that character set as well.

- `connect [db_name [host_name]], \r [db_name [host_name]]`

  Connect (or reconnect) to the given database on the given host. If you omit the database name or hostname, the most recently used values from the current `mysql` session are used.

- delimiter *str*, \d *str*

  Set the statement delimiter. The default delimiter is the semicolon (';'). The stored program parser recognizes only the semicolon as the statement delimiter, so this command can be used to redefine the delimiter for `mysql` while defining a stored program. For an example, see Section 4.2.1, "Compound Statements and Statement Delimiters."

  It's best to avoid using backslashes in the delimiter because MySQL treats backslash as an escape character.

- edit, \e

  Edit the current statement. `mysql` attempts to determine what editor to use by examining the `EDITOR` and `VISUAL` environment variables. If neither variable is set, `mysql` uses `vi`. This option is unavailable under Windows.

- ego, \G

  Send the current statement to the server and display the result vertically.

- exit

  Same as `quit`.

- go, \g, ;

  Send the current statement to the server and display the result.

- help [*topic*], \h [*topic*], ? [*topic*], \? [*topic*]

  Display a help message describing the available `mysql` commands.

  If the help tables in the `mysql` database have been loaded, you can use `help` to get server-side help: Use `help contents` to get a list of help categories, `help` *category* for help on a particular category, or `help` *keyword* for help about the particular keyword (such as `SELECT` or `UPDATE`). For instructions on loading the help tables, see Section A.3.6, "Initializing Other System Tables."

- nopager, \n

  Disable the pager and send output to the standard output. This command is unavailable under Windows.

- notee, \t

  Stop writing to the tee file.

- nowarning, \w

  Stop automatically displaying any warnings generated by each statement.

- pager [*program*], \P [*program*]

  Send output through the paging program specified by *program*, or through the program specified in the `PAGER` environment variable, if that variable is set and *program* is not given. This command is unavailable under Windows.

- print, \p

  Display the current statement (the text of the statement itself, not the results obtained by executing it).

- prompt [arguments], \R [arguments]

  Redefine the primary mysql> prompt. Everything following the first space after the prompt keyword becomes part of the prompt string, including other spaces. The string can contain special sequences, as described in Section F.4.5, "mysql Prompt Definition Sequences." To revert the prompt to the default, specify prompt or \R with no arguments.

- quit, \q

  Quit mysql.

- rehash, \#

  Recalculate the information needed for database, table, and column name completion. See the description for the --auto-rehash option.

- source file_name, \. file_name

  Read and execute the statements contained in the named file. For Windows filenames that include backslash ('\') pathname separators, double them or specify them using slash ('/') instead.

- status, \s

  Retrieve and display status information from the server. This is useful for checking the server version, default database, SSL cipher, and so forth.

- system command, \! command

  Execute command using your default command interpreter. This command is unavailable under Windows.

- tee [file_name], \T [file_name]

  Copy output to the end of the named file. The previous file is used if you omit file_name.

- use db_name, \u db_name

  Select the given database to make it the default database.

- warnings, \W

  Automatically display any warnings generated by each statement.

F.4.5   mysql Prompt Definition Sequences

The MYSQL_PS1 environment variable, the --prompt option, or the prompt command can be used to redefine the primary mysql> statement prompt that mysql prints. For example, to include the name of the default database in the prompt, use the prompt command as follows, then select different databases to see how the prompt follows the current selection:

```
% mysql
mysql> prompt \d>\_
PROMPT set to '\d>\_'
(none)> USE sampdb;
Database changed
sampdb> USE test;
Database changed
test>
```

Follow the prompt keyword with the prompt definition string. Within the definition, escape sequences that begin with backslashes indicate special prompt options. The \d and _ sequences signify the default database name and a space. (If you set the prompt using the environment variable or the --prompt option, you might find it necessary to double the backslashes when specifying the prompt string.) The following table shows the available options.

Sequence	Meaning
\c	Current input line number
\d	Default database name, or "(none)" if no database is selected
\D	Full date and time
\h	Current host
\l	Current delimiter
\m	Minute
\o	Month number
\O	Month name, three letters
\p	Current port number, or socket, named-pipe, or shared-memory name
\P	am or pm indicator for time values
\r	Hour (12-hour time)
\R	Hour (24-hour time)
\s	Second
\S	Semicolon
\t	Tab
\u	Current username, without hostname
\U	Current username, including hostname
\v	Server version
\w	Weekday name, three letters
\y	Year (two-digit)
\Y	Year (four-digit)
\'	Single quote

Sequence	Meaning
\"	Double quote
_	Space character
\	Space character (the sequence is backslash-space)
\\	Literal '\'
\n	Newline (linefeed)
\x	Literal 'x' for any 'x' not otherwise listed

F.5 `mysql.server`

`mysql.server` starts and stops the `mysqld` server by invoking `mysqld_safe`. `mysql.server` is a shell script and is available on Unix.

`mysql.server` understands a command-line argument of `start` or `stop`:

```
mysql.server start
mysql.server stop
```

Normally, `mysql.server` is installed in a run-level directory on Unix systems that use such directories under `/etc`. (The installed version typically is named `mysql` rather than `mysql.server`.) The system starts the server by invoking the script with an argument of `start` at system boot time. The system shuts down the server by invoking the script with an argument of `stop` at system shutdown time. The script also can be invoked by hand with the appropriate argument to start or stop the server.

F.5.1 Options Supported by `mysql.server`

Support by `mysql.server` for standard MySQL options is limited. It does not read any standard options from the command line. Within the `[mysql_server]` and `[mysql.server]` groups in option files, it reads `basedir`, `datadir`, and `pid-file` options and passes them to `mysqld_safe`. It also reads `service-startup-timeout`, which takes a numeric value that indicates how long in seconds the script should wait for the server to start. The default is 900. A value of 0 means "do not wait" and negative values mean "wait forever."

F.6 `mysql_config`

The `mysql_config` utility aids development of MySQL-based programs written in C. It can be invoked to obtain the proper flags needed to compile C source files or link in MySQL libraries:

```
mysql_config [options]
```

For an example of usage, see Section 7.1, "Compiling and Linking Client Programs."

F.6.1 Options Specific to `mysql_config`

- `--cflags`

  Display the include-directory flags needed to access MySQL header files and other C compiler flags that might be necessary.

- `--cxxflags`

  Like `--cflags` but for the C++ compiler. This option was introduced in MySQL 5.6.4.

- `--embedded`, `--embedded-libs`

  These options are synonyms for `--libmysqld-libs`.

- `--include`

  Display the include-directory flags needed to access MySQL header files.

- `--libmysqld-libs`

  Display the library flags needed to link in `libmysqld`, the embedded server library.

- `--libs`

  Display the library flags needed to link in the client library.

- `--libs_r`

  Display the library flags needed to link in the thread-safe client library.

- `--plugindir`

  Display the default plugin directory.

- `--port`

  Display the default TCP/IP port number.

- `--socket`

  Display the default Unix socket file pathname.

- `--variable=`*var_name*

  Display the value of *var_name*, which can be `pkgincludedir`, `pkglibdir`, or `plugindir`.

- `--version`

  Display the MySQL version string.

F.7 `mysql_install_db`

The `mysql_install_db` script creates the server's data directory, initializes the `mysql` database that contains the grant tables, and creates an empty `test` database:

```
mysql_install_db [options]
```

`mysql_install_db` populates the grant tables with initial accounts for the `root` and anonymous users. See Chapter 12, "General MySQL Administration," for details on these accounts and how to secure your installation by establishing passwords.

`mysql_install_db` is unavailable on Windows, but unnecessary because Windows distributions include a preinitialized data directory.

F.7.1   Standard Options Supported by `mysql_install_db`

```
--help        --user        --verbose
```

For general descriptions of these options, see Section F.2.1, "Standard MySQL Program Options."

On Unix, the `--user` option runs the server using the login account of the named user. Specify this option if you invoke `mysql_install_db` as the Unix `root` user, to ensure that any directories and files created by the server are owned by this user.

F.7.2   Options Specific to `mysql_install_db`

You can use the options mentioned in this section on the command line, and you can set the values for many of them by placing appropriate entries in the `[mysqld]` group of an option file. The script also reads the `[mysql_install_db]` option group, which is useful for options such as `--ldata` and `--force` that are understood only by `mysql_install_db` and not by `mysqld`.

`mysql_install_db` passes any unrecognized options to `mysqld`.

- `--basedir=dir_name`

  The pathname to the MySQL base directory.

- `--datadir=dir_name`, `--ldata=dir_name`

  The pathname to the MySQL data directory.

- `--force`

  Run even if the current hostname cannot be determined. The IP address of the host is used to create grant table entries instead, which means that to use client programs, you'll need to specify the IP address rather than the hostname except for connections to `localhost`.

- `--skip-name-resolve`

  Use only IP addresses in the grant tables rather than hostnames. This option might be necessary if you don't have a working DNS server.

F.8 `mysql_upgrade`

This program should be used after you upgrade MySQL to a newer version. By default, it connects to the local server as the MySQL `root` user, so invoke it with the `root` password:

```
% mysql_upgrade --password=rootpass
```

`mysql_upgrade` checks databases for a MySQL installation to find incompatibilities with the new version and fixes them if possible. This includes upgrading the tables in the `mysql` database (for example, to handle new privileges), and repairing tables containing data in formats that might cause problems for the new server. After you run `mysql_upgrade`, restart the server so it takes advantage of any changes that were made.

`mysql_upgrade` invokes `mysqlcheck` to perform check and repair operations. See the description of that program for more information about its capabilities.

F.8.1 Standard Options Supported by `mysql_upgrade`

`--character-sets-dir`	`--default-character-set`	`--port`
`--compress`	`--help`	`--protocol`
`--debug`	`--host`	`--shared-memory-base-name`
`--debug-check`	`--password`	`--socket`
`--debug-info`	`--pipe`	`--user`
`--default-auth`	`--plugin-dir`	`--verbose`

For general descriptions of these options, see Section F.2.1, "Standard MySQL Program Options." `mysql_upgrade` also supports the standard SSL options listed in Section F.2.1.1, "Standard SSL Options."

The default `--user` value is `root`, unlike most MySQL programs. The `--verbose` option is enabled by default; use `--skip-verbose` to disable it.

F.8.2 Options Specific to `mysql_upgrade`

- `--basedir=dir_name`, `-b dir_name`

  This option is unused.

- `--datadir=dir_name`, `-d dir_name`

  This option is unused.

- `--force`, `-f` (*boolean*)

  Force an upgrade even if `mysql_upgrade` has been executed for the current version of MySQL.

- `--tmpdir=dir_name`, `-t dir_name`

  The pathname of the directory to use for temporary files.

- `--upgrade-system-tables, -s` (*boolean*)

  Upgrade only tables in the `mysql` database.

- `--write-binlog` (*boolean*)

  Write to the binary log those SQL statements issued while `mysql_upgrade` executes. Use this option to cause the statements to be replicated.

F.9 `mysqladmin`

The `mysqladmin` client communicates with the MySQL server to perform administrative operations. You can use `mysqladmin` to obtain information from the server or control its operation, set passwords, and create or drop databases:

```
mysqladmin [options] command ...
```

F.9.1 Standard Options Supported by `mysqladmin`

`--bind-address`	`--default-character-set`	`--protocol`
`--character-sets-dir`	`--help`	`--shared-memory-base-name`
`--compress`	`--host`	`--silent`
`--debug`	`--password`	`--socket`
`--debug-check`	`--pipe`	`--user`
`--debug-info`	`--plugin-dir`	`--verbose`
`--default-auth`	`--port`	`--version`

For general descriptions of these options, see Section F.2.1, "Standard MySQL Program Options." `mysqladmin` also supports the standard SSL options listed in Section F.2.1.1, "Standard SSL Options."

`--silent` causes `mysqladmin` to exit silently if it cannot connect to the server. For a few commands, the `--verbose` option causes `mysqladmin` to print more information.

F.9.2 Options Specific to `mysqladmin`

- `--count=n, -c n`

  The number of iterations to make when `--sleep` is given. If `--sleep` is given but `--count` is not, `mysqladmin` iterates forever (or until you interrupt it).

- `--force, -f` (*boolean*)

  This option has two effects. First, it causes `mysqladmin` not to ask for confirmation of the `drop db_name` command. Second, when multiple commands are specified on the command line, `mysqladmin` attempts to execute each command even if errors occur. Normally, `mysqladmin` exits after the first error.

- `--no-beep, -b` (*boolean*)

  Suppress production of beeps when errors occur.

- `--relative, -r` (*boolean*)

  Show the difference between the current and previous values when used with `--sleep`. This option works only with the `extended-status` command.

- `--sleep=n, -i n`

  Execute the commands named on the command line repeatedly with a delay of *n* seconds between each repetition.

- `--vertical, -E` (*boolean*)

  Like `--relative`, but format output vertically.

- `--wait[=n], -w[n]`

  The number of times to wait and retry if a connection to the server cannot be established. The default value of *n* is 1 if no value is given. If *n* is specified after `-w`, there must be no intervening space or the value will not be interpreted correctly.

F.9.3 Variables for `mysqladmin`

The following `mysqladmin` variables can be set using the instructions given in Section F.2.1.2, "Setting Program Variables."

- `connect_timeout`

  The number of seconds to wait before timing out when attempting to connect to the server. The default is 43,200.

- `shutdown_timeout`

  For `shutdown` commands, the number of seconds to wait for a successful shutdown. The default is 3,600.

F.9.4 `mysqladmin` Commands

Following any options on the command line, you can specify one or more of the following commands. Each command name can be shortened to any unambiguous prefix. For example, `processlist` can be shortened to `process` or `proc`, but not to `p`.

Several of these commands have an equivalent SQL statement, as noted in the descriptions. See Appendix E, "SQL Syntax Reference," for more information about the meaning of these statements.

- `create db_name`

  Create a new database with the given name. This command is like the CREATE DATABASE *db_name* statement.

- `debug`

  Instruct the server to dump debugging information to the error log.

- `drop` *db_name*

  Remove the database with the given name, and any tables that may be in the database. `mysqladmin` asks for confirmation of this command unless the `--force` option was given. This command is like the `DROP DATABASE` *db_name* statement.

- `extended-status`

  Display the names and values of the server's status variables. This command is like the `SHOW STATUS` statement.

- `flush-hosts`

  Flush the host cache. This command is like the `FLUSH HOSTS` statement.

- `flush-logs`

  Flush (close and reopen) the log files. This command is like the `FLUSH LOGS` statement.

- `flush-privileges`

  Reload the grant tables. This command is like the `FLUSH PRIVILEGES` statement.

- `flush-status`

  Clear the status variables. (This resets several counters to zero.) This command is like the `FLUSH STATUS` statement.

- `flush-tables`

  Flush the table cache. This command is like the `FLUSH TABLES` statement.

- `flush-threads`

  Flush the thread cache.

- `kill` *id,id,...*

  Kill the server threads specified by the given identifier numbers. If you specify multiple numbers, the ID list must contain no spaces so that it will not be confused for another command following the `kill` command. To find out what threads are currently running, use `mysqladmin processlist`. This command is like issuing a `KILL` statement for each thread ID.

- `old-password` *new_password*

  This command is like the `password` command except that it causes the password to be stored in the password-hashing format used prior to MySQL 4.1.

- `password` *new_password*

  Change the password for the account that the server authenticates you as when you connect. (Being able to connect to the server using this account serves as verification that you know the current password.) The password is set to *new_password*. This command is like the SET PASSWORD statement.

On Unix, you can use either single quotes or double quotes in the `mysqladmin` command to quote the password if it contains characters that your command interpreter considers special. On Windows, you should use only double quotes. Windows command interpreters do not recognize single quotes as argument-quoting characters, so if you use them, they become part of your password!

As of MySQL 5.5.3, if `password` is the last command on the command line, the *new_password* value is optional and `mysqladmin` prompts for it if it is missing.

- `ping`

  Check whether the MySQL server is running.

- `processlist`

  Display a list of currently executing server activities. This command is like the SHOW PROCESSLIST statement, or, with `--verbose`, like SHOW FULL PROCESSLIST.

- `refresh`

  Flush the table cache and the grant tables, and close and reopen the log files. If the server is a replication master server, the command tells it to delete the binary log files listed in the binary log index file and to truncate the index. If the server is a slave server, the command tells it to forget its position in the master binary log.

- `reload`

  Reload the grant tables. This command is like the FLUSH PRIVILEGES statement.

- `shutdown`

  Shut down the server.

- `start-slave`

  Start a replication slave server. This command is like the START SLAVE statement.

- `status`

  Display a short status message from the server.

- `stop-slave`

  Stop a replication slave server. This command is like the STOP SLAVE statement.

- `variables`

  Display the names and values of the server's variables. This command is like the SHOW GLOBAL VARIABLES.

- `version`

  Retrieve and display the server version information string. This is the same information returned by the VERSION() SQL function.

F.10   `mysqlbinlog`

The `mysqlbinlog` program displays the contents of a binary log file in readable format:

```
mysqlbinlog [options] file_name ...
```

By default, `mysqlbinlog` reads local log files directly without connecting to a server. It is also possible to connect to a server and ask it to send log files over the connection. See the description for the `--read-from-remote-server` option.

The format of the binary log has changed from time to time. To avoid compatibility problems, you may find it necessary to use a version of `mysqlbinlog` that is at least as recent as your server version.

`mysqlbinlog` also reads relay log files created by replication slave servers because the binary and relay logs have the same format.

F.10.1   Standard Options Supported by `mysqlbinlog`

`--bind-address`	`--help`	`--shared-memory-base-name`
`--character-sets-dir`	`--host`	`--socket`
`--debug`	`--password`	`--user`
`--debug-check`	`--plugin-dir`	`--verbose`
`--debug-info`	`--port`	`--version`
`--default-auth`	`--protocol`	

For general descriptions of these options, see Section F.2.1, "Standard MySQL Program Options."

The `--verbose` option causes `mysqlbinlog` to display row events as commented SQL statements. Given twice, the option also produces comments to describe column metadata.

F.10.2   Options Specific to `mysqlbinlog`

- `--base64-output=value`

  Control how to display output as `BINLOG` statements in base-64-encoded form. Such statements typically are used for row events not described in terms of SQL. These option values are permitted:

  - `AUTO` or `UNSPEC`: Automatically use `BINLOG` statements when necessary.

  - `NEVER`: Do not produce `BINLOG` statements, and exit with an error if a row event is encountered that cannot be displayed other than with `BINLOG`.

  - `DECODE_ROWS`: For use when `--verbose` is also given, this value is like `NEVER` but does not exit with an error.

  - `ALWAYS`: Always display `BINLOG` statements if possible. This option value is no longer available as of MySQL 5.6.1.

Option values are not case sensitive. If this option is not given, the default is AUTO, which is also the only value that is safe if you plan to re-execute the output of mysqlbinlog. Other values should be considered for debugging or testing only.

- `--binlog-row-event-max-size=`*n*

The maximum permitted size for row-based events. mysqlbinlog attempts when possible to group rows into events no larger than this value. The value is truncated to the nearest nonzero multiple of 256. The default is 4GB. This option was introduced in MySQL 5.6.0.

- `--database=`*db_name*, `-d` *db_name*

Extract statements from the log file only for the named database. This option works only when reading local logs.

- `--disable-log-bin`, `-D` (*boolean*)

Include statements in the output that disable binary logging of the update statements in the log. This prevents the statements from being logged again if they are re-executed.

- `--force-if-open`, `-F` (*boolean*)

Read binary log files even if they were not closed properly (or are currently in use). This option is enabled by default. To disable it, use `--skip-force-if-open`.

- `--force-read`, `-f` (*boolean*)

This option controls what mysqlbinlog does when it reads an unrecognizable event from the binary log. By default, it stops. If this option is enabled, mysqlbinlog continues after logging a warning and discarding the event.

- `--hexdump`, `-H` (*boolean*)

Include a hexadecimal/ASCII event dump in the output.

- `--local-load=`*dir_name*, `-l` *dir_name*

The directory in which to create to create temporary data files for processing LOAD DATA LOCAL statements. mysqlbinlog does not delete these files because you might not re-execute its output immediately and the files are needed at re-execution time. Delete the files manually when they are no longer needed.

- `--offset=`*n*, `-o` *n*

Skip the first *n* events in the log file.

- `--raw` (*boolean*)

This option is used with `--read-from-remote-server` to request binary log files from a given server in their original binary format rather than the default text format. One use for this is to make a backup of a server's binary log files. (In this case, `--result-file` can be used to control output file naming.) This option was introduced in MySQL 5.6.0.

- `--read-from-remote-server, -R` (*boolean*)

Read binary log files by making a network connection to a server and asking it to send the logs over the connection. To do this, use the `--read-from-remote-server` option and give the `--host`, `--password`, `--port`, `--protocol`, `--socket`, and `--user` options as necessary to specify connection parameters. Without `--read-from-remote-server`, those options are ignored.

- `--result-file=file_name, -r file_name`

Write output to the named file, if `--raw` is not specified. With `--raw`, this option indicates how to name the local copies of binary log files transferred from the server. In this case, the output files have the same name as the master log files, with any prefix given as the `--result-file` option value. The value can begin with a directory to write files in that directory. For example, backup files made on 2012-01-28 might be labeled as such using `--result-file=2012-01-28-` and the output filenames will begin with that date in the current directory. To write the files in `/var/backup` instead, use `--result-file=/var/backup/2012-01-28-`.

- `--server-id=n`

Dump only events created by the server with this ID.

- `--set-charset=charset`

Include a SET NAMES statement in the output.

- `--short-form, -s`

Show only the statements that are present in the log; omit any extra information in the log that is associated with the statements and do not show row-based events.

- `--start-datetime=date_time`

Start reading binary log events beginning with the first event that has a time at or later than the given `date_time` value. `date_time` should be specified in a legal DATETIME format in the time zone local to the host on which you run `mysqlbinlog`. Quote the value if necessary for your command interpreter.

- `--start-position=n, -j n`

Start reading binary log events at the given position in the first log file named on the command line.

- `--stop-datetime=date_time`

Stop reading binary log events beginning with the first event that has a time at or later than the given `date_time` value. `date_time` should be specified in a legal DATETIME format in the time zone local to the host on which you run `mysqlbinlog`. Quote the value if necessary for your command interpreter.

- `--stop-never` (*boolean*)

The option is used with `--read-from-remote-server` to stay connected to the server. It can be used to display log events as the server writes them, or with `--raw` to make a continuous live log backup. This option was introduced in MySQL 5.6.0.

- `--stop-never-slave-server-id=server_id`

  The server ID to report to the server when `--stop-never` is used. The default ID is 65535, but it might be necessary to specify an ID explicitly if a slave server or another instance of `mysqlbinlog` is using that ID. This option was introduced in MySQL 5.6.0.

- `--stop-position=n`

  Stop reading binary log events at the given position in the last log file named on the command line.

- `--to-last-log, -t` (*boolean*)

  When reading log files from a server (which requires the `--read-from-remote-server` option), this option causes binary log files to be read through the last log file of the server, rather than at the end of the last requested log file. To make sure that you have obtained all binary log information from the server, use `--to-last-log`. (However, if you are sending the events to the same server to be processed, this can lead to an infinite loop.)

- `--verify-binlog-checksum, -c` (*boolean*)

  Enable verification of checksums in events. This option was introduced in MySQL 5.6.1.

F.10.3 Variables for `mysqlbinlog`

The following `mysqlbinlog` variables can be set using the instructions given in Section F.2.1.2, "Setting Program Variables."

- `open_files_limit`

  The number of file descriptors to reserve. The default is 64.

F.11 mysqlcheck

`mysqlcheck` is a client program for checking and repairing tables. It presents a command-line interface to these administrative statements: CHECK TABLE, ANALYZE TABLE, OPTIMIZE TABLE, and REPAIR TABLE.

All `mysqlcheck` options are supported for MyISAM tables. `mysqlcheck` also can check and analyze InnoDB tables.

`mysqlcheck` can be run in any of three modes:

```
mysqlcheck [options] db_name [tbl_name] ...
mysqlcheck [options] --databases db_name ...
mysqlcheck [options] --all-databases
```

In the first case, `mysqlcheck` checks the named tables in the given database. If no tables are named, `mysqlcheck` checks all tables in the database. In the second case, all arguments are taken as database names and `mysqlcheck` checks all tables in each one. In the third case, `mysqlcheck` checks all tables in all databases.

F.11.1 Standard Options Supported by `mysqlcheck`

--bind-address	--default-character-set	--protocol
--character-sets-dir	--help	--shared-memory-base-name
--compress	--host	--silent
--debug	--password	--socket
--debug-check	--pipe	--user
--debug-info	--plugin-dir	--verbose
--default-auth	--port	--version

For general descriptions of these options, see Section F.2.1, "Standard MySQL Program Options." `mysqlcheck` also supports the standard SSL options listed in Section F.2.1.1, "Standard SSL Options."

F.11.2 Options Specific to `mysqlcheck`

`mysqlcheck` supports the following options to control how it processes tables. Following this list you'll find a description of the equivalences between these options and the SQL statements to which they correspond.

- --all-databases, -A (*boolean*)

  Process all tables in all databases.

- --analyze, -a

  Perform table analysis by issuing an ANALYZE TABLE statement. (For example, this analyzes the distribution of key values.) The results of the analysis can help the query optimizer perform index-based lookups and joins more quickly.

- --all-in-1, -1 (*boolean*)

  Without this option, `mysqlcheck` issues separate statements for each table. This option causes `mysqlcheck` to group tables by database and name all tables within each database in a single statement.

- --auto-repair (*boolean*)

  If any checked tables are found to have problems, run a second phase to repair them after the check phase has finished.

- --check, -c

  Issue a CHECK TABLE statement to check for errors. This is the default action if no action is specified explicitly.

- --check-only-changed, -C

  Check only tables that have changed since they were last checked or that have not been closed properly.

- `--check-upgrade, -g`

  Check whether tables are compatible with your current version of MySQL. With `--auto-repair`, automatic table repair is attempted if incompatibilities are found. This option enables the `--fix-db-names` and `--fix-table-names` options.

- `--databases, -B` (*boolean*)

  Interpret all arguments as database names and check all tables in each database.

- `--extended, -e` (*boolean*)

  Perform an extended table check. If used with `--repair`, use a more extensive but slower repair method than is used for `--repair` by itself.

- `--fast, -F` (*boolean*)

  Check only tables that have not been closed properly.

- `--fix-db-names` (*boolean*)

  Check database names and convert them per name-encoding changes that were made between MySQL 5.0 and 5.1.

- `--fix-table-names` (*boolean*)

  Check table and view names and convert them per name-encoding changes that were made between MySQL 5.0 and 5.1.

- `--force, -f` (*boolean*)

  Continue execution even if errors occur.

- `--medium-check, -m`

  Perform table checking using a method that is faster than `--extended` but slightly less thorough. This check mode should suffice for most circumstances.

- `--optimize, -o`

  Perform table optimization by issuing an OPTIMIZE TABLE statement.

- `--quick, -q` (*boolean*)

  For table checking, this option skips checking links in the data rows. Used with `--repair`, this option repairs only the index file and leaves the data file untouched.

- `--repair, -r`

  Perform table repair by issuing a REPAIR TABLE statement. This repair mode should correct most problems except the occurrence of duplicate values in an index that should contain only unique values.

- `--tables`

  Override `--databases` to cause any following arguments to be interpreted as table names.

- `--use-frm` (*boolean*)

  When used with `--repair`, perform a table repair operation that uses the table's `.frm` file to reinitialize the index file and to determine how to interpret the contents of the data file so the indexes can be rebuilt. This can be useful if the index has become lost or irrecoverably corrupted. However, it should be treated as a last resort and used *only* if your current version of MySQL is the same as that used to create the table. Otherwise, you risk further damage to the table.

- `--write-binlog` (*boolean*)

  Write `ANALYZE TABLE`, `OPTIMIZE TABLE`, and `REPAIR TABLE` statements to the binary log (which means they will be sent to replication slaves). This option is enabled by default. To disable it, use `--skip-write-binlog`.

The following tables show the relationship between `mysqlcheck`'s options and the SQL statements that it issues.

Table checking options (InnoDB and MyISAM tables only):

Option	Corresponding Statement
`--check`	`CHECK TABLE tbl_list`
`--check-only-changed`	`CHECK TABLE tbl_list CHANGED`
`--extended`	`CHECK TABLE tbl_list EXTENDED`
`--fast`	`CHECK TABLE tbl_list FAST`
`--medium-check`	`CHECK TABLE tbl_list MEDIUM`
`--quick`	`CHECK TABLE tbl_list QUICK`

InnoDB does not support different types of checks, so for InnoDB tables, `mysqlcheck` treats all options in the preceding table as `--check`.

Table analysis options (InnoDB and MyISAM tables only):

Option	Corresponding Statement
`--analyze`	`ANALYZE TABLE tbl_list`

Table repair options (MyISAM tables only):

Option(s)	Corresponding Statement
`--repair`	`REPAIR TABLE tbl_list`
`--repair --quick`	`REPAIR TABLE tbl_list QUICK`
`--repair --extended`	`REPAIR TABLE tbl_list EXTENDED`
`--repair --use-frm`	`REPAIR TABLE tbl_list USE_FRM`

Table optimization options (MyISAM tables only):

Option	Corresponding Statement
--optimize	OPTIMIZE TABLE *tbl_list*

F.12 `mysqld`

`mysqld` is the MySQL server. It provides database access to client programs, so it must be running or clients cannot use databases administered by the server. When `mysqld` starts, it opens network interfaces on which to listen and then waits for client connections. `mysqld` is multi-threaded—it provides concurrency among clients by using multiple threads to process client connections.

The usual invocation sequence is simply the server name followed by any desired options:

```
mysqld [options]
```

On Windows, a server can be installed to run as a service. For example, the server might be installed to run automatically at system startup, or removed as a service as follows:

```
C:\> "C:\Program Files\MySQL\MySQL Server 5.5\bin\mysqld" --install
C:\> mysqld --remove
```

The install command uses the full pathname to the server. If your server is installed in a different location, modify the pathname accordingly. The default service name is MySQL. You can provide a service name following the option (type each command on a single line):

```
C:\> "C:\Program Files\MySQL\MySQL Server 5.5\bin\mysqld" --install
        service_name
C:\> mysqld --remove service_name
```

This enables multiple servers to be run under different service names. With no *service_name* argument or a service name of MySQL, the server uses MySQL as the service name and reads the [mysqld] group from the standard option files. With a *service_name* argument different from MySQL, the server uses that name as the service name and reads the [mysqld] and [*service_name*] groups from the standard option files.

A --defaults-file option following the service name is permitted to specify an additional file of options for the server to read at startup (type the command on a single line):

```
C:\> "C:\Program Files\MySQL\MySQL Server 5.5\bin\mysqld" --install
        service_name --defaults-file=file_name
```

In this case, the *service_name* argument is not optional.

The preceding remarks about --install apply to --install-manual as well.

F.12.1 Standard Options Supported by `mysqld`

```
--character-sets-dir    --port                    --user
--debug                 --shared-memory-base-name --verbose
--help                  --socket                  --version
```

For general descriptions of these options, see Section F.2.1, "Standard MySQL Program Options." `mysqld` also supports the standard SSL options listed in Section F.2.1.1, "Standard SSL Options."

The `--help` option by itself displays only a brief usage message. To see the full help message, use this command:

```
% mysqld --verbose --help
```

The verbose help message also displays system variables that can be set on the command line. For descriptions of these variables, see Appendix D, "System, Status, and User Variable Reference."

Although `--socket` is supported, the corresponding short form (`-S`) is not. On Windows, `--socket` sets the pipe name if the server supports named-pipe connections.

On Unix, if the `--user` option is given, it specifies the username or numeric user ID of the account to use for running the server. In this case, when the server starts, it looks up the user and group ID values of the account from the password file and then changes its user and group IDs to match. In this way, the server runs with the privileges associated with that user, not `root` privileges. (The server must be started as `root` for the `--user` option to be effective. Otherwise, it cannot change its user ID and issues a warning.)

F.12.2 Options Specific to `mysqld`

Of all MySQL programs, `mysqld` has the most extensive set of options. However, if you compare the output from `mysqld --verbose --help` with the list of options described here, you'll notice that the help output contains many items that are missing from this list. That's because the help output also includes "options" that are really system variables that can be set at server startup. In the interest of conserving space, if an option has the same name as a system variable, I omit the option here. If you don't see a server option here that you're looking for, check for it in Appendix D, "System, Status, and User Variable Reference." For example, the `mysqld` help message lists a `--general-log` option to enable the general query log. You can find information about it in the description of the `general_log` system variable.

The first list of options here describes general options. It is followed by lists of options specific to Windows and to replication.

- `--allow-suspicious-udfs` (*boolean*)

  Enable the server to load older user-defined functions (UDFs) that might define only the symbol corresponding to the function name and not any of the related standard support-routine symbols. This capability is disabled by default as a precaution against loading functions that might not be true UDFs.

- `--ansi, -a`

  Tell the server to use standard SQL behavior for certain types of syntax, rather than MySQL-specific syntax. This option can be used to make the server more standards-compliant.

  This option is equivalent to setting the `sql_mode` system variable to include the `REAL_AS_FLOAT`, `PIPES_AS_CONCAT`, `ANSI_QUOTES`, `IGNORE_SPACE`, and `ONLY_FULL_GROUP_BY` mode values.

- `--archive[=state]`

  Control the activation state of the `ARCHIVE` storage engine plugin, if it is included with the MySQL distribution. For a list of permitted `state` values, see the description for `--plugin_name`.

- `--basedir=dir_name, -b dir_name`

  The pathname of the MySQL installation root directory. Many other pathnames are resolved in relation to this directory if they are given as relative pathnames.

- `--bind-address=addr`

  Bind to the given IP address to listen for TCP/IP client connections. As of MySQL 5.6.6, the default is `*` (listen on all IPv4 and IPv6 interfaces). Before 5.6.6, the default is `0.0.0.0` (listen on all IPv4 interfaces). For more information, see Section 12.2.4, "Controlling How the Server Listens for Connections."

- `--binlog-row-event-max-size=n`

  The maximum permitted size for row-based events. `mysqld` attempts when possible to group rows into events no larger than this value. The value is truncated to the nearest nonzero multiple of 256. The default is 8KB as of MySQL 5.6.6, 1KB in earlier versions.

- `--blackhole[=state]`

  Control the activation state of the `BLACKHOLE` storage engine plugin, if it is included with the MySQL distribution. For a list of permitted `state` values, see the description for `--plugin_name`.

- `--bootstrap`

  This option is used by installation scripts when you first install MySQL.

- `--character-set-client-handshake` (*boolean*)

  Tell the server to use character set information provided by the client. This option is enabled by default; `--skip-character-set-client-handshake` causes the information to be ignored, which is the behavior in MySQL 4.0.

- `--character-set-server=charset, -C charset`

  The server's default character set.

- `--chroot=`*`dir_name`*`, -r `*`dir_name`*

  Run the MySQL server anchored to the given directory as its root directory. See the `chroot()` Unix manual page for more information on running in a `chroot()`-ed environment.

- `--collation-server=`*`collation`*

  The default collation for the server's default character set.

- `--core-file`

  When a fatal error occurs, cause the server to generate a core file before exiting.

- `--datadir=`*`dir_name`*`, -h `*`dir_name`*

  The pathname of the MySQL data directory.

- `--default-time-zone=`*`tz_name`*

  Set the server's default time zone to *`tz_name`*. Time zone values are described in Section 12.6.1, "Configuring Time Zone Support." This option sets the `time_zone` system variable, not `system_time_zone`.

- `--delay-key-write[=`*`val`*`]`

  Set the mode used by the server for handling delayed key writes for MyISAM files. *`val`* can be `ON` (delay key writes on a per-table basis, according to any `DELAY_KEY_WRITE` value specified when tables were created; this is the default if no option value is given), `OFF` (never delay key writes for any MyISAM table), or `ALL` (delay key writes for all MyISAM tables). `OFF` and `ALL` enforce a policy that is applied regardless of how individual tables were defined when they were created.

- `--des-key-file=`*`file_name`*

  The name of the file that holds DES keys for the `DES_ENCRYPT()` and `DES_DECRYPT()` functions. For a description of the file format, see the entry for `DES_ENCRYPT()` in Appendix C, "Operator and Function Reference."

- `--exit-info[=`*`n`*`], -T[`*`n`*`]`

  Cause the server to produce debugging information when it terminates. If *`n`* is specified after `-T`, there must be no intervening space or the value will not be interpreted correctly.

- `--external-locking` (*boolean*)

  Enable external locking (filesystem locking) for systems such as Linux, where external locking is off by default.

  External locking is problematic because it doesn't work reliably on some systems, and is effective only for operations that only read tables, such as table checking.

- `--federated[=`*`state`*`]`

  Control the activation state of the `FEDERATED` storage engine plugin, if it is included with the MySQL distribution. For a list of permitted *`state`* values, see the description for `--`*`plugin_name`*.

- `--gdb`

Set up signal handlers that are useful for debugging with `gdb`.

- `--ignore-db-dir=dir_name`

Specify the name of a directory in the data directory not to be treated as a database directory by `SHOW DATABASES` or `INFORMATION_SCHEMA` tables. This option can be given multiple times. Directories so specified are available at runtime as the value of the `ignore_db_dirs` system variable, except that specifying this option with an empty value clears the list, overriding any earlier instances. This option was introduced in MySQL 5.6.3.

- `--innodb[=state]`

Control the activation state of the `InnoDB` storage engine plugin. For a list of permitted `state` values, see the description for `--plugin_name`. Because InnoDB is the default storage engine, it is enabled by default. To disable it if you don't use InnoDB tables, use `--innodb=OFF`. In this case, you must also set the `default_storage_engine` system variable (and also `default_tmp_storage_engine` as of MySQL 5.6.3) to specify a different default engine or the server will not start; see Section 12.5.2, "Selecting a Default Storage Engine."

- `--innodb-status-file` (*boolean*)

Write `SHOW INNODB STATUS` information to a file named `innodb_status.nnnnnn` in the data directory periodically. *nnnnnn* is the server process ID number. These status files are not removed except for clean shutdown. Occasionally, you should remove those that no longer are needed.

- `--innodb-xxx`

Many other InnoDB parameters are available as system variables that can be set at server startup; see Section D.1.1, "InnoDB System Variables."

- `--language=lang_name, -L lang_name`

The language for error messages. This option is obsolete. Use the `lc_messages` and `lc_message_dir` system variables instead to specify the error message locale and file location.

- `--log[=file_name], -l[file_name]`

Enable the general query log. This option is deprecated and is removed in MySQL 5.6. Use the `general_log` and `general_log_file` system variables instead.

- `--log-bin[=file_name]`

Enable the binary log. `file_name` specifies the basename for the binary log files. If not given, the log filename is `HOSTNAME-bin.nnnnnn` in the data directory, where `HOSTNAME` is the name of the server host and *nnnnnn* is a sequence number that the server increments by one each time it opens a new log file. If `file_name` is given as a relative path, the server interprets it relative to the data directory.

- `--log-bin-index=file_name`

  Enable the binary log index file. If `file_name` is not given, the default name is the same as the basename of the binary log files, with an `.index` extension. If `file_name` is given as a relative path, the server interprets it relative to the data directory.

- `--log-isam[=file_name]`

  Enable index file logging. This is used only for debugging MyISAM operations. If you specify no name, the default is `myisam.log` in the data directory.

- `--log-raw` (*boolean*)

  Suppress rewriting of statements written to the general query log, slow query log, and binary log to prevent passwords from appearing as clear text. This is intended for debugging and testing; normally you do not want passwords to be exposed in server logs. This option was introduced in MySQL 5.6.3.

- `--log-short-format` (*boolean*)

  Write less information to the binary log and slow query log if those logs are enabled.

- `--log-slow-admin-statements` (*boolean*)

  Administrative operations such as those performed by ALTER TABLE or OPTIMIZE TABLE might be slow, but by default are not logged to the slow query logs. This option causes them to be logged if they are slow.

- `--log-slow-queries[=file_name]`

  Enable the slow query log. This option is deprecated and is removed in MySQL 5.6. Use the `slow_query_log` and `slow_query_log_file` system variables instead.

- `--log-tc=file_name`

  The pathname to the transaction coordinator log file (for XA transactions). This option is unused.

- `--log-tc-size=n`

  The size of the transaction coordinator log file.

- `--log-warnings[=n]`, `-W[n]`

  Write certain noncritical warning messages to the error log. This option is on by default. Give the option with no value to enable warnings, or with a value of 0 or 1 to disable or enable warnings. Give the option with no value twice or specify it with a value of 2 to enable logging of aborted connections and access-denied errors. If `n` is specified after `-W`, there must be no intervening space or the value will not be interpreted correctly.

- `--memlock` (*boolean*)

  Lock the server in memory if possible. This option is effective only on systems such as Solaris or Linux that can lock processes in memory, and may require that you run the server run as `root`.

- `--myisam-block-size=size`

  The block size for MyISAM table index blocks.

- `--old-style-user-limits` (*boolean*)

  MySQL accounts can have limits placed on their activities, as described in Section 13.2.2.5, "Limiting an Account's Resource Consumption." Limits for an account are assessed ignoring which particular host the account connected from, but `--old-style-user-limits` can be used to enable the old method of assessing limits. (Before MySQL 5.0.3, limits were assessed separately per host from which the account connected.)

- `--plugin-load=plugin_list`

  Load the plugins indicated by the option value, which is a list of one or more semicolon-separated `plugin_name=lib_name` or `lib_name` specifiers. Naming a plugin and library causes the server to load only that plugin from the library. Naming a library without a plugin name causes the server to load all plugins from the library. `--plugin-load` resets the list of plugins to be loaded, so if you specify it multiple times, only the last instance has any effect. For more information, see Section 12.4, "The Plugin Interface."

- `--plugin-load-add=plugin_list`

  Similar to `--plugin-load` but add to the list of plugins to be loaded without resetting the list first. This option was introduced in MySQL 5.6.3.

- `--plugin_name[=state]`

  If the server will load a plugin at startup because it was built in, registered in the `mysql.plugin` table, or specified using the `--plugin-load` or `--plugin-load-add` option, it is possible to control the plugin's activation state. To do this, use an option named after the plugin. For example, `--innodb` provides activation control of the InnoDB storage engine. The permitted `state` values are `OFF` (do not activate), `ON` (activate, the default if `state` is omitted), `FORCE` (activate and fail startup if an error occurs), and `FORCE_PLUS_PERMANENT` (like `FORCE`, but also prevent plugin unloading at runtime). For additional information about plugin loading, see Section 12.4, "The Plugin Interface."

- `--port-open-timeout=n`

  How long in seconds the server should wait for its TCP/IP port to become available at startup. The default is 0 (no wait).

- `--safe-mode`

  This option is obsolete.

- `--safe-user-create` (*boolean*)

  Prohibit account creation by users who do not have `INSERT` access to the `mysql.user` grant table.

- `--skip-grant-tables` (*boolean*)

Disable use of the grant tables for verifying client connections. This gives any client full access to do anything. It also disables the `CREATE USER`, `DROP USER`, `RENAME USER`, `GRANT`, `REVOKE`, and `SET PASSWORD` statements, and prevents the server from loading any plugins registered in the `mysql.plugin` table. You can tell the server to begin using the grant tables again by issuing a `FLUSH PRIVILEGES` statement or a `mysqladmin flush-privileges` command, or by restarting it without `--skip-grant-tables`.

- `--skip-host-cache`

Disable use of the hostname cache. As of MySQL 5.6.5, this has an effect similar to setting `host_cache_size=0`, except that, with `--skip-host-cache`, the cache cannot be re-enabled at runtime.

- `--skip-stack-trace`

Skip stack-trace printing when failure occurs.

- `--symbolic-links`, `-s` (*boolean*)

For Unix, enable symbolic linking for MyISAM table data and index files (using the `DATA DIRECTORY` and `INDEX DIRECTORY` table creation options). For Windows, enable symbolic linking of database directories. These techniques are discussed in Chapter 11, "The MySQL Data Directory." Database symlinking support on Windows is enabled by default. To disable it, use `--skip-symbolic-links`.

- `--sysdate-is-now` (*boolean*)

`SYSDATE()` returns the date and time at which it is invoked, whereas `NOW()` returns the time at which the statement began executing. `--sysdate-is-now` causes `SYSDATE()` to behave like `NOW()`.

- `--tc-heuristic-recover=str`

This option is unused.

- `--temp-pool` (*boolean*)

With this option, the server uses a small set of names for temporary files, rather than creating a unique name for each file. This avoids some caching problems on Linux, which is the only system to which it applies. This option is enabled by default. To disable it, use `--skip-temp-pool`.

- `--tmpdir=dir_name`, `-t dir_name`

The pathname of the directory to use for temporary files. The option value can be given as a list of directories, to be used in round-robin fashion. Under Unix, separate directory names by colons; under Windows, separate them by semicolons.

- `--transaction-isolation=level`

Set the default transaction isolation level. The permitted *level* values are `READ-UNCOMMITTED`, `READ-COMMITTED`, `REPEATABLE-READ`, and `SERIALIZABLE`.

- `--transaction-read-only` (*boolean*)

  Whether the default transaction access mode is read only. This option is disabled by default, which means the default access mode is read/write. This option was introduced in MySQL 5.6.5.

F.12.2.1 Windows Options

The options in this section are available only for servers running under Windows. Service names and named-pipe names are not case sensitive. Shared-memory names are case sensitive.

- `--console` (*boolean*)

  Display a console window for error messages. If `--log-error` is given as well, error messages go to the log file rather than the console.

- `--install` [`service_name`]

  Install the server as a service that runs automatically when Windows starts. If `service_name` is not given, the default service is named `MySQL`.

- `--install-manual` [`service_name`]

  Install the server as a service that does not run automatically when Windows starts. You must explicitly start the service yourself. If `service_name` is not given, the default service is named `MySQL`.

- `--named-pipe` (*boolean*)

  For MySQL servers that include named-pipe support, named-pipe connections are disabled by default. This option enables named-pipe connections. The default pipe name is `MySQL`. The name can be changed with the `--socket` option.

- `--remove` [`service_name`]

  Remove the server as a service. If `service_name` is not given, the default service is named `MySQL`.

- `--shared-memory` (*boolean*)

  Enable shared-memory connections. The default shared-memory name is `MYSQL`. The name can be changed with the `--shared-memory-base-name` option.

- `--standalone`

  Run the server as a standalone program rather than as a service.

F.12.2.2 Replication Options

The options in this section pertain to MySQL's replication capabilities.

The `--show-slave-auth-info` option affects the output of `SHOW SLAVE HOSTS` on the master, as described in Appendix E, "SQL Syntax Reference."

- `--abort-slave-event-count=n`

  This option is used by the MySQL test suite for replication testing.

- `--binlog-do-db=db_name`

  Tell a replication master to log updates only for the named database. No other databases will be replicated. To log updates for multiple databases, repeat the option once for each database.

- `--binlog-ignore-db=db_name`

  Tell a replication master not to log updates for the named database. To ignore updates for multiple databases, repeat the option once for each database.

  Note that use of this option causes the binary log to contain no information that could be used for recovery of the named database if a crash occurs. To avoid this problem, use `--replicate-ignore-db` on the slave server instead.

- `--disconnect-slave-event-count=n`

  This option is used by the MySQL test suite for replication testing.

- `--master-info-file=file_name`

  For a replication slave, the name of the file that stores information about the current replication state. The contents of this file are the replication coordinates (master binary log filename and position), master host, username, password, port number, connection retry interval, and SSL option values. The default name for this file is `master.info` in the data directory. If `file_name` is given as a relative path, the server interprets it relative to the data directory.

- `--master-retry-count=n`

  For a replication slave, the number of times to attempt a connection to a master server before giving up. In MySQL 5.6, this option is obsolete. Use the `MASTER_RETRY_COUNT` option of the `CHANGE MASTER TO` statement instead.

- `--max-binlog-dump-events=n`

  This option is used by the MySQL test suite for replication testing.

- `--relay-log=file_name`

  For a replication slave, this option specifies the basename of the relay log files. (The slave I/O thread stores updates read from the master in the relay log, and the SQL thread reads the relay log for statements and executes them.) By default, relay log filenames are `HOSTNAME-relay-bin.nnnnnn` in the data directory, where `HOSTNAME` is the name of the server host and `nnnnnn` is a sequence number that the server increments by one each time it opens a new log file.

- `--relay-log-index=file_name`

  For a replication slave, the name of the relay log index file. The default name is `HOSTNAME-relay-bin.index` in the data directory, where `HOSTNAME` is the name of the server host. If *file_name* is given as a relative path, the server interprets it relative to the data directory.

- `--relay-log-info-file=`*file_name*

For a replication slave, the name of the relay log information file. The default name is `relay-log.info` in the data directory.

- `--replicate-do-db=`*db_name*

Tell a replication slave to replicate only the named database. To restrict replication to a set of databases, repeat the option once for each database.

- `--replicate-do-table=`*db_name.tbl_name*

Tell a replication slave to replicate only the given table, which should be named in *db_name.tbl_name* format. To restrict replication to a set of tables, repeat the option once for each table.

- `--replicate-ignore-db=`*db_name*

Tell a replication slave not to replicate the named database. To ignore multiple databases, repeat the option once for each database.

- `--replicate-ignore-table=`*db_name.tbl_name*

Tell a replication slave not to replicate the named table. To ignore multiple tables, repeat the option once for each table.

- `--replicate-rewrite-db=`*master_db->slave_db*

Tell a replication slave to treat one database as another. Updates made to the original database *master_db* on the master server are replicated as updates to the database *slave_db* on the slave server. The rewrite applies only when *master_db* is the default database and only to statements that operate on tables in that database. When given on the command line, the option value should be enclosed within quotes to prevent the command interpreter from treating the '>' character as an output redirection operator. This option can be given multiple times. The server tries them in order and uses the first rule for which the *master_db* value matches.

This option is applied before actions specified by other `--replicate-`*xxx* options are tested, so if you use it, those options should use *slave_db* as the database name.

- `--replicate-same-server-id` (*boolean*)

If this option is enabled, the server will not skip replication events that contain its own server ID. This option is disabled by default to prevent replication loops, but can be enabled in certain special circumstances.

- `--replicate-wild-do-table=`*pattern*

Tell a replication slave to replicate only tables with names that match the given pattern. To restrict replication to a set of patterns, repeat the option once for each pattern.

- `--replicate-wild-ignore-table=`*`pattern`*

  Tell a replication slave not to replicate tables with names that match the given pattern. To ignore multiple patterns, repeat the option once for each pattern.

- `--show-slave-auth-info` (*boolean*)

  Cause a master server to display slave server usernames and passwords in the output of the `SHOW SLAVE HOSTS` statement.

- `--skip-slave-start`

  Cause the server not to start the slave threads automatically. They must be started manually by issuing a `START SLAVE` statement.

- `--sporadic-binlog-dump-fail` (*boolean*)

  This option is used by the MySQL test suite for replication testing.

F.12.3 Variables for `mysqld`

To see the full help message that displays the system variable values that `mysqld` will use by default, use this command:

```
% mysqld --verbose --help
```

To see what system variable values the currently executing `mysqld` is using, use this command:

```
% mysqladmin variables
```

You can also check the current system variable values by issuing a `SHOW VARIABLES` statement or checking the `INFORMATION_SCHEMA` tables named `GLOBAL_VARIABLES` and `SESSION_VARIABLES`. Individual system variables are described in Appendix D, "System, Status, and User Variable Reference." System variable values can be set at startup using the instructions given in Section F.2.1.2, "Setting Program Variables." In addition, many system variables can be modified dynamically; see Section 12.3.1, "Checking and Setting System Variable Values," and the entry for the `SET` statement in Appendix E, "SQL Syntax Reference."

F.13 `mysqld_multi`

The `mysqld_multi` script makes it easier to run several `mysqld` servers on a single host. It enables you to start or stop servers, or determine whether they are running:

```
mysqld_multi [options] command server_list
```

command is one of `start`, `stop`, or `report`. As of MySQL 5.6.3, `reload` (stop and restart) is permitted as well. The *server_list* argument indicates which servers to manipulate. For further instructions on using `mysqld_multi`, see Section 12.9.4, "Using `mysqld_multi` for Server Management."

F.13.1 Standard Options Supported by `mysqld_multi`

```
--help        --silent      --verbose
--password    --user        --version
```

For general descriptions of these options, see Section F.2.1, "Standard MySQL Program Options."

`mysqld_multi` passes the `--user` and `--password` option values to `mysqladmin` when it needs to stop servers or determine whether they are running. For the `--password` option, the password value is not optional, unlike most MySQL programs.

F.13.2 Options Specific to `mysqld_multi`

- `--example`

  Display a sample option file that demonstrates option file groups suitable for use with `mysqld_multi`.

- `--log=file_name`

  The name of the log file where `mysqld_multi` should log its actions. Output is appended to the log if it already exists. The default log file is named `mysqld_multi.log` in the data directory. To disable logging, use `--no-log`.

- `--mysqladmin=file_name`

  The pathname to the `mysqladmin` binary to use. This can be useful if `mysqld_multi` cannot find `mysqladmin` by itself, or to use a particular version.

- `--mysqld=file_name`

  The pathname to the `mysqld` binary to use. This can be useful if `mysqld_multi` cannot find `mysqld` by itself, or to use a particular version. It is permitted to specify a pathname to either `mysqld` or `mysqld_safe` as the value of this option.

- `--no-log`

  Display log output rather than writing it to a log file. To see output on the screen, you must use this option, because the default is to log to a file.

- `--tcp-ip`

  By default, `mysqld_multi` attempts to connect to a server using a Unix socket file. This option causes the connection attempt to use TCP/IP instead. It can be useful when a server is running but its socket file has been removed and the server is accessible only over TCP/IP.

F.14 `mysqld_safe`

`mysqld_safe` starts the `mysqld` server and monitors it:

`mysqld_safe [options]`

If the server dies, `mysqld_safe` restarts it. `mysqld_safe` is a shell script and is available on Unix.

F.14.1 Standard Options Supported by `mysqld_safe`

`--help`   `--plugin-dir`

For general descriptions of these options, see Section F.2.1, "Standard MySQL Program Options."

F.14.2 Options Specific to `mysqld_safe`

If you specify options on the command line that `mysqld_safe` does not support, it passes them to `mysqld`.

`mysqld_safe` understands the following options of its own:

- `--basedir=dir_name`

  The pathname to the MySQL base directory.

- `--core-file-size=n`

  Limit the size of core files to n bytes if the server crashes.

- `--datadir=dir_name`

  The pathname to the MySQL data directory.

- `--ledir=dir_name`

  The "libexec" directory in which to look for the server.

- `--log-error[=file_name]`

  The file to use for the error log. This option is interpreted the same way that `mysqld` interprets the value for the `log_error` system variable.

- `--malloc-lib[=lib_name]`

  The library that `mysqld` should use for its `malloc()` implementation rather than the system library. This option modifies the `LD_PRELOAD` environement variable to affect dynamic linking for `mysqld`. For Linux, the `lib_name` value can be `tcmalloc` to use the implementation of that library bundled with MySQL distributions. If the option value is a directory pathnmame, `mysqld_safe` modifies `LD_PRELOAD` by adding that directory to the beginning of its value.

- `--mysqld=file_name`

  The path to the `mysqld` program.

- `--mysqld-version=suffix`

  The value of this option is a suffix string. If the option is given, the suffix is added to the basename `mysqld`, with a dash in between, to produce the name of the server that `mysqld_safe` should start.

- `--nice=N`

  Use the `nice` program to set the server scheduling priority to `N`.

- `--open-files-limit=n`

  The number of file descriptors that `mysqld` should reserve.

- `--pid-file=file_name`

  The name of the `mysqld` process ID file.

- `--port=port_num`

  The port number on which the server should listen for TCP/IP connections.

- `--skip-kill-mysqld`

  Do not try to kill any currently running `mysqld` process before starting a new one. This can be useful if you are running multiple instances of a given `mysqld` binary. It is effective only on Linux.

- `--skip-syslog`

  Specify that error output should not be sent to `syslog`; a log file is used instead. The default is to use a log file.

- `--socket=file_name`

  The pathname of the Unix socket file.

- `--syslog`

  Specify sending error output to `syslog`, for systems that have the `logger` program.

- `--syslog-tag=tag`

  When error output is sent to `syslog`, messages from `mysqld_safe` and `mysqld` are tagged with the program name as a prefix. The `--syslog-tag` option modifies the prefix to be `mysqld_safe-tag` and `mysqld-tag`, respectively.

- `--timezone=tz_name`

  Set the server system time zone to `tz_name`. This might be useful if the server cannot determine the system time zone automatically.

- `--user=user_name`, `--user=uid`

  The username or numeric user ID of the account to use for running the server.

F.15 `mysqldump`

The `mysqldump` program writes the contents of database tables into text files. These files can be used for several purposes, such as database backups, moving databases to another server, or setting up a test database based on the contents of an existing database.

By default, output for each dumped table consists of a `CREATE TABLE` statement that creates the table, followed by a set of `INSERT` statements that load the contents of the table. If the `--tab` option is given, the table contents are written to a data file as tab-separated values, one line per row, and the table-creation SQL statement is written to a separate file.

`mysqldump` can be run in any of three modes:

```
mysqldump [options] db_name [tbl_name] ...
mysqldump [options] --databases db_name ...
mysqldump [options] --all-databases
```

In the first case, `mysqldump` dumps the named tables in the given database. If no tables are named, `mysqldump` dumps all tables in the database. In the second case, all arguments are taken as database names and `mysqldump` dumps all tables in each one. In the third case, `mysqldump` dumps all tables in all databases. If `--databases` or `--all-databases` is used, the output contains `CREATE DATABASE IF NOT EXISTS` and `USE` statements preceding the statements for the tables in each database.

One common way to use `mysqldump` is as follows:

```
% mysqldump db_name > backup_file
```

To import the backup file back into MySQL, use `mysql` rather than with `mysqlimport`:

```
% mysql db_name < backup_file
```

`mysqldump` ignores and does not dump the `INFORMATION_SCHEMA` database unless you name it explicitly on the command line. In this case, you must also specify `--skip-lock-tables`.

F.15.1 Standard Options Supported by `mysqldump`

`--bind-address`	`--default-character-set`	`--protocol`
`--character-sets-dir`	`--help`	`--shared-memory-base-name`
`--compress`	`--host`	`--socket`
`--debug`	`--password`	`--user`
`--debug-check`	`--pipe`	`--verbose`
`--debug-info`	`--plugin-dir`	`--version`
`--default-auth`	`--port`	

For general descriptions of these options, see Section F.2.1, "Standard MySQL Program Options." `mysqldump` also supports the standard SSL options listed in Section F.2.1.1, "Standard SSL Options."

F.15.2   Options Specific to `mysqldump`

The following options control how `mysqldump` operates. Section F.15.3, "Data Format Options for `mysqldump`," describes options used in conjunction with the `--tab` option to indicate the format of data files.

- `--add-drop-database` (*boolean*)

  Add a `DROP DATABASE IF EXISTS` statement before each `CREATE DATABASE` statement.

- `--add-drop-table` (*boolean*)

  Add a `DROP TABLE IF EXISTS` statement before each `CREATE TABLE` statement.

- `--add-drop-trigger` (*boolean*)

  Add a `DROP TRIGGER IF EXISTS` statement before each `CREATE TRIGGER` statement. This option was introduced in MySQL 5.6.0.

- `--add-locks` (*boolean*)

  Add `LOCK TABLE` and `UNLOCK TABLE` statements around the set of `INSERT` statements for each table.

- `--all-databases, -A` (*boolean*)

  Dump all tables in all databases. This option also causes the dump output to include `CREATE DATABASE IF NOT EXISTS` and `USE` statements for each database.

- `--all-tablespaces, -Y` (*boolean*)

  Dump all tablespaces. Relevant only for MySQL Cluster.

- `--allow-keywords` (*boolean*)

  Permit the creation of column names that are keywords.

- `--apply-slave-statements` (*boolean*)

  This option is used in conjunction with `--dump-slave`. It causes the dump output to include `STOP SLAVE` before the `CHANGE MASTER` statement and `START SLAVE` at the end. This option was introduced in MySQL 5.5.3.

- `--comments, -i` (*boolean*)

  Include additional informational comments in the output, such as the `mysqldump` version, which tables each set of `INSERT` statements applies to, and so forth. This open is enabled by default. To disable it, use `--skip-comments`.

- `--compact` (*boolean*)

  Generate more concise output that does not include comments, including version-specific comments that set system variables. This option also enables the `--skip-add-drop-table`, `--skip-set-charset`, `--skip-disable-keys`, and `--skip-add-locks` options.

- `--compatible=`*mode*

This option causes `mysqldump` to modify its output to be compatible with standard SQL, other database servers, or older versions of MySQL server. The *mode* value specifies a compatibility mode. It can be given using one or more of the following values as a comma-separated list.

Option	Compatibility Meaning
ANSI	ANSI-compatible
DB2	Compatible with DB2
MAXDB	Compatible with MaxDB
MSSQL	Compatible with MS SQL Server
MYSQL323	Compatible with MySQL 3.23
MYSQL40	Compatible with MySQL 4.0
ORACLE	Compatible with Oracle
POSTRESQL	Compatible with PostgreSQL
NO_FIELD_OPTIONS	Suppress MySQL-specific column-related options
NO_KEY_OPTIONS	Suppress MySQL-specific index-related options
NO_TABLE_OPTIONS	Suppress MySQL-specific table-related options

This option has no effect with servers older than MySQL 4.1.

- `--complete-insert, -c` (*boolean*)

Write `INSERT` statements that name each column to be inserted.

- `--create-options, -a` (*boolean*)

Include additional information in the `CREATE TABLE` statements that `mysqldump` generates, such as the storage engine, the beginning `AUTO_INCREMENT` value, and so forth. This is the information that you can specify using *table_option* values in the `CREATE TABLE` syntax. (See Appendix E, "SQL Syntax Reference.")

This option is enabled by default. To disable it, use `--skip-create-options`.

- `--databases, -B` (*boolean*)

Interpret all arguments as database names and dumps all tables in each database. This option also causes the dump output to include `CREATE DATABASE IF NOT EXISTS` and `USE` statements for each database.

- `--delayed-insert` (*boolean*)

Write `INSERT DELAYED` statements rather than `INSERT` statements. If you are loading a dump file for MyISAM tables into another database and want to minimize the impact of the operation on other statements that may be taking place in that database, `--delayed-insert` is helpful for achieving that end.

- `--delete-master-logs`

  Delete the binary log files on the server and begin a new one by issuing a `FLUSH MASTER` statement after generating the dump output. Don't use this option unless you're sure you want the existing binary logs to be wiped out. This option enables `--master-data`.

- `--disable-keys, -K` (*boolean*)

  Add `ALTER TABLE ... DISABLE KEYS` and `ALTER TABLE ... ENABLE KEYS` statements to the output, to disable updates to nonunique indexes while `INSERT` statements are being processed. This speeds up index creation for each MyISAM table by causing it to happen all at once after the table is loaded.

- `--dump-date` (*boolean*)

  Add a comment indicating the dump date to the end of the output.

- `--dump-slave[=n]`

  This option is like `--master-data`, but is used for dumping a replication slave server and produces a `CHANGE MASTER` statement in the output that indicates the binary log coordinates of the slave's master, not those of the slave itself. See the description of `--master-data` for a description of how the option argument is used. The `--dump-slave` option was introduced in MySQL 5.5.3.

- `--events, -E` (*boolean*)

  Include Event Scheduler events in the dump output.

- `--extended-insert, -e` (*boolean*)

  Write multiple-row `INSERT` statements. These can be loaded more efficiently than single-row statements.

- `--flush-logs, -F` (*boolean*)

  Flush the server log files before dumping tables. By default, the logs are flushed for each database to create a checkpoint. This makes it easier to perform restore operations because you know that binary log files created after the checkpoint time were made after the backup for a given database. In conjunction with `--lock-all-tables` or `--master-data`, the logs are flushed only after all tables have been locked. This option requires the `RELOAD` privilege.

- `--flush-privileges` (*boolean*)

  If the dump includes the `mysql` database, include a `FLUSH PRIVILEGES` in the output after dumping that database.

- `--force, -f` (*boolean*)

  Continue execution even if errors occur.

- `--hex-blob` (*boolean*)

  Dump `BINARY`, `VARBINARY`, and `BLOB` columns as hexadecimal constants. For example, with this option, `mysqldump` writes "MySQL" as `0x4D7953514C`.

- `--ignore-table=`*`db_name.tbl_name`*

Skip dump output for the named table or view. To ignore multiple tables, repeat the option once for each table.

- `--include-master-host-port` (*boolean*)

For the `CHANGE MASTER` statement in output produced with `--dump-slave`, include `MASTER_HOST` and `MASTER_PORT` options that specify the hostname and port number of the slave's master. This option was introduced in MySQL 5.5.3.

- `--insert-ignore` (*boolean*)

Write `INSERT IGNORE` statements rather than `INSERT` statements.

- `--lock-all-tables`, `-x` (*boolean*)

Use `FLUSH TABLES WITH READ LOCK` to lock all tables across all databases. This option disables `--single-transaction` and `--lock-tables`.

- `--lock-tables`, `-l` (*boolean*)

For each dumped database, use `LOCK TABLES ... READ LOCAL` to obtain locks for all dumped tables before dumping them. This option is good for MyISAM tables because a `READ LOCAL` lock enables concurrent inserts to proceed while the dump is in progress. For InnoDB tables, `--single-transaction` is preferable.

- `--log-error=`*`file_name`*

Write warning and error messages to the end of the named file.

- `--master-data`[`=`*`value`*]

This option helps make a backup that can be used to set up a slave server. With this option, `mysqldump` sends a `SHOW MASTER STATUS` statement to the server to get its current binary log filename and position, and uses the results to write a `CHANGE MASTER` statement to the output that contains the same filename and position. The effect is that when you load the dump file into a slave server, it synchronizes the slave to the proper replication coordinates of the dumped server to begin replicating at the point when the dump was made. This option has no effect unless the server has binary logging enabled.

By default, the `CHANGE MASTER` statement is written in noncommented form. `--master-data` takes an optional value to explicitly control commenting of the statement. A value of 1 produces a noncommented statement, and a value of 2 produces a commented statement.

`--master-data` requires the `RELOAD` privilege. This option automatically enables `--lock-all-tables` if `--single-transaction` is not given.

- `--no-autocommit` (*boolean*)

Write the `INSERT` statements for each table within a transaction. The resulting output can be loaded more efficiently than executing each statement in autocommit mode.

- --no-create-db, -n (*boolean*)

  Cause CREATE DATABASE statements not to be written. (Normally, these are added to the output automatically when --databases or --all-databases are used.)

- --no-create-info, -t (*boolean*)

  Cause CREATE TABLE statements not to be written. This is useful to dump only table data.

- --no-data, -d (*boolean*)

  Cause table data not to be written. This is useful to dump only the CREATE TABLE statements.

- --no-set-names, -N

  A synonym for --skip-set-charset.

- --no-tablespaces, -y (*boolean*)

  Cause tablespaces not to be dumped. Relevant only for MySQL Cluster.

- --opt

  Optimize table dumping speed and write a dump file that is optimal for reloading speed. This option turns on --add-drop-table, --add-locks, --create-options, --disable-keys, --extended-insert, --lock-tables, --quick, and --set-charset. This option is enabled by default. To disable it, use --skip-opt.

- --order-by-primary (*boolean*)

  Dump table rows in order of the primary key or the first unique index if there is one. This produces sorted dump output for each table at a cost in performance.

- --quick, -q (*boolean*)

  By default, mysqldump reads the entire contents of a table into memory and then writes it out. This option causes each row to be written to the output as soon as it has been read from the server, which is much less memory intensive. However, if you use this option, you should not suspend mysqldump. Doing so causes the server to wait, which can interfere with other clients.

- --quote-names, -Q (*boolean*)

  Quote table and column names by enclosing them within backtick ('`') characters. This is useful if names are reserved words or contain special characters. --quote-names is enabled by default. To disable it, use --skip-quote-names.

- --replace

  Produce REPLACE statements instead of INSERT statements.

- --result-file=*file_name*, -r *file_name*

  Write output to the named file. This option is intended for Windows, where it prevents conversion of linefeeds to carriage return/linefeed pairs.

- `--routines`, `-R` (*boolean*)

Include stored functions and procedures in the dump output.

- `--set-charset` (*boolean*)

Write a `SET NAMES` `charset` statement to the output, where `charset` is `utf8` by default. The character set can be changed using the `--default-character-set` option. The `--set-charset` option is enabled by default. To disable it, use `--skip-set-charset`.

- `--single-transaction` (*boolean*)

This option enables consistent dumps of InnoDB tables. The idea is that all the tables are dumped within a single transaction. `mysqldump` uses the `REPEATABLE READ` transaction isolation level to produce a consistent dump without causing other clients to block. (For nontransactional tables, changes might still occur during the dump operation.) This option disables `--lock-all-tables`.

- `--skip-opt`

This option has the opposite effect of `--opt`, which is enabled by default.

- `--tab=`*dump_dir*, `-T` *dump_dir*

This option causes `mysqldump` to write two files per table, using *dump_dir* as the location for the files. The directory must already exist. For each table *tbl_name*, a file *dump_dir*/*tbl_name*`.txt` is written containing the data from the table, and a file *dump_dir*/*tbl_name*`.sql` is written containing the `CREATE TABLE` statement for the table. You must have the `FILE` privilege to use this option.

By default, data files are written as newline-terminated lines consisting of tab-separated column values. This format may be changed using the options described under Section F.15.3, "Data Format Options for `mysqldump`."

The effect of the `--tab` option can be confusing unless you understand precisely how it works:

- Some of the files are written on the server host and some are written on the client host. *dump_dir* is used on the server host for the `*.txt` files and on the client host for the `*.sql` files. If the two hosts are different, the output files are created on different machines. To avoid any uncertainty about where files are written, it is best to run `mysqldump` on the server host when you use this option so that all files are created on the same machine.

- The `*.txt` files are owned by the account used to run the server, and the `*.sql` files are owned by you. This is a consequence of the fact that the server itself writes the `*.txt` files, whereas the `CREATE TABLE` statements are sent by the server to `mysqldump`, which writes the `*.sql` files.

- `--tables`

Override `--databases` to cause any following arguments to be interpreted as table names.

- `--triggers` (*boolean*)

  Include triggers in the dump output. Triggers are included by default. To exclude them, use `--skip-triggers`.

- `--tz-utc` (*boolean*)

  Set the time zone to UTC after connecting to the server and include a `SET TIME_ZONE='+00:00'` statement in the output. The effect is to suppress conversion to and from the local time zone when dumping and reloading data so that `TIMESTAMP` values do not change if the reload occurs in a time zone different from the dump. This option is enabled by default. To disable it, use `--skip-tz-utc`.

- `--where=where_expr`, `-w where_expr`

  Dump only rows selected by the `WHERE` condition given by *where_expr*. You should enclose the condition in quotes to prevent your command interpreter from treating it as multiple command-line arguments.

- `--xml`, `-X`

  Generate output in XML format rather than as a set of SQL statements.

F.15.3 Data Format Options for `mysqldump`

If you specify the `--tab` or `-T` option to generate a separate data file for each table, several additional options apply. You might need to enclose the option value in appropriate quoting characters. These options are analogous to the data format options for the `LOAD DATA` statement. See the entry for `LOAD DATA` in Appendix E, "SQL Syntax Reference."

- `--fields-enclosed-by=char`

  Specify that column values should be enclosed within the given character, usually a quote character. The default is to not enclose column values within anything. This option precludes the use of `--fields-optionally-enclosed-by`.

- `--fields-escaped-by=char`

  Specify the escape character for escaping special characters. The default is no escape character.

- `--fields-optionally-enclosed-by=char`

  Specify that column values should be enclosed within the given character, usually a quote character. The character is used for nonnumeric columns. The default is to not enclose column values within anything. This option precludes the use of `--fields-enclosed-by`.

- `--fields-terminated-by=str`

  Specify the column value separation character or characters to use for data files. By default, values are separated by tab characters.

- `--lines-terminated-by=`*`str`*

  Specify the character or characters to write at the end of output lines. The default is to write newlines.

F.15.4   Variables for `mysqldump`

The following `mysqldump` variables can be set using the instructions given in Section F.2.1.2, "Setting Program Variables."

- `max_allowed_packet`

  The maximum size of the buffer used for communication between the server and the client. The default is 24MB and the maximum is 1GB.

- `net_buffer_length`

  The initial size of the buffer used for communication between the server and the client. This buffer may be expanded up to `max_allowed_packet` bytes long. The default is slightly less than 1MB.

F.16   `mysqlimport`

The `mysqlimport` client program is a bulk loader for reading the contents of text files into existing tables. It presents a command-line interface to the LOAD DATA SQL statement, and is an efficient way to enter rows into tables:

```
mysqlimport [options] db_name file_name ...
```

The *db_name* argument specifies the database that contains the tables into which to load data. The tables to load are determined from the filename arguments. For each filename, any extension from the first period in the name is stripped off and the remaining basename is used as the name of the table into which the file should be loaded. For example, `mysqlimport` loads the contents of a file named `president.txt` into the `president` table.

`mysqlimport` reads data files only. It is *not* intended for reading SQL-format dump files produced by `mysqldump`. Use `mysql` for that.

F.16.1   Standard Options Supported by `mysqlimport`

`--bind-address`	`--default-character-set`	`--protocol`
`--character-sets-dir`	`--help`	`--shared-memory-base-name`
`--compress`	`--host`	`--silent`
`--debug`	`--password`	`--socket`
`--debug-check`	`--pipe`	`--user`
`--debug-info`	`--plugin-dir`	`--verbose`
`--default-auth`	`--port`	`--version`

For general descriptions of these options, see Section F.2.1, "Standard MySQL Program Options." mysqlimport also supports the standard SSL options listed in Section F.2.1.1, "Standard SSL Options."

F.16.2   Options Specific to mysqlimport

The following options control how mysqlimport processes input files. Section F.16.3, "Data Format Options for mysqlimport," describes options used to indicate the format of the data in the input files.

- --columns=*col_list*, -C *col_list*

  Specify the list of columns in the table to which columns in the data file correspond. mysqlimport loads values in input rows into the named columns, and sets other columns to their default values. *col_list* lists one or more column names separated by commas.

- --delete, -d (*boolean*)

  Empty each table before loading any data into it.

- --force, -f (*boolean*)

  Continue loading rows even if errors occur.

- --ignore, -i

  When an input row contains a value for a unique key that already exists in the table, keep the existing row and discard the input row. The --ignore and --replace options are mutually exclusive.

- --ignore-lines=*n*

  Ignore the first *n* lines of the data file. This can be used to skip an initial row of column labels, for example.

- --local, -L (*boolean*)

  By default, mysqlimport lets the server read the data file, which means that the file must be located on the server host and that you must have the FILE privilege. Specifying the --local option tells mysqlimport to read the data file itself and send it to the server. This is slower but works when you're running mysqlimport on a different machine than the server host, as well as on the server host even if you don't have the FILE privilege.

  This option is ineffective if the server has been configured to prohibit use of LOAD DATA LOCAL.

- --lock-tables, -l (*boolean*)

  Lock each table before loading data into it.

- --low-priority (*boolean*)

  Use the LOW_PRIORITY scheduling modifier on statements generated to load data into the table.

- `--replace, -r` (*boolean*)

  When an input row contains a value for a unique key that already exists in the table, replace the existing row with the input row. The `--ignore` and `--replace` options are mutually exclusive.

- `--use-threads=`*n*

  Use *n* threads to load files in parallel.

F.16.3   Data Format Options for `mysqlimport`

By default, `mysqlimport` assumes that data files contain newline-terminated lines consisting of tab-separated values. The expected format may be altered using the following options. You might need to enclose the option value in appropriate quoting characters. These options are analogous to the data format options for the LOAD DATA statement. See the entry for LOAD DATA in Appendix E, "SQL Syntax Reference."

- `--fields-enclosed-by=`*char*

  Specify that column values are enclosed within the given character, usually a quote character. By default, values are assumed not to be enclosed by any character. This option precludes the use of `--fields-optionally-enclosed-by`.

- `--fields-escaped-by=`*char*

  Specify the escape character used to escape special characters. The default is no escape character.

- `--fields-optionally-enclosed-by=`*char*

  Specify that column values may be enclosed within the given character, usually a quote character. This option precludes the use of `--fields-enclosed-by`.

- `--fields-terminated-by=`*str*

  Specify the character or characters that separate column values. By default, values are assumed to be separated by tab characters.

- `--lines-terminated-by=`*str*

  Specify the character or characters that terminate input lines. By default, lines are assumed to be terminated by newline characters.

F.17   `mysqlshow`

`mysqlshow` lists databases, tables within a database, or information about columns or indexes within a table. It provides a command-line interface to the SHOW SQL statement:

```
mysqlshow [options] [db_name [tbl_name [col_name]]]
```

If no database name is specified, `mysqlshow` lists all databases on the server host. If a database name but no table name is specified, all tables in the database are listed. If database and table names are specified, but no column name is specified, it lists the columns in the table. If all the names are specified, `mysqlshow` shows information about the given column.

The final argument may contain the '%' and '_' SQL wildcard characters, which have the same meaning as for the `LIKE` operator. Output is limited to values that match the wildcards. If the final argument contains the '*' or '?' shell wildcard characters, they are treated as '%' and '_', respectively.

F.17.1 Standard Options Supported by `mysqlshow`

--bind-address	--default-character-set	--protocol
--character-sets-dir	--help	--shared-memory-base-name
--compress	--host	--socket
--debug	--password	--user
--debug-check	--pipe	--verbose
--debug-info	--plugin-dir	--version
--default-auth	--port	

For general descriptions of these options, see Section F.2.1, "Standard MySQL Program Options." `mysqlshow` also supports the standard SSL options listed in Section F.2.1.1, "Standard SSL Options."

The `--verbose` option causes additional columns to be included in the output (tables per database, rows per table, and so forth). The option may be given multiple times.

F.17.2 Options Specific to `mysqlshow`

- `--count` (*boolean*)

  Include the number of rows per table in the output. Counting the rows may be slow for some storage engines.

- `--keys, -k` (*boolean*)

  Display information about table indexes in addition to information about table columns. This option is meaningful only if you specify a table name argument.

- `--show-table-type, -t` (*boolean*)

  Include an output column showing the type for each table (either BASE TABLE or VIEW), as in the output from SHOW FULL TABLES.

- `--status, -i` (*boolean*)

  Display the same kind of table information displayed by the SHOW TABLE STATUS statement.

F.18 `perror`

`perror` displays error messages for error codes:

```
perror [options] [err_code] ...
```

You can use it to determine the meaning of errors returned by MySQL programs.

```
% perror 142
MySQL error:  142 = Unknown character set used
```

F.18.1 Standard Options Supported by `perror`

```
--help        --silent      --verbose      --version
```

For general descriptions of these options, see Section F.2.1, "Standard MySQL Program Options."

The `--silent` option causes only the error message and not the code to be displayed. The default is `--verbose`, which displays both the code and the message.

`--info` and `-I` are synonyms for `--help`.

Index

Symbols

+ (addition operator), 58, 241, 766

& (AND) operator, 242, 773

&& (AND) operator, 241, 773

\ (backslashes), strings, 184

, (comma) join operator, 138

/ (division operator), 57, 241, 767

$ (dollar signs), PHP, 492

... (ellipsis), operators/functions, 764

= (equal to operator), 57, 243, 769

<=> (equal to operator), 57, 243

^ (exclusive-OR operator), 242, 773

> (greater than operator), 57, 243, 770

>= (greater than or equal to operator), 57, 243, 770

< (less than operator), 57, 243, 770

<= (less than or equal to operator), 57, 243, 770

% (modulo operator), 57, 241, 767

* (multiplication operator), 57, 241, 767

~ (negation operator), 774

! (NOT) operator, 241, 772

!= (not equal operator), 57, 243, 770

< > (not equal to operator), 57, 243

<=> (null-safe equality operator), 770

| (OR operator), 242, 773

|| (OR operator), 241-242, 773

( ) (parentheses), 401

; (semicolons), 27, 266

#! (shebang), 396

<< (shift left operator), 242, 773

>> (shift right operator), 242, 773

[ ] (square brackets), operators/functions, 764

- (subtraction operator), 57, 241, 767

!= (unequal) operator, 770

|| (vertical bars), operators/functions, 764

% (wildcard character), 244

_ (wildcard character), 244

A

aborted_clients status variable, **881**

aborted_connects status variable, **881**

ABS() function, **784**

absence table, **45, 49**

access control, **540**

   administrative-only, setting, 649-651

      data directory exception, 651

      directories outside base directory, 651

      Innodb directory, 651

      servers, running, 652

      symlinks, 651

   authentication plugins, 676-679

      proxy users, creating, 677-679

      server connections, 677

      server side/client side, 677

      specifying, 676

   base directory insecurities, checking, 648

   clients, 686-687

   column information structures, 364

   CREATE USER statements

      account operations, 655

      selecting, 656

   data directory, 546-547, 648

   DROP USER statement, 656

   external risks, 646

   grant tables

      administrative privilege columns, 680

      authentication columns, 680, 684

      listing of, 680

      object privileges, 681-682

      privilege columns, 683-684

      privilege tables, 683

      resource management columns, 680, 685-686

      scope-of-access columns, 680-681, 683

      SSL-related columns, 680, 685

      user table authentication, 680

   internal risks, 645

   metadata, 130

      command line, 135

      INFORMATION_SCHEMA database, 132-135

   multiple-user benefit, 13

   option files, 653-654

   overview, 646-647

   privileges

      account administering, enabling, 669-670

      administrative, 661-663, 666

      ALL specifier, 661, 666

      combining, 665

      database-level, 666

      displaying, 671

      global, 666

      granting, 660-661

      level-specifiers, 665

      no privileges, 668

      object, 663-665

      ON specifier, 665

      PROXY, 667

      quoting, 667

      revoking, 671-672

      secure connections, requiring, 668-669

      stored routines, 667

      table/column level, 667

      USAGE specifier, 661

   remote, 13

   RENAME USER statement, 656

   resource consumption limits, 670-671

   risks, 673-676

      ALTER privilege, 676

      anonymous-user accounts, 673

      FILE privilege, 674-676

      GRANT OPTION privileges, 674

      insecure accounts, 673-674

      mysql database privileges, 674

      passwords in old hash format, 673

      PROCESS privileges, 676

      RELOAD privileges, 676

      SUPER privileges, 674, 676

   scope columns

      case sensitivity, 689

      column_name, 688

      Db, 688

      host, 687-689

      listing of, 687-689

      matching order, 690-691

      routine_name, 688

      table_name, 688

      user, 688

server table, preventing, 701
  internal locking, 702-703
  locking all tables at once, 705
  read-only locking, 703-704
  read/write locking, 704-705
  shutting down servers, 702
statement access verification, 689-690
stealing data example, 647
Unix socket file, 652-653
user accounts
  account-management statements, 654-655
  authentication, 659-660
  grant tables, upgrading, 655
  matching host values to DNS, 658-659
  names, 656-658
  passwords, changing/resetting, 672
user table row matching example, 691-694
accessor macros, Web: 1087-1088
account clause
  account-management statements, 656
  GRANT statement, 660
accounts
  administrator, creating, 24
  anonymous-user
    deleting, 568-569
    passwords, assigning, 567-568
    security risk, 673
  initial user, 564-569
    available on all platforms, 566
    client program connections, 566
    displaying, 565
    passwords, assigning, 567-569
    platform specific, 567
  login, creating, 738-739
  mysqld login, 571-572
  root passwords, 567-569, 582-583
  user. *See* user accounts
ACID (Atomic, Consistent, Isolated, and Durable) properties, 157
ACOS() function, 784
action parameter, 513
activation state (plugins), 592
add_new_event() function, 517-518
ADDDATE() function, 803
addition (+) operator, 57, 241, 766
ADDTIME() function, 803

administration
  access control, 540
  databases
    backups, 540
    migration, 541
    preventive maintenance, 540
    recovery, 541
    replication, 541
  default character set/collation, 603-604
  error message language, setting, 604
  initial user accounts, 564-569
    available on all platforms, 566
    client program connections, 566
    displaying, 565
    passwords, assigning, 567-569
    platform specific, 567
  locale, 604-605
  logs
    age-based expiration, 625
    binary, 618, 622-623
    enabling, 619
    error, 618, 620-621
    expiring, 629-631
    fixed-name, rotating, 626-629
    flushing, 626
    general query, 618, 621
    listing of, 617-618
    maintenance, 539
    output destination, selecting, 624-625
    relay, 618, 624
    replication-related expiration, 625
    rotating, 625
    slow query, 618,
    table truncation/rotation, 625
    tables, 625, 631
  multiple servers, 539, 632
    client programs, running, 641
    configuring, 635
    directory options, 633
    error log file names, creating, 634
    InnoDB log location, 634
    issues, 632-635
    login account options, 635
    network interface options, 633
    replication slave options, 634
    startup options strategies, 636-637

status/log file names options, 634
Unix, 637-639
Windows, 639-641
mysqld
  configuration and tuning, 539
  connections, listening, 579-580
  restarting manually, 581-582
  root password, resetting, 582-583
  startup/shutdown, 539, 577-579
  stopping, 580-581
mysqld on Unix
  running, 570
  starting, 572-574
  unprivileged login account,
    configuring, 571-572
mysqld on Windows, 575
  running as Windows service, 576-577
  running manually, 575
new server passwords, setting, 569
plugins
  activation state, 592
  case sensitivity, 591
  displaying, 592
  interface components, 590
  library suffix, 590
  loading at runtime, 591
  loading at startup, 591
  operations, 590
  uninstalling, 592
software updates, 539
status variables
  displaying, 584
  overview, 584
  values, checking, 588-589
storage engines
  available, displaying, 593
  default, selecting, 594
  status/startup options, 593-594
system variables, 584-585
  displaying, 583
  overview, 583
  setting at runtime, 587-588
  setting at server startup, 586-587
  values, checking, 585-586
time zones, 602-603
updates, 641-643
user account maintenance, 539

administrative functions
  C, Web: 1117-1119
  Perl DBI, Web: 1147-1148
administrative-only access, configuring,
  649-651
  data directory exception, 651
  directories outside base directory, 651
  innodb directory, 651
  servers, running, 652
  symlinks, 651
administrative privileges, 661-663, 666, 680
administrator accounts, creating, 24
advisory locking functions, 824-826
AES_DECRYPT() function, 821
AES_ENCRYPT() function, 821
aliases
  case sensitivity, 100
  quoting with identifiers, 98
ALL specifier, 146-147, 661, 666
ALTER DATABASE statements, 107, 898
ALTER EVENT statements, 898-899
ALTER FUNCTION statements, 899
ALTER privilege, 663, 676
ALTER PROCEDURE statements, 899
ALTER ROUTINE privilege, 663
ALTER TABLE statements, 899-904
  action values, 899-903
  benefits, 127-128
  clauses
    CHANGE, 128
    CHARACTER SET, 128-129
    ENGINE, 129
    MODIFY, 128
    RENAME, 129-130
  indexes, adding, 124
  partitioning options, 904
  resequencing existing columns, 237
  sequence columns, adding, 236
  syntax, 128
  table files, 549
ALTER VIEW statements, 905
ANALYZE TABLE statements, 905
AND (&) operator, 57, 773
AND (&&) operator, 241, 774
anonymous-user accounts
  deleting, 568-569
  passwords, assigning, 567-568
  security risk, 673

ANSI_QUOTES mode, 96, 182, 863

ANSI SQL mode, 96

ANY subqueries, 146-147

Apache

configuring, 460-461

APIs

C. *See* C client programs

Perl DBI. *See* Perl DBI API

PHP. *See* PHP API

selecting, 314

development time, 316-317

execution environment, 315

performance, 315-316

portability, 317

SSL capabilities, 698

app_type member (my_option structures), 341

approximate-value numbers, 181-182

architecture

data directory, 545

Perl DBI API, 311-312

pluggable, 589-590

storage engines, 108

terminology, 21-22

ARCHIVE storage engine, 108, 112

arg_type member (my_option structures), 341

arguments

connect() function, 399-400

expression functions, 240

fetch() function, 502-503

undef, 422

vectors, processing, 342

arithmetic operators, 57, 766-767

addition, 766

DIV, 767

division, 767

listing of, 241

modulo, 767

multiplication, 767

NULL values, 246

rules, 766

subtraction, 767

ASCII conversions, 254

ASCII() function, 254, 790

ASIN() function, 784

ATAN() function, 785

ATAN2() function, 785

Atomic, Consistent, Isolated, and Durable
(ACID) properties, 157

attributes. *See also* clauses

account, 660

collation, 102-103

columns, 35, 660

global, 747

Perl DBI, Web: 1149

database-handles, Web: 1149

dynamic, Web: 1155

general handle, Web: 1149-1150

MySQL-specific database handle,
Web: 1150-1152

MySQL-specific statement handle,
Web: 1154-1155

statement-handles, Web: 1152-1153

PDO database-handles, Web: 1173-1174

PrintError, 403

privileges, 660

RaiseError, 403

temporal data types, 223

TraceLevel, 428

what, 660

auth_info clause

CREATE USER statement, 659-660

GRANT statement, 661

authentication

columns (grant tables), 684

plugins, 676-679

proxy users, creating, 677-679

server connections, 677

server side/client side, 677

specifying, 676

user accounts, 659-660

AUTO_INCREMENT clause, 202

AUTO_INCREMENT columns, 230

adding to tables, 235-236

creating, 47

member table column example, 36

nonpositive numbers, 235

properties

general, 230-232

InnoDB, 234

MEMORY, 234-235

MyISAM, 232-234

ranges, 235

resequencing existing columns, 236-237

resets, 235

unsigned, 235

auto_increment_increment system variable,
    836
auto_increment_offset system variable, 836
autocommit system variable, 836
automatic_sp_privileges system variable, 270,
    837
automating
    initialization, 224-226
    log expiration, 630-631
    update properties, 224-226
auto-recovery, 706
    failure, 725-726
    performing, 700
available_drivers() function, Web: 1132
availability
    character sets, 103-104, 185-186
    collations, 103-104, 185-186
    result set metadata, 359
    SSL support, 370
    storage engines, 108-109
average values summaries, 76
AVG() functions, 76, 818

B

back_log system variable, 837
backslashes (\), strings, 184
backups, 707-709
    best practices, 709
    binary, 714-715
        complete, 714-715
        logs, 623
        partial, 715
    databases, 540
    InnoDB tables, 715-716
    selecting, 708
    slave, creating, 732-733
    storage engine portability, 709-710
    text, 711-714
        all tables from all databases, 711
        compressing, 712
        database transfers, 716-717
        individual files, 711
        mysqldump options, 712-714
        mysqldump output, 711-712
        table subsets into separate files,
            creating, 712
    types, 708

bail_out() function, 405
banner advertisement tables example, 19
basedir system variable, 837
Basic Multilingual Plane (BMP), 104
BEGIN...END statements, 988
BEGIN statement, 905
begin_work() function, Web: 1137
beginTransaction() function, Web: 1162
BENCHMARK() function, 829
BETWEEN operator, 243
big_tables system variable, 837
BIGINT data type, 193, 750-751
    ranges, 197
    storage requirements, 197
BIN() function, 200, 790
binary backups, 714-715
    best practices, 709
    complete, 714-715
    defined, 708
    partial, 715
    text-format backups, compared, 708
binary character sets, 216
binary data
    printing, 353
    statements, 367-368
BINARY data types 204, 207
binary logs, 556, 618
    administration, 622-623
    expiring, 629-630
    formats, 731
    index file, 623
    post-backup statements, re-executing,
        723-725
    system backups, 623
binary protocol
    disadvantages, 378
    prepared statements, 377
        executing, 378-379
        inserting rows and retrieving them
            program, writing, 379-388
        parameterizing, 377-378
binary strings, 194, 755-756
    BINARY, 755
    BLOB, 755-756
    conversions, 255
    defined, 185
    LONGBLOB, 756

MEDIUMBLOB, 756
nonbinary strings, compared, 188-189
sorting properties, 186
TINYBLOB, 755
VARBINARY, 755
BINARY str operator, 773
bind_address system variable, 765
bind_col() function, 421, Web: 1142
bind_columns() function, 421, Web: 1142
bind_param() function, Web: 1142
bind_param_array() function, Web: 1143
bindColumn() function, 503, Web: 1166
bindParam() function, Web: 1166-1167
bindValue() function, Web: 1167
BINLOG statement, 906
binlog_cache_disk_use status variable, 881
binlog_cache_size system variable, 837
binlog_cache_use status variable, 881
binlog_checksum system variable, 837
binlog_direct_non_transactional_updates system variable, 838
binlog_format system variable, 838
binlog_row_image system variable, 838
binlog_rows_query_log_events system variable, 838
binlog_stmt_cache_disk_use status variable, 881
binlog_stmt_cache_size system variable, 838
binlog_stmt_cache_use status variable, 881
biographical information table, creating, 32, 34-35
BIT_AND() function, 818
BIT_COUNT() function, 829
BIT data types, 193, 197, 200-201, 752
ranges, 197
storage requirements, 197
bit-field numbers, 182
BIT_LENGTH() function, 829
bit operators
AND, 773
exclusive-OR, 773
listing of, 242
negation, 774
NULL values, 246
OR, 773
shift left, 773
shift right, 773, 818
BIT_OR() function, 818

BIT_XOR() function, 809
BLACKHOLE storage engine, 108, 112
BLOB data types
indexes, 207
overview, 207-208
query optimization, 298
size, 204, 207
special care, 208
storage requirements, 204
BLOB strings, 194, 755-756
block_size member (my_option structures), 341
BMP (Basic Multilingual Plane), 104
boolean mode searches, 170, 174-175
boolean values, 192
bulk_insert_buffer_size system variable, 838
bytes_received status variable, 881
bytes_sent status variable, 882

C

C client programs, 311
accessor macros, Web: 1087-1088
client library, 320
compiling/linking, 321, Web: 1074-1075
connect1, 323-326
connect2, compared, 347
establishing connections, 324-325
header files, 324
initialization macro, 326
initializing client library, 326
running, 326
shortcomings, 326
source file, 323-324
terminating client library, 326
terminating connections, 325
variables, declaring, 324
connect2, 327, 344-348
connect1/show_opt programs, compared, 347
connection parameters, specifying, 348
error-checking, 330
running, 347
source file, 344-347
connection parameters at runtime, specifying, 331
command-line option-handling, 335-343

option files, reading, 332-335
parameter formats, 331
data structures, Web: 1075
nonscalar. *See* nonscalar data structures
scalar data types, Web: 1075-1076
error-checking, 327-330
example resources, 320
functions
administrative, Web: 1125-1126
client library initialization/termination, Web: 1088-1089
connection management, listing of, Web: 1089-1100
debugging, Web: 1127
error-reporting, Web: 1101
information, Web: 1113-1116
multiple result sets, Web: 1113
parameter names, Web: 1087-1088
prepared statement construction/execution, Web: 1118-1120
prepared statement error-reporting, Web: 1117-1118
prepared statement result set processing, Web: 1120-1125
prepared statements, Web: 1116-1117
result sets processing, Web: 1104-1113
statement construction/execution, Web: 1102-1104
threaded clients, Web: 1126-1127
transaction control, Web: 1116
header files, 320
interactive statement-execution, 368-369
Makefiles, 322-323
multiple servers, running, 641
new client, 348
prepared call, 390-393
output, 393
parameter setup, 390-391
prepared statement handler, initializing, 390
results, processing, 391
retrieval loop, 392
server versions, verifying, 390
prepared statements, 377
executing, 378-379
inserting rows and retrieving them program, writing, 379-388
parameterizing, 377-378

result sets
metadata, 359-364
returning, 351-353
row-modifying, 350
sending to server functions, 349
special characters, 365-366
SSL support, 370-374
availability, 370
enabling, 696
holding option values variables, 372-373
options, adding, 370-372
passing SSL option information to client library, 374
statements, handling, 348-350
alternative approaches, 356-357
binary data, 367-368
causes of failures, 349
character-escaping operations, 349
general-purpose statement handler, 354-355
multiple-statement execution, 375-377
mysql_store_result() *versus* mysql_use_result() functions, 357-359
result sets, returning, 351-353
row-modifying, 350
sending to server functions, 349
special characters, 365-366
CACHE INDEX statement, 906
CALL prepared statements, 389-393
output, 393
parameter setup, 390-391
prepared statement handlers, initializing, 390
results, processing, 391
retrieval loop, 392
server versions, verifying, 390
CALL statement, 906
CAs (Certificate Authorities), 695
cascaded deletes, 164, 167-168
cascaded updates, 164, 168
CASE [*expr*] WHEN *expr1* THEN *result1* ... [ELSE *default*] END operator, 771
case sensitivity, 881
aliases, 100
columns, 100
database names, 100
filenames, 100

forcing lowercase, 100
functions, 99
index names, 100
keywords, 99
LIKE operator, 244
MySQL utilities, 1001
Perl DBI scripts, 400
plugins, 591
scope columns, 689
SQL statements, 29, 99-101
stored program names, 100
strings, 100, 183
system variables, 836
table names, 100
trigger names, 100
view names, 100
CASE statements, 988
CAST() function, 253, 783-784
cast operators, 775-776
category columns, creating, 47
CEIL() function, 781
CEILING() function, 785
certificate files (SSL), 695
CGI scripts, 459-460
    functions
        HTML structure, 461
        importing, 461
        object-oriented interface, 461-462
    HTML
        text, escaping, 464-465
        versus XHTML, 464
    input parameters, 462
    multiple-purpose pages, writing, 465-468
    output, generating, 462-464
    portability, 463
    URL text, escaping, 464-465
CHANGE clause, 128
CHANGE MASTER statement, 907-908
CHAR data types
    size/storage requirements, 204
    VARCHAR data types, compared, 206
CHAR() function, 254, 790
CHAR strings, 194, 756-757
CHAR_LENGTH() function, 790
character data, retrieving, 56
CHARACTER_LENGTH() function, 786

CHARACTER SET clause
    ALTER TABLE statement, 128-129
    CREATE DATABASE statement, 106
    rules, 102-103
character_set_client system variable, 838
character_set_connection system variable, 838
character_set_database system variable, 839
character_set_filesystem system variable, 839
character_set_results system variable, 839
character_set_server system variable, 102, 603, 839
character_set_system system variable, 839
character sets
    availability, 103-104, 185-186
    columns, editing, 128-129
    conversions, 254
    current, displaying, 104
    default, setting, 603-604
    features, 101-102
    mixing, 102
    setting, 102-103
    strings, 214-216, 753-754
        binary, 188-189, 216
        CONVERT() function, 187-188
        displaying, 215
        example, 214
        introducers, 187-188
        nonbinary, 188-189
        rules, 214
        selecting, 215
        variables, 189-191
    Unicode support, 104-105
    variables, 189-191
character_sets_dir system variable, 839
CHARSET clause
    CHARACTER SET statement, 102-103
    string data types, 214-216
        character sets, displaying, 215
        example, 214
        rules, 214
CHARSET() function, 790
charset notation, 187
_charset str operator, 773
check_pass() function, 533
check_response() function, 527
CHECK TABLE statement, 719-720, 909-910

checking tables
    CHECK TABLE statement, 719-720
    InnoDB, 718
    MyISAM, 719
    mysqlcheck utility, 720-721
CHECKSUM TABLE statement, 910
chk_mysql_opt_files.pl script, 653-654
clauses. *See also* attributes
    auth_info, 659-661
    AUTO_INCREMENT, 36, 202
    CHANGE, 128
    CHARACTER SET, 106, 128-129
    CHARSET, 102-103, 214-216
    COLLATE, 102-103, 106, 214-216
    CREATE DATABASE statement, 106
    data types, 201-203, 214-216, 747
    DEFAULT, 203
    DEFINER, 276
    ENGINE, 46-47, 129
    FROM, 54-56, 149
    GRANT statement, 660-661
    GROUP BY, 74-76
    IDENTIFIED WITH, 676
    IF NOT EXISTS, 106
    LIKE, 131, 585, 589
    LIMIT, 63-64, 475
    MODIFY, 128
    NOT NULL, 216, 223
    NULL, 216, 223
    numeric data types, 749
    ON DELETE CASCADE, 166-167
    ON DELETE SET NULL, 169
    ON UPDATE CASCADE, 166-167
    ON UPDATE SET NULL, 169
    PARTITION BY, 120-121
    RENAME, 129-130
    REPLACE, 232
    REQUIRE
        GRANT statement, 661
        GRANT USAGE statement, 697
        secure connections, 668-669
    RETURNS, 268
    ROLLUP, 77
    SELECT statements, 956-957
    SIGNED, 201
    TEMPORARY, 115-116
    UNSIGNED

        AUTO_INCREMENT, 235
        numeric data types, 201
    UPDATE, 232
    WHERE
        COUNT() function, 72
        DELETE statement, 85
        query optimizer, 288-289
        SELECT statement, 56
        SHOW statement, 131
        SHOW STATUS statement, 589
        SHOW VARIABLES statement, 585
        UPDATE statement, 86
    WITH
        GRANT statement, 661
        resource consumption limits, 670
    WITH GRANT OPTION, 669-670
    WITH ROLLUP, 77-78, 263
    ZEROFILL, 201-202
client access, 686-687
    scope columns
        case sensitivity, 689
        column name, 688
        Db, 688
        host, 687-689
        listing of, 687-689
        matching order, 690-691
        proxied_host, 689
        proxied_user, 689
        routine_name, 688
        routine_type, 688
        table_name, 688
        user, 688
    statement access verification, 689-690
    user table row matching example,
        691-694
client programs. *See* C client programs
clone() function, Web: 1137
CLOSE statements, 992
closeCursor() function, Web: 1168
COALESCE() function, 790
COERCIBILITY() function, 791
col_prompt() function, 451
COLLATE clause, 102-103
    CREATE DATABASE statement, 106
    string data types, 214-216
        collations, displaying, 215
        example, 214
        rules, 214

collation attribute, 102-103

collation_connection system variable, 839

collation_database system variable, 839

COLLATION() function, 255, 787

collations

    availability, 103-104, 185-186

    current, displaying, 104

    default, setting, 603-604

    names, 186

    setting, 102-103

    strings, 753-754

        binary *versus* nonbinary, 188-189

        displaying, 215

        example, 214

        rules, 214

    suffixes, 186

    type conversions, 255

collation_server system variable, 102, 603, 839

column_name columns, 688

columnCount() function, Web: 1168

columns

    aliases, quoting with identifiers, 98

    attributes, 35

    AUTO_INCREMENT, 36

        adding to tables, 235-236

        creating, 47

        member table column example, 36

        nonpositive numbers, 235

        properties, 230-235

        ranges, 235

        reséquencing existing columns, 236-237

        resets, 235

        unsigned, 235

    category, creating, 47

    character sets, editing, 128-129

    contents, retrieving, 54-56

    currency information, 258

    data types

        editing, 128

        specifying, 193-195

    date

        creating, 47

        information, 258-259

        values, 35

    deleting, 85-86

displaying, 131

enumeration, creating, 46

expiration, creating, 36

grant tables

    administrative privilege, 680

    authentication, 684

    object privilege, 682-681

    privilege columns, 683-684

    resource management, 685-686

    scope. *See* scope columns

    scope-of-access, 680-681, 683

    user table authentication, SSL, resource management, 680

height information, 257-258

identical data types, comparing, 288

identifiers, 99

indexing, selecting, 281-285

    badly performing queries, identifying, 285

    cardinality, 282

    comparisons, matching to index types, 284-285

    overindexing, 284

    prefixes, 283-284

    short values, 283

individual values, retrieving, 503

information, displaying, 135

INFORMATION_SCHEMA database, displaying, 134

information structures, accessing, 364

integer, creating, 46, 48

joined table references, qualifying, 138-139

member_id, creating, 36

names

    case sensitivity, 100

    views, 263-264

output

    restrictions, 37

    values, naming, 64-66

PRIMARY KEY clauses, 36

privileges, 667

references, 240

scope. *See* scope columns

sequence

    adding to tables, 235-236

    creating, 47, 237-239

    general properties, 230-232

InnoDB characteristics, 234
MEMORY characteristics, 234-235
MyISAM characteristics, 232-234
nonpositive numbers, 235
ranges, 235
resequencing existing, 236-237
resets, 235
unsigned, 235
unsetting, 87
updating, 86
values, specifying, 196
variable-length, 35, 46
columns attribute, 660
columns_priv table, 680
com_xxx status variable, 882
comma (,) join operator, 138
command line
metadata access, 135
mysqld startup options, 578
option-handling, 335-343
argument vector, processing, 342
option information, defining, 339-341
show_opt, invoking, 342-343
show_opt program, 336-338
SSL options, 697
system variables, setting, 586
commands
input editing, 90-91
mysql utility, 1026-1028
mysqladmin client, 1035-1037
mysqlshow, 135
perldoc, 743
comments
my_option structures, 340
Perl DBI scripts, adding, 398
syntax, 996-997
commit() function, Web: 1137, Web: 1162
COMMIT statement, 910-911
comparison functions, 781-783
comparison operators, 57, 768-772
CASE [expr] WHEN expr1 THEN result1 ... [ELSE default] END, 771
equal, 769
expr BETWEEN min AND max, 770-771
expr IN (value1,value2,...), 772
expr IS, 772

expr IS NULL/expr IS NOT NULL, 772
expr NOT BETWEEN min AND max, 770-771
expr NOT IN (value1,value2,...), 772
greater than, 770
greater than or equal to, 770
less than, 770
less than or equal to, 770
listing of, 243
NULL values, 247
null-safe equality, 769
rules, 768-769
unequal, 770
comparisons
data types, 748
index type matching, 284-285
complete binary backups, 714-715
completion_type system variable, 839
composite indexes, 233
compound statements, 266-267, 987-996
condition-handling, 992-996
control structure, 987-989
cursor, 991-992
declaration, 989-991
COMPRESS() function, 821
compressing dump files, 712
compression functions, 821-824
compression status variable, 882
CONCAT() function, 248, 253, 791
CONCAT_WS(), 792
concurrency
problems, preventing, 156
storage engine locking levels, 303-305
concurrent_insert system variable, 840
condition-handling statements, 992-996
configuring
administrative-only access, 649-651
data directory exception, 651
directories outside base directory, 651
innodb directory, 651
servers, running, 652
symlinks, 651
character sets, 102-103
collations, 102-103
full-text searches, 176-177
InnoDB tablespace, 595-598
auto-extend increments, 596

file pathnames, 596
file specification syntax, 596
per-table, 599-600
raw partitions, 597-598
regular files, 597
system variables, 595
Windows, 598
master-slave replication, 728-731
master server settings, 728-729
master.info file, 730
separate slave accounts, 730
server ID values, assigning, 728
slave settings, 729-730
statements, 730-731
threads, starting/stopping, 731
multiple servers, 635
MYSQL_BIND arrays
insert_rows() function, 384
select_rows() function, 385-388
mysqld, 539
SQL mode, 96-97
SSL, 695-698
accounts requiring SSL, creating, 697-698
certificate/key files, 697
client programs SSL support, enabling, 696
command-line options, 697
language APIs, 698
option files, 697
server SSL support, enabling, 695-696
SSL-related server status variables values, displaying, 697
system variables
runtime, 587-588
server startup, 586-587
tablespaces, 111
time zones, 602-603
unprivileged mysqld login accounts, 571-572
utility variables, 1006-1007
Web servers, 460-461
connect() function, Web: 1132-1136
connection parameters, 432, Web: 1135-1136
driver options, Web: 1133-1135
Perl DBI scripts, 399-400
connect_cached() function, Web: 1136

connect_timeout system variable, 840
connect1 client program, 323-326
client library
initializing, 326
terminating, 326
connect2, compared, 347
connections
establishing, 324-325
terminating, 325
header files, 324
initialization macro, 326
running, 326
shortcomings, 326
source file, 323-324
variables, declaring, 324
connect2 client program, 327, 344-348
connect1 program, compared, 347
connection parameters, specifying, 348
error-checking, 330
new client programs based on, writing, 348
running, 347
show_opt programs, compared, 347
source file, 344-347
connection_errors_xxx status variable, 882
CONNECTION_ID() function, 829
CONNECTION_USER() function, 830
connections
databases (Perl DBI scripts), 312, 400
handlers, 325
management functions, Web: 1088-1099
mysql utility, 87
option files, 87-88
shell aliases/scripts, 89
shell command history, 88
mysqld
restarting manually, 581-582
root password, resetting, 582-583
parameters, specifying
C client programs, 331, 336-341
command-line option-handling, 335-343
connect2 program, 348
option files, reading, 332-335
parameter formats, 331
Perl DBI, 423-426
secure, requiring. See also SSL, 668-669

servers
    authentication plugins, 677
    establishing, 25-26
    PHP scripts, 490-491
    programs. *See* connect1 client
        program; connect2 client program
    terminating, 26-27
    Web scripts, 468-469
TCP/IP
    listening (mysqld), 579
connections status variable, 882
constants (PDO), Web: 1173-1174
    general database-handle attributes,
        Web: 1173-1174
    fetch-mode values, Web: 1174
    parameter-type values, Web: 1174
constructor (PDO), Web: 1159-1161
Content-Type: header, 463
control structure statements, 987-989
CONV() function, 792
CONVERT() function, 187-188, 254-255, 784
CONVERT_TZ() function, 803
copying
    databases to other servers, 716
        text backup files, 716-717
        writing directly to other server,
            717-718
    tables, 117-120
core_file system variable, 840
correlated subqueries, 148
COS() function, 785
costs (indexing), 281
COT() function, 785
COUNT() function, 819
    GROUP BY clause, 74-76
    ROLLUP clause, 77
    summaries, 72-76
    WHERE clause, 72
    WITH ROLLUP clause, 77-78
counters, incrementing, 238-239
counting summaries, 72-76
    distinct non-NULL values, 73
    groups, 74-76
    minimum/maximum/total/average
        values, 76
    non-NULL values, 73
    number of rows clause matches, 72
    number of rows selected, 72

overall count of values, 73
    summary, 77-78
CRC32() function, 785
CREATE DATABASE statement, 30, 106-107,
    130, 547, 911
CREATE EVENT statement, 274, 912-913
CREATE FUNCTION statement, 268, 913-915
CREATE INDEX statement, 915-916
CREATE privilege, 664
CREATE PROCEDURE statement, 268, 913-915
CREATE ROUTINE privilege, 664
CREATE TABLE statement, 113-114, 916-926
    AVG_ROW_LENGTH option, 115
    column definitions, 926
    data type keywords, 918-919
    ENGINE clause, 46-47, 114
    foreign key support, 922-923
    IF NOT EXISTS modifier, 115
    index clauses, 919
    MAX_ROWS option, 115
    options, 919-922
    PARTITION BY clause, 120-121
    partitioning, 923-925
    student table, 45-46
    table files, creating, 549
    TEMPORARY keyword, 115-116
CREATE TABLE...LIKE statement, 117-118
CREATE TABLE...SELECT statement, 117-119
CREATE TABLESPACE privilege, 664
CREATE TEMPORARY TABLES statement, 664
CREATE TRIGGER statement, 272, 926-927
CREATE USER privilege, 661
CREATE USER statements, 927-928
    account operations, 655
    account value, 656
    auth_info clause, 659-660
    IDENTIFIED WITH clause, 676
    selecting, 656
CREATE VIEW privilege, 664
CREATE VIEW statement, 928-929
created_tmp_disk_tables status variable, 882
created_tmp_files status variable, 882
created_tmp_tables status variable, 882
CSV storage engine, 108, 112, 710
CURDATE() function, 68, 803
currency information, storing, 258
CURRENT_DATE() function, 803

CURRENT_TIME() function, 803
CURRENT_TIMESTAMP() function, 804
CURRENT_USER() function, 276, 816
cursor statements, 991-992
CURTIME() function, 804

D

damages (tables)
  checking
    CHECK TABLE statement, 719-720
    InnoDB tables, 718
    MyISAM, 719
    mysqlcheck utility, 720-721
  overview, 718
  repairing
    InnoDB, 718
    MyISAM, 719
    mysqlcheck utility, 720-721
    REPAIR TABLE statement, 720
data
  adding to tables
    data files, 52-53
    INSERT statement, 50-52
  binary
    printing, 353
    statements, 367-368
  C API structures, Web: 1075
    nonscalar. See nonscalar data
      structures
    scalar data types, Web: 1075-1076
  format options, 1067-1068
  loading efficiency, 300-303
    dropping/deactivating indexes,
      302-303
    index flushing, reducing, 301-302
    INSERT statement, 301
    LOAD DATA statement, 300-301
    mixed query environments, 303
    shorter statements, 302
  recovering. See recovery
  retrieving
    column values, naming, 64-66
    criteria, specifying, 56-59
    dates, 57, 66-69
    multiple tables, 78-85. See also joins;
      subqueries
    NULL values, 60-61

numeric ranges, 56
  pattern matching, 69-70
  Perl DBI script. See dump_members.pl
    script
  PHP script, 497-499
  SELECT statements, 54-56
  several individual values, 59
  string values containing character
    data, 56
  summaries, 72-78
  table contents, displaying, 54
  user-defined variables, 71
data directory
  access
    control, 546-547
    exception, 651
  architecture, 545
  defined, 539
  file representations
    databases, 547
    tables, 548
    triggers, 549
    views, 549
  files, 545
  grant tables. See grant tables
  identifier constraints, 550-551
  initializing, 740-741
  insecurities, checking, 648
  location, 544-545
  log files, 554-556
  maximum table size, 551-553
  performance, 553-554
  permissions, displaying, 650
  PID files, 555
  relocating, 556-557
    assessing, 558-559
    entire directory, 559
    function, selecting, 557
    individual databases, 559-560
    individual tables, 560
    InnoDB tablespace, 561
    precautions, 558
    startup option, 557
    status/log files, 561-562
    symlink, 557
  status files, 554
  table operations statements, 549-550
  Unix, 543

data_sources() function, Web: 1136
data types
    attributes, 747
    character sets
        features, 101-102
        mixing, 102
        setting, 102-103
    characteristics, 192
    collations, 102-103
    columns
        editing, 128
        specifying, 193-195
    comparisons, 748
    conversion, 247-251
        binary/nonbinary strings, 255
        character sets, 254
        collations, 255
        comparisons, 251
        CONCAT() function, 248
        dates, 254
        explicit, 247
        floating-point and integer values, 248
        forcing, 253-255
        hexadecimal, 248-249, 253
        illegal values, 248
        implicit, 247
        operands to operator expected types,
            249
        string-to-number, 249-250
        temporal values, 251
        testing, 252-253
        time parts, 254
        values into strings, 253
    date. See temporal data types
    default values, 748
    ENUM, 297
    explicit, 179
    global attributes, 747
    implicit, 95
    length, 748
    MYSQL_ROW, 352
    names, 747
    numeric, 193, 748-749
        attributes, 201-203, 749
        BIT, 197, 200-201, 752
        exact-value, 197-199
        fixed-point, 751

        floating-point, 197, 200, 751-752
        improper values, 228
        integer, 749-751
        listing of, 193
        NULL/NOT NULL values, 203
        ranges, 197
        selecting, 203, 257-258
        storage requirements, 197-198
Perl DBI. See handles
query performance, selecting, 296-298
    BLOB/TEXT, 298
    ENUM, 297
    NOT NULL, 297
    numbers, 296
    PROCEDURE ANALYSE() function,
        297
    smallest types, 296-297
    strings, 296
    tables, defragmenting, 297
ranges, 748
scalar, Web: 1075-1076
selecting, 255-256
    currency, 258
    dates, 258-259
    height information, 257-258
    performance/efficiency, 256
    ranges, 256, 259-260
    storage size, 256
    value types in column, 256-259
storage, 748
string, 193, 204, 753-754
    attributes, 214-216
    binary, 204-205, 207, 755-756
    BLOB, 207-208
    CHAR/VARCHAR, 206
    character sets/collations, 753-754
    ENUM, 208-213, 758
    improper values, 228
    lengths, 205, 753
    listing of, 194
    nonbinary, 204-205, 756-758
    selecting, 217-218
    SET, 208-213, 759
    size, 204
    storage requirements, 204
    TEXT, 207-208
    trailing pad values, 218, 754
    VARBINARY, 207

temporal, 193, 759
    attributes, 223
    automatic initialization/update
        properties, 224-226
    DATE, 220-221, 760
    DATETIME, 221, 760
    fractional seconds, 223-224
    improper values, 228
    input dates, 220
    listing of, 193
    MySQL 5.6 improvements, 218
    ranges, 218-219
    storage requirements, 219, 759
    temporal values, 226-227
    TIME, 221, 760-761
    TIMESTAMP, 221-222, 761-762
    two-digit years, 227-228
    YEAR, 222-223, 762
    zero values, 220
type conversions
    ASCII, 254
    binary/nonbinary strings, 255
    character sets, 254
    collations, 255
    comparisons, 251
    CONCAT() function, 248
    dates, 254
    explicit, 247
    floating-point and integer values, 248
    forcing, 253-255
    hexadecimal, 248-249, 253
    illegal values, 248
    implicit, 247
    operands to operator expected types,
        249
    string-to-number, 249-250
    temporal values, 251
    testing, 252-253
    time parts, 254
    values into strings, 253
variable-length characters, creating, 35
zero values, 748
data values
    boolean, 192
    columns, specifying, 196
    improper handling, 228-230
    NULL, 192

numeric, 181-182
permitted lists, defining, 209
spatial, 191-192
strings. *See* strings, values
temporal, 191
DATABASE() function, 830
databases
    access interfaces (PHP), 485-486
    backups, 540, 707-709
        best practices, 709
        binary, 714-715
        selecting types, 708
        storage engine portability, 709-710
        text, 711-714
    browser script, 471-475
        data limits, 475
        empty values into nonbreaking
            spaces, converting, 475
        HTML table, creating, 475
        initial page, generating, 472-473
        main body, 471-472
        security warning, 471
        table contents, displaying, 473
        tbl_name parameter, 472
    connections, 400
    copying to other servers, 716
        text backup files, 716-717
        writing directly to other server,
            717-718
    crash recovery. *See* recovery
    creating, 30-31, 106-107
    data, loading, 300-303
        dropping/deactivating indexes,
            302-303
        index flushing, reducing, 301-302
        INSERT statement, 301
        LOAD DATA statement, 300-301
        mixed-query environments, 303
        shorter statements, 302
    data directory, relocating, 559-560
    default, setting, 30-31
    definition, displaying, 106-107
    deleting, 107
    editing, 107
    file representations, 547
    handles
        attributes, Web: 1149
        functions, Web: 1137-1142

MySQL-specific attributes,
Web: 1150-1152
PDO attributes, Web: 1173-1174
identifiers, 98
INFORMATION_SCHEMA
columns, displaying, 134
displaying, 132
metadata access, 132-135
tables, 133-134
integrity, maintaining
auto-recovery, 706
preventive maintenance, scheduling,
707
listing, 38, 130, 135
metadata, accessing, 130
command line, 135
INFORMATION_SCHEMA database,
132-135
SHOW statement, 130-132
migration, 541
mysql privileges, 673-674
names, case sensitivity, 100
preventive maintenance, 540, 699-700
privileges, 666
recovering, 541, 722
replication, 541
compatibility guidelines, 727-728
master-slave, 728-731
overview, 727
resetting to known state, 53-54
selecting, 105-106
server connectivity, 312, 400
tables, listing, 37
types, 708
datadir system variable, 840
DATE() function, 804
DATE_ADD() function, 68, 254, 804-805
date and time
columns, creating, 47
data types. *See* temporal data types
differences between, 68
expiration columns, creating, 36
formats, 226
functions, 802-821
ADDDATE(), 803
ADDTIME(), 803
CONVERT_TZ(), 803

CURDATE(), 803
CURRENT_DATE(), 803
CURRENT_TIME(), 803
CURRENT_TIMESTAMP(), 804
CURTIME(), 804
DATE(), 804
DATE_ADD(), 804-805
DATE_FORMAT(), 806
DATE_SUB(), 807
DATEDIFF(), 807
DAY(), 808
DAYNAME(), 808
DAYOFMONTH(), 808
DAYOFWEEK(), 808
DAYOFYEAR(), 808
EXTRACT(), 808-809
FROM_DAYS(), 809
FROM_UNIXTIME(), 809
GET_FORMAT(), 809-810
HOUR(), 810
LAST_DAY(), 810
listing of, 802-821
LOCALTIME(), 810
LOCALTIMESTAMP(), 810
MAKEDATE(), 810
MAKETIME(), 811
MICROSECOND(), 811
MINUTE(), 811
MONTH(), 811
MONTHNAME(), 811
NOW(), 811
PERIOD_ADD(), 812
PERIOD_DIFF(), 812
QUARTER(), 812
SEC_TO_TIME(), 812
SECOND(), 812
STR_TO_DATE(), 813
SUBDATE(), 813
SUBTIME(), 813
SYSDATE(), 813
TIME(), 813
TIME_FORMAT(), 813
TIME_TO_SEC(), 814
TIMEDIFF(), 814
TIMESTAMP(), 814
TIMESTAMPADD(), 814
TIMESTAMPDIFF(), 814

TO_DAYS(), 815
TO_SECONDS(), 815
UNIX_TIMESTAMP(), 815
UTC_DATE(), 815
UTC_TIME(), 815
UTC_TIMESTAMP(), 816
WEEK(), 816-817
WEEKDAY(), 817
WEEKOFYEAR(), 817
YEAR(), 817
YEARWEEK(), 817
locale, selecting, 604-605
operations supported, 66
parts, retrieving, 67-68
retrieving, 27, 57
specific, searching, 66-67
syntax, 66
tables, linking, 41
two-digit years, 227-228
type conversions, 254
values, 191
zero value errors, 229
DATE data type, 35, 193, 221, 760
DATE_FORMAT() function, 806
date_format system variable, 840
DATE_SUB() function, 69, 807
DATEDIFF() function, 807
DATETIME data type, 193, 221, 760
automatic initialization/update
properties, 224-226
current timestamp, 221
date values, 221
formats, 221, 226-227
time values, 221
datetime_format system variable, 840
DAY() function, 808
DAYNAME() function, 808
DAYOFMONTH() function, 67, 808
DAYOFWEEK() function, 808
DAYOFYEAR() function, 808
db_browse.pl script, 471-475
display_table_contents() function,
473-475
display_table_names() function, 472-473
HTML table, creating, 475
LIMIT clause, 475
main body, 471-472

nonbreaking spaces, 475
security warning, 471
tbl_name parameter, 472
Db columns, 688
db table, 680
DBI_DRIVER environment variable, Web: 1156
DBI_DSN environment variable, Web: 1156
DBI_PASS environment variable, Web: 1156
DBI_TRACE environment variable, 429,
Web: 1156
DBI_USER environment variable, Web: 1156
DEALLOCATE PREPARE statement, 929
debug system variable, 840
debugging
functions, Web: 1119-1120
Perl DBI scripts, 426
print statements, 428
tracing, 428-429
DECIMAL data type, 193, 751
ranges, 197
storage requirements, 197
DECLARE statements, 989-991
DECODE() function, 822
decreasing number sequences, creating, 238
def_value member (my_option structures), 341
DEFAULT attribute, 203
DEFAULT() function, 830
default databases, setting, 30-31
default_storage_engine system variable, 840
default_tmp_storage_engine system variable,
840
default_week_format system variable, 840
DEFINER clause, 276
definer privileges, 276
defragmenting tables, 297
DEGREES() function, 786
delay_key_write system variable, 841
delayed_errors status variable, 882
delayed_insert_limit system variable, 841
delayed_insert_threads status variable, 882
delayed_insert_timeout system variable, 841
delayed_queue_size system variable, 841
delayed_writes status variable, 882
DELETE privilege, 664
DELETE statement, 929-930
multiple tables, 154-155
rows, 85-86

deleting
    anonymous-user accounts, 568-569
    cascaded deletes, 164, 167-168
    columns, 85-86
    databases, 107
    rows, 85-86
        events, 275
        multiple tables, 154-155
        preserving sequencing, 235
    tables, 121-122
delimiters (compound statements), 266-267
DES_DECRYPT() function, 822
DES_ENCRYPT() function, 822-823
DESCRIBE statement, 36-37, 930-931
development releases, 643
directories
    creating (Perl DBI), 436-442
        plain text, 439-440
        RTF version, 440-442
    online, creating, 455-458
    sampdb distribution, 735-736
        Perl DBI scripts, 476-477
        PHP, 514-515
dirty reads, 162
disaster planning. *See* recovery
disconnect() function, Web: 1137
display_cell() function, 516
display_column() function, 535
display_entry() function, 531-533
display_events() function
display_form() function, 525-526
display_login_form() function, 530
display_login_page() function, 530
display_scores() function, 477-479, 518-519
display_table_contents() function, 473-475
display_table_names() function, 472-473
displaying
    character sets available, 185-186
    collations available, 185-186
    columns, 131, 134
    CREATE DATABASE statement, 130
    current character sets/collations, 104
    database definitions, 106-107
    databases, 130, 135
    errors, 170
    foreign keys, 170

help messages (utilities), 1000-1001
indexes, 131
INFORMATION_SCHEMA database, 132
initial user accounts, 565
plugins, 592
privileges, 671
result set metadata, 360-364
    column display width, 361-362
    final code, 362-364
    printing
        boxed column labels, 362
        values, 362
row storage formats, 300
SSL-related server status variable values, 697
statement results, 28
status variables, 584
storage engines available, 593
system variables, 583, 836
tables, 130
    contents, 50, 54
    structure, 36-37
distinct non-NULL values, counting, 73
DIV (integer division) operator, 57, 241, 767
div_precision_increment system variable, 841
division by zero errors, 229
division (/) operator, 57, 241, 767
DNS, account name host values, matching, 658-659
do() function, 406-407, Web: 1137-1138
DO statement, 931
dollar signs ($), PHP, 492
DOUBLE data type, 193
    ranges, 197
    storage requirements, 197
double-quoting strings (qq), 417-418
DROP DATABASE statement, 107, 547, 931
DROP EVENT statement, 932
DROP FUNCTION statement, 932
DROP INDEX statement, 127, 302, 932
DROP privilege, 664
DROP PROCEDURE statement, 932
DROP TABLE statement, 121-122, 549, 932
DROP TRIGGER statement, 932-933
DROP USER statement, 656, 933
DROP VIEW statement, 933
dropping. *See* deleting

dump_members.php script, 497-499
  display values, encoding, 498
  error handling, 498
  home page link, creating, 498-499
  installing/accessing, 498
  result set, returning, 498
dump_members.pl script, 397-398
  case sensitivity, 400
  comments, adding, 398
  connect() function arguments, 399-400
  connections, 400
  disconnecting, 402
  finish() function, 402
  result sets, retrieving, 400-401
  row-fetching loop, 401-402
  statement terminators, 401
  use DBI statement, 399
  use strict statement, 399
  use warnings statement, 399
  warnings, 401
dump_members2.php script, 499-500
dump_members2.pl script, 404-405
dump_results() function, Web: 1143
dynamic attributes (Perl DBI), Web: 1145-1155

E

edit_member() function, 452
edit_member.php script
  editing form, 533-534
  framework, 529-530
  member login page, 530-531
  null values, 535-536
  password verification, 531-533
  updating entries, 534-535
edit_member.pl script, 448-454
editing
  columns
    character sets, 128-129
    data types, 128
  databases, 107
  rows
    storage formats, 300
    with statements, 350
  tables
    storage characteristics, 114-115
    structure, 127-130

user account passwords, 672
U.S. Historical League member entries
  command-line script, 448-454
  online, 527-536
ellipsis (...), operators/functions, 764
ELT() function, 779
empty values, 475
ENCODE() function, 823
ENCRYPT() function, 823
ending
  server connections, 26-27
  statements, 27-28
  transactions, 160
ENGINE clause
  ALTER TABLE statement, 129
  CREATE TABLE statement, 46-47
enter_scores() function, 520-521
entering statements, 27
  case-sensitivity, 29
  function syntax, 29
  multiple-lines, 28
  multiple statements on single line, 28-29
ENUM data type, 208-213
  creating, 46, 208
  improper values, 228
  numeric form, 210-211
  permitted value lists, defining, 209
  query optimization, 297
  SET data type, compared, 208
  size/storage requirements, 204
  sorting/indexing, 212-213
ENUM strings, 194, 758
environment variables
  DBI_TRACE, 429
  PATH, configuring, 739-740
  Perl DBI, Web: 1156
  utility options, checking, 1011-1012
eq_range_index_dive_limit system variable, 841
equal to (=) operator, 57, 243, 769
equal to (<=>) operator, 57, 769
err() function, Web: 1146
error_count system variable, 842
error handling
  foreign keys, displaying, 170
  improper values. See improper values
  message language, setting, 604
  PDO exceptions, 491

Perl DBI, 402-405
   automatic, 403-404
   checking, 400
   default error messages, replacing, 404
   default settings, 403
   dump_members2.pl script example, 404-405
   manually checking/printing, 403
   PrintError attribute, 403
   RaiseError attribute, 403
PHP, 507-509
prepared statement functions, Web: 1112-1113
reporting functions, Web: 1099
error logs, 556, 620-621
   defined, 618
   event scheduler, 274
   levels, selecting, 620
   multiple servers, 634
   Unix, 620
   Windows, 621
errorCode() function, 508, Web: 1162, Web: 1168
ERROR_FOR_DIVISION_BY_ZERO, 863
errorInfo() function, 508, Web: 1163, Web: 1168
errstr() function, Web: 1146
escape_demo.pl script, 464-465
escape sequences
   strings, 183
   utility option files, 1010
escapeHTML() function, 464-465
EVENT privilege, 664
event_scheduler system variable, 842
events, 274-275
   creating, 274
   defined, 274
   deleting old rows from table example, 275
   enabling/disabling, 275
   IDs, 41-42
   one time only, 275
   privileges, 274
   scheduler
      enabling, 274
      logging, 274
      starting/stopping at runtime, 274
      status, verifying, 274
   security, 276

exact-value data types, 197-199
exact-value numbers, 181-182
exception functions, Web: 1172-1173
exclusive-OR (XOR) operator, 773
exec() function, Web: 1163
   prepared statements, 505
   row-modifying statements, 501
exec_stmt program, 368-369
exec_stmt_ssl.c, creating, 370-374
   availability, 370
   holding option values variables, 372-373
   options, adding, 370-372
   running, 374
execute() function, Web: 1143, Web: 1168
execute_array() function, Web: 1143
EXECUTE privilege, 664
EXECUTE statement, 933
EXISTS subqueries, 147-148
EXP() function, 786
expiration column, 36
expire_logs_days system variable, 629, 842
expiring logs, 625, 629-631
   automating, 630-631
   binary, 629-630
   relay, 630
EXPLAIN statement, 290-296, 933-936
explicit data types, 179
EXPORT_SET() function, 792
expr BETWEEN *min* AND *max* operator, 770-771
expr IN (*value1,value2,...*), 772
expr IS operator, 772
expr NOT BETWEEN *min* AND *max* operator, 770-771
expr NOT IN (*value1,value2,...*) operator, 772
expressions, 239-240
   NULL values, 246-247
   operators, 241-243
      arithmetic, 241
      bit, 242
      comparison, 243
      logical, 241-242
      precedence, 246
   pattern matching, 243-245
      LIKE operator, 243-244
      REGEXP operator, 244
   type conversions, 247-251
      ASCII, 254

binary/nonbinary strings, 255
character sets, 254
collations, 255
comparisons, 251
CONCAT() function, 248
dates, 254
explicit, 247
floating-point to integers, 248
forcing, 253-255
hexadecimal, 248-249, 253
illegal values, 248
implicit, 247
operands to operator expected types, 249
string-to-number, 249-250
temporal values, 251
testing, 252-253
time parts, 254
values into strings, 253
writing, 240-241
column references, 240
functions/arguments, 240
scalar subqueries, 241
writing styles, selecting, 290-292
external locking, 702
external security risks, 646
external_user system variable, 842
EXTRACT() function, 808-809
EXTRACTVALUE() function, 828

F

FEDERATED storage engine, 108, 113
fetch() function
arguments, 502-503
example, 501
Perl DBI, Web: 1143
PDO, Web: 1168-1169
PHP data-retrieval script, 498
FETCH statements, 992
fetchAll() function, 504, Web: 1169
fetchall_arrayref() function, 415, Web: 1144
fetchall_hashref() function, Web: 1144
fetchColumn() function, 491, Web: 1169
fetchObject() function, Web: 1169
fetchrow_array() function, 401, 408-409, Web: 1144

fetchrow_arrayref() function, 409-410, Web: 1145
fetchrow_hashref() function, 410-411
FIELD() function, 779
FIELDS clause, 943-944
FILE privilege, 662, 674-675
files
data, loading, 52-53
data directory, 545
.frm
defined, 548
MEMORY tables, 548
MyISAM tables, 548
views, 549
include, 491-497
InnoDB tablespace, 595-598
adding, 599
auto-extend increments, 596
file specification syntax, 596
pathnames, 596
raw partitions, 597-598
regular files, 597
startup failure, troubleshooting, 598
system variables, 595
Windows, 598
log. See logs
Makefiles, 322-323
master.info, 730
MYISAM table, 548
names
case sensitivity, 100
identifier constraints, 550
option, 1008
connection parameters, reading, 424
logging, enabling, 619
mysql utility connection parameters, 87-88
mysqld startup, 578
plugins, loading, 591
reading, 332-335
securing, 653-654
SSL, 697
system variables, setting, 586
Unix, 1007
utility, 1007-1011
Web script security, 470-471
Windows, 424-425, 1008

PID, 555
retrieving images and storing in tables, 367-368
sampdb distribution, 735-736
source
    connect1.c, 323-324
    connect2, 344-347
    show_opt, 336-338
SSL status, 695-696
    listing of, 554
    multiple servers, 634
    relocating, 561-562
statements, storing, 29
table-specific, 109-110
TRG, 549
TRN, 549
Unix socket, securing, 652-653
filesystem security, 540
FIND_IN_SET() function, 793
finish() function, 402, Web: 1145
fixed-length string types, 205
fixed-name logs, rotating, 626-629
fixed-point types, 751
flip_flop.pl script, 467-468
FLOAT data type, 193
    ranges, 197
    storage requirements, 197
FLOAT[(M,D)] type, 752
FLOAT(p) type, 751
floating-point data types, 197, 200, 751-752
    FLOAT[(M,D)], 752
    FLOAT(p), 751
FLOOR() function, 253, 786
flush_commands status variable, 882
FLUSH PRIVILEGES statement, 583
FLUSH statement, 936-937
flush system variable, 842
FLUSH TABLES statement, 302, 703
flush_time system variable, 842
flushing logs, 626
footers, 495-497
forcing type conversions, 253-255
foreign_key_checks system variable, 842
foreign keys
    absence table example, 49
    benefits, 164
    cascaded deletes

        creating, 166-168
        testing, 167-168
    cascaded updates
        creating, 166-168
        testing, 168
    defining in child table, 164-165
    deletes/updates, 164
    displaying, 170
    errors, displaying, 170
    guidelines, 166
    insertion, verifying, 167
    null values, 168-170
    parent/child values, 164
    referential integrity, 164
    row entries, 164
    score table example, 48
    unique indexes, creating, 169
FORMAT() function, 793
format_entry() function, 455
formats
    binary logs, 731
    row storage
        displaying/editing, 300
        InnoDB, 299-300
        MEMORY, 299
        MyISAM, 299
forms
    hidden fields, creating, 525-526
    text input fields, 530
FOUND_ROWS() function, 830
.frm files
    defined, 548
    MEMORY tables, 548
    MyISAM tables, 548
    views, 549
FROM clause
    SELECT statements, 54-56
    subqueries, 149
FROM_BASE64() function, 793
FROM_DAYS() function, 809
FROM_UNIXTIME() function, 809
ft_boolean_syntax system variable, 842
ft_max_word_len system variable, 842
ft_min_word_len system variable, 843
ft_query_expansion_limit system variable, 843
ft_stopword_file system variable, 843

full-text searches
  boolean mode, 174-175
  characteristics, 171
  configuring, 176-177
  natural language, 172-174
  query expansion, 175-176
  types, 170
FULLTEXT indexes, **124**, **126**
  configuring, 176-177
  creating, 171-172
  Web table searches, 482-483
func() function, Web: **1147-1148**
functions
  add_new_event(), 517-518
  advisory locking, 824-826
  ASCII(), 254, 790
  AVG(), 76, 818
  bail_out(), 405
  BENCHMARK(), 829
  BIN(), 200, 790
  bind_col(), 421
  bindColumn(), 503
  bind_columns(), 421
  BIT_COUNT(), 829
  BIT_LENGTH(), 829
  C API
    administrative, Web: 1125-1126
    client library initialization/
      termination, Web: 1088-1089
    connection management, listing of,
      Web: 1089-1100
    debugging, Web: 1127
    error-reporting, Web: 1101
    information, Web: 1113-1116
    multiple result sets, Web: 1113
    parameter names, Web: 1087-1088
    prepared statement construction/
      execution, Web: 1118-1120
    prepared statement error-reporting,
      Web: 1117-1118
    prepared statement result set
      processing, Web: 1120-1125
    prepared statements, Web: 1116-1117
    result sets processing, listing of,
      Web: 1104-1113
    statement construction/execution,
      Web: 1102-1104
    threaded clients, Web: 1126-1127
    transaction control, Web: 1116

cast, 783-784
CAST(), 253, 783-784
CGI.module, 462
CGI.pm
  HTML structures, 461
  HTML/URL text, escaping, 464-465
  importing, 461
  object-oriented interface, 461-462
  output, 462-464
CHAR(), 254, 790
check_pass(), 533
check_response(), 527
col_prompt(), 451
COLLATION(), 255, 787
comparison, 781-783
compression, 821-824
CONCAT(), 248, 253, 791
connect()
  connection parameters, 423
  Perl DBI scripts, 399-400
CONNECTION_ID(), 829
CONNECTION_USER(), 830
CONVERT(), 187-188, 254-255, 784
COUNT(), 819
  GROUP BY clause, 74-76
  ROLLUP clause, 77
  WITH ROLLUP clause, 77-78
  summaries, 72-76
  WHERE clause, 72
CURDATE(), 68, 803
CURRENT_USER(), 276, 816
DATABASE(), 830
date and time, listing of, 802-821
DATE_ADD(), 68, 254, 804-805
DATE_SUB(), 69, 807
DAYOFMONTH(), 67, 808
DEFAULT(), 830
display_cell(), 516
display_column(), 535
display_entry(), 531-533
display_events()
  Perl DBI, 476-477
  PHP, 514-515
display_form(), 525-526
display_login_form(), 530
display_login_page(), 530
display_scores(), 477-479, 518-519

display_table_contents(), 473-475
display_table_names(), 472-473
do(), 406-407
edit_member(), 452
enter_scores(), 520-521
errorCode(), 508
errorInfo(), 508
escapeHTML(), 464-465
exec()
    prepared statements, 505
    row-modifying statements, 501
expressions, 240
fetch()
    arguments, 502-503
    example, 501
    PHP data-retrieval script, 498
fetchAll(), 504
fetchall_arrayref(), 415
fetchColumn(), 491
fetchrow_array(), 401
finish(), 402
FLOOR(), 253, 786
format, 763
format_entry(), 455
FOUND_ROWS(), 830
getCode(), 508
getMessage(), 508
handle_options(), 342
header(), 463
HEX(), 201, 253
hidden_field(), 526
html_begin(), 495-497
html_end(), 495-497
html_format_entry(), 456, 481
htmlspecialchars(), 498
insert_rows(), 381-385
interpret_argument(), 445
IP address, 826-828
is_null(), 504
LAST_INSERT_ID(), 237-239, 831
li(), 473
load_defaults()
    defined, 332
    security, 335
    show_argv program example,
        332-333
LOAD_FILE(), 831

load_image(), 367
MASTER_POS_WAIT(), 831
MAX(), 76, 820
MIN(), 76, 820
MONTH(), 67, 811
MONTHNAME(), 67, 811
my_init(), 326
mysql_affected_rows(), 350
mysql_close(), 325
mysql_errno(), 328
mysql_error(), 328
mysql_fetch_row(), 351-352
mysql_free_result(), 351
mysql_init(), 325
mysql_library_end(), 326
mysql_library_init(), 326
mysql_more_results(), 375
mysql_next_result(), 375
mysql_query(), 349
mysql_real_connect(), 325, 375
mysql_real_escape_string(), 365
mysql_real_query(), 349
mysql_set_server_option(), 375
mysql_sqlstate(), 328
mysql_stmt_close(), 388
mysql_stmt_fetch(), 388
mysql_stmt_free_result(), 388
mysql_stmt_init(), 380
mysql_store_result(), 351, 357-359
mysql_use_result(), 351, 357-359
NAME_CONST(), 831
names
    case sensitivity, 99
    identifiers, 98
new PDO(), 490
notify_member(), 446
numeric, 784-789
OCT(), 201, 797
ORDER BY RAND(), 523
param(), 462
parentheses, 401
password_field(), 531
PDO, Web: 1159
    constants, Web: 1173-1174
    exceptions, Web: 1172-1173
    PDO class, Web: 1159-1166
    statement handles, Web: 1166-1172

Perl DBI
    administrative, Web: 1147-1148
    %attr hash argument, Web: 1130
    calling sequence, Web: 1130
    database-handle, Web: 1137-1142
    DBI class, Web: 1132-1136
    general handle, Web: 1146
    statement-handle, Web: 1142-1145
    utility, Web: 1148-1149
prepare(), 505
present_question(), 525
print_dashes(), 362
print_error(), 329-330
PROCEDURE ANALYSE(), 297
process_call_result(), 392
process_multi_statement(), 376
process_real_statement(), 356-357
process_result_set() function, 352-353
process_statement(), 355
prompt(), 451
query(), 491
quote(), 418-419, 505-506
radio_button(), 526
read_file(), 445
remove_backslashes(), 512
ROUND(), 253, 788
ROW_COUNT(), 831-832
rowCount(), 505
row-fetching
    fetchrow_array(), 408-409
    fetchrow_arrayref(), 409-410
    fetchrow_hashref(), 410-411
    listing of, 407
SCHEMA(), 832
script_name(), 516
script_param(), 512
search_members()
    ushl_browse.pl script, 480
    ushl_ft_browse.pl, 482-483
security, 821-824
select_rows(), 385-388
selectrow_array(), 413
SESSION_USER(), 832
SLEEP(), 832
solicit_event_info(), 516-517
spatial, 828

start_html(), 463
stored, 268-271
    creating, 268
    defined, 268
    integer-valued parameter representing
        a year example, 268
    multiple values, 269
    names, 269
    privileges, 270-271
    security, 276
    tables, updating, 270
STR_TO_DATE(), 66, 813
string, listing of, 789-802
submit_button(), 526
SUM(), 76, 820
summary, listing of, 817-821
syntax, 29, 764, 780
SYSTEM_USER(), 832
table(), 475
td(), 475
text_field(), 530
textfield(), 481
th(), 475
TIMESTAMPDIFF(), 68, 814
TO_DAYS(), 68, 815
trace(), 428
undef argument, 422
USER(), 832
UUID(), 832
UUID_SHORT(), 833
VALUES(), 833
VERSION(), 833
XML, 828

G

gen_dir.pl script
    entry-fetching loop, 439
    format selection code, 438-439
    HTML format, 456-458
    switchbox, 437-438
general_log system variable, 621, 843
general_log_file system variable, 621, 772
general-purpose statement handlers, 354-355
general query logs, 556, 618, 621
GET_BOOL var_type, 340
GET DIAGNOSTICS statements, 992-994

GET_DISABLED var_type, 340
GET_DOUBLE var_type, 340
GET_ENUM var_type, 340
GET_FORMAT() function, 809-810
get_info() function, Web: 1138
GET_INT var_type, 340
GET_LL var_type, 340
GET_LOCK() function, 825
GET_LONG var_type, 340
GET_NO_ARG var_type, 340
GET_SET var_type, 340
GET_STR_ALLOC var_type, 340
GET_STR var_type, 340
GET_UINT var_type, 340
GET_ULL var_type, 340
GET_ULONG var_type, 340
getAttribute() function, Web: 1163, Web: 1170
getAvailableDrivers function, Web: 1163
getCode() function, 508
getColumnMeta() function, Web: 1170
getMessage() function, 508
global attributes, 747
global privileges, 666
GLOBAL qualifier
    SHOW STATUS statement, 589
    SHOW VARIABLES statement, 586
global variables, 97
globalization
    default character set/collation, 603-604
    error message language, 604
    internationalization, 601
    locale, 604-605
    localization, 601
    time zones, configuring, 602-603
grade_event table
    creating, 40, 47
    linking with score table
        dates, 41
        event IDs, 41-42
grade-keeping project, 17
    above-average scores for a grade event,
        finding, 145
    absences
        finding, 145
        summarizing, 82-83
        table, creating, 45, 49
    grade_event table, 40, 47

gradebook example, 39
incorrectly entered grades, swapping,
    160-161
linking tables, 41
missing tests/quizzes for students,
    finding, 141-143
online score-entry application, 510-511
    action input parameter, 513
    editing scores, 520-522
    event table cells, generating, 516
    events, displaying, 514-515
    framework, 513-514
    hyperlink URLs, 516
    new event entry form, 516-517
    scores, entering, 517-518
    scores for selected events, displaying,
        518-519
    security, 522
    transactional data-entry operations,
        520
perfect attendance, 84, 145
quiz/test scores for given date,
    retrieving, 78-81
rows, adding
    from files, 52-53
    INSERT statement, 50-52
scores
    browser, creating, 475-479
    retrieving, 43-44
    table, creating, 39-40, 48-49
    total score per student at end of
        semester, 82
student table, creating, 44-47
tables, linking, 41-42
test/quiz statistics view, 264-265
GRANT OPTION privilege, 662, 669-670, 674
GRANT statements, 938-943
    clauses, 660-661
        ON, 939-940
        REQUIRE, 668-669, 941
        WITH, 941-942
    examples, 942-943
    privileges, revoking, 672
    privileges to be granted, 938-939
    selecting, 661
grant tables
    account-management statements
        affected, 654-655

accounts, 564-569
    available on all platforms, 566
    client program connections, 566
    displaying, 565
    passwords, assigning, 567-569
    platform specific, 567
administrative privilege columns, 680
columns
    authentication, 684
    privilege, 683-684
    resource management, 685-686
    scope. *See* scope columns
    SSL-related, 685
initializing, 740-741
listing of, 680
object privileges, 681-682
privilege tables, 683
source, 566
statement access verification, 689-690
upgrading, 655
user tables
    authentication, 680
    row matching example, 691-694
GRANT USAGE statement, 697
greater than (>) operator, 57, 243, 770
greater than or equal to (>=) operator, 57, 243, 770
GREATEST() function, 779
GROUP BY clause, 74-76
GROUP_CONCAT() function, 819-820
group_concat_max_len system variable, 843
groups
    operators, 765-766
    option, 578
    values, counting, 74-76

H

handle_options() function, 342
HANDLER statement, 943
handler_commit status variable, 882
handler_delete status variable, 883
handler_external_lock status variable, 883
handler_mrr_init status variable, 883
handler_prepare status variable, 883
handler_read_first status variable, 883
handler_read_key status variable, 883
handler_read_last status variable, 883
handler_read_next status variable, 883
handler_read_prev status variable, 883
handler_read_rnd status variable, 883
handler_read_rnd_next status variable, 883
handler_rollback status variable, 883
handler_savepoint status variable, 883
handler_savepoint_rollback status variable, 884
handler_update status variable, 884
handler_write status variable, 884
handles, 397
    database
        attributes, Web: 1149
        functions, Web: 1137-1142
        MySQL-specific attributes, Web: 1150-1152
        PDO attributes, Web: 1173-1174
    general
        attributes, Web: 1149-1150
        functions, Web: 1146
    names, 397
    PDOStatement, 501
    statements
        attributes, Web: 1152-1153
        functions, Web: 1142-1145
        MySQL-specific attributes, Web: 1154-1155
        PDO functions, Web: 1166-1172
HASH indexes, 124-125
have_compress system variable, 843
have_crypt system variable, 843
have_dynamic_loading system variable, 843
have_geometry system variable, 843
have_openssl system variable, 844
have_query_cache system variable, 844
have_rtree_keys system variable, 844
have_ssl system variable, 844
have_symlink system variable, 844
header() function, 463
headers
    connect1 client program, 324
    Content-Type:, 463
    html_begin() function, 495-497
height information, storing, 257-258
hello world script examples, 487-488
help messages, displaying, 1000-1001
HEX() function, 201, 253, 793

hexadecimal notation
  conversions, 248-249
  strings, 184
hidden_field() function, 526
hidden fields (forms)
  creating, 525-526
  security, 528
HIGH_NOT_PRECEDENCE, 863
host access
  limited, 657
  matching host values to DNS, 658-659
  single, 657
  unlimited, 657
host_cache_size system variable, 844
host columns, 687-688
hostname system variable, 844
HOUR() function, 810
HTML
  escaping, 464-465
  structure, 455-456
  tables, creating, 475
  XHTML, compared, 464
html_begin() function, 495-497
html_end() function, 495-497
html_format_entry() function, 456, 481
htmlspecialchars() function, 498
hyperlinks, creating, 499-500

I

id (my_option structures), 339
IDENTIFIED WITH clause, 676
identifiers, 97
  aliases, 98
  columns, 99
  constraints
    MySQL, 550
    operating systems, 550-551
  database, 98
  function names, 98
  length, 98
  qualified names, 99
  qualifiers, 98
  quoting, 97-98
  tables, 98
  unquoted, 97
  views, 98

identity system variable, 844
IF() function, 779
IF statements, 988
IF NOT EXISTS clause, 106
IFNULL() function, 779
ignore_builtin_innodb system variable, 870
ignore_db_dirs system variable, 844
IGNORE_SPACE, 863
images, retrieving from files and storing in
  tables, 367-368
implicit data types, 179
importing CGI.pm functions, 461
improper values, handling, 228-230
  division by zero errors, 229
  strict mode
    turning on, 230
    weakening, 230
  transactional/nontransactional tables,
    229
  warnings, 229
  zero date errors, 229
IN operator, 59, 243
IN subqueries, 145-146
include files (PHP)
  benefits, 491-493
  Historical League example, 495
  locations, establishing, 493-504
  referencing, 494
increasing number sequences, creating,
  237-238
INDEX privilege, 664
indexes, 278
  benefits, 278-281
    multiple tables, 280
    single-table queries, 279
  binary logs, 623
  BLOB/TEXT data types, 207
  case sensitivity, 100
  columns, selecting, 281-285
    badly performing queries,
      identifying, 285
    cardinality, 282
    comparisons, matching to index
      types, 284-285
    overindexing, 284
    prefixes, 283-284
    short values, 283
  composite, 233

costs, 281
creating
    column prefixes, 126
    existing tables, 124
    FULLTEXT, 126
    HASH, 125
    new tables, 125
    unique, 124-125
data loading efficiency
    dropping/deactivating, 302-303
    flushing, reducing, 301-302
deleting, 127
displaying, 131
ENUM/SET data types, 212-213
flexibility, 122
FULLTEXT
    configuring, 176-177
    creating, 171-172
    Web table searches, 482-483
ID numbers, generating, 36
information, displaying, 135
query efficiency, 292-296
storage engine characteristics, 123
synthetic, 298
tables, 122-123
types, 123-124
INET_ATON() function, 826
INET_NTOA() function, 826
INET6_ATON() function, 827
INET6_NTOA() function, 827
information functions, Web: 1109-1111
INFORMATION_SCHEMA database
    columns, displaying, 134
    displaying, 132
    metadata access, 132-135
    tables, 133-134
init_connect system variable, 844
init_file system variable, 845
init_slave system variable, 845
initial user accounts, 564-569
    available on all platforms, 566
    client program connections, 566
    displaying, 565
    passwords, assigning, 567-569
    platform specific, 567
inner joins, 137-138

InnoDB storage engine, 108
    auto-recovery, 706, 725-726
    backing up, 715-716
    checking/repairing tables, 718
    data, representing, 548
    features, 110
    innodb directory access mode, setting, 651
    locking levels, 303
    portability, 710
    row storage formats, 299-300
    sequence characteristics, 234
    status variables, listing of, 888-891
    system variables, listing of, 870-880
    tablespace
        auto-extend increments, 596
        components, adding, 599
        configuring, 595-598
        contents, 595
        file pathnames, 596
        file specification syntax, 596
        individual (per-table), 599-600
        maximum size, 552
        overview, 111
        raw partitions, 597-598
        regular files, 597
        relocating, 560
        startup failure, troubleshooting, 598
        system variables, 595
        Windows, 598
    transaction isolation levels, 162-163
    variables, 600-601
innodb_adaptive_flushing system variable, 870
innodb_adaptive_flushing_lwm system variable, 870
innodb_adaptive_hash_index system variable, 870
innodb_adaptive_max_sleep_delay system variable, 870
innodb_additional_mem_pool_size system variable, 871
innodb_autoextend_increment system variable, 596, 871
innodb_autoinc_lock_mode system variable, 871
innodb_available_undo_logs status variable, 888
innodb_buffer_pool_dump_at_shutdown system variable, 871

innodb_buffer_pool_dump_now system variable, 871

innodb_buffer_pool_dump_status status variable, 888

innodb_buffer_pool_filename system variable, 871

innodb_buffer_pool_instances system variable, 871

innodb_buffer_pool_load_abort system variable, 871

innodb_buffer_pool_load_at_startup system variable, 871

innodb_buffer_pool_load_now system variable, 872

innodb_buffer_pool_load_status status variable, 888

innodb_buffer_pool_pages_data status variable, 888

innodb_buffer_pool_pages_dirty status variable, 888

innodb_buffer_pool_pages_flushed status variable, 888

innodb_buffer_pool_pages_free status variable, 888

innodb_buffer_pool_pages_latched status variable, 888

innodb_buffer_pool_pages_misc status variable, 888

innodb_buffer_pool_pages_total status variable, 889

innodb_buffer_pool_read_ahead status variable, 889

innodb_buffer_pool_read_ahead_evicted status variable, 889

innodb_buffer_pool_read_requests status variable, 889

innodb_buffer_pool_reads status variable, 889

innodb_buffer_pool_size system variable, 600, 872

innodb_buffer_pool_wait_free status variable, 889

innodb_buffer_pool_write_requests status variable, 889

innodb_change_buffer_max_size system variable, 872

innodb_change_buffering system variable, 872

innodb_checksum_algorithm system variable, 872

innodb_checksums system variable, 873

innodb_commit_concurrency system variable, 873

innodb_concurrency_tickets system variable, 873

innodb_data_file_path system variable, 595, 873

innodb_data_fsyncs status variable, 889

innodb_data_home_dir system variable, 595, 873

innodb_data_pending_fsyncs status variable, 889

innodb_data_pending_reads status variable, 889

innodb_data_pending_writes status variable, 889

innodb_data_read status variable, 889

innodb_data_reads status variable, 889

innodb_data_writes status variable, 889

innodb_data_written status variable, 890

innodb_dblwr_pages_written status variable, 890

innodb_dblwr_writes status variable, 890

innodb_doublewrite system variable, 873

innodb_fast_shutdown system variable, 873

innodb_file_format_check system variable, 873

innodb_file_format_max system variable, 874

innodb_file_format system variable, 873

innodb_file_io_threads system variable, 874

innodb_file_per_table system variable, 111, 599, 874

innodb_flush_log_at_trx_commit system variable, 874

innodb_flush_method system variable, 874

innodb_flush_neighbors system variable, 874

innodb_force_load_corrupted system variable, 875

innodb_force_recovery system variable, 875

innodb_ft_xxx system variable, 875

innodb_have_atomic_builtins status variable, 890

innodb_io_capacity system variable, 875

innodb_io_capacity_max system variable, 875

innodb_large_prefix system variable, 875

innodb_lock_wait-timeout system variable, 875

innodb_locks_unsafe_for_binlog system variable, 875

innodb_log_buffer_size system variable, 600, 876

innodb_log_file_size system variable, 601, 876

innodb_log_files_in_group system variable, 601, 876

innodb_log_group_home_dir system variable, 601, 876

innodb_log_waits status variable, 890

innodb_log_write_requests status variable, 890

innodb_log_writes status variable, 890

innodb_lru_scan_depth system variable, 876

innodb_max_dirty_ages_pct_lwm system variable, 876

innodb_max_dirty_pages_pct system variable, 876

innodb_max_purge_lag system variable, 876

innodb_max_purge_lag_delay system variable, 876

innodb_mirrored_log_groups system variable, 877

innodb_monitor_disable system variable, 877

innodb_monitor_enable system variable, 877

innodb_monitor_reset system variable, 877

innodb_monitor_reset_all system variable, 877

innodb_num_open_files status variable, 890

innodb_old_blocks_pct system variable, 877

innodb_old_blocks_time system variable, 877

innodb_open_files system variable, 877

innodb_os_log_fsyncs status variable, 890

innodb_os_log_pending_fsyncs status variable, 890

innodb_os_log_pending_writes status variable, 890

innodb_os_log_written status variable, 890

innodb_page_size status variable, 890

innodb_page_size system variable, 877

innodb_pages_created status variable, 890

innodb_pages_read status variable, 890

innodb_pages_written status variable, 891

innodb_print_all_deadlocks system variable, 877

innodb_purge_batch_size system variable, 877

innodb_purge_threads system variable, 877

innodb_random_read_ahead system variable, 878

innodb_read_ahead_threshold system variable, 878

innodb_read_io_threads system variable, 878

innodb_replication_delay system variable, 878

innodb_rollback_on_timeout system variable, 878

innodb_rollback_segments system variable, 878

innodb_row_lock_current_waits status variable, 891

innodb_row_lock_time status variable, 891

innodb_row_lock_time_avg status variable, 891

innodb_row_lock_time_max status variable, 891

innodb_row_lock_waits status variable, 891

innodb_rows_deleted status variable, 891

innodb_rows_inserted status variable, 891

innodb_rows_read status variable, 891

innodb_rows_updated status variable, 891

innodb_sort_buffer_size system variable, 878

innodb_spin_wait_delay system variable, 878

innodb_stats_method system variable, 878

innodb_stats_on_metadata system variable, 879

innodb_stats_persistent_sample_pages system variable, 879

innodb_stats_sample_pages system variable, 879

innodb_stats_transient_sample_pages system variable, 879

innodb_strict_mode system variable, 879

innodb_support_xa system variable, 879

innodb_sync_spin_loops system variable, 879

innodb_table_locks system variable, 879

innodb_thread_concurrency system variable, 880

innodb_thread_sleep_delay system variable, 880

innodb_truncated_status_writes status variable, 891

innodb_undo_directory system variable, 880

innodb_undo_logs system variable, 880

innodb_undo_tablespaces system variable, 880

innodb_use_native_aio system variable, 880

innodb_use_sys_malloc system variable, 880

innodb_version system variable, 880

innodb_write_io_threads system variable, 880

innodb_xxx status variable, 884

input editing commands, 90-91

input line editing, 90-91

input parameters
    CGI.pm function, 462
    PHP, 511-512

INSERT() function, 794

INSERT privilege, 664

INSERT statement, 943-946
    data loading, 301
    double-quoting strings in Perl DBI, 417-418
    rows, adding, 50-52

insert_id system variable, 845

insert_rows() function, 381-385
INSTALL PLUGIN statement, 591, 946
install_driver() function, Web: 1136
installed_drivers() function, Web: 1136
installing
    MySQL, 737-739
        data directory, initializing, 740-741
        grant tables, initializing, 740-741
        login accounts, creating, 738-739
        PATH environment variable,
          configuring, 739-740
        system tables, initializing, 742-743
        Unix, 739
        Windows, 739
    PDO, 743
    Perl DBI software, 743
    PHP, 743-745
INSTR() function, 794
INT data type, 193, 750
    ranges, 197
    storage requirements, 197
integer columns, creating, 46, 48
integer data types, 749-751
    BIGINT, 750-751
    INT, 750
    MEDIUMINT, 750
    SMALLINT, 750
    TINYINT, 749
integer division (DIV) operator, 57
interactive online quizzes, creating, 522-527
    checking user responses, 527
    creating questions, 523-525
    form hidden fields, creating, 525-526
    presenting questions, 525
    user response submissions, 526
interactive statement-execution program,
    368-369
interactive_timeout system variable, 845
interfaces
    database-access (PHP), 485-486
    plugin
        activation state, 592
        case sensitivity, 591
        components, 590
        displaying plugins, 592
        library suffix, 590
        loading plugins at runtime, 591
        loading plugins at startup, 591
        operations, 590
        uninstalling plugins, 592
internal locking, 702-703
    all tables at once, 705
    read-only access, 703-704
    read/write, 704-705
    single sessions, 703
    statements, 703
internal security risks, 645
internationalization
    default character set/collation, 603-604
    defined, 601
    error message language, 604
    locale, 604-605
    time zones, configuring, 602-603
interpret_argument() function, 445
INTERVAL() function, 779
inTransaction() function, Web: 1164
introducers, 187
invoker privileges, 276
IP address functions, 826-828
IPv4/IPv6 addresses, 657
IS_FREE_LOCK() function, 826
IS_IPV4() function, 827
IS_IPV4_COMPAT() function, 827
IS_IPV4_MAPPED() function, 827
IS_IPV6() function, 828
IS NOT NULL operator, 243
IS NULL operator, 243
is_null() function, 504
IS_USED_LOCK() function, 826
ISNULL() function, 779
ITERATE statements, 988

J

join_buffer_size system variable, 845
joins
    column references, qualifying, 138-139
    inner, 137-138
    LEFT, 82
    multiple tables example, 78-83
    outer, 139-143
    query optimizer support, 289
    SELECT statements, 955-956

single table, 83-84
STRAIGHT_JOIN, 287
subqueries, converting, 149
 matching values, 149-150
 nonmatching values, 150

K

keep_files_on_create system variable, 845
key_blocks_not_flushed status variable, 884
key_blocks_unused status variable, 884
key_blocks_used status variable, 884
key_buffer_size system variable, 845
key_cache_age_threshold system variable, 846
key_cache_block_size system variable, 846
key_cache_limit system variable, 846
key_read_requests status variable, 884
key_reads status variable, 884
key_write_requests status variable, 884
key_writes status variable, 884
keywords (Web table searches), 479-482
KILL statement, 946

L

language system variable, 846
languages, error message, selecting, 604
large_files_support system variable, 846
large_page_size system variable, 846
large_pages system variable, 846
LAST_DAY() function, 810
LAST_INSERT_ID() function, 831
 AUTO_INCREMENT columns, 231
 sequences, creating, 237-239
last_insert_id system variable, 846
last_query_cost status variable, 884
last_query_partial_plane status variable, 884
lastInsertId() function, Web: 1164
latin1 character set, 104
lc_messages system variable, 604, 846
lc_messages_dir system variable, 604, 846
lc_time_names system variable, 604, 846
LCASE() function, 794
LEAST() function, 779
LEAVE statements, 989
LEFT() function, 794
left joins, 82, 139-143

length
 data types, 748
 identifiers, 98
 string data types, 205
LENGTH() function, 753, 794
less than (<) operator, 57, 243, 770
less than or equal to (<=) operator, 57, 243, 770
li() function, 473
license system variable, 847
LIKE clause
 SHOW statements, 131
 SHOW STATUS statement, 589
 SHOW VARIABLES statement, 585
LIKE/NOT LIKE operators, 243-244, 776-777
LIMIT clause
 db_browse.pl script, 475
 query results, limiting, 63-64
limiting query results, 63-64
LINES clause, 944
Linux, log rotating, 628
live hyperlinks, creating, 499-500
LN() function, 786
LOAD DATA statement, 300-301, 946-951
 data files, loading, 52-53
 data formats, 948
 FIELDS clause options, 948-949
 LINES clause, 949-950
 LOCAL keyword, 947
 special characters, 948
LOAD INDEX INTO CACHE statement, 951
LOAD XML statement, 951-952
load_defaults() function
 defined, 332
 security, 335
 show_argv program example, 332-333
LOAD_FILE() function, 831
load_image() function, 367
loading
 data, 300-303
 dropping/deactivating indexes, 302-303
 index flushing, reducing, 301-302
 INSERT statement, 301
 LOAD DATA statement, 300-301
 mixed-query environments, 303
 shorter statements, 302

plugins
    runtime, 591
    startup, 591
LOCAL keyword, 941
local_infile system variable, 847
locale, selecting, 604-605
localization
    default character set/collation, 603-604
    defined, 601
    error message language, 604
    locale, 604-605
    time zones, configuring, 602-603
LOCALTIME() function, 810
LOCALTIMESTAMP() function, 810
LOCATE() function, 794
LOCK TABLES privilege, 664
LOCK TABLES statement, 304, 702, 952-953
lock_wait_timeout system variable, 786, 847
locked_in_memory system variable, 847
locking
    advisory functions, 813-814
    all tables at once, 705
    levels, 303-305
    overview, 702-703
    read-only access, 703-704
    read/write, 704-705
    single sessions, 703
    statements, 703
    tables, 303-305
LOG() function, 783
log system variable, 847
LOG2() function, 787
LOG10() function, 787
log_bin system variable, 847
log_bin_basename system variable, 847
log_bin_index system variable, 847
log_bin_trust_function_creators system
  variable, 847
log_error system variable, 847
log_output system variable, 848
log_queries_not_using_indexes system variable,
  848
log_slave_updates system variable, 848
log_slow_queries system variable, 848
log_throttle_queries_not_using_indexes system
  variable, 848

log_warnings system variable, 620, 848
logical operators, 772
    AND (&&), 773
    listing of, 57, 241-242
    natural language distinctions, 59
    NOT (!), 772
    NULL values, 247
    OR (||), 773
    XOR, 773
login accounts, creating, 738-739
logrotate utility, 628
logs
    age-based expiration, 625
    binary, 556, 618
        administration, 622-623
        expiring, 629-630
        formats, 731
        index files, 623
        post-backup statements, re-executing,
        723-725
        system backups, 623
    enabling, 619
    error, 556, 620-621
        defined, 618
        event scheduler, 274
        levels, selecting, 620
        multiple servers, 634
        Unix, 620
        Windows, 621
    expiring, 629-631
        automating, 630-631
        binary, 629-630
        relay, 630
    fixed-name, rotating, 626-629
    flushing, 626
    general query, 556, 618, 621
    listing of, 554, 617-618
    maintenance, 539
    multiple servers, 634
    output destination, selecting, 624-625
    relay, 618, 624, 630
    relocating, 561-562
    replication-related expiration, 625
    rotating, 625-629
    security, 556
    slow query, 618

tables
    rotating, 625, 631
    truncating, 625, 631
    writing to, 625
long_query_time system variable, 848
LONGBLOB data type, 204, 207-208
LONGBLOB strings, 194, 756
LONGTEXT data type, 204, 207-208
LONGTEXT strings, 194, 758
looks_like_number() function, Web: 1148
LOOP statements, 989
low_priority_updates system variable, 849
LOWER() function, 795
lower_case_file_system system variable, 849
lower_case_table_names system variable, 100, 849
LPAD() function, 795
LTRIM() function, 795

M

mailing lists, 80
maintenance
    backups, 707-709
        best practices, 709
        binary, 714-715
        InnoDB, 715-716
        selecting, 708
        slave, creating, 732-733
        storage engine portability, 709-710
        text, 711-714
        types, 708
    checking tables
        CHECK TABLE statement, 719-720
        InnoDB tables, 718
        MyISAM tables, 719
        mysqlcheck utility, 720-721
    databases
        backing up, 540
        crash recovery, 541
        preventive, 540
    logs, 539
    preventive
        auto-recovery, 706
        databases, 699-700
        scheduling, 707
        server cooperation, 700-701
        tables, 700
        tools, 700
        Unix login, 701
    repairing tables
        InnoDB tables, 718
        MyISAM tables, 719
        mysqlcheck utility, 720-721
        REPAIR TABLE statement, 720
    replication
        binary logging formats, 731
        compatibility guidelines, 727-728
        master-slave, 728-731
        overview, 727
        slave backups, creating, 732-733
    server interference, preventing, 701
        internal locking, 702-703
        locking all tables at once, 705
        read-only locking, 703-704
        read/write locking, 704-705
        shutting down servers, 702
    user accounts, 539
MAKE_SET() function, 795
MAKEDATE() function, 810
Makefiles, 322-323
MAKETIME() function, 811
master_info_repository system variable, 849
MASTER_POS_WAIT() function, 831
master-slave replication, 728-731
    master server settings, 728-729
    master.info file, 730
    relay logs, 731
    separate slave accounts, 730
    server ID values, assigning, 728
    slave settings, 729-730
    statements, 730-731
    threads, starting/stopping, 731
master_verify_checksum system variable, 850
master.info file, 730
MATCH() function, 796-797
MATCH operator, full-text searches
    boolean mode, 174-175
    natural language, 172-174
    query expansion, 175-176
MAX() function, 76, 820
max_allowed_packet system variable, 850
max_binlog_cache_size system variable, 850
max_binlog_size system variable, 850

max_binlog_stmt_cache_size, 850

max_connect_errors system variable, 850

max_connections system variable, 850

max_delayed_threads system variable, 850

max_error_count system variable, 851

max_heap_table_size system variable, 851

max_insert_delayed_threads system variable, 851

max_join_size system variable, 851

max_length_for_sort_data system variable, 851

max_prepared_stmt_count system variable, 851

max_relay_log_size system variable, 624, 630, 851

max_seeks_for_key system variable, 852

max_sort_length system variable, 852

max_sp_recursion_depth system variable, 852

max_tmp_tables system variable, 852

max_used_connections status variable, 884

max_user_connections system variable, 852

max_value member (my_option structures), 341

max_write_lock_count system variable, 852

maximum value summaries, 76

MD5() function, 823

MEDIUMBLOB data type, 204, 207-208

MEDIUMBLOB strings, 194, 756

MEDIUMINT data type, 193, 750
    ranges, 197
    storage requirements, 197

MEDIUMTEXT data type, 204, 207-208

MEDIUMTEXT strings, 194

member_id columns, creating, 36

member table, 33
    creating, 35-38
    expiration column, 36
    member_id column, 36

membership
    list tables, creating, 33
    renewal notifications, sending, 443-448
    tables, creating, 35-38

MEMORY storage engine, 108
    data, representing, 548
    locking levels, 304
    overview, 111-112
    portability, 710
    row storage formats, 299
    sequence characteristics, 234-235

MERGE storage engine, 108, 113, 304

metadata
    accessing, 130
        command line, 135
        INFORMATION_SCHEMA database, 132-135
        SHOW statement, 130-132
    result sets
        C client programs, 359-364
            availability, 359
            column information structures, accessing, 364
            defined, 359
            displaying, 360-364
            result set data processing decisions, 359
        metadata, displaying, 364
        Perl DBI scripts, 430-434

metadata_locks_cache_size system variable, 852

methods. See functions

MICROSECOND() function, 811

MID() function, 797

migrating databases, 541

MIN() function, 76, 820

min_examined_row_limit system variable, 852

min_value member (my_option structures), 341

minimum value summaries, 76

MINUTE() function, 811

mixed format logging, 731

MOD() function, 787

MODIFY clause, 128

modules (CGI.pm), 459-460
    HTML
        structures, 461
        text, escaping, 464-465
        XHTML, compared, 464
    importing functions, 461
    input parameters, 462
    multiple-purpose pages, writing, 465-468
    object-oriented, 461-462
    output, generating, 462-464
    portability, 463
    URL text, escaping, 464-465

modulo (%) operator, 57, 241, 767

MONTH() function, 67, 811

MONTHNAME() function, 67, 811

multiple-client environments, 156
multiple-data retrieval
    joins, 138-139
    subqueries, 144
multiple-line SQL statements, 28
multiple-purpose pages, writing, 465-468
multiple servers, 632
    administration, 539
    client programs, running, 641
    configuring, 635
    error log file names, 634
    InnoDB log location, 634
    issues, 632-635
    new servers, passwords, 569
    options
        directory, 633
        login accounts, 635
        network interface, 633
        replication slaves, 634
        startup, 636-637
        status/log file names, 634
    Unix, 637-639
    Windows, 639-641
multiple-statement execution, 375-377
    enabling, 375
    process_multi_statement() function, 376-377
    result retrieval functions, 375
multiple-tables
    deletes, 154-155
    queries, 78-84
    retrievals
        joins. See joins
        subqueries. See subqueries
        UNION statements, 151-154
    updates, 155-156
multiple-user access benefit, 13
multiplication (*) operator, 57, 241, 767
my_init() function, 326
my_option structures, 339
    app_type, 341
    arg_type, 341
    block_size, 341
    comment, 340
    def_value, 341
    id, 339
    max_value, 341

min_value, 341
name, 339
sub_size, 341
typelib, 340
u_max_value, 340
value, 340
var_type, 340-341
my_print_defaults program, 1011
MyISAM storage engine, 108
    auto-recovery, 706
    checking/repairing tables, 719
    data, representing, 548
    features, 111
    locking levels, 304
    portability, 710
    row storage formats, 299
    sequence characteristics, 232-234
    table maximum size, 552
myisam_data_pointer_size system variable, 852
myisam_max_sort_file_size system variable, 853
myisam_mmap_size system variable, 853
myisam_recover_options system variable, 853
myisam_repair_threads system variable, 853
myisam_sort_buffer_size system variable, 853
myisam_stats_method system variable, 853
myisam_use_mmap system variable, 853
myisamchk utility
    defined, 538
    maintenance advantages, 719
    options
        specific to myisamchk, 1015-1018
        standard, 1014
    overview, 1013-1014
    table maintenance, 700
    variables, 1018-1019
MySQL
    benefits, 11-12
        availability, 14
        capabilities, 14
        client/server architecture, 22
        connectivity, 22
        cost, 17
        easy, 16
        flexible output format, 13
        flexible retrieval order, 13

multiple-user access, 13
open distribution/source code, 21
portability, 16
query language support, 20
record filing time reduction, 13
record retrieval time reduction, 13
remote access, 13
security, 22
speed, 13
Web-based inventory searches, 14
installing, 737-738, 739
   data directory, initializing, 740-741
   grant tables, initializing, 740-741
   login account, creating, 738-739
   PATH environment variable,
     configuring, 739-740
   system tables, initializing, 742-743
   Unix, 739
   Windows, 739
mailing lists, 80, 642
needs scenarios, 12
pronunciation, 22
reference manual website, 7
server. *See* mysqld
software, updating, 539
Workbench website, 21
mysql database privileges, 673-674
MYSQL structure, Web: 1076
mysql utility, 21
   commands, 1026-1028
   connections, 87
     option files, 87-88
     shell aliases/scripts, 89
     shell command history, 88
   databases, resetting, 53
   defined, 538
   invoking, 25-26
   options
     specific to mysql, listing of,
       1021-1025
     standard, 1021
   overview, 1019-1021
   prompt definition sequences, 1028-1029
   statements
     case-sensitivity, 29
     ending, 27-28
     entering, 27

function syntax, 29
multiple-lines, 28
multiple statements on single line,
   28-29
reading from files, 29
results, displaying, 28
table structure, displaying, 36-37
typing less, 90-93
typing tips
   copy/paste, 92
   script files, 92-93
variables, 1025-1026
MySQL Workbench program, 21
mysql_affected_rows() function, Web: 1104
mysql_autocommit() function, Web: 1116
MYSQL_BIND arrays
   configuring, 384
   select_rows() function, 385-388
MYSQL_BIND data structure, Web: 1082-1086
   input values, Web: 1085
   member purpose, Web: 1083-1084
   output values, Web: 1083-1085
   public members, Web: 1082-1083
mysql_change_user() function, Web: 1090
mysql_character_set_name() function,
   Web: 1113
mysql_close() function, 325, Web: 1090
mysql_commit() function, Web: 1116
mysql_config utility
   defined, 1030
   options, 1030-1031
mysql_data_seek() function, Web: 1106
mysql_debug() function, Web: 1127
mysql_dump_debug_info() function, Web: 1127
mysql_errno() function, 328, Web: 1101
mysql_error() function, 328, Web: 1101
mysql_fetch_field() function, Web: 1106
mysql_fetch_field_direct() function, Web: 1107
mysql_fetch_fields() function, Web: 1106-1107
mysql_fetch_lengths() function,
   Web: 1107-1108
mysql_fetch_row() function, 351-352,
   Web: 1108
MYSQL_FIELD data structure, Web: 1076-1080
mysql_field_count() function, Web: 1108-1109
mysql_field_tell() function, Web: 1110
mysql_field_seek() function, Web: 1109
mysql_free_result() function, 351, Web: 1110

mysql_get_character_set_info() function,
    Web: 1090

mysql_get_client_info() function, Web: 1114

mysql_get_client_version() function, Web: 1114

mysql_get_host_info() function, Web: 1114

mysql_get_proto_info() function, Web: 1114

mysql_get_server_info() function, Web: 1114

mysql_get_server_version() function,
    Web: 1114

mysql_get_ssl_cipher() function, Web: 1091

mysql_hex_string() function, Web: 1102

mysql_info() function, Web: 1114-1115

mysql_init() function, 325, Web: 1091

mysql_insert_id() function, Web: 1110-1111

mysql_install_db script, 1031-1032

    specific to mysql_install_db, 1032
    standard options, 1032

mysql_library_end() function, 326, Web: 1089

mysql_library_init() function, 326, Web: 1089

mysql_more_results() function, 375,
    Web: 1113

mysql_next_result() function, 375, Web: 1113

mysql_num_fields() function, Web: 1111

mysql_num_rows() function, Web: 1111

mysql_options() function, Web: 1091-1096

    example, Web: 1092
    options, Web: 1092-1095
    reading option files options,
        Web: 1095-1096

mysql_ping() function, Web: 1096

mysql_query() function, 349, Web: 1102

mysql_real_connect() function, 325, 375,
    Web: 1097-1099

    client connection protocols, Web: 1097
    flags values, Web: 1097-1099
        specific to mysql_upgrade, 1033-1034
        standard options, 1033

mysql_real_escape_string() function, 365,
    Web: 1103-1104

mysql_real_query() function, 349, Web: 1104

mysql_refresh() function, Web: 1125-1126

MYSQL_RES data structure, Web: 1080

mysql_rollback() function, Web: 1116

MYSQL_ROW data type, 352, Web: 1080-1082

mysql_row_tell() function, Web: 1112

mysql_row_seek() function, Web: 1112

mysql_select_db() function, Web: 1100

mysql_server_end() function, Web: 1089

mysql_server_init() function, Web: 1089

mysql_set_character_set() function, Web: 1100

mysql_set_server_option() function, 375,
    Web: 1126

mysql_shutdown() function, Web: 1126

mysql_sqlstate() function, 328, Web: 1101

mysql_ssl_set() function, Web: 1100

mysql_stat() function, Web: 1115

MYSQL_STMT data structure, Web: 1082

mysql_stmt_affected_rows() function,
    Web: 1120

mysql_stmt_attr_get() function, Web: 1120

mysql_stmt_attr_set() function, Web: 1121

mysql_stmt_bind_param() function, Web: 1118

mysql_stmt_bind_result() function, Web: 1121

mysql_stmt_close() function, 388, Web: 1118

mysql_stmt_data_seek() function, Web: 1122

mysql_stmt_error() function, Web: 1117

mysql_stmt_errno() function, Web: 1117

mysql_stmt_execute() function, Web: 1118

mysql_stmt_fetch() function, 388, Web: 1122

mysql_stmt_fetch_column() function,
    Web: 1122

mysql_stmt_field_count() function, Web: 1122

mysql_stmt_free_result() function, 388,
    Web: 1123

mysql_stmt_init() function, 380, Web: 1118

mysql_stmt_insert_id() function, Web: 1123

mysql_stmt_next_result() function, Web: 1123

mysql_stmt_num_rows() function, Web: 1123

mysql_stmt_param_count(), Web: 1124

mysql_stmt_prepare() function, Web: 1119

mysql_stmt_reset() function, Web: 1119

mysql_stmt_result_metadata() function,
    Web: 1119

mysql_stmt_row_tell() function, Web: 1124

mysql_stmt_row_seek() function, Web: 1124

mysql_stmt_send_long_data() function,
    Web: 1120

mysql_stmt_sqlstate() function, Web: 1117

mysql_stmt_store_result() function, Web: 1124

mysql_store_result() function, 351, 357-359,
    Web: 1112

MYSQL_TIME data structure, Web: 1086-1087

mysql_thread_end() function, Web: 1126

mysql_thread_id() function, Web: 1116

mysql_thread_init() function, Web: 1126

mysql_thread_safe() function, Web: 1127

mysql_upgrade utility, 1033

mysql_use_result() function, 351, 357-359,
    Web: 1112

mysql_warning_count() function, Web: 1116

mysqladmin utility, 1034
  commands, 1035-1037
  defined, 538
  options
    specific to mysqladmin, 1034-1035
    standard, 1034
  variables, 1013-1035

mysqlbinlog utility, 622
  options
    specific to mysqlbinlog, 1038-1041
    standard, 1038
  overview, 1038
  variables, 1041

mysqlcheck utility
  checking/repairing tables, 720-721
  defined, 538
  maintenance, scheduling, 707
  options
    specific to mysqlcheck, 1042-1044
    standard, 1041-1042
    table analysis, 1044
    table checking, 1044
    table optimization, 1044-1045
    table repair, 1044
  overview, 1041
  table maintenance, 700

mysqld, 21
  administration
    configuration and tuning, 539
    log maintenance, 539
    multiple servers, 539
    MySQL software updates, 539
    startup/shutdown, 539
    user account maintenance, 539
  client access control, 686-687
  connections, listening, 579-580
  data directory access, 546-547
  defined, 538
  login accounts, 571-572
  maintenance interference, preventing, 701
    internal locking, 702-703
    locking all tables at once, 705
    read-only locking, 703-704
    read/write locking, 704-705
    shutting down mysqld, 702
  options
    replication, 1053-1056
    specific to mysqld, listing of, 1046-1053
    standard, 1045-1046
    Windows, 1053
  overview, 1045
  restarting manually, 581-582
  root password, resetting, 582-583
  security, 540
  starting, 741
    Unix, 741
    Windows, 742
  startup options, 577-579
  stopping, 580-581
  Unix
    connections, listening, 579
    running, 570
    starting, 572-574
    unprivileged login account, configuring, 571-572
  variables, 1056
  Windows, 575
    connections, listening, 580
    running as Windows service, 576-577
    running manually, 575

mysqld_multi script, 637-639, 1056
  specific to mysqld_multi option, 1057
  standard options, 1056-1057

mysqld_safe, 1058
  specific to mysqld_safe option, 1058-1059
  standard options, 1058

mysqldump utility, 21, 135
  data format options, 1067-1068
  database maintenance, 700
  defined, 538
  options, 712-714
    specific to mysqldump, 1061-1067
    standard, 1060
  overview, 1060
  text dump files
    all tables from all databases, 711
    compressing, 712
    creating, 711-714
    individual files, 711
    output, 711-712

table subsets into separate files, creating, 712

variables, 1068

mysqldumpslow utility, 621

mysqlimport utility

data files, loading, 53

options

data format, 1070

specific to mysqlimport, 1069-1070

standard, 1068

overview, 1068

mysql.server utility, 1029-1030

mysqlshow utility, 38, 135

options

specific, 1071

standard, 1071

overview, 1070-1071

mytbl.frm file, 548

mytbl.MYD file, 548

mytbl.MYI file, 548

N

NAME_CONST() function, 831

named_pipe system variable, 853

names

aliases

case sensitivity, 100

quoting with identifiers, 98

case sensitivity

aliases, 100

columns, 100

databases, 100

files, 100

functions, 99

indexes, 100

stored programs, 100

tables, 100

triggers, 100

views, 100

collations, 186

columns, 64-66, 263-264

data types, 747

files, 550-551

functions, 98

my_option structures, 339

Perl DBI handles, 397

Perl DBI non handle variables, 397

PHP scripts, 486

qualified, 99

stored functions, 269

system variables, 836

tables, 32

files, 109

renaming, 129-130

temporary, 116

triggers, 272

user accounts, 656-658

account value, 656

hostnames, 656-657

IPv4/IPv6 addresses, 657

localhost, 658

matching host values to DNS, 658-659

quoting, 658

usernames, 657

wildcards, 657

variables, Web: 1131

Windows file paths, 424-425

natural language searches, 170, 172-174

NDB storage engine, 108, 112

neat() function, Web: 1148

neat_list() function, Web: 1148-1149

need_renewal.pl script, 443-444

negation operator (~), 774

net_buffer_length system variable, 854

net_read_timeout system variable, 854

net_retry_count system variable, 854

net_write_timeout system variable, 854

network interface options (multiple servers), 633

new PDO() function, 490

new system variable, 854

nextRowset() function, Web: 1170-1171

NO_ARG arg_type, 341

NO_AUTO_CREATE_USER, 863

NO_AUTO_VALUE_ON_ZERO, 863

NO_BACKSLASH_ESCAPES, 863

NO_DIR_IN_CREATE, 863

NO_ENGINE_SUBSTITUTION, 864

NO_FIELD_OPTIONS, 864

NO_KEY_OPTIONS, 864

NO_TABLE_OPTIONS, 864

NO_UNSIGNED_SUBTRACTION, 864

NO_ZERO_DATE, 864
NO_ZERO_IN_DATE, 864
nonbinary strings, 756-758
    binary strings, compared, 188-189
    CHAR, 756-757
    conversions, 255
    defined, 185
    LONGTEXT, 758
    MEDIUMTEXT, 758
    sorting properties, 186
    TEXT, 757-758
    TINYTEXT, 757
    VARCHAR, 757
nonbreaking spaces, 475
non-NULL values, counting, 73
nonrepeatable reads, 162
nonscalar data structures (C API),
    Web: 1076-1087
    MYSQL, Web: 1076
    MYSQL_BIND, Web: 1082-1086
        input values, Web: 1085
        member purpose, Web: 1083-1084
        output values, Web: 1083-1085
        public members, Web: 1082-1083
    MYSQL_FIELD, Web: 1076-1080
    MYSQL_RES, Web: 1080
    MYSQL_ROW, Web: 1080-1082
    MYSQL_STMT, Web: 1082
    MYSQL_TIME, Web: 1086-1087
nontransactional tables, 229
NOT BETWEEN operator, 243
not equal to (!=, < >) operators, 57, 243
NOT EXISTS subqueries, 147-148
NOT IN subqueries, 145-146
NOT LIKE operator, 243
NOT NULL values
    data types for query optimization, 297
    numeric data types, 203
    string data types, 216
    temporal data types, 223
NOT (!) operator, 57, 241, 774
NOT REGEXP operator, 243
not_flushed_delayed_rows status variable, 885
notify_member() function, 446
NOW() function, 811
N'str' notation, 187

null-safe equality operator (<=>), 769
NULL values, 60-61, 192
    AUTO_INCREMENT columns, 231
    column sort, 62
    directory membership updates, 535-536
    expressions, 246-247
    foreign key relationships, 168-170
    numeric data types, 203
    result sets, checking, 416, 504
    sequence columns, 231
    string data types, 216
    temporal data types, 223
NULLIF() function, 780
numbers
    hexadecimal, 253
    sequences. *See* sequences
    string conversions, 249-250
numeric data types, 193, 748-749
    attributes, 201-203, 749
    BIT, 197, 200-201, 752
    exact-value, 197-199
    fixed-point, 751
    floating-point, 197, 200, 751-752
        DOUBLE, 752
        FLOAT[(M,D)], 752
        FLOAT(p), 751
    improper values, 228
    integer, 749-751
        BIGINT, 750-751
        INT, 750
        MEDIUMINT, 750
        SMALLINT, 750
        TINYINT, 749
    listing of, 193
    NULL/NOT NULL values, 203
    query optimization, 296
    ranges, 197
    selecting, 203, 257-258
    storage requirements, 197-198
numeric functions, 784-789
numeric values, 181
    approximate, 181-182
    bit-field, 182
    exact, 181-182
    retrieving, 56

O

object privileges, 663-665, 681-682
OCT() function, 201, 797
OCTET_LENGTH() function, 797
old system variable, 854
old_alter_table system variable, 854
OLD_PASSWORD() function, 823
old_passwords system variable, 854
ON clause, 937-938
ON DELETE CASCADE clause, 166-167
ON DELETE SET NULL clause, 169
ON specifier, 665
ON UPDATE CASCADE clause, 166-167
ON UPDATE SET NULL clause, 169
online score-entry script. See score_entry.php
    script
ONLY_FULL_GROUP_BY, 864
open_files status variable, 885
open_files_limit system variable, 854
Open Geospatial Consortium Web site, 191
OPEN statements, 992
open_streams status variable, 885
open_table_definitions status variable, 885
open_tables status variable, 885
opened_files status variable, 885
opened_table_definitions status variable, 885
opened_tables status variable, 885
operand conversions, 187
operating systems, identifier constraints,
    550-551
operators
    IN, 145-146
    ALL, 146-147
    ANY, 146-147
    arithmetic, 57, 766-767
        addition, 766
        DIV, 767
        division, 767
        listing of, 241
        modulo, 767
        multiplication, 767
        NULL values, 246
        rules, 766
        subtraction, 767
    bit
        AND, 773
        exclusive-OR, 773

listing of, 242
negation, 774
NULL values, 246
OR, 773
shift left, 773
shift right, 773
cast, 775-776
comparison, 57, 768-772
    CASE [expr] WHEN expr1 THEN
        result1 ... [ELSE default] END, 771
    equal, 769
    expr BETWEEN min AND max,
        770-771
    expr IN (value1,value2,...), 772
    expr IS, 772
    expr IS NULL/expr IS NOT NULL, 772
    expr NOT BETWEEN min AND max,
        770-771
    expr NOT IN (value1,value2,...), 772
    greater than, 770
    greater than or equal to, 770
    less than, 770
    less than or equal to, 770
    listing of, 243
    NULL values, 247
    null-safe equality, 769
    rules, 768-769
    unequal, 770
EXISTS, 147-148
format, 763
grouping, 765-766
IN(), 59
logical, 772
    AND (&&), 774
    listing of, 57, 241-242
    natural language distinctions, 59
    NOT (!), 772
    NULL values, 247
    OR (||), 773
    XOR, 773
MATCH
    boolean mode, 174-175
    natural language, 172-174
    query expansion, 175-176
NOT EXISTS, 147-148
NOT IN, 145-146

pattern-matching, 776-780
  LIKE/NOT LIKE, 776-777
  REGEXP/NOT REGEXP, 777-780
  RLIKE/NOT LIKE pattern, 780
precedence, 246, 764-765
relative comparison, 144-145
SOME, 146-147
syntax, 764
OPT_ARG arg_type, 341
optimization, 277
  data loading, 300-303
    dropping/deactivating indexes, 302-303
    index flushing, reducing, 301-302
    INSERT statement, 301
    LOAD DATA statement, 300-301
    mixed-query environments, 303
    shorter statements, 302
  data types, selecting, 296-298
    BLOB/TEXT, 298
    ENUM, 297
    NOT NULL, 297
    numbers, 296
    PROCEDURE ANALYSE() function, 297
    smallest types, 296-297
    strings, 296
    tables, defragmenting, 297
  indexing, 278
    benefits, 278-281
    columns, selecting, 281-285
    costs, 281
  query optimizer, 286-290
    alternative forms of queries, testing, 289
    EXPLAIN output, 290-296
    hints/overrides, 287
    identical data type columns, comparing, 288
    joins versus subquery support, 289
    operation, verifying, 287
    restrictive tests, 286
    stand alone indexed columns in comparison expressions, 288-289
    table order, forcing, 287
    tables, analyzing, 287
    type conversions, 289-290

row storage formats, 299
  displaying/editing, 300
  InnoDB, 299-300
  MEMORY, 299
  MyISAM, 299
scheduling policies, 303
storage engine locking levels, 303-305
OPTIMIZE TABLE statement, 953-954
optimizer_prune_level system variable, 855
optimizer_search_depth system variable, 855
optimizer_switch system variable, 855
optimizer_trace_xxx system variable, 855
option files
  connection parameters, reading, 424
  logging, enabling, 619
  mysql program connection parameters, 87-88
  mysqld startup, 578
  plugins, loading, 591
  reading, 332-335, 424
  securing, 653-654
  SSL, 697
  system variables, setting, 586
  Unix, 1007
  utility, 1007-1011
    escape sequences, 1010
    leading spaces, 1010
    read directives, 1010-1011
    user-specific option privacy, 1011
  Web scripts security, 470-471
  Windows, 424-425, 1008
options
  CHANGE MASTER statement, 907
  CHECK TABLE statement, 909
  command-line, 335-343
    argument vector, processing, 342
    option information, defining, 339-341
    show_opt, invoking, 342-343
    show_opt program source file, 336-338
  connect2 program, 344-348
    connect1/show_opt programs, compared, 347
    connection parameters, specifying, 348
    running, 347
    source file, 344-347

CREATE TABLE statement, 916-918
FLUSH statement, 933-934
groups, 578
myisamchk utility
    specific to myisamchk, listing of,
        1015-1018
    standard, 1014
mysql utility
    specific to mysql, listing of,
        1021-1025
    standard, 1021
mysql_config utility, 1030-1031
mysql_install_db script
    specific, 1032
    standard, 1032
mysqladmin client
    specific to mysqladmin, 1034-1035
    standard, 1034
mysqlbinlog
    specific to mysqlbinlog, 1038-1041
    standard, 1038
mysqlcheck
    specific to mysqlcheck, 1042-1044
    standard, 1041-1042
    table analysis, 1044
    table checking, 1044
    table optimization, 1044-1045
    table repair, 1044
mysqld
    replication, 1053-1056
    specific to mysqld, listing of,
        1046-1053
    standard, 1045-1046
    Windows, 1053
mysqld_multi
    specific to mysqld_multi, 1057
    standard, 1056-1057
mysqld_safe
    specific to mysqld_safe, 1058-1059
    standard, 1058
mysql_upgrade
    specific options, 1033-1034
    standard, 1033
mysqldump utility, 712-714
    data format, 1067-1068
    specific to mysqldump, 1061-1067
    standard, 1060

mysqlimport
    data format, 1070
    specific, 1069-1070
    standard, 1068
mysql.server utility, 1030
mysqlshow
    specific to mysqlshow, 1071
    standard, 1071
option files, 332-335
perror, 1072
SELECT statements, 954-955
SSL, adding to clients, 370-372
utilities
    case sensitivity, 1001
    checking, 1011
    escape sequences, 1010
    group names, 1009
    leading spaces, 1010
    long-form/short-form, 1001
    option-file processing, 1008-1009
    option files, 1007-1011
    processing features, 1002
    quoting, 1010
    read directives, 1010-1011
    SSL, 1006
    standard, 1003-1005
    user-specific option privacy, 1011
    variables, 1006-1007
values, holding, 372-373
OR operator (||), 57, 241-242, 773
ORD() function, 797
ORDER BY RAND() function, 64, 523
outer joins, 139-143
output
    CGI.pm generating, 462-464
    column values, naming, 64-66
    format flexibility, 13
    query optimizer EXPLAIN statements,
        290-296
        efficiency with indexes, 292-296
        expression writing style, selecting,
            290-292
overall count of values, counting, 73
overindexing, 284
override parameter, 481
ownership
    administrative-only, setting, 649-651
    base directory, displaying, 650

P

PAD_CHAR_TO_FULL_LENGTH, 865
param() function, 462
parameters
    action, 513
    binding (Perl DBI), 421-423
    connection, specifying
        C client programs, 331
            command-line option-handling,
            335-343
            connect2 program, 348
            option files, reading, 332-335
        Perl DBI, 423-426
    input
        CGI.pm, 462
        PHP, 511-512
    mysql_real_connect() function, 325
    override, 481
    prepared statements, 377-378
    tbl_name
        checking, 473
        db_browse.pl script, 472
    types (stored procedures), 271-272
parentheses ( ), 401
partial binary backups, 715
PARTITION BY clause, 120-121
partitions, creating, 120-121
PASSWORD() function, 823-824
password_field() function, 531
passwords
    Historical League member entries online
        editing script, 527-529
    initial user accounts, assigning, 567-569
    new servers, setting, 569
    old hash format security risk, 673
    root accounts, resetting, 582-583
    user accounts, 672
PATH environment variable, 739-740
pattern matching, 69-70, 243-245
    NULL values, 247
    operators, 776-780
        LIKE/NOT LIKE, 243-244, 776-777
        REGEXP/NOT REGEXP pattern,
        777-780
        RLIKE/NOT LIKE pattern, 780
    Web table searches, 479-482

PDO (PHP Data Objects) extension, 314
    classes, Web: 1158
    errors
        exceptions, 491
        handling, 507-509
    functions, Web: 1159
        constants, Web: 1173-1174
        exceptions, Web: 1172-1173
        PDO class, Web: 1159-1166
        statement handles, Web: 1166-1172
    installing, 743
    placeholders, 506-507
    statements, handling, 500-501
        result sets, 501-504
        row-modifying, 501
    transaction processing, 520
    Web site, 486
PDOStatement statement handle, 501
performance
    APIs, selecting, 315-316
    data directory, 553-554
    optimizing. See optimization
    queries, identifying, 285
performance_schema xxx status variable, 885
performance_schema_xxx system variable, 855
PERIOD_ADD() function, 812
PERIOD_DIFF() function, 812
Perl DBI API, 311-312
    architecture, 311-312
    attributes, Web: 1149
        database-handles, Web: 1149
        dynamic, Web: 1155
        general handle, Web: 1149-1150
        mysql-specific database-handle,
            Web: 1150-1152
        mysql-specific statement-handle,
            Web: 1154-1155
        statement-handles, Web: 1152-1153
    database server connections, 312
    defined, 310
    environment variables, Web: 1156
    functions
        administrative, Web: 1147-1148
        %attr hash argument, Web: 1131
        calling sequence, Web: 1131
        database-handle, Web: 1137-1142
        DBI class, Web: 1132-1136

general handle, Web: 1146
statement-handle, Web: 1142-1145
utility, Web: 1148-1149
portability, 312
scripts, writing. *See* Perl DBI scripts
variable names, Web: 1131
Web site, 395,

Perl DBI scripts, Web: 1130
case sensitivity, 400
characteristics, 396
comments, adding, 398
connect() function arguments, 399-400
connections, 400, 425-426
parameters, specifying, 423-426
data-retrieval script, 397-398
debugging, 426
print statements, 426-428
tracing, 428-429
disconnecting, 402
error handling, 402-405
automatic, 403-404
default error messages, replacing, 404
default settings, 403
dump_members2.pl script example, 404-405
manually checking/printing, 403
PrintError attribute, 403
RaiseError attribute, 403
finish() function, 402
function parentheses, 401
handles, 397
names, 397
nonhandle variables, 397
invoking, 396
option files, securing, 653-654
parameter binding, 421-423
placeholders, 419-421
prepared statements, 421
quoting special characters, 416-419
requirements, 395
result sets
metadata, 430-434
retrieving. *See* result sets, Perl DBI scripts
row-fetching loop, 401-402
row-modifying statements, 406-407
software, installing, 743

statement terminators, 401
transactions, 434-436
undef argument, 422
U.S. Historical League
directory, generating, 436-442
member entries, editing, 448-454
membership renewal notices, sending, 443-448
members with common interests, finding, 454-455
online directory, creating, 455-458
use DBI statement, 399
use strict statements, 399
use warnings statement, 399
warnings mode, 401
Web-based, 459
CGI.pm module. *See* CGI scripts
database browser, 471-475
grade-keeping project score browser, 475-479
security, 470-471
server connections, 468-469
table searches, 479-483
Web server, configuring, 460-461
where-to-find-Perl indicator, 398
Perl modules Web site, 743
perldoc command, 743
permissions
administrative-only, setting, 649-651
base directory, 650
data directory, 650
perror utility
options, 1072
overview, 1072
phantom rows, 162
PHP API
client host that requested the page IP address, displaying, 313
database interfaces, 314, 485-486
defined, 310
functions, Web: 1159
constants, Web: 1173-1174
exceptions, Web: 1172-1173
PDO class, Web: 1159-1166
statement handles, Web: 1166-1172
installing, 743-745
PDO. *See* PDO
scripts, writing. *See* PHP scripts

tag styles, Web: 1157-1158
up-to-the-minute information to visitors script, 313
Web site, 486, 743
PHP scripts
data-retrieval, 497-499
  display values, encoding, 498
  error handling, 498
  home page link, creating, 498-499
  installing/accessing, 498
  result set, returning, 498
directory member entries, editing online, 527-536
  editing form, 533-534
  framework, 529-530
  member login page, 530-531
  null values, 535-536
  passwords, 527-529, 531-533
  updating entries, 534-535
error handling, 507-509
headers/footers functions, 495-497
hello world examples, 487-488
home page, 488-491
include files
  benefits, 491-493
  Historical League example, 495
  locations, establishing, 493-494
  referencing, 494
input parameters, 511-512
interactive online quiz, 522-527
  checking user responses, 527
  creating questions, 523-525
  form hidden fields, creating, 525-526
  presenting questions, 525
  user response submissions, 526
live hyperlinks, creating, 499-500
names, 486
online score-entry, 510-511
  action input parameter, 513
  editing scores, 520-521
  event table cells, generating, 516
  events, displaying, 514-515
  framework, 513-514
  hyperlink URLs, 516
  new event entry form, 516-517
  scores, entering, 517-518
  scores for selected events, displaying, 518-519

transactional data-entry operations, 520
online score-entry application, 522
overview, 487
PDO error exceptions, 491
placeholders, 506-507
prepared statements, 505
quoting special characters, 505-507
row-modifying statements, 501
rows, retrieving, 501-504
  all at once, 504
  arrays, 503
  calculated columns, 503
  default fetch mode, setting, 502
  individual column values, 503
  NULL values, checking, 504
  row-fetching loop, 501-503
  statement handle, 501
samples, installing, 486-487
security, 491
server connection, 490-491
standalone, 489
statements, handling, 500-501
tag styles supported, Web: 1157-1158
variables, 492
Web site
welcome message with membership count home page, 491
PI() function, 787
PID (Process ID) files
overview, 555
relocating, 561-562
pid_file system variable, 855
ping() function, Web: 1138
PIPES_AS_CONCAT mode, enabling, 242
PIPES_AS_CONCAT SQL mode, 96, 865
placeholders
Perl DBI scripts, 419-421
PHP, 506-507
plain text directories, creating, 439-440
pluggable architecture, 589-590
plugin_dir system variable, 855
plugins
activation state, 592
authentication, 676-679
  proxy users, creating, 677-679
  server connections, 677

server side/client side, 677
specifying, 676
case sensitivity, 591
displaying, 592
interface
components, 590
library suffix, 590
operations, 590
loading
runtime, 591
startup, 591
uninstalling, 592
port system variable, 855
portability
APIs, selecting, 317
CGI.pm module, 463
Perl DBI API, 312
storage engines, 709-710
POSITION() function, 798
POSIX character class constructions, 778
POW() function, 787
POWER() function, 787
precedence (operators), 246, 764-765
prefixes (indexing), 283-284
preload_buffer_size system variable, 855
prepare() function, 505, Web: 1138,
    Web: 1164
PREPARE statement, 954
prepare_cached() function, Web: 1138
prepared statements, 377
C client programs
call. See CALL prepared statements
executing, 378-379
inserting rows and retrieving them
    program, writing, 379-388
parameterizing, 377-378
functions, Web: 1112
construction/execution,
    Web: 1113-1114
error-reporting, Web: 1112-1113
result set processing, Web: 1114-1117
Perl DBI, 421
PHP, 505
prepared_stmt_count status variable, 885
pres_quiz.php script, 522-527
checking user responses, 527
creating questions, 523-525
form hidden fields, creating, 525-526

presenting questions, 525
user response submissions, 526
present_question() function, 525
president table, creating, 32, 34-35
preventive maintenance
auto-recovery, 706
backups, 707-709
best practices, 709
binary, 714-715
InnoDB, 715-716
selecting, 708
storage engine portability, 709-710
text, 711-714
types, 708
databases, 699-700
scheduling, 707
server cooperation, 700-701
server interference, preventing, 701
internal locking, 702-703
locking all tables at once, 705
read-only locking, 703-704
read/write locking, 704-705
shutting down servers, 702
tables, 700
tools, 700
Unix login, 701
PRIMARY KEY clause, 36
primary keys
absence table example, 49
converting to unique indexes, 169
defining, 166
score table example, 48
print statements, 427-428
print_dashes() function, 362
print_error() function, 329-330
PrintError attribute, 403
printing binary data, 353
privileges
account administering, enabling,
    669-670
administrative, 666
combining, 665
database-level, 666
definer, 276
displaying, 671
events, 274
global, 666

grant tables
  administrative, 682
  object, 682-681
invoker, 276
no privileges, 668
object, 663-665
PROXY, 667
quoting, 667
resource consumption limits, 670-671
revoking, 671-672
secure connections, requiring, 668-669
specifiers
  ALL, 666
  ALL/USAGE, 661
  levels, 665
stored functions/procedures, 270-271
stored routines, 667
super, 276, 673-674
table/column level, 667
triggers, 273
user accounts
  administrative, 661-663
  granting, 660-661
views, 263
privileges clause, 660
PROCEDURE ANALYSE() function, 297
procedures (stored)
  creating, 268
  defined, 268
  example, 269
  invoking, 269
  parameter types, 271-272
  privileges, 270-271
  security, 275-276
  tables, updating, 270
Process ID files. See PID files
PROCESS privilege, 662, 674-675
process_call_result() function, 392
process_multi_statement() function, 376-377
process_real_statement() function, 356-357
process_result_set() function, 352-353
process_statement() function, 355
processing statements, 348-350
  alternative approaches, 356-357
  binary data, 367-368
  causes of failures, 349
  character-escaping operations, 349

general-purpose statement handler, 354-355
multiple-statement execution, 375-377
mysql_store_result() function, 357-359
mysql_use_result() function, 357-359
prepared statements, 377
  executing, 378-379
  inserting rows and retrieving them
    program, writing, 379-388
  parameterizing, 377-378
quoting special characters, 365-366
result set metadata, 359-364
  availability, 359
  column information structures,
    accessing, 364
  defined, 359
  displaying, 360-364
  result set data processing decisions,
    359
result sets, returning, 351-353
row-modifying, 350, 406-407
sending to server functions, 349
procs_priv table, 680
prompt definition sequences, 1028-1029
prompt() function, 451
protocol_version system variable, 856
proxied_host columns, 689
proxied_user columns, 689
proxies_priv table, 680
PROXY privilege, 662, 667
proxy_user system variable, 856
proxying authentication plugins, 677-679
pseudo_thread_id system variable, 856
PURGE BINARY LOGS statement, 730, 954-955

Q

Qcache_free_blocks status variable, 891
Qcache_free_memory status variable, 891
Qcache_hits status variable, 891
Qcache_inserts status variable, 892
Qcache_lowmem_prunes status variable, 892
Qcache_not_cached status variable, 892
Qcache_queries_in_cache status variable, 892
Qcache_total_blocks status variable, 892
Qcache_xxx status variable, 885
qq (double-quoting strings), 417-418

qualifiers
    identifiers, 98
    joined table column references, 138-139
QUARTER() function, 812
queries
    alternative forms, testing, 289
    badly performing, identifying, 285
    criteria, specifying, 56-59
    dates, 57
        differences between, 68
        operations supported, 66
        parts, retrieving, 67-68
        specific, searching, 66-67
        syntax, 66
    expansion searches, 170, 175-176
    multiple tables. *See* joins; subqueries
    NULL value, 60-61
    numeric ranges, 56
    optimizer, 286-290
        alternative forms of queries, testing,
            289
        EXPLAIN output, 290-296
        hints/overrides, 287
        identical data type columns,
            comparing, 288
        joins *versus* subquery support, 289
        operation, verifying, 287
        restrictive tests, 286
        stand alone indexed columns in
            comparison expressions, 288-289
        table order, forcing, 287
        tables, analyzing, 287
        type conversions, 289-290
    pattern matching, 69-70
    results
        binding to variables, 421-423
        limiting, 63-64
        sorting, 61-63
    several individual values, 59
    string values containing character data,
        56
    summaries
        counting, 72-76
        unique values present in a set of
            values, 72
    table contents, displaying, 54
    terminology, 20-21
    user-defined variables, creating, 71

query() function, 491, Web: 1164-1165
query_alloc_block_size system variable, 856
query_cache status variables, listing of,
    891-892
query_cache_limit system variable, 856
query_cache_min_res_unit system variable,
    856
query_cache_size system variable, 856
query_cache_type system variable, 856
query_cache_wlock_invalidate system variable,
    856
query_prealloc_size system variable, 857
questions status variable, 885
quote() function, 418-419, 505-506, 798,
    Web: 1139, Web: 1165
quote_identifier() function, Web: 1139
quoting
    C client programs, 365-366
    identifiers, 97-98
    options, 1008-1009
    Perl DBI, 416-419
    PHP, 505-507
    privileges, 667
    user account names, 658

R

RADIANS() function, 787
radio_button() function, 526
RAND() function, 787-788
rand_seed1 system variable, 857
rand_seed2 system variable, 857
range_alloc_block_size system variable, 857
ranges
    data types, 748
    numeric data types, 197
    sequence columns, 235
    temporal data types, 218-219
RasieError attribute, 403
raw data values, loading, 52-53
raw partitions, 597-598
RDBMS (relational database management
    system), 18
    banner advertisement table example, 19
    defined, 18-19
READ COMMITTED isolation level, 162
READ UNCOMMITTED isolation level, 162
read_buffer_size system variable, 857

read_file() function, 445
read_only system variable, 857
read-only table locking
    all tables at once, 705
    individual tables, 703-704
read_rnd_buffer_size system variable, 857
reading option files, 332-335
    connection parameters, 424
    Windows, 424-425
read/write table locking, 704-705
REAL_AS_FLOAT, 865
records
    filing time benefit, 13
    multiple-user access, 13
    remote access, 13
    retrieval benefits, 13
recovery, 722
    auto-recovery, 700, 706
    backups, 707-709
        best practices, 709
        binary, 714-715
        InnoDB, 715-716
        selecting, 708
        storage engine portability, 709-710
        text, 711-714
        types, 708
    binary log file statements, re-executing,
        723-725
    databases, 541, 722
    InnoDB auto-recovery failure, 725-726
    tables, 723
REFERENCES privilege, 664
referential integrity, 164. See also foreign keys
REGEXP/NOT REGEXP operators, 243-244,
    777-780
regular expressions
    pattern matching, 775-778
    POSIX character class constructions, 778
regular indexes, 123
relational database management system. See
    RDBMS
relative comparison operators, 144-145
relay_log system variable, 857
relay_log_basename system variable, 857
relay_log_index system variable, 857
relay_log_info_file system variable, 857
relay_log_info_repository system variable, 858

relay_log_purge system variable, 858
relay_log_recovery system variable, 858
relay_log_space_limit system variable, 858
relay logs, 618, 624
    expiring, 630
    master-slave replication, 731
RELEASE SAVEPOINT statement, 955
RELEASE_LOCK() function, 825
RELOAD privilege, 662, 676
relocating data directory contents, 556-557
    assessing, 558-559
    entire directory, 559
    function, selecting, 557
    individual databases, 559-560
    individual tables, 560
    InnoDB tablespace, 560
    precautions, 558
    startup option, 557
    status/log files, 561-562
    symlink, 557
remote access, 13
remove_backslashes() function, 512
RENAME clause, 129-130
RENAME TABLE statement, 955
RENAME USER statement, 656, 955
renaming tables, 129-130
renewal notices, sending, 443-448
renewal_notify.pl script, 444
REPAIR TABLE statement, 720, 956
repairing tables
    InnoDB, 718
    MyISAM, 719
    mysqlcheck utility, 720-721
    REPAIR TABLE statement, 720
REPEAT() function, 798
REPEAT statements, 989
REPEATABLE READ isolation level, 162
REPLACE attribute, 232
REPLACE() function, 798
REPLACE statement, 956-957
replication
    binary logging formats, 731
    compatibility guidelines, 727-728
    databases, 541
    master-slave, 728-731
        master.info file, 730
        master server settings, 728-729

relay logs, 731
separate slave accounts, 730
server ID values, assigning, 728
slave settings, 729-730
statements, 730-731
threads, starting/stopping, 731
mysqld options, 1053-1056
overview, 727
slave backups, creating, 732-733
REPLICATION CLIENT privilege, 662
REPLICATION SLAVE, 663
report_host system variable, 858
report_password system variable, 858
report_port system variable, 858
report_user system variable, 858
REQUIRE clause
GRANT statement, 661, 938
GRANT USAGE statement, 697
secure connections, 668-669
REQUIRED_ARG arg_type, 341
requirements
data type storage
string, 204
temporal, 219
sample database, 23-24
software, 736-737
storage, 197-198
RESET statement, 957
resetting
databases to known state, 53-54
user account passwords, 672
RESIGNAL statements, 994-995
resource management columns (grant tables),
685-686
restarting mysqld, 581-582
result sets
memory, releasing, 388
metadata, 359-364
availability, 359
column information structures,
accessing, 364
defined, 359
displaying, 360-364
Perl DBI scripts, 430-434
result set data processing decisions,
359
multiple, Web: 1108-1109

Perl DBI scripts, 400-401
entire sets, returning at once,
413-415
null values, checking, 416
number of rows returned, counting,
411
row-fetching loops, 407-411
PHP, 501-504
all rows at once, 504
arrays, 503
calculated columns, 503
default fetch mode, setting, 502
individual column values, 503
NULL values, 504
row-fetching loop, 501-503
statement handle, 501
processing functions, Web: 1103-1108,
Web: 1114-1117
returning (statements)
C client programs, 351-353
Perl DBI. See result sets, Perl DBI
scripts
single-row, 411-413
results
binding to variables, 421-423
limiting, 63-64
retrieving, 54-56
column values, naming, 64-66
criteria, 56-59
dates, 66-69
multiple tables, 78-85
NULL values, 60-61
pattern matching, 69-70
summaries, 72-78
table contents, 54
user-defined variables, 71
sorting, 61-63
subqueries, testing, 143-144
retrieving
data
column values, naming, 64-66
criteria, specifying, 56-59
dates, 57, 66-69
multiple tables. See joins; subqueries
NULL values, 60-61
numeric ranges, 56
pattern matching, 69-70
SELECT statements, 54-56

several individual values, 59

string values containing character data, 56

summaries, 72-78

table contents, displaying, 54

user-defined variables, 71

rows

all at once, 413-415, 504

arrays, 503

calculated columns, 503

default fetch mode, 502

individual column values, 503

null values, checking, 416, 504

number returned, counting, 411

Perl DBI, 401-402

PHP, 501-504

row-fetching loops, 407-411, 501-503

single-row results, 411-413

RETURN statement, 268, 989

RETURNS clause, 268

REVERSE() function, 798

REVOKE statement, 671-672, 957-958

revoking privileges, 671-672

RIGHT() function, 798

right joins, 139-143

RLIKE/NOT RLIKE operators, 780

rollback() function, Web: 1139, Web: 1165

ROLLBACK statement, 958-959

ROLLUP clause, 77

root accounts passwords

assigning, 567-569

resetting, 582-583

rotate_fixed_logs.sh script, 626

rotating logs, 625

fixed-name, 626-629

tables, 631

ROUND() function, 253, 788

routine_name columns, 688

routine_type columns, 688

row-based logging, 731

ROW_COUNT() function, 831-832

row-fetching loops

Perl DBI, 407-411

fetchrow_array() function, 408-409

fetchrow_arrayref(), 409-410

fetchrow_hashref(), 410-411

functions, listing of, 407

PHP, 501-503

rowCount() function, 505, Web: 1171

rows

adding

data files, 52-53

INSERT statement, 50-52

deleting, 85-86

events, 275

preserving sequencing, 235

modifying statements, 350

Perl DBI, 406-407

PHP, 501

multiple-table

deleting, 154-155

updates, 155-156

phantom, 162

randomly selecting, 64

retrieving

all at once, 413-415, 504

arrays, 503

calculated columns, 503

default fetch mode, 502

individual column values, 503

null values, checking, 416, 504

number returned, counting, 411

Perl DBI, 401-402

PHP, 501-504

row-fetching loops, 407-411, 501-503

single-row results, 411-413

storage formats, 299

displaying/editing, 300

InnoDB, 299-300

MEMORY, 299

MyISAM, 299

updating, 86

rows() function, Web: 1145

RPAD() function, 799

RTF directories, creating, 440-442

RTRIM() function, 799

S

sampdb distribution

files/directories, 735-736

unpacking, 735

Web site, 735

sampdb_pdo.php script, 495

sample databases
  administrator accounts, creating, 24
  databases
    creating, 30-31
    listing, 38
  distribution, 23
  grade-keeping. *See* grade-keeping project
  requirements, 23-24
  resetting to known state, 53-54
  rows, adding, 50-52
  server connections
    establishing, 25-26
    terminating, 26-27
  statements
    case-sensitivity, 29
    ending, 27
    executing, 27-30
    function syntax, 29
    multiple-lines, 28
    multiple statements on single line, 28-29
    reading from files, 29
    results, displaying, 28
  tables, listing, 37
  U.S. Historical League. *See* U.S. Historical League project
SAVEPOINT statement, 161, 959
savepoints, 161
scalar data types (C API), Web: 1075-1076
scalar subqueries, writing, 144, 241
scheduler (events)
  enabling, 262
  logging, 274
  starting/stopping at runtime, 274
  status, verifying, 274
scheduling
  policies, 303
  preventive maintenance, 707
SCHEMA() function, 832
scope columns, 683
  case sensitivity, 689
  column_name, 688
  Db, 688
  host, 687-689
  listing of, 687-689
  matching order, 690-691

  proxied_host/proxied_user, 689
  routine_name, 688
  routine_type, 688
  table_name, 688
  user, 688
score table
  creating, 39-40, 48-49
  linking with grade_event table
    dates, 41
    event IDs, 41-42
score_browse.pl script, 475-479
  display_events() function, 476-477
  display_scores() function, 477-479
score_entry.php script, 510-511
  action input parameter, 513
  add_new_event() function, 517-518
  display_cell() function, 516
  display_events() function, 514-515
  display_scores() function, 518-519
  enter_scores() function, 520-522
  framework, 513-514
  PDO transaction processing, 520
  script_name() function, 516
  security, 522
  solicit_event_info() function, 516-517
script_name() function, 516
script_param() function, 512
scripts
  C client. *See* C client programs
  Perl DBI. *See* Perl DBI scripts
  PHP. *See* PHP scripts
  stored
    benefits, 261-262
    compound statements, 266-267
    defined, 261
    events, 274-275
    security, 275-276
    single statement example, 266
    stored functions, 268-271
    stored procedures, 268-272
    triggers, 272-273
  Web-based. *See* Web-based scripts
search_members() function
  ushl_browse.pl script, 480
  ushl_ft_browse.pl script, 482-483

searches
full-text
boolean mode, 174-175
characteristics, 171
configuring, 176-177
natural language, 172-174
query expansion, 175-176
types, 170
tables, 479-483
SEC_TO_TIME() function, 812
SECOND() function, 812
secure_auth system variable, 858
secure_file_priv system variable, 858
Secure Sockets Layer. *See* **SSL**
security
access control risks, 673-676
ALTER privilege, 676
anonymous-user accounts, 673
FILE privilege, 674-676
GRANT OPTION privilege, 674
insecure accounts, 673-674
mysql database privileges, 673-674
passwords in old hash format, 673
PROCESS/SUPER privileges, 674-675
RELOAD privilege, 676
superuser privileges, 673-674
db_browse.pl script, 471
external risks, 646
filesystem access, 540
administrative-only, setting, 649-651
base directory insecurities, checking, 648
data directory insecurities, checking, 648
overview, 646-647
stealing data example, 647
functions, 821-824
hidden fields, 528
Historical League member entries online editing script, 527-529
initial user accounts, 564-569
available on all platforms, 566
client program connections, 566
displaying, 565
passwords, assigning, 567-569
platform specific, 567
internal risks, 645

load_defaults() function, 335
log files, 556
mysqld, 540
new server passwords, 569
online score-entry script, 520-521
option files, 653-654
PHP, 491
SSL
benefits, 694
configuring, 695-698
storage engine locking levels, 303-305
stored programs, 275-276
Unix socket file, 652-653
user-specific options (programs), 1011
views, 275-276
Web-based scripts, 470-471
SELECT privilege, 665
SELECT statements, 959-965
clauses
FROM, 54-56
FOR UPDATE, 964
GROUP BY, 963
HAVING, 963
INTO, 964
LIMIT, 963
LOCK IN SHARE MODE, 964
ORDER BY, 963
PROCEDURE, 963
WHERE, 56
data, retrieval, 54-56
examples, 964-965
indexes, 962
joins, 961-963
column references, qualifying, 138-139
inner, 137-138
outer, 139-143
NULL values, checking, 504
number of rows returned, 411
options, 960
overview, 954-958
results, writing to files, 964
single-row results, retrieving, 412-413
subqueries, 143-144
ALL/ANY/SOME, 146-147
correlated, 148
FROM clause, 149

EXISTS/NOT EXISTS, 147-148
IN/NOT IN, 145-146
relative comparison operators, 144-145
rewriting as joins, 149
uncorrelated, 148
syntax, 136
select_full_join status variable, **886**
select_full_range_join status variable, **886**
select_range status variable, **886**
select_range_check status variable, **886**
select_rows() function, **385-388**
select_scan status variable, **886**
selectall_arrayref() function, Web: **1140**
selectall_hashref() function, Web: **1140**
selectcol_arrayref() function, Web: **1140**
selecting
  APIs, 314--314
    development time, 316-317
    execution environment, 315
    performance, 315-316
    portability, 317
  columns for indexing, 281-285
    badly performing queries, identifying, 285
    cardinality, 282
    comparisons, matching to index types, 284-285
    overindexing, 284
    prefixes, 283-284
    short values, 283
  data types, 255-256
    currency, 258
    dates, 258-259
    height information, 257-258
    performance/efficiency, 256
    ranges of values, 256, 259-260
    storage size, 256
    string, 217-218
    value types in column, 256-259
  data types for query optimization, 296-298
    BLOB/TEXT, 298
    ENUM, 297
    NOT NULL, 297
    numbers, 296
    PROCEDURE ANALYSE() function, 297

smallest types, 296-297
strings, 296
tables, defragmenting, 297
databases, 105-106
error message language, 604
expression writing style, 290-292
GRANT statements, 661
locale, 604-605
numeric data types, 203, 257-258
rows, 64
storage engines, 594
selectrow_array() function, **413**, Web: **1141**
selectrow_arrayref() function, Web: **1141**
selectrow_hashref() function, Web: **1141**
semicolons (;), statements, **27**, **266**
sequences, **230**
  adding to tables, 235-236
  arbitrary values, creating, 238
  AUTO_INCREMENT properties
    general, 230-232
    InnoDB, 234
    MEMORY, 234-235
    MyISAM, 232-234
  creating without AUTO_INCREMENT, 237-239
  decreasing numbers, creating, 238
  increasing numbers, creating, 237-238
  incrementing counters, 238-239
  multiple independent, creating, 233
  mysql prompt definition, 1028-1029
  nonpositive numbers, 235
  ranges, 235
  resequencing existing columns, 236-237
  resets, 235
  unsigned, 235
SERIALIZABLE isolation level, **162**
server_id system variable, **858**
server_uuid system variable, **858**
servers
  connections
    authentication plugins, 677
    establishing, 25-26
    Perl DBI API, 312
    PHP scripts, 490-491
    programs. *See* connect1 client program; connect2 client program
    terminating, 26-27
    Web scripts, 468-469

database transfers, 716
  text backup files, 716-717
  writing directly to other server, 717-718
maintenance interference, preventing, 701
  internal locking, 702-703
  locking all tables at once, 705
  read-only locking, 703-704
  read/write locking, 704-705
  shutting down servers, 702
multiple, 632
  administration, 539
  client programs, running, 641
  configuring, 635
  directory options, 633
  error log file names, 634
  InnoDB log location, 634
  issues, 632-635
  login account option, 635
  network interface options, 633
  replication slave options, 634
  startup option strategies, 636-637
  status/log file names, 634
  Unix, 637-639
  Windows, 639-641
MySQL. *See* mysqld
new passwords, setting, 569
option groups, 578
replication
  compatibility guidelines, 727-728
  master-slave, 728-731
  overview, 727
running as administrator, 652
shutting down, 702
SQL mode, 96-97
  setting, 96-97
  values, 96
Web, configuring, 460-461
SESSION qualifier
SHOW STATUS statement, 589
SHOW VARIABLES statement, 586
SESSION_USER() function, 832
SET data type, 208-213
creating, 209
ENUM data type, compared, 208
improper values, 228

numeric form, 211-212
permitted value lists, defining, 209
size/storage requirements, 204
sorting/indexing, 212-213
SET PASSWORD statement, 567-568, 966-967
SET statement, 159-160, 965-966
SET strings, 194, 759
SET TRANSACTION statement, 967-968
setAttribute() function, Web: 1165, Web: 1171
setFetchMode() function, Web: 1171-1172
SHA() function, 824
SHA1() function, 824
SHA2() function, 824
shared_memory system variable, 859
shared_memory_base_name system variable, 859
shebang (#!), 396
shells
aliases, 89
command history, 88
scripts, 89
shift left (<<) operator, 773
shift right (>>) operator, 773
SHOW BINARY LOGS statement, 969
SHOW BINLOG EVENTS statement, 969-970
SHOW CHARACTER SET statement, 970
SHOW COLLATION statement, 970-971
SHOW COLUMNS statement, 37, 131, 971
SHOW CREATE DATABASE statement, 106-107, 130
SHOW CREATE statement, 972
SHOW DATABASES privilege, 663
SHOW DATABASES statement, 38, 130, 547, 972
SHOW ENGINE statement, 972
SHOW ENGINE INNODB STATUS statement, 170
SHOW ENGINES statement, 108-109, 593, 973
SHOW ERRORS statement, 973
SHOW EVENTS statement, 973
SHOW FULL COLUMNS statement, 37
SHOW FUNCTION STATUS statement, 973
SHOW GRANTS statement, 671, 974
SHOW INDEX statement, 131, 974-975
SHOW MASTER STATUS statement, 975
SHOW OPEN TABLES statement, 975
SHOW PLUGINS statement, 976
SHOW PRIVILEGES statement, 976

SHOW PROCEDURE STATUS statement, 973

SHOW PROCESSLIST statement, 976

SHOW RELAYLOG EVENTS statement, 976

SHOW SLAVE HOSTS statement, 977

SHOW SLAVE STATUS statement, 730, 977-979

SHOW statement, 969
   LIKE pattern clause, 131
   metadata, accessing, 130-132
   WHERE clause, 131

SHOW STATUS statement, 979-980
   GLOBAL/SESSION qualifiers, 589
   LIKE/WHERE clauses, 589
   status variables, displaying, 584

SHOW TABLE STATUS statement, 131, 980-981

SHOW TABLES statement, 37, 130, 981

SHOW TRIGGERS statement, 981

SHOW VARIABLES statement, 982
   GLOBAL/SESSION qualifiers, 586
   LIKE clause, 585
   system variables, displaying, 583
   WHERE clause, 585

SHOW VIEW privilege, 665

SHOW WARNINGS statement, 982

show_argv program, 332-335

show_opt program
   connect2 program, compared, 347
   invoking, 342-343
   overview, 336
   source file, 336-338

SHUTDOWN privilege, 663

shutting down
   mysqld, 539
   servers, 702

SIGN() function, 789

SIGNAL statements, 995-996

SIGNED attribute, 201

SIN() function, 789

single-row result sets, returning, 411-413

size
   BLOB/TEXT data types, 207
   string data types, 204
   tables, 551-553

skip_external_locking system variable, 859

skip_name_resolve system variable, 859

skip_networking system variable, 859

skip_show_database system variable, 859

slave_allow_batching system variable, 859

slave backups, creating, 732-733

slave_checkpoint_group system variable, 859

slave_checkpoint_period system variable, 859

slave_compressed_protocol system variable, 860

slave_exec_mode system variable, 860

slave_heartbeat_period status variable, 886

slave_last_heartbeat status variable, 886

slave_load_tmpdir system variable, 860

slave_max_allowed_packet system variable, 860

slave_net_timeout system variable, 860

slave_open_temp_tables status variable, 886

slave_parallel_workers system variable, 860

slave_pending_jobs_size_max system variable, 860

slave_received_heartbeats status variable, 886

slave_retried_transactions status variable, 886

slave_running status variable, 886

slave_skip_errors system variable, 860

slave_sql_verify_checksum system variable, 860

slave_transaction_retries system variable, 861

slave_type_conversions system variable, 861

SLEEP() function, 832

slow query logs, 618,

slow_launch_threads status variable, 886

slow_launch_time system variable, 861

slow_queries status variable, 886

slow_query_log system variable, 193, 621,

slow_query_log_file system variable, 861 750, 861

SMALLINT data types
   ranges, 197
   storage requirements, 197

socket system variable, 861

software required, 736-737

solicit_event_info() function, 516-517

SOME subqueries, 146-147

sort_buffer_size system variable, 861

sort_merge_passes status variable, 886

sort_range status variable, 887

sort_rows status variable, 887

sort_scan status variable, 887

sorting
    ENUM/SET data types, 212-213
    properties (strings), 186
    query results, 61-63
SOUNDEX() function, 799
source files
    connect1.c, 323-324
    connect2 program, 344-347
    show_opt, 336-338
SPACE() function, 799
spatial functions, 828
SPATIAL indexes, 124
spatial values, 191-192
special characters
    C client programs, 365-366
    LOAD DATA statements, 942-943
    Perl DBI, 416-419
    PHP, 505-507
specifiers
    ALL, 666
    privileges
        ALL/USAGE, 661
        levels, 665
SQL (Structured Query Language), 20
    case sensitivity, 99-101
        aliases, 100
        column names, 100
        database names, 100
        filenames, 100
        forcing lowercase, 100
        function names, 99
        index names, 100
        keywords, 99
        stored program names, 100
        string values, 100
        table names, 100
        trigger names, 100
        view names, 100
    fluency, 538
    identifiers, 97
        aliases, 98
        columns, 99
        database, 98
        function names, 98
        length, 98
        qualified names, 99

        qualifiers, 98
        quoting, 97-98
        tables, 98
        unquoted, 97
        views, 98
SQL mode, 96-97
sql_auto_is_null system variable, 861
sql_big_selects system variable, 861
sql_buffer_result system variable, 862
sql_log_bin system variable, 862
sql_log_off system variable, 862
composite modes, 862-866
    setting, 96-97
    values, 96, 862-865
sql_mode system variable, 96, 862-866
    composite modes, 865
    values, 862-865
sql_notes system variable, 866
sql_quote_show_create system variable, 866
sql_safe_updates system variable, 866
sql_select_limit system variable, 866
sql_slave_skip_counter system variable, 866
sql_warnings system variable, 866
SQRT() function, 789
square brackets ([ ]), operators/functions, 764
SSL (Secure Sockets Layer)
    benefits, 694
    client support, 370-374
        availability, 370
        holding option values variables, 372-373
        options, adding, 370-372
        passing SSL option information to client library, 374
    configuring, 695-698
        accounts requiring SSL, creating, 697-698
        certificate/key files, 697
        client programs SSL support, enabling, 696
        command-line options, 697
        language APIs, 698
        option files, 697
        server SSL support, enabling, 695-696
        SSL-related server status variable values, displaying, 697
    grant table columns, 685

program options, 1006
requiring, 668
status variables, 892-894
ssl_accept_renegotiates status variable, 892
ssl_accepts status variable, 892
ssl_callback_cache_hits status variable, 892
ssl_cipher status variable, 892
ssl_cipher_list status variable, 892
ssl_client_connects status variable, 892
ssl_connect_renegotiates status variable, 892
ssl_ctx_verify_depth status variable, 893
ssl_ctx_verify_mode status variable, 893
ssl_default_timeout status variable, 893
ssl_finished_accepts status variable, 893
ssl_finished_connects status variable, 893
ssl_server_not_after status variable, 893
ssl_server_not_before status variable, 893
ssl_session_cache_hits status variable, 893
ssl_session_cache_misses status variable, 893
ssl_session_cache_mode status variable, 893
ssl_session_cache_overflows status variable, 893
ssl_session_cache_size status variable, 893
ssl_session_cache_timeouts status variable, 893
ssl_sessions_reused status variable, 893
ssl_used_session_cache_entries status variable, 893
ssl_verify_depth status variable, 894
ssl_verify_mode status variable, 894
ssl_version status variable, 894
ssl_xxx status variable, 887
ssl_xxx system variable, 867
standalone PHP scripts, 489
START SLAVE statement, 731, 983
START TRANSACTION statement, 157-158, 983-984
start_html() function, 463
starting mysqld, 539, 741
    options, 577-579
    Unix, 572-574, 741
    Windows, 742
startup
    character set/collation, setting, 603
    InnoDB tablespace failure, 598
    logging options, 619
    multiple server options, 636-637
    mysqld options, 577-579

plugins, loading, 591
storage engines status change options, 593-594
state
    databases, resetting, 53-54
    plugin activation, 592
statements
    ; (semicolons), 27
    access verification, 689-690
    account-management, 654-655
    ALTER DATABASE, 107, 898
    ALTER EVENT, 898-899
    ALTER FUNCTION, 899
    ALTER PROCEDURE, 899
    ALTER TABLE, 899-904
        action values, 899-903
        benefits, 127-128
        CHANGE clause, 128
        CHARACTER SET clause, 128-129
        ENGINE clause, 129
        indexes, adding, 124
        MODIFY clause, 128
        partitioning options, 904
        RENAME clause, 129-130
        resequencing existing columns, 237
        sequence columns, adding, 236
        syntax, 128
        table files, 549
    ALTER VIEW, 905
    ANALYZE TABLE, 905
    BEGIN, 905
    binary logging, 731
    BINLOG, 906
    CACHE INDEX, 906
    CALL, 906
    case-sensitivity, 29, 99-101
        aliases, 100
        column names, 100
        database names, 100
        filenames, 100
        forcing lowercase, 100
        function names, 99
        index names, 100
        keywords, 99
        stored program names, 100
        string values, 100
        table names, 100

triggers, 100
view names, 100
CHANGE MASTER, 907-908
CHARACTER SET, 102-103
CHECK TABLE, 719-720, 909-910
CHECKSUM TABLE, 910
client programs, 348-350
    alternative approaches, 356-357
    binary data, 367-368
    causes of failures, 349
    character-escaping operations, 349
    general-purpose statement handler,
        354-355
    mysql_store_result() functions,
        357-359
    mysql_use_result() functions, 357-359
    quoting special characters, 365-366
    result set metadata, 359-364
    result sets, returning, 351-353
    row-modifying statements, 350
    sending to server functions, 349
COLLATE, 102-103
comments, adding, 996-997
COMMIT, 910-911
compound, 266-267, 987-996
    condition-handling, 992-996
    control structure, 987-989
    cursor, 991-992
    declaration, 989-991
construction/execution functions,
    Web: 1099-1102
CREATE DATABASE, 30, 106-107, 130,
    547, 911
CREATE EVENT, 274, 912-913
CREATE FUNCTION, 268, 913-915
CREATE INDEX, 915-916
CREATE PROCEDURE, 268, 913-915
CREATE TABLE, 113-114, 916-926
    AVG_ROW_LENGTH option, 115
    column definitions, 926
    data type keywords, 918-919
    ENGINE clause, 46-47, 114
    foreign key support, 922-923
    IF NOT EXISTS modifier, 115
    index clauses, 919
    MAX_ROWS, 115
    options, 919-922
    PARTITION BY clause, 120-121

partitioning, 923-925
student table, 45-46
table files, creating, 549
TEMPORARY keyword, 115-116
CREATE TABLE ...LIKE, 117-118
CREATE TABLE ...SELECT, 117-119
CREATE TRIGGER, 272, 926-927
CREATE USER, 927-928
    account operations, 655
    account value, 656
    auth_info clause, 659-660
    IDENTIFIED WITH clause, 676
    selecting, 656
CREATE VIEW, 928-929
date/time retrieval, 27
DEALLOCATE PREPARE, 929
DELETE, 85-86, 154-155, 929-930
DESCRIBE, 36-37, 930-931
DO, 931
DROP DATABASE, 107, 547, 931
DROP EVENT, 932
DROP FUNCTION, 932
DROP INDEX, 127, 302, 932
DROP PROCEDURE, 932
DROP TABLE, 121-122, 549, 932
DROP TRIGGER, 932-933
DROP USER, 656, 933
DROP VIEW, 933
ending, 27-28
entering, 27
    multiple-lines, 28
    multiple statements on single line,
        28-29
    typing less, 90-93
EXECUTE, 933
EXPLAIN, 290-296, 933-936
FLUSH, 936-937
FLUSH PRIVILEGES, 583
FLUSH TABLES, 302, 703
function syntax, 29
GRANT, 938-943
    clauses, 660-661
    examples, 942-943
    ON clause, 939-940
    privileges, revoking, 672
    privileges to be granted, 938-939
    REQUIRE clause, 668-669, 941

selecting, 661
WITH clause, 941-942
GRANT USAGE, 697
HANDLER, 943
handles. *See* handles
identifiers, 97
    aliases, 98
    columns, 99
    database, 98
    function names, 98
    length, 98
    qualified names, 99
    qualifiers, 98
    quoting, 97-98
    tables, 98
    unquoted, 97
    views, 98
INSERT, 943-946
    data loading, 301
    double-quoting strings in Perl DBI, 417-418
    rows, adding, 50-52
INSTALL PLUGIN, 591, 946
interactive statement-execution client, 368-369
KILL, 946
LOAD DATA, 300-301, 946-951
    data files, loading, 52-53
    data formats, 948
    FIELDS clause options, 948-949
    LINES clause, 949-950
    LOCAL keyword, 947
    special characters, 948
LOAD INDEX INTO CACHE, 951
LOAD XML, 951-952
LOCK TABLE, 304, 702, 952-953
master-slave replication, 730-731
multiple, executing, 375-377
    enabling, 375
    process_multi_statement() function, 376-377
    result retrieval functions, 375
OPTIMIZE TABLE, 953-954
ORDER BY RAND(), 64
Perl DBI
    entire result sets, returning at once, 413-415
    null values, checking, 416

number of rows returned, 411
placeholders, 419-421
prepared, 421
quoting special characters, 416-419
result sets, returning. *See* result sets, Perl DBI scripts
row-fetching loops, 407-411
row-modifying, 406-407
single-row results, returning, 411-413
PHP, 500-501
    NULL values, checking, 504
    prepared, 505
    quoting special characters, 505-507
    row-modifying, 501
    rows, retrieving, 501-504
PREPARE, 954
prepared. *See* prepared statements
print, 426-428
PURGE BINARY LOGS, 954-955
reading from files, 29
RELEASE SAVEPOINT, 955
RENAME TABLE, 955
RENAME USER, 656, 955
REPAIR TABLE, 720, 956
REPLACE, 956-957
RESET, 957
result sets, returning, 351-353
results, displaying, 28
RETURN, 268
REVOKE, 671-672, 957-958
ROLLBACK, 958-959
row-modifying, handling
    C client, 350
    Perl DBI, 406-407
SAVEPOINT, 161, 959
SELECT, 959-965
    data retrieval, 54-56
    examples, 964-965
    FOR UPDATE clause, 964
    FROM clause, 54-56
    GROUP BY clause, 963
    HAVING clause, 963
    indexes, 962
    INTO clauses, 964
    joins syntax. *See* SELECT statements, joins
    LIMIT clause, 963

LOCK IN SHARE MODE clause, 964

nesting with another SELECT statement. *See* subqueries

NULL values, checking, 504

number of rows returned, 411

options, 960

ORDER BY clause, 963

PROCEDURE clause, 963

results, writing to files, 964

single-row results, retrieving, 412-413

subqueries. *See* SELECT statements, subqueries

syntax, 136

WHERE clause, 56, 963

SET, 159-160, 965-966

SET PASSWORD, 567-568, 966-967

SET TRANSACTION, 967-968

SHOW, 969

LIKE pattern clause, 131

metadata, accessing, 130-132

WHERE clause, 131

SHOW BINARY LOGS, 969

SHOW BINLOG EVENTS, 969-970

SHOW CHARACTER SET, 970

SHOW COLLATION, 970-971

SHOW COLUMNS, 37, 131, 971

SHOW CREATE, 972

SHOW CREATE DATABASE, 106-107, 130

SHOW DATABASES, 38, 130, 547, 972

SHOW ENGINE, 972

SHOW ENGINE INNODB STATUS, 170

SHOW ENGINES, 108-109, 593, 973

SHOW ERRORS, 973

SHOW EVENTS, 973

SHOW FULL COLUMNS, 37

SHOW FUNCTION STATUS, 973

SHOW GRANTS, 671, 974

SHOW INDEX, 131, 974-975

SHOW MASTER STATUS, 975

SHOW OPEN TABLES, 975

SHOW PLUGINS, 976

SHOW PRIVILEGES, 976

SHOW PROCEDURE STATUS, 973

SHOW PROCESSLIST, 976

SHOW RELAYLOG EVENTS, 976

SHOW SLAVE HOSTS, 977

SHOW SLAVE STATUS, 977-979

SHOW STATUS, 979-980

GLOBAL/SESSION qualifiers, 589

LIKE/WHERE clauses, 589

status variables, displaying, 584

SHOW TABLE STATUS, 131, 980-981

SHOW TABLES, 37, 130, 981

SHOW TRIGGERS, 981

SHOW VARIABLES, 982

GLOBAL/SESSION qualifiers, 586

LIKE clause, 585

system variables, displaying, 583

WHERE clause, 585

SHOW WARNINGS, 982

START SLAVE, 983

START TRANSACTION, 157-158, 983-984

STOP SLAVE, 984

synonyms, 898

syntax, 897

table file operations, 549-550

table locking, 703

TRUNCATE TABLE, 984

UNINSTALL PLUGIN, 592, 984

UNION, 151-154, 985

UNLOCK TABLE, 304, 703, 985

UPDATE, 986-987

multiple-table, 155-156

root/anonymous-user passwords, 568

rows, 86

USE, 987

use DBI, 399

use strict, 399

use warnings, 399

status files

listing of, 554

multiple servers, creating, 634

relocating, 561-562

status variables, 881

case sensitivity, 881

displaying, 584

general, listing of, 881-888

InnoDB, listing of, 888-891

overview, 584

query cache, listing of, 891-892

SSL, 892-894

values, checking, 588-589

STD() function, 820
STDDEV() function, 820
STDDEV_POP() function, 820
STDDEV_SAMP() function, 820
stealing data example, 647
STOP SLAVE statement, 731, 984
stopping mysqld, 580-581
storage
   data type requirements
      numeric, 197-198
      temporal, 219
   data types, 204, 748
   images from files, 367-368
   row formats, 299
      displaying/editing, 300
      InnoDB, 299-300
      MEMORY, 299
      MyISAM, 299
   SQL statements in files, 29
   temporal data types, 759
storage_engine system variable, 867
storage engines
   ARCHIVE, 112
   auto-recovery, performing, 700
   availability, 108-109
   BLACKHOLE, 112
   converting tables to different, 129
   CSV, 112, 710
   default, selecting, 594
   default status/startup option, 593-594
   defined, 46
   displaying available, 593
   FEDERATED, 113
   file representations, 548
   grade-keeping student table example, 46-47
   index characteristics, 123
   InnoDB
      auto-recovery, 706, 725-726
      backing up, 715-716
      checking/repairing tables, 718
      data, representing, 548
      features, 110
      innodb directory access mode, setting, 651
      locking levels, 303
      portability, 710

      row storage formats, 299-300
      sequence characteristics, 234
      status variables, listing of, 888-891
      system variables, listing of, 870-880
      tablespace. *See* tablespaces (InnoDB)
      transaction isolation levels, 162-163
      variables, 600-601
   listing of, 108
   locking levels, 303-305
   MEMORY
      data, representing, 548
      locking levels, 304
      overview, 111-112
      portability, 710
      row storage formats, 299
      sequence characteristics, 234-235
   MERGE, 113, 304
   MyISAM
      auto-recovery, 706
      checking/repairing tables, 719
      data, representing, 548
      features, 111
      portability, 710
      row storage formats, 299
      sequence characteristics, 232-234
      table maximum size, 552
   NDB, 112
   pluggable architecture, 108
   portability, 709-710
   specifying for tables, 114
   table-specific files, 109-110
stored functions, 268-271
   creating, 268
   defined, 268
   integer-valued parameter representing a year example, 268
   multiple values, 269
   names, 269
   privileges, 270-271
   security, 276
   tables, updating, 270
stored procedures
   creating, 268
   defined, 268
   example, 269
   invoking, 269
   parameter types, 271-272

privileges, 270-271
security, 275-276
tables, updating, 270
triggers, 273
stored_program_cache system variable, 867
stored programs
benefits, 261-262
case sensitivity, 100
compound statements, 266-267
defined, 261
events, 274-275
creating, 274
defined, 274
deleting old rows from table
example, 275
enabling/disabling, 275
enabling scheduler, 274
logging, 274
one time only, 275
privileges, 274
scheduler status, verifying, 274
security, 276
starting/stopping scheduler, 274
security, 275-276
single statement example, 266
stored functions, 268-271
creating, 268
defined, 268
integer-valued parameter representing
a year example, 268
multiple values, 269
names, 269
privileges, 270-271
tables, updating, 270
stored procedures
creating, 268
defined, 268
example, 269
invoking, 269
parameter types, 271-272
privileges, 270-271
security, 275-276
tables, updating, 270
triggers
actions, 273
benefits, 272
creating, 272

defined, 272
names, 272
privileges, 273
security, 276
stored routines
defined, 262
privileges, 667
security, 276
update_expiration(), 270
str COLLATE collation operator, 773
str NOT REGEXP pattern, 775-778
STR_TO_DATE() function, 66, 813
STRAIGHT_JOIN, 287
STRCMP() function, 780
strict mode
division by zero errors, 229
transactional/nontransactional tables,
229
turning on, 230
weakening, 230
zero date errors, 229
STRICT_ALL_TABLES SQL mode, 96, 865
STRICT_TRANS_TABLES SQL mode, 96, 865
strings, 182-184, 193
binary/nonbinary, 255
case sensitivity, 100
character data, retrieving, 56
converting to numbers, 249-250
data types, 204, 753-754
attributes, 214-216
binary, 755-756
binary/nonbinary corresponding
types, 204-205
BINARY/VARBINARY, 207
BLOB, 207-208
CHAR/VARCHAR, 206
character sets/collations, 753-754
ENUM, 208-213, 758
improper values, 228
length, 205
lengths, 753
nonbinary, 756-758
query performance, improving, 296
selecting, 217-218
SET, 208-213, 759
size, 204
storage requirements, 204

TEXT, 207-208
trailing pad values, 218, 754
types, listing of, 194
escape sequences, 183
functions, listing of, 789-802
quoting characters
C client programs, 365-366
Perl DBI, 416-419
PHP, 505-507
surrounding quotes, 182-183
values
backslashes, turning off, 184
binary, 185
binary *versus* nonbinary, 188-189
character set variables, 189-191
CONVERT() function, 187-188
escape sequences, 183
hexadecimal notation, 184
introducers, 187-188
length, 188
nonbinary, 185
quote characters, including, 183-184
sorting properties, 186
surrounding quotes, 182-183
structural terminology, 18-19
Structured Query Language. *See* **SQL**
student table
columns, creating, 46
creating, 44-47
sub_size member (my_option structures), 341
SUBDATE() function, 813
submit_button() function, 526
subqueries, 84-85, 143-144
ALL/ANY/SOME, 146-147
correlated, 148
correlated/uncorrelated, 144
defined, 78
EXISTS/NOT EXISTS, 147-148
FROM clause, 149
IN/NOT IN, 145-146
query optimizer support, 289
relative comparison operators, 144-145
results, testing, 143-144
rewriting as joins, 149
matching values, selecting, 149-150
nonmatching values, 150

scalar, 144, 241
types, 143
uncorrelated, 148
SUBSTR() function, 799
SUBSTRING() function, 799-800
SUBSTRING_INDEX() function, 800
SUBTIME() function, 813
subtraction operator (-), 57, 241, 766
SUM() function, 76, 820
summaries, 72-78
counting, 72-76
distinct non-NULL values, 73
groups, 74-76
minimum/maximum/total/average values, 76
non-NULL values, 73
number of rows, 72
overall count of values, 73
summary, 77-78
functions, listing of, 817-821
unique values present in a set of values, 72
SUPER privilege, 663, 673-674
definer privileges, setting, 276
security risks, 674-675
switchboxes, 437-438
symlinks, 557, 651
sync_binlog system variable, 867
sync_frm system variable, 867
sync_master_info system variable, 867
sync_relay_log system variable, 867
sync_relay_log_info system variable, 867
synthetic indexes, 298
SYSDATE() function, 813
system tables, initializing, 742-743
system_time_zone system variable, 602, 867
SYSTEM_USER() function, 832
system variables, 584-585, 835-836
character_set_server, 603
collation_server, 603
displaying, 583, 836
error message language selection, 604
expire_logs_days, 629
general, listing of, 836-870
general_log, 621
general_log_file, 621
InnoDB, listing of, 870-880

innodb_autoextend_increment, 596

innodb_data_file_path, 595

innodb_data_home_dir, 595

innodb_file_per_table, 599

lc_time_names, 604

log_warnings, 620

max_relay_log_size, 624, 630

names, 836

overview, 583

setting, 764

   runtime, 587-588

   server startup, 586-587

slow_query_log, 621

time zones, 602-603

values, checking, 585-586

T

table() function, 475

table handlers. *See* storage engines

table_definition_cache system variable, 868

table_locks_immediate status variable, 887

table_locks_waited status variable, 887

table_name columns, 688

table_open_cache, 868

table_open_cache_hits status variable, 887

table_open_cache_instances system variable, 868

table_open_cache_misses status variable, 887

table_open_cache_overflows status variable, 887

tables

   absence, 45, 49

   aliases, 98

   backups

      best practices, 709

      binary, 714-715

      InnoDB, 715-716

      selecting, 708

      storage engine portability, 709-710

      text, creating, 711-714

      types, 708

   banner advertisement example, 19

   columns. *See* columns

   contents, displaying, 50, 54

   copying from other tables, 117-120

   creating, 113-114

      CREATE TABLE statement, 45-46

      if it doesn't already exist, 115

      from other tables/query results, 117-120

      partitions, 120-121

      storage characteristics, 114-115

      temporary, 115-116

   damages

      checking with CHECK TABLE statement, 719-720

      checking with mysqlcheck utility, 720-721

      InnoDB, checking and repairing, 718

      MyISAM, checking and repairing, 719

      overview, 718

      repairing with mysqlcheck utility, 720-721

      repairing with REPAIR TABLE statement, 720

   data directory, relocating, 560

   default database, listing, 37

   defragmenting, 297

   deleting, 121-122

   descriptive information, displaying, 131, 135

   file representations, 548

   files created by storage engines, 109-110

   grade_event

      creating, 40, 47

      linking with score table on dates, 41

      linking with score table on event IDs, 41-42

   grants. *See* grant tables

   HTML, creating, 475

   identifiers, 98

   indexes, 122-123

      column prefixes, 126

      deleting, 127

      existing tables, 124

      flexibility, 122

      FULLTEXT, 126

      HASH, 125

      ID numbers, generating, 36

      new tables, 125

      storage engine characteristics, 123

      types, 123-124

      unique, 124-125

INFORMATION_SCHEMA database, 133-134
linking
    dates, 41
    event IDs, 41-42
listing, 130, 135
locking, 303-305
    all at once, 705
    overview, 702-703
    read-only access, 703-704
    read/write, 704-705
    single session, 703
    statements, 702
logs
    rotating, 631
    truncating, 625, 631
    rotation, 625
    writing to, 625
multiple
    deleting rows, 154-155
    queries, 78-84
    retrievals. *See* joins; subqueries
    updating rows, 155-156
names, 32, 100
operations statements, 549-550
partitions, creating, 120-121
preventive maintenance, 700
privileges, 667
recovering, 723
renaming, 129-130
rows. *See* rows
score
    creating, 39-40, 48-49
    linking with grade_event table on dates, 41
    linking with grade_event table on event IDs, 41-42
sequence columns, adding, 235-236
server access, preventing, 701
    internal locking, 702-703
    locking all tables at once, 705
    read-only locking, 703-704
    read/write locking, 704-705
    shutting down servers, 702
size, 551-553
storage characteristics, editing, 114-115
storage engines, converting, 129

structure
    displaying, 36-37
    editing, 127-130
student
    columns, creating, 46
    creating, 44-47
system, initializing, 742-743
temporary
    creating, 115-116
    names, 116
transactional/nontransactional
    mixing, 163
    strict mode, 229
updating, 270
U.S. Historical League, creating, 31
    member, creating, 35-38
    member table, 33
    president, 32, 34-35
Web searches, 479-483
    FULLTEXT indexes, 482-483
    pattern matching, 479-482
tables_priv table, **680**
tablespaces (InnoDB), **548**
    components, adding, 599
    configuring, 111, 595-598
        auto-extend increments, 596
        file pathnames, 596
        file specification syntax, 596
        raw partitions, 597-598
        regular files, 597
        system variables, 595
        Windows, 598
    contents, 595
    defined, 111
    individual (per-table), 599-600
    relocating, 560
    startup failure, troubleshooting, 598
TAN() function, **789**
tbl_name parameter
    checking, 473
    db_browse.pl script, 472
tc_log_max_pages_used, **887**
tc_log_page_size status variable, **887**
tc_log_page_waits status variable, **887**
TCP/IP connections, listening, **579**
td() function, **475**

temporal data types, 193, 759
  attributes, 223
  automatic initialization/update
    properties, 224-226
  DATE, 220-221, 760
  DATETIME, 221, 760
  formats, 226
  fractional seconds, 223-224
  improper values, 228
  input dates, 220
  listing of, 193
  MySQL 5.6 improvements, 218
  ranges, 218-219
  storage requirements, 219, 759
  TIME, 221, 760-761
  TIMESTAMP, 221-222, 761-762
  two-digit years, 227-228
  values, 191, 226-227
    temporal data types, 226-227
    type conversions, 251
  YEAR, 222-223, 762
  zero values, 220
TEMPORARY clause, 115-116
temporary tables
  creating, 115-116
  names, 116
terminology
  architectural, 21-22
  query language, 20-21
  structural, 18-19
testing
  alternative forms of queries, 289
  cascaded deletes, 167-168
  cascaded updates, 168
  subquery results, 143-144
  type conversions, 252-253
text backups
  all tables from all databases, 711
  binary backups, compared, 708
  compressing, 712
  creating, 711-714
  database transfers, 716-717
  individual files, 711
  mysqldump options, 712-714
  output, 711-712
  table subsets into separate files, creating,
    712

TEXT data type
  indexes, 207
  overview, 207-208
  query optimization, 298
  size, 204, 207
  special care, 208
  storage requirements, 204
text-format backups
  best practices, 709
  defined, 708
text input fields, 530
TEXT strings, 194, 757-758
text_field() function, 530
textfield() function, 481
th() function, 475
thread_cache_size system variable, 868
thread_concurrency system variable, 868
thread_handling system variable, 868
thread_stack system variable, 868
threaded client functions, Web: 1119
threads_cached status variable, 887
threads_connected status variable, 887
threads_created status variable, 887
threads_running status variable, 888
TIME data type, 193, 221, 228, 760-761
time formats, 226
TIME() function, 813
TIME_FORMAT() function, 813
time_format system variable, 868
TIME_TO_SEC() function, 814
time_zone system variable, 602, 868
time zones, configuring, 602-603
timed_mutexes system variable, 880
TIMEDIFF() function, 814
TIMESTAMP() function, 814
TIMESTAMP data type, 193, 221-222, 761-762
  automatic initialization/update
    properties, 224-226
  current timestamp, 222
  formats, 226-227
  ranges, 222
  time zones, 222
timestamp system variable, 868
TIMESTAMPADD() function, 814
TIMESTAMPDIFF() function, 68, 814
TINYBLOB data type, 204, 207-208
TINYBLOB strings, 194, 755

TINYINT data type, 193, 749
  ranges, 197
  storage requirements, 197
TINYTEXT data type, 204, 207-208
TINYTEXT strings, 194, 757
tmp_table_size system variable, 868
tmpdir system variable, 869
TO_BASE() function, 800
TO_DAYS() function, 68, 815
TO_SECONDS() function, 815
total value summaries, 76
trace() function, 428, Web: 1146
trace_msg() function, Web: 1146
TraceLevel attribute, 428
TRADITIONAL SQL mode, 96
trailing pad values, 218, 754
transaction_alloc_block_size system variable, 869
transaction_prealloc_size system variable, 869
transactional tables
  mixing, 163
  strict mode, 229
transactions
  ACID properties, 157
  commit/rollback capabilities, 156
  concurrency problems, preventing, 156
  control functions, Web: 1112
  defined, 156
  ending, 160
  incorrectly entered grades, swapping example, 160-161
  isolation, 162-163
  performing
    SET statements, 159-160
    START TRANSACTION statement, 157-158
  Perl DBI scripts, 434-436
  processing, 520
  savepoints, 161
  transactional/nontransactional tables, mixing, 163
TRG files, 549
TRIGGER privilege, 665
triggers
  actions, 273
  benefits, 272
  creating, 272
  defined, 272
  example, 273

  file representations, 549
  names, 100, 272
  privileges, 273
  security, 276
TRIM() function, 800
TRN files, 549
troubleshooting
  InnoDB tablespace startup failure, 598
  multiple server issues, 632-635
  mysqld connectivity
    restarting manually, 581-582
    root password, resetting, 582-583
  table damages, 718
    checking with CHECK TABLE statement, 719-720
    InnoDB, checking and repairing, 718
    MyISAM tables, 719
    mysqlcheck utility, 720-721
    repairing with REPAIR TABLE statement, 720
TRUNCATE() function, 789
TRUNCATE TABLE statement, 984
truncating tables, 631
tuning mysqld, 539
tx_isolation system variable, 869
tx_read_only system variable, 869
typelib member (my_option structures), 340
typing tips
  copy/paste, 92
  input line editing, 90-91
  script files, 92-93

U

u_max_value (my_option structures), 340
UCASE() function, 801
ucs2 character set, 104
unary minus (-) operator, 241
UNCOMPRESS() function, 824
UNCOMPRESSED_LENGTH() function, 824
uncorrelated subqueries, 148
undef argument, 422
unequal operators, 770
UNHEX() function, 801
Unicode character sets, 104-105
UNINSTALL PLUGIN statement, 592, 984
uninstalling plugins, 592
UNION statements, 151-154, 985

unique indexes, **123**
  creating, 124-125
  primary key conversions, 169
unique values present in a set of values summary, 72
unique_checks system variable, 869
Universal Coordinated Time (UTC), 222
Unix
  compressing dump files, 712
  database relocation, 559
  error logs, 620
  initial user accounts, 567
  input editing commands, 90-91
  logs, rotating, 626-628
  multiple servers, 637-639
  MySQL, installing, 739
  mysqld
    connections, listening, 579
    running, 570
    starting, 572-574, 741
    stopping, 580-581
    unprivileged login account, configuring, 571-572
  PATH environment variable, configuring, 739
  preventive maintenance login, 701
  program option files, 1007
  socket file, securing, 652-653
  symlinks, 557
UNIX_TIMESTAMP() function, 815
UNLOCK TABLE statement, 304, 703, 985
unpacking sampdb distribution, 735
unquoted identifiers, 97
unsetting columns, 87
UNSIGNED attribute
  AUTO_INCREMENT, 235
  numeric data types, 201, 749
updatable_views_with_limit system variable, 869
UPDATE privilege, 665
UPDATE statement, 986-987
  AUTO_INCREMENT columns, 232
  multiple-table, 155-156
  root/anonymous-user account passwords, 568
  rows, 86
update_expiration() routine, 270

updates
  automatic, 224-226
  cascaded, 164, 168
  columns, 86, 155-156
  deciding to upgrade or not, 641-643
  grant tables, 655
  MySQL software, 539
  rows, 86, 155-156
  tables, 270
  views, 265
UPDATEXML() function, 828
UPPER() function, 801
uptime status variable, 888
uptime_since_flush_status status variable, 888
URL text, escaping, 464-465
USAGE privilege, 668
USAGE specifier, 661
use DBI statement, 399
USE statement, 105-106, 987
use strict statements, 399
use warnings statement, 399
user accounts
  access control risks, 673-676
    ALTER privilege, 676
    anonymous-user accounts, 673
    FILE privilege, 674-676
    GRANT OPTION privilege, 674
    insecure accounts, 673-674
    mysql database privileges, 674
    passwords in old hash format, 673
    PROCESS/SUPER privilege, 676
    RELOAD privilege, 676
    superuser privileges, 673-674
  account-management statements, 654-655
  anonymous
    deleting, 568-569
    passwords, assigning, 567-568
    security risk, 673
  authentication, 659-660
  authentication plugins, 676-679
    proxy users, creating, 677-679
    server connections, 677
    server side/client side, 677
    specifying, 676
  CREATE USER statement
    account operations, 655
    selecting, 656

DROP USER statement, 656
grant tables, upgrading, 655
initial, 564-569
    available on all platforms, 566
    client program connections, 566
    displaying, 565
    passwords, assigning, 567-569
    platform specific, 567
login, creating, 738-739
maintenance, 539
names, 656-658
    account value, 656
    hostnames, 656-657
    IPv4/IPv6 addresses, 657
    localhost, 658
    matching host values to DNS,
      658-659
    quoting, 658
    usernames, 657
    wildcards, 657
passwords, changing/resetting, 672
privileges
    account administering, enabling,
      669-670
    administrative, 661-663, 666
    ALL specifier, 661, 666
    combining, 665
    database-level, 666
    displaying, 671
    global, 666
    granting, 660-661
    level-specifiers, 665
    no privileges, 668
    object, 663-665
    ON specifier, 665
    PROXY, 667
    quoting, 667
    revoking, 671-672
    secure connections, requiring,
      668-669
    stored routines, 667
    table/column level, 667
    USAGE specifier, 661
RENAME USER statement, 656
resource consumption limits, 670-671
root
    passwords, assigning, 567-569

    resetting passwords, 582-583
    SSL required, creating, 697-698
USER() function, 832
user table, 680
    authentication columns, 680, 684
    privilege columns, 683
    resource management columns, 680,
      685-686
    SSL-related columns, 680, 685
users
    accounts. See user accounts
    column values, 688
    defined variables, 71, 894-895
    proxy, creating, 677-679
U.S. Historical League project, 15-17
    common-interest Web searches
        FULLTEXT indexes, 482-483
        pattern matching, 479-482
    creative ideas, 15-16
    directory, generating, 436-442
        HTML format, 455-458
        plain text version, 439-440
        RTF version, 440-442
    directory member entries, editing
      online, 527-536
        editing form, 533-534
        framework, 529-530
        member login page, 530-531
        null values, 535-536
        password verification, 531-533
        passwords, 527-529
        updating entries, 534-535
    displaying current membership count to
      visitors script, 313
    home page, 488-491
    interactive online quiz, creating,
      522-527
    member entries, editing, 448-454
    members with common interests,
      finding, 454-455
    membership renewal notices, sending,
      443-448
    membership updates, 270
    objectives, 15
    practical questions, 16-17
    president born first, finding, 144-146
    presidents born before Andrew Jackson
      subquery, 84

tables, creating, 31
   member, 33, 35-38
   president, 32, 34-35
ushl_browse.pl script, 479-482
ushl_ft_browse.pl script, 482-483
UTC (Universal Coordinated Time), 222
UTC_DATE() function, 815
UTC_TIME() function, 815
UTC_TIMESTAMP() function, 816
utf8 character set, 104
utf8mb4 character set, 105
utf16 character set, 105
utf16le character set, 105
utf32 character set, 105
utilities
   environment variables, checking,
     1011-1012
   functions, Web: 1148-1149
   help messages, displaying, 1000-1001
   my_print_defaults, 1011
   myisamchk
     defined, 538
     maintenance advantages, 719
     options specific to myisamchk, listing
      of, 1015-1018
     overview, 1013-1014
     standard options, 1014
     table maintenance, 700
     variables, 1018-1019
   mysql. *See* mysql utility
   mysql_config
     defined, 1030
     options, 1030-1031
   mysql_install_db
     specific options, 1032
     standard options, 1032
   mysql.server, 1029-1030
   mysql_upgrade, 1033
     specific options, 1033-1034
     standard options, 1033
   mysqladmin
     commands, 1035-1037
     defined, 538
     options, 1034-1035
     variables, 1013-1035
   mysqlbinlog, 622
     overview, 1038

     specific options to mysqlbinlog,
      1038-1041
     standard options, 1038
     variables, 1041
   mysqlcheck
     checking/repairing tables, 720-721
     defined, 538
     maintenance, scheduling, 707
     overview, 1041
     specific options to mysqlcheck,
      1042-1044
     standard options, 1041-1042
     table analysis options, 1044
     table checking options, 1044
     table maintenance, 700
     table optimization, 1044-1045
     table repair options, 1044
   mysqld_multi
     specific options to mysqld_multi,
      1057
     standard options, 1056-1057
   mysqld_safe, 1058
     specific options to mysqld_safe,
      1058-1059
     standard options, 1058
   mysqldump, 135
     data format options, 1067-1068
     database maintenance, 700
     defined, 538
     options, 712-714
     overview, 1060
     specific options to mysqldump,
      1061-1067
     standard options, 1060
     text dump files, creating, 711-714
     variables, 1068
   mysqldumpslow, 621
   mysqlimport
     data files, loading, 53
     data format options, 1070
     overview, 1068
     specific, 1069-1070
     standard options, 1068
   mysqlshow, 38
     overview, 1070-1071
     specific options, 1071
     standard options, 1071

options
  case sensitivity, 1001
  checking, 1011
  escape sequences, 1010
  group names, 1009
  leading spaces, 1010
  long-form/short-form, 1001
  option files, 1007-1011
  processing features, 1002
  quoting, 1010
  read directives, 1010-1011
  SSL, 1006
  standard, 1003-1005
  user-specific privacy, 1011
  variables, 1006-1007
perror
  options, 1072
  overview, 1072
rotate, 628
UUID() function, 832
UUID_SHORT() function, 833

V

value member (my_option structures), 340
values
  account, 656
  boolean, 192
  columns, specifying, 196
  data types
    default, 748
    zero, 748
  empty, 475
  improper, handling, 228-230
    division by zero errors, 229
    transactional/nontransactional tables, 229
    turning on strict mode, 230
    warnings, 229
    weakening strict mode, 230
    zero date errors, 229
  MYSQL_BIND array parameters, assigning, 385
  NOT NULL
    data types for query optimization, 297
    numeric data types, 203
    string data types, 216
    temporal data types, 223

NULL, 192
  AUTO_INCREMENT columns, 231
  column sort, 62
  directory membership updates, 535-536
  expressions, 246-247
  foreign key relationships, 168-170
  numeric data types, 203
  result sets, checking, 416, 504
  sequence columns, 231
  string data types, 216
  temporal data types, 223
numeric, 181
  approximate, 181-182
  bit-field, 182
  exact, 181-182
options, holding, 372-373
permitted lists, defining, 209
scope columns, 687-689
  column_name, 688
  Db, 688
  host, 687-689
  proxied_host, 689
  proxied_user, 689
  routine_name, 688
  routine_type, 688
  table_name, 688
  user, 688
spatial, 191-192
sql_mode system variable, 862-865
SSL-related server status variables, displaying, 697
status variables, checking, 588-589
strings, 182-184
  backslashes, turning off, 184
  binary, 185, 188-189
  case sensitivity, 100
  character set variables, 189-191
  CONVERT() function, 187-188
  escape sequences, 183
  hexadecimal notation, 184
  introducers, 187-188
  length, 188
  nonbinary, 185, 188-189
  quote characters, including, 183-184
  sorting properties, 186
  surrounding quotes, 182-183

system variables, checking, 585-586
temporal, 191
    temporal data types, 226-227
    type conversions, 251
trailing pad, 754
type conversions, 247-251
    ASCII, 254
    binary/nonbinary strings, 255
    character sets, 254
    collations, 255
    comparisons, 251
    CONCAT() function, 248
    dates, 254
    explicit, 247
    floating-point and integer values, 248
    forcing, 253-255
    hexadecimal, 248-249, 253
    illegal values, 248
    implicit, 247
    operands to operator expected types,
        249
    string-to-number, 249-250
    temporal values, 251
    testing, 252-253
    time parts, 254
    values into strings, 253
VALUES() function, 833
VAR_POP() function, 821
VAR_SAMP() function, 821
var_type member (my_option structures),
    340-341
VARBINARY data type
    overview, 207
    size/storage requirements, 204
VARBINARY strings, 194, 755
VARCHAR data type
    CHAR data types, compared, 206
    columns, creating, 35
    size/storage requirements, 204
VARCHAR strings, 194, 757
variable-length character data types, 35
variable-length string types, 45-46, 205
variables
    automatic_sp_privileges, 270
    character set, 189-191
    character_set_server, 102
    collation_server, 102

connect1 client program, declaring, 324
connection handlers, 325
DBI_TRACE, 429
environment
    PATH, 739-740
    Perl DBI, Web: 1156
    program options, checking,
        1011-1012
global, 97
InnoDB storage engine, 600-601
innodb_file_per_table, 111
lower_case_table_names, 100
myisamchk utility, 1018-1019
MySQL programs, setting, 1006-1007
mysql utility, 1025-1026
MYSQL_BIND array parameters,
    assigning, 385
mysqladmin client, 1013-1035
mysqlbinlog, 1041
mysqld, 1056
mysqldump, 1068
option values, holding, 372-373
Perl DBI, 397, Web: 1131
PHP, 492
query results, binding, 421-423
sql_mode, 96
SSL-related server status values,
    displaying, 697
status, 881
    general, listing of, 881-888
    InnoDB, listing of, 888-891
    overview, 584
    query cache, listing of, 891-892
    SSL, 892-894
    values, checking, 588-589
system, 584-585, 835-836
    character_set_server, 603
    collation_server, 603
    displaying, 583, 836
    error message language selection, 604
    expire_logs_days, 629
    general, listing of, 836-870
    general_log, 621
    general_log_file, 621
    InnoDB, listing of, 870-880
    innodb_autoextend_increment, 596
    innodb_data_file_path, 595

options
    case sensitivity, 1001
    checking, 1011
    escape sequences, 1010
    group names, 1009
    leading spaces, 1010
    long-form/short-form, 1001
    option files, 1007-1011
    processing features, 1002
    quoting, 1010
    read directives, 1010-1011
    SSL, 1006
    standard, 1003-1005
    user-specific privacy, 1011
    variables, 1006-1007
perror
    options, 1072
    overview, 1072
rotate, 628
UUID() function, 832
UUID_SHORT() function, 833

V

value member (my_option structures), 340
values
    account, 656
    boolean, 192
    columns, specifying, 196
    data types
        default, 748
        zero, 748
    empty, 475
    improper, handling, 228-230
        division by zero errors, 229
        transactional/nontransactional tables, 229
        turning on strict mode, 230
        warnings, 229
        weakening strict mode, 230
        zero date errors, 229
    MYSQL_BIND array parameters, assigning, 385
    NOT NULL
        data types for query optimization, 297
        numeric data types, 203
        string data types, 216
        temporal data types, 223

    NULL, 192
        AUTO_INCREMENT columns, 231
        column sort, 62
        directory membership updates, 535-536
        expressions, 246-247
        foreign key relationships, 168-170
        numeric data types, 203
        result sets, checking, 416, 504
        sequence columns, 231
        string data types, 216
        temporal data types, 223
    numeric, 181
        approximate, 181-182
        bit-field, 182
        exact, 181-182
    options, holding, 372-373
    permitted lists, defining, 209
    scope columns, 687-689
        column_name, 688
        Db, 688
        host, 687-689
        proxied_host, 689
        proxied_user, 689
        routine_name, 688
        routine_type, 688
        table_name, 688
        user, 688
    spatial, 191-192
    sql_mode system variable, 862-865
    SSL-related server status variables, displaying, 697
    status variables, checking, 588-589
    strings, 182-184
        backslashes, turning off, 184
        binary, 185, 188-189
        case sensitivity, 100
        character set variables, 189-191
        CONVERT() function, 187-188
        escape sequences, 183
        hexadecimal notation, 184
        introducers, 187-188
        length, 188
        nonbinary, 185, 188-189
        quote characters, including, 183-184
        sorting properties, 186
        surrounding quotes, 182-183

system variables, checking, 585-586

temporal, 191

    temporal data types, 226-227

    type conversions, 251

trailing pad, 754

type conversions, 247-251

    ASCII, 254

    binary/nonbinary strings, 255

    character sets, 254

    collations, 255

    comparisons, 251

    CONCAT() function, 248

    dates, 254

    explicit, 247

    floating-point and integer values, 248

    forcing, 253-255

    hexadecimal, 248-249, 253

    illegal values, 248

    implicit, 247

    operands to operator expected types, 249

    string-to-number, 249-250

    temporal values, 251

    testing, 252-253

    time parts, 254

    values into strings, 253

VALUES() function, 833

VAR_POP() function, 821

VAR_SAMP() function, 821

var_type member (my_option structures), 340-341

VARBINARY data type

    overview, 207

    size/storage requirements, 204

VARBINARY strings, 194, 755

VARCHAR data type

    CHAR data types, compared, 206

    columns, creating, 35

    size/storage requirements, 204

VARCHAR strings, 194, 757

variable-length character data types, 35

variable-length string types, 45-46, 205

variables

    automatic_sp_privileges, 270

    character set, 189-191

    character_set_server, 102

    collation_server, 102

connect1 client program, declaring, 324

connection handlers, 325

DBI_TRACE, 429

environment

    PATH, 739-740

    Perl DBI, Web: 1156

    program options, checking, 1011-1012

global, 97

InnoDB storage engine, 600-601

innodb_file_per_table, 111

lower_case_table_names, 100

myisamchk utility, 1018-1019

MySQL programs, setting, 1006-1007

mysql utility, 1025-1026

MYSQL_BIND array parameters, assigning, 385

mysqladmin client, 1013-1035

mysqlbinlog, 1041

mysqld, 1056

mysqldump, 1068

option values, holding, 372-373

Perl DBI, 397, Web: 1131

PHP, 492

query results, binding, 421-423

sql_mode, 96

SSL-related server status values, displaying, 697

status, 881

    general, listing of, 881-888

    InnoDB, listing of, 888-891

    overview, 584

    query cache, listing of, 891-892

    SSL, 892-894

    values, checking, 588-589

system, 584-585, 835-836

    character_set_server, 603

    collation_server, 603

    displaying, 583, 836

    error message language selection, 604

    expire_logs_days, 629

    general, listing of, 836-870

    general_log, 621

    general_log_file, 621

    InnoDB, listing of, 870-880

    innodb_autoextend_increment, 596

    innodb_data_file_path, 595

innodb_file_per_table, 599
lc_time_names, 604
log_warnings, 620
max_relay_log_size, 624, 630
names, 836
overview, 583
setting, 587-588, 836
slow_query_log, 621
time zones, 602-603
values, checking, 585-586
user-defined, 71, 894-895
VARIANCE() function, 821
verifying
event scheduler status, 274
query optimizer operation, 287
VERSION() function, 833
version system variable, 869
version_comment system variable, 870
version_compile_machine system variable, 870
version_compile_os system variable, 870
vertical bars (||), operators/functions, 764
viewing. See displaying
views
column names, 263-264
defined, 261-263
file representations, 549
grade-keeping project test/quiz statistics example, 264-265
identifiers, 98
names, 100
privileges, 263
referring to columns, 263
security, 275-276
updating, 265
WHERE clauses, 263

W

wait_timeout system variable, 870
warning_count system variable, 870
warnings (Perl DBI), 401
Web
HTML documents, 455-456
input parameters, checking, 462
integration, 309
inventory searches, 14
multiple purpose pages, writing, 465-468

online directory, creating, 455-458
output, generating, 462-464
servers, configuring, 460-461
Web-based scripts, 459
CGI
HTML structure functions, 461
HTML/URL text, escaping, 464-465
HTML versus XHTML, 464
importing functions, 461
input parameters, 462
multiple-purpose pages, writing, 465-468
object-oriented interface, 461-462
output, generating, 462-464
portability, 463
database browser, 471-475
data limits, 475
empty values into nonbreaking spaces, converting, 475
HTML table, creating, 475
initial page, generating, 472-473
main body of script, 471-472
security warning, 471
table contents, displaying, 473
tbl_name parameter, 472
grade-keeping project score browser, 475-479
displaying events as a table, 476-477
scores for specified event, listing, 477-479
Perl DBI scripts, 459-460
PHP
data-retrieval, 497-499
error handling, 507-509
headers/footers functions, 495-497
home page, 488-491
include files, 491-495
input parameters, 511-512
interactive online quiz, 522-527
live hyperlinks, creating, 499-500
member entries online editing, 527-536
NULL values, checking, 504
online score-entry. See PHP scripts, online score-entry
placeholders, 506-507
prepared statements, 505
quoting special characters, 505-507

row-modifying statements, 501
rows, retrieving, 501-504
security, 470-471, 491
statements, handling, 500-501
servers, connecting, 468-469
table searches, 479-483
    FULLTEXT indexes, 482-483
    pattern matching, 479-482
Web server, configuring, 460-461
Web sites
MySQL
    mailing list, 80, 642
    reference manuals, 7
    Workbench, 21
Open Geospatial Consortium, 191
PDO, 486
Perl DBI, 395
Perl modules, 743
PHP, 486, 743
sampdb distribution, 735
WWW security FAQ, 471
XPath, 816
WEEK() function, 816-817
WEEKDAY() function, 817
WEEKOFYEAR() function, 817
WEIGHT_STRING() function, 801-802
WHAT clause, 660
WHERE clause
COUNT() function, 72
DELETE statement, 85
query optimizer, 288-289
SELECT statement, 56
SHOW statement, 131
SHOW STATUS statement, 589
SHOW VARIABLES statement, 585
UPDATE statement, 86
views, 263
where-to-find-Perl indicators, 398
WHILE statements, 983-984, 989
wildcards
LIKE operator, 244
REGEXP operator, 244
user account names, 657
Windows
compressing dump files, 712
database relocation, 560
initial user accounts, 567

InnoDB tablespace, configuring, 598
input editing commands, 90-91
logs, 621, 628
multiple servers, 639-641
MySQL, installing, 739
mysqld, 575
    connections, listening, 580
    options, 1053
    running as Windows service, 576-577
    running manually, 575
    starting, 742
    stopping, 581
PATH environment variable,
    configuring, 740
program option files, 1007-1008
WITH clause
GRANT statement, 661, 938
resource consumption limits, 670
WITH GRANT OPTION clause, 669-670
WITH ROLLUP clause, 77-78
writing expressions, 240-241
column references, 240
functions/arguments, 240
NULL values, 246-247
operators, 241-243
    arithmetic, 241
    bit, 242
    comparison, 243
    logical, 241-242
    precedence, 246
pattern matching, 243-245
    LIKE operator, 243-244
    REGEXP operator, 244
scalar subqueries, 241
writing scripts
APIs. *See* APIs
benefits, 307-308
C client. *See* C client programs
goals, 308
Perl DBI, Web: 1130
    case sensitivity, 400
    characteristics, 396
    comments, adding, 398
    connect() function arguments,
        399-400
    connection parameters, specifying,
        423-426
    connections, 400, 425-426

debugging. *See* debugging, Perl DBI scripts

disconnecting, 402

dump_members.pl, 397-398

entire result sets, returning at once, 413-415

error handling, 402-405

finish() function, 402

function parentheses, 401

handles, 397

invoking scripts, 396

nonhandle variables, 397

null values, checking, 416

number of rows returned, 411

parameter binding, 421-423

placeholders, 419-421

prepared statements, 421

quoting special characters, 416-419

requirements, 395

result set metadata, 430-434

result sets, displaying, 400

row-fetching loops, 401-402, 407-411

row-modifying statements, 406-407

single-row results, returning, 411-413

statement terminators, 401

transactions, 434-436

undef argument, 422

use DBI statement, 399

use strict statements, 399

use warnings statement, 399

U.S. Historical League examples. *See* Perl DBI scripts, U.S. Historical League

warnings mode, 401

Web-based. *See* Perl DBI scripts, Web-based

where-to-find-Perl indicator, 398

PHP, Web: 1157-1158

data-retrieval, 497-499

database-access interfaces, 485-486

error handling, 507-509

headers/footers functions, 495-497

hello world examples, 487-488

home page, 488-491

include files, 491-495

input parameters, 511-512

interactive online quiz, 522-527

live hyperlinks, creating, 499-500

member entries online editing, 527-536

names, 486

NULL values, checking, 504

online score-entry. *See* PHP scripts, online score-entry

overview, 487

PDO classes, Web: 1158

PDO error exceptions, 491

placeholders, 506-507

prepared statements, 505

quoting special characters, 505-507

row-modifying statements, 501

rows, retrieving, 501-504

samples, installing, 486-487

security, 491

server connections, 490-491

standalone, 489

statements, handling, 500-501

variables, 492

Web site, 486

Web integration, 309

WWW security FAQ Web site, 471

X

X509, 668

XHTML, 464

XML functions, 828

XOR operator, 57, 241, 773

XPath, 816

Y

YEAR data type, 193, 222-223, 762

YEAR() function, 817

YEARWEEK() function, 817

Z

zero date errors, 229

ZEROFILL attribute, 201-202, 749

zero values, 748